P9-EDG-677

The Encyclopedia of
PSYCHIATRY,
PSYCHOLOGY,
· A N D ·
PSYCHOANALYSIS

Editors

Benjamin B. Wolman, Ph.D.
Editor in Chief

Jean E. Wolman
Managing Editor

CONSULTING EDITORS

Leah J. Dickstein, M.D.
Psychiatry

Gregory A. Kimble, Ph.D.
Joseph M. Notterman, Ph.D.
Experimental, Physiological, and Comparative Psychology

George Stricker, Ph.D.
Social, Developmental, and Clinical Psychology

Samuel Ritvo, M.D.
Albert J. Solnit, M.D.
Psychoanalysis and Related Systems

EDITORIAL ASSISTANTS

Paul David Boyer
Debra Duchin

The Encyclopedia of

PSYCHIATRY, PSYCHOLOGY, ·AND· PSYCHOANALYSIS

◆ ◆ ◆

Benjamin B. Wolman

EDITOR IN CHIEF

HENRY HOLT AND COMPANY · NEW YORK

Henry Holt and Company, Inc.
Publishers since 1866
115 West 18th Street
New York, New York 10011

Henry Holt ® is a registered trademark of Henry Holt and Company, Inc.

Copyright © 1996 by Aesculapius Publishers, Inc.
All rights reserved.

Published in Canada by Fitzhenry & Whiteside Ltd.,
91 Granton Drive, Richmond Hill, Ontario L4B 2N5.

Distributed outside of the United States
and Canada by Macmillan Publishers:
ISBN 0-333-692-977

Library of Congress Cataloging-in-Publication Data
The Encyclopedia of psychiatry, psychology, and psychoanalysis/
Benjamin B. Wolman.—1st ed.
p.   cm.
Includes bibliographical references and index.
1. Psychiatry—Encyclopedias. 2. Psychology—Encyclopedias.
3. Psychoanalysis—Encyclopedias. 4. Clinical psychology—Encyclopedias.
I. Wolman, Benjamin B. II. Series.
RC437.E49   1996
616.89'003—dc20   95-41116
                                                      CIP

ISBN 0-8050-2234-1

Henry Holt books are available for special
promotions and premiums. For details contact:
Director, Special Markets.

First Edition—1996

Designed by Victoria Hartman

Printed in the United States of America
All first editions are printed on acid-free paper. ∞

3   5   7   9   10   8   6   4   2

Contents

FOREWORD TO THE 1977
EDITION BY JEAN PIAGET   IX

PREFACE   XI

AUTHOR ACKNOWLEDGMENTS   XIII

AUTHORS   XV

ENTRIES   1

Foreword to the 1977 Edition

BY JEAN PIAGET

When I was young (quite a while ago), the great psychologists who dominated the scene, such as Thorndike, Spearman, Köhler, Binet, Claparède, and many others, could have still flattered themselves that they knew all the fields of psychology. One could speak with them about perception, intelligence, learning, interests, or affects, and so on. They were up to date on the main works, and they read all the essentials pertaining to these areas besides. They possessed a reciprocal general knowledge in neurology and psychiatry. The great specialists in neurology and psychiatry knew psychology. The only disquieting barrier that one could observe was the one that separated psychoanalysts from experimental psychologists in the sense that the first harbored some misapprehension for "academic psychology," while the reverse was less true, for few psychologists readily understood the general basis of psychoanalysis (such as the importance of the unconscious and its roots in infancy, repression, etc.).

At that distant time, an encyclopedia that encompassed the different aspects of the human mind, like the present one that I have the honor to preface today, would have been a rather small volume and would not have been of great significance, since every scholar could have acquired general knowledge of whatever was of importance.

However, at the present time (that is, sixty years after the period I have just described), the situation is totally different. Even in regard to psychology, I think that no psychologist has a complete mastery of all areas in the science. For my part, I believe that I know the principal tendencies of contemporary psychology, but if I had to pass an examination on the entirety of works inspired by Skinner's work or on the multiple aspects of psycholinguistics, and so on, I think that my examiners would judge me very severely and I would not receive a passing mark. Even in the field of perception, which I studied for years (see my work *Les Mécanismes Perceptifs*), I am no longer completely up to date on the numerous recent works. Nevertheless, I continue to work and write every day. But to read all that appears is a totally different matter! I recall a visit that I made around 1954 to a renowned Scandinavian colleague because I was told about similarities between our respective works. He accepted me very kindly, and afterward he made several visits to Geneva at the times of our annual *Symposia*. His first words were the following: "You have certainly never read anything of mine, and never will. As far as I am concerned, I have not read anything of yours, and this will not change. We should find devoted young collaborators who would inform each of us of the works of the other!"

In regard to neurological and psychiatric knowledge of psychologists and psychological knowledge of neurologists and psychiatrists, they are more and more incomplete because of the growing complexity of these different fields and scarcity of truly interdisciplinary works. As a matter of fact, true interdisciplinarity requires "multicompetence" from each one of the participants and not only competence in his own domain.

It is therefore evident that in the presence of this alarming situation, Dr. Benjamin B. Wolman has rendered a very great service to our different disciplines by conceiving the ambitious but infinitely useful project of the *International Encyclopedia of Psychiatry, Psychology, and Psychoanalysis*. This collective work renders the greatest service by presenting a picture of the totality of our knowledge of man—his nervous system and the functions of his mind, his development, and his pathological deviations. By consulting the innumerable articles devoted to every particular question, not only beginners or students, but also qualified experts will learn much that has been done in this subject. Also, and this is probably essential, in addition to those problems that preoccupy them, they will discover the multitude and complexity of those they had not even thought about.

In concluding this brief preface, allow me to be presumptuous and to speak on behalf of future readers in thanking and congratulating Dr. Benjamin B. Wolman, the authors, editors, and other participants, for rendering us all the greatest of services by providing us with this great work.

Jean Piaget
Geneva, October, 1976

Preface

The twelve-volume International *Encyclopedia of Psychiatry, Psychology, Psychoanalysis, and Neurology* was published in 1977. In 1983 the thirteenth Progress Volume was published. The present one-volume *Encyclopedia of Psychiatry, Psychology, and Psychoanalysis* is an outgrowth of two major needs: to update the Encyclopedia and to make it available to researchers, graduate students, and practitioners in the mental health field.

The editors of this new Encyclopedia have checked every single entry in the thirteen volumes and decided which ones should be omitted, which abridged, and which updated. We have come to realize that the thirteen-volume Encyclopedia is too expensive for individual faculty members, clinicians, researchers, and graduate students; thus, we abridged most entries. We have decided that neurology will warrant a separate volume, and there is not urgent reason to include it in this Encyclopedia. Also, a description of current developments in other countries is omitted. Biographical entries were reduced in size, and, to save space, the number of references were cut to a minimum.

The present Encyclopedia offers an authoritative, complete, and up-to-date description of research, theory, and practice in the sciences and professions that deal with the human mind and its ills. The Encyclopedia is written for the professions of psychiatry, psychology, psychoanalysis, clinical social work, and related areas. It is intended to serve as a basic reference book for graduate, doctoral, and postdoctoral programs. The Encyclopedia is an indispensable source of information for physicians in private practice, pediatricians, neurologists, guidance workers, social workers, public health officials, nurses, and other professionals involved in mental health and human mind problems. No point of view, no new idea, no area of research has been omitted.

I was fortunate to secure the efficient cooperation of my wife, Jean Evans Wolman, in the task of managing editor. She organized and supervised the entire work. I was fortunate also to get the cooperation of Leah J. Dickstein, M.D., as the consulting editor of *Psychiatry*; Gregory A. Kimble, Ph.D., and Joseph M. Notterman, Ph.D., as consulting editors of *Experimental, Physiological, and Comparative Psychology*; George Stricker, Ph.D., as consulting editor of *Social, Developmental, and Clinical Psychology*; and Albert J. Solnit, M.D., and Samuel Ritvo, M.D., as consulting editors of *Psychoanalysis and Related Systems*.

I have read and edited every article and checked for accuracy and presentation in close cooperation with the consulting editors.

May I express my gratitude to all our authors, consultants, coworkers, and assistants, especially Paul David Boyer and Debra Duchin.

I am profoundly grateful to Kenneth Wright, editorial director of Henry Holt Publishers, to Robert Markel, president of Markel Associates, and to Mary Kay Linge, editor of Henry Holt Reference Books, for their unswerving support and guidance.

Benjamin B. Wolman

Author Acknowledgments

The following authors wish to acknowledge the assistance they received in preparing their articles:

Linda Wilson Craighead and **W. Edward Craighead** wish to express their appreciation to K. Daniel O'Leary, Ph.D., for his comments on an earlier draft of their manuscript.

Bruce P. Dohrenwend acknowledges the support of National Institute of Mental Health research grant no. MH-10328 and Research Scientist Award K5-MH-14663 from the United States Public Health Service.

Carl H. Frederiksen, **Edward Harris**, and **Richard P. Duran** acknowledge support by the National Science Foundation, grant no. NSF-GS-40203. In addition, the authors are grateful to Charles R. Zubrizycki for calling attention to pertinent materials on semantic memory.

Henry U. Grunebaum and **Justin L. Weiss** acknowledge that their article was supported by the Milton Fund of Harvard University and the National Institute of Mental Health, grant no. 5R11-MH-01272-02.

Alan Hein acknowledges the support of the Spencer Foundation, the National Institutes of Health, and National Aeronautics and Space Administration.

John Money acknowledges that the writing of his article was supported in part by United States Public Health Service grants MD00325 and MD07111.

Howard A. Moss wishes to acknowledge his affiliation with the National Institute of Mental Health.

Joseph M. Notterman wishes to express appreciation to Joseph Farley, Jeffrey S. Hrapsky, George Miller, Michelle Millis, and Daniel R. Tufano for their careful reading of his manuscript. The research described in his article was supported by the Army Research Institute under grant DAHC19-G0012 and contract MDA903-79-0426.

Abraham Tesser wishes to acknowledge that preparation of his entry was supported in part by the National Science Foundation, grant no. DBS-9121276 and the John D. and Catherine T. MacArthur Foundation, grant no. 8900078.

Robert A. Wicklund acknowledges that the writing of his article was supported in part by National Science Foundation grant no. GS-31890.

Leon J. Yarrow wishes to acknowledge his affiliation with the National Institute of Mental Health.

Edward F. Zigler acknowledges that preparation for his article was supported by the National Institute of Child Health and Human Development research grant no. HD-03008. He wishes to extend thanks to Sally Styfco for her assistance.

Authors

Jules C. Abrams, Ph.D.
Richard Abrams, M.D.
Sigurd H. Ackerman, M.D.
James F. Adams, Ph.D.
Paul L. Adams, M.D.
Robert Ader, Ph.D.
Helmut E. Adler, Ph.D.
Kurt A. Adler, M.D.
Leonore Loeb Adler, Ph.D
Ian E. Alger, M.D.
Vernon L. Allen, Ph.D.
Earl A. Alluisi, Ph.D.
François E. Alouf, M.D.
Irwin Altman, Ph.D.
Teresa M. Amabile, M.A.
Scarvia B. Anderson, Ph.D.
Klaus Angel, M.D.
John Annett, D.Phil.
Adrienne P. Applegarth, M.D.
Mortimer Herbert Appley, Ph.D.
Ruben Ardila, Ph.D.
David Arenberg, Ph.D.
Robert Athanasiou, Ph.D.
Norman Atkins, M.D.
John W. Atkinson, Ph.D.
Kurt W. Back, Ph.D.
Lynne Baker-Ward, M.A.
Paul B. Baltes, Ph.D.
Albert Bandura, Ph.D.
Edwin M. Banks, Ph.D.
Allan G. Barclay, Ph.D.
John K. Bare, Ph.D.
George W. Barlow, Ph.D.
Robert P. Barrell, Ph.D.
Linda May Bartoshuk, Ph.D.
Francis D. Baudry, M.D.

William E. Baxter, M.A., M.S.
Colin Gordon Beer, D.Phil.
Michael Beer, Ph.D.
Diane Beeson, M.A.
W. D. Alan Beggs, Ph.D.
Allan Beigel, M.D.
Leonard Berkowitz, Ph.D.
Daniel E. Berlyne, Ph.D.
Leo H. Berman, M.D.
Walter Bernard, Ph.D.
Arnold Bernstein, Ph.D.
Jerome C. Bernstein, Ph.D.
Ellen S. Berscheid, Ph.D.
Vytautas J. Bieliauskas, Ph.D.
Henry B. Biller, Ph.D.
Robert Charles Birney, Ph.D.
Benjamin Blackman, M.D.
Colin B. Blakemore, Ph.D.
Gertrude Blanck, Ph.D.
Anne R. Bloom, Ph.D.
Harold P. Blum, M.D.
June E. Blum, Ph.D.
Herman T. Blumenthal, M.D.
James A. Blumenthal, Ph.D.
Medard Boss, M.D.
Lawrence R. Boulter, Ph.D.
Gordon H. Bower, Ph.D.
L. Bryce Boyer, M.D.
Robert M. Boynton, Ph.D.
David L. Bradford, Ph.D.
Leland P. Bradford, Ph.D.
Jack W. Brehm, Ph.D.
Charles Brenner, M.D.
Jean L. Bresnahan, Ph.D.
Peter D. Bricker, Ph.D.
Marie H. Briehl, B.A.

Walter Briehl, M.D.
Stanley L. Brodsky, Ph.D.
Crittenden E. Brookes, M.D.,
   Ph.D.
Henry W. Brosin, M.D.
S. Joyce Brotsky, Ph.D.
Alan Brown, M.D.
Judson S. Brown, Ph.D.
Josef Brožek, Ph.D.
Hilde Bruch, M.D.
James H. Bryan, Ph.D.
Milton Budoff, Ph.D.
Harvey Burdick, Ph.D.
Gordon M. Burghardt, Ph.D.
John C. Burnham, Ph.D.
Ewald W. Busse, M.D.
Laura Butkovsky, M.S.
Karla Butler, Ph.D.
Thomas C. Cadwallader, Ph.D.
William S. Cain, Ph.D.
Victor Calef, M.D.
Robert Cancro, M.D.
Morton B. Cantor, M.D.
Patrick J. Capretta, Ph.D.
Patricia Carrington, Ph.D.
Daniel H. Carson, Ph.D.
Desmond S. Cartwright, Ph.D.
Arthur Centor, Ph.D.
James L. Chapel, M.D.
Antony J. Chapman, Ph.D.
Stella Chess, M.D.
David A. Chiriboga, Ph.D.
David A. Chiszar, Ph.D.
Roger W. Cholewiak, Ph.D.
Gerard Chrzanowski, M.D.
Eve V. Clark, Ph.D.

Dale L. Clayton, Ph.D.
Lynwood G. Clemens, Ph.D.
Victor B. Cline, Ph.D.
Glynn D. Coates, Ph.D.
Charles N. Cofer, Ph.D.
Leslie B. Cohen, Ph.D.
John D. Coie, Ph.D.
Robert Coles, M.D.
Sheila Coonerty, Ph.D.
Alan B. Cooper, M.D.
Joel Cooper, Ph.D.
Emory L. Cowen, Ph.D.
Linda Wilson Craighead,
　Ph.D.
W. Edward Craighead, Ph.D.
Elliot M. Cramer, Ph.D.
Rue L. Cromwell, Ph.D.
Charles R. Crowell, Ph.D.
Lee R. Crowley, M.A.
Ralph M. Crowley, M.D.
Leon Cytryn, M.D.
Helen B. Daly, Ph.D.
Richard H. Dana, Ph.D.
Robert S. Daniels, M.D.
John McCannon Darley, Ph.D.
Kenneth H. David, Ph.D.
Isabel S. Davidoff, B.A.
Anthony Davids, Ph.D.
Gerald C. Davison, Ph.D.
Max Day, M.D.
William DeJong, M.A.
Herman C. B. Denber, Ph.D.
Florence L. Denmark, Ph.D.
Joseph de Rivera, Ph.D.
Donald A. Dewsbury, Ph.D.
Leah J. Dickstein, M.D.
Ronald C. Dillehay, Ph.D.
Leonard Diller, Ph.D.
Bruce P. Dohrenwend, Ph.D.
Margaret E. Donnelly, Ph.D.
T. Wayne Downey, M.D.
Thomas W. Draper, Ph.D.
David J. Drum, Ph.D.
Charles P. Ducey, Ph.D.
Richard P. Duran, M.A.
Samuel F. Dworkin, Ph.D.
Morris N. Eagle, Ph.D.

Gustav Eckstein, M.D., D.D.S.,
　L.H.D.
Adele Edwards, B.A.
Allen Jack Edwards, Ph.D.
Richard L. Edwards, Ph.D.
David Ehrenfreund, Ph.D.
Samuel Eisenstein, M.D.
Rudolf Ekstein, Ph.D.
Jeffrey W. Elias, Ph.D.
Merrill F. Elias, Ph.D.
Albert Ellis, Ph.D.
Henry C. Ellis, Ph.D.
Harmon S. Ephron, M.D.
Phillip S. Erdberg, Ph.D.
Walter B. Essman, Ph.D.
C. L. Estes, Ph.D.
Rand B. Evans, Ph.D.
Sheila M. Eyberg, Ph.D.
Robert M. Fagen, Ph.D.
Joseph Farley, Ph.D.
Dana L. Farnsworth, M.D.
Saul Feldman, D.P.A.
Lucy Rau Ferguson, Ph.D.
Norma Deitch Feshbach, Ph.D.
Seymour Feshbach, Ph.D.
Frank W. Finger, Ph.D.
Stephen K. Firestein, M.D.
Ira J. Firestone, Ph.D.
Charles Fisher, M.D.
Leonard D. Fitts, Ed.D.
Frederic F. Flach, M.D.
Stephen Fleck, M.D.
Raymond D. Fowler, Ph.D.
James L. Fozard, Ph.D.
Allen J. Frances, M.D.
Shervert H. Frazier, M.D.
Carl H. Frederiksen, Ph.D.
Aharon H. Fried, Ph.D.
Richard C. Friedman, M.D.
Mindy Thompson Fullilove, M.D.
Laurel Furumoto, Ph.D.
Eugene Galanter, Ph.D.
Eileen A. Gavin, Ph.D.
John E. Gedo, M.D.
Ivan B. Gendzel, M.D.
Margaret Joan Giannini, M.D.
Robert W. Gibson, M.D.

Sanford Gifford, M.D.
Alan L. Gilchrist, Ph.D.
Barbara Jean Gillam, Ph.D.
Mark B. Ginsburg, Ph.D.
Amedeo Giorgi, Ph.D.
Abraham Givner, Ph.D.
Albert J. Glass, M.D.
David C. Glass, Ph.D.
Bernard C. Glueck, M.D.
Philip A. Goldberg, Ph.D.
Leo Goldberger, Ph.D.
Marvin R. Goldfried, Ph.D.
Marion Zucker Goldstein, M.D.
Lawrence Goodman, M.S.W.
Leonard D. Goodstein, Ph.D.
Frederick K. Goodwin, M.D.
Norma V. S. Graham, Ph.D.
Donald C. Greaves, M.D.
Alyce M. Green, B.A.
Elmer E. Green, Ph.D.
Barrie Sanford Greiff, M.D.
John H. Greist, M.D.
William W. Grings, Ph.D.
Martin Grotjahn, M.D.
Philip M. Groves, Ph.D.
Howard E. Gruber, Ph.D.
Gerald E. Gruen, Ph.D.
Henry U. Grunebaum, M.D.
J. P. Guilford, Ph.D.
Joan S. Guilford, Ph.D.
Harold O. Gulliksen, Ph.D.
Barry J. Gurland, M.R.C.P.
　(London), M.R.C.Psych.
Thomas G. Gutheil, M.D.
Arthur Gutman, Ph.D.
Karl L. Hakmiller, Ph.D.
Judy E. Hall, Ph.D.
David L. Hamilton, Ph.D.
Craig Haney, Ph.D., J.D.
Peggy Hanley-Hackenbruck,
　M.D.
Douglas B. Hansen, M.D.
Beatrice Harris, Ph.D.
Edward Harris, B.A.
Ross Harrison, Ph.D.
Peter Hartocollis, M.D.
Albert H. Hastorf, Ph.D.

William H. Hays, Ph.D.
William W. Haythorn, Ph.D.
Fritz Heider, Ph.D.
Madeline E. Heilman, Ph.D.
Alan Hein, Ph.D.
Joseph B. Hellige, Ph.D.
Robert Louis Helmreich, Ph.D.
Harry Helson, Ph.D.
Mary Henle, Ph.D.
Maurice Hershenson, Ph.D.
Harold Hiatt, M.D.
Elaine Hilberman, M.D.
John R. Hinrichs, Ph.D.
Ebbe Curtis Hoff, Ph.D., M.D.
Lois Wladis Hoffman, Ph.D.
Robert Hogan, Ph.D.
Dennis H. Holding, Ph.D.
Edwin P. Hollander, Ph.D.
Jack F. Hollis, Ph.D.
Wayne H. Holtzman, Ph.D.
Donald C. Hood, Ph.D.
Verne Bennett Horne, A.B.
Irwin A. Horowitz, Ph.D.
Mardi J. Horowitz, M.D.
Robert A. Horwitz, Ph.D.
C. I. Howarth, D.Phil. (Oxon.)
William C. Howell, Ph.D.
Barry H. Hughes, M.A.
Charles L. Hulin, Ph.D.
Portia Bell Hume, M.D.
John D. Hundleby, Ph.D.
Raymond G. Hunt, Ph.D.
Paul E. Huston, M.D.
Marvin A. Iverson, Ph.D.
Raymond L. Jackson, M.A.
Durand F. Jacobs, Ph.D.
Leo I. Jacobs, M.D.
Theodore J. Jacobs, M.D.
Lissy F. Jarvik, M.D.
Jerald M. Jellison, Ph.D.
M. Antoinette Jenkins, Ph.D.
George A. Jervis, Ph.D.
Ann I. Johnson, Ph.D.
Isaac Jolles, M.A.
Cindy Jones, Ph.D.
Edward E. Jones, Ph.D.
James M. Jones, Ph.D.

Stanley E. Jones, Ph.D.
Boaz Kahana, Ph.D.
Eva Kahana, Ph.D.
Edwin Kahn, Ph.D.
Edith Kaplan, Ph.D.
Ira T. Kaplan, Ph.D.
Stephen B. Karpman, M.D.
Irwin Katz, Ph.D.
Raymond A. Katzell, Ph.D.
Judith Kaufman, Ph.D.
Lloyd Kaufman, Ph.D.
Alan E. Kazdin, Ph.D.
Patricia Keith-Spiegel, Ph.D.
Henry Kellerman, Ph.D.
John M. Kennedy, Ph.D.
Geoffrey Keppel, Ph.D.
Beth Kerr, Ph.D.
M. Masud R. Khan, M.A.
Charles A. Kiesler, Ph.D.
Gregory A. Kimble, Ph.D.
Dorothy McBride Kipnis, Ph.D.
David Klahr, Ph.D.
Devra G. Kleiman, Ph.D.
Majorie H. Klein, Ph.D.
Thomas W. Klein, Ph.D.
Hans J. Kleinschmidt, M.D.
Peter H. Klopfer, Ph.D.
Richard P. Kluft, M.D.
Edward H. Knight, M.D.
Paul A. Kolers, Ph.D.
Bernard M. Kramer, Ph.D.
Beatrice J. Krauss, Ph.D.
Herbert H. Krauss, Ph.D.
Alan Kraut, Ph.D.
Kenneth Kressel, Ph.D.
Wolfgang Kretschmer, M.D.
Anton O. Kris, M.D.
Daniel M. Landers, Ph.D.
Harold A. Lando, Ph.D.
Robert J. Langs, M.D.
Donald G. Langsley, M.D.
Richard I. Lanyon, Ph.D.
Kathie G. Larsen, Ph.D.
Henry P. Laughlin, M.D., Sc.D.
Joseph C. LaVoie, Ph.D.
J. Wayne Lazar, Ph.D.
Richard S. Lazarus, Ph.D.

Robert L. Leahy, Ph.D.
Zigmond M. Lebensohn, M.D.
Sondra Leftoff, Ph.D.
Henry Leland, Ph.D.
Richard M. Lerner, Ph.D.
Alan I. Levenson, M.D.
Sidney Levin, M.D.
Harry Levinson, Ph.D.
Marguerite F. Levy, Ph.D.
Norman J. Levy, M.D.
Robert Paul Liberman, M.D.
Joseph D. Lichtenberg, M.D.
Robert M. Liebert, Ph.D.
Lewis P. Lipsitt, Ph.D.
Leopold Liss, M.D.
Susan A. Locke, Ph.D.
Gregory R. Lockhead, Ph.D.
Peter Loewenberg, Ph.D.
Frank A. Logan, Ph.D.
Karen L. Lombardi, Ph.D.
Harvey London, Ph.D.
Steven Regeser López, Ph.D.
Maurice Lorr, Ph.D.
Albert J. Lott, Ph.D.
Bernice Lott, Ph.D.
Reginald S. Lourie, M.D., M.Sc.D.
David Loye, Ph.D.
Elinore E. Lurie, Ph.D.
Dorothy E. McAllister, Ph.D.
Wallace R. McAllister, Ph.D.
Raymond J. McCall, Ph.D., Ph.D.
Robert B. McCall, Ph.D.
John B. McConahay, Ph.D.
John F. McDermott, Jr., M.D.
John Bourke McDevitt, M.D.
William J. McGuire, Ph.D.
Frank McKinney, Ph.D.
Ronald William McNichol, M.D.
Marion White McPherson, Ph.D.
Paul McReynolds, Ph.D.
John M. MacDonald, M.D.
Avram Mack, M.D.
Arthur C. MacKinney, Ph.D.
John F. Maher, M.D.
Michael J. Mahoney, Ph.D.
James C. Mancuso, Ph.D.
Irwin M. Marcus, M.D.

Elliott L. Markoff, M.D.
Elizabeth Warren Markson, Ph.D.
Ronald G. Marteniuk, Ed.D.
Rainer Martens, Ph.D.
Christina Maslach, Ph.D.
Aaron S. Mason, M.D.
Michael J. Mattioli, Ph.D.
Bernard Mausner, Ph.D.
Gene R. Medinnus, Ph.D.
Robert D. Mehlman, M.D.
John H. Meier, Ph.D.
William W. Meissner, S.J., M.D.
Roy W. Menninger, M.D.
Frank J. Menolascino, M.D.
David R. Metcalf, M.D.
Herbert H. Meyer, Ph.D.
Roger E. Meyer, M.D.
Charles D. Michener, Ph.D.
Henry H. W. Miles, M.D.
Steven M. Mirin, M.D.
Walter Mischel, Ph.D.
Henryk Misiak, Ph.D.
Arnold H. Modell, M.D.
George Moeller, Ph.D.
John A. Molino, Ph.D.
John Money, Ph.D.
Rolf H. Monge, Ph.D.
Gary Robert Morrow, Ph.D.
Julian P. Morrow, M.A.
Robert S. Morrow, Ph.D.
Howard A. Moss, Ph.D.
David J. Muller, M.D.
Bernard I. Murstein, Ph.D.
Herman Musaph, M.D.,
　F.R.C.Psych.
Hyman L. Muslin, M.D.
Paul H. Mussen, Ph.D.
David F. Musto, M.D.
Paul D. Nelson, Ph.D.
S. Joseph Nemetz, M.D.
Peter B. Neubauer, M.D.
Karl M. Newell, Ph.D.
Lottie M. Newman, B.A.
Russell Newman, J.D., Ph.D.
Clyde Everett Noble, Ph.D.
Joseph M. Notterman, Ph.D.

Jum C. Nunnally, Ph.D.
Maureen O'Connor, J.D.
K. Daniel O'Leary, Ph.D.
Thomas H. Ollendick, Ph.D.
Marvin K. Opler, Ph.D.
Jesse Orlansky, Ph.D.
Anna Ornstein, M.D.
Paul H. Ornstein, M.D.
Lida Orzeck, Ph.D.
Edna O'Shaughnessy, B.Phil.
David W. O'Shea, Ph.D.
Asher R. Pacht, Ph.D.
David S. Palermo, Ph.D.
Stanley R. Palombo, M.D.
Robert Paluck, Ph.D.
Erwin Randolph Parson, Ph.D.
H. McIlvaine Parsons, Ph.D.
Darhl M. Pedersen, Ph.D.
Charles A. Perfetti, Ph.D.
Paul A. Pilkonis, Ph.D.
Robert Plutchik, Ph.D.
George H. Pollock, M.D.,
　Ph.D.
Erving Polster, Ph.D.
Miriam Polster, Ph.D.
John A. Popplestone, Ph.D.
Karl H. Pribram, Ph.D., M.D.
Patricia N. Prinz, Ph.D.
Sally Provence, M.D.
Albert I. Rabin, Ph.D.
John D. Rainer, M.D.
Craig T. Ramey, Ph.D.
Patricia M. Raskin, Ph.D.
Richard G. Ratliff, Ph.D.
Bertram H. Raven, Ph.D.
Diane Frances Reardon, Ph.D.
Joel Redfield, Ph.D.
Pamela C. Regan, Ph.D.
William R. Reich, Ph.D.
F. Theodore Reid, Jr., M.D.
Manuel Riklan, Ph.D.
Lucille B. Ritvo, Ph.D.
Samuel Ritvo, M.D.
Trevor W. Robbins, Ph.D.
Elizabeth Anne Robertson-
　Tchabo, Ph.D.

Charles Edward Robins, S.T.D.,
　Ph.D.
Daniel Nicholas Robinson, Ph.D.
Robert L. Robinson, M.A.
Irvin Rock, Ph.D.
James P. Rodgers, Ph.D.
Milton Rokeach, Ph.D.
May Ethel Romm, M.D.
Maj-Britt Rosenbaum, M.D.
Max Rosenbaum, Ph.D.
Miriam B. Rosenthal, M.D.
Norman Rosenzweig, M.D.
Lee Ross, Ph.D.
Mathew Ross, M.D.
Ruth Ross, M.A.
Julian B. Rotter, Ph.D.
Donald K. Routh, Ph.D.
James E. Royce, S.J., Ph.D.
Donald B. Rubin, Ph.D.
David L. Rubinfine, M.D.
Bertram A. Ruttenberg, M.D.
John P. Sabini, Ph.D.
Barbara Jacquelyn Sahakian,
　A.B.
William S. Sahakian, Ph.D.
Bruce D. Sales, Ph.D., J.D.
Jonathan Sandoval, Ph.D.
Allan Sapolsky, Ph.D.
S. Stansfield Sargent, Ph.D.
Robert A. Savitt, M.D.
Earl S. Schaefer, Ph.D.
Marshall D. Schechter, M.D.
Albert E. Scheflen, M.D.
Karl E. Scheibe, Ph.D.
Richard L. Schiefelbusch, Ph.D.
Elliot Schildkrout, M.D.
Herbert J. Schlesinger, Ph.D.
Arthur H. Schmale, M.D.
Gertrude Schmeidler, Ph.D.
Richard A. Schmidt, Ph.D.
Jerome M. Schneck, M.D.
Marie-Louise Schoelly, M.D.
Clarence G. Schultz, M.D.
Duane P. Schultz, Ph.D.
Hans-Henning Schulze,
　Dr.Rer.Nat.

John J. Schwab, M.D.
John Paul Scott, Ph.D.
Melvin Seeman, Ph.D.
Hanna Segal, M.B., Ch.B.,
   F.R.C.Psych.
Martin E. P. Seligman, Ph.D.
Elvin V. Semrad, M.D.
Frank T. Severin, S.J., M.A.
Virginia Staudt Sexton, Ph.D.
Alvin P. Shapiro, M.D.
Arthur K. Shapiro, M.D.
Elaine Shapiro, Ph.D.
Evelyn Shaw, Ph.D.
Jack Edward Sherman, Ph.D.
Murray H. Sherman, Ph.D.
Edwin S. Shneidman, Ph.D.
Franklin C. Shontz, Ph.D.
Richard A. Shweder, Ph.D.
Miguel Siguan, Ph.D.
Reuben J. Silver, Ph.D.
Rune J. Simeonsson, Ph.D.
Marianne L. Simmel, Ph.D.
Bennett Simon, M.D.
Jerome L. Singer, Ph.D.
Melvin Sinowitz, Ph.D.
Gary N. Siperstein, Ph.D.
Faye D. Siskel, Ph.D.
Florence R. Skelly, A.B.
Theodore M. Skolnik, M.A.
Yitzchok Skolnik, B.A.
Joseph W. Slap, M.D.
Arnold M. Small, Ph.D.
Charles Philip Smith, Ph.D.
Edward E. Smith, Ph.D.
Judith L. Smith, Ph.D.
Richard W. Smith, Ph.D.
Charles W. Socarides, M.D.
Albert J. Solnit, M.D.
Leonard Solomon, Ph.D.
Richard L. Solomon, Ph.D.
James E. Spar, M.D.
Charles Paul Sparks, M.A.
Donald E. Spiegel, Ph.D.
Charles D. Spielberger, Ph.D.
Vann Spruiell, M.D.
Jeanne Spurlock, M.D.

Leo Srole, Ph.D.
Ross Stagner, Ph.D.
Calvert Stein, M.D.
Donald G. Stein, Ph.D.
George E. Stelmach, Ed.D.
Walter G. Stephan, Ph.D.
John A. Stern, Ph.D.
David A. Stevens, Ph.D.
Tommy T. Stigall, Ph.D.
Allen W. Stokes, Ph.D.
Robert J. Stoller, M.D.
William E. Stone, M.D.
Arnold E. Stoper, Ph.D.
Edward M. Stricker, Ph.D.
George Stricker, Ph.D.
Charles F. Stroebel, Ph.D., M.D.
Hans H. Strupp, Ph.D.
Peter Suedfeld, Ph.D.
John J. Sullivan, Ph.D.
John D. Sutherland, C.B.E.,
   F.R.C.P.E.
Brian Sutton-Smith, Ph.D.
Clifford H. Swensen, Ph.D.
Robert A. Swoap, Ph.D.
Arnold S. Tannenbaum, Ph.D.
Allan Tasman, M.D.
Edward H. Taylor, Ph.D.
Shelley E. Taylor, Ph.D.
Abraham Tesser, Ph.D.
Alexander Thomas, M.D.
David R. Thomas, Ph.D.
Kenneth W. Thomas, Ph.D.
Albert S. Thompson, Ph.D.
Nicholas S. Thompson, Ph.D.
William C. Thompson, M.D.
William R. Thompson, Ph.D.
James L. Titchener, M.D.
David M. Todd, Ph.D.
David A. Tomb, M.D.
Donald A. Topmiller, Ph.D.
Edison J. Trickett, Ph.D.
Don A. Trumbo, Ph.D.
Eugene E. Trunnell, M.D.
Read D. Tuddenham, Ph.D.
Geoffrey F. W. Turner, M.S.
Janet Turner, M.S.

Thomas E. Twitchell, M.D.
Robert L. Tyson, M.D.
Julius E. Uhlaner, Ph.D.
Montague Ullman, M.D.
Richard Umansky, M.D.
J. Thomas Ungerleider, M.D.
William R. Uttal, Ph.D.
Steven G. Vandenberg, J.D.,
   Ph.D.
Adrian van Kaam, Ph.D.
John Van Praag, M.A.
Thom Verhave, Ph.D.
Joseph Veroff, Ph.D.
W. Edgar Vinacke, Ph.D.
Charles William Wahl, M.D.
Charles J. Walker, Ph.D.
Edward L. Walker, Ph.D.
Douglas M. Wardell, Ph.D.
Judith A. Waters, Ph.D.
Luke S. Watson, Jr., Ph.D.
Wayne S. Watson, M.S.
Wilse B. Webb, Ph.D.
Charles P. Webel, Ph.D.
John J. Weber, M.D.
Henry Wechsler, Ph.D.
Annemarie P. Weil, M.D.
Herbert Weiner, M.D.
Irving B. Weiner, Ph.D.
Edward M. Weinshel, M.D.
Justin L. Weiss, Ph.D.
A. T. Welford, Sc.D. (Cantab.)
Charles Wenar, Ph.D.
Marion A. Wenger, Ph.D.
Frank Wesley, Ph.D., Dr. Phil.
Jack C. Westman, M.D.
Robert B. White, M.D.
Roy M. Whitman, M.D.
Robert A. Wicklund, Ph.D.
Arthur N. Wiens, Ph.D.
Jerry S. Wiggins, Ph.D.
Edwin P. Willems, Ph.D.
Leslie R. T. Williams, Ph.D.
Richard H. Willis, Ph.D.
Sherry L. Willis, Ph.D.
G. Terence Wilson, Ph.D.
Glenn D. Wilson, Ph.D.

Wilma A. Winnick, Ph.D.
Earl G. Witenberg, M.D.
Michele Andrisin Wittig, Ph.D.
Eric D. Wittkower, M.D.
Milton Wittman, D.S.W.
Joachim F. Wohlwill, Ph.D.
Lewis R. Wolberg, M.D.
Ernest S. Wolf, M.D.

Benjamin B. Wolman, Ph.D.
David M. Wright, M.D.
Melvin D. Yahr, M.D.
Daniel Yankelovich, M.A.
Leon J. Yarrow, Ph.D.
Richard M. Yarvis, M.D.
Paul Thomas Young, Ph.D.
Abraham Zaleznik, D.C.S.

Alvin F. Zander, Ph.D.
Steven Zavodnick, M.D.
David Zeaman, Ph.D.
Edward F. Zigler, Ph.D.
Philip G. Zimbardo, Ph.D.
Carl B. Zuckerman, Ph.D.

· A ·

Abortion: Psychiatric Aspects

E. Smith reported the findings of a follow-up study that was conducted of 125 women who had contacted a problem-pregnancy counseling service in Missouri, where abortion had not been legalized. The 80 women studied ranged from lower to upper class; the majority were single, white, Protestant (27% were Catholic), and not initially psychiatrically disturbed. At one year or more postabortion, their psychological state appeared related to a number of factors, particularly age (most of those who had experienced moderate to severe psychological discomfort were teenagers) and ambivalence about the decision to obtain an abortion. Conversely, many of the women viewed the abortion experience as maturing and growth producing.

A committee chaired by Dr. Mildred Mitchell-Bateman and appointed by the National Academy of Sciences to make an objective analysis of available abortion facts (1975) found no measurable increase in mental upsets provoked by abortion. Other pertinent findings of the committee: (1) an estimate of postabortion psychosis ranged from 0.2 to 0.4 per 1,000 legal abortions; (2) postabortion depression and guilt feelings were usually mild and of short duration; (3) one in four women obtaining abortions were married; and (4) one-third of the women were younger than 20; another one-third were between the ages of 20 and 25.

The subject of abortion continues to be a controversial matter, as are the findings pertaining to postabortion psychological effects. The most common negative effects—depression, guilt, and anxiety—have usually been transient. Often, psychiatric symptoms occur in women with a history of previous emotional instability. In such instances it cannot be ruled out that the psychiatric symptoms would have appeared in this group if the pregnancy had continued to full term.

Jeanne Spurlock

Abraham, Karl (1877–1925)

Abraham, the first German psychoanalyst, was an outstanding contributor to psychoanalytic literature and an organizer of German and international psychoanalysis. In 1910 he founded the first psychoanalytic society and institute in Berlin. Abraham was a pioneer in the study of libido development, character formation, schizophrenia, manic-depressive psychosis, alcoholism, and drug addiction. He was the first to describe the levels of mental development, which he divided into oral, anal, and phallic phases.

Martin Grotjahn

Abreaction and Catharsis: Freud's Theory before 1897

Sigmund Freud's definition of the cathartic method of treating hysteria appeared in a short encyclopedia article in 1924: "The cathartic method was the immediate predecessor of psycho-analysis, and in spite of every extension of experience and of every modification of theory, is still contained within it as its nucleus." In this same paper, Freud shared responsibility with Josef Breuer for the term *catharsis*, saying "the authors gave this procedure the name 'catharsis' (purging, setting free of a strangulated affect)." But throughout Freud's portions of the

Studies on Hysteria (1895/1955), and in all of his historical accounts of the development of analysis, the term was carefully attributed to Breuer as "Breuer's cathartic method," "Breuer's technique of investigation under hypnosis," and "Breuer's method of treating hysterical symptoms by an investigation and an abreaction of them under hypnosis."

In their first use of "catharsis" and "abreaction," still in inverted commas as if they were quoting each other, Breuer and Freud meant the adequate discharge of painful emotions at the time of the original traumatic event. Later, in their *Preliminary Communication* and in Freud's final chapter in the *Studies on Hysteria*, both terms were used more easily and frequently to indicate the therapeutic methods by which these repressed memories and "strangulated affects" were recovered under "light hypnosis." Together, they made a careful distinction between the "cathartic method," in which hypnosis is used to penetrate the hysterical amnesia and reconstruct the traumatic events, and the use of hypnosis by Jean-Martin Charcot and their other predecessors to remove the hysterical symptoms by suggestion.

In rereading *Studies on Hysteria* today, one is invariably struck by two contrasting impressions. First, one is reminded of how many elements of later psychoanalytic theory were already foreshadowed in rudimentary but recognizable form: a dynamic theory of repression, a concept of unconscious forces seeking expression, of resistance and defense in the therapeutic process, and a recognition of the "personal relationship" between patient and physician, then still perceived as an interfering factor. But one is also reminded, as in the preanalytic history of catharsis, how close the thinking of both Breuer and Freud was to the ancient traditions of Hippocratic medicine, and to its still earlier antecedents in religious and magical concepts of ritual defilement and purification, sin and atonement, and the exorcism of evil spirits from the disordered mind. Thus Breuer and Freud, like Aristotle before them, chose the general term *catharsis* and gave it a specialized psychological meaning, derived partly from its everyday meaning of "cleansing" and partly from its medical sense of removing alien or pathogenic matter. Freud wrote figuratively about the relief of symptoms by the cathartic method as the removal of a "foreign body," and Breuer compared the "talking away" of symptoms to the Roman Catholic confessional.

Two final questions remain to be answered: (1) How much does Breuer and Freud's term *catharsis* owe to Aristotle? and (2) Is our loose, ubiquitous everyday use of "catharsis" in nonscientific writing derived from Aristotle, Breuer, or Freud, or a popular mixture of all? As to the second question, in its current, all-purpose usage, *catharsis* has been applied to everything from a political outcome to a satisfactory sexual experience. There is also a proliferation of popular psychotherapies derived from oversimplifications and perversions of psychoanalytic concepts and resembling the anti-intellectual healing cults that arose during the last centuries of Greco-Roman civilization. But the first question is of concern because, it has been pointed out, Jacob Bernays, a prominent Aristotelian scholar, was the uncle of Freud's wife, Martha Bernays.

Sanford Gifford

Abstinence: The Psychoanalytic Rule

In Sigmund Freud's first statements the rule of abstinence was aimed at the danger that analysts might attempt to gratify the patient's transference wishes rather than interpret their substitutive nature. To respond with some kind of gratification or rejection rather than interpret the transference neurosis would not only diminish the patient's motivation for treatment but would also subvert the basic purpose of psychoanalysis.

The rule of abstinence is closely connected with the concept of the analyst's neutrality, the nonjudgmental and nonpreferential way of listening and responding that permits full expression of the patient's story. It is also connected with the analyst's relative anonymity, silence, and location outside the patient's view, all of which contribute to the development of the transference as much as they provide conditions for interpretation and resolution.

From the first, Freud emphasized the sympathetic understanding and interest required of the analyst in order to enlist the patient's cooperation: "The patient's cooperation becomes a personal sacrifice, which must be compensated by some substitute for love. The trouble taken by the physician and his friendliness have to suffice for such a substitute" (Breuer & Freud 1895, p. 301).

At times, the rule of abstinence has been unwisely used as the rationale for restrictive demands placed upon the patient outside the analysis. Where "dilution" or acting out threaten to interfere with development or resolution of the transference, it is more profitable to view them as violations of the rule of free association, both as substitute expressions and as resistances, and to base recommendations to the patient for restrictions on that premise.

Anton O. Kris

Acculturation

The acculturation process can be viewed within the broad framework of crosscultural psychology. The assimilation of a newcomer (i.e., an immigrant or sojourner) into a foreign culture is highly dependent on the development of understanding between the recent arrival and his or her hosts. Crucial to the development of such understanding is the effective exchange of information between the new arrival and his hosts, that is, intercultural communication.

The difficulty that a newcomer commonly encounters during the assimilation process is sometimes referred to as "culture shock." Problems in a newcomer's social-psychological adjustment (i.e., culture shock) occur when she is unable to communicate with her hosts. Not only is there a lack of understanding between the newcomer and people of the host culture, but there are misunderstandings that tend to result in conflict, withdrawal, hostile acts, and other nonadaptive behaviors.

The assimilation of the newcomer in the host culture is affected by (1) situational factors in the host culture, (2) background factors of the newcomer, and (3) the learned cognitions and behaviors of the newcomer.

Kenneth H. David

Achievement Motivation: Development

Achievement motivation can be defined as a need or motive to excel in a wide variety of situations. When the motive is aroused, it is expressed in driving energy directed toward attaining excellence, getting ahead, improving on previous work, doing things better, faster, and more efficiently, and finding solutions to difficult problems that require ingenuity and persistence. People with high achievement motivation generally are self-confident individuals who function best in situations where they assume personal responsibility and can control what happens to them. They set challenging but realistic goals demanding maximum effort; they are not satisfied with the automatic success that comes from easy goals, nor do they try to do the impossible. They take pride in their accomplishments and derive pleasure in striving for the challenging goals that they set for themselves.

The answer to the origin and development of achievement motivation lies in the style of parenting for any one individual and, more generally, in the styles of parenting across cultures. Mothers of highly motivated children, in comparison with mothers of less-motivated children, insist more on autonomous functioning during their offspring's early years: they reward this independence with more affection and recognition, and while they insist on observance of rules earlier, these rules are not as numerous as for children with low motivation. In short, the greater the child-centered self-reliance, the higher the achievement motivation.

Thomas H. Ollendick

Achievement Tests

In educational settings, achievement tests have assumed at least eight functions: (1) to aid in the assignment of grades that are based upon standardized and objective measurements of learning; (2) to identify students who need remediation because of educational deficiencies, and to measure improvement once remediation is undertaken; (3) to facilitate learning for all students by giving periodic feedback regarding areas of strength and weakness;

(4) to assist placement and classification of students in educational settings where homogenous grouping is used or where there are special enrichment, acceleration, or remediation programs; (5) to help teachers to gauge teaching methods and content to the needs and abilities of students; (6) to evaluate the effectiveness of teaching; (7) to assist the counseling of students in educational and vocational planning; and (8) to select students for admission to colleges, graduate schools, professional schools, and a wide variety of jobs.

The classification of achievement measures includes a differentiation between survey and diagnostic tests. The former assess general levels of achievement in some area of study, usually reading or arithmetic. The latter analyze more specifically the strengths and weaknesses in knowledge and skills that contribute to the overall level of performance.

Diagnostic tests vary in at least three respects: whether they are administered on a group or individual level; the number and range of grade levels tested; and the number of subtest scores yielded. Usually, the most intensive diagnostic measures are individually administered and provide a multifaceted performance profile. The largest number of diagnostic tests measure reading and language skills, such as comprehension, vocabulary, auditory discrimination, syllabication, and reading rate.

While originally designed for educational purposes, achievement tests have been developed to evaluate mastery of highly specialized information and skills. However, A. Anastasi (1988) maintains that the achievement tests are rather related to developing abilities than to achievement.

Susan A. Locke

Achievement Tests in Psychology and Education

Validity

In many cases, achievement tests can be used to predict some later form of success, such as using high school achievement tests to predict success in college. However, forecasting future events is not their major purpose. The worth of achievement tests is determined mainly by content validity, not by predictive validity or construct validity. Rather than determine content validity after tests are constructed, validity should be ensured by the plan and procedures of construction. To take a simple example, content for an achievement test in spelling for fourth-grade students could be obtained from a random sampling of words in specified textbooks, followed by a sensible procedure for transforming the words into test form.

Types of Achievement Tests

Achievement tests can be classified in three important categories. First, the tests are categorized in terms of the topics that they cover. Tests are available for a myriad of topics, ranging from knowledge of Hebrew to proficiency in shorthand. A second classification is construction—whether a test is highly standardized or is constructed informally. Examples of informally constructed achievement tests are classroom examinations that teachers prepare for their students. Although such tests may be valid for particular purposes, they usually are not based on any formal research, and their validity is limited to the particular teacher and particular unit of instruction. On the other extreme are the highly standardized achievement tests produced by commercial testing firms. A great deal of work goes into the components of the test to ensure content validity, including (1) interviewing knowledgeable people about appropriate content, (2) formulating an explicit statement of the intended content, (3) performing statistical methods of item analysis to select the best items, (4) gathering norms for thousands of students, (5) careful writing of items, and (6) careful composition of detailed test manuals.

Among highly standardized achievement tests, a third important classification concerns the breadth of content coverage. On one extreme, there are standardized, commercially distributed tests for measuring progress in individual school topics, such as high school chemistry. At the other extreme, comprehensive test series are available for measuring overall progress in schools, industrial training, government work, and other areas. Most widely used in this respect are the comprehensive tests that measure overall achievement in the elementary school grades.

A typical series for the fourth grade would contain separate tests for reading comprehension, reading speed, arithmetic, mechanics of expression, and language usage. Jum C. Nunnally (1972) discusses the relative advantages and disadvantages of tests for special topics as opposed to comprehensive tests.

Professional Uses

Achievement tests are helpful to classroom teachers. They facilitate the grouping of students for instruction into several levels in terms of overall ability. The members of each group work together, are provided instruction tailored to their level of overall ability, and are given readings and exercises that may differ from those given to students at other levels. Another classroom use is in planning day-to-day instruction. Regardless of the educational setting, experienced teachers have on many occasions had the experience of completing a unit of instruction and then later having a new class of students starting fresh with the subject. How well have the students mastered their previous training? If comprehensive achievement tests were administered before the instruction got under way, the results would go a long way toward providing the teacher with the necessary information to deal effectively both with the class as a whole and with individual students.

A clinical psychologist will find test scores useful in diagnosing the problems of an apparently bright boy who is performing far below average in school. If the student is average in most school topics but far below average in one or more of them, such as reading or mathematics, in-depth achievement tests in those particular topics might provide considerable information helpful to the clinical psychologist.

A neurologist will find achievement test scores informative with respect to a brain-damaged teenager. For example, if the teenager has no difficulty in reading aloud but has very low scores in tests concerning memory for what had been read previously, this can provide hints as to the locus and extent of brain damage.

A psychiatrist can make use of achievement tests with a child who has become severely disturbed as the result of a broken home. For example, if the child performed well above average in the fourth and fifth grades, but his scores have dropped markedly in the two years following the breakup of the home, the psychiatrist would have useful information in working with the child and his parents.

Jum C. Nunnally

Acting Out

The term *acting out* was first used by Sigmund Freud in his essay *Remembering, Repeating and Working Through* (1914), though the concept of repeating, instead of recalling, arose in his reflections on the Dora case (1905). Freud described acting out, in contradistinction to remembering, as the compelling urge to repeat the forgotten past, revived within the analytic setting, by unconsciously reliving repressed emotional experiences and transferring these experiences onto the analyst and to all other aspects of the current life situation.

Acting out frequently is an attempt to turn passivity into activity in order to master the affects related to passive and dependent situations, such as traumatic experiences of infancy and early childhood. This disposition to activity is a prominent feature of personality types called "acting-out characters," who seem especially predisposed to acting out. Their difficulties appear to be related to developmental ego disturbances, reflecting the effects of chronic and acute traumatic situations in which they were passive participants.

Acting out always offers the potential for serving as a resistance and may occur to some degree in every analysis. It is fostered by the "tilted" relationship between the analyst and the analysand that is structured into the analytic situation. The analytic situation facilitates acting out by its characteristic of abstinence and the basic rule of free association.

Of the three techniques known for the management of acting out—interpretation, prohibition, and strengthening the ego—interpretation is by far the most useful. In patients with insufficient ego strength, a properly timed interpretation of transference needs and anxieties related to both libidinal and aggressive impulses and to fears of passivity and helplessness can be quite effective both in reducing the acting out and in facilitating insight.

Norman Atkins

Acting Out: Post-Freudian Approach

The patient's attitude toward the analyst in the analytic work may be modeled after attitudes toward authority figures in the past. When acting out occurs in relationship to the analysis, it is termed acting out within the transference neurosis.

P. Greenacre (1950) suggests oral fixation and high narcissistic need play an important role in the eti-ology of acting out.

As an analysis progresses and resistance develops, acting out may increase outside analysis, and the resistance may not be as accessible for interpretation by the analyst in the course of working through. Should a major life change be involved in acting out, it may produce serious resistance to the analytic work.

Anna Freud (1936) has suggested, "The ego continues to function freely or if it makes a common cause with the id and simply carries out its behest, there is little opportunity for endopsychical displacement and the bringing to bear of influence from without." She notes that repetitive acting out cannot be analyzed; it inhibits dealing with the underlying structural material and prevents successful completion of an analysis.

Alan B. Cooper

Activity Drive/Deprivation

The concept of an activity drive has been posited to account for behavior that occurs in the apparent absence of any other drive. Thus, for example, a sexually immature rat is observed to run in the revolving wheel even though food and water are freely available and all other environmental conditions seem to be optimal for survival. If it is assumed that drive or need is a necessary antecedent of all activity, the conclusion suggested is that there must be an activity drive or need to be active to account for the behavior.

Results of activity-deprivation experiments are presented as validation of this concept. Most often these involve the recording of behavior in the wheel or other device traditionally said to measure "general activity." Since increases of general activity are usually found to accompany states said to be characterized by high drive—for example, during prolonged food deprivation—the logical extension is that if there is a drive for activity, deprivation of the opportunity to be active should be followed by increased running.

Frank W. Finger

Activity, Spontaneous

The term *spontaneous activity* refers to the preponderance of normal behavior that appears to the casual observer to spring from unidentifiable internal sources. The reference is better identified by the neutral term *general activity*. The concept appears most frequently in discussions of biological rhythms and motivation.

With respect to motivation, "spontaneous activity" is a convenient label for behaviors not easily identified as directly instrumental to attainment of specific goals, but which nevertheless are affected by motivating events.

The concept of biological rhythm is founded on the assumption that total activity varies regularly over time in response to internal events. Spontaneous activity in this instance is some measure taken as an index of total activity. In infrahumans, distance run in an activity wheel, amount of motion transmitted to home cage mounting (stabilimeter), and total distance traversed in an open field are a few such indices. The validity of any partial measure representing the whole should be demonstrated rather than presumed. For example, C. Cofer and M. H. Appley (1964) note that "measures from the activity wheel and stabilimeter are neither highly correlated nor similarly affected by presumed common causal events."

Methodologically, the techniques developed to measure spontaneous activity have been important to the study of motivation for their presumed special characteristics: continuous availability for measurement over extended periods; high data rate; sensitivity to most kinds of motivating events; and occurrence as a natural behavior that does not have to be formally taught. These special characteristics also make spontaneous activity an important tool in attempts to identify the neural substrate common to all motivating events.

George Moeller

Act Psychology

Act psychology is best seen in contrast to German content psychology, which emanated from Wilhelm Wundt and his students at the University of Leipzig. While the focal point of content psychology was mental elements (sensation, feeling, etc.), *Aktpsychologie* (psychology of act) focused on the act of intending; that is, reference to objects was seen in terms of underlying psychic processes. The act psychologists saw experience as a way of acting, but the content psychologists (or "structuralists," as they came to be known) treated experience as a structure.

Brentano's Act Psychology
In his *Psychologie vom Empirischen Standpunkt* (Psychology from an empirical point of view; 1874), Franz Clemens Brentano views phenomena as active; that is, as the acts of an individual. By regarding mental processes as acts, he introduced act psychology. The three primary mental acts are sensing (ideation), judging, and feeling. For Brentano, intentionality acquires importance because without the intended object of thought, there can be no thinking; there is no desire without its object. Therefore, Brentano characterizes the mental as a "reference to a content" or "direction upon an object."

Von Ehrenfels's Gestalt Qualities
Brentano's pupil, Christian Freiherr von Ehrenfels (1859–1932), inspired by Ernst Mach, developed a theory of form qualities in his classic paper, *Über Gestaltqualitäten* (On gestalt qualities; 1890). Accepting form qualities as genuine perceptual contents, he observes that the same melody is perceptible even when transposed into a different key with a different group of notes; "If the melody were nothing else that the sum of notes, different melodies would have to be produced." New qualities or syntheses arise while the gestalt remains the same, notwithstanding variations of the elements of which it is composed.

William S. Sahakian

Act, Pure Stimulus

Pure stimulus act is a concept used by Clark L. Hull in his attempts to develop an S-R (stimulus-response) account of foresight and purpose. The reference is to the r_g–s_g mechanism by which fractional anticipatory goal responses (r_g) are capable of eliciting some sort of representation of the goal (s_g). More specifically, r_g is a pure stimulus act, because it has no effect upon the environment and its only purpose appears to be that of eliciting s_g. Occasionally Hull uses the concept to refer to other behavior whose only function is to provide informative stimulation.

Gregory A. Kimble

Adaptation-Level (AL) Theory of Motivation

The theory of adaptation level (AL) provides a natural frame of reference for the explanation of the chief phenomena of motivation, a concept that has been assigned many contradictory roles. It is sometimes regarded as an external, sometimes as an internal, source of behavior. Distinctions have been made between primary and secondary, innate and learned, extrinsic and intrinsic, organic and social sources of motivation. It has been said that it is necessary to initiate behavior and also that it has to be reduced to make learning possible. According to some authors, motivators are highly specific; according to others, all stimulation is motivating. A theory of motivation must provide for these meanings of the concept, or at least for the nontrivial phenomena to which they refer.

Because all stimuli, almost without exception, can be ordered on continua having positive, negative, and indifferent zones, it follows that the concept of level applies equally well to sensory, affective, cognitive, and motivational behavior. With recent emphasis on the role of contextual stimuli in such different fields as memory, achievement motivation, and communication, it is evident that the concept of AL applies to verbal and cognitive stimuli, as well as to effects of physical stimuli. Tying contextual effects to ALs defined as weighted by log or arithmetic means makes possible quantitative evaluation of their contributions to level. Reference to contextual and residual stimuli without quantitative specification leaves these important determinants of behavior in the vague qualitative domain of so many psychological terms.

Motivation does not rise or fall at a constant rate, nor does it necessarily remain constant over long periods of time. It waxes and wanes and is subject to changes in goal objects. The social, as well as organic and physiological, bases of motivations have been recognized by many writers. The influence of background and residual factors in the operation of physiological factors is now becoming better understood. We now know that the expression of sex, eating habits, and achievement motivation can be socially conditioned. The stud will often not perform in unfamiliar surroundings, and food may be rejected under improper illumination. In such cases, there is an interplay of focal, contextual, and residual factors recognized in AL theory.

Harry Helson

Adaptive Behavior Measurement

Adaptive behavior was first introduced as a classification dimension in the area of mental retardation in 1959, when the American Association of Mental Deficiency (AAMD) published its *Manual on Terminology and Classification in Mental Retardation* (Heber 1959).

In 1977, the AAMD adopted the following definition of adaptive behavior: "The effectiveness or degree with which an individual meets the standards of personal independence and social responsibility expected for an age and cultural group" (Grossman 1977, p. 11).

State departments, agencies, and programs have begun to develop their own checklists, inventories, and other types of scales in an attempt to measure adaptive behavior through the use of rapid screening tools. There has also been a flow of research and some discussion of those efforts, as well as continued research by the authors of the original scales.

Adaptation is represented by three behavioral formations:

1. Independent functioning, defined as the ability to successfully accomplish those tasks or activities demanded by the community in terms of survival demands for that community and in terms of expectations for specific age groups.
2. Personal responsibility, defined as both the willingness of individuals to accomplish those critical tasks they are able to accomplish (generally under some supervision) and their ability to assume individual responsibility for personal behavior. This ability is reflected in decision making and choice of behavior.
3. Social responsibility, defined as the ability of the individual to accept responsibility as a member of a community group and to carry out appropriate behaviors in terms of group expectations. This is reflected in levels of conformity, social adjustment, and emotional maturity. It is further analyzed in terms of the acceptance of some level of civic responsibility leading to complete or partial economic independence.

The main criterion of adaptive behavior for the mentally retarded is whether the patient's behavior can be tolerated by the community. If it can, the individual is able to survive and, in some instances, even to succeed. Such an individual does not need to be considered retarded regardless of the level of intellectual or academic functioning. Conversely, failing to demonstrate appropriate coping strategies, and so becoming a constant annoyance to those on whom a person is most dependent, often means failing to function successfully in the community. The patient in this situation may require care in a more specialized setting.

Henry Leland

Adler, Alfred (1870–1937)

Adler was associated with Sigmund Freud from 1902 to 1911. He was the editor of the *Psychoanalytic Journal*, and in 1910 he was the president of the Psychoanalytic Society. After leaving the Psychoanalytic Society in 1911, Adler founded the Society for Free Psychoanalytic Research, later renamed the Society for Individual Psychology.

Expanding the idea of "organ inferiority and its compensation," Adler developed the theory that it was the feeling of inferiority, which every newborn infant can be said to have, that compels a striving for mastery, called by Adler "striving for superiority." Adler's idea was that this natural striving for better adaptation was the driving force in human life. According to Adler, heredity, environment, and experiences are the only available materials from which the child constructs his unique, individual personality. Adler called his personality theory "individual psychology."

Adler continued to develop his theory and added the concept of "social interest." This concept implies the feeling of being at one with people, of being part and parcel of the community, of belonging and being co-responsible for the welfare of individuals in one's society and in the world. Social interest exists as a potential in everyone, but it has to be cultivated in the child in order to flower. The degree to which social interest has developed is the surest and, perhaps, the only true measure of the mental health of an individual.

Kurt A. Adler

Adler's Theory

Alfred Adler's individual psychology is a cognitive ego psychology. Its basic assumption is, "Life is movement, which must endlessly strive for a better adaptation to the environment." Adler assumed that the striving for better adaptation to the environment is a constant quality of all life. This means that all living creatures strive to satisfy all their needs; that they strive for comfort when they feel uncomfortable; that they strive for better security when they feel insecure; for orientation when they feel disoriented;

and so on. Any failure in this attempt at adaptation is experienced as a feeling of inadequacy, of inferiority, of being in an unsatisfactory situation—and the individual, straining all its available functions, will go to any length to establish or reestablish a situation or a position of satisfaction, of being well adapted, of superiority. The child uses her heredity, instincts, and physical and social environment as building materials to construct her personality according to an individual perception of all these factors. In order to escape feelings of inferiority, generated by difficulty in achieving a better adaptation, the child constructs for herself a goal of ideal adaptation, toward which all thinking, wishing, and acting is directed; in this way she creates an idealized goal of greatness, perfection, and superiority. By constantly repeating what she deems to be the best method toward ideal adaptation, she develops a lifestyle that will characterize her for the rest of her life and which is comparatively fixed by the age of four or five. Stressing his ego psychology, Adler wrote, "More important than predisposition, environment, and objective experience is their subjective evaluation," and further, "We do not think objectively, but in accordance with our goal and style of life that we have created."

Instincts have been in any case greatly weakened in humans, since they have become a hindrance for developing brainpower and mastery of nature. The term *instinctoid needs*, used for humans, denotes needs that are not determining as are instincts in animals. This corresponds to Adler's assertion, that the instincts behave the way the ego directs and are not determining. Learning and training therefore become an absolute necessity for human beings, where other animals use their instincts. According to Adler, "Instincts would be a pitifully poor guide through the complexities of our world; only goal-directed man can find his way." Adler insisted that humans are relentlessly striving forward toward a self-created ideal goal of perfection, mastery of nature, and superiority.

The principle of goal-directedness is also known as the principle of teleology, which follows a soft determinism; it proposes that the mind is guided or governed by purposes, values, and interests, which are created uniquely by every individual. Adler insisted that the way humans desire the future to be influences very strongly the way they act. This concept of teleology, as seen epistemologically, had been very much denied in the natural sciences and in theology, but has been totally accepted in the social sciences, especially in recent years. This principle of goal-directedness or teleology rescues psychology and personality theory from their mechanistic bondage, puts humanity into them, and gives humans and their minds the dignity and autonomy of which drive psychology, reflexology, and behaviorism had threatened to rob them. It also negates completely the superficial comparisons and conclusions drawn from animal experiments.

Adler emphasized the role of social factors. He believed that humankind could only have developed through cooperation and not through competition, and that cooperation was a necessity for its survival. Mastery of nature could only be achieved by cooperation between individuals, and this ability has been developed from the first relationship of the child with its mother. Newborn human beings are creatures who are striving for adaptation. It is, of course, impossible to describe in words what has never been formulated in words by the infant—namely, the feelings of dissatisfaction, neediness, and the urge to overcome them, to achieve a better and more satisfying situation. But it is one of the first hypotheses of Adler's individual psychology that the infant behaves "as if" she had such feelings of inadequacy and "as if" she were striving with all available powers to overcome this feeling of inadequacy and reach a goal of ideal adaptation, of adequacy, of superiority. Adler maintains that such a hypothesis allows us to explain behavior better and more comprehensibly, and to test it in actual practice. As the infant herself has poor faculties of perception, discrimination, and judgment and lacks the ability to put desires into actions, she is very apt to misinterpret reality and to make mistakes effecting a better adaptation. Therefore the infant will constantly grope, in neverending trial and error, for even the smallest satisfaction and adaptation, repeating her efforts over and over again until she seems to have found the best way.

It is the mother's task to develop the necessary cooperative behavior with the child and then to spread this cooperative behavior to the rest of the family, giving the child a feeling of a friendly world. In those cases where such cooperative behavior and such feelings of belonging to the human race and seeing people as friends rather than enemies are not developed, the child is missing the development of social interest (*Gemeinschaftsgefühl*) and will later mismanage her life, professionally, romantically, and in friendships. In such cases it is probable that, to maintain a semblance of self-esteem and prestige, the individual will develop a variety of symptoms by which to rescue self-esteem and avoid responsibility for failures; the symptoms are always purposely, though unconsciously, constructed and are what Adler calls "safeguarding devices."

In therapeutic treatment Adler used early recollections of a patient as a method of providing as deep insights as free associations do. In addition, early recollections are easily elicited, since they are considered by the patient to be mere trivial incidents. These recollections do not have to be true of events that happened in the past, but they indicate the patient's attitude to the present, according to his lifestyle. The fictional goals of superiority or self-aggrandizement tend to estrange the individual from reality. Social feelings, on the other hand—feelings of belonging to the human community—anchor the individual in reality, because reality is, in the main, social reality; social feelings counteract the irrationality of the fictional goal. According to Adler, "It is almost impossible to exaggerate the value of an increase of one's social feelings. One's mind becomes improved, because intelligence is a social function. One's self-worth and self-value is heightened, giving one courage and an optimistic view of the world." True social interest contains both self-interest and interest in others, because when one feels a part of others, interest in others will be felt as part of one's self-interest; thus, the contradiction between egoism and altruism is resolved.

Adler's commitment to the social nature of human life was definite. He stated that reason, logic, ethics, and esthetics can only originate through human communal life, and are the bonds that hold the community together and uphold culture and civilization.

Adler's stress on interpersonal relations also led him to investigate birth order in the family and to develop its use for the investigation of a person's lifestyle as well as for therapy. The position that the child feels she has in the family with siblings and parents influences her feelings about herself and other people.

According the Adler, "The honest psychologist cannot shut his eyes to social conditions which prevent the child from becoming a part of the community and from feeling at home in the world, and which allow him to grow up as though he lived in an enemy country. We should be concerned to create and foster those environmental influences which made it difficult for a child to get a mistaken notion of the meaning of life and to form a faulty style of life. Therefore, parents perpetrate great damages to children, when they set an example of striving for personal power over others by showing the child the gratification and the exalted position that can be gained from the possession of power. It makes the child also desire power over others, as much or more power as the father or mother have. This striving for power over others, however, is a fateful delusion and poisons the communal life of people. Whosoever wants a peaceful, social life without malice, envy, killing and domination, must renounce the striving for power over others."

Adler extended this view to the equality of men and women: "The power of men over women robs both of the highest enjoyments of erotics, and must, in a more developed culture, bring women to rebellion against their female role. . . . Also love is full of those deceptions, and demands from the partner excessive submission."

Adler developed the often-misunderstood concept of the "masculine protest" as a metaphorical expression of our society's exalted concept of masculinity, which, for thousands of years, has attributed such positive qualities as strength, wisdom, activity, greatness, and benevolence only to men, while passivity, helplessness, submission, coyness, and lack of wisdom have been attributed to women. As a result, the "masculine" qualities have been acclaimed by men and women as goals of superiority, frequently causing destructive competition between the sexes. If not exaggerated, the striving for the positive "masculine" qualities can also be used for positive achievements by men and women. The diminution and eventual abolition of attributing these concepts only to men is an important next step that society must take to develop a more peaceful social life between the sexes.

According to Adler, dreams express problems that the dreamer does not know how to solve. Therefore, to assuage feelings of inferiority around the unsolved problem, she solves the problem in dreams by asocial or unrealistic methods, which can easily be done, since in dreams logic and social sense are greatly diminished. The dream, therefore, points to the problem of the dreamer, which then has to be discussed and demonstrated to the patient in therapy.

Philosophically, Adler saw the history of humans as the activity of striving for mastery of nature and for greater freedom, while rejecting the concept of being determined by instincts. Civilization and culture and art and science are created to forward striving toward ever greater accomplishments. But he warned that humankind might be doomed unless it develops more social feelings, nationally and internationally, and that "the belief that the cosmos ought to have an interest in the preservation of life, is scarcely more than a pious wish."

Kurt A. Adler

Adler's Treatment Method

The main emphasis in Adlerian therapy is on the relationship between the patient and the therapist. The therapist, from the very first, must see to it that the patient feels at ease and that he is an indispensable collaborator.

Since the competitive nature of our society is bound to influence the patient's attitude toward the therapist, the therapist must continuously stress the importance and necessity of their cooperation. She must emphasize that her services will be rendered futile if the patient does not cooperate. In this way, the competitiveness and expected negativism of the patient lose a great deal of ground, since much of these are based on the patient's fear of appearing inadequate or inferior.

The fellowship that the therapist offers is frequently a great relief to the patient, who has been involved in battles with significant people and views all relationships competitively. Since the patient naturally hates to feel inferior, he either strives strenuously to be superior, or if convinced of his inferiority, spends time in constructing excuses for not being superior. Otherwise he constructs symptoms that are designed to make it clear, both to himself and others, that it was after all impossible to be superior. Most patients at first have a strong inclination to depreciate the therapist. In their competitive battle to be superior, they often try to prove that they are not being helped.

Adlerian personality theory maintains that neuroses and psychoses are purposefully, though unconsciously, constructed so as to avoid a confrontation with social problems. Thus, the patient hopes to prove that she is not being helped in order to depreciate the therapist. The therapist's task is to show the patient that her way of perceiving the therapist is inappropriate. One way to show this to the patient is by using the face-to-face setting instead of the patient lying on a couch and the therapist sitting lordlike behind her. The therapist must constantly impress on the patient that she considers the patient a collaborator, an equal, and a partner because without the patient's collaboration therapy will never succeed. Also, the patient laying on the couch sees only the ceiling, which invites fantasies, while the therapist wants the patient to accept more reality. Regarding countertranference, the therapist will see her patients much as she has generally seen people since childhood, unless she has been able—through deep insight in her own therapy—to alter her attitudes.

Many patients, when they are convinced of the inappropriateness of the neurotic methods they are using, will often use other methods that are equally inappropriate, but which they hope will lead to success without endangering their sense of prestige and their idealized self-image. Again, the therapist will have to show the patient how he tries to uphold his self-image with his new methods, instead of dealing with people in a realistic, cooperative way; collaborating with them, instead of competing, is to both their advantages. It is a mistake of the therapist to moralize about the necessity of becoming less self-centered. The patient must, however, be apprised of the fact that only by bringing his justified self-interest into harmony with the interest and welfare of others will he develop more self-confidence and become a self-actualizing person, leading a life that is more satisfactory.

* * *

The cognitive method that Adler used in all cases is especially useful in the treatment of depression. The patient may have found in his childhood that by being sick and helpless, or by crying, he could get attention and affection, and get his way. Carrying this lifestyle into adulthood, such patients demand and coerce constant support from people at whom they are in fact angry, but they do not dare to express this anger even to themselves, since they depend on this support. Characteristically, they express guilt feelings for being such a burden on others, since their self-image demands they be considered noble and benevolent. These guilt feelings are never real remorse but are intended only to whitewash for themselves their unreasonable demands. Adler showed that every depressive has one main opponent with whom he has vied for dominance since childhood. Silvano Arieti has called this "the significant other."

Suicide in depression is also seen as developing from childhood, where the child hurts herself in order to hurt her main opponent. The adult suicide always believes her opponent will be shattered by her act and will suffer from guilt feelings for it. She also believes that she will be considered noble, while her opponent will be seen as mean and base. An additional bonus is that she will not have to face the problems of life, which she fears she is unable to handle.

Cognitive therapy is directed toward showing the patient this revenge motive and that people will be mainly angered with suicides and try to forget them, considering them utterly self-centered. The false grandeur and heroics with which the suicide tries to impress himself and others has to be completely smashed in therapy. In that and many other ways the act of suicide is made "ego-alien" for the patient, so as to make it veritably impossible for him to commit suicide, since it would threaten to destroy his self-image. Those who protest that they, by attempting suicide, only want to free their relatives of the burden they are have to be told that they really only want to depreciate their relatives and hold themselves up as noble. Those who state that it is, after all, their privilege to decide if they want to live or die have to be shown that they only want to hurt themselves in order to hurt somebody else. A mild form of expressing this in childhood is bed-wetting (enuresis), where the child does something to herself demanding attention, even at night, and attacking usually the mother for not giving in to her wishes; statistically there is a great number of suicide attempters amongst former bed-wetters.

In anxiety, too, the patient mobilizes this feeling by conjuring up and demonstrating the most anxiety-provoking thoughts, pictures, memories, or fantasies from his life experience in the hope of getting comfort and attention. In phobias, the process is essentially the same, except that there is a more urgent claim for dependency, especially when the patient fears to lose the attention of her caretaker.

The purpose of obsessive-compulsive neuroses is to demonstrate, to himself and to others, that the patient must deal with a "sideshow" in which he feels trapped and therefore cannot be expected to deal with the "main show," which contains all the problems he is afraid of; he substitutes compulsions for volition. Even paranoid conditions are treated by showing the patient that she needs her paranoid ideas, saying, in fact, how important she must be, since people are always after her. With schizoid, schizophrenic, and psychotic personalities, the treatment is necessarily much slower; a relationship with these patients first has to be achieved. The goal, to make the patient accept the therapist as a friend, is often a lengthy and arduous endeavor, but without that, improvement can hardly be expected. One must be careful to avoid anything that the patient may interpret as depreciation or humiliation.

The use and abuse of drugs is seen in Adlerian therapy as a method chosen by people who refuse to face and deal with the difficulties of life and want to make everything easier. Many street drugs, as well as alcohol, accomplish this by diminishing perception to the point where the problems users have and are afraid of are made to disappear. Basically, therefore,

they pamper themselves and refuse to confront the normal difficulties of life. In therapy these patients must be encouraged to deal with their difficulties and not be so afraid of possible failures.

The borderline personality disorder was not a diagnostic category in Adler's time; nevertheless, we find that he discusses therapy with patients possessing many of the symptoms of the classic borderline. He writes that it is the therapist's goal to become a constant friend so that it is difficult for the patient to see the therapist in an "antithetical mode of apperception." This is how Adler denotes "splitting," since splitting is the patient's way of seeing everybody and everything, including the therapist.

The therapist must always lead the patient from irrational thinking to more rational attitudes, and she must hold the patient back if she sees that the patient wants quick success. She has to explain to the patient that he has developed his erroneous ways slowly and over a long period of time, and therefore cannot expect to change quickly. The therapist must not be unsettled by the patient's occasional heights nor by his frequent depressions, but must point out how both are due to unrealistic self-concepts. The goal is for the patient to accept himself where he is at present, and to understand that he can only progress from that point.

Adler (1929) admonishes the therapist with the following words:

> The therapist must lose all thoughts of himself and all sensitivity about his own ascendance, and he must never expect anything of the patient. Since he is a belated assumption of maternal functions he must work with a corresponding devotion to the patient's needs.
>
> *Kurt A. Adler*

Adolescence, Adjustment to

Early adolescence is marked by a sequence of growth changes that within a few years transform physically immature preadolescents into teenagers who have attained most of their adult height and virtually all of their adult physical sex characteristics.

For girls, there is a two-year period starting at around age 11 during which the hips become rounded, the breasts begin to develop, height increases rapidly, and, at an average age of 13, the first menstruation occurs.

Boys usually begin their period of rapid physical changes a little later than girls, around age 13. They experience a sudden spurt in height, broadening of the shoulders, increase in the size of their genitals, development of axillary and pubic hair, first growth of beard, and deepening of the voice.

Because of the rapid and visible physical changes taking place in them, early adolescents go through periods of feeling uncomfortable with their bodies.

Middle adolescence corresponds roughly to the high school years, after the major growth changes have occurred but before any major focus on consolidating personal identity. This era is characterized mainly by concerns with being independent and learning to handle heterosexual relationships. With regard to independence, all young people of high school age experience pressing needs to establish themselves as competent, self-reliant individuals who can and should be allowed to govern their own lives, independent of parental restriction or intrusion.

Heterosexual interests develop gradually with the onset of pubescent growth changes and are expressed through a graduated sequence of socializing activities that bring teenagers into increasingly closer contact with each other. Middle adolescence figures prominently in this sequence because it is usually the time when the informal boy–girl parties, group dating, and casual relationships of earlier years give way to individual dating and more intimate and binding relationships than have previously existed.

Late adolescence begins when a youngster has passed the peak of his or her earlier concerns about reaching out for psychological independence and heterosexual relationships and starts to think through the nature of his or her long-range values, aspirations, and commitments. It is in this sense that the key developmental task of late adolescence is the consolidation of a sense of personal identity, that is, a reasonably consistent and gratifying sense of who

one is, what one believes in, and where one is going in life.

Late adolescents confront the task of finding an identity for themselves by experimentation. When late adolescents cannot deal with the challenges of identity formation, they sometimes develop an identity crisis. An identity crisis is neither a normative nor an inescapable aspect of the adolescent years, and it does not refer to the mild, transient anxiety and uncertainty that always accompany the process of identity formation. Rather, identity crisis refers to an abnormal overreaction to the stress of seeking an identity.

Irving B. Weiner

Adolescence: Psychopathology

Comparisons between adolescent and adult psychopathology based on epidemiological surveys are difficult to interpret. Nevertheless, it seems fairly clear that in comparison with adult patients, adolescent psychiatric patients are less likely to be given diagnoses of schizophrenia and depressive reaction and more likely to be designated as "transient situational personality disorders."

However, if there are unique developmental processes, demands, and stresses in adolescence, it is inevitable that the interaction of such factors with predispositions set in motion before adolescence will have consequences for adolescent psychopathology. Second, some of the major fundamental psychiatric syndromes (e.g., manic-depressive psychosis, reactive depression, and schizophrenia) occur infrequently before adolescence and more frequently during and after this developmental phase.

Schizophrenia
In contrast to the infantile or developmental psychoses, which are sometimes termed "schizophrenia," classical schizophrenia is rare in childhood. Schizophrenia is diagnosed with increasing frequency throughout the adolescent and early adult years. The common adolescent and postadolescent onset of schizophrenia suggests a particular vulnerability at these ages.

Alcoholism and Drug Addiction

The epidemiology of alcohol and drug abuse among adolescents affects their mental health and interpersonal relations. It is closely related to the present-day psychosocial climate of excessive permissiveness.

Depression

The relationship of depressive diagnoses to age follows a pattern similar to that of schizophrenia: relatively uncommon in childhood and increasing in frequency throughout adolescence. The relationship to age is somewhat complicated by a theoretical position that holds that depression occurs frequently in childhood and early adolescence but is "masked" and expressed through depressive equivalents.

Marshall D. Schechter
David M. Wright

Adolescent Psychoanalysis

In the analytic method, a workable relationship, or *therapeutic alliance*, must be established within which the therapist can progress from interventions of the type that promote the alliance and foster the analytic situation to those that are transference interpretations and etiological (genetic) reconstructions. The latter two forms of communication (transference and reconstructions) are usually referred to as the "interpretations." The departure from the standard techniques of communication and behavior familiar to those doing adult analysis are broadly divided into *adaptations*, a term proposed by Marianne Kris, and *parameters*.

Adaptations refer to the modifications in technique that create an effective therapeutic climate for the observable developmental and neurotic ego levels of function or alterations stimulated by a progressive change in development. Parameters, on the other hand, are deviations required by the severe nature of the patient's psychopathology (extent of ego regression, low tolerance for frustration, acting out, etc.).

The adolescent is psychologically, socially, and biologically different as he or she progresses through adolescence from the early subphases (12–14 years of age), into middle (14–16) and late (16–18) subphases. In our culture, with prolonged dependency and extended schooling, late-adolescent features in the personality may be observable up to 21 years of age, or even a couple of years beyond.

The early adolescent is most difficult to involve in analysis. The group identifications are active and are coupled with a diminished interest in maintaining the earlier childhood attachments and dependency needs on the parents and other meaningful adults. Oedipal reactions have been repressed, and certain defenses, such as the reaction formations, are lessened so that behavior is less acceptable to the adult environment.

Anna Freud (1936) has described the middle phase, in which biological changes are considerable and sexual pressures are now strong. The ego is besieged by these impulses, and there is difficulty in integrating and mastering aggressive and sexual needs.

During the spontaneous consolidation stage, the analyst is usually impressed with the limitations of interpretations aimed at transference or resistance (defense). The analyst who observes this process can attempt to limit his or her interpretative activities to avoid too much supportive relief from anxiety.

The transference neurosis (when present) during adolescence is not identical to that of the adult patient with a structured adult neurosis. The analyst is at times a transference object and then again a real person, as in child analysis.

The interpretive work during the course of an analysis, which repetitively demonstrates certain gained insights about the adolescent's life in various connections (experiences, behavior, emotions), is the working-through process. In this regard, the data from transference are a significant, but not exclusive, source of insight in analyzing children and adolescents. Reexperiencing the variety of attitudes in the transference situation allows clarification and interpretation to educate the patient as to the significance of the past conflicts and their influence upon the reality of the present.

Irwin M. Marcus

Adolescents: Runaway Behavior

Most studies on primary runaways focus on identifying personality and family characteristics that differentiate them from adolescents who do not run away. Samples are drawn from mental health clinics, youth service agencies, the police, and the courts. Runaways have shown poorer school performance and more troubles with adults, but no differences in peer and sibling relationships. Runaways also show other delinquent behaviors to a greater extent than the comparison groups.

Studies of the antisocial group also focus on personality variables that differentiate runners from nonrunners, but in addition attempt to consider the relative importance of environmental variables as they affect running from training schools. Two studies examining antisocial runaways from home followed up on the adults who as children came to the attention of the police and child guidance clinics. The studies revealed that children who ran away from home had a higher incidence of antisocial and psychiatric disturbances as adults than did a comparison group of nonrunaways.

Most of the work on antisocial runaways is concerned with escapes from training schools. Studies have described the personality profiles of delinquents who fit the diagnostic category of runaway reaction (whether from home or the school is not clear). A runaway reaction group and those diagnosed with unsocialized aggressive reaction showed more elevated profiles on the Minnesota Multiphasic Personality Inventory than did "more normal" boys diagnosed as socialized delinquent.

A study of girls who ran away from an inpatient psychiatric service placed them in five categories: angry defiance; psychotic disorganization; escape; desire to be on one's own; and fusion with parents. When runaways are compared to nonrunaways, there is no difference in family disorganization, but there are more adopted children in the runaway group.

Karla Butler
Diane Frances Reardon

Adult-Gerontological Intelligence and Learning

Research and theorizing regarding intellectual development suggest that adult intelligence exhibits both quantitative and structural changes. Such a perspective is based on (1) a multidimensional model of intelligence derived from factor-analytic studies of the relationships among mental abilities and (2) differential age-related, developmental changes with regard to various intellectual abilities.

Quantitative Change

Quantitative changes in adult intelligence appear to be multidirectional and differential for various cognitive abilities. In general, it has been shown that the earliest and greatest age-related performance decrements are associated with memory and spatial and reasoning abilities, while performance tends to be maintained into advanced age for mental abilities involving verbal and social knowledge.

Deficits in learning performance include failure to produce and use mediators and to recognize and apply problem-solving strategies; rigidity or difficulty in changing sets; interference in learning; and decrements in information-processing and organizational skills. There is empirical evidence that some decrement in adult intellectual performance is caused by extraneous performance variables such as fatigue, cautiousness, test-taking sophistication, and attitudes, rather than by decrements in intellectual competence or potential by themselves.

The increasing evidence for the impact of cumulative and immediate environmental factors suggests that adult intellectual development must be studied with a focus on both biological and psychological factors. The significance of psychological factors is highlighted by evidence of cohort-related variability in adult intellectual performance and by growing evidence of the effectiveness of intervention research.

Paul B. Baltes
Sherry L. Willis

Affects: Freud's Theory

In the early cathartic phase of psychoanalysis, Freud did not specifically refer to the term *instinct*; the concept was incorporated in his description of affects and psychic energy. That is to say, he made no distinction between affects and instincts.

Instincts cannot be known directly; instead they are known by means of their representatives, which are ideas and affects. These two instinctual representatives are treated differently by the process of repression.

Implicit in the notion of affects as an instinctual representative is the belief that a somatic process such as an instinct is perceived not directly but only through some intermediary. That intermediary is the ego, the agency of the mind that controls perceptual processes.

The ego uses affects themselves in a more direct way for defensive purposes. This was first observed by E. Jones (1929), who described what he called the "layering" of affects. For example, guilt or anxiety may be defended against by an outburst of anger; or anxiety itself may be disguised as erotic excitement.

Arnold H. Modell

Affects: Therapeutic Aspects in Psychoanalysis

Mechanisms underlying the phenomenon of affect have reference to an organismic, ultimately mental disequilibrium that the person tries to correct without recourse to action. The awareness of fluctuations in central excitation, corresponding to conflictual wishes or ego-dystonic self- and object-representations, is experienced either as arousal or as drowsiness. How much of an arousal is going to occur at any given moment depends on the degree of organization of the ego, the degree of ego integration, and the ego strength.

Beyond their basic quality of pleasure or unpleasure, human affects contain, necessarily, an element of time. The experience of time as slow or fast—time as duration—is a function of a person's ability to be in tune with his or her affects or to experience affects at all. When the sense of time comes to dominate the subject's attention, the experienced affect defines a pathological mental state, a stressful situation, or both. While anxiety seems to be just an affective state calling for defensive action, depression, guilt, and boredom are defensive in a primary sense.

Peter Hartocollis

Affiliation, Interpersonal

Affiliation serves stimulation functions, providing the interest and informational challenge necessary for cognitive growth and a more comprehensive understanding of the world. Most intrinsically social are the ego-enhancing functions of affiliation. Lack of acceptance and warmth in interpersonal relations during childhood has often been suggested as a precursor of various mental disorders. The approval and support, comfort and consensual validation, and status and prestige provided in the context of deeper interpersonal involvements are essential for the maintenance of self-identity.

Affiliation in adults continues to be directed toward similar others. Life-cycle compatibility becomes a determinant of the social friendship of families. Proximity in dwelling and similarity of social background and personal style are effective in the initiation of acquaintance, especially for working-class and less mobile persons, such as homemakers and the elderly. Similarity in interests, beliefs, and values dominates proximity in the deepening of relationships, especially for middle-class people.

Affiliation increases in importance from middle age on as successive discontinuities of role loss, such as the departure of children, retirement from work, and death of a spouse, are experienced. However, elderly persons may be less overtly active in seeking affiliation than the middle-aged, though they have ample time and need for substitute involvements. Coping with the anxieties of isolation and loneliness, failing competence, and health are factors that favor interdependence, which is the basis for affiliation.

Ira J. Firestone

Aged, Psychotherapy with the

Psychiatrists often treat noninstitutionalized elderly patients in once- or twice-a-week psychotherapy sessions. Length of treatment may range from a few sessions to as many as a hundred. Recovery or marked improvement occurs in a high percentage of aged patients; recovery rate is dependent on the selection process of the therapist and the diagnosis of the patient. The majority of aging patients fit into two prominent diagnostic categories of depression or hypochondriacal patterns. If the patient is younger than 75 years old and there is no demonstrable organic disease, other than the normal processes of senescence, a 75% improvement rate has been reported. Drug therapy may be ancillary to psychotherapy but is not considered the primary mode of therapy in this recovered group.

Many older patients protest that after all the years of their lives, someone has taken advantage of them. Therapy may reveal a lifelong pattern of self-defeat, misuse by family members, or smothered creative potential.

Harold Hiatt

Aggression in Children

An aggressive response can be seen as a habit that is learned in the same way that other habits are acquired. The work of Albert Bandura and his associates on the imitation of aggressive models has provided significant insights into the processes by which a child acquires aggressive response patterns from parental, teacher, peer, and other models. (Bandura, Ross, & Ross 1961; Portuges & Feshbach 1969).

During the early years of a child's life, parents control the child's experiences of frustration and gratification, determine whether he or she is reinforced for aggressive or nonaggressive behavior, and serve as models for the child to imitate.

There is a close relation between the determinants of aggression and the means for controlling aggression. For example, the effects of punishment and violence in the mass media and the consequences of imitation can be examined either as potential causes of aggression or as potential regulators of aggression. Laboratory results indicate that punishment has a temporary suppressing effect on aggressive responses. However, in the long term, punishment, particularly physical punishment, appears to enhance aggression rather than inhibit it.

A child with a strong conscience will refrain from carrying out a socially prohibited act, including an aggressive act, even when she knows she will not be discovered and need not fear punishment by external authority figures. The development of conscience is related to such factors as parental warmth and parental use of reasoning as a technique of discipline.

Associated with conscience development, but theoretically distinct from it, is the acquisition of self-control. Several studies have shown that preschool children high in self-control were less aggressive than children who displayed weak capacities for self-control.

Seymour Feshbach
Norma Deitch Feshbach

Aggression in Human Beings

Konrad Lorenz and other ethologists have insisted that we are not as different from our animal relatives as we would like to believe. Man, we are at times told, is basically only a "naked ape," who is supposedly driven to gain and defend property by the same instincts that operate in other species and is even remarkably similar to the greylag goose in the way he shows his love, jealousy, and competition for positions of dominance.

Most discussions of the animal origins of human social behavior, from Charles Darwin (1873) to the present, see action as impelled primarily by spontaneously generated "instinctual" energy. Following this concept, both Konrad Lorenz and Sigmund Freud have traced aggression to an internally engendered drive pushing man to attack other people.

Most probably the frustration-aggression relationship is just one example of the connection between aversive stimuli and aggression. Thwartings are noxious, and pain is a fairly reliable stimulus to fighting in many animal species. It is possible that social fighting has evolved from defensive reactions to pain. Even though frustrations can be operationally differentiated from insults, and all aversive events do not have exactly the same consequences (Bandura, 1986), both frustrations and insults can increase the chances of an aggressive reaction to the extent that they are unpleasant.

Many psychologists believe it advisable to distinguish between at least instrumental aggression, where someone is attacked largely in order to achieve certain nonaggressive ends rather than to hurt him, and hostile aggression, which is controlled primarily by expectations of the injurious consequences.

A person's reaction to a painful event is also influenced by her interpretation of the cause of the occurrence. In line with attribution theorizing, she is more likely to act violently if she believes that the frustrater had intended to hurt her than if she regards the thwarting as accidental.

Leonard Berkowitz

Aggression: Power and Acceptance Theory

The factors that serve survival—oxygen, water, food, rest—can be put together under the name *basic needs*. Power is the ability to satisfy needs. The more power one possesses, the better are one's chances for survival.

No one is powerful enough to fight his adversaries singlehandedly. Even at the peak of power one depends on allies, and the weaker one is, the more help one needs. To be accepted by people is therefore an important need, although the stronger one is, the less urgent this need is.

One may hypothesize that there is a universal drive, the lust for life. There is one general biochemical energy, but that energy can be transformed into mental energy in any fashion, and the discharge of energy can go in any direction. It can be eros and libido, whenever it supports life, and libido can be cathected in self or others in a sexual or a desexualized way. Whenever there is a threat to life, the hostile and aggressive impulses take over.

The universality of aggressive behavior aimed at survival has given rise to the belief that it is genetically transmitted. There is, however, the possibility of its modification, mollification, and redirection.

Ethological studies point to the fact that intraspecies fights rarely occur and are merely ritualistic. Animals kill to eat and thus to survive. Intraspecies fighting to kill rarely occurs in vertebrates. The human race is an exception; human belligerence has resulted in the deaths of 59 million human beings in wars and from persecution between the years 1820 and 1945.

Perception of one's weakness—that is, one's inability to satisfy one's own needs—leads to fear, which further leads to offensive or defensive aggression. Hungry wolves that fear they may have nothing to eat are offensive; sheep who fear being eaten are defensive.

The weaker one is, and the more one is aware of weakness, the more hostile one tends to be. Hostility is an attitude; aggression is acting out hostility. Hatred is often related to the perception of oneself as weak and of others as strong (Wolman, 1987). Those who are powerful and have no reason to fear, don't hate. Wolves eat sheep but don't hate them; sheep hate wolves.

Benjamin B. Wolman

Aggression: Psychoanalytic Theory

Sigmund Freud defined an instinctual drive as a stimulus to the mind coming from the body. He accordingly maintained that purely psychoanalytic or, more generally, purely psychological data alone cannot furnish an adequate basis for a theory of drives. For this reason, when he introduced aggression as an instinctual drive (1920), he felt it necessary to relate it to a nonpsychological somatic process. He therefore postulated a death drive or instinct, which, he asserted, is characteristic of all protoplasm. All living matter, he said, is driven by a tendency to return to the inorganic state (Thanatos).

The source of the aggressive drive is, at present, assumed to be the same as that of psychological processes in general; that is, both the genetically determined and functional characteristics of the brain that are responsible for psychological phenomena of every sort. The idea is that a compulsion to repeat is a characteristic of the instinctual drives. Freud found it necessary to make this assumption in order to explain the lack of connection he postulated between aggression and the pleasure principle.

At present, most analysts agree that derivatives of aggression play a role in psychic conflict that is at least comparable to that played by derivatives of the libidinal drive. One may argue whether they are equal, but they seem to most observers to be comparable.

The aims of aggression are of considerable interest. Despite some sharp disagreements and occasional cautious reservations, psychoanalysts in general accept the view that the aim of the aggressive drive is "destruction of the object."

One may say that the aims of aggression change along with changes in libidinal development, changes in ego development, and as a function of the events and memories that are unique for each child, as well as his or her thoughts and fantasies about them.

Charles Brenner

Aging

Aging is generally considered to include changes in structure and function that occur during the lifetime of an organism. These changes are universal in all species and are progressive, decremental, and intrinsic. Because aging and the associated increasing probability of death are inevitable, the term "normal aging" is generally applied. However, aging appears to proceed at different rates in different species and even among individuals within a species. There are also differences in the rate of aging in various organ systems of the same individual.

It seems that certain biological changes impair health and can bring death with the mere passage of time. All of us get old almost at the same age as Moses and Pharaoh. The advance of medicine and civilization enables people to survive to old age.

Theories of Aging

There are almost as many theories of aging as there are biologists engaged in research on aging. In the broadest context, however, they can be divided into "why" and "how" theories. "Why" theories relate to the influence of evolution on aging. For example, light is thrown on the aging-disease relationship by the observation that in mammals a plot of mortality rate compared to age yields two peaks, a minor one before age 15, approximately, with a trough roughly between ages 15 and 30, followed by an ascending curve.

The "how" theories are generally directed at the cellular level, where several older theories describe time-related phenomena, such as age-related changes of intercellular colloids, including the cross-linking of collagen molecules, as well as the accumulation within cells of a variety of metabolically inert substances that may impair cell function, such as lipofuscin, calcium and other insoluble mineral salts, denatured proteins, and other forms of so-called cellular garbage.

Several studies suggest that the immune system loses efficiency at a rate similar to that of other organ systems, and that the cells of the immune system are also as prone to misspecification.

Every organism may possess a "biological clock," which may determine the rate of aging and may also set the time that the diseases of aging appear.

Herman T. Blumenthal

Aging and Convalescence

Despite the apparent sanguinity with which most old people take the decrement in health linked with the aging process, occurrence of illness is nonetheless a significant psychological and social life event. Convalescence means to regain one's health, and this is often a physical impossibility for the elderly. The outcome of convalescence in old age is a function of the interactions among biological capacity, social elements, expectations for recovery or decline, and self-expectations.

For the elderly person who has outlived his or her peers and career, the sick role may be particularly seductive. Old age generally has a devalued status in

American society, and there is evidence to suggest that "feeling old" is marked both by a sense of physical or behavioral change in one's self and by awareness of ill health, disability, and weakness.

Most old people view hospitals as a "last resort" for treatment of medical problems, and they fear institutionalization as a prelude to death. Yet a lengthy convalescence invites placement in a nursing home or other extended-care facility from which the major mode of release is death. In an institution the elderly are even more isolated, spatially, socially, and psychically, from the realm of everyday life and are dependent on their caretakers for their most elementary life functions and social needs.

An attitude of therapeutic nihilism too often prevails in facilities caring for the sick and convalescing elderly. There is some indication that old people are more likely to die from even minor ailments in a nursing home or institution than if they are left to live in the community, even with adverse home conditions.

Elizabeth Warren Markson

Aging, Learning, and Problem Solving

Age differences in performance are typically substantial on recall tasks, in which subjects are required to search the memory store to produce a response. In contrast, age differences in performance are small in recognition tasks, which minimize search requirements as the subject is presented with an item and required to decide whether or not the item had been presented previously.

Age-related decrements in learning performance are usually attributed to an increased susceptibility to interference, although the mechanism of interference proneness is rarely specified. Previous habits are among the most potent sources of interference for older subjects in learning new information. Frequently, older people initially misinterpret the instructions in a learning experiment.

Some studies have attempted to minimize the memory component of the task. Even when all the information was available for review, the elderly typically did not solve as many problems or found less effective solutions compared with young adults.

There are, however, some older individuals whose performance is indistinguishable from that of young adults. Furthermore, other factors, such as health status and education, which are correlated with age have marked effects on performance.

Elizabeth Anne Robertson-Tchabo
David Arenberg

Aging: Nonorganic Disorders

Nonorganic psychological disorders (neuroses and psychoses), rather than being unique, represent at old age syndromes and lifelong defense patterns mitigated or exacerbated by the aging process.

The most prevalent disorder among the elderly is hypochondriasis. The primary system of focus for the older patient is the gastrointestinal tract. Psychodynamically, the ailments can provide an acceptable explanation for reduced efficiency, and the return of concern for bodily functions is indicative of ungratified dependency needs and an indirect call for succorance.

Anxiety, which is expressed psychophysiologically, is a common symptom in an older person who is more vulnerable to life stresses and/or age changes.

Compulsive disorders involve character traits that in late life become the last bastion of personality defense. These traits limit self-expression and may be exasperating to the patient.

Depression

Psychodynamically, the mild depressive episodes of the elderly are more concerned with the loss of narcissistic supplies than with the guilt and anger turned against the self that is seen in depressed younger people (Busse & Pfeiffer 1973).

The increased incidence of depression in the later years, particularly in older women, has been noted etiologically in terms of environment and endogenous involvement. Among the latter, the role of biological aging is being reexamined in relation to the finding that monoamine oxidase levels rise with age, which, in the catecholamine theory of affective disorder, could explain the predisposition of older adults to depressive reactions.

Schizophrenias—Paranoid Psychoses of Late Life

Some elderly psychotics are late survivors of early-onset schizophrenia. In old age, early-onset schizophrenics usually show a chronic state of defective affect and motivation, with less prominence of the delusions and hallucinations that colored earlier years (though these may flare up again under stress). Life span does not seem to be shortened in this group, and dementia is no more common than in the general population of corresponding age.

In contrast to people with organic psychoses, the life span of patients with functional psychosis is comparable to that of normal elderly persons in the population at large. However, a sample of late-onset paranoid disorders that do not show organic psychiatric features is known to include at least 5% that prove on follow-up to have an underlying cerebral disease and a resultant shorter life span.

June E. Blum

Aging and Organic Mental Disorders in the Elderly

Primary degenerative dementia may specifically affect cholinergic neurons, as indicated by decreased amounts of acetylcholinesterase and choline acetyltransferase (the enzymes responsible for catabolism of acetylcholine, and synthesis of acetylcholine by acetylation of choline, respectively) in brain areas harboring large numbers of neurofibrillary tangles and senile plaques (the characteristic lesions of primary degenerative dementia). Moreover, both the density of these histopathological lesions and the degree of enzyme depletion correlate with measurement of dementia.

The most important step is accurate diagnostic differentiation of dementias for which specific treatments are available (e.g., thyroid dysfunctions, electrolyte imbalance, drug reactions) from those that can be treated only symptomatically at this time. Patients in the latter category can benefit from a program of titrated psychosocial stimulation and support; correction of dietary and metabolic imbalances; and judicious use of antidepressant, neuroleptic, and, in the case of multi-infarct dementia,

possibly anticoagulant medication (e.g., aspirin for prevention of further infarcts).

Lissy F. Jarvik
James E. Spar

Aging and Organic Psychoses

The cardinal features of organic psychoses are (1) impairment of memory, particularly registration of new impressions; (2) confusion, progressing to disorientation in time and space; (3) intellectual decline, especially in comprehension, reasoning, judgment, learning, and calculation; and (4) deterioration sufficiently severe to interfere grossly with the ability to meet the ordinary demands of life, including self-care, often resulting from a distortion of reality.

Syndromes

The acute organic brain syndromes or acute confusional states are characterized by recent onset (often rapid) and fluctuating severity with clouding of consciousness, impaired concentration and attention, disorientation, and perplexity. Sleep pattern is often reversed. The term *delirium* is used when a confusional state is marked by increased motor restlessness, hallucinations, and preoccupation with imaginary experiences. Elderly patients with acute organic brain syndromes have a high immediate death rate (about 40%).

The chronic organic brain syndromes (OBS) or dementias are insidious in onset and tend to progress relentlessly toward global deterioration of intellect, memory, and personality. The great majority are irreversible, but it must be remembered that a few dementias are reversible, at least in part, with treatment; for example, those due to hypothyroidism, vitamin B_{12} deficiency, or normal pressure hydrocephalus.

Arteriosclerotic dementias tend to show a stepwise course (deterioration following each cerebrovascular accident) rather than the continuous downhill progression of senile dementias.

Senile dementias tend to have a later and more gradual onset, usually appearing in persons over 80 years old who show physical signs of aging in all systems. Current evidence indicates that, like arteriosclerotic dementia, senile dementia is a separate entity from normal aging. It is more frequent in women, and a genetic predisposition is likely, according to United States and Swedish data. Mortality is high, with 58% dying within six months after diagnosis and five-year survival being rare. The cause of death is usually vague (e.g., "senile debility"). Pathology includes diffuse cortical atrophy, loss of neurons (both total cell loss and the number of neurons that have lost horizontal dendrites are significant), and formation of senile plaques, with a central core of amyloid, surrounded by degenerating neural process.

Lissy F. Jarvik

Aging: Physiological Aspects

Aging is normally accompanied by many somatic changes; some changes are quite visible, such as the loosening of the skin, graying of the hair, and decline in overall muscle mass and strength. Other changes are less visible; the body's metabolism slows and shifts slightly in the direction of breakdown of tissue proteins rather than synthesis of new tissues.

Brain

Many of the surviving neurons in the aged central nervous system (CNS) show evidence of structural changes under light microscopy. There is often a decrease in neuron size and in the amount of Nissl substance inside the cell (Nissl substance is considered to be the visible form of the protein-synthesizing machinery of the cell). There is an increased deposition of lipofuscin, a golden-brown pigment that accumulates inside the cell, which can occupy as much as 20% of the internal cell space.

Cerebrovascular changes are generally small and uncorrelated with the mild intellectual impairment seen in neurologically normal elderly individuals. However, in those suffering from various cerebral pathologies, (e.g., organic brain syndrome [OBS]), greater reductions in brain oxygen uptake and blood-flow levels are generally observed. The large

decrements in mental abilities in OBS patients are reported to correlate well with these two cerebrovascular measures.

Not all electroencephalogram (EEG) changes in elderly subjects and patients can be related to mental function; both the appearance of large focal slow waves in the senescent EEG (as recorded from highly localized temporal sites) and the increased appearance of fast EEG activity (beta waves, 20 to 40 cps) in elderly women are variables that fail to correlate with psychometric test scores.

As a result of nighttime sleep impairments, many older persons later become sleepy and prone to take daytime naps. The slow wave (SW) stages of sleep are characterized by the varying abundance of EEG slow activity (delta range, 1 to 3 cps) of high amplitude (75 to 350 V [microvolts] in young subjects). With aging beyond 50 years, there is a progressive decline in the number and amplitude (10 to 150 V in healthy elderly) of EEG slow waves.

Patricia N. Prinz

Aging: Sensation and Perception

Responses to minimal sensory stimulation, as well as the ability to discriminate between changes in stimuli, decrease with older age. In addition, there are age-related differences in complex perceptual judgments. The decreases in sensory sensitivity reflect age-related changes in the physiological composition of the sense organs and the nervous system, as well as the effects of life experiences, illness, and long exposure to environmental insult.

Vision

Sensitivity to light. At low levels of illumination the sensitivity of the eye to light is determined by the responses to light by the rods of the retina. The practical consequences of changes in sensitivity to light with older age include a restriction in vision at night and in twilight. In the latter, levels of ambient illumination cross between values required for rod and cone vision. In such circumstances, color vision and depth perception are both impaired.

Depth perception. Information about the distance

of an object from a viewer comes from cues available to either eye—such as relative position, shadows and haze, and changes with distance in the distinctiveness of the details of objects—and from information available to both eyes (i.e., retinal disparity and convergence).

Color vision. Because the lens yellows with age, it acts as a filter for shorter wavelengths, which are experienced as hues of violet and blue. The ability to discriminate among these hues declines relatively more with older age than that for reds and yellows.

Temporal factors. The older person requires more time to identify a single letter or other acuity target. Extracting information from such a visual display depends upon the time that it is present plus the time that the positive afterimage persists. The age effect occurs partly because, with aging, the afterimage lasts a shorter time, and partly because the central nervous system operates at a slower scanning rate in taking in information.

The magnitude of hearing loss with age may be overestimated by some testing procedures. When the subjects are tested with a procedure that requires them to indicate their confidence in their judgments, it is seen that older persons, in comparison to young adults, require relatively greater levels of sound intensity in order to reach the same level of certainty in their judgments.

Clinical evidence suggests that pain sensitivity decreases with age. However, pain of the skin, as measured by responses to thermal stimulation to the forehead, shows no consistent change with age.

James L. Fozard

Aging and Sexuality

Alterations in characteristics related to sex that occur concomitantly with advancing age in humans include those of a physiological nature and those that manifest themselves behaviorally. Among the most basic is a change in the levels of gonadal steroids in both males and females. Circulating androgens in middle life assume approximately one-third the values found earlier. Urinary ketosteroids steadily decline with age. The origin of these decreases, however, is now thought to be principally

adrenocortical, inasmuch as they are seen in both men and women. Greatly depressed levels of estrogen are characteristic of aging in women; ovarian estrogen production decreases gradually from ages 30 to 60 and virtually ceases around the time of the climacteric. Males show similar decreases in specific estrogen groups, but overall estrogen levels do not show as pronounced a drop as they do in women.

From age 60 on, the frequency of intercourse decreases with advancing age for both men and women; at about age 80, this frequency approaches zero. In every age group, men are more sexually active than women. In general, married men and women are more sexually active than their single cohorts.

Both males and females display a decrease in the degree of sexual interest with increasing age—the probability of giving the response "strong" to questions regarding interest in sexual activity decreases significantly from ages 46 to 71. In one study no male respondents of ages 80 to 90 gave this response, but 50% of them answered "moderate" or "mild."

Ann I. Johnson

Aging and Skill

It is possible that the psychomotor decline that accompanies aging is a result of another well-known consequence of aging: reduced performance of the sense organs. Early studies indicated a slight decline in simple reaction time for both vision and hearing from 20 to 80 years of age. Later studies have shown no significant age differences in the latency of the pupil of the eye in response to light or in the response of the retina. Dark adaptation, visual acuity, accommodation, and auditory acuity are known to decline with age and to adversely affect performance.

Industrial studies of older individuals functioning in jobs show that, in many respects, older workers experience no difficulties. Investigations by K. F. H. Murrell of lathe workers reveal that older workers do their work faster than younger workers. Older workers in a laboratory setting were initially slower than younger subjects, but the two groups performed at equivalent levels after several days of practice.

A general slowing in reaction time is known to occur with aging. Early studies indicated a lengthening of simple reaction time (RT) with visual and auditory stimuli for persons from 20 through 80 years of age. Auditory RT was always less than that for vision, because this relationship is not affected by age. RT was later measured for three different reactors (finger, jaw, and foot) with a sound stimulus. An increase in the RT was again found with age for all three reactors.

The general slowing of psychomotor behavior that accompanies the aging process may be influenced by a change in central information processing: either a qualitative change in method or strategy of approaching a motor task and/or a decline in the speed with which incoming stimuli are processed. There is mounting evidence that the decline in motor behavior that accompanies aging is concomitant with a decline in the processing time of the central nervous system.

Arnold M. Small
M. Antoinette Jenkins

Aichhorn, August (1878–1949)

Aichhorn was an educator and an expert in the education of wayward and delinquent youths. In 1920, Aichhorn joined the Viennese Psychoanalytic Association, and in 1946, after World War II, he became the president of the reopened association.

Rudolf Ekstein

Alexander, Franz (1891–1964)

Alexander founded the Chicago Psychoanalytic Institute and was its director for 25 years; he was also the director of research at Mt. Sinai Hospital in Los Angeles. He was opposed to rigid, standardized, and formal psychoanalysis and advocated flexible analytic techniques, leading to a "corrective emotional experience." Alexander was a pioneer in psychosomatic diseases, viewing them not as an attempt to express an emotional conflict in conversion hysteria but rather as a physiological concomitant of constant or periodical recurring emotional states. Alexander and his team investigated the dynamics of hypertension, bronchial asthma, and gastrointestinal diseases, including ulcerative colitis. His analysis of asthma as a repressed cry for help from one's mother and an expression of fear of separation has become an analytic classic.

Martin Grotjahn

Alienation

The idea of alienation, like a number of other concepts in the social sciences (e.g., attitudes and social role), stands at the intersection of a variety of disciplinary interests. The six related but distinguishable versions, or dimensions, of alienation sketched below have received the bulk of attention, both in the traditional literature and in recent empirical work.

1. *Powerlessness.* The feeling, belief, or expectancy that one's own behavior cannot control the occurrence of events (some would say "reinforcements"), whether these events involve positive or negative outcomes, or outcomes of global or intimate scale (e.g., international war or a personal vendetta).
2. *Meaninglessness.* Sometimes thought of in the grand existential manner (the "absurdity" of life) but also conceivable, in a more restricted way, as simply a sense of incomprehensibility in social affairs.
3. *Normlessness.* High expectancies for, or commitment to, socially unapproved means in the achievement of given goals; that is, the view that one is not bound by conventional norms in the pursuit of what may be quite conventional goals.
4. *Cultural estrangement.* The individual's rejection of commonly held values in the society (or subsector thereof), the typical image here being that of the alienated artist or intellectual who rejects the current standards.
5. *Social isolation.* The individual's low expectancy for inclusion and social acceptance,

expressed in feelings of loneliness or repudiation, typically found among minority members, the aged, or the physically disabled.

6. *Self-estrangement.* This focuses on the discrepancy between one's ideal self and one's actual self-image (a discrepancy that some people think psychotherapy resolves, especially those who advocate the "client-centered" Rogerian approach).

Melvin Seeman

Allee, Warder Clyde (1885–1955)

Allee was a pioneer in ecological and ethological research. His work provided information on the disadvantages of under- and overcrowding. Allee defined *protocooperation* as a basic property of animals leading to both unconscious and conscious cooperation in higher animals. He was an ardent promoter of studies of animal behavior and sociology.

Edwin M. Banks

Allelomimetic Behavior

Allelomimetic behavior is defined as a kind of social behavior in which two or more members of the same species do the same thing at the same time with some degree of mutual imitation. It is limited to those animals that have adequate sensory capacities and live in environments that permit constant intercommunication and coordination. With a few exceptions among arthropods, such as army ants, it occurs chiefly in vertebrates, where it may be developed into a major system of behavior in a variety of orders. Where well developed, it results in the maintenance of a social group, often very large. Such groups have received specialized names in popular terminology, such as schools of fishes, flocks of birds, herds of hoofed mammals, packs of wolves and some other carnivores, troops of primates, and crowds of people.

Little attention has been paid to this major motivational system in humans except in connection with social facilitation. Generalizing from other animals

to humans, one would predict that strong social attachment must result in allelomimetic behavior for that contiguity to be maintained. Thus, motivation associated with allelomimetic behavior has the properties of a general social drive. Interference with this drive, as in cases of separation induced by death or migration, frequently results in severe depressive symptoms.

John Paul Scott

Allport, Gordon W. (1897–1967)

Allport stressed the idiographic approach in the study of personality; his personality theory emphasized the concept of functional autonomy and personality traits. The Allport scale measures the incidence of ascendance and submission traits. The Allport-Vernon-Lindzey scale measures individuals' attitudes.

James F. Adams

Altruism, Development of

Infants may be attached to their mothers or other caretakers and, in that sense, care about them, but they can hardly be expected to show authentic altruism or commitment. They are too egocentric, too narrow in their perspective, and too concrete in their thinking to act altruistically.

The nature of parent-child interactions during the preschool years also has a strong impact on the development of caring for others. For example, among youngsters attending nursery school, those who express warmth toward and concern for their peers are the children of parents whose child-rearing practices are characterized by a good balance of warmth, love, support, and encouragement.

Empathy, another essential ingredient of altruism, increases markedly between ages 5 and 8. This may be a particularly sensitive period for the development of empathy and, perhaps, for effective training for the promotion of this characteristic (Feshbach & Roe 1968). Six- and 7-year-old boys who rate high in empathy tend to rate high in generosity and low in overt hostility and aggression.

Among children between 10 and 12 years of age, observation of adult models behaving generously results in increased altruism toward strangers. In one experiment, an adult model gave some of the money he won in a game to a fund for "children who have no toys." Many of the children who observed the altruistic model imitated his charitable behavior.

During preadolescence, as in earlier childhood, altruistic behavior is related to personality structure and to the quality of parent-child relationships. Highly altruistic children of 11 or 12 generally manifest high ego strength and self-esteem: they are self-confident, satisfied with their peer relationships, and assured about their own sociability, popularity, dependability, leadership qualities, and independence.

Paul H. Mussen

Altruism and Helping Behavior

Customarily, an altruistic act is defined as an act that benefits the recipient and produces no benefit to the giver. One obvious conclusion from the dominant hedonic orientation of human nature is that truly altruistic acts are not committed. People do not commit actions from which they expect to gain no benefit. As can be expected from the prevalence of this image of humanity as self-interested, relatively little theoretical or empirical attention has been paid to the study of altruism in psychology, as compared to other topics such as aggression or violence. One theme represented in altruism research is the search for the elusive "pure" altruistic act, which cannot be accounted for by any possible benefit to its initiator.

Investigations seeking to validate the concept of a central personality trait of "helpfulness" possessed in different amounts by different people have been frequently unsuccessful, although persons who generally ascribe action responsibilities to themselves have been found to be more likely to help in specific concrete situations (Schwartz & Clausen, 1970).

John McCannon Darley

Alzheimer's Disease

Alzheimer's disease affects the cells of the brain. It was called presenile dementia when it was believed that it affected people below the age of 65, but at the present time it is known that it also affects older people. Alzheimer's disease occurs in 2 to 3% of the population. The main symptoms are a serious decline of memory, especially of recent experiences, inability to form rational judgment, frequent states of confusion, poor motor coordination, irritability, and delusions. There is a loss of weight within the brain, and neurofibrillary tangles appear. Alzheimer's patients experience withdrawal from social contacts, neglect their appearance, and exhibit far-reaching personality changes. As the disease progresses, the patients lose their sense of identity, forget where they live and who they are, and become totally disoriented and unable to take care of themselves.

The causes of Alzheimer's are unknown. A great deal of research is going on, and several new hypotheses are being reported.

Benjamin B. Wolman

American Board of Professional Psychology

The mission of the American Board of Professional Psychology (ABPP) is to promote excellence in the practice of professional psychology, specifically in the application of psychological theory and scientifically derived knowledge and techniques. To fulfill its mission, the ABPP has instituted a credentials review and examination process in recognized specialty practice areas, which assesses individual applicants for advanced competence. Those who qualify receive a diploma and are given the status of diplomate. To further promote excellence, the ABPP has developed a set of procedures for officially recognizing emerging specialty practice areas, and it assists emerging specialties in the development of credentialing standards and examination procedures through which advanced competence within the specialty can be determined. The focus of the ABPP is on the individual practitioner: it neither evaluates nor accredits training programs in psychology.

The ABPP was established during the late 1940s, when it became apparent that there was a pressing need for an institutional mechanism to certify psychologists for practice. The first indication of such a need became apparent during World War II, when the value of applying psychological knowledge toward solving important personnel and societal dilemmas was recognized. It also became evident that trained psychologists could function independently of medical supervision. At the same time, the knowledge base of the discipline was expanding rapidly, resulting in the development of intervention techniques that drew psychology toward becoming an applied science, with psychologists directly serving people's needs. As any discipline moves from the laboratory to practice, a gap grows between researchers producing knowledge and practitioners applying that knowledge. With that gap comes the need for regulation. Consumer-protection interests require that the discipline monitor those who apply the science and assure their capacity to do so.

Broader social forces have also contributed to the need to establish certification procedures for psychologists. An increased awareness of mental health problems in society followed World War II. Business and industry discovered that the application of psychological knowledge could have remarkable effects on employee productivity and satisfaction. As a result, society's stake in determining who was competent to provide what psychological service was increasing. During this period, a minority of state legislatures began authorizing state-run psychologist licensure and certification boards for the first time. It would be two decades, however, before all states passed certification and licensure acts to govern the practice of psychology.

Notwithstanding the importance of the above-mentioned influences, the greatest impetus to establish the ABPP came from within the profession. In 1946, the American Psychological Association's Council of Representatives appointed a committee to determine the best way to certify professional psychologists. The committee recommended incorporating a separate organization specifically dedicated to this purpose. The council adopted the recommendations and granted seed money to establish such a board. In 1947, the American Board of Examiners in Professional Psychology was incorporated in the District of Columbia; subsequently, the name was changed to the American Board of Professional Psychology.

The ABPP's incorporation came at an interesting time in the history of psychology, when it was difficult to determine the shape that the independent practice of psychology would eventually take. In 1946, there was no existing approval process within the discipline for granting accreditation to training or internship programs in psychology. Only one state had certification procedures for psychologists, and little was known about the best procedure for credentialing professional psychologists. The attitude held by many in the medical community that psychologists should not be allowed to practice unless supervised by a licensed physician only added to these uncertainties.

Since the ABPP was founded when no model existed for certification procedures, its initial decision regarding professional practice had a profound effect in shaping the credentialing process in use today for the discipline. Some examples of early policy include:

- setting the doctoral degree as an important threshold for certification of specialty practitioners;
- requiring supervised experience for eventual certification to practice;
- linking examination of core knowledge and professional skills to certification of readiness to practice; and
- recognizing and defining specialty practice areas for the profession.

Before the ABPP could begin certifying psychologists in specialty practice areas, it first had to determine what areas were then in existence. The two primary criteria used to identify practice areas as specialties were a consensus among psychologists and the existence of doctoral training programs in an area. The ABPP initially identified three specialty practice areas that are known today as Clinical, Counseling, and Organizational/Industrial Psychology. After identifying these areas, the ABPP did not concern itself with defining boundaries, scope, or unique techniques used on populations served by these initial specialties. Rather, it turned its attention to certification of specialty practitioners.

Over the next 45 years, the ABPP became the premier credentialing body for psychologists. As has been true from its inception, it awards diplomas in its specialty areas based on demonstrated advanced competence in the area of specialization. The ABPP currently awards diplomas and confers the status of diplomate in nine areas of specialty practice: Clinical Psychology, Clinical Neuropsychology, Counseling Psychology, Industrial/Organizational Psychology, School Psychology, Forensic Psychology, Family Psychology, Behavioral Psychology, and Health Psychology. Two additional specialty practice areas—Psychoanalytic Psychology and Group Psychology—currently are seeking affiliation with the ABPP.

Organizational Structure

The ABPP Board of Trustees (BOT) is comprised of representatives from each of the nine specialty areas, one public member, and the past president of the BOT. Each specialty practice has an incorporated board, which performs specialty-specific credentials review, examination, and appeals functions. Specialty boards are charged to develop, administer, evaluate, and revise specialty-specific examinations; to meet minimum credentialing standards set by the ABPP, and set additional standards unique to the specialty; and to communicate to the ABPP issues of relevance regarding the specialty.

The ABPP serves as a forum for exchanging information and ideas across specialties; for establishing procedures for official recognition and subsequent affiliation of new specialties; for establishing minimum education and experience standards for all specialties; and for conducting other important quality assurance activities. It also maintains an administrative headquarters to keep diplomates' records and to act as a unitary organization of behalf of its diplomates with the public, related professions, and health care organizations.

Pursuit of Specialty Certification

Pressure upon practitioners to specialize intensifies as the knowledge base, applicable techniques, service settings, problems encountered, and range of people served expands. Also, as with other disciplines, certification and regulation of specialists remain within the profession, with the involvement of governmental bodies limited primarily to issuance of general-practice licenses.

Since the ABPP is the body that has carried out the certification and regulation of specialty practitioners within psychology, it might be helpful to outline that process. Achieving board certification through the ABPP typically involves three steps: becoming a candidate, developing a work sample, and successfully completing an oral examination. Eligibility to become a candidate for the ABPP diploma requires that the applicant meet the following minimum requirements:

- an earned doctoral degree in psychology from a regionally accredited institution;
- three years of experience relevant to the specialty or successful completion of an accredited postdoctoral program in the specialty;
- two years of supervised postdoctoral experiences relevant to the practice of the specialty or successful completion of an accredited postdoctoral program in the specialty (a predoctoral internship may be counted as partial fulfillment of this requirement); and
- an appropriate state, provincial, or territorial license to practice psychology.

Along with these minimum eligibility requirements common to all specialties, each specialty may hold specialty-specific candidacy requirements.

Once admitted to candidacy, most specialties require that candidates develop a work sample to demonstrate advanced competence within the specialty. Guidelines for acceptable work samples are available, as is a description of the procedures to be followed and the format for its development. Several specialty boards require successful completion and acceptance of the work sample before allowing an applicant to sit for the examination; other boards integrate the work sample evaluation into the oral examination.

The final step in earning the status of diplomate is successful completion of the oral examination. The oral examination varies in length from four to six hours and typically is designed to demonstrate a candidate's strength in assessment and diagnosis of a problem, skills in constructive intervention, knowledge of the specialty, and integration of ethical behavior into practice. For most of its 45 years of operation, the ABPP used a uniform examination across specialties. The current practice, however, recognizes specialty-specific variables and allows greater latitude in examination methods and format. Although each specialty board develops the most relevant and thorough examination for its specialty area, the ABPP retains oversight authority. In this way, the ABPP assures that each board's examination meets or exceeds its minimum standards.

Need for Specialty Certification in Psychology

Providing specialty certification in any profession— be it law, medicine, or psychology—serves two fundamental purposes. First, it elevates standards of practice by establishing criteria to which practitioners can aspire. For example, the medical profession's success in having large numbers of practitioners achieve board certification in specialty practice areas has demonstrated to the public the relationship between board certification and quality of care. Consumers have become increasingly attuned to the connection between specialty certification and competence of the health care provider. Certification of advanced competence and the desire to attain it clearly lead practitioners to sharpen and enhance their professional skills. The second purpose of specialty certification is to aid potential consumers in determining which practitioners among many have pursued and attained more than minimum training and experience, and have integrated the knowledge, skills, ethics, and values of the profession into peer-recognized, highly competent specialized practice.

Specialty certification also has the advantage of making the practitioner more competitive in the health care marketplace. Because psychology programs, as well as those of allied mental health disciplines, are producing far more practitioners today than even a decade ago, there is increasing competition in the marketplace. Whenever this has occurred in the past (and in other professions), the practitioner who possesses the highest and most relevant

credential remains positioned to be considered a valued provider of services. When an excess of providers exists, consumers can choose the best qualified among many.

Managed care competition has also accelerated interest in specialty credentials. It will increasingly become the case (assuming relatively equal cost) that acceptance into provider panels or sole source provision contracts will be based upon credentials that attest to advanced or specific competence. Providers who have earned the highest and most relevant specialized credentials present less risk overall to health care organizations. Sharpened focus to quality surveillance in service delivery within health care organizations will require that practitioners have the credentials to fortify their contention that they are competent and well-trained professionals. As malpractice costs for organizations rise and standards of quality care become clearly articulated, those who demonstrate the most promise for helping organizations meet those standards will become the most valued. Requiring board certification of its health care providers is one method an organization can use to demonstrate its commitment to quality service.

Over the past decade, the practice of psychology has been evolving in a way that makes the ABPP central to the profession. The discipline and practice of psychology has become more sophisticated and differentiated, witness the addition of five new ABPP-recognized specialty certification areas and the burgeoning number of practitioners seeking specialty training beyond the doctoral program. This increased involvement and interest in postdoctoral training has brought a greater need for specialty certification for the practitioners and trainers. Given the current pace of inquiry the ABPP is receiving from nonrecognized specialties, it is conceivable that within the next five years the ABPP will add several more specialty practice areas. Because in virtually all cases training in the newly added specializations occurs postdoctorally and even past initial licensure, the ABPP will be needed to develop and conduct examinations and set practice standards for certification in these areas, making its role in professional psychology even more essential.

David J. Drum

American Psychiatric Association (APA)

In 1844 the Association of Medical Superintendents of American Institution for the Insane formed. In 1921 the association became the American Psychiatric Association. Progress in psychiatry between 1900 and 1940 was found in the growing acceptance of psychoanalytic theory and therapy, which encouraged the development of private practice. By 1940 mental hospital superintendents and other mental hospital physicians no longer dominated the membership of the association. In 1934, by which time the membership had grown to about 1,500, the association played an instrumental role in establishing the American Board of Psychiatry and Neurology, which symbolized the acceptance of psychiatry as a bona fide specialty of medicine.

Reorganization of the APA

The establishment of a headquarters in Washington, D.C., for the first time provided the association's officers and components with the professional staff support they needed to carry out new programs and policies. The staff grew from 4 people in 1948 to 120 in 1976, and at the same time the budget expanded from about $100,000 to $4.5 million a year.

Joint Commission on Mental Illness and Health

In 1955, the association took the initiative in forming the Joint Commission on Mental Illness and Health and securing a passage by Congress of the Mental Health Study Act of 1955. The comprehensive survey of mental health resources conducted by the commission over the next five years led to the famous action report, *Action for Mental Health*, published in 1961. That report influenced President Kennedy to deliver his special message to Congress on mental illness and retardation in 1963, which in turn led to the federally funded community mental health center movement in the 1960s and 1970s. The association played a similar role in the launching of the Joint Commission on Mental Health of Children in the 1960s.

The Structure of the APA

The powers of the association are vested in a board of trustees elected by the voting members. The trustees include the president, president-elect, two vice presidents, secretary, treasurer, speaker of the Assembly of District Branches, three immediate past presidents, three trustees elected at large, and one trustee elected by each of the seven geographical areas of the assembly.

The substantive studies and findings that underly the programs and policies of the association originate in the work of twelve councils, each of them with committees and task forces that serve under their aegis. The titles of the twelve councils reflect the major areas of concern to the association: addiction psychiatry; aging; children, adolescents, and their families; economic affairs; internal organization; international affairs; medical education and career development; national affairs; professions and associations; psychiatric services; psychiatry and law; and research. Well over a hundred committees, task forces, boards, commissions, and ad hoc groups study and report to the councils in these topic areas. The councils, in turn, report to the board of trustees through a Reference Committee.

Robert L. Robinson

American Psychiatric Association: Recent Developments

After 1945, the American Psychiatric Association was reorganized. Among the many reforms that occurred was the establishment of a central office in Washington, D.C., under the management of a medical director. Daniel Blain, M.D., was selected to be the first medical director, and served from 1948 until 1958. Under his leadership the APA became a national force, advocating on behalf of patients and psychiatry. Since 1948, membership in the organization has increased exponentially, reaching nearly 39,000 by 1993.

Through the 1960s, advances continued to be made in the treatment of the mentally ill. These improvements in treatment, the promise of further improvements, and the social climate of the "Great Society" programs led to passage of the Community Mental Health Centers Act in 1963. In simple terms, this act opened the door to community care for the mentally ill; unfortunately, this was at the expense of the old state mental hospitals. For the next thirty years, patients were released in a movement called "deinstitutionalization." This rapid release of patients became the social crusade of the 1970s. Patients won in court a number of cases that limited how long they could be confined to a mental hospital and established their rights to refuse to be admitted at all and to refuse medication. Improved therapeutic techniques allowed many more patients to leave the hospitals; limited funds led the states to force the rest out. This wholesale emptying of state mental hospitals created many problems, the most obvious of which is today's large population of homeless mentally ill. These unfortunate people are caught in the trap of lacking the money to care for themselves, while claiming the legal right to refuse care offered. The significant reductions in resources available to the mentally ill during the 1980s has led to rapid increases in the numbers of homeless people. Many states have decided to close their hospitals completely, releasing their remaining patients to some sort of community care, which is likely to be underfunded, or directly to the streets.

Through its members, the APA seeks to advance its objectives: to improve the treatment, rehabilitation, and care of the mentally ill, the mentally retarded, and the emotionally disturbed; to promote research, professional education in psychiatry and allied fields, and the prevention of psychiatric disabilities; to advance the standards of all psychiatric services and facilities; to foster the cooperation of all who are concerned with the medical, psychological, social, and legal aspects of mental health and illness; and to make psychiatric knowledge available to other practitioners of medicine, to scientists in other fields, and to the public.

Organized psychiatry's role in the 1990s will be to educate society and government that mental illness is like any other illness, that it warrants the full range of treatment options that other illnesses have, and that every member of society has the right to treatment.

As the American Psychiatric Association prepares to celebrate its sesquicentennial, it finds itself in a situation similar to that of 1844—that is, educating society about the need to care for the mentally ill and to develop better methods to diagnose and treat these patients. The massive growth of the APA in recent years reflects the success of its efforts to provide national leadership in dealing more effectively with all aspects of mental illness.

William E. Baxter

American Psychological Association (APA)

The American Psychological Association (APA) is the world's largest and oldest national psychology organization, having celebrated its 100th anniversary in 1992. The APA advances psychology as a science, as a profession, and as a means of promoting human welfare.

Origins

The first organizational meeting of the American Psychological Association was held on July 8, 1892, at the home of G. Stanley Hall, the APA's first president. Later that year, the APA's first annual convention was held at the University of Pennsylvania. At the end of the meeting, the APA had 31 members.

The APA began as a learned society in which scholars and scientists could meet and exchange information and research findings. After World War II, the association experienced phenomenal growth and the rapid rise of applied areas of psychology. Today the membership is comprised of both academicians, who teach and conduct research, and practitioners, who provide services in the health and mental health fields. Over the years, a dynamic tension between the academicians and the practitioners has been instrumental in shaping the structure and the goals of the association.

Membership

The minimum standard for election to full member status is the doctoral degree, based in part on a psychological dissertation or on other evidence of proficiency in psychological scholarship. The doctoral degree must be received from a program primarily psychological in content. Other membership categories include *fellows* and *associates*. Fellows are members nominated by sponsoring divisions (see below) for their outstanding contributions to the field. Associate members must have completed two years of postbaccalaureate study in psychology at a recognized graduate school and be engaged in work or study that is primarily psychological in nature, or they must have received a master's degree in psychology and completed one full year of professional work in psychology. Individuals may become affiliates of the association in one of the following categories: international, student, and high school teacher.

Divisions

The many specialized interests of the members are represented through the APA's forty-eight divisions. In 1945, nineteen charter divisions were created to facilitate groupings within the APA of psychologists whose interests were becoming more and more diverse. As the interests of psychologists have expanded, the number of divisions has grown. Division topics reflect the diversity of psychology: general, teaching, experimental, developmental, social, clinical, industrial and organizational, educational, school, counseling, consumer, women-related, health, law, family, gay and lesbian–related, media, sports, and peace psychology are a few of the areas. The divisions have played a significant role in unifying the APA and in developing psychology as a discipline.

State Associations

The expanding role of practitioners in the APA has been paralleled by an increasingly active role played by state and provincial psychological associations (SPPAs). Unlike the divisions, SPPAs are independent entities that voluntarily affiliate with the APA. The SPPAs vary greatly in size, although many have evolved from small groups of volunteers into fairly complex professional organizations with central offices, executive officers, and active programs of advocacy for professional psychology. With consultation and assistance from the APA, the SPPAs have become a powerful national network to promote the applications of psychology at the state level.

Governance/Organizational Structure

The APA bylaws establish the following major structural units: the Council of Representatives, the Board of Directors, the officers, the standing boards and committees, and the Central Office with the chief executive officer. The Council of Representatives is the major legislative and policy-setting body, with the sole authority to set policy or appropriate funds. Approximately 120 council members are elected by the divisions and state associations to represent them at two annual meetings. The Council elects the Board of Directors, treasurer, and recording secretary and approves the selection of a chief executive officer by the Board of Directors. The president, who is elected by the membership, chairs the board and council. The board oversees the business of the association, subject to periodic approval by the council. Much of the work of the association is done on a volunteer basis by members of boards and committees.

The substantive areas of psychology—science, practice, public interest, and education—are represented in the central office by four directorates, each of which has at least one oversight board. Policy recommendations from these boards and their committees are forwarded through the Board of Directors to council for final determination.

Central Office

EXECUTIVE OFFICE

The chief executive officer is responsible for the operation of all aspects of the central office and for coordinating the activities of the four directorates and three major program areas: Central Programs, Communications, and Finance and Administration. In addition, the offices of Board and Council Affairs and Legal Affairs operate directly out of the Executive Office.

DIRECTORATES

As the association has grown, the central office has been restructured to meet the needs of its increasingly diverse membership. In 1987, the directorate system was established to give more direct representation to the various constituencies. Science, Practice, and Public Interest were the initial directorates, and Education was developed in 1990.

The Science Directorate is the focal point of the APA's effort to expand the recognition of psychology's scientific achievements in Congress, the federal agencies, and the larger scientific community. Working with the Public Policy Office, the Science Directorate has successfully promoted legislation to increase funding for the major federal agencies that support psychological research. It has also developed guidelines for research with human and animal subjects and coalitions with other science organizations. The Science Directorate sponsors a traveling psychology exhibition that travels to museums across the United States; university-based research conferences; awards programs; science programs at the annual convention; a newsletter; a research support network; and electronically delivered research funding information.

The Practice Directorate promotes the practice of psychology through legislative and judicial advocacy, education, and public relations and marketing efforts. It also helps to develop the policies, standards, and guidelines for the delivery of psychological services, as well as educational documents about the profession for psychologists and the public. The Practice Directorate has succeeded in enacting Medicare legislation, enabling beneficiaries to receive psychological care, gaining hospital privileges for psychologists, gaining access to psychoanalytic training, and building a strong advocacy network at the state level.

The Public Interest Directorate promotes the application of the science and practice of psychology in the public interest. Priority issues include the psychological impact of discrimination, poverty, mental illness, victimization, violence, and homelessness. The programs of the directorate focus on children, families, and lifespan development. Major projects include the Commission on Violence and Youth, the HIV Office for Psychology Education, the Office on AIDS, and conferences. Working with the Public Policy Office, the directorate informs Congress and the federal agencies of psychology's concerns and influences legislation on behalf of underrepresented groups.

The Education Directorate develops policy in education and training for the science and practice of psychology. The directorate effectively advances psychology in educational institutions through its programs in accreditation and continuing education. It supports and advocates funding of education and training in psychology from the precollege to the postgraduate level. The directorate promotes the applications of psychology to educational reform and provides leadership in the development of educational policies. It also conducts research related to education in psychology and disseminates results for the professional and public good.

CENTRAL PROGRAMS
This newly formed program area is composed of offices that have an impact on all of the APA membership rather than a particular constituency. Offices included in this area are Ethics, Division Services, Public Policy, *American Psychologist*, International Affairs, Public Communications, APA Graduate Students, Affirmative Action, Board and Committee Operations, and Convention Services.

COMMUNICATIONS
The APA is the world's largest publisher in psychology. The APA Knowledge Dissemination Program is operated through the Office of Communications. It consists of APA journals, APA books, and PsycINFO (which is the APA abstract service). APA journals and abstracts are distributed to more than 300,000 individuals and institutions worldwide. The APA publishes twenty-one major international journals, the *Psychological Abstracts*, and five other secondary abstract periodicals. The APA books program publishes over forty-five scholarly books each year, including the *APA Style Manual*, the major international style guide in psychology and related fields. The PsycINFO abstract system is available online as PsycINFO and on CD-ROM products as PsycLIT.

OFFICE OF FINANCE AND
ADMINISTRATION
The Office of Finance and Administration develops and manages the APA budget and coordinates all financial and business affairs, including administrative services, property development, management information services, human resources, and printing.

Priority Issues
Some of the major issues faced by the association now and in the future include the following: funding

for basic scientific research; the role of psychologists in national health care reform; the effect of managed care on the independent practice of psychology; the feminization of the field; and the discovery of new ways to meet the needs of both the academic and practice communities within one united association.

Raymond D. Fowler

American Psychological Society (APS)

The American Psychological Society (APS) was founded on August 12, 1988, by a vote of the membership of the then-year-old Assembly for Scientific and Applied Psychology (ASAP), an organization of some 450 scientifically oriented psychologists interested in advancing scientific psychology and its representation as a science at the national level. Today, the APS has a membership of over 15,000.

The ASAP itself was founded in May 1987 as an interim society primarily to promote the incorporation of scientific interests and a science agenda in the framework of the 100-year-old American Psychological Association (APA). The APA's political and organizational structure had increasingly evolved, since the 1960s, to that of a guild for practitioners, with less emphasis on scientific interests and participation. Numerous unsuccessful attempts had been made over the years prior to the ASAP's formation to enhance the status and voice of science in the APA. Ultimately, after a year of pressure from the scientific community, the ASAP-initiated effort to reorganize the APA also proved unsuccessful, having been rejected by a vote of the APA membership in August 1988. This failure sparked the birth of the APS, as the ASAP's bylaws stipulated that a new society devoted to science be formed upon the failure of the effort to reorganize the APA. The mail ballot of the ASAP's membership approved the measure 419 to 13. (APS newsletter, October 1988).

The APS has grown in four years as a nonprofit society to become the foremost national organization devoted to scientific psychology. Its growth has been phenomenal, reaching over 15,000 members and making it perhaps the fastest-growing scientific society in the world. At the same time, the APS headquarters office consists of a small staff, which helps fulfill one of the APS's goals, of keeping its bureaucracy to a minimum.

The society's mission is to promote, protect, and advance the interests of scientifically oriented psychology in research, application, teaching, and the improvement of human welfare. To date, the APS has met the demands of its mission because of its strong and committed leadership, a minimal bureaucracy, and a sense of urgency in the scientific community that representation of scientific psychology had been neglected for too long. The APS has also met its mission in spite of its limited funds and the pressures of a particularly harsh economic environment in its early formative years.

APS members include psychologists across the entire spectrum of scientific, applied, and teaching specialties, as well as psychologists outside the United States. Requirements of membership are a doctoral degree or evidence of sustained and significant contributions to scientific psychology; student affiliates are also accepted. Distinguished contributions are recognized by Fellow status or by specific awards (e.g., James McKeen Cattell Award, William James Fellow Award) in cases of superior accomplishment.

Impetus for the Society's Creation

The impetus for creating the APS came from the recognition that (1) the needs and interests of scientific, applied, and academic psychologists are distinct from those of psychologists whose sole or primarily interest is in clinical practice; and (2) there is a strong need for a society to advance the interests of the discipline in ways that specialized organizations are not intended to do.

One clear indication that the APS was an organization just "waiting to happen" has been its tremendous membership growth, surpassing 5,000 members in its first six months of existence. Other indications are the numerous strides APS has made in unifying and strengthening the science of psychology.

The APS serves its members and pursues its mission through a variety of activities administered or overseen by its Washington, D.C., headquarters staff.

Publications

The APS publishes two bimonthly scholarly journals, *Psychological Science* and *Current Directions in Psychological Science*. *Psychological Science* presents the latest developments in psychological science for the purposes of promoting interdisciplinary knowledge among psychologists. *Current Directions in Psychological Science* publishes invited mini-review articles spanning the range of cutting-edge psychological research and explaining scientific psychology to psychologists and nonpsychologists alike. The society also publishes the *APS Observer*, a member newsletter that features the current activities of the society, national and international events affecting the society or psychology, noteworthy psychological research, announcements, and monthly employment listings.

Annual Convention

A three-day annual meeting featuring the latest in scientific research and theory is held each June (meeting site varies from year to year). Invited addresses and symposia explore major issues in psychological science from a variety of perspectives; poster presentations highlight specific research questions and findings; and exhibits offer the latest in publications, and teaching and research equipment and technology. In addition to the APS convention, the APS annual meeting has begun to attract satellite meetings of other, related organizations, who hold meetings either before or after the APS event. These have included the Society for Personality and Social Psychology, the American Association for Applied and Preventive Psychology, the Society for Text Processing, and the Society for Chaos Theory in Psychology, among others.

Student Caucus

The APS offers its student affiliates the opportunity to serve in leadership roles within the society. The APS Student Caucus (APSSC) elects its own officers and advocates who advise the Board of Directors on issues of student membership recruitment, retention, and conversion, as well as academic accreditation and employment concerns. The APSSC also oversees the formation of student chapters and administers a mentorship program, guest lecture program, and a student travel award fund.

Summits

One of the society's first activities was to convene the Summit of Scientific Psychological Societies in January of 1989 at the University of Oklahoma (*APS Observer*, January 1989). Attendees representing more than forty psychological organizations discussed the role of science advocacy at the national level, enhancing the identity of psychology as a coherent scientific discipline, protecting scientific values in education and training, using science in the public interest, and scientific values in psychological practice.

Subsequent summit meetings have involved representatives of seventy organizations and culminated in the publication of the Human Capital Initiative (HCI), a national behavioral science research agenda. The document targets six critical contemporary problems facing America as a nation, as well as its communities and families. Psychological science can assist in alleviating the direct and indirect consequences of these problems: worker productivity, schooling and literacy, the aging society, drug and alcohol abuse, mental and physical health, and violence in American society. The HCI is intended as a guide to Congress and federal research agencies in planning behavioral science research activities. Future APS-convened summits will help formulate specific research initiatives to address these crosscutting national concerns.

Alan Kraut

Angell, James R. (1869–1949)

Angell developed the theory of functionalism, stating that it was psychology's task to study the function of consciousness in adapting the individual to the environment, rather than personality's structure.

Thomas C. Cadwallader

Anokhin, Pyotr Kusmich (1898–1974)

Anokhin followed I. P. Pavlov's study of "higher nervous activity." In his research of conditioned reflexes, Anokhin used electroencephalograph and microelectric mapping. He wrote intensively and successfully on his conception of the architecture of conditioned reflexes.

Gustav Eckstein

Anorexia Nervosa and Bulimia

The term *anorexia nervosa* refers to a state of emaciation, the result of self-inflicted starvation, although the patient suffers no true loss of appetite. Instead of the lethargy and exhaustion commonly associated with severe malnutrition, the anorexic has a marked drive for activity and defends her extreme thinness as being "just right," and the only protection against the dreadful fate of being fat (Bruch 1973).

Body Image Disturbances
Anorexics are identified by their skeleton-like appearance, their denial of its abnormality, and their insistence on maintaining it. Excess weight precedes the illness in only about 15 to 20% of cases; most anorexics are initially of normal weight and a few are on the thin side, but all feel they are "too fat" and start dieting.

Ineffectiveness
Underneath their spirited facade, anorexics suffer from a deep sense of ineffectiveness, a conviction of acting not on their own initiative but only in response to the demands of others.

Family Transactions
The families of anorexics are usually socially ambitious and financially successful, and present themselves as "happy"; on first encounter, they appear to be stable.

Anorexia nervosa occurs conspicuously less often in males than in females. In females, thinness is the leading motive in the primary picture with similar family constellations of overcompliance and excep-

tional performance during childhood. The illness becomes manifest when the assured status of superiority is threatened by new demands or changes in the environment. Rigid self-starvation or eating binges followed by self-induced vomiting bring about severe weight loss.

Bulimia
Anorexia nervosa is frequently associated with bulimia, periods of compulsive overeating followed by self-induced purging by vomiting or laxatives. Bulimic individuals are obsessed with their body image and fear of gaining weight.

Hilde Bruch

Anthropology and Psychiatry

Human societies have evolved at different rates with historical and regional variations throughout the world. Some cultures retrogressed, some advanced, and some were entirely wiped out. Aside from the small percentage of mental illnesses that have clearly definable organic causes, the much larger proportion of disorders rooted in psychosocial conditions has increased in the modern world as well as among peoples of nonliterate cultures affected by colonialism and modernization. Indeed, European nations and the American continents show increasing amounts of the most serious types of disorders, especially in modern times.

Social psychiatry emphasizes the importance of new diagnostic categories that more accurately reflect the effects of cultural conditions. In the modern scene, these include the conditions within ethnic groups, subcultures, and social classes that determine the type and incidence of the mental disorders. While such conclusions were not reached in the earlier collaborations of leading anthropologists with the leading psychiatrists whom they influenced, one can nevertheless note their limited progress in this direction. These collaborators include, for example, anthropologist Ruth Benedict and psychiatrist Karen Horney, Edward Sapir and Harry Stack Sullivan, Clyde Kluckhohn and Henry A. Murray, and M. K. Opler and Thomas A. C. Rennie.

Frequent physical illness is commonly associated with high incidence of psychiatric disorder, and since psychoneurotic and psychosomatic ailments occur in clusters within certain families, psychiatry in its more preventive role has moved its researches to communities and cultural groups.

As Clyde Kluckhohn once put it, anthropology holds up a vast mirror for man of his past vicissitudes and accomplishments, as well as his current successes and failures. Rather than fatal acquiescence and nihilistic hopelessness in the face of tremendous human spoilage in the modern world, anthropology can point the way to better means of psychiatric prevention and intervention.

Marvin K. Opler

Anthropology and Psychoanalysis

The principle thesis of Sigmund Freud's *Totem and Taboo* (1913/1955) is that, at some point in paleohistory, both totem and taboo had their origin in a hominid horde in which the strong, jealous, and tyrannical male dominated the female and drove his sons off as they approached maturity. His dispossessed offspring one day united, killed and ate their father, and took the women—their mother and sisters—for themselves. At this point, as guilt and remorse led the brothers to renounce the ill-gotten females, as well as any future partaking of father-displacing totem symbols, both totem and taboo arose.

Géza Roheim, as the first anthropologist involved in the serious study of psychoanalysis, appreciated its relevance to cross-cultural studies. His contributions to anthropology, mythology, folklore, and applied psychoanalysis were highly regarded by psychoanalysts, but they have been almost ignored by anthropologists, with the exceptions of G. Devereux, W. LaBarre, Margaret Mead, and Edward Sapir.

Culture and personality studies began essentially in the 1930s at Yale University when Sapir and John Dollard collaborated, and Clyde Kluckhohn considered that to Sapir "more than any other single person must be traced the growth of psychiatric thinking in anthropology."

In the latter half of the nineteenth century, European scientists stressed the hereditary factor in personality organization. Later, a contradictory viewpoint was held for a period in America. Then, many anthropologists and neo-Freudian psychoanalysts believed that cultural environmental influences were predominantly responsible for the shaping of personality organization.

The first major collaboration between a psychoanalyst and anthropologists, which resulted in major theoretical advances, was between Abraham Kardiner, R. Linton, C. DuBois, and Karl Withers, who together used the pseudonym James West. The concept of the *basic personality* was developed from their studies.

Kardiner's work introduced an important methodological shift. Previously, psychoanalysts had limited their crossdisciplinary work almost solely to the interpretation of anthropological field data. Kardiner was also involved in the actual planning of the anthropological acquisition of such information. Collaborative fieldwork involving members of both disciplines commenced with the work of Erik Erikson (1950).

There has been a gradual expansion of the involvement of anthropologists in the study of psychoanalysis in order to use its hypotheses to understand personality development and expressive culture. The methodological applications of psychoanalysis have varied. Following the lead of Kardiner and his coworkers, some have involved analysts in their planning of field work. Others, like H. Muensterberger and G. Devereux, followed Roheim's lead and used the recounting of myths, stories, and dreams and the questions of their informants as "free associations," which enabled them to understand not only the meanings and uses of such data by individuals and other members of their cultures but also the nature of the interrelationships among id, ego, and superego operations—that is to say, the character structure—of their informants. Those who have contributed are Sidney Axelrad, Ruth M. Boyer, George DeVos, Alan Dundes, Arthur E. Hippler, Hazel Weidman, and Derek Freeman, among others.

L. Bryce Boyer

Antigone Principle

The idea of self-sacrifice, as developed by Benjamin B. Wolman, has been called the "Antigone Principle" (1965). Wolman distinguishes three types of interindividual relations. When an individual enters a relationship with the aim of having her own needs satisfied, it is an instrumental relationship; when she intends to give and to get, it is mutual; when she intends to give without expecting anything in return, it is vectorial. The extreme in giving is self-sacrifice.

One of the outstanding features of the Antigone Principle is the willingness to accept pain and injury. Injury means damage to the tissues, whereas pain is a psychological experience. As a rule, pain accompanies injury.

One should distinguish three main levels of functioning: (1) the prehedonic and subdolorific, (2) the pain-pleasure hedonic and dolorific, and (3) the postdolorific and posthedonic. The functions of division, growth, and decline of cells, glandular secretion, growth of hair and nails, growth of bones and muscles, and tumors (in their initial stages) do not produce pleasure or pain sensations. They are prehedonic. Sucking, eating, drinking, rhythmical movements, sexual intercourse, hugging, and kissing are hedonic actions. Deprivation of food is painful. However, deprivation of important nutritional elements, even when harmful for the organism, may not be painful.

Heros or heroines are neither masochists nor supermen or superwomen. They are mutual in friendship and sex and vectorial in relation to their children and to those they feel they have to protect. They do not profess heroism, nor are they self-styled martyrs. Antigone ate and drank, and hoped some day to be happily married to Haemon.

Benjamin B. Wolman

Antisocial Behavior

Antisocial behavior has been variously defined as behavior that is antagonistic, hostile, unfriendly, irresponsible, and opposed to the principles on which society is based, and that violates the personal or property rights of others or the rules developed by society to maintain group cohesiveness. The American Psychiatric Association's *Diagnostic and Statistical Manual* (DSM-III-R 1984, p. 359) refers to antisocial behavior as either due to a mental disorder (e.g., antisocial personality disorder, conduct disorder, or impulse disorder) or not due to a mental disorder (such as the behavior of some professional thieves, or drug dealers). The American Psychological Association's *Psychological Abstracts* sorts publications under the antisocial behavior subheadings of child abuse/neglect, crime, elder abuse, emotional abuse, homicide, juvenile delinquency, partner abuse, physical abuse, rape, sexual abuse, terrorism, theft, and torture. We shall use antisocial behavior to refer to behavior that has been declared unacceptable in a given social or cultural setting.

There are few behavior sequences that would be universally regarded as intrinsically antisocial. Whether a specific action is to be regarded as socially acceptable depends largely on the social purposes it serves. In many cultures, a person has a right to use whatever degree of force is necessary to protect his own life and property, because the preservation of life and property has been accorded a high social value. Although taking another's life is considered unacceptable, it may be considered warranted, even expected, in some situations (e.g., killing an armed attacker or intruder, an enemy soldier in battle, or a prisoner on death row if one is an executioner).

Most people engage in antisocial behavior at some time in their lives, in response to a variety of situations. Antisocial behavior may vary with genetic endowment and the social learning and conditioning of the individual and may be colored by the interaction of a number of variables so that its precise causal basis is almost impossible to isolate. A primary instigator of antisocial behavior may be the very complexity of modern society, with its technological and social variations, which place people in perplexing situations that seem to require nonstandard behavioral responses, some of which may be regarded as serving no legitimate social purpose.

Antisocial behavior occurs primarily when certain conditions of the person and the social situation exist that stimulate antisocial acts. Not only does society define what is antisocial, but it discriminates among people in terms of age and sex, sexual orientation, appearance, socioeconomic status, and race as to what behaviors will be sanctioned in a given setting. The peer culture and the availability of instruments to facilitate antisocial behavior are powerful determinants of behavior as well. Such activities as gang rape, murder, drug dealing, or carjacking may be positively viewed by gang members, while being abhorrent to outsiders. Peer-group-sanctioned criminal behavior among young people may result in part from disillusionment with the perceived personal benefits of following adult social norms.

Etiology of Antisocial Behavior

A variety of hypotheses have been advanced regarding the underpinnings of antisocial behavior. Some are attempts to account for specific types of socially troublesome behavior, and others are derived from complex theories of human development and behavior.

PSYCHOANALYTIC

Classical psychoanalysis views antisocial proclivities as innate but constrained by the ego and superego. One view holds that psychopathic behavior arises from unconscious conflict and a sense of guilt. Another view is that some parents have unconscious antisocial impulses, and without realizing it work deliberately and persistently to influence their child to carry out irresponsible activity in order to gain for themselves a vicarious satisfaction they do not dare seek directly. Quite often, the child is induced by the rejecting parent into a career of self-defeating antisocial behavior (Wolman, 1987).

MODELING

Social learning theories assume that antisocial behavior in a child may result from modeling another person's antisocial behavior. If parents are distant and cold, or if there is continuing parental discord, the child goes not learn how to relate to others with closeness and warmth. If parents are inconsistent in providing rewards and punishments, the child has no consistent model to imitate, and consequently her concept of appropriate and inappropriate behavior tends to remain diffuse and inconsistent. If a child is frequently promised rewards that are not delivered, she may in turn make promises she does not keep. If parental models show little capacity to delay gratification, the child may expect immediate gratification of her needs and desires. A child who has been abused by a parent may later tend to abuse her own children.

CONDITIONING FAILURE

A child gradually acquires moral knowledge—an awareness of the rules of society—through concept formation and cognitive learning. One view holds that moral feelings (shame, remorse, guilt) are acquired through classical conditioning, whereas moral behavior results from instrumental and imitative learning. Moral feelings may be too poorly conditioned in some children (e.g., the sociopath) to inhibit antisocial behavior. In other children, the problem is not conditioning failure but conditioning source. One view is that the socialized or dyssocial criminal may have strong feelings and good conduct, according to the standards of his own subculture; he has simply learned a set of rules that is contrary to those of society at large. Antisocial behavior is also believed by some to result from punishment applied at the wrong time in relation to the improper behavior, or punishment applied without attempting to make sure the child understands the reason for it.

SELF-CONCEPT

If a parent condemns a child for an original incident of antisocial behavior, the child may see herself as a bad or unlovable person. If she adopts a view of herself as bad or unlovable, she will tend to behave as a bad or unlovable child. Her deviant behavior will bring further social rejection and reinforce her negative self-concept.

GENETICS

There is a recurring hypothesis that genetic endowment determines how destructive or aggressive a child may become. Some parents may be subjected to unwarranted criticism for instigating antisocial behavior in a child when, in fact, the child is congenitally hyperaggressive or destructive and elicits what is actually reasonable and necessary force, punishment, or restraint under the circumstances. The

XYY chromosomal type has also been accused of being genetically predisposed to antisocial acts, but there is little convincing data to support this notion.

EMOTIONAL CONTROL

Although temper tantrums are common in young children, by the age of 5 most children have gained relatively good control of their emotions. Some people, on the other hand, continue to suffer from rage attacks into adulthood, developing emotionally labile or explosive personalities in which they become "fighting mad" or destructive to property when even slightly frustrated. Criminal law recognizes that even a person of ordinary temperament may, under certain circumstances, be provoked to kill intentionally and impulsively, without reflection. Thus, there is a distinction in law between crimes of voluntary manslaughter (occurring in the heat of passion) and murder (involving deliberate suspension of control and malice aforethought). Mob violence is a special situation in which emotionally uncontrolled reactions of one person seem to release a chain reaction of similar responses in other persons.

DISORDERED PERSONALITY

Antisocial acts are believed to arise out of mental disorder in some people, as, for example, in response to auditory hallucinations, where a person does what he is told by the "voices" that command him, fearing to disobey them. Such inner directives may have resulted in cult disasters such as those that occurred in Jonestown and Waco, Texas. Antisocial behavior may result from the temporary or permanent impairment of mental or intellectual abilities, rendering a person unable to distinguish whether an act is normally right or wrong or impelling him irresistibly to act from a sudden loss of self-control.

INTENTIONAL

Antisocial acts may arise out of an intention to injure a person or a person's property. Willful or deliberate harm may be inflicted by an individual attempting to retaliate for perceived wrongs done to her, or because she holds the life or property of others of little value and believes she can execute an offense without suffering negative consequences. The

behavior of sociopaths is believed by some to be based on willful and deliberate disregard for law and the moral standards of society (Wolman 1987).

NEGLIGENCE

Many people suffer injuries to themselves or property arising out of the carelessness or recklessness of others. Many modern cultures expect adult behavior to be governed by mature judgment and reason. Tort law in the United States asserts that everyone has a duty to exercise due care so as not to subject others to the unreasonable risk of harm. It is expected that a reasonable person will foresee that certain actions might cause harm to others and forego them. Much of the antisocial behavior of children and youths arises from their lack of mature judgment and their inability to foresee that certain acts might injure another person or property.

INTOXICATION

Antisocial acts frequently occur while an individual is intoxicated by alcohol or drugs, which temporarily reduce his capacity for rational control of aggressive or sexual impulses or cloud his judgment. Chronic alcoholism has sometimes been considered a legal defense to disorderly conduct or breach of the peace, because the chronic alcoholic presumably does not drink by choice.

ADDICTION

Antisocial behavior may arise from an induced need to support a drug habit. This is an instance in which one type of antisocial behavior (illegal drug use) leads in a circular fashion to another (theft, prostitution, etc.) in order to continue the first.

MISCELLANEOUS

Antisocial behavior may result from a variety of other internal or external conditions. It may occur as an adaptive attempt to solve a problem, such as stealing when one is hungry. It may occur out of necessity, as a choice between two evils, as when a ship's crew mutinies because they fear their drunken captain will destroy the ship. It may occur under duress, as when a person is coerced into participating in a bank robbery under the threat that if she does not, her kidnapped child will be killed. Antisocial behavior may also be induced through the "bad influence" of others.

Research

Many research studies have shed light on the characteristics and backgrounds of people who engage in antisocial behavior. Much of the most recent research on antisocial behavior has focused on hate-motivated crimes (Berk, Boyd, & Hamner 1992); sociomoral development (Berkowitz, Guerra & Nucci 1991); the antisocial personality (Dinitz, 1986); the sociopathic personality (Wolman 1987); etiology of antisocial behavior (Hawkins & Lishner 1987); epidemiology of antisocial behavior (Offord, Boyle & Racine 1991); antisocial behavior and social distress (Rieber & Green 1989); antisocial behavior and depression (Snyder & Huntley 1990); predicting antisocial behavior from childhood behavior (Trimblay 1992); antisocial behavior of persons suffering from mental disorders (Hodgins 1988); and prevention of antisocial behavior (Wurmser 1987).

Donald E. Spiegel

Anxiety in Children: Clinical Syndromes

Current diagnostic classification, as represented by American Psychiatric Association's *Diagnostic and Statistical Manual* (*DSM-III*), specifies three anxiety disorders of childhood. These three—separation anxiety disorder, avoidant disorder, and overanxious disorder—have characteristic clinical presentations. *Separation anxiety disorder* is characterized by excessive anxiety on separation from primary attachment figures, or from the home surrounding. This anxiety may be manifested through "shadowing," where the child physically follows the parent as if he were the parent's shadow, through clinging behavior, or through refusal to leave the house and/or the parent. Although *DSM-III* distinguishes between "true" school phobia (fear of school itself) and school refusal as a function of anxiety at separation from the parent, school phobia is thought by many (Bowlby, 1973) to be a subset of separation anxiety. Associated features include somatic complaints, travel phobias, and preoccupations with death and dying.

Avoidant disorder is marked by a shrinking from contact with strangers and acquaintances to a degree that significantly interferes with social functioning. Such children are to be distinguished from those who are schizoid or depressively withdrawn, as they demonstrate a clear and intense desire for warmth and contact with others. The picture here is more one of pathological shyness than of withdrawal. Such children tend to experience a painful lack of self-confidence, are unassertive, and are incapacitated by the sorts of competition that children experience in ordinary school and social environments.

Overanxious disorder is characterized by chronic anxious worrying about concerns or events that are not directly related to separation. Anxiety tends to center around concerns of not meeting expectations; for example, worries about not doing well on examinations, about not doing chores, not meeting deadlines, or about the perceived dangers of anticipated situations. There are tendencies to perfectionism, obsessive self-doubt, and a pathological need for approval. This disorder may be difficult to distinguish from obsessive-compulsive neurosis, particularly in its obsessive aspects.

Other anxious states that may appear in childhood include various simple phobias, which are thought by some researchers (Gittelman 1986; Orvashel & Weissman 1986) to be age-appropriate and not pathological markers; obsessive-compulsive neurosis; and post-traumatic stress disorder, which is precipitated by special circumstances, such as rape, war, or natural disaster, that are catastrophic in nature.

Etiology of Anxious States in Childhood

While recent empirical studies rather consistently suggest a relationship between childhood anxiety and parental anxiety or depression (Berg 1976; Moreau et al. 1989; Weissman et al. 1984), the inferences drawn by researchers tend to be split between those who implicate genetic factors on a biochemical basis and those who see the social and emotional history, and specifically a psychological sensitivity to separation, as the crucial factors. Ethological studies demonstrate that anxiety exists in nonhuman primates (Harlow 1958; Suomi 1986), and also present evidence that validates attachment and relational models, as opposed to genetic and biochemical models, as the primary models for the etiology of anxiety. Even individuals who are identifiably physiologically reactive do so under conditions of stress, which are interpersonal in nature.

Developmental Issues in Anxiety

Anxiety once was considered an endogenous state, which developed internally in the individual as a reaction to repressed desires, or as a signal of impending danger from without (Freud 1926). Current theorizing tends to stress the interpersonal or object-relational etiology of anxiety. Such normally appearing developmental markers as stranger anxiety (Spitz 1965), characterized in the 7- or 8-month-old infant by some expression of distress when a nonfamiliar person is encountered, suggest that the prototype of anxiety centers around the loss of primary objects, and indicate the need for a smoothly flowing dialogue between infant and mother and/or other important objects for the establishment of a sense of personal security and continuity (Sandler 1977). Depressive anxiety, a cornerstone of Kleinian theory (Melanie Klein 1935), occurs developmentally at about the same time as stranger anxiety and corresponds to the infant's increasing ability to relate to the mother (and other primary objects of attachment) as a whole person. Depressive anxiety is relational in nature, involving concern regarding the destructive impulses of the child toward the people she most loves and depends upon. More contemporary theorists (Bowlby 1973) and developmental researchers (Ainsworth et al. 1978; Main et al. 1985) postulate that anxiety is a primary response due to a rupture in the attachment to the mother. Children who have difficulties in the quality of the original tie to the mother (as well as to the father and other primary caregivers) have characteristic difficulties in the management of rather ordinary daily separations and reunions, and with the regulation of anxious affects. The child's original tie to the mother and other primary objects is threatened not simply by literal physical separation but by words, affects, and attitudes that communicate the tenuousness of that tie. For example, a mother who holds her child close and cries as she rocks him or her, or a parent who says "You'll be the death of me" when the child fails

to be compliant, will eventually communicate to the child something of the tenuousness of their relationship. Anxiety states stand in contradistinction to the development of security in the sense of relatedness that develops between child and primary caregivers.

Karen L. Lombardi

Anxiety and Conditioning

Some of the most important work on the effect of anxiety upon conditioning brings together two important branches of psychology, individual differences and Hullian theory. This work was carried out by Kenneth W. Spence (1958) and various colleagues who made the explicit assumption that anxiety is a state of drive.

In Hullian theory, the effect of drive (D) is to multiply habit strengths ($_sH_r$) to heighten performance. Thus, if strong anxiety means high drive, a high level of anxiety should improve performance under certain circumstances. The conditions where this should not happen are considered below. Tests of this general idea were made with experimental subjects differing in their levels of anxiety.

This straightforward outcome is theoretically predictable only for simple learning situations; it should be understood that complexity usually implies the existence of competing response tendencies in the situation. For subjects learning a complex maze, for example, each choice point requires the individual to select between the competing tendencies to turn right or left. In such cases, predicting the effects of anxiety upon performance requires knowledge of (1) which of the competing tendencies is correct and (2) which is stronger.

Gregory A. Kimble

Anxiety, Fear, and Depression

One must draw a distinction among the emotions of depression, fear, and anxiety. Depressive people feel weak, worthless, and helpless and blame themselves for these feelings. They tend to be passive, and their loneliness and isolation aggravates their depression. Fear is a reaction to a true or imaginary external threat. When one believes that his resources are inadequate in the face of a threat, fear leads to flight.

Anxiety is not related to an external threat. Anxiety is a state of expecting an impending disaster. Fear is a momentary reaction to danger; anxiety is a lasting expectation of danger.

Depression is related to the past, anxiety to the future. When one blames oneself for past inadequacies and errors, one is depressed. When one anticipates impending gloom, one is in an anxiety state. All these emotions indicate feelings of being weak, helpless, and hopeless.

Benjamin B. Wolman

Anxiety: Psychoanalytic Theory

Sigmund Freud grouped together anxiety neurosis, neurasthenia, and hypochondriasis under the term *actual neuroses*, as distinguished from hysterical and obsessional states, which are more specifically psychological in origin. The basic model of the actual neuroses is a reflex involving merely physical or physiological processes; excessive sexual stimulation produces a quantitative energic accumulation because of inadequate discharge, a subsequent transformation of energy, and finally discharge of a toxic agent responsible for the anxiety symptoms.

It is not until the chapter on anxiety in the *New Introductory Lectures* (1933) that Freud finally abandons the notion of anxiety as transformed libido, which he had clung tenaciously to for nearly 40 years as the last vestige of the basically physiological origins of his thinking, enunciated so clearly in his "Project for a Scientific Psychology" (1895/1950). The reorganization of his thinking makes the ego the seat of anxiety; anxiety is seen specifically as a response of the ego to dangerous situations.

Opting for the signal theory, Freud shifted his emphasis away from the economic base of his anxiety theory, according to which repression produces anxiety, to a clear emphasis on the ego's use of anxiety to produce repression and other defenses. The signal function of the ego places greater emphasis on the elements of meaning and information transfer inherent in the notion of "signal."

A developmental dimension is also introduced to the theory of anxiety, which reintroduces the complex interplay of subjective and objective factors in the emergence of anxiety. Thus, castration anxiety and separation anxiety play a distinct, if related, role in the psychic economy. The threat of castration or the threat of separation may not be present in the real developmental situation, but they are nonetheless inherent risks in the psychology of these respective developmental phases.

William W. Meissner

Anxiety: Theory and Research

The concept of anxiety-as-process usually implies a temporally ordered sequence of events that are initiated by a stressful external stimulus or by an internal cue that is interpreted as dangerous or threatening. Cognitive appraisals of danger are immediately followed by an anxiety-state reaction, or by an increased intensity of the anxiety state. Thus, anxiety as an emotional state is at the core of the anxiety process.

Because intense anxiety reactions are experienced as unpleasant or painful, an individual will initiate cognitive or behavioral operations that serve to reduce or minimize the discomfort. The individual may reappraise the stressful circumstances that initiated the anxiety process and identify appropriate coping mechanisms for escaping or avoiding the stress. If the individual is unable to cope with or reduce the stress, he or she may resort to intrapsychic maneuvers (psychological defenses) that serve to eliminate the anxiety state or to reduce its level of intensity.

Anxiety-as-process also implies a theory of anxiety that includes stress, cognitive appraisal, threat, state anxiety, and psychological defense mechanisms as fundamental constructs or variables. The terms *stress* and *threat* are used to denote different aspects of a temporal sequence of events, which results in the evocation of an anxiety state. *Stress* refers to stimulus situations or environmental conditions that are characterized by some degree of objective danger. Objectively stressful situations are likely to be perceived as dangerous by most people. Whether or not a stressful situation is regarded as threatening by a particular individual will depend on his or her own cognitive appraisal of that specific situation. It should also be noted that an objectively stressful situation may not be appraised as dangerous or threatening by a particular individual, and conversely, that nonstressful situations may be appraised as threatening by people who, for reasons generally based on past experience, interpret such situations as potentially harmful or dangerous.

The intensity and duration of state anxiety reactions in response to both psychological stress and physical danger will be in proportion to the amount of threat the situation poses for the individual and the persistence of his or her interpretation of the situation as personally threatening. It should be noted, however, that the appraisal of a particular evaluative situation as threatening is also influenced by the individual's skills, abilities, and past experience, as well as his or her level of trait anxiety. Furthermore, frequently encountered stressful situations may lead to the development of effective coping responses that quickly eliminate or minimize the danger, or to the activation of defensive processes that serve to reduce or mitigate the intensity of the state-anxiety reaction.

Early research on anxiety and learning assumed that people with high scores on measures of trait anxiety were chronically more anxious than individuals low in trait anxiety, and therefore higher in drive level. The results of more recent experiments indicate that people who differ in trait anxiety show differences in learning only when the conditions of learning involve some degree of psychological stress. Individuals high in trait anxiety respond to psychological stress with greater elevation in state anxiety than do people with low trait anxiety.

Contemporary research on anxiety (Wolman and Stricker 1994) deals also with several hypothetical issues, including genetics, biochemical factors, and biopsychobehavioral aspects, and relates the treatment of anxiety to family and group psychotherapy.

Charles D. Spielberger

Appraisal and Coaching of Personnel

Periodic appraisal of an employee's performance by his or her manager, with a follow-up feedback interview, is a widely practiced personnel activity in large organizations.

Experience and some research have shown that the success of appraisal interviews for coaching purposes is likely to be enhanced if the manager follows these guidelines:

1. Prepare in advance, even to the point of deciding how a suggestion for improvement will be phrased.
2. Ask the subordinate to also prepare in advance by assessing his or her own performance and thinking through any issues or problems he or she would like to bring up in the interview.
3. In discussing performance, confine evaluative comments to performance actually observed, and avoid imputing personal shortcomings based on observed performance.
4. Use a nondirective approach as much as possible. That is, encourage the subordinate to discuss his or her own performance and to present suggestions or plans for improvement.
5. Do not bring up deficiencies that are not within the individual's control.
6. Emphasize strengths to build on rather than focusing on weaknesses.
7. Translate suggestions for improvement into specific work plans and goals.

Herbert H. Meyer

Aptitudes and Aptitude Testing

One important kind of worker characteristic is the pattern of aptitudes possessed. An aptitude is a set of characteristics regarded as symptomatic of an individual's ability to acquire with training some (usually specified) knowledge, skill, or set of responses. Aptitudes thus differ from skills or proficiencies in that the latter measure present performance while the former predict future performance. Being able to type 50 words a minute is a skill; being able to learn easily and quickly how to type requires aptitude for typing.

Research on aptitude measurement has had two major purposes: (1) to identify the basic aptitudes that differentiate people, and (2) to predict success and satisfaction in some relevant activity in a socio-economic system.

Because most aptitude-test situations involve measuring more than one simple function, the most common measure resulting from the test battery is a test profile, showing the relative strengths and weaknesses of the individual on the functions measured by the test or tests.

In general, aptitude tests have three main uses. First, they are research tools useful in studying individual differences and occupational requirements. Second, they are career-planning aids that help the individual understand himself or herself better and thus make more appropriate career plans. Third, they are useful in personnel situations where administrative decisions, such as hiring, placement, admission, transfer, or promotion, are involved and where objective data are needed to supplement other personnel data, such as work history, supervisor ratings, or educational background (Ghiselli 1973).

The basic rationale underlying an aptitude test is that the individual's present performance on some task is predictive of his or her future performance on a similar or related task. However, if a given individual has had limited or different experiences, his or her test results are apt to compare unfavorably with the test results of the "norm group." In recognition of a possible unfairness when tests are applied routinely to groups different from those on whom the test was originally standardized, the government has recently set up guidelines for test usage, which are designed to provide equal employment opportunity for subgroups of the labor force such as minorities, older workers, and women.

Albert S. Thompson

Archives of the History of American Psychology

The Archives of the History of American Psychology was established in 1965 at the University of Akron (Ohio) to protect, catalog, and make accessible to scholars materials relevant to the history of psychology. The repository holds both manuscript collections (the unpublished papers of individuals) and archives (the unpublished records of organizations). Additional holdings include oral histories and tape recordings; films and photographs; laboratory apparatus, manuals, and floor plans; and psychology-department histories, curricula, and inventories. A locator file lists materials held by other institutions and by private individuals.

Finding aids are of two varieties: inventories and card files. The former consists of an inventory of the contents of each accession. There are five varieties of card files, which specify the in-house location of all psychometric and other tests, photographs, pieces of historic apparatus, organizations and agencies, and all psychologists reflected in the documentary deposits. Except for the inventories and the listing of laboratory equipment, there is no topical classification, and the retrieval system is organized around the names of individuals and groups.

Discretion mandates the restriction of certain items, but the staff endeavors to provide access to as many materials as is possible without violating donor agreements. Inquiries about resources and on-site research visits are welcomed.

John A. Popplestone
Marion White McPherson

Arieti, Silvano (1914–1981)

Arieti's research encompassed several fields related to clinical work, as well as to psychology of personality and psychopathology. Arieti studied cognitive processes, creativity, and volition in normal and abnormal individuals. His main work was devoted to schizophrenia. Arieti wrote *Intrepretation of Schizophrenia* (1950) and he was the editor-in-chief of the voluminous *American Handbook of Psychiatry*.

Benjamin B. Wolman

Art and Psychoanalysis

Several ego needs are served by the push to create; the search for complete acceptance, and hence ideal love, as well as the justification of feelings of uniqueness and the restitution of lost love objects. Furthermore, the creative endeavor is also an attempt to master aggressive impulses, which threaten to overpower the ego.

Gratification as a result of a finished creation is short-lived, since no work of art can fulfill all restorative ego needs, all narcissistic or aggressive strivings, or all omnipotent fantasies. A feeling of letdown sets in, of having fallen short of one's expectations and ambitious aims. The artist complains of being totally drained of creative energy and imagination. This phase of discouragement, even depression, due to the injury to the artist's narcissism can only be resolved through renewed creative activity.

Works of art have form and style, which distinguish them from dreams. Creative activity has been compared to dream work, and analysts have been fond of approaching artworks like dreams, interpreting the subject matter as symbolic expression of the artist's conflicts, love life, and character structure.

The complexity of the creative process would seem to be bound up with the particular accessibility to the artist of the primary process, of the unconscious and preconscious systems. Many possible levels of integration of life experience with cognitive mechanisms are lying side by side, as it were, which may be the secret of their availability to the artist.

Hans J. Kleinschmidt

Art Therapy

Art therapy uses the visual and enactive modes of communication, rather than the typically verbal modes of psychotherapy, and it can be used in the context of any theoretical orientation or treatment aim. To understand the basic dimensions of art therapy, it is wise to place image formation in the context of other modes of thought, examine the advantages and disadvantages of graphic communication, and consider the variety of styles and interventions used with this technique.

When therapists encourage some form of graphic communication instead of talking with patients, they do so usually for one or more of these reasons: to obtain more information; to establish more closeness with the patient; to evoke emotional expressions and work through feeling states; or to transform the patient's mood or attitude.

The need for nonverbal communication is much greater in patients who are mute, severely withdrawn, or simply mistrust talking relationships. While some therapists remain physically present but silent with such patients until they are willing or able to talk, other therapists believe they can reach a patient by a nonlexical approach such as attempting to draw with them.

Because image formation is closely linked with emotion, images can be used to change mood or attitude. This process is complex in actual practice and not without hazards, but a simple illustration is when a depressed person is asked to draw a happy scene. If she cooperates, her mood may lift (temporarily), and the experience may indicate to her that it is possible to feel better, thus supplying hope.

Individual therapists vary in how they use graphic communication. Some prefer to use the experience much like art, hence the name. The patient is encouraged to express inner feelings and ideas, and also to achieve an aesthetically pleasing or at least satisfying expression.

Art therapy techniques can also be used in group settings. The most common use is with psychiatric inpatients, where the graphic production can be used to foster social communication in group psychotherapy.

The therapist may deliberately instruct a patient to draw recurrent intrusive images repeatedly, on the grounds that through such repetition the patient may learn control of the image and complete cognitive processing of the relevant ideational and affective associations, so mastering a previously overwhelming experience or fantasy.

Art therapy is also used with children. It helps them to express graphically what they are unable to express verbally.

Mardi J. Horowitz

Artistic Aptitude: Measurement Methods

The measurement of artistic aptitude involves several components. For producing works of art, there are probably some underlying abilities that cut across different times and different cultures. Most painting requires the ability to make line drawings, to combine colors, and to achieve properties of "balance." In musical ability, the basic sensory skills of tonal memory, sense of pitch, and recognition of rhythms to some extent cut across different kinds of musical production. Tests can also be made concerning how well the individual can actually produce works of art, this being more easily done with graphic art than musical art.

Musical Aptitude

SEASHORE MEASURES

One of the oldest and most widely used musical tests is the Seashore Measures of Musical Talents. The test stimuli are reproduced on phonograph records, which can be used for the testing of moderate-sized groups of subjects. The battery includes the following subtests:

1. *Pitch discrimination.* The subject is asked whether the second of two tones is higher or lower than the first. The items are made progressively more difficult by decreasing the difference in pitch between the pairs of tones.
2. *Loudness discrimination.* The subject judges which of two tones is louder.
3. *Time discrimination.* One tone is presented for a longer period of time than another. The subject judges which of the two tones is longer.
4. *Rhythm judgment.* The subject judges whether two rhythmic patterns are the same or different.
5. *Timbre judgment.* The subject judges whether or not two tones are of the same musical quality.
6. *Tonal memory.* Two series of notes are played. In the second series one of the notes is altered. The subject judges which of the notes is different.

WING TESTS

The Wing Standarized Tests of Musical Intelligence were designed to evaluate the skills required for musical production and appreciation. Like the Seashore Measures, the Wing Tests use phonograph recordings. The following seven functions are tested:

1. *Chord analysis.* The subject judges the number of notes in a chord.
2. *Pitch change.* The subject judges the direction of change of notes in a repeated chord.
3. *Memory.* The subject judges which note is changed in a repeated melodic phrase.
4. *Rhythmic accent.* The subject judges which performance of a musical phrase has the better rhythmic pattern.
5. *Harmony.* The subject judges which of two harmonies is better for a particular melody.
6. *Intensity.* The subject judges which of two pieces has the more appropriate pattern of dynamics, or emphasis.
7. *Phrasing.* The subject judges which of two versions has the more appropriate phrasing.

Graphic Art

MEIER TEST

The Meier Art Judgment Test is by far the most widely used test of art appreciation. It also uses the altered-version type of item. In this test only one alternative version is given for each original work of art, and the items concern relatively timeless art masterpieces. The items are all in black and white. The altered version of each masterpiece is meant to destroy its aesthetic organization. In a typical altered version, one figure is moved to the side in such a way as to change the balance of the painting.

GRAVES TEST

The Graves Design Judgment Test consists entirely of abstract designs, which makes it as independent as possible of traditional and contemporary art values. Each test item consists of either two or three versions of the same basic design. The altered version or versions were constructed to violate accepted aesthetic principles. The judgments of art teachers and art students were used to select the best 90 items from an original list of 150. Although the Graves Test gives promise of being a useful measure, only a small amount of empirical work has been done with it.

WORK SAMPLE TESTS

A number of tests have been designed to measure how well individuals can actually produce graphic art. Typical of these is the Horn Art Aptitude Inventory, which includes the following subtests:

1. *Scribble exercise.* The subject makes outline drawings of twenty simple objects.
2. *Doodle exercise.* The subject makes abstract compositions out of simple geometric forms.
3. *Imagery.* The subject works from a given set of lines to a completed composition.

Other tests that are concerned largely with the production of art are the Knauber Art Ability Test and the Lewerenz Tests in Fundamental Abilities of Visual Art.

Jum C. Nunnally

Associationism: A Historical Review

For analytical convenience, we distinguish the history of psychology as consisting of three major phrases: (1) a classical period, lasting from about 400 B.C. to the end of World War I, in which psychology was primarily an adjunct of some philosophical system; (2) from World War I to the end of World War II, which can be called a transitional systematic phase; and (3) a contemporary period, lasting roughly from 1950 to the present, in which the field expanded out of academic cloisters and into the world of both general science and humanistic concerns. In each of these periods, the doctrine of associationism has had a peculiar and distinctive career.

Classical Psychology

Plato (429–347 B.C.) mentions the phenomena of association (in *Phaedo* 73–74) in an amplification of the discussion in *Meno* that learning is recollection. In *Phaedo*, the argument is that things conjoined often in experience tend to recall one another. The

sight of Simmias recalls that memory of his friend Cebes, who is usually inseparable from him. Then the dialogue moves to another argument: not only does like recall like, but it also recalls unlike. Thus physical objects, which are particulars, may recall universals, which are the Platonic forms. The Platonic forms are innate, acquired by perceptual context in another life of the psyche, and are elicited in thought by their corresponding physical objects. This is an early expression of the notion of association by frequency of past experiences and by a cognitive similarity. For Plato, this notion of similarity does not refer to the similarity between two perceptual objects, as it does for the empiricists; rather, for Plato, it refers to the similarity between a perceptual object and an independently existing form, an idea of which was innate in the perceiver. In other words, a person's situation is simply an occasion for the recall of innate ideas or forms.

In Aristotelianism, all psychic functions have potential and actual employments and passive-active aspects. In perception, *sight* as potentiality is distinguished from *seeing*, which is the actualization of sight. *Memory* is a potentiality, as distinguished from *recollection*, which is the act of going through trains of memories in search of something that one believes one has in memory. In the act of thinking, a relation is made between elements of perception or memory on the basis of some logical consideration. In perception and memory of the passive-receptive type, relations between content elements are formed on the basis of sequences of experience and the frequency and similarities of these experiences. In passive mind, connections occur by association; in active mind, connections occur by reason or by a free construction of the human intellect.

L. M. Brennan, in *Thomistic Psychology*, has pointed out the strong naturalistic tendency in Thomistic doctrine: it conceives that things we experience are naturally similar to one another, naturally opposed to each other, or naturally close to each other. In memory, these experiences are related by the same bonds: likeness, contrast, propinquity. The laws of reminiscence within a Thomistic framework can be conceived of as laws of syllogistic memory. For example: (1) Plato reminds one of Socrates because both are philosophers; (2) Hector reminds one of Achilles because they fought opposite each other in the Trojan War; and (3) father and son are naturally placed together. Reason is particularly needed for the formation of connection of the second type, for such a relation depended upon an abstraction of the opponencies of a relationship.

In the *Sixth Meditation on First Philosophy*, René Descartes recognizes the phenomena of association, but since these are fundamentally embedded in sensory phenomena, he distrusts these associations because they involved confused (sensory) ideas. He uses the argument of association, however, to make a strong case for the close association of mind and body. According to Descartes, mind in body is not like a sailor on a ship, for when the body is injured there is an internal feeling of pain. However, when the hull of a ship is injured, the sailor sees this situation cognitively.

In the Aristotle-Aquinas tradition, Benedict de Spinoza also notes that there are not only associations of external experiences determined by the history of experiences of the individual but also "associations which arises from the order of the intellect, whereby the mind perceives things through their primary causes, and which is in all men the same." The Aristotelian heritage here is strong, for one can see the passive and active intellect distinction. It is also apparent that the intellect, which is the same in all persons, is related to the Aristotelian-Cartesian notion that the distinguishing characteristic of man (his essence) is the possession of an intellect (or soul), which has the capacity of reasoning.

David Hume has been called the most "psychological" of philosophers. In *A Treatise of Human Nature* (1739), he says of the principle of association, "Here is a kind of attraction, which in the mental world will be found to have as extraordinary effects as in the natural, and to show itself in as many and as various forms."

James Mill's *Analysis of the Phenomena of the Human Mind* (1829) has been called the high point of the associationistic doctrine. For Mill, the idea of a house is composed of a number of duplex (complex complex) ideas, which in turn are composed of complex ideas, which in turn are composed of simple ideas.

Systematic Psychology

For the most part, the early systematic psychologists had been trained by philosophers whose empirical interests were in theories of mind. These psychologists constructed rather broad theories based on remote philosophical models. Sigmund Freud studied with Franz Clemens Brentano, Wolfgang Köhler with C. Stumpf, Edward L. Thorndike with William James, John Broadus Watson with John Dewey and J. R. Angel, E. C. Tolman with J. W. Perry, and R. R. Holt, and Clark L. Hull was strongly influenced by the logical positivists. The basic element in each of the standard systems was either a relation or structure (gestalt), an impulse with ideational and libidinal aspects (Freudian), or an association of some sort, usually of either two stimuli (S-S), two responses (R-R), a stimulus and response (S-R), or combinations of stimuli and responses (S-R)–(S-R).

Contemporary Psychology

In the modern, "scientific" phase of psychology, the system of ideas associated with associationism has come under new development and old criticisms. The basic ideas of associationism have been formulated as a terminal metapostulate (TMP) by T. G. Bever, J. A. Fodor, and J. F. Garrett.

The controversy over the present status of a strictly defined (positivistic) statement of the principle of association reflects a basic difference between phenomenal and physicalistic patterns of explanation. Phenomenalistically, one only experiences temporal and spatial relations, and this is the ultimate reduction base of science. In a strict phenomenal description of sequences of experience, explanations are of an elementary law type (as distinguished from deductions from a theory) and require the specification of precise antecedent conditions of any behavioral event of interest. Given the individual and his adaptive machinery, this may or may not be a realistic research program. Certainly, precise control of antecedent and contemporary conditions is a major rationale of experimental research.

John J. Sullivan

Attention and Conditioning

Attention can be assessed by two different procedures. In one case, a sharper generalization gradient along some stimulus dimension (such as wavelength or color, frequency or pitch, brightness, loudness, etc.) is taken as evidence of greater attention to the stimuli of that dimension. In the second case, facilitation of the acquisition of a discrimination based on some stimulus dimension is assumed to indicate greater attention to the stimuli of that dimension. Of course, both of these procedures provide only relative measures of attention, as between different treatment groups, and in no way indicate the absolute value of attention. In mathematical models, attention may be assigned some specific value, but that value is dependent on the specification of some arbitrary scale.

Overshadowing

Overshadowing refers to the finding that when two (or more) redundant (equally predictive) stimuli signal reinforcement, only one stimulus, the salient one, gains control of responding. Salience, in essence, refers to the attention inherently commanded by a stimulus and is a function of such variables as intensity and sensory modality; thus, a bright light is more salient than a dim one and, for pigeons—which rely heavily on vision—a visual stimulus is more salient than an auditory stimulus. The attentional interpretation of overshadowing proposes that the stimulus attended to, that is, the most salient stimulus, is the one that acquires control over responding. (A nonattentional interpretation asserts that a particular reinforcer will support only so much conditioning, and associative strength accrues to the salient stimulus so much more rapidly than to the less-salient stimuli that the limit of conditioning is reached before any significant amount of associative strength has accrued to the less-salient stimuli.)

Blocking

Blocking refers to the finding that when a redundant stimulus (B) is added to an already conditioned stimulus (A), B fails to acquire any control of responding. The attentional interpretation is that because attention is already directed to A at the time B is introduced, the subject fails to learn about the signaling properties of B. (A nonattentional interpretation proposes that because A has acquired all of the associative strength that the reinforcer can support, there is no associative strength left to accrue to B. Consistent with this notion is the finding that if the magnitude of the reinforcer is increased at the time of B's introduction, B does acquire some control of responding.)

A final line of evidence for attentional processes comes from experiments on reversal learning, in which the stimulus signaling reinforcement (S+) is reversed with the stimulus signaling nonreinforcement (S−); that is, S+ becomes S− and S− becomes S+. The overtraining reversal effect (ORE) refers to the finding that subjects overtrained beyond a certain criterion learn the reversal more rapidly than subjects trained only to that criterion. The serial reversal learning effect refers to the finding that after several successive reversals, subjects come to respond correctly after the second or third trial of each reversal. The assumption is that the effect of overtraining or multiple reversals is to focus the subject's attention on the relevant dimension so that learning about the signaling properties of specific stimuli is very rapid.

James P. Rodgers

Attention Research in Social Psychology

One of the most widely accepted generalizations in attitude research has been that the individual's prior attitude leads him or her to selectively prefer exposure to contexts in which support of their attitude is probable, and to prefer to avoid contexts in which information that contradicts their attitude is likely to be displayed.

The process by which a message alters the individual's attitude has been construed by some theorists as consisting of a series of successive stages. Specifically, these stages have been said to include attention, comprehension, yielding, retention, and expression. If the individual is to change from his or her premessage attitude to some new enduring attitude, he or she must first attend to the message, comprehend its content, yield to a new position by accepting some or all of that content, and retain an altered position for expression in later behaviors toward the referent of the attitude.

Several studies have reported differences in comprehension of the message as a function of attention or distraction manipulations.

More traditional manipulations of attention have used shadowing of irrelevant material presented simultaneously with target material, or counting backward immediately following presentation of target material.

Karl L. Hakmiller

Attitude Development and Change: Theories

The definition of attitude has always been somewhat elastic, and its precise usage varies with both the writer and the area of discourse. Traditionally, attitude is an enduring organization of motivational, emotional, perceptual, and cognitive processes with respect to some aspect of the individual's world. An attitude can be positive or negative in varying degrees and is related to one's predispositions to act consistently toward some object, whether the "object" is an idea, a person, or a political party. Other definitions put more or less emphasis upon physiological variables involved in the readiness to act, the affective nature of attitudes, and their various dimensions (such as complexity, extremity, intensity, and connectedness to other attitudes). The tripartite threads of feeling, thinking, and action run through almost all definitions. All investigators agree that although attitudes are enduring, they are also learned or, more broadly, changed through experience.

Theoretical approaches to attitude change can be divided into four major but not mutually exclusive categories: consistency theories, learning and conditioning theories, functional theories, and judgmental theories.

Consistency Theories

The most important consistency theories are balance theory and dissonance theory (Abelson et al. 1968). These represent slightly different approaches, but in each it is assumed that people strive to perceive their world in a consistent manner—that a lack of consistency makes one uncomfortable and leads to attempts to "rearrange" one's psychological world so that it is more consistent. This rearrangement typically takes the form of attitude change.

F. Heider, in his balance theory (1958) emphasizes the relationship among three things in a person's phenomenological world; the person (P); another person (O); and some object (X). Either a liking or a unit (a belonging or gestalt) relationship can exist within each pair of the three, and this relationship can be either positive or negative. If all three relationships are positive or two negative and one positive, the state is balanced. All other arrays are imbalanced.

L. Festinger (1957) emphasizes cognitive elements and the consequences when elements are inconsistent or dissonant with one another. Cognitive elements are defined as bits of knowledge, or opinions or beliefs about self, one's behavior, or one's environment. Any pair (or cluster) of elements can be irrelevant, consonant, or dissonant with one another. It is emphasized that inconsistency need not be logical. Theoretically, dissonance is a state of psychological tension that leads to efforts to reduce it. Ways to reduce dissonance include changing cognitive elements, all of which may be said to involve attitude change.

As R. B. Zajonc has pointed out, consistency theories emphasize human rationality, but the ways that one maintains and achieves consistency emphasize the irrational side of human nature.

Learning Theories

Many people assume that most attitudes are learned, but paradoxically, relatively little experimental research underlies this claim. Probably many important attitudes are developed in childhood through single significant, often traumatic experiences. Other attitudes are developed through restrictive experiences, such as the greater contact one has with parents over other adults, or with particular points of view through television and newspapers in a given culture or subculture.

Functional Theories

The functional approach to attitude development and change recognizes that certain attitudes can satisfy the psychological needs of the individual. For example, extremely patriotic (or other chauvinistic) attitudes can provide structure for an individual whose need for orderliness and fear of rejection are important ingredients of his authoritarian personality.

Judgmental Theories

Judgmental theories, especially those of M. Sherif and H. Helson, emphasize that people develop standards of comparison into which new information must fit. Just as the judgment of physical objects is affected by the breadth and quality of one's previous experience with similar objects, so can one's attitudinal judgments of people and ideas be influenced by previous experiences. It has been suggested that people develop latitudes of acceptance and rejection into which new information must be placed.

There are a variety of theories of narrower scope regarding attitude development and change, but most of them fall into one or the other of the four categories described above. The concept of attitude is intimately concerned with the way we see and interpret our world and how we act toward it. As such, it has provoked considerable empirical and theoretical attention in social psychology.

Charles A. Kiesler

Attitudes and Opinions

Attitudes and opinions are concepts that refer to implicit responses regarding almost any entity, e.g., persons, objects, or ideas. These implicit responses are usually assumed to be of three varieties: affective, cognitive, and behavioral. Affective responses are positive or negative feelings, such as liking or disliking. Closely related to affect is the notion of evaluation, the extent to which something is judged to be good or bad. Although affect and evaluation are conceptually distinct, in practice they are often lumped together. Cognitive responses refer to the beliefs we hold about an entity, e.g., its properties, like color and age and the likelihood that the entity will promote or block our own goals and values. Behavioral responses can be well articulated, involving a script of many actions over time, but often, in practice, they refer simply to one's positive or negative tendencies regarding the entity. Positive tendencies would include things like promoting, voting for, endorsing; negative tendencies include things like opposing, fighting, interfering with, denigrating. Opinions are distinguished from attitudes in that opinions reflect, for the most part, cognitions or beliefs, whereas attitudes more strongly reflect affective/evaluative responses. Both opinions and attitudes are frequently assumed to be related to behavior.

Measurement

The most common way of measuring an individual's attitude is by asking him or her about it. There have been several methods devised to do this. For example, in L. L. Thurstone's method of equal appearing intervals, an individual is confronted with a list of about twelve items, which differ in their favorability to an attitude object, e.g., the game of baseball. A very favorable item might be "Baseball is the single most interesting sport." A more neutral item might be "There is nothing intrinsically good or bad about the game of baseball." An unfavorable statement might be "Too much time on television is currently devoted to baseball." Each of these statements has a scale value reflecting its positivity to baseball. (These scale values would have been established on the basis of previous research.) An individual's attitude score is the average scale value of the items he or she endorses.

A more popular way of measuring attitudes is the method of summated ratings, or the Likert scale (Likert 1932). In this approach, individuals are given a large number of statements that are clearly favorable or unfavorable regarding the attitude object. For each statement, the individual selects the option that best reflects his or her own level of agreement with the statement: strongly agree, agree, undecided, disagree, or strongly disagree. If the statement is favorable to the attitude object then the response options are scored 5, 4, 3, 2, 1, respectively; if the statement is unfavorable to the attitude object then response options are scored 1, 2, 3, 4, 5, respectively. Thus, strong agreement with a positive statement or strong disagreement with a negative statement is scored 5; agreement with a positive statement is scored 4; agreement with a negative statement is scored 2. An overall attitude score is derived by summing the individual's score on each item.

There are a number of other paper-and-pencil techniques for measuring attitudes. Paper-and-pencil or self-report measures are useful and relatively easy to use, but it is easy for people to distort their responses. For example, they can give responses that are "socially desirable," or they can easily provide answers even if they have no well-developed attitudes. Therefore, some investigators have attempted to measure attitudes by measuring physiological responses to the attitude object, such as skin conductance, heart rate, pupil dilation, and the contractions of facial muscles involved in smiling and frowning. Still others have attempted to infer attitudes from behaviors. While paper-and-pencil measures are the most widely used approach, the other approaches provide valuable additional information.

Functions

Why do people hold particular attitudes? What functions do they serve? These fundamental questions have been addressed by a number of theorists (Katz 1960). Perhaps the function that has received the most research attention is the knowledge or object appraisal function. Attitudes that serve this function help us to decide what to do with respect to various objects. When situations are ambiguous, information is changing quickly, or there is more information than we can assimilate, the attitudes that we bring to the situation can help us to decide (with the expenditure of minimal cognitive resources), whether to approach the situation with openness or to withdraw. Research has shown, for example, that having easily accessible attitudes reduces the stress of decision making (Fazio, Blascovich, & Driscoll 1992).

Ego-defensive attitudes help us defend against unwanted thoughts and beliefs about ourselves. For example, the belief that members of an outgroup are aggressive can serve as a way of rationalizing our own aggressive (but unacceptable) impulses toward that group. A third function that attitudes can serve is a utilitarian, instrumental, or social-adjustive function. Attitudes that serve this function are held because they are useful in obtaining other desired goals. Agreeing with one's employer can sometimes be an example of this. Altering one's attitude as a way of fitting in better with members of desirable groups is another example. Some attitudes serve a value-expressive function. These attitudes provide the individual with a way of expressing core aspects of the self or her most important values. Steele (1988) has shown that simply asserting one's important values can reduce the impact of other threats to self-esteem.

Attitudes and Behavior

Attitudes are often of interest because they are believed to be important predictors of overt behavior. Although this belief has the intuitive ring of validity, some very early work has produced dramatic instances of inconsistencies between self-reported attitudes and measures of overt behavior. These demonstrations have resulted in a substantial amount of work trying to find the conditions under which attitudes would or would not predict behavior.

One solution is psychometric. For example, attitudes toward the environment might be used to predict the extent to which individuals recycle plastic. Ajzen and Fishbein (1980) point out that this prediction is likely to be disappointing because of a discrepancy in generality of measurement. As in this example, attitude measures are usually quite general, while behaviors are usually quite specific. If the attitude could be measured more specifically—e.g., attitudes toward recycling—or if the behavior could be made more general—e.g., by including a variety of behaviors such as signing petitions about clean air and donating money to environmental organizations—the prediction of behavior from attitude will improve. Fishbein and Ajzen also suggest that behavior might also be predicted from attitudes toward the behavior rather than toward the attitude object. For example, to predict who will go see a particular movie, one should measure attitudes about *going* to the movie rather than attitudes about the *movie*.

Some approaches to the problem of when attitudes will predict behavior are more psychological. Ajzen and Fishbein (1980) suggest that behaviors may be predictable from attitudes toward the behavior and the perceived norms regulating the behavior. This *theory of reasoned action* has become one of the most popular approaches to predicting behavior from attitudes. Fazio (1986) suggests that attitudes vary on a continuum from nonattitudes to strongly held attitudes. Attitudes that are strongly held because, for example, they are based on personal experience or because they have been frequently used might be identified by the speed with which they are accessed. Such strongly held attitudes are better predictors of behavior than are nonattitudes.

A more complex view of the relation between attitudes and behavior has been offered by Millar & Tesser (1992). Their mismatch model relies on the implicit responses underlying the attitude measurement and the goals of the behavior. A consummatory behavior is engaged in for its own sake, e.g., eating a candy bar; an instrumental behavior is engaged in in order to obtain a more distal goal, e.g., studying for a required course in order to get a good grade. Affective responses (feelings) predict consummatory behavior; cognitive responses (beliefs) predict instrumental behavior. Thus, if an attitude measure primarily reflects affective responses it will predict consummatory behaviors better than instrumental behaviors; if an attitude measure primarily reflects cognitive responses it will predict instrumental behavior better than consummatory behavior.

Behavior Sometimes Causes Attitudes

Two very powerful social-psychological theories make the counterintuitive suggestion that it is behavior that affects attitudes rather than vice versa. Leon Festinger's (1957) theory of cognitive dissonance posits that individuals have a drive to be consistent. The experience of inconsistency is aversive, and the individual will do something to reduce that inconsistency. For example, suppose you are a liberal and you agree to your best friend's request to put a sign on your lawn advertising his conservative candidacy

for town counsel. Putting a conservative sign on your lawn is inconsistent with being liberal, but there is strong justification—helping a friend is a virtue that you strongly endorse. In the face of this justification, there is little dissonance. Suppose, however, the conservative candidate is a stranger and you agree to plant the sign on your lawn. Here, there is very little external justification, and you would experience the discomfort of dissonance. To make things consistent, you could change your attitude or your behavior. Since the behavior is visible and very difficult to deny, you are likely to change your attitude and become more conservative.

Daryl Bem's (1972) self-perception theory explanation for this phenomenon is different from dissonance theory. According to Bem, people have very few internal cues regarding implicit states like attitudes. Often, when asked, people have to figure out what their attitudes are. Figuring out one's own attitude is just like figuring out someone else's attitude. If I want to infer how liberal my neighbor is, I would watch his relevant behaviors. If I see him put a conservative sign on his lawn but know he is doing it as a favor for a good friend, I wouldn't know what to infer. (Is he doing it because he is conservative, or is he doing it to help a friend?) Putting the sign on the lawn is quite revealing, however, if the candidate is a stranger: the sign is there because my neighbor is conservative. When people are asked for their attitude or opinion they often figure it out for themselves just as they figure it out for others. They report their attitudes as consistent with their behavior when there is little external justification for the behavior.

Abraham Tesser

Attraction, Interpersonal

The theoretical statements relevant to predicting interpersonal attraction generally fall into three somewhat overlapping categories: (1) theories that have predictive implications for a number of social phenomena, including attraction; (2) theories that focus exclusively on interpersonal attraction of all varieties and intensities and across all situations; and (3) theoretical statements that are addressed principally to specific varieties of attraction (e.g., romantic love) and/or to phenomena commonly believed to be closely related to attraction (e.g., mate selection).

Newcomb and Heider

T. M. Newcomb (1956) proposes that our attraction for one another, defined as a positive attitude toward that other, is a function of the frequency with which that other rewards us. The likelihood of our receiving rewards from another, in this view, varies with the frequency with which we reward her.

Fritz Heider's balance theory predicts both the antecedents and the consequences of interpersonal attraction, focusing on two kinds of relationships that may exist between a person, another person, and X (which may be a third person or other entity): (1) sentiment relationships (e.g., liking and disliking), and (2) unit relationships (e.g., belonging together or nonbelonging).

Cognitive Theories

The theory of cognitive dissonance has also contributed to an understanding of interpersonal attraction, perhaps most importantly by stimulating experiments that demonstrate that our attraction toward another may be influenced by our behavior toward him and vice versa. One way that dissonance may be reduced is by derogating a person whom one has harmed so that, cognitively, he becomes deserving of the injury. Support for this hypothesis has stimulated further investigations in this area, including the "just world" research of M. J. Lerner and his colleagues.

Social Exchange Theories

Theories of social exchange have also been influential in attraction research. One such theory represents an application of B. F. Skinner's theory of operant behavior to the prediction of social behaviors. Two prominent hypotheses relevant to interpersonal attraction in this theory are that (1) the more a person values an activity another emits, the greater the esteem he or she will accord the other, and (2) if the frequency of interaction between two or more people increases, their attraction to one another will also increase.

Another theory introduces the concept of "comparison level" (which represents the standard against which the relationship of the moment is evaluated) and of "comparison level for alternatives" (the standard a person uses in deciding to stay in or leave the relationship).

Conditioning

Conditioning has been viewed as attraction within the attitude-acquisition framework provided by Hullian learning theory. The central proposition is that attraction to another will result when an individual experiences reward in the presence of that other, regardless of the relationship between the other and the rewarding state of affairs.

Research has stressed the role of affect and of classical conditioning in the development of attraction: "One likes others who reward one because they are associated with one's own good feelings."

Mating and Love

The concept of a "field of eligible spouse-candidates" has been elaborated by Theodore Kirchhoff, who has analytically explored the degree to which the field of eligibles is a "field of availables" and/or a "field of desirables." Other theoretical statements of mate selection include the "stimulus-value-role" theory and the "matching hypothesis" initially formulated and tested by G. W. Walster and her colleagues.

Drawing on Schachter's two-component theory of emotion, E. S. Berscheid and Walster propose that individuals will experience romantic love whenever two conditions coexist: that they are intensely aroused physiologically and that situational cues indicate that "romantic love" is the appropriate label for their arousal.

Ellen S. Berscheid

Attribution Theory

Attribution theory is concerned with the attempts of ordinary people to explain and draw inferences from the events they witness. It deals with the assumptions and working hypotheses that comprise the "naive psychology" of "the man in the street" as he interprets his own behavior and the actions of others. The term *attribution* is appropriate in two senses, for investigators and theorists in this area of psychology have been concerned both with the process by which individuals explain or attribute events and the process by which they make judgments about the stable properties or attributes of individuals, objects, and situations. Attribution theorists have specified the questions of "psychological epistemology" that confront men and women as they seek to understand, predict, and control their environment and the behavior of their fellows. These questions correspond closely to the broad questions that social scientists pursue through controlled observation, experimentation, and formal methods of data analysis.

Causality

The task of delineating the problems and concerns of contemporary attribution theory, however was largely accomplished by Fritz Heider (1944, 1958), whose work foreshadowed and provided an important foundation for the increasingly "cognitive" orientation of social-psychological theory in the decades that followed. Heider stresses the extent to which processing the evidence of one's social environment is more than a simple, objective matter of storage and retrieval. He characterizes the attempts of social perceivers to detect, and even to impose, order and coherence upon the "data"—to construct a view of the world that offers internal consistency, stability, and predictability. In describing this search for coherence and predictability, he focuses on the perception of cause and effect.

Exploration of Individual Differences

Julian Rottner and others have designed personality scales to measure individual differences in expectancies or beliefs about the factors that control reinforcements. The Rottner scale distinguishes two personality types: (1) those who chronically attribute outcomes, positive and negative alike, to "internal" factors (i.e., the actor's abilities and efforts), and (2) those who consistently see outcomes and events as the product of unpredictable and uncontrollable

"external" or situational factors (i.e., luck or fate). Researchers have offered speculation and some data about the reinforcement histories and the socioeconomic, cultural, and ideological factors that might determine such stable attributional tendencies. They have also demonstrated the predictive power of the Rottner scale and other individual difference measures; for instance, their capacity to predict information-seeking behavior, political participation, and responses to external persuasion and self-persuasion paradigms. More recently, investigators have attempted through factor analysis to augment and clarify the components of Rottner's internality-externality dimension.

Commonsense Attributional Principles

The most comprehensive and formal models for such rational or logical processing of attributional evidence have been proposed by Harold Kelley (1967, 1973). These models assume that social observers implicitly use two principles: the covariation principle (when a person has multiple observations on which to base her attribution) and the discounting principle (when only single observations are available).

The covariation principle states that attributors attempt to discover the covariation, or consistent association, of possible causes and effects in a given data matrix. In this attempt, the attributor implicitly performs operations analogous to formal statistical procedures. For instance, he attributes a given response to a particular environmental object or "entity" rather than to the actor or attendant circumstances, to the extent that the response shows (1) distinctiveness to the entity (i.e., similar responses are not made to other entities), (2) consistency (i.e., the responses are made on different occasions and in a variety of circumstances), and (3) consensus (i.e., many different actors respond similarly to the entity in question).

Most evidence for the use of logical principles or rational schemata has come primarily from questionnaire studies in which subjects read anecdotes about the responses of actors to specified entities under specified circumstances. Such studies make it clear that attributors can and probably frequently do make use of these principles to some degree. However, the precise degree of correspondence between these implicit, intuitive schemata and the formal, logical rules of which they are reminiscent remains unresolved.

Self-Perception

Social scientists from several traditions have considered the process by which individuals make inferences about their own feelings, dispositions, attitudes, and actions. Research both on the "labeling" of emotional experience and on the effects of "role playing" and "forced compliance" upon attitude change has been particularly concerned with attributional processes. Daryl Bem (1972), proceeding from a radical behaviorist perspective, has proposed that self-perception processes are essentially similar to social perception and interpersonal attribution processes. This proposal provides the basis for a provocative reinterpretation of several classic results obtained in research on the theory of cognitive dissonance. Later attribution theorists, however, have challenged Bem's contention and attempted to illustrate motivational, informational, and perceptual factors, which may lead actors and observers to different casual interpretations of the same event. E. I. Jones and R. I. Nisbett, in particular, have marshaled evidence that differences in available information and in perspective lead actors to "situational" explanations and attributions, but lead observers to "dispositional" interpretations of outcomes and behaviors. One intriguing experiment showed that actor's and observer's attributions of an event can be reversed through "videotape replays," which shift each attributor's perspective of the event.

Attributional Bias and Error

Early researchers assumed the operation of a motivational bias through which attributors selectively assign credit and blame to maintain or enhance their own self-esteem. Research paradigms focusing on the attributions of successful and unsuccessful teachers have pursued this suggestion vigorously, but with mixed results; it now appears that no consistent self-enhancement tendency exists. More recent investigators have concentrated on perceptual and informational biases.

Lee Ross
Teresa M. Amabile

Auditory Communication

Auditory communication is social behavior, though elaborate physical systems may intervene between transmitting and receiving persons and may even separate their functions in time.

The primary determinants of systems design are the functional requirements, that is, what is to be accomplished by the transmission of messages. It is useful to classify the functions for which humans use auditory communication into five types, arranged hierarchically according to the demands they place on communication systems. The simplest type is that of *releasing functions*, in which an auditory signal serves to elicit a well-defined behavior at a particular point in time. The school bell and the starter's pistol are examples of sounds used in this way. The next, more complex function is *identification*, in which each of the signals in an ensemble is assigned a unique referent. An example of a set of auditory signals used for identification is the ensemble of tones that a telephone user might encounter after dialing a number. Each tone identifies a particular state of affairs, such as "ringing" or "busy." At the third level are *linguistic functions*, which make use of a natural language capable of encoding an infinite variety of messages, as opposed to the limited message set involved in identification functions. Examples are radio broadcasts and recorded announcements. The fourth type, called *interactive functions*, includes situations in which two or more persons exchange messages, alternating in the roles of sender and receiver. Finally, there are *affective functions* that are performed by auditory communication such as music and paralanguage. These are least understood, and are placed last here arbitrarily, as their place in the hierarchy is not clear.

Systems Design

Systems design does not proceed in a straight-forward manner from the specification of functional requirements, because there is no one-to-one correspondence between facilities and functions. Systems that carry electronically coded acoustic signals may be classified according to their capacity as low (suitable for tonal signaling), medium (conveying the essential information of speech), or high (covering the full range of hearing, as high-fidelity music systems), but the capacity of physical systems can be specified much more precisely than that. Since the mathematical theory of communication appeared in the mid–twentieth century, it has been possible to measure the channel capacity of any communication system on a common continuous scale. This same measure, the units of which are bits per second, has been applied to various human communication behaviors.

Sensory Limitations

Parameters of auditory signals useful for identification coding include frequency, intensity, repetition rate, direction, duration, modulation parameters, and spectral parameters affecting timbre. No more than four or five steps per dimension can be used for absolute identification. Listening conditions such as noise level and distortion must be better when identification is required than for the mere detection of presence or absence of a signal.

In face-to-face conversation, talkers signal that they wish to hold or yield the floor in various ways, some visible, some audible. Listeners signal their attention, agreement, or desire to speak in similar ways. In strictly telephonic conversations, all of these messages must be carried by auditory signals, yet conversation goes on. There is evidence that both form and substance are somewhat different: utterances are longer on the telephone, and the outcomes of negotiation experiments tend to be more favorable toward parties with stronger initial cases over the telephone than face-to-face. It is recognized that face-to-face interaction involves sensory channels other than auditory, such as visual, thermal, and olfactory, but it is not clear what their role in interactive function is. Since the addition of a video channel at present requires 300 times the capacity of audio, the visual role is especially the subject of current research.

Recent research maintains "that the ability to perceive certain nonnative phonetic contrasts is not due to a sensory-based loss, but instead derives from a reorganization of perceptual abilities in terms of the native tongue."

Peter D. Bricker

Auditory Psychophysics

The task of auditory psychophysics is to study the relation between acoustic stimuli and judgments of subjects about these stimuli. As in other fields of psychology, it is important to specify the stimulus. The stimuli for hearing are sound waves that strike the eardrum. The pressure waveform at the eardrum is a description of the stimulus. This is difficult to obtain in a natural environment, because reflected and scattered waveforms interfere with the original sound wave. Therefore, most of the auditory experiments are performed either in an anechoic room or with earphones. The most important terms needed to specify acoustic signals will be summarized below.

The intensity of a sound is defined by the average power per unit area (unit dyne/cm^2). Intensity (I) is usually expressed relative to the reference intensity of I_O=0.0002 dyne/cm^2, which corresponds to the intensity of a just-audible tone.

A sound of intensity I is said to have a sound pressure level (SPL) of x decibels (dB) re .0002 dyne/cm^2 if $x - 10 \log (I/I_O)$. The most elementary waveforms used in psychoacoustic experiments are sinusoidal signals referred to as pure tones. These are functions of the form $p(t) - A \sin(2wft+O)$, where $p(t)$ is the instantaneous pressure at time t, f is the frequency in cycles per second (often the abbreviation Hz for hertz is used), A is the amplitude, and O is the phase angle. The period T is the reciprocal of the frequency.

According to a theorem by Jean-Baptiste Fourier, periodic signals for which $p(t)=p(t-T)$ can be represented by a sum of sinusoids with frequencies that are integer multiples of the fundamental frequency

I/T. The amplitudes and phases of the components can be computed from the waveform. They specify the discrete spectrum of the signal.

When the signal is not periodic, it is represented by a continuous spectrum. An example of a non-periodic signal often used as a masking stimulus is white noise. This stimulus contains equal energy at all frequencies, while the relative phases of the components are random. Often it is desirable to produce noise with energy concentrated in a particular region of the spectrum. This is called "bandpass filtered noise."

Hans-Henning Schulze

Auditory Space Perception

Shortly after J. W. S. Rayleigh's work, the first parametric experiments conducted in 1876, Silvanus Thompson inaugurated a second theory to explain auditory localization at low frequencies—the phase theory. In a series of two experiments, Thompson first observed binaural beats when the sounds from one tuning fork and from another fork slightly mistuned were led to different ears by rubber tubes. When both a high-frequency and a low-frequency fork were played through a single tube branching to both ears, he observed that if the low-frequency fork was rotated around its axis, thereby changing its phase relative to the high-frequency fork, the lower frequency tone tended to migrate from one side of the head to the other.

The systematic experiments of Rayleigh and Thompson concentrated mainly upon the spatial perception of sustained pure tone sources. The exception was Rayleigh's initial demonstration study, with his laboratory assistants speaking to him from different directions. In this instance, the most accurate and unequivocal localization judgments were realized. The speech signal that he used may best be characterized as a fluctuating envelope of intensity forming a sequence of brief transient sounds. Thus, information on the perception of transient sounds has a bearing on explaining this exceptional performance. In 1849, Joseph Henry made a series of observations on the perception of brief echoes from a perpendicular wall. In his simplest method, Henry clapped his hands while approaching the wall and listening for the echo.

Methods and Findings

Several methods have been developed for indicating the response of the subject. Earlier methods traditionally required the subject to point, but this procedure was limited by the accuracy with which the subject could position his hand. Contemporary experimenters tend to use one of three more modern methods: (1) A pointer stimulus may be employed such that it can be positioned in the direction of the perceived sound source. The pointer may be a puff of air to the face or a different auditory signal with independently manipulated parameters. (2) A centering method may be used whereby one interaural stimulus difference, say an intensity difference favoring the right ear, is offset or canceled by another interaural stimulus difference, say a phase difference favoring the left ear. The two conflicting cues, when presented simultaneously, can be adjusted so that the resulting sound source image will appear to be straight ahead or in the very center of the head. (3) The centering technique may be made more sensitive by adding a null measurement feature. In the nullity method, the signals to the right and to the left earphones are regularly switched or commutated, so that each ear alternately listens to its own signal and to the one for the opposite ear. The subject's task is to minimize any perceived difference when the signals are so commutated.

Scientists have also addressed the issue of how much of the decoding information must be learned and how much is innate. On the one hand, newborns will instantly turn toward the direction of a click sound-source only hours after birth. On the other hand, predictable distortions and reorientation of spatial attributes can be achieved by using pseudophones (moderate displacement) or tilting or rotating subjects so as to alter the referents provided by other sensory modalities. Thus, while parts of the auditory localization mechanism must be innate, other parts must be learned and are subject to adaptation. Still other psychophysical investigations have enriched the realm of auditory spatial perception with autokinetic motion and figural aftereffects.

Models and Applications

The modern physiological model has evolved along somewhat different lines. G. von Békésy proposed that the brain contains a nucleus that is innervated by both ears. Neural impulses from the right and left can tune the various cells in this nucleus, and the number of cells so tuned can be decoded as direction. This model did not accord with modern concepts of neural functioning, however. Thus Jeffress devised a model that permits the representation of time differences as different loci of coincidental neural firing in the nervous system. The model postulates two neural delay lines arranged in parallel but transmitting in opposite directions, with a series of comparator cells monitoring both lines along the entire length. Depending upon the arrival time difference of neural impulses to the two delay lines, a coincidence of neural firings will occur at different places along the pair of lines. The delay-line model cannot in itself account for intensity differences, however. The neural latency explanation advanced by B. H. Deatherage must be evoked in this regard. It is well known that the nerve impulses resulting from intense sensory stimulation travel faster up the neural pathways than do those resulting from mild sensory stimulation. In the extreme case, then, all intensity information could be transformed into temporal information to be processed by the same neural delay line. But much psychophysical data contradicts this extreme position. Consequently, W. A. Van Bergeijk proposed a more sophisticated model, relying more heavily upon physiological and histological data; he suggests that each cochlear nucleus may send inhibitory nerve fibers to the ipsilateral olivary nucleus and excitatory ones to the contralateral olivary nucleus. The balance of excitation and inhibition in these nuclei can then be processed to yield spatial information.

John A. Molino

Authoritarianism and the Authoritarian Personality

The Authoritarian Personality (T. W. Adorno, E. A. Frenkel-Brunswik, D. J. Levinson, & F. M. Sanford 1950) presented the classical research on anti-Semitism, ethnocentrism, politico-economic conservatism, and authoritarianism. Authoritarianism was analyzed into nine variables comprising a syndrome: conventionalism, authoritarian aggression, authoritarian submission, anti-intraception, superstition and stereotype, power and toughness, destructiveness and cynicism, projectivity, and sex. T. W. Adorno et al. developed the F scale as an indirect measure of prejudice and a measure of prefascism in the personality.

Milton Rokeach (1960) developed the concept of dogmatism as general authoritarianism, or closed-mindedness, encompassing not only prefascists but other political adherents who accept only narrowly defined political positions, broadly reject and condemn other people who differ, and are insusceptible to influence to change their views. The D scale for dogmatism is commonly interpreted as measuring general authoritarianism free of sociopolitical coloration. Evidence exists, based on relationships with other tests and comparisons of known groups, that the F and D scales do measure somewhat different but correlated personality characteristics.

Abundant controversy has arisen over methods in the research of Adorno and his colleagues and in the F scale (Christie & Jahoda 1954; Kirscht & Dillehay 1967, pp. 7–29). Potential shortcomings in the methods leading to the conceptualization of the syndrome have been overshadowed by attention to acquiescence response bias in the scales surrounding the early work: all the original instruments, including an anti-Semitism scale, an ethnocentrism scale, the politico-economic conservatism scale, and the F scale, are worded in such a way that agreement indicates the psychological characteristic of interest; the same is true for the D scale.

Ronald C. Dillehay

Autism, Infantile

Infantile autism must be differentiated from hyperkinesis; deafness and blindness; rumination and failure to thrive; anaclitic depression; early stimulus deprivation syndrome/maternal deprivation; early infant abuse; aphasia and other developmental language disorders; mental retardation; general developmental delay; specific organic brain disorders and metabolic disorders; atypicality; symbiotic psychosis; and early childhood schizophrenia. Metabolic disorders, encephalopathies, congenital rubella, and major sensory deficits have been associated with autistic behaviors.

Autism is the most primitive adaptation to internal and external deficits or disorders that allows survival. Autistic infants may withdraw, but they do not become apathetic. They remain defensively alert and focus on nonhuman stimuli and objects. Their early history is one of relationship problems and lack of response to humans. There is no cuddling, no anticipatory posture, no social smile. However, they accept nourishment, and they do not waste away and die.

Rutter (1978b) cited a cognitive deficit to be operative in infantile autism and that the severe language disorder found in autism is part of the deficit. The comprehension defect is more severe in autism than in aphasia, and it includes an impairment in social usage; in autism, the developmental disorder is more pervasive.

Symbiotic psychosis starts after the second year of life, usually not until 2.5 or 3 years of age. Frequently, autistic children develop a symbiotic relationship with their mothering caretakers while maintaining an autistic stance with the rest of the world, particularly teachers, peers, and others who require contact and cognitive performance. The symbiosis associated with autism is one of controlling manipulation to keep the person at hand rather than the clinging and melting-into behavior typical of symbiotic disorders. The differential history reveals the earlier onset of the autistic symptoms.

Bertram A. Ruttenberg

Autism, Infantile: Differential Diagnosis

The BRIAAC (Behavior Rating Instrument for Autistic and Atypical Children) (Ruttenberg et al. 1978) rates these children developmentally in eight key areas and ten levels of function. Autistic children generally fall in the lowest three levels; the atypical, in levels two through five; the symbiotic, in levels five through eight; and schizophrenic children fall in the highest three levels and beyond. This is a gross differentiation, but it adds support to the concept that these disorders are roughly on a continuum of developmental disorder.

Hyperkinesis and disorders of motor integration, particularly developmental delay or dysfunction of the vestibular system, may be contained within and act as predisposing factors in certain types of autistic syndrome.

Deafness and Blindness
Congenital or early acquired deafness or blindness can precipitate severe emotional reaction, bizarre behaviors, and developmental arrest in infants and young children. Some autistic children under 1 year of age can be found in pediatric hearing clinics because they were thought to be deaf.

Rumination and Failure to Thrive
The ruminating infant returns stomach contents to the mouth without vomiting. The contents may stay in the mouth, may be rechewed and swallowed, or may dribble out. Failure to thrive is seen within the first weeks or months of life. Unless there is congenital neurophysiological disorder interfering with the infant's capacity to activate or respond, it is caused by emotional factors (over 50%).

Anaclitic Depression
Anaclitic depression is a response to the loss of a relationship already established with a specific mothering source that is not easily replaceable by another mothering source. There is an autistic-like withdrawal and eventually marasmus and failure to thrive.

Early Stimulus Deprivation Syndrome/Maternal Deprivation
Hospital observations of deprived, abused, neglected, and abandoned infants usually point to their being different from autistic children.

Early Infant Abuse
Abused children may develop flinching and avoidance symptoms, but not withdrawal and autism unless the battering has produced brain damage and mental retardation. Infantile neglect with actual star-

vation can cause reduction in brain cells and retardation and lead to an autistic-like picture.

Aphasia and Other Developmental Language Disorders

The comprehension defect is more severe in autism than in aphasia, and it includes an impairment in social usage; in autism, the developmental disorder is more pervasive.

Mental Retardation

Severely and profoundly mentally retarded children are frequently referred to as autistic because of their bizarre hand movements, self-destructive behavior, and lack of language and relationship development.

Early Childhood Schizophrenia

Classical schizophreniform symptomatology is not reported before the age of 3. The distinguishing features are the evidence of a thought disorder and the relative presence of language ability and relationship, though both are disordered. Reports of onset of schizophrenia before the age of 4.5 or 5 are rather infrequent. E. M. Ornitz and S. Ritvo (1976), in support of their belief that there is a continuum between autism and childhood schizophrenia, cite cases where children clearly autistic at age 3 or 4 have developed schizophrenic behavior at the ages of 5 to 8. B. A. Ruttenberg (1971) reports similar cases but stresses the difference between autism and schizophrenia in early stages and prodromal symptoms.

Bertram A. Ruttenberg

Autistic Children: Therapy

There are three stages in psychoanalytically oriented relationship therapy with autistic children. The first involves forming a positive relation with the child through warmth, consistency, patience, understanding, and meeting her needs. Specific techniques utilized are feeding, holding, rocking, and pleasurable visual and aural stimulation. The establishment of a differentiated self is facilitated by reciprocal and mirroring activities, such as reflecting vocalizations and playing patty-cake. In the final phase, explo-

ration, mastery, and the acquisition of skills are stressed.

According to Benjamin B. Wolman (1970), autism is one of the phases of childhood schizophrenia. He advises avoiding emotional countertransference and advocates a matter-of-fact, directive, and realistic approach that allays the autistic child's fears.

Behavior therapists regard the autistic child's behavioral repertoire as impoverished, but with the possible exception of speech, no different in content from that of the normal child. More important, the child spends an inordinate amount of time engaging in simple activities that have no environmental consequences (e.g., rocking or twirling a shoestring).

Certain therapies are predicated on the assumption that autistic children have not received adequate sensory stimulation. Some experts maintain that the deficiency results from a pathologically high threshold for sensory receptivity; others conceptualize it as a failure to make the transition from proximal to distal sense receptors. Lacking adequate stimulation, the autistic child has not been able to define his or her body as an entity and to make the basic differentiation between his or her self and the external world. As a remedy, the therapist provides the kinds of body sensations that would aid the child in establishing such a body identity. Proprioceptive, kinesthetic, and tactile stimulation are provided typically in a gamelike atmosphere.

Establishing a warm emotional relationship with autistic children is a prerequisite for preventing their tendency to isolate and/or hurt themselves, and increases the chance of successful treatment.

Charles Wenar

Autonomic Conditioning: Perceptual Factors

Observations of stimulus-compounding emphasize the fact that conditioning and transfer behavior with an electrodermal response is determined to an important extent by the subject's verbal-perceptual activity. Individual differences in outcome can be traced to differences in orientation to the task and the way in which the subjects perceive the stimulation sequence. Some are relatively passive, while others strive diligently to perceive some relation among stimuli. Such variation should be accounted for in a more systematic way than has been done in the past, where the emphasis was on instructions intended to mislead the subject into an assumption that some neutral form of physiological measurement was being made.

Awareness

Increasing concern for the role of the subject's perception of stimulus relations as a variable in the electrodermal situation has led to a variety of investigations. The general question is whether conditioning performance is different for subjects who are not aware of stimulus contingencies than for those who are. Several experimental arrangements have been developed to examine the question. In one, subjects were interviewed after conditioning to determine whether or not they were aware of any conditioned stimulus–unconditioned stimulus (CS-US) relations. Almost without exception, persons who were aware showed better conditioning than those who were not. Refinements of methods for evaluating awareness have been made in the form of recognition tests, intertrial reports, and continuous monitoring of subjective expectations. Awareness is manipulated in these tests by special instructions and by masking tasks, which require the subject to utilize the stimuli but keep her busy so that she cannot focus on the conditioning relations. Most studies conclude that conditioning is better with awareness, and some argue that awareness is necessary before conditioning will occur.

Stimulus Contrast

Another approach uses the notion of positive and negative contingencies, as related to concepts of excitation and inhibition, to vary degree of correlation between CSs and USs, ranging from positive (where CS is predictive of US) and negative (where CS is predictive of no US) to unrelated (where CS is randomly distributed with reference to US). In a multiple-stimulus sequence (where more than one type of CS-US contingency operates), electrodermal performance suggests the development by the subject of relational perceptions depending upon the kinds of contingencies operating at the time. For

example, anticipatory response to a CS that is negatively correlated with a US (i.e., that predicts safety) is smaller when that stimulus is in a sequence containing a CS that is positively correlated with US occurrence than when it is in a sequence containing only CSs that are unrelated to US occurrence (with the US probability density the same overall in both cases). Such data suggest that perception of stimulus relations is determined by variables such as stimulus contrast and adaptation level.

William W. Grings

Autoshaping

Autoshaping is the term assigned to a procedure and phenomenon first reported by P. L. Brown and M. A. Jenkins (1968). In their original experiment, the pecking key of a conventional pigeon-operant conditioning chamber was illuminated 8 seconds prior to each 4 seconds' availability of grain. In the course of 160 response-independent keylight-food pairings, all 36 subjects began pecking the key when it was lighted; the mean trial of the first key peck was 45. It is important to note that the only pretraining received by the subjects was to eat from the hopper when the grain tray was raised. While in Brown and Jenkins's experiment pecks to the lighted key produced immediate reinforcement (4 seconds' access to grain), the first key peck emerged in the absence of any explicit training in the response-reinforcer contingency. Futhermore, keypecking is maintained even when pecking has no consequence on the availability of grain. (Wasserman & Molina 1975).

Classical Conditioning

A factor critical to the acquisition and vigor of a classically conditioned response is the correlation between the conditioned stimulus (CS) and unconditioned stimulus (US). Two important variables are P(US/CS) (read "the probability of the unconditioned stimulus given the occurrences of the conditioned stimulus") and P(US/CS) (read "the probability of the US given no CS"). If the former is greater than the latter, excitatory conditioning occurs, while if the reverse is true, inhibitory conditioning results; the magnitude of the difference controls the rate of conditioning and the vigor of the conditioned response (CR).

James P. Rodgers

Aversion Therapy

Aversion therapy is an attempt to either associate a target behavior with noxious stimulation or to make the noxious stimulation contingent upon the behavior. The objective in either case is to create a new link that will be effective in suppressing the undesirable response.

Despite theoretical ambiguities, aversion therapy has been successfully applied to a variety of target behaviors. Many practitioners stress the desirability of rewarding incompatible behaviors as an adjunct to aversive conditioning. They emphasize that enduring changes in behavior are much more likely if clear alternatives are made available.

The wisdom of attempting to coerce behavioral change can be questioned on pragmatic as well as ethical grounds. Wilson and Davison (1974) question whether any behavioral change can be imposed upon unwilling clients.

Harry A. Lando

Avoidance Procedure; Sidman's

The Sidman avoidance procedure, invented by Murray Sidman (1953), is a free-responding procedure that employs neither warning signals nor, in the usual sense, trials. The animal to be conditioned is placed in the experimental apparatus, where two physical realities exist: (1) electric shock is administered on some regular schedule, perhaps every 30 seconds; (2) a response by the organism postpones shock by a certain interval, perhaps 15 seconds. These two arrangements define what are called (1) the shock-shock interval, and (2) the response-shock interval.

Gregory A. Kimble

· B ·

Balance Theory

Balance theory belongs to a group of what have been called "consistency theories" (Abelson 1968; Feldman 1966). It treats the cognitive, affective, and motivational consequences of certain constellations of attitudes and unit relations. By "attitude" is meant a positive or a negative relation between a person, often designated as p, and another person, o, or an impersonal entity, x, the latter being a situation, an event, an idea, or an object. Examples of attitudes are liking, loving, esteeming, valuing, and their opposites. "Unit relations" include similarity, causality, membership, possession, or belonging. The statement that p is in a unit with o or x (often expressed by pUo or pUx) can therefore mean that p belongs to the group x, p owns x, p caused x, and so on. Other relations, which in many ways seem to function like units, are p is familiar with, is used to, or knows o or x well.

A number of experimental studies have dealt with the triadic p-o-x constellation. It involves three relations arranged in a closed loop, p to o, o to x, p to x. A balanced state exists, for instance, when p likes o and when p and o have similar attitudes toward an impersonal entity x, or toward a third person. Though the possible combinations are numerous, one can suggest the following general rule for conditions of balance with triads: A balanced state exists if all three relations are positive, or if one is positive and two negative. The state is imbalanced if two relations are positive and one negative. The case of three negative relations is somewhat indeterminate, and its status in regard to balance seems to depend on the interpretation of the configuration.

Fritz Heider

Balint, Michael (1896–1970)

Balint emphasized the importance of transference in psychoanalysis in terms of object relations. He emphasized how much and what kind of satisfaction is needed by the patient *and* by the analyst to keep the tension in the psychoanalytic situation at an optimal level. According to Balint, the analyst functions as a need-satisfying object, almost as a part of the patient's psychic structure. Balint stressed the importance of preoedipal reactions between child and mother.

In 1933, Balint was director of the Budapest Psychoanalytic Clinic.

Roy M. Whitman

Bateson, Gregory (1904–1980)

Bateson's main contributions are to 1) the theory of social relations, 2) communication, and 3) schizophrenia. Bateson revised Margaret Mead's and H. S. Sullivan's theories and added the structural frame of reference and cybernetic concepts. Bateson drew a distinction between simple communication and metacommunicational description that regulates interpersonal communication. Bateson's theory of schizophrenia, developed jointly with D. D. Jackson, J. Haley, and J. Weakland, stressed the double-bind pattern in parent-child communications as a relevant etiological factor.

Benjamin B. Wolman

Beard, George Miller (1839–1883)

Beard was a neurologist who, in 1869, described a new clinical entity, *neurasthenia* (defined as "nervous exhaustion"), which for generations afterward was an important nosological category. Beard was concerned with the protection of the insane and the prevention of insanity.

John C. Burnham

Beaunis, Henri (1830–1921)

Beaunis was a French physiologist and psychologist who organized the first physiological laboratory in France. Together with Alfred Binet, he founded the first French journal of psychology, *L'Année Psychologique*.

Margaret E. Donnelly

Behavior Modification: Techniques in the Classroom

Most successful behavior modification programs have used contingent positive reinforcement procedures to modify academic and social behaviors, such as generating language repertoires, articulation skills, and reading skills, fighting, and withdrawal. The most common of these procedures is the token economy, in which tokens or some other material reinforcer that have been earned for emitting appropriate behavior are exchanged for designated positive reinforcers, that is, free play, money, food, and special privileges.

Systematic desensitization and other relaxation techniques have been used to reduce anxiety levels and phobic reactions. Assertiveness training has been used successfully with withdrawn children. However, serious ethical, legal, and procedural issues germane to aversive techniques and other forms of control have been raised (Franks and Wilson 1975; Stolz, Wienckowski, & Brown 1975).

Abraham Givner

Behavior Modification with the Mentally Retarded and Psychotics

The main types of reinforcement used with mentally retarded and psychotic individuals are edible and manipulatable social privileges and tokens. Edible and manipulatable social reinforcements are used primarily with young children as well as severely, or profoundly, retarded or extremely psychotic individuals, while tokens and social privileges (or social reinforcement) are usually used with the trainable mentally retarded (TMR) or educable mentally retarded (EMR), or less psychotic persons. The primary function served by reinforcement is to energize the person to engage in the training program or activity.

One area of great concern in behavior modification is eliminating disruptive behavior. This can be accomplished in two ways: eliminate the cause of the disruptive behavior, that is, the stimuli producing it; or directly deal with the behavior itself.

Self-help skill training involves toilet training and teaching individuals to eat with utensils, undress, dress, shower, shave, and so on. Toilet-training technology is one of the best examples of the development of behavior modification methodology in this area. It began with simple shaping-reinforcement procedures and progressed from more detailed step-by-step program development into a highly sophisticated quick training procedure (Foxx & Azrin 1973).

Complex or comprehensive behavior modification programs require a sophisticated management system if they are to be effective, particularly in residential institutions. Budde has developed such a model using systems technology (Budde & Menolascino 1971), which enables administrators to design and implement effective behavior modification programs. Watson (1976) also has developed a similar management system for use in parent-training programs, where severely retarded or psychotic children are the clients in an intensive-comprehensive habilitation program, and in habilitation programs in residential institutions.

Luke S. Watson, Jr.

Behavior Therapy: An Overview

Behavior therapy primarily involves applications of principles derived from research in experimental and social psychology to alleviate human suffering and enhance human functioning. Behavior therapy emphasizes a systematic monitoring and evaluation of the effectiveness of these applications.

In terms of its historical development, behavior therapy can be viewed as a confluence of several relatively distinct trends. The first, represented by and large by the work of Joseph Wolpe and Arnold Lazarus in South Africa in the 1950s, as well as by experimental and clinical work at the Maudsley Hospital in London by M. B. Shapiro and Hans J. Eysenck, tended to emphasize Hullian learning theory, as well as Pavlovian conditioning.

Related to the largely British tradition in behavior therapy was the work of Andrew Salter in the United States. In 1949, Salter published a polemical yet cogent book called *Conditioned Reflex Therapy*, in which he proposed that human neurotic problems result from an excess of cortical inhibition. His theoretical framework was largely Pavlovian.

Regardless of the concepts used or procedures proposed, the common denominator in all behavior therapy theorizing and research is the insistence on rigorous standards of proof and a commitment to an experimental analysis of therapeutic processes.

It is often assumed that behavior therapists place no emphasis on the therapist-client relationship. This is not the case, nor can one find much support in the experimental literature for this radical viewpoint. The simple fact of the matter is that all clinical procedures take place within an interpersonal context, and this interpersonal context itself is amenable to a scientific analysis.

Gerald C. Davison

Behavior Therapy in Groups

There are two general categories of behavioral approaches to group therapy: unstructured and structured.

Behavioral Methods in Unstructured Group Therapy

In a controlled study of two matched therapy groups of nonpsychotic outpatients, Liberman (1971) found that an experimental group led by a therapist who systematically reinforced intermember expressions of cohesiveness and solidarity experienced faster improvement of symptoms than a comparison group led by a therapist in a more intuitive, psychodynamic fashion. The patients in the experimental group also showed significantly greater cohesiveness, measured sociometrically, as well as changes on personality tests that assessed dimensions of interpersonal competence and comfort. In both groups, whether or not the therapist was aware of the contingencies of reinforcement, a lawful positive relationship was evident between the group members' expression of cohesiveness and the therapist's activity in prompting and acknowledging this dimension of group dynamics.

Studying dyads of chronic psychotic patients, it has been demonstrated that reinforcement contingencies, but not information, increase conversational behavior, defined here as talk between the dyads about a specific topic of general interest, with eye contact at least once every 15 seconds. Providing the two patients with information about the specified topics just prior to the sessions was ineffective in generating conversations.

Behavioral Methods in Structured Group Therapy

Systematic desensitization, one of the first of the behavioral therapies, is used for patients with avoidance problems based upon fear or anxiety, such as phobias. Desensitization has been applied in group settings for patients with various anxiety reactions.

Assertiveness training is a generic term that includes any structured group situation that facilitates the acquisition of emotionally expressive behaviors. Behavioral goals can include learning how to "stand up for yourself," say "no" to people who are exploiting you, and express affection, anger, tenderness, or sadness.

Personal effectiveness (assertiveness) training is the keystone of treatment for a mixed group of psychotic and marginally functioning patients at the day treatment program of the community mental health center. Patients referred to the day treatment program as an alternative to hospitalization have major deficits in their repertoires of emotional expressiveness and instrumental role. Many of them are passive and withdrawn and reluctant to stand up for their rights. They fail to generate reinforcers from their families and work settings, but instead allow the world to ignore or exploit them. Some patients are deficient in expressing affection, anger, or sadness. Expressing these emotions, with convincing nonverbal correlates, is the goal of personal effectiveness training.

Robert Paul Liberman

Behavioral Approaches to Personality and Psychopathology

Dollard and Miller and Instrumental Learning

The first major effort at conceptualizing personality in behavioral terms was that of J. Dollard and M. E. Miller (1950). The purpose of their effort was to integrate three widely differing influences—Clark L. Hull's learning theory, Sigmund Freud's psychoanalysis, and anthropology's emerging stance that cultural factors play a significant role in personality development. More precisely, their effort was to redefine Freudian concepts in behavioral terms and to reduce the system of psychoanalysis to a set of propositions that could be both operationally defined and empirically verified.

Dollard and Miller hoped to explain the acquisition of all personality traits in terms of drive, cue, response, and reward. Taking some liberty with early Hullian definition, they define drive as any strong stimulus event that impels the organism to action. Such stimuli include both innate or biological drives, such as hunger or thirst, and secondary or learned drives, such as fear or anxiety, which are derived from primary drives and are unusually critical in motivating neurotic behavior.

In addition, Dollard and Miller use the concepts of extinction, discrimination, generalization, and gradients of reinforcement to further refine their system. Thus, failure of discrimination and overgeneralization account for much of the socially inappropriate behavior manifested by neurotic persons, while the concept of gradients of reinforcement helps to account for the peculiar timing and out-of-sequence responses given by many neurotic personalities.

Beyond the general paradigm for the acquisition of neurotic behavior, Dollard and Miller define neuroses as characterized by miserable, maladaptive, and symptomatic behavior. First, the neurotic is miserable because if he takes the ordinary steps in life he becomes anxious, tense, and fearful of following through on his plans. Second, neurotic behavior is maladaptive because such behavior often leads to punishment rather than to reward. Third, neurotic behavior is characterized by symptoms that the neurotic regards as his neurosis, but that Dollard and Miller regard as symbolic of an unconscious conflict.

Eysenck and Classical Conditioning

According to Hans I. Eysenck, all neuroses can be classified as either overconditioning or underconditioning, which he calls Type I and Type II disorders. There are three steps in the development of Type I disorders. In the first step, a person experiences either a single traumatic event or a series of subtraumatic events, which give rise to strong, unconditioned sympathetic reactions in the autonomic nervous system. Depending on the intensity or duration of the trauma and the physiological response responsivity of the individual, the autonomic reactions of the individual may be sufficient to disorganize behavior. At the second stage of development, previously neutral cues become associated with the unconditioned stimuli that elicit severe emotional reactions. Through the association of the previously neutral stimuli with autonomic arousal, both the original unconditioned stimulus (trauma) and the conditioned stimuli (previously neutral stimuli) will elicit the emotional, disorganized, and maladaptive behavior that is often characteristic of the neurotic. If the conditioned responses are again elicited without contingent trauma, then the responses are extinguished.

Eysenck assumes that people are genetically predisposed to varying degrees of autonomic lability. Associated with high autonomic lability is high excitation, a process that facilitates the cortical activities of learning, conditioning, remembering, and performing. Associated with low autonomic lability is cortical inhibition, a process that interferes with, or inhibits, such processes. High degrees of cortical excitation (hence, high conditionability) are associated with introversion, while high degrees of cortical inhibition (hence, low conditionability) are associated with extroversion. Thus, introverts condition readily while extroverts condition slowly. Finally, there is a close relationship between personality type (i.e., introversion and extroversion), autonomic lability, and personality disorder. That is, the trait of neuroticism is related to introversion-extroversion in that those high in both neuroticism and introversion will condition readily and will develop Type I disorders (e.g., oversocialized behavior, anxiety, obsessions). Those high in neuroticism and extroversion condition slowly and will develop Type II disorders (e.g., undersocialized behavior, hysteria, sociopathy).

Social Learning Theory

The basic assumption of social learning theory is that large segments of human behavior are acquired through imitative learning. The two essential components of imitative learning are a model to perform the behavior and an observer to learn it. Imitative learning is unusually efficient because the modeled behavior is acquired as a total unit and neither shaping nor practice trials are necessary for learning to occur. Further, the observer, or learner, need not be directly reinforced to promote performance of the modeled behavior. All that is necessary for imitative performance is for the learner to observe the model being reinforced. That is, vicarious reinforcement is as effective in producing performance of modeled behavior as is direct reinforcement. Thus, the necessary components for imitative learning are a model performing some act and an observer to imitate that act. Under these conditions, learning occurs on an all-or-nothing basis, while vicarious reinforcement is sufficient to induce the observer to perform the act.

Albert Bandura and R. H. Walters (1963) cite evidence that the success of social reinforcement varies with the prestige of the reinforcing agent and that high prestige models are more likely to serve as sources of imitative behavior. Thus, in overview, the effects of social reinforcement and the degree of social learning vary meaningfully with a variety of social and biological factors, such as history of social reinforcement, sex, and type of physical characteristics, none of which are considered to be important sources of variance in the more traditional learning paradigms.

Richard G. Ratliff

Behavioral Assessment in Behavior Therapy

Behavior therapists view the concept "personality" as an abstraction that one can make only after observing the way in which an individual actually behaves. As M. R. Goldfried and R. N. Kent (1972) have suggested, "personality may be construed as an intervening variable that is defined according to the likelihood of an individual manifesting certain behavioral tendencies in the variety of situations that comprise his day-to-day living."

In using behavioral observation procedures, certain methodological problems must be controlled so as to ensure a nonbiased assessment. Among such problems are the reactivity of the observer (i.e., a person may behave differently if he knows he is being observed) as well as various sources of unreliability among observers.

Behavioral assessment represents a crucial first stage before the implementation of behavior therapy (Goldfried & Davison 1976). Unlike other therapeutic approaches, which typically use the same procedure for all individuals, the behavior therapist has at her disposal numerous techniques. As a result, the assessment is used as a means of making some decision regarding which technique would be most appropriate in any given case. Following any one of the above strategies for her data collection, the behavior therapist attempts to focus on situational antecedents, organismic variables (physiological as well as self-statements or thoughts), and response consequences, including various dimensions of the response itself, such as frequency, magnitude, and pervasiveness.

Marvin R. Goldfried

Behavioral Ecology

Behavioral ecology is a general orientation, a set of values and assumptions, that leads one to view behavior, behavior change, and research on behavior in distinctive ways. The central theses of behavioral ecology are (1) that behavior must be viewed in terms of complexity, which is quite atypical in behavioral science; (2) that the complexity lies in the relationships that link person, behavior, social environment, and physical environment; (3) that such behavior-environment systems have properties that change and unfold over long periods of time; and (4) that the focal challenge is to achieve enough understanding of such systems so that the effects of interventions can be anticipated in comprehensive fashion.

The Ecological Strategy

The ecologist sees a world characterized by complexity rather than simplicity, a world that obeys laws of balance, reciprocity, and interdependency rather than a world in which independent events occur in isolated fashion, a world in which environment and organism are linked inextricably, a world in which many crucial events and their relations evolve over time. Because of the nature of the problems they study and the way they view the problems, there is a distinctly pluralistic strategic structure of thrust to the way ecologists work. The parts of this strategic thrust are (1) documenting the distribution of the phenomena in nature; (2) taxonomic research; (3) searching for basic processes and principles; (4) testing specific hypotheses; (5) formulating principles of organization and interdependency within systems; (6) predicting effects within systems over time; and (7) systematically assessing various kinds of effects.

Edwin P. Willems
Lee R. Crowley

Behavioral Medicine

Hippocrates wrote that he "would rather know what sort of person has a disease than what sort of disease a person has." Behavioral medicine is a new interdisciplinary field associated with cognitive behavioral therapies representing a collection of methods that stress the patient's active role in self-awareness, in changing beliefs, and in carrying out prescribed activities as a vehicle to new learning.

Illness is a blow to body integrity and to overall well-being. In behavioral medicine, the following is considered characteristic of illness:

1. It creates changes in the patient's sense of self.
2. It disturbs emotional and cognitive balance.
3. It creates distortions in social systems.
4. It sets up a variety of illness-related roles and functions involving the patient, family, significant others, and health care staff and institutions.

Biological, psychological, and social factors are involved in common disorders, especially in insomnia, pain, tension, and irritability. Usually the internist diagnoses these symptoms as psychosomatic and refers the patient to the mental health clinic. Quite often, however, the medical problem begins with the internist who prescribes tranquilizers or antidepressants.

Research studies in biofeedback, cognition, and "the sick role" have led behavioral medicine to emphasize the adaptive and maladaptive functions of the system, i.e., the mind-body connection.

Stress contributes to the way people act and experience being ill, and to their beliefs about disease. It challenges or even exceeds the adaptive resources of the individual. Maladaptive behavior evolves from maladaptive thinking. The patient must become aware and take an active role in correcting his or her cognition.

An important determinant of pain experience is the meaningfulness of the illness to the sufferer, and its likely consequences and their context. Despair, and not the disease, is the greatest enemy.

Essential factors in behavioral medicine interventions include:

1. assessment,
2. formulation in initiating treatment, which must distinguish between acute and chronic disorders,

3. promoting a sense of personal competence or self-efficacy in the patient,
4. emphasizing management by goals-setting,
5. attending to compliance and its management,
6. the patient's and the physician's attitudes about illness and about treatment.

Self-efficacy and self-control are determined by beliefs conditioned by personality and life experiences, the patient's ability to cope with illness, the patient's degree of activity or passivity in self-control, and the patient's level of motivation. The patient must define relevant goals clearly and agree on them with the physician.

Behavioral medicine approaches its goals gradually. It starts with self-monitoring with a journal, self-evaluation, self-reinforcement, and reward. The behavioral-medicine physician must respond to patient's questions and act as a teacher. The physician reinforces positively, involves significant others, and creates a partnership. The patient is encouraged to practice self-monitoring in medicine, meals, symptoms, signs, blood pressure, and temperature.

Relaxation procedures (Benson 1975) most commonly used in behavioral medicine, as main or adjunctive treatment with and without medication, are:

1. Physical relaxation response: training procedures, progressive muscle relaxation, Jacobson techniques, physical exercise, and other methods.
2. Imaginal exercise: imagery, autogenic training, sensory awareness, passive progressive pain, relaxation, and meditation.
3. Hypnosis: therapist- or self-directed.
4. Biofeedback-assisted methods: electromyography (EMG), temperature, pulse, EEG, galvanic skin response (GSR), and visceral monitor.

Leah J. Dickstein

Behaviorism, Classical

Classical behaviorism crystallized in 1919, when John Broadus Watson (1878–1958) published his manifesto *Psychology from the Standpoint of a Behaviorist*. Each of the several doctrines set forth in this historic paper had identifiable precursors; Watson's contribution was to bring the propositions together in one statement and energetically promote the resulting system, which subsequently came to be known as Watsonian or classical behaviorism. Psychology as Watson the behaviorist viewed it was an objective and experimental branch of natural science; its goal was the prediction and control of behavior.

To Watson, it appeared that if psychology ever wanted to take its place in the world as a natural science, it would have to "discard all reference to consciousness" and "no longer delude itself into thinking that it is making mental states the object of observation." Psychology, he maintained, should dispense with consciousness in a psychological sense. A psychologist should use consciousness in the "naive sense," that is, in the same way that other natural scientists employ it, as an instrument or tool, without making it a special object of observation.

The new system that Watson proposed based itself first on "the observable fact that organisms . . . adjust themselves to their environment by means of hereditary and habit equipments." Second, it proposed that certain stimuli lead organisms to make responses. It then followed for Watson that "in a system of psychology completely worked out, given the response the stimuli can be predicted; given the stimuli the response can be predicted."

Watson described the conditioned-reflex methods devised by the Russian physiologists Ivan Petrovich Pavlov and Vladimir M. Bekhterev, and maintained that Bekhterev's conditioned-motor-reflex technique provided an especially promising method for studying reactions to a variety of stimuli in humans.

Although repudiation of hereditary influences in human behavior is probably the most well known feature of classical behaviorism, this emerged as a relatively late development in Watson's system and was not one of its pivotal principles. The essential aspects of classical behaviorism were rather an emphasis on psychology as a science of observables, whose goal was the prediction and control of behavior and boundless faith in the proposition that everything worth studying in psychology would ultimately yield to a behavioristic analysis in terms of stimulus and response.

Laurel Furumoto

Behaviorism, Operant

The movement in psychology variously called operant behaviorism, operant conditioning, reinforcement theory, and—the expression most preferred by workers in this field—the experimental analysis of behavior has its origins in the work of B. F. Skinner in the early 1930s. The principles of operant behaviorism have remained essentially unchanged since they were first presented in Skinner's *Behavior of Organisms* in 1938. In operant conditioning the reinforcement is contingent on the occurrence of the response.

Before the middle 1940s, the historical development of operant behaviorism is largely synonymous with Skinner's work at Harvard, the University of Minnesota, and Indiana University. During this time, he engaged in basic research on positive reinforcement and, with W. K. Estes, on aversive control. He also began to apply the techniques of operant conditioning to practical matters, such as his project using pigeons to guide missiles and his controlled-environment "baby box." After World War II, operant behaviorism emerged as a cohesive movement. F. S. Keller and W. N. Schoenfeld, at Columbia, organized an undergraduate psychology curriculum based on an operant conditioning point of view. The first conference on the experimental analysis of behavior was convened in 1946 at Indiana University. Skinner returned to Harvard as a faculty member in 1948, the same year as the publication of *Walden Two*, his novel of a utopian community structured on the principles of positive reinforcement.

In 1953, Skinner published *Science and Human Behavior*, a rather complete statement of his extension of the principles of operant conditioning to the more complex behavioral contingencies that occur in education, psychotherapy, and societal control. In 1957, C. B. Ferster and Skinner published the results of five years of research as *Schedules of Reinforcement*. During this decade, researchers began to adopt operant technology to investigate phenomena heretofore associated with other disciplines of psychology. The effects of psychopharmacological agents, brain lesions, and intracranial electric stimulation were studied with operant techniques. The sensory capacities of nonverbal organisms were determined by operant discrimination procedures. Skinner himself popularized teaching machines and programmed instruction. Other psychologists began to transfer their laboratory skills to clinical settings, to teach mental retardates and psychotics.

Jean L. Bresnahan

Bekhterev, Vladimir M. (1857–1927)

Bekhterev made two important contributions to psychology and other behavioral sciences: (1) he broadened the application of conditioning methodology by including leg and finger flexion, cardiac responses, and respiratory responses, and (2) he insisted on a strictly objective approach to the study of behavior.

Gregory A. Kimble

Beritov Beritashvili, Ivan S. (1885–1972)

Beritov's early research focused on the role of the spinal cord in controlling the motor behavior of hands and legs. He has made significant discoveries concerning the labyrinth and jugular tonic reflexes, reciprocal inhibition of skeleton muscles, and other inhibitory functions.

Beritov conducted research on neuropsychological orientation mechanism in men and animals in space travel, on image-motivated psychophysiological activity of the brain, and on emotional and perceptual factors in memory.

Beritov was director of the Sechenov Institute of Physiology in Moscow and a member of the Soviet Academy of Medical Sciences and of the Georgian Academy of Science.

Benjamin B. Wolman

Berne, Eric (1910–1970)

Berne was the founder of transactional analysis (TA), a direct and active group psychotherapy method. In 1965, Berne formed the International Transactional Analysis Association (ITAA).

Stephen B. Karpman

Bernfeld, Siegfried (1892–1953)

Bernfeld tried to combine Freudian and Marxian thinking. He studied infants from a psychoanalytic point of view and was interested in war victims, orphans, and displaced children. In 1922, Bernfeld became a psychoanalyst.

Rudolf Ekstein

Bertalanffy, Von Ludwig (1901–1972)

Bertalanffy, the author of *General Systems Theory*, maintained that biological and psychological systems are open systems. The second law of thermodynamics, that of entropy, is a general law of nature, whereas the self-organizing and adaptive capabilities of the open systems enable them to attain equilibrium without becoming static.

Benjamin B. Wolman

Bilingualism

Bilingualism is usually produced by home and/or by the social environment; two examples are:

1. The child who learns to speak two different languages at the same time.
2. Cultural adaptation, such as with new immigrants.

Language and Thought
The fact that an individual can express the same thought process in two different languages or in two different codes of the same language can be understood if we realize that the processes of thinking are not confounded with their verbal expression.

Problems of the Bilingual Individual
Quite often, the bilingual person belongs to a linguistic minority that is considered socially inferior, and she uses the "weak" language. She may lack sufficient knowledge of the "strong" language that the dominant society expects her to use. The problems of the bilingual in this case often are related to her acculturation and to her difficulties with integration. Insufficient knowledge of the "strong" language may cause her to be discriminated against and often misunderstood.

A member of a national linguistic minority group or an immigrant may claim loyalty to his own language and feel frustrated at the same time, because he gives up the possibilities of being accepted by the dominant linguistic group or society. He may give up his own language and adopt the "strong" one in order to integrate and move upward into the established society.

Miguel Siguan

Binet, Alfred (1857–1911)

Under the influence of the English associationists James and John Stuart Mill, the English psychologist Francis Galton, and the French neurologist Jean Charcot, Binet developed a new theory of reasoning. He organized a psychology laboratory in Paris for child study in 1900. Binet published the *Experimental Study of Intelligence*, based on the psychological investigation of his two daughters. In 1894 Binet became the director of the physiological laboratory at the Sorbonne and cofounded the first French psychological journal, *L'Année Psychologique*. He wrote extensively on experimental psychology, reasoning, individual differences, intelligence, suggestibility, and hypnosis. In the years 1905–11 Binet developed in cooperation with Théodore Simon a new intelligence scale, the Binet-Simon intelligence scale, which was published in English in 1913.

Benjamin B. Wolman

Biochemistry of Learning and Memory

In 1959, H. Hydén succeeded in developing microchemical methods for the measurement of chemical activity in single cells removed from the mammalian brain. The emerging theoretical proposal was that ribonucleic acid (RNA) and changes in its base ratios may constitute a biochemical substrate for the process of memory. The RNA bases, it was reasoned, may be influenced by the electrochemical events that attend the pattern of nerve impulses accompanying stimulus input and stimulus elaboration in the learning and remembering organism. Alterations in one or more of the bases of the RNA molecule may lead, thereby, to a coded RNA molecule that is capable of synthesizing a new protein. This protein, in turn, may then act to facilitate the release of a potential neurotransmitter molecule, once the coded impulse pattern arrives at a site where appropriate stimulation provides for transmitter molecule release. This theory gave rise to empirical studies in which cell-specific RNA changes were related to the acquisition process in learning. Hydén and his colleagues demonstrated RNA changes specific to the neuron and reciprocated by changes occurring in adjacent glial cells. Perhaps one point of significance in the theoretical and empirical work contributed by this group was the impetus that it provided for further studies concerned with the RNA molecule. Some investigators have suggested that an increase in the availability of RNA alone might facilitate learning memory. This rationale governed studies that found general improvement in memory ability in geriatric patients and also in rats. The latter, injected with yeast-derived RNA, showed a more rapid acquisition and a slower rate of extinction of an escape response conditioned to shock. Studies such as these have been extensively criticized in the literature, largely because of their failure to explain, in terms of any existing model, a potential basis for the presumedly observed effect. Systematically administered RNA probably never enters the central nervous system, either because the molecule may be rapidly degraded following its entry into the circulation, or because it simply fails to cross the blood-brain barrier. For either or both of these reasons, it may well be that the effects observed in experiments such as those cited may represent either peripheral effects, effects of impurities in crude commercially available RNA preparations, or the effects of breakdown products of the RNA molecule.

Macromolecular Events in Learning and Memory

A pioneering hypothesis for dealing with relationships between specific behaviors and macromolecular phenomena suggested the specific role of RNA and its mediation of subsequent protein synthesis. Alterations in the ionic equilibrium within the cell cytoplasm presumably occur as a consequence of frequency-modulated inputs to the central nervous system. The stability of the nitrogenous bases of the RNA molecule as a specific site is, therefore, affected by such an equilibrium change. Alterations in the base configuration of the RNA molecule and subsequent alterations in its molecular structure in turn constitute a basis upon which RNA-dependent, newly synthesized proteins can interact with molecules of complementary structure. The release of transmitter molecules will result from such an interaction, providing an appropriate time has elapsed. This general hypothesis raises methodological as well as conceptual issues. The required nuclear localization of the RNA molecule is rather difficult to reconcile with the changes in those neurotransmitter molecules stored, released, and subject to other influences at the presynaptic nerve ending.

Another approach to the relationship between macromolecular synthesis and behavioral change employs radioactively labeled precursors of nucleic acids, which are incorporated into macromolecules. Such incorporation has been measured during learning in studies with rats and mice. A training situation provides for acquisition of a conditioned active avoidance response in one animal, whereas a control animal receives only comparable stimulation and handling that results in no acquisition. Incorporation of radioactive precursors C^{14}-uridine or H^{3}-uridine into the RNA molecule is carried out using a double-labeling procedure with intracranially injected isotopes. The amount of the C^{14} and H^{3} label in the RNA isolated from fractions of nuclei, ribosomes, and supernatant material is analyzed to reveal that the trained animal shows greater uridine incorporation into RNA in the nuclei and ribosome than does its untrained control. This finding only obtains, however, for animals killed immediately after the training experience. It is not observed when animals are killed 30 minutes after training. This effect is specific to brain, inasmuch as it could not be demonstrated in other peripheral tissues; it furthermore suggests that the labeling of RNA in animals undergoing specific training for new-task acquisition occurs at a greater rate than the labeling of the RNA molecule in animals that receive stimulation equivalent to that of the trained rats but are not undergoing training.

The nucleo-protein-based lattice representing a memory trace constitutes the beginnings of attention to proteins and their synthesis as a basis for learning and memory. If the synthesis of new proteins is indeed the basis upon which the acquisition of new information, the storage of such information, and the retrieval of such stored information is dependent, then one obvious approach would involve the blocking of newly synthesized proteins. Such an approach has indeed been adopted; the effects of such inhibitors of protein synthesis as puromycin are illustrative. Puromycin is found to be more potent as a source of behavioral disruption than that produced by another agent, acetoxycyclohexamide. The latter, although able to inhibit protein, does not produce the complete depression of EEG activity characteristic during peak inhibition of protein synthesis with puromycin. At comparable levels of inhibition of protein synthesis, acetoxycyclohexamide produces only slight alterations in EEG voltage and, similarly, does not alter the course of learned information as is the case with puromycin.

Cholinergic Functions in Learning and Memory

The impact of environmental stimuli upon cholinergic mechanisms in the brain has been extensively explored. A number of rodent species have been investigated, and the effects of environmental stimulation have been compared to those of environmental impoverishment. The results of such comparisons have suggested that small changes occur in the activity of cholinergic enzymes in the brain, providing provisional support for the notion that an increased availability of acetylcholine at cholinergic synaptic endings might allow facilitation of the acquisition

and perhaps retention of behavior. The activity of acetylcholinesterase in the cerebral cortex has been found to decrease as a consequence of environmental "enrichment," with an increase in the activity of "pseudo"-cholinesterase in the same region. These findings, while suggestive of facilitated cholinergic activity in the cerebral cortex, also suggest a possible proliferative effect of such stimulation, reflected in noncholinergic nerve cells or glia. This view is complicated by a number of methodological as well as conceptual issues. The basic issue is whether an environmentally stimulated animal becomes more easily adaptable and therefore a more efficient learner as a result of such stimulation, or whether the effects are solely due to the cholinergic system.

The use of agents that combine irreversibly with cholinesterase seems to point to a specific cholinergic mechanism operative in learning and memory. The administration of diisopropylfluorophosphate (DFP) by direct injection into the hippocampus produces amnesia for an acquired habit. If the same habit has been forgotten, the injection of DFP results in an enhancement of memory. Such studies support the view that the drug-induced prevention of the destruction of acetylcholine promotes depolarization of the postsynaptic membrane, wherein low levels of synaptic conduction prevail. Synaptic conductance is presumably increased by training leading to the acquisition of new behavior; therefore, one result of learning is an increased synaptic conductance. Forgetting or weakening of the learned material weakens synaptic conductance, and a forgotten habit may be facilitated by such agents as DFP, which prevent the destruction of acetylcholine. The increased levels of acetylcholine, superimposed upon a hypothetically low level of synaptic conductance, thereby act to facilitate the response. Enhanced recall of a partially learned habit has also been demonstrated with drugs such as DFP, lending further support to the suggestion that the facilitation of learning may occur through alterations in synaptic transmission.

Serotonin, Learning, and Memory

Prevailing evidence from a large series of experiments implies that lowered levels of brain serotonin (5-HT) are associated with facilitation of learning and/or memory, whereas elevation of this amine by a number of means, including drugs, electrical stimulation of the central nervous system, or a wide range of stimuli that serve as amnesic agents or events, leads to decreased learning efficiency and impaired memory storage or retrieval. Particularly in the latter regard, several studies have shown that such agents or events as anaesthetic doses of diethyl ether, hypothermia, electroconvulsive shock, pentylenetetrazol-induced convulsions, spreading cortical depression, cerebral hypoxia, CO_2 inhalation, and hepatic coma—all of which produce either a retrograde or anterograde amnesia in a variety of animal species—lead to an elevation in regional or whole-brain levels of serotonin. The magnitude of such elevation and the time course over which it occurs varies, of course. However, these treatments hold in common the fact that serotonin is elevated. Studies have further indicated that the depletion of brain serotonin with such agents as p-chlorophenylalanine, an inhibitor of tryptophane hydroxylation that interferes with the synthesis of serotonin, provides for facilitation of several types of behavioral acquisition by rodents.

Catecholamines, Learning, and Memory

The relationship between brain catecholamines, their alteration, and their relationship to specific aspects of either learning and/or memory, has been given only limited consideration. One of the problems is that most of the pharmacological agents that modify brain catecholamines also have transient or concurrent effects upon other amines, notably serotonin. One avenue that has been explored is the use of the tyrosine hydroxylase inhibitor alpha-methyl-tyrosine, which leads to a decreased rate of formation of 3-4-dihydroxyphenylalanine, the molecule from which dopamine and norepinephrine are formed. In studies where this treatment has been used to reduce these catecholamines, response has decreased. The extent of behavioral disruption depends upon the extent to which catecholamines are, in fact, depleted.

Concluding Observations

One of the many problems in formulating a relationship between the biochemistry of brain cells and the processes of learning and/or memory is defining the species of both ingredients. The biochemical focus appears to rest upon the selection of macromolecules, synthesized or transformed in the brain as a consequence of learning or new experience, so that these constitute molecular bases for subsequent retrieval of newly acquired information. There is also a growing interest in the specific role of macromolecules that are implicated in increasing numbers in the mediation of transmission across the multiple synapses involved with sensory input in the central nervous system.

Walter B. Essman

Biofeedback

Biofeedback, a term coined in 1969 at the founding meeting of the Biofeedback Research Society, means giving a person immediate ongoing information about his or her own biological processes or conditions, such as heart behavior, temperature, brain waves, or muscle tension. Information is usually "fed back" by a needle on a meter, a light, or a sound, or by allowing the person to watch the physiological record as it emerges from monitoring equipment. Biofeedback training is the self-directed process by which a person uses the biological information voluntarily to control a specific body process or function.

The limbic structure of the subcortical brain has been intensely studied in both animals and humans in the years since J. W. Papez's historic paper (1937) outlined the emotional functions of the limbic system. J. H. Masserman demonstrated in animals that sham rage can be elicited by electrophysiological stimulation of subcortical structures, and R. G. Heath and his group have demonstrated similar behavior in humans. D. D. MacLean coined the phrase "visceral brain" for the limbic system, and others have referred to it as the emotional brain. Such research has demonstrated that induced emotional changes are often reflected in, or can be correlated with, electrophysiological changes in the limbic system; conversely, induced electrical changes in the limbic system are often reflected in, or can be correlated with, emotional changes.

In learning voluntary control of normally unconscious processes, we do not become directly aware of the neural pathways and specific muscle fibers involved, any more than we become aware of what cortical and subcortical nerves are involved in hitting a golf ball. But analogous to the golf ball example, when we get external objective feedback of inside-the-skin events, we can learn to modify "internal" processes and bring about biological changes in the desired direction.

Elmer E. Green
Alyce M. Green

Biological Constraints on Learning

Perceptual Constraints

Jacob von Uexkull (1934) was the first behavioral scientist to emphasize the role of perceptual mechanisms in the manufacturing of meaning and reality. He insisted that the phenomenal world (*Umwelt*) of an organism was a nonarbitrary product of its biologically predisposed perceptual and effector interaction with the environment, and that stimuli derive their taxon-specific meanings through these interactions. Hence, von Uexkull would have argued that an important locus of control of learning resides in these interpretive processes.

Reinforcer-Induced Constraints on Stimuli and/or Responses

There are at least two kinds of reinforcer-induced constraints that can lead to nonarbitrary learning. First, the availability of some responses for conditioning in particular situations may be strongly influenced, because the test animal is predisposed by the reinforcer to behave in certain predictable ways. The second category of reinforcer-induced constraint involves the availability of stimuli. Normally (in arbitrary events paradigms), stimuli, responses, and reinforcers must follow one other in close temporal proximity, with separations of even a few seconds or minutes causing severe retarding effects on rate of conditioning.

Age Constraints

The final class of biological constraints on learning contains a number of cases that illustrate that animals are better able to acquire a response or be more generally influenced by a specific experience at some particular (usually early) age than at other times of life. The importance for song learning in many birds and of hearing the species-specific song during sensitive periods is well known. Equally well known is the phenomenon of imprinting. The young of various species of precocial birds begin the process of filial-attachment formation during a sensitive period that spans the first hours or days of life. Moreover, sensitive periods are known or suspected for aspects of socioemotional development in rodents, dogs, and primates, including humans. The combined weight of this evidence argues for the existence of special epigenetically controlled associative processes that subserve adaptive, nonarbitrary learning mechanisms, which are probably not isomorphic with those known from traditional learning paradigms.

David A. Chiszar

Biological Drives

Biological drives (primary drives) are defined as transitory or reversible tissue conditions that tend to modify the speed, intensity, amplitude, persistence, or direction of behavior. Some drives involve deviation from a physiological state essential for the individual's well-being and survival. Most frequently included in this category are general reduction of food supply, deficiency of a specific dietary element, water deficit, oxygen lack, temperature extreme, excessive stimulation in any modality ("pain"), interference with the normal cycle of activity and rest, and eliminative pressures. A second class of biological or primary drives are those crucial for the survival of the species, particularly sexual and parental. These are associated with behaviors sometimes termed instinctive, that is, complex patterns that are relatively consistent within and across the normal individuals of a species and that appear in their approximately final form with little prior opportunity for practice.

If the general understanding of drive itself has

been elusive, significant progress has been made in elucidating the related behaviors of eating, drinking, and sexual activity. Current attention is focused on the empirical examination of neurological, hormonal, sensory, and experiential factors that control these patterns. Even with the lower animals studied, the picture that emerges is one of increasing complexity. It is obvious that only the sketchiest outline of the place of biological drives in human behavior can at present be delineated.

Frank W. Finger

Biological Psychology

The biological contribution to psychology has emanated from three major nineteenth-century influences: the rise of sensory physiology; the increasing interest in psychology shown by clinical neurologists and psychiatrists; and, perhaps most significantly, the emergence of evolutionary theories. There are two themes characterizing these contributions: first, the search for mechanistic explanations of psychological phenomena, grounded in the physiological functioning and anatomical organization of the brain, and second, the realization that behavior must aid a species in its survival and adaptation to changing environmental conditions. The latter theme reflects an essentially biological as opposed to physical and chemical influence on psychological theory, derived from Charles Darwin's theory of evolution (1859), which contends that the variety of living forms can be explained by genetic mechanisms of natural selection and random variation.

Darwin's implication of phylogenetic continuity suggests a similarity rather than a dichotomy between behavior in man and in animals. This has made research into animal behavior potentially more interesting and laid down the foundations of comparative and animal psychology.

The importance of biological adaptation has eventually been recognized by physiological psychologists. The analysis of which features of stimuli are necessary to fire neurons at various stages in the processing of sensory information has shown that these features are likely to be of biological relevance to the animal. Thus cells in the retina of the frog have been noted that would be useful for detecting small moving objects, such as bugs, which form a major part of the frog's diet.

The study of behavior and the brain functions of organisms in this biological context has given rise to the science popularly called biopsychology.

Trevor W. Robbins

Biopsychology

Biopsychology concerns the influence of the functions of the three major biological systems of the body on behavior. These are the nervous system, particularly the brain, the endocrine system, and the immune system. It is also concerned with the effect of psychological conditions on biological functions.

In vertebrates, the nervous system consists of two major divisions: the central nervous system, brain, and spinal cord, and the peripheral nervous system. The latter is divided into the autonomic nervous system, which controls such functions as heartbeat, digestion, and other involuntary functions, and the somatic nervous system, which gathers information from the sense organs and conveys commands to the muscles and glands.

The endocrine system consists of a number of glands pouring their product directly into the blood. Each controls major bodily activities. Examples are the pineal gland, which regulates sleeping-waking cycles; the anterior pituitary, which controls many other endocrine glands; and the posterior pituitary, which is concerned with blood pressure. There are also the thyroid, which affects metabolism; the adrenals; and the pancreas, which regulates hunger and satiation. Finally, there are the gonads, the male and female sex organs, which are important sources of sexual behavior.

The behavioral implications of the immune system are a fairly recent discovery (Ader 1981). This consists of a specialized system of white blood cells: some (the B-cells) are manufactured in the bone marrow; others (the T-cells) migrate from there to the thymus gland. Other types of cells are known as macrophages, helper T-cells, and killer cells. Their function is to recognize and destroy foreign cells, including invading bacteria, viruses, and cancer cells.

The relationship of these bodily systems and behavior raises a theoretical and philosophical question: What is the connection of mind and body? The first theory to attempt to answer this question from a scientific point of view was posited by René Descartes, who thought that the pineal gland in the center of the brain might be the connecting link. Later developments have centered on the brain, but there is as yet no complete answer to this question.

The study of the brain and nervous system by physiologists advanced our knowledge of their function. Hermann Ludwig Ferdinand von Helmholtz established that the speed of the nerve impulse is much slower than the almost-instantaneous conduction of electricity, as had been conjectured. Johannes Müller showed that, while all nerve conduction is alike, specific nerves connected to a specific area carry the meaning of the message. He called this the "doctrine of specific nerve energies." The "stars" you see when you are hit in the eye are your nervous system's interpretation of the mechanical stimulation of the optic nerve.

When psychologists started to study behavior with experimental methods, they called their new science *physiological psychology*, because physiology was the epitome of an experimental approach. Gradually, the more specific term *experimental psychology* prevailed, leaving physiological psychology for the more biologically oriented studies. Current usage has settled on the synonymous *biopsychology* to emphasize the biological nature of this approach. Psychobiology and biological psychology are equivalents also in use. The term *neuroscience* refers to a more interdisciplinary study of the brain and behavior, in which psychologists cooperate with other disciplines in studying brain function.

That the brain acts as a whole was hypothesized by Karl S. Lashley (1890–1958). He proposed three principles. That of *mass action* posited that learning depends on total brain mass available, rather than location, based on experiments with rats tested on maze learning after systematic removal of brain material. The second principle, that of *equipotentiality*, claims that one part of the brain can substitute for another. Finally, the principle of *vicarious functioning* assumes that if one part of the brain is destroyed, another part can be trained to take over its function.

Modern technology has solved some of these questions. The functioning brain has been studied with noninvasive techniques, such as electroencephalograms (EEGs), CAT (computerized axial tomography) scans, PET (positron emission tomography) scans, and MRI (magnetic resonance imaging). Both localization and general functions have been found. In addition, differences in processing of information have been discovered between the two hemispheres of the cortex. The left hemisphere is responsible for verbal and analytic processing, whereas the right hemisphere is specialized for nonverbal, spatial, and synthetic processing.

Much progress has been made in understanding the working of the individual nerve cells, the neurons, and their interaction with one another via their junction, the synapse. According to estimates, the adult human brain has approximately 100 billion neurons. Most of them have multiple synapses with other neurons, and each has only two states, active and inactive. Because of the close parallel, the brain has been compared to the hardware of a computer, but it is obvious that the brain's complexity still exceeds by many orders of magnitude that of even the largest and most complex computers.

The nerve impulse is propagated as an action potential of about 80 millivolts, mediated by an exchange of sodium ions and potassium ions across the cell membrane. Regardless of the magnitude of stimulation, each neuron responds with the same action potential once it is set off. This is known as the *all-or-none law*. Stimulus magnitudes are signaled by the frequency of nerve discharge, but even this is limited by the capacity of an individual neuron. Neurons differ in size and speed of conduction. The larger and faster neurons are insulated by a layer of fatty tissue, the myelin sheath.

Further control of the flow of information occurs at the synapse. This junction represents a minute discontinuity, the synaptic cleft, which must be bridged by the nerve impulse via a chemical transmitter system. There are many neurotransmitter substances; they are manufactured within the neuron and released when an action potential reaches the synapse. When they have stimulated the adjacent neuron, they are either neutralized or reabsorbed. Both excitatory and inhibitory synapses exist. Different neurotransmitters also have specific effects. The synapse is therefore the key to the functioning of the nervous system. A good example of the importance of synaptic transmission is the effect of various psychoactive drugs on synaptic pathways. Cocaine, for example, blocks the reuptake of excitatory transmitters, thus increasing stimulation. Curare, the Indian arrow poison, paralyzes by blocking the synaptic transmitter.

The brain is divided into the hindbrain, the midbrain, and the forebrain. The hindbrain, the continuation of the spinal cord, contains the medulla, the center for a life-support system of vital reflex functions, such as heart rate, breathing, swallowing, vomiting, coughing, and sneezing. Also in the hindbrain is the cerebellum, a large structure with many folds, somewhat off the direct line of connection from lower to higher centers. It controls fine movement, and it is also concerned with some types of learning. The midbrain is a way station for sensory information. It is less important in humans than in birds, reptiles, amphibians, and fish. The forebrain is the most prominent part of the mammalian brain. The outer, convoluted layer is known as the cortex; below it lie the thalamus, hypothalamus, and other subcortical structures. The cortex is divided into two hemispheres and four so-called lobes. The hindpart is called the occipital lobe and is primarily concerned with vision. The parietal lobe receives sensation from the body, and the temporal lobe below it primarily deals with hearing. The frontal lobe controls movement, language, and other complex behavior. Emotions are mediated by a series of subcortical structures known as the limbic system. From an evolutionary point of view, these are the older parts of the brain. The limbic system works in close cooperation with the endocrine system.

Whereas the nervous system is responsible for behavior that is short-term and immediate, such as activity, sensory perception, thought, and language, the endocrine system controls slower but longer-lasting processes. As in the case of the synapse, communication in the endocrine system is chemical, and often the same chemicals that act as neurotransmitters will also act as hormones in the endocrine system.

The adrenal glands have two separate functions. The interior, called the medulla, produces epinephrine, also known as adrenaline. It prepares the body for emergencies as it increases heart rate and blood pressure and reduces digestive action. Epinephrine is also the neurotransmitter in the sympathetic part of the autonomic nervous system, which becomes most active in fight-or-flight situations. The exterior of the adrenals, known as the cortex, produces a number of hormones, generally called steroids, which include cortisone and the sex hormones, androgen and estrogen.

Sex hormones are also produced by the gonads, the male and female sex organs. They play a crucial role in sexual development and, in animals at least, control sexual behavior. As in many other biological processes, humans are under less direct control of their hormones, as cultural factors assume a larger role. Animal experiments have shown that sex hormone production is also controlled by external cues, such as temperature, available breeding grounds, social dominance in the group, and the presence of receptive females. These affect parts of the brain, particularly the hypothalamus. The hypothalamus, in turn, controls the anterior pituitary gland, which produces gonadotropic hormones, which regulate the release of sex hormones by the gonads.

Feedback circuits of this type are common. Regulation of body temperature is a good example. When body temperature falls, thyroid-stimulating hormone (TSH) is released by the anterior pituitary under the control of the hypothalamus. The thyroid gland releases thyroxin, which increases the metabolism, creating body heat. The rise in body temperature inhibits the release of TSH, causing less thyroxin to be released. This mechanism is supplemented by constriction of peripheral blood vessels, shivering, and movement to warmer environment. Many bodily functions are thus regulated to stay within optimum limits in a process known as *homeostasis*.

The discovery of the role of the immune system was a serendipitous byproduct of an experiment to condition food aversion. When the body is under stress, the immune system is suppressed. Both nervous system and endocrine involvement in the immune system have been noted, and it may also be true that the immune system affects the nervous and endocrine systems. The new field of psychoneuroimmunology studies these effects.

Immune suppression as the effect of stress has now been demonstrated in medical students facing examinations, widowed spouses, and people living near the Three Mile Island nuclear power plant, even six years after the accident. Since both cancer and AIDS involve the immune system, it is hoped that, although they involve different aspects, positive consequences may be gained from a better understanding of the behavioral factors involved.

Helmut E. Adler

Biorhythms

Circadian Cycles

Biological rhythms have been demonstrated with periods ranging from fractions of seconds to several years. This discussion will be directed primarily toward the more commonly studied circadian (*circa*: about; *dian*: daily) cycles. The observation that period lengths generally correspond to cycles of the environment has led to questions about the endogenous–exogenous (internal-external) nature of biological rhythms. The majority of researchers accept the concept of an endogenous mechanism capable of measuring time intervals without consulting external time cues. This position is based primarily on features of free-running circadian cycles. A behavior that continues to cycle in constant conditions is said to be running free of external time cues, that is, free running.

Zeitgebers

Light stimuli are the most common and effective *zeitgebers* (literally, timegivers) or entraining agents. Other stimuli capable of entraining biorhythms include temperature, feeding schedules, noises, tidal changes, and social encounters. The effectiveness of zeitgebers is somewhat dependent upon their intensity, duration, and certain other parameters. For example, light cycles with graded transitions (i.e., dawn and dusk) are capable of entraining organisms

to longer and shorter periods than are cycles with sharp on-off transitions. In humans and many other organisms, if the imposed period deviates markedly from 24 hours (e.g., shorter than 18 or longer than 30 hours), entrainment breaks down and the biorhythm reverts back to a near-24-hour period. The limits can be extended markedly by the use of twilights in some if not all animals.

Amplitude

The amplitude (difference between the maximum and mean values) of a rhythmic phenomenon is generally reduced or fades out completely when placed in constant conditions. Fade-out occurs, as a rule, more rapidly in constant light than in constant darkness. Some rhythms are fairly labile in constant conditions, while others may persist for several months. The apparent absence of an overt rhythm does not always mean that the oscillations are absent. The fade-out may be due to a gradual desynchronization of component rhythms within the body so that the overt expressions are not obvious.

Dale L. Clayton

Bleuler, Eugen (1857–1939)

Bleuler, the Swiss psychiatrist, objected to the term *dementia praecox* in schizophrenia. He wrote in 1911, "As the disease need not progress as far as dementia and does not always appear praecociter, i.e. during puberty or soon after, I prefer the name schizophrenia." According to Bleuler, the disruption of continuity of personality and withdrawal and emotional disturbances are the main features of schizophrenia. Bleuler maintained that schizophrenia is not a single disease, but a group of diseases. Certain symptoms of schizophrenia are psychogenic and some are organic. The organic symptoms are disintegrative.

Benjamin B. Wolman

Borderline Personality Disorder

Borderline personality disorder (BPD) is one of the most common mental disorders, more frequent in females than in males. People afflicted by borderline personality disorder fail to establish their own identity and develop life plans. They are emotionally unbalanced and impulsive, have frequent temper tantrums, and are almost constantly angry. They have poor self-control and may spend more money than they can afford, buying things they don't need. They tend to go to extremes in their social relationships, shifting from great admiration to total rejection. They are often self-harmful, illogical, and paranoid. They have a low self-image, are frequently depressed, and fear loneliness but are unable to develop lasting relationships in marriage and career. People with BPD tend to be accident-prone and to be careless drivers, and they sometimes practice self-mutilation. They may indulge in petty crimes such as cheating and shoplifting. Usually underachievers, they are overdependent on and overdemanding of their friends and relatives, whom they try to manipulate. Many become drug and alcohol addicts, or have no self-discipline in eating. Many borderline patients threaten suicide; some of them are suicidal.

Etiology

The borderline personality disorders are related to genetic predisposition. There is no clearly established hereditary transmission of this disorder, but most probably some individuals are born with a predisposition to poor stress tolerance and inadequate ability for self-control. Children with this kind of predisposition are extremely sensitive to parental attitudes. If the child's parents, expecially the mother, act in a self-contradicting manner, shifting from overprotection, attachment, and affection to hateful and punitive behavior, the child develops feelings of overattachment and admiration for the mother, combined with frequent resentment and depression. The child is prevented from developing a persistent self-image and self-control, and is at the mercy of the accepting-rejecting mother.

Psychotherapy

Therapists must be aware of these patients' continuous and unjustified angry moods, blaming of others for true or imaginary misery, lack of social relations, extreme fear of separation and loneliness, and self-defeating and self-mutilating behavior, all of which are symptoms of borderline personality disorder.

People afflicted with borderline personality disorder are difficult patients. They frequently regress, are very demanding and sometimes suicidal, an often elicit negative feelings in their psychotherapists.

Psychotherapy with borderline patients needs to be supportive and reality oriented, preventing regression and suicide attempts. Quite often psychotherapy with borderline patients becomes more guidance than therapy.

Benjamin B. Wolman

Brain and Language

On the basis of observations made in the clinic, large portions of the central part of the cerebral cortex have been shown to be involved in the interpretation and expression of language in humans. In broad outlines, the relationship between a variety of brain systems and aspects of language has been reliably established. Nonetheless, many specifics of these relationships remain obscure due to individual differences and to incomplete knowledge.

Before the relationship between brain and language can be explored, it is necessary to define what is meant by language. Animals are often able to communicate fairly precise messages. Such communications have been referred to as language, e.g., the language of the bees or ape language. Also, though the term *language* is derived from the Latin root "lingua," referring to tongue, gestural sign language has been studied extensively, and comparisons have been made between such productions in apes and humans. On the other hand, linguists, whose domain is the study of human language, insist on a more restricted definition, in which the structure of the communication becomes the central interest.

Definition is important. Thus, if one is primarily concerned with communication or its loss due to brain injury, one finds a region surrounding the sylvian fissure of the left hemisphere of the brain that, when damaged, results in communication difficulties. Some localization within this territory can be ascertained: toward the front of the region, difficulties are apt to be with expression; toward the rear, they are more likely to entail comprehension.

The linguist can refine these rather gross relations. Linguistic analysis shows that lesions in the anterior part of the region superior to the sylvian fissure are apt to produce difficulties in processing function words (words that make fluency possible in constructing sentences). By contrast, lesions of the posterior part of the region inferior to the sylvian fissure impair comprehension because of a loss in the ability to process content words (words that refer to objects and events).

Language as studied by linguists has other attributes: semantic, pragmatic, and syntactic. The semantic aspects are concerned with ostensive definitions: what utterances designate in the world of objects and events. Damage to the part of the cerebral cortex behind and above the sylvian fissure has been shown to impair the semantic aspects of language, leaving intact comprehension dependent on the internal meaning of utterances (e.g., "a knife is used to cut with" is understood, but when given the word and asked to select a picture of a knife, the patient is unable to make the connection).

The pragmatic aspects of language deal with rhetoric, with prosodics, and with the social effectiveness with which the language is used. The term *prosodics* refers to intonation and to pauses used for effectiveness. Intonation has been shown to be related to the right hemisphere; impaired expression anteriorly, and impaired comprehension posteriorly. Appropriate pausing appears to be processed by the left hemisphere, anteriorly, and is related to fluency and the use of function words.

The syntactic aspects of language are programmed by the centrally located region of the cerebral somatosensorymotor cortex that surrounds the Rolandic fissure. It is syntax that brings together the semantic and pragmatic aspects of language. Syntactic procedures provide the skill necessary to make language comprehensible and fluent.

All of the above is most applicable to ordinarily right-handed males raised in a culture of Indo-European languages. Left-handers may adhere to this scheme or may reverse or scramble hemispheric localization. Females suffering from strokes show more rapid and complete recovery, suggesting that their language processes are less restrictedly localized than those of males.

A persistent problem in localization has been delineating the location of the lesion responsible for expressive aphasia. Initially, Pierre Paul Broca pointed to the third frontal convolution of the left cerebral hemisphere, anterior to the localization of the representation of the tongue. However, an increasing number of patients with disturbances in fluency have been found whose left third frontal convolution is intact. Ordinarily, such patients can be shown to have a fairly deep lesion in the neighborhood of the third frontal convolution or somewhat more posteriorly, invading the territory of the tongue representation. Several possible explanations present themselves: expressive aphasia is due to (1) a combination of impaired regulation of tongue and throat movement (dysarthria) plus a more extensive frontal involvement in processing function words, leading to loss of fluency and rhetoric; (2) an involvement of the uncinate fasciculus, which connects the inferior part of the frontal lobe with the polar part of the temporal lobe, including the amygdala; or (3) critical involvement of the basal ganglia (head of the caudate nucleus, and/or the nucleus accumbens).

This particular problem is but one of many of this type. Thus, despite a good deal of knowledge regarding the relation of brain and behavior, serious gaps in knowledge remain. Emphasis has been placed by neurologists on "disconnection syndromes" to account for some of these gaps. The idea is that complex symptomatology is produced by disconnections between cortical areas, due to severing of corticocortical fiber tracts. In monkeys, however, even radical disconnections of corticocortical tracts produce remarkably few, if any, effects. By contrast, disconnecting the cortex from the basal gaglia results in dramatic difficulties, mirroring those obtained by extensive resections of that cortex. Surprisingly disconnection from or destruction of relevant thalamic structures does not produce such an effect.

It may well be that effective corticocortical connections are what make human linguistic and other cultural processes possible. Nevertheless, it is worth considering that these processes rely on the relationship between the cerebral cortex and the basal ganglia. Explorations of the role of the basal gaglia (e.g., by electrical stimulation) in language have yet to be undertaken.

Karl H. Pribram

Brain, Motivation, and Emotion

To understand the relation between brain systems and feelings and their expression, it is necessary to distinguish emotion from motivation. Emotions are to a large extent processes occurring within the organism, while motivations extend the relationship of the organism to its environment through intended or expressed action. Synonyms for *emotion* are *affect* and *feeling*. When emotions are expressed, they reflect the internal process by facial and other nonverbal designations or by the prosodics of language. Such expressions are used by organisms as signals to guide social intercourse.

By contrast, motivations initiate planned, intended action. Aggression (agonistic behavior) provides an example of the difference between emotion and motivation. Emotional aggression results from frustration. It is characterized by an outburst of poorly organized behavior, directed at whatever happens to be in the vicinity. Motivated aggression is carried out with consummate skill, as when a lioness stalks and succeeds in bringing down her prey. Similarly, emotional love is passionate; when expressed, it reflects an internal state of the lover. Motivated love is directed toward the well-being of the loved one. Romantic, passionate love resulted, during the period of the Crusades, in incarcerating the loved person in a tower and forcing her to wear a chastity belt! Today, passionate involvement often leads to frustration, anger, and occasional violence against the loved one. Better not to be the recipient of this

sort of extreme passionate love; rather, passion should be leavened with motivated caring and commitment.

The diencephalon of the brain contains two reciprocally acting regions. One centers on the ventromedial nucleus of the hypothalamus; the other is known as the far lateral hypothalamic region. Electrical stimulation of the region of the ventromedial nucleus produces a series of responses graded as a function of the amount of current in the stimulus. Mild stimulation produces alerting and the cessation of ongoing activity, including that of eating and drinking. The region has thus become known as critical to the orienting reaction and as a satiety center. More intense stimulation will produce signs of irritation and, in the extreme, "sham" rage, an example of aggression directed at whatever is close at hand.

The far lateral region of the hypothalamus is made up of fiber tracts and contains few nerve cells. Some of these tracts connect the amygdala with the ventromedial hypothalamic region. The amygdala is a basal ganglion, which has been shown to modulate ventromedially initiated orienting, satiety, and aggression.

By far the majority of fibers coursing through this lateral diencephalic region are tracts that connect the substantia nigra with the corpus striatum and globus pallidus. These connections mediate the dopaminergic activity of the basal ganglia involved in the control of posture and other attitudinal aspects regulating behavior. Here lie the neural substrates of motivation, the substrates of motivated aggression, love, and commitment. Unfortunately, as of now the details of the manner in which these motivational processes operate are not as carefully worked out as those that modulate emotions by the activity of the amygdala.

One of the clearest ways to understand the processes mediated by brain systems is to investigate, whenever possible, the sensory input to the system. With respect to the processes regulated by the amygdala, the modalities of pain and temperature have been found to be critical. In the spinal cord, the nerve fibers carrying pain and temperature sensation travel together in the ventral spinothalamic tract. However, only about one-third of these fibers find their way directly to the thalamus. The remainder of the pain and temperature input reaches the region of the amygdala and surrounding cortex by way of the periaqueductal gray matter of the mesencephalon.

Pain comes in two distinct modes: (1) a sharp sensation localized in time and place, and (2) an aching sensation that seems to wax and wane and is difficult to locate. The fibers mediating the sharp sensation find their way to the parietal cortex via the dorsal thalamus; intractable aching is relieved by orbitofrontal lobotomy, which disrupts its uncinate connections to the amygdala.

Temperature discrimination has a similar dual relationship. Only very fine temperature discriminations have been shown to be disrupted by parietal lobe resections. For the most part, disruption of temperature sensibility occurs when the amygdala system is stimulated electrically or is excised.

From this analysis of the difference between sensory input to the parietal convexity and that of the amygdala system and its connections, a distinction between an epicritic and a protopathic aspect of somatic sensation can be drawn. Epicritic sensations show local sign; they can be precisely located in time and space. Protopathic (the term is related to the Greek *pathos*, from which *pathological*, as begetting compassion, is derived) sensations provide hedonic tone. The hedonic tone of pain is aching discomfort; that of temperature is comfort. Comfort reflects normally operating metabolism, which is anchored, in warm-blooded animals, by basal temperature.

The results of lobotomy indicate that modulation of the pain/temperature process involves higher-order regulation of the amygdala system. In addition to the orbital part of the frontal lobe, its dorsal part, through connections with the cingulate gyrus and thus the hippocampal system, has been shown to play an important role in mediating between emotional and motivational processes. Motivations are regulated via connections with the striatum. Mediation takes effort and prevents the hedonic process from becoming hung up in passion or in blind commitment.

In summary, by distinguishing emotions from motivations and both from epicritic processes, brain systems regulating the hedonic foundations of experience and behavior have been identified.

Karl H. Pribram

Brentano, Franz Clemens (1838–1917)

Brentano's work encompasses several areas in philosophy and psychology; he defines psychology as the "science of the soul." The act of perceiving, not the content of what is perceived, is the subject matter of Brentano's psychological system.

Benjamin B. Wolman

Breuer, Josef (1842–1925)

An Austrian physician and physiologist whose work was a precursor to Freudian psychoanalysis, Breuer developed the cathartic treatment method, based on suggestion and hypnosis. Breuer and Sigmund Freud believed that "hysterics suffer mainly from reminiscences." A psychological trauma may lead to a discharge of energy, whereas hysteria blocks discharge. The accumulation of the blocked mental energy, which causes hysterical symptoms, must be unblocked and discharged. Hypnosis enables unblocking, and a release called *catharsis* restores mental health. Breuer treated a young woman with serious hysterical symptoms by encouraging her to talk freely in an autohypnotic state. Freud compared the cathartic method to an incision and drainage of an abscess; the open pathway permitted the discharge of accumulated energy and a cure.

Benjamin B. Wolman

Brigham, Amariah (1798–1849)

Brigham was one of the thirteen founders of the American Psychiatric Association. In 1842, he organized and became head of the new State Lunatic Asylum in Utica, New York, where he put into practice mild and "moral" (psychological and milieu) therapy. Brigham was an advocate of phrenology.

John C. Burnham

Brill, Abraham Arden (1874–1948)

Brill was the first psychoanalyst in the United States and the first translator of Sigmund Freud's writings. Between 1908 and 1910, Brill was the only psychoanalyst in the United States. In 1911, Brill organized the New York Psychoanalytic Association. In 1933, he became the first chairman of the program on psychoanalysis given by the American Psychoanalytic Association.

May Ethel Romm

Broca, Pierre Paul (1824–1880)

Broca was interested in anthropology and conducted anthropometric and craniometric research. Broca founded the Société d'Anthropologie and the *Revue d'anthropologie* and became a member of the Institut d'Anthropologie. In 1861, he demonstrated a circumscribed lesion in the frontal lobe of the brain of a patient who suffered from aphasia, thus confirming the hypothesis that frontal lobe lesions cause disturbances in speech.

Marie-Louise Schoelly

Brogden, Wilfred John (1912–1973)

Brogden's work on neural structures contributed to the understanding (1) that conditioning is a function of the central nervous system and occurs independently of peripheral processes, and (2) that such conditioning can occur subcortically. Brogden's interest in the incentive properties of unconditioned stimuli led to an important work on avoidance learning.

Gregory A. Kimble

Bühler, Charlotte (1893–1974)

Bühler was one of the pioneering women in the field of psychology. Along with her early research on children, Bühler introduced a new theory: Growth versus decline represents the processes of expansion and restriction; the second organizing principle is homeostasis versus self-realization. According to Bühler, there are four basic human tendencies: (1) need satisfaction; (2) self-limiting adaptation; (3) creative expansion; and (4) upholding and restoring the inner order.

Patricia Keith-Spiegel

Bykov, Konstantin Mikhailovich (1886–1959)

There are two principal points in Bykov's research: (1) the function of interoceptors, studied by the method of conditioned reflexes, cortical control of autonomic functions, and the effects on the central nervous system (CNS) of the afferent signals of the state of inner organs; and (2) the corticovisceral theory of pathology. Bykov was a protagonist of orthodox Pavlovianism. From 1850, Bykov was the director of the I. P. Pavlov Institute of Physiology.

Josef Brožek

Bystander Intervention

The social-psychological inquiry into bystander intervention has focused on those conditions that elicit spontaneous helping on behalf of individuals in immediate need of assistance. Research interest in bystander intervention has been in direct response to several incidents widely reported by the media in which people were raped, murdered, or brutalized while their fellow citizens were unwilling to intervene.

Attempts at defining personality traits of interveners in emergencies have not met with any notable success (Krebs 1970). Harvey London (1970), in his study of individuals who helped Jews escape from Nazi Germany, found that one characteristic common to all these individuals was that each had one altruistic parent. Helping individuals in distress is, in part, an act prescribed by ethical norms and precepts.

Irwin A. Horowitz

· C ·

California Psychological Inventory

The California Psychological Inventory (CPI) is a paper-and-pencil personality test that can be administered individually but ordinarily is given in groups. While no time limit is imposed, most subjects complete the form in about an hour. Since only fourth-grade reading ability is required, the test can be administered to subjects ranging in age from 12 to 70. However, some of the items are not appropriate for elementary or junior high school students.

The CPI's scales fall into four broad categories. Class I represents measures of poise, ascendancy, and self-assurance: dominance (Do), capacity for status (Cs), sociability (Sy), social presence (Sp), self-acceptance (Sa), and sense of well-being (Wb). The Class II scales measure socialization, maturity, and responsibility: they include responsibility (Re), socialization (So), self-control (Sc), tolerance (To), good impression (Gi), and communality (Cm). The Class III scales, regarded as measures of achievement potential and intellectual efficiency, are: achievement via conformance (Ac), achievement via independence (Ai), and intellectual efficiency (Ie). The last, Class IV, constitutes measures of intellectual and interest modes: psychological-mindedness (Py), flexibility (Fx), and femininity (Fe). Of these eighteen scales, three (Wb, Gi, and Cm) constitute validity measures that also have interpretive value. Factor analysis of the eighteen variables indicates that Class I and II roughly correspond to the first and second factors. A number of investigators have devised other CPI-based scales, such as those measuring empathy and anxiety.

Perhaps the only first-order factor study based on CPI items was performed by H. D. Hase (Hase & Goldberg 1967). Hase assembled eleven factor-based scales from an analysis of items data. (Item listings appear in the Appendix of Megargee's *Handbook*.) The eleven scales were labeled (1) extraversion-introversion; (2) harmonious childhood; (3) surgency; (4) conformity-rebelliousness; (5) ascendance-submission; (6) superego strength–neuroticism; (7) orthodoxy-flexibility; (8) self-confidence in public; (9) amiability-irritability; (10) serenity-depression; and (11) ego strength–psychoticism. Thus, at least eleven first-order factors are measured by the CPI.

The favorable features of the CPI may be summarized as unusually large norms, extensive validity studies, and high test-retest reliabilities. Another positive feature is the continued revision of the CPI manual to keep it up to date.

Maurice Lorr

Cannon, Walter Bradford (1871–1945)

Cannon developed the principle of homeostasis, stressing the need to adjust to changes in the environment. Homeostasis is defined as the coordinated physiological processes that maintain most of the steady states of the organism. According to Cannon, living beings are stable; they must be so "in order not to be destroyed, dissolved or disintegrated by colossal forces, often adverse, which surround them." Cannon believed that homeostasis enables people to be "free to develop new ideas and interests, and to work and play." Mental disorders demonstrate failure in homeostasis.

Benjamin B. Wolman

Cardiovascular Diseases: Psychosomatic Aspects

Cardiovascular diseases account for one of every two deaths in the United States.

Anxiety

Anxiety can affect the functions of the cardiovascular system in a number of ways. Chiefly through the autonomic nervous system, anxiety can cause increased pulse rate, increased cardiac output, and, by means of peripheral vasoconstriction, an increased afterload on the heart. Norepinephrine released from sympathetic nerve endings and epinephrine released from the adrenal glands are the major mediators of these phenomena, and considerable effort has been put into attempting to establish that predominance of one or another is equated with different behavioral states.

Although the autonomic nervous system is perhaps the major factor in producing the psychophysiologic manifestations of emotionally derived stimuli, almost any of the mechanisms that mediate acute change in the organism can similarly be called into play by such stimuli. To the extent that any or all of these affect cardiovascular function, they therefore can play a role in heart disease.

Personality and Behavior in Coronary Artery Disease

One of the most fascinating chapters in the area of coronary artery disease has been the increasing recognition and acceptance of the "coronary personality." Before the middle 1950s, a number of psychiatrists, most notably Flanders Dunbar (1943), had commented on the seeming preponderance of "hard-driving, goal-directed individuals seeking refuge in work" who displayed coronary artery disease. It remained, however, for M. Friedman et al. (1968) to begin to put these observations together in a fashion that has led to a number of prospective studies. M. Friedman and R. H. Rosenman have designated two types of behavior patterns, Type A and Type B. "Type A" denotes overambitious, competitive, restless, hyperassertive, intolerant, and irritable behavior.

It was found that subjects who while living exhibited the Type A pattern succumbed to coronary artery disease six times more frequently than subjects who exhibited the Type B pattern. The Type A subject also exhibited, irrespective of the actual cause of death, more severe basic coronary atherosclerosis that did the Type B subjects.

Behavioral Mechanisms in Hypertensive Disease

The importance of emotional factors in understanding hypertensive vascular disease has long been apparent. Blood pressure, by several of the mechanisms described earlier, is easily influenced by noxious stimuli of behavioral origin and probably represents the major cause for the marked variability in blood pressure seen even in the hypertensive patient. A number of studies in animals have demonstrated a model in which long-lasting emotional stress alone may result in hypertensive disease with accompanying pathological findings.

One of the most important recent developments in hypertension has been a number of studies investigating the question of perception and cognition in hypertensive patients. It has been suggested that the hypertensive subject, who is well known to be a "blood pressure hyperreactor" to any type of stimulus, may somehow be behaviorally aware of this hyperreactivity and "shield" himself from environmental events that would stimulate him.

Alvin P. Shapiro

Carmichael, Leonard (1898–1973)

Carmichael's main experimental research was devoted to the prenatal development of sensory processes and behavior in mammals. Together with J. J. Jasper, Carmichael devised an apparatus for electroencephalograms. Carmichael's research covered visual fatigue, electrophysiology of the eye and other visual tests, and developmental psychology. Carmichael was president of the American Psychological Association and of the American Philosophical Society.

Benjamin B. Wolman

Cattell, James McKeen (1860–1944)

Cattell contributed to several areas in psychology, especially to clinical and experimental psychology, to the study of individual differences, and to mental testing. In 1894 he cofounded the *Psychological Review* and became the editor of *Science*. Under his guidance Teacher's College of Columbia University has become the center of psychological testing. Cattell stressed that psychological treatment of mental disorders should start with trait diagnosis, based on a thorough research of psychological traits.

Benjamin B. Wolman

Cattell's Trait Theory

Factor Analysis

Factor-analytic procedures, while exceedingly complex in practice, are essentially simple in principle. In fact, factor analysis is a simple mathematical model resembling our inductive efforts to discover how things work in everyday life. As applied by James McKeen Cattell and his colleagues, factor analysis involves finding a set of hypothetical constructs to account for the covariation among a large number of behavioral variables. The factor-analytic model requires that the constructs be linearly related to the behavior, additively contributive to it, and noninteractive. While these constraints are often restrictive, Cattell and others have demonstrated that factor analysis appears to be fairly robust to naturally occurring violations of its assumptions.

Intelligence

In the area of abilities and intelligence, for example, Cattell's analyses over more than 30 years have revealed that intellectual traits are arranged hierarchically, from lower order acquired abilities ("agencies") given names such as inductive and deductive reasoning, associative memory, and memory, which are subsumed by provincial powers such as more general (but still localized) factors of reasoning and memory, in turn subsumed by higher order constitutional capacities such as basic undifferentiated fluid intelligence. General intelligence is seen as a surface trait based on two source traits, fluid and crystallized intelligence, the latter representing the total investment of undifferentiated fluid intelligence in acquired abilities. Cattell has developed relatively culture-neutral intelligence tests to measure fluid intelligence exclusive of culture-specific influences on its investment. Many of the implications of the theory of fluid and crystallized intelligence have been developed by Cattell's associate and former student, John Horn.

Motivation

By analyzing the covariation among a large number of different attitudes, Cattell found that the resultant factors could be bifurcated into acquired sentiments (e.g., sentiment toward self or career) and innate urges (e.g., sex or fear urge). Thus, attitudes could be represented in a lattice, subsidiated to sentiments with those sentiments subsidiated in turn to urges. The way in which urges contribute to sentiments and sentiments to attitudes in a dynamic lattice can be very idiosyncratic. With this framework, and the development of the Motivation Analysis Test for assessment, possibilities for the analysis and measurement of adjustment and conflict in clinical settings (what Cattell has termed "quantitative psychoanalysis") are now being realized.

Temperament

A major contribution of Cattell and his coworkers in the domain of temperament has been the extension of empirically based train theory. Objective test devices have been designed to minimize the self-evaluation and faking often present in questionnaires and ratings, while better representing personality as it appears in actual behavior. They include psychophysiological measurements (e.g., galvanic skin response), paper-and-pencil tests (e.g., miniature situations), and devices that are ostensibly ability, perceptual, motor, and social-evaluative tests.

R- and P-Techniques

Cattell has developed and used factor-analytic techniques that can be applied quite flexibly to trait theory. While factor analysis is used typically to discover traits of individuals through the covariation of tests (R-technique), it is also possible to discover moods or states of a single individual from the covariations of tests across occasions (P-technique).

Cattell has relied almost exclusively on multivariate research methods, in particular, factor analysis. He has been an incisive critic of the premature operationism of ad hoc personality measurement and the trial-and-error piecemeal development of personality theory exclusively through bivariate procedures. Although personality theory itself is still in its infancy, Cattell is committed to the idea that its potential development is assured through a stable basis of personality constructs that can, in principle, be assessed. The principles of psychometrics, according to Cattell, should be based on personality theory, rather than vice versa.

Douglas M. Wardell

Character Analysis

There have been numerous schools based on departures from Freud's theories and practices. Wilhelm Reich, in his book *Character Analysis* (1933), although it was a later contribution to Freudian psychoanalytic technique, has never been outside of the mainstream of its theory and practice. It has been an important link in the evolving and developing chain of technique from the methods of catharsis, free association, interpretation, resistance and defense analysis, and ego analysis.

Sandor Ferenczi's treatment concept (1920) is in complete accord with Reich's work in character analysis in 1933 and later. Ferenczi's active therapy artifice consists, for example, of urging and prevailing upon a phobic patient to face and experience the rationalized anxiety-precipitating object of his or her fears, irrespective of the degree of the anxiety.

Character-analytic technique, as distinguished from the more classical symptom technique, emphasizes the significance of this armor and applies itself, metaphorically speaking, to its penetration and its dismemberment. Only when this objective is accomplished, following many difficult hours dealing with negative transference phenomena, is the patient really able to associate repressed material consistently and with the feeling and the emotion originally present. Reich averred that at the beginning of treatment there never exists a genuine positive transference. He was dubious of the therapeutic value of abundant "content" material—the associations of the trifles of everyday life and material emotionally uncathected, irrespective of whether the associations were of libidinal, ego, superego, or topical nature.

In confronting the patient with his character resistances, Reich cautioned against pushing the patient to a degree of negative transference that could jeopardize further treatment. It could take months of consistent, persistent, and carefully moderated interventions and interpretations, with periods of working through, to remove the armor, layer by layer, which should then permit each symptom, with its appropriate affect, to surface unencumbered by defensive devices. With this "preanalytic" task accomplished, free association (the basis of analytic therapy) can proceed with greater spontaneity toward its therapeutic objective.

Walter Briehl

Charcot, Jean-Martin (1825–1893)

Charcot was one of the founders of modern neurology. He organized and directed the famous neurological clinic at the Salpetrière Hospital in Paris. In 1885 Sigmund Freud studied in Charcot's clinic and was inspired to use hypnosis in the treatment of hysteria.

Benjamin B. Wolman

Chemoreception

Taste
Modern psychophysical taste studies use some of the classic techniques, which originated in the nineteenth century, for determining thresholds. However, a group of procedures known as the ration-scaling methods, developed by S. S. Stevens and his colleagues at Harvard in the 1950s, have replaced the Fechnerian scaling methods. The most commonly used is direct magnitude estimation. The subject tastes a series of stimuli and assigns each a number, so that a stimulus that tastes twice as strong as another is assigned a number twice as large.

Taste receptor cells are slender, oval cells that combine somewhat like the segments of an orange into globular clusters known as taste buds. Most taste buds are buried within taste papillae, although taste buds can be found in the mouth in areas without papillae. The tops of some of the taste cells are elongated into filament-like processes and project into a space called the taste pore. When solutions are placed on the tongue, they enter the taste pores and come into contact with the elongated processes at the tops of the cells, which are believed to contain the sites giving rise to taste sensations. There are three kinds of taste papillae: fungiform or mushroom-shaped papillae on the front of the tongue, foliate papillae, which look like parallel ridges on the sides of the tongue, and circumvallate papillae, large moundlike structures arranged in an inverted **V** on the rear of the tongue. In infrahuman species, the three kinds of papillae differ somewhat from those in humans.

A number of often-quoted facts about taste have been contradicted by modern psychophysical research. Despite anecdotal reports, the effects of smoking on taste and smell are surprisingly small. Sensitivity to the four basic tastes has been believed to vary on different tongue areas; however, taste thresholds for the four qualities are actually fairly uniform across the tongue. Taste intensity grows with concentration at different rates on different tongue areas. In particular, bitterness increases with concentration faster for the posterior tongue than for the anterior tongue. This accounts for the common experience of noting that a bitter compound tastes more bitter on the back than the front of the tongue.

Olfaction

The psychophysical methods used to study olfaction are identical in a formal sense to those used to study taste. Modern experiments deal primarily with suprathreshold functioning and rely heavily on ration-scaling procedures, such as magnitude estimation.

Perceived odor magnitude (ψ) typically grows as a power function of concentration (ϕ), that is, $\psi = k\phi\beta$. The exponent (β) of the function ranges from less than 0.2 to about 0.7, depending on the properties of the odorant. Accordingly, a hundred-fold change in concentration may produce a thirty-fold change in the perceived intensity of some odorants and only a threefold change in the intensity of others. Substances that yield low exponents tend also to yield the lowest thresholds, often less than one part per billion. The electro-olfactogram also grows as a power function of concentration.

The most salient attribute of odors seems to be the hedonic attribute, and consequently, olfactory stimuli can have strong motivating properties. Substances known as pheromones are particularly potent in this regard. These are natural chemical signals transmitted from one member of a species to another. An example is the sex attractant emitted by female insects. The females themselves may be insensitive to the attractant, but males may be exquisitely sensitive, often possessing receptor cells sensitive specifically to the attractant. There have been numerous successful attempts to identify and synthesize the active constituents of the attractants emitted by various species, and a number of the synthesized substances are now used in ingenious pest-control programs.

Linda May Bartoshuk
William S. Cain

Chiarugi, Vincenzo (1759–1820)

The Italian psychiatrist Chiarugi's most notable departure in practice was his insistence on extensive personal intervention by the physician and on treating the hospital as a therapeutic institution.

John C. Burnham

Child Abuse

The abuse of children assumes diverse expressions, which include physical and sexual abuse, neglect, and emotional abuse.

Definitions and Nature of Abuse

There is no common definition of child abuse: Its perception varies with the reporting person or agency, the age of the child, current child-rearing fashion, and cultural assumptions. This ambiguity has led to unreliable statistics and confusion regarding forms and incidence of abuse, outcome, the need for treatment, and the effectiveness of treatment.

Physical abuse of a child is viewed by some as strict or appropriate discipline. Increasingly, however, experts and the public concur that repeated hitting of a child with an open or closed hand or with an object, particularly about the face or head and particularly if physical damage (bruises, cuts) results, constitutes abuse. More obvious trauma leaves little doubt: burns, broken bones, serious head trauma.

Sexual abuse is equally problematic: Although forced or unforced touching of the genitals or actual intercourse is uniformly condemned, a gray zone exists of hugging, kissing, and general stroking of the child. Correctly distinguishing sexual abuse from affection is crucial not only for the child but also for the adult involved, because the results of mistakes can range from failing to protect a child from ongoing abuse to unfairly exposing a well-meaning adult to stigma and even criminal liability.

Neglect results from acts of omission rather than commission and frequently goes unrecognized except in its most extreme forms. Children whose daily needs for food, shelter, and protection are not met, who may be unnecessarily exposed to physical harm, or who are abandoned or expelled from the home suffer from physical neglect. Even though this is the most commonly reported type of neglect, it may be much less common than the emotional neglect of a caretaker who meets basic physical needs but provides little or no attention to the child's interests, fears, education (educational neglect), and other psychological needs. This seems to be the mechanism at work in producing psychopathology as diverse as that seen in nonorganic failure to thrive, some "latch-key children," and some runaways.

Epidemiology of Child Abuse

Incidence and prevalence data are notoriously unreliable in all forms of child abuse, not only because definitions differ and many accounts are the retrospective reports of past abuse by adults, but also because an unknown but presumably large number of cases go unrecognized because the parents (or neighbors or friends) fail to report the abuse, professionals and legal authorities overlook it, the child denies it (out of fear, ignorance, youth, or confusion), and society all too often feels it's "a family matter." Certainly, however, abuse and neglect are significantly underreported.

The incidence of child abuse of all types varies with the age and sex of the child. Preschool and preadolescent boys, who tend to be active and obstreperous, are at a modestly increased risk for physical and emotional abuse compared to girls, an equivalent risk for neglect, and a decreased risk for sexual abuse. On the other hand, teenage boys, who are increasingly capable of fighting back successfully or leaving home, have a lower risk for physical abuse than girls, a much lower incidence of sexual abuse, because teenage girls are the most likely group to be victimized, and an equivalent risk for neglect and emotional abuse. Overall, approximately 20% of all children are abused at some point, and many of those children are abused in multiple ways. Nearly 20% of girls and 5% of boys are sexually abused at some time, while 2 to 4% of both sexes are physically abused, 2 to 3% are emotionally abused, and 3 to 5% suffer neglect. However, these numbers are uncertain, vary widely with the population, are skewed toward cases of severe abuse, and are likely to be underestimates.

Other factors that increase the likelihood for abuse include the presence of psychiatric disorders such as ADHD (attention deficit–hyperactive disorder), learning disorders, mental retardation, and conduct disorders, as well as the personality styles of being overly affectionate and needy (risk for sexual abuse) or loud, active, and stubborn (risk for physical abuse). Environmental factors that increase the risk of abuse include low socioeconomic status, low parental education, and a dysfunctional family and/or community. Common parental factors include a depressed mother or a mother of borderline intelligence, a violent and antisocial father, alcoholism and/or drug abuse by either parent, and a father who is a pedophile (sexual abuser of younger children). Familial factors include the relationship of a dominant, violent father with a passive, dependent mother, in which the mother turns a blind eye to the abuse to escape the father's attention. The reverse pattern is a dominant wife and a passive husband, in which the father finds affection from the daughter that he fails to receive from the wife, and a single-parent home with a live-in boyfriend or a home with a stepfather. The other feature common to abusive homes, and particularly those characterized by sexual abuse, is forced family isolation: little contact with neighbors or peers is encouraged or permitted.

Almost 90% of physical and emotional abuse takes place in the home at the hands of parents, with mothers more likely to abuse younger children and fathers more likely to abuse teenagers. Sexual abuse differs in that it is done mostly by men; rarely by strangers, however: siblings account for about 40% of sexual abuse; fathers and stepfathers, another 20%; other relatives, 10 to 15%; and nonrelative acquaintances, 10 to 15%. The vast majority of sexual abuse involves teenage girls.

Effects of Abuse

Knowledge about the effects of the spectrum of abuse is flawed primarily because it depends upon either the outcome of cases referred for treatment, which usually constitute the most severe cases of abuse, or on retrospective accounts of childhood abuse by adults who are experiencing current emotional troubles. The symptoms experienced by the vast majority of children subjected to moderate, chronic abuse are documented only anecdotally. However, several general patterns of responses are seen frequently.

The effects of physical abuse are somewhat unpredictable but seem to cluster into two groups. Some children react to beatings, kickings, chronic uncertainty, and even terror with anxiety and withdrawal. They become clingy and isolated and increasingly dependent on those who are abusing them for shreds of healthy nurturance. Some suffer subtle brain damage. As they mature into their teenage years, low self-esteem and depression emerge, along with poor peer relations and low motivation. An alternate pattern seen in the physically abused child is hyperactive, aggressive acting out (Livingston 1987), laced with defiance toward individuals both at home and in the community (particularly school). As they enter their teen years, a more classic con-

duct-disordered picture frequently emerges, particularly in boys; generalized delinquency, substance abuse, running away, and occasionally very violent behavior (the vast majority of violent delinquents have been abused as children). Research continues to support the concept of the intergenerational transmission of violent behavior: approximately 30% of physically abused children later abuse their own children (Kaufman & Zigler 1987). Although the former pattern occurs more frequently (2:1 to 3:1), the groups overlap in that both sets of children display poor self-esteem, low motivation and poor school performance, a limited ability to form close friendships, and an increased suicide potential.

Children who have endured neglect (lack of care and a general disinterest) and emotional abuse (rejection, denigration, threats) are more likely to respond primarily with depression, low self-esteem, isolation from peers and other adults, limited concern for others, and impaired enthusiasm and productivity, all of which may be lifelong. This also may produce a form of intergenerational transmission as these children attempt to raise children of their own.

Reactions to sexual abuse in childhood and adolescence is perhaps the most confused and contested area in child abuse. Many acute and long-term responses seem to depend upon the particulars of the abuse: age of occurrence, duration, perpetrator, form of abuse. Clearly, some children show little effect from sexual abuse. This is particularly true of those abused at a young age, by a peer, only once, and without force or physical trauma. On the other hand, those abused frequently and chronically, over their objections, sometimes painfully, by someone formerly trusted, with destructive effects on the family, and with personal stigmatization, are likely to suffer from acute and long-lasting psychological symptoms. The range of symptoms of serious and chronic sexual abuse in childhood and adolescence is particularly diverse and includes chronic depression and low self-esteem, guilt, difficulty with trust and impaired peer relations, a sense of being "damaged goods," acting out (e.g., substance abuse, criminal activities, sexual misbehavior and hypersexuality, and running away), bulimia, somatization, sleep disturbance, symptoms of post-traumatic stress disorder, loss of motivation and a sense of self-mastery, school failure, role confusion (when treated as the father's partner), distorted sexual identity and interests, and suicidal interests. If untreated, many of these symptoms continue so that, as adults, these individuals are at risk for chronic difficulty with healthy interpersonal relationships (both sexual and nonsexual), depression with self-destructive impulses, borderline and dissociative pathology, and a lifelong inability to reach their human potential (Herman 1992).

Treatment of the Abused Child

The first requirement, always, is to stop the ongoing abuse. No treatment will be of value without providing the child safety and care. In addition, several other reality issues must be addressed. Environmental factors may contribute to the abuse (poverty, peculiar housing arrangements) and demand correction. This often means working extensively with public agencies. The legal system frequently becomes involved, particularly in sexual abuse cases. It is essential to separate treatment from legal issues, even though this is difficult due to the high level of emotion involved in some abuse cases, conflicts between parents, conflicts between the parents and the public system, pressures on children to "help get at the truth" (which may be profoundly damaging, particularly in the case of false accusations, [Yates 1988]), and strong feelings on the part of the professionals. Physical and sexual abuse may generate therapist countertransference (excessive anger, rescue fantasies, overidentification) more commonly than in any other area of work with children.

Individual therapy forms the mainstay of treatment, focusing on issues of lack of safety, failure of the other parent to protect, betrayal, abandonment, anger, anxiety, stigmatization, shame, and guilt. Because the issues are so emotionally charged, denial is often the major defense the therapist must confront. Adolescents frequently will profit from group therapy, particularly if members of the group have had similar experiences.

Family therapy is commonly essential, even if the family is not going to stay together. This difficult work, where various members of the family often have different, competing, and strongly felt agendas, attempts to produce a more supportive, protective environment for the child by identifying (or cultivating) strengths and eliminating threats. Sometimes focusing therapy on the parents may be the key to successful treatment. Unfortunately, family therapy in abuse cases has a high dropout rate. There has been a recent appropriate shift in emphasis to prevention by the development of media campaigns, hotlines, and parenting classes, the creation of shelters for abused spouses and their children, and the targeting of high-risk groups for preventive attention.

David A. Tomb

Child Development: Anna Freud's Concept of Developmental Lines

In her work on child development, Anna Freud proposes the use of developmental lines as a method of describing the child that can help to address developmental issues and disturbances more effectively in practice. She discusses the need for assessments that are not limited to scales or sequences and that define circumscribed aspects of the child's personality, but that integrate what is (or can be) known into a totality. Her focus is upon basic interactions between the id and the ego and their various developmental levels, as well as age-related sequences of these interactions, comparable to the gradual unfolding of ego functions and to the maturational sequence of libidinal stages.

The child who is developing in a healthy manner will progress along the developmental lines, but not necessarily at a uniform rate. Some disequilibrium in the rate or level of development is frequent and may result only in the many variations of normality that are encountered. However, severe or prolonged disharmony among the various parts of the developing personality indicates a disturbance that requires attention.

Sally Provence

Child Psychiatry

Child psychiatric activities take place in a number of different settings, and under a number of different administrative auspices. These include private practice, community mental health centers, university teaching centers, public health and state hospital systems, consultative work with specialists in pediatrics, juvenile and family courts, and school systems. Involvement in cooperative consultative work with child care agencies in the community is an essential part of child psychiatric practice, based on the principle that primary prevention and early intervention greatly increase the chances of successful child development.

Following a three- or four-year medical school program leading to the M.D. degree, the future child psychiatrist spends one year in a hospital internship program emphasizing medicine or pediatrics. She then moves to a psychiatric residency program, generally spending two years in adult-oriented training, both outpatient and inpatient, and two years in specialized child psychiatric training. The child psychiatry training program offers a well-balanced patient load, which includes work with preschool and school-age children and adolescents, supervised diagnostic treatment, and consultative work with children and their parents. The clinical experience provides not only a wide range of problems of varying types and degrees of severity but also diversification of age, socioeconomic status, and sex.

Studies of normal populations are changing our view of adolescence, which is becoming better understood as a developmental period with less turmoil and turbulence than previously thought, from a clinical viewpoint. On the other hand, while the average adolescent may be described as adjusting without undergoing serious personality disruption, what have been considered "delinquent" behaviors occur so frequently in normal populations as to be considered modal, or part of this period.

John F. McDermott, Jr.

Chomsky, A. Noam (1928–)

Chomsky's main contribution was to psycholinguistics, in which he revised the transformational grammar and emphasized the phrase structure of grammar. Chomsky's science of semiology, the study of signs and symbols, built a bridge between psy-

cholinguistic research and clinical psychology, psychotherapy, and psychoanalysis.

Benjamin B. Wolman

Classical Studies and Psychoanalysis

From the earliest days of psychoanalysis, there was an easy affinity between psychoanalytic thought and classical antiquity. Sigmund Freud and other early analysts, well schooled in classical and humanistic studies, naturally turned to classical antiquity as a source for naming important concepts in the developing body of psychoanalysis (e.g., catharsis, eros, libido, narcissism, Oedipus complex). Even more important, Freud, Karl Abraham, Otto Rank, and others responded to the quality of "psychological-mindedness" that is so impressive in the work of Greek antiquity, particularly in the great Greek tragedies. When Freud, in *The Interpretation of Dreams*, discussed *Oedipus Rex*, he not only utilized the play's plot as an exemplar of what he later termed the Oedipus complex but also correctly saw the parallel between the construction of the plot and the psychoanalytic processes of the lifting of repression.

Psychoanalytic studies of classical antiquity reflect the significant changes in theory and emphasis within psychoanalysis from Freud's early writings to the present. Thus *Oedipus Rex*, the source of the term *Oedipus complex*, has become over the years the vehicle for exploring various preoedipal factors, especially the nuances of the mother-child dyad. The play has become the medium for exploring parental aggression and conflict as they influence the child's conflicts, as well as exploring the relationship between an individual's conflict with society and his or her own intrapsychic conflicts.

Bennett Simon

Classification, Nosology, and Taxonomy of Mental Disorders

Purposes and Uses

The major functions of a psychiatric classification are to facilitate communication about psychiatric abnormality with other mental health professionals (e.g., in textbooks, lectures, case records, and consultations); memorization and recall of clinically relevant material (e.g., appropriate treatment for a given abnormality); collection and analysis of statistics on the number, location, and fate of persons with various psychiatric abnormalities; and the generation of new knowledge about the categories of abnormalities through clinical experience or experimental methods.

Historical Development

Descriptions of psychiatric abnormalities may be found in the observations of Hippocrates (third century B.C.) and of Artaeus (second century A.D.), but psychiatric classification was not well developed until the early nineteenth century, at which time numerous highly theoretical systems of classification abounded. Before the nineteenth century, psychiatric abnormalities were often ascribed to mystical forces or personal malice warranting redemption, exorcism, or punishment, rather than treatment.

In 1863, Karl Ludwig Kahlbaum proposed to replace theoretical schemata with a system of classification depending on "methods found most suitable in the natural sciences and empirical medicine" (Lewis 1970), namely clinical observation and investigation into causes. Following these same principles, in 1892 Emil Kraepelin published a classification that drew also on the work of J. P. Falret, J. Baillarger, and E. Hecker, taking into account what was known about the relationship between psychiatric abnormality and gross brain pathology and dividing the remaining severe abnormalities on the basis of their patterns and course over long periods of time. Refinements to this method of descriptive or phenomenological psychiatry were added by, among others, Eugen Bleuler (1911), who emphasized psychological functions rather than only symptoms or signs as a means of classification; Karl Jaspers (1963), who argued for a precise understanding and description of symptoms; and Kurt Schneider (1959), who identified crucial or pathognomonic symptoms for diagnosis of the functional psychoses. Benjamin Wolman (1973) has traced three historic principles of phenomenology, namely, reliance on empirical observations as valid data, establishment

of logical connections between these observations, and formulation of hypotheses to permit precise description and prediction of such observations.

Current Alternatives

Most widely accepted psychiatric classifications today are based on descriptive phenomenology, the cross-sectional and longitudinal patterns of symptoms (subjective complaints), and signs (observations) of abnormal behavior, feeling, or thinking. At a stage of experimental development are classifications based upon biochemical or physiological concomitants of psychiatric abnormalities (Holzman et al. 1974; Schildkraut 1974), or upon the response of a patient to a pharmacological agent (Lehmann & Ban 1968).

Bellak's (1973) classification, based on ego strength, attempts to classify persons with psychiatric abnormality in a manner that is compatible with psychoanalytic theory and treatment. Another system, based on balance of cathexes, was proposed by Wolman (1973).

Barry J. Gurland

Classroom as a Social System

A focus on systematic features of the classroom environment, that is, the classroom as an organized social system with an evaluation of how its members are affected by the forms of that organization, considers the question of the effects of that system's properties on learning and teaching (Dunkin & Biddle 1974).

Within the system, the key feature is its members. Each member has a role consisting of behavior patterns, which are characteristic of one or more individuals. Each role within the system is tied to the other, leading to the generation and setting of activity and communication patterns.

Research indicates that the most fruitful way to consider classroom leadership and to generate positive interactive patterns is to view the classroom system as an interpersonal process rather than as an attribute of a single individual, on which traditional teacher training focused (Dunkin & Biddle 1974; Wolman 1958). Teachers and other school personnel certainly have legitimate power conferred by the formal organization. However, it is important to establish interpersonal influence relationships based on perceived power relationships.

Judith Kaufman

Clinical Child Psychology

Clinical child psychology is among the most highly specialized areas of psychology today, with a long and rich history within the United States. In his fascinating volume *Clinical Psychology since 1916: Science, Practice and Organization* (1994), Donald K. Routh notes that the field of clinical psychology was primarily concerned with children before World War II and that C. M. Louttit, who authored the book *Clinical Psychology: A Handbook of Children's Behavior Problems* (1936), was probably the first clinical child psychologist according to our contemporary understanding of the term. Interestingly though, Lightner Witmer, the founder of clinical psychology, established a psychology clinic in 1896 that, as it developed, was especially concerned with children and with mental development and retardation.

What is a contemporary clinical child psychologist? We suspect there may be as much controversy in defining clinical child psychology as there is in defining clinical psychology today. Clinical psychology is considered "the application of psychology" and, as such, represents a field of study rather than a specialty (Resnick 1991). Clinical child psychologists have been described primarily as clinical psychologists, but with a special interest in working with children (Routh 1991). Clinical child psychology may also be defined, directly or indirectly, through the activities of clinical child psychologists and the products of their professional organizations, e.g., training guidelines.

By extrapolation from a definition of clinical psychology put forth by the American Psychological Association's Division on Clinical Psychology (Resnick 1991), the clinical child psychologist integrates science, theory, and practice to understand, predict, and alleviate maladjustment, disability, and discomfort, as well as to promote safe and healthy adaptation, adjustment, growth, and development in children, youths, and families. Clinical child psychology focuses on the intellectual, emotional, biological, psychological, social, and behavioral aspects of individual and family functioning of children from infancy through adolescence, in varying cultures, and at all socioeconomic levels.

Training in Clinical Child Psychology
An earned doctorate from a clinical psychology program represents the basic entry level for the provision of clinical child psychology services. Unique to clinical psychology training is the requirement of substantial course work in the areas of personality and psychopathology, resulting in a comprehensive understanding of normal and abnormal adjustment and maladjustment across the life span. The Hilton Head Conference on Training Clinical Child Psychologists (Tuma 1985) has emphasized the importance of including material on life-span developmental psychology in the training of all professional psychologists. There has been concern that all professional psychologists have a minimum competence in assessment, psychopathology, and intervention methods to serve children, youths, and families, rather than emphasizing specialty training in clinical child psychology (Routh 1991).

What Do Clinical Child Psychologists Do?
The clinical child psychologist is educated and trained to generate and integrate scientific and professional knowledge and skills so as to further psychological science and the professional practice of child psychology. Clinical child psychologists are involved in research, teaching and supervision, professional training at the graduate, internship, and postdoctoral level, program development and evaluation, consultation, public policy, professional practice, and other activities that promote psychological health in infants, children, adolescents, and families, as well as groups and organizations dedicated to the health, education, and welfare of children. Their work can range from prevention of and early intervention in minor problems of adjustment to dealing with the adjustment and maladjustment of children whose disturbance requires them to be institutionalized. Clinical child psychologists work throughout

the United States in a variety of settings, some of which include individual practice, mental health clinics, managed health care organizations, hospitals, legal systems, schools, and universities.

Researchers in clinical child psychology conduct assessment, intervention, prevention, and explicative studies of children and families who are developing along a normal or abnormal continuum, and through their publications document the empirical base of clinical child psychology. There exist over a hundred journals that publish articles on aspects related to children and youth from a psychological perspective (Roberts, Lyman, Breiner, & Royal 1982). The *Journal of Clinical Child Psychology*, the official journal of the Section on Clinical Child Psychology of the Division of Clinical Psychology of the American Psychological Association, and the *Journal of Abnormal Child Psychology*, the official journal of the Society for Research in Child and Adolescent Psychopathology, are among those most representative of the field. Practitioners of clinical child psychology work directly with children at all developmental levels (infants to older adolescents), as well as groups (families, patients of similar psychopathology, and organizations), using a wide range of assessment and intervention methods to promote mental health and alleviate discomfort and maladjustment.

Assessment in clinical child psychology involves determining the nature, causes, and potential effects of personal distress; of developmental, social, school, and work dysfunctions; and the psychological factors associated with physical, behavioral, emotional, nervous, and mental disorders. Examples of assessment procedures are parent and child interviews, behavioral observations, parent and teacher rating scales, sociometric measures, and the administration and interpretation of tests of intellectual abilities, academic achievement, developmental progress, aptitudes, personality characteristics, and other aspects of human experience and behavior relative to disturbance.

Interventions in clinical child psychology are directed at preventing, treating, and correcting behavior problems, emotional conflicts, personality disturbances, psychopathology, and the skill deficits underlying social and personal distress or dysfunc-

tion. Examples of intervention techniques include parent training, play therapy, individual psychotherapy, behavior therapy, family therapy, peer modeling, group therapy, biofeedback, relaxation training, cognitive retraining and rehabilitation, and environmental consultation and design. The goal of intervention is to promote satisfaction, adaptation, social order, and health.

Clinical Child Psychology and the American Psychological Association

The Section on Clinical Child Psychology (Section 1 of the Division of Clinical Psychology of the American Psychological Association), founded by Alan O. Ross in 1962, has a distinguished history of supporting and encouraging the evolution and development of clinical child psychology as both a science and a profession. Its goals are to advance scientific inquiry, training, and professional practice in clinical child psychology as a means of furthering knowledge, welfare, and mental health of children, youth, and families. The landmark Hilton Head Conference on Training Clinical Child Psychologists (1985) resulted in a comprehensive set of recommendations for training at the graduate, internship, and postdoctoral level (Tuma, 1985). These recommendations continue to guide training and ultimately define the field of clinical child psychology.

Sheila M. Eyberg

Clinical Psychology

Clinical psychologists provide assessment, intervention, and consultation regarding the mental, emotional, and behavioral problems of adults and children as well as of couples and families. They also provide help in resolving the psychological and social aspects of physical health problems. Compared to other mental health professionals who practice independently, clinical psychologists have the most extensive training in the behavioral sciences and in research methods, and often have direct experience carrying out research. However, unlike psychiatrists, clinical psychologists are trained in graduate schools rather than medical schools and emphasize psychological approaches to treatment rather than medication or surgery. Clinical psychologists often do cooperate with physicians in order to provide a more comprehensive approach than either profession could provide alone. Unlike social workers and marriage and family therapists, clinical psychologists traditionally have focused on helping individuals rather than systems or groups. Clinical psychologists usually spend four years in graduate school plus a one-year full-time clinical internship before receiving the doctoral degree, which may be a Ph.D., Psy.D., or Ed.D. Their academic training includes basic courses on the biological, social, and cognitive and affective bases of human behavior and individual differences, and advanced courses on personality and psychopathology. One further year of full-time supervised experience and an examination are required before the psychologist may be licensed by a state or province in North America. In other countries, training and licensure requirements differ somewhat.

The most definitive published description of clinical psychology was one adopted in 1990 by two organizations in the field (Definition and Description of Clinical Psychology, 1991). The following excerpts from this definition provide further details of the way the field is conceptualized by its own practitioners:

1. Assessing and/or diagnosing the nature and causes and predicting the effects of subjective distress; of personal, social, and work dysfunctions; and of the psychological and emotional factors involved in, and consequent to, physical disease and disability. Procedures may include but are not limited to interviewing, behavioral assessment, administering and interpreting tests of intellectual and cognitive abilities, aptitudes, emotions, motivations, personality characteristics, and other aspects of human experience and behavior relative to disturbance (p. 7).

2. Intervening at the primary, secondary, and tertiary levels. This includes interventions directed at preventing, treating, and correcting the psychopathology, emotional conflicts, personality disturbances, and skill deficits underlying a person's distress and/or dysfunction. It

also includes interventions to promote health and adjustment. Interventions may reflect a variety of theoretical orientations, techniques, and modalities. These may include, but are not limited to, psychotherapy, psychoanalysis, behavior therapy, marital and family therapy, group therapy, social learning approaches, biofeedback, cognitive retraining and rehabilitation, and environmental consultation and design. Psychopathology is intended here to be interpreted broadly to include and transcend traditional categories of mental illness (e.g., the disorders of the American Psychiatric Association's *Diagnostic and Statistical Manual*). Included are all areas of mental, emotional, behavioral, and psychological patterns that produce distress, dysfunction, disorder, or disease. Clinical psychological intervention promotes satisfaction, adaptation, social order, and health (pp. 7–8).

3. Professional consultation, program development, supervision, administration, and evaluation of clinical psychological services (p. 8).

4. Analysis, development, and implementation of public policy in all areas relevant to the field of clinical psychology (p. 8).

Clinical psychologists are not the only psychologists trained and licensed to provide health services to the public. Counseling psychology and school psychology are related professions. In contrast to clinical psychologists, counseling psychologists are more likely to work with basically normal individuals, such as college students trying to decide upon a vocation, or in rehabilitation centers for persons with, for example, spinal cord injuries. School psychologists, as their name implies, are more likely to work within school systems and to be concerned with youngsters' academic difficulties or classroom misconduct. However, these three areas of professional activity (clinical, counseling, and school psychology) overlap heavily and are sometimes characterized collectively as human service psychology or health service psychology.

The field of clinical psychology was organized at the University of Pennsylvania less than a century ago, in 1896, and the first clinical psychology organization was founded in 1917. Early clinical psychologists were primarily concerned with developing and applying tests and other assessment procedures, such as the Stanford-Binet and Wechsler intelligence tests, and personality measures, such as the Rorschach inkblot test and the Minnesota Multiphasic Personality Inventory. It was not until after World War II that most clinical psychologists ventured into the area of psychotherapy as well, and they were the first to subject psychotherapy to rigorous scientific evaluation. The main impetus to the growth of clinical psychology as a profession was the need of returning veterans and their families for mental health services. At this time, the U.S. Veterans Administration and the National Institute of Mental Health provided a large amount of funds to support the training and employment of clinical psychologists in the public sector. The first state licensing laws for psychologists engaged in independent practice began to be enacted in 1945 (now all states and provinces in the United States and Canada have such laws). Many clinical psychologists were prominently involved in the development of behavior therapy and cognitive behavior therapy, beginning in the 1960s. Within recent years, clinical and other applied psychologists have expanded into many other areas, such as forensic psychology, health psychology, neuropsychology, and marriage and family therapy. The Division of Clinical Psychology (Division 12) of the American Psychological Association now has over 6,000 members. The current interest groups within Division 12, the principal clinical psychology organization in the United States, include children, the aging, scientific research in clinical psychology, the clinical psychology of women, the psychology of children's health problems, and ethnic minority issues. As these interests make clear, clinical psychologists work with all age groups from infants to geriatric patients. They are concerned with the full range of health and mental health, from normal individuals to those with chronic or life-threatening disease or psychosis. The service settings where they work include individual practice, mental health clinics, managed care organizations, hospitals, schools, universities, counseling centers, business organizations, legal systems, government organizations, and the military services.

Clinical psychologists generally feel a strong obligation to base their practice upon current research findings. The primary research journals developed by the field include the following, listed in the order in which they emerged historically: *Journal of Abnormal Psychology, Journal of Consulting and Clinical Psychology, British Journal of Clinical Psychology, Journal of Clinical Child Psychology, Journal of Pediatric Psychology*, and *Psychological Assessment*.

A person who wishes to seek the services of a clinical psychologist might begin by asking for a referral from a family physician or other primary health care provider, thus relying upon this person's knowledge of the local professional community. An alternative method would be to look under the heading of "psychologists" in the yellow pages. In doing this, one should at least make sure that the individual is identified as a licensed psychologist. However, it is often difficult to tell from listings in the telephone book which practitioners are clinical psychologists. About the only way to be sure would be to limit the search to those who are listed as diplomates in clinical psychology of the American Board of Professional Psychology. This organization, analogous to medical specialty boards, identifies those individuals who have met its standards of training in clinical psychology (and other specialty areas) and have passed a thorough examination of their professional competence by a committee of qualified examiners.

Donald K. Routh
George Stricker

Clinical and Statistical Prediction

Practitioners of clinical psychology, psychiatry, and neurology are frequently called upon to predict a patient's future performance or state of health on the basis of present signs, symptoms, or psychological test data. Although the content of such predictions varies widely from one field to another, the predictions all involve attempts to forecast future performance on the basis of fallible input data. Input data may be thought of as any kind of potentially quantifiable information that is thought to be relevant to the prediction task.

Clinical versus Statistical Prediction

From the standpoint of clinical practice, theories of clinical and statistical prediction are less important than empirical studies that contrast the relative accuracy of the two methods. For a proper scientific evaluation of the relative merits of the two methods, it is necessary to design studies in which all factors are held constant except the method of data combination.

Studies reviewed by Meehl have covered a variety of prediction situations, including success in academic or military training, recovery from psychosis, and medical diagnosis. The input data utilized for prediction have also varied widely, from interview impressions to objective test scores. It should not be concluded from Meehl's review that input data based on human judgment (interviewer's impressions) are less useful in prediction than objective test scores, such as the Minnesota Multiphasic Personality Inventory.

A surprising finding is that in all studies, unit weighting of variables (i.e., simply adding them up) results in predictions superior to those generated by random models, paramorphic models, and the judges themselves. In fact, in some of the studies, the unit-weighting model has outperformed the statistically optimal model. This result has important implications for both clinical and statistical prediction. In situations in which the ratio of observations to variables is relatively low, regression weights tend to be unstable, and unit weighting is preferable.

Jerry S. Wiggins

Coalition Formation

Coalition formation is a process whereby individuals combine to control outcomes. The theory typically assumes a conflict of interest or competition for rewards. Because members must agree among themselves, the coalition requires an allocation of rewards, or a deal. Negotiation to reach deals is an essential feature of coalition formation.

Minimum power theory, based on game-theoretic assumptions, invokes the concept of pivotal power, or the proportion of times that a member's resources can convert a losing into a winning coalition.

Bargaining theory (Komorita & Chertkoff) emphasizes the role of negotiation. Each member seeks to maximize his or her gains but also assesses what he or she can expect to receive. Norms may be invoked to reach a solution: an equality norm for the weaker members, a parity norm for the strongest.

"Psychological" theories, (especially those treatments by W. Edgar Vinacke [1969]), stress the perceptions of the participants and the attitudes (or strategies) that influence their behavior. In this respect, exploitative and accommodative strategies have been distinguished.

W. Edgar Vinacke

Cocaine

The mechanism of action of cocaine is based on its ability to block the generation and transmission of neuronal impulses. This effect is rapidly reversible, accounting for the brief duration of cocaine activity. Cocaine sensitizes the sympathetic nerve endings by inhibiting the reuptake and destruction of norepinephrine.

The long-term use of cocaine leads to periods of depression, which are "cured" by readministration of the drug. Cocaine does not produce physical dependence, since physiological withdrawal symptoms do not occur upon the abrupt discontinuation of cocaine.

The predominant physical effects of cocaine include widely dilated pupils, increased cardiac and respiratory rates, heightened body temperature, pilo-erection, fine motor tremors, diaphoresis, rhinorrhea, and tearing. According to recent studies 61% of cocaine addicts have mood disorders, 35% have attention deficit disorder, and 21% have anxiety disorder (Rousanville et al. 1991).

Alan Brown
J. Thomas Ungerleider

Cognition and Intelligence

The study of factors influencing the development of intelligence and cognition centered at one time around the relative contributions of nature and nurture. More recently, the organism has been assumed to both influence and be influenced by the total environment in an interactional or transactional manner.

Early social interaction, particularly mother-infant interaction, is recognized as an important determiner or correlate both for affective and cognitive development, and the early maternal behavior toward a premature infant can be compared to the interaction of the mother with a full-term baby. The mother-child interaction of retarded 3- to 7-year-olds is more neutral and less active than for nonretarded 4- to 5-year-olds.

The physical-psychological environment includes those stimuli that constitute "aliment," or input for cognition. Jean Piaget's cognitive-developmental analysis makes the assumption that the developing child's genetic makeup acts upon the environment in an adaptive fashion, resulting in transitions from lower to higher stages.

DEVELOPMENTAL COMPETENCY
The progression of retarded children from dependent to increasingly independent environmental settings is one of the axioms of the normalization principle. Closely aligned to this is the Piagetian focus on demonstration of specific competencies at varying developmental levels.

INDEPENDENT-DEPENDENT VARIABLE SHIFTS
Traditionally, the psychometric value of a particular group has been the independent variable for predicting performance of a particular task. From the trends already described, the performance of a task itself becomes more often the independent variable. Accordingly, it becomes a basis for making decisions about the child.

Rune J. Simeonsson
Rue L. Cromwell

Cognitive-Behavior Therapy

Although the roots of behavior therapy are frequently traced to John Broadus Watson's early twentieth-century work with conditioning and fears in children and the Mowrers' use of the bell-and-pad procedure to correct enuresis, extensive applications

of behavioral procedures began in the late 1950s and the 1960s (Craighead, Craighead, & Ilardi 1994; Kazdin 1978). During the period from 1950 to 1969, behavior therapy or behavior modification focused largely on applied learning theory: B. F. Skinner's (1953) principles of operant conditioning and Joseph Wolpe's (1958) use of counterconditioning, usually conceptualized within a classical conditioning model, in the description and employment of systematic desensitization to treatment of anxiety problems. At that point, behavior therapy was characterized by (1) its employment of principles of basic psychology (primarily principles of learning); (2) the utilization of experimental methods to validate the effectiveness of clinical procedures derived from the utilization of the principles of "basic" psychology (also called *methodological behaviorism*); and (3) a focus on overt, observable behaviors (as opposed to "inferred" states) as the target of clinical interventions (Mahoney, Kazdin, & Lesswing 1978).

Applications of Operant Conditioning
Early and successful applications of operant conditioning principles included classroom management for regular and special classes by Bijou, Baer, Becker, O'Leary and others (Bijou & Baer 1961; O'Leary & O'Leary 1977). Procedures evolving from this research are now widely used in educational settings. Operant procedures were also utilized with difficult clinical problems, such as autism, mental retardation, and schizophrenia; although these disorders, which appear to have a major biological diathesis, were not "cured," the power of individualized contingency management programs and comprehensive token economics to increase adaptive behaviors was clearly established, and the quality of life was improved for many of these chronic patients (see Paul & Lentz 1977, for example). Similar procedures were also employed to reduce undesirable behaviors (such as aggression and stealing) and recidivism and to promote prosocial behavior (e.g., attending school) among delinquent and conduct-disorder adolescents (Kazdin 1994).

The term *applied behavior analysis* evolved to refer to this type of intervention program. The use of single-subject research designs (Hersen & Barlow

1976) allowed behavior analysts to focus on observable, individual behaviors and concurrently to use experimental methodologies to establish that an intervention was responsible for the obtained behavioral change. The relatively straightforward nature of such applications made it possible to train paraprofessionals and institutional ward staff to implement these types of programs.

Applications of Classical Conditioning

Wolpe developed and described several behavioral procedures of psychotherapy based on the learning principle of reciprocal inhibition (1958). His human applications were presented as having been derived from his and others' laboratory work, conducted under the general rubric of classical conditioning with nonhuman species (particularly cats), in which several responses incompatible with anxiety were paired with a previous anxiety-arousing stimulus; the nonanxious response "inhibited" the anxiety response, and thus the anxiety was overcome. In clinical work with humans, the most widely used nonanxious response became a modified, shortened version of P. J. Jacobson's progressive muscular-relaxation procedure, which was combined with the use of imagery of anxiety-provoking situations; over time, the term *systematic desensitization* evolved as the label for these procedures. Based on the work of Lang and others and his own research, G. L. Paul (1969) concluded that systematic desensitization was an effective anxiety treatment.

These early behavioral interventions, occurring in the historical context of the prevailing psychodynamic model, were claimed to be a passing fad and even to be detrimental, in that they would result in "symptom substitution." That they were not a fad is apparent, and there have been little or no data supporting either the occurrence or the deleterious effects of symptom substitution (Kazdin & Wilson 1978).

Development of Cognitive-Behavior Therapy

The 1970s and 1980s witnessed two major developments in behavior therapy: (1) procedures derived from learning principles, at least used metaphorically, were developed to treat an increasingly wide range of clinical problems; and (2) as basic psy-

chology underwent a cognitive revolution (Dember 1974), the conceptual basis for clinical applications became more cognitive (Craighead, Craighead, Kazdin, & Mahoney 1994). The integration of rational emotive therapy (Ellis 1962) and cognitive therapy (Beck 1976) with behavioral procedures and the emphasis on evaluation of the efficacy of those integrated models and procedures has been felicitously titled "cognitive-behavior therapy" (CBT). In addition to the development of cognitive therapy and clinical procedures based on findings from basic cognitive psychology, there were two other major influences in the development of cognitive-behavior therapy: social learning theory and self-control therapies.

SOCIAL LEARNING THEORY

The importance of cognitive variables as causal factors in the development, maintenance, and change of behavior was highlighted by the work of Albert Bandura (1969) and his colleagues, who established the basic principles of observational learning. *Behavioral rehearsal*, the general term used to refer to the clinical procedures derived from this model (essentially instruction and/or modeling and practice with feedback), has become a standard method for teaching new skills in a wide variety of domains. Behavioral rehearsal employs graduated levels of performance difficulty, and it is frequently combined with prompting, shaping, and positive reinforcement (i.e., operant procedures) to provide motivation for performing the newly acquired skills. These procedures have been applied to many different clinical problems, ranging from rehabilitation of the chronically mentally ill to college students with few dates. These procedures have formed the basis for interventions commonly labeled *assertion training*, *social skills training*, and *problem-solving training*.

Bandura (1977) later developed his theory of self-efficacy, which further emphasized the role of cognitive variables. Self-efficacy refers to situation-specific (as opposed to global) expectations about one's ability to perform a particular behavior and one's perception of the likelihood that this behavior will result in a desired outcome. These self-efficacy expectations determine whether coping behavior is initiated, as well as the degree of effort expended to maintain active coping behavior when obstacles are encountered.

SELF-CONTROL

While the initial conceptualizations of operant principles focused on contingency management by external agents, the development of self-control (self-management) paradigms (Mahoney & Thoresen 1974) employed Bandura's (1969) notion of reciprocal determinism, i.e., that a person could initiate changes in the environment to alter the probability of his or her own behaviors. Self-management programs typically include both stimulus control procedures (altering cues in the environment) and self-managed contingencies (standard setting, self-evaluation, and self-reinforcement/punishment). These procedures have been most extensively applied in the treatment of obesity and addictions (Brownell 1989; Marlatt & Gordon 1985). The notion of teaching specific relapse-prevention skills has been a major contribution from this area. Self-instructional training, which emphasizes the utilization of verbal statements (gradually faded) to direct one's own behavior, is another important innovation (Meichenbaum 1975). It has proved useful for modifying various impulsive behaviors of children and for anger control in both children and adults.

Examples of Cognitive-Behavioral Interventions

MAJOR DEPRESSION

Cognitive-behavior therapy is a psychosocial treatment for major depression. The treatment of depression illustrates both the utilization of behavioral procedures with a wide range of problems and the utilization of clinical cognitive therapy (Beck 1976) and cognitive therapy derived from cognitive psychology (Bandura 1969; Mahoney 1974). Major depression was one of the later major clinical problem areas to be studied by traditional behaviorists. Although a few behaviorists had addressed the topic of depression (Ferster 1973; Lewinsohn 1974), and Aaron T. Beck had described a cognitive therapy for depression (1970, 1976), it was the comparative effectiveness of Beck's cognitive-behavior therapy (Beck, Rush, Shaw, & Emery 1979) to a widely used

tricyclic antidepressant (Rush, Beck, Kovacs, & Hollon 1977) that called major attention to this therapeutic approach. Beck and his colleagues drew upon his cognitive therapy background in the development of their treatment manual, but they also made extensive use of the rapidly developing fields of cognitive psychology, attribution theory, and behavioral and cognitive depression psychopathology in the development of their critically evaluated and clinically useful standardized treatment manual for major depression.

Partially due to the development of Beck's program and partially due to the general development of cognitive and social-cognitive psychology, other previously behavioral (learning-theory oriented) mental health professionals working in the area of depression became more cognitive in their description of the etiology of depression (e.g., the learned-helplessness theory was reformulated [see Abramson, Seligman, and Teasdale 1978]) and in their treatment and prevention of depression (see Lewinsohn, Clarke, Hops, & Andrews 1990). It is expected that the next decade will witness the integration of these CBT models and treatments with the more somatic-based models and treatments of biological psychiatry (Hollon, DeRubeis, Evans, et al. 1992; Craighead 1990).

ANXIETY DISORDERS

The increasing breadth and cognitive focus of behavioral applications is also illustrated well in the treatment of anxiety disorders. As earlier noted, Joseph Wolpe developed systematic desensitization, which was used successfully to treat phobias, speech anxiety, and test anxiety (Paul 1969). As anxiety disorders were further delineated (e.g., APA 1980) different procedures were developed to address the specific nature of the various problem areas defined by the label "anxiety." For example, "exposure" and "response prevention," derived from the learning concept of extinction, were developed as effective treatments for obsessive-compulsive disorder (Salkovskis & Kirk 1989). Similarly, intensive exposure (sometimes used concurrently with relaxation training) is the behavioral treatment of choice for post-traumatic stress disorder (PTSD) in combat survivors (Keane, Fairbanks, Caddell, & Zimering

1989) and rape survivors (Foa, Rothbaum, Riggs, & Murdock 1991). The treatment of PTSD, in which the patient has experienced repeated trauma, such as that which may occur in familial sexual abuse (frequently a major developmental factor in co-morbid borderline personality disorder) includes major behavioral components but has also incorporated cognitive and emotional components into its programs, such as the one developed by Linehan (1993). Although progressive muscular relaxation has remained a major part of the treatment for generalized anxiety disorder, incorporation of cognitive procedures for "worry" is a significant aspect of the most effective treatments (Borkovec, Shadick, & Hopkins 1991). Perhaps the clearest integration of behavioral and cognitive therapies for anxiety disorders is D. H. Barlow's treatment (Barlow & Cerny 1988) for panic disorder. This well-evaluated and highly effective treatment includes progressive muscular relaxation (with an emphasis on deep breathing), exposure, and cognitive-restructuring procedures (Barlow, Craske, Cerny, & Klosko 1989).

OTHER PROBLEM AREAS

Traditional behavior therapy procedures have been successfully employed in the treatment of marital discord (Beach, Sandeen, & O'Leary 1990; Jacobson & Margolin 1979). Like most other forms of behavior therapy, with the increasing recognition that cognitive factors affect marital interaction styles (Fincham, Bradbury, & Scott 1990) behavioral marital therapy has become increasingly more cognitive by emphasizing the role of a partner's standards, expectations, and attributions regarding the other's behavior (Baucom & Epstein 1990). Moreover, marital therapy has been used to treat other disorders (e.g., major depression) within the context of the marriage (Beach & O'Leary 1992).

Eating disorders is another major area in which behavioral procedures have been successfully integrated with cognitive interventions. Early behavioral programs for obesity developed out of the self-control paradigm and focused primarily on altering eating habits and increasing exercise. Adding a greater focus on cognition (i.e., cognitive restructur-

ing) did not significantly improve weight loss, but this is likely related to biological constraints, because extending the length of treatment did improve results. Unfortunately, even with relapse-prevention strategies, long-term maintenance of weight loss has been disappointing (Brownell, 1989; Craighead, Craighead, & Kirkley 1994). However, as behaviorists began treatment of bulimia and anorexia nervosa, the importance of cognitive components became more obvious. Therapy utilizes behavioral self-management strategies to reinstate normalized eating patterns, but cognitive restructuring is used extensively to challenge directly the maladaptive beliefs about weight and shape, which are seen as central to these disorders. (Fairburn, Jones, Peveler, Hope, & O'Connor 1993).

In addition to the treatment of traditional mental health problem areas, CBT has begun to have a major impact on problems of social significance, which have an impact on health and mental health adaptive functioning. For example, CBT techniques have been a major component of community education programs for individuals at risk for exposure to HIV and AIDS (Kelly, St. Lawrence, Hood, & Brasfield 1989). Behavioral procedures, first evaluated empirically, have been incorporated on a widespread basis to facilitate the wearing of seatbelts (Geller, Paterson, & Talbott 1982). CBT programs are currently being evaluated to determine if they can reduce marital and family violence (O'Leary & Neidig 1993) and prevent social and self-destructive aggression in young males (Conduct Problems Prevention Research Group 1993). Finally, cognitive-behavior therapists are working with physicians and medical personnel to assist in the prevention and treatment of a wide range of health problems, such as diabetes, cardiovascular disease, cancer (to prolong and improve quality of life), and chronic pain in both children and adults (Keefe & Beckham 1994; Oyama & Andrasik 1992; Peterson, Sherman, & Zink 1994). The combination of medical and psychological procedures in the treatment of both general health and mental health problems (e.g., panic, depression, manic-depression) holds great promise and should receive extensive study during the next few years. The role of emotion in these disorders and their treatment within the individual and family contexts is another major topic that warrants serious study and systematic evaluation in the near future.

W. Edward Craighead
Linda Wilson Craighead

Appreciation is expressed to K. Daniel O'Leary, Ph.D., for his comments on an earlier draft of this manuscript.

Cognitive Consistency Theories

There are several reasons why individuals might strive for cognitive consistency. Regarding perception of the external environment, one's ability to cope effectively with the environment depends upon one's ability to predict external events. If, for example, one did not characterize situations or people in any way, then life would become difficult indeed, with each setting or interactant approached warily without regard for previous learning. We organize our thoughts about people and events and, unless that organization is extremely complex, it must by necessity have a certain degree of consistency. It is also known, however, that any such organization affects the way we subsequently perceive these events or people.

Heider's balance theory emphasizes the relationships among self, other people, and objects (or events) in the world. Two types of relationships are stressed: sentiment and unit, either of which may be positive or negative. The sentiment relationship roughly corresponds to liking. The unit relationship is related to the gestalt: "Briefly, separate entities comprise a unit when they are perceived as belonging together. For example, members of a family are seen as a unit; a person and his deed belong together" (Heider 1958, p. 176).

Festinger's dissonance theory (1957) represents the opposite pole from Heider on several dimensions. The theory is more formal; its proponents have been very productive in experimental research; and some of the research has been controversial because of the "nonobvious" findings.

Festinger emphasizes that the implicative relationship between cognition is psychological rather than simply logical. That a relationship is logically inconsistent does not necessarily mean that people see it as psychologically dissonant.

Research has concentrated on discrepancies between attitudes and behavior and on consequences of decisions. In the former case, the issue is the consequences of acting inconsistently with one's beliefs.

How people perceive their world, organize those perceptions, and when and how they change them are the general questions addressed by cognitive consistency theories.

Charles A. Kiesler

Cognitive Dissonance Theories

Cognitive dissonance theory, first postulated by Leon Festinger (1957) and elaborated by J. W. Brehm and A. R. Cohen (1962), has had a continued impact on social psychological thinking since its inception. There are probably two reasons for this impact: the theory implies a number of counterintuitive, unique effects; and it applies to a broad domain of behaviors studied by psychologists of other theoretical traditions.

Cognitive dissonance is a motivational state, and is said to lead the person to reduce dissonance. Here is where the theory becomes unique relative to all other theories of cognitive balance: dissonance reduction is postulated to take place through change in whatever cognitive elements are least resistant to change, and as Festinger notes, the primary source of resistance to change is a cognition's correspondence with reality.

Applications

Virtually all research generated from dissonance principles has involved the person's making a decision, and it has been assumed that the behavior of deciding to take a certain course of action is highly resistant to change.

Attitude Discrepancy

An important application of dissonance theory is to the effects of attitude-discrepant behavior. In one experiment by Cohen and Latané (Brehm & Cohen 1962, pp. 88–91), subjects who had indicated opposition to compulsory religion at Yale were asked to make a public statement in favor of a mandatory religion course. Subjects in one condition were offered a choice whether or not to participate; in another condition, subjects were given no choice. Because the commitment to make a speech is a cognition highly resistant to change, cognitive dissonance theory would predict that the subjects in the choice condition would change their attitude. Subjects in the no-choice condition, on the other hand, would not be expected to change their attitude. The attitude change results bore out this reasoning.

Selective Exposure

Dissonance theory also has implications for other motivational states, such as thirst, hunger, and pain.

Expectancy

Although most applications of dissonance theory assume a recent behavioral commitment to be the cognition most resistant to change, there has been at least one paradigm that takes exception. In a study by Aronson and Carlsmith (1962) some subjects were given a strong expectancy that they would continue to perform poorly on a test of personality judgment. The authors proposed that a person who has a firm conception of himself will experience dissonance when that expectancy is violated, and as a result, there will be efforts to realign events with that prior expectancy.

Robert A. Wicklund

Cognitive Factors in Classical Conditioning: An Information-Processing Stage Analysis

Here, classical conditioning is viewed as a complex information-processing task composed of several processing stages in an attempt to show how these various cognitive variables would be expected to influence performance.

Stage Analysis of Classical Conditioning

Cognitive or information-processing approaches to psychology typically analyze an experimental task into a series of processing stages or steps that intervene between the onset of a stimulus and the onset of an appropriate response. At each stage, information made available by earlier stages is further analyzed and transformed into a more abstract form that is useful for performing the experimental task. It is instructive to consider what sorts of information-processing operations intervene between the onset of the conditioned stimulus (CS) and the onset of an appropriate response on any particular conditioning trial. The stages to be considered involve CS detection, CS recognition, memory comparison, response decision, and response execution. Such stages are typical of those commonly included in general cognitive processing models.

CS DETECTION

It seems reasonable to suppose that a CS must be above the observer's sensory threshold for it to elicit an appropriate response. Therefore, the first stage of analysis on a conditioning trial can be thought of as providing a registration that some stimulus has been presented. According to most information-processing models, this process of stimulus detection requires very little time, so that CS detection should be almost immediate upon the presentation of suprathreshold CS.

CS RECOGNITION

Evidence from perceptual information-processing experiments indicates that the presentation of a stimulus initiates a recognition process that examines the information contained in the stimulus in an attempt to determine exactly which of many potential stimuli has been presented. The process of stimulus recognition takes considerably more time than the process of detection, so CS recognition is not immediate.

MEMORY COMPARISON

If an appropriate response is to be given on a particular conditioning trial, then the information processor must be able to determine whether an unconditioned stimulus (US) is likely to follow the now-recognized CS. That is, the recognized CS must be compared with some memory representation of the CS-US contingencies so that some estimate of the probability of a US occurrence can be made. The CS-US associations, or memory representations, can be influenced by many variables. Certain cognitive factors also seem to influence the actual comparison of the recognized CS with the memory representation.

RESPONSE DECISION

Once the memory-comparison stage determines whether a US is likely to occur, a response decision process must either initiate or withhold a conditioned response (CR). Such variables as facilitatory versus inhibitory response instructions and US intensity can influence the overall probability of CR occurrence—presumably by influencing this response decision process. Because an observer can be aware of the correct CS-US contingencies and still not give appropriate CRs, it is necessary to realize that overt CR performance is not always an accurate indicator of the state of CS-US contingency learning.

RESPONSE EXECUTION

When the response decision is positive, a CR must be programmed and executed.

Joseph B. Hellige

Cognitive Map

In the theory of E. C. Tolman, the "cognitive map" was one way of referring to the conception that learning involved the acquisition of knowledge about "what leads to what" in the environment.

Gregory A. Kimble

Cognitive Style in the Classroom

The research of H. R. Gardner et al. has been directed toward the relationship between cognitive style and defense selection, using adults as subjects of study. Research, using Gardner's constructs, has not been directed to the classroom. The research

using the constructs of Kagan and Witkin has been, in contrast, developmental, using children as subjects and studying the relation between cognitive style and performance relevant to the educational experience (J. Kagan & N. Kogan 1970).

The work of Witkin et al. focuses on the cognitive styles of *field independence* and *field dependence*. Other names given to the dimension are *field articulation*, as opposed to *diffuseness*, and *analytic* as opposed to *global* functioning.

J. E. Robinson and J. L. Gray's (1974) investigation into the relationship between cognitive style and school learning of fifth-grade children has identified three cognitive styles among children (Kagan 1966). Of the three styles—categorical, descriptive, and relational—the descriptive style is most important in the prediction of school learning. This style has been called analytic, because the individual deals with similarities among the concrete detail of stimuli.

Beatrice Harris

Cognitive Theories in Social Psychology

Cognitive theories may be divided into at least two types. Some focus upon the way that cognitions are organized, for it is through such organized structures that we make sense out of an otherwise chaotic environment. Other theories examine the interaction among cognitions and the dynamic forces for change that arise therefrom.

In Krech and Crutchfield's (1948) terms, there is a noncognitive, structural process such that properties of the stimulus evoke certain neural activities in the perceiver. But equally important is a functional process, in which a decision is made by the perceiver as to the meaning of the environmental stimuli.

J. S. Bruner (1957), one of the leading proponents of the importance of cognitive processes in perception, proposes that a person responds to an object or event by trying to relate it to an appropriate cognitive category. The individual is in an active position, matching the events to various cognitive structures until a suitable fit is achieved.

J. E. Jones and K. E. Davis (1965), following the lead of Fritz Heider (1958), discuss the cognitive rules that we use for the processing of information about other people. According to their theory of correspondent inferences, judgments about the stable properties of other persons derive from an analysis of their behavior and its effects.

An alternate set of rules for processing information about other persons (Kelley, 1967) proposes that people who witness an actor behaving in a social situation attribute a behavior either to properties of the social field (external attribution) or to the properties of the actor (internal attribution).

Psychological balance. Heider (1946) proposes that there are two types of relationships between entities—units and sentiments. The former are relationships of belonging, while the latter are relationships of liking (L) and disliking (DL). It is the sentiment relationship that forms the crux of the balance approach.

Theory of cognitive dissonance. Leon Festinger (1957) proposes that inconsistency among cognitions creates an uncomfortable tension state, called dissonance. Like other drives, dissonance demands reduction. One of the assets of Festinger's theory is its ability to estimate differential magnitudes of tension. In general, the magnitude of dissonance is said to be directly proportional to the number and importance of inconsistent cognitions a person holds, and inversely proportional to the number and importance of consistent cognitions.

Most of the research in dissonance theory has been conducted in the paradigm of forced compliance. In this paradigm, an individual is induced to behave in ways that are at variance with his or her private attitude. For example, Festinger and Carlsmith (1959) had subjects participate in a boring experimental procedure. They were then asked to tell a waiting subject that the procedure was in fact interesting and enjoyable. The public statement was inconsistent with subjects' private beliefs and therefore aroused the tension state of dissonance.

Joel Cooper

Cognitive Therapy

During the last two decades, the cognitive therapy model advanced by Aaron T. Beck has gained ascendancy in the field of psychotherapy. Initially, Beck's

work as a traditional psychoanalytic therapist led him to conclude that depression was not due to repressed anger, as Sigmund Freud had proposed, but rather to a pervasive predisposition toward negative cognitions. Beck proposed that depression is characterized by the *negative triad*—that is, a negative view of the self, experience, and the future.

Cognitive Assessment

The cognitive model proposes that there are three levels of cognitive assessment—specifically, automatic thoughts, maladaptive assumptions, and schemas (about self and others). Each of these levels of cognition is largely conscious and relatively accessible to inquiry. Automatic thoughts are thoughts that occur spontaneously, appear plausible, and are associated with negative affect (such as anxiety, depression, anger, or hopelessness). These thoughts may prove to be accurate or inaccurate. The cognitive therapist categorizes the thoughts according to their apparent cognitive distortions. These distortions include mind reading, personalizing, fortune telling, overgeneralizing, catastrophizing, and mislabeling. In addition to the automatic thought distortions, the therapist helps the patient identify underlying maladaptive assumptions. These assumptions include the "if-then" rules or "should" statements that contribute to depressive vulnerability. Examples of maladaptive assumptions are "I should always do a perfect job" or "I need everyone's approval to feel worthwhile." At a more central level of information processing are the individual's schemas or concepts of self and others. The depressive schemas include thoughts that the self is worthless, helpless, ugly, evil, or empty. Negative schemas of others reflect the belief that others may be rejecting, untrustworthy, controlling, abandoning, or punitive.

Cognitive Specificity

The cognitive model is fundamentally an information-processing model of psychopathology. According to this model, information consistent with the underlying schema(s) is selectively attended to and recalled in memory. This schematic processing accounts for the "resistance" of depressive and anxious cognitive styles.

According to Beck's model, each area of psychopathology involves specific cognitive content. Depression involves themes of loss, failure, and emptiness; anxiety entails danger and imminent threat; and anger involves insult and personal injury, often reflecting a moralistic evaluation.

Cognitive specificity is an important component of Beck and Derek Freeman's model of personality disorders. According to this model, each personality disorder reflects a specific cognitive content for schemas. For example, the avoidant personality sees the self as socially inept and views others as critical and demeaning. The dependent personality views the self as needy, weak, and helpless and sees others (in an idealized state) as nurturant, supportive, and competent.

Intervention Strategies

Cognitive therapy differs from traditional psychoanalytic therapy in several ways. The emphasis is largely on current, conscious thoughts and behavior; each session has an agenda; the therapist and patient engage in a collaborative "Socratic" dialogue to elicit, test, and challenge thoughts and behavioral patterns; the duration of treatment is relatively short term; there is accountability for effectiveness as measured by targeted symptoms or behaviors; patients are encouraged to complete self-help homework assignments; and the therapist actively engages in challenging the patient's dysfunctional thinking. In addition to the in-session structuring of sessions, patients are encouraged to use bibliotherapy to supplement their therapy, with popular books such as David Burns's *Feeling Good* as an important element in the patient's self-help program.

The cognitive therapist integrates behavioral techniques with cognitive techniques. Because depression is associated with a decrease in rewarding activities, patients are asked to monitor mood fluctuations associated with various activities and to increase scheduling of pleasurable and challenging activities. In addition, avoidant and anxious patients are encouraged to construct a hierarchy of anxiety-provoking situations and to gradually engage in exposure to these situations. Other behavioral interventions include assertiveness training, communication training, and problem solving.

Specific cognitive techniques include eliciting and identifying automatic thoughts, evaluating the evidence for and against negative thoughts, examining the costs and benefits of thoughts and assumptions, actively challenging the logic underlying the thought, arguing back at the thought through role playing in which the therapist takes the counterpoint to the thought, examining the double standard of the underlying assumptions, and setting up behavioral experiments, either to test out the thought or to act in opposition to the thought. Imagery-induction techniques are utilized to access "deeper" negative thoughts and fantasies. These thoughts and fantasies are then tested utilizing many of the techniques outlined above.

Obsessive patients are encouraged to set aside "worry time" in order to limit worrying to a specific time and place. These worries are then submitted to an evaluation as to how "catastrophic" the consequences are likely to be for each worry. In addition, behavioral techniques—such as relaxation training or breathing exercises to reduce hyperventilation—are often used in the treatment of anxiety and obsessiveness.

Homework assignments are designed to generalize the techniques that are used in session outside of therapy. The assumption is that self-help is an essential component of therapy—that is, the patient does not improve simply by gaining insight or catharsis or resolving transference issues with the therapist. Rather, improvement is established through actively challenging the negative assumptions in the real world outside of therapy. In fact, outcome studies demonstrate that compliance with homework is one of the best predictors of improvement in cognitive therapy and in maintaining the gains of therapy one year later.

The cognitive model of panic disorder illustrates the importance of integrating cognitive and behavioral strategies. Panic disorder is conceptualized as an overinterpretation of anxiety symptoms—that is, the panic patient excessively self-monitors his symptoms and then interprets these symptoms as predictive of catastrophic consequences (i.e., "I'll go crazy" or "I'll be unable to catch my breath"). The therapist assists the patient in understanding the physical nature of anxiety (e.g., the consequences of hyperventilation) and the catastrophic interpretations that the patient is making. The therapist may guide the patient through a self-induced panic attack in the session and then show the patient how the panic attack can easily and quickly be diminished. This in vivo exposure has proven to be extremely effective in rapidly decreasing panic attacks and in helping agoraphobic patients successfully confront feared stimuli and reduce their anticipatory anxiety.

Marital Therapy

The cognitive model has also been extended by Baucom and Epstein to marital therapy. Marital dysfunction is conceptualized in a multimodal fashion as involving deficits or differences in mutual reward, the use of punishment or withdrawal, communication style, ineffective listening, and lack of mutual problem solving. In addition, distressed couples often have unrealistic expectations and maladaptive assumptions and tend to engage in the same cognitive distortions that depressed and angry patients use. For example, one spouse may misinterpret the other's behavior as personally directed against him or as evidence of an unchangeable and awful trait that makes any intervention appear hopeless to the distressed spouse. These cognitive distortions and maladaptive assumptions are challenged using the techniques described above. In addition, there is a strong emphasis on communication training and behavioral intervention with couples.

Outcome Evaluation

Numerous studies have indicated that cognitive therapy is as effective as antidepressant medication in the treatment of depression. Furthermore, compared to patients receiving medication, cognitive therapy patients are more likely to maintain their improvement on one- and two-year follow-up after treatment has been terminated. In addition, cognitive therapy has proven to be especially effective in reducing suicidal risk. For the treatment of panic disorder, cognitive therapy has been shown to be very effective over the course of a ten-week intervention. Research on marital discord indicates that cognitive therapy is as effective as traditional behavioral interventions.

The use of cognitive therapy is not inconsistent with biological interventions such as medication. The addition of medication for severely depressed patients may facilitate the therapeutic intervention. However, in milder or moderate cases of depression, or in the treatment of panic disorder, the patient may be unclear as to whether the improvement is due to the medication or to the use of cognitive therapy. Recent research on treatment effectiveness has focused on "process" variables, such as the patient's compliance with homework assignments and attitude toward "personal resourcefulness," that is, an attitude conducive to personal change. Although several recent authors have argued that cognitive therapy may be effective with personality disorders, there are no studies that specifically address the treatment efficacy for these patients.

Robert L. Leahy

Collective Behavior and Crowd Behavior

Criterion

Collective behavior may be distinguished from other types of social processes in terms of the number of participants and the level of organization. Dyadic relationships are clearly outside the range of collective activity. Small group functions, however, may sometimes fall within the field, since the definition of what constitutes a "small group" is often difficult to determine operationally. In general, collective behavior is associated with many persons, especially those who are experiencing unrest and a desire for change.

Determinants

N. Smelser (1963) has proposed a complex and systematic theory that delineates the determinants of certain types of collective behavior and can be applied to the panic, the craze, the hostile outburst, or the norm-oriented social movement.

Structural conduciveness refers to the existing social conditions that permit a given form of collective behavior. Terrorization of certain subgroups within a society, for example, occurs when there are sharp class distinctions, norms of violence, and also when the target group conceives of itself as powerless and consequently does not retaliate. It was in such a milieu that the Ku Klux Klan and the night riders of the Old South operated at the turn of the century in America. Should the oppressed group fight back, the event becomes a riot or civil war.

Leaders may emerge from within the group by dint of activity level alone (Freedman, Carlsmith, and Sears 1974), or they may come from outside the group. A frequent complaint of authorities in an institution beset by unrest and agitation is that the dissatisfaction expressed is often due to the influence of "outside agitators" who were not originally members of the protesting group.

Brown (1965) has separated the concept of collective behavior into two basic categories: the active and the passive crowd. Active crowds are labeled "mobs." Mobs are further divided into four subcategories according to the behavior typically exhibited by each:

1. *Aggressive crowds*, such as lynch mobs, rioters, and groups that terrorize.
2. *Escape groups*, which generally demonstrate some degree of panic.
3. *Acquisitive crowds*, such as those involved in hoarding panics during times of potential deprivation, as well as looters.
4. *Expressive crowds*, such as those observed in religious revival meetings or political rallies.

Crowds, as with individuals or other groups, may follow normative patterns, but it depends on the payoff matrix at hand within the situation. The more intangible benefits afforded ordinarily for following societally prescribed behavior may be forsaken for the more immediate tension release obtained in subscribing to the influence of a dynamic but malevolent leader.

Judith A. Waters

Color Constancy

Color constancy refers to the strong tendency of surface colors to be correctly perceived despite wide variations in the kind and amount of light those surfaces reflect to the eye. It is one example of a group of phenomena called the perceptual constancies, so

named because some aspect of the physical world (size or shape, for instance) is perceived as constant regardless of changes in the corresponding aspects of the stimulation of the sense organs (size and shape of the image projected onto the eye) that result from changes in viewing conditions (such as distance, illumination, or orientation in space).

Color Perception

Color perception is the culmination of a process that can be separated into four stages: (1) light is emitted from some source; (2) it strikes various surfaces, which absorb some and reflect the rest of the light; (3) a pattern of light from all the surfaces in the field of view reaches the eye and is focused into an image; and (4) that image creates a pattern of excitation within the nervous system, which (after various transformations) results in the experience of seeing surfaces with specific colors.

Wallach's Studies

In 1948, H. Wallach proposed a remarkably simple explanation of lightness constancy that sidesteps the difficulties of Hermann Ludwig Ferdinand von Helmholtz's idea that illumination is taken into account. Wallach proposed that equal *ratios* of light intensity at the eye produce equal shades of gray. He supported that proposal with the following demonstrations:

A homogenous disk of light is projected onto a screen. A second projector is used to project a ring of light, the inner contour of which coincides with the outer contour of the disk. The ring and the disk are equal in area, but each is independently variable in intensity. By simply varying the intensity of the ring, the disk can be made to appear any color from white to black, even though its own intensity remains constant. When the ring is approximately half the intensity of the disk, the disk appears white. When the ring is twenty times the intensity of the disk, the disk appears black. All the shades of gray appear between these extremes. Thus, the relative nature of black and white becomes clear.

Wallach's *ratio-concept* immediately provides an explanation for the classic phenomenon known as simultaneous brightness contrast. A piece of medium-gray paper looks darker on a white background than on a black background. The grays appear different because the ratio of each gray to its surround is different.

Lateral Inhibition

T. N. Cornsweet (1970) has developed a widely accepted model to account for lightness constancy based upon lateral inhibitory interactions. When the level of illumination on an array is raised, the level of neural excitation corresponding to each surface in the array will remain approximately constant, a result of lateral inhibition.

Hue Constancy

Sensory theories emphasize contrast mechanisms. Hue contrast is illustrated by the fact that a neutral surface appears to acquire a color complementary to the color of a surface on which it is placed. For example, a gray disk on a green background will appear reddish.

Alan L. Gilchrist

Color Vision

The stimulus for color vision is surprisingly complex. Not only does light exist in an infinite variety of wavelengths, but a uniformly colored surface typically stimulates the eye not with light of just one wavelength but rather with light of every wavelength. Surfaces of different color provide light that is concentrated in different regions of the spectrum.

Electromagnetic Spectrum

The visible part of the electromagnetic spectrum consists of photons whose energy varies from about 5.23 to 2.65 picoerg, corresponding to wavelengths ranging from 380 nm to 750 nm. When a "white" light containing most or all of these wavelengths is allowed to shine upon a surface that is "colored," the color of that surface is physically based upon its spectrally selective reflection. A "red" surface, for example, strongly favors the reflection of the longer wavelengths. Similarly, a "red" signal light is typically produced by projecting a white light through a transmitting filter that selectively absorbs the shorter

wavelengths while transmitting the remainder. In neither of these examples is the redness of a light just a matter of physics; rather, it depends for its perception upon a human observer who has normal color vision.

The receptors in the retina of the eye that mediate color perception are the cones. These operate at photopic retinal illuminances in excess of a few million photons per sec per mm^2, corresponding to white paper in moonlight. Although vision is possible at lower levels than this, such scotopic vision is mediated by rods and is colorless. Cones have been shown to be of three types, often called (loosely) blue (B), green (G), and red (R). This means, for example, that if R cones are the ones primarily stimulated, the resulting sensation is that of redness. For this to happen, however, signals triggered by these cones must be further processed and delivered through the optic nerve to the brain. It is activity in the brain and not the eye that finally underlies visual perception.

Photoreceptors

The signals that photoreceptors generate are graded potentials without evidence of spikes. These signals result from the inhibition by light of an active process of depolarization that otherwise occurs continuously in total darkness. Relative to their state in the dark, vertebrate photoreceptors become hyperpolarized. These signals contain no information about the wavelength of the light that elicits them, because many combinations of radiances and wavelengths prove capable of sustaining exactly the same signals. Color is therefore encoded, at the photoreceptor stage, in terms of the relative degree of activation of the three cone types. This explains why a mixture of three spectral primaries can imitate any intermediate color.

Color perception that depends upon the activity of R and G cones is associated with relatively large signals from such receptors. Relatively greater activity of the G receptors encodes greenness, and a shift of activity in the R direction encodes redness.

R, G, and B Cones

Only a limited range of color experience is mediated by R and G cones. To round out the picture, the activity of the B cones must also be considered. These have a peak sensitivity at about 440 nm, well separated from that of the other two types. B cones also differ from the other kinds of cones in at least the following respects: (a) there are probably far fewer of them; (b) when operating in isolation, they mediate the perception of only coarse spatial detail; (c) they are sluggish in their temporal responsiveness; and (d) they contribute signals that can markedly alter the color balance of a percept with very little change in brightness.

Where the color code is concerned, cells in the lateral geniculate nucleus (the principal relay station between retina and brain) behave similarly to retinal ganglion cells. A wide variety of cells are found in the visual cortex, some of which respond only to narrow spectral regions.

Metameric Match

Metameric matches occur whenever two stimuli excite the R, G, and B cones in exactly the same way; an extreme example is a pair of white lights, one of which is comprised of an equal energy spectrum and the other of a superposed mixture of red, green, and blue "primaries." The concept of luminance has been adopted to describe subjective intensities that appear equal in the absence of an exact match. Established for practical reasons in 1931 by the International Commission of Illumination (CIE), mainly by the method of flicker photometry, it turns out that two stimuli of equal luminance probably produce the same sum of activity from the R and G cones. Luminances established in this way are reflexive, additive, and transitive, so that a single equation permits calculations of luminance according to the relation,

$$L = K \int N\lambda \, V\lambda \, d\lambda$$

where $N\lambda$ is the radiant power of the stimulus in watts, $V\lambda$ is the CIE luminous-efficiency function (standardized in 1931), K is a constant (680 lumens/watt), and the integration is done in equal intervals of wavelength across the visible spectrum. Colors of equal luminance are roughly of equal brightness for the normal observer, but not exactly so, because of individual differences and the tendency for the more saturated (highly colored) member of a color pair, at equal luminance, to appear brighter.

Robert M. Boynton

Communication in Clinical Practice

Psychotherapy is a variant of communication that features self-expression. The therapist is supposed to make inferences about psychological processes and about the special characteristics of her patient, although making inferences is but one of many psychological processes in communication.

Four common kinds of furniture placement are employed in various schools of psychotherapy. In psychoanalysis, a couch is located for the patient, and a chair for the therapist is placed behind or next to the couch. This virtually precludes face-to-face engagement. In one-on-one psychotherapy, two chairs or more face each other so that some measure of mutual face and eye behavior is mandatory. In family therapy, a square or rectangle of chairs and sofas is often used. The therapist or therapists each claim a chair, while family members sit side by side on the sofa. A seating arrangement common in American family life is thus replicated. Group therapy commonly employs a circle of straight chairs, as is traditional in informal meetings where an egalitarian relation is supposed to prevail.

A participant in a session maintains a running commentary on his behavior. He stops to explain or rationalize what has just been said and criticize himself, and his facial expression conveys anger, contempt, or amusement. In this way participants clarify, modify, and qualify their own part in the communication. In Gregory Bateson's term, these running commentaries constitute *metacommunication*.

Participants in psychotherapy can fail to achieve rapport or intellectual understanding even though they try to do so, and even though none of them behaves in a deviant or pathological way. This does not refer to disagreement, which can occur in high involvement and with excellent mutual comprehension, but to situations in which participants are unable to resolve their communicational differences.

Albert E. Scheflen

Communication Theory

Formal communication theory in psychology and psychiatry is based upon the idea that communicative behavior is expressive. The assumption is that speech and body movement reveal personality, cognition, affect, or motive. The organismic scientist observes communicative behavior as a basis for making inferences about traits and intraorganismic processes.

Expression theory underlies much traditional research in the psychological sciences. In psycholinguistics, the speaking style is the basis of psychological inferences. In psychokinesics, qualities of posture and gesture are the basis of psychoanalytic inferences.

In a sociological approach, a group of people is visualized as a whole. Hence, an institution can be thought of as behaving communicatively.

In social psychology, action-reaction models are combined with concepts of expression. Sometimes the traits of participants are classified on the premise that mutual responses express one's personality traits. Thus psychodynamic paradigms are introduced into interactional theory. The behavior of each participant is seen as both a response and an expression.

R. L. Birdwhistell (1970) employs a structural approach to study body movement in communication, which he calls *kinesics*. In the early years of kinesics, emphasis was upon gesture and other speech-related behavior; other modalities of movement, such as touch, gaze, interpersonal distance, and posture, also received attention. To the structuralist, nonlanguage behavior is as communicative as language. Customary units of gesture, facial display, posture, touch, and distance have evolved in each culture and are recognizable and meaningful to other members of that culture.

In forming a simple classification of traditional theories Scheflen (1973) employs two distinctions:

Object-centered and field epistemologies. One can begin to study some phenomena by looking first at the objects or people in a field of observation, then describing what these things or people do, and finally postulating how and why they do it. One can also focus on relationships among events—behavioral events, for instance—and describe them in terms of space and time. Only then does a field theorist become concerned with the people who act and move in such a field.

Levels of complexity and organization. People and behaviors are organized in increasingly complex relationships. In either epistemology an observer can focus on single entities or multiple interrelations. For example, one can focus upon the nervous system and ignore other organ systems, or one can focus upon a single person or look at a whole group. In general systems theory, these differences in the scope of the observational field allow an observer to visualize different levels of organization.

Toward a Holistic Theory of Communication

Gregory Bateson distinguishes between communicational and metacommunicational behavior. The first term can refer to the rather automatic performance of traditional coded sequences; the latter is used to describe behavior that clarifies, qualifies, modifies, and otherwise regulates the processes of human communication.

Albert E. Scheflen

Communicative Interaction in Psychoanalysis

The therapist's interventions may be termed "adaptive contexts" (adaptation-evoking or intervention contexts) and constitute communicative stimuli with manifest and latent implications to which the patient responds adaptively and maladaptively. Investigations have shown that the interventions of the therapist are the major stimuli for the patient's neurotic reactions and for those communicative responses that most clearly illuminate his or her neurosis.

Among the many possible dimensions of a particular intervention, several important categories may be identified:

1. accuracy or validity;
2. the extent to which intervention deals with the analytic interaction or sets it aside;
3. the degree to which it identifies the adaptation-evoking context to which the patient is responding, and gives fair attention to both unconscious fantasies and unconscious perceptions;
4. the extent to which it is based entirely on the patient's material in a given session, as compared to the introduction of material from other hours or from the therapist's own associations or reactions;
5. the extent to which it denies valid unconscious perceptions and erroneously translates the patient's material into distorted unconscious fantasies; and
6. the degree to which the intervention is interpretive rather than noninterpretive or manipulative.

A full comprehension of the unconscious implications of the therapist's interventions fosters the identification of the patient's many valid unconscious perceptions and introjects of the implications of the therapist's work. Pathological introjects tend to evoke retaliatory and hurtful, as well as curative and corrective, efforts by the patient, which can be identified only through a full understanding of the spiraling communicative interaction itself.

Among the many ramifications of the study of the communicative interaction between patient and analyst, two seem especially pertinent. The first is the realization that the assigned role and function of the patient and therapist, their designated places in the treatment relationship, must be distinguished from the manner in which each participant is actually *functioning* from moment to moment in the unfolding therapeutic experience.

In terms of the spiraling communicative interaction, we may identify two therapeutic modalities that exist on a continuum:

- *truth therapy*, in which the therapist intervenes in terms of the spiraling communicative interaction: the unconscious implications of the adaptive context of his or her interventions and the patient's responsive, derivative response; and

- *lie therapy*, in which the therapist's interventions depart from this model and therefore serve functionally to cover over or falsify the actualities of the unconscious communicative interaction as they pertain to the patient's neurosis.

The approach to psychotherapy and psychoanalysis that places the communicative interaction at the center of the treatment process is highly responsive to the patient's actual adaptive reactions and the true meanings and functions of his or her associations and behaviors. This approach has led to an understanding of the patient in analysis that stresses his or her unconscious resources, while mindful of their pathological reactions.

Robert J. Langs

Community Mental Health and Community Mental Health Centers

Historical Perspectives

Dorothea Dix was the first "mental health reformer" to seek federal legislation that would provide assistance through the development of state and territorial facilities. The legislative mechanism she proposed was similar to the federal land grant program for public colleges, and she lobbied intensively for the passage of an act to turn over to the individual states and territories land for use as sites for mental hospitals. In 1847, although the bill was finally adopted by both houses of Congress, it was vetoed by President Franklin Pierce.

As the years passed, the federal government did assume some responsibility in regard to special problem areas relevant to mental health. For example, two federal narcotic hospitals were established during the 1930s, and in 1946 the National Mental Health Act was passed, authorizing the creation of the National Institute of Mental Health. The NIMH initially directed its attention toward research and education, and it was not seen as a source of support for service programs.

The experiences of World War II brought about the recognition of a societal problem involving the care of the mentally ill; other events during that period brought forward the potential for solution.

The treatment methods developed and used by military psychiatrists dealt with mental disorders as acute problems and sought to utilize short-term treatment methods. Every effort was made to treat acutely mentally ill servicemen in hospitals located as close as possible to the site of battle instead of returning them to the United States for hospitalization. When many psychiatrists returned home after the war, they were eager to find and develop civilian applications for new techniques.

In response to different forces pressing for change in the mental health delivery system after the end of World War II, Congress took an unprecedented step. It passed the Mental Health Study Act of 1955, which established the Joint Commission on Mental Illness and Health. With representation from a wide variety of professional and citizen organizations, it conducted a series of exhaustive studies, which led to the first full-scale analysis of the nation's mental health requirements and capabilities and the publication in 1960 of *Action for Mental Health*.

Action for Mental Health emphasized that a local orientation to the delivery of services was critical, if they were to be maximally effective. Mental health services must be readily available when and where they are needed, without isolating the patient from people and surroundings that are familiar.

The Community Mental Health Centers Act also emphasized prevention and the need to develop programs to prevent mental illness as well as to treat it. It was recognized that some methods were already available and that others could be developed to achieve more effective prevention of many mental disorders.

The concept of local service and community orientation was implemented through the introduction of the "catchment area" concept. The emphasis on local services required a means of identifying a community to be served, and effectively the catchment area was defined as the focal community. In the original federal program, a catchment area was a designated geographical area having no fewer than 75,000 and no more than 200,000 people. These lower and upper limits were chosen because they appeared to provide a basis for effective programming.

Continuity of care was defined in terms of those program elements most likely to create linkages between or among various services of a center. These linkages were viewed in terms of people and information. People, both staff and patients, had to be able to move from one service to another, and in a like manner, it had to be possible for information to follow them.

During the initial years of the program, centers struggled continuously to achieve financial balance. Most had great difficulty in obtaining financial support from other than public governmental agencies. The availability of fees to support programs has been minimal because of the absence of a national health insurance program and the failure of many third-party payers to reimburse centers for the variety of services required to treat mental illness effectively.

Allan Beigel
Alan I. Levenson

Community Mental Health Centers: Legislation

The Community Mental Health Centers Act of 1963 and its subsequent amendments included provisions for two kinds of federal support. Grants were made available to assist both in the construction of community mental health centers and in meeting their costs for staffing. In both instances, matching funds were required from the applicant.

To qualify for receipt of construction funds, each state was required to develop a plan for community mental health centers and to designate a single state agency responsible for the preparation of this plan. The state was to indicate the relative need for community mental health centers in different areas of the state, with priority being determined on the basis of such factors as the number of mentally ill persons, the existence of mental health service facilities, and other indices, such as socioeconomic criteria.

The Community Mental Health Center Amendments of 1970 made several significant changes to these mechanisms of financial support. First, the amendments made it possible for those centers serving poverty areas to receive higher levels of construction support. Furthermore, the poverty areas were also authorized to receive preferential staffing support beginning at a level of 90% of eligible costs. In addition, the period of eligibility was increased from 51 months to 96 months for all centers, with the level of support for poverty centers never falling below 70%. For other centers, staffing support remained at 30% during the final 4 years of the 8-year period.

The Mental Health Systems Act of 1980

The recommendations of the president's Commission on Mental Health were studied by a task force of the Department of Health, Education and Welfare (now the Department of Health and Human Services), culminating in the introduction by the president, in early 1979, of a proposed Mental Health Systems Act, which contained numerous provisions designed to address the critical problems identified by the commission.

Over an 18-month period, this proposed legislation was studied thoroughly by both the House and the Senate and revised considerably. Finally, legislation emerged that was acceptable to Congress and endorsed by the mental health constituency groups. The legislation was signed into law by President Carter in October 1980.

While the Mental Health Systems Act calls attention to deinstitutionalized chronic mentally ill persons, the ultimate success in meeting their needs will depend on increased attentiveness to this population by other human service agencies. Principal among these are housing agencies, which need to develop additional community residences; nursing homes, which have been an important resource for those persons discharged from state hospitals; vocational rehabilitation programs, which have not satisfactorily provided for the specialized needs of this population; and income support programs, which—while recognizing that many of these patients need ongoing financial support—have often created rules and regulations that present unnecessary barriers to effective rehabilitation. Current research aims to develop prevention programs focused on specific stressful issues.

Allan Beigel
Alan I. Levenson

Community Psychology: Research

The action focus of community psychology has dominated its research; much work has taken the form of initiating a project or intervention and describing or evaluating its process and impact. Thus, evaluative research has emerged as an important research task in community psychology. At times, the issue of evaluation has focused on the overall effectiveness of a program (e.g., Head Start), while other efforts have been more closely linked to testing a more specifiable action research hypothesis.

Nonprofessionals in mental health roles. The Zax and Cowen project approached the task of early intervention through a widely used strategy in the field of community psychology, the use of nonprofessionals in mental health roles. Many reasons for the use of nonprofessionals have been offered, including the need to increase manpower to fill social needs, the unique ability of nonprofessionals to reach segments of the population suspicious of or antagonistic toward "the helping establishment," and the importance of developing new careers for persons with unique and underutilized interpersonal or programmatic skills.

One area of research relevant to promoting positive development involves differing approaches to the conceptual and empirical assessment of human environments. Various terms, including social ecology, human ecology, and ecological psychology, have been used to describe, in a broad sense, alternative approaches to this question.

J. G. Kelly's (1967) elaboration of the "ecological analogy," through a longitudinal study of adolescent adaptation to high school, highlights this kind of question more directly. In studying how adolescents cope with differing kinds of school environments, several general hypotheses about behavior have been made.

The process of community research mediates between the research problem and the research act. Often, in community psychology, both the definitions of the problem and the nature of the subsequent research are heavily influenced by the community in which the research occurs. How the researcher-community relationship is formed, how the different parties perceive each other, and what aspects of both persons and social settings interact to facilitate or constrain the research process are important substantive questions for learning about the dynamics of community processes.

Edison J. Trickett
David M. Todd

Comparative Psychology

Modern comparative psychology stems from two sources. One is the age-old quest to understand the functioning and behavior of the animal world around us. This tradition goes back to Aristotle's *Historia Animalium*, subsequent natural histories and medieval bestiaries, and more recent attempts at a comparative psychology analogous to other comparative studies, such as comparative anatomy, comparative physiology, comparative neurology, and comparative linguistics. The other source is driven by evolutionary considerations, working toward an understanding of the phylogeny of behavior. Darwinian theory stands at the beginning of this approach; ethology and sociobiology are parallel trends in the study of animal behavior and zoology.

The first text on comparative psychology was published in 1866 by Carl Gustav Carus (1789–1869), a physician and author of texts on comparative anatomy as well as developmental psychology. He assumed a progressive scale of complexity of mental life from primitive organisms to humans. Despite this apparent progressive change, he did not believe in evolution.

When Charles Darwin published his *On the Origin of Species* (1859), its implications for the continuity of behavior became clear. Comparative psychology had a unifying theme in the effect of behavior on the origin and evolution of the characteristics of different species of animals.

In its early days, the evidence for an evolutionary progression was based on casual observation. This anecdotal method laid the foundation of modern comparative psychology. For example, George J. Romanes (1848–1894) was handpicked by Darwin, a personal friend, to explore animal behavior, as summarized in his *Animal Intelligence* (1882). C. Lloyd Morgan (1852–1936) objected to Romanes's excessive anthropomorphizing. His "canon," an application of the law of parsimony, admonished students of animal behavior not to attribute a more complex explanation to the observed behavior when a simpler principle would do. Morgan's *Introduction to Comparative Psychology* (1894) set the standard and fixed the name of the new science.

Morgan introduced comparative psychology to the United States when he lectured at Harvard in 1896. Edward L. Thorndike, who was in the audience, began his animal learning experiments the next year. Margaret Floy Washburn's *Animal Mind* (1908) went through many editions. She summarized experimental results as they became available. Her first edition had 476 references, her second (1917) 841, and, the third edition (1926) had grown to 1,135 items. Her approach was essentially functional, contrary to the impression that may be created by her title. Robert M. Yerkes (1876–1956) was a major figure in the development of comparative psychology. He analyzed problem-solving abilities in different species with his multiple-choice apparatus. Later, he was the founder of the primate facilities at Orange Park, Florida. These were eventually relocated to the Yerkes Regional Laboratory of Primate Biology in Atlanta, Georgia, under the auspices of Emory University. (The early history of comparative psychology is exhaustively summarized in the three-volume work by Warden, Jenkins and Warner, 1935–1940; for the history of later work in America see *Hilgard*, 1987.)

Subsequent to these developments, most research with animals focused on studies of learning, primarily in the white rat and pigeon, except for a small core of devoted comparative psychologists. Meanwhile, in Europe, a new approach to animal behavior originated, spearheaded by Nobel Prize winners Konrad Lorenz (1903–1989) and Nicholaas Tinbergen (1907–1988), which assumed the name of *ethology* (Tobach, Adler & Adler 1973). Lorenz held that activities could be treated like structures of the body, subject to evolutionary pressures and fixed in species-specific expression. He did not deny the importance of learning and, in fact, was the first to consider imprinting (a rapid learning of response patterns during a sensitive period, such as newly hatched ducklings following their mother), but he stressed the instinctive elements of behavior. This notion of instinct attracted strong criticism in the 1950s from American comparative psychologists, particularly T. C. Schneirla and D. S. Lehrman.

Tinbergen, a Dutchman, became attracted to Lorenz's ideas. His classic studies of the courtship of the stickleback, displays in herring gulls, orientation in wasps, and the behavior of grayling butterflies provided an experimental basis for Lorenz's theories. His *Study of Instinct* (1951) provided the first exposition of ethology to the English-speaking world.

Comparative psychology was compelled to spend more time on the issues of adaptation, evolution, and testing animal behavior in its natural setting, in response to the challenge of ethology. A further challenge to comparative psychology came with the publication of E. O. Wilson's *Sociobiology* (1975). Wilson, a Harvard expert on social insects, stressed the evolutionary importance of behavior that would increase an individual's genes in the population. A key concept of sociobiology is the evolution of altruism, shown, for example, in the self-sacrifice of a honeybee willing to die for the defense of the hive by stinging an aggressive predator. The theory holds that, because she is closely related to her sisters (the other workers), her sacrifice permits the survival of the closely related genes in the colony. Although this pattern holds particularly for ants, bees and wasps, due to their peculiar genetic makeup (haplodiploidy), it holds also for animals—such as termites and even a mammal, the naked molerat—who have a set of genes from each parent (diploidy). Wilson claimed that sociobiology would eliminate comparative psychology. Comparative psychologists responded that their field had an identity of its own; it rejected the all-inclusive claims of sociobiology and advanced solutions of a psychological nature (Wyers et al. 1980).

Comparative psychologists study a wide range of phenomena, starting with the functions of the nervous system and the sense organs. It can be shown, for example, that the hunting bat's sonar clicks elicit neural responses in the moth's nervous system that allow it to avoid capture. Complex navigational systems have been detected in insects and birds. The honeybee can use the sun's position in the sky as an aid to navigation and to communicate the direction of a food source to its hivemates by means of a special dance language. Homing pigeons and migrating birds also use the sun as a navigational aid. In addition, they appear capable of using the earth's magnetic field and possibly olfactory cues (Adler, 1971).

The development of behavior has been studied intensively. Harry F. and Margaret K. Harlow's experiments on infant rhesus monkeys have demonstrated the need for contact with other monkeys in early infancy. Placed in isolation with the choice of a surrogate "wire mother" offering a bottle of milk but constructed purely of bare wires, and a "cloth mother" that offers no milk but to which the baby could cling as it would to its real mother, the baby stays with the cloth mother in preference to the food source. After reaching adulthood, its physical development is normal, but its social behavior is greatly disturbed; it is terrified of other monkeys and unable to form sexual relationships.

Animals have a time sense that regulates their behavior. The behavior patterns that depend on the 24-hour period of day and night typically have been found to vary from this period when no cues were available, resulting in the so-called circadian rhythm, which may be shorter or longer than twenty-four hours. This free-running rhythm can be synchronized with the actual time by regularly occurring events, such as sunrise or nightfall. In an experiment intended to measure the accuracy of time sense, starlings were placed in lightproof and soundproof compartments. One starling, under constant light and free access to food, showed a typical circadian rhythm, being active in what would be daytime and inactive at nighttime, except that her activity shifted about one-half hour earlier every day, so that it no longer coincided with the actual day-night cycle. The other bird was given access to food for one hour, four times daily, at fixed times. This sufficed to coordinate her daily activities with clock time, and her accuracy was about 10 to 15 minutes.

In recent years, comparative psychologists have shown an increased interest in animal cognition

(Roitblat, Bever & Terrace 1984). These studies have involved, among others, communication with animals, self-recognition, and tests of complex intellectual tasks. Although still controversial, ape language communication started when Beatrice and Allen Gardner succeeded in teaching their chimp Washoe American Sign Language. Later experiments followed, attempting communication with other chimpanzees, a gorilla, and even a gray African parrot. Work continues at the Yerkes Primate Center in Atlanta, Georgia, but skeptics still need to be convinced that these animals are actually capable of language use.

The study of self-recognition, initiated by Gordon Gallup, has also generated considerable debate (Povinelli 1993). Chimpanzees were observed as to whether they recognized their mirror image as themselves, indicating a self-concept. While anesthetized, red paint had been smeared on their faces. If they touched themselves at the spot that had been painted when they saw their image, this was evidence of a self-concept. Orangutans also show this evidence of a self-concept; gorillas and other monkeys do not, but are nevertheless said to show mirror competence. Whether self-recognition is the best criterion for animal consciousness has not been answered decisively, but this fact does not deter many from laboring toward this goal.

Complex problem solving in animals has a history that goes back to the early days of comparative psychology. In recent years, the goal has been to obtain comparable data of cognitive functions in various species, in particular, different species than the white rat, pigeon, monkeys, and chimpanzees. Dolphins have been considered to have superior abilities, so an experiment with dolphins matching to sample is typical of this approach (Adler & Adler 1990). The task for the dolphins is to match objects such as a fish or a ball with their names, written in English letters and Chinese characters. The dolphins, after appropriate training procedures, respond between 95 and 100% correctly. While this experiment does not prove that the dolphins use mental imagery in solving the problem, it does indicate a superior level of cognitive functioning.

Comparative psychology, through a long and complex history, has maintained its focus on comparison and evolution of behavior. By noting similarities and differences in various species, it will approach its ultimate goal: to put human behavior in its proper perspective.

Helmut E. Adler

Competency: Social Competency and Its Development

One of the most complete definitions of social competency is offered by Anderson and Messick (1974) and is based on the deliberations of a distinguished panel of child development experts. A number of underlying conceptual problems are reviewed, and twenty-nine facets of competency are specified. These facts, briefly summarized, are as follows:

1. differentiated self-concept and consolidation of identity;
2. concept of self as an initiating and controlling agent;
3. habits of personal maintenance and care consistent with common peer-group standards;
4. realistic appraisal of self, accompanied by feelings of personal worth;
5. differentiation of feelings and appreciation of their manifestations and implications;
6. sensitivity and understanding in social relationships;
7. positive and affectionate personal relationships;
8. role perception and appreciation;
9. appropriate regulation of antisocial behavior;
10. morality and prosocial tendencies;
11. curiosity and active exploration of the environment;
12. control of attention, as a function of situational or task requirements;
13. perceptual skills—visual, auditory, tactile, and kinesthetic;
14. fine motor skills;
15. gross motor skills;
16. perceptual-motor skills (coordination of visual, auditory, and motor behavior);
17. language skills—productive and receptive;

18. categorizing skills;
19. memory skills;
20. critical thinking skills;
21. creative thinking skills;
22. problem-solving skills;
23. flexibility in the application of information-processing strategies;
24. quantitative and relational concepts, understandings, and skills;
25. general knowledge (of health and safety, social environment, physical environment, practical arts, consumer behavior, sports, art, music, literature, etc.);
26. competence motivation;
27. facility in the use of resources for learning and problem solving;
28. some positive attitudes toward learning and educational experiences; and
29. enjoyment of humor, play, and fantasy.

Efforts to foster social competency that derive from learning or contingency theories are likely to stress the more "academic" competency goals, direct instruction, and specific reward systems. Formal measurement may play a significant role in the process. Stage-development theorists would allow children to achieve social competence at their own rate and introduce educational interventions mainly to avoid stage retardation (rather than to accelerate stages) and/or to stimulate horizontal decalage, the spread of generalization of concepts or actions across a given stage.

Scarvia B. Anderson
Thomas W. Draper

Computerized Testing

Automation and Computerization
A test is automated to the extent that some type of device performs some or nearly all aspects of the measurement operations, including providing instructions, presenting items (using the word *item* to refer to any stimulus requiring a response), scoring each item, computation of overall test scores, and complete statistical analysis of results. Frequently, tests have been automated and computer-ized as an incidental aspect of investigating some applied or basic research issue in psychometrics.

The Potential Advantages of AC Tests
(AC) tests have a marked advantage when repeated measurements are required. If the items are of a kind that usually appear on printed tests, one approach is simply to store a very large number of items in the computer and call up a random number of these (or a more complex strategy could be employed, as in adaptive testing).

ADAPTIVE TESTING
Because of the ability to sample from large numbers of items, with these either being composed and stored or computer generated, one is in an ideal position to examine the effectiveness of various proposals for adaptive or tailored testing.

ANALYSIS OF RESULTS
One of the cardinal advantages of an AC approach to testing is that it provides an extremely easy use of all of the programs for statistical analysis that customarily are available in computer centers. It is a simple matter to obtain overall test scores, scores for each item, scores for any designated subpart of the test, and a variety of kinds of scores (e.g., both number correct and average latency of response).

Jum C. Nunnally

Conditioning and Age

Neonates
E. R. Siqueland and L. Lipsitt, in a series of studies, have demonstrated that newborns will acquire a head-turning response under appropriate reinforcing circumstances. In one of these studies, newborns developed differential conditioning in the short period of one-half hour, such that the sounding of one tone followed by a touch to the cheek produced increased head-turning in that direction if followed by the opportunity to suck, while a tone-touch combination involving a different tone, not followed by reinforcement, yielded no increased responding.

Newborns are especially sensitive by constitution to environmental manipulation of mouthing behavior. It has been shown that the two major facets of sucking behavior, the expression or squeeze component and the suction component, are to some extent plastic in that reinforcing of one component such as suction as opposed to expression (the two are not perfectly correlated) will result in suction being enhanced while expression remains the same or diminishes.

Infants

A number of studies (see Lipsitt 1963) have shown motor activity and sucking-response "adjustments" over the first ten days of life suggestive of learning, in that babies tended to settle into patterns of sleep and wakefulness, and of active periods versus quiet, depending upon the feeding schedule to which they were subjected. Supporting the conditioning supposition is the fact that Marquis's three-hour-schedule subjects, when shifted to four hours, demonstrated great protest, as if a frustration of expectation was involved.

In a straight operant head-turning rather than an elicited head-turning procedure, Siqueland reinforced thirty-four newborns with a non-nutritive nipple each time their heads turned in either direction a distance of 10 degrees. Whether the infants were reinforced on a ration or a continuous schedule, their head-turning behavior increased reliably, and a comparison group that was reinforced for holding their heads still (rather than turning) went down in incidence of head turns. When all reinforcement was withheld for all groups, the ratio group extinguished more slowly than the continuous reinforcement group, while the pause group reinstituted its baseline head-turning frequency.

Lewis P. Lipsitt

Conditioning, Classical

Classical, or Pavlovian, conditioning refers to a procedure in which two stimuli are presented to an organism independently of its behavior. These stimuli are generally selected so that one stimulus consistently elicits a behavioral response while the other is neutral with respect to that elicited behavior. Suc-cessful conditioning is said to occur when the previously neutral stimulus evokes a change in behavior as a consequence of its temporal sequencing with the other stimulus.

When discussing the conditioning procedure in a more general sense, the stimuli and their attendant responses are described in terms of their "conditioned" status. The stimulus (food) that elicits some behavioral response prior to conditioning is called the unconditioned stimulus (US), and the response (saliva) it elicits is called the unconditioned response (UR). The initially neutral stimulus (tone) is called the conditioned stimulus (CS), and the response (saliva) it comes to evoke is called the conditioned response (CR). The US is often described as the "reinforcer" in classical conditioning, following the terminology of Pavlov, because it is the stimulus that produces the CR to the CS. The CS is said to acquire associative strength to the extent that it develops the capacity to elicit the CR.

Conditioned stimuli. The essential consideration in selecting a stimulus as a CS is that it be neutral with respect to the response elicited by the US. Additionally, the CS must be of relatively weaker motivational significance than the US. For example, if a severe electric shock is employed as the CS and food is presented to a moderately hungry animal as the US, a salivary response will not occur to the shock. However, a mild shock can be an effective CS in eliciting salivation if it is paired with food for a very hungry animal.

Unconditioned stimuli. The US is generally selected from one of two categories referred to as either *appetitive* or *aversive* USs. These two classes of USs are distinguished in terms of the organism's instrumental behavior toward them. Appetitive USs are those that an organism will work for or do nothing to avoid. Aversive USs are those that an organism will avoid or escape from. Food, water, or access to a sexual partner are examples of appetitive USs, while electric shock, acid, or a puff of air to the eye are examples of aversive USs.

USs may also be interoceptive as well as exteroceptive. For example, if an exteroceptive CS is paired with a diuretic agent (US) during conditioning when the CS is presented alone the subject demonstrates the urge to urinate (Bykov, 1957). If either the CS or US are interoceptive stimuli, the procedure is called "interoceptive conditioning."

CS-US relationships. When a positive relationship exists between the CS and US such that the US is presented only if the CS has been presented, conditioning is described as "excitatory." Conversely, when a negative relationship exists between the CS and US so that the occurrence of the CS predicts the absence of the US, the procedure is described as "inhibitory conditioning."

With human subjects, a popular technique for studying classical conditioning is to follow a CS with a noxious puff of the air to the eye; the CR is the eye blink. Another technique often employed is galvanic skin response (GSR) conditioning. The GSR is a change in skin resistance that occurs when a person anticipates electric shock. When a CS is paired with shock, a conditioned GSR will occur to the CS.

What is learned? The question of what is learned, or associated, in classical conditioning has been an issue of historical as well as contemporary concern. Two outstanding positions have emerged. One is that an association develops between the CS and US. The CR reflects a general anticipation or expectancy about the occurrence of the US when the CS is presented.

Significance of process. Classical conditioning provides the basis by which neutral stimuli may gain emotional significance, thereby acquiring the capacity to reward or punish instrumental behavior. Conditioned emotional states are thought to underlie such instrumental behavior as avoidance. Indeed, the interaction between classical and instrumental conditioning is extensive.

Jack Edward Sherman

Conditioning, Higher Order

In the higher order conditioning experiment, the conditioned stimulus (CS) from one phase of the experiment becomes the unconditioned stimulus (US) in another, later, phase. In one demonstration of the process reported by Pavlov, the salivary response was first conditioned to an auditory CS.

When the salivary conditioned reflex (CR) was thoroughly established, a black square was presented just before the auditory stimulus. After ten such pairings of the black square and the auditory stimulus, a salivary CR occurred to the black square. This is an example of second-order conditioning. In a few cases, Pavlov was able to demonstrate third-order conditioning. In the example under discussion, this would involve presenting a third CS just before the black square. Fourth- and still higher order CRs could not be established.

The theoretical importance of higher order conditioning is that this phenomenon shows that the CS in an experiment acquires reinforcing powers. It becomes a *secondary reinforcer*, to use more modern terminology.

Gregory A. Kimble

Conflict

The psychology of conflict is the study of the effects of the simultaneous arousal of two or more mutually incompatible motives, aims, attitudes, or reactive tendencies.

Kurt Lewin's conceptions proved more exciting to stimulus-response psychologists than to his fellow field theorists. Clark L. Hull, in particular, was quick to show that the cardinal concepts of vector theory could be translated with profit into his own goal-gradient, stimulus-response notation. Experimental studies bearing on these conceptual advances were followed by N. E. Miller's (1944) classic treatise, which, more than any other, set the stage for subsequent theorizing and experimentation. Hull's (1952) detailed and inventive exposition and subsequent minor extensions of the theory to temporal conflicts (Brown 1957), and to the problem of alcohol-induced conflict resolution (Brown & Crowell 1974) owed much to Miller's comprehensive account.

Approach-avoidance conflict. This variety of conflictive situation is marked by the simultaneous instigation of tendencies both to approach and to avoid a given region in the environment. Suppose, for example, that a hungry rat has repeatedly approached a goal box at the end of a straight runway and has been fed there. Such reinforcement should strengthen the animal's tendency to approach, and the strength of the tendency should increase with nearness to the goal. If the rat is punished when it approaches the same goal, an antagonistic avoidance tendency will be established. This tendency is also expected to be strongest at the point where punishment has been administered and to weaken with distance from it. Avoidance gradients such as this are assumed to be characteristically steeper than the approach gradient for a variety of reasons (Miller 1944, 1959). (Essentially, these same assumptions have been made by Lewin, Hull, and Miller.)

A state of conflict engendered by competitions may be accompanied by, or may generate, distinctive afferent events that could serve as conditioned or discriminative stimuli in mediating the transfer of responses from one situation to another.

It is also possible that the conflict state itself may be conditionable to contiguous stimuli. Thus, on subsequent occasions a conditioned form of conflict would be evoked by those cues, perhaps in the absence of competitive tendencies.

Conflict resolution. Usually, conflicts can be resolved either by increasing the difference between the incompatible tendencies or by weakening their absolute strengths, or both. Some writers, however, have suggested that approach-avoidance conflicts, in particular, are resolved simply by variables that lead the organism to approach more closely to the bivalent goal.

Conflicts can be produced in situations where spatial distance is not a factor by requiring the individual to learn a discrimination between, say, two tonal frequencies or two visual patterns. After the positive and negative stimuli have become conditioned cues for incompatible responses, a discriminative conflict can be induced by simultaneously presenting both stimuli, by presenting a single stimulus that is intermediate between the original cues, or by increasing the similarity of the discriminanda.

Charles R. Crowell
Judson S. Brown

Conflict Management in Industry

Conflict management is largely concerned with establishing constructive conflict-handling behavior among conflict parties. Schemes for classifying this conflict behavior have varied. However, variations of one two-dimensional scheme have prevailed since the 1960s. Kenneth W. Thomas (1976) interprets the scheme as combining the dimensions of assertiveness (attempting to satisfy one's own concerns) and cooperativeness (attempting to satisfy the other party's concerns).

Robbins (1974) has listed a number of general conflict management strategies and cataloged them for usefulness in reducing or stimulating conflicts from three sources—poor communications, structural variables, and "personal-behavioral" factors. Kilmann and Thomas (1976) group conflict-management interventions into four general influence strategies. Interaction management strategies mediate and control the overt behavior of conflicting parties—usually to control escalation and steer discussion toward problem solving. Consciousness-raising strategies address the conflict parties' subjective views of the conflict—to aid their understanding of ongoing conflict dynamics, make them aware of alternatives, and help them clarify their objectives. Contextual modification strategies adjust external conditions that shape the conflict—to change competitive incentives, social norms, negotiation procedures, and policies. Selection and training strategies change relatively stable characteristics of people within an organizational role—by recruiting or promoting individuals who generate fewer conflicts and have skills to manage conflicts, and by training managers in new skills.

In the 1960s, studies began to document the transactions, negotiations, and conflicts between departments. A number of integrative mechanisms have been used to facilitate collaboration in these interdepartmental negotiations: (1) broadened performance criteria for departments, to prevent narrowness of objectives and provide common goals; (2) managerial evaluation procedures that explicitly consider the quality of a manager's relations with other work units; (3) regular meetings between interdependent work units to facilitate coordination;

(4) special coordinating units to manage the interface between large departments; (5) job rotation practices to increase familiarity with other departments; (6) managerial training programs to develop skills relevant to interdepartmental conflicts; and (7) providing behavioral consultants.

Kenneth W. Thomas

Conformity, Theories of

People seek both to be right and to be accepted. If these two goals are incompatible, how is the conflict resolved? In particular, how will public behavior be related to private beliefs and attitudes? One answer is that people's public behavior will be determined by social rewards and punishments, while their private views will be determined by the sources of information that define reality for them. This answer is not satisfactory, however. Not infrequently people express unpopular opinions quite deliberately, sometimes even in the face of threats of extreme punishment.

In addition to public compliance or conformity, and private acceptance or internalization, H. Kelman (1961) found the need for a third category, identification. Identification occurs when the individual adopts behavior or an attitude derived from a person or a group, not because of rewards and punishments administered, but because it is associated with a satisfying self-defining relationship to the person or group.

A potentially broad theory of conformity is based on an amalgam of economic exchange theory and social exchange theory, outlined by W. R. Nord (1969). Overt conformity is considered as a "commodity" or service that can be bought and sold, so to speak, in such social marketplaces as a group or organization. Previous treatments of conformity have been close to an exchange theory, but usually deal only with the supply side of the market.

The *diamond model* of movement conformity was proposed by Willis (1965). The model is a mapping model, and as such, its concern is not with explanation or prediction but rather with the description of that which is to be explained or predicted. Such description is obtained by mapping the possible combinations of values among dependent variables. A prototype of a mapping model exists in sensory psychology, namely, the color solid that schematically represents all possible color combinations of hue, brightness, and saturation.

The logic and experimental results both show that one does not always need the whole diamond. If anticonformity and self-anticonformity tendencies are negligible, a unidimensional conformity-independence model suffices.

Richard H. Willis

Connoly, John (1794–1866)

The British psychiatrist John Connoly was the champion and spokesman of the campaign against physical restraint of mental patients. He was one of the founders of what has become the British Medical Association.

John C. Burnham

Consciousness, Altered States, and Imagery: Psychoanalytic Research

Studies of imagery have shown that information from perception may be incorporated into ongoing thought without any memory for episodes of conscious expression of that information. The most popular method for such research has been to study the return of dim, brief, or peripheral perceptions in the contents of subsequent dreams, reveries, or other pictorializations.

Image systems involve a quasi-sensory expression of meanings in any of the subsystems of visual, auditory, gustatory, olfactory, or tactile-kinesthetic sensation. Image systems thus represent both perception and thought; they have a dual input of information.

Psychoanalytic research by Arlow, Knapp, Warren, Kanzer, Stern, and others has demonstrated that intrusive images are not meaningless, even though their meaning may escape the person who has the surprising episode of conscious experience. Instead, the contents often contain an amalgam of warded-off memories, feelings, wishes, and fears, as well as compensatory (even restitutional) ideas. Careful psychoanalytic study of such sudden alterations in state of consciousness and emergence of images once again confirms how decisions about what reaches consciousness awareness are made at an unconscious level of information processing.

Early developmental experiences are believed to provide cognitive structures that affect the way a person thinks throughout life. The degree to which cognitive styles are innate dispositions and the degree to which they evolve from experiences with the environment is uncertain. It is known that drastically understimulated infants seem to have maldeveloped cognitive capacities.

Some persons experience recurrent intrusive images. These range from hallucinations to more frequently occurring episodes of vivid thought images that may upset a person but are not mistaken for reality.

Mardi J. Horowitz

Consumer Psychology

Applications
Consumer psychology serves economists, social psychologists, sociologists, social historians, and other behavioral scientists, proving an important element for both analysis and forecasting. The most significant and widespread application of consumer psychology, however, is its use by marketers of consumer goods and services. Over the past several decades, marketers have become increasingly aware of the value of consumer psychology for guiding new products or service development; identifying markets (for example, identifying the type of person who will be most responsive to a particular product or service); developing marketing strategies (for example, advertising, brand names, packaging, and pricing); and selecting appropriate retail outlets. Virtually all major marketers currently use consumer psychology data in their decision making.

There is wide agreement among practitioners, however, that theories and principles can be abstracted for a given product category—even if not for the full range of all consumer behavior. Even theories about consumer psychology for a specific and narrow product category are seriously questioned by many important practitioners on the grounds that the dynamics of the marketplace make any such efforts quickly obsolescent. In other words, any new entry into a product category can quickly require the need for a revision in any theory advanced to explain the consumer psychology of that category.

Despite the reluctance on the part of the field to see the value of—let alone do the work to develop—a theory or set of principles governing consumer psychology, some practitioners have tried to evolve a few independent general principles, not yet leading to a unified theory. Among these general principles:

1. Personality traits are not usually the key factor underlying general consumer attitudes and behavior, although such traits may account for behavior with respect to some product classes.
2. Consumer motives and behavior are not necessarily consistent from product category to product category. Status needs may, for example, play a key role in the purchase of one appliance and no role at all in the purchase of another.
3. The sociological categories of age, social class, and (to a lesser degree) sex frequently are more germane to consumer behavior than are unconscious motives.
4. The importance of the product category to the consumer (often a function of acculturation) will often transcend such demographic characteristics as age and social class in determining consumer behavior.
5. The specific values (i.e., the goals, aspirations, and beliefs) of the society or of subgroups within the society may be more relevant to understanding consumer psychology than are theories of motivation drawn from general psychology and psychoanalysis.
6. Increasingly, fragmentation of consumers into ever-smaller subgroups is more common than generalizations that subsume all consumers.

Daniel Yankelovich
Florence R. Skelly

Contact Need

Research by Harry F. and Margaret F. Harlow, beginning in the 1950s, has demonstrated a need for contact by immature primates. Extensive contact is maintained by rhesus monkeys for the first two or three months of life with available objects: real mothers, surrogate mothers, or agemates. For the first two or three weeks, this contact results from reflexive grasping, and then it becomes volitional. Compressibility (softness) is an important factor; surrogate mothers made of cloth-covered foam rubber are preferred over those made of wire mesh, regardless of which provides nourishment. Thus comfort, not hunger reduction, determines choice. The incentive value of these soft objects has been further established by showing the learning of an instrumental task with sight of the objects as the reinforcer.

David A. Stevens

Contrast Mechanisms

The perceived brightness of light is not merely a function of its physical intensity. Even if two sources of light emit the same average number of quanta of the same wavelengths per unit time, under diverse circumstances one light may appear to be much brighter than the other. Many factors may produce such differences in apparent brightness. If, for example, an image of one of the equivalent lights should fall on a part of the retina that had previously been stimulated by a bright adapting light, then the lowered sensitivity of that portion of the retina would result in the test light looking dimmer. This occurs largely because of the fact that there is less photopigment available in the receptors for catching the quanta emitted by the test light after adaptation.

There are formal similarities between metacontrast and simultaneous brightness contrast. The effect is most pronounced when the contours of the masking stimulus are nearly adjacent to those of the test stimulus. The effect is stronger if the mask has greater luminance. One major difference between metacontrast and simultaneous brightness contrast, however, is that the latter is largely retinal

in origin, while metacontrast can be very pronounced even if the test stimulus is presented to one eye and the masking stimulus to the other eye. This argues for the cortical origin of the phenomenon.

Lloyd Kaufman

Control and Authority in Organizations

Control in complex organizations conforms to the hierarchic pattern, and this pattern has been the subject of criticism and debate (Tannenbaum et al. 1974)

Leadership that is supportive and that builds trust and favorable attitudes is presumed to be more effective than control based on coercion or pure authority (Likert 1960). Positive reinforcement is superior to negative reinforcement as a means of eliciting "voluntary" accession to influence attempts and as a way of contributing to a feeling of freedom on the part of members (Skinner 1971).

Research concerning these "human relations" and participative approaches to control in organizations is not conclusive. It does suggest, however, that these approaches can be effective in contributing to high levels of morale among members, in reducing absenteeism and turnover, and in maintaining high levels of performance.

Arnold S. Tannenbaum

Convulsive Therapy

Convulsive (or electroconvulsive) therapy is a biological method for treating mentally ill patients by the induction of cerebral seizures under medically controlled conditions. Ladislas von Meduna invented convulsive therapy while working in Berlin in 1935.

The primary indication for convulsive therapy is in patients with affective disorders, including manic-depressive illness, involutional melancholia, and psychotic depression. The best therapeutic effects are seen in patients with the syndrome of endogenous depression, characterized by early-morning insomnia, anorexia and weight loss, psychomotor retardation or agitation, and unrealistic or delusional notions of guilt, sin, self-reproach, worthlessness, and hopelessness.

Convulsive therapy is given under general anesthesia and therefore requires a routine pretreatment medical examination, including a medical history, physical examination, urinalysis, complete blood count, and chest X ray. For patients over the age of 40, an electrocardiogram is also obtained.

Bilateral electroconvulsive therapy (ECT) is the original method of Cerletti and Bini, in which an electric current is passed through the brain from a pair of stimulating electrodes placed over the fronto-temporal areas on both sides of the head. Depending on the particular treatment apparatus used, the applied current ranges from 300 to 900 milliamperes, which is sufficient to induce a generalized cerebral seizure, with its motor components more or less modified by the muscle-relaxant drug. The seizure generally lasts from 30 to 90 seconds and terminates spontaneously.

Amnesia, disorientation, and confusion are the most prominent unwanted secondary effects of conventional bilateral ECT and flurothyl convulsive therapy, and although they are temporary, they may be distressing to the patient and his or her family. Both a retrograde and an anterograde amnesia occur and are directly related to the number and frequency of induced seizures and to the age of the patient. The retrograde amnesia is for events immediately preceding the first treatment and may extend backward in time for days, weeks, or months if sufficient treatments are given. Once the course of convulsive therapy is terminated, however, the retrograde amnesic gap shrinks rapidly and is usually gone by two to six weeks after the final treatment.

Richard Abrams

Cooperation and Competition

Laboratory research on cooperation and competition has focused primarily on the antecedents and consequences of cooperative and competitive behavior.

Empirical methods have been used to study the effects of within-group and between-group cooperation and competition on interpersonal relations. The evidence indicates that cooperation between groups improves relations both between and within groups, while within-group cooperation leads to increased cohesion among group members. The experimental evidence indicates that competition between groups has adverse effects on the groups' relations to one another.

M. Deutsch has hypothesized that cooperation facilitates role differentiation within the group, substitutability of behaviors between group members, greater influence of members upon one another, and high amounts of helping. Competition is hypothesized to lead to a concern with individual efforts, an unwillingness to allow another individual's actions to substitute for one's own, a resistance to specialization of functions, a resistance to influence attempts from other members, and a lack of interest in helping other group members.

A number of field studies have explored the effects of cooperation and competition on variables such as prejudice and on learning and interpersonal relations in the classroom. Successful cooperation among equal status members of minority and majority groups generally leads to reductions in prejudice.

Walter G. Stephan

Coping Psychology

Coping has been mainly a lay term referring to the way we manage the demands and crises of living. The word also has been used informally by biosocial scholars and scientists for a long time, because of its obvious general importance in adaptation and human functioning; recently there have been signs of more systematic usage, especially in the health sciences.

Coping in the psychological sense refers both to specific behavioral adaptations or single acts, as when an individual evades or escapes an immediate danger or scans the scene for clues about what to do, as well as complex patterns of acts extended over a period of time, as in coping with bereavement.

A rudimentary taxonomy might include two major categories, direct actions and palliative modes. Direct actions consist of any behavioral effort to alter the troubled relationship with the environment;

for example, active searching for information on which to predicate coping actions, preparing against anticipated harm, avoidance and escape, or instrumental attack on an agency of harm. Palliative coping, on the other hand, consists of all efforts to relieve the bodily disturbance or psychological distress that accompanies an appraisal of harm or threat.

The interrelationship between direct action and palliative modes of coping are of special significance for the adaptive outcome. The traditional psychiatric view has treated defensive distortion of reality, as in the case of denial, for example, as pathological or maladaptive. Such a view is supported by observations showing that many women with undiagnosed lumps in their breasts endanger their lives by denying the danger and failing to seek prompt medical attention. On the other hand, denial often has very positive adaptive consequences, such as in preserving hope and tiding a person over the early stages of a health crisis when her physical and psychological strength does not permit a more realistic appraisal nor any useful direct coping actions. Palliative modes of coping are damaging primarily when they prevent essential direct actions demanded by the situation. These modes can be useful in preserving the overall morale and well-being of the person, however, and thus helping to maintain their basic integration under conditions otherwise likely to encourage psychological breakdown.

Richard S. Lazarus

Correlational Analysis of Psychological Tests

Correlational analysis is absolutely essential for basic research on individual differences between people. A typical study involves the investigation of six tests of reasoning ability. It is hypothesized that three of the tests concern mainly deductive reasoning and that the other three tests concern mainly inductive reasoning. These hypotheses could be tested by administering the six measures to a large group of persons and applying correlational analyses to the resulting six sets of scores. Support for the hypotheses would be obtained if (1) the three tests supposedly concerning deduction correlated highly, and (2)

the three tests supposedly concerning induction correlated highly, but (3) the tests concerning induction had only low correlations with the tests concerning deduction.

Interpretation of Correlation Coefficients

A negative correlation means that there is an inverse relationship between the two measures. Persons who rank high on the first measure tend to rank low on the second measure and vice versa for persons who rank low on the first measure. A good example of a negative correlation would be between school grades and days absent from school. Generally, it would be expected that students who were absent a considerable number of days would, on the average, make somewhat lower grades than those who were seldom absent. A correlation of -1.00 means a perfect inverse relationship. Correlations between zero and -1.00 indicate varying degrees of inverse relationship.

The correlation coefficient is used for many purposes in addition to that of measuring the correspondence between two tests. One important use is that of determining the predictive validity of aptitude tests, such as those used to select students for college. Each year, millions of high school students are required to take such college aptitude tests as part of the admissions requirements of colleges and universities. Being predictor tests, their validity depends upon the extent to which test scores are predictive of overall grades earned later in higher education. Most typically, what is done is to correlate test scores with grade-point averages earned over four years of college.

Correlations found in psychological research tend to be even smaller than those found in measuring predictive validity. For example, one would expect only rather low correlations, if any, between muscular coordination and intelligence and between grades and amount of time spent in study. Such variables are quite complex, and it is unreasonable to expect high correlations among them. The major question at issue is whether there is a perceptible correlation. In this context, correlations as low as .20 often are quite interesting, and correlations as high as .30 or .40 are sometimes considered major findings.

Correlation and Causation

The correlation coefficient is not necessarily a measure of causation. For example, there is a positive correlation between the number of books in homes and the grades of students. It would be wrong to conclude from this that students make better grades because books are in the home.

Statistical Significance and Confidence

The two important characteristics of any sample are that it be unbiased and that sufficient numbers of persons be involved. If the sample is unbiased, the precision with which the sample correlation estimates the real population correlation varies with the number of persons involved. Correlations based on 100 persons provide more accurate estimates than those based on 10 persons. Correlations based on 1,000 persons would provide much better estimates. When the sample is as large as 10,000, estimates are so accurate as to be exactly correct for all practical purposes.

Before any effort is made to interpret a particular correlation, some assurance must be obtained that the coefficient is significantly different from zero. Otherwise, the correlation may represent a chance sampling of people from a population in which the true value is zero. One way to gain some confidence is particular correlations is to learn the odds, or the probability, with which the correlation could have been obtained by chance alone. If the probability is very low, say 1 in 100, or at the .01 level as it will be called, then it is relatively safe to assume that the correlation is not merely a chance relationship.

After testing for statistical significance, it usually also is important to investigate statistical confidence. Even if the correlation is statistically highly significant (e.g., beyond the .01 level), the correlation should not be considered an exact point but rather as lying in a range extending above and below the obtained value. If, for example, a correlation of .50 is found in a sample of 100 persons, the proper view is that the real correlation lies in a region centering on .50, perhaps being as high as .70 or as low as .30. Such a region is referred to as a *confidence band*, a region in which we feel confident that the real (population) correlation lies. For this purpose, a 95% confidence band is often employed, which means

essentially that the odds are 95 out of 100 that the population correlation is somewhere within the band.

Jum C. Nunnally

Counseling Psychology

According to the fourth edition of the *Dictionary of Occupational Titles* (U.S. Dept. of Labor, 1977), counseling psychologists provide individual and group counseling services to assist people in achieving more effective development and adjustment. They collect data through interview, case history, and observational techniques and select and interpret psychological tests, evaluating test data to identify problem causes and determine the advisability of counseling or referral. They conduct interviews, provide occupational and educational information, and assist in educational and occupational planning and follow-up results.

History

The term *counseling psychology* and the job title of counseling psychologist first entered our occupational lexicon in 1951. At that time, sixty leading psychologists who were interested in vocational guidance and counseling attended a meeting at Northwestern University, chaired by C. Gilbert Wrenn, the then-president of the Division of Counseling and Guidance of the American Psychological Association.

The origins of counseling psychology can be found, in the United States, in the vocational guidance movement, which in turn owes its beginnings to the concerns of philanthropists interested in improving postschool vocational adjustment. Soon, psychologists interested in measurement joined with guidance specialists who were providing occupational information and orientation, as they had hopes of providing tests for vocational counseling as well as selection (aptitude testing). The Great Depression added still more reasons; now placement and retraining were added as functions. By this time, the National Vocational Guidance Association numbered among its members educators, psychologists, social workers, and representatives from business and government. By the end of the 1930s counselors and guidance specialists were also interested in psychotherapy because they had become aware of individual personality differences, and that adjustment difficulties in one domain often had correlates in others. Counseling psychology, in its current form, incorporates the streams of guidance, community service, education, assessment, and psychotherapy into its armamentarium, and these domains help to distinguish it from both education (not concerned with therapy) and clinical psychology (not concerned with guidance or vocational choice).

Philosophy

The objective of counseling psychology is to help the normal individual to achieve better integration and to find greater satisfaction through appropriate outlets than she or he otherwise might. Even when the clients of counseling psychologists are disabled in some way, the work is focused on the normal developmental concerns they present rather than physical or psychological challenges. The term *hygiology* (as opposed to *pathology*) has been used to describe the domain of interest to counseling psychologists, emphasizing the focus on the strengths and assets individuals possess rather than their infirmities. The themes that bring together the diverse activities that occur within the profession and help to differentiate counseling psychologists from other professions and specialized psychologists are: (1) the theme of focus on the intact personality; (2) the focus on people's assets and strengths regardless of degree of disturbance; (3) the use of relatively brief interventions; (4) an emphasis on person-environment interactions; and (5) a focus on the educational and career development of individuals and on educational and vocational environments. These themes and philosophies represent central tendencies. There is great variation among individual practitioners along each thematic continuum.

Settings

Counseling psychologists can be found in a variety of settings, such as colleges, universities, hospitals, rehabilitation facilities, nursing homes, large corporations, schools, and community agencies: "wherever people need help in mobilizing their personal resources and in using the environment in order to make better adjustments" (Super 1980, 20). They also increasingly work in private settings. Within these various settings, counseling psychologists occupy a range of roles: direct service (counseling), administrative, and/or academic. Indeed, many counseling psychologists engage in more than one of these roles in more than one setting. For example, there are many counseling psychologists who hold administrative positions in college counseling centers, maintain small independent practices, supervise counseling trainees, teach one or two courses a year, and consult to organizations other than their primary work setting. In a recent survey, almost 44% worked primarily in college or university academic departments, almost 22% in independent practice, and almost 18% in university counseling centers.

Functions

Counseling psychology has traditionally been concerned with three functions: remedial or rehabilitative, preventive, and educative. In the remedial role, counseling psychologists typically help clients to move into educational settings, enter the work force, and identify appropriate retraining opportunities, or to overcome obstacles in doing so. Examples of interventions in this function are crisis intervention, personal/social counseling, and psychotherapy with individuals, couples, and groups. In the preventive role, clients are helped to "anticipate, circumvent, and, if possible, forestall future difficulties" (Jordaan, Myers, Layton & Morgan 1968, 1), to improve their decision-making skills, to understand their environments and resources, and to make good choices about their futures. Interventions designed at this level can sometimes be termed "psychoeducation," and might include, for example, workshops for students, residence hall advisors, and supervisors on specific topics such as alcoholism, drug abuse, suicide prevention, and team building. When counseling psychologists engage in developmental or educative counseling, individuals are helped to use their resources, both environmental and personal, to obtain maximum benefit from their experiences in order to discover and develop their potential. Skill-training interventions, relationship-enhancing groups for couples, personal growth groups for individuals, and insight-oriented psychotherapy for well-functioning clients are examples of interventions serving this purpose. Counseling psychologists can be engaged in a range of activities serving these purposes: counseling, psychotherapy, consultation, testing, assessment and evaluation, research and writing, teaching, training and supervision, and administration.

Clientele

Although historically the clients of counseling psychologists have been adolescents, especially late adolescents in college, this base is broadening. More and more adults are making significant career changes midlife and are seeking help individually, in groups, and in organizations in doing so. As the population ages, counseling psychologists are helping clients to plan for and adjust to retirement, to cope with lateral or downward mobility, and to forge new relationships within families as they develop. They also help individuals and organizations manage diversity. Counseling psychologists are often called in to consult with small and large groups who wish to empower and value traditionally underserved populations. So, too, are counseling psychologists increasingly involved with younger clients, especially in helping school-age girls and boys with career education.

Preparation

Counseling psychologists are trained at the doctoral level, and may hold a Ph.D., Ed.D. or Psy.D. There are more than fifty APA-approved training programs in the United States, housed in either colleges of education or departments of psychology. The basic training model in the field is that of the scientist practitioner. Training occurs both in counseling and in research and does not differ widely from program to program. Completion of training results in eligibility for licensure and/or certification in all states, as well as eligibility for membership in the National Register for Health Service Providers. Experienced practitioners can become certified by the American Board of Professional Psychology. In most doctoral programs, students are expected to have had either prior training or related work experience or both, although that is not universally the case.

Organizations

Many counseling psychologists are members of Division 17 of the American Psychological Association; some also join other divisions, depending on their specific interests; many are also members of the American Counseling Association or the American Educational Research Association.

Patricia M. Raskin

Counterconditioning

The term *counterconditioning* refers generally to the circumstances where, following the conditioning of one response to a particular conditioned stimulus (CS), a second, incompatible response is conditioned to the same CS. The idea is of fundamental importance to several applications. The first of these is explanation of extinction, where the suggestion has been made, for example, by E. R. Guthrie, that extinction of the initial response occurs only when a second response to the CS replaces it.

Gregory A. Kimble

Countertransference

Few topics in analysis and analytic therapy have been the focus of as much discussion and debate in recent years as the issue of countertransference. Questions have been raised about the definition and usefulness of the term, about the nature of countertransference phenomena, and about whether such reactions on the part of therapists constitute impediments in treatment or valuable contributions to it.

This keen interest in countertransference is a comparatively recent development. Countertransference was once regarded as a problem of the analyst's that interfered with his ability to analyze. It was a shortcoming in him that he needed to eliminate either through additional analysis or by means of his self-analytic efforts.

With countertransference reactions viewed in this manner, it is not surprising that few analysts spoke openly about them. Privately, every analyst knew how important countertransference reactions are in treatment and how powerful a force they can be in shaping and influencing the analytic process. Publically, and in print, little was acknowledged.

The first change in the prevailing attitude toward countertransference phenomena in this country took place following the publication by P. Heimann (1950), M. Little (1951), and L. E. Tower (1956) of their now-classic papers. Having had considerable experience working with quite troubled patients and knowing well the intense countertransference responses regularly stimulated by such work, these authors pointed out that such reactions, rather than being an impediment to treatment, could be used productively as a pathway to understanding the inner experiences of the patient.

Heimann believed that countertransference phenomena could best be understood as direct responses to unconscious communications from the patient. As such, they gave the analyst a great deal of useful information about his patient's unconscious fantasies and conflicts.

Little not only concurred in this view but believed that it was useful at times for the analyst to share certain of his countertransference responses with the patient. Such self-revelation, she believed, had the salutory affect of confronting the patient with the impact that her attitudes and behavior have on another individual. This kind of confrontation, she believed, helps the patient come into closer contact with certain unconscious forces in herself, including certain warded-off impulses and character traits, and to recognize the effect that they may have on others. Tower believed that countertransference was intrinsic to every analysis, developed as a part of the unconscious interaction of patient and analyst, and could neither be dispensed with nor "analyzed out." It needed, rather, to be understood, for the patient's capacity to resolve the transference depended in large measure on the analyst's ability to resolve her own countertransference neurosis.

To many classically trained analysts, the views of these authors courted danger. They presented the issue of countertransference in a deceptively positive light, the traditionalists argued. Instead of recognizing it for the problem it was, they elevated countertransference to a position of unwarranted importance and value. Anne Reich (1951, 1960, 1966) became the spokesperson for this point of view. In a series of important papers, she argued that countertransference responses, although inevitable and perhaps necessary in treatment, nonetheless constitute an impediment to analytic work. Because she was a leader in the field and a highly respected clinician who spoke within the Freudian tradition, Reich's works carried much weight. For some years thereafter, her position became the position of most classically trained analysts in this country. Because it emphasized the problematic aspects of countertransference and the difficulties to which they can lead, it had a dampening effect on further exploration of the complexities and possibilities inherent in them.

While this situation existed in America, matters were quite different elsewhere. Early on, Melanie Klein and her followers had emphasized the importance of the analyst's feelings as a guide to understanding the projections and projective identifications that, in her view, play so central a role in human psychology. Winnecott (1949), too, stressed the value of understanding countertransference reactions. In certain cases, he pointed out, such reactions occur in response to actual qualities in the patient, and it is important to distinguish such objective countertransference reactions from the more subjective variety. Writing from an object-relations perspective, W. R. Bion (1962) and H. Guntrip (1961) demonstrated how the analyst's experience of the patient, as well as the reverse, shed light on the patient's inner world of objects. In more recent times, H. Segal (1969), B. Joseph (1983) and J. Klauber (1987), among others have discussed the central role that countertransference reactions play in decoding the patient's unconscious communications. J. McDougall (1979) pointed out that in the treatment of certain traumatized individuals who are unable to express their feelings verbally, the analyst's countertransference reactions provide the only reliable clue to what they are attempting to communicate.

For these psychoanalysts, countertransference responses are conceptualized within a larger context, as one element in the stream of unconscious communications that takes place between patient and analyst. The recognition and exploration of such communications becomes for them an essential, if not the central, task of analysis.

This development, along with the work of Heimann and Little, which was rediscovered by a number of American analysts, has had the effect of legitimizing countertransference and stimulating investigation of its role in the analytic process. This interest, in turn, has led to exploration of a larger and more complex issue; the psychology of the analyst and the way that it resonates and interdigitates with the psychology of the patient. This perspective came about as a result of a shift in thinking about the analytic situation that has evolved over the past 20 years. Formerly conceptualized as an in-depth investigation of the psychology of one individual under the guidance of a relatively objective and neutral analyst, analysis is now recognized as inevitably involving the psychology of two individuals. Being in constant interaction, the two participants exert a continual influence on each other. Thus, transference and countertransference are seen as being a dialectic relationship, each affecting and helping to shape the form, content, and mode of expression of the other.

Pivotal in this view of countertransference and its relationship to the patient's transference is the work of Heinrich Racker (1968), an Argentinian analyst of the Kleinian school who, in the late 1960s, published a comprehensive and highly sophisticated study of countertransference phenomena. Making useful distinctions between various types of countertransference responses, in this work Racker shows how certain of these reactions result from the analyst's identification with the patient's internal objects, while others develop as a consequence of his identification with the patient's drives or ego states. The latter phenomena he terms *concordant identifications,* the former, *complementary identifications.* Racker also distinguishes between direct and indirect countertransference reactions. Direct reactions are those that are stimulated by the patient. Indirect countertransference responses arise as more complex phenomena. They represent the analyst's emotional reactions to supervisors, teachers, colleagues, or other significant individuals who exert an influence on his way of perceiving and working with his patient. Racker also recognizes that the analyst may be influenced in important ways by his reactions to individuals in the patient's world about whom he

hears and who evoke memories and fantasies in him. A male analyst, for instance, may develop feelings of rivalry vis-à-vis the spouse of a female patient, and in subtle, or not so subtle, ways this reactivation of his oedipal conflicts may unconsciously influence his perception of the patient. A similar situation may arise when preoedipal conflicts are stimulated in the analyst by the patient's interaction with mothering figures in her life. Racker's recognition of these indirect, but important, dimensions of countertransference has opened the way to further exploration and investigation of a phenomena and to the appreciation of the fact that countertransference is a highly complex reaction that condenses and expresses wishes, fantasies, memories, defenses, and superego prohibitions in a multidetermined way.

Charles Brenner (1985) has expressed his view of countertransference, noting that it, like symptoms, character traits, and transference itself, represents a intrapsychic compromise formation. How that compromise formation affects the analyst's capacity to listen, understand, and respond to his patient depends on the balance of forces contained within it and whether those forces impede or enhance the analyst's functioning and his analytic instrument. Brenner views countertransference as essentially the analyst's transference. It is for that reason that the usefulness of the term *countertransference* has been questioned. Noting that the term, with its suggestion of a problem of the analyst, still carries negative connotations, a number of analysts prefer to speak simply of the mutual transference of patient and analyst as a central feature of the analytic situation.

This mutuality and its exploration has taken center stage in the recent literature on the transference-countertransference issues. J. Sandler (1976) writes of the way that the patient's wish to impose a particular role on the analyst often leads to the latter's enacting that role. For Sandler, such a role responsiveness on the part of the analyst is an inevitable and necessary part of her functioning. Focus on this kind of interaction between patient and analyst, he points out, often leads to productive work in analysis. Warren Poland (1986), too, has emphasized the dyadic nature of the analytic situation. The analyst's insight and his communications to the patient develop out of interweaving two psychologies, two lives in interaction, and can only be understood in this context. The analyst's memories and his life experiences, including his experiences with other patients, form a reservoir into which he dips continually as he listens to and processes material from his patient. It is this reservoir that provides the psychological basis for his capacity to understand the unconscious of another person. H. Blum (1980) speaks of the analyst's past as being inevitably evoked by her work with patients and of the analyst's self-analysis needing to proceed in a way that is parallel with that of the patient.

J. E. Gardner (1983) illustrates how the analyst's fantasies and memories can be used creatively as a vehicle for grasping the patient's unconscious communications, and Silverman (1987) shows how the countertransference response may be used to unlock logjams in treatment. Jacobs (1992) also focuses on the analyst's use of himself as an integral and potentially valuable force in the analytic situation. Emphasizing the importance of the analyst's listening to the psychic reality of her patient, Schwaber (1981) demonstrates how personal concerns and anxieties, as well as theoretical positions held by the analyst, can disrupt the listening process. McLaughlin (1981), in a series of papers, shows how old conflicts of his have been stirred by work with his patients and how the evocation and reexamination of his problems have been essential to his ability to help patients work through familiar difficulties.

More recently, we have seen significant changes in the concept of countertransference. No longer viewed primarily as an obstacle to effective analytic work, countertransference is now seen as part of the analyst's analyzing instrument and as an indispensable vehicle for understanding the unconscious communications of the patient. Transference and countertransference are recognized as being a dynamic interaction, one influencing the other in constantly shifting and evolving ways. While it is necessary for the analyst to monitor her responses in order to recognize those aspects of her countertransference reactions that may distort her ability to listen to and respond to her patients, modern technique also emphasizes the importance of the analyst's ability to tune into and utilize her psychological reactions as they arise in treatment. Stud-

ies of countertransference phenomena over the last two decades have shown conclusively that such reactions are invaluable in opening up pathways to understanding the inner world of the patient; pathways that, in certain cases, are available to the analyst through no other means.

Theodore J. Jacobs

Creativity: Measurement Methods

Test items can be composed to measure students' abilities to see unusual uses for objects and methods. For example, students can be asked, "What are some uses that can be made of empty tin cans?" Both the number and quality of answers are important. The noncreative student will think of "carry water," "plant flowers," and "hold marbles" and then be at a loss to provide more answers. The really creative child will produce a flood of answers, suggesting not only ordinary uses such as those mentioned above but also such clever ones as "cut out the tops and bottoms and weld them together to make a stove chimney," "put them in the ground to make golf cups," and "cut holes in the bottoms and use them to spread grass seed." Similar items can be composed relating to screwdrivers, paper clips, bottle caps, and many other objects. Tests relating to "unusual uses" are included on the Torrance Tests of Creative Thinking.

Fluency

Apparently, one aspect of creativity is the sheer fluency with which words, ideas, and solutions to problems are produced. Tests of verbal fluency are used very widely in this regard. An illustrative item would require students to produce as many words beginning with the letter *s* as possible in two minutes' time. Although word fluency is only moderately well correlated with conventional measures of intelligence, it apparently does go along to some extent with measures of creativity.

Tests of various aspects of verbal and ideational fluency are present on the Torrance Tests of Creative Thinking. An interesting approach to the measurement of some aspects of verbal fluency is the Remote Associates Test (RAT) of Mednick and

Mednick. On each item, the subject is given three words and asked to supply a fourth word that relates to the others. An example would be the words *blue*, *cottage*, and *rat*; an appropriate response would be *cheese*. Like most supposed measures of different aspects of creativity, the RAT is still highly experimental.

Creative Productions

In order to validly score products relating to creativity, it is necessary to obtain judgments from people who recognize creativity when they see it. This is not much of a problem with students in the elementary grades. What would be creative responses for most of them are not difficult for teachers and other persons to recognize.

Perceptual Tests

One type of perceptual problem that has been studied in relation to creativity concerns embedded figures. An example would be a triangle that is hidden in the midst of surrounding distracting figures. The person is shown the simple figure and required to select one from a number of other figures in which the simple figure is embedded. In order to mark the correct figure, it is necessary to "see through" the maze of distracting lines and competing figures within the complex pattern.

Comprehensive Batteries

There are no comprehensive, well-standardized batteries of tests to measure a wide spectrum of traits relating to creativity. Among other reasons, this is because (1) the study of creativity is not well advanced, (2) the issues are complex and there is much controversy surrounding them, (3) there is a wide variety of traits that are thought to be related to creativity, and (4) much more effort and time will be required in order to develop excellent tests relating to creativity. The Torrance Tests of Creative Thinking consist of two batteries, one verbal and one pictorial. The verbal battery provides measures of fluency, flexibility, and originality. In addition to these three traits, the pictorial battery is purported to measure a fourth trait, that of elaboration.

Jum C. Nunnally

Creativity: An Overview

Creativity is essentially a function of the whole personality that permits one to view and understand whatever he may be considering in such a way that it can assume new and unexpected form and meaning.

Four Steps

Various attempts to define the creative act not only broaden the concept of creativity beyond the limits of artistic or scientific production but also highlight the various steps involved in the process of original thinking itself. Hermann Ludwig Ferdinand von Helmholtz was one of the first to divide the creative process into stages: *preparation*, or saturation with the subject; *incubation*, or allowing the problem to rest; and *illumination*. Henri Poincaré added a fourth and vital stage: *verification*, during which the ideas that have occurred are tested in real life to determine their significance, value, and effectiveness.

Gestalt

The Gestalt school of psychology has added a further dimension to understanding the creative process. *Insight* is the term used by this group to describe an imaginative way of learning or problem solving, as opposed to the trial-and-error method. *Closure* is the process of structuring an insight. Closure itself is a basic property of the mind—the ability to combine parts into a whole, or to identify parts in the whole and to shift from one whole to another.

Stimulating Creativity

Two important techniques for stimulating creativity are redefining the problem and distancing. A simple example of redefining is to ask a question in a different way, with a new focus. For instance, instead of asking, "Should I write this particular article or book?" ask, rather, "What is the message I wish to deliver, and what is the most effective way of doing so?"

One of the formal techniques for putting some distance between the problem and the problem solver is called *synectics*, originated by W. J. J. Gordon (1961), and involves the use of metaphors and analogies. The problem must be changed in some way—to "make the strange familiar and make the familiar strange"—before creative work can begin on it. M. I. Stein (1974) summarized the steps in this process thus: First, state the problem. Then give a short analysis of it. Verbalize the solutions that have already occurred, to get rid of them and make way for new ones. Finally, restate the problem and move to the use of metaphors and analogies.

Groups

In groups, interpersonal interactions become critical in determining the creative viability of the group; common purpose, trust, openness of feeling and communication, and mutual respect will facilitate innovation; on the other hand, competitiveness, distrust, lack of involvement, confusion as to goals, and absence of the necessary knowledge and experience input will defeat it.

Frederic F. Flach

Creativity: Psychoanalytic Studies

Sigmund Freud was very careful to acknowledge the limitations of the psychoanalytic understanding of creativity. Psychoanalysts generally agree that the principle of the complementary series holds in all personality development. Any given psychic organization is a product of constitutional and experiential factors varying together. However, constitutional factors cannot be assessed by psychoanalytic method alone; in the case of creativity, it is usually assumed that creators are born with certain gifts, although the exact nature of these gifts is difficult to determine.

Kurt R. Eissler's study of Johann Wolfgang von Goethe (1963) led him to conclude that, although genius is a form of madness, the problems of geniuses are essentially different from those of ordinary neurotics or psychotics. While Eissler regarded Goethe as a paranoid schizophrenic, he was thought to be unlike other paranoid schizophrenics.

From a very different point of view, Lawrence Kubie (1958) emphasizes the preconscious system, and Benjamin B. Wolman (1967) stresses the access to unconscious processes. Creativity may mean the ability to use preconscious and unconscious processes effectively. Such an ability implies that a creative individual is not bound by reality, conformity, logical processes, or repetitive unconscious difficulties. If the creative act is associated with neurotic processes, it is apt to become stereotyped, as in the artist who repeats the same picture or the novelist who rewrites the same book. According to Wolman, creative artists, capable of delving into their own unconscious, have more in common with psychoanalysts than with patients. Kubie argues that the concept of sublimation is not really needed to provide a psychoanalytic explanation of creativity.

Creators are individuals who have been able to set up an unusual ego organization. They are able to coordinate both the primary and secondary processes of thinking (Giovacchini 1960; Kris 1952). During periods of inspiration the ego has access to content that is ordinarily unconscious.

The ego operations of a creative individual show a strong tendency to action relating to a love relationship with an object. The object representation does not, however, refer to a real person but rather to parts of the real or imaginary world that become synthesized as an alternative to a real person, a "collective alternate" (Greenacre 1957).

Vann Spruiell

Crisis Intervention

Crisis intervention is a term applied to brief immediate treatment in acute behavioral disturbances in individuals, families, and groups. Crisis techniques use pharmacotherapy and a variety of psychosocial therapies. The goal is to return to the level of adaptation that existed prior to the crisis. Crisis is viewed as a reaction to a precipitating hazard, which may be external or internal.

Crisis intervention is time-limited therapy. It should be immediately available on a 24-hour basis. The therapist generally considers the presenting problem as a function of a recent precipitating stress. Though she may want to place the crisis in the context of some brief overview of the individual, the family, and the social situation, the questions are more likely to be directed toward recent change and current upsets.

The goals of treatment are symptom relief, amelioration of the immediate problem, and the restoration of the patient to the level at which he was functioning before the crisis. Crisis intervention is not meant to change long-term problems of maladaptive behavior, but the therapist must be prepared to make recommendations about further treatment needs.

Evaluation and treatment in a hospital emergency room has traditionally been the responsibility of a psychiatrist. As crisis intervention became concerned with ambulatory treatment, other mental health professionals began to develop and use such skills. In the management of acute psychotic disorders, a mental health team approach was found to be exceedingly useful. The clinical skills necessary for crisis intervention have been taught to psychiatrists, clinical psychologists, social workers, mental health nurses, and paraprofessionals.

Donald G. Langsley
Richard M. Yarvis

Cross-Cultural Psychology

Cross-cultural psychology has been established and accepted only since the early 1970s. Within the discipline of psychology, cross-cultural psychology is an important area of specialization. It concentrates on comparing human behavior in different cultures, investigates the customs and manners of people in a variety of ecologies, and studies patterns of behavior of different ethnic groups. Recently the research orientation has included multicultural and multi-ethnic groups in industrial and nonindustrial environments.

It is one of the goals of cross-cultural psychology and cross-cultural research to make culture-bound individuals aware of the differences between cultures by reducing their ethnocentricity. However, cross-cultural research not only centers on differences in behaviors, which are often easily noticeable, but also on similarities, where the background or bases of actions and interactions are more obscure. Therefore, the discovery of similarities across cultures may be more meaningful than the findings of differences cross-culturally (L. L. Adler 1977). When the same or similar characteristics are found

to occur in several different and distant cultures, cross-cultural psychologists engage in research to look for some underlying universal phenomena or schema. Emphasis is given to methodological issues and research techniques, as well as to theoretical issues and evaluations.

Two major foci are employed in cross-cultural research, which set the stage for observation of the behavior of people in specific cultural or ethnic environments. First, the etic approach is truly cross-cultural research and is the most frequently used method of investigation. With this method, the investigator can observe several populations for comparison from the vantage point of another culture. The scientist can collect data in many different ecologies at the same time, or one at a time, and thereby provide an extensive basis for comparisons between the various cultures.

While the etic (culture-general) orientation looks at other cultures from an outsider's point of view, the second approach, the emic (culture-specific) method, looks at the culture from within, which is—strictly speaking—not a cross-cultural method, because it only studies the culture from an insider's point of view. Using both approaches together provides the most information by assessing people's behaviors from within a culture and then comparing the same behaviors between different cultures. The *International Handbook on Gender Roles* (L. L. Adler 1994) is a case in point. Each chapter is written from an insider's (emic) life-span perspective; however, it is up to the reader to compare the various geographical locations (etic approach). Recently it has been suggested that the term *emic* be replaced with "culture-specific" and *etic* with "universal." So far, the terms *emic* and *etic* still remain in frequent use.

Other terms are important for a fuller understanding of cross-cultural psychology. While socialization is an important process in the development of young children, *enculturation* is a broader term for what can be called vertical cultural transmission, when parents (or other adults) transmit to their offspring their own cultural values, beliefs, attitudes, accepted gender roles, and appropriate manners and behaviors. Enculturation is the automatic process of accepting or complying with cultural prerogatives, without thought or question. The persons enculturated in their cultural environment are not aware of differences or similarities to other cultures (unless they are made aware of behaviors in different cultures), and thus usually have an entirely ethnocentric point of view, accepting their own cultural background and lifestyle as their standard.

The term *acculturation* has a completely different meaning; it refers to the gradual change, both cultural and psychological, that occurs when individuals leave one cultural environment to live more or less permanently in a different one. Acculturation has no developmental limitations but can occur at any time during the life span after long-term contact with another cultural or ethnic group has been established. The acculturation changes occur gradually and imperceptibly to the individual in areas of values, beliefs, attitudes, self-perception, manners, and personal interactions, among others. Another goal of cross-cultural research is to examine intercultural relationships in new cultural environments or in multicultural communities; it seeks to discover specific features that can lead to some generalization of the long-term effects directly due to the new culture contact and change (Berry et al. 1992). Acculturation may not always be a smooth process, and it may lead to acculturation stress. In recent years there has been an increase in migration around the world. Many countries are aware of this situation, mostly evident in the presence of ethnic minorities in the workplace and in the multicultural classroom.

Many of the areas worthy of study in psychology are pertinent fields, as well, for investigations of cross-cultural psychology. Some topics have been more intensively studied worldwide (Adler and Gielen 1994).

Following is a brief overview of some of the areas in cross-cultural psychology:

1. *Life-span development* not only takes the cultural environment into consideration but focuses also on ecology and biological variables with cultural interactions (L. L. Adler 1994).

2. *Child-rearing practices* from infancy through the school years are observed and studied in modern and traditional environments—both industrial and nonindustrial—as well as in rural and urban communities.

3. *Children's drawings* are used in investigations of attitudes toward traditionalism and modernization in terms of the value hypothesis and the familiarity hypothesis.

4. *Cognition.* There also exists an interaction between ecological and cultural factors. The research in this area frequently follows Jean Piaget's investigations of his stage theory of cognitive development for cross-cultural comparisons. Frequently, other investigations focus on the differences among the cognitive process, competence, and performance (see Dasen in L. L. Adler 1982).

5. *Moral reasoning* is widely studied in terms of the theory of moral development, and it has generated many cross-cultural studies with children and young adolescents. The attainment of the highest level of moral reasoning has been, and still is, a basis of controversy.

6. *Personality development* is investigated with a reliance on the social learning theories, as well as several trait theories. This topic includes emotional expressions and nonverbal communications found in different cultural and ethnic groups.

7. *Visual perception* has long been a target of cross-cultural research. Investigations on different continents have focused on pictures, visual patterns, and illusions. As a basis of explanation, the "carpentered-world hypothesis" as well as the "foreshortening hypothesis" have been advanced. With both these hypotheses the three-dimensional effects in the interpretation of two-dimensional figures result in visual illusions. If, however, no experience with three-dimensional perceptions exist, no such visual illusions occur.

8. *Gender roles*—for example, marital lifestyles such as monogamy, polygamy, and polyandry—are based mainly on cultural prerogatives, and are therefore enculturated early in life. Some gender roles, as well as appropriate patterns of behavior, change during the life span in most cultural settings. In recent years changes in status have followed on the indus-

trialization of third world and developing countries and, in modern societies, new career opportunities for women.

9. *Aging and old age* has long been neglected in research. However, during the last few decades both governmental and private agencies in modern countries have contributed to support the elderly, though mostly in urban areas. In traditional and rural environments, the elderly are still mainly taken care of by their children. Whether this duty is performed by the son or the daughter is mostly based on traditional or customary tenets.

10. *Psychopathological conditions* have been analyzed and researched extensively for many years. While often symptoms and diagnoses are the same or similar, treatments for and acceptances of these conditions vary among cultures and countries (see L. L. Adler 1989).

Cross-cultural research is being conducted in many other areas. Among these are multicultural and multiethnic studies in education; multinational investigations in the international business world; electronic bases in intercultural communications; and cross-cultural advertisement. The field of cross-cultural psychology is expanding rapidly, and it is hoped that it will reach some of its goals in the near future, and improve understanding and harmonious interactions with people cross-ethnically and cross-culturally.

Leonore Loeb Adler

Culture and Thought

Investigations of culture and thought pose two fundamental questions. First, how does what one learns as a member of a cultural community influence thinking (e.g., making inferences, retrieving information, constructing explanatory theories, estimating likelihoods)? And second, how is thinking distributed across cultural communities?

Lucien Lévy-Bruhl has noted that "primitives" are perfectly capable of logical and scientific thinking. They are also not confused; their intellectual procedures are not incompetent applications of the canons of logic and science. Quite the contrary, Lévy-Bruhl argues; the "primitive mentality" accepts the authority of methods of thought so different that logical models are inappropriate for their evaluation and inadequate for their description. The primitive mentality is prelogical, not illogical; mystical, not irrational.

Thinking: Its Cultural Environment

Rules (or norms) are standards (often unconscious but always recognized in their breach) for how something is to be done if it is to count as an instance of a certain kind of activity (e.g., speaking English, playing chess, being reasonable). One can, of course, utter any pattern of sound, move pieces of wood in any direction across a checkered board, or claim that just about anything "follows" from your mother's conditional threat. But if one is to speak English, or play chess, or reason logically (e.g., in terms of the propositional calculus), most of these possible behaviors are either wrong or beside the point. Rules define the limits within which much that we call thinking (e.g., word coining, game playing, inference drawing) has its life.

Beliefs. Beliefs are understandings about how objects and events fall into categories and how categories relate to one another. The objects and events do not usually insist; they don't sort themselves out. For example, in a recent legal case, a doctor was tried for "aborting" (or is it "murdering"?) a "product of conception" (or is it a "child"?). A dispute arose between the defense and prosecuting attorneys over terms to be used in arguments. Shall it be "the product of conception" or "the child," "the fetus" or "the offspring," "the patient" or "the mother"; that is, shall we talk in a language for things or a language for persons? Pointing couldn't settle the issue; the attorneys couldn't point at personhood.

Beliefs and Reasoning

Beliefs also influence reasoning. A logic has been defined as a system "in which formulae may be transformed into new formulae according to certain rules governing the manipulation of symbols." There are many such systems; not all of them have been formalized. There is a recent recognition among psychologists (e.g., P. Wason and P. Johnson-Laird) that the meaning and cultural context surrounding what one reasons about can be decisive for which system of logic is brought to bear on a proposition, and that no current formalized system of logic is capable of representing these meaning-laden judgments of what follows from a proposition.

Thinking: Its Cross-Cultural Distribution

Cultures differ in their performance on a sample of tasks categorized as indicators of intelligence in our schooled culture (i.e., on standard IQ tests), but interpretations of such differences are usually equivocal. Typically, there is as little reason for concluding that the test is a measure of a superior gift of intellect as there is for attributing the chess grandmaster's perfect recall of game positions to a superior capacity to recollect visual imagery. All cultures are grandmasters of their own intellectual skills. Not surprisingly, the introduction of culturally meaningful materials often has a massive augmenting effect on intellectual performance (e.g., M. Cole et al. 1971).

Richard A. Shweder

explored (through visual and manipulatory behaviors) as the various aspects of the event are encoded in relation to other stored experiences. Following this process of transformational thinking, play activities dominate the child's interaction with the stimulus, followed, in turn, by a more active search for new stimulation.

Children of all ages visually explore incongruous and unfamiliar stimuli at greater length than congruous and familiar objects. In contrast to the trends for complexity research, however, age differences are not found for the effects of novelty on curiosity behavior. Older and younger subjects explore novel stimuli with equal intensity and duration.

The relationship between curiosity and cognitive competence is reciprocal: the motive to explore certainly advances competency, which in turn determines both capacity for investigation and play and the targets of investigation. For the more advanced child there is less need to explore other events because the child is able to recognize the incongruity or paradox in them.

John D. Coie

Curiosity: Development in Children

Daniel E. Berlyne (1960) argued that organisms require an optimal level of stimulation. Thus, excessive stimulation leads to avoidance and withdrawal, whereas insufficient stimulation leads to approach and exploration. This part of the theory emphasizes the internal status of the organism and leads to a research focus on the stimulus history of the organism. The question then arises as to which aspects of the stimulus field are most likely to be explored by an "under-aroused" organism. Berlyne's answer to this question lies in the category of collative properties. These are stimulus characteristics, such as novelty, surprisingness, or incongruity—properties that evoke cognitive conflict within organisms. With this conflict comes heightened arousal, the motivational state for exploratory behavior.

Jum C. Nunnally (1973) has related specific and diversive exploration in a time-sequence analysis of curiosity: initial orienting responses are made to a stimulus with collative properties. This stimulus is

Curiosity, Exploration, and Aesthetics

Exploratory behavior can take many forms. It invariably involves receptor-adjusting responses, that is, postural and physicochemical changes that direct sense organs toward particular objects or events and enhance their sensitivity. These are not infrequently preceded by locomotor exploration (i.e., approach movements) and by investigatory behavior (i.e., responses that act on, or modify, objects so as to draw stimulation from them that they would not otherwise yield). This latter category includes the artistic efforts of human beings, who radically transform, or can even be said to create, portions of their environments in accordance with aesthetic values. It also includes the steps taken by human beings to inspect the artistic products of their conspecifics.

Locomotor Exploration and Investigatory Behavior

Locomotor exploration has been studied most often either by recording how much animals (usually rats) move about in an open field or maze or by studying how likely they are to move toward sources of novel stimulation. Several investigators have found that lesions in the hippocampus will reduce novelty seeking, as well as slowing down the decline in locomotion that generally sets in as an environment becomes more and more familiar.

The Orientation Reflex

Investigators from the former Soviet Union, notably E. N. Sokolov, have reported that, when stimuli exceed a particular strength, the orientation reaction is replaced by the defensive reflex, whose components act to reduce the impact of stimulation. Western researchers have had some difficulty in confirming the findings on which this view is based, but there have recently been suggestions that it could be related to J. I. Lacey's observations showing heart rate to decrease when human subjects are receptive to external stimulation, and to increase when they are motivated to exclude it.

The orientation reaction is evoked most readily by novel or surprising stimuli, whatever form they may take. Its occurrence must presumably be governed by neural units characterized by input from several sensory modalities, by diffuseness of output, and by sensitivity to novelty as revealed through a decline in sensitivity when a stimulus is repeated. Neurons corresponding to this description have been located in the limbic system and throughout the neuroaxis. The hippocampus has also been implicated by experiments showing slow electrical waves to be derivable from it during the orientation reaction. There is now evidence that another limbic structure, the amygdala, is especially responsible for registering environmental novelty and signaling when habituation of responses associated with novelty can occur.

Exploratory Behavior and Arousal

Although exploratory responses can be affected by many factors, external and internal, their strength and direction are determined most powerfully by the collative stimulus properties, i.e., variations along familiar-novel, expected-surprising, simple-complex, congruous-incongruous, and clear-ambiguous dimensions.

Aesthetic Behavior

Much of the behavior centering on works of art and other objects of aesthetic appreciation can be recognized as exceptionally elaborate, peculiarly human forms of exploratory behavior. This holds for the professional activities of the creative artist and the interpretative artist. It applies also to the behavior of the appreciator while looking at, listening to, or reading artistic products, as well as to the highly diversified exertions that lead up to contact with a work of art. On the other hand, some portions of aesthetic behavior, namely, the internal and overt reactions that follow exposure to aesthetic stimulation, are not classifiable as exploration and raise different though related problems.

Daniel E. Berlyne

·D·

Darwin, Charles R. (1809–1822)

Darwin developed three theories: (1) struggle for survival, (2) biological variation, and (3) survival of the fittest. Darwin's theories marked the beginning of the functionalist movement in psychology.

Patrick J. Capretta

Day Hospitals and Night Hospitals

Day hospitals and night hospitals are important parts of comprehensive community psychiatric services. They provide opportunities for treatment almost as complete as that provided by the full-time hospital. Among possible therapeutic services are individual psychotherapy, small group psychotherapy, milieu therapy, pharmacological therapy, electroconvulsive therapy, occupational therapy, and the full range of activities in the recreational therapies.

Issues commonly presented are the effectiveness of part-time care; the cost; the dangers of extensive patient freedom; the intimacy of interpersonal relationships; the changing of traditional staff roles; and the apparent abdication of authority on the part of physicians.

Treatment Functions of the Day Hospital
The treatment functions of a day hospital may be summarized as follows:

1. as a definitive treatment center for many patients now treated in full-time hospitals
2. as a gradual transition when discharge from the full-time hospital is likely to result in increased symptoms or regression
3. as a transition into a full-time hospital when patient and family cannot tolerate immediate total separation
4. as a training center to reestablish work patterns and to facilitate rehabilitation
5. as a treatment center for patients who, after a course of individual therapy, need additional treatment emphasizing interpersonal relationships
6. as a treatment center where contact with family is maintained and made the focus of treatment

The Night Hospital
The night hospital offers therapeutic advantages in the following situations:

1. as a temporary intermediate residence between full-time hospitalization and total discharge
2. as a temporary residence for the patient who lacks family and other environmental support
3. as a temporary residence for the patient who is trying to separate from his or her family of origin
4. as a treatment center where functioning at work, school, or home may be continued

The night hospital is a valuable facility for that group of patients where daytime functioning can be maintained. It permits the patient to continue with his or her usual daytime activities, which increases self-esteem and discourages regression. Simultaneously, extensive treatment can be provided.

Robert S. Daniels

Day Health Centers for the Elderly

A day health (or day care) center is a facility for the frail elderly, offering the participants health care supervision and therapeutic regimens, in addition to social activities and one or more meals. Although direct medical and health services care by a physician is often not provided, a health professional may monitor chronic diseases, such as diabetes and hypertension, referring the participant to medical care when appropriate. Therapeutic regimens are designed for the needs of each participant, and therapies may include reality therapy, reorienting the participant to time, place, and person; counseling about personal and family problems or problems of living, such as financial management; and occupational, physical, and speech therapies. In addition, recreational activities are usually provided, and social interaction among participants is encouraged.

Day health centers should be seen as part of the spectrum of services needed by elderly people; they enable participants to continue community residence rather than requiring institutional care.

Elinore E. Lurie

Death and "Death and Dying"

Death

Death—the concept as well as the troubling reality—has never budged from the center of concern for psychiatry, psychology, and psychoanalysis in continental Europe. Sigmund Freud wrote that his greatest achievement, *The Interpretation of Dreams* (1900), was a direct reaction to the death of his own father. In his second preface to that work, he writes that "the death of one's father" is the most important event, the most decisive loss (*der entschneidendster Verlust*) in a person's life." His early clinical studies on hysteria point in large measure to the same unsettling reality: an unmourned death, usually that of a parent, lurks repressed in the shadows, strangling the patient, especially in his or her sexuality. In *Fetishism* (1905), Freud openly wonders, How could these two young men who did not mourn their "beloved fathers" *not* have become psychotic? Freud's preoccupation with death was vast,

as one can glean from scanning the hundreds of citations to "death" in the index of his *Standard Edition*. But perhaps he is best known for his insistence on the concept of a "death drive" (*Todestriebe*), even when it was not at all popular among his fellow analysts, especially those who migrated to England and the United States and came to a favor a "conflict-free" ego. The resistance to Freud's concept can be demonstrated by looking up "death drive" in the index of the English-version *Standard Edition*: First, "death drive" is not listed as such, but as "death instinct" (Freud did not use the word "instinct" in German!). Then the reader is immediately directed to "*see also* Aggressiveness; Destructive impulses; Ego instincts; Masochism; Sadistic impulses," and only after that are the volume and page numbers for the death instinct given. The death drive is related to but not at all graspable from studying one of its expressions, for example, "aggressiveness," and much less "ego instincts." In *Beyond the Pleasure Principle* ("beyond eros, the life drives"), Freud (1955) insists that "the aim of all life is death" and that the death drive, as the drive "to return to the inanimate state," is the first to arise; the life instincts (eros) come later. Freud insisted on this position to the end, to the dismay of his collaborators in England and the United States, who were embarrassed by his "European pessimism" and more interested in "optimistic object relations" and "conflict-free egos," untrammeled by the troublesome presence of death. In England, however, the psychoanalytic school of Melanie Klein did retain and develop Freud's concept of the death drive, calling it Thanatos.

Historically, the roots of psychoanalysis in Continental Europe were nourished from philosophy and religion: their concern was with death. From philosophy came Michel Eyquem de Montaigne's famous dictum, which is also attributed to Lucius Seneca, "Philosophy means learning how to die," and from Georg Wilhelm Friedrich Hegel, "The only absolute master is death." From religious thought, we recall that "remembering death" was the Christian's prime duty, because soon, at death, his soul would be judged by God. ("*Memento Mori*," Thomas More's motto, meant both his remembering his own death and his desire that God remember him.) In this regard, it is of interest that Freud himself perdured in using the religious word "soul" (*Seele*) to denote the personal subject (when Dora broke down, he writes that "her soul was shattered" when he could have used "psyche" or other available German words).

Psychiatry and psychology in England, on the other hand, was rooted in empirical, "objective" experimental science, wherein death and the dying subject were not central concerns. The *Standard Edition*, for example, betrays its empiricist bias by translating Freud's "soul" as "mental apparatus"! This is not to say that the theme of death is not recognized in English culture: on the contrary, Shakespeare is an acknowledged master at weaving death throughout his plots. But that was not the tradition that nourished the development of the psychological sciences in England (and, of course, in the empiricist-influenced United States).

Man's struggle with death was always a central concept for existentialist philosophers, beginning with Soren Kierkegaard (1813–1855). For Martin Heidegger (1889–1976), authentic human existence (*Dasein*) arises only on the horizon of our "being-unto-death" (*Sein zum Tode*); in other words, the anticipation of one's death "pushes existence into its finitude," its authentic state. Once one has grasped the finitude of one's existence—only then—is one capable of full life and of full speech. Heidegger's influence was decisive on European psychiatrists and psychoanalysts, notably Freud's friend Ludwig Binswanger and Medard Boss in Switzerland, Jacques Lacan in France, and Rollo May in the United States. Heidegger- and Karl Jaspers–inspired existentialism also had no small influence on the theologians like R. Bultmann, P. Tillich, K. Barth, and J. Pieper, who helped disseminate the existentialist credo into popular European and American psychology. It should also be noted that, in the United States, Harold Searles recognized "the existential anxiety of death" as playing a critical role in the etiology of schizophrenia in his *Schizophrenia and the Inevitability of Death* in 1961. Quoting Heidegger, he concludes that at base the schizophrenic patient is unwilling to face any loss whatsoever, but most of all the loss of death, since infantile fantasies of personal omnipotence demand immor-

tality. Two other American clinicians who have written widely on death and the effects of unmourned deaths are Irvin Yalom and George Pollock. Others who championed a position for death in American psychology and on American campuses were Norman O. Brown, Edith Wyschograd, and Ernest Becker.

Currently, it is Jacques Lacan's (1981) clinical theory that most conspicuously celebrates death as one of the central concepts in psychoanalysis, which profoundly disturbs us because it is "all too real," that which, when we are confronted with it, leaves us speechless. Death as a necessary loss must be faced: the alternative may be psychosis. The neurotic lives in fear under the law of death; the psychotic is free of that law, but free of symbolic roots, too. In every treatment, Lacan writes, Death is always present—like "the Dummy" in a game of bridge (*Le mort*, "death" in French). Silent Death is present as our partner whether we like it or not, gaping at us, stirring us out of our lethargy, impelling us to start living our lives because "it is already too late." It was when this Death poisoned his mother and then pricked his own arm that Hamlet was finally able to take action, writes Lacan. Human subjectivity is awakened in the face of death. Lacan thus continues Freud's emphasis on the death drive (in fact, he terms his entire work "a return to Freud") and, like Freud, bemoans the developments of psychoanalysis in England and America that purport to offer a kind of happiness or fulfillment far removed from life on the razor's edge of the death drive.

"Death and Dying"

On the American scene, the name popularly associated with the topic "death and dying" is that of the psychiatrist Elisabeth Kübler-Ross. In her tremendously popular 1969 book, *On Death and Dying*, she sets forth a series of five stages that terminally ill patients often go through in accepting the reality of their own imminent death. In her preface, she hopes to encourage people "not to shy away from the hopelessly sick" because "we can learn much about the functioning of the human mind." She further states that the need for denial of death is "in direct proportion to the doctor's need for denial."

The first stage of dying is denial and isolation:

most patients usually respond with temporary shock and disavowal of the fact that they are dying ("Not *me!*") and sometimes even seek a different diagnosis from other doctors who will support their denial. Finally, when the patient drops his denial, he enters the second stage of dying, anger. Now he becomes "the difficult patient," and because of his rage, is often avoided by hospital staff as well as by family members. Now the patient is asking "Why *me*?" and displacing his anger onto staff, family members, his physician, and God. Kübler-Ross writes that patients must be encouraged to express their anger during this stage, and not deny it; in this way, they work their way through their anger and are ready to start the next stage. However, if patients are not allowed to express their anger, or if they are made to feel guilty because of it, they remain stuck in this second stage. It is here that psychotherapists can be of great benefit to the dying.

Bargaining is the third stage. The patient now prays to be spared in exchange for good deeds, giving up alcohol, dedicating his life to others, etc. Now, the patient admits that he is dying, but at least has a brief "moment of truce" before he must face the inevitable. "Most bargains are made with God and kept secret," Kübler-Ross writes. The fourth stage is depression. Now the patient faces the certainty that his life is ending, that everything and everyone he has lived for—not just physical health—will be lost. The patient now becomes silent and withdrawn, experiencing "preparatory grief" or mourning, according to Kübler-Ross. Soon he will want only significant others around; it is too late for new acquaintances. The fifth and final stage is that of acceptance, and is attainable only if the patient has had enough time and enough encouragement to work through the preceding stages. If not, the patient may still be fighting in denial, or will resign herself to death in thrashing, bitter resentment. By contrast, the patient in the stage of acceptance will be able to contemplate his coming end with a "certain degree of quiet expectation," be "almost void of feelings." "He may just hold our hand and ask us to sit in silence. . . . We may just let him know it is all right to say nothing." Kübler-Ross's point is that "the harder they struggle, the harder they deny, then the more difficult it is for them to reach the final stage with peace and dignity." Her writings reflect the optimistic words of ego psychologist Erik Erikson: "Healthy children will not fear life if their elders have integrity enough not to fear death."

What is important throughout all these stages, writes Kübler-Ross, is the persistence of hope. "If a patient stops expressing hope, it is usually a sign of imminent death." The merits of Kübler-Ross's work surely lie in her isolating definable stages in the process of dying and her encouragement of psychotherapists to work with the dying. However, it is not surprising, owing to her insistence on the patient's having hope and the therapist's encouraging some kind of hope for recovery or continued existence, that in the years after her best-seller she became a proponent of "after-life phenomena," in which she professed strong belief.

Death and "death and dying" were in vogue on American campuses in the 1970s: thanatology courses and even how-to manuals for self-burial were widespread. Ingmar Bergman's screenplay *Cries and Whispers*, a vivid portrayal of a young woman becoming a corpse, was published in the *New Yorker* in 1972. The film's unforgettable images of the heavy-bosomed Anna cradling the dying Agnes are imprinted on the imaginations of a whole generation of Americans and Europeans. The consciousness of death was further enhanced by global concern for nuclear destruction in the 1970s, renewed interest in the Holocaust in the 1980s, and the diffusion of the "new wars" like Granada, Panama, and the Persian Gulf. The American psychiatrist Robert J. Lifton has been most prolific in writing of these events (e.g., 1990).

Most recently, the AIDS epidemic has cast the shadow of death over the work of hospital psychiatrists, psychologists, and social workers. Psychotherapists from every discipline, including the new medical psychologists, are actively conducting individual and group psychotherapy with these terminally ill patients. Elisabeth Kübler-Ross and Irvin Yalom continue to be two of the most prolific contributers to and encouragers of psychotherapy for this population.

Charles Edward Robins

Decision Making

Decision theory has been aptly described as a complex body of knowledge developed by mathematicians, statisticians, economists, and psychologists attempting to prescribe how decisions should be made and to describe systematically the variables that affect decision making. The prescriptive or normative approach has a long history, dating back at least to the seventeenth- and eighteenth-century mathematicians who advised gamblers in the French court. The descriptive approach is of more recent origin, having developed within the framework of behavioral science as part of the effort to understand human behavior in general. Decision-making or choice behavior obviously plays a significant role in humans' attempts to deal with their environment. Thus it is important to learn how people function in this capacity and to explore ways to improve their decision capability.

One can approach the problem of filling out the matrix in several ways, each of which has both theoretical and empirical implications. First, one might try to arrive at independent scale values for both value and likelihood, then apply these measures either to deduce combination rules from choice behavior or to prescribe choice behavior with the aid of preselected theoretical combination rules.

Measurement

In the case of value, it has long been recognized that the subjective worth of an outcome to the decision maker (i.e., its utility), not its value on any objective scale, is the appropriate index for either descriptive or prescriptive purposes. Therefore, utility must be measured for each decision maker over each set of outcomes. Ways for doing this include all the standard scaling procedures from rank ordering to paired comparisons to direct magnitude estimation.

A second approach to the problem of measurement involves simultaneous scaling of utility and uncertainty—together with verification of composition rules—through analysis of choices among selected gambles. Choice situations are constructed such that a number of combinations of value and likelihood are sampled. Although the choice data themselves are only ordinal, proper design and analytic treatment permit inferences about scale properties and composition rules. One such procedure is known as conjoint measurement. Test conditions are constructed such that various orders of preference rule out specific decision axioms.

Subjectively Expected Utility

Conjoint and functional measurement, then, represent a direct attack upon the processes that underlie decisions (in contrast to working through independent measurement of value and likelihood). Let us consider now the principal models that have been proposed to represent these decision processes. By far the most pervasive notion is that DM attempts to maximize subjectively expected utility (SEU) in choice behavior (SEU model).

Most of the other descriptive models can be regarded as special cases of SEU or as applicable to very specific decision problems. H. A. Simon (1990), for example, has proposed that real-life decision makers do not try to optimize anything but rather accept the first alternative that exceeds some internal standard of acceptability (i.e., "satisfies"). The additive difference model seeks to account for intransivities in choice behavior. The minimax model suggests that the decision maker's only concern is avoiding the least desirable outcome (hence uncertainty considerations are irrelevant), while L. Hurwicz's model permits an indexing of the decision maker's degree of pessimism with respect to desirable or undesirable outcomes. None of these models has seriously challenged SEU as a general theory of human decision behavior.

Baye's Rule

The principal model of opinion (or subjective probability) revision is Baye's theorem, the mathematically optimum rule for modifying prior probabilities on the basis of observed data. A simple form of Baye's rule is

$$P(H/D) = \frac{P(D/H)\, P(H)}{P(D)}$$

where $P(H)$ is the prior probability of the hypothesis or outcome or interest, $P(D)$ is the probability of an observed diagnostic event or datum, $P(D/H)$ is the probability of the datum conditional upon the hypothesis, and $P(H/D)$ is the posterior probability of the hypothesis conditional upon the observed datum. Thus, the decision maker's prior opinion as to the truth of some hypothesis should be revised, upon the observation of an item of data, by multiplicative combination of that prior opinion with the diagnostic impact of the datum on that hypothesis. Although other forms of Baye's theorem are more congenial to research, the logic of the model is apparent in this simple version.

Various practical applications of the Bayesian information-processing model have been suggested and, in a few cases, put to some form of test. Medical diagnostic systems and military command-and-control systems are two examples. One popular suggestion (known as PIP, probabilistic information processing) is to limit human judgment to estimates of diagnostic impact, $P(D/H)$, and to leave the aggregation process to computing machines. This presumes that human conservatism is largely a matter of misaggregation—an as-yet-unproven position.

William C. Howell

Decision Theory in Social Psychology

Decision making is generally conceived to involve the processes of weighting positive and negative attitudes toward, or evaluations of, decision alternatives, and then selecting the most satisfying alternative. A specialized and highly mathematical subarea of psychology has developed, which focuses on these processes of weighting and selecting alternatives (Rapoport and Wallsten 1972).

Dissonance theory predicts that following a decision, the relative difference in the attractiveness of the chosen and unchosen alternatives will be increased. This phenomenon, known as postdecisional spreading of the alternatives, has been shown to be stronger when the alternatives are relatively similar in attractiveness before the decision than when they are dissimilar.

The process of selective exposure to information has been reconceptualized by J. S. Mills (1968) to include both predecisional and postdecisional infor-

mation-seeking behavior. In Mills's choice-certainty theory, it is assumed that when choosing to take an action, people want to be certain that the preferred action is better than the available alternative actions. If an individual is uncertain, she will seek information that supports the preferred alternative and avoid information likely to decrease her certainty that the preferred alternative is best.

As a result of a paper by M. Steiner (1970) and the popularity of attribution theory, there is a growing literature on the determinants of perceived choice, or perceived freedom. This research examines the characteristics of decisions that give rise to feelings or perceptions of high choice.

Jerald M. Jellison

Deculturation and Disinhibition

There are several aspects of behavior disorders, such as disturbances in cognitive processes, social adjustment, and emotional responses. However, the inability to control one's behavior is an outstanding sign of a severe behavior disorder. One can find in back wards of mental hospitals totally disinhibited individuals who practice sexual freedom and act out aggressive impulses.

A tree cannot go back and become a sapling, and a sapling cannot become a seed. An adult who regresses to an infantile mode of behavior does not become an infant but, rather, a severely disturbed adult. Mental disorder is often a failure to grow up.

Disinhibited behavior, similar to severe psychosis, can be found in animals and in human neonates. A retrospective look into the phylogenetic and ontogenetic aspects of human evolution discovers the roots of psychosis. Judging by comparative-evolutionary standards, psychotic behavior is regressive—that is, as "natural" as the behavior of animals—and resembles infantile modes of behavior. When all ego and superego inhibitions are removed, individuals do not exercise control over their bowels and bladder; they do not practice any sort of self-restraint; they bite when hungry; they rape or masturbate when sexually aroused; they attack when annoyed—in short, their "spontaneous" behavior knows no limits.

In times of crisis and despair, men and women have tried to find ways of escape from fears. The first road of escape was represented by Diogenes, the second by mystics; the first was carpe diem, the second, sub specie aeternitatis. The third and most frequent road has been violence, for violent behavior gives the illusion of power. It takes hundreds of skilled workers to build a bridge, but one deranged individual can throw a bomb and wreck it.

The weaker one is, the more secure one feels in a mob, no matter whether the mob is led by religious fanatics, chauvinistic demagogues, or radical zealots. It's easier to fight for peace, religion, social justice, and any other slogan than to work for them. Violence and destruction give one the illusion of power; creative efforts make one aware of the limitations of one's power. Roaming mobs, screaming senseless slogans, give one as much feeling of power as one experiences in a collective temper tantrum in a kindergarten.

It seems that the present-day social climate fosters sociopathic personality distortions and encourages antisocial moral values. The two extremes, the very wealthy and the very poor, have somehow managed to occupy the main streets of our cities and impose their ways of life. The upper classes and the so-called jet set practice their selfish ways of life, and the government stands behind them, ready to bail out a corrupt bank or corporation with the taxpayer's money. The poorest don't look for productive life, for the welfare system has turned many of them into passive receivers of public handouts. These two extremes seem to be the main resources of antisocial, parasitic, and criminal behavior.

Benjamin B. Wolman

Defenses and Defense Organization, Psychoanalytic Theory of

Defense operates unconsciously. The ego uses any of its normal functions, such as directing attention or the formation of identifications, in its defensive efforts. In addition, the ego employs specific techniques in its struggles against the emergence of the threatening wishes; these techniques are called the mechanisms of defense. Sigmund Freud (1914) wrote that the theory of defense "is the corner-stone on which the whole structure of psycho-analysis rests." He accorded defense much importance because conflict was, and is to this day, central to the psychoanalytic understanding of neuroses and psychoses.

In his paper on repression (1915), Freud declared that *"the essence of repression lies simply in turning something away, and keeping it at a distance, from the conscious"* [his italics]. He differentiated between primal repression, which denies access to consciousness to the representative of the instinct, and repression proper, which defends against derivatives of the repressed material or such trains of thought that have come into association with it. Thus, the term *repression proper* replaced *secondary defense.* He here took up "the mechanisms of repression," raising the question "whether perhaps each of the psychoneuroses is distinguished by a mechanism of repression peculiar to it" (154).

In 1936 Anna Freud published *The Ego and the Mechanisms of Defense*, a monumental work that synthesized what had gone before, integrated defense theory with the structural theory, and made important new contributions. She established the concept of mechanisms of defense, which her father had presaged; she took the position, which initially met with resistance, that the defenses are a legitimate object of analysis and not merely a hindrance to access to instinctual material.

From 1939 through 1964, the work of Heinz Hartmann (1939, 1964) and Hartmann, Kris, and Lowenstein (1964) provided the organizing influence on psychoanalytic theory. A crucial addition was the proposition that the ego is in part conflict-free. Some ego structures are autonomous from the start, while some conflict-born structures undergo a change in function and achieve secondary autonomy.

The Mechanisms of Defense

This list is arbitrary, because there is no official or universally accepted roster of defense mechanisms. Only the gist of their functioning is presented here.

Altruistic surrender. An individual barred from a

source of gratification (e.g., a desirable man or woman), by virtue of the reality situation or internal conflict, actively aids a rival toward success. He gains satisfaction through identification with the beneficiary of his altruism and from the sense of control in determining who wins the desired object.

Conversion. Fantasies, barred from consciousness, are expressed symbolically in sensory or motor symptoms. Conversion is to be distinguished from psychophysiologic reactions in that it has symbolic meaning, involves voluntary musculature, defends against anxiety, and does not lead to organic disease.

Displacement. One object, activity, or part of the body is substituted for another, less acceptable counterpart with which it is associatively connected. In this way, a fantasy may achieve a measure of expression and gratification. A common example is hostility to peers at school or work displaced from siblings.

Identification. Identification refers to a normal maturational process whereby an individual tries to become like another in one or several respects; it is essential to learning and the acquisition of interest and ideals. Identification often is combined with other mechanisms: In denial in fantasy, the subject often identifies with a figure with the desired attributes; in identification with the aggressor, the subject assumes the role of an object who has, or who she fears will, hurt her.

Introjection. Whereas identification has the meaning of being like an object in one or several respects, introjection involves a fantasy of taking in and containing an object. Being inhabited by a dybbuk is an example of an introjection that defends against the pain of conflict involved in the death of an important object.

Isolation. This mechanism involves the sequestering of memories and thoughts from associational connections. In this way, the traumatic impact or significance for conflict of the particular mental content is not perceived, and anxiety is thus avoided.

Isolation of affect. Here, the memory or thought, while conscious, is separated from its painful affect, which remains unconscious.

Projection. Disavowed impulses, feelings, or aspects of the self are attributed to an external object. For example, a man who is defending against

the impulse to be unfaithful may come to suspect his wife is cheating.

Rationalization. A reasonable explanation is given for some attitude, intended action, or completed behavior; this explanation, while reasonable, masks the true reason, which, if recognized, would produce anxiety or other painful affect.

Reaction formation. One of a pair of attitudes is exaggerated while its opposite is kept unconscious. For example, a father defending against erotic feelings for his teenage daughter may become severely critical of her because her room is messy or because of her study habits; thus, he proclaims, "It is not true I lust for my daughter; actually, I dislike her."

Regression. Defensive regression involves avoidance of anxiety at the phallic-oedipal level by regression to prephallic levels. Ego regression may also be employed defensively; for example, one may appear confused or incompetent in order to appease a feared adversary and thus avoid his vengeance. Progression may be used as a defense, as in the case of adolescents who act pointedly grown-up in order to mask infantile yearnings.

Repression. Dangerous or traumatic material consisting of impulses, memories, and fantasies is barred from consciousness. Primary repression is the initial exclusion of the material from consciousness, while repression proper keeps the repressed material and its derivatives unconscious.

Splitting. Positive images of the self in relationship with good objects are kept separate from negative images of the self in relationship with frustrating, despised objects. Such splitting is a defense that channels aggression in one direction, permitting the possibility of experiencing love in the other.

Sublimation. A forbidden instinctual trend becomes acceptable, even socially useful, by modification of its aim. For example, an individual with strong aggressive trends may become a valuable surgeon or military officer as interest in cutting or weaponry evolves into these professional pursuits.

Turning against the self. An impulse, generally of an aggressive nature, is turned against the self. For example, some individuals when rejected handle their rage by cutting or burning themselves.

Undoing. An action is performed in order to magically cancel a thought or action that has aroused guilt. Lady Macbeth's hand-washing is a classic example of undoing.

The defensive organization refers to the totality of the defensive processes, including the defense mechanisms, operating within the ego of a particular individual. The need for such a concept becomes apparent with the recognition that lists and definitions of defense mechanisms focus on restricted, atomized aspects of defensive functioning.

Psychoanalysts have tended to stress distinctions between defense mechanisms and other cognitive processes, although there have been acknowledgments of common genetic relationships. Referring to similar opinions of Freud and Anna Freud, Hartmann (1950) wrote that certain defense mechanisms "may be patterned after some autonomous [conflict-free] preliminary stages of ego functions and after processes characteristic of the ego apparatus." J. E. Gardner et al. (1960) have demonstrated experimentally that there are cognitive controls that regulate attention and memory in a manner similar to the defense mechanisms of isolation and repression.

Joseph W. Slap

Delay of Reinforcement

The term *delay of reinforcement* refers to one of the basic parameters of learning, the time between the occurrence of a to-be-learned response and the presentation of reward or punishment. The basic experimental question concerns the effect of this variable upon learning. In general, long delays of reinforcement interfere with acquisition. The early history of experimentation on the effect of this variable was one of an effort to bring procedures under better control in order to obtain an uncontaminated picture of the function involved. The point was to eliminate secondary reinforcement, the argument being that stimuli and situations associated with primary reinforcement could serve as immediate secondary reinforcers and thus extend the delay period over which learning could occur.

Gregory A. Kimble

Delirium

Delirium is a symptom complex of multiple etiology. Clouding of consciousness is the paramount feature, and disorientation, bewilderment, delusions, illusions, and hallucinations are common to all its forms. Maniacal excitement may occur. The electroencephalogram (EEG) is characteristically slowed except in atypical variants such as delirium tremens (DTs). The EEG abnormalities correlate with the severity of the delirium, the EEG being slowest when awareness is lowest. Delirium may be caused by endogenous factors, exogenous factors, or a combination of both.

In early stages of delirium, psychogenic depression or low intelligence is often misdiagnosed. As the disease progresses, there may be periods of coarse tremulous agitation, including asterixis and multifocal myoclonus, stereotyped movements, florid hallucinations, disorientation for place and person, memory defects, loss of contact with the environment, fragmentation of sleep pattern, delusional thinking, excretory incontinence, masturbation, obscenities, and incoherent cries and singing. In this stage, functional psychoses may be misdiagnosed. Lastly, seizures, weakness, stupor, and coma may occur and are often mistaken for gross structural brain disease.

Therapy

The treatment of delirium includes three primary considerations:

1. etiologic factors—this includes inquiry into all causative factors as well as secondary physiological and/or biochemical defects of diseases
2. supportive care of all major functions
3. sedation and restraint where specifically indicated

The patient should be in a hospital under constant surveillance. The treatment environment should provide constant, low-level stimuli. All medical and nursing procedures should include a careful, simple explanation to reduce the patient's feeling of helplessness, confusion, and terror, no matter how "out of contact" the patient appears to be. Visitors should be limited to a few close relatives and friends.

* * *

Delirium tremens (DTs) was first named and described by Thomas Sutton in 1813, although Hippocrates is reported to have said, "If the patient be in the prime of life, and . . . if from drinking he has trembling hands, it may be well to announce beforehand either delirium or convulsion." Sutton stressed the presence of "tremors," "rapid pulse," "picking at the bed clothes," and "heat of skin" in making the diagnosis.

Ronald William McNichol

Delusions

Delusions are one of the most characteristic symptoms of psychotic reactions. They represent a failure of reality testing and are defined as false beliefs that are impervious to reason. They are maintained with inflexible tenacity by those patients who are unable to discriminate between reality and fantasy. Organic brain syndromes may give rise to delusions.

Delusional ideation includes ideas of influence, ideas of reference, hypochondriacal ideas, fanaticisms, and animistic beliefs. They vary in intensity from mere prejudices and secret suspicions to apostolic ecstasies that may last from a few moments to a lifetime.

Persecutory delusions may vary from fleeting episodes of persecutory anxiety to gross delusions of persecution, relentlessly immune to logic and reason. The former occur in otherwise normal individuals under stressful circumstances. They suspect sinister forces at work and believe the circumstances have been hatched with cruel intent. After the crisis, although one would classify the belief as delusional, it may not interfere with one's subsequent adjustment. Because life is filled with stressful circumstances, many fall victim to this form of thinking, at least occasionally. Others resort to delusional thinking so frequently that their subsequent adjustment is maladaptive to an extreme degree.

Animism is a prime example of a cultural determinant that must be taken into account when considering delusions. Those who were raised in an environment that believes that animal spirits reside in trees, rivers, mountains, and the like, though suffering from false beliefs according to our view, would be coping adequately according to their own social climate.

Delusions of grandeur are thought to arise from a restitutive attempt to heal a narcissistic wound. Patients who feel profoundly inadequate, unloved, and without hope of winning recognition in the real world may overcompensate mentally by replacing such painful thoughts with grandiose ideas. Convictions that one is a president or emperor serve to soothe the battered ego of one who feels despairingly lost.

The fate of delusions vary with each patient. Although some "morbid" delusions may last for only a few seconds, representing a momentary regression in an otherwise healthy individual, most false beliefs remain throughout the course of an acute psychotic state, varying only in degree and intensity with the course of the illness itself.

Therapy

The treatment of delusions is encompassed by the treatment of the primary illness itself. In the case of organic brain syndromes, delusions are symptomatic of that state and will diminish and disappear as the treatment progresses in the same way that a fever, symptomatic of an infectious process, will diminish and disappear as the infection is cured.

Benjamin Blackman

Dementia in the Elderly

There are about seventy different dementias that can afflict both young and old, including the two most commonly occurring dementias in the elderly. Hence, we no longer speak globally or generically of senility or organic brain syndrome (OBS) but can define the complex nature of cognitive and behavioral manifestations that occur in the course of one of these dementias in considerably more precise etiologic terms. Primary degenerative dementia of the Alzheimer's type with or without depression, delusions, or delirium; multi-infarct dementia with or without these complications; or a combination of these two are the most commonly occurring dementias in the elderly (American Psychiatric Association

1987; Read 1991). A conservative estimate is that four million Americans suffer from Alzheimer's disease and related dementias (ADRD). In old age, increased age is a risk factor for developing dementia. Because the "oldest old," those eighty-five years old and over, are the fastest growing segment in our population, it is anticipated that the estimated prevalence of ADRD will rise to over 6 million by 2040. Estimates of incidence and prevalence depend very much on the source of the sample studied: (1) community, (2) hospital, (3) nursing home or other, (4) severity of the disorder, (5) diagnostic tools used clinically or in research protocols, and (6) availability and technique of postmortem studies (Braye 1993). These diseases are not only major public health problems but take an inordinate toll on the individual, family, and other caregivers, intrapsychically, socially, and financially, during their long and varied continuum—which can last up to twenty years (G. Cohen 1989; Goldstein 1989; Jarvik and Winograd 1988; Zarit 1989).

Evaluation, Assessment, Diagnosis

The National Institute of Neurological and Communication Disorders and Stroke (NINCDS) and the Alzheimer's Disease and Related Disorders Association (ADRDA) have established criteria by which the predictive value of probable Alzheimer's disease was 88% and possible Alzheimer's disease 78% (McKhann et al. 1984).

The Consortium to Establish a Registry for Alzheimer's Disease (CERAD) is a group of more than twenty cooperating centers, including the federally funded Alzheimer's Disease Research Centers (ADRCs), which coordinates procedures used for neuropsychological assessments, brain imaging studies, and neuropathologic evaluation to arrive at standardized methods of data collection. The long-range goal is to influence standards of clinical practice, as well as clinical and epidemiologic research.

Clinical evaluation of an elderly patient with cognitive, mood, thought, behavioral, or personality changes needs to be quite comprehensive and include physical, emotional, familial, neuropsychological, social, financial, and legal issues (M. Z. Goldstein 1989). The differential diagnosis includes "normal" aging, delirium, depression, schizophre-nia, endocrine disorders, infectious diseases, and organ system impairments. Neurological impairments, such as mass lesions, vascular lesions, and hydrocephalus, need to be ruled out, and disorders of movement, such as Huntington's chorea, Parkinson's disease, and progressive supranuclear palsy, need to be considered, as well as the primary dementias of Alzheimer's, Pick's, and the rapidly progressing Creutzfeldt-Jacob disease.

In order to arrive at a diagnosis of progressive dementia, the minimal laboratory workup needs to include a blood count; urine analysis; blood chemistries (including electrolytes); glucose, renal, liver, and thyroid function studies; B-12 and folate levels; a syphilis test; EKG; EEG; and CT scan of the head to rule out reversible conditions. Minimally, administration of a Mini-Mental State Examination (MMSE) and/or a clock-drawing test should be integrated in the interview (Tuokko et al. 1992). A score on the MMSE indicating dementia (below 24/30) with losses in scoring for orientation registration, attention, calculation, recall, language, and/or visuospatial orientation needs to be explored for other causes. Loss of points in scoring may reflect inability but also may point to depression with lack of interest (primary or secondary to the dementia), effort, and concentration; possible sensory deficits in hearing and/or vision; or mobility restrictions due to arthritis. Level of education is also an important factor to be considered in interpreting the score. The behavioral clinical presentations of cognitive deficits can be so varied and have been present but not recognized as pathological for such an extended period of time that inclusion of objective testing is of utmost importance at six-month intervals for diagnostic and prognostic reasons. The Hachinski test is useful in determining multi-infarct dementia with its stepwise course and possible measures, which can be taken to lengthening the intervals between declines by treating blood pressure, high cholesterol levels, and other risk factors for infarcts (Hachinski, Iliff, and Zika 1975). CT scans of the head can also help with the differential diagnosis by revealing the presence of cerebellar atrophy with ventruculomegaly, with or without lacunar infarcts or vice versa.

The patient history is, of course, of utmost diagnostic importance and needs to be supplemented with collateral information. Because of the complexity and varied clinical presentations of dementia, objective scales, which are valid, sensitive, and specific, should be used in the office or bedside along with other traditional diagnostic tools. Scales should include an assessment of activities of daily living, such as grooming, bathing, dressing, toileting, and feeding, as well as instrumental activities of daily living, such as shopping, telephoning, cooking, getting places, and money management.

Treatment and Approaches

Dementia is a devastating disease, and the patient and informal and formal support systems need extensive education and ongoing support in order to cope as effectively as possible and preserve quality of life for all concerned. While maximum autonomy and safety need to be preserved for the patient, in a predictable familiar environment with communications and activities appropriate to area and level of decline, family and caregivers need therapeutic and supportive interventions to sustain the long goodbye. The demented elderly need help to preserve self-respect and self-esteem in an environment that prevents abuse, neglect, and exploitation and that provides a supportive community for the caregivers in the family, respite, or long-term care setting (M. Z. Goldstein 1993a, 1993b).

Marion Zucker Goldstein

Density and Crowding

Problems introduced by increased population growth; urban population concentrations; and requirements for planning our living, working, and recreation facilities with increasingly limited resources have stimulated research on the effects of density and crowding on human behavior.

Effects of density on pathology as represented by mortality, suicide, disease, crime, delinquency, and illegitimacy are mediated by socioeconomic status (SES), education, and cultural variables. Among the population of Honolulu, controlling for SES and education exposed an effect due to persons per net acre, but no effect due to persons per room. In Hong Kong, neither measure of population density

related to pathology, and this result is attributed largely to strict social control among Chinese families. However, the overall effects of density on human behavior, and particularly on pathology, derived from ecological analysis require many qualifications to avoid such inconsistencies, which may be attributed to the insensitivity of physical measures of density at this level of analysis to many social structural variables.

The effects of alterations in density on cognitive, emotional, and attitude changes have been studied in natural settings and laboratories. Natural settings maintain the integrity of the setting and minimize interference with behavior. Direct and unobtrusive observation is used, sometimes over relatively long periods of time. Uncontrolled correlates of density are not easily separated in the analysis of effects found in natural settings.

When people are strongly task oriented, variations in social or spatial density account for very little variation in performance, unless densities are sufficient to limit physical movement. High density has no direct effects on the performance of cognitive and perceptual tasks, especially over periods as short as 4 hours. Even for periods up to 12 weeks, performance on cognitive tasks in an academic program is unrelated to variations in density.

Daniel H. Carson

Depersonalization

The experience of depersonalization alienates the observing self from the experiencing self. Delusions of depersonalization result in a perception that major changes have taken place within oneself, so much so that the person believes he or she has lost vital organs or even the entire body.

The process of dehumanization is generally defined as one that produces a decreased awareness of the human attributes of others and a loss of humanity in interpersonal interactions. People stop perceiving others as having the same feelings, impulses, thoughts, and purposes in life that they do and thus psychologically eliminate any human qualities that these others might share with them.

A theoretical model has been offered for the

process by which conditions of deindividuation (initiating stimuli or events) create an experiential state of deindividuation and result in deindividuated behaviors that violate established norms of social appropriateness.

Philip G. Zimbardo
Christina Maslach

Depression: Psychotherapy

Treatment of severe psychotic depression usually requires hospitalization because of the danger of suicide, the inability of the patient to care for his needs alone, the disruption in family life created by the presence of the patient, and the need to regulate his antidepressant medication properly or to administer electroconvulsive therapy. Milder psychotic depressions do not require hospitalization and are treated in the office or outpatient clinic.

Many milder endogenous depressions do not appear psychotic in that these patients do not show a definite break with reality by having delusions, hallucinations, marked distortions of interpersonal relationships, or an inability to function in routine activities. Some of these cases, particularly of the endogenous depressive type, respond completely to antipsychotic drugs or to two or three electroconvulsive treatments. Supportive psychotherapy also helps these patients but, so far as is known, does not shorten the duration of a depression.

Depressive Neurosis

Psychotherapy of depressive neurosis contains the elements of supportive psychotherapy, which are directed toward building and maintaining the patient's self-esteem. But the focus of treatment is directed toward the alleged cause of the depression. Why the patient reacted to her loss with such intensity is a basic question. Answers to this involve the relationship of the lost object to the patient, its meaning for her not only in cognitive but also in feeling terms.

In all these cases, the internal conflict is largely conscious in the mind of the patient. He feels depressed and anxious. His sleep is broken, and he may have disturbing dreams. His appetite may be poor, or, less frequently, he may overeat. Tension marks his daytime as well, and he may use sedatives for sleep and alcohol to relax and elevate his flagging spirits. A wide variety of other somatic complaints appears as well.

But if the nature of the conflict is not entirely clear, or the relationship to a precipitating cause is absent or doubtful, then it is possible that the roots of the conflict date back to early childhood experiences. To uncover these long-repressed experiences requires deeper probing.

Depression Following Common Human Losses

There are a number of common human losses that may initiate depressive feelings for which psychotherapy is helpful. One of the most universal of these is the grief reaction. Following the death of a spouse, there are periods of grief, anxiety, restlessness, poor appetite and sleep, crying, and a wide variety of autonomic disturbances and somatic complaints.

The physician should be familiar with the various parameters of grief reaction and must be ready to counsel and assist the bereaved. She should be supportive, understanding, and reassuring, and should gently urge the patient to prepare for the future. The bereaved—for example, a widow with children and limited financial resources—may have many practical problems. Other persons may have to be called in to help her.

Depressive reactions are common in the elderly and vary from milder forms, lasting only a few days or weeks, to more severe psychotic or more protracted forms. Old age is a period of loss of physical vigor and stamina, of good health, and of relatives and friends, all of which contribute to social isolation and loneliness. Mandatory retirement and reduced income produce a loss of self-worth. The high suicide rate in the aged (nearly 30 percent of all suicides occur in persons over age 60) bears more heavily on men, who at age 70 or older show a fourfold greater suicide rate than do women.

Psychotherapy should be appropriate to the loss of function and its meaning for the patient. Its purpose is to assist the patient to avoid or minimize the unhealthy reactions and to accept the changes in life that the impairment imposes upon him. Former aspirations now are unachievable, and interpersonal relationships are disrupted. The individual is therefore encouraged to convert his lifestyle to one that permits him to live with the impairment, while maintaining a feeling of self-worth and acceptance by others.

Paul E. Huston

Depression: Somatic Therapies

An approximate specificity may be described between depressive syndromes and somatic therapies. Patients with milder major depression, dysthymia, and atypical (i.e., anxious) depression respond to specific serotonin reuptake inhibitors (SSRIs) and to monoamine oxidase inhibitors (MAOIs). Tricyclic antidepressants (TCAs) are most effective in nonbipolar, nonpsychotic depressions of moderate severity. The most severe depressions, including those with associated psychotic symptoms, respond best to electroconvulsive treatment (ECT) or to TCA-neuroleptic combinations. Bipolar depression may respond to lithium salts.

Tricyclic Antidepressants

The efficacy of tricyclic antidepressants (TCAs) in the treatment of acute depression and the prevention of relapse has been well demonstrated. Patients with acute unipolar depression of at least moderate intensity constitute the core group responding to these agents, with reported rates of improvement ranging from 65 to 90 percent. Response to TCAs is less clear at both extremes of the spectrum of severity, with bipolar depression, and with chronic depressions. Tricyclic antidepressants and doses are listed in table I. These drugs are of similar chemical structure. The dose range of these drugs is 150–300 mg daily, with the exception of nortriptyline and protriptyline, which are given in one-half and one-fifth of the usual dose respectively. Drug dosage is a critical variable in the clinical use of TCAs. Underdosing is the most common error, perhaps because of the difficulty many patients encounter in tolerating the side effects of the more sedating, hypotensive, and anticholinergic drugs of this group. A figure of 3.5 mg/kg has been suggested for drugs with a 150–300 mg range, yielding an average daily dose of well over 200 mg/d. Plasma drug levels may be helpful in allowing for variability in patients' ability to metabolize TCAs. With nortriptyline, a better drug response has been associated with plasma levels between 70 and 140 ng/ml; responsiveness is reduced both below and above this therapeutic window. Improvement with imipramine has been associated with blood levels of imipramine plus desipramine over 225 ng/ml.

TABLE 1

Tricyclic Antidepressants

	Range of Daily Dosage (mg)
amitriptyline	150–300
nortriptyline	75–150
protriptyline	30–60
imipramine	150–300
desipramine	150–300
chlorpramine	150–300
trimipramine	150–300
doxepin	150–300

Response to antidepressant drugs of all types is usually not seen until three or four weeks after the therapeutic dose is reached. There is little reason to continue TCAs alone beyond six weeks if response has not been forthcoming. At this point, the addition of an adjunctive agent such as lithium or triiodothyronine or an alternative antidepressant should be considered.

Drug side effects frequently present a limiting factor. A patient's inability to tolerate sedative, hypotensive, or other autonomic effects may interfere with the goal of achieving a satisfactory clinical response. While there is no difference in efficacy among the TCAs, reduced side effects and better understanding of the relationship between plasma level and patient response may render the secondary amines nortriptyline and desipramine the agents of choice.

Central nervous system side effects include sedation, induction of psychosis, confusional states, and tremor.

Peripheral anticholinergic effects include blurred vision, dry mouth, constipation, and urinary difficulties. Hypotension related to adrenergic blockade, heart rate increases with anticholinergic (antivagal) effects, and a quinidine-like effect consisting of antiarrhythmic actions at lower plasma levels with increasing degrees of conduction blockade at higher dose levels are seen. The secondary amine TCAs seem to be safer, as hypotensive and anticholinergic effects are less with these agents. Plasma-level monitoring may help in determining the lowest effective doses to use.

TCA overdose should be treated with caution. Attention to suicidal ideation and intent is important in prescribing, since a 10-day supply of medication at usual doses may be lethal. Symptoms of overdose include delirium, mydriasis, flushing, dry mucosae, decreased bowel and bladder activity, cardiac arrhythmia, seizure, and coma. Patients should be treated in an intensive setting with cardiac monitoring for a 24- to 48-hour period. Physostigmine 1–2 mg intravenously can produce dramatic, rapid reversal of central and peripheral anticholinergic toxicity with a duration of about two hours.

Monoamine Oxidase Inhibitors

While there is some overlap in the efficacy of MAOIs and TCAs, there are subpopulations of patients who seem to respond preferentially to MAOIs. Two diagnoses for which specific MAOI responsiveness has been suggested are atypical depression and dysthymia. Some patients with the diagnosis of major depression respond to MAOIs. Another use of MAOIs has been in patients with bipolar depression, in the hope—as yet unsubstantiated—that the tendency of TCAs to induce mania or rapid cycling in this patient might be avoided.

Greater awareness of the effective dose range of these compounds (see table 2) has contributed to their resurgence in clinical practice. It has been reported that 80% or greater inhibition of platelet monoamine oxidase is associated with a higher rate of response. As the measurement of platelet MAO inhibition is not generally available in routine clinical laboratories, the practical application has been an upward movement in the doses prescribed. The dose range of phenelzine is 60–90 mg daily, and of tranylcypromine 40–60 mg daily, in order to attain this level of MAO inhibition. There has been interest in more specific MAOIs, with preferential affinity

for one of several enzymatic subtypes. To date, the hopes for either reduced toxicity or enhanced clinical response have not been realized. Questions remain about efficacy and whether in vitro specificity is retained at the clinical doses required. Central nervous system side effects of MAOIs include insomnia, sedation, nervousness, and psychotoxicity. MAOIs may exacerbate symptoms of schizophrenia and induce mania or hypomania in bipolar patients. Hypotension is the most frequent side effect encountered in routine MAOI use. This may be a limiting factor in treatment. The risk of syncope, falls, and related injuries is a serious consideration.

TABLE 2

Monoamine Oxidase Inhibitors

Drug	Dose (mg / d)
isocarboxazid	40–60
phenelzine	45–90
tranylcypromine	30–60

Dry mouth, blurred vision, and constipation are seen with MAOIs. The mechanism of this is obscure. Anorgasmia, ejaculatory inhibition, paresthesia, and myoclonus are dose-related and reflect autonomic and peripheral nervous system toxicities.

Inhibition of monomine oxidase in the gut may expose patients to effects of dietary pressor amines with a risk of hypertensive crisis and rare cerebrovascular hemorrhage. With proper education, most patients are able to observe an MAOI diet, which reduces the risk of severe hypertensive crisis.

Food to be avoided include most forms of cheese, preserved meats and fish, liver, fava beans, brewer's yeast products (not baked goods), red wines, and dark beers. Important interactions with medications include all sympathomimetic amines (decongestants, appetite suppressants, stimulants) and meperidine. TCAs should be avoided in combination with MAOIs except with special experience and close monitoring. Symptoms of hypertensive crisis include pounding headache, sweating, pallor, and palpitations. Patients should be directed to the nearest medical setting for blood pressure monitoring and possible intervention. Dietary and medication precautions should be continued for two weeks after MAOIs are discontinued, as these are irreversible enzymatic inhibitors and the additional time is required for new enzyme synthesis. SSRIs and MAOIs are contraindicated in combination, as severe serotonin-mediated toxicity may result. A 5-week interval is recommended when switching from SSRIs to MAOI treatment.

Specific Serotonin Reuptake Inhibitors

Specific serotonin reuptake inhibitors (SSRIs) have been most widely tested in outpatient populations with a diagnosis of major depression of mild to moderate severity (dosages in table 3). In these patients, their efficacy is comparable to TCAs. The mechanism of action is thought to involve a specific alteration of serotonergic neurotransmission with little effect on acetylcholine, norepinephrine, or dopamine, as well as alteration of postsynaptic receptor sensitivity. Clinical experience suggests positive responses in patients with dysthymia and atypical depression as well. The advantages of this category include clinical benefit in some patients who fail to respond to TCAs, markedly reduced side effects, and minimal overdose toxicity. Side effects include nausea, nervousness, insomnia, mild sedation, and inhibition of orgasm. Fluoxetine seems to be the agent most likely to cause nervousness and insomnia. It is difficult to delineate clear-cut differences in therapeutic action between the members of this class at the present time; however, it is possible that these drugs are not entirely interchangeable. Because the percentage of patients responding is the same (though not necessarily the same patients), the safety and side effect advantage of SSRIs has led some clinicians to consider them the drugs of choice in the treatment of depressed outpatients.

TABLE 3
Specific Serotonin Reuptake Inhibitors (SSRIs)

Drug	Dose (mg / d)
fluoxetine	20–80
sertraline	50–200
paroxetine	10–50
fluvoxamine	100–300

Second-Generation Antidepressants

During the 1980s, a series of unrelated, nontricyclic, non-MAOI antidepressants were introduced (Table 4). These have been referred to as heterocyclic or second-generation antidepressants, although neither term is particularly informative.

TABLE 4
Second-Generation Antidepressants

Drug	Dose (mg)
amoxapine	150–300
maprotiline	75–225
trazodone	150–300
bupropion	200–450

Amoxapine is a demethylated derivative of the neuroleptic drug loxapine. The pharmacology, efficacy, and side effect profile of amoxapine is similar to the TCAs, with the addition of acute extrapyramidal effects. It appears to be no safer than TCAs in overdose.

Maprotiline is described as a tetracyclic antidepressant. The pharmacology is rather like that of desipramine, with specific effects on norepinephrine reuptake and postsynaptic receptors. Efficacy, side effects, and overdose lethality are quite similar to those of the TCAs.

Trazodone is structurally and pharmacologically distinct. A triazolopyridine, it may be viewed as a mixed serotonin agonist-antagonist. Side effects for trazodone are limited to sedation and occasional gastrointestinal discomfort. Priaprism is an infrequent side effect. Overdose lethality is low.

Bupropion is a novel antidepressant drug that has structural similarities to the psychomotor stimulants. The mechanism of action is thought to involve dopamine, setting it apart from SSRIs, TCAs, MAOIs, and other second-generation antidepressants. This drug has been as effective as TCAs in trials involving inpatient and outpatient groups with major depression. Clinical experience suggests that there are patients who respond to this agent after failing to improve with other drugs. Side effects are usually not problematic and are quite similar to those seen with fluoxetine—occasional nervousness, insomnia, headache, or nausea—although the drugs and mechanisms of action are dissimilar.

Lithium

Lithium salts are generally considered to be either second-line or adjunctive agents in the treatment of unipolar patients. Evidence for lithium's ability to prevent the recurrence of depression in the maintenance treatment of bipolar patients is clear. There is some support for the use of lithium as an acute antidepressant in bipolar patients, in maintenance treatment of recurrent unipolar depressions, and occasionally in the acute treatment of unipolar depression. There is little published work on the use of lithium in atypical depression or dysthymia. An area that has excited considerable interest in recent years is the addition of lithium to standard antidepressant treatment in patients who initially appear to be treatment-refractory. Patients responding have included a small number with psychotic symptoms, a group who may not respond well to TCAs alone. Lithium doses were in the 900–1200 mg daily range, with few additional side effects seen and no correlation between serum lithium levels and clinical response. It is not clear how long to continue combined treatment after a positive response; some patients maintained their improvement after the early discontinuation of lithium. In view of the low risk and the usual need for a four- to six-week trial when switching from one failed antidepressant treatment to another, an intervening two-week period of adjunctive lithium therapy seems a reasonable second step prior to initiating a new antidepressant in any patient not responding to the first drug selected.

Maintenance treatment for the prevention of recurrent depression as been described with lithium levels 0.5–0.8 mEq/1. Side effects include tremor, thirst, polyuria, and possibly some of the subtler central nervous system complaints, such as decreased concentration and memory. Suppression of thyroid function and occasional hypothyroidism are to be expected with chronic treatment. Lithium intoxication is the most severe problem to be encountered with the use of this agent. Symptoms are a combination of gastrointestinal and central nervous system toxicities: nausea, vomiting, diarrhea combined with coarse tremor, incoordination, dysarthria, or drowsiness. The serum lithium is usually above the range of 1.0–1.5 mEq/1. The diagnosis of lithium intoxication should be made clinically. Early recognition and discontinuation of lithium treatment leads to resolution of symptoms in a few days without sequelae.

Thyroid Potentiation

Thyroid potentiation with triiodothyronine has been found useful in converting TCA nonresponders to responders and in shortening the lag period for TCA response. This treatment is not dependent upon a diagnosis of frank or subclinical hypothyroidism. In euthyroid depressed patients, the dose range for antidepressant potentiation is usually 25 to 50 mcg triiodothyronine daily in the morning. Response may be seen within two weeks, and supplemental thyroid medication is usually discontinued after a month. Side effects may include sympathetic nervous system overactivity and cardiac arrhythmia.

Electroconvulsive Therapy

Electroconvulsive therapy (ECT) was first used by Ugo Cerletti in 1938. Severe depressions—including those in patients with psychotic symptoms or catatonia, acutely suicidal depressed patients, and patients failing to respond to drug treatment—constitute the main indication for ECT. ECT is generally not used for mild, atypical, or chronic depression. The response rate to ECT often exceeds 80%. The main drawbacks to the use of this treatment are availability and relapse. Relapse is a major issue in treatment of all patients with affective disorders. In a review of maintenance treatment in depression, it was shown that over 50% of treated patients suffer relapse within a few months without continuation of treatment. A similar number of patients experience relapse after a successful course of ECT. The clinician is left the choice of attempting maintenance treatment with a drug whose efficacy is uncertain or maintenance ECT.

The addition of barbiturate anesthesia and muscle relaxation agents 20 years ago reduced the subjective distress and physical trauma associated with older convulsive techniques. Recent modifications include unilateral ECT treatments, reduction in the electrical stimulus used, close physiological monitoring, and electroencephalographic monitoring during treatments.

The main side effect of ECT is the acute confusional state, which is related to the number of treatments, age, and whether the stimulus is administered to the dominant cerebral hemisphere. Memory dysfunction is minimal with unilateral, nondominant hemisphere ECT. With bilateral treatments, the severity of anterograde amnesia usually increases with the number of treatments. Memory function is typically recovered one to two months after the cessation of ECT, although recall for events occurring during the amnestic period is lost. Delirium during the immediate post-ECT, postanesthesia recovery period may be encountered. This typically resolves spontaneously. Transient elevation in blood pressure and cardiac arrhythmias are usually managed quite easily by anesthesia personnel. Fatalities with ECT are rare. L. B. Kalinowsky (1975) cited a series greater than 100,000 treatments with a death rate of 0.003% despite the fact that many patients were elderly with concomitant cardiovascular and other medical problems.

Steven Zavodnick

Depression: Wolman's View

Depression can be defined as a feeling of helplessness and blaming oneself for being helpless. Depression is self-directed hatred usually associated with hatred directed toward others. By definition depression is endogenous, for it comes from within, and as such it is clearly distinct from emotional exogenous reactions to misfortunes.

Depression can occur in a variety of situations, and it is not limited to the classic syndrome of unipolar depressive or bipolar manic-depressive psychosis. People afflicted by a physical disease can feel pain, loneliness, and unhappiness without hating themselves. However, if they blame themselves, they are depressed.

One may relate Freudian concepts of cathexis to observational categories of overt behavior and distinguish four categories of human relations: hostile (H), instrumental (I), mutual (M), and vectorial (V). A hostile attitude is destructive. An instrumental attitude aims at using others for one's own benefit: infants are takers; their attitudes are instrumental. Through growth and learning they will acquire the mutual attitude of giving and taking: in mature sex and marriage, one is usually mutual. When one becomes more mature, one may be capable of giving without taking: mature parents display a vectorial attitude to their children.

Observing mental patients in hospitals or in private offices, one can't help noticing three distinct patterns of behavior. Some patients are hyperinstrumental, loving only themselves and exploiting others. At the other extreme are the hypervectorials, who love others too much at their own expense. The third category are the dysmutuals, who swing from one extreme to another. The hyperinstrumental sociopaths are extremely selfish, the hypervectorial schizophrenics are too unselfish, and the dysmutual manic-depressives go from one extreme to the other. The hypervectorial schizoprhenics love others too much; thus, no love is left for themselves, and they often hate themselves for not loving enough. When their defense mechanisms fail, they may break loose in catatonic fury. The dysmutual depressives swing from being very friendly to being very hostile.

One may distinguish five levels of severity of mental disorder: neurosis, character neurosis, latent psychosis, manifest psychosis, and total collapse. Dysmutual neurotics are usually absentminded, forgetful, and careless. In elated moods, they are hyperactive and tend to confuse wish and reality. In depressed moods, they are sluggish, passive, apathetic, and procrastinating.

One may distinguish three clinical syndromes: depressive, dissociative, and conversion (i.e., conversion-hysteria) reaction. Depressive neurosis is a state of continuous anxiety, inferiority feeling, accident-proneness, and self-defeating behavior. The dissociative syndrome is associated with memory losses, fugue states, depersonalization, and loss of identity. Hysterical symptoms imitate every possible physical disease.

Benjamin B. Wolman

Depression and Mania: Psychoanalytic Theories

In 1911, Karl Abraham drew a parallel between the way anxiety is related to fear and the way depression is related to grief. By this, he meant that depression is a consequence of an unconsciously experienced loss, and grief a reaction to a known loss.

Sigmund Freud (1917), starting from Abraham's comparison of mourning and melancholia and the inference that the subject's sadistic attitudes toward the lost object are turned upon the ego, adds a crucial clinical observation, that is, that the self-reproaches in depression seem to apply to the lost object.

Bertram D. Lewin's clinical studies of hypomania led him to the assumption that elation serves as a screen defense (denial) against threatening infantile aspects of reality, with their accompanying affects of anxiety and depression. Elation would thus repeat the oral triad of wishes: the wish to eat, the wish to be eaten, and the wish to sleep (die).

Abraham (1916) observes that depressively predisposed people are enormously dependent on oral gratification; that is, they are orally fixated. Noting the symptoms of refusal of food and fear of starvation, he concludes that in the manic-depressive psychoses the libido has regressed to the oral, cannibalistic stage, in contrast to the sadistic desires of the obsessional neurotic, in whom the dominant pleasure is to retain and master his objects.

The present-day theory of depression is based on the notion that the superego punishes the subject for the oral-sadistic cannibalistic incorporation of the object. This explanation is not Freud's but is derived from a single textual reference in *Mourning and Melancholia* by Abraham and later by Otto Fenichel.

Abraham (1924) adds further clinical observations bolstering the unconscious equation by depressed patients of the lost object with feces. The depressed patient's associations demonstrate the experience of object loss as a defecation, that is, anal expulsion and murder.

Sado Rado (1926) published a paper on drug addiction in which he suggests that the ecstasy of drug-induced states is a replication of the experience of "fusing with the mother that takes place during the nursing at the breast," and is like an "alimentary orgasm." In 1928, comparing depressive patients to drug addicts, Rado comments on their constant and overwhelming craving for narcissistic gratification. Maintenance of self-esteem in such patients depends on a constant supply of love rather than on genuine accomplishment.

G. Gero (1936) found in the detailed study of two depressed patients that there is a fixation to infantile narcissistic cravings for love. He emphasizes the consequences of the introjection of ambivalently regarded objects with all the corresponding oral and anal sadistic fantasies and the resulting guilt and lowering of self-esteem.

Melanie Klein (1935) conceives of the "depressive position" as a crucial milestone in infant development. Her theory of subsequent depressive illness is based on the failure to achieve and resolve the infantile depressive position and thus form intrapsychic "whole objects" with good and bad qualities whose threatened loss would produce anxiety and whose loss would be mourned.

Otto Fenichel (1945) stresses both libidinal and ego regression in the genesis of depressive illness. Not only is there a regression to the oral libidinal phase, with its intensified need for oral supplies, but the ego regression to a primal narcissistic state is characterized by the incapacity to distinguish the self from the nonself.

E. Jacobson (1953, 1971) defines narcissistic identification as partial or total fusion of self and object representations in the systems ego. Jacobson assumes that the regressive movement, arising from a failure of narcissistic supplies and a drop in self-esteem, brings about a blurring and fusion of self and object representations.

E. Bibring (1953) conceives of depression as an intrasystemic phenomenon—as a "basic affective state of the ego." He saw inhibition of the ego as a ubiquitous characteristic of the depressive state. Regression in depression, for Bibring, is not simply to an oral fixation point but is primarily an ego regression to an ego state, that is, it is a reactivation of a primal state.

The work of René A. Spitz (1936) tends to support Bibring's formulation. This too-early self-experience of the infantile ego's helplessness is the most frequent factor predisposing to depression.

David Rapaport (1959) points out that Bibring's comparison of boredom and depression alerts us to the fact that in boredom there is also a lack of supplies. Fenichel (1934) used the term "stimulus hunger" to characterize this state.

J. Sandler and his associates (1960, 1960, 1963, 1965) and David L. Rubinfine (1968) have addressed themselves to different aspects of this problem. Sandler, in his paper *The Background of Safety* (1960), suggests that there is an affective state of well-being that seems to subsume a number of concepts, including self-esteem. He terms this affective state "feelings of safety."

Rubinfine (1968), reasoning somewhat along the same lines, conceptualized this "ideal" state of well-being as a state of narcissistic unity with the mother, and theorized that a premature disruption of this state results in a too-early awareness in the infant of its separateness from the mother, threatening the investment of both mother and self with aggression.

John Bowlby (1960, 1969, 1973) assumes a given inborn set of mechanisms in the infant, which result in attachment behavior when the mother is available. If the mother becomes unavailable, "protest" behavior and separation anxiety result. He postulates that mourning occurs in infants, and that later depressive illnesses are a consequence of such pathological mourning reactions. Classical psychoanalytic theory (A. Freud 1960) assumes that true mourning cannot occur before clear-cut distinction between self and nonself is established and a stage of object constancy achieved. This position seems to gain support from the work of the Robertsons (1971).

Summary

Freud's theory of depression has been criticized because this theory is linked so inextricably to the theory of narcissism, which was devised before the development of the structural viewpoint, and has never been integrated with it or with the concept of the undifferentiated phase (Hartmann et al. 1964). The concept of ego was not defined in the framework of the paper on narcissism; it was regarded there as the original reservoir of libido, and is often used interchangeably with "self."

David L. Rubinfine

Deutsch, Helene (1884–1982)

Helene Deutsch's contributions to psychoanalysis were directed toward two main areas; (1) the clinical and theoretical aspects of the science and (2) the organization of training and of educational facilities. Deutsch was the first psychoanalyst who constructed a comprehensive psychology of the life cycle of women.

Marie H. Briehl

Developmental Psychology

Research in developmental psychology attempts to elucidate the processes underlying the transformation of sperm and egg united at conception into an individual with a mind capable of the perceptual, emotional, social, language, and cognitive capacities that we take for granted as adults. While some of these capacities will be discussed individually below, it is recognized that the child develops as a whole organism within whom each of these identified parts interacts and influences all of the others throughout the developmental process.

There are a number of conceptual questions that unite the field of developmental psychology, regardless of the subdiscipline involved (e.g., cognitive development, social development). For example, is development influenced more by nature or nurture? Few developmentalists adhere to either extreme position, but questions continually arise as to how heredity and environment contribute to development, and most importantly, how these two forces interact. A second question relates to whether the developmental progression is best characterized as discrete or continuous. While some developmental differences appear to progress through qualitative steps, others would appear to reflect smooth quantitative transitions.

Research techniques ranging from unobtrusive naturalistic observations to tightly controlled experiments have been used to gain insight into these and many other issues. The central goal of developmental research is to assess the processes underlying the changes we observe as the child grows older. Therefore, research relies heavily upon both cross-sectional designs (which gather observations from different samples of children at multiple developmental levels taken at one point in time) and longitudinal designs (which follow a single group of individuals across several developmental levels). Each method has its advantages and disadvantages. Multiple methods are often employed to address questions concerning age-related change because they offer the opportunity for converging evidence.

Perception

While infants were formerly considered perceptually deficient, it is now generally recognized that they possess remarkable perceptual powers, though all of these processes are not mature until near the end of the second year. Neonates appear to be capable of distinguishing light from dark and tracking moving objects that are in focus. Newborns also show a preference for patterned objects over uniform ones. Research has shown that color vision and depth perception are available 2 to 3 months after birth, and complex patterns are favored over simpler ones at about the same age. Additionally, infants demonstrate preferences for pictures of human faces over pictures with jumbled facial features.

Auditory perception has been measured prenatally, and is more advanced than visual perception at birth. Neonates have the ability to discriminate human voices from other sounds. Within a few days of birth, infants can tell their own mother's voice from that of a stranger.

Intermodal perception between visual and auditory stimuli has also been observed soon after birth. Neonates have the capability of localizing a sound, and by 4 months a general coordination between sight and sound is in place.

Less is known about newborns' senses of taste and smell. Within a few hours of birth, neonates can differentiate between sweet, sour, and bitter tastes but prefer sweet. Within the first week of life children are capable of distinguishing between the smell of their mother and that of a stranger. While great

advancements in the perceptual systems are made in the first 2 years, infants are perceptually quite complex even at birth.

Language Development

Language learning involves four distinct aspects: phonology (the ways in which sounds are combined in a language), semantics (the meaning of words), syntax (the complex rule system that governs how sentences are constructed), and pragmatics (social guidelines involving appropriate language use). Infants are very sensitive to the sounds of speech and are able to make fine discriminations between phonemes (basic sound units of speech). The sequence of language acquisition proceeds very quickly and in an orderly progression. The infant's vocal communication advances from crying in the newborn to cooing in the 6- to 8-week-old, and babbling in the 3- to 6-month-old. Infants are likely to utter their first word between 12 and 20 months of age, although new words are acquired slowly during this early stage of speech. However, at approximately 18 months, infants exhibit a vocabulary spurt, and during this period they may learn as many as 20 words per week! Throughout the period of language acquisition, it is important to note that children's receptive language is often more advanced than their productive language. At approximately 2 years of age, children will begin to combine words into two-word utterances. Throughout the preschool period, children will begin to learn new words and incorporate those words into increasingly complex sentences. By the time children reach 5 years of age, they have mastered most of the complexities of their native language.

Several theories have been advanced to explain children's acquisition of language; however, most language researchers assume that an interaction between environmental and biological factors contributes to language development. The interactionist view suggests that humans may have certain cognitive abilities that aid the rapid acquisition of language, even though environmental contributions (e.g., quality of a parent's speech to a child) and biological predispositions to learn language are important.

Cognitive Development

The study of cognitive development is probably most closely associated with the work of Jean Piaget. His constructivist view of cognitive development focuses on the increasingly sophisticated mental structures children acquire through interaction with the environment. At each level of development, these mental structures both grow out of preceding structures and provide the foundations for more advanced structures, which follow.

Central to Piaget's theory are the processes of assimilation and accommodation as they relate to the mechanism of development, equilibration. Assimilation refers to the child's ability to integrate novel objects and situations into existing schemes or representations. Accommodation, on the other hand, refers to the adaptation of schemes to better fit the circumstances encountered by the child. This back-and-forth cycle of assimilation and accommodation results in more and more stable mental states. This tendency toward stability or equilibration drives advancement.

Piaget organized cognitive development into four sequential stages with rough age norms. The sensory-motor period, which lasts from approximately birth to age 2, is characterized by schemes that are tied to direct actions and perceptions. The preoperational period is marked by the attainment of symbolic reasoning, where symbols, such as words, can represent other entities. This period extends to about age 6. From approximately age 6 to 11, children make great strides in logical thought, yet thinking is still tied to concrete objects. By about age 12, cognitive development has reached Piaget's final stage: formal operations. With the attainment of formal operational thought, reflective, abstract thinking becomes possible, and operations themselves become objects of thought.

Within the last decade, however, researchers have suggested that knowledge plays a larger role than Piaget recognized. Increasing evidence suggests that children possess theories within specific domains of inquiry, which organize their knowledge. As children's theories, or casual-explanatory frameworks, are restructured through knowledge acquisition, logical reasoning abilities become more sophisticated, but only within specific domains. The infer-ences children make about objects, the metaphors they understand, and the category distinctions they make can all be understood in terms of their naive theories. This shift in emphasis from structure to content has modified the view that children possess general abilities in favor of one in which children are seen as having mental structures that are more specific to particular cognitive domains.

To a lesser extent, other investigators have focused on the contributions of working memory, attention, and speed of processing on children's cognitive advancement in ways similar to adult information-processing theorists. This avenue of exploration focuses more heavily on the quantitative changes seen in childhood.

Moral Development

Research concerning children's morality has centered around three major theoretical viewpoints. Social learning theory, proposed by Albert Bandura, posits that children's moral behavior is shaped by the behaviors adults model, especially parents. There is evidence to suggest that parents who demonstrate aggressive behaviors are more likely to have children who behave aggressively. Similarly, parents who display helping behaviors tend to have children who exhibit helping behaviors as well. This theory has been criticized, however, because it fails to account for children's reasoning about moral issues.

Cognitive theories of morality, like that of L. Kohlberg (1984), stress invariantly ordered, hierarchical stages of morality. In this scheme, differences in reasoning about the perspectives, needs, and feelings of others define the different developmental stages. Kohlberg's research has been faulted for its potential cultural and gender biases.

In addressing the issue of sex differences between male and female moral levels of development, C. Gilligan (1982) has argued that females are socialized in ways that emphasize relationships and caring over justice. Morality based on different ethical standards, according to Gilligan, are not comparable within the same moral framework. She proposed that different moral schemes be used for males and females. Data in support of her conclusions, however, have been equivocal. Cognitive explanations of moral development have met with criticism because of the difficulty linking moral reasoning to moral behavior.

J. C. Turiel's view of morality attempts to describe moral behavior in terms of interactions between children's knowledge in three domains: moral, societal, and psychological. These distinctions appear to provide more accurate links between behavior and thought.

Emotional Development

Emotions are multifaceted behaviors, comprised of physiological, expressive, and experiential components. Emotions are often classified into two categories. Basic emotions (e.g., anger, joy, fear) are those emotions that appear relatively early in life and are thought to have some biological basis. Complex (or social) emotions (e.g., guilt, pride) require more sophisticated cognitive abilities, such as an understanding of self and an appreciation of the perspective of others. Although the precise age at which infants are capable of expressing certain emotions is still in dispute, most researchers agree that the basic emotions are evident within the first year of life. It is not until the second year of life that children begin to display complex emotions. Emotional development continues throughout childhood, as advances in cognitive development continue.

Theories of emotional development often disagree on the extent to which they emphasize the biological and universal aspects of emotions or the cognitive construction and social acquisition of emotions. These views are not necessarily incompatible, and current theories are attempting to integrate these ideas. Most current theories of emotional development agree that emotions are integral to both intrapersonal functioning and interpersonal relations and are, therefore, crucial to the organization of adaptive human behavior.

While it is widely assumed that infants have access to the full range of emotions, individual differences in temperament will determine the manner in which emotions are expressed. Temperament refers to relatively stable, constitutionally based characteristics, which are evident early in life. Although there is disagreement regarding which specific characteristics should be considered temperamental, important

dimensions include emotionality, self-regulation, activity level, and sociability.

Social Development

Attachment, the relationship between an infant and his or her caregiver(s), is often thought to be the most important relationship in an individual's life. The attachment relationship is formed gradually, during the course of the first year of life. In the first months of life, young infants show evidence of indiscriminate attachments; they are likely to greet people with social signals such as crying and smiling. However, by 7 or 8 months of age the infant becomes more selective and will form specific attachments, most often to the primary caregiver(s). Several behaviors indicate the formation of specific attachments, including stranger anxiety (distress responses to unfamiliar people) and separation anxiety (distress over separation from the primary caregiver).

Much of current research on attachment draws on the ethological theory of John Bowlby, who believed that attachment serves an adaptive function in the evolutionary history of the human species. M. D. S. Ainsworth (1978) extended Bowlby's ethological theory with the development of the Strange Situation, a laboratory procedure that assesses the quality of the attachment relationship. Research has documented an association between characteristics of the caregiver (e.g., sensitivity) and the quality of the attachment relationship. The attachment relationship may have long-lasting implications for development. For example, a secure attachment in infancy, which is considered to be most optimal, is correlated with social competence in the preschool years.

Other issues related to children's social development include the influence of parenting styles. Styles of parenting are often described with regard to two attributes: the amount of warmth or nurturance parents display toward their children and the amount of control parents attempt to exert over their children's behavior. Parenting styles are associated with many aspects of children's development. Children of authoritative parents (parents who set limits on behavior, yet display substantial warmth) are likely to be independent, achievement oriented, and cooperative with adults and have good relations with peers. Children of authoritarian parents (those who

TABLE 1

Erikson's Eight Psychosocial Phases

	A Psychosocial Crises	B Radius of Significant Relations	C Related Elements of Social Order	D Psychosocial Modalities	E Psychosexual Stages	F Basic Virtues
I	Trust vs. mistrust	Maternal person	Cosmic order	To get To give in return	Oral-respiratory sensory-kinesthetic (incorporative modes)	Drive and hope
II	Autonomy vs. shame, doubt	Parental persons	"Law and Order"	To hold (on) To let (go)	Anal-urethral, muscular (retentive-eliminative)	Self-control and willpower
III	Initiative vs. guilt	Basic family	Ideal prototypes	To make (=going after) To "make like" (=playing)	Infantile-genital, locomotor (intrusive, inclusive)	Direction and purpose
IV	Industry vs. inferiority	"Neighborhood," school	Technological elements	To make things (=completing) To make things together	"Latency"	Method and competence
V	Identity and repudiation vs. identity diffusion	Peer groups and outgroups; models of leadership	Ideological perspectives	To be oneself (or not to be) To share being oneself	Puberty	Devotion and fidelity
VI	Intimacy and solidarity vs. isolation	Partners in friendship, sex, competition, cooperation	Patterns of cooperation and competition	To lose and find oneself in another	Genitality	Affiliation and love
VII	Generativity vs. self-absorption	Divided labor and shared household	Currents of education and tradition	To make be To take care of		Production and care
VIII	Integrity vs. despair	"Mankind," "my kind"	Wisdom	To be, through having been To face not being		Renunciation and wisdom

Source: Reprinted from *Identity and the Life Cycle* by Erik H. Erikson. By permission of W. W. Norton & Company, Inc. Copyright © 1959 by International Universities Press, Inc.

are highly controlling, but provide little warmth), children of permissive parents (those who exert little control, yet demonstrate considerable warmth), and children of uninvolved parents (those who are emotionally distant and indifferent to their child) have less optimal outcomes.

The vast majority of research on children's social development has focused on the mother-child relationship. This focus is probably the result of historical theories, which assumed the mother played the most significant of other relationships, both within and outside the family. For example, it is now widely accepted that fathers are a different, yet equally important, source of influence on child development. Similarly, children's friends and peers play a unique role in children's development. Only when interacting with their peers can children experience truly reciprocal relationships.

Laura Butkovsky
Geoffrey F. W. Turner
David S. Palermo

Developmental Tasks, Phase-Specific

Erikson

Erik Erikson described a sequence of eight psychosocial phases (table 1) that span the whole life cycle. These phases are correlated with the stages of psychosexual development described by Sigmund Freud (1905). Each phase is characterized by a specific development task. These tasks are described in terms of the extreme successful and unsuccessful solutions of the phase-specific developmental task.

Failure in one developmental phase interferes with successful resolution in subsequent phases. Likewise, an earlier failure can, at times, be partially compensated for through success in a subsequent phase.

Mahler

Margaret S. Mahler has written about the separation-individuation phase, which follows what she labels the "symbiotic phase," the period from about the 4th or 5th month of life to the 30th to 36th month. The phase-specific task is the child's psychological separation and increasing physical independence from her mother, and corresponds in part to the phases of basic trust versus basic mistrust, autonomy versus shame and doubt, and initiative versus guilt, as described by Erik Erikson.

Like all other developmental phases, the phase of separation-individuation is never complete but "reverberates throughout the life cycle" and may be reactivated at a later time (Mahler 1972, 333).

Blos

Peter Blos (1967) has conceptualized the second individuation stage of adolescence. He defines the developmental task as a restructuralization of the ego resulting from the disengagement of libidinal and aggressive cathexes from the internalized infantile love and hate objects.

Eugene E. Trunnell

Deviational Children and Their Treatment

With regard to deviational children, three types of problems are in the foreground in varying proportions: problems of social-emotional adaptation; problems of manageability; and neurotic symptoms. In some instances, poor social-emotional adaptation is evinced by indiscriminate outgoingness befitting a much younger child; in others, by lack of relationships. The latter at times may even be accompanied by paranoid trends.

"Neurotic" symptomatology is characterized by the overload of tension and anxiety expressed diffusely in driven restlessness, sleeplessness, and/or inability to concentrate. Due to continuing hypersensitivity in these spheres, often there are still fears connected with sound and light phenomena (also the hark response; P. Greenacre 1941). In others, anxiety in relation to changes dominates the picture: changes in the environment, in routines, and fear of new things and new people.

The neurotic-like symptomatology is often fused or interwoven with neurotic manifestations, and panic anxiety has fused with or intensified conflict anxiety.

Annemarie P. Weil (1973) conceptualized the disturbance in deviational children in metapsychological terms and stated that the most prominent features are intersystemic and intrasystemic imbalances:

- imbalance between ego and drives
- imbalance within the ego (this relates to the often unusually high intelligence and apparatus skills in contrast to the poor development of ego functioning)
- imbalance between libido and aggression with aggression prevailing
- imbalance between nonhostile and hostile aggression

The fundamental therapeutic approach can be characterized by diminishing imbalances, that is, helping integration by furthering ego development, promoting structure formation, and helping to resolve the intertwined neurotic symptomatology, thus freeing the ego to develop its fullest potential.

The therapy of such children begins with teaching parents to understand and follow their somewhat imbalanced infant's needs, and to help with the poorly integrated facets of their functioning—for example, between excitability and tension discharge—so that a fairly satisfactory symbiotic phase can take place.

Some deviational children have relatively good access to past events (Mahler and Gosliner 1955), but even in the light of good memory, reconstruction of the past is generally most fruitful and effective when it is implemented in association with neurotic and basic transference material. As in the case of neurotic children, interpretations may also relate to the early and told past (told to the child and to the analyst by the parents).

Annemarie P. Weil

Dewey, John (1859–1952)

John Dewey outlined his theory of functional psychology in 1896. Dewey rejected the idea of separation of nature and nuture variables and stressed the organism-environment interaction.

Richard M. Lerner

The Diagnostic and Statistical Manual of Mental Disorders, Fourth Edition

DSM-IV (American Psychiatric Press, 1994) is the official nomenclature of mental disorders developed by the American Psychiatric Association. It includes a set of diagnostic criteria and a descriptive text for each disorder. The texts include the following headings: diagnostic features; associated features and disorders; specific age, cultural, or gender-related features; prevalence and incidence; course; complications; familial pattern; and differential diagnosis. The main sections of DSM-IV are: disorders usually first diagnosed in infancy, childhood, or adolescence; delirium, dementia, amnesiac, and other cognitive disorders; mental disorders due to a general medical condition; substance-related disorders; schizophrenia and other psychotic disorders; mood disorders; anxiety disorders; somatoform disorders; factitious disorders; dissociative disorders; sexual and gender identity disorders; eating disorders; sleep disorders; impulse control disorders not elsewhere classified; adjustment disorders; personality disor-

ders; and other conditions that may be a focus of clinical attention.

DSM-IV is intended primarily for clinical, research, and educational purposes, but it is also used in forensic and disability deliberations to document the need for insurance reimbursements and for statistical data collections. It is used by a wide range of individuals (including psychiatrists, other physicians, psychologists, nurses, social workers, rehabilitation therapists, trainees, students, administrators, record room librarians, insurance companies, disability boards, and lawyers); in a wide range of settings (including educational, inpatient and outpatient hospitals, clinics, private practice, primary care, and public health).

Historically, the Diagnostic and Statistical Manuals were developed because of a need for a consistent system for recording and reporting statistical and epidemiological data. DSM-I was published in 1952, in coordination with the sixth edition of the *International Classification of Diseases* (ICD-6) and included 106 categories. DSM-II, published in 1968 in correlation with the release of ICD-8, was similar in format to DSM-I but included 182 categories.

DSM-III was published in 1980 in coordination with ICD-9. DSM-III instituted several major innovations in methods for classifying the mental disorders. An atheoretical view of the etiology of mental disorders was presented, allowing clinicians of varying theoretical orientation to use the manual and communicate with one another. Explicit diagnostic criteria were included to guide clinicians, improve diagnostic reliability, and facilitate the integration of findings for research and clinical interface. A multiaxial system with five axes was introduced in order to help clinicians plan and predict the outcome of treatment and to ensure thorough clinical assessment. Axis I was for noting most clinical syndromes, Axis II for personality and specific developmental disorders, Axis III for physical disorders and conditions, Axis IV for severity of psychosocial stressors, and Axis V for highest level of adaptive functioning, past year. DSM-III listed 265 categories of mental disorders.

A revision of DSM-III, known as DSM-III-R, was published in 1987 in order to resolve a number of technical inconsistencies in DSM-III. The major innovations of DSM-III were maintained, and only minor changes were made to the nomenclature. The total number of categories was increased to 292.

DSM-IV was published in 1994 in coordination with the publication of ICD-10. The major advance of DSM-IV was the careful process of empirical review and documentation that informed the various decisions that were made. While previous versions of DSM reflected current theories in the field of mental disorders, there was little archival account of how they had been developed. Much of the content of DSM-III and DSM-III-R was the result of expert consensus without a systematic review of the rationale and empirical support for the decisions. DSM-IV is the first well-documented psychiatric nosology. A three-stage process of comprehensive literature reviews, reanalyses of data sets, and field trials has provided the empirical support for the changes that were made in the text and criteria sets of DSM-IV. This process was carried out by thirteen work groups, each of which had responsibility for a specific section of the manual.

The first stage consisted of a review of the existing literature and was performed following a methodical, objective, and comprehensive process. The reviewers were instructed to provide an explicit statement of the issue(s) and their relevance to clinical practice and research, an objective and descriptive summary of the existing literature on the subject, and recommendations for solutions with the advantages and disadvantages for each option. The reviews were then critiqued by the appropriate DSM-IV work group members and advisers (some 1,000 participants in all) in order to ensure accuracy, coverage, and unbiased interpretation of the literature.

The second stage of data reanalysis addressed a number of issues that could not be resolved through the extensive literature reviews. Previously unpublished data sets were reanalyzed to compare current available criteria sets and algorithms (DSM-III, DSM-III-R, and ICD-100 systems) and to generate and evaluate alternative proposals for new criteria sets for DSM-IV.

The third stage of field trials examined some of the questions that had not been completely resolved by the literature reviews and data reanalyses, com-

pared alternative DSM-III, DSM-III-R, ICD-10, and proposed DSM-IV options, and evaluated the impact of suggested changes. Carefully designed and monitored studies focused on twelve separate topics: antisocial personality disorder; autism and related pervasive development disorders; disruptive behavior disorders; insomnia; major depression and dysthymia; mixed anxiety-depression; panic disorder; obsessive-compulsive disorder; posttraumatic stress disorder; schizophrenia; somatization disorder; and substance use disorders. Each field trial was conducted across five to twelve sites (including international sites in some cases) with 350 to 1,000 patients to represent the array of disease in the various arenas in which DSM-IV was to be used. These field trials provided information on the acceptability, feasibility, coverage, generalizability, reliability, and validity of proposed criteria sets and algorithms for DSM-IV.

The empirical support for DSM-IV and the rationale for the decisions that were made appear in the five-volume *DSM-IV Sourcebook* (American Psychiatric Press 1994). The results of the literature reviews are described in volumes 1–3, the data reanalyses in volume 4, and the field trials and final decisions in volume 5.

DSM-IV is basically a descriptive system of diagnosis. It is hoped that the availability of a reliable psychiatric classification will facilitate clinical work, education, and the research necessary to develop a deeper understanding of mental disorders.

Allen J. Frances
Cindy Jones
Avram Mack
Ruth Ross

Differential Diagnosis

Differential diagnosis in psychology and psychiatry consists of identifying types of disturbance that are preventing people from functioning effectively and enjoying their lives. Sometimes these disturbances involve distressing symptoms, such as pervasive sadness, irrational fears, or an inability to think clearly and logically. At other times they involve maladaptive personality styles that undermine achievement striving and preclude rewarding interpersonal relationships. The goal of differential diagnosis is to relate whatever patterns of disturbance are present to some cohesive and recognizable form of psychopathology, such as depressive disorder or passive-aggressive personality disorder.

Differential diagnosis is based on four types of criteria for classifying psychological disturbance into different forms. One type of criteria classifies disorders phenomenologically, according to manifest symptoms, as in diagnosing bipolar disorder, in part, on the basis of observable mood swings. A second type classifies disorders etiologically, according to causation, as in diagnosing post-traumatic stress disorder, in part, on the basis of a person's having experienced an unusually distressing event. A third type classifies disorders dynamically, according to inferred personality processes, as in diagnosing borderline personality disorder, in part, on the basis of indications that a person has a disturbed sense of identity. The fourth type of criteria classifies disorders prognostically, according to outcome or treatment response, as in diagnosing chronic schizophrenia, in part, on the basis of persistence of the condition without remission. The best known and most widely used psychopathology classification scheme, the *Diagnostic and Statistical Manual of Mental Disorders* of the American Psychiatric Association (DSM-III-R and the new DSM-IV), stresses differential diagnosis on the basis of manifest symptomatology. However, both DSM and clinicians in practice frequently draw as well on aspects of causation, inferred personality processes, and treatment outcome in formulating diagnostic impressions.

Differential diagnosis, when properly employed, facilitates treatment planning and aids subject selection in psychopathology research. With respect to treatment planning, identifying the types of disturbance that people have helps to determine the kinds of intervention that are likely to benefit them. Classification allows therapists to draw on cumulative knowledge concerning which treatment methods work best to alleviate certain kinds of symptoms or to modify certain kinds of personality characteristics. Guidance from diagnostic formulations that identify similarities among types of psychologically disturbed individuals spares clinicians from having to devise treatment plans from scratch every time they see a new patient.

In psychopathology research, differential diagnosis holds the key to obtaining meaningful results. Advances in knowledge concerning what a condition consists of, why it occurs, what its outcome is likely to be, and how to treat and prevent it can occur only when comparisons can be made between some research subjects who display that condition and other subjects who display some other condition or no condition at all. Only with adequate methods of differential diagnosis can subjects be reliably designated as displaying one condition or another, and a reliable system of classifying disorders is a necessary starting point for being able to conduct systematic research on their nature.

Despite the important purposes that differential diagnosis serves, it is at times criticized as being a dehumanizing and stigmatizing procedure that puts people in pejorative pigeonholes, exposes them to devastating experiences of prejudice and rejection, and gives professionals unseemly power to pass judgment on their patients. From a humanistic perspective, in particular, it has been asserted that people should be considered in their own uniqueness and individuality and not be stripped of their dignity by being assigned classificatory labels that are shared by groups of people.

Although personality classification and diagnostic labeling can be used in ways that stigmatize or disadvantage people, such outcomes represent a misuse of differential diagnosis rather than any misanthropy intrinsic to its procedures. Moreover, individually oriented and group-centered approaches to working with people are not mutually exclusive in clinical practice. In the eyes of caring clinicians, an individual's uniqueness surely survives her being identified as sharing certain characteristics with other people. How people are alike and how they differ from each other are, in fact, complementary bits of information that clinicians can and should use together in their efforts to understand and help their patients. If they do so conscientiously, their differential diagnoses can leave humanistic values unscathed.

In arriving at differential diagnoses of psychological disturbance, clinicians draw on four sources of data; (1) presenting symptoms, which comprise the patient's reported or manifest complaints and concerns; (2) a case history of the patient's past and current life experiences, including the circumstances in which she grew up, the nature of her interpersonal relationships and accomplishments in academic and work situations, and the extent and course of any prior psychological difficulties; (3) behavioral observations of the patient's appearance, affect, bodily movements, language usage, and style of relatedness; and (d) the patient's performance on relevant psychological tests. To illustrate these data sources, schizophrenic disorder might be indicated by complaints that other people are controlling the patient's mind (presenting symptom) in a man with long-standing social withdrawal (case history) who displayed inappropriate affect while being interviewed (behavioral observations) and an impaired sense of reality on psychological tests.

Interviewing and psychodiagnostic testing are the two primary methods used by mental health professionals to develop the sources of data used in differential diagnosis of psychological disturbance. It is mainly in interviews that clinicians learn about patients' current concerns and personal history and have an opportunity to observe their behavioral style. Psychologists and psychiatrists typically talk with their patients in an open-ended fashion intended to encourage spontaneity and elaboration. In diagnostic interviews, however, some modicum of structure is required to ensure that certain kinds of information, such as evidence of suicidal tendencies or a history of substance abuse, are obtained in sufficient detail. In particularly complex cases or for research purposes, clinicians may even employ a specific set of questions that structure the interview in considerable detail. Frequently used structured interview guides include the Schedule of Affective Disorders and Schizophrenia (SADS), the Diagnostic Interview Schedule (DIS), and the Structured Clinical Interview for DSM-IV (SCID).

Many clinicians also include in their diagnostic interviews a mental status examination, which consists of some brief questions to determine whether patients are oriented and alert (e.g., "What year is this?"; "Who is president now?") and some simple tasks to assess their attention, concentration, memory, and abstract thinking capacities (e.g., repeating digits; explaining the meaning of proverbs). This kind of examination serves initial screening purposes in identifying mental incapacity or disorganization. When information that is crucial to arriving at a differential diagnosis cannot be obtained readily from interviews, even with the inclusion of a mental status examination, then formal psychodiagnostic testing may be employed.

Psychodiagnosis consists of the clinical use of psychological tests to facilitate personality and cognitive assessment. When psychodiagnostic testing appears to be indicated, psychologists select a battery of tests tailored to the diagnostic questions at issue. If a psychodiagnostic consultation relates to possible brain dysfunction, for example, extensive testing of cognitive and perceptual-motor functions will be conducted using such well-known measures as the Wechsler Adult Intelligence Scale and the Halstead-Reitan Neuropsychological Test Battery. If a referral question concerns differential diagnosis or treatment planning in relation to psychotherapy, a broad-based assessment of personality structure and dynamics will be undertaken using such well-known measures as the Minnesota Multiphasic Personality Inventory and the Rorschach Inkblot Test.

Irving B. Weiner

Dilthey, Wilhelm (1833–1911)

Wilhelm Dilthey rejected the *Naturwissenschaften* (natural sciences) approach to psychology. He suggested the humanistic, mental social sciences *Geisteswissenschaften* approach, directed toward understanding (*Verstehen*) psychology.

Eileen A. Gavin

Discourse Structure and Discourse Processing

Linguists, influenced by L. Bloomfield, have focused on the most observable aspect of the process of linguistic communication by seeking to characterize surface regularities of utterances without reference to either meaning or context. They have sought to do this by identifying regularities in the distribution of linguistic units (e.g., phonemes, grammatical morphemes) in natural language sentences. Edward Harris extended this approach to connected discourse. With Noam Chomsky, the goals of linguistics began to shift away from simply describing the primary linguistic data (word strings) and centered instead on the problem of formulating explicit rules that are capable of accounting for observed regularities in the distribution of grammatical morphemes in sentences. Chomsky sought to define a system of grammar that is capable of generating all of the grammatical sentences of a language by means of a finite set of phrase structure rules and grammatical transformations. A sentence, in Chomsky's system, is generated by a succession of phrase structure rules, which result in a terminal string of grammatical categories into which lexical items are inserted. The resulting string is called the kernel sentence.

Chomsky's system of grammar begins with the notion that a sentence may be represented by a tree structure consisting of an initial symbol S (for sentence), a set of nonterminal nodes branching from S and labeled by grammatical categories, and a set of terminal nodes labeled by lexical items. This tree structure, called the *deep structure*, represents the derivation of the kernel sentence using the phrase structure rules of the grammar.

Presupposition

C. Fillmore has demonstrated that many sentences are uninterpretable without reference to the extralinguistic factors mentioned above (technically called deixis). For example, the sentence "I will come there tonight" can only be used appropriately if the listener is "there" now or will be "there" tonight. Such purely semantic judgments as contradiction ("I am not here") must be made on the basis of diectic categories. Similarly, G. Leech has indicated that the position of the speaker must be considered in the interpretation of propositions of relative location such as *above* or *beyond*.

Semantic Memory

Experimental research on memory for sentences has led to the conclusion that when a subject is exposed to a sentence embedded in a text, information concerning the surface form of the sentence is not retained, but rather, some more abstract semantic or conceptual information is retained. The primary experimental evidence for this conclusion rests on studies of confusions among alternative sentence paraphrases in choice-recognition studies, in which a subject is tested at varying intervals after a sentence has been presented. Thus, there is reason to believe that there is a long-term semantic or conceptual memory store, distinct from other short- or intermediate-term memory stores.

Semantic networks frequently have been represented as data structures in computer programs. Computationally, semantic networks so represented can be viewed as functions or procedures to be executed. For example, semantic relations could be defined as generating functions that would eventually produce an adequate syntactic structure. The significance of this observation is that it has extended the notion of a static semantic memory to include active procedural information. Thus, there is no formal distinction between data structures and procedures operating on them, and it is possible to formulate memory models that include stored "procedural" information as well as "structural" information.

Discourse Processing and Modes

The consideration of active relational models for semantic memory naturally leads to a further investigation of the processing of natural language inputs. What is required is a detailed account of the levels and types of processing involved in generating semantic information from textual inputs. At present, relatively little is known about the processes involved in discourse comprehension. Theoretical models that have been proposed have yet to achieve implementation as well-specified process models in any form that is adequate from either a linguistic or a psychological perspective. However, attempts to construct computer models of natural language processors have helped to identify specific problems and issues, which will have to be treated by an adequate model of discourse processing.

The conceptual dependency system of R. Schank was implemented as a set of computer programs modeling human language understanding at the sentence level. Schank's system is based on a verb-centered stratificational approach to language structure, in which comprehension is regarded as a process of mapping from grammatical and lexical information contained in input sentences to "conceptual dependency networks." Thus, in Schank's system, lexical verbs are transformed or decomposed into primitive case networks containing slots, which can be filled by concepts corresponding to input lexical items or by other stored concepts. These networks consist of labeled binary semantic relations connecting primitive nonverbal "acts," "picture producers" (objects), and "modifiers." The network is generated from a syntactic parsing of an input sentence and from knowledge about the context of an utterance.

Carl H. Frederiksen
Edward Harris
Richard P. Duran

Discrimination Learning

Ivan Petrovich Pavlov and subsequent Russian investigators have used a wide variety of stimuli including visual, auditory, tactile, noxious—in fact, just about any stimulus for which the subject has an appropriate sense organ. Studies from the former Soviet Union have shown the importance of context or background to an extent not heretofore appreciated. The usual emphasis has been on the conditioned stimulus (CS), with the assumption that a constant background contributes little or nothing to the conditioned response (CR). But, in switching experiments, the same CS paired with different unconditional stimuli (USs) will evoke different CRs if the pairing takes place in different rooms or even in the same room at different times with different experimenters. Thus, a metronome, the CS, paired with a food US in the morning but with an electric shock to a paw US in the afternoon with a different experimenter, will evoke salivation in the morning and leg flexion in the afternoon.

Two Types of Presentation

In the instrumental situation, some gross motor response or movement is required, such as running down an alley, pressing a lever, pushing or jumping against a card, choosing a door or box, and so forth. The relevant stimuli may be present successively or simultaneously. The successive presentation is one of two types. Type I—called go-no-go—is analogous to the arrangement in classical conditioning. When S$^+$ is presented, an approach or manipulative response is rewarded. When S$^-$ is presented, the response is followed by no reward (or punishment). The apparatus for the Type II successive stimulus presentation is the same as for the two-choice simultaneous presentation. In both, the subject is faced with a display having two cards, alleys, and so on, side by side.

Theories

The earliest use of two-choice discrimination was predominately for sensory and perceptual problems, in which a series of studies by Karl S. Lashley was influential. There were a few studies dating from the early part of this century, such as those by G. V. Hamilton and Robert M. Yerkes, which contained descriptions of the nature of the response, but it wasn't until the early 1930s that there emerged systematic and formal attempts at theorizing about the nature of the response. The most powerful, influential, and enduring theory was set forth in a series of papers by Kenneth W. Spence (1960). Was it a one- or two-stage process? Most are agreed that two stages are usually required. As Spence put it, it is first necessary to learn "what to look at," and then it is possible to develop differential responses to these cues.

The Gestalt view in its traditional form described the response as being to the total configuration, and therefore made no distinction between the Type II successive presentation and the two-choice visual simultaneous presentation. In the former, the subject is faced with black-black versus white-white, which should be easier than the latter, which displays a black-white versus white-black configuration. From the Gestalt view, both arrangements involve successive presentation. With either arrangement the subject is rewarded by consistently choosing one side for one configuration and the other side for the other configuration. The evidence is strongly against the Gestalt view: (1) simultaneous two-choice is easier than Type II successive; (2) mutilating the configuration—replacing S$^-$ with a different and novel stimulus—does not disrupt correct responding.

David Ehrenfreund

Discrimination Reversal in Conditioning

This term refers to any experiment in which subjects first learn a particular discrimination with a particular reinforcement contingency (e.g., black positive, white negative), and then the contingency is reversed (black negative, white positive). The most important application of the method in an effort to resolve a theoretical problem has been to the continuity-noncontinuity issue. In these experimental applications, the subjects have often been rats learning a black-white discrimination of the type suggested above. The animals learn the discrimination in a simple, single-choice maze with black on one side and white on the other.

The test of these alternatives involves the discrimination reversal experiment. Specifically, if positive and negative stimuli are switched during the presolution period, this manipulation, according to the noncontinuity theorists, should have no effect. According to the continuity theorists, of whom Kenneth W. Spence was the most important, the reversal should slow up mastery of the discrimination, because it would be necessary for the animal to unlearn the developing habit to go to the now-incorrect stimulus.

Gregory A. Kimble

Disgust

The pattern of rejection because of disgust is basically a form of riddance reaction by which the organism tries to eliminate a substance or object that has been incorporated. As the individual gains experience with objects, this pattern of behavior may occur in abbreviated form to the sight or smell of the object as a conditioned reaction. Although this is a basic protective mechanism and has considerable survival value for the individual, it has not been systematically studied.

The psychoanalyst Wilhelm Reich (1949) described vomiting as a biological expressive movement, which acts convulsively to expel body contents. It is based on a peristaltic movement of the stomach and esophagus in the direction opposite to its normal function. In infants, vomiting is sometimes accompanied by diarrhea, another form of ejection.

Robert Plutchik

Divorce: Psychological Aspects

Given the millions of persons directly affected by divorce, and the additional millions of parents, other relatives, and friends who are indirectly involved, the psychosocial consequences of divorce become of major concern for society.

The most frequent approach to examining the health of divorced persons has dealt with prevalence rates for various indicators of dysfunction. Compared with other marital categories, the separated and divorced manifest higher rates of admission into psychiatric facilities, higher suicide and homicide rates, a higher rate of alcoholism, and a greater likelihood of motor vehicle accidents. The separated and divorced also manifest higher morbidity and mortality rates.

Children and Divorce

If the psychological consequences for adults are marked, those for children are often devastating. A number of factors mediate the impact of divorce for children, including especially the mental health of parents, the characteristics of the single-parent household, the developmental level of the child, and the potential opposition in the goals of divorcing parents and their children.

The custodial parent, frequently the mother, is often faced with reduced income; alimony and/or child support (if provided) may need to be supplemented via work-related activities that absent the parent from the house. The parent also faces the demand to be both mother and father to the children and to run the household while reestablishing his or her life.

The long-term adaptation of children is generally less affected by developmental level than by such factors as whether the parents have resolved their own problems, how custodial and noncustodial parents function in their altered parenting roles, the child's basic mental health, and the availability of social support. Of particular importance is the quality of the relationship with the same-sex parent. Some research also suggests that mothers have a more disturbed relationship with their sons than daughters, and that this disturbance may lead to a slower recovery of boys from the divorce.

During the transition from one lifestyle to another, the individual faces an escalation of divorce-related stressors, the initial separation prompting secondary stressors in the areas of finances, family, friends, work, the law, and so on.

David A. Chiriboga

Dix, Dorothea Lynde (1802–1887)

Dorothea Dix advocated "moral treatment" of the mentally ill, and she worked for better conditions for the poor insane.

Leo H. Berman

Dreikurs, Rudolf (1897–1972)

After Alfred Adler's death, Rudolf Dreikurs was the leading exponent of individual psychology. Dreikurs developed and systematized Adler's theories, particularly the dynamics of family constellation, the techniques of family counseling, psychotherapy, and the lifestyle assessment.

Janet Turner

Drive

The term *drive* was introduced into psychology by R. S. Woodworth in his *Dynamic Psychology* (1918). According to Paul Thomas Young, Woodworth took the term from mechanics, the idea there being that the mechanisms of a machine must be activated by a source of energy in order to operate. Woodworth thought that there could be a number of sources of drive, including biological ones like hunger and thirst and activities already under way. The term came into general use in the next decade, especially among psychologists interested in animal behavior, and it was extended to the human. Sigmund Freud had used the word *Trieb*, which can be translated as "drive," although the common translation actually employed was instinct.

Biological drive, in the typical case, is defined by the result of deprivation (for example, periods of time without food or water in the case of hunger and thirst) and by behavioral consequences of deprivation. Such consequences include consummatory behavior like eating, periodic restless or "spontaneous" activity, and action to overcome an obstacle in order to obtain an incentive or goal object. The effectiveness of reinforcers or rewards in studies of learning has been found to be related to prior deprivation, so evidence of learning is counted as testimony to the presence of drive.

Drivelike conceptions of human motives, such as achievement, affiliation, aggression, and the like, have turned out to be too simple. In accounting for the behavior appropriate to these motives, it is necessary to consider a number of factors aside from the measured motive strength itself (Weiner 1990). Situational factors as well as subjective and cognitive evaluations seem to be involved, as illustrated by current emphasis on attribution theory.

Charles N. Cofer

Drug Abuse Rehabilitation

Opiate Addiction and Its Treatment
The most common symptoms of heroin overdose include pupillary constriction, respiratory depres-

sion, obtundation, and pulmonary edema. Since 1965, a precipitous rise in the incidence of heroin use has provided considerable experience in the outpatient detoxification of dependent patients, many of whom present themselves for treatment when the amount or quality of heroin in the street declines, thus making it difficult to maintain their physical dependence and allay symptoms of withdrawal. The severity of withdrawal symptoms in any given patient will depend on the drug used, the duration of use, the degree of tolerance that has been developed, the time elapsed since the last dose, and the psychogenic overlay each patient attaches to his symptoms.

The treatment of opiate withdrawal is carried out primarily with the use of methadone, a synthetic opiate with pharmacologic properties qualitatively similar to heroin and morphine. In addition to its cross-dependence with other opiate drugs, methadone is more slowly metabolized than heroin or morphine, and thus can be more easily withdrawn over a period of ten days or less.

The heroin epidemic of the late 1960s prompted the development of a range of treatment modalities, from the outpatient detoxification described above to prolonged placement in residential "therapeutic communities." Patients have also been offered a choice of high- or low-dose methadone maintenance or treatment with narcotic blocking drugs.

As a treatment modality, methadone maintenance evolved out of the recognition that total abstinence from opiate drugs may be impossible for some individuals, and that abstinence may not be the only criterion for successful treatment.

Methadone maintenance boasts the highest retention rate (50–80%) of any treatment program for opiate addiction. For patients in treatment, heroin use is markedly decreased, though approximately 20% of all subsequent examinations reveal the use of other illicit drugs. Criminal behavior is also diminished, though it does not disappear completely.

Though methadone alone does not represent a panacea in the treatment of opiate addiction, it does represent an important adjunct to successful treatment. Generally, the level of heroin use and antisocial behavior declines in patients maintained on methadone, but adequate social rehabilitation requires the concurrent use of a broad range of services, including job training, supplementary education, and legal, financial, and psychiatric help.

Narcotic antagonists are structurally similar to the opiates and may occupy the same receptor sites in the central nervous system, thus exerting their antagonistic effect through competitive inhibition. In sufficient doses they will completely block the pharmacologic effects of subsequently administered heroin. However, if given after opiate dependence has already developed, they will precipitate an acute abstinence syndrome. Some antagonists (e.g., cyclazocine and nalorphine) have agonistic effects of their own, while others, like naloxone and naltrexone, appear to be pure antagonists.

Abuse of Hypnotic Sedative Drugs

Pharmacologic agents with widely varying chemical structures share the ability to produce sedation or sleep in therapeutic doses. Included in this group are the barbiturates, chloral hydrate, paraldehyde, glutethamide, methyprylon, ethchlorvynol, meprobamate, methaqualone, and the minor tranquilizers (i.e., benzodiazepine derivatives). In general, these drugs depress the central nervous system, including the cerebral cortex, limbic system, hypothalamus, and ascending reticular formation. They may inhibit both the release of neurotransmitters and the latter's effect at the postsynaptic membrane.

In severe overdose, there may be impairment of cardiorespiratory function. Cheyne-Stokes breathing, hypoxia, respiratory acidosis, and paralytic dilation of the pupil. In terminal cases, the patient is in shock and the electroencephalogram reveals varying amounts of rhythmic, fast (20–30 cycles per second) or mixed fast and slow activity.

Frequently, sedative overdose is the result of large-scale ingestion with suicidal intent. In some cases, however, confusion after ingestion of normally therapeutic doses leads to "drug automatism," in which the patient, forgetting that she has already taken the drug, ingests a second, third, or even fourth dose, with resultant overdose.

Withdrawal from central nervous system (CNS) depressants can, in severe cases, be accompanied by a significant mortality rate. For this reason, treatment is usually carried out in a hospital setting. Onset depends on the duration of action of the particular drug abused. In the case of the short-acting barbiturates, withdrawal symptoms may be manifest 12 to 16 hours after the last dose. Withdrawal of the longer-acting hypnotic sedatives may not result in symptoms until 7 days after the last dose.

Early manifestations of abstinence include agitation, tremor, postural hypotension, diffuse anxiety, and vomiting. As withdrawal progresses, the patient may develop hyperactive reflexes and a gross resting tremor. There is also an increase in the duration of rapid eye movement (REM) sleep, nightmares become more frequent, and sleep duration is shorter. In the case of the short-acting barbiturates, symptoms characteristically peak two or three days after the last dose and generalized seizures may occur within this period, either singly or as *status epilepticus*.

Treatment with barbiturates will suppress the sedative withdrawal syndrome only in its early stages. Once delirium has developed, 24 to 72 hours of barbiturate treatment may be required before it clears.

Amphetamine Dependence and Its Treatment

Acute amphetamine-induced psychosis has been found responsive to treatment with major tranquilizers, such as chlorpromazine or haloperidol, both of which have also been shown to block amphetamine effects in laboratory animals. A test dose of 25 mg of chlorpromazine can be followed by 50 mg by mouth four times per day until the psychosis is resolved, usually within 48 hours. Intramuscular administration can be considered if severe agitation or aggressivity is a problem, provided the patient can be monitored for the development of hypotension. As the psychosis resolves, treatment is next focused on the depression accompanying amphetamine withdrawal, with special attention to the patient's suicide potential.

An inpatient setting is desirable both from the standpoint of conservative management and as a base from which to evaluate the patient and his needs to promote long-term rehabilitation. The presence or absence of existent schizophrenic pathology should be determined, and appropriate treatment instituted in such cases. Recently behavioral couple-therapy and various methods of family therapy have proven to be more effective than other methods (Lebow and Gurman 1995).

Steven M. Mirin
Roger E. Meyer

Drug Problems and the School Psychologist

It is estimated that every three out of four young people enrolled in schools have had some contact with nonmedically prescribed drugs. Schools have responded to the drug problem with a diversity of measures. Four basic approaches have been identified: (1) policy, (2) awareness, (3) curriculum, and (4) programs.

The National Association of School Psychologists has raised the issue of drugs in schools, and a special committee on drug abuse was appointed. At the annual meetings, workshops were developed to ascertain the viewpoint of the school psychologist on drugs and discover how she could be helpful.

Because of her training and contact with the school, the school psychologist is of maximum assistance in responding to the drug problem. Training in the behavioral sciences, clinical skills, learning, motivation, and group dynamics provides a composite of basic skills needed to function successfully in drug abuse prevention.

Leonard D. Fitts

Dying Patients and the Physician

The primary goal in treating the terminally ill patient is to assure the terror of death in the patient, and to enable the patient, if need be, to die with dignity and serenity in the fullest possession of her human faculties that her stature permits. The task of the physician is usually to strengthen and buttress the natural and ever-present defenses of denial.

It is important also that the patient not be isolated, either from friends, relatives, or the staff. Regularity and predictability of contact with the physician implies continuity.

The patient should be touched, because the

touch, the caress, is the most archaic preverbal way we possess of communication, solace, and comfort. Frequent backrubs and massages, therefore, engender not only physical well-being but psychic as well. Also, cosmetic care of the patient should not be neglected.

The patient should not be treated as if he had no future. All patients should be encouraged to plan for the future for themselves and for their relatives and children, and initiative should be encouraged.

It is very important to convey to the families of patients that in any dying person a whole series of retrogressive traits of behavior may appear. The ill patient usually manifests aspects of character that, under other circumstances, would be characterized as selfish, petulant, fractious, or ungrateful.

Charles William Wahl

Dynamic Psychology

The term *dynamic psychology* has generally referred to the approach of R. S. Woodworth, who for more than 50 years (from approximately 1910 to 1960) encouraged the discovery and exploration of how and why psychological activity occurs as it does. Although Woodworth's own program was "neither new nor revolutionary" (1926, 111)—steeped as it was in the already dynamic roots of functional psy-

chology, of physiology as a sister science, and of evolutionary doctrine—it merits the title *dynamic psychology* because of its long-standing, emphatic, influential, and truly dynamic aim: to describe psychological processes as they actually occur; to discover their antecedents and consequents; to assess the conditions under which they occur; and to find their causes and effects.

Woodworth's dynamic psychology stressed several major conceptions, including mechanism and drive, and individual as basic unit. These concepts found support in his own rigorous scientific work, in his open attitude toward psychological exploration, and in his abiding awareness not only of what he knew but also of the limits of existing knowledge.

According to Woodworth, mechanisms under certain circumstances may become transformed into drives. In a sequence of activities that prepares for a consummatory response, such as eating, one mechanism (as aroused drive) may become a drive for another mechanism that will carry the preparatory sequence further. A mechanism may in this case become a drive by facilitating another mechanism. In other instances, an external stimulus that had activated a particular mechanism and that had therefore been a drive may eventually be needed no longer. Now the mechanism may become a drive in its own right.

Eileen A. Gavin

· E ·

Early Experience: An Overview

The area of early experience has an experimental-predictive orientation. It attempts to specify the results in adulthood of some treatment (naturally occurring or experimentally applied) undergone by an organism early in life. It departs from the standard stimulus-response (S-R) behaviorist program, inasmuch as it accords a special significance to the variable of development. Thus, this orientation assumes that an input experience incurred by a young organism will have effects that will differ in degree and kind from those ensuing from the same input applied to an adult subject. The exact reasons for assuming such differences, however, have not always been very clearly elucidated. As a substantive field early experience is rather loosely defined and involves studies using a variety of types of subjects, methods, and variables.

Animal Research: Issues and Findings
In birds and primates, it appears that the formation of appropriate early attachments is of great importance for normal adult behavior. This has been clearly shown by Harry F. Harlow and Margaret K. Harlow (1958) using rhesus monkeys. Motherless or surrogate-reared young show pathological behavior during development and also deviant sexual and maternal behavior later on. However, this may not apply to all primate genera. In the case of birds, nonattachments do not produce marked or obvious abnormalities. Nevertheless, it is widely supposed that mate choice may well be influenced by the characteristics of the imprinting object.

Human Research: Issues and Findings
We may group under the category of environmental deficit all institutions or circumstances in which a child gets less than a "normal" amount of stimulation, inanimate or interpersonal. Therefore, all orphanages, foundling homes, and similar institutions are candidates for inclusion but cannot be included necessarily. Although aberrations or at least alterations in the behavior of children reared in such institutions have been reported by some studies, others have found few major effects. Thus, institutional rearing does not always involve environmental deficit and hence does not always produce behavioral pathology (W. R. Thompson and J. Grusec 1970).

William R. Thompson

Early Experience and Mild Mental Retardation

Early stimulation has been assigned considerable importance for intellectual as well as socially adaptive development. Investigations with animals have revealed that variations in experience, particularly early experience, affect both the organization and the biological bases of subsequent behavior.

The cumulative nature of development, rather than the presence of critical periods for the effects of early stimulation, however, still renders the early years of human life highly significant for later intellectual functioning. Skills and competencies attained early in life affect the child's ability to respond effectively to later situations requiring complex behavioral organization and adaptation.

Preschool day-care intervention. Data from the

Consortium of Longitudinal Studies (Lazar et al. 1977) supports the contention that high-quality, intensive preschool intervention can also have persistent positive effects on the academic performance of disadvantaged children. The consortium consisted of twelve investigators who conducted experimental preschool programs during the early 1960s. These programs served children at risk for psychosocial retardation, had included control groups, and had conducted standardized intelligence testing. When the children who had originally attended the programs were junior and senior high school students, about 80% were successfully relocated and reevaluated. The results of this effort revealed a lower incidence of special education placement and grade retention and higher levels of mathematics achievement among children who had attended the preschool programs. IQ scores, however, did not differ between the experimental and control groups. These results suggest that preschool programs may have more lasting effect on measures more ecologically valid than IQ scores.

The day-care intervention also altered the correlations between the mothers' and children's IQs in the treated and untreated groups. Beginning at 3 years of age and continuing at ages 4 and 5, the IQ correlations in the control group approximated the .50 predicted by a polygenic model of intellectual development. The relationship between mother and child IQ in the experimental group, however, was close to 0 (Ramey and Haskins 1981). This finding affirms the importance of environmental stimulation in preventing psychosocial retardation and encourages optimism regarding the potential for reaching the lower segment of the disadvantaged population through a day-care format.

The relationship between early stimulation and later intellectual functioning is a complex one, affected by the continuing quality of the fostering environment. The cumulative nature of human development, however, renders the skills and competencies acquired during the early years of life of major importance to later functioning. Early intervention programs that provide increased stimulation to disadvantaged children have been shown to be effective in attenuating the decline in intellectual development associated with poverty.

Craig T. Ramey
Lynne Baker-Ward

Educational Psychology: Brief History and Current Status

Definition and the Influence of Values

Although it is easier to say what educational psychology is not than to indicate what it is, there is virtually complete agreement on one issue: educational psychology goes beyond the mere *application* of psychological theory. (For an extensive treatment of matters related to this entry, see Notterman and Drewry 1993).

For example, Mathis, Menges, and McMillan (1977) hold that educational psychology consists of multiplicative interaction among the following variables: (1) basic knowledge of the behavioral sciences (not neglecting social psychology, developmental psychology, and personality), (2) formal and informal educational processes ("informal" because not all education takes place in the classroom), and (3) theoretical and practical research methods that have been developed to illuminate the interaction.

Turning to the influence of values upon the kind of educational psychology that emerges among different nations, it is clear that the values characteristic of the former Soviet Union, and still dominant in several of its former states, place a premium upon group ownership and endeavor. These values are taught in schools. Individual initiative and creativity are retained only by the exceptional person.

Education and Evolving Psychological Positions

If only to maintain a balance in regard to the relation between psychology and education, one must consider the evolution of psychological viewpoints. In so doing we keep our perspective by not embracing as new that which has long been known, or—alternatively—disregarding the lessons of the past simply because they are not fashionable. We begin with functionalism.

FUNCTIONALISM AND DEWEY'S PROGRESSIVE EDUCATION

Functionalism addressed itself to the same concerns as today's psychology, with the exception that it emphasized the importance of adaptation through learning. William James and William McDougall held that the ability to adapt through learning is manifested through an organism's goal-directed behavior, which, in turn, permits the inference of purpose.

As a philosopher, John Dewey (who accepted purposivity) is known as a pragmatist. Pragmatism is defined as the pursuit of truth or knowledge through evaluation of the consequences of an act. Dewey's educational philosophy of "learning by doing" fits squarely into the ideas of both purpose and pragmatism. It also relates to sociological conditions. He asserted that children are naturally inclined to action, communication, and exploration; the teacher's task is to capitalize on these attributes through creating the proper physical and interpersonal classroom environment. Dewey sharpened his ideas at the University of Chicago, where he established a Lab School devoted to his "progressive education," a term that implies that education is a continuing, adaptive process.

Dewey's views are as current as today's debates about how to improve education in the United States. We should assume that children are curious, active, malleable, and influenced for better or worse by the conditions of the particular society they experience.

ASSOCIATIONISM AND THORNDIKE'S CONNECTIONIST LAW

Edward Lee Thorndike developed his ideas of connectionism and the law of effect from associationism. He initially used cats as subjects. According to Benjamin B. Wolman (1989, 72), connectionism is "the doctrine that the basis of all behavior and learning are connections of stimulus and response which are strengthened to produce stability." The way that connections are strengthened (or weakened) is by means of the law of effect. Wolman describes Thorndike's principle as follows: "[The law states] that annoyance weakens and satisfaction strengthens a stimulus-response connection" (198).

It is evident that associationism and connectionism (less its anthropomorphic overtones) laid the foundation for American behaviorism and its educational offshoot, programmed instruction. Connectionist networks have even found their way into cognitive psychology.

BEHAVIORISM: SKINNER'S EXTENSION FROM OPERANT CONDITIONING TO PROGRAMMED INSTRUCTION

Operant conditioning involves teaching an organism, human or animal, to operate upon the environment, and thereby to acquire some new behavior. The experimenter (or teacher) creates circumstances leading to the emission of the desired behavior. Care is taken to include one or more stimuli as part of the triggering prior circumstances. When the response appears, the person in charge promptly reinforces the behavior. The behavior may be an act, a movement, an utterance, an answer to a workbook problem, and so on. Once the initial operant is acquired, it can readily be produced under the appropriate circumstances, which now include the original stimuli serving as cues. The researcher or instructor can then connect new links to the first one. All that is necessary is for the new link to produce the signal for the initially acquired operant, which, as before, leads to reinforcement. Depending upon the skill of the researcher or teacher, the aptitude of the organism, and the kinds of responses involved, many such links can be successively attached, so as to lead to the original operant. This procedure is called *chaining*. The establishment of cues leading to the serial emission of each of the links, one after the other, is called *discrimination*. The alteration of the responses to fit some standard is called *shaping*. Underlying the entire procedure is the principle of reinforcement, derived from Thorndike's law of effect. The reinforcement need not be regular; it may be, and usually is, intermittent, but frequent enough to maintain the desired behavior. Chaining, discrimination, shaping, and intermittent reinforcement are vital to programmed instruction, of which computer-aided instruction is an offshoot.

F. S. Keller developed his Personalized System of Instruction (PSI) as a way of combining technology with the art of teaching (1968). His idea was to use the teacher as a way of providing interaction with the student's use of a program. The teacher not only makes himself or herself available but intrudes sufficiently to ensure that the students are using the program thoughtfully, and not merely mechanically. It is noteworthy that "the single most significant conclusion to be reached from research on innovatory teaching methods in higher education is that the Keller Plan is clearly superior to other methods with which it has been compared. Indeed, the Keller Plan has been so consistently found superior that it must rank as the method with the greatest research support in the history of research on teaching" (Dunkin and Barnes 1986, 759). Along similar lines, J. R. Anderson et al. (1973) have developed ACT (Adaptive Control of Thought). The computer is employed as an "intelligent tutor," with the teacher standing by to interact with the student as necessary or desirable.

Computer-aided instruction owes its rationale to programmed instruction, which in turn goes back to Skinner's form of laboratory behaviorism, operant conditioning. However, it is not a panacea. The good teacher remains an essential element in the educational process.

GESTALT PSYCHOLOGY AND INSIGHT THINKING

When Wolfgang Köhler (1969) asserted that "the whole is different than the sum of its parts," he implied that the *solution* is different than the sum of its parts. He thus engaged the "aha" (insight) experience, an unusual situation involving thinking, one in which we suddenly experience the solution to a problem. Insight is related to productive thinking.

Max Wertheimer's book *Productive Thinking* presents a clear example of productive or creative thought, one involving how children generalize from computing the area of a rectangle to that of a parallelogram (Notterman and Drewry 1993, 107–8).

FREUD ON EDUCATION

Freud asserted that educators were generally hostile to his description of psychosexual development: "almost all infantile sexual activities are forbidden or

made disagreeable to the child; the ideal has been to make the child's life asexual; . . . The children alone take no part in this conversation; . . . and demonstrate persistently that they have yet to learn their 'purity' " (1957, 321).

These remarks are as timely as today's pros and cons concerning sexual education in the schools, including topics such as the prevalence and seriousness of AIDS and the distribution of condoms for prevention of illness and pregnancy (see B. B. Wolman and J. Money 1993).

Freud considered psychoanalysts to be master teachers, whose task was to counter the consequences of the "purity" approach. He stated, "The labor of overcoming the resistance is the essential achievement of the analytic treatment; the patient has to accomplish it and the physician makes it possible for him to do this by suggestions which are in the nature of *education*. It has been truly said therefore, that psychoanalytic treatment is a kind of *re-education*" (1957, 459; emphasis in the original). In the same spirit, the American Academy of Psychoanalysis sponsored a panel discussion on "The Art of Psychoanalysis as a Technology of Instruction" (J. M. Notterman 1987).

COGNITIVE PSYCHOLOGY AND EDUCATION

The resurgence of interest in the mind occurred in conjunction with the development of the binary digital computer, with the latter coming to serve as a metaphor for the former. The are two major ways in which the metaphor works: (1) as a model of how the mind operates on different types of information, and (2) as a model for studying memory. Both of these aspects of the computer metaphor are of relevance to education, but we are here concerned only with the first.

OPERATION ON DIFFERENT TYPES OF INFORMATION

Motor action. There are two opposing views about how motor action unfolds. William James and Charles Scott Sherrington championed the position that peripheral feedback from the action itself guides the movement. R. S. Woodworth argued that central governance takes control. John Dewey fell in between, by asserting the practice led from reliance upon peripheral feedback to direct, central guidance (i.e., motor programs). The interaction of and compromise between the two views are of importance to any educational endeavor related to sports, aging, and rehabilitation. (See Newell 1991 for an overview of motor skills acquisition; Gianutsos and Notterman 1987 on feedback data of relevance to rehabilitation.)

J. H. Flavell (1977, 16) provides a fine example of how cognitive psychology uses the foregoing ideas in connection with infant cognition. Along the way, he relates his thesis to motor programs in the adult:

> His [the five month old infant's] is an entirely unconscious and self-unaware, nonsymbolic . . . know-how type of cognition. . . . It is . . . the kind that you yourself exhibit when performing many actions which are characteristically nonsymbolic and unthinking by virtue or being overlearned and automatized—e.g., brushing your teeth, starting the car. . . . It is . . . intelligence as inherent and manifest in organized patterns of sensory and motor action, and hence Piaget's description of infant cognition as presymbolic, prerepresentational, and prereflective "sensory-motor intelligence."

Biological maturation. We have already presented certain Piagetian views, as perceived by Flavell. In general, Jean Piaget held that every person goes through four principal stages of genetic epistemology (intellectual development), the last being the formal operational stage (11 to 15 years). In this stage, symbols (including numbers) and language can be used without dependence upon the physical environment. It is at this crucial adolescent phase of life that constructive education may provide the last opportunity to extend or to change the individual from leading an unproductive life to leading one that is beneficial to her and to society. Unfortunately, just because a student is chronologically in the formal stage, it does not necessarily follow that she will be logical in language, thought, or behavior.

Rule learning. Cognitive psychologists have reinvigorated the debate concerning associationism versus rationalism. They have done so in the context of artificial intelligence involving connectionist networks (associationism) as against the acquisition of rules (rationalism), as being basic to the learning of language.

The Future of Psychology in the United States

Joseph M. Notterman and H. N. Drewry (1993, 246–50) identify six issues that they believe will dominate the interaction between education and psychology in the next decade.

1. The perception that our educational system will continue to fail to meet society's needs. Among the reasons for this perception are: (a) other countries have outpaced us in publicly available education; (b) there is considerable variation in quality of education from one district to another, let alone across states; (c) there is a basic lack of agreement within society as to what the goals of education should be.

2. There will be continuing debate as to the need for educational reform, a consequence of the perception that society is not meeting its educational requirements. Whether anything of note will emerge "may depend more on a host of economic, social, and political issues than on the educational merits of the case" (248).

3. Society may gradually accept "de facto separation of school districts along racial lines" (248). "Middle-class black and Hispanic parents appear increasingly to respond, like other middle class parents, by moving to suburban or other areas where schools are perceived as 'better,' or to send their children to nonpublic schools (Statistical Abstract of the United States, 1991)" (249).

4. The teaching profession will increasingly attract a higher quality of college graduates. This phenomenon cuts across the different ways in which potential teachers are trained.

5. Efforts will be made by parents and other groups of citizens to reduce conflicts between school boards and teacher organizations.

6. Educational services will be extended to both younger and older populations. In the younger direction, "Growth in the number of single-parent homes and families raises questions about the welfare of children in the first four or five years of life" (250). However, "at the

other end of the age continuum, the expansion of available years has not been matched by improvement in the quality of life" (250).

Joseph M. Notterman

Effectance Motivation

Effectance motivation designates the motivational aspect of competence. Competence indicates the capacity of an organism to interact effectively with its environment, and effectance refers to its motivation to do so. White's position was that behaviors in which the organism is attempting to exercise or extend its mastery over its environment (an infant learning to crawl, or a child building with blocks) cannot adequately be explained by drive or tension reduction models of motivation. He argued, largely on the basis of bringing together the work of a number of other investigators, that higher animals and human beings are inherently motivated to seek mastery over immediate aspects of their environments, that is, to exercise competence. Because competence behavior is basically different from consummatory behavior, it is useful, he suggests, to have a special term for its motivational component. This term is *effectance*, though the term *competence motivation* is also used.

The concepts of competence and effectance have been influential in emphasizing the importance of taking account in motivation theory of an organism's ongoing interactions with its environment. Though suffering from a lack of precision, they have nevertheless stimulated considerable research.

Paul McReynolds

Ego Involvement

Level of ego involvement specifies the salience of portions of a person's cognitive systems, particularly those frames of reference that relate the person to his or her social ecology. Thus, levels of ego involvement correspond basically to levels of motivation. The concept fits best into psychological theories that focus on individual, experientially developed cognizing systems, that is, perspectivist or constructivist theories. The concept has its roots in the work of social theorists of the early twentieth century, such as C. H. Cooley and G. H. Mead, who formulated the idea of self as social role.

M. Sherif and H. Cantril (1947) proposed that ego involvement describes situations wherein events are related to personal frames of reference. From these premises they went on to adduce the principle that psychological activity represents a striving to maintain or to enhance the ego. Further, Sherif et al. proceeded to specify the conditions relating to the tensions of ego invalidation, particularly to the invalidation of an attitude matrix that has high priority in the person's overall self system, that is, to attitudes high in ego involvement. Further, these investigators devised formulations by which they could predict the effects of discrepant information and disconfirmation in relation to levels of ego involvement.

The concept of ego involvement has been elaborated by specific reference to self-role definition. On the assumption that self-constructions are developed and validated in social interactions, one can propose that certain roles acquire superordinancy. Thus, though a person's psychological processes are channeled by anticipations of validations of each role she enacts, her behavior reflects greater involvement in enactments of specific roles within the repertoire of her developed roles.

James C. Mancuso

Emergency Management in Psychiatry

Suicide and homicide are almost invariably the first associations that one makes with the term *psychiatric emergency*. These acts or aborted attempts are generally preceded by prolonged feelings of hopelessness and of a seemingly needless despair, which finally results in loss of aggression control, faulty impulse control, and sociopathy.

Acute or chronic brain syndromes include intoxication from alcohol and/or drugs and delirious episodes. Psychotic syndromes are manic-depressive manifestations, manic excitement, and schizophrenic turmoil. Anxiety, panic, fugues, postconcussive confusion, and aggressive behavior come under the rubric of nonpsychotic syndromes. Components of acute depression and severe anxiety can be found in each of the categories, along with elements of aggressive, assaultive, and bizarre behavior. Excessive fears or phobic reactions are also found in each of these categories.

General Principles of Management

1. The sine qua non of responding to a psychiatric emergency is prompt, immediate action, appropriate to the particular emergency.
2. The disturbed, excited, panicky, or unruly patient must be accepted as he is, rather than being scolded, punished, or ignored. A noncondemnatory attitude is a requisite before the physician can proceed to obtain the patient's history. A history is most important, so that the precipitant of the emergency can be determined.
3. Supportive human and humane contact should be provided for the patient by talking quietly and staying with her until others are assigned to do so.
4. It is usually better to do too much rather than too little. Most patients in acute upsets have regressed to a childlike level, so that they are without the use of many of their usual coping capacities. This regression may not be recognized if the patient is well known to the person who is with him; the usual error in such cases is to expect more from the patient than he is capable of handling.
5. Instill into the interpersonal relationship you are creating some flavor of "tender loving care."

Aggressive and bizarre behaviors are often found as symptoms in schizophrenia, and with severely disturbed patients prompt and effective sedation is in order.

The psychiatrist should have an assistant of the opposite sex in attendance, because such a combination will often mollify the patient.

Patients in an acute anxiety state, or in hysterical excitement, are likely to be in severe physical distress. They have difficulty in breathing and swallowing, which in turn increases their anxiety and causes intense feelings of fear, accompanied by palpitation, dyspnea, tremor, sweating, and restlessness. Such patients do not present great difficulty in management, which should consist primarily of firm and calm reassurance.

Those who have made a suicide attempt have an increased likelihood of repeating it, not infrequently with greater determination. History taking is essential, and questioning should be assiduous to obtain all clues about suicidal ideation.

Vigilance is the key word in the management of suicidal patients. An exquisite sensitivity to covert or nonverbal behavior must be maintained during the entire treatment course.

All psychiatry resident-training programs should include education in the techniques and procedures for handling psychiatric emergencies.

Shervert H. Frazier

Emotion, Theories of

Charles Darwin
Darwin's basic conclusion, consistent with his general ideas about evolution, is that emotional expressions have two fundamental characteristics. The first is that they have survival value and have developed as an adaptation to certain environments. The second is that they have communication or signal value.

William James
The commonsense view of what happens during an emotion, James said, is that we perceive a situation (e.g., an animal coming at us); then we feel the emotion (e.g., fear); and then we sweat, tremble, and try to run away (action). James believed that this sequence was not correct, and he proposed a change: We perceive a situation as one of danger; then we sweat, tremble, and try to run; and then we feel afraid. In his words, "We do not run because we are afraid, but rather we are afraid because we run."

Sigmund Freud
What is basic to the Freudian view of emotion is that emotions may be unconscious, and an individual may be totally unaware of his own emotional states.

Thus Freud, in contrast to William James, largely deemphasized the feeling aspect of emotion. In addition, he concluded that infants also show emotions, even if they cannot tell us about them. In other words, an emotion is a basic biological fact that is part of the inheritance of man. Freud relied heavily upon dreams, free associations, slips of the tongue, postures, facial expressions, voice quality, and so forth in order to arrive at inferences about a person's repressed emotions.

Cognitive Theories of Emotion

Several views have been presented that emphasize the cognitive aspects of emotion. For example, Arnold (1960) assumes that it is always necessary that an individual evaluate or interpret a stimulus before an emotional response can occur. If the evaluation leads to the conclusion that the stimulus is "good," according to Arnold, then the person feels a tendency to approach the stimulus. If the evaluation results in the conclusion that the stimulus is "bad," then the person feels a tendency to avoid the stimulus. Another illustration of a cognitive approach is found in the work of R. S. Lazarus (1968). His basic assumption is that each emotional response is the result of a particular kind of appraisal of a situation.

Emotion as Activation

D. B. Lindsley suggests that emotion is associated with activity of the reticular activating system (RAS), which is a part of the brain stem. This area is referred to as an activating system partly because electrical stimulation of the RAS will wake a sleeping cat or produce a change typical of alert wakefulness in the electroencephalogram (EEG). The idea that emotion can be associated with activity of the RAS is rather vague and, in addition, does not even attempt to deal with any of the basic psychological questions dealing with the nature of emotion.

Behavioristic Theories of Emotion

Watson. In 1924 J. B. Watson, in his *Psychology from the Standpoint of a Behaviorist*, defined emotion as "an hereditary pattern-reaction involving profound changes of the bodily mechanism as a whole, but particularly of the visceral and glandular systems."

This view, as developed, implies that emotion is always disruptive of organized activity and that the basic pattern of emotional reaction is unlearned.

Tolman. E. C. Tolman emphasizes that emotion cannot be defined by responses alone or by stimuli alone but only in terms of the relations between the two. In emotion, the responses of an individual are designed to change the stimulus situation. For example, in fear, most of the responses may be thought of as acting to protect the individual in some way; in anger, most of the responses act to destroy the stimulus. Emotions, therefore, may be defined as "a drive or tendency toward a particular type of behavior result, of response-as-affecting-stimulus; e.g., in the case of fear, protection from the stimulus, in the case of anger, destruction of the stimulus, and in the case of love, encouragement or enticement of the stimulus."

Skinner. B. F. Skinner's view of emotion is presented mainly in two sources, *The Behavior of Organisms* (1938) and *Science and Human Behavior* (1953). In the earlier work, he points out that "emotion is not primarily a kind of response at all but rather a state of strength comparable in many respects with a drive." The way an individual judges the existence of emotion in another person is not by checking his blood pressure or level of adrenaline but simply by observing changes in the appearance of certain learned responses, such as rate of talking or overall approach or avoidance.

Tomkins's Theory of Emotion

Silvan Tomkins (1970) assumes that there are eight basic emotions (or affects, as he prefers to call them). The positive ones are (1) interest, (2) surprise, and (3) joy. The negative ones are (4) anguish, (5) fear, (6) shame, (7) disgust, and (8) rage. These basic emotions are "innately patterned responses" to certain types of stimuli, and are expressed through a wide variety of bodily reactions, but particularly through facial responses. For each distinct affect there are assumed to be specific "programs" stored in subcortical areas of the brain. There is, therefore, a genetic, species-related basis for the expression of the basic emotions.

Plutchik's Theory of Emotion

Robert Plutchik attempts to show that emotion languages have certain systematic relations to one another, as well as within each language. He develops a three-dimensional model that looks like a cone to express the relations of intensity, similarity, and polarity. A number of psychometric tests have been developed on the basis of the theory, and many studies have been reported.

Robert Plutchik

Emotional Disturbances in the Mentally Retarded

The Severely Retarded

Several studies on severely retarded children with the rubella syndrome and on the multiply handicapped–severely retarded clearly document the high vulnerability of these children to psychiatric disorders. It has been noted that without active and persistent interpersonal, special sensory, and educational stimulation (including active support of the parents) these youngsters fail to develop any meaningful contact with reality ("organic autism").

The Moderately Retarded

The moderately retarded's slow rate of development and specific problems with language elaboration and concrete approaches to problem-solving situations present both unique and marked vulnerability for adequate personality development. T. G. Webster (1970) viewed these vulnerabilities as stemming from their characteristic postures toward interpersonal transactions (i.e., in the family and in a developmental day care center). He reported the following clinical features: a nonpsychotic autism (i.e., selective isolation), inflexibility and repetitiousness, passivity, and a simplicity of the emotional life.

The Mildly Retarded

The entire range of mental illness symptoms have been noted in the mildly retarded. Most frequently, one notes neurotic depression, character disorders, and the symptom clusters that flow from the reaction-formation type of defense. It has been frequently noted that the mildly retarded experience repeated negative motivational and social reinforcement from their peers and teachers and that they have had many experiences at failure or unfavorable comparisons.

Mental Retardation and the Severe Emotional Disturbances

Clinical descriptions of the childhood psychoses have drawn psychiatric attention to the issue of pseudoretardation. The young child who displays bizarre gestures and postures, whose speech is uncommunicative, who exhibits few (if any) relationships to peers, who shows marked negativism, and who makes little or no discrimination between animate and inanimate objects represents the severe emotional disturbance termed "childhood psychosis." On the first score, these children clearly have ushered in a prolonged reexamination of the interreactions of cognitive and affective development in early life, and they have cast new light on the possible interrelationships of the early determinants of the symptoms of both mental retardation and emotional disturbance.

Neurotic Reactions

F. Menolascino (1970) notes neurotic reactions in the mildly retarded, but rarely in any other levels of the mentally retarded. For example, Menolascino (1965) studied a group of community-based Down's syndrome youngsters and noted a fairly high incidence of mental illness. In a later study of an institutionalized sample of Down's syndrome youngsters (1974), he noted that many of them "appeared" happy and overly friendly, and would literally swarm around a visitor on the ward. On reflection, the bulk of stereotyped "Prince Charming" behavior in this particular subgroup of the mentally retarded appears to be secondary to affect hunger, and a far different set of diagnostic considerations and treatment challenges emerge, in contrast to the initial impression given by this behavior.

Frank J. Menolascino

Emotionally Disturbed Children and the Role of the School Psychologist

Identification and screening of the emotionally handicapped remains an integral part of the school psychologist's role, (Bower, 1972; Freehill, 1972; Herron et al., 1970; Meyers et al., 1974 and Valent, 1963). However, the scope of assessment extends far beyond diagnosis and the assignment of the label "emotionally disturbed" to the child. The school psychologist has the responsibility of utilizing screening and evaluation techniques in addition to the traditional IQ measures for educational placement and planning. To merely indicate that a child does or does not belong in one class or another is not sufficient. The psychologist must become directly involved with establishment of special classes when necessary, decisions concerning curricula and materials for utilization in these classes, and evaluation of programs to determine whether they serve the individual needs of the children.

The role of the school psychologist encompasses the treatment function as seen from many different perspectives, particularly that of the mental health consultant in the school, and extends to the primary prevention area. Treatment seen from the traditional perspective—that is, intensive counseling services with disturbed pupils—may be desirable, but is often not feasible. Short-term treatment may be more possible.

A primary prevention and intervention model is essential when considering the incidence of emotional disturbance in the population at large. Teachers and parents should be made aware of and trained to recognize general symptoms of emotional disturbance. Such training may be considered as part of the school psychologist's function. Psychologists can exert the greatest leverage for mental health practices and the establishment of intervention practices on the primary level. The school can become an important agency in the primary prevention of emotional and mental disorders. School psychologists can play a vital role in the utilization of these resources through the creation of innovative mental health programs and the coordination of available facilities.

Judith Kaufman

Emotions: Emergency Theory

The emergency theory of emotion was formulated during World War I, when the distinction between war and peace was obvious. The discharge across the sympathetic network, Walter B. Cannon stated, puts the organism on a wartime basis. This discharge during stress mobilizes the energy reserves of the body and prepares the organism to face an emergency. In times of peace, Cannon argues, the parasympathetic nerves control conservative and upbuilding functions of anabolism. The peacetime functions of the parasympathetic nerves are antagonistic to and incompatible with the sympathetico-adrenal discharge, and thus do not occur simultaneously with the emergency reaction.

Paul Thomas Young

Emotions: Measurement

Several different methods have been developed for measuring emotional states. One is based upon self-reports of feelings or moods. Its major use is with human adults. A second method depends upon ratings of behavior. This method can be used with lower animals, as well as with humans. A third approach to measuring emotions depends on an assessment of correlated but indirect behaviors, such as handwriting or fantasies. The fourth method that has been used depends on the indirect expression of emotional states through physiological changes, as shown for example in the "lie detector."

Self-Report Measures of Emotion

Examples of such measures include the Taylor Manifest Anxiety Scale (MAS) and the Nowlis Mood Checklist. In the MAS, the subject is asked to respond true or false to such statements as: I frequently find myself worrying about something; I sometimes feel that I am about to go to pieces.

Some investigators have been concerned with the existence of response biases and social desirability sets. As a result, several forced-choice-type measuring instruments have been developed. An example of such a test is the Emotions Profile Index (EPI) developed by Robert Plutchik and Henry Kellerman (1974).

Behavior Rating Scales

There are four types of populations with which behavior rating scales for emotion have been used: mental patients; mentally retarded patients; children and infants; and animals.

Robert Plutchik

Emotions and Autonomic Physiology

Use of the term *automatic nervous system* (ANS) always implies (1) two groups of bipartite motor nerves with intervening ganglia—hence the terms *preganglionic* and *postganglionic neurons*; (2) chemical mediation of neural action; (3) control of smooth muscles, cardiac muscle, and duct glands; and (4) at least partial control of two kinds of endocrine glands, the adrenal medullae and the islet cells of the pancreas. Sometimes the afferent return from ANS end organs is regarded as part of the system.

The preganglionic neurons of one portion of the ANS emanate from thoracic and lumbar vertebrae and, for the most part, synapse in two interconnected chains of ganglia lying bilaterally to the spinal cord. Some synapse in outlying ganglia and some synapse directly on the adrenal medullae and activate them to liberate adrenaline (epinephrine) and small amounts of its precursor, noradrenaline (norepinephrine). This activation, and that of all postganglionic neurons in the ANS, occurs via the neurotransmitter acetylcholine; however, most postganglionic neurons of this thoracico-lumbar branch secrete and liberate noradrenaline, which in turn activates the target organs.

This branch of the ANS is commonly called the sympathetic nervous system (SNS). It lends itself well to mass action for several reasons; (1) the interconnections among the ganglia; (2) the fact that neither adrenaline nor noradrenaline break down quickly in the body; and (3) that the former, in particular, circulates in the blood and serves to maintain and reinforce many of the actions already initiated by noradrenaline.

The other portion of the ANS arises from some cranial and some sacral nerves at each end of, or "beyond," the SNS, and thus it is most commonly referred to as the parasympathetic nervous system (PNS). Structurally, it differs from the SNS in having long preganglionic processes that synapse in noninterconnected ganglia, which lie close to or on the target organs.

Partial SNS Activation

Selective activation within the SNS system is well known in other areas, entirely apart from the differential liberation of adrenalin and noradrenalin. Perhaps most spectacular is the difference between the adaptive heat-retention and heat-loss patterns in low and high ambient temperatures. Both involve mixed SNS responses. The first requires vasoconstriction in peripheral blood vessels, decreased sweating, and increased striated muscle action; the second requires peripheral vasodilatation, increased heat-regulatory sweating or panting (to facilitate heat loss through evaporation), and relaxation of striated muscles with a consequent reduction in internal heat production.

One other sign of selective SNS activation is known to all—the blush of embarrassment. It is attributed by some to SNS vasodilator neurons, by others to acetylcholine in postganglionic SNS neurons (Burn 1963). According to Burn, stronger stimulation results in pallor.

Marion A. Wenger

Environmental Psychology: An Overview

The field of environmental psychology has become crystallized in the last few decades. Among the trends that can be discerned as having had an impact on the field, the following may be cited: (1) the architectural profession has become highly sensitive to the functional adequacy of buildings and other man-made structures; (2) from an entirely different perspective, the field of behavioral geography has sprung into being, through the efforts of a growing number of geographers; (3) the growing concern over the population problem, both as a national and an international issue; (4) the concerns of conservationists and of environmentalists more generally, with problems of pollution, wilderness preservation, conservation of natural resources, and energy consumption. The physical environment represents a constellation of stimulus conditions that create the context and background for behavior.

Cutting across the diverse approaches, influences, and trends discussed above are certainly more general conceptual and methodological issues, which workers in this field have had to face. Perhaps the most pervasive is, paradoxically enough, how much and what sort of role should be accorded the physical environment as an influence on behavior. Much of the thinking and research in this field has laid stress on the role of the individual as a mediator of the environment-behavior relationship. Accordingly, concepts such as mental maps, personal space, environmental meanings and values, and theoretical frameworks, such as those of cognitive-developmental and personal-construct theory, have been invoked to handle phenomena in this field. Similarly, methodologies, such as factor analysis of semantic differential ratings and the like, have been applied to deal with individual-difference variables and factors in the individual's response to the environment based in the organism, rather than the environment.

Joachim F. Wohlwill

Epidemiological Research in Social Psychiatry

A pioneering study by Faris and Dunham in Chicago in the 1930s sparked investigators' efforts to uncover social processes causing mental disorders. From an analysis of state hospital admissions they found that schizophrenics came predominantly from a deteriorated inner-city area, while manic-depressives came from all parts of the city. These investigators hypothesized that the area producing the schizophrenics, "hobohemia," was pathogenic. The poverty, deprivation, and social isolation, if not a relative degree of social disorganization in the inner-city area, probably accounted for the high frequency of schizophrenia.

In the 1950s, Hollingshead and Redlich (1958) gathered data on almost all of the inhabitants of New Haven, Connecticut, who were obtaining mental health care. In *Social Class and Mental Illness* they reported that, generally, lower-social-status patients were more likely to have serious mental disorders, while the upper were more likely to have milder forms of mental illness, for example, neurotic depressions.

The large-scale field studies that provided first-hand information have been carried out in North America. In the Stirling County Study in Nova Scotia, D. C. Leighton et al. (1963) interviewed a random sample of the adult population to test their social disintegration hypothesis. According to established criteria, certain communities in the county were placed on a socially integrated-disintegrated continuum. Mental illness and impairment rates were found to be higher in the disintegrated than in the more-integrated communities.

In the Midtown Manhattan study, almost 2,000 randomly selected adults were interviewed in their homes (Langner and Michael 1963). Less than 25% of the sample was found to be well—free from impairment. As in the Stirling County study, which reported that only about 40% of the sample was judged to show little or no evidence of a psychiatric disorder, mental illness and impairment rates were higher in the elderly and in the poor than in the younger or more affluent. The investigators in the Midtown Manhattan study formulated a stress-strain model of illness; stress was defined as noxious or potentially noxious factors, while strain was the resultant personality deformation.

Findings from epidemiologic studies using either patient or survey data indicate generally that mental disorders are more common in the elderly than in the young, and in females than in males.

Generally accepted definitions of mental illness not only change from era to era but also connect and expand. As D. W. Dunham (1973) explains, the widening of the definition may be responsible for the marked differences in the results of field studies conducted in the United States and northern Europe before and after World War II. The percentages reported ill in the 1920s and 1930s ranged from 1.1 to 7.5% of the populations studied, in contrast to a range from 3.4 to as high as 60% and more after the war.

Notwithstanding research difficulties, epidemiologic studies have produced certain findings of importance for social psychiatry. The most significant are the broadening of the definition of mental illness, the impact of rapid social change, and the association between poverty and the greater frequency of mental disorders.

John J. Schwab

Erikson, Erik Homburger (1902–1994)

Erik Erikson developed new psychoanalytic conceptual systems related to the concepts of identity, identity crisis, and psychosocial moratorium. In *Childhood and Society*, published in 1950, Erikson analyzed the relationship between the individual and his or her social, economic, or historical environment. In *Young Man Luther* (1958), Erikson showed how youths tried to settle within themselves various conflicts and develop into strongminded, intricate, and powerful personalities. In *Ghandi's Truth* (1969), Erikson showed how Ghandi worked through his life to find a way of living up to certain ideals. In his later works Erikson linked psychoanalysis to ethology, history, political science, philosophy, and theology.

Robert Coles

Ethical Principles of Psychologists and Code of Conduct

Ethical guidelines used by psychologists are published as the *Ethical Principles of Psychologists and Code of Conduct* by the American Psychological Association (APA) (1992). According to the preamble, the code "has as its primary goal the welfare and protection of the individuals and groups with whom psychologists work. It is the individual responsibility of each psychologist to aspire to the highest possible standards of conduct." Six general principles labeled *A* through *F* precede the main code. They are: *A:* competence; *B:* integrity; *C:* professional and scientific responsibility; *D:* respect for people's rights and dignity; *E:* concern for others' welfare; and *F:* social responsibility.

The code is then divided into eight sections, the first of which is labeled "General Standards"

because it is thought to be "potentially applicable to the professional and scientific activities of all psychologists." Under this section are found requirements for competence, i.e., that psychologists are to provide services only in specialties for which they are properly trained. They are enjoined to maintain their level of expertise "and undertake ongoing efforts to maintain competence in the skills they use." When providing services, they are expected to explain in advance "the nature of such services and appropriate information later about results and conclusions." Discrimination is prohibited. Sexual harassment is carefully defined and enjoined against. A psychologist must prevent personal problems from interfering with professional duties, and must prevent her influence or the results of her work from being misused. The manner in which relationships should be conducted with clients, colleagues, students, subordinates, and others are also specified.

The second section is labeled "Evaluation, Assessment, or Intervention." This section covers every essential assessment procedure in which psychologists may normally become involved, whether it be diagnosing of psychopathology or psychological testing in a school, business, or career counseling situation. "Psychologists perform evaluations, diagnostic services, or interventions only within the context of a defined professional relationship." Psychologists must make certain that both their assessment procedures and the ensuing results are not misused. Assessment techniques that are outdated must not be used. There are standards for scoring and interpreting test results, including a requirement that they be appropriately explained.

Section three is labeled "Advertising and Other Public Statements." Psychologists are expected to prevent or correct deceptive statements made by others with regard to their work. They must not "make public statements that are false, deceptive, misleading, or fraudulent," and may only "claim as credentials . . . degrees that (1) were earned from a regionally accredited educational institution or (2) were the basis for psychology licensure by the state in which they practice."

Section four, "Therapy," spells out the standards for a doctor-patient relationship within a therapeutic setting. Psychologists must "discuss with clients or patients ... the nature and anticipated course of therapy, fees, and confidentiality" and "avoid apparent misunderstandings about therapy." The phrase "Psychologists obtain appropriate informed consent to therapy or related procedures," is followed by a definition of what constitutes informed consent. "Psychologists do not engage in sexual intimacies with current patients and clients," and "do not accept as therapy patients or clients persons with whom they have engaged in sexual intimacies." The psychologist must also "provide for orderly and appropriate resolution of responsibility ... with paramount consideration given to the welfare of the patient or client" when interruption of service occurs.

Section five, "Privacy and Confidentiality," requires psychologists "to respect the confidentiality rights of those with whom they work or consult," and to minimize any intrusions on privacy. "Psychologists disclose confidential information without the consent of the individual only as mandated by law, or where permitted by law for a valid purpose." Confidentiality of information entered into computer files and databases must be protected. When their research is written about or lectured on, psychologists are expected to protect the privacy of patients, organizations, and research participants, and are expected to "disguise confidential information concerning such persons or organizations so that they are not individually identifiable to others."

Section six is labeled "Teaching, Training Supervision, Research, and Publishing." "Psychologists who are responsible for education and training programs seek to ensure that the programs are competently designed" and "seek to ensure that there is a current and accurate description of the program content, training goals and objectives." "When engaged in teaching or training, psychologists present psychological information accurately and with a reasonable degree of objectivity." Psychologists must "plan their research so as to minimize the possibility that results will be misleading," and "conduct research competently and with due concern for the dignity and welfare of the participants." Psychologists are expected to comply with the law at the federal and state level "as well as professional standards governing the conduct of research." Again,

rules for obtaining informed consent are carefully spelled out. With regard to the use of deception in research, "Psychologists do not conduct a study involving deception unless they have determined that the use of deceptive techniques is justified by the study's prospective scientific, educational, or applied value and that equally effective alternative procedures that do not use deception are not feasible." There are also extensive specifications regarding the use of animals in research.

Section seven, "Forensic Activities," spells out rules for the giving of testimony or provision of evidence in a legal proceeding. "Psychologists' forensic assessments ... are based on information and techniques ... sufficient to provide appropriate substantiation for their findings." And "psychologists provide written or oral forensic reports or testimony of the psychological characteristics of an individual only after they have conducted an examination of the individual adequate to support their statements or conclusions." "In forensic testimony and reports, psychologists testify truthfully, honestly, and candidly and, consistent with applicable legal procedures, describe fairly the bases for their testimony and conclusions."

Section eight, the final section, is titled "Resolving Ethical Issues." It declares that "psychologists have an obligation to be familiar with this Ethics Code, other applicable ethics codes, and their application to psychologists' work. Lack of awareness or misunderstanding of an ethical standard is not itself a defense to a charge of unethical conduct." The section concludes by requiring psychologists to report violations of the ethics code and to cooperate when such violations are investigated.

Benjamin B. Wolman
Paul D. Boyer

Ethics, Principles of Medical and Psychiatric

Ethical guidelines for psychiatry are specified in the *Principles of Medical Ethics with Annotations Especially Applicable to Psychiatry*, published by the American Psychiatric Association (APA) (1993). They are taken directly from the *Principles of Medi-*

cal Ethics of the American Medical Association. As stated in the preamble, "The medical profession has long subscribed to a body of ethical statements developed primarily for the benefit of the patient." These ethical statements "are not laws but standards of conduct, which define the essentials of honorable behavior for the physician." They contain seven sections; each of the seven is accompanied by a set of annotations especially applicable to psychiatry.

Section 1: A physician shall be dedicated to providing competent medical service with compassion and respect for human dignity.

This section defines the doctor-patient relationship as one that ought to enable the patient to have complete faith and confidence in the psychiatrist, coupled with an effort to guarantee access to mental health services by every member of society. The first annotation includes the words, "The patient may place his/her trust in his/her psychiatrist knowing that the psychiatrist's ethics and professional responsibilities preclude . . . exploiting the patient. The psychiatrist shall be ever vigilant about the impact that his/her conduct has . . . upon the well being of the patient." The second declares that "a psychiatrist should not be a party to any type of policy that excludes, segregates, or demeans the dignity of any patient because of ethnic origin, race, sex, creed, age, socioeconomic status, or sexual orientation."

Section 2: A physician shall deal honestly with patients and colleagues, and strive to expose those physicians deficient in character or competence, or who engage in fraud or deception.

This section specifies what is required to maintain an honest level of interaction between psychiatrist and patient. The first annotation states that "the requirement that the physician conduct himself/herself with propriety in his/her profession . . . is especially important in the case of the psychiatrist because the patient tends to model his/her behavior after that of his/her psychiatrist by identification. . . . Sexual activity with a current or former patient is unethical." The second includes the words, "The

psychiatrist should diligently guard against exploiting information furnished by the patient and should not use the . . . therapeutic situation to influence the patient in any way not directly relevant to the treatment goals."

Section 4: A physician shall respect the rights of patients, of colleagues, and of other health professionals, and shall safeguard patient confidences within the constraints of the law.

The rules of doctor-patient confidentiality are spelled out in the annotations to this section. The first includes the sentence "Confidentiality is essential to psychiatric treatment." The second begins, "A psychiatrist may release confidential information only with the authorization of the patient or under proper legal compulsion." In the ninth we are told that "the right of the patient to confidentiality and, by extension, to unimpaired treatment, should be given priority." Possible exceptions to the rule of confidentiality are specified in the eighth annotation: "When in the clinical judgment of the treating psychiatrist the risk of danger is deemed to be significant, the psychiatrist may reveal confidential information disclosed by the patient." Thus there is a provision granting the psychiatrist the right to violate the rule of confidentiality under special circumstances.

Sections 1, 2, and 4 seek to establish a standard of quality for the doctor-patient relationship. The relationship must be conducted with "compassion and respect," the psychiatrist must "deal honestly with patients" and must not be a party to any form of discrimination, must observe confidentiality, etc. All of these provisions go directly to the core of the one-on-one interchange within the therapeutic situation.

Other provisions of the code spell out a plethora of issues, including the contractual nature of mental health services, an enjoinment against fee splitting, the right to protest against social injustice (especially when something is deemed "contrary to the best interests of the patient"), standards for research, professional conduct in a training situation, how to interact with other mental health professionals, how to deal with other psychiatrists who are no longer competent to practice or who violate this code, responsibility when interviewing someone charged with a crime, the responsibility to improve the community in which they practice, and much more. Section 5, annotation 1, reads, "Psychiatrists are responsible for their own continuing education and should be mindful of the fact that theirs must be a lifetime of learning." It is thus a primary ethical responsibility of the psychiatrist to keep abreast of advancements in the field.

Benjamin B. Wolman
Paul D. Boyer

Ethological Motivation Theory

Classical ethologists hypothesized the existence of fixed action patterns (called "instincts") whose performance was inherently satisfying and each of which was motivated by a unique energy source called action-specific energy. The fixed action patterns themselves were thought to be invariant unified behavior patterns.

Classical ethological motivation theory explains vacuum and displacement activities as the result of overaccumulations of action-specific energy such that the energy forces the innate releasing mechanism and spontaneously flows out into behavioral channels. In the case of vacuum activities, the overaccumulation occurs as a result of the absence of the appropriate releaser, and the energy overflow is into the appropriate or autochthonous channel. In the case of displacement activities, the overaccumulation is the result of equal and simultaneous accumulation of action-specific energy appropriate to behavior that cannot be performed simultaneously, such as flight and incubation; the energy flow in this case is into an inappropriate or allochthonous channel.

Nicholas S. Thompson

Ethology

Classified ethology started with the observation that animal behavior can sometimes be regarded in the same way as animal morphology: just as features of form characterize and distinguish mockingbirds and house wrens, or mallard ducks and sheld ducks, so too do features of song or courtship movements. Moreover, the similarities and differences of form upon which taxonomy and judgments of phylogenetic affinity rely have, in comparisons of some groups, been found to have correlated similarities and differences in behavior.

Feedback

The notion of feedback implicit in this last observation was introduced to ethology by von Holst and Mittelsteadt in 1950 in their reafference principle, which states that initiation of movement may entail setting up "expectation" (*Sollwert*) of the stimulus change that should result from the movement, subsequent behavior depending upon "comparison" between this expectation and the stimulus change actually fed back (reafference). Since then there have been numerous attempts to apply the notion of feedback, and other concepts from cybernetics, to particular mechanisms of animal behavior, or in theoretical models of such mechanisms (e.g., McFarlane, 1973).

Heredity and Ontogeny

The evidence that behavior traits can be genetically inherited is sufficient to put the fact beyond doubt, especially for fruit flies and rodents. Particular behavioral traits have been associated with particular genes, and artificial selective breeding has been used to shift the behavioral characteristics of strains in predicted directions, even to the point of erecting barriers to breeding between strains that initially hybridized freely.

In many developmental studies it has been found that for experience of a certain sort to have an influence, it must be had within a certain limited period or phase of a growing animal's early life. Such critical or sensitive periods occur in many species of birds as part of a phenomenon called *imprinting*. A newly hatched gosling, for example, will follow the first moving object it sees, which from then on will be the "mother companion" for the gosling; such a gosling is said to be imprinted on the object. Normally, the first moving object a gosling sees is its mother, so the imprinting effects social attachment, and also, according to Konrad Lorenz (1935), teaches the gosling what another member of its species looks like, knowledge that it will need later when it comes to choose a mate.

Adaptive Significance

Much animal behavior poses questions about utility. Especially for the postures adopted and the sounds uttered in social situations, the question arises: What are they for? A first approach to this kind of question is little different from that to questions about causation: observation of what follows what, to discover the immediate consequences that performance of the behavior in question might have. The results of such observation may be checked experimentally by adding or subtracting in the relevant situation. In these ways, for example, Nicholas Tinbergen (1951) investigated what turned out to be threat and courtship signaling behavior of three-spined sticklebacks.

Colin Gordon Beer

Existential Analysis (*Daseinsanalyse*)

The terms *Analysen des Da-seins* and *Daseinsanalysen* first appear in Martin Heidegger's epoch-making work *Sein und Zeit* (Being and Time), published in 1927. There they refer solely to the philosophical exposition of the fundamental characteristics or *Existentialien* (in English sometimes referred to as "existentials" or "existential characteristics") on which the unity of human existence is based. Heidegger describes a number of such fundamental characteristics: the primary and all-founding world-openness of "human nature"; the primordial temporality and spatiality of the human being; one's attunement-to-world, which includes one's moods, disposition, temper, humors, and passions; being together with other beings of one's own kind in a common world; one's bodiliness (or better, one's bodyhood); and one's having to die (mortality).

As early as 1941, Ludwig Binswanger designated a new method of investigation as "psychiatric Daseinsanalysis." This method enables the concrete, particular, immediately sensorily perceptible psy-

chopathological symptoms and syndromes to be understood and described phenomenologically.

As a result of Heidegger's teaching, Medard Boss was able to emulate his thinking in the field of psychopathology and so develop his new insights into a *Grundriss der Medizin und der Psychologie*—fundamentals of medicine and psychology.

The daseinsanalytic approach is phenomenological. In other words, it consists of the simple practice of an undistorted seeing of that which reveals itself in what is seen.

The human *Da-sein* has then first to be characterized as an open worldly realm of the ability to perceive what it encounters. As such, it primordially spans the breadth of a world whose limits are there, where the most distant beings of that world engage the *Da-sein*. In this sense, the human *Da-sein* is fundamentally and characteristically "ek-static," and can, as a totally immaterial perceptivity—not, however, as a material body—always be "here" as well as "there," and so dwell in a free open place vis-à-vis whatever encounters it out of the openness of its world. The human being is not only capable of choosing knowingly which possibilities of relating to which of the multitudinous present beings he will actualize; he *has* to make such choices in every moment of his existence him*self*. The fundamental and unique selfness of human beings is founded in this.

Human existence is then always present as an already-being related to those beings engaging it from an immediate closeness, or to other beings that are distant and leave it indifferent. This constant already-taking of position and direction in the relationships to the close and distance entities of her world constitutes the nature of the primordial spatiality of the human being.

The basic state of the healthy human being is characterized as her ability to dispose freely over all her given possibilities for relating to whatever appears to her in the openness of her world. The character of all illness is correspondingly unitary. It consists solely of a restriction of "human freedom of movement," however this restriction may be structured. For this reason, the question that science has to direct to each ill person is threefold: In which way are which possibilities of relating to which range of encountered beings distorted? This basic way of questioning leads to a new general pathology, one that is adequate and appropriate to the human being understood as *Da-sein*.

Daseinsanalytic insights into the basic constitution of human beings not only make possible a new and more adequately human understanding of the different modes of illness but are also of preeminent practical therapeutic significance. As compared with the techniques suggested by the Freudian and Jungian schools of thought on the basis of their theories of dreams and transference, these new insights allow a quite different therapeutic application of dreams and a no-less-important change in the way of dealing with the patient-doctor relationship.

Medard Boss

Existential Psychology and Therapy

Existential psychology is but one expression of a cultural movement of reaction against psychological reductionism, idealism, rationalism, physicalism, and mechanistic determinism. At times, notably in some existentialistic philosophies, it became an overreaction giving rise to excessive subjectivism.

Existential Psychology
The following features tend to underlie most forms of existential psychology: (1) It is not a special school of psychology; representatives of different fields and schools try by means of the existential attitude and method to restore or increase within their own field a scientific interest in the human and experiential aspects of human psychology. (2) The study of measurable behavior should be complemented by a study of experience by means of scientific methods, among them the phenomenological. It is unscientific to allow assumptions of any school of philosophy, psychology, or psychiatry to affect the primary exploration of experience. (3) The results of phenomenological methods should be validated by methods of intersubjective validation and, if possible, complemented by traditional research. (4) The human dimension embraces the following characteristics:

a. Humanity is not only determined by its situation, but also has some freedom from it which can increase and be fostered therapeutically.

b. This freedom entails responsibility and, therewith, the possibility of the development of a scale of values and of authentic guilt to be distinguished from inauthentic guilt.

c. Psychology should also research basic human experiences, such as hope, joy, despair, anxiety, creativity, ego transcendence, playfulness, love, hate, envy, and originality.

d. Humanity must be understood in terms of interaction with the world and the situation in which it finds itself.

Main Features of Existential Therapy
Existential therapy aims at the development of existential commitment: the client's willingness to live a project of life that, according to her own insight, is in tune with the demands of reality. It also aims at the client's acceptance of herself, implying self-respect, a standing up for her own rights, and relative independence from parental figures and her environment.

Adrian Van Kaam

Expectancy and Aspiration

The act of estimating one's score in the research of Kurt Lewin and his associates in the 1920s and 1930s generated considerable research concerned with a subject's reactions to failure, success, and various patterns of outcome. An aspiration carries the implication of striving toward a goal level, as well as the more motivationally neutral idea of an objective estimate of one's chances.

In *Purposive Behavior in Animals and Men* (1932), E. C. Tolman expressed his concern for cognition as well as drive in the explanation of purposive behavior. Clark L. Hull was prepared to use anticipatory goal response in his analysis of rodent learning, but these were responses, however fractional. Tolman insisted that there were cognitive processes, utilizing perceptual and experiential contributions to create new cognitions, which guided behavior.

The use of expectancy in formal theories has led

to a general category known as expectancy-value theories. These have in common the use of probability estimates of outcome, and some way of designating outcome values as the critical variables to be included in formulations of behavioral choice, strength, onset, or direction.

Robert Charles Birney

Experimental Design: An Overview

Experimental design denotes a category of research that permits the inference of cause and effect. This is possible because differences observed in behavior can be directly related to differences in treatment that are under the explicit control of the experimenter.

Research Plan

Research hypothesis. The first step in a research plan is the formulation of a testable research hypothesis. These hypotheses flow directly from past work and usually represent logical deductions from theory. In this sense, research hypotheses are tests of the theory from which they are derived.

Independent variable. An independent variable refers to the differences among the treatment conditions that are systematically varied by the experimenter. These differences are often referred to as the levels of an independent variable. Independent variables may represent either qualitative differences (e.g., a comparison of the effect of different types of drugs on behavior) or differences along a quantitative dimension (e.g., the effects of varying amounts of a particular drug on behavior).

In choosing the levels of an independent variable, a researcher will usually attempt to include a representative sampling of the relevant dimension. For a qualitative variable this might mean including examples of all major categories that comprise the variable; for a quantitative variable this might mean the systematic sampling of the entire range of variation of the dimension.

More than one independent variable may be manipulated by means of a factorial design. In a factorial design, the experimenter includes every possible combination of the levels of the two (or more) independent variables. Such a design allows a determination of the effects of each variable averaged over the levels of the other (called main effects). Two variables are said to interact when the behavioral effects of one of the variables changes at the different levels of the second variable.

Dependent variable. That aspect of behavior that is observed and recorded during the administration of the experimental treatments is called the *dependent variable* or the *response measure*. Any aspect of behavior that can be counted or measured reliably can serve as a dependent variable.

Statistical analysis. One major use of statistics is in the summary or description of the discrete observations that constitute the results of an experiment. The most common descriptive statistics are measures of central tendency (average performance), measures of variability (degree to which a set of scores is variable), and measures of correlation (degree to which two or more response measures are related). Two other major functions of statistics are inferential in nature, allowing the extension of findings obtained in an experiment to a much larger population of subjects, of which those included in the experiment are considered a sample. In order to make inferences from a sample concerning features of the population, two types of operations are performed, estimation and hypothesis testing.

The mere presence of differences among treatment conditions on a response measure does not mean that they were necessarily produced by the differences in treatment. The usual random assignment of subjects to treatment conditions, for example, might have resulted in ability differences among the conditions that existed before the start of the experiment and which would account completely for the differences observed during the experiment. To assess this possibility, a ratio is formed that compares the variation among the treatment conditions that may be due to treatment effects and to chance factors, by the variation due to chance factors alone. (In the analysis of variance, this ratio is the F statistic.) If it is hypothesized that there are no treatment effects (the null hypothesis), the numerator term now represents only chance variation (treatment variation is assumed to be absent under the null hypothesis), and the ratio should approximate unity.

On the other hand, if the null hypothesis is false and there are "real" treatment effects (the alternative hypothesis), this ratio should be greater than unity. At this point the researcher applies a decision rule that specifies the circumstances under which the null hypothesis will be rejected in favor of the alternative hypothesis. While an application of the rule will still result in errors of statistical inference, they can be dealt with in the sense that they can be controlled and estimated.

Experimental control. An extremely large number of independent variables vary during the conduct of an experiment. Many of these will be irrelevant or ineffective in influencing the behavior under study, and need not be controlled. Many others, on the other hand, either will be known to influence or will have the potential to influence the behavior being investigated. Because these independent variables are not of systematic interest to the researcher, they will be termed extraneous. The operation of extraneous variables must be brought under some sort of control, however. If they are not controlled, one or more may vary systematically with the variations in the independent variable under manipulation, and a confounding of extraneous and treatment variables will exist. When this occurs, it may be impossible to determine the independent influence of the confounded variables.

Types of Experimental Design

In completely randomized design (or independent-groups designs), subjects are assigned at random to the different treatments or treatment combinations. Each subject serves in only one condition, and the analysis is based upon a single score provided by each subject. (Additional response measures may be analyzed separately or by multivariate procedures.) These designs are relatively simple to analyze, require the fewest statistical assumptions, and are the most common type of design observed in the literature. Randomized block designs introduce a matching variable in a factorial arrangement. The subjects from each matching block (e.g., low, medium, or high IQ) are still assigned randomly to the treatment conditions, however. The advantage of this design is in the reduction of error variability and the opportu-

nity to determine the interaction, if any, of the blocking variable and the experimental variables.

Geoffrey Keppel

Experimental Neurosis

As used by Ivan Petrovich Pavlov, the term *neurosis* referred to a chronic disturbance of the behavior of a dog, which might last for weeks, months, or even years. Such disturbances could be produced in a variety of ways: using CSs that were too strong or too complex, creating a strain on the inhibitory process by using a conditioned stimulus-unconditioned stimulus (CS-US) interval that was too long, castration, or producing a "collision" between excitatory and inhibitory neural mechanisms.

In America, research on experimental neuroses was carried on by H. S. Liddell and Jules H. Masserman, working with sheep and cats respectively. In a general way, Liddell was able to confirm Pavlov's observations both as to the means of producing experimental neuroses and the behavioral symptoms. Of particular importance was the fact that Liddell found experimental neuroses to be very persistent, lasting for a period of 13 years in one case.

Gregory A. Kimble

Experimental Psychology

Experimental psychology is the use of the methods of science to establish and test the general principles (or laws) of the behavior and experience of humans and the behavior of animals. It manipulates (where possible) the antecedent conditions under which the behavior occurs and observes any subsequent changes in behavior; it examines correlations between events and behavior; it proposes theories and tests them; and it adopts well-supported theories as principles. Historically, it has examined sensing, perceiving, motivation, learning, remembering, problem solving, and thinking. Its present concerns range from genetics to consciousness, and its scope is as broad as everything that humans and animals do.

Experimental psychology can be contrasted with

those areas of psychology in which the principles are applied to particular problems, namely, clinical, educational, industrial, organizational, social, and political psychology. But the contrast can be overdrawn; these problem-solving areas in turn help in the examination of the principles and suggest new principles for study.

John K. Bare

Experimental Psychology: An Overview

For about a quarter of a century (roughly 1940–1965), B. F. Skinner's behaviorism was the most visible intellectual force in American psychology. Its power originated in a much-needed reminder to psychologists that human behavior cannot be adequately accounted for by "explanations" that rest upon reification of the phenomena under inquiry.

Along with the burgeoning of research, theory, and application, problems inevitably arose that did not lend themselves to explanations consistent with paradigms and rules acceptable to operant behaviorists. Some of the problems originated within the laboratory itself. Unexpected limitations were uncovered in the control of animals' behavior by instrumental reinforcement contingencies. The distinctions among operant, reflexive, and species-specific behaviors began to encounter difficulties. Other problems arose in applied areas. These observations were interpreted as indicating that organisms were capable of behaving in ways that could not be predicted exclusively from experimenter manipulations of reinforcement, drive, discriminative stimuli, or from plausible past conditioning histories.

Joseph M. Notterman
Joseph Farley

Extinction

The essential condition for the establishment of a classical or operant conditioned response (CR) is reinforcement. The removal of reinforcement after a response is conditioned leads to its gradual disap-

pearance or extinction. The process of extinction is complex, but there is reason to argue for at least the following contributing processes:

Generalization decrement. The elimination of reinforcement represents a physical change in the experimental situation, and the response is weakened because of this change.

Counterconditioning. The general idea here is that a new form of conditioning replaces the original conditioning. Stimulus-response (S-R) theorists argue that the interfering mechanism is the conditioning of a new response to the conditioned stimulus (CS). Stimulus-stimulus (S-S) theorists believe that what is involved is the creation of a new expectancy.

Loss of motivation. In any conditioning situation one of the effects of the unconditioned stimulus (US) is motivational. This effect may be positive if the reinforcer is a positive reinforcer, or negative if the reinforcer is an aversive one. In either case, the removal of the US lowers motivation and consequently lowers performance.

Inhibition. In particular, the phenomenon of disinhibition shows that the extinguished response is not destroyed but merely inhibited.

Loss of habit strength. It is impossible to say whether this is any different from counterconditioning. It depends upon the particular position the theorist takes. The reference is to a weakening of the connection between CS and CR.

Gregory A. Kimble

Extrinsic Motivation

Extrinsic motivation, in general, refers to motivation for behavior that is neither inherent in the behavior itself nor representative of goals established by the behaving person. That is, extrinsic motivation is, in a sense, imposed from without. For example, when a child's performance at a piano lesson is rewarded with a gold star, this reward has nothing inherently to do with playing the piano. In school, the child may have no goal for achievement, so that an external reward or punishment system may be introduced to assure that the child studies and attempts to master the subject matter. Extrinsic motivation, then, can refer to rather arbitrary rewards and goals, in contrast to the inherent reward of an act itself, or to self-determined goals that characterize intrinsic motivation.

Charles N. Cofer

Eysenck, Hans J. (1916–)

Hans J. Eysenck's work covered several areas in psychology, including personality, psychotherapy, intelligence, and testing methods. His personality trait theory distinguishes between introversion and extroversion, and between stability and neuroticism. Eysenck's Personality Inventory (EPI) includes twenty-four yes-no items for the extraversion scale, twenty-four items for the neuroticism scale, and nine items for the lie scale. Eysenck combined classical conditioning with his factor-analytic description of personality traits.

According to Eysenck, neurotic behavior is a learned behavior, caused by overconditioning (Type I) or underconditioning (Type II). Anxiety, phobias, and obsessive-compulsive disorders belong to Type I. Type II disorders caused by underconditioning are related to the failure to condition positive and adaptive habits. Eysenck's method of behavior therapy is based on Ivan Petrovich Pavlov's and Clark L. Hull's theories.

Benjamin B. Wolman

Eysenck's Personality Inventory (EPI)

This is a personality test that has three measures: (1) introversion-extroversion; (2) neuroticism-stability; and (3) lie. It is essentially an upgraded version and revision of Eysenck's earlier Maudsley Personality Inventory (MPI). There are two equivalent A and B versions for subjects or individuals of ninth-grade education or above; the availability of two equivalent forms should be especially useful for those who may be doing research with the instrument.

Item selection on the EPI's two primary scales, E (extroversion-introversion) and N (neuroticism-stability), has been improved to reduce and elimi-

nate the modest correlations that were present on the older MPI between these scales. While the N and E dimensions are now uncorrelated on the EPI, the correlations between the two E scales (on the MPI and EPI) and the two N scales on both instruments are as high as the reliability of either of the two instruments.

Much research on the EPI centers on predictions that Eysenck makes about the influence of the E and N factors on other personality characteristics and behaviors of the individual.

In a study by Harrison and McLaughlin (1969), it was found that self-ratings of extroversion and neuroticism were highly correlated with scores obtained on the EPI on these respective dimensions (with correlations of .72 and .56).

Victor B. Cline

Eysenck's Trait Theory

Eysenck's most substantial contribution to trait theory is in the area of personality. He assumes a hierarchical model with the following levels of generality distinguished: (1) specific responses, for example, approaching a stranger at a cocktail party; (2) habitual responses, for example, repeatedly approaching strangers; (3) traits, for example, sociability; and (4) types, for example, extroversion. "Type" is used to refer to the highest level of generality, and is not meant to imply exclusive categories.

Eysenck has put forward a biological theory of temperamental differences. He postulates that the extroversion-introversion dimension reflects variations in the function of the ascending reticular activating system. According to neurophysiologists, this functions to produce nonspecific arousal in the cerebral cortex in response to external stimulation, and Eysenck postulates that arousal is higher for introverts than extroverts, given identical conditions of stimulation. This difference in arousal is thought to underlie all the experimentally observed differences between extroverts and introverts. For example, introverts acquire conditioned responses more quickly than extroverts; thus, introverts develop dysthymic symptoms because of their overready conditioning to normally neutral stimuli. Hysterical and pyschopathic behavior are more common in extroverts, because they represent a failure of the conditioning that constitutes the normal socialization process.

In *The Psychology of Politics* (1955), H. J. Eysenck identified two major attitude factors: radicalism versus conservatism and tough-mindedness versus tender-mindedness. Because these two factors were orthogonal, the recurrent problem of left-wing authoritarianism was resolved. Authoritarianism as measured by the California F scale turns out to be tough-minded conservatism; members of Communist groups turn out to be tough-minded radicals. Thus, Fascists and Communists are widely separated on the R dimension but very similar on the T dimension. Further research revealed that R is based largely on class interests, while T correlates with "masculine" personality characteristics, such as psychoticism and aggressiveness.

Glenn D. Wilson

· F ·

Facial and Body Deformity in Children: Psychological Effects

Physical features are assumed to influence social behavior in one or more ways: (1) differential expectations are elicited for persons of differing levels of attractiveness; (2) the process of social exchange is influenced; (3) social images resulting from social exchange are modified; and (4) interpersonal behavior patterns of physically attractive persons are likely to be more positive and to display more self-confidence. Evidence supporting the assumption that social exchange and social images are influenced by physical features can be found in the literature on peer relations.

Facial attractiveness is a salient determinant in the perception of and dispositional attribution toward others and in interactive behavior. Therefore, facial disfigurement ought to severely hamper adjustment. The effect of facial disfigurement in children has not been studied very extensively, but the studies that have examined the problem indicate that the area around the mouth has the greatest impact because it is the focal point during conversation.

A major factor in the individual's adjustment to disfigurement seems to be the time at which the deformity occurred. According to A. C. Redmond et al. (1980), children who have severe craniofacial malformations from birth experience stressful family lives.

Many of the physiological reactions of burned children result from the pain accompanying the injury. M. K. Savedra (1976, 1977) identifies six strategies used by children: reduction of threat, postponement, bypass, constructing a distance between self and threat, diverting attention, and sleep with-drawal. Postponement of treatment associated with the pain was the most common strategy.

Some evidence for personality change in handicapped children appeared in a study comparing a group of handicapped children with a matched group of nonhandicapped children (Harper 1978).

The child with a facial or physical deformity must face an enormous task in terms of coping with this disability. Not only must the child reestablish the body image and self-concept that were distorted as a result of a birth defect, a disease, or an accident, but this child also faces probable social isolation and stereotyping. The reconstruction of a physical identity is the most immediate and crucial task, because disfigurement of a part of the body is generalized by the child to the entire body. Even though the child eventually comes to terms with this facial or physical disability, he or she still faces the problem of social acceptance.

Joseph C. LaVoie

Factor Analysis of Psychological Tests

Factor analysis is a class of statistical methods for combining scores on a relatively large number of variables into a smaller set, which contains most of the information in the larger set. The variables usually are psychological tests of aptitude and personality, but the logic applies to any variables.

Advantages of Factor Analysis
The major advantages of factor analysis are in terms of parsimony in (1) employing psychological tests in applied situations, (2) performing statistical analyses

of test scores and their relationships to other variables, and (3) helping to understand psychological abilities, personality characteristics, and other traits. In essence, what one attempts to do is to boil down a rather miscellaneous collection of variables into a smaller and more important set of factors.

Data Matrix

Factor analysis concerns a rectangular table of data, such as that illustrated in table 1. A data matrix (or "score matrix," as it frequently is called) will be symbolized as S. The matrix contain the scores of N persons on k measures. Thus, a_1 is the score of person 1 on measure a; a_2 is the score of person 2 on measure a; and k_n is the score of person N or measure k. It is assumed that scores on each measure are standardized. Then, the sum of scores in any column of the table is zero, and the variance of scores in any column is 1.0. The term *measures* is used in a very general sense to refer to any set of attributes that can be quantified.

TABLE 1

Data Matrix

		Measures						
		a	b	c	.	.	.	k
	1	a_1	b_1	c_1	.	.	.	k_1
	2	a_2	b_2	c_2	.	.	.	k_2
	3	a_3	b_3	c_3	.	.	.	k_3
	4	a_4	b_4	c_4	.	.	.	k_4
Persons	.	.	.	.	.	.	.	.
	.		.	.	.	.	.	.
	.	.	.	.	.	.	.	.
	N	a_n	b_n	c_n	.	.	.	k_n

Source: J. C. Nunnally, *Psychometric Theory*, New York: McGraw-Hill, 1967.

Linear combinations. Any linear combination of the variables in a data matrix is said to be a factor of that matrix. That is all there is to it. Any linear combination (A) would be as follows;

$$A = w_a a + w_b b + w_c c + \ldots + w_k k$$

If, for example, the weight for variable a (w_a) is .80, the scores for each person on measure a are multiplied by .80. The weights can be either all the same or different. Some can be positive and some can be negative. Different methods for deriving factors are defined in terms of the ways that weights are used for obtaining linear combinations. Any consistent method, whether it makes sense or nonsense, for determining such weights is the basis for a particular type of factor analysis. For example, the centroid method requires that all weights be either +1 or -1.

Factor correlations. After a factor is obtained, scores on the factor can be correlated (PM formula) with scores on each of the individual variables in the data matrix.

Successive factoring. In most problems it is important to go beyond one factor and see what, if any, other factors are involved in the data matrix. The number of factors to be obtained is suggested by the first set of factor loadings. If these are very high, it suggests that only one factor is needed. If they are near zero, it suggests that there are no common factors. If they are moderately high (e.g., around .50), it suggests that more factors may be needed.

The matrix of factor loadings. A matrix of factor loadings is shown in table 2. Variables a, b, and c tend to have substantial loadings only on factor A; d, e, and f have substantial loadings only on factor B; and g, h, and i have substantial loadings only on factor C. There are some principles concerning the properties of matrices of factor loadings that form the basis for interpreting results. The square of any factor loading tells the proportion of variance explained in a particular variable by a factor. The correlation of a variable with a factor has the same interpretation that any correlation coefficient does. Thus, since variable a has a loading of .60 on factor A, it can be said that factor A explains 36% of the variance of a.

The sum of squares in any column of the factor matrix indicates the total amount of variance explained by that factor for the variables as a group. More important, the average square loadings (V_i) in a column is the proportion (without the decimal, a percentage) of variance of the variables as a group explained by that factor. Thus, factor A explains 19% of the total variance in the original data matrix X. The sum of average squared loadings for the several factors (V) indicates the percentage of variance explained by the factors, which provides an indica-tion of the extent to which a set of factors does a good job of explaining the original variables.

TABLE 2

Matrix of Factor Loadings

		Factors			
		A	B	C	h2
	a	.60	-.06	.02	.36
	b	.81	.12	-.03	.67
	c	.77	.03	.08	.60
	d	.01	.65	-.04	.42
Variables	e	.03	.80	.07	.65
	f	.12	.67	-.05	.47
	g	.19	-.02	.68	.50
	h	.08	-.10	.53	.30
	i	.26	-.13	.47	.31
Sum of squared loadings		1.76	1.56	.98	
	V_i	.19	.17	.77	$V(V_i)$=.47

Source: J. C. Nunnally, *Psychometric Theory*, New York: McGraw-Hill, 1967.

The correlation matrix. It frequently is said that one "factors a correlation matrix." In previous sec-tions it was stated that it is more appropriate to think of factoring the data matrix. For two reasons, however, correlations among the variables play important parts in factor analysis. Preparatory to any factor analysis, the first step is to compute the full matrix of correlations among variables. The first important part played by the correlation matrix is in determining the signs and sizes of coefficients in the linear combinations that produce factors. For exam-ple, if all the correlations are positive, which tends to indicate that all the variables have something in common, it might be decided to give all variables positive weights in the first linear combination. If, on the other hand, some of the variables tend to corre-late negatively with the others, it might be decided to give negative weights to those. If, instead of assigning weights on some a priori basis, one derives weights mathematically in a way that optimizes some property of the data, the correlation matrix indicates how that optimization is to be done. Thus, the corre-lation matrix is very useful in determining the signs and sizes of coefficients in linear combinations.

Hypothesis testing with factor analysis. In some instances factor analysis is employed when the inves-tigator has definite hypotheses about the clustering of tests. For example, in investigating the realm of reasoning abilities, the investigator may hypothesize that there are four types of reasoning ability, which he attempts to measure. He develops four tests to measure each of the types of reasoning ability, result-ing in sixteen tests in all. After the tests are adminis-tered to subjects, a 16x16 matrix of correlations is obtained.

Exploratory factor analysis. In most uses of factor analysis, hypotheses have not been conducted so as to guide the way in which factors are determined. An example is a situation in which an investigator has collected a large number of tests that supposedly concern some aspect of reasoning ability. Although the investigator has some hunches about at least some of the clusters of factors that might be involved, these hunches are not sufficient to guide the type of hypothesis-testing factor analysis described previously. What investigators do in that case is to let the statistics speak for themselves, as evidenced in some standard procedure of factor analysis. The first step is usually to apply a method of condensation; this boils down the collection of tests to a smaller number of arbitrarily chosen fac-tors. The factors are arbitrarily chosen in the sense that they are required to fit a statistical principle rather than being obtained with respect to a theory. The most frequently used method of condensation in modern times is referred to as the "method of principle axes." With this method, each successive factor is obtained in such a way as to explain as many as possible of the correlations in the matrix. The first factor explains as much as possible of the variance—the sum of squared correlations. After the influence of the first factor is partialed from the orig-inal correlation matrix, the second factor is extracted in such a way as to explain the maximum possible variance in the residual matrix, and so on for subsequent factors.

Jum C. Nunnally

Faculty Psychology

Plato (427–347 B.C.) divided the soul into three strata: the rational or thinking part, seated in the head; the volitional part or will, based in the heart; and the appetites or desire, located in the abdomen (perhaps the liver?). Will functioned as a mediator between reason and desire, and Plato gave considerable place to the irrational in man. Freud's id, ego, superego, and unconscious seem thus to be foreshadowed here. Augustine (354–430 A.D.) spoke of man's reason, memory, will, and imagination in a rather Platonic vein.

Aristotle (384–323 B.C.) divided human functions into three levels: vegetative, sensory or animal, and rational. Each of these was further classified into several subdivisions, notably the latter two into cognitive and appetitive. Thomas Aquinas (1225–1274) was to use these divisions with minor refinements, but, as will be noted, neither of these philosophers conceived of man's powers as separate faculties in the later understanding of the term.

Christian von Wolff (1679–1754) in Germany and Thomas Reid (1710–1796) of the Scottish school are considered the chief proponents of the modern concept of faculty psychology. Reid spoke of "intellectual powers" and "active powers" of man, reason, memory, emotion, and will.

Immanuel Kant (1724–1804) held an elaborate system of mental faculties in man. His basic tripartite division was into cognitive, desire, and feeling (pleasure or displeasure); cognitive in turn was subdivided into understanding, judgment, and reason. Faculty theory in its eighteenth-century form declined with the rise of scientific psychology and even became an object of ridicule. The empirical approach of both the structural and functional schools of psychology demanded experimental correlates rather than hypothetical entities. P. Flourens and later Karl S. Lashley showed that the brain was to some extent equipotential; even the specific localizations by Pierre Paul Broca, Ramon y Cajal, and others did not confirm either phrenology or facultism.

For Jim Locke, as for the scholastics, man's powers were qualities, not substances. And for both, man is born with the capacity or ability to function,

not with actual function or content (ideas). In this more plausible form, the notion of operative powers stresses that knowledge is not mere passive reception of impressions but is active in ways suggestive of Gestalt and other perceptual approaches, and of psychologies that use such concepts as ego strength, choice behavior, and self-actualization.

James E. Royce

Failure: The Tendency to Avoid It

In contemporary theory of achievement motivation, the tendency to avoid failure—which opposes, blocks, dampens, that is, subtracts from the tendency to achieve success—is conceived as the behavioral effect of anxiety or fear of failure (Atkinson and Raynor 1974).

The general idea that an expectancy of some negative outcome (e.g., punishment, failure, rejection, etc.) of an activity will produce a specific tendency not to undertake that activity is one of the heuristic hypotheses of decision theory (W. Edwards 1954). If one always chooses so as to maximize subjectively expected utility (SEU) from among the available alternatives, and

$$SEU = P_1 U_1 + P_2 U_2 + \ldots + P_n U_n$$

where P_1 is the subjective probability of consequence 1 and U_1 is its value (positive or negative) to the individual, it is clearly implied that the product of $P_n U_n$ will be negative if the expected consequence of a particular activity is negative. If a positive product is taken to imply "do it," one cannot escape the implication that a negative product implies "don't do it."

John W. Atkinson

Fairbairn, W. Ronald (1890–1964)

W. Ronald Fairbairn believed that Freud's libido theory should be replaced by a theory of personality development founded on ego structure, created out of experience with objects. According to Fairbairn, libido is the innate, object-seeking tendency of the

TABLE 1

Levels of Familial Transmission

A. Cellular and subcellular	B. Biopsychological organizaiton	C. Relational guidance	D. Socialization

1. Genetic
  a. Fixed chromosomal defects
  b. Accidental one-generational aberrations of genes
2. Prenatal environmental
  a. Mechanical
  b. Metabolic—nutritional
	1. Transmission through maternal behavior (e.g., anxiety)
	  a. Autonomic stabilization and integration
	  b. Special foci—locus of least resistance (e.g., through bowel training)
	2. Body image and self-boundary conceptualization
	  a. Attachment behavior (e.g., symbiotic)
	  b. Identifying and labeling of feelings
	  c. Helping child develop self-sense (vs. engulfment)
	3. Language and thought ordering
	  a. Content
	  b. Form
	  c. Abstraction
		1. Modeling—gender identity and affectivity
		2. Culture-appropriate repression—incest taboo and psychosexual moratorium
		3. Peer environment provisions and guidance
			1. Communication competence regarding linguistic and interactional symbols and abstract thought
			2. Adolescence—tolerance for identity experiments
			3. Fostering and regulating peer intimacy
			4. Emancipation from family of origin

ego. Aggressive behavior is reactive to frustration, and anxiety is a direct innate response to an absence of an object or to its loss. The activity of the super-ego refers to a complex process involving the ego ideal, the antilibidinal ego, and the antilibidinal object.

John D. Sutherland

Family in the Etiology of Mental Disorders

The role of the family in the transmission of essential human characteristics should be considered on four levels. On all levels transmission risks are twofold: one is that the transfer mechanisms may be defective, and the other that pathogenic and pathological items pass from parents to children. Defective transmission could occur prenatally; for instance, if there is insufficient oxygenation of fetal blood or deficiency in nutrients reaching the fetus due to placental abnormalities, aberrant nurturance and communication of many types could take place. Chromosomal or cellular aberrations, inherited or caused by damaging drugs crossing the placenta, and indoctrination in deviant sociocultural concepts after birth exemplify transfers of abnormal conditions or information. The four levels of transmission concern (1) cellular and subcellular elements, (2) psychobiological organization, (3) basic human roles

TABLE 2

Family System Deficiencies in Psychiatric Disorders

Level	Schizophrenia	Psychopathy	Affective Illness	Psychophysiological Disorders	Neuroses
Cellular	Undefined inherited factor (?)	Possible preparanatal embarrassment	Undefined inheritance factor	(?) Specific organ system vulnerability	—
Psychobiological Organization	Nurturance and weaning disturbed	Perfunctory nurturance; (?) dificient affectivity	Overly rigid, with emphasis on developmental achievement	Overemphasis on particular body function and/or insufficient autonomical nervous system stabilization	Possible stress on particular body function
Personality Development	Disturbance in all areas—e.g., leadership, communication, affectivity, and boundary development	Overemphasis on appearance; disregard for feelings of self and others	Intolerance for hostile and sad affects; inculcation of shame and guilt	Bodily expression of conflicts; (?) body image disturbance	Selective repression of conflicts; parental modeling of neurotic solutions
Socialization	Emancipation handicapped by previous deficiencies	Defective communication and family-community boundary	—	—	—

and relationships, and (4) socialization in, and emancipation from, the nuclear family.

The first function in family organization is the establishment of the marital coalition, defined as those interactional patterns that spouses first develop for their mutual needs and satisfaction. Later, in the evolving structure and dynamics of the family, especially the isolated nuclear family, this coalition must serve the children and their age-appropriate needs.

Emancipation of offspring from the parental family is the final evolutionary task of the nuclear family system. To be accomplished succcessfully, this final separation cannot be abrupt; it must be the culmination of many forms of increasing psychosocial separateness between parents and child. The first step in this evolution is weaning, followed by many partial steps of emancipation and vectorial independence, which the family must abet and effect as the child moves through later developmental stages. Among such steps are the first school entrance, camp or other living-away-from-home experiences, peer relationships, dating, job or college, and the offspring's final achievement of a solid identity and capacity for self-direction, culminating ideally in marriage and parenthood.

A chromosomal deficiency—for instance, of phenylalaninase—can lead to mental retardation or psychosis, but need not, if dietary adjustments and special training are provided in good time. Although this metabolic defect is genetically transmitted (i.e., familial in etiology on the subcellular level), the clinical expression of this defect varies even when untreated, and no specific data are available correlating various clinical manifestations with postnatal events, except for dietary adjustments.

On the cellular and subcellular levels there is statistical evidence of a genetic component, although which cell activity or neurochemical system is affected by what genetic aberration is not clear for either phenotypic schizophrenia or affective disorders. In either instance, the postnatal familial influences seem crucial in the prevention or development of phenotypical clinical expression. The same principles apply to "minimal brain dysfunction" in many disturbed children and severe psychopaths and possibly some schizophrenic patients.

Genetic factors are also implicated in affective disorders, more so in the bipolar than in the unipolar type; but in addition, affective and even material deprivations have been found, as well as deficient separation mastery. In anaclitic types of depression, failure to impart a sense of object constancy has been noted.

Although, in general, the family system defects in sociopaths do not seem as global as in the backgrounds of schizophrenics, shallow affectivity, ineffectual weaning and discipline, and serious communication problems have been found. These last consist of the almost exclusive use of language to produce desired effects at the expense of communication in the service of affective expression or interaction and of interpersonal accounting. Moreover, nurturance is probably defective, because underneath the sociopathic phenotype one often finds severe anaclitic depression, rooted in the perfunctory manner in which these patients seem to have been handled since infancy.

Stephen Fleck

Family Influences on Socialization

The characteristics of parent-child interaction—the priority, continuity, duration, amount, intensity, and range of the interaction—suggest the importance of family influence on socialization, with socialization defined as the process of developing patterns of socially relevant behavior through social interaction (Zigler and Child 1973). Because of these characteristics, the major mechanisms of socialization—identification, modeling, reinforcement, and mediated learning—operate most powerfully within the family.

Continuous bipolar dimensions of child behavior, which have been identified in several reviews of personality research, support the feasibility of a focus upon competence and adjustment. Two major replicated dimensions of child adjustment are sym-

pathy, considerateness, and helpfulness versus hostility and aggression; and extroversion, gregariousness, and expressiveness versus introversion, withdrawal, and inhibition. Major dimensions of child competence, particularly in the classroom, are: task orientation, perseverance, and industry versus hyperactivity and distractibility; and intelligence versus mental retardation.

Evidence that family relationships are influenced by social supports and stresses and by professional and institutional policies and practices indicates the possibility of influencing family socialization of the child. Intervention research supports that hypothesis and suggests that a major goal of the professions should be to strengthen and support family care of the child rather than to supplement and inadvertently supplant it. Thus, the development of an ecological perspective on socialization, which emphasizes the network of family relationships and the effects of informal support by the community and formal support by the professions upon those relationships, has contributed to intervention programs that significantly influence both child adjustment and competence.

Earl S. Schaefer

Family and Mental Health

Since the 1950s, there has been a tremendous upswing in family therapy; the families of the severely mentally ill, however, especially those of patients in public hospitals, receive no more therapeutic attention from physicians or mental health professionals than they did years ago. Family therapy seems to have concentrated, and continues to concentrate increasingly, on the families seen in outpatient settings and offices.

The leadership of the family is usually vested in the biological parents, and always so in the bigenerational or nuclear family residing apart from the parents' progenitors or other relatives. The leadership, therefore, is exercised by two people, whether formally married or not, and it has been found that children with only one parent are often handicapped or at risk with regard to their mental development and ultimate state of mental health.

Communication in the family is one of the best indicators about family functioning, because without it the system cannot function properly. Communication is also the tool for clinical examination and family interviews, and communication styles have been found to be highly indicative of family dysfunction.

Affectivity in the family is observable in group sessions with the family as well as assessable by historical accounts. Affectivity in the modern and isolated nuclear family is the major cement that holds the family together, in contrast to earlier bonds of economic necessity or ritual prescription. Affectivity concerns most of all a sense of feeling wanted on the part of all family members, a sense that their cohesion and interdependence outweigh conflict and crises in intrafamilial relationships.

With the birth of the first child the family becomes a triad, and each subsequent child forms a different triad with the parents (in addition to sibling relationships). No two children, not even twins, grow up in the same family in this narrow sense, not only because each triad is unique, but also because the family and individuals involved change during the birth intervals.

Once the child has developed body competence, including control over the sphincter, and has begun to learn to speak and use language on a concrete level, the family enters the stage of relationship learning and relationship ordering in the basic triangle, another critical phase in the development of mental health or ill health, designated by Sigmund Freud (1932) as the "oedipal period."

With puberty, the adolescent family phase begins. Unlike the previous stage, this one is not altogether harmonious and peaceful. The children's rapid physical growth and changes and their equally incisive drives toward becoming more social beings, with intense interest in relationships with the opposite sex and sexual impulsion in general, bring issues of dependence and independence within the family to the fore; and these issues can assume conflict intensity.

At the postparental phase, the parents often have to live as a dyad again. This transition depends very much on the nature of their original marital coalition as well as their ability to change this coalition, in connection with not only parental roles but also age-typical issues. The transition is more critical for women than for men, because men usually continue in their occupation or profession whether children live at home or not, although midlife issues may also bring difficulties for the male spouse (Levenson 1978).

Stephen Fleck

Family, Single-Parent

The single-parent family must reorganize its domestic and economic responsibilities and its system of affectional and emotional support (Marotz-Bader 1979; Biller 1974), along nontraditional lines. In single-parent families the mother is often the sole parent, and is frequently the sole provider as well. These mothers must work to support the family, and in a great many cases the children are left in an empty home with no one to relate to.

In 1960 5% of children lived in single-parent homes with the mother as head of household. In 1970 12% of American families were single-parent households with the mother as the head. In 1993 the mother was the sole parent in 26% of families in the United States. The problem is more severe in African-American families. In 1970 33% of African-American families had the mother as the sole parent, whereas by 1993 the number had risen to 58%. Single parenthood is on the rise and is providing children with less economic support, less attention, less protection, and much less adult guidance.

Time magazine (June 28, 1993) described the situation as follows: "At the present time more children will go to sleep tonight in a fatherless home than ever in the nation's history. Talk to the experts on crime, drug abuse, depression, school failure, and they can point to some study somewhere blaming those problems on the disappearance of fathers from the American family. . . . The Census Bureau can document the 70 million mothers age 15 or older in the U.S.A. but has scant ideas how many fathers there are. . . . It's a non-existent category. It's the ignored half of the family."

Benjamin B. Wolman

Family Therapy

Nathan Ackerman, considered by many the "father of family therapy," applied psychoanalytic insight to family dynamics. John Bell derived his techniques from the analytically oriented family work of John Bowlby at the Tavistock Clinic in London.

Ackerman (1966) pointed out that conjoint sessions can either be the sole method of treatment or can be used in conjunction with individual sessions. He emphasizes the need for "flexible accommodation" to the unique features of each disorder and the need to "discover a good fit between the style of a given family and the style of a particular therapist" (110–11). As with other forms of psychotherapy, the effectiveness of family therapy for a particular problem seems to depend less on the specific symptom than on the clinical skill and judgment of the therapist.

While family therapy approaches have been utilized in a wide variety of clinical situations, several conditions have received particular attention in recent years. These include: (1) anorexia nervosa and other psychosomatic disorders; (2) adolescent separation difficulties, including running away, delinquency, schizophrenia, and suicide attempts; and (3) drug and alcohol abuse.

Increasing the number of therapists. Multiple impact therapy (MIT), an approach developed by D. M. MacGregor et al. (1974), involves an interdisciplinary team of mental health professionals who meet in a series of conferences with various individuals and subgroups from the family, as well as the family as a whole, over a marathon 2-day period.

Increasing the number of family members. Speck and Attneave's (1973) Family Networks method involves as many as 40 to 50 people in the identified patient's social network (friends, neighbors, work or school associates, etc.) who are gathered together for a series of 4-hour meetings with a therapist team to explore the stresses and supports available to the patient and to build a framework for continuing resolution of problems in the future.

Nonverbal techniques. Most family therapy approaches recognize the importance of nonverbal communication within sessions, including seating arrangements, physical contact between family members, and exchanges of facial expressions; but several writers have stressed the value of utilizing nonverbal techniques as a treatment strategy. S. Minuchin's (1974) structural approach often involves the therapist rearranging the seating in a family session in order to demonstrate the need for different boundaries and coalitions. Speck and Attneave (1973) suggest that nonverbal encounter-group exercises (holding hands, jumping, screaming in unison) can be useful in building cohesion within the family network.

Robert A. Horwitz

Fathers and Children

Research has revealed that many infants form strong attachments with their fathers during the first year of life. These attachments are clearly reflected in the infant's interest in the father's behavior. For example, infants who are attached to their fathers spend much time looking at their fathers, react animately when their fathers enter or leave the room, and often make movements indicating a desire to be close to their fathers. The extent of such attachment is highly related to the quality of the father's involvement with the infant.

"Well-fathered" infants are more secure and trustful in branching out in their explorations. There are also indications that their development in terms of crawling, climbing, and manipulating objects is advanced. Some fathers, when they are involved, tend to be more tolerant than mothers of physical explorations by infants and to actively encourage physical mastery. Another factor in the early facilitation of the infant's explorations of her environment is that the father provides an additional attachment figure.

Fathers are the basic representatives of men for most boys and girls. Some researchers believe that the quality of the father-child relationship is a primary determinant of the child's ability to trust, respect, and relate to men. The father has a particularly significant influence on the sex role development of both his male and female offspring. He tends to differentiate considerably more than the mother between sons and daughters and rewards children's sex-appropriate behavior more than she does. The father thus helps to delineate his child's sex role and reward children's positive evaluation of their sexuality.

Presently we are witnessing a growing participation of fathers, partially as a result of modern concepts of equal responsibility of fathers and mothers, and partially as a result of the increasing role of mothers in supporting the family.

Henry B. Biller

Fatigue and Motor Performance

The term *fatigue* continues to be used both in the popular language and in the technical terminology of experimental psychology to represent three classes of phenomena: (1) decreasing ability to perform a given task, believed to be mediated by a (2) changing state of the performing organism, which may be consciously experienced as (3) feelings related to both— all three occurring as performance of the task continues over time. The task itself may be either simple or complex, and in either case it may be primarily physical (muscular) or mental (involving relatively little physical energy).

The performance decrement in simple muscular tasks is called objective fatigue. Physiological fatigue refers to a changed state of the organism associated with the decreased capacity of the muscle following continued contraction or repeated contractions: it results from a combination of the muscle contraction's use of fuel (e.g., glycogen) and oxygen, and accumulation of waste products (e.g., carbon dioxide and lactic acid) at the cellular level.

The feelings of subjective fatigue in simple motor tasks range from pain, ache, and tiredness localized in the specific muscle group used in the task, to awareness of elevated pulse, raised temperature, and sweating; if the task is continued through several such fatiguing cycles, more general feelings of weariness or whole-body tiredness may be reported.

Fatigue in Complex Tasks
Following the suggestions of Bartley and Chute (1947), many subsequent writers have used the term *fatigue* to mean the experiential aspect of the phenomenon of subjective fatigue. Likewise, they have used the term *impairment* to refer to physiological fatigue, the physiological tissue changes that reduce the ability of a muscle to take part in the molar activities of work or skill performance. Work output has been used to represent the overt aspects of the activity that here have been called *performance decrements* or *objective fatigue*.

The current view with regard to objective fatigue in work situations is that performance decrements will occur in the form of reduced productivity, increased variability of work-output quantity and quality, reduced average quality of output (in part a function of reduction in the subjective standard of acceptability on the part of the fatigued worker), losses in the accurate timing of elements in complex tasks, and a general tendency toward a smaller span of apprehension (e.g., in losing the "big picture" or perceptual frame, and elements in complex tasks such as radar air-traffic control).

Factors Associated with Objective Fatigue
Elements of the worker's total work environment that have been shown to affect performance decrements or objective fatigue may still be classified into the four areas classically identified as temporal, situational (work- or task-related), environmental, and organismic (or personal) factors. The work decrement or inferred state of fatigue is not a simple function of any one of these factors but rather a result of the complex interaction of all of them. Thus, although there may be, in concept, a single general fatigue function related to work decrements, in practicality, there is a family of functions, the parameters of which are specific conditions of the temporal, situational, environmental, and organismic variables involved in any specific work domain.

Earl A. Alluisi
Glynn D. Coates

Fear as Motivation

Learning
In N. E. Miller's study (1951), the two motivational roles of fear (energizing and reinforcing) are both

operative in determining the learning of the instrumental response. However, it is possible with the acquired-drive paradigm to study the reinforcing role independent of the energizing role. After giving identical fear-conditioning treatment, the amount of fear elicited by the stimuli in the nonshock compartment after the instrumental response can be manipulated (e.g., by varying the similarity of the stimuli in the two compartments), thereby manipulating the amount of fear reduction. In this manner, increases in the amount and percentage of reinforcement have been found to be directly related to escape-from-fear performance (McAllister and McAllister).

The energizing role of fear, separate from its reinforcing role, may be demonstrated by the manner in which fear affects an unlearned response tendency. The magnitude of a startle response is often directly related to the amount of fear present when the startle response was elicited by a loud noise.

Avoidance Learning

Regardless of the nature of the reinforcement mechanism, it seems incontrovertible that neutral stimuli can, through conditioning, come to elicit fear and that, in its presence, organisms will be motivated to change this state of affairs. This conviction is a basic assumption of many modern psychotherapists who believe that many of the fears and anxieties of humans, particularly phobias, are conditioned, also, that many of the neurotic symptoms of humans are learned as responses because they lead to fear reduction.

Wallace R. McAllister
Dorothy E. McAllister

Feature Detection

Perceptual psychology has, in the last hundred years, moved from the concept of a simple representation of the outside world to a much more dynamic model of perceptual processing—a model in which the brain is thought of as struggling to extract only the most important scraps of information from the barrage of sense data presented to it by its sense organs.

Evidence from Sensory Physiology

In the 1940s and 1950s, sensory physiologists produced one remarkable discovery after another. Ganglion cells of frogs and cats were shown to have receptive fields with an antagonistic surrounding zone where light inhibits the responses produced by the appropriate pattern falling in the central region. Thus, the necessary stimulus is an event restricted in space as well as time. The inhibitory surround ensures that each ganglion cell will only respond optimally for a stimulus of a particular size and at a particular position in the visual field. The basic type of concentric receptive field has either a central region where illumination produces a response when turned on, and a surrounding area within which light causes inhibition and there is a response when it turns off (ON center, OFF surround), or the opposite arrangement (OFF center, ON surround).

J. Y. Lettvin and his collaborators reexamined the receptive fields of frog retinal ganglion cells with the intention of defining them purely in terms of the natural trigger features that would make them respond best. They were able to classify the cells into five types:

1. *sustained edge detectors,* which respond to a stationary or moving dark-light contrast
2. *convex edge detectors,* which respond best to dark convex objects (about the size of a fly at snapping distance) moving within the receptive field
3. *changing contrast detectors,* which respond well to a moving contrast
4. *dimming detectors,* which respond to any sudden reduction of overall intensity
5. *dark detectors,* which discharge impulses at a rate inversely related to steady light intensity

It seems that the ganglion cells of all animals can be classified into a similar concise set of feature detectors, and many other retinas have been studied, from goldfish to squirrels, from pigeons to monkeys. In general, it seems to be true that animals with their eyes placed on the side of the head, and hence panoramic vision, perform a fuller and more complex feature analysis in their retinas. On the other hand, animals (usually predatory) with the eyes directed forward, and hence a large area of binocular visual field, tend to have rather simpler kinds of retinal ganglion cells, usually of the concentric type.

Feature Processing beyond the Retina: Serial and Parallel Models for Perception

Most neurons in the visual cortex are orientation selective and many are direction selective, too. In fact, the new principle that has emerged from D. H. Hubel and T. N. Wiesel's now-classic studies of the visual cortex is that neurons can have a combination of feature selectivities, and that the combination may increase in complexity from each cell to the next in the chain. Cortical neurons can be selectively sensitive to the width of a moving bar, as well as its orientation and direction of movement, to the velocity of movement, to its three-dimensional distance, and in the monkey, even to its color.

There is some evidence that certain neurons have very particular stimulus requirements. C. G. Gross has recorded activity from the infero-temporal area of the monkey's cerebral cortex, to which information eventually projects after its analysis in the striate cortex and other areas in the occipital lobe.

Colin B. Blakemore

Federn, Paul (1871–1950)

Paul Federn was the fourth physician, after Alfred Adler, W. Stekel, and R. Reitler, to join Freud's inner circle and form the group of psychoanalytic pioneers. Federn was mostly interested in psychology and treatment of psychotics. His *Ego Psychology and Psychosis* was published after his death.

Martin Grotjahn

Fenichel, Otto (1897–1946)

According to Otto Fenichel, a leading psychoanalyst, depression stems from the superego's punishment for his or her oral-sadistic incorporation of the object. Fenichel believed that the self-respect of depressed people depends on approval and love given to them from without; depression represents a regression to a primal narcissistic state. He main-

tained that interpretation and strengthening of the ego are the most effective methods of coping with acting out. Affects, according to Fenichel, are "unconscious dispositions" that express themselves in personality development, in dreams, and in symptom formation. Fenichel's main work was *The Psychoanalytic Theory of Neurosis*.

Benjamin B. Wolman

Ferenczi, Sandor (1873–1933)

Sandor Ferenczi introduced far-reaching modifications in psychoanalytic technique, calling his method "active analytic therapy." Ferenczi gave advice, suggestions, and sometimes commands to his patients. In his book *Thalahassa: The Theory of Genitality* (1924), Ferenczi interpreted the sexual act as a regressive move, a return to the uterus.

Martin Grotjahn

Feuchtersleben, Ernst Freiherr Von (1806–1849)

Ernst Feuchtersleben, an Austrian psychiatrist, was a spokesman for the so-called romantic medicine in the field of psychiatry. He believed in the unity of mind and body and advocated psychotherapy, which he conceptualized as reeducation.

John C. Burnham

Field Theory

The subject of study in Kurt Lewin's theory (1936) is not the person as person, as is ordinarily understood—as an organism that exists independent of its environment. Rather, the subject of psychology, the actor, is an entity that may be called a "life space." A life space is an individual being that consists of two interdependent parts: a person and the person's environment. These parts cannot be isolated from one another. That is, the "person" exists only as a part of his situation and cannot be adequately described independently of this situation; and the "environment" is a personal environment that cannot be described independently of the person. The whole that is formed from these parts, the life space, is the reality that is the fundamental unit of psychology. Behavior—whether it be the movement of a person relative to her environment, a temporary restructuring of the person or of the environment, or the development of the life space—is a change in a life space.

To establish the validity of his theory, Lewin used a method that might be termed "experimental phenomenology." That is, he and his students would create conditions in the laboratory designed to create specified conditions in the life space of a subject. By the use of meticulous observation and careful description of the behavior and the experience of the individual subject, they described a variety of conditions that may occur in the life space and a number of laws that appear to govern its changes.

We may distinguish three broad areas of development within the general rubric of field theory: first, the development within social psychology of "miniature" theories that follow the general method of field theory and are consonant with the theoretical points outlined above, but which apply to limited domains of behavior and have not yet been systematically related to each other or to the body of field theory (e.g., Leon Festinger's theory of cognitive dissonance, Richard M. Lerner's "just world" hypothesis); second, the development of approaches in other areas of psychology, which are compatible with field-theoretic principles but have not yet been integrated with Lewin's field theory (e.g., Karen Horney's version of psychoanalysis, Friedrich Perls's principles of Gestalt therapy, E. Goffman's approach to sociological analysis); third, attempts to develop basic field theory in ways that will enable it to encompass the complete range of psychological phenomena.

While Lewin's formula

$$\text{Behavior} = f(\text{Life space})$$

emphasizes the fact that the current life space determines behavior, from an existential point of view it is possible to write the formula

$$\text{Life space} = f^{-1}(\text{Behavior})$$

thus emphasizing the person's choice and responsibility for the organization of the field. Such an interpretation may open the possibility of developing a systematic psychology of the emotional choices that confront persons and the consequences within the life space that necessarily follow from how these choices are made.

Joseph De Rivera

Flournoy, Theodore (1854–1920)

Theodore Flournoy was a psychologist interested in history and the philosophy of science. He analyzed religion, occult phenomena, and parapsychology.

Margaret E. Donnelly

Forensic Psychiatry

The term *forensic* owes it etymologic origin to *forum*, an open space where discussions can take place, disputes can be resolved, and conflicts can be settled. Note that the word *court* in the sense of courtyard has identical origins.

Originally, forensic psychiatry was the province of "alienists" who guided the court as to the mental state of individuals caught up in the legal system. In modern usage, however, forensic psychiatry—while continuing to have the sense of performing such consultative services to the legal system—has acquired a second connotation: legal issues forming a regulatory context around the practice of psychiatry. Hence, forensic psychiatry currently embraces both the psychiatry of law and the law of psychiatry (see below). First, some general remarks may provide a context for this discussion.

The Adversary System
Adversary proceedings are at the core of the American legal system, and the English one before it. Truth is considered best discovered by placing the data upon the rack: pulled and probed by direct examination and cross-examination, the evidence will yield up its nugget of truth.

This model fits badly with clinical psychiatric work, which depends so heavily on the nonadversarial therapeutic alliance. In addition, while the dynamic psychiatrist listens to "everything" (and sometimes with the analytic "third ear" to boot!), the law defines some evidence as inadmissible according to sometimes elaborate schemes based on principles of justice. Forensic psychiatrists realize that to enter the courtroom is to adopt and to adapt to a new set of rules.

These rules include: given that one is working for the court as well as the patient ("dual agency"), the examinee must be informed of this in advance; the treater should not testify as a forensic expert witness because of the incompatibility of those roles; the forensic witness renders opinions, but the judge or jury makes the ultimate finding or decision.

Note also that—while the treater tries to see the world "through the patient's eyes" in an empathic, even credulous manner—the forensic psychiatrist must enter the case with appropriate skepticism about self-serving goals in the examinee, must be alert to malingering, and must perform extensive examination of external sources of observations and data to corroborate or discorroborate the examinee's report.

The Psychiatry of Law

CRIMINAL ISSUES

Competence to stand trial. Individuals appearing before the court have long been recognized as varying in their ability to take part in the legal process. Three categories of individuals have historically been identified as experiencing some incapacity to participate, that is, to be of suspect competence to play a comprehending role in the proceedings. These are children, "idiots," and "lunatics" (as they were first described); or, in more modern idiom, minors, the mentally retarded, and the mentally ill. While judges make the final determination, psychiatric input is commonly sought.

The forensic psychiatrist serves as an evaluator to offer an opinion as to whether the accused defendant possesses the requisite abilities for such competence. These abilities include knowledge of the nature and object of court proceedings; the roles of the personnel; the charges; penalties and options for pleadings; and the ability to cooperate with an attor-

ney in the defense. The fact that such competence may exist intact, in the presence of even severe mental illness, demonstrates the need for professional evaluation in this area.

Criminal responsibility (insanity defense). This perhaps most controversial of forensic evaluations appears to exist because of the legal system's need to be perceived as fair. This "perception of fairness" in turn appears based on the society's view that certain individuals should not be held as accountable for their crimes as others. Closely related to this issue is the fact that certain crimes are defined in terms that require a particular mental state, e.g., specific intent to commit that crime.

Once again, mental illness, though necessary for this assessment, is not determinative. The forensic evaluator is charged with arriving at an opinion as to whether the particular manifestations of the "mental disease or defect" (i.e., mental illness or organic impairment) reach the threshold of the statutorily defined criteria for insanity or nonresponsibility for the crime. With some jurisdictional variation, these criteria usually focus on the defendant's incapacity to appreciate the wrongfulness of the conduct in question and sometimes to be able to conform his or her conduct to the requirements of the law. Each of these elements could be affected, theoretically, by the symptoms of an illness or organic impairment.

Origins of criminality. Although this emphasis of forensic psychiatry has declined somewhat, the theoretical approaches to the origins of criminality and their respective treatments are a legitimate concern of the field. These theories include: sociological theories based on socioeconomic factors, factors that were, for a time, reflected in the term *sociopath* for such offenders; object relations and self-psychology theories, which emphasize abuse, failures of empathy, and alienation; dynamic systems theories, which emphasize superego lacunae in the parents and acting out of parental impulses; and biological theories, which stress brain damage and its subsequent impact on recidivism through the inability to learn from experience and autonomic hyporeactivity, which leads to thrill-seeking, danger-courting behavior in the effort to generate intense feelings.

Note that criminality and mental illness tend to be independent variables; the previously criminal are likely to repeat, and mental illness drops out as a factor in controlled studies.

Other criminal issues. Additional areas of forensic psychiatric relevance include competence of a witness to testify, defendants' diminished capacity, sentencing issues, competence to be executed, and emotional effects on victims (victim impact data).

CIVIL ISSUES

Civil commitment. For centuries, in American law and the English law that precedes it, provisions have been made by lawmakers for the uncommon possibility that the mentally ill will be dangerous to self or others. Under these provisions, certain agencies in society, most commonly the courts (and, on a very short-term basis, mental health professionals), have been given the right to hospitalize an individual against his will, a step called "involuntary commitment." Courts often draw upon forensic testimony as to the potential for violence (dangerousness).

Civil competencies. Adults are assumed to have the capacity to make reasonable decisions (whether they make them or not!); this capacity or ability is termed "competence," and it is considered present until proven otherwise.

Forensic psychiatrists may be asked to assess competence in a number of civil contexts. These include:

1. competence to make a will or contract
2. competence to consent to medical treatment
3. competence to marry or divorce
4. competence to be a parent or have child custody (sometimes called "fitness")
5. competence to manage one's assets, property, or financial affairs

In the event of a finding of incompetence, a judge or guardian usually takes over the relevant decision making.

Other civil issues. Forensic psychiatrists may also evaluate (and, far less commonly, testify about) issues of the presence of, and damages from, psychiatric malpractice; questions of informed consent to medical and psychiatric treatments; emotional injuries from various sources, including general medical malpractice; and compensation questions, such as psychiatric disability and workers' compensation.

The Law of Psychiatry

Forensic psychiatrists commonly play consultative roles in a number of areas that cross the interface between psychiatry and the law and often relate to legal regulation of clinical practice. Examples include issues of confidentiality, where various tensions bear upon the clinician: to keep material from the treatment secret or to breach confidentiality for a good cause (e.g., matters subject to mandated reporting or the existence of a possible emergency). Issues of documentation and record keeping form a related area of possible need for forensic consultation. Finally, forensic psychiatry includes treatment of offenders in prisons and forensic settings and evaluation of ethics complaints and ethical standards, as well as consultation to professional licensing boards.

Thomas G. Gutheil

Form Perception

Gestalt

When we listen to speech we experience auditory units—that is, separate words. But in the stream of speech there are few pauses between words. The segmentation into separate words of the acoustic waveforms that reach the ear must be accomplished by the listener. In this case, it is clear that unit formation is a result of learning. When one listens to a foreign language speaker, a jumble of sounds is heard: segmentation is not achieved.

Max Wertheimer arrived at a number of "grouping principles" or "laws of organization," which determine what is seen as belonging together and at the same time as segregated from other regions in the field. In addition to (1) proximity, there are (2) similarity—elements alike in color, brightness, and size are grouped together (grouping by similarity is the basis of several tests for color blindness); and (3) direction (usually referred to as "good continuation"); (4) common fate—elements (e.g., a flock of birds) that move together in the same direction with the same speed appear as a unit. G. Johannson has explored the influence of this factor in the organization of motion configurations. The principles of grouping determine what goes with what, what belongs together and is separated from other regions; in other words, they account for the segmentation of the visual field.

We are in a position to summarize the main features of the Gestalt theory of form perception. Gestalt psychologists agree with traditional views that retinal stimulation has to be supplemented in order to arrive at perceptual structures. But they argue that it is not memory or learning processes that integrate the sensory data; the segmentation of the visual field and the shape imparting function of the contour are products of "sensory organization."

Hebb's Theory

Hebb (1949) proposes a theory of form perception, which relies heavily on eye movements. He assumes the existence of "primitive unity"—a kind of figure-ground separation that leads to some kind of amorphous percept, similar to what we experience in the peripheral field, a "something." What Hebb calls the property of "identity" has to be gradually built up. For example, the perception of a triangle as a specific shape beyond the primitive unity requires a long process of learning in the infant (or for a newly operated congenital cataract patient). Eye movements comprise the necessary factor, which integrates simpler elements such as lines and corners (which Hebb considers to be partly innate in perception) into the final perception of a triangle.

Carl B. Zuckerman

Foster Homes for the Mentally Ill

New York State has developed a system of foster homes under the leadership of Hester Crutcher as an alternative to the state mental hospital. This method was elaborated by Henrietta DeWitt in Maryland. In both cases, the institution of foster care became established as a systematic means whereby patients were carefully selected for placement outside the institution into homes that were themselves intact and able to provide a suitable physical and psychological environment for the mentally ill person.

A number of surveys have indicated that varying types of results have been obtained from foster care placement. These placements tend to be more difficult when the patients concerned are older patients who have less flexibility and more immediate need for nursing care. Not all foster homes are able to provide this, and readmission to institutions becomes necessary. The maintenance of patients in the community becomes more effective when adequate control over use of drugs is established.

Most patients in the community are adult patients in remission. Many of them have regular opportunities for intermittent therapeutic sessions back at the hospital or in regional centers close to their homes or their foster homes. The introduction of day care and halfway houses with day-care facilities has considerably changed the burden for the careholder or foster parent. It is quite possible now for patients to spend five days a week in a day center, where they are engaged in recreational or educational activities. Most community mental health centers offer day care as one of the means of offering partial hospitalization.

Milton Wittman

Fractional Anticipatory Goal Response

This is the theoretical concept that fractional components of a goal response (e.g., a consummatory response) can generalize to various aspects of the situation in which they occur and, through their proprioceptive stimuli, provide a mechanism that allows the organism to "think ahead."

Gregory A. Kimble

Franz, Sheperd Ivory (1874–1933)

Contrary to views current at that time, Franz found a lack of precise brain localization of functions in animals and humans. He rehabilitated cerebrum-damaged individuals by reeducation and "reinforcement" techniques.

J. Wayne Lazar

Free Association and the Psychoanalytic Method

The method of free association is widely recognized to be the cornerstone of the psychoanalytic process and the major contribution that the patient makes to the work of analysis. The requirement of free association has thus become the fundamental rule of clinical psychoanalysis. In addition, the development of the technique of free association played a central role in the emergence of Sigmund Freud's clinical methodology and, subsequently, of psychoanalytic theory itself.

Only after several years did Freud abandon the so-called pressure technique and shift gradually from the use of such forms as suggestion toward an increasing emphasis on the relaxation of the patient's censorship and the more-or-less free and spontaneous expression of associations. Sigmund Freud's interest in dreams and his growing familiarity with them eventually convinced him of the usefulness of the free-association technique, and by the time of the publication of *The Interpretation of Dreams* (1900), the free-association technique had been solidly established.

As Freud relied more and more on the associative technique, his awareness of the patient's resistances and the role they played in the analysis grew apace. The further analysis of such resistances and the further application of the principles of associative determination underlie Freud's theory of the dream work and the evolution of his dynamic, economic, and genetic point of view.

William W. Meissner

Freud, Anna (1895–1982)

Anna Freud was the only one of Sigmund Freud's children to take up psychoanalysis as a profession. She initiated the application of psychoanalysis to the treatment of children (child analysis) and to education. In 1938, she left Vienna for London, where she founded the Hampstead Child-Therapy Course and Clinic.

Anna Freud believed in a close connection between theory and practice. Her major contri-

bution is the central organizing concept of developmental lines.

Anna Freud was the editor of the journal *Psychoanalytic Study of the Child* all her life. Her main works are: *The Ego and the Mechanisms of Defense* (in seven volumes) and *Normality and Pathology in Childhood*.

Lottie M. Newman

Freud, Sigmund (1856–1939)

Sigmund Freud's original training was in neurology. After studying with Jean-Martin Charcot in Paris, Freud accepted Charcot's physiological explanations of hypnosis and of neurotic symptoms. In cooperation with Josef Breuer, Freud published the *Studies in Hysteria* (1893–1895).

At almost the same time, Freud became preoccupied with the unconscious. He started to utilize free association techniques instead of a recall under hypnosis. Freud became increasingly concerned with resistance to free association and began to concentrate on analyzing resistance that protected pathogenic material. He described transference phenomena in 1895, and countertransference in 1910.

In the 1890s, Freud came to believe that pathogenic experiences were sexual in nature. His clinical practice led him to an emphasis upon sexuality and sexual behavior in the etiology of neuroses. During the period from 1894 to 1895, Freud theorized that dreams represent the fulfillment of wishes, and in 1897 he developed his theory of the Oedipus complex.

Freud described his theories in his *General Introduction to Psychoanalysis* (1916–1917). In 1920 he described his idea of the death instinct in *Beyond the Pleasure Principle*, and in 1923 he described the three mental structures of id, ego, and superego in *The Ego and the Id*. In later years Freud wrote about sociocultural issues and religion.

John C. Burnham

Freud's Economic Hypothesis

Under the strong influence of Herman Ludwig von Helmholtz, several young scientists dedicated themselves to rooting out all scientific explanations that rested upon concepts of vitalism and that presupposed some intellective principle at work. They resolved to restrict themselves to explanations in physical-chemical terms. Among this group was Ernst Brücke, in whose institute Freud worked for several years and who had a most important formative influence on Freud.

As the discoveries in neuroanatomy and neurophysiology unfolded over a number of years, there was considerable optimism and excitement over the possibilities of understanding brain function in physical and chemical terms. Although Freud left this field, his interest in such possibilities obviously remained, as shown in his *Project for a Scientific Psychology*, and his thinking continued to be influenced by these ideas even when ostensibly he had given up specific neurological speculations.

As Freud chose to derive all the energies from instinctual drives, he had to account for activities of a diverse and noninstinctual nature being powered by energy of an instinctual character. He introduced the idea of "desexualization," a process carried out in the ego by which the energy was stripped of its instinctual character and put at the disposal of the ego.

In the ego and the id, Freud laid the groundwork for the modern expansion of the economic hypothesis by developing the idea that libidinal energy could be stripped of its instinctual character—that is, sublimated—and then made available to the ego for use in its various functions. He referred to this energy as "neutral" and also postulated that some of it could be shifted to reinforce one instinctual current or another, thus, for example, accounting for the change of love into hate or the reverse. It was also available for the various ego activities.

The process of defense received special attention in Heinz Hartmann's theories. On intuitive grounds, defense seemed to have some flightlike quality and was therefore considered to be powered by relatively neutralized aggressive energy. The processes of maturation and development were also seen as entailing progressive growth of the capacity to neutralize energy.

David Rapaport (1960) exercised important influence in the modern development of energy theory. He attempted to make the theory more systematic and clarified many concepts and their relationship to the rest of metapsychology. He clearly regarded as essential to analytic theory the basic model of drive energy leading to action designed to satisfy the drive, leading in turn to discharge and reduction of energy.

Adrienne P. Applegarth

Freud's Ego Concept, 1897–1923

In Sigmund Freud's *Studies in Hysteria* (1893–1895), the ego is defined as the dominant mass of ideas, and it has the capacity to defend itself by repudiating (repressing) an incompatible idea. In *The Interpretation of Dreams* (1900), Freud presents a far more complex analysis of the functioning of the high-level or rational agencies. These ego features are presented as attempting to regulate the passage through mental apparatus of the incompatible ideation of the dynamic unconscious.

In his 1900 theory, Freud had indicated a group of mental activities, which he later redefined, systematized, and conceptualized under the unifying term *the ego*.

Along with his exploration into the defensive activities, Freud developed a theory of the reality-adaptive activities of the mind. Pleasure (discharge) as a sole regulatory principle is supplemented by the reality principle. Consciousness as a sense organ learns to comprehend the sensory qualities of perception. Attention meets the sense impressions in an active way guided by memory. Motor discharge is employed intentionally, as actions aimed at the appropriate alteration of reality.

By the early 1920s, Freud arrived at a conception of mental functioning that was profoundly rich in its details, and the contradictions inherent in the topographic and ego-instinct theories became apparent. Using the quality of consciousness as the principle criterion of topographic systems resulted in such irreconcilable confusions as: the primary process, a property ascribed to the Ucs (the system unconscious), occurs commonly in consciousness as in fantasy; secondary process contents may be repressed and unconscious; and defenses, ascribed to the Pcs (the system preconscious) and/or Cs (the system conscious), are in fact unconscious.

Joseph D. Lichtenberg

Freud's Structural Model

The structural model refers to the last phase of Sigmund Freud's theorizing about the nature of mental activity. Freud assumed the existence of a mental apparatus that carried out the various aspects of mental activity with which he was concerned as a psychoanalyst. On the basis of his first discoveries concerning the psychology of the psychoneuroses, dreams, jokes, and what he called the psychopathology of everyday life (such as slips of the tongue, of the pen, and of memory), he suggested a division of the mental apparatus into several parts, which he called "systems." One he called the system unconscious (Ucs); a second, the system preconscious (Pcs); and a third, the system conscious (Cs).

Freud subsequently altered some of his ideas about the mental apparatus. The major work devoted to an exposition of these changes in theory was *The Ego and the Id* (1923). The revised theory is what is called the structural theory or model.

The most obvious innovation was the introduction of a new terminology. Instead of Ucs, Pcs, and Cs, Freud in 1923 proposed to divide the mental apparatus into id, ego, and superego. The change in names is of far less importance, however, than the change in emphasis, namely, that in the new theory it is not accessibility to consciousness that is the most important criterion for the division into systems but rather the grouping of mental elements in situations of psychic conflict. In the new theory, it is recognized that the three systems merge into one another and form a cooperative whole, except when there is conflict (A. Freud, 1936).

The new theory takes into account that repressed fantasies from later childhood and adolescence may be decisively important among instinctual derivatives. Finally, in the new theory, *instinctual* is no longer synonymous with *libidinal*. By the time it was

formulated, Freud had introduced a dual theory of instinctual drives, according to which aggression is posited to be a drive along with libido.

In an early monograph, Heinz Hartmann (1939) developed the role of the ego in adaptation, an idea that he expanded in a long series of subsequent papers. Another influential contribution to ego theory is that of R. Waelder (1930). The fundamentally important contributions to an understanding of the relationship of conflict to anxiety and to ego defenses are *Inhibitions, Symptoms, and Anxiety* (Freud 1926), and *The Ego and the Mechanisms of Defense* (A. Freud 1936).

The superego is defined as the group of mental functions having to do with ideal aspirations and with moral commands and prohibitions. It originates as a consequence of the oedipal phase of development through identification with the ethical and moral aspects of one's parents.

Joseph D. Lichtenberg

Freud's Theory of Instinctual Drives

Freud proposed that the instincts are composed of two classes, the sexual instincts and the ego instincts—or put another way, instincts that subserve the preservation of the species and instincts that subserve the preservation of the individual. That these two kinds of instinct are often in opposition is clear from daily clinical experience. Thus, from the outset, Freud's formulations concerning the nature of the instincts was a dual one, rooted in the idea of conflict, which plays so prominent a role in his understanding of the neuroses.

For the dynamic manifestations of the sexual drive Freud adopted the term *libido*. Using a terminology that reflected both his previous neurophysiological interests as well as a long-standing desire to be able to comprehend and conceptualize the phenomena of psychology in physical terms, Freud conceived of libido as an energic force that, like its counterpart in physics, was capable of multiple shifts and transformations within the psychic system.

Freud was not content simply to postulate the existence of an aggressive drive in man that could help account for certain facts of human behavior, a theory that, with some exceptions, psychoanalysts have found valuable. Freud went on to hypothesize the existence of two fundamental instincts or biological principles that are intrinsic to all living matter—a life instinct and a death instinct. The life instinct, eros, is equated with sexuality, while the death instinct, sometimes called Thanatos, is associated with aggression.

The majority of analysts, while finding the notion of a distinct aggressive drive a useful and indeed necessary explanatory concept, have not endorsed the idea of a primary drive toward death. Their reservations are echoed by many biologists and ethologists who find no evidence for such an instinct in the animal world. The present situation with regard to this hypothesis remains essentially as it was 60 years ago, when Ernest Jones concluded that it "represents a personal train of thought rather than a direct reference from verifiable data."

Theodore J. Jacobs

Freud's Topographic Model

To grasp Sigmund Freud's rationale for dividing mental life into two (or three) systems distinguishable in terms of the relations of their contents to consciousness, it is necessary to review the observational data at his command at the time he was formulating this concept.

In his 1915 revision of the topographic theory, Freud noted that even in adult life some psychic processes originating in the Ucs (the system unconscious) are not repressed or otherwise turned back by censorship but freely pass into consciousness. The implication of this amendment of the theory is that the mind is not accurately represented by a model of two entirely separate systems divided from each other by an intact barrier of defenses.

In a paper published in 1911, "Formulations on the Two Principles of Mental Functioning," Freud completed his differentiation of primary from secondary processes by postulating that they are characterized by two differing regulatory principles. Primary processes operate in accord with the "unpleasure principle"; in this mode of behavior, the person will not perceive anything unpleasant. This

automatic avoidance of unpleasure is the prototype of repression. It is acquisition of the capacity to cathect even unpleasurable memories that marks the beginning of secondary process thinking, which is regulated by the reality principle.

Although Freud proposed the topographic model in an effort to cover a wide array of observational data, he was cautious enough to indicate the limits of its applicability to various types of primitive mental functioning. In addenda of 1919 to *The Interpretation of Dreams*, he indicated that these limits extend beyond the mental life of young children and of psychotics. In discussing anxiety dreams and those of punishment, Freud demonstrated that the wishes fulfilled in these unpleasurable dreams do not belong to the repressed but to the critical agency that determines voluntary behavior, an agency that he now called "the ego."

With the revival of interest in metapsychological problems, these issues have been reexamined by various authors, e.g., M. Gill (1963), Arlow and Brenner (1964), and Goldberg (1973).

John E. Gedo

Fromm-Reichmann, Frieda (1889–1957)

Frieda Fromm-Reichmann, though deeply devoted to psychoanalytic principles, developed her own method of treatment for schizophrenia. Her book, *Principles of Intensive Psychotherapy* (1950), expressed her concepts and their application to therapy.

Hilde Bruch

Frustration

When an organism is not rewarded in the presence of stimuli previously paired with reward, an internal motivational response called frustration is aroused. Frustration has been shown to have three effects on the behavior of an organism: (1) inhibitory—avoidance responses aroused by conditioned frustration counteract approach responses; (2) excitatory—responses following the arousal of frustration are more vigorous; and (3) reinforcing—

responses allowing escape from frustration-arousing stimuli are learned.

Primary frustration is presumed to be a drive and thus energizes any behavior occurring in its presence. To measure the energizing effect, an organism is first trained to make two appetitive instrumental response in a row (running down two alleys in tandem, with a food reward at the end of each one). Reward is then no longer given at the end of the first alley, and the effects of primary frustration aroused in the first goal box increase running speed in the second alley (the "frustration effect"; Amsel 1971).

The effects of frustration have also been demonstrated during acquisition of an appetitive instrumental response reinforced on a partial reinforcement (PRF) schedule (subjects receive rewards on some trials and not on others), and during discrimination learning. In both situations nonreward occurs in the presence of stimuli that arouse an expectancy for reward. On rewarded trials during training on a PRF schedule, an expectancy for reward is conditioned, and on subsequent nonrewarded trials frustration is aroused and conditioned.

Nonreward in the presence of a generalized expectancy for reward is experienced during discrimination learning, and thus frustration is aroused. The expectancy for reward conditioned in the presence of the rewarded stimulus generalizes to the nonrewarded stimulus, resulting in the typical increase in responding in the presence of the nonreinforced stimulus early in discrimination training. However, when reward is not received, frustration is aroused and becomes conditioned.

Helen B. Daly

Functional Autonomy of Motives

Though the term *functional autonomy* is properly associated with G. W. Allport, the essence of the concept—that an activity that earlier was instrumental to some given end may become functionally separate and independent—has a longer history. The best-known previous statement of the principle is R. S. Woodworth's (1918) axiom that behavioral mechanisms may become drives. Similar notions can be found in the writings of Aristotle, James McCosh, William Stern, and E. C. Tolman.

Paul McReynolds

Functionalism

American functionalism, which flourished during the early part of the present century, developed in part out of certain trends in nineteenth-century English biology and psychology, notably Darwinism in its psychological repercussions. In the United States, William James might be considered a forerunner of functionalism, if not in fact its spiritual father. Functionalism provides an American parallel to German act psychology, which is in marked contrast to the content psychology of Wilhelm Wundt. Whereas in Germany the school of Franz C. Brentano, the principal rival of the Leipzig group, was empirical and rational rather than experimental, functional psychology in America has stressed the adaptive role of mental processes, has been more practical in orientation, and in the course of its development has extended the range of psychological research and application.

John Dewey's principal contribution is the famous article "The Reflex Arc Concept in Psychology" (1896), which forthrightly attacks elementarism in all its forms, including the concept of stimulus and response. Sensorimotor reactions are not a double-component system but a causal continuum, he argues, "one uninterrupted, continuous redistribution of mass in motion." The customary distinctions may be made only as functional divisions in the total act.

Some of the historical significance of functionalism derives from its relationship to behaviorism. Behaviorism could be interpreted as a radical deviation from functional psychology. The change from mental content to mental function led by easy stages to the study of behavioral functions. Thus, "mentalistic" functionalism has given rise to, as well as given way to, "objective " behaviorism.

Ross Harrison

· G ·

Ganser Syndrome

Ganser syndrome is a rare dissociative state usually associated with hysterical symptoms of auditory and visual hallucinations, spatial and time disorientation, amnesia, delusions, and inability to face usual life situations. Patients afflicted with Ganser syndrome fail to answer simple questions. Their answers are not related to what they were asked, although they seem to have understood the question.

The etiology of Ganser syndrome is not clear. Some researchers believe that it is a hysterical symptom, while others regard it as an organic state of confusion. The syndrome doesn't last very long, and is usually treated by psychotherapy and tranquilizers. Ganser syndrome was described in 1898 by S. J. M. Ganser.

Benjamin B. Wolman

Gender Identity

Core gender identity is a conviction that the assignment of one's sex is anatomically, and ultimately psychologically, correct. It is the first step in the progress toward one's ultimate gender identity, usually established around age 2 or 3, and is the nexus around which masculinity and femininity gradually accrete. Core gender identity has no implication of role or object relations. Efforts to shift it in later years will probably fail.

The biological "force." Without the addition of fetal androgens, in all mammals, including humans, anatomical maleness cannot occur. This is true whether the chromosomes are male (XY) or female (XX). But if these fetal androgens are present at the

right time and in the right amount, and if they are of the right chemical structure, both anatomical maleness and postnatal masculinity will be possible regardless of chromosomal maleness or femaleness.

Although it is argued that the boy's first love is heterosexual, there is an earlier stage in gender identity development where the boy is merged with the mother. Only after some months does the mother gradually emerge as a clearly separate object. Sensing oneself a part of mother—a primeval and thus profound part of character structure (core gender identity)—lays the groundwork for an infant's sense of femininity.

Robert J. Stoller

General Adaptation Syndrome

Hans Selye (1959) defined systematic stress as the state of the organism when homeostatic mechanisms fail. The general adaptation syndrome (GAS), consisting of all nonspecifically induced biologic system changes, is a manifestation of the stress state. The GAS consists of three stages: an alarm reaction, a stage of resistance, and a stage of exhaustion.

In the early stage (shock phase) of the alarm reaction, the organism typically shows increased autonomic excitability, adrenalin discharge, and heart rate, temporary blood-sugar elevation followed by a drop (and the reverse for blood leukocyte count), anemia, acidosis, lowered body temperature and muscle tone, and, if extended, gastrointestinal ulcers. Continuation of the alarm reaction unabated (into its countershock phase) may lead to hyperactivity, adrenocortical enlargement, and thymus and lymph node involution. Presence of these symptoms ordinarily indicates a stress state, according to Selye, though their absence does not rule out such a state.

Mortimer H. Appley

Generalization in Conditioning

Stimulus generalization is the tendency for stimuli similar to a stimulus in whose presence a particular response has been learned to evoke the same response. Usually this tendency is an orderly function of the similarity between test stimuli and the training stimulus; the less similar a test stimulus is to the training stimulus, the less is the tendency to respond.

Generalization Test and Gradient

If the absolute number of responses (or some other measure of response strength) to each value of the set of test stimuli is plotted as a function of its position on the stimulus dimension, the figure is an absolute generalization gradient. If response strength at each value is plotted as a fraction or percent of the total responses to all values or as a fraction of the responses to the training stimulus, the figure is a relative generalization gradient.

A typical procedure to investigate the generalization of inhibition is to reinforce responding in the absence of a stimulus, and extinguish responding in the presence of the stimulus. The inhibitory gradient is obtained by measuring the response rate, in extinction, in the presence of stimuli differing in similarity to the unreinforced training stimulus.

Theories of Generalization

Ivan Petrovich Pavlov asserted that generalization is a fundamental process that occurs as an integral part of conditioning. According to this position, the training stimulus excites not only the cortical site representing the training stimulus but also, to a lesser extent, nearby cortical sites, which represent similar stimuli. Thus, by the same processes through which the training stimulus becomes associated with the learned response, the stimuli similar to the training stimulus come to be associated, perhaps less strongly, with the response.

Karl S. Lashley and Wade have advanced a theory of generalization known as the "failure of discrimination." They assert that responding generalizes to stimuli other than the training stimulus to the extent to which the subject fails to discriminate the test stimulus from the training stimulus.

Discrimination Training

In explicit discrimination training, different stimuli signal different reinforcement contingencies. In interdimensional discrimination training, training is conducted between stimuli from different stimulus dimensions. In extradimensional discrimination training, the subject is trained in a discrimination on one dimension, for example, color. In intradimensional discrimination training, the generalization test is performed along the same dimension as discrimination training.

Generalization Decrement

The term *generalization decrement* refers to the reduction of response strength as a result of a change from the training stimulus to a different stimulus. When the object of study is not stimulus generalization, the stimulus change may not be well specified.

James P. Rodgers

Genetic Influences on Personality Development

One of the most influential demonstrations of the importance of hereditary factors for personality was probably the study by A. Heston (1966) of children placed in a foster home or adopted because their mothers were schizophrenic when they delivered their babies. Many years later, he was able to find forty-seven of these individuals—thirty of them males—and to interview them personally, as well as obtain information from their military and medical records. He also obtained Menninger mental health ratings on the basis of the interviews. Heston was able to compare these forty-seven persons "at risk" for schizophrenia with fifty who had also been in foster homes years ago, but not for psychiatric reasons.

Broad heritability may be estimated by twice the

difference between the monozygous and dizygous concordance: $2(r_{mz} - r_{dz})$. It cannot be stressed enough that heritability estimates will vary between studies due to differences between samples, conditions at the time of examination, testing procedures, and other factors. Therefore, it is close to meaningless to speak of *the* heritability of a trait, as if there exists a certain fixed "true" value.

There is some support for the idea that consistent achieving and vigorous activity are, in part, due to genetic factors. Somewhat similar findings have been reported for mice (G. E. McClearn and J. C. DeFries 1973) and for dogs (J. C. Scott and J. L. Fuller 1965). S. W. Gray (1973) had speculated on possible causal (i.e., neurophysiological) mechanisms underlying such general personality traits.

Steven G. Vandenberg

Genetics and Psychopathology

Great conceptual and technical advances in genetics have been made in the past decade, so that the nature and function of the gene have increasingly been revealed and efforts made toward the detection of genes related to psychiatric disorder. More than ever, it is necessary to consider the overall role of genetics in human health and disease and the particular care required in considering the relation of genetics to psychiatry.

Without research based on careful and unbiased ascertainment of patient and control populations using reliable diagnostic criteria, and without informed attention to prenatal and postnatal environmental influences, genetic findings may be spurious, of only limited application, or of limited use in counseling and prevention.

Having noted these cautions, it can be said that both genetics and psychiatry have come a long way in reaching a rapprochement on a new level of scientific sophistication. Human genetics has become the science not only of heredity but also of human development, the controlled expression of the coded information in the genes (DNA molecules) in continuous reponse to and interaction with the environment. This interaction takes place on all levels, from the molecular and cellular to the organis-

mic, the familial and social, and then to the entire natural and human-made world in evolutionary perspective. It has long been the feeling of thinkers in psychiatry and in psychoanalysis (Sigmund Freud, Ernest Jones, and Sador Rado) that some of their most difficult problems await solution in the area of genetics.

With the stage thus set for giving genetics its unifying place in psychiatry, it has remained for the ever-accelerating technical advances of recent years to make the relation of genetics to psychiatry more concrete and to bring them more closely together. The understanding of the genetic code, the visualization of human chromosomes, the detection of gene-produced enzymes in human cells in health and disease, the refinement of methods of finding gene locations by linkage analysis and of the genetic study of populations, the delineation of an increasing number of genetic syndromes and the actual isolation of genes in a significant number of these, and the association of genetics with psychopharmacology by searching for genes coding for neuroreceptors—these are some of the areas, from the most basic to the more applied, that command the attention of psychiatrists.

Schizophrenia

One main area of consideration in the application of genetics to psychiatry is the role of genetics in the etiology of mental disorder, particularly in the major psychoses. It can be said at once that, at the time of writing (May 1993), definitive breakthroughs have not yet been achieved in the complete genetic understanding of schizophrenia and affective psychosis. Nevertheless, recent large-scale studies of twins and families and investigations of adoptees have mirrored the picture furnished by some earlier classic investigations, while combined efforts on the national and international scale are aimed at refining population-genetic and linkage analyses.

Thus, the line of evidence for a heritable predisposition to schizophrenia, going back to studies of Franz J. Kallmann (1946) and others, has been more recently confirmed using current diagnostic criteria, showing about a tenfold increase in risk among first-degree relatives of probands. Studies of twins have consistently noted a 40 to 50% concordance in monozygotic pairs, versus about 10% in dizygotic twins.

Studies of schizophrenic patients reared in adoptive homes have failed to show increased psychopathology in adoptive families commensurate with that found in biological families. Conversely, persons taken as children from schizophrenic mothers and reared in foster, nursing, or adoptive homes have shown a high rate of schizophrenia and related symptoms compared with control groups of similarly reared children of nonschizophrenic mothers.

The data thus far assembled are not able to specify a mode of transmission, although a recessive pattern seems unlikely. The search for linked genetic markers, close to a gene or genes for schizophrenia, has to date yielded only some apparently false leads, but more powerful methods and continued research by a consortium of investigating teams continues to hold promise. Diagnostic heterogeneity remains a major problem. Nonhereditary factors still require clarification; the high proportion of unaffected monozygotic twins of affected individuals, and brain-imaging defects in the affected as opposed to the nonaffected twin, point in this direction. Longitudinal observations of offspring of affected parents (a high-risk group) are revealing defects in neurological signs, as well as information handling and attention deficits.

Affective Psychoses

As in schizophrenia, recent family, twin, and adoption studies have corroborated genetic transmission. First-degree relatives of bipolar probands have a risk of about 18% compared with 6% in relatives of controls, and the data seem consistent with a dominant form of inheritance. The genetic mode of transmission in unipolar recurrent depression is less clear, with polygenic inheritance possible. Evidence for X linkage, based on presumed closeness of a gene to the color-blindness locus on the X chromosome, has been weakened by recent gene marker study, and that for linkage on chromosome 11 was similarly diminished when larger diagnosed pedigrees were included. Heterogeneity may account for some of the difficulty in genetic marker studies.

Nevertheless, if hereditary studies can help to divide the depressive syndrome into biological subentities, it not only will have nosological and prognostic importance but may be of great value when it comes to treatment. Drug response (e.g., to lithium) may vary with the basic nature of the illness.

Other Psychiatric Disorders

Statistical findings suggesting genetic factors in panic disorder, anorexia, obsessive-compulsive disorder, and Tourette's syndrome have yet to be substantiated by gene localization. Studies in alcoholism, particularly adoption studies but also twin studies, suggest that both nongenetic and genetic factors play a role. Some adoptive studies, for example, seem to demonstrate the additional pathogenic role of the adoptive families, while the concordance in twin studies shows less difference between monozygotic and dizygotic twins than found in the major psychoses. Alcoholism may indeed be heterogeneous, with some cases having a greater genetic causation than others.

Chromosomal Abnormalities

Before techniques of molecular biology focused attention of geneticists on the search for DNA markers and eventually for the genes coding for psychiatric disorder, the excitement in psychiatric genetics began in the area of chromosomal anomalies. With the determination in the mid-1950s of the normal human genome, with forty-six chromosomes visualized in twenty-two pairs of autosomes and the XY pair of sex chromosomes, the stage was set for the rapid discovery of chromosome variations involving aneuploidy (incorrect number) and translocation (of part of one chromosome to another). The trisomic state in Down's syndrome (extra chromosome 21) and sex-chromosome anomalies (Klinefelter's syndrome, a male with an extra X chromosome; Turner's syndrome, a female with a missing X chromosome) were soon described.

Aside from their value in genetic counseling after amniocentesis or chorionic villus analysis, these and similar chromosomal variations have more recently pointed the way for molecular biological studies of particular chromosomes or particular regions in the search for DNA markers and genes.

Neuropsychiatric Disorders

Recently, among the most successful results of molecular genetic analysis have been advances in the understanding of neuropsychiatric disorders. The dramatic pinpointing of the gene for Huntington's chorea culminated a ten-year period of frustrating research that followed its localization on chromosome 4 by linkage methods. The gene turned out to be characterized by repeated sequences in a long DNA molecule, with normals having up to thirty-four repeats and patients, forty-two or more; higher number of repeats are apparently associated with earlier age of onset.

Another important advance has been the localization of a gene for spinal muscular atrophy on chromosome 5, with both forms of this childhood disease apparently traced to the same region.

Duchenne muscular dystrophy, an X-linked disease, has been traced to a gene whose product is under study, and cystic fibrosis, a common autosomally inherited condition, is currently in the stage of therapeutic trial based on gene replacement.

Genetic Counseling

An area of increasing importance in psychiatric genetics is genetic counseling. With the increase of knowledge, making possible more specific answers, comes increasing responsibility to provide usable information and avoid doing harm. Chromosomal examination of cells in amniotic fluid obtained by amniocentesis or in chorionic villi studied in early pregnancy can determine chromosomal or enzymatic abnormalities associated with disease, and also determine the sex of the fetus. This process opens up many potentially beneficial as well as many controversial areas.

In the major psychiatric illnesses, without knowledge of the exact mode of inheritance and without localization of the responsible gene or genes, risks of recurrence are currently based on empirical data collected from experience with other families. These data may be modified by the severity of the proband's illness, the presence of the illness in other relatives, and the presence of assortative mating. Counseling has to take account of the uncertainties inherent in our state of knowledge, and also of the burden and treatability of the disease in question.

In other conditions, such as Huntington's chorea, it is actually possible to determine the presence or likelihood of abnormal genes. The implication of such knowledge, especially in an illness whose onset may be at a future date, requires careful preparation of the individual and family. It is becoming increasingly important to realize that advice regarding parenthood or marriage must be given with understanding, with humility, and with consideration of the impact on the couple seeking help and their families.

All aspects of individual and family dynamics come into view during genetic counseling. In discussing these matters, weight must be given not only to the genetic risk but also to the mental health and social responsibility of the prospective parents and the anticipated home environment. Persons offering genetic counseling must be versed in methods of interviewing and methods of counseling and in the many factors involved in adoption, family planning, therapeutic abortion, artificial insemination, and the like.

Social and Ethical Issues

The misuse of genetics for political or economic discrimination has been an unfortunate theme in world history. Policies regarding genetic screening at birth or before marriage, sperm banks, eugenic considerations, and questions of population, both qualititative and quantitative, have generated heated discussion. The project to map and eventually sequence the entire human genome will have a profound impact on clinical medicine. The relation of genetic risk to insurability under health plans is an increasing concern. As in any other science, there is opportunity for unsocial or unpsychological thinking in genetics. It may very well have to be the job of some psychiatrists and psychologists to have a voice in the larger issues and to prepare themselves either to do genetic counseling or at least to be concerned, to supervise, and to be involved with it.

John D. Rainer

Genius

Francis Galton's genetic and statistical studies offered the first quantitative studies of human abilities. He made the assumption that these abilities are distributed in the form of a bell-shaped curve, with genius represented at one extreme end of the continuum. He further argued that these high natural gifts would express themselves in visibly achieved eminence through varied accomplishments. Such eminence is achieved only by one individual in 4,000 (or .025% of 1%) of the general population.

In 1921, Louis M. Terman and his associates began an extensive project, studying 1,528 children from California schools, ranging in IQ from 135 to 200, and in age from 2 to 19. These were labeled, according to Terman's classification, as genius or "near" genius. In comparing their experimental group to the control groups, the gifted children were found to be superior in medical and physical indicators and in accelerated educational accomplishments, and displayed a wider range of interests outside of their school achievement and an active play life. Moreover, they came from privileged families, as measured by socioeconomic indices, with the numbers of eminent relatives and ancestors far exceeding that which would be expected by chance. The frequency of insanity in these families was lower than average, with only 0.4% of the parents showing any record of mental illness.

Studies of the lives of many creative geniuses indicate that the average age for first productions is between 21 and 25 years of age (i.e., Sigmund Freud at 21 and Albert Einstein at 22). Their productive years were extensive, averaging more than 30 years (i.e., Freud, Einstein, Charles Darwin, Pablo Picasso, etc., all more than 50 years). Also, when eminent scientists, mathematicians, and psychologists were compared with matched controls in their fields, the ones identified as the more creative outnumbered their controls very significantly in terms of quality and quantity of productions.

Anne R. Bloom

Geriatric Psychiatry

The immune system is a primary defense mechanism that is essential for the preservation of life. However, it may also play a significant role—either passively or actively—in senescence and in termination of life. The capabilities of defense by the immune system decline throughout the life span. In addition, it appears that cells become genetically diverse with time. They then may become antigenic and stimulate antibody production, producing autoimmune disease with injury to normal cells.

Three mental disorders are frequently observed in elderly people: organic brain disease, depressive reactions, and hypochondriacal reactions. Although the occurrence of organic brain disease rises sharply after the age of 75, it appears that 4 to 6% of the population age 65 and over suffer from definite organic brain syndrome, and that an additional percent suffer from milder degrees of impairment.

Organic Brain Syndromes

Organic brain syndromes are likely to be accompanied by important alteration in the person's thinking and behavior. The so-called cognitive functions, which include comprehension, calculation, problem solving, learning, and judgment, are impaired. Memory is spotty, and orientation for time, place, and person is faulty. Emotional responses are easily elicited and are disproportionate or inappropriate to the stimulus.

Cerebrovascular disease is another serious and common problem in late life. Dementia associated with cerebral arteriosclerosis frequently appears before the age of 70. Rarely does the disease appear in individuals as young as 45. It is more common in males than in females.

Depression

Depressive symptoms are not unusual in patients with organic brain disease. The majority of the clinical studies indicate that depressive symptoms are more common in cerebral arteriosclerosis and other types of cerebrovascular disease than in senile dementia. Depressed elderly patients occasionally present a clinical picture of pseudodementia. Such patients appear to be severely perplexed and disoriented, and memory defects are associated with frequent approximate answers.

In the elderly, depressive episodes are commonly associated with losses—social, financial, and physical. The elderly individual is very much aware of his or her loss of self-esteem.

Hypochondriasis

Hypochondriasis is ubiquitous but is particularly common in elderly people seeking help as outpatients. It is generally accepted that hypochondriasis is not a disease entity but a syndrome consisting of anxious preoccupation with the body or a portion of the body, which the patient believes is either diseased or not functioning properly.

Ewald W. Busse

Gestalt Psychology

The first formulations of Gestalt psychology were made in 1912 by Max Wertheimer, who, together with Wolfgang Köhler and Kurt Koffka, founded the new movement. It was to become a major revolution in psychological thinking.

Perception

Except under special conditions, the characteristics of a perceived whole cannot be derived from those of its components, considered in isolation. Indeed, the nature and function of a part depend, rather, upon the whole or context in which it is found. Apparent (stroboscopic) movement—whose investigation by Wertheimer launched Gestalt psychology—cannot be explained by reference to the independent "stills" that give rise to it. A melody cannot be derived from the characteristics of its component notes; no more can the form of an object be explained in terms of the corresponding local retinal stimulation.

An important advance was Wertheimer's investigation of perceptual organization, of the fact that our perceptual world is not a composite of individual sensations but consists of things and of groups, with spaces between them. How is it that some items belong together and form wholes or groups, which are segregated from other such structures? Wertheimer studied the factors that determine which parts of a visual field belong together. (The same problem presents itself in other modalities.) He found that, other things being equal, similar items form groups, as do items in proximity; he demonstrated closure, good continuation, and other factors of organization. Visual wholes, he found, tend to be as simple and regular as the prevailing conditions permit. All these facts suggest that selective interactions determine the organization of the perceptual field.

Isomorphism

In perception we find only the products of the above-mentioned selective interactions, which must, therefore, occur in another realm. Gestalt psychology posits that psychological events are structurally similar to the corresponding physical processes in the brain. This is the hypothesis of psychophysical isomorphism. According to it, interactions, especially those in the cerebral cortex, produce functional wholes whose correlates are structured psychological events.

Isomorphism, especially as Köhler developed it, became a powerful heuristic. It became possible, from observation of perceptual facts, to make hypotheses about the corresponding neurological events. Such hypotheses should have consequences for new perceptual facts, which could then be tested in direct psychological experiments. This procedure of working back and forth between psychological observation and physiological hypothesis led Köhler to the study of figural aftereffects; from these he deduced the kind of process that must correspond to all organized perceptions, and he was finally led to first demonstrations of the cortical currents that accompany perceptual processes.

Thinking and Problem Solving

The role of logical requiredness in thinking has been studied by Mary Henle. When the premises that go into a given thinking process are fully understood, many apparently faulty deductions are found not to transgress the rules of the syllogism. Rudolf Arnheim, by showing the "intelligence" of perception, evidenced particularly in perceptual abstraction, has made clear the natural relation between perception and thinking.

The concept of insight is associated with Gestalt psychology, which has emphasized its importance in thinking. Insight is simply the awareness of relations, which are seen as following from the characteristics of the related material. However, it must not be supposed that, for Gestalt psychology, thinking is no more than insight. The correct relations must be found—often they suddenly present themselves—before they can be understood, that is, before insight can occur. Thus, once more, we are led to a realm that transcends the phenomenal realm, that of physical processes in the cerebral cortex.

Work on the nature of recall shows it to involve an interaction between a present process and a memory trace, based on the similarity of the two. Such an interaction may be prevented if the process and trace in question do not show distinctive similarity but are merely members of a monotonous series of similar items. Under such conditions of "crowding," recall is much impaired. Crowding, in turn, depends upon interactions among similar items in a trace field. Thus, recall and the disturbance of recall are subsumed under the same principle, a principle previously shown to operate in perceptual organization.

Learning

A natural extension of Gestalt theories of perception and thinking has been Arnheim's work in the psychology of art and his formulation of a theory of expression. The latter rests on an extension of the principle of isomorphism.

Gestalt psychology is an experimental psychology. It differs from certain other experimental psychologies in its preference for starting with phenomenological observation in advance of specific experimental research. This term is used here to refer to the attempt to get a good look at the phenomena one is going to investigate, as free as possible from bias and from any assumptions about them, before undertaking experimental manipulations. In certain areas—such as the study of the fac-

tors determining organization, the observation of Ehrenfels properties, the analysis of value, and much of the work on thinking—simple observation or demonstration alone has so far been employed. But phenomenological observation is used, where possible, as a preliminary to experimentation.

Mary Henle

Gestalt Therapy

Gestalt therapy is a phenomenologically rooted existential psychotherapy. It accepts the responsibility of each person for the creation of his or her own life, for its dilemmas as well as its eventual resolutions. The core of the Gestalt therapy process is itself a paradigm for a life richly lived—full experience of the present moment, then movement into another engrossing experience.

Central to the ability to move easily and confidently into contact is the process of awareness. Awareness is a mobilizing, arousing, orienting recognition of that which is oneself and that which is not. It is a constant assertion of one's own separateness, one's own boundaries, so that one may mitigate the fear of being overwhelmed or swept up by the compelling flow of the environment.

In working with awareness, the therapist may attend to the individual's awareness of sensations, wants, actions, feelings, and values, concentrating on these components of experience and staying with them, accentuating and amplifying them until expressive action occurs organically. This process of amplification underlies the native movement toward the completion of the previously unfinished situation. The expressive possibilities earlier repressed are freed to ripen into resolution. This cycle may have to be repeated many times in order to lay the unfinished business at last to rest. Each time, the process of amplification must lead to a fresh occurrence, not merely a stale rehash.

Basic to this dedication to reclaiming and reworking avoided or absent aspects of the patient's life is the process of amplifying and supporting the contact possibilities. Dialogue, movement, bodily recovery, and imagery are all valuable actions, which can foster a surge into the completion of experience. The experiment must be an organic outgrowth of what the patient is doing or feeling at any particular moment in therapy. It is not a facile technique to be applied indiscriminately, irrespective of person or timing. The reciprocal components of safety (support) and emergency (risk) call for careful attention, so that the patient is neither blasted into experiences that are too threatening for her nor allowed to stay in safe, but infertile, territory.

Miriam Polster
Erving Polster

Glover, Edward (1888–1972)

Glover was one of the pioneers of psychoanalysis in England and played a crucial role in the formation of the British Psychoanalytic Society in 1924.

M. Masud R. Khan

Goal Gradient

Clark L. Hull (1932) used the goal gradient hypothesis to explain thirteen different features of maze learning:

1. The animal will choose the shorter of two paths to a goal.
2. The greater the difference between the lengths of the two paths, the more readily will the short path be chosen.
3. The relative rather than the absolute difference determines the ease of discrimination between the two paths.
4. Animals will eliminate blind alleys.
5. Long blind alleys will be eliminated more readily than short ones.
6. Blind alleys will be eliminated in a backward order.
7. Long mazes will be harder to learn than short ones.
8. Speed of running will increase as the animal approaches the goal.
9. If there are two alternative paths to a goal,

one longer than the other, the animal will run more slowly in the first part of the long route than in the first part of the short one.
10. Speed will be about equal in the final parts of the two paths referred to in the ninth deduction.
11. After a blind alley has been eliminated, animals will tend to pause at its entrance before proceeding through the maze.
12. Pure stimulus act sequences will drop out of behavioral sequences with practice.
13. Fragments of goal reactions will intrude into sequences of instrumental acts.

Six years later, Hull (1938) used the goal gradient hypothesis as a part of his treatment of "some field-force problems of young children." In this paper, he set forth the main ideas that were to become the most important theory to account for approach-avoidance conflict.

Gregory A. Kimble

Goldstein, Kurt (1878–1965)

Goldstein viewed behavior as the unified activity of the whole organism, whose motive is optimum self-actualization. Study of brain-injured patients reveals the general change within which specific symptoms occur. According to Goldstein, aphasia is the language manifestation of impairment of the abstract attitude. Impairment of abstract appears in certain psychotic processes. Goldstein maintained that mental functions and some mental defects can be localized in the brain.

Marianne L. Simmel

Grandparenthood

Grandparents generally attribute a positive value to their role and show strong affectional ties with their grandchildren. Actual interactional patterns tend to be more variable. Specific activities shared with grandchildren are rather infrequent. Thus, on the average, grandparents report shared activities with their grandchildren only a few times a year (Wood and Robertson 1975). Grandparents do not express a great deal of commitment to grandchildren but derive vicarious satisfaction from their successes and accomplishments.

The majority of studies on the family that specifically include the grandparent generation center on intergenerational relations within the family. Intergenerational continuity in personality, in values, and in orientation have been examined. Rather than confirming the existence of a generation gap within a family or demonstrating great similarities among generations, these studies reveal selective continuity and differences.

Social class, cultural and racial factors, kinships, and residence all play an important role in shaping grandparents' role performance (B. Kahana and E. Kahana 1971). Thus, maternal grandmothers have been found to portray special closeness and warmth toward their grandchildren. They are more likely to view grandchildren as like their own children and to approve of their grandchildren's upbringing than are paternal grandparents. Consideration of social class factors reveals more consistent helping patterns among middle-class than among lower-class grandparents, even though need for grandparental help may be greater in lower-class families (Shanas 1968). Black grandparents, especially grandmothers, often assume major responsibility for care of grandchildren. Thus, 44% of black grandmothers and 82% of black grandparents under age 50 were involved in providing care for their grandchildren. This trend represents a more prevalent pattern than that observed in studies of white grandparents.

Boaz Kahana
Eva Kahana

Graves' Disease: Emotional Factors

Graves' disease is a syndrome of endogenous thyrotoxicosis related to overfunction of the thyroid gland. Many female patients, prior to the onset of illness, have been forced (at times prematurely) to assume a caretaking role and domestic responsibilities. They describe themselves as mature and self-sufficient (G. C. Ham, F. Alexander, and H. T.

Carmichael 1951). Their sensitivity to bereavement and their childlike fears of death, isolation, and abandonment are the expressions of an underlying (unconscious) dependent relationship to one person. The illness begins when the bonds of a key relationship are either threatened or disrupted.

T. Lidz studied fifteen hospitalized patients with thyrotoxicosis but formulated their personal problems in more general terms (T. Lidz and J. C. Whitehorn 1950). The patients (twelve women and three men) had untreated thyrotoxic disease; in one patient the illness was complicated by diabetes mellitus. They were intensely dependent upon the affection and the slavish devotion of other people.

B. M. Mandelbrote and E. D. Wittkower (1955) compared patients to members of a comparison group and found evidence of differences in depression, anxiety, diminished assertiveness, sexual adjustment, confusion about sexual role, and anxiety about sexual fantasies, which preoccupied them. Conflicts over eating and biting were in evidence. The patients with Graves' disease harbored strong feelings of having been rejected; they were insecure in their relationships to others and yearned to remain dependent on their mothers.

P. Cushman reported that a patient had a recurrence of Graves' disease following surgical biopsy of a benign breast tumor. Prior to surgery, the T_3 suppression test had been normal.

Herbert Weiner

Griesinger, Wilhelm (1817–1868)

Wilhelm Griesinger, a German psychiatrist, was primarily interested in physiology and internal medicine. He insisted on combining mental hospital and neurological clinic. In 1845, he wrote the textbook *Pathology and Therapy of Mental Diseases.*

John C. Burnham

Groddeck, Georg (1866–1934)

German psychiatrist Groddeck, who called himself "a wild analyst," wrote about men's envy of mothers. Groddeck believed in the patient's wish to return to the womb. He considered himself not a scientist but an artist who interpreted the unconscious.

Martin Grotjahn

Group Cohesiveness

G. C. Homans (1961), using a general theory of human exchange, views cohesiveness as simply the value of different kinds of rewards available to members of a group. Lott and Lott (1974) propose that rewards for human beings must be relative to an individual's motivational state, preceding experiences, and the social context in which they are received, all of which must be taken into account before a stimulus or an event can be deemed rewarding.

J. W. Thibault and H. H. Kelley (1959) have offered a theory of interdependence that defines a viable interpersonal relationship as one where members of a collectivity (group) affect one another's outcomes (rewards, payoffs, etc.). Group cohesiveness is defined in terms of rewarding outcomes.

Steiner (1972) has suggested that while attraction to a group is a positive function of all expected gains, cohesion ultimately depends on who is attracted to the group, and how much. Through this qualification Steiner is attempting to take into account the fact that certain group members are usually more central to a group's success and permanence than others.

Albert J. Lott

Group Dynamics: An Overview

Group dynamics began as a special topic for investigation in the late 1930s through the stimulation of Kurt Lewin, whose life and contributions are recounted by Alfred Marrow (1969).

Studying Group Preferences

Perceiving a set of persons to be a unit. When specifiable conditions exist, a collection of individuals are likely to perceive themselves to be a unit, a group. If they do see themselves as a group, but a comparable set do not see themselves as such, and some event has an impact upon each set, that event will have a stronger effect upon the participants in the more unified set than on those in the less unified one.

Group goal. Sooner or later, members of a group establish a preferred objective and develop procedures to attain that end. This group goal, and the path to accomplish it, may be clear or muddy, and members may (or may not) know what they are to do and how they are to do it.

Desire for group success. When a group's goal has been established and work has been done toward its attainment, those who are in the group develop a desire to have their group succeed.

Leadership. The effect of a group's leadership cannot be sharply separated from other aspects of group process because often the initiative in a group's operations are shared by members who are not designated as primary or central officers. A leader's impact on the group depends not only on his or her skills but also on the power assigned to that role, the amount of respect members accord him or her, and the degree to which the group's task is appropriate for the leader's personal disposition.

Alvin F. Zander

Group Ecology

Ecological Theories

I. Altman (1969) presents an ecological theory of the functioning of social groups. In this theory, social processes involve an interaction between man and his environment; social behavior functions as a system, with the various levels of behavior operating as a holistic, integrated entity through time. In these time-linked relationship changes, individuals engage in communications via a multichannel system.

E. T. Hall (1966) describes four distance zones, which are appropriate for various kinds of social interaction: (1) intimate, (2) casual-personal, (3) social-consultative, and (4) public. Interpersonal distance is the link between the self and the social environment.

General Systems Theory

Personal space is similar to Hall's casual-personal zone. It is the distance a person customarily places between himself and others. D. M. Pederson and L. M. Shears (1973) treat personal space in terms of general system theory: the person is viewed as a system. The person system responds to other people, things, and space in its environment. As a system, the person's objective is to maintain a steady state in his body.

Darhl M. Pedersen

Group Homes

At the present time there are in the United States more than 1,500 day treatment centers that are partial hospitalization houses. They offer psychotherapy, group psychotherapy, family psychotherapy, vocational rehabilitation, and other mental health and psychosocial services, depending upon the needs of the patients.

Benjamin B. Wolman

Group Psychotherapy: A Historical Review

Group therapy was initiated in 1905 in internal medicine by Joseph H. Pratt in treatment of tuberculosis. In 1919 the psychiatrist L. Cody Marsh applied Pratt's method to the treatment of institutionalized mental patients. He was followed by the psychiatrist E. W. Lazell, who lectured to schizophrenic patients about their disorder. Gradually the idea of bringing patients together and combining therapy with the process of socialization won many supporters. Today there are several group psychotherapy methods, and all of them reduce the feeling of isolation, using the group interaction as a therapeutic factor.

Alfred Adler

Adler, a socialist, was deeply concerned about the problems of the working class. Because of this he tried to adapt techniques of individual psychotherapy to large groups of people.

J. L. Moreno

Moreno arrived in the United States in 1925. Before his arrival he had used group methods in Vienna and he originated the term *group therapy* in 1931. He was demonstrating his methods publicly by 1929, and in 1932 his techniques were described at the annual conference of the American Psychiatric Association.

Moreno is identified with psychodrama, which he introduced into the United States in 1925. According to him, psychodrama is the "science which explores truth by dramatic methods. The psychodramatic method uses mainly five instruments—the stage, the subject or patient, the director, the staff of therapeutic aides or auxiliary egos, and the audience."

Louis Wender

In 1929, Wender began to use psychoanalytic concepts in group therapy when he treated borderline patients in a private mental hospital. Wender's groups consisted of six to eight patients of the same sex who met two or three times each week for one-hour sessions.

P. Schilder

Sigmund Freud's monograph on groups was speculative, but is still valued by many group therapists. His observations referred primarily to leader-led groups, although he knew that groups could exist without leaders. Freud called the leader a representative of the father figure, while P. Schilder (1940) conceived of the group leader as both a mother and a father symbol.

T. L. Burrow

Burrow became interested in the biological principles underlying group behavior after 1932. He stated that man is part of a group, and the analysis of the individual can never be completed without real study of the group of which he is an essential part. His technique of group analysis was his contribution to group psychotherapy and psychoanalysis.

Samuel Slavson

During the 1930s Slavson trained as an engineer, and he later entered group work and group education and began working with activity group therapy at the Jewish Board of Guardians in the United States. He combined progressive education, group work, and psychoanalytic theory in activity group therapy where the therapist is permissive and accepting as patients interact with one another.

Carl Rogers

After World War II, Rogers's students practiced group psychotherapy with adults, using an approach directed toward interaction rather than insight. Rogers's phenomenological approach focuses on resolution of situational conflicts on conscious levels. The client is believed able to cure herself in a permissive setting where she can discuss her problems.

More Recent Trends

A. Wolf published a lengthy paper in the United States describing his psychoanalysis of groups (1949). He began his work in 1938, stimulated by the work of Schilder and Wender. By 1940 he was working with five groups of patients, and he continued his work with groups during his four years of service in the U.S. army during World War II. After the war he trained many psychotherapists. He applied the principles of individual psychoanalysis—free association, dreams, transference, and historical development—to the therapy group.

Married couples are often treated in groups. Cotherapy, joint therapy, multiple therapy, and cooperative psychotherapy are different names for the technique of using more than one therapist at one time in group psychotherapy.

The "here and now" is stressed in the practice of Gestalt therapy and Gestalt group therapy. The goal of Gestalt therapy is for the patient to form figures and grounds and to destroy old gestalts. In this way, aggressive feelings can be used in a healthy fashion. The patient is supposed to carry out his own therapy.

Eric Berne set forth three forms of ego function—parent, child, and adult. In the transactional practice of group therapy the patient's behavior is investigated as a transaction going on within her—among the ego states of parent, child, and adult.

In 1963, a sensitivity training group that met in California agreed to continue meeting over the weekend. This extended session, later called "marathon" group therapy, was used by more and more therapists who emphasized the here and now approach.

The students of Wilhelm Reich developed a bioenergetic method of group psychotherapy, which explores feelings by analysis of posture, breathing, and body musculature. Patients in the group observe and react to one another's body movements and are encouraged to maintain physical contact such as touching and caressing (Pierrakos 1974).

Max Rosenbaum

Guilford's Structure of Intellect

J. P. Guilford's classification scheme implies that all forms of intellectual functioning can be categorized with respect to subdivisions of three major characteristics. The most important characteristic is that of the psychological process apparently involved in any test, the process spoken of as the type of operation that subjects perform. 1) One operation is that of cognition, or "knowing," examples of which are knowing the meaning of the word "tangible" and knowing the product of 12 and 12. Memory involves the operation of retaining information that is briefly presented, such as recalling a phone number heard on the radio or a randomized list of nine letters presented on a screen for four seconds. 2) Divergent thinking consists of producing a variety of ideas that lead in different directions, such as thinking of unusual uses for common objects or of numerous words that rhyme with "peal." In divergent thinking, there is no one best solution; rather, what is at stake is the production of many clever ideas in some class.

In contrast to divergent thinking, 3) convergent thinking concerns finding the right solution to the problem or to accept the best possible solution. Outstanding examples of items involving convergent thinking are those concerning arithmetical reasoning and verbal analogies, where the subject must supply the one word that completes the analogy.

The classification scheme developed by Guilford

has been modified on a number of occasions to take account of the accumulating evidence and his own theorizing about human abilities. One problem that has been mentioned by numerous persons is that the model leads to an appallingly large number of factors, which makes it difficult to provide a simple outlook on human abilities. However, it maybe necessary first to look at human abilities in terms of all their complexities and then later pare the model down to only essential factors. Even if his model is supplanted by a very different one later, Guilford will have made a major contribution by attempting to classify all factors of human ability.

Jum C. Nunnally

Guilford-Zimmerman Temperament Survey

The Guilford-Zimmerman Temperament Survey (GZTS) was based upon a number of years of research, which first attempted to determine by factor analysis the dimensions of personality involved in Carl Jung's construct of introversion-extroversion and was later broadened to include neurotic dispositions. For example, the id does not cover all aspects of personality, or even its temperamental compo-

nents. The ten well-discriminated traits that it was designed to assess are characterized as follows:

G General activity versus slowness and lack of energy

R Restraint or seriousness versus arrhythmia and impulsiveness

A Ascendance and social boldness versus submissiveness and timidity

S Sociability and social interest versus reclusiveness and shyness

E Emotional stability and optimism versus instability and depression

O Objectivity versus subjectivity and hypersensitivity

F Friendliness and agreeableness versus hostility and belligerence

T Thoughtfulness or reflectiveness versus unreflectiveness

P (Good) personal relations and cooperativeness versus criticalness and intolerance

M Masculinity of interests and emotions versus femininity

J. P. Guilford
Joan S. Guilford

· H ·

Habit

As used by most psychologists, *habit* is a rough equivalent for the term *learning*. For Clark L. Hull, however, habit is a carefully defined theoretical concept. In Hull's theory the magnitude of habit s^Hr is defined as a negatively accelerated positive growth function of the number of reinforcements. The upper limit to which a habit can grow is further specified as a positive function of the amount of reinforcement, a negative function of the delay of reinforcement in instrumental conditioning, and a nonmonotonic function of the interstimulus interval in classical conditioning. Habit is distinguished carefully from performance.

Gregory A. Kimble

Habit-Family Hierarchy

Habit-family heirarchy is a concept invented by Clark L. Hull (1934) as a way of beginning to deal with the complexity of behavior. The general proposition is that in most situations where there is a goal to be attained, the organism has at its disposal many different acts (a habit family) that it may use to attain that goal. At the same time, however, these several habits vary in strength (form of hierarchy). The strength of the habit determines the probability that it will be used.

One of the most straightforward applications of the concept of habit-family hierarchy is to the explanation of selective learning. In these terms the process becomes one of reordering the strengths of the various available habits. Because the situation is a learning situation, by definition the strongest habit in the learning situation is not the correct one.

Gregory A. Kimble

Habituation

Habituation is characterized in all organisms by a decrement in response to a repetitive stimulus; the recovery of response if the repetitive stimulus is withheld for some period of time is termed *spontaneous recovery*. In the single-celled organism Stentor coeruleus, for example, mechanical stimulation will provoke a vigorous contraction of the cell. If the stimulus is repeated, the contractions will wane and eventually fail to occur. If the stimulus is then withheld, contraction will recover to its original strength (Wood 1970). In higher organisms, habituation may be defined by a variety of additional characteristics (Thompson and Spencer 1966). The flexion reflex—a reflexive withdrawal of the limb from a noxious stimulus such as a shock to a foot, which will occur in many experimental animals with the spinal cord completely disconnected from the brain—demonstrates all of the common characteristics of habituation and has been studied in some detail as a "model system" for understanding the characteristics of habituation and their possible physiological mechanisms (Groves and Thompson 1970).

Philip M. Groves

Habituation of Attention in Infants

The demonstration of subtle discriminative abilities in the human infant indicates the sophistication of visual attention and perception even by 4 or 5 months of age. Some evidence suggests that as early as 14 months of age, infants may habituate to conceptual characteristics of a visual event. In one experiment, infant fixation times were first habituated to a scene in which a boy moved a table from left to right.

The close correspondence between habituation and cognition is also apparent when one examines how the infant is able to habituate at all. By definition, if the infant habituates, her response does not decrease to all stimuli but only to that stimulus, or class of stimuli, that has been repeatedly presented. More specifically, the infant looks less at a pattern on a later trial because she has seen that particular pattern before, because it is becoming familiar.

When the infant habituates, he is demonstrating his ability not only to perceive or process information but also to remember that information.

One might expect rate of habituation or preference for novelty to be predictive of other important individual differences. Some studies have shown little preference for novelty in premature or mentally retarded infants. Other studies have found rate of habituation to be related to an infant's Apgar score at birth, his or her socioeconomic status, and even the IQ at 44 months. New multiple assessment devices or tests to distinguish "normal" from high-risk infants are currently under development. These tests include measures of infant habituation and visual attention.

Leslie B. Cohen

Halfway Houses

Halfway houses are full-time residential facilities, which provide room, board, and assistance in the activities of daily living to individuals with special problems and needs. Among the special groups served by halfway houses are the emotionally disturbed, the mental retarded, juvenile delinquents, drug and alcohol abusers, prisoners and parolees, or combinations of these.

In the United States, the halfway house movement for individuals with emotional disorders received its major impetus in the 1950s and 1960s. During that time, the number of operating halfway houses increased from 3 in 1953 to 209 in 1973. The historical roots of the movement and its growth from the period of the mid-1950s can be traced to several factors. These reflect many of the new directions that characterized the mental health field since World War II and that, in many areas, altered the delivery of mental health services from the traditional medical model to a social model.

The Community Mental Health Centers Act, enacted by Congress in 1963, became a major vehicle for implementing these new approaches. Among its primary goals was the provision of a range of services as alternatives to inpatient care. This helped demonstrate that many people with mental health problems could be helped in settings other than hospitals. It also showed that where hospitalization was essential, the length of stay could be minimized, particularly when alternative living facilities were available.

Viewed retrospectively, halfway houses were originally conceived as facilities that would bridge the gap between institutionalization and the community. Halfway houses are described in the literature of the 1950s as one of a number of newly developed transitional facilities between the closed mental hospital and the open community. Their major goal was to prepare individuals to move from their dependence on the sheltered environment of hospitals to the community, either with families or in other residential arrangements.

Two-thirds of halfway houses accept both men and women as residents. Other admission requirements relate to age, diagnosis, and prognosis. Age restrictions are most frequently stated in terms of a minimum age of 17 for acceptance. Diagnostic restrictions generally result in the resident population having a history of emotional problems only, though some halfway houses also accept alcoholics and mentally retarded people.

Saul Feldman
Isabel S. Davidoff

Hall, G. Stanley (1844–1924)

The American psychologist G. Stanley Hall applied psychology to education, maintaining that each individual psychological development recapitulates that of the human race. He believed that the study of children would uncover the development of the mind throughout its evolution.

Hall was the founder of psychological journals and of the America Psychological Association.

Thomas C. Cadwallader

Hallucinations

Hallucinations are errors of perception that occur when an internal sensory image is mistaken for a nonexistent external object, or when a sensation is experienced in the absence of the usual stimuli. They may arise from a variety of organic (endogenous and exogenous) and psychological factors. Because they may be associated with illusions, delusions, and delirium, they may occur in any of the numerous circumstances that occasion these states.

Hallucinations have three major characteristics: (1) perceptualization of the concept; (2) projection to the external world of the inner experience; and (3) the difficult corrigibility of the experience.

The perceptualization of the concept is the most specific characteristic of hallucinations. Before this stage of complete perceptualization is reached, intermediate stages may be experienced, such as hypnagogic hallucinations. The second important characteristic of hallucinations is projection. This quality is also present in dreams; the dreamer believes that the dream actually takes place outside herself.

Experimentally induced stresses, including sensory isolation, have been shown to induce acute hallucinations in previously healthy subjects. When healthy persons are isolated, with vision and hearing diminished by the use of patches and earplugs and with mobility limited, after several hours they experience anxiety and a desire for external stimulation and motor activity, as well as difficulty in concentration, reduction in motivation, and progressive difficulty with directed thinking. After 72 hours they develop delusional and visual hallucinatory experiences.

Ronald William McNichol

Hallucinogens

Hallucinogens are substances capable of producing profoundly distorted perceptions of internal and external stimuli and altered states of consciousness. These substances may be of either natural or synthetic origin. Hallucinogens have been known to humans throughout recorded history, and natural or synthetic substances have been used by every studied culture to alter the awareness of the members of that culture.

Hallucinogens may be roughly divided according to the neurotransmitter through which they appear to act. Phenylethylamines are hallucinogens related in chemical structure to epinephrine and are biochemically based on the catechol nucleus. This group includes mescaline and amphetamine-like hallucinogens such as MDA (methylenedioxyamphetamine) and STP (dimethyloxymethylamphetamine). The anticholinergic hallucinogens are related to parasympathetic chemistry. They occupy the acetylcholine receptor sites but do not activate them. In this way, they block the action of the parasympathetic nervous system. These agents include the belladonna alkaloids. Hallucinogens with an indole nucleus are related to the neurotransmitter serotonin. Lysergic acid diethylamide (LSD), psilocybin, morning glory seeds (ololiuqui), and dimethyltryptamine (DMT) are the principal representatives of this group of hallucinogenic agents.

Mescaline is derived from the peyote cactus (Lophophora williamsii) or is synthesized directly. This cactus is indigenous to South and Central America. Of the eleven or more alkaloids in the peyote cactus—an ancient plant used by Central American Indians—that affect the mind, mescaline is the most potent in producing hallucinations.

MDA (also called "Mellow Drug of America") is chemically related to both mescaline and STP. MDA is a relatively new drug that is produced synthetically; it is not known to occur in nature.

The anticholinergic hallucinogens are unique

among hallucinogenic agents in that they produce periods of amnesia and delirium. The active alkaloids that produce these effects are atropine and scopolamine. These alkaloids are available in datura (locoweed, jimsonweed), belladonna (deadly nightshade), mandrake root, and many over-the-counter cold remedies and sleeping mixtures.

The effects of these anticholinergic agents are somewhat different from the effects of the indole- and catechol-based hallucinogens in that their effects may persist as long as 48 hours or longer and include retrograde amnesia, psychological depression, toxic delirium, and generalized lethargy.

Psilocybin occurs in the sacred mushroom of Mexico, *teonanacatl*. These mushrooms are most often dried and eaten. Synthetic psilocybin is available as a white powder. Psilocybin has a long history of ceremonial and religious use in Central America. Other than LSD, psilocybin is the hallucinogen that has attracted the most scientific and lay attention.

DMT (dimethyltryptamine) is chemically related to both psilocybin and LSD. It is a colorless crystal, which is usually soaked into parsley or tobacco, dried, and smoked. The LSD-like effects of this drug last from 30 minutes to 2 hours, with an immediate onset when smoked or injected.

J. Thomas Ungerleider
Alan Brown

Hartmann, Heinz (1894–1970)

From an early age Heinz Hartmann took on leadership roles in psychoanalysis. He was a training analyst and faculty member in Vienna, Paris, and New York psychoanalytic institutes. He was the president of the New York Psychoanalytic Society from 1952 to 1954 and president of the International Psycho-Analytic Association from 1951 to 1957 and its honorary president from 1959 to 1970. His main works were *Die Grundlagen der Psychoanalyse* (1927) and *Ego Psychology and the Problem of Adaptation* (1930).

Albert J. Solnit

Haslam, John (1764–1844)

The English physician John Haslam's first major work was *Observations on Insanity* (1798). He advocated improvement in the conditions of mental patients.

John C. Burnham

Hate

René Descartes and Thomas Hobbes considered hate to be a basic passion, while Benedict de Spinoza related hate to the idea of sorrow associated with external causes. Other authors have postulated that hate is related to sorrow, anguish, anger, or even love. William McDougall conceived of hate as a mixed state consisting of anger, fear, and disgust.

The sequence distinguishing the verbal expression of hate from the motoric in D. Stanley-Jones's hypothesis is consistent with the Freudian concept of acting out. The congruence of Stanley-Jones's theory and the psychoanalytic theory of acting out appear to be that the presence of language results in a non-acting-out resolution of hate, while the absence of language may produce overt acting out.

G. Bychowski implies that the hated object is so repulsive that the mechanism of projection is called upon to keep the hated object as something alien. This correlation between the mechanism of projection and the emotion of disgust suggests the hypothesis that just as displacement manages anger and repression manages fear, so too does projection manage feelings of disgust and hate.

The defense syndrome of hate may be clearly seen in the development of the classic paranoid paradigm. The paranoid condition is characterized by excessive criticality, as well as by hatred. In his development, the paranoid person generally ends up saying "she hates me" or "they hate me." The sequence of psychological dynamics that operate in this paranoid development generally includes repression, projection, displacement, and reaction formation.

On an individual psychological level, hate may lead to the feeling of being "eaten up inside," implying the deteriorating effect of hatred. Sociologically, hate constitutes a basic threat to civilization. It is obvious that the emotions intimately connected with hate and the defense mechanisms involved in maintaining it point to the destructive consequences of hate in social living.

Henry Kellerman

Health Services in Psychology: The *National Register*

The Council for the National Register of Health Service Providers was established by the American Board of Professional Psychology (ABPP) in 1974 at the request of the board of directors of the American Psychological Association (APA). The *National Register of Health Service Providers in Psychology* is the publication listing those licensed psychologists whose education, training, and experience have been determined to meet the requirements for being defined as a health service provider, as follows:

A Health Service Provider in Psychology is defined as a psychologist, certified/licensed at the independent practice level in his/her jurisdiction, who is duly trained and experienced (meeting criteria for registration) in the delivery of direct, preventive, assessment and therapeutic intervention services to individuals whose growth, adjustment, or functioning is actually impaired or is demonstrably at high risk of impairment.

Psychology professionals are not typically licensed by specialty designation, just as physicians, dentists, and lawyers are not licensed in areas of specialty practice. Psychologists listed in the *National Register* have degrees in psychology and specialize in many areas. Regardless of specialty area of the degree (for example, clinical, counseling, school psychology), each has met the criteria for registration as a health service provider in psychology. ("Currently licensed, certified or registered" as a psychologist "at the independent practice level" means currently, actively licensed, certified, or registered for psychology practice generally, with no material limitations, conditions, or restrictions (e.g., supervision or

other conditions or limitations on practice) required by a state, provincial, or territorial board or governmental body.)

The original purpose of the *National Register* was to provide a voluntary mechanism to identify psychologists who meet the jurisdictional standards for practice *and* who are specifically educated and trained to serve the public's health service needs. The *National Register* is used for reimbursement purposes by private insurers and managed care organizations, such as HMOs, PPOs, and EAPs; for granting of staff privileges by hospitals and other facilities; for identification of qualified providers by state and federal government programs that include psychologists in their service delivery system (Medicare, CHAMPUS, disability, civil commitment, workers' compensation, etc.); and for referral purposes by peers, other health care professionals, and the public. In recent years several states have amended their legislation to identify health service providers among the larger group of licensed psychologists, using criteria similar to or identical to the criteria for listing in the *National Register*.

Criteria for Listing in the **National Register**

1. currently licensed, certified, or registered by a state/provincial board of examiners of psychology at the independent practice level of psychology
2. a doctoral degree in psychology from a regionally accredited educational institution
3. two years (3,000 hours) of supervised experience in health services in psychology, of which one year (1,500 hours) is an internship or organized health service training program and one year (1,500 hours) is postdoctoral supervised experience

Listing goes beyond licensure and identifies, for reimbursement and other purposes, those psychologists who have applied and whose education and experience have been determined to meet the criteria for registration.

Other Criteria Developed by the **National Register**
Where possible and appropriate, collaborative efforts have been undertaken by the Board of Directors of the National Register in support of psychology as an independent health profession and in support of the public interest in health services provided by psychologists. As indicated in a recent antitrust case (*MacHovec v. Council for the National Register*), the federal district court concluded, "The National Register serves the public interest in efficiently disseminating information to the marketplace with respect to the training and experience of healthcare providers."

The Board of Directors, the policy-making body responsible for the management of the corporation, is composed of eight psychologists and three public members, each serving a 4-year term, renewable once. A formal liaison relationship exists between the National Register and the Association of State and Provincial Psychology Boards (ASPPB) and with the Canadian Register of Health Service Providers in Psychology. One outcome of the relationship with ASPPB is the development and formal approval of criteria for identifying those training programs that could be designated as doctoral programs in psychology for purposes of licensure and credentialing (see criterion 2 above). The designation criteria, developed at the 1976–77 credentialing conferences jointly sponsored by the APA, the National Register, and the American Association of State Psychology Boards (former name of ASPPB), led to the decision to review doctoral programs to determine if they met those criteria. The yearly review and designation of doctoral programs was initiated first in 1981 by the National Register and became a joint effort of the National Register and Association of State and Provincial Psychology Boards in 1987. At that time, Canadian doctoral programs also were included in the review for designation purposes. This publication, *Doctoral Programs Meeting Designation Criteria* (ASPPB, 1993), is a valuable professional resource for educational institutions, prospective graduate students, state and provincial licensure boards, and credentialing bodies. As of a 1993 survey by this author, all of the fifty jurisdictions in the United States (with the exceptions of California and Vermont) rely on the publication to identify doctoral programs that will meet their criteria for licensure or include some or all of the criteria in their statute or rules and regulations as the definition of an acceptable doctoral program in psychology for licensure purposes.

In 1980, the Appeal Board of the National Register, a group of psychologists and public members who review the decisions made regarding denial of listing and delisting, recommended that the National Register develop criteria that could be used to identify health-service training programs in psychology. The "Guidelines for Defining an Internship or Organized Health Service Training Program in Psychology" were based upon or derived from several sources, including the Directory of the Association of Psychology Internship Centers (APIC), the Criteria for Accreditation of Internship Programs (APA), and experience gained from the review of applications for listing in the *National Register*. Those criteria have helped clarify the standards so that potential applicants for listing can make informed decisions regarding choice of an internship site or in designing an organized training program.

In 1982, the Board of Directors of the National Register approved criteria that would permit dropping any registrant from listing who had been found guilty of a crime, been expelled from membership in a state or national psychological association, or had his or her license revoked, suspended, or restricted by a state or provincial board of examiners and therefore no longer satisfies the criteria for continued listing. Furthermore, similar action occurs if it is determined that the person significantly misrepresented his or her credentials. Psychologists affirm their adherence to ethical and professional standards by completing an attestation form at the time of application and yearly at the time of their renewal of listing. Adherence to professional standards is required by the "Guidelines Concerning Removal from Listing in the *National Register*" which became policy in 1982. This type of effort by the National Register and by other professional organizations in psychology, each acting independently, represents psychology's concern with the maintenance of standards of conduct and interest in recognizing the profession's responsibility to the public welfare.

Publication

From an initial listing of approximately 7,000 registrants in 1975, the *Register* has grown to over 16,000 psychologists. In the past, the *National Register* was published every 2 years, followed by two supplements at 8-month intervals. The eleventh edition, published late in 1993, summarizes changes to the listing from January 1, 1992, through August 31, 1993. Each subsequent publication updates annually all listing information. Interim updates are provided in the *Register Report*, a quarterly newsletter published by the National Register for its registrants and subscribers to the *National Register*. Each year approximately 700 psychologists apply for listing, and 3% retire or are not listed for other reasons (disabled or deceased).

The National Register also publishes in the area of current legal issues for psychologists, including *The Psychologist's Legal Handbook* (C. Stromberg et al., 1988) and, in 1993, quarterly legal updates, all written by attorney Clifford Stromberg.

Development of a Database on Practice

"The National Register Survey: The First Comprehensive Study of All Licensed/Certified Psychologists" (D. H. Mills, A. Wellner, & G. R. Vandenbos 1979) was the first national survey of licensed psychologists. Late in 1990, a survey of registrants was mailed, to which 12,000 of the 16,000 registrants responded. The second part of that survey occurred in 1993. Taken together, part I and part II of this survey analyze a typical practice period of 60 days and indicate for each registrant responding (1) highest degree in psychology, date awarded, and name of granting institution, (2) classification by site of the two years of experience submitted to the National Register, (3) five areas of expertise based on a self-assessment of education, training, and experience, as well as the number of hours per week engaged in those areas of expertise, (4) primary and secondary theoretical orientations, (5) ages and groups served, (6) language fluency, (7) ABPP and ABPH diplomates, and (8) active licenses held.

At the same time, a new application for listing makes possible a detailed analysis of the training of psychologists who apply for listing in the *National Register*. For both the internship and postdoctoral year, the applicant indicates the percentage of time spent in specified activities, age groups served, and diagnostic categories (based on DSM-IV) of clients served.

A separate credentialing procedure assists psychologists listed in the *National Register* in documenting staff membership in a hospital or similar facility. Copies of the hospital staff bylaws, staff appointment letter, and the list of delineated privileges submitted by the appointing hospital credentialing officer verifies hospital staff membership. Those registrants who document satisfactorily these privileges have a special designation (HSM) added to their alphabetical listing.

Maintenance of this up-to-date database on psychologists listed in the *National Register* helps describe the aggregate characteristics of national registrants' education and training, special expertise, health service experience, and practice patterns.

Direct Verification of Credentials

To maintain accuracy of the information provided, the National Register works closely with the sixty-one regulatory bodies in the United States and Canada. Because the National Register verifies licenses yearly before publication (many registrants hold more than one license), an automatic licensure-verification computer-matching procedure, established in 1991, assists in the matching of the licensure information obtained directly from those jurisdictions to that information in the National Register database. Half of the regulatory bodies provide this information on a computer floppy or tape.

Graduate education is verified by requiring official transcript(s) directly from the degree-granting institution. The two years of health service experience is verified on forms submitted to the National Register by the supervising psychologist(s) or other qualified professional(s). Psychologists hired by the National Register conduct the multi-step application review process. All decisions to list are based solely on the documentation, with ample opportunity given to clarify questions about the application. Any psychologist denied listing may appeal to the Appeal Board or may reapply for listing at any time.

Conclusion

The activities of the staff and the Board of Directors of the National Register, in concert with the information provided in the *National Register of Health Service Providers in Psychology*, together help promote the identification and involvement of health care services by psychologists in today's health care marketplace. Given that this is a changing marketplace, it is likely that the National Register will continue to expand its initiatives into related areas and to refine and improve the implementation of the credential review process. Because the National Register is the most successful of all credentialing organizations in psychology, based on the number of those psychologists who have voluntarily applied to have their education, training, and experience reviewed, its future is assured by maintaining its emphasis on a quality-assessment process.

Judy E. Hall

Hedonic Theories of Motivation

Paul Thomas Young has conducted experimental work on the problem of hedonic tone since the early 1920s, eventually settling on the variable of food palatability in rats as his primary research technique. Palatability refers to the hedonic value of a foodstuff, as reflected by the animal's preferences in a free-choice situation. Extensive work by Young and his associates, which showed conclusively that rats will learn and perform for saccharin-solution rewards—which are without food value—has proved very influential in convincing psychologists that drive reduction is not necessary to motivate behavior and, further, that hedonic conceptions can be scientifically studied. Young conceives of a bipolar hedonic (affective) continuum ranging from extreme distress to extreme delight. Organisms tend to repeat behaviors leading to positive affective arousal, and to avoid those leading to negative affect. This naturally requires learning, and Young accepts a contiguity conception of learning. Affective processes are considered motivational in the sense that they both energize and determine the course of behavior. Affects, as well as sensory stimuli, are seen as being subject to classical conditioning, and on this basis the organism learns new motives.

The affective arousal theory proposed by David McClelland and associates in 1953, in a manner not unlike Young's formulation, conceives that motives are the learned results of the association of neutral cues with affective states. Thus, positive affects can lead to the development of approach motives, and negative affects to the development of avoidance motives.

Paul McReynolds

Hedonism, Psychological

The term *psychological hedonism* (*hedonism* is derived from the Greek word for "pleasure") designates the doctrine that acts are motivated by preferences for pleasure and aversions to displeasure. It is to be distinguished from *ethical hedonism*, which asserts that pleasure is intrinsically good or desirable and that displeasure is intrinsically undesirable. Considerable confusion can result from a failure to distinguish between these two conceptions. A theorist may accept either, neither, or both. Among the more eminent psychological hedonists have been Epicurus (341–270 B.C.) and Jeremy Bentham (1748–1832), both of whom also espoused ethical hedonism.

Psychological hedonism has often been criticized (B. B. Wolman 1965), yet it seems to survive and to undergo periodic renaissance in spite of the criticisms. These criticisms have taken two main forms. First, behaviorists, beginning with John Broadus Watson, have argued that feelings of pleasure and displeasure are mentalistic concepts and, hence, not appropriate subjects for study. And second, the tendency of some writers to define pleasure and displeasure in terms of an animal's behaviors—pleasure being inferred from approach behaviors and displeasure from avoidance behaviors—and then to use these concepts in order to explain the same behaviors has led to a charge of tautology.

Paul McReynolds

Heinroth, Johann Christian August (1773–1843)

Heinroth, a German psychiatrist, attributed all mental disturbances to sins and advocated punishment and severe restraint.

John C. Burnham

Helplessness

Learned helplessness has been suggested as a model of reactive depression in humans, because it has been observed, experimentally and anecdotally, that both helpless and depressed subjects show passivity, difficulty seeing response as effective, low mood, lowered aggression, loss of appetite drives, and catecholamine depletion. Both may centrally involve the belief in the futility of active responding and may be reversed and prevented by experiences with mastery. Learned helplessness has also been implicated in augmented stress, developmental failure, and sudden psychosomatic death.

Martin E. P. Seligman

Herbart, Johann Friedrich (1776–1841)

According to German psychologist Johann Friedrich Herbart, the human soul is a Kantian "thing-in-itself," thus inaccessible to empirical cognition, but its actions are observable. The main force of the soul is inertia, which is resistance to change. Herbart called the defensive discharges of energy "Vorstellungen" (presentations, ideas). Inhibited ideas are repressed and become unconscious. Acceptance of new ideas was called "apperception." According to Herbart's educational psychology, apperception elicits interest, which is a prerequisite for successful learning.

Benjamin B. Wolman

Hilgard, Ernest R. (1904–   )

The American psychologist Ernest Hilgard became best known for his expository textbook *Conditioning and Learning* (with Donald Marquis, 1940), *Theories of Learning* (1948), and *Introduction to Psychology* (1953). Hilgard conducted experimental research on hypnosis and was the editor of *American Psychology in Historical Perspective* (1978).

Gordon H. Bower

History of Psychiatry

Most present-day mental illnesses were known in antiquity; Hippocrates' writings (fifth and fourth centuries B.C.) dealt with phobic reactions, mania, melancholia, postpartum psychoses, mental confusion after hemorrhage, delirious states associated with tuberculosis and malaria, paranoia, obsessive-compulsive problems, and hypochondriasis. Classifications were eventually modified, but *melancholia* remains one of the oldest terms in medicine.

The transition between the Greek and Roman period and the Middle Ages was gradual. Empiricism declined, theological and metaphysical influences expanded, and demonology took hold. The medieval period witnessed masochistic flagellants, dancing manias, and the growth of witchcraft cults. Concurrently, general hospitals were established with sections for the mentally ill. In 490 A.D., a psychiatric hospital was founded in Jerusalem.

During the Inquisition, witches were sought as causative agents in sexual dysfunctions and mental deterioration. Treatment continued to involve purgatives and narcotics, mercury for impotence, and gold and silver for melancholia.

In the eighteenth century, writings on mental illness increased. The authors usually practiced general medicine with a neurological orientation. But, in 1779, Franz Anton Mesmer developed the idea of "animal magnetism," along eighteenth-century concepts of disease due to disharmony or disturbances of nervous fluid (*Mémoire sur la découverte du magnétisme animale*).

Psychiatry as a specialty was developed in England with William Battie's clinical demonstrations of patients in St. Luke's Hospital for Lunatics in 1753 constituting an important step. Electrotherapy was used in Middlesex Hospital, St. Bartholomew's, and an asylum in Leicester, and in 1793 a London Electrical Dispensary was organized.

Early nineteenth-century phrenology overlapped mesmerism and influenced psychiatrists and general physicians, with stress on a crude cortical localization of mental faculties. Franz Joseph Gall, anatomist and neurologist, saw the cerebral cortex as the physical substrate of the mind and apparently intended his phrenology to be a psychophysiology. He suggested that mental functions were rooted in special areas of the brain.

In 1885 Sigmund Freud was influenced by Jeane-Martin Charcot in Paris and, in 1889, by H. Bernheim, whose experiments impressed Freud with the possible existence of strong unconscious forces influencing patients. Freud collaborated with Josef Breuer in Vienna in hypnotic investigations and with him coauthored a preliminary paper in 1893, followed by *Studien über Hysteria* in 1895. Freud eventually found it necessary to discontinue the use of hypnotism and proceeded to develop psychoanalytic concepts and treatment. Concurrently, Pierre Janet in France and Morton Prince in the United States investigated many aspects of personality functioning.

J. C. Prichard published his *Treatise on Insanity and Other Disorders Affecting the Mind* in England in 1835, presenting a concept of "moral insanity" that was eventually incorporated into descriptions of "antisocial personality."

In 1911 Eugen Bleuler, in Switzerland, published *Dementia Praecox oder die Gruppe der Schizophrenien.* He introduced the terms *schizophrenia* and *ambivalence*, noted disharmony of affect and alterations in the thinking process, and observed a group of reactions rather than one specific disease. He described the psychogenesis of secondary symptoms and dereistic and autistic thinking. Concurrently, Morton Prince studied manifestations of hysteria and supplied descriptions of multiple personalities.

Freud presented the dynamic unconscious in its complex manifestations, with theoretical and clinical presentations of unusual depth and range. His psychological insights introduced new or additional perspectives to sociology, anthropology, literature, and history.

Carl Jung and Alfred Adler deviated from Freud's views early in the second decade of the century and developed analytical psychology and individual psychology, respectively. Jung was identified with a "collective unconscious" and the spiritual components in personality makeup. Adler stressed the feelings of inferiority and organ inferiority, the masculine protest in women, and the drive toward power. Among neo-Freudians, Karen Horney stressed "the struggle toward self-realization" in her view of neurosis. Harry Stack Sullivan is identified with the fundamental importance of interpersonal relations and their disturbances in personality development. By mid-century, pharmacotherapy had moved into a prominent position for treatment of neuroses and psychoses, and new medications continued to appear with varying claims of success.

The second half of the twentieth century has witnessed child psychiatry, which stresses essentially the care and training of the mentally disabled, while "child study" stresses education. Focus on children and delinquency appeared between 1909 and 1919. William Healy promoted the idea of child guidance clinics and founded the Chicago Juvenile Psychopathic Institute in 1909.

Group therapy, hypnotherapy, behavior therapy, and numerous other therapies and modifications of conventional psychotherapy blossomed, especially after World War II. Concurrently, psychologists, social workers, and then a variety of psychotherapists moved directly into the private practice of psychotherapy or into institutional positions. Non-physicians started to play a more significant role in psychiatric settings, including hospitals.

Jerome M. Schneck

History and Psychology

The man who elevated psychology to a focal role in history was Wilhelm Dilthey. Dilthey rejected Immanuel Kant's transcendental ethics and H. Rickert's and H. Windelband's neo-Kantian notion of a priori values. According to Dilthey, values are expressions of human emotions and desires. He also rejected Windelband's categorization of nomothetic natural sciences and idiographic sciences of culture and history. According to Dilthey, geography, astronomy, natural history, economics, comparative psychology, philology, and even history have both idiographic and nomothetic aspects. Dilthey proposed instead to distinguish between natural sciences and humanities (*Geisteswissenschaften*). Human studies, which include the mind and its products, have a special interest in the individual case. Whenever we study the individual (psychology), or the arts, or history, it is always the study of our inner processes, while the natural sciences look at their subject matter from without.

In 1880 Dilthey described the limitations of psychology. While the British associationistic psychology was patterned after contemporary physics, psychology was still far from operating with the precision of mathematical inferences. Nor could experimental psychology cover the entire area of the human mind. Psychological laws, wrote Dilthey, "are pure laws of form; they deal with the formal side of human actions and dispositions; they do not deal with the content of the human mind." If mathematics is the foundation for all natural sciences, psychology has to play an analogous role in human studies.

Dilthey suggested a new psychological system called "understanding psychology" (*verstehende Psychologie*). The contemporary explanatory, experimental psychology was unable to see what history, art, and religion see. The new understanding psychology was to serve as a foundation for all human studies. Psychological analysis "illuminates" human relations. "Without reference to the mental system on which their relations are grounded, the human studies are an aggregate, a bundle, not a system."

History as a Study of Behavior

The search for more complex phenomena in the higher evolutionary levels is a legitimate scientific task; according to Benjamin B. Wolman (1971), however, such discoveries must be made rather than taken for granted. The fact that at a certain evolutionary level a certain species became capable of communicating with the use of symbolic signs is highly important, but as such does not necessarily herald a radical change in behavioral patterns of the particular species. Too often, history records a description of lives that pretend to be more than they really were.

Comparative psychology, sociology, and anthropology bear witness to the fact that the so-called progress and alleged changes in human behavior have not been so large and significant as some thinkers would like them to be. There have been substantial changes in the technique and tools used in production of food, housing, and clothing, but today people toil for food, clothing, and shelter as they did 100,000 years ago. Atomic warheads and ballistic missiles are not exactly a copy of a dagger or bow and arrow, but ultimately they serve the same purpose. Regardless of the Pill, human beings are born as a result of the method of sexual intercourse, and they grow, mature, decline, and die as ever. Cavemen and high-rise dwellers, lonely prehistorical shepherds and ultramodern private jet owners, are born, eat, drink, and die in practically the same way, and all of them fear death.

It seems, therefore, that the only way of seeing the past in an objective way is to dethrone the human species, "depedestal" history, and finally accept the Copernican point of view. Man is not the center of the universe, and he had better take care lest his magnificent progress turn against him and destroy him together with his pretentious aspirations. The entire history of the human species is just a small segment of natural history and comprises historical events that follow the causal rules pertinent to other natural phenomena. The fact that humans build houses and bridges does not make human history less natural, nor does it exclude historical science from the group of biological sciences. Birds build nests, and beavers build dams; some fish and wolves live in families, and the rebellion against parental authority is not a particularly human privilege.

Benjamin B. Wolman

History, Psychoanalytic

A psychoanalytical history has three essentials:

1. It seeks the function of the unconscious in human behavior as evidenced by lifestyles, adaptations, creativity and subliminations, character, slips of speech, hearing and writing, dreams, neuroses and psychoses, and human action or inhibition.
2. It emphasizes, as does all history, the importance of origins, antecedents, and patterns of repetition. Therefore, it stresses the significance of the infancy and childhood of man but it is also a dynamic psychology, recognizing that the present reality interacts at all times and is related to the personal and social past in the unconscious.
3. It gives due place to the aggression, sexuality, passions, fantasy, and other emotional states of the inner world of its subjects, while rejecting the myth of the asexuality and innocence of child or adult, man or woman.

Peter Loewenberg

Hoarding

Most readily observed in rodents, hoarding is the accumulation of food supplies beyond the animal's immediate needs. Thus, a rat will carry large numbers of food pellets to the home cage from an external location. The amount of hoarding usually increases with a decline in ambient temperature, and in some species it is a precursor to hibernation.

Frank W. Finger

Hoffer, Willi (1897–1967)

Austrian psychologist, Willi Hoffer moved from education to psychoanalysis and psychoanalytic research. He was concerned with psychoanalytic education, ego psychology, and integration of mouth and hand.

Rudolf Ekstein

Holism

Holistic psychology views the individual as a complete whole in biological, psychological, and sociological terms. To fragmentize a person and her behavior is to corrupt her essence, thus making a true understanding of her impossible. This approach to gaining knowledge about humans and their behavior is in direct opposition to reductionism. The reductionist investigates phenomena on a molecular level; he breaks the whole down to examine the parts. In psychology, reductionism is seen as the analysis of behavior in stimulus-response terms, and human behavior is viewed mechanistically.

Holism has had a great impact on the field of learning. Its effects can be seen whenever a gross change or restructuring is hypothesized to be necessary before problem solving can occur. Holism rejects stimulus-response connections as the basic process underlying learning. This position is best exemplified by the theories of E. C. Tolman and of the Gestalt psychologists.

Barbara Jacquelyn Sahakian

Holtzman Inkblot Technique

The HIT (Holtzman Inkblot Technique) consists of two parallel sets of inkblots, each containing forty-five test blots preceded by two trial blots, X and Y, that are identical in both forms A and B. Unlike its predecessor, the Rorschach, the HIT subject is asked to give only one response per card, and a simple standardized inquiry immediately follows the response in order to ascertain where the percept is seen and what qualities of the blot suggested it. Because the two parallel forms were constructed concurrently using psychometric methods of test development, they are truly equivalent forms that can be considered interchangeable for most purposes.

The ninety-two inkblots comprising the two parallel forms are the best of thousands of inkblots constructed over a period of four years with the help of a professional artist. Systematic variation in symmetry, form, color, and shading result in a much richer set of stimulus variables than those characterizing the ten Rorschach plates. The first thirty inkblots in each form are carefully paired on both stimulus and response characteristics to enhance the equivalence of the two parallel forms. The last fifteen blots are balanced across the two forms, although they are not precisely matched.

Standardized inkblot protocols were obtained for over 1,400 cases in populations ranging from 5-year-old normal children to superior adults, from mentally retarded individuals to chronic schizophrenic patients. The scoring system developed for the HIT includes twenty-two different variables that cover many aspects of an individual's response to an inkblot. The more important systems for scoring the Rorschach were carefully taken into account in defining these variables so that most Rorschach scores could be easily derived from the basic elements in them.

Interscorer agreement, internal consistency reliability, and test-retest stability using alternate forms are generally very high regardless of the population or variable employed. Interscorer agreement is exceptionally high for a projective technique; only penetration and integration fall below reliabilities of .95, while in many cases the reliability approaches 1.00.

Wayne H. Holtzman

Homeostasis

The term *homeostasis*, defined as "the coordinated physiological processes which maintain most of the steady states in the organism," dates from an article by Walter B. Cannon in 1929. The concept has received widespread attention since the publication of *The Wisdom of the Body* (Cannon 1932). However, not surprisingly, the principle, if not the concept, has a long history. Alcmaeon of Crotona (circa 500 B.C.) proposed that disease is due to a deficit of some bodily humor and that the body has an automatic restorative mechanism, which reestablishes equilibrium and health. Hippocrates and Galen adopted versions of this view. In more recent years, W. Bernard, E. Pflüger, C. P. Richter, and others have ascribed great importance to this principle in explaining motivation.

Physiological homeostasis is essential to survival. Cannon showed evidence that the sequence described above is relevant to equilibria such as osmotic pressure, temperature, fats, glucose, calcium, pH, and others. Research since that time has led to the identification of additional factors that can trigger the same motivational pattern. The discrepancy-detecting, energy-arousing, and satiation mechanisms are part of a final common path. Homeostasis is a generalized process, not simply a collection of specific reflexes.

The principle of homeostasis must also be extended by taking account of the principle of anticipation. The organism does not sit placidly waiting for disequilibrium to occur. If a given steady state is disturbed regularly (by metabolism or by some external event), the organism anticipates this discrepancy before it passes the threshold magnitude required for reflex action. Humans anticipate possible cold, discomfort, and thirst; they take forestalling action (security actions) to prevent the discrepancy from occurring. A formal statement of this process would be the following: Every discrepancy arouses anxiety and tension. Cues signaling discrepancy become signals for anxiety. Action is taken to prevent or reduce the anxiety.

The Role of External Cues
The exteroceptive system (visual, auditory, olfactory) also plays an important part in homeostatic controls. These cues indicate the availability of substances that can restore equilibrium; thus, they identify objects that acquire positive value and are protected as an extension of the body. These cues also identify dangers—threats of disturbance of equilibrium—and guide defensive behavior. Finally, they often play a role in the satiation mechanism. It is well established, for example, that a dog deprived of water for a specified time will drink an amount appropriate to that degree of deprivation. Because he stops drinking long before the water can dilute the blood stream, it is obvious that the moistening of membranes, lapping, and so forth have signaled impending satiation (Pribram 1971). The satiation mechanism is essential to prevent excessive dilution of the blood. Typically, this feedback process is of the deviation-reducing type: as the magnitude of the

discrepancy from normal decreases, behavioral activity also slows down. This means that the restorative process zeroes in on the target value and ceases when the discrepancy vanishes.

Psychological Homeostasis

The most important role of psychological homeostasis in motivation theory involves the establishment of new steady states, which are then defended and restored in the same fashion as biological study states. For example, primitive people anticipating winter might accumulate furs, erect a shelter, and make other preparations. They then would protect these, just as they protect themselves against basic biological disturbances. The so-called territorial imperative (which is sometimes observed in humans as well as among animals) may be considered as an instance of a protective device reducing such dangers as food deprivation or sexual deprivation.

That constancy of the self is vigorously defended is attested by varied research on dissonance, on social comparison processes, and on relative deprivation. Self-esteem is always relative to some comparison, just as pride in family or in possessions has to be relative to comparisons. Thus, one may attempt to restore equilibrium not by raising the level of the self but by denigrating the persons who might be compared to the self.

Basic Processes

Karl H. Pribram (1971) has asserted that these complex varieties of equilibratory behavior can be conceptualized physiologically. Thus, one form of behavioral hierarchy is that in which a new homeostat is set to control a simpler, more primitive homeostat. A very elementary example is that of having a schedule for eating. One may feel disturbed (discrepancy of input from steady states) when a mealtime is missed, even though the more fundamental steady state (glucose) does not yet report a discrepancy. It is possible that these complex phenomena, such as defending one's property, one's family, or one's ego, are instrumental to more fundamental equilibria.

The homeostatic approach to motivation, with its focus on discrepancy of input from a recorded steady state, can readily be expanded to incorporate the phenomena ascribed to "dissonance" by George A. Kelly, Leon Festinger, and others. As noted above, the organism develops perceptual constancies. If an input offers cues that conflict with the established image of the hypothetical object "out there," the person experiences tension and tries to eliminate the discrepancy, either by denying the presence of some incoming cues or by restructuring the established image. (Jean Piaget calls the former process assimilation, and the latter accommodation.) A wide range of experiments has demonstrated that dissonance has motivational value. Homeostasis appears to provide the indispensable link between such energy mobilization and biological processes.

Ross Stagner

Homing

Homing is the act, observed in numerous species at many phyletic levels, of returning to a familiar area, such as the nest, either after a foraging trip or after having been transported to a relatively distant point of release. While experience improves performance in at least the more complex organisms, there is clearly a strong innate component.

Frank W. Finger

Homosexuality

Homosexuality came into the purview of Western medicine and science as recently as the last century. That it was viewed as an illness was a vast improvement on the pervading religious and moral understandings of it as a form of depravity. Scientific investigation since then has led to the consensus in Western psychiatry and psychology that homosexuality, per se, is *not* a mental illness. Further, homosexuality, per se, does not impair individuals' appropriate and productive functioning in society. In 1973 and 1974 the American Psychiatric Association and the American Psychological Association, respectively, made official statements adopting these understandings. Homosexuality was removed as a pathological condition from the DSM in 1973 and from the WHO International Classification of Diseases in 1991. The shift from the disease concept to the understanding of homosexuality as a normal variant was the result of study and research in the social sciences as well as psychiatry and psychology.

Prior to the 1950s, research and theory about homosexuality was based on patients or prisoners. Since then nonpatient and cross-cultural populations have been studied. The A. C. Kinsey studies of 1948 and 1953 were groundbreaking in several respects in the understanding of homosexuality. The incidence of homosexual fantasies, attractions, and behavior were much more prevalent in the general population than previously thought. Furthermore, Kinsey found that sexual orientation exists on a continuum from exclusive heterosexuality to exclusive homosexuality, with mixtures of homosexual and heterosexual fantasies, attractions, and behavior between the two pole positions.

Accurate information on the incidence of homosexuality has been impossible to obtain. Prejudice and stigma associated with homosexuality lead people to hide their orientation (even to themselves at times) and/or to be unwilling to identify themselves to researchers. Keeping this caveat in mind, the Kinsey studies found that for at least 3 years, 4% of the men sampled were exclusively homosexual, 50% were exclusively heterosexual, and 46% were between the extremes. The statistics on women were similar but somewhat lower for exclusive homosexuality and higher for exclusive heterosexuality. A number of studies since then and reevaluations of the Kinsey data have, in general, paralleled these findings with somewhat lower percentages for homosexuality. While exact percentages are impossible to determine, these studies indicate that millions of people in the population experience exclusive or periodic homosexual sexuality.

A great deal has been learned about gay men and lesbians and homosexuality since the Kinsey studies. Societal attitudes greatly influence the experiences and identities of gay men and lesbians. Because of stigma and prejudice regarding homosexuality, individuals may refrain from ever acting on their homosexual desires. Conversely, homosexual behavior in sex-segregated settings, such as prisons, may reflect factors unrelated to homosexual desire (such as power and domination in the prison setting).

The term *homosexual*, used either as a noun or adjective to refer to an individual, still carries pejorative connotations for many people. Many men and women, especially those who have come to a positive acceptance of their homosexual orientation, prefer to be called gay (especially men) or lesbian (women only).

While most of the current research has been on white male Americans, the gay and lesbian population is as diverse in all ways as the heterosexual community. Homosexuality is both a personal (individual) and social identity. In many Western countries, gay men and lesbians have developed rather loose and diverse communities. The bonds of these communities are based on the commonality of having same-sex attraction and being different from and stigmatized by the dominant heterosexual culture. A multifaceted gay and lesbian culture has developed to express the communities' shared social identities. Gay and lesbian communities are diverse and are neither highly cohesive nor entirely inclusive of all gay men and lesbians.

Homophobia, the fear and hatred of or prejudice against homosexuality and gay/lesbian people, is a pervasive attitude in North America and many other societies. Homophobia affects all people and shapes the lives and experiences of gay men and lesbians. Homophobia is reflected in the pejorative myths and stereotypes about gay/lesbian people. These negative beliefs, myths, and stereotypes exist at all levels of the society, from institutions and organizations to individuals. Individuals tend to internalize these cultural values, and they become "internalized homophobia."

Internalized homophobia and societal homophobia greatly influence the developmental process that gay men and lesbians experience as they integrate sexual orientation into their individual and social identity. Coming to awareness of homosexuality internally and eventually acknowledging it to others is called "coming out." For most people, coming out is a developmental process, which lasts years and encompasses a common definable sequence. It often spans the years from earliest awareness of same-sex attraction, acknowledgment to oneself, and questioning of societal attitudes about homosexuality to full integration into personal and social identity.

Homophobia (internalized and external) often causes anxiety, fear, shame, and identity confusion in this process. Individuals who come through this process to a positive acceptance of their orientation have been found to be emotionally healthier and happier than those who cannot overcome their own and society's negative attitudes.

Homosexuality touches all phases of the life cycle for gay men and lesbians. For many people, earliest awareness of same-sex feelings or romantic attraction began in childhood and adolescence. There is no single pathway of sexual identity development in children, although most researchers agree that the factors that determine adult sexual orientation are probably in place by age 2 or 3. Recent research in brain morphology, genetic coding, monozygotic twin concordance, and family constellations has yielded positive information about the biological aspects of homosexuality. These factors and their interactions with life circumstances probably account for the great variation in expression of sexual orientation in people. Homosexuality, and sexual orientation in general, is undoubtedly best understood in the context of the biopsychosocial model.

By adolescence, some young people are consciously aware of persistent homosexual interests and responses. They are equally aware of societal attitudes. Not all youth who are aware of homosexual interests will become gay, lesbian, or bisexual adults. Those who do have to struggle with their own and society's homophobia at a particularly sensitive developmental stage. The support of family is often lacking. Recent research has shown that these youths are at a significantly higher risk for suicide than other adolescents. Peer and community support resources are available in many of the larger North American cities at this time.

Many individuals do not "come out" during adolescence. They may be aware of same-sex feelings for many years and postpone "coming out" until well into adulthood. Others, especially some women, may first become aware of these feelings at some point in adulthood.

Family members also go through a process similar to "coming out." This often takes several years and involves challenging and changing their beliefs about homosexuality and accepting their gay or lesbian family member's changed identity. Children of gay men and lesbians go through this process about their parents as well.

Studies of gay men and lesbians have shown no significant differences in psychological adjustment and functioning from that of heterosexuals. Chemical dependency may be somewhat higher in certain subpopulations of the gay/lesbian community (older people), although methodological problems interfere with the accuracy of these findings. The aging lesbian and gay population has been found to fall into two general groups: those who are happy and integrated into their gay/lesbian communities and those who are isolated and do not have a positive gay/lesbian identity.

The AIDS epidemic has had a profound impact on the gay male community especially. Many community organizations have developed to meet the needs of afflicted people and their loved ones and friends. The sick and the well have been affected by this disease and the fact of death and dying in a generally younger, healthy population. The incidence of HIV disease in the North American gay population has recently begun to drop as a result of effective education, community awareness, and activism.

Although homosexuality has often been condemned by the world's major religions, religion and spirituality thrive among gay men and lesbians. They belong to and are active (often invisibly) in all major religions. In North America, the ordination of "out" gay men and lesbians is allowed in a few Protestant denominations and the more liberal Jewish congregations. The AIDS epidemic has catalyzed strong interest in spiritual and religious issues for many gay men and lesbians.

Lesbians

Women's experience and expression of homosexuality differ significantly from that of men. Women whose primary emotional and sexual bonds are with other women are called female homosexuals, gay women, or lesbians. The term *lesbian* is used by those women who are often highly accepting of their orientation. It has a feminist political connotation as well. The word *lesbian* comes from the name of the Greek island, Lesbos, where the ancient poet, Sappho lived and wrote of her same-sex love.

Numerous studies of lesbians confirm that they are more similar to other women, psychologically, than to gay men and that lesbians do not differ from heterosexual women in overall psychological adjustment and functioning. Several studies have found that lesbians tend to be more independent and self-sufficient and have greater job and relationship satisfaction than heterosexual women.

Myths and stereotypes are not validated when this diverse population is actually studied. Lesbians neither hate men nor wish to be men. They value relationships as much as other women do. Lesbian couples tend not to act out husband and wife roles but divide chores and responsibilities based on preferences and skills. They tend to be egalitarian in relation to power and to cherish closeness and communication. They also tend to be monogamous.

Many women come to awareness of their being lesbian initially through falling in love with another woman rather than primarily through sexual feelings, fantasies, or experiences outside a relationship. Many lesbians have had heterosexual experiences as well and do not become aware of same-sex feelings until they have had homosexual ones. Apparently unlike men, women frequently become aware of same-sex orientation as adults or even late in life.

While lesbians may be less visible than gay men, they represent a significant minority of the female population. They frequently have children from previous heterosexual marriages or through alternative insemination technologies, adoption, or foster parenting (the same is true of gay men). Numerous studies show that lesbians (and gay men) are good parents and raise well-adjusted children. Several studies have shown that lesbian and single heterosexual mothers are comparable in adjustment, attitudes toward parenting, and parenting skills. Children raised by lesbian mothers (and gay fathers) do not differ significantly in adjustment or sexual orientation from children raised by heterosexual mothers. Lesbians (and gay men) form stable and loving families. Many lesbians are subjected to discrimination or harassment, however, because their lifestyle is contrary to expected feminine role behavior. Their lives are organized around and dependent upon their relationships with other women, rather than with men as is expected in most cultures and societies.

Peggy Hanley-Hackenbruck

Hopelessness

Hopelessness is the subjective state of despair or futility, in which no desirable expectations exist. It normally occurs only after both situational or task-oriented and ego-defensive coping responses have failed (or have been perceived to fail or to be likely to fail) in the face of demand(s) for action. Such transituational helplessness is tantamount to a withdrawal from reality into energy-conserving inactivity. Coping failure is more likely to lead rapidly from situational helplessness to a general state of hopelessness and depression when ego strength is low or is weakened by the removal of social and cultural support structures.

Mortimer H. Appley

Hormic Psychology

Viewing behavior as a purposive striving, rather than as intellectual foresight, characterizes William McDougall's hormic psychology. In concert with his predecessors, McDougall espouses an anti-intellectualism (and antimaterialism) in the view that cognitive powers or the organism are subservient (or at best guides) to striving. Purposive or hormic psychology is "autonomous," unbound by the principles of physical science, and holds that "active striving towards a goal is a fundamental category of psychology" (1930, 4).

Out of a primal urge to live, differentiated hormic tendencies as striving capacities emerge. McDougall (1927) favored Jean-Baptiste Lamarck's theory of the transmission by inheritance of acquired characteristics. While lecturing in 1906, McDougall was struck with the realization that "the energy displayed in every human activity might in principle be traced back to some inborn disposition" (1961, 208). McDougall identified these natural primary motives, transmitted through heredity, as instincts. While human instincts undergo modification with respect to their afferent and motor aspects, their central portions, responsible for the emotional tone of consciousness, remain unalterable. In *An Introduction to Social Psychology* (1908), McDougall identified eleven instincts, or inborn urges, charged with emotional energy. However, by the time of his *Energies of Men* (1932) he had increased them to eighteen. He subtitled this work "A Study of the Fundamentals of Dynamic Psychology," thus allying hormic psychology with the dynamic school. Furthermore, by this time he had abandoned the provocative term *instincts* for the less controversial *propensity*.

By the early 1920s, McDougall had developed a personality theory out of his hormic psychology, comprised of the following principal factors of constructs: disposition (instinctive tendencies); temper (operations of conative impulses); temperament (metabolic or chemical effects); and mood (resultant or persistent emotions). A combination of instincts directed toward the same object results in a sentiment, which in turn contributes to the formation of character. The crowning sentiment, self-regard, is principally a social outgrowth. Character, when coupled with intellect, comprises the human personality.

William S. Sahakian

Horney, Karen (1885–1952)

Karen Horney introduced several new ideas to psychoanalytic theory and therapy. She rejected Freud's theories of libido and death instinct, emphasized the role of sociocultural influences on personality development, and stressed three basic needs in human interaction, namely: 1) moving toward people, 2) moving against people, and 3) moving away from people. Horney rejected Sigmund Freud's rule of abstinence; she believed that acting out is an important phenomenon in the psychoanalytic situation, since the patient dares to act in a manner that she was never permitted to do before. In contradistinction to Freud, she stressed the importance of the present, actual neurotic difficulties, and she believed that self-assertion and aggression are usual traits of mature individuals. Horney organized the Association for the Advancement of Psychoanalysis.

Benjamin B. Wolman

Horney's Psychoanalytic Technique

Using a holistic model, Karen Horney (1950) stated that curative forces are inherent in the mind as they are in the body, and the physician's task is to give a helping hand to remove the harmful and to support the healing forces. Technique refers to the what and how of the analyst's behaviors. The analyst's aim is to help the patient experience wider and deeper knowledge of herself, weakening the obstructive forces of the pride system while giving the constructive forces of the real self an opportunity to grow.

Psychoanalysis is a process in which two people are one, in the sense that they are helping the analytic situation unfold. At the same time, they are two to the degree that either participant can be moving the other toward more clarity. In this sense, the patient sometimes can be the therapist and the analyst the patient. One may question whether the patient can grow in his analytic experience without the analyst growing as well.

The task of formulating general rules about how the analyst should act in every situation becomes overwhelming when we add to the uniqueness of each analytic situation the uniqueness of the person of the analyst, the uniqueness of the patient, and the fact that both are engaged in a uniquely human cooperative venture guided by a theory that is constantly evolving, holistic, and open-ended.

Horney focused on the quality of the analyst's attention and understanding. She felt that were our understanding complete, we would need no books on technique. The understanding cannot be complete because each patient confronts the analyst with problems that he has not encountered before in that specified form and combination.

The necessary quality of the analyst's attention includes three aspects: wholeheartedness, comprehensiveness, and productiveness. *Wholeheartedness* is the ideal state of observing with all one's capacities and faculties. It involves listening, seeing, and feeling with intuition, undivided interest, reason, curiosity, and specialized knowledge, including all that one is aware of in the particular patient, without being distracted by one's own deeper problems or by situations that may be disturbing. The *comprehensiveness* of attention refers to striving for an ideal of being flexible enough to take in everything without focusing exclusively on a limited set of factors. Horney summarized the *productiveness* of attention as constantly asking ourselves, "Is what is going on now leading to self-awareness and bringing us closer to self-realization?" (Cantor 1959).

The patient's original motivation for therapy may be to remove a symptom or to dissolve the anxiety resulting from a conflict in which his previous attempts at solution no longer allow him to live comfortably. To the extent that he is neurotic, he wishes to bolster his pride system (Horney 1950) and to perfect his idealized self. He may not be aware of his anxiety or that there is a conflict going on within himself. All the patient may know is that he is experiencing physical or psychological discomfort or having difficulties in his interpersonal relationships or in his work, or that there is a feeling of not knowing who he is or what he wants to do in life. From all this, the patient may want the immediate relief of "answers," with the implication that "knowing" will automatically solve the difficulties or that the analyst has the magic cure.

The analyst's objectives range from the immediate to the intermediate to the long-range ultimate that the patient be without pretense, emotionally sincere, and able to put the whole of herself into her feelings, work, beliefs, and relationships. The more specific objectives shift as the analyst moves along with the patient, always beginning first with where the patient is and with whatever has the most immediacy at the time.

One might begin helping the patient with a particular problem regarding work or human relationships or with the specific symptom that brings him into therapy, or try to allay his overwhelming anxiety or to focus on helping him feel more integrated when he feels that he is falling apart. The analyst may focus on building a trusting, mutually respectful, and working relationship. Although the latter is an essen-

tial precondition of all work, with some patients this may be the only initial objective for quite some time.

The specific objectives turn to emphasizing the actually existing inner conflicts underlying the reasons for which the patient has sought therapy, what her attempts have been to solve them, her anxiety, and the defenses she has built up against experiencing it. How much one can do depends on the patient's ability to "let go" of some of her externalizing, her rigid idealizing, and her self-hatred. With the analyst's evaluation and sense of where the patient is, the analyst is constantly measuring the patient's motivation and availability for forward motion.

The initial interview is a unique opportunity for starting the relationship off in a constructive direction and creating an attitude of trust. In addition to presenting the immediate concerns, the patient is telling how he experiences his present life situation and historical background on infinite multidimensional levels, as well as his future aspirations and attitudes toward them.

The analyst diagnoses and prognoses. The prognosing depends on the ongoing diagnosing; it involves evaluating how rigidly the patient is using her particular type of attempted solution, how many satisfactions she has, and her ability to live and work with another human being. The analyst assesses the patient's degree of aliveness, hopefulness, openness, her ability or willingness to experience her own feelings; how well she can present her own thoughts, see cause-and-effect relationships, and think psychologically, abstractly, and symbolically.

Horney is most emphatic in seeing the initial interview as pregnant with therapeutic possibilities. The patient is meeting, perhaps for the first time in his life, another human being who is interested in him, and who can listen in a spirit that allows him to express what he never dared to previously. The analyst can show the patient the contradictions in his desires and discrepancies in the way he is living, and bolster his need to seek help. By not being shocked or frightened by the pathology and by seeking to elicit the patient's past and present assets and accomplishments, the analyst is indicating a hopeful attitude. By suggesting possible connections between past and present or different aspects in his present life, the analyst is aiding the patient to dispel an attitude of mystery about his condition and implying that these things have meaning, can be understood, and, therefore, can be changed.

Three analytic sessions per week are optimal. Double sessions may be more effective at times when patients whose literalness, circumstantiality, or anxiety takes them longer to get started, or with patients whose available time precludes their coming on three separate days. In some instances, once a week may be all that is necessary to introduce the patient to therapy.

As regards the vis-à-vis position or the couch, the question is not which is better, but which is more effective in moving therapy in a constructive direction at a particular time in a particular analysis and for each unique combination of patient and therapist. Vis-à-vis is generally better for the early periods of therapy, as it gives both an opportunity to get a clearer picture of and feel for one another. It becomes more valuable to maintain or return to when the patient is elusive, evasive, compulsively intellectualizing, feeling isolated, floundering, approaching panic, or escaping into fantasy.

The value of the couch lies in promoting meditation, aiding the patient to experience both her tension and her relaxation, enhancing her use of the analyst for transferential neurotic fantasies, and helping her to free-associate more easily, thus providing for fuller utilization of dreams and allowing for variations in states of consciousness, such as hypnagogic reveries and states of depersonalization. On the couch, the patient has a better opportunity to learn to discriminate sick feelings of aloneness, loneliness, and isolation from healthier feelings of being alone. She can begin to recognize the analyst's silence as less of a disturbance and distraction, and appreciate the constructive value of her own silence. In becoming better acquainted with her own boundaries, she may begin to know herself as an autonomous entity and a self-responsible agent in her own life, while experiencing her connectedness with others.

The analyst's questions become a form of communication, whether by verbalizations, intonations, facial expressions, or gestures, which aid the patient to become more productive in the therapeutic process. They are a way of confronting the patient, helping to create a juxtaposition that promotes creative tension through raising doubt, through reflection, and through independent searching.

Horney emphasizes that in dreams we are closer to the reality of ourselves, and through understanding them we get the best help in seeing how the patient attempts to deal with conflicts in healthy and neurotic ways. In dreams the patient may find a unique world in which he may feel more real to himself than the illusion in which he actually lives. This is especially true of the constructive forces that the patient has so little awareness of in his waking life.

Because self-realization is never complete, the notion of total "cure" is impossible in holistic process terms. One can see how much progress the patient has made in terms of experiencing herself as a more authentic person. She becomes more capable of taking responsibility for her own actions when she becomes more genuine with other people and respects them as people apart from her own needs. This includes "resolving the transference" on the part of the analyst. The patient also begins to recognize how much analytic work she has been able to do without help from the analyst, and will welcome the opportunity to continue to do so on her own. The patient is assisted in the separation by the knowledge that if she should need help in the future, the analyst will still be available (Cantor 1967).

Morton B. Cantor

Horney's Theory

Karen Horney played a unique role in the history of psychoanalysis from many standpoints. While appreciating Sigmund Freud's undebatable contributions, she was among the first psychoanalysts to organize and present her theoretical objections based on her dissatisfaction with clinical results (Horney 1939). She was also the first psychoanalyst to question Freud's concepts of feminine psychology, as early as the 1920s. Horney was also the first psychoanalyst to strongly stress the role of cultural forces (Horney 1937). Her writings led the way for the first expansion of American psychoanalysis beyond the orthodox Freudian American Psychoanalytic Association into the other various schools of psychoanalytic thought, which eventually came together in 1956 and formed the American Academy of Psychoanalysis. Many of her ideas may not seem so unusual today because of what has followed since, with the works of Harry Stack Sullivan, Frieda Fromm-Reichmann, Ralph Greenson, Heinz Kohut, and so many others.

Horney's primary interest was not in formulating a theory of personality but in therapy by delineating the neurotic process, and out of this her theory was derived. This theory is holistic, considering the whole human being in all aspects of her being—how she was in sickness and in health, her physical and psychological processes as a social and spiritual being (interpersonal and intrapsychic), in work and in leisure, as an individual, and with others as part of the cosmos. She saw individual and environment mutually influenced by and influencing each other.

In Horney's theory, neurosis is seen as a special form of human development that, because of the resulting waste of constructive energies, made it antithetical to human growth. In essence, the neurotic process moves along with the growth process. Growing in a healthy way means the liberating of evolutionary constructive forces inherent in humans that urge them forward to realize their given potentialities (the real self). No matter how impressed we may be with the evidence of pathology, Horney emphasizes that we must never forget that also present, however buried or inactive, are these potentials for healthier growth.

This optimistic, positive, life-affirming approach led to Horney's concept of "a morality of evolution." Rather than seeing humans as by nature sinful or ridden by primitive instincts, they are seen as neither good nor evil but with the moral obligation and privilege of evolving toward self-realization by ever-increasing awareness and understanding of themselves, by being truthful to themselves, by being active and productive, by relating themselves to others in the spirit of mutuality, and by assuming responsibility for themselves (Horney 1950).

In her early emphasis on the role of culture, Horney felt that neurosis must be viewed sociologically as well as psychologically, because each culture determines its norms, which vary within the culture.

The person is considered to the degree to which he deviates from the pattern common to his culture. The four main ways we use to escape anxiety are by rationalizing it, denying it, narcotizing it, and by avoiding thoughts, feelings, impulses, and situations that might arouse it. Hostile impulses are a main source of neurotic anxiety, and because they are so frequent and dangerous, they must be repressed, which leads to more anxiety (Horney 1937).

The evolution of the neurotic process begins early in infancy, as the child begins to feel a lack of genuine warmth and affection, and senses that she is not being accepted as herself. The actions and attitudes of the parents arouse a "basic hostility," which has to be repressed. This leads to an insidiously increasing feeling of being isolated and helpless in a hostile world. This "basic anxiety," one of the essential concepts in Horney's theory, is inseparably interwoven with the basic hostility and lies unconsciously at the core of the neurotic process.

The child's normal experience of immediacy leads him to organize his behavior by moving toward, against, or away from others. How these functions are used depends on the shifting way he feels about himself. Healthy children who feel loved and accepted are able to move toward another person when they need contact or support. They are also able to oppose others and move away to be alone with themselves (but not lonely) when they feel that they can depend on themselves and can depend on others being there for them when they return. These fundamental ways of relating can be spontaneous and interchangeable and can allow for a sense of integration and genuine satisfaction within oneself and in relation to one's environment (Horney 1945).

To the extent that children are operating under the effects of basic anxiety, they can no longer orient themselves freely for satisfaction based on their inner needs, wishes, and feelings. They are driven to pursue the direction of safety in ways that are compulsive, indiscriminate, and insatiable. These ways become rigid characterological attitudes (trends), each related to a specific aspect of the basic anxiety. Healthy moving toward people becomes compulsive compliance, as children accept their helplessness and try to cope with it by clinging, submitting, and obeying. Healthy moving against others becomes compulsive aggressiveness, as the hostility around them is taken for granted and they have to defy and rebel against others. Healthy moving away from others becomes compulsive detachment, in which their isolation becomes accepted and they try to avoid either belonging or fighting by secrecy, uninvolvement, and distancing.

Horney (1945) saw four kinds of automatic, unconscious attempts at solution of this conflict. First, the child may repress two of the drives while streamlining the third so that he now becomes predominantly organized around this one set of needs, qualities, sensitivities, and inhibitions in an attempt to gain a sense of value and identity. This entails radical changes in personality and the development of a gestalt.

A second attempt to deal with the basic conflict is to withdraw as much as possible from relating to others so as not to have to confront the conflict. To do away with the feelings of being divided, weak, and confused, a third attempted solution is to unconsciously create an idealized image of oneself. The child's compulsive submissiveness may become saintliness, her compulsive disparagement of others becomes strength and honesty, her compulsive detachment becomes independence. In her last book, *Neurosis and Human Growth* (1950), K. Horney expanded on the consequences of the idealized image as the essential intrapsychic process within the neurotic development.

The fourth attempted solution of the basic conflict is externalization, the experiencing of inner processes as if they were external ones. This shifts to the aims of actualizing the idealized self, which molds the whole personality and may be entirely unconscious. Because it becomes a total plan of behavior around which a person organizes all functions of his life compulsively, Horney refers to it as the comprehensive solution of the search for glory. To reinforce one's search for glory, needs become neurotic claims, which are irrational because they assume an entitlement that does not exist in reality and are made without regard for the possibility of their fulfillment.

Whereas neurotic claims delineate the search for glory in terms of the outer world, the person is simultaneously trying to mold herself into her image

of perfection by a system of "shoulds" and "should nots," which Horney called "the tyranny of the shoulds." These inner dictates comprise all that the neurotic should be able to do, to be, to feel, to know—and taboos on how and what she should not be. She operates with a supreme disregard for the feasibility of these dictates, the conditions under which they could be fulfilled, and her own physical and psychic condition.

For all these efforts, the neurotic does not get what he needs most—self-confidence and self-respect—and is left with neurotic pride, which is vulnerable, easily hurt because it is based on such shaky foundations, and always threatening to prove the falseness of his idealized self. The inevitable consequence here is self-hate, with its merciless self-accusations, self-contempt, self-frustration, self-torment, and self-destructiveness. Neurotic pride and self-hate belong inseparably together as one process, which Horney called the pride system.

The culmination of all Horney's previous works was contained in her final volume, *Neurosis and Human Growth* (1950). She focused on the real self as the central inner force common to all human beings.

In an attempt to find a sense of wholeness and identity, the person's idealized image becomes an idealized self, which becomes more real to her than her real self, not primarily because it is more appealing, but because it seems to answer all her stringent needs. This transfer of one's center of gravity is in the core of one's being, one's feeling about oneself, the perspective from which one looks at and measures oneself.

Something of an emcompassing character is necessary to give form and direction to the whole personality, to deal with the intrapsychic conflict of how the person identifies with his glorified or despised self. There are three major solutions to this conflict. The major solutions are more properly directions of development, which determine the kinds of satisfactions attainable, what is to be avoided, the hierarchy of values established, and how the person will relate to himself and others.

In the first major solution, the expansive solution, the individual identifies predominantly with the glorified self and is driven by the appeal of mastery.

Horney delineated three kinds of expansiveness: the narcissistic, the perfectionistic, and the arrogant-vindictive types. The narcissist dedicates her life to being adored for her idealized image and is unable to tolerate otherwise. The perfectionist identifies with his standards, is constantly striving to be respected for them, rather than adored, and looks down on others with contempt. The arrogant-vindictive type is primarily identified with pride in controlling others, being more powerful, and feeling free to express her hostility, with vindictiveness becoming her way of life.

In the second major solution, the self-effacing person identifies with the despised self and is driven by the appeal of love. He can only live under the shadow of others, creating the dilemma of desperately needing to be loved while feeling unworthy and not trusting the positive feelings of others.

In the third major solution, resignation, the person attempts to immobilize herself and withdraw from the conflict between identifying with either her glorified or her despised self. Her greatest appeal is for a freedom from and not for active living. With independence and maintaining the status quo as her credo, she becomes hypersensitive to any kind of influence, coercion, and especially change.

Morton B. Cantor

Hospital Therapy of Adolescents

The severely psychotic youngster, frightened into panic or assaultive behavior, requires the control, the security, and the opportunity for restraint that only the hospital can offer and provide. The adolescent who attempts suicide should be admitted for psychiatric evaluation and the development of a treatment plan. Severe episodes of manic behavior can lead to exhaustion and even death, unless hospitalization is employed with its structure and the capacity to initiate proper and appropriate pharmacological treatment. Young women, and the rare young man, suffering from anorexia nervosa frequently require hospital treatment in order to forestall progressive and possibly fatal emaciation.

Between the ages of 13 and 17, the adolescent is in compulsory school attendance from early morning to midafternoon for three-quarters of each year. During these hours, the teenager is removed from family and home and accepts, to varying degrees, an entirely different set of performance standards, behavioral codes, and authority figures with whom identifications are possible. Other than in this structured setting, the culture and society do not afford many opportunities for gainful employment, healthy peer relationships, or the development of constructive social skills that contribute to orderly maturation.

The extent to which the hospital can recreate the best parts of this atmosphere will be a measure of the effectiveness of treatment away from the home setting. The adolescents carefully distributed throughout the adult hospital provide, during those parts of the day when school is not in session, an atmosphere that more closely resembles the family structure than one would have on a unit devoted entirely to adolescents. This distribution of patients can provide certain role models and an arena in which to work out problems in group living. It can also assist in the necessary task of avoiding destructive gang formations.

With adolescents, restraints, seclusion, and isolation policies require special attention in formulation, interpretation, and usage. Even these words are traditionally linked to punitive rather than therapeutic attitudes. Impulsivity, mischievous play, and confrontation with "the establishment" are a normal part of growth but, in excess, can be most irritating to adult staff and patients alike. Staff, therefore, must be selected carefully to represent a healthy tolerance for these actions and a capacity to set limits.

It is frequently helpful to explain these policies to adolescent patients in advance of the need for urgent action. It is often reassuring to disturbed young people to know about sanctions and the circumstances of their use. It is not unusual, when that is done, for an adolescent to ask for restraint when he or she becomes more anxious or is threatened by the urge to act on impulses. Therapists may favor having a room where patients may request seclusion or isolation on a voluntary basis.

As soon as the patient has made sufficient progress in psychotherapy that a good adaptation to a more realistic environment can be made, discharge should be arranged. Under varying conditions, this discharge may be to the patient's home, to a foster home, to a boarding school, or to one of the schools equipped to provide a good environment for children with emotional difficulties. In most cases, a suitable means of continuation of psychotherapy should be insured.

Donald C. Greaves

Hospitals: Psychiatric Units

The first psychiatric unit in the United States was established in 1902 by Dr. J. M. Mosher at the Albany (New York) Medical Center "for the detention and care of persons afflicted with nervous and mental disorders." One of the outstanding pioneers in the general hospital movement was A. E. Bennett, who wrote extensively on the subject in the 1940s and 1950s.

By the 1970s, medical and public acceptance of general hospital psychiatry had reached an all-time high. As a result, there arose in all parts of the country a great demand for psychiatrists with special interest in this area to spearhead the development of new units and to direct and work in the new departments of psychiatry.

The number of beds on the psychiatric unit varies not only with the size of the hospital but also with the needs of the community and availability of staff. General hospitals having fewer than 100 beds have an average of 15 beds in each of their psychiatric units; hospitals with 750 or more beds average 91 beds devoted to psychiatry. Approximately 9% of the beds of all general hospitals with psychiatric units are devoted to psychiatric care.

Special facilities usually (but not always) found on the well-equipped psychiatric unit are a day room, a room for physical examination and/or somatic treatments, a separate occupational therapy area, a dining room, and a gymnasium. Units vary enormously in this regard, influenced chiefly by the total bed capacity of the unit, the treatment philosophy of the department, and the availability of funds.

Day room. The day room or multipurpose lounge is an almost indispensable part of the psychiatric unit. In a 1963 survey, 97% of the units had one,

and all units built since then probably include a day room. The current tendency is to have a day room large enough and so furnished as to serve a wide range of functions, such as group therapy, games, exercises, viewing movies and TV, and visiting.

Occupational therapy. Occupational therapy (OT) is playing an increasingly important role in psychiatric treatment programs in general hospitals. The OT department may vary in size, depending on the size of the unit and department policy. Some small units make do with a volunteer or a part-time occupational therapist. In general hospitals, occupational therapy is practiced in one of three places: (1) at the bedside; (2) on the psychiatric unit, usually in the day/dining room; or (3) in a special part of the hospital separate from the unit (56% of the 1963 survey). Some such areas are quite elaborate and are equipped with lathes, kilns, potters' wheels, and woodworking equipment.

The composition of the psychiatric staff varies greatly from unit to unit, depending upon the number of psychiatrists in the community, the regulations of the hospital, and the practice in other departments of the general hospital. The composition of the staff of the psychiatric unit of many university teaching hospitals tends to be greatly influenced by the background and training of the chief of the department. This tends, in turn, to determine the treatment philosophy followed and the treatment modalities made available. In hospitals patterned after the private practice medical model and staffed by privately practicing psychiatrists, a wide variety of treatment modalities and treatment philosophies are offered.

Psychiatric units are able to offer a wide variety of modern psychiatric therapies and are organized to provide rapid intervention in emergencies. Most good units lay proper stress on the establishment of a therapeutic milieu. Psychotherapy of all varieties—analytic, supportive, individual, eclectic, and group therapy—have been observed on existing units. Psychopharmacology is frequently used because the illnesses treated on a psychiatric unit are usually acute and of short duration.

Zigmond M. Lebensohn

Hovland, Carl I. (1912–1961)

The American psychologist Carl I. Hovland's chief contribution to the field of conditioning was a series of studies of stimulus generalizations.

Gregory A. Kimble

Hull, Clark L. (1884–1952)

The basic framework of the American psychologist Clark L. Hull's system is the reinforcement theory of learning. Under the impetus of need or drive, the organism acts, and its response brings a reduction of the particular need or drive. Behavior is goal directed; according to Hull's goal-gradient hypothesis, the nearer the organism is to the goal, the better and faster it learns.

Hull's drive reduction theory is the core of his work. His *Principles of Behavior* (1943) and *Behavior System* (1952) further examined his ideas.

Walter Bernard

Human Factors

The study of human factors is concerned with five human-machine-environment considerations. One is design: how should machines, tools, equipment, systems, and environments be designed to take into account human capabilities and limitations? What are these capabilities and limitations—sensory, perceptual, psychomotor, and cognitive—in such contexts? Closely related are the processes of establishing and describing the procedures for using the various elements of technology. A third activity is evaluation of human-machine combinations and systems, through analysis and experimental testing of their effectiveness. A fourth human factors concern is training: research in training techniques, development of training devices, and adaptation of training methods to new areas. The fifth is the selection and allocation of personnel.

The psychologists who devote themselves to design, procedures, and evaluation (and training devices) generally come from the subdiscipline called engineering psychology and engage in the multidisciplinary field called human factors engineering or human engineering, which is the largest subdivision of human factors and is often equated with it. Psychologists interested in training and personnel are more likely to come from industrial and social psychology, though many specializing in training and personnel do not regard themselves as within the human factors field. Most of the behavior investigated in human factors consists of performance at work—as might be expected in view of the focus on machines and equipment. In Europe, the field is called ergonomics; its earlier emphasis on the physiological effects of work has shifted to include the American emphasis on performance.

H. McIlvaine Parsons

Human Figure Drawing

The subject is asked to draw a person. The whole person should be drawn, rather than just the head or bust. As the subject draws, the examiner may record any comments made by the subject as well as the sequence she uses in making her drawing. When this step is completed, the subject is asked to draw a person of the sex opposite to that which has been drawn. At this point, if she has not already done so, J. N. Buck (1966) suggests requesting the subject to draw the groundline and also the sun.

All facets of the drawing are used in interpretation: the drawing as a whole, its placement on the page, the line quality, the details of the person, and extraneous details. Perspective and proportion are also factors affecting interpretation. Finally, the postdrawing interrogation or association not only clarifies some aspects of the drawing, but also serves as a projective interview, which can reveal much about the subject's thinking, his attitudes, and his feelings.

Proportion represents the values the subject assigns to things, situations, persons, and so on, which parts of the drawing may represent. For example, very short arms may indicate absence of striving with feelings of inadequacy or even castration feelings or fears; a small head may indicate the subject's need to minimize intellectual activity, perhaps as a defense against his learning problems.

The sex of the drawn person represents the subject's own sexual identification. The clinician gains further information about this aspect of the subject's personality through the subject's drawing of a person of the opposite sex.

Extraneous details may have significance. Earrings are frequently drawn by subjects with sexual preoccupations of an exhibitionistic type. A very carefully clothed person may be indicative of clothing or social narcissism in an infantile, egocentric subject. Items such as a cigarette, cigar, or pipe, when drawn significantly, may represent phallic symbols.

Isaac Jolles

Human Immunodeficiency Virus and Acquired Immunodeficiency Syndrome

The Threat of AIDS

The epidemic of acquired immunodeficiency syndrome (AIDS) was first recognized in 1981, when apparently healthy young gay men in three major urban centers—New York, San Francisco, and Los Angeles—became ill with pneumocystis carinii pneumonia, an illness typically seen only among patients with compromised immune systems. The medical community quickly realized that these young men did, indeed, have immune system failure caused by an infectious agent, identified in 1984 as the human immunodeficiency virus (HIV). Even before the virus was identified, epidemiologists established that there were four primary routes of transmission: infected blood products; contaminated syringes; sexual intercourse with exchange of semen or vaginal fluids; and during pregnancy from infected mother to fetus.

Several factors have combined to give this epidemic worldwide importance. First, this is a new epidemic. Not only did AIDS appear to threaten large numbers of people but also there was nothing known about the course of disease or about either appropriate treatments or reliable methods of prevention. Moreover, there was almost no body of information or experience upon which prevention and intervention strategies might be developed. The fact that the virus attacked the immune system—the body's natural means of defense against illness—added to the gravity of the situation.

Second, despite the rapid growth in information about HIV and its related illnesses, the epidemic has been difficult to control. Since 1981, cases of AIDS have been reported from 164 countries around the world. The global report *AIDS in the World* estimated that, by early 1992, 219 million people (including 4.7 million women, 7.1 million men, and 1.1 million children) had been infected with HIV. Of those with HIV, one-fifth had developed AIDS. Of those with AIDS, 90% had died. This new epidemic has been characterized as volatile, dynamic, and unstable. In no part of the world already affected has the epidemic been brought under control. Further, no part of the world currently unaffected can consider itself safe from future incursions of the virus.

Third, HIV infection has disproportionately affected young adults, striking during that period in life when young people are beginning to assume their roles as parents and/or workers. The loss of so many young people poses a substantial threat to the economy and functioning of many countries around the world, and has already created a substantial number of orphans whose care must fall to relatives or government agencies.

AIDS Epidemiology

In the United States, AIDS was first recognized among homosexual men, but the list of "risk groups" quickly expanded to include intravenous drug users, recipients of blood and blood products, heterosexual partners of those in risk groups, and infants born to mothers infected with HIV. In the United States the epidemic has disproportionately affected men, who constitute more than 85% of the adults diagnosed with AIDS to date, and African-Americans and Hispanics, who, though 20% of the U.S. population, constitute 44% of those diagnosed with AIDS to date.

As AIDS has spread in numbers and through risk groups, it has also spread geographically. From the major urban centers where it was first identified, AIDS was spread through hierarchical diffusion (from larger communities to subordinate or smaller communities), through spatial contagion (from the core of an epidemic's epicenter outward to surrounding areas), and through network diffusion (through personal, domestic, and community social networks). For example, AIDS spread from major cities to smaller cities connected by transportation routes. AIDS also spread within the commuting fields of each of the affected cities, extending outward from local epicenters. Though AIDS has affected all states and most counties in the United States, it has hit certain urban centers with particular force. As of May 1993, four urban centers accounted for 27% of the 289,320 reported cases of AIDS in the United States: San Francisco, with 209 cases per 100,000 reported between April 1992 and March 1993; New York, with an annual case rate of 116; San Juan, Puerto Rico, with an annual case rate of 89; and Miami, with an annual case rate of 85.

The pattern of AIDS cases observed in the United States is typical of industrialized countries. These Pattern I countries include the United States, Canada, and Mexico. In these areas, large numbers of gay men and intravenous drug users were infected with the virus as early as the 1970s. A second pattern of cases can be observed in Haiti and other parts of the Caribbean and much of sub-Saharan Africa. In those Pattern II countries, the spread of infection began in the late 1970s. However, the transmission of the virus has occurred primarily through heterosexual intercourse, and the ratio of male-to-female cases is approximately 1-to-1. Pattern III countries, which include sections of Eastern Europe and North Africa, were affected by the epidemic in the mid- to late 1980s; to date, the number of cases in these nations is small. Pattern IV countries, including parts of Central and South America, are those nations that have reported that cases have shifted from those affecting predominantly homosexual men to those concentrated among heterosexuals and children.

Risk and Prevention

HIV infection is spread through specific behaviors, particularly sexual intercourse without barrier protection and sharing of contaminated needles. The most vigorous and successful prevention efforts have been those conducted within large, urban gay communities. Begun early in the AIDS epidemic, these efforts were largely responsible for a substantial reduction in rates of gonorrhea infection by 1985. However, there is a substantial amount of sexual risk taking in the general population, with little adoption of preventive behaviors in evidence. In 1991 and 1992, Catania and colleagues at the University of California, San Francisco, conducted a national probability study of the general heterosexual population of the United States. They found that condom use among those surveyed was relatively low. Only 17% of those with multiple sexual partners, 12.6% of those with risky sexual partners, and 10.8% of untested transfusion recipients used condoms all the time.

Sharing of drug injection equipment, the other major risk behavior, is concentrated among those who use illicit drugs, particularly heroin, cocaine, and amphetamines. Because of the illegal nature of drug use, drug users function within well-hidden subcultures, mostly located in poor communities in urban centers. The occult, self-contained nature of these subcultures has posed a substantial challenge for HIV prevention. Because of the difficulty drug users have in controlling their addiction, the incorporation of prevention behaviors was presumed to be equally difficult. This has not proven to be the case, however. Drug users have decreased needle sharing and increased use of disinfectants and needle exchange programs. Taken together, an assessment of many of the more successful prevention efforts suggests that forceful efforts can be effective in producing at least modest changes, particularly if they are supported by widely held community perceptions of the need to reduce HIV risk (Coates 1990).

The Clinical Course of HIV Infection

Observations of cohorts of people infected with HIV have provided data on the natural history of disease progression. Primary infection with HIV is followed in 50 to 75% of patients with an acute mononucleosis-like syndrome, which develops approximately 3 to 6 weeks after initial infection. HIV is widely disseminated throughout the body during this period. There is also a high level of viremia, which declines markedly or disappears weeks to months after the acute syndrome subsides. That change is temporally associated with the emergence of an HIV-specific immune response.

After the primary infection subsides, most patients enter an ostensibly latent period, characterized by gradual, but clinically asymptomatic, deterioration of systems. This asymptomatic period can last for many years. Many estimates place the median duration of this period at approximately 10 years. However, the inevitable outcome of the progressive deterioration of the immune system is clinically apparent disease; once this stage is reached, death usually ensues within two years. Among the clinical manifestations of HIV disease are lymphadenopathy, neurological impairment, opportunistic infections, and neoplasms. The most severe of these medical conditions are classified as AIDS-defining conditions. The AIDS diagnosis, which signals advanced HIV disease, is based on criteria established by the U.S. Centers for Disease Control and Prevention, as well as international health agencies. The criteria for the AIDS diagnosis have been altered on several occasions to reflect increasing knowledge of HIV disease.

During the course of a decade of intensive effort, it has become clear that psychiatric and neuropsychological problems play an important role in HIV/AIDS. Patients may experience psychiatric illnesses, such as affective disorders or anxiety disorders. These psychiatric conditions may represent a primary manifestation of HIV disease. HIV-infected patients who present with the new onset of serious mental illness—mania, for example—may have developed the illness as a part of their HIV disease. Psychiatric illness may also represent an emotional reaction to HIV/AIDS. For example, symptoms of depression appear to increase transiently after patients are notified of HIV-positive status, receive an AIDS-defining diagnosis, or experience serious loss of functioning due to progression of illness. In such cases, the psychiatric illness might be considered a reaction to HIV disease. Finally, the psychiatric illness may be a comorbid condition. For example, HIV infection is common among the chronically mentally ill. Though the original mental illness is neither caused by nor a reaction to HIV disease, the management of that psychiatric condition will be essential to proper care of the HIV-infected patient.

A wide range of neuropsychological problems have also been reported as part of HIV disease. These problems range from mild disorientation and memory impairment to dementia. The presence of mild neuropsychological complications may be an early manifestation of HIV illness, occurring long before immunological measures or clinical symptoms provide evidence of disease progression. Dementia and other severe neuropsychological problems appear to be associated with late, if not terminal, stages of illness.

The assessment and treatment of psychiatric and neuropsychological problems can be an important part of patient care, though standard practice may need to adapted to meet the needs of those with HIV disease. For example, as compared to many other psychiatric patients, patients with HIV infection may require lower doses of psychoactive medications, more psychosocial support, and more detailed evaluation to ascertain a correct diagnosis.

Stigma and Denial in Response to the AIDS Epidemic

Perhaps no issue more naturally falls to behavioral scientists and clinicians than the study of stigma and denial as responses to the AIDS epidemic. As the National Commission noted in its 1991 report, *America Living with AIDS: Transforming Anger, Fear and Indifference into Action*,

> We must, as a society, find a way to convert anger, fear, and indifference into informed action. We must deal effectively with discrimination and prejudice, overcome present governmental inertia, rededicate ourselves to maintaining a necessary intensity of research endeavor, educate the public to replace panic with an informed awareness of what is needed to prevent infection, and coordinate our resources to meet the urgent health care needs of the sick in cost-efficient ways that take full advantage of our powerful science. (p. 3)

These tasks carry tremendous importance, for the affects noted by the commission have created major obstacles to national action. There is little question about the importance of the AIDS epidemic. But because its force has hit marginalized groups first and foremost, policy makers have felt both justified and secure in allowing the epidemic to follow its course. Understanding the nuances of epidemic response and proposing appropriate interventions are critical tasks for behavioral scientists and clinicians, which pose important challenges for the future management of this unstable epidemic.

Mindy Thompson Fullilove

Human Information Processing

Human information processing (HIP) is an approach to investigating and explaining human thought and behavior that relies heavily on models of information and its acquisition, representation, and manipulation by the human mind (Reed 1988; Wickens 1992). In this approach, research is conducted using tasks designed especially to identify the unobservable mental structures and operations that are responsible for observed performance. The mental elements are usually conceptualized in terms of the metaphor of computers or other information-handling systems. Hypotheses derived from these models are tested empirically using behavioral, physiological, or self-report measures—sometimes in combination. The resulting data serve to advance understanding of the inferred cognitive mechanisms as well as prediction of performance on similar tasks.

Emphasis on the computer metaphor has produced an important symbiosis between psychological and computer science, as evidenced by the emergence of new fields such as cognitive science and artificial intelligence (AI). More generally, the information-processing metaphor has served to unite psychological researchers and design professionals via disciplines such as engineering psychology and human factors. Finally, HIP is virtually synonymous with cognitive psychology as it appears today. However, cognitive psychology does not depend exclusively on information-processing concepts, and its origin predates the appearance of such notions by at least a half-century. In sum, HIP is not a field or psychological specialty; rather, it is an approach and perspective that is fundamental to many disciplines, most notably, modern cognitive psychology.

Background

The "cognitive revolution" in psychology closely paralleled developments in computer and information science (J. Gardner 1985). Hence, the HIP approach and its associated models were instrumental in psychology's shift from a predominantly behavioristic to a predominantly cognitive paradigm.

Among the earliest of these developments was a general theory of information and its measurement conceived by communications engineers of the late 1940s to enable the precise evaluation of communication systems. Information theory thus constituted the first comprehensive model of HIP and, together with a closely related signal detection model, dominated the human performance research literature for the next several decades. Its popularity began to wane by the early 1970s due to its demonstrated limitations as a literal representation of human cognition, coupled with the evolution of the more powerful metaphor afforded by the digital computer. Nevertheless, the measures provided by information theory and signal detection theory continue to serve as a useful means of quantifying certain stimulus, response, and human performance characteristics. And some generalizations from this line of research, such as Miller's (1956) insight that temporary "working memory" is limited to about seven items of information, remain as cornerstones of modern cognitive theory.

Other important contributions to the evolution of the HIP perspective included D. E. Broadbent's (1958) "filter theory" of attention and serial processing stages; N. L. Miller, E. Galanter, and K. H. Pribram's (1960) model of the processing involved in planned behavior; J. W. Atkinson and M. Shiffrin's (1968) theory of memory components and their interaction; J. F. Collins and M. R. Quillian's (1969) model of organization in memory; Anderson's (1976) ACT model of knowledge and its acquisition; and M. Shiffrin and E. L. Schneider's (1977) distinction between automatic and controlled processing modes.

Illustrative Concepts

A plethora of HIP models, in addition to those mentioned above, has appeared in recent years, only a few of which can be presented here as illustrations. The reader is referred to Massaro and Cowan (1993) for a more comprehensive account. The present sample includes early and current examples.

Information theory. Information is conceptualized as the reduction of uncertainty that occurs when an event happens (typically a signal, message, or stimulus). The uncertainty in a state lottery with its millions of possible outcomes, for example, is much greater than in the Kentucky Derby with its dozen or so horses. When a winner is announced, therefore, the message conveys considerably more information in the former case. Uncertainty can thus be quantified in terms of the number of alternative events that *could* occur, weighted by their respective probabilities (formally, $H = \overset{i}{\Sigma} p_i \log_2 p_i$, where H is amount of information in a set of i events, and p_i is the probability of the ith event).

This metric makes it possible to calculate how much information-conveying potential exists in any stimulus set or message source, how much capability the receiving party has to register it, and, when a message has been sent, how much information was actually transmitted from source to receiver. Furthermore, by including temporal considerations (such as reaction time, RT), one can express the performance of the medium or "communication channel" over which the information was conveyed as a transmission rate, H/sec. Now, if the human is regarded as a communication channel (or series of channels), one has a powerful means of determining (and analyzing) how effectively that channel (or its components) processes information.

The information model produced several robust laws of human performance besides the aforementioned generalization about working memory capacity (Wickens 1992). The Hick-Hyman law, for example, holds that human choice RT increases as a linear function of the information (uncertainty) in the stimulus. Similarly, Fitts' law holds that the difficulty of tasks involving simple directed movement is a function of distance moved and size of target—in essence, the uncertainty in response selection.

Modern stage models. Based on models such as those cited earlier, a consensus view is that HIP occurs in stages as stimuli (or information-bearing events) are acted upon by a succession of mental components that comprise the functional system. Wickens (1992, 17) offers a representation in which boxes denote principal processing structures and functions, and arrowed lines, the primary routes of information flow. Large bodies of research and numerous detailed models underlie each of the components depicted. Overall, however, information is received and stored very briefly by the sensory systems, interpreted by perceptual mechanisms with the help of stored knowledge (long-term and working memory) plus invested attentional resources, and acted upon only after consideration of feasible response options and selection of one (again, with the help of attention and memory).

Memory and attention thus constitute key processes that exercise important controlling functions over all other system components. How information is prepared for storage, represented and maintained in storage, and retrieved from storage have been focal research issues from the beginning. Interest in attentional mechanisms, on the other hand, has been more recent, and controversy continues over its precise function. One popular view is that it consists of a limited "resource pool" that can be allocated to other mental functions in part at the discretion of the processor. Another is that it acts like a "searchlight," highlighting selected stimuli or memories in its beam while others remain only dimly in view.

The generic stage model implies that information is operated on serially, and is largely stimulus-driven (a property referred to as "bottom-up" processing). For this reason, response accuracy, RT, and H/sec have been popular dependent variables in HIP research. Indeed, techniques for decomposing components of RT have often been used to identify and describe the functioning of component processing stages. F. C. Donders's subtraction method and S. Sternberg's additive factors method were two such techniques (S. Sternberg 1969). It has long been recognized, however, that some processing occurs concurrently (i.e., "in parallel" rather than "in series"), and that the observer has some control over the input (i.e. "top-down" rather than exclusively "bottom-up" processing). Research interest has increased recently in both parallel and top-down processing (Howell 1993).

Automatic versus controlled processing model. First introduced by Shiffrin and Schneider (1977), this model illustrates several recent trends in HIP research. Basically, it suggests that some information processing occurs without the investment of attentional resources (automatically, or without thinking) while other kinds must draw heavily on this limited resource pool (controlled or conscious processing). Highly overlearned skills can become automated and, therefore, can be performed in parallel with serial controlled processing. Research has focused on issues such as the conditions that produce automatic processing, dual-task performance, and practical implications of the two processing modes.

William C. Howell

Humanistic Psychology

Humanistic psychologists believe that psychologists must not, as in the past, rely almost exclusively on the methods of natural science. These methods were devised for the study of the physical world and, because inanimate objects lack both consciousness and autonomy, no provision was made for exploiting these sources of data. Research with human beings should focus on experience and its meaning to the individual as the primary data, rather than on behavior or other derivatives of it. Humanistic psychologists are convinced that any approach that restricts the study of the person to experimenters observing him from the outside while minimizing or altogether neglecting what that person thinks, feels, and intends, can scarcely be called a human science.

Humanistic psychologists insist that humans, both as a species and as individuals, are unique. They cannot be adequately understood in terms of research on lower animals, nor is personality reducible to standardized traits or conditioned responses.

Frank T. Severin

Hunger

Metabolism in tissues requires continuous supplies of utilizable fuel, which may be derived from carbohydrate, fat, or protein. Hunger is a strong motivation to seek, obtain, and consume food that derives from the need for these metabolic fuels.

VMH Center

For several decades, hunger has been attributed to increased neuronal activity in a lateral hypothalamic (LH) "feeding center." This change was presumed to reflect decreased inhibition from an adjacent ventromedial hypothalamic (VMH) "satiety center." In support of this dual-center model are the familiar findings that following VMH lesions, animals eat much more food than controls and become obese, whereas following LH lesions they refuse to eat and will die of starvation despite the presence of familiar and nutritious foods.

In its role as a satiety center, the VMH was believed to influence food intake by providing for the long-term constancy of body weight. Thus, unlesioned starved animals permitted access to food ate unusually large amounts and quickly reattained previous body weights. However, it now appears that the fat content in adipose tissue is autoregulated and influences hunger only indirectly, by varying the supply of fuels available to body tissues; when animals are lean, a greater portion of ingested calories are deposited as fat than occurs normally, whereas fat is less readily stored when animals are relatively heavy.

The Liver

Sensory input into the brain appears to course through modality-specific primary projections, as well as through collateral polysensory pathways that serve a general activational role. Central dopaminergic fibers appear to be part of the latter group. Thus, destruction of these fibers, by LH lesions or by extrahypothalamic lesions, results in akinesia that precludes not only feeding but other motivated activities, such as drinking, maternal, and thermoregulatory behaviors.

Social-Psychological Factors

Aside from homeostatic considerations, a great variety of social and psychological variables are known to influence food intake so that animals (especially, people) with nutritional needs may not choose to eat while animals with no such needs may eat anyway. Indeed, these variables are likely to have a predominant effect in determining how much is eaten as well as which foods are consumed and when.

Specific Hungers

The specific hungers for water and sodium appear to be innate, as are complementary endocrinological mechanisms that help to conserve these nutrients. The special behavioral and physiological capacities for maintenance of water and sodium balance are not unexpected, since these are the two nutrients (aside from oxygen) that animal organisms can least afford to do without. In contrast, the need for vitamins and other minerals occurs much less often, and specific hungers for these nutrients appear to be learned adaptations.

Edward M. Stricker

Hunger and Instincts

Sigmund Freud made a theory of instinct (or libido theory) the cornerstone of his teaching. He defined instinct as "a borderland concept between the mental and the physical, being both the mental representative of the stimuli emanating from within the organism and penetrating to the mind, and at the same time a measure of the demands made upon the energy of the latter in consequence of its connection with the body" (1914).

Lawrence Kubie (1956) emphasized the complexity of instinctual development and maintained that a proper understanding required recognition of the influence of the symbolic processes on instinctual processes. Kubie ranked different bodily needs in order of complexity, according to the possibility of their immediate satisfaction or their dependence on intervention by others. For the gratification of the inherent needs of the infant for water and food, the aid of the mother or nurse is essential, and the time lag between tissue deprivation or the warning signals and the gratification is important for the behavioral elaboration of the instinct of nutrition.

My hypothesis is that hunger awareness is not innate biological wisdom, but learning is necessary for this biological need to become organized into recognizable patterns (Bruch 1961). The success of this learning will depend upon how appropriately an infant's needs are fulfilled and how consistently her gradually maturing brain will receive information so that she can learn to perceive and distinguish different needs, including hunger, and to express them and take proper steps to their satisfaction.

The human infant starts life unable to differentiate himself from others, and his biological needs are not more than unidentified and unidentifiable states of tension and discomfort.

Jean Piaget (1954) speaks of these processes as accommodation, the transformations induced in the child's perceptual schemata and behavioral patterns by the environment, and assimilation, the incorporation of objects and characteristics of the environment into the child's patterns of perception and behavior, with corresponding transformations of these objects.

Konrad Lorenz observed that goslings would not become attached to a substitute mother (an artificial goose with silk feathers, a warm underside, and a large beak) if the dummy was installed with a mechanism that produced continuous goose noise. If, however, the same dummy mother produced instead of a continuous noise, a sound only in response to a gosling's weeping, then a strong attachment would be formed.

Hilde Bruch

Hypnosis

Hypnosis may be used in psychotherapy as an adjunct with all types of patients and problems. It is particularly indicated when one wishes rapidly to establish rapport with a patient, as in short-term psychotherapy, and to reinforce authoritative suggestions for symptom relief or removal.

Hypnosis permits the reexperiencing in fantasy of

real life experiences that have consistently provoked avoidance reactions. Gradually, patients become immunized to the traumatic events in their everyday lives and learn to dampen fantasies of anticipated catastrophic happenings. They are enabled to talk more freely about them and to strip them of their terrorizing connotations. The therapist may encourage the patient to reenact scenes that stimulate painful emotions. In those patients who cannot remember dreams, hypnosis often helps break through the resistance, and they begin to talk about even the more repressed elements. As the patient successfully copes with his fantasies of aggression, assertiveness, and sexuality, he is less burdened with a need to suppress and repress; energy is released for more constructive activities.

A rich background in psychotherapy is an essential prerequisite for hypnotherapy. Preferably the therapist should have been schooled in a variety of approaches, including psychoanalytically oriented psychotherapy and behavioral modification. Psychotherapy is essentially a learning process in which maladaptive patterns are gradually replaced by those that promote an effective and realistic adjustment.

Sometimes the mere induction of a trance will bring out the fundamental problems and defenses of the patient. The patient's reactions to the hypnotic situation—the induction process, the suggestions made—and to the therapist are more important than beneficial responses to therapeutic suggestions.

Hypnosis is a fluctuating state, the adumbrations of which vary rapidly with shifts in the individual's physiological and psychological status. The situation under which hypnosis is induced and the motivations of the patient fashion the data under investigation. On the other hand, it may be possible, through the use of hypnosis, to study such processes as dreams, defense mechanisms, emotions, and psychopathological phenomena (Wolberg 1948).

Lewis R. Wolberg

Hypothetico-Deductive Method

In an early presentation of this hypothetico-deductive method, Clark L. Hull (1935) described the program in these terms:

1. The definitions and postulates of a scientific system should be stated in a clear and unambiguous manner, they should be consistent with one another, and they should be of such a nature as to permit rigorous deductions.
2. The labor of deducing the potential implications of the postulates of the system should be performed with meticulous care and exhibited, preferably step by step and in full detail. It is these deductions that constitute the substance of a system.
3. The significant theorems of a truly scientific system must take the form of specific statements of the outcome of concrete experiments or observations. The experiments in question may be those that have already been performed, but of particular significance are those that have not previously been carried out or even planned. It is among these latter, especially, that the crucial tests of a theoretical system will be found.
4. The theorems so deduced, which concern phenomena not already known, must be submitted to carefully controlled experiments. The outcome of these critical experiments, as well as all previous ones, must agree with the corresponding theorems making up the system.

Gregory A. Kimble

· I ·

Id: The Role of the Id in the Psychoanalytic Structural Theory

The id is the great source of mental energy for the whole of the mental apparatus. The wishes of the id press for gratification, and in doing so they impel the ego to action, action that may be of various kinds, because the ego, in the structural theory, includes the function of executant for the drives, as well as their opponent in situations of psychic conflict. The ego serves the functions of drive discharge and of countercathexis or opposition to the drives.

By the time he had formulated the mental apparatus in terms of id, ego, and superego—the structural theory—Sigmund Freud had introduced aggression as an instinctual drive on a footing roughly comparable to that of the erotic or libidinal drive. The introduction of this concept necessarily complicated his conceptual framework.

Freud assumed that the repetition compulsion represented a tendency in psychological life that he believed is present in all living matter—that is, in all protoplasm—namely, to repeat past events. Thus the death drive expresses the tendency of living matter to return to an inorganic state, according to Freud; or, in other words, the tendency to repeat what it once was.

One can summarize the concept of the id in the structural theory or model by saying that its elements are derivatives of the aggressive and libidinal drives, always mixed in varying proportions; that, as such, it is the great source of energy or motivational impulsion for the whole of the mental apparatus; that it operates according to the pleasure principle; and that the ego serves to mediate between id and external world, both as executant and opponent or modifier.

Charles Brenner

Ideology, Belief Systems, Values, and Attitudes

By the time we become adults we may have developed tens of thousands of beliefs and thousands of attitudes, but only several dozen of instrumental values and only a handful of terminal values. This difference in numbers suggests a hierarchically connected system of attitudes and values distinguished by content or structure. If it is content we are interested in, we might focus on whether a person is liberal or conservative, anti-Semitic or anti-Communist. If it is structure we are interested in, we would focus on the study of the central-peripheral dimension of belief systems, its degree of differentiation, breadth or narrowness, isolation, time perspective, simplicity-complexity, and the like.

T. W. Adorno. One of the most influential books in modern social psychology is *The Authoritarian Personality* (Adorno et al. 1950). This study was a melding of two social concerns—the desire to better understand how the threat of fascism could arise during the 1930s, which shaped its focus on "the authoritarian personality," and how prejudice against Jews and other minorities arose. These underlying objectives then shaped the operational emphasis of the Adorno group on four sets of psychological variables: (1) anti-Semitism, (2) ethnocentrism, (3) political-economic conservatism, and (4) the authoritarian personality, for which the famous F scale (*F* for fascism) was developed.

Rokeach. Problems with the Adorno study motivated Milton Rokeach to carry out the work summarized in *The Open and Closed Mind* (1960). What struck Rokeach was the imbalance in equating the authoritarian personality solely with fascism. To measure general processes, Rokeach developed the dogmatism scale to measure general authoritarianism and the opinionation scale to measure general intolerance. His main finding was that dogmatism and opinionation are characteristics of all forms of authoritarianism, more or less independent of one's position on the left-right continuum: neither rightists nor leftists have a monopoly on authoritarianism and intolerance.

Eysenck. Hans J. Eysenck subjected 22,000 statements of attitude bearing on left-right ideology to factor analysis and found not one but two factors, accounting for a major portion of the variance: liberalism-conservatism and a new second factor reminiscent of William James's observation of people as being tough-minded or tender-minded.

Tomkins. Silvan Tomkins was the first to handle left and right as both one-dimensional and two-dimensional, to add a clear articulation of middleness as a third major division, and to further add a fourth dimension of the nonideological. This theoretical patterning was expressed in the first radically new measure for the field, the Tomkins polarity scale (1964). The measures used by practically all other investigators were of the Likert type, which reduces the variety of a person's ideology to a single score. Tomkins's measure, however, presented the respondent with four choices: right, left, both, or neither. Scoring was then, as with the Rorschach, a profile of scores, with the ratios of their relationships expressing the meaning for personalized interpretation.

Tomkins's work has been extended by David Loye in studies designed to advance the measurement and theory of ideology through an integration of Tomkins's thought with various sociological, historical, and psychological works (Loye 1971, 1975). Advancements by David Loye included the demonstration of a significant relation of liberal activism to norm maintaining.

David Loye
Milton Rokeach

Illusions

Activity theories attribute illusions to responses an individual makes, or plans to make, to certain stimuli. Although illusions can occur without eye movements, a theory has emerged that attributes illusion to the readiness to make saccadic eye movements (efferent readiness theory). These eye movement programs are sometimes off target, according to the theory, because of a tendency to fixate the center of gravity of a set of contours in the interest of acuity. Perception of target position is biased accordingly. Jean Piaget's theory belongs to this category. He proposes that illusions depend on which parts of figures are centrated, or attended to (Over 1968). However, critics point to the lack of an independent criterion for the processes supposed to underlie the illusions.

Functional theories treat illusions as adaptive responses that help give an accurate view of the world under normal viewing conditions and are therefore reinforced. During the last century, A. Thiery explored two-dimensional representations of three-dimensional scenes with considerable success in order to find the well-known illusory configurations. He showed, as others have done since, that the same distortions that are called illusions in a sketchy drawing would tend to produce veridical perception if applied to the same elements in a three-dimensional scene.

In summary, it seems unlikely that illusions can all be explained by a single process, or that they will be explained at all until perception in general is much better understood and the different approaches converge. The study of illusions may itself contribute to this end.

Barbara Gillam

Imaginative Development in Childhood

There is increasing evidence that by the age of two, children are already able to treat an empty cup as if it were full, to play "as if" they were drinking, or to feed a toy horse with a spoon, behaving as if the horse were a child.

Jean Piaget described the constant interplay

between the efforts of the child to accommodate to environmental stimulation by physically reaching or touching and by vocalizing imitation of sounds or words, and by motorically mimicking movements of the adults around her. In privacy, the child continues the accommodation, but now she must try to assimilate these movements and actions to her limited range of cognitive skills in order to make some kind of match or fit. In this assimilative effort, the child plays and replays bits and pieces of her encounters with adults and with the physical world, and inevitably creates novel situations to which she must further respond.

The research carried out indicates that children by the ages of three and four show a moderate amount of time, during free-play periods sampled, in which they engage in behavior that can be described as "make-believe." These include examples of introducing characters not in the immediate environment, for example, "Bat Man"; transforming plastic toys into objects not immediately present or into completely different functions, for example, taking a plastic giraffe and making it into a human baby, or a plastic cowboy into a spaceman.

Evidence of the earliest origins of imaginative behavior have come from a series of studies by L. G. Fein and various collaborators. These studies indicate that as early as 18 months of age, children already show evidence of transformations of objects that can only be interpreted as make-believe or pretending.

S. Smilansky (1968) and J. L. Singer (1973) have outlined a large number of specific advantages to the child in the course of development of imaginativeness. These include heightened capacity for imagery, which has been shown in studies to increase the effective use of language. In addition, there are indications that imaginative play is associated with greater exploration of the environment and, hence, acquisition of additional learning.

There is some evidence suggesting that training in imaginative play could have beneficial effects as an ameliorative or therapeutic orientation for disturbed and impulsive children.

Jerome L. Singer

Impotence Therapy

Impotence is a man's inability to obtain and maintain a sufficient erection to successfully engage in coitus. Primary impotence refers to the male's life-long failure in his attempts to have sexual intercourse. Secondary impotence implies at least one successful past instance of coitus. When a man's failure to achieve coital connection approaches 25% of his opportunities, the diagnosis of impotence is in order.

Virginia Masters and William H. Johnson identify the male's pronounced fear of sexual failure as the crucial immediate cause of psychogenic impotence (1970). In the patient population studied at the Reproductive Biology Research Foundation in St. Louis, they found various psychosocial influences that may contribute to the incidence of impotence. They describe maternal seductiveness and dominance, paternal dominance, religious orthodoxy, homosexuality, adverse experiences with prostitutes, and a history of premature ejaculation and acute alcoholic episodes.

At the onset of treatment, the therapists impress on the patient that no man can will an erection. It is pointed out that this is as impossible a task as for a woman to achieve vaginal lubrication through sheer willpower.

Sensate focus exercises are prescribed. The couple is asked to take turns, at home in the nude, receiving and giving tactile pleasure, and to communicate to each other what sensory experiences are most pleasurable. Any attempt at coitus and direct contact with the genitals are initially prohibited during these intimate sessions of mutual body caressing. A high level of erotic ecstasy is quickly reached as this non-demand interaction leads to a heightened awareness of tactile, visual, olfactory, and auditory inputs. The male, to his surprise, will develop erections without direct genital stimulation.

The next instruction is for both partners to stroke each other's pelvic area. Again, taking turns, they guide the caressing partner through verbal instructions, body movement, sounds, facial expression, or manual direction, so as to maximize the intensity of this sensual experience.

The team directs the couple to go on, in their sessions at home, to penetration. The woman places herself in the female-superior position, straddling her partner with her knees at or below his nipple line. She manually stimulates his penis to erection, and then proceeds to manually insert the penis into her well-lubricated vagina, while continuing to stimulate the shaft.

H. S. Kaplan describes how the therapist can help the couple reach the first coital experience, which is a sensitive and critical landmark in the treatment of impotence. He or she can recommend that the male immerse himself in a favorite sexual fantasy to overcome obsessive doubts regarding the permanence and firmness of his erections. The therapist may prescribe manual stimulation of the penis and rapid penetration as soon as the point of ejaculatory inevitability is reached. Other males may benefit from timing penetration to take advantage of their morning erections. To be effective, psychotherapy has to help the couple reach interpersonal intimacy based on an egalitarian relationship between two individuals who trust each other.

The treatment of primary impotence is particularly difficult. Conjoint psychotherapy is frequently impossible, because the male does not have a sufficiently involved or concerned partner. Individual psychotherapy is often indicated to resolve serious intrapsychic conflicts, such as the patient's maturational failure to move from the primary identification with his mother to a stable male identity, his fear of losing his identity in a close relationship with a woman, or his unconscious equation of coitus with rape within the context of his rage at an invasive mother.

Leo I. Jacobs

Incentive Factor

The symbol K was introduced by Clark L. Hull when he abandoned his earlier approach, which assumed that the conditions of reinforcement affect learning. This concept was presaged by E. C. Tolman as a sign-gestalt-expectation.

Subsequently, Kenneth W. Spence identified K

with the stimulus-intensity dynamism associated with the fractional anticipatory goal response $(r_g - s_g)$. His notion was that organisms begin to make components of the consummatory response before receiving the reward, and the feedback from such expectations excites them into more vigorous behavior.

Frank A. Logan

Incentive and Learning

The term *incentive* refers to the motivational properties of reinforcement, and as a process it stands in sharp opposition to the concept of drive reduction. Motivators are also drive inducers. The drive-reduction theory of reinforcement argues that reinforcers serve to promote learning because they reduce drives. Some do. Food reduces hunger; water reduces thirst; copulatory behavior reduces the sexual drive; and so on. But these same objects and activities also arouse the organism. Put food, water, or a female in heat in the presence of a male rat and make it inaccessible, and the rat shows arousal rather than inactivity, as would be expected from a decreased level of drive. Moreover, such arousal can be reinforcing. A male rat, for example, will learn a response when the reward is the opportunity to copulate with a receptive female (arousal) but not to ejaculate (drive reduction).

Gregory A. Kimble

Incentive Theory of Motivation

A controversy developed in the 1930s and 1940s between reinforcement theorists, who contended that the amount of reward determines the degree of learning, and contiguity theorists, who contended that practice alone determines learning. Among the many studies intended to resolve this controversy, those on latent learning are most exemplary. It was found that if rats were allowed to explore a maze without any explicit reward, the later introduction of food into the goal box led to a dramatic change in their performance: they now ran directly to the goal box. This learning was considered to be latent because it was not apparent until reward was introduced to motivate the rats to exhibit what they had learned from their earlier explorations.

Incentive theories of motivation can be traced back as far as hedonism. To put that view most simply, the pleasures of the body are paramount: eat when hungry, drink when thirsty, engage in sexual activity when aroused, and relieve oneself from pain when hurt. In the parlance of hedonism, these may all be done to excess in order to languish in luxury. Although current incentive theories acknowledge the potency of these goals, the notion of secondary reinforcement has also been introduced. Social approval, praise, achievement, and respect are among the rewards toward which humans aspire and may provide even greater motivation than biological rewards. Any event that an organism values produces motivation to receive it. Be it a peanut or a pearl, its reward value to the organism determines its potential for exciting incentive motivation.

Frank A. Logan

Independence in Children

Independence, like other characteristics that have their roots in early childhood, has been studied with techniques that include interviews with parents and teachers, ratings based on observations of the child in a naturalistic setting or in the laboratory, self-reports, and projective techniques (Hartup 1963). After observing the play of preschool children, Beller (1955) reasoned that both independence and dependence consist of a number of different components, which may or may not be correlated.

Although independence training tends to encourage mature behavior in social, intellectual, and emotional performance, its primary focus is on permitting the child to make her own choices, direct her own behavior, and feel responsible for the effects of her behavior.

There may be differences in the kind of environment that fosters independence in a boy or in a girl. D. Baumrind (1973) examined the children from authoritarian, permissive, nonconforming, and au-

thoritative (a good deal of parental control with encouragement of independence and individuality) homes. Although girls from authoritative homes were above average in independence in each of three studies, the results were not as clear for boys.

S. Joyce Brotsky

Individual Differences in Conditioning

Trait versus State Anxiety

The most studied between-individual difference variable in conditioning is trait anxiety. Most studies of the effects of trait anxiety on conditioning involve a comparison of individuals who are high or low in anxiety as determined by scores on a standard test. The most common conditioning procedure has been eyelid conditioning. The most common result has been that high-anxiety subjects condition to a higher level (and more quickly) than low-anxiety subjects.

Some investigators have had great difficulty in obtaining this most common result. Although the definitive experiments have not been done, scattered evidence suggests that the procedures of these unsuccessful experiments may have failed to create a temporary state of anxiety in the individuals who were prone to it by reason of their trait. In some of these same unsuccessful experiments, postexperimental reports of anxiety level during the experiment (state anxiety) have correlated highly with conditioning ($r=+.70$), while trait anxiety had no effect at all. Thus, it appears that anxiety must be considered as a within-individual difference and that low-trait-anxiety people can exhibit high trait anxiety under certain circumstances.

Age and Conditioning

The one individual difference variable related to inhibitability on which some work has been done is that of chronological age. Research in this area has demonstrated quite convincingly that classical conditioned reflexes (CRS) can be established before birth, and that conditionability continues into old age. Somewhat surprisingly, conditioning probably occurs more readily in children than it does in young adults or especially in the aged, where conditioning is sometimes difficult. It is this last point that puts age differences in conditionability in touch with the topic of inhibition.

Voluntary and Conditioned Responders

One of the most suggestive individual differences is that between voluntary and conditioned responders in the classical eyelid-conditioning experiment. In that context, and on the basis of characteristic response form, it is possible to identify some individuals who respond predominantly with what have been called voluntary (or V-form) responses and others who produce predominantly conditioned (or C-form) responses. Careful studies of these two groups indicate that they differ in ways that suggest that V-form and C-form responders may process stimuli in fundamentally different ways. These experiments provided strong evidence that the Vs are left-hemisphere dominated, and that the Cs are right-hemisphere dominated.

Gregory A. Kimble

Individuality: Emergence

Alexander Thomas and Stella Chess's methods of data collection and analysis have been reported in a number of publications and are described in detail in Thomas et al. (1963) and Thomas, Chess, and H. G. Birch (1968). Nine categories of temperament have been defined by inductive content analysis of the infant behavior protocols. Each is scored on a three-point scale and can be identified clearly at 2 to 3 months of age and at subsequent age periods. The nine categories are:

1. *Activity level*—the motor component present in a given child's functioning and the diurnal proportion of active and inactive periods. Protocol data on the child's motility when she is being bathed, fed, dressed, and handled, as well as information concerning her sleep-wake cycle and reaching, crawling, walking, and play patterns, are used in scoring this functional category.

2. *Rhythmicity* (biological regularity)—the pre-dictability and rhythmicity and/or the unpredictability and arhythmicity in time of any function. This is analyzed in relation to the child's sleep-wake cycle, his hunger or feeding patterns, and his elimination schedule.

3. *Approach-withdrawal* (positive-negative initial responses)—the nature of the child's initial response to a new or altered stimulus, be it a new food, a new toy, or a new person.

4. *Adaptability*—the nature of a child's responses to new or altered situations with respect to the ease with which they are modified in a desired direction, irrespective of the initial response.

5. *Intensity of reaction*—the energy level or vigor of a child's responses, independent of its direction (either a negative or a positive response can be mild or intense). Responses to stimuli, to preelimination tension, to hunger, to repletion, to new foods, to attempts at control, to restraint, to dressing, and to diapering all provide scorable items for this category.

6. *Threshold of responsiveness*—the intensity level of stimulation necessary to evoke a discernible response, without regard to the specific form that the response may take or the sensory modality affected. The behaviors used are responses to sensory stimuli, environmental objects, and social contacts.

7. *Quality of mood*—the amount of pleased, joyful, and friendly behavior versus the amount of displeased, crying, and unfriendly behavior is determined; that is, does the child show more smiling and laughing or more fussing and crying behavior?

8. *Distractibility*—the ease with which a child can be diverted from an ongoing activity by extraneous peripheral stimuli.

9. *Attention span and persistence*—two related categories. Attention span is the length of time a particular activity is pursued by the child. Persistence refers to the continuation of an activity by the child in the face of obstacles to the maintenance of the activity direction.

Temperamental individuality in itself does not determine the outcome of development in terms of personality structure, behavior disturbance, academic achievement, or socialization.

Alexander Thomas
Stella Chess

Industrial Mental Health

There is a heavy contemporary emphasis on management education by a wide range of methods, both in companies (as well as governmental organizations) and outside them. These have largely to do with recognizing the range and importance of human feelings and the interpersonal and organizational issues that have negative effects on them and, therefore, on health. Those methods include variants of group dynamics, like the Managerial Grid, transactional analysis, the application of psychoanalytic theory to management problems, and in some cases, learning theory.

Much attention has been given to style of management and its impact on people's feelings. W. J. McGregor (1960) offers the thesis that there are two basic theories about motivation, Theory X and Theory Y; the former is authoritarian and the latter allows for a great deal more self-control. This thesis has been pushed particularly by Rensis Likert (1961), who uses the principle of supportive relationship as the major device for relating the organization to the individual and defines organizational units as overlapping sets of groups. Chris Argyris (1964) contends that organizations foster dependency and submissiveness, which impair the development toward self-fulfillment. F. Herzberg, J. J. Mausner, and B. Snyderman (1959) define what they differentiate as hygienic factors versus motivating factors, indicating that when hygienic factors are not adequately present, there is stress. D. Blake and P. Mouton (1964) report from their small-groups studies that organizations that have equal concern for people and production do better.

The field is marked by limited research, limited theoretical generalizations, and attempts to apply descriptive conceptions to situations that demand explanatory concepts to have action taken on them. There is a general skepticism among most people in executive ranks about mental health issues, particularly about their need for understanding and consultation. Simultaneously, there is a growing awareness of the importance of psychological factors in health and illness, as well as in management and motivation.

Harry Levinson

Industrial and Organizational Psychology

This is an area of both psychological science and practice. Its scientific aspect is concerned with understanding the behavior of people as workers. The professional practice applies that knowledge to furthering the adaptation and effectiveness of those workers. "Worker" refers here to employees of all kinds of organizations and occupying all kinds of jobs, including managers, professionals, and rank-and-file blue-collar and white-collar employees. It is estimated that there are some 3,000 industrial and organizational (I-O) psychologists in the United States alone, a large majority of whom have a Ph.D. degree. Reflecting the dual nature of the field, about one-third of them are employed on university faculties, with the remainder working as practitioners in industry, government, or consulting.

Raymond A. Katzell and J. T. Austin (1992) have described the development of the field since its origin around the beginning of the twentieth century. Two of its founding figures were Walter Dill Scott, an American, and Hugo Münsterberg, a German, who later moved to Harvard University as professor of psychology. Another early leader was Walter V. Bingham, who in 1915 headed the Division of Applied Psychology at what is now Carnegie-Mellon University.

World War I provided major impetus to the field. Psychologists attached to the army developed group tests of mental ability for use in screening and classifying army recruits, a checklist for detecting psychoneurotic symptoms, scales for rating performance, and a system for analyzing military job requirements.

Those efforts fostered the growth of what eventually became known as the "industrial" or "I" focus of industrial and organizational psychology. That aspect of the field, also sometimes called personnel psychology, focuses on fitting workers to their jobs by means of proper selection and training, with an associated armamentarium of concepts and techniques.

What has become labeled as the "organizational" or "O" focus of the field emphasizes adapting organizational practices and conditions to human requirements. That approach got under way in the 1930s, stimulated by the famous Hawthorne studies which illuminated the importance of social factors, and by the seminal work on group dynamics by Kurt Lewin and his associates.

Those two foci are by no means separate, for the optimum arrangement entails the mutual adaptation of workers to their work and the work environment to the workers. The modern approach therefore conceives of workers and the employing organization as interacting parts of a system, which even takes into account their embeddedness in a broader socio-economic and cultural context. For purposes of expository convenience, however, contemporary research and practice in I-O psychology will be described below in terms of that dichotomy.

It should be noted first that research in all areas of I-O psychology is conducted by methods common to the rest of scientific psychology. About half of that research is conducted in the laboratory, where subjects perform tasks under conditions that aim to represent some of those present in organizational settings, and about half of the research is done in the field. Many of the field studies involve action research conducted with the active collaboration of members of the client organization. Controlled changes in one or more variables are introduced in much of the research done in the field and virtually all done in the laboratory. However, many field studies employ designs that correlate measurements of naturally occurring rather than contrived variations, as, for example, when observed differences in employees' working conditions are correlated with measures of their job satisfaction. Laboratory experiments obviously have the advantage of greater precision, whereas field research benefits from greater veridicality; however, there is evidence that the find-ings of well-designed laboratory research can generalize to field settings.

The topics of contemporary concern in the area of industrial or personnel psychology include the refinement and improvement of techniques for selecting, placing, and promoting workers. Among those techniques are psychological tests, interviews, biographical data questionnaires, and assessment centers. The latter aim to obtain a comprehensive picture of the candidate's aptitudes, skills, personality, and motivation, utilizing such techniques as tests, interviews, discussion groups, and work simulations. Research efforts focus on establishing the validity of those methods, including the extent to which validity may be generalized across different jobs, organizations, and demographic groups.

Psychological aspects of training and development programs include analysis of training needs, design of methods of instruction, and evaluation of program outcomes. There are programs of individual training, team development, and organization development. Affirmative action programs typically include specialized training and counseling both of minority workers and of their supervisors and coworkers. Programs of stress reduction and health improvement also often feature relevant training.

Because how well workers perform their jobs serves as a basis for compensation and promotion, as well as a criterion for evaluating selection and training programs, the subject of performance appraisal is another of major interest. Improvement in the fairness and accuracy of performance ratings is of ongoing concern.

Interest in the organizational or "O" segment of the field burgeoned after World War II. Among the subjects of major attention has been that of leadership. Research is addressed to measuring attributes of successful leaders, to analyzing how their behavior differs from that of less successful ones, and to ways in which those properties are contingent on characteristics of the work setting. Applications of such research include methods of selecting and training people for managerial jobs.

In addition to leadership patterns, other properties of work groups also affect their performance. These include structural properties such as their size, composition, and distribution of responsibilities. Equally important are psychosocial factors, like communication patterns, power distribution, inter-member attractiveness, and behavior norms. Intergroup relations, including conflict and cooperation, also are subjects of attention. Information on those subjects is used in the design and staffing of work teams and in team development efforts.

The effects of leadership and group relations are explained to a large extent by their effects on worker motivation, which has itself become a major focus of organizational psychology. Research on that subject has led to the formulation of principles that are conducive to high levels of motivation, and a number of practices have been evolved to implement each of them:

- workers' motives and values must be appropriate to the nature of the work, e.g., by motive training
- jobs must be attractive, interesting, and satisfying, e.g., by enlarging the scope of responsibilities
- performance must be appropriately reinforced, e.g., by merit pay plans
- work goals must be clear and challenging, e.g., by quality circles
- personal and material resources must be adequate, e.g., by improved work methods
- interpersonal and group processes must support goal attainment, e.g., by norm building
- personal, social, and technological parameters must be harmonious, e.g., by sociotechnical system design

Raymond A. Katzell and R. A. Guzzo (1983) reviewed 207 field experiments in which those and similar programs were introduced; productivity improvements were reported in 87% of the experiments, and most also resulted in more positive attitudes on the part of the workers.

In addition to research addressed to understanding individual and group factors in workers' behavior, I-O psychologists consider the broader sociocultural context. Such concerns include the effects of organizational climate and culture, advanced technology, unemployment, and values and norms in different national locations.

In sum, the field of industrial and organizational psychology seeks to understand how personal, group, organizational, and cultural factors affect the behavior, feelings, performance, and well-being of people at work, and to apply those understandings to the welfare of the workers and of their employing organizations. There is strong evidence that those efforts are often effective.

Raymond A. Katzell

Infancy: Personality Development

Because personality functioning is often evaluated in the context of social interactions and communications, certain infant behaviors that reflect the potential for interactions, such as smiling, vocalizing, visual behavior, and protesting, seem relevant to the ontogenesis of personality. Most of the studies dealing with these variables, however, are aimed at gathering normative data, determining age of onset, and identifying the conditions that produce and maintain these behaviors.

Vocal behavior among infants appears to be associated with both endogenous and environmental factors. One study has demonstrated a similar developmental course in the frequency of vocalizations among infants born to both deaf and hearing parents. Also, deaf infants show similar qualities in their vocalizations to those of hearing infants. These findings suggest an endogenous or built-in basis for early vocalizations. On the other hand, social conditioning has been proven effective in altering the vocal behavior of 3-month-old infants.

The visual system plays a primary role in many aspects of human experience. The assimilation of interpersonal stimuli is particularly dependent on vision. The visual apparatus is well developed at an early age. It has been established that infants are capable of discriminating movement and intensity of light during the early days of life, can distinguish different visual patterns by two weeks of age and, by four months, show a preference for the human face over other stimuli. The visual system is instrumental in facilitating early social experiences through eye contact with others.

The cry is a highly expressive and compelling signal by which the infant communicates distress (needs) and imperiously influences the behavior of those around her. The evidence is quite persuasive as to the potency of the cry as a determinant of parental behavior and as a central response linking parent and infant. Considerable variability exists among infants concerning the intensity, duration, and quality of their crying behavior (H. A. Moss 1974).

R. M. Thomas et al. (1963) have found stability between infancy and early childhood for a series of temperamental characteristics. These characteristics include activity level, rhythmicity, adaptibility, approach avoidance, intensity of reaction, threshhold of responsiveness, mood, distractibility, attention, and persistence. Furthermore, because they have found stability in crying behavior, they assert that irritability may be an enduring personality characteristic.

Based upon her observations of a sample of infants, S. K. Escalona (1968) also has stressed the pervasive effect of activity level in being associated with and influencing many aspects of development. For instance, she considers activity level to contribute to visual attentiveness, oral activity, responsiveness to stimulation, and interaction with inanimate and social objects.

John Bowlby (1958) has proposed that there are five instinctual responses in the behavioral repertoire of the infant that bind it to its mother. These responses are sucking, clinging, following, crying, and smiling. Sucking, clinging, and following are considered to occur mainly through the active initiation of the infant, with only a minimal response from the mother being necessary, whereas crying and smiling depend for their affect on maternal behavior.

Howard A. Moss

Infant Perception

Soon after birth, the human infant is able to respond differentially to various aspects of the visual environment. Intensity differences are differentially attractive, and this ability to discriminate increases rapidly over the first few months of life. Hue discrimination has been reported for infants in a number of carefully controlled studies.

Coordinated head and eye movements are demonstrated in infants in the first month of life. Four looking patterns have been observed: a shift pattern, in which a saccadic movement of the eyes is integrated with a smooth and fairly rapid movement of the head; a search pattern, in which a slow displacement of the head is coordinated with a series of eye fixations and saccades; a focal pattern, in which the head is stable while a series of small saccades and fixations cover a limited portion of the visual field; and a compensation pattern, in which the eyes and head move slowly and continuously in opposite directions and then return to their original positions.

The data from experiments on infants strongly suggest that infants see objects arranged in space, maintaining their size and shape as they change position and orientation. Not only are objects ordered in visual space but the space and the objects possess a metric for the perceiving adult. Perceptual development may be related to the acquisition of this metric.

Maurice Hershenson

Information Processing in Children

Information processing (IP), in the present context, refers to the perception, encoding, recoding, storage, retrieval, and manipulation of information by the brain.

Sensory development (Pick and Pick 1970) is substantially complete by age 5—the age at which our analysis starts. Moreover, at the level of abstraction and encoding with which the IP theories are stated, such development plays a minor role: it does not appear to affect the processing of information in any fundamental way. However, R. H. Pollack (in Farnham-Diggory 1972) demonstrates the effect of physiological aging upon the strength of certain optical illusions, and there are some that increase with age, reflecting noncognitive factors at the initial sensory stage of processing.

When we look up a telephone number and then consciously rehearse it on our way to the telephone we are using our short-term memory. Short-term-memory (STM) capacity is measured in terms of the number of items in an ordered list that we can repeat immediately after hearing or seeing them. If the items are digits, STM capacity is described in terms of "digit span." It ranges from two or three digits at age 2 or 3, to seven or eight items in adults. Spans obtained by 5-year-olds and adults, repectively, are approximately 4.3 and 8 for digits; 3.7 and 7.2 for letters; 4.3 and 5.9 for concrete words; and 4.2 and 5.3 for geometric figures. Notice that children's span is relatively unaffected by differences in materials, while adults' span for digits is almost 60% greater than their span for geometric figures.

Similar to children's strategic deficit, with respect to the formation and rehearsal of STM chunks, is their apparent lack of powerful attentional strategies. Attentional processes determine which aspects of the sensory buffers will be transmitted to STM, and which items, once in STM, will be transferred further to long-term memory (LTM). H. A. Simon (in Farnham-Diggory 1972) postulates a fixed fund of attention: attention cannot be increased or diminished, it can only be reallocated. Children have as much of it as adults, but they lack adequate allocation strategies. This view is consistent with the research on incidental learning and visual scanning in children.

David Klahr

Ingenieros, José (1877–1925)

The Argentinian psychologist José Ingenieros introduced positivism and behaviorism in Argentina. He considered psychology a natural science, which studies the psychological functions of living organisms.

Ruben Ardila

Ingratiation

There are four major classes of ingratiation tactics that have received research attention: other-enhancement, opinion conformity, favor rendering, and self-preservation. We can try to make others like us by flattering them, agreeing with them, doing things for them, or describing ourselves in an appealing way. In various experiments these responses have been viewed either as antecedent or consequent conditions.

One theoretical analysis of the conditions giving rise to ingratiation (E. E. Jones 1964) holds that ingratiation is a function of three factors: the incentive value of attraction, the subjective probability of obtaining it, and the perceived legitimacy of the attainment attempt. The first two factors are assumed to be multiplicative. The greater the incentive value of the attraction solicited, and the greater the subjective probability of successfully eliciting attraction, the greater the likelihood of ingratiation. Perceived legitimacy may serve as a threshold factor, providing a go or stop signal for ingratiation, once the value of incentive times probability reaches a certain strength.

Edward E. Jones

Innate Releasing Mechanism in Animals

This is a hypothesized perceptual mechanism elaborated in 1935 by Konrad Lorenz in his famous "Kumpan" article. Here he proposes an array of such mechanisms in the central nervous system, each of which responds selectively only to a specific stimulus. Furthermore, each such mechanism is said to be linked with a specific pattern of response, called a *fixed* or *modal action pattern*.

The innate releasing mechanism acts as the receiver and decoder. It is a selective filter, eliminating all but the relevant stimulus. When the input is "correct," the releasing mechanism "releases" the proper response. Lorenz hypothesizes that this is accomplished by activating, or disinhibiting, the appropriate motor coordinating system. Thus, when a female pigeon is confronted with a displaying male, at some point she squats; squatting in turn releases treading in the male, which releases in the female moving the tail out of the way and averting the cloaca, and so on. Likewise, in the stickleback, the male's red belly triggers attack in a territorial male, or sexual responses in a female close to spawning.

The releasing mechanism in many animals may reside in part, at least, in the peripheral nervous system, not just in the brain. Much coding of stimuli is known to occur in the eyes of frogs, rabbits, and cats. The same applies to acoustical stimuli that are filtered in the auditory nerves of bats and bullfrogs.

George W. Barlow

Instinctive Behavior Patterns

Behavior is a process, not an entity to be transmitted from generation to generation. If a fixed pattern of muscle action is not required for the performance of stereotyped acts, how are these to be coded by the genome? In fact, geneticists are increasingly prone to reject the notion of the genes as a biochemical homunculus, that is, a repository of all the information needed to construct the constituent organism. Rather, they see genes as information-generating devices, which feed upon their ordered environment. Thus, gene A produces a substance that, upon interacting with particular other substances in its environment, forms a new compound. This may, in turn, modify the activity of gene A, repressing it and stimulating another gene, B, into action. Thus, the ultimate end product is no more to be attributed to gene A than to the substance in the substrate—it is the product of their interaction.

There are patterns of behavior that characterize mice but not cats; just as a given form and color may serve to define a particular species, so may a given behavior pattern. Indeed, in spiders and ducks, behavior patterns may be more useful for classification than morphologic characters (Heinroth 1910; Petrunkevitch, 1926).

Instincts are processes that derive from a series of interactions commencing with fertilization. In an ordered and predictable environment, the final outcomes have a degree of sameness and inevitability. Instincts are better regarded as sequences of movements and perceptions. These must be analyzed with a view to unraveling a skein of interactions that tie together particular stimuli (a red spot), and particular movements (a peck).

Peter H. Klopfer

Instruction, Individualized

Individualized instruction, or personalized systems of instruction (PSI), has been used with varying degrees of success from the primary and high school levels to the college level and beyond. There are five essential characteristics of such programs:

1. One must arrange the environment so that the student makes the desired response.
2. The instructor should be available to give immediate feedback.
3. The student should proceed in small steps, with each successive item constructed so that the student uses and incorporates former learning to answer a new question.
4. The student should proceed at his own rate.
5. There must be continuous feedback to the instructor indicating how effective are procedures, so that modifications in the program can be made immediately.

William R. Reich

Instrumental (Operant) Conditioning

Law of Effect
Instrumental conditioning refers to any change in behavior that is the result of a contingency between a response and a stimulus event.

Two fundamental paradigms for the study of learning have evolved in psychology laboratories. The first, classical or Pavlovian conditioning, is a change in behavior that is the result of a contingency between two stimuli. Typically, a "neutral" stimulus called the conditioned stimulus (CS), which evokes no particular response of its own accord, is followed by some motivationally significant stimulus, called the unconditioned stimulus (UCS), which "automatically" evokes an unconditioned response (UR or UCR); after several pairings of the CS and US, the CS alone may elicit the response, now called the conditioned response (CR), previously evoked only by the US. When this occurs, classical conditioning has been demonstrated.

Instrumental Procedures

The second fundamental paradigm—instrumental, operant, or Thorndikean conditioning—is a change in behavior produced by a contingency between a response (R) and a reinforcing stimulus (S^r). Six different instrumental procedures can be identified by combining two types of reinforcer: appetitive ("satisfiers": food, water, or any stimulus normally thought of as a reward) or aversive ("annoyers": electric shock, extreme cold, or any stimulus normally thought of as a punisher), with three kinds of response outcome: presentation, removal, or prevention of the reinforcer. The result may be either an increase or decrease in rate, vigor, probability, or any other measure of response strength.

Reward Training

Drive has a profound effect on performance, with higher drive levels producing faster response rates. An important issue is whether drive increases the rate at which a response is acquired or simply the vigor with which it is performed. In some experiments two groups of animals have learned the same response, one at a high drive level, the other at a low drive level; then both have been tested at an intermediate level. The former high-drive group has performed better than the low-drive group, suggesting that drive affects both learning and performance.

Reward magnitude affects performance, larger rewards producing higher response rates. Whether reward magnitude affects learning is not easily answered. When reward magnitude is decreased from a high to an intermediate level, response rates decline below response rates for a group that has always received a reward of intermediate magnitude; this phenomenon is termed *negative contrast*.

Omission Learning

Omission training has the effect of reducing response rates. Most omission experiments require that an animal withhold responding—usually responses of the sort discussed above, initially established by reward training—in order to receive an appetitive reinforcer. Besides suppressing responding, the transition from reward to omission can elicit aggressive behavior, such as attacks on another member of the same species, if such a target is available.

Punishment

Several theories of punishment have been proposed. According to the conditioned response (CR) theory, the stimulus situation in which punishment occurs becomes a classically conditioned CS (conditioned stimulus) for the responses elicited by the punishing stimulus, which acts as a US (unconditioned stimulus).

A special case of punishment is the development of taste aversions. Animals have the remarkable ability to form aversions to tastes followed by illness as long as eight hours after ingesting the food. As might be expected, taste aversions develop more readily to novel foods than to familiar foods. While taste aversions are often analyzed in terms of classical conditioning, where the taste is the CS for the US of illness and, as such, comes to be avoided (the CS, taste, acquires some of the aversive properties of the US, illness), they can also be thought of as a case of discriminated punishment; that is, the response of eating in the presence of the discriminative stimulus of a particular taste is punished by a subsequent aversive reinforcer, illness.

Escape Training

In escape training, also known as negative reinforcement (not to be confused with the negative law of effect), an animal's response terminates an aversive reinforcer. Responses studied in escape include all those mentioned in the discussion of reward training; while loud noises and blasts of air have been used, electric shock is the aversive reinforcer most commonly employed. Shock intensity is an important determinant of the rate of acquisition and latency to perform the escape response. Carefully conducted investigations have revealed that the significant quantity is the percentage reduction in intensity produced by an escape response rather than the absolute reduction.

Avoidance

In avoidance training, a response prevents the occurrence of an otherwise scheduled aversive reinforcer.

The responses studied in avoidance include lever pressing, wheel running, wheel turning, one-way shuttling (in which the subject moves from one compartment to another, usually past an obstacle such as a hurdle), two-way shuttling (in which an animal leaves the compartment and reenters), jumping out (onto a "safety ledge"), panel pressing, and traversing a runway. The aversive reinforcer most frequently employed is electric shock.

Two theories treat avoidance responses as anticipatory escape responses. According to the S-R theory, avoidance responses are first learned as escape responses reinforced by shock offset in the presence of the CS. Eventually, the CS comes to elicit the response prior to the shock. Two serious problems for this theory are that avoidance can be learned with shocks too brief to be escaped, and avoidance can be learned when the required avoidance response is different from the required escape response. The Pavlovian or classical theory of avoidance as anticipatory responses claims that the signal is a CS for the US of shock, which in turn unconditionally evokes certain unconditioned responses. After several pairings of the CS and shock, the CS alone evokes the responses as anticipatory CRs, which just happen to meet the experimenter's requirement for an avoidance response.

The two-factor or two-process theory of avoidance asserts that instrumental learning and classical conditioning (the two processes or factors) are both involved in avoidance learning. The theory rests on three proposals:

1. The signal for shock and any interoceptive feedback stimuli generated by any response other than the avoidance response, by virtue of the fact that they are always followed by shock, become classically conditioned CSs for the CR of fear, a drive state unconditionally evoked by shock.
2. Termination of the signal for shock and any interoceptive stimuli generated by performance of the avoidance response, which are never followed by shock, become conditioned inhibitors (CSs) of fear.
3. The avoidance response is reinforced by a

reduction in fear resulting from the removal of the CSs for fear or the institution of CSs for fear.

According to expectancy theory:

1. The signal for shock and any interoceptive feedback stimuli generated by responses other than the proper avoidance response are aversive, because they are followed by shock.
2. Absence of the signal for shock and interoceptive stimuli generated by the performance of the avoidance response are less aversive, because they are not followed by shock.
3. Avoidance responses are reinforced by the transition from an aversive state to a less aversive state.

James P. Rodgers

Intellectual Abilities: Individual Differences

Alfred Binet's contemporary, Charles Spearman, measured the correlation between a test and an abstract, theoretical variable g, or general intelligence, for estimating the amount of "general intelligence" that a child possessed.

Spearman's successors have broadened his method to disclose dimensions narrower than general intelligence, yet broad enough to have utility for predicting talent in specialized areas. L. L. Thurstone formulates seven primary ability factors: verbal, number, spatial, memory, reasoning, word fluency, and perceptual speed. The most elaborate and comprehensive model of intellectual abilities is Guilford's "Structure of the Intellect," a tridimensional scheme of contents, operations, and products to provide a $4 \times 5 \times 6$ or 120 distinct factors, 82 of which are alleged to have been demonstrated.

David Wechsler (1969) has collated data on the range of human traits, both those measurable by physical scales, and those only quasi-quantifiable with respect to a reference group. The results in the two cases are surprisingly similar.

Individual differences in learning abilities imply corresponding differences in interests and in educational needs. Homogeneous grouping by ability or tracking has often been adopted in the schools as a means of coping with individual differences.

Read D. Tuddenham

Intelligence, Heredity, Race, and Environment

Heredity and Intelligence

One of the pioneers in this area was Francis Galton, who in 1869 published his epic study on genius. He studied the biographies of famous men and their families and concluded that greater-than-chance within-family prominence was due to heredity. Galton was the chief proponent of the eugenics or selective-breeding movement. At the other end of the intellectual scale are the studies of mental retardation by R. L. Dugdale (1877) on the Jukes family and H. H. Goddard (1912) on the Kallikaks. Dugdale's investigation showed that a many members of the Jukes clan were mental and moral degenerates, and this was attributed to heredity. Goddard studied about 500 descendants of Kallikak's family.

W. Shockley (1972) and A. R. Jensen (1972) are among the foremost supporters of the so-called genetic theory of intelligence. Their conclusions are based mostly on the analysis of data from 122 pairs of identical twins representing four studies from the United States, England, and Denmark, where the twins were separated at birth or shortly thereafter.

Environment and Intelligence

Laboratory experimentation with rats and other animals tends to support the hypothesis that a stimulating environment facilitates intelligence, while deprivation militates against proper intellectual development. M. R. Rosenzweig and D. Krech and their colleagues (1968) have shown that rats who were reared in superior environments had better developed brains and learned better than those rats who were reared in inferior or deprived atmospheres of stimulation. L. J. Yarrow et al. (1972) have found that infants benefit intellectually from the amount and kind of stimulation they receive from their mother.

Race and Intelligence

Few issues in psychology have stirred more controversy than that of the relationship between race and intelligence. Foremost at present is the question of difference between the so-called black and white races. There have been times, however, when for political, especially immigration, purposes, studies were reported on the various white groups alone. For example, Karl Pearson and M. Moul (1925) in England reported that Jews, who were migrating there, were innately inferior in intelligence. H. H. Goddard (1913), using his tests of mental ability, preceded Pearson by "scientifically" reporting the following high percentages of feeblemindedness among immigrants tested at Ellis Island: Russians 87%, Jews 83%, Hungarians 80%, and Italians 79%. Goddard believed these groups to be genetically inferior. Louis M. Terman (1916) claimed that "Indians, Mexicans and Negroes" were genetically inferior. Contemporary replication studies comparing Jews and non-Jews in intelligence as reviewed by Benjamin B. Wolman (1951) and reported in many other studies indicate Jews to be equal to and not superior to non-Jewish groups.

The Colorado Adoption Project, which started in 1975, reported some data in 1994 (DeFries et al. 1994), the Twin Study (Bouchard and Gropping 1993) and other recent studies stress the combined role of genetics and environment. However, there is no conclusive evidence either way.

Robert S. Morrow
Julian P. Morrow

Intelligence Tests: Developmental Changes

Infancy. There is very little relation between global measures of parental education and socioeconomic status (SES) and infant test performance, although some studies have reported relations between specific parental behaviors and general or specific aspects of test performance.

Childhood. In contrast to the infancy period, there is a moderate correlation (e.g., .25 to .50) between global indices of parental education or SES and childhood IQ. This rise from infancy to childhood coincides with the increase in cross-age correlation, heritability, and the predominance of verbal and symbolic test items. Developmentally, profiles that show increases in IQ through the childhood period are associated with higher levels of parental education, whereas essentially declining patterns are related to lower parental SES.

A developmental perspective suggests that the nature of the mental performance assessed by omnibus IQ tests changes markedly during the first 6 years, and that these differing skills are under the control of genetic and changing environmental factors. During the first year of life, infant tests basically represent an assessment of neuromotor behavior and sensorimotor alertness.

Data from the W. C. Fels longitudinal study, the Berkeley growth study, and a longitudinal study by I. C. Uzgiris (1976) blend with the theorizing of Jean Piaget to suggest several major qualitative transitions during the first 2 years of life in the very fabric of mental ability.

At approximately 8 months, the infant becomes capable of distinguishing means from ends—she discovers that her hand is different from the rattle, for example. This permits a more systematic exploration of the environment. By approximately 13 months, the infant comes to understand that objects are not only distinguishable from actions with them but exist independently of the infant and even carry their own dynamic properties.

At approximately 21 months, the infant begins to relate objects symbolically, such as understanding a locative proposition (e.g., put the block *on* the table). Now, two-word utterances are possible, as well as elementary creative thinking.

Robert B. McCall et al. (1973) attempt to discern groups of individuals from the Fels longitudinal study who display contrasting developmental patterns in IQ as reflected on seventeen Binet assessments between 2.5 and 17 years of age. Five patterns of IQ change over age are described.

Two major points emerge. First, although the cross-age stability of mental test performance is quite high after the first 2 years of life, substantial and meaningful changes in relative performance do occur during childhood. Individuals are not necessarily "locked into" a given IQ. Second, if we are to understand the development of mental functioning,

we must look at developmental changes in the very nature of mental behavior and acknowledge that growth functions for some specific abilities will be different than for other skills.

Robert B. McCall

Intelligence Theories

Two-Factor Theories

Charles Spearman (1904) proposed his two-factor theory of intelligence. The two factors consist of g (the general intelligence factor, which accounts for the positive intercorrelations among the tests) plus s (the specific factors for special abilities, such as number concepts, arithmetic reasoning, word knowledge, verbal reasoning, memory, and so on). These specific factors contribute in varying amounts to the global g factor. Those functions, such as vocabulary, that correlate highly with overall intelligence scores are regarded as being more saturated with g than the functions that have low correlations with general intelligence, such as sensory discrimination.

Three commonly used intelligence tests have been influenced by Spearman's two-factor theory. In the various scales developed by David Wechsler, the full scale IQ represents g as a general reasoning or educative factor, and the eleven subtests are the s_s. Verbal and performance IQs are the overlapping group factors. These clinical contentions are supported by factor-analytic studies on the various Wechsler scales.

Also, Raven's Progressive Matrices Test is constructed according to the Spearman concept that abstract reasoning in fitting the pattern correctly is the best measure of g. The s_s involve spatial aptitude, inductive reasoning, perceptual accuracy, and so on.

R. B. Cattell claims to have been influenced by Spearman's two-factor theory in the development of his Culture-Fair Intelligence Test. Actually, Cattell (1971) in his factor-analytic research has isolated two g's rather than one. These are identified as g_c and g_f. The g_c factor is labeled "crystallized general ability." While g_c is primarily verbal (i.e., vocabulary tests) and acquired by cultural experience, it also involves numerical skills, memory, and mechanical knowledge. Each of these represents a skill that has been acquired by educational and cultural experiences. The g_f factor represents fluid ability, which is more culture-free. It is involved in perceptual and performance tests dealing with spatial judgment and inductive reasoning, including matrices, analogies, and classifications.

Donald O. Hebb (1942) has developed a theory of intelligence along similar lines by structuring intelligence in terms of two levels or concepts, intelligence A and B. Intelligence A is the innate biological potential, and intelligence B is the later development of that intelligence by the environment, mostly to the stage or level where it can be observed and measured.

Multiple Factors Theories

L. L. Thurstone was one of the pioneers in the development of factor analysis. In using this technique to analyze tables of intercorrelations among various intelligence tests, he discovered many factors that caused him to disagree with Spearman's theory of a general intelligence factor. According to his theory, multiple group factors comprise intelligence rather than the general and specific factors.

J. P. Morrow (1941) applies multiple-factor analysis to the intercorrelations among a number of intelligence and aptitude tests. The factors that he obtains are interrelated rather than independent. P. E. Vernon (1965) proposes a hierarchical model with g at the top, followed by two broad group factors, which are identified as verbal-educational and practical-mechanical. These are further subdivided into so-called minor group factors, such as verbal, number, spatial, and manual. At the lowest level, the specific factors are enumerated.

J. P. Guilford (1967) has postulated still another psychometric structure of intelligence, which he develops from the technique of factor analysis. His structure of intellect model consists of a cube in which each of three interacting dimensions contains a number of functions. The operations dimension consists of five thinking processes or operations: evaluation, convergent thinking, divergent thinking, memory, and cognition.

Qualitative Analysis

In contrast to psychometric theories stands Jean Piaget's qualitative analysis of intelligence. As explained by H. Ginsburg and S. Opper (1969), his is a developmental approach that evaluates intelligence as a global construct through different stages or periods. It involves the interaction between biological adaptation and environmental adaptation and involves performance of the total organism with respect to its physical, cognitive, and emotional capacities.

Julian P. Morrow
Robert S. Morrow

Interests: Measurement Methods

The purpose of the interest inventory is to determine which occupations most closely match an individual's interests, by asking him about his preferences for a wide range of relatively specific activities, such as mending a clock, preparing written reports, and talking to groups of people. A fundamental assumption in the use of interest inventories is that people in different occupations have at least partially different interests. Otherwise, there would be no way in which interest tests could be used successfully to advise people to consider one occupation rather than another.

The Strong Vocational Interest Blank

One of the earliest and still most widely used measures of interests is the Vocational Interest Blank (VIB) by E. K. Strong. (Separate forms are available for men and women.) The VIB employs 400 questions, mostly about relatively specific activities. On most of the items the subject indicates his preferences by marking one of three categories: like, indifferent, and dislike. Some illustrative items from the men's form are as follows:

Buying merchandise for a store	L	I	D
Adjusting a carburetor	L	I	D
Interviewing people for a job	L	I	D

The Kuder Preference Record

The Kuder Preference Record and the Strong VIB are the two most widely used interest inventories. The two inventories present an interesting contrast in procedures of test development. Instead of using the VIB "like/indifferent/dislike" response categories, the Kuder inventory presents items in triads. The subject picks from three activities the one that he likes most and the one that he likes least. Two illustrative item triads are as follows:

Visit an art gallery	_____
Browse in a library	_____
Visit a museum	_____
Collect autographs	_____
Collect coins	_____
Collect butterflies	_____

Uses of Interest Inventories

In vocational guidance, interest inventories are used for two related purposes: to predict satisfaction in the work and to predict successful performance. The criterion keying on the Strong inventory provides some supporting evidence that interest tests can predict future satisfaction on the job. Another type of evidence is that follow-up studies of individuals who completed the VIB in college show a strong tendency for people to enter occupations related to their expressed interests. Both these pieces of evidence also tend to support the hypothesis that interests are predictive, at least to some extent, of job performance.

Jum C. Nunnally

Interests and Interest Testing

The latest form of the Strong interest measure, the Strong-Campbell Interest Inventory (SCII), attempts to provide an all-purpose measure useful in a variety of situations with both men and women. The development of one form appropriate for both sexes reflects the current pressure for breaking down sex discrimination in career planning.

The Minnesota Vocational Interest Inventory by K. E. Clark is designed to measure interests in occu-

pations below the college level. It thus complements the Strong.

The Ohio Vocational Interest Survey (OVIS) is organized around the classification of occupations of the Department of Labor's *Dictionary of Occupational Titles*. It is designed for use at the secondary level and relates the individual's career interests to the world of work.

The Work and Values Inventory, developed by D. E. Super, deals not with specific interests but with the characteristics that people consider important in their work. The person taking the test rates the importance of work in which "you help others," "you create something new," "you make your own decisions," and so on. The responses are scored in terms of the relative importance of fifteen work values, such as independence, prestige, security, and associates.

Albert S. Thompson

Intergroup Relations

J. Harding, H. M. Proshansky, B. Kutner, and I. Chein (1969) state that the most prevalent usage "applies the term 'intergroup behavior' to the behavior of a person toward some member or members of an ethnic group other than his or her own, *whether or not this behavior is influenced by the person's ethnic attitudes*" (6).

Major contributions to the theory have come from Sherif (1967), who concludes that, contrary to the psychodynamic theory of prejudice, it is not the deviant member but the relatively better-adjusted majority who is more likely to exhibit hostility toward outgroups.

In a comprehensive review of the topic, J. M. LeVine and D. T. Campbell (1972) attempt to integrate major theoretical work and supporting data from all of the social science disciplines under the following headings: realistic group-conflict theory, social-structural theories of conflict in anthropology, reference group theory, theories of psychoanalytic origin, perceptual theories, cognitive-congruity theories, and transfer and reinforcement theory.

Marguerite F. Levy

International Relations and Psychiatry

As Henry Kissinger has noted, we live in a world of military bipolarity but political multipolarity. In the absence of some internationally agreed-upon concept of order, it is potentially possible for a conflict between two small, even insignificant nations to begin a chain of events that could end with the destruction of civilization as we know it. The growing sensitivity to and awareness of this destructive potential has given a spirit of urgency to the efforts of psychiatrists to influence international relations.

In 1932, in response to Albert Einstein's request that the knowledge of the human mind developed by psychoanalysis be applied to finding a means to eliminate war, Sigmund Freud replied that, while civilization had to some extent tamed man's instincts, it was unrealistic to expect that man was ready to renounce his instincts in favor of reason.

In 1935, a group of 339 psychiatrists from 30 countries signed a declaration, which became known as the Netherlands Manifesto, which claimed that psychiatry was "sufficiently advanced" as a science to understand militarism and appealed to national leaders around the world to "understand their own attitude toward war. By self-knowledge a world calamity may be prevented." While officials of nineteen nations replied to the manifesto, psychiatric insights did not forestall World War II.

On the initiative of Benjamin B. Wolman, in 1970 a group of psychiatrists, psychologists, and other behavioral scientists formed the International Organization for the Study of Group Tensions (IOSGT).

The greatest challenge that faces a psychiatry of foreign relations, therefore, is that of helping the national leaders on both sides to change, to relinquish their defensiveness, and to increase their receptivity to searches for new approaches.

Norman Rosenzweig

Interoceptive Conditioning

Interoceptive conditioning is a form of classical conditioning in which the conditioned stimulus (CS) or unconditioned stimulus (US) is inside the body. The following example, described by Gregory Razran (1961), is illustrative. An intestinal loop was brought to the outside of the body of a dog and sutured there. The exposed segment of intestine was brushed with a feather (CS), and this was followed by the administration of shock (US). The dog developed a pronounced cardiac conditioned response (CR) to stimulation of the intestine. One test for the effectiveness of the conditioning procedure was of particular interest. The dog was fed, and when the food reached the section of intestine involved in the conditioning experiment, the cardiac response occurred. The significance of this demonstration is that it shows a possible mechanism for the development of disturbances internal to the body of a type that might be involved in behavioral disorder.

Gregory A. Kimble

Interpersonal Behavior

Personality theorists have long concerned themselves with identifying the motivational factors in an individual's behavior. Henry A. Murray (1938) developed a list of twenty manifest needs, fifteen of which were then incorporated in the Edwards Personal Preference Schedule (1959) to provide a research instrument that has gained wide usage. Neopsychoanalytic theorists—for example, Benjamin B. Wolman (1974)—developed the power and acceptance theory, related to the ability to satisfy needs (power) and the willingness to do so (acceptance). Other neoanalysts (Karen Horney, Erich Fromm) have focused on psychological processes that are basically interpersonal in origin or expression. Harry Stack Sullivan (1953) advanced a theory of interpersonal relationships and social communication, while orthodox Freudians have sought to conceptualize the development of "object" relationships.

D. P. Schutz's fundamental interpersonal relations orientation (FIRO) theory claims that the interpersonal need areas of inclusion, control, and affection represent the prime determiners of interpersonal behavior. How people wish to be responded to, and how they respond to others, in each of these three need areas constitutes the basis for an understanding of the interpersonal behavior that develops. His theory is intimately related to a measuring instrument, the FIRO-B, which is a Guttman-scaled questionnaire that is constructed to yield two measures, expressed behavior and behavior wanted from others, in regard to each of the need areas of inclusion, control, and affection.

Fritz Heider (1958) placed major emphasis on humans' constant need to predict the world around them. Thus, making predictions about other people becomes a crucial ingredient in the development of interpersonal relationships.

Allan Sapolsky

Interpretive Process in Psychoanalysis

An overview of the development of interpretation (and its changing function) as a conceptual and therapeutic tool can best be highlighted in relationship to resistance, transference, and reconstruction.

Resistance. Once the importance of the resistances was discovered, Sigmund Freud's attention was almost exclusively drawn to this aspect of the treatment. The "removal" of resistances by systematic interpretations contrasted with the effect that could be achieved either by avoiding or circumventing them with hypnotic suggestions. Remembering and abreacting with the help of hypnosis receded into the background, and instead the analyst began to study whatever presented itself in the patient's free associations.

Transference. A microscopic analysis of the interpretive process related to transference affects is most convincingly described by James Strachey (1934). In his close attention to the technique of transference interpretation, Strachey puts particular emphasis on the economic aspects of interpretations and on the economic aspects of structural change.

Reconstruction. The reconstruction of genetically significant childhood memories gives psychoanalytic treatment its unique dimension. The fate of the childhood memories and their reconstruction in the analysis is best understood from a developmental point of view; early childhood memories become distorted by later life experiences and are given additional meaning.

With the widening scope of psychoanalysis, suitability for analysis was extended to patients with pregenital and narcissistic psychopathology, and along with this extension the process of interpretation also acquired new dimensions. It was primarily, but not exclusively, in relation to these extensions of psychoanalysis that the issue of deliberately noninterpretive interventions, or nonverbal interventions, was considered, by some, as a technical necessity.

Clinical and Theoretical Advances Affecting Interpretations

The view of narcissism as a developmental driving force, rather than merely as a pathological fixation upon early development phases, led H. Kohut (1971) to the recognition of two specific forms of narcissistic transference: the mirror transference and the idealizing transference. Both are revivals of the earliest cohesive infantile narcissistic constellations, just as the classical transference neurosis is a revival of the infantile oedipal constellation.

Empirical data derived from the analyses of narcissistic transferences led Kohut to a crucial theoretical step: the assumption that narcissism has a developmental line of its own, largely separate from that of object love, thus permitting the analysis of narcissistic transferences in their own right, as direct expressions of the core psychopathology and not merely as defensive precursors of the oedipal transference neurosis.

The Concept of the Interpretive Process

The concept of interpretation has always been inextricably interwoven with the theory of psychopathology and the theory of cure. Interpretation (in its technical sense) refers to the details of understanding and explaining the patient's experiences during the analytic process (including, of course, the genetic meaning of those experiences) and to the verbal communication of such understanding and explaining for the various phase-specific purposes of the analysis.

L. Macalpine (1950) stresses those elements in the psychoanalytic situation that induce regression and trigger the development of transference. The analyst's personality and her attitudes, manner of relating, and countertransferences will all be part of the analytic situation in relation to which the transference becomes crystallized.

With the widening scope of indications for psychoanalysis, interpretation in general, and mutative interpretation (Strachey 1934) in particular seemed to account less satisfactorily for all of the analyst's complex and multilayered contributions to the psychoanalytic process.

A tentative working definition of the interpretive process can now be offered (Ornstein and Ornstein 1975): interpretation should be viewed as a process evolving over time, with a changing function, responsive to the dynamic shifts in the analytic process. "To give interpretations" is to offer (unconscious or preconscious) meanings or a sequence of connected (unconscious or preconscious) meanings to the patient's experiences in the analysis. However, these meanings will cumulatively, rather than individually, enhance the achievement of insight, recollection, working through, and transmuting internalization, in whatever mode they are communicated. Thus, all of the analyst's communications are part of the interpretive process.

Anna Ornstein
Paul H. Ornstein

Interstimulus Interval Function

This term refers to the function relating level of conditioning to the time separating conditioned stimulus (CS) and unconditioned stimulus (US) in classical conditioning. If the CS precedes the US, the arrangement is called forward conditioning, and the time values involved are assigned positive numbers. If the CS follows the US, the arrangement is called backward conditioning, and the time values are assigned negative numbers.

It has begun to seem clear that the interstimulus interval function is actually less general than at first supposed. The basis for such a conclusion is that we now know that the GSR and certain responses to poison and irradiation can be conditioned at very long intervals. Apparently, the explanation for the

early data showing that the GSR was most easily conditioned at a shorter interval was that the actual conditioned response (CR) in these experiments was not the GSR but some skeletal response that mediated the autonomic reaction.

Gregory A. Kimble

Isolation and Confinement

Sensory Deprivation

In addition to in situ studies of natural settings, extensive laboratory research has also been undertaken with a view to identifying more precisely the relevant variables and their effects in an isolation and/or confinement situation. Laboratory studies have been addressed to so-called sensory and perceptual deprivation, and to small groups in isolation and confinement. Generalizations have often been difficult to establish due to the wide variety of field and laboratory settings examined, the different lengths of time involved (ranging from a few minutes in some studies of extreme sensory deprivation up to many months in some field settings), the wide variety of variables examined in the research, and great diversity in research methodologies and measurement techniques used to conduct the research.

Hallucinatory phenomena have been reported in numerous other studies, with more recent literature avoiding the "hallucination" label and substituting for it the phrase "reported visual sensations" (RVS). M. Zuckerman and G. Cohen have proposed a classification of RVS into two categories: A for flashes of light, dots, and geometric forms; and B for meaningful objects, people, scenes, and so on.

Subjective Experiences

In addition to reported visual sensations, individuals in conditions of stimulus and/or perceptual deprivation often report other unusual subjective experiences, including an inability to concentrate, a heightened sense of fear and anxiety with no apparent external reference, changes in body image, boredom, a sense of irreality, and positive contemplation (for some individuals). A number of factor analyses of an isolation-symptomology questionnaire developed by P. G. Myers and others have yielded three independent factors: irreality stress, fear and anxiety, and positive contemplations. Perceptual deprivation, according to J. P. Zubek (1969), results in greater impairment of cognitive functioning than does sensory deprivation, with the former generating significant impairment on arithmetic problems, numerical reasoning, verbal fluency, space visualization, abstract reasoning, and recognition tests.

Physiological Factors

Early research at McGill University on the electrical activity of the brain during isolation found a progressive slowing of mean alpha wave frequency with increasing duration of isolation. This result has been confirmed in other laboratories and occurs whether subjects are in conditions of extreme perceptual deprivation or under less extreme conditions, such as those of two or three men confined together for up to 3 weeks.

Interpersonal Behavior

In addition to these intraindividual phenomena (perceptual experiences, emotional reactions, physiological changes), a considerable amount of research has also been addressed to behavioral changes in isolation, and in the case of groups, to changes in interpersonal behavior. Circadian rhythm has been found to change after several days.

Extensive laboratory studies of small groups (two to three men) in soundproof, lightproof rooms for varying periods of time have been conducted at the Naval Medical Research Institute in Bethesda, Maryland. These studies have consistently found subjective reports of emotional experiences similar to, although generally less intense than, those reported by subjects in sensory or perceptual deprivation conditions. Reports of visual sensations are rare in group settings.

Observation of individuals in natural isolated settings, such as Antarctic weather stations, Sealabs, and isolated farms in Noway, suggests that the effects reported in sensory and perceptual deprivation experiments and laboratory group studies are also detectable in these larger group settings with greater stimulus variety, but diminishing in degree or intensity as the group/environment context increases in social and environmental complexity, variety, and change.

William W. Haythorn

· J ·

James, William (1842–1910)

William James's psychological theory is known as the James-Lange theory of emotion, because C. Lange formulated a similar theory at about the same time, in 1884. James was twice president of the American Psychological Association, and his two-volume *Principles of Psychology* (1890) was an enormously influential work.

Thomas C. Cadwallader

Janet, Pierre (1859–1947)

Pierre Janet introduced the concept of the unconscious independently of Sigmund Freud. Janet defined neuroses as a type of mental disorder that included phobias and anxieties. He maintained that hysteria is psychogenic and an outcome of suggestion; and advocated hypnosis as the chief method of treatment for mental disorders.

Benjamin B. Wolman

Jaspers, Karl (1883–1969)

In 1913, Karl Jaspers published his work on psychopathology, where he emphasized humanism, existentialism, and understanding rather than causation.

Leo H. Berman

Job Analysis

There are three basic approaches to job analysis—observation, consultation, and performance—each of which can be further subdivided. The observation techniques consist of having the job analyst (this term will be used to identify anyone carrying out a job analysis) observe a sample of workers through several cycles of the job.

In industrial behavioral science, the consultation techniques are basic. These procedures, which for the purposes of this discussion will be subdivided into the interview and the questionnaire approaches, seek information by consultation with job incumbents and/or job supervisors.

Interview approach. Interviews for gathering job information may be carried out either with individuals or groups; use of groups is somewhat more typical and probably preferable in order to reduce the risk of distortion. One common approach is to use a committee of incumbents and supervisors to discuss and write the job description, which is then circulated among members of the larger group for additions and amendments.

Questionnaire approach. Perhaps the most widely used example of this approach is the "Position Analysis Questionnaire" developed by McCormick and his coworkers (PAQ, form B). This tool consists of 194 "job elements" or task statements of several types: information input, mental processes, work output, relations with other persons, and job context.

Performance approach. Under some unusual but only occasional circumstances, it may make sense to have the job analyst work on the job under study in order to carry out an analysis of that job. This is not a procedure for common use because it is time-consuming and costly.

Given information about the context of the job, a logical next step is to inquire about what characteristics of the worker are needed for them to perform that job. This is the process typically referred to as "job specification," or more accurately and simply, establishing job or worker requirements. The purpose is to identify characteristics of job incumbents that will differentiate between good and poor performance.

Arthur C. MacKinney

Jones, Ernest (1879–1958)

English psychoanalyst Ernest Jones wrote a three-volume biography of Freud (1953, 1955a, 1955b) and several other books and papers on psycho-analysis.

Robert L. Tyson

Jung, Carl Gustav (1875–1961)

Carl Jung was born in Basel, Switzerland, in 1875, and he received his M.D. degree from the University of Basel in 1902. He worked at the Burghölzli Hospital under Eugen Bleuler from 1900 to 1907. It was there that Jung developed his word-association technique to discover unconscious groups of autonomous wishes and ideas, which he called complexes. Jung's reputation was established with the publication of a book in 1906, *The Psychology of Dementia Praecox*.

Jung's relationship with Sigmund Freud started in 1907, when Jung and his wife traveled to Vienna for a visit with Freud and his family. Freud and Jung became closely associated and maintained active communication by mail. The first evidence of a rift came on the trip to Clark University in 1909. After the visit to the United States, Freud and Jung seldom met socially, although they still communicated by mail. In 1912 Jung published *The Psychology of the Unconscious*, later renamed *Symbols of Transformation*. This book presented a written statement of points on which Jung's opinion differed from Freud's, and was a catalyst in the slowly developing disagreement between the two men. In Munich, the real differences were brought to the surface. In 1913, at the first meeting of the International Psycho-Analytic Association, the break between Jung and Freud was evident. This was the last time the two men ever met.

From 1913 to 1917, Jung went through a period of deep and intensive self-analysis; he was no longer "Freudian," and he had to establish what he did believe. His thinking during this period led to his own full theory of analytic psychology. Two important papers written during this wartime period illustrate the direction of Jung's psychology. In "On the Importance of the Unconscious in Psychology" he emphasizes his concept of a balance between the virtues and defects of the conscious and unconscious. "The Transcendent Function," written in 1916 but not published until 1917, tells of a method, "active imagination," designed to reach the unconscious. "New Paths in Psychology," written in 1912, is the earliest statement of the collective psyche, the psychological types, and the "pairs of opposites." Jung's work *Psychological Types* is the culmination of his theoretical development. In it he puts forth his classification of healthy personalities—the introverts and the extroverts; he also speaks of the four functions—thinking, feeling, sensing, and intuition.

Jung spent his later years pursuing a variety of interests. His theory of collective unconscious led him into an anthropological study of peoples of Africa and of the Navajo Indians of America. He became interested in mythology and religion. An illustration of the diverse fields of thought in which Jung lingered is the difference in topics of two of his later books. *Aion* (1950) puts forth reflections of unusual psychological phenomena and discusses the archetypal history of the mind in the Christian aeon. *Psychology and Alchemy* draws an analogy between the two fields of study mentioned in the title.

Vytautas J. Bieliauskas

Jungian School: Analytic Theory

Jung's theoretical system, which (together with his writings on therapy) he termed "analytical psychology," involves a description of the structure and dynamics of the psyche, defined as the totality of all mental (as opposed to physical) processes, both conscious and unconscious. Jung based his work on the central idea of the ontological reality of the psyche. This concept holds that the psyche exists as an objective fact, and therefore can be studied scientifically. In Jung's view, a religious idea is as "real" as, say, a sexual fantasy. His position is that the error of biological determinism is (in this instance) to attach a greater reality to a sexual fantasy than to a religious idea, when from the viewpoint of the psyche both have equal reality. The idea that the psyche is more than a mere epiphenomenon of the neurobiological processes of the central nervous system must be clearly understood in order to give full significance to Jungian thought.

Jungian psychological science is phenomenological. Its raw data are subjective experiential reports, objectifiable in the sense that they consist of describable and repeatable themes found in the artistic rendering of images and in the telling of stories and myths as recorded in anthropological and historical reports, as well as in individual descriptions of dreams and other productions of fantasy and subjectively colored life experience.

The science that emerges is a thematic exploration of similarities among the diverse kinds of data mentioned above, and is more like the descriptive science of Carolus Linnaeus or Charles Darwin, or like the recent speculations of theoretical physics, than it is like the measurement-oriented sciences of Newtonian physics or of experimental psychology. Jung collated his data into thematic categories, and his theoretical system is formed from a series of inferences about the structure of a psyche that could produce such data.

To the extent that phenomenological data are generalizable from individual to individual, from culture to culture, and from historical epoch to historical epoch, Jung inferred the existence of a collective human psyche, which appears to underlie individual psychology and which has both conscious and unconscious components. Jung focused most of his attention on that aspect of the collective psyche that he called the "collective unconscious." He likened the collective psyche to the rhizome of a plant, which remains below ground and sends shoots to the surface. From above ground the shoots appear to be individual plants, but in actuality they are individual aspects of a larger plant, most of

which lives underground. Similarly, individual psyches are rooted in collective or "rhizomal" unconscious elements.

Identifiable similarities among his diverse data led Jung to the inference that the collective psyche is composed of archaic thematic elements, which he called "archetypes." These phenomena, much like atomic particles, are never directly seen. Jung likened the archetype to the capacity of supersaturated solutions to produce crystals, prior to actual crystal formation. What is seen are archetypal images, which are analogous to the appearance of the crystal once it is formed, while the archetype itself is analogous only to the original solution's capacity, as opposed to the manifestation of that capacity (i.e., crystal formation). Archetypal images present themselves as symbols produced in dream, fantasy, myth, and artistic production.

The spontaneous production of archetypal symbols reveals a purposive or teleological dynamic of the psyche. The symbol brings into consciousness something from the unconscious psyche, which is as yet not fully known. *Symbol* may be defined as a fantasy production in the form of image or idea—rich in meaning but both open-ended and directional—which is referencing an area of experience that is still emerging or evolving out of the unconscious into consciousness. *Symbol* does not stand for a specific thing that is already known—Jung used the term *sign* to designate an image or idea that stands for a known entity.

Jung called the process of symbol formation by the psyche the "transcendent function." The term *transcendent* denotes a transition from one state of consciousness to another, not a metaphysical quality. For Jung, the psyche as a totality is constantly evolving or emerging from indeterminate archetypal roots.

A sense of the meaning and context of Jungian ideas can be maintained if it is remembered (1) that each structural concept is archetypally based, and (2) that each corresponds to a universal characteristic of human experience, although a particular form of the experience may be individual and idiosyncratic.

Jung pointed out that the psyche possesses the qualities of polarity and enantiodromia. *Polarity* indicates that human life is experienced dualistically or in terms of opposites, while the Greek term *enantiodromia* adds that anything that is experienced in extreme form will inevitably turn into its opposite, through activation of its (polarized) unconscious component. Consequently, dream process, arising as it does from the unconscious, is often compensatory to a strongly held attitude of consciousness.

Polarity dictates that many of the archetypes will be described in dualistic terms. The archetype *anima/animus* (soul) underpins the androgynous nature of the psyche, and refers to much of the feminine element in a man's psyche (anima), and to the masculine element in a woman's psyche (animus). "Soul" is used because Jung observed that the contrasexual element often appears in dream or fantasy as a guide to deeply unconscious experience.

This "regression to the archetype" is accompanied by a quality of affect that Jung called "numinosity," a feeling described as awesome, mysterious, magical, or religious/spiritual, and often imbued with a powerful quality of meaning. Numinosity accompanies the regression of consciousness to a reconnection with archetypal elements. When an archetype is activated in dream and fantasy, the phantasmagoric images are often "larger than life," accompanied by numinous affect. The concept of numinosity is Jung's contribution to the theory and description of human affect.

Regression to the archetype, usually triggered by intense psychic conflict (duality), marks the first stage of the transcendent function. This function is completed when the archetype thus activated produces a new "living symbol," charged with numinous energy. If accepted by the ego as an internal and highly personal experience (rather than being externalized), a new attitude of consciousness is created. The archetype of the self, which Jung felt to be the central organizing principle of the psyche, provides the motive power for symbol formation.

Father/mother and *puer/puella* mark additional archetypal elements involved with human androgyny. Undifferentiation from the parental image is a major characteristic of neurotic persons. Such individuals often identify with the *puer/puella*, which fixates both conscious and unconscious experience and behavior at the level of "the eternal child," leaving the contrasexual component unavailable for participation in full adult development.

The *puer/puella* polarizes against the *senex* archetype—that is, the energy or naïveté of youth, as opposed to the wisdom or constriction of old age. This exemplifies that any archetypal element can be constellated (given form or image by experience) in either positive (functional) or negative (dysfunctional) ways.

Jung described the ego as the center of consciousness, which arises from the capacity of the ego to make discriminations. Once consciousness is established, the problem of the opposites (duality and conflict) must be dealt with. The ego is the center of the conscious personality, of subjective identity or "I." It has the capacity to observe the psyche, but because of its conservative nature it tends to resist new material rising from the unconscious.

Jung developed a psychological typology, which both differentiates among individual styles of ego function and provides a modus operandi through which such functions take place. The "attitudes" have to do with the flow of psychic energy (libido). Extroversion involves energy flow from ego toward external objects. Introversion involves energy flow from ego toward internal objects (the archetypal images that bring substantiality to the inner psyche). The ego is also at the center of four "functions" that have to do with apprehension. Sensation tells one that something exists. Thinking establishes what something is, what it is called. Feeling apprehends the value of something, and intuition determines the possibilities inherent in something.

The ego faces the inevitability of its own dissolution in death, and from a developmental viewpoint must give over its connection with individual identity to the larger and deeper self-archetype, which Jung called the archetype of "wholeness," co-identical with the larger psyche and source of the driving force of psychic evolution and change. The self is the ordering and unifying center of the total psyche, and individuation or self-realization is the process of moving from limited ego identity to idiosyncratic self-identity during the course of personal development. It involves a reuniting of the opposites, to which Jung gave the alchemically related name *coniunctio oppositorum*. Jung's studies of medieval alchemy were based on his view that alchemical writings were actually psychological treatises involved with a symbolic tracing of the individuation process.

The ego is closely connected with the persona, the mask that the individual wears before the world; the social roles played. It is also connected with the shadow, which consists of the "personal unconscious," those elements of personal experience and awareness that are unacceptable to ego-consciousness and, therefore, repressed. The trickster archetype is a creative aspect of the shadow, reminding ego-consciousness of its own limitations.

Jung held that the psyche follows its own laws, rather than the Newtonian laws of space, time, and causality. His principle of synchronicity holds that psychic events are not connected causally, as are events in the physical universe, but rather by "meaningful coincidence." The principle of synchronicity allows for extrasensory events and so-called psi phenomena, but also for simple meaningful psychic occurrences in everyday life, which often cannot be repeated or shared with others.

The concept of complexes, introduced by Jung during his early studies of word association, introduces his theory of psychological pathology. A complex is a cluster of closely associated ideas, images, affects, and behaviors, interconnected by a central archetypally based theme. Thus the ego itself is a complex, not necessarily pathological. On the other hand, a "mother complex" indicates that the individual remains tied to those aspects of the mother archetype that were constellated (given form) by her own mother, as well as fascinated by those aspects of the mother archetype that remain unconstellated and, therefore, appear in dream and fantasy as highly charged archetypal images.

Elaboration and additional development of the theoretical system by Jungian writers was already under way prior to Jung's death in 1961, and has continued at a more rapid pace in recent years. Brief space does not allow acknowledgment of many seminal contributions, but a few especially noteworthy examples can be included. Eric Neumann's classic work (1954) details the course of the archetypally driven development of the collective psyche, and

finds the recapitulation of that development in the psychic development of each individual. Michael Fordham (1970), greatly influenced by the work of Melanie Klein, Donald W. Winnicott, and related non-Jungian writers, has tied Jungian archetypal theory to contemporary theories of child development and mother-child interaction. James Hillman (1975) has amplified Jung's psychological definitions of "soul" into a vision of "soul making" as the central dynamic of the development of consciousness. Nathan Schwartz-Salant (1989) has developed theoretical concepts that allow some resolution of the split between physical and spiritual (psychic) reality. This sets the stage for a review of the nature and dynamics of healing during the therapeutic encounter.

Crittenden E. Brookes

Jungian School: Therapy

Carl Jung did not outline a precise model for psychotherapy or analysis. This would have been inconsistent with his open-ended view of the psyche. However, his numerous remarks on the process of therapy provide a series of coherent themes. These themes elaborate and give further definition to Jung's theoretical work.

Some knowledge of the Jungian conceptual system is necessary for an understanding of the therapeutic approach.

Views of the nature of therapy derive from what the therapist looks for and attends to. Jungian therapists, like most therapists, are alert to such phenomena as transference and countertransference, quality of and fluctuation in ego strength, defensive operations and style, nature and origin of conflicts, insight potential, and response to intervention. However, Jung contributed some unique elements to the therapeutic repertory:

1. Jung's respect for both the power and the creative potential of the unconscious made him particularly sensitive to the relationship between the unconscious and the ego. If the ego protects itself too well from unconscious

activity, the enrichment that the larger psyche brings to consciousness is lost, and a rigid, barren, and uncreative life ensues. Character disorder provides a major example of this phenomenon. On the other hand, if the ego becomes overly fascinated with the inner world, inflation and even inundation of the ego are possible. This encompasses not only the possibility of psychosis, but also the recently discovered borderline and narcissistic disorders.

2. The concept of androgyny, which is central to Jungian thinking, alerts therapist and patient to the nature of the patient's relationship with his or her contrasexual psyche. In our present culture, with its rigid definitions of masculine and feminine roles, much psychological pathology stems from polarization and denial of opposite-sex characteristics. The current prevalence of homophobia in our culture provides a case in point. Jung found it helpful to have patients either simultaneously or serially work with both male and female analysts, as a way of activating contrasexual elements of the psyche during therapy.

3. Jung was perhaps more interested in what those who consulted him found meaningful in life than he was in their neurotic and self-protective behavior. His attention to the numinous aspects of human experience inspires therapists to evaluate their clients' potential for creativity and change, and to honor manifestations of such potential during the course of therapy.

4. Jung saw death as a natural aspect of life itself. The problem that death poses for the individual is a function of the degree to which the individual is able to move from limited ego identity to the larger identity that Jung called "self." For Jungian therapists, many late-life neuroses stem from the inability to move beyond a rigid identity, and the therapy of such difficulties is inevitably involved with establishing connection between ego-consciousness and the deeper aspects of the self.

Jung's elaboration of the nature of therapy necessarily constructs an "ideal" picture of the therapeutic process. Jung himself was more than respectful of the psyche, and as it were of the "right" of the patient to have a less-than-complete experience of her analysis or therapy. Another way of saying this is that there are times when resistances should be respected. Therefore, it should be acknowledged that few if any patients go through all of the kinds of experiences to be discussed.

A requirement of individual development is that ego-consciousness must separate itself from the collective psyche. Failures of such separation can become nodal points for mental pathology early in life, just as failure to give the ego over to a larger identity can produce pathology in later life. It follows that neurosis (used in a generic sense) derives from a dysfunctional attitude of the ego, and that such an attitude often involves an overidentification of the ego with some archetypal element, with its associated images, affects, and behaviors. This is the central idea of Jung's theory of pathological complexes. In this view, the oedipal complex is only one of many possible complexes. When activated, each complex functions autonomously, almost as if it were a "separate personality" within the psyche. The attention of the ego is captured by the complex, and creative adaptation is no longer possible. The task of separating ego-consciousness from the complex is a central aspect of Jungian therapy.

Because human neurosis is psychogenic (that is, derived from processes of the psyche), it is an illness of the entire personality. Diagnosis is somewhat irrelevant, except for a broad distinction among psychosis, neurosis (Jung would probably include the borderline and narcissistic conditions), and possibly character disorder. A specific diagnosis may lead to therapy by application of technique, which to Jung is antithetical to the proper treatment of psychogenic conditions.

The primary tool of the therapy of the psychogenic neuroses is the whole personality of the doctor, as it interacts with the whole personality of the patient. A dialectical procedure is necessary, which results in a transformation of the personalities of both parties. The cure is defined by the acquisition of new meaning by the patient, and for that matter by the doctor also. This involves a shift in the originally dysfunctional attitude of the ego, as it views the inner and outer psychic worlds.

The process of therapy or analysis proceeds with doctor and patient face to face, in relational mode. Jung acknowledged the value of a regressive couch analysis, but saw it as, at best, a preparation for further prospectively oriented dialectic work with the psyche. His outline of the process of analysis includes the following stages: (1) confession or catharsis, (2) elucidation or interpretation, both of the transference and of the infantile psyche, (3) education to new ways of adaptation, and (4) transformation or individuation, in which the patient discovers and develops his or her own unique pattern of being-in-the-world. Jung also referred to the latter stages of analysis as "education as a social being."

An educative approach is central to therapy because individuals must often be "reeducated" to an awareness of the unique reality of their own psychic processes, while at the same time learning to "impersonalize" archetypal experience. The distance between ego-consciousness and the Scylla and Charybdis of inner and outer worlds is distorted in one direction or another in the neuroses, and learning the proper ego-distance from each often requires a process of intense education. This education is provided by the relational dialectic of the therapy process.

During such a process, the patient has the opportunity to learn the deeper meaning of his inner androgyny and to reconnect with the spiritual dimension of the psyche, finding in that reconnection an attitude that provides a correction for the entrapment of ego-consciousness by specific complexes. Spiritual connection—defined by Jung as an activation of the numinous, archetypal layer of the psyche—produces new symbols that are experienced by the patient in dream and fantasy, then applied to daily experience and behavior. In Jungian terms, a full analysis reactivates the transcendent function of the psyche through the production of new symbols and the consequent resolution of dualism and conflict.

Although the relationship between analyst and patient must be maintained on a level of mutual reality, transference and countertransference elements are necessarily present in the process and must be attended to. The patient transfers onto the analyst not only the infantile conflicts that are as yet unresolved (transference neurosis) but also the unrealized aspects of the psyche (unconstellated archetypal elements). These transferential (and countertransferential) events are dealt with in the context of the "symbolic friendship" that develops between analyst and analysand. In both its inner and outer aspects, the analysis approximates the coming together of the opposites—Jung's *mysterium coniunctionis*.

Jung saw fixed methods or "techniques" in therapy as dysfunctional. However, certain quasi-technical considerations are particularly applicable to Jungian therapy:

1. The interpretive stance tends to be synthetic-hermeneutic and prospective rather than analytic-reductive. The movement of libido or psychic energy in the former is in the direction of growth and development, whereas the movement of libido in the latter is toward fixation on infantile reminiscences.

2. The analyst often takes part in an elaboration of the material brought to therapy by the patient. At the same time, the analyst often encourages active imagination on the patient's part as one aspect of the elaboration of material. This "telling a story" around specific events is much like the elaborative process of projective testing, but is itself therapeutic rather than merely diagnostic. Sand play (Kalff 1971) is a technical application of active imagination to the clinical setting.

3. Work with dreams may be a major aspect of Jungian therapy, if access to such material is available. The dream is approached mutually by analyst and patient through a process of amplification of the dream material. As symbolic productions, dreams are metaphoric in nature, and bringing such metaphors to consciousness further activates the production of unconscious material. Synchronistic phenomena are often revealed by the interaction of dream and outer event, and recognition of

them aids in establishing a new ego attitude. Jung's view of the meaning of dreams is quite broad, and includes his own concept of compensation for distorted attitudes of consciousness, as well as Freud's wish fulfillment. More generally, dreams are seen as "the final common pathway" for all processes of the psyche, both known and unknown. The central idea is that dreams have meaning, and that they can add to conscious knowledge. They should be interpreted in the context of the patient's life as a whole. With each new dream, theoretical dream formulations should be abandoned, to allow viewing each dream image as a new and idiosyncratic production of the psyche.

4. Jungian typology may be useful in the interpretive and elaborative aspects of analytic work, especially in cases of low self-esteem, as well as with marital and relationship difficulties.

A few points on Jung's view of the training of the analyst should be mentioned. Jung was the first to insist that each analyst-in-training undergo a personal analysis. In addition, he was concerned that the technical education of the physician often left her unprepared to deal with the broad ramifications of the psyche. Jung favored training the therapist in the humanities rather than excessive technological and scientific training. On the other hand, he was precise in stating that the lay analyst should always work in conjunction with a physician, whom he felt was better qualified to identify and deal with problems of incipient psychosis.

Since Jung, Jungian views on the therapeutic process have developed into a number of identifiable viewpoints, which in turn derive from the theoretical orientations of the analysts who hold them. S. Samuels (1985) divides the post-Jungians into three groups, each with a particular theoretical orientation and a particular emphasis for therapy. The classical group (Matoon 1992) most closely approximates Jung's theory and views on therapy as previously outlined. The developmental group (Fordham 1978) emphasizes the effect of early childhood experiences and favors a regressive personal analysis, while continuing to see archetypal patterns in developmental processes. James Hillman's archetypal group (Hillman 1972, 1975) has moved so far beyond clinical emphasis and toward symbolism as to question the legitimacy of psychotherapy as it is traditionally practiced.

Crittenden E. Brookes

Juvenile Delinquents: Psychotherapy

The challenge of the psychotherapist in treating the youthful offender is to develop a multisystem diagnostic understanding of the delinquent and design a program that will stimulate a desire for a different lifestyle, help him fully recognize his self-destructive qualities, gain release from pathological family and social forces, and provide for the development of the coping and vocational skills needed for gratifications that outweigh the frustrations of social living. Delinquents need help in living with both themselves and others. The essence of treatment is to foster personal maturation and resolve inner conflict.

The crucial issue is establishing a viable therapeutic contract, a special challenge with an unmotivated, hostile, compulsively symptomatic youth whose current life provides competing pleasures (S. R. Slavson 1965). The prospect of lengthy, painful, and stigmatized treatment evokes only avoidance by the youth. To enter treatment is to capitulate to resented adult authority. From the delinquent's viewpoint there is nothing to gain and everything to lose.

When treatment has begun, testing of the therapist's limits brings symptomatic acting-out behavior into the purview of treatment. The hospital can be a useful instrument for separating the youth from the family and providing a stable environment.

The concept of a therapeutic alliance as a specialized form of therapeutic relationship has particular value in adolescent psychotherapy because it highlights the need to create a cooperative stance of enquiry between members of disparate generations predisposed to conflict. Not only does the adolescent lack the perspective of an established place in society, but the delinquent in particular does not share the values held by the therapist.

Concomitant with individual meetings with the youth, varying mixtures of family, parent, and allied professional conferences and treatment sessions are helpful. The general aim is to educate adults in contact with the youth in behavioral management and offer them opportunities for catharsis. The extent of parental pathology determines the degree to which objectives for them involve basic or superficial changes.

When the youth views the therapist as a friend and as a potential agent of change, a more psychotherapeutic relationship can develop. When this point is reached, the youth can be involved in educational and career-oriented activities that offer the prospect of moving away from her family and peer group.

The essence of treatment is related to the therapists' ability to establish themselves as a model for the youth and to convert his milieu to promoting rather than impeding personal growth. With attention to the youth's developmental need for establishing self-identity, the later course of psychotherapy can concentrate on interpreting and working through defenses.

Jack C. Westman

· K ·

Kahlbaum, Karl Ludwig (1828–1899)

Kahlbaum's *Classification of Mental Illness and the Divisions of Emotional Disturbances* (1863) was based on the age of onset, biological transition, and organic conditions.

Leo H. Berman

Kallmann, Franz J. (1897–1965)

Franz Kallmann wrote a pioneering work on genetics of mental illness, particularly on schizophrenia. His main works include *The Genetics of Schizophrenia* (1938) and *Heredity in Health and Mental Disorder* (1953).

Leo H. Berman

Kant, Immanuel (1724–1804)

According to Immanuel Kant, the cognitive faculty is based on sensation. There are two main senses: the inner sense provides the perception of time, while the external sense involves partial perceptions of sight, touch, smell, taste, and hearing. Kant rejected the traditional idea of a soul as a substantive entity, and he introduced the concept of ego or self (*Ich*), representing the unity of consciousness.

Benjamin B. Wolman

Kelman, Harold (1906–1977)

Kelman was the author of numerous papers on neuropathology, clinical neurology, psychoanalysis, phenomenology, existentialism, Eastern philosophy, and general systems theory—extending the concepts of Sigmund Freud and Karen Horney. Kelman published two collections of articles on Horney's theory and technique. His major work, *Helping People*, appeared in 1971.

Norman J. Levy

Kinesthesis

Kinesthesis is the sensory modality concerned with the perception of movement. Kinesthetic receptors are a narrower class of receptors that subserve proprioception, which, according to Charles Scott Sherrington (1906), include those that respond to stimuli arising in the "deep field" of the body as opposed to the "surface field." These deep-field receptors include the visceral, muscular, arthrodial, and vestibular afferent systems.

Mechanoreceptors

Except for the pattern of motor innervation, all other sources of kinesthetic information arise from mechanoreceptors, where a signal is initiated by the deformation of their endings. The various mechanoreceptors that have been identified include the spray-type (Ruffini) endings and the paciniform corpuscles in the joint capsule, the Golgi-type ending within ligaments, and the cutaneous receptors. The spray endings and Golgi-type endings are slow-adapting receptors and signal joint angle, while being independent of movement, direction, and speed. The paciniform corpuscles, on the other hand, are fast adapting, are independent of joint angle, and are dependent upon the velocity, acceleration, and direction of limb movement.

Experimental Evidence for Afferent and Efferent Views of Perception of Movement

A number of experimental techniques have been employed to study the contributions of the joint receptors, the muscle spindles, and the pattern of innervation to the perception of movement. They have revolved around anesthetizing joints so that no afference can arise from movement of the joints, but sparing the afferents to the muscles acting at the joint; anesthetizing both muscle and joints so that no afferent information can arise from either class of receptors; and recording discharges by electrophysiological procedures as the limb is moved.

Kinesthetic Judgments

In general, judgments about active movements are made with more precision than those about passive movements. Several studies demonstrate that blind movements actively made to a predetermined end point result in less error of reproduction than movements that have been passively induced. One explanation for the greater accuracy of the active movements is that they include the firing of the muscle spindles, whereas they are not active during pure passive movement.

Kinesthesis and Motor Performance

For almost all types of motor performance, feedback is necessary for the accurate attainment of the performer's goal. It is this type of closed-loop control where kinesthetic feedback can be used to detect errors of movements. A number of investigators have attempted to delineate the role that kinesthesis plays in the ongoing regulation of movement. Much of this work has a common theme in that it describes a hierarchical movement-control system.

Several studies demonstrate the importance of kinesthetic feedback in motor performance. These studies attempt to manipulate the quality of kinesthetic feedback available in both pursuit and compensatory tracking. In general, it has been found that pressure control results in more accurate tracking when compared to free-moving (amplitude) control, indicating that kinesthetic feedback in the former

condition, which is isometric in nature, is both of a higher quality and can be used more rapidly than feedback resulting from isotonic contractions. However, amplitude cues have also been shown to add to tracking ability. When various degrees of elasticity, viscous damping, and inertia to performance were kept constant between a movable control stick and an isometric one, the additional kinesthetic cues resulting from movement produced superior tracking (J. M. Notterman 1975; J. M. Notterman and P. N. Page 1962).

Kinesthesis and Motor Learning

Learning of any motor skill is a complex process. One aspect of this process is the ability to control the temporal ordering of a pattern of movements. R. A. Schmidt (1971) argues that the capacity to order the temporal sequence of movements, which he calls timing, depends upon kinesthetic feedback. This "input theory" suggests that kinesthetic feedback received from early parts of a movement is used for timing later portions. Through extensive practice of a skill, a learner acquires specific stimulus characteristics that cue succeeding portions of the task. Schmidt supports this theory by noting several studies that show that by adding kinesthetic feedback to a movement, usually in the form of rising tension, the learning of these movements is facilitated as compared to movements that were not practiced under the increased tension.

Ronald G. Marteniuk

Kirchhoff, Theodore (1853–1922)

In 1880, Theodore Kirchhoff became director of an insane asylum, where he abolished restraints for agitated patients. He became instrumental in founding and modernizing other mental hospitals. He developed the concept of *biotonus*, subdivided into muscle tonus, nerve tonus, and serum tonus.

Marie-Louise Schoelly

Klein, Melanie (1882–1960)

Melanie Klein investigated the early childhood personality processes. According to Klein, the fundamental structure of the ego and object relations is laid in the first few months and years of the individual's life. Early object relationships not only lay the roots of the superego but modulate the character of the ego by processes of projective-introjective identification. Klein introduced the concept of "position," distinct from Freud's oral, anal, and phallic stages. The early positions are the paranoid-schizoid, followed by the depressive position.

Edna O'Shaughnessy

Klein's Contribution to Psychoanalysis

Melanie Klein introduced the concept of position as distinct from stages or phases of development, such as oral, anal, and phallic. By "position" she meant a characteristic constellation of the state of the ego, the nature of the object relations, and the prevailing anxiety and defenses. Both positions are rooted in the oral stage—the depressive position succeeding the paranoid-schizoid—but both are active at any time of the individual's life, determining her personality, the nature of her object relations, and the structure of her neurosis or psychosis. In the paranoid-schizoid position, which starts at birth, the ego is not fully integrated and is subject to splitting and fragmentation.

In the depressive position, the ego is integrated and capable of ambivalence without splitting itself. The object is whole and separates from the self. It is depended on and simultaneously loved and hated. With introjection, it becomes a more integrated superego, perceived as an internal object inducing feelings of guilt when aggression is directed toward it. The anxiety is of a depressive nature about injury to the loved object and its loss.

The working through of the depressive position depends on reparative mechanisms. The pain experienced in the fear of the loss of the object and the guilt mobilizes love and reparative wishes toward the object, resulting in a drive to restore the good internal and external objects. Successful reparation of the internal object, in turn, promotes the growth of the ego.

The paranoid-schizoid and depressive positions are only partly developmental concepts. In fact, if one thinks of the working through of the depressive position as the achieving of maturity, this state is probably never fully achieved, and every step in development that awakens a feeling of loss arouses depressive anxieties anew, with the possibilities of regression to paranoid-schizoid defenses. Thus the depressive, infantile anxieties are reawakened and have to be worked through at different levels at all stages of development, such as weaning, the overcoming of the Oedipus complex, adolescence, midlife crises, and finally old age and facing death. With adequate working through in a creative way, each step leads to the enrichment of the internal world, growth, and increasing maturity.

The Kleinian analyst is probably tuned in to the nonverbal elements in the patient's communication, because it is often in nonverbal behavior that primitive and charged feelings and fantasies find expression. Usually those nonverbal elements are not interpreted until the pattern of behavior becomes clear and convincing. The Kleinian analyst pays more attention to her own countertransference, as, again, it is often the more primitive nonverbal aspects of the patient's behavior that are most likely to affect the countertransference.

Klein's views have been applied to such fields as aesthetics (Segal 1973), philosophy (Money-Kyrle; Wolheim), and social studies (W. R. Bion; Jacques).

Hanna Segal

Koffka, Kurt (1886–1941)

Kurt Koffka, with Max Wertheimer and Wolfgang Köhler, was a cofounder of Gestalt psychology. In the *Psychological Bulletin* of 1922, Koffka introduced Gestalt psychology to American psychologists. His *Principles of Gestalt Psychology* was published in 1935.

Mary Henle

Köhler, Wolfgang (1887–1967)

Wolfgang Köhler, with Max Wertheimer and Kurt Koffka, was a cofounder of Gestalt psychology. Köhler's studies of problem solving by chimpanzees (1917) provided a new direction for psychology of thinking. Köhler wrote about theory of values. His physiological research and examination of the evolutionary theory pointed to the invariant dynamics that the organism shares with all of nature.

Mary Henle

Kohut, Heinz (1913–1981)

Heinz Kohut's psychoanalytic theory introduces a new concept of self. According to Kohut, the self is the person's center of the psychological universe, and it represents the totality of inner experiences at a certain point in time. Kohut distinguishes two poles of the self: 1) the pole of ambitions, which covers childhood assertiveness and its adult neutralization; and 2) the pole of ideals, which includes the person's totality of ideals. Human beings are motivated by ambition and talent, and by skill and ideals. The continuum of ambition and ideals is the basis for the cohesive self, which enables the person to conduct a mature and productive life. According to Kohut, an inadequate cohesiveness of the self is the main cause of psychopathology. Kohut distinguishes between the following psychopathological types: 1) narcissistic personality and narcissistic behavior disorder, caused by deficiencies in the poles; 2) borderline conditions, caused by deficiencies in the self-object environment; 3) schizoid and paranoid personalities, who defend themselves against a total collapse of self; and 4) psychoses caused by inability to develop any cohesiveness of the self. Kohut's treatment method stresses the development of self-object transferences, which lead to mature self-object relationships.

Benjamin B. Wolman

Kohut's Self Psychology

In Heinz Kohut's view, man is knowable by the process of empathic cognition of his self. The self is to be viewed as the center of the psychological universe; it comprises the total body of experiences of which the person is aware at any given time; thus, it can only be ascertained through "empathy," the process of thinking and feeling oneself into the inner life of another person. Appreciation of the self of a person represents the beginning and end of all psychological investigations; i.e., to understand the inner mental life means not to understand the drives the person is struggling with nor the type of his relationship with objects but to comprehend the collection of inner experiences called the self.

Developmental Considerations

The developing self of an individual requires a specific milieu of empathic caretakers who, as a result of their empathic recognition of the needs of the infant and child, foster the growth of the self. The early development of the child requires a caretaker, ordinarily the mother, who by her confirming-approving (mirroring) presence aids in the establishment of the child's grandiosity, which is later to become the pole of ambitions.

The quality of self-selfobject relationships changes from infancy to adulthood. In infancy, as the self is accreting the functions of the mirroring selfobject and idealized parent, the nature of the tie is a merger. In later life, the self-selfobject relationship constitutes an empathic resonance; i.e., the self's contact with a selfobject in adulthood is an empathic experience of being recognized, appreciated, and admired, but not in the childhood inner experience of fusion (archaic merger). Kohut's version of the intact or cohesive self is that this cohesive self continues to need and maintain self-selfobject ties (both archaic and mature) throughout life.

Psychopathology of the Self

Narcissistic personality and narcissistic behavior disorders. These people have ordinarily had deficient experiences resulting in two out of the three areas of the self (pole of ambitions; pole of ideals; talents and skills) being defective. The primary deficiency in mirroring is sometimes compensated by a good relationship with an idealized parent.

The self in the neurotic disorders. When the self needs are not responded to by the environment and cohesiveness of the self is lost, preoccupation with and fixations on drives become manifest. If the phase-appropriate selfobject supports at the oedipal phase are missing or distorted (competitive behaviors, punitiveness), the child will experience a breakup of her self, and fear her love feelings or assertiveness.

Hyman L. Muslin

Konorski, Jerzy (1903–1973)

The U.S. psychologist Jerzy Konorski's main contributions were the formulation of two-factor theory and the investigation of the interaction between classical and instrumental conditioning. Konorski's major publications include the book *Conditioned Reflexes and Neuron Organization* (1948).

Gregory A. Kimble

Kraepelin, Emil (1856–1926)

The German psychiatrist Emil Kraepelin's chief influence and legacy come through his textbook of psychiatry. He based his neurological system on etiology, prognosis, and distinguishable clinical examinations. In 1899 he elucidated two major "endogenous" processes, namely dementia praecox (renamed "schizophrenia" by Eugen Bleuler) and manic-depressive insanity.

John C. Burnham

Krafft-Ebing, Richard (1840–1902)

The Austrian neuropsychiatrist Richard Krafft-Ebing is the founder of modern sexual pathology. In his book *Psychopathia Sexualis* he describes various sexual dysfunctions and introduces the words *sadism* and *masochism*.

Leo H. Berman

Kretschmer, Ernst (1888–1964)

The German psychiatrist Ernst Kretschmer's study of bodily and mental signs of hospitalized patients led to the following basic categories: pyknic manic-depressives, and leptosomic and athletic schizophrenics. Kretschmer advanced a character theory based on the study of reflexes. According to Kretschmer, "character" means a sort of mind-body combination manifested through modes such as asthenic-sthenic, sensitive-expansive, primitive, hysterical, and compulsive. His main work is *Physique and Character* (1925).

Wolfgang Kretschmer

Kubie, Lawrence (1896–1973)

The United States psychiatrist and psychoanalyst Lawrence Kubie's main works were *Practical and Theoretical Aspects of Psychoanalysis, Psychoanalysis as Science,* and *The Neurotic Distortions of the Creative Process.* Kubie was president of the New York Psychoanalytic Society and the American Psychosomatic Society.

Robert W. Gibson

· L ·

Lacan, Jacques (1901–1981)

Jacques Lacan emphasized the need for an increased attention to the use of language in psychoanalysis. Lacan called his method "textual analysis" and maintained that the understanding of oneself depends on one's analysis of his or her language.

Benjamin B. Wolman

Language and Cognitive Development

The child first begins to use language between 12 and 24 months, and soon afterward starts to combine single words to form longer utterances. In so doing, she is beginning to construct a grammar for the specific language she has been exposed to. Before she can work on language properly, though, the child has to be able to "cognize the physical and social events that are encoded in language," and she also has to be able to "process, organize and store linguistic information" (Slobin 1973).

During the first 18 or 24 months—the sensorimotor stage of development—the child amasses information about what he can do to or with different objects (adaptive behavior), and his relations in space both to himself and to others as well as their temporal properties (e.g., object constancy). He begins to organize this knowledge acquired through exploration of his environment. Piaget wrote of the child's action patterns providing the input for the organization of knowledge during the sensorimotor period: these action patterns include both physical movements, such as grasping, reaching, and manipulating on the part of the child, and also visual explo-ration of the child's surroundings (Jean Piaget 1967).

Overextensions seem to fall into six main classes, where the criterial features involve shape, size, movement, sound, texture, and taste (Clark 1973). There is also one other class that seems to involve reference to actions rather than to objects, for example, a child who overextends *open* from opening and shutting the door, to taking off her shoes, to peeling an orange. While the similarities between the situations are obvious in the latter case, it is harder to pin down exactly what characteristic of the situations the child is using as the meaning of *open*. Overextensions appear to be the result of the child's hypothesis about the meaning of a particular word—that it refers to some salient feature of an object (Clark 1974).

The sensorimotor period appears to build up the child's cognitive knowledge about his surroundings, and it is this knowledge that he uses when he begins to acquire language. His ability to recognize objects and their properties, as well as similarities among objects, plays a basic role in learning reference in language.

D. I. Slobin (1973) has approached the language-cognition issue from a slightly different viewpoint, after considering an extensive collection of cross-linguistic data on first-language acquisition. There appears to be a regular order of appearance for certain linguistic distinctions (e.g., plurality), both within and across languages. Slobin argues that the ordering is the result of prior cognitive development of the distinction in question. Thus, if the child has not yet developed a particular cognitive distinction, that distinction is clearly not available for mapping into some linguistic form.

H. Sinclair–de Zwart (1967), working within a Piagetian framework, makes one of the few attempts to examine this question carefully. As a test of whether language can affect cognitive development, she asks whether nonconserving children can acquire conservation as a result of purely verbal training on the kinds of descriptions used spontaneously by conservers. She finds that children who pass the conservation tests use comparatives (e.g., "more" and "less").

Eve V. Clark

Latent Learning

One of the most important early lines of evidence for the learning/performance distinction was the phenomenon of latent learning. In a typical latent-learning experiment motivated rats are run through a maze for several trials without reinforcement. After many such trials, food or water is introduced into the goal box of the maze. This typically leads to a very rapid improvement in performance—as if the animal had learned the maze, but the learning remained "latent" until a good reason to display it (the reward) became available.

Gregory A. Kimble

Laughter

The research of developmental psychologists has contributed most to our understanding of laughter, although by and large their conclusions are not unequivocal. Some of the ontogenetic analyses of "humorous laughter" appear to be in direct conflict, and this is because of inherent and unresolved definitional problems. It is clear that laughter maturationally precedes humor appreciation, being first manifested at around 4 months of age, but it has been argued that infants as young as 7 months experience humor when incongruous events are presented in safe situations.

One observation that meets with consistent and unqualified support from various quarters is that humor is rarely, if ever, sufficient to cause an explosive, overt response. In other words, it can engender internal amusement, but not laughter. For the emission of "humorous laughter" there is widespread acceptance that a "playful mood" has to run through the proceedings (P. E. McGhee 1979). However, at the same time, no one disputes that there is a basic distinction between laughing *at* and laughing *with* another, and the former presumably derives from hostile rather than amicable intentions.

As well as operating as an attention-avoiding/arousal-dissipating device, laughter can be used in a converse manner, to attract and maintain attention and so promote increments in social arousal within individuals. Hence, interactants who concur in their tacit desire to advance social intimacy rapidly can capitalize on laughter and joke telling: for example, they can stare continuously at one another, and they can reduce interpersonal distance. It is especially at such times that laughter itself can induce and augment laughter in others.

Antony J. Chapman

Law of Effect

The law of effect was first expressed by Edward Lee Thorndike as a result of his studies of human and animal learning. In one form, now frequently referred to as the "empirical law of effect," it is the generalization that an animal or person learns, and is likely to repeat in a given situation, responses that have satisfying consequences in that situation. This generalization has provided both the name and the format of instrumental learning: responses are learned in a situation to the extent that they are instrumental in producing a satisfying state of affairs.

Thorndike's view that the law of effect works because satisfiers strengthen an associative bond between the situational stimuli and the instrumental response has convincingly been challenged. Current reviews of relevant research appear to favor the view that what is learned are relevant contingencies; these may be contingencies between stimuli of importance; between responses; between stimuli and responses; or between stimuli, responses, and reinforcers.

Lawrence R. Boulter

Leadership: An Overview

In the first half of this century, a great deal of attention in psychology was directed to the "traits" of leaders. However, the trait approach proved to be quite inadequate, as Ralph M. Stogdill (1948) found in his literature survey. He did report one neither surprising nor psychodynamically vital finding, namely, a tendency for leaders to be slightly more intelligent than followers. The failings of the trait approach gave impetus to the development of a situational approach to leadership, especially in the 1950s.

In both the trait and situational approaches to leadership, there is an implicit assumption of a demarcation between those who lead and those who follow. Indeed, followers are essentially viewed as a residual category of nonleaders. This simplistic notion denies reality, however. All leaders, some of the time and in varying degrees, are followers; and followers are not immutably cast in nonleader roles, because they can and at times do become leaders.

The effectiveness of leadership depends upon a transaction between the leader and followers. This transaction provides the potential for changes in influence, for counterinfluence, and for determining who may take on the leader role. In contrast with earlier approaches, the more dynamic orientation of this transactional approach places greater weight on the followers' perception of the leader, including her source of authority, competence, motivations, success in achieving favorable outcomes, and continued "legitimacy" in her role.

There are, in fact, two broad categories of leadership, each diverse within itself. The first encompasses basic executive, managerial, and supervisory roles within organizational frameworks. The second involves emergent leadership, in which the leader achieves his role by the willing support of followers, as exemplified in the political realm, and also in freely functioning informal groups.

Another approach to leadership is represented in "contingency models," the most notable of which is F. E. Fiedler's (1967). He predicts varying levels of effectiveness for differing combinations of the leader's and situation's characteristics. The primary leader attribute is the orientation to coworkers, which comes down to a matter of style (i.e., a human relations orientation versus a task orientation). In Fiedler's model, leader effectiveness is predicted to be a function of the fit of the leader's orientation to the patterning of three situational variables (i.e., the quality of leader-member liking, the degree of task structure, and the position power of the leader).

In another contingency model, V. Vroom and P. Yetton (1973) deal with some of this complexity. They are specifically concerned with leader styles in processes of organizational decision making. The broad problem that they address is the specification of situational factors calling forth particular styles of decision making, and then the relationship of those styles to criteria of organizational effectiveness. Their model differentiates three main styles for arriving at the solution to group problems (autocratic, consultative, and group), arrayed by the degree of potential participation allowed to subordinates.

Edwin P. Hollander

Leadership, Power, and Acceptance

Leadership can be defined as an interpersonal relationship in which the activities of some (the followers) are initiated, stimulated, and to some extent controlled by another (the leader). Forced obedience, as at gunpoint or under slavery, is not an example of leadership: D. Hartley (1952) suggests the term *headship* for this kind of relationship. Within the framework of voluntary relationships, leadership depends upon the willingness of followers to accept the guidance and/or control of a leader.

The reason for acceptance of leadership is obvious: we are aware of certain needs and of our inability to take care of all of them. Thus, we accept guidance from individuals whom we perceive as strong (that is, capable of satisfying our needs) and friendly (that is, willing to do so)—and this is what makes us followers.

In a study of classroom discipline by Benjamin B. Wolman (1949), attention is given to the rating of teachers by students in the above-mentioned dimensions of power (strong versus weak) and acceptance (friendly versus hostile). Teachers who are rated weak and hostile cannot control their classes. These teachers constantly report discipline problems, and most of them desperately and unsuccessfully struggle with unruly students.

Practically no disciplinary problems are noted in classes taught by strong and friendly teachers. Their instructions are implemented thoroughly, with almost no objections. Students do not dare or wish to alienate their "powerful friends."

A method of rating the dimensions of power and acceptance has been developed by B. B. Wolman (1958) using a special tool called the "statogram."

Benjamin B. Wolman

Learning: Classical Theories

During the period from about 1930 to about 1950, the psychology of learning was dominated by the views of four important theorists, E. R. Guthrie, Clark L. Hull, B. F. Skinner, and E. C. Tolman. These theorists shared certain broad commitments, but they also differed on many points. Within broad guidelines the classical theorists differed on certain basic issues:

1. the number of forms of learning that must be discriminated, one or more than one;
2. what is learned, S-R associations or S-S expectancies;
3. the role of rewards in learning, essential, or nonessential; and
4. the role of practice.

Some of these theorists believed that learning is a sudden, all-or-none process; others, following Thorndike, believed that learning is gradual.

Guthrie's Theory
E. R. Guthrie believed that there is only one form of learning, specifically, classical conditioning. He maintained that learning consists in the development of S-R associations, that contiguity rather than reward is the essential condition, and that learning is complete in a single trial.

Hull's Theory
With Guthrie, C. L. Hull maintained that there is only one kind of learning, but he identified instrumental conditioning as the basic form. Learning, he maintained, consists of the gradual strengthening of S-R connections, and the essential requirement is that of reward or reinforcement, which he interpreted in terms of need, drive, or drive-stimulus reduction at different times in his career.

Skinner's Theory
B. F. Skinner's work concentrated on operant conditioning. In that context he believed that learning consists of strengthening S-R connections, that the process is a cumulative one, and that reward is necessary.

Tolman's Theory
The positions most characteristic of E. C. Tolman are his various statements of expectancy theory. In these he treats learning in terms of the development of sign-gestalt expectations—a proposition on the part of the learner that, given a sign (stimulus), following such and such a behavior route will lead to a certain further stimulus or significate. On the basis of such statements it is sometimes said that, for Tolman, learning consisted of acquiring a knowledge of "what leads to what" in the environment. Another way of putting it in Tolman's terms is that learning consists of the development of cognitive maps.

Gregory A. Kimble

Learning among the Mentally Retarded

The mentally retarded are not a homogeneous group. Using severity of handicap as the criterion for dividing the population of mentally retarded persons, one finds the great majority to be borderline and mildly retarded. These individuals are predominantly from poor and/or minority group backgrounds. A small proportion of the mildly retarded come from middle-class backgrounds. These persons invariably have demonstrable organic damage or serious personality difficulties.

A major explanatory construct for understanding the learning behavior of the mentally retarded is the concept of mental age. The hypothesis is that mentally retarded persons develop more slowly and that mental age indicates their current expected competencies, because this construct is keyed to the ages at which the normally developing child exhibits particular competencies, as calculated by intelligence tests.

Differences between retardates and normals have been described as a function of treatment conditions such as massed versus spaced practice, high versus low incentive, meaningful versus nonmeaningful material presented, and instruction or cueing to enhance learning performance versus no instructions (i.e., spontaneous grasp of a principle). The group-by-treatment design seeks to establish that IQ or mental age is related to task performance and that the laws governing the relationship between the treatment variables and performance among normals differ from the relationships evident among the mentally retarded.

Two tasks have been most commonly employed: paired associates and serial learning. In paired-associates learning, the subject is presented with a list of words, for each of which she must learn another word as an associate. She sees the stimulus word, has a few seconds to deliver the associated response word, and then is shown the correct response word. In rote serial learning, the subject tries to learn the words on a list in order. He or she sees the first word on the list, has a few seconds to say the second word, is then shown the second word, tries to guess the third word, and so forth.

Studies of the perceptual motor learning capabilities of mental retardates have employed such tasks as exposed and shielded mazes, rotary pursuit, mirror drawing, coding, card sorting, form board, and even athletic games. The two critical factors across all of these tasks, which should be considered when comparing normals and retardates, are the level of task difficulty and the degree of practice allowed the person.

Some psychologists and educators tend to identify lack of intelligence with incapacity to learn; the two are not identical, although they are related. For example, low-IQ children perform poorly on academic tasks, which comprise the major indicator of validity for the intelligence test score. By contrast, retarded adults can learn laboratory learning tasks efficiently when certain conditions have been fulfilled.

Milton Budoff
Gary N. Siperstein

Learning Disability

The pioneering work of Alfred Binet, through its theoretical basis and system of classification, provided the early impetus for the development of special education for the mentally retarded and focused the school psychologist's attention on psychoeducational evaluation, instructional recommendations, and special class assignment.

Over the years, emphasis has shifted from causative diagnosis to functional or descriptive evaluation. A comprehensive psychological evaluation generally involves integrating the information obtained from tests, behavioral observations, interviews, records, and reports. The objective is to describe as accurately as possible the child's specific skill inventory.

The purpose for both individual psychological evaluation and screening programs is to provide for instructional recommendations. The school psychologist has become increasingly knowledgeable about learning processes and curriculum and uses this skill for more direct intervention in the classroom through the teacher.

Michael J. Mattioli

Learning Set

In animals ranging from rats to humans there is evidence that the ability to master a particular form of learning problem increases with the individual's experience with the type of problem involved. That is, the organism acquires a set to learn: the subject "learns how to learn."

Possibly the most impressive demonstration of learning sets came from a series of studies by Harry F. Harlow (1949, 1950) at the University of Wisconsin. In these experiments monkeys were required to master a series of several hundred discrimination-learning problems. The objects to be discriminated were changed on each problem. After 200 to 300 problems, the monkeys were able to make the discrimination perfectly after just one trial. That is, at first, upon the presentation of a new problem the animals made an initial choice that was right about half the time and wrong half the time, but on the second trial the choices were consistently correct. They had developed a learning set.

Gregory A. Kimble

Legal and Criminal Justice: The Role of Psychologists

Psychologists try to bring objectivity and detachment from the adversary process to the courtroom. This posture is maintained successfully in three procedures. The first is the determination of whether the act itself was committed, or scientific study related to *actus reus*. Psychologists often study memory, eyewitness reliability, and accuracy of perception under given stimulus conditions, related to whether the accused offender was guilty.

A second role is in mental health clinics attached to juvenile, family, or criminal courts. These clinics undertake both assessment and treatment, although the major legal involvement is in assessment outcomes.

Third, state hospitals and independent practitioners often assess competency to stand trial. An individual must be mentally as well as physically present in the courtroom; this means that he must understand the charges, be aware of the nature of the court proceedings, and be able to assist the attorneys in his own defense.

Adversary Roles
The most publicized adversary role is that of expert witness on an insanity plea in a murder trial. Only in murder or another serious crime does an individual plead not guilty by reason of insanity. The criteria typically include whether the person knew the nature and quality of her act, and if so, if she had some awareness of whether the act was wrong. In some states, this cognitive test is supplemented by an affective test of whether the person was mentally disordered and irresistibly, impulsively driven to commit this act.

Legal Regulation of Psychological Methods and Practices
In some states psychologists are given absolute privilege of confidentiality for clients in psychotherapy; in others no protection, or an intermediate privilege, is given.

In contested child custody cases, expert witnesses are subpoenaed to testify about parental suitability or needs of the child. These examples are indicative of the extent to which psychologists may experience substantial legal issues and contact in their previously cloistered and autonomous practices.

The Psychologist in the Correctional Setting
The prison psychologist typically operates on the principle that the prison replicates free living, with opportunities for reward and advancement, and punishment and failure. Clinical goals are then identified as providing help to those individuals who want it and encouraging individuals who need help to seek it out.

Stanley L. Brodsky

Lerner, Karl Edward (1903–1964)

Karl Lerner conducted pioneer work on salivary conditioning in the dog. He conditioned salivary responses to a bell.

Gregory A. Kimble

Level of Aspiration

The history of studies on the effects of success and failure upon changes in a subject's stated goals can hardly begin with the first major research in which the term *level of aspiration* was used. Previous experimental studies on success and failure were related to this subject, as were clinical descriptions by Alfred Adler.

Hoppe

Current investigations can be clearly traced, however, to the work begun by students of Kurt Lewin who were interested in formulating laws concerning goal responses. These studies were begun by F. Hoppe in 1930. Hoppe, however, failed to distinguish clearly between implicit and explicit goals, although he recognized that the subject's immediate or momentary goal was different from her "ideal" goal. The reality of the ideal goal could be changed by experiences of success and failure. He noted also that failure depressed and success elevated the immediate goal. As Hoppe was not primarily concerned with individual differences, he failed to consider the effect of different tasks or different instructions upon the changes in level of aspiration, although he noted that vast individual differences existed in what his subjects considered success and failure.

Hausmann

In 1933, M. F. Hausmann veered from the theoretical approach of Hoppe and concerned himself with the technique "as a test to evaluate some personality traits." He changed the instructions so that a "bid" was made before each trial; the subject was penalized if he fell below this bid and received no extra credit if he scored higher than the bid.

Frank

J. D. Frank was concerned both with the theoretical value of the results of studies using this technique and with the possibilities of the technique itself as a method of studying personality. He was among the first to begin the standardization and quantification of results so that they would be amenable to further investigations. Frank defined level of aspiration operationally as "the level of future performance in a familiar task which an individual, knowing his level of past performance in that task, explicitly undertakes to reach."

Group Studies

General findings for group studies of adults in American culture provide the following reasonably well replicated results:

1. In general, people tend to raise their stated goals following success in a task and to lower them following failure.
2. In setting explicit goals in a series of repeated trials, people tend to be affected more by recent experience than by earlier experience. However, the effect of earlier experience is reinstated if there is a long period of delay between trials.

Individual Differences

The first theoretical rationale for the instrument as a measure of individual personality characteristics was made by Kurt Lewin et al. (1944). Generally, they attribute level of aspiration behavior to three kinds of factors or influences: (1) the seeking of success, (2) the avoiding of failure, and (3) the cognitive factor of probability judgment.

Rotter's Level of Aspiration Board

A variety of techniques have been used for personality assessment, including asking subjects to estimate future grades, dart throwing, selecting mazes of varying difficulty, and a variety of motor coordination and intellectual tasks. The Rotter Level of Aspiration Board (J. B. Rotter 1954) is a widely used standardized procedure for investigating individual differences. For twenty trials, the subject hits a steel ball down an alley, trying to use the right amount of force so that the ball stops in a high-numbered groove. Instructions emphasize realistic expectancies.

Behavior on the Level of Aspiration Board has also been related to a variety of personality characteristics, including authoritarianism and conformity. Level of aspiration behavior is, additionally, clearly related to work on need achievement and has been found to be related to attitudes of internal versus external control of reinforcement. J. B. Rotter and Jensen, and D. Cassells have also produced standardized level of aspiration techniques adapted for group administration.

Julian B. Rotter

Lewin, Bertram David (1896–1971)

Bertram Lewin wrote on dreams and dream screening, affective disorders and sleep, psychoanalytic and medical education. He was cofounder and editor of the *Psychoanalytic Quarterly*.

Henry W. Brosin

Lewin, Kurt (1890–1947)

Kurt Lewin's major contributions are in the areas of personality theory, experimental studies of human motivation, and social psychology. His basic formula was that behavior is a function of the person and the environment. Lewin's early representations made use of the concepts of topology. His fundamental concepts for the environment were cognitive structure, valence, and force, and for the person, structure and tension.

Lewin's psychology, which is frequently referred to as "field theory," is related to Gestalt psychology. His book *Field Theory in Social Science* was published in 1951.

Mary Henle

Lie Detection

The technique of lie detection uses a structured interview with about ten questions, designed to be either relevant or neutral to the purpose of the inquiry. The questions are discussed prior to the formal interrogation, and should be modified, as required, to remove any possible ambiguity. The subject is told to answer only "yes" or "no." The set of questions will be repeated once or twice.

Polygraph examiners claim that lie detection has a high validity (accuracy of 90–100%) but have published no substantiating data. P. J. Bersh (1969) found an agreement of 92% between the judgment of polygraph examiners in 157 cases and that of a panel where four lawyers judged the guilt or innocence of subjects from information available in the case files.

Jesse Orlansky

Listening Process in Psychoanalysis

It is advisable for the therapist to enter each session without desire, memory, or understanding (Bion 1970), so that she maintains an openness to all possible levels of meaning and implication of the patient's communications. It is also advisable to allow each session to be its own creation, so that silent formulations developed in a particular hour are maintained only if supported by ongoing material from the patient in that session. Basic to this approach is the therapist's use of free-floating attention and role- and image-responsiveness, as well as her capacity to contain and metabolize (understand) the patient's projective identifications.

The communicative approach to the listening/experiencing process postulates basic adaptive responses within the patient and focuses on the ongoing spiraling conscious and especially unconscious communicative interaction between the patient and the therapist. This approach considers all of the patient's material in light of the therapeutic relationship. It makes use of the me/not me interface, through which the patient's associations are first understood as referring to the therapist and then as referring to the patient. In the former instance, the material is taken as a reflection of an unconscious perception and introject of the therapist based on her interventions, while the latter involves the patient's unconscious fantasies and memories.

Valid interventions organized around activated adaptive contexts provide the patient with insight into the truth of the therapeutic interaction as it has mobilized his unconscious perceptions and fantasies.

Robert J. Langs

Literature and Psychoanalysis

In his *Autobiographical Study*, Sigmund Freud (1925) differentiated the dream from the work of art, contrasting the narcissistic nature of the former and the role of the receptive audience in the latter, that is, the basic function of art as communication and the wish of the artist to arouse interest.

Other ventures of Freud in the area of literature included a paper, "The Three Caskets" (1913), comparing a theme from Shakespeare's *Merchant of Venice* with its probably mythological origins and connections with universal fantasies. In a subsequent paper, "The Exceptions," Freud (1916) deals with the character of Richard III as illustrating a special character type claiming exemption from the general rules and mores demanded by society. Freud's final contribution specifically devoted to literature was a paper on Fyodor Dostoyevsky and the theme of parricide (1928).

There are two possibilities for using psychoanalysis as a tool for literary criticism. One type (the so-called endopoietic approach) was defined by Kurt Eissler (1968) as "deliberately avoiding the use of elements outside the work itself, viewing each detail within it in the light shed by the whole work in terms of the aggregate of those details of which the work consists and their interpretations." The second (exopoietic) approach attempts to explain a literary piece by seeking connecting factors outside the work, whether these be processes in the author's mind or elements in the author's environment—economic, social, or cultural.

The contribution of analysis to the psychology of the artist has evolved along with the development of psychoanalytic theory. In its early stages, analysis was concerned with the concepts of drive and defense; hence, there was interest in relating mature forms to early instinctual derivatives (oral, anal, phallic) and an overriding preoccupation with the unconscious.

Through its vast clinical pool, analysis is in a position to make a hypothesis about the influences of such factors as object loss, separations, and other traumas of early childhood (consider the influence on Keats's work of the loss of his mother at an early age) or to reconstruct the antecedents of certain mental illnesses coexisting with creativity (Vincent van Gogh, Gerard de Nerval) or even to appreciate the impact of certain physical infirmities (Henri de Toulouse-Lautrec) and their ramifications on the creative function.

P. Greenacre (1957) has concluded that the basic characteristics of creative talent include—whether inborn or not is hard to say—the following: (1) greater sensitivity to sensory stimulation, (2) unusual capacity for awareness of relations between various stimuli, (3) predisposition to an empathy of wider range and deeper vibration than usual, and (4) intactness of sufficient sensorimotor equipment to allow the building up of projective motor discharge for expressive functions.

Psychoanalysis provided a whole new dimension and impetus to psychological literary criticism. It now became possible to make in-depth studies of the psychological evaluation of characters in novels and plays, demonstrating how the writer's genius unconsciously describes her keen knowledge of the human mind.

Analysis is in a position to make some contribution to the history of the evolution of literary styles and schools. It may elucidate the prevalence or avoidance of certain themes or conflicts in a given period or in a particular artist.

Francis D. Baudry

Locus of Control Scale

The Locus of Control Scale (Rotter 1966) was developed to measure the construct, locus of control, that was derived from Julian B. Rotter's social learning theory. Social learning theory holds that most behavior is learned in a social situation and is fused with needs that are largely satisfied through other people. The scale measures the degree to which people perceive the events in their own lives as being largely the consequence of their own actions, and thus under their own control (internal control), or as being largely unrelated to their own behavior and thus beyond their own personal control (external control).

The scale is composed of twenty-nine paired-choice items in which the subject selects the one of two paired items with which he most agrees. The reported reliabilities of the scale have varied from .49 to .83.

A wide range of studies has been conducted with this scale, and a variety of alternative scales designed to measure the same construct have been developed, some of them for use with specific populations, such as schoolchildren. Factor-analytic studies suggest that there may be two factors contained within the scale: personal control and ideological beliefs.

Clifford H. Swensen

Love

Love has long been of theoretical interest, but empirical research on love is relatively recent and grew out of social-psychological theory and research on interpersonal attraction (e.g., Berscheid 1985). Many taxonomies of love have been offered. Of all the proposed varieties of love, romantic love has received the most attention, partly because it is strongly associated with marriage in Western culture (see Berscheid 1985).

Romantic love was initially believed to be simply a strong form of such milder sentiments as liking, with essentially the same, albeit stronger, antecedents. It became apparent, however, that increases in liking do not always lead to love, especially romantic love, and early investigators began to empirically and theoretically distinguish between these two forms of attraction. For example, as noted by Ellen S. Berscheid (1985), in 1970 D. C. Rubin empirically developed Love and Liking Scales that appeared to differentiate between the two sentiments, and in 1978 Berscheid and E. Walster theoretically distinguished between companionate love (i.e., the affection we feel for those with whom our lives are deeply intertwined) and romantic or passionate love (i.e., a state of intense absorption in another). E. Hatfield and J. Sprecher (1986) have recently developed a Passionate Love Scale that appears to reliably measure this type of love. In 1974 Berscheid and Walster also proposed a two-factor theory of love that states that romantic love will often be experienced when the individual is strongly aroused physiologically and when situational cues indicate that "romantic love" is the appropriate label for the arousal. Under most circumstances, the source of arousal is correctly attributed to the romantic partner, but some research indicates that fear-induced arousal may be, under conducive circumstances, misattributed and

also interpreted as romantic attraction to another. Other research suggests that extraneous arousal alone, even when not misattributed to the other, may be sufficient to facilitate romantic attraction (for additional discussion see Berscheid 1985, 1994).

The past decade has seen a resurgence of interest in love (Berscheid 1994). Many new theories have been offered, with several theorists taking an evolutionary approach. D. M. Buss (see R. J. Sternberg and C. D. Barnes 1988), for example, views love as a syndrome of actions that have evolved to facilitate reproductive success (e.g., display of resources), and has found evidence for a sex difference in mate selection preference such that men are more likely to emphasize physical attractiveness, a function of youth and health, in potential martial partners, while women are more likely to emphasize economic status factors.

Inspired by John Bowlby's theory of attachment, C. Hazan and P. R. Shaver (R. J. Sternberg and C. D. Barnes 1988) also take an evolutionary approach to love. Self-endorsement by adults of one of three descriptive paragraphs designed to be analogues of the three primary types of infant attachment (i.e., secure, avoidant, anxious/ambivalent) has been found to be associated with individuals' reports of experiences in their most important romantic relationship, as well as with beliefs about romantic love and retrospective self-reports of childhood relationship experiences. Subsequent research has suggested that adult attachment style may reflect a general security and trust orientation toward all social relationships, rather than romantic relationships exclusively. M. D. S. Ainsworth (1989) also has discussed several implications of Bowlby's attachment theory for sexual pair bonding beyond infancy. She speculates that the reproductive or sexual behavior system proposed by Bowlby may be important initially in the pair bonding characteristic of adult romantic relationships, but then, as sexual attraction wanes, the attachment and caregiving behavioral systems may become more important in sustaining the relationship. No evidence relevant to this proposition is yet available.

Other investigators recently have attempted to empirically develop a taxonomy of love varieties by drawing upon the concepts and methods of cognitive psychology. For example, B. Fehr and J. A. Russell (1991) have used a prototype approach to examine the centrality of different types of love in the natural language category "love." Although "maternal love" appears to be regarded as the most prototypical example of love and "infatuation" as the worst, these investigators join many others by concluding that "the folk definition of love is complex and provides no sharp boundary between love and other, related experiences" (435).

Many investigators are currently taking a psychometric approach to love, attempting to identify the dimensions that underlie self-reported experiences of individuals involved in heterosexual dating or romantic relationships. For example, based on consideration of previous social–psychological theory and research on love and liking in young adults and factor analyses of self-reports of dating experiences, R. J. Sternberg (see R. J. Sternberg and C. D. Barnes 1988) proposes a "triangular" theory of love, in which all forms of love are viewed as combinations of three components: intimacy, decision/commitment, and passion. For example, companionate love is believed to result from a combination of the intimacy and decision/commitment components, and romantic love, from a combination of passion and intimacy. Also taking a psychometric approach to love, Lee (see Sternberg and Barnes 1988) examines the contents of interviews and other data and proposes three primary "love styles"—*Storge*, affectionate, committed love; *Eros*, romantic love; and *Ludus*, sexually cynical, game-playing love—and numerous secondary love styles resulting from combinations of these. C. Hendrick and S. S. Hendrick (1986) have developed a Love Attitudes Scale to reliably assess each of these styles in a specific relationship and have examined their correlates (e.g., relationship satisfaction in heterosexual couples appears to be positively correlated with the "Erotic" love style).

Recent research suggests that the psychometric approach has not been able clearly to differentiate between different types of love. Hendrick and Hendrick (1989), for example, examine five popular love scales and conclude that love "means different things to different people in different relationships at different points in time" (793). Unfortunately, current theories of love do not sufficiently elaborate the characteristic manifestations, contemporary and historical antecedents, and individual and interpersonal consequences of different love experiences to guide empirical investigation of the several types of love so many theorists have presumed to exist (see Berscheid 1994).

Interest in cultural differences in love experiences has increased in recent years. K. K. Dion and K. L. Dion (see Sternberg and Barnes 1988), for example, review a number of theories that suggest that the concept of romantic love is compatible with the individualistic Western cultural perspective, with its emphasis on self-sufficiency and personal autonomy, but not with the collectivist Eastern (e.g., Chinese) cultural perspective, with its focus on traditional kinship-related obligations and tacit disapproval of public expressions of intimacy and affection. E. Hatfield and R. L. Rapson (1987), however, argue that romantic love is a pancultural experience, and current studies, including those conducted by anthropologists interested in romantic love (e.g., I. Jankowiak and G. W. Fischer 1992), appear to show more cross-cultural similarities than differences.

Ellen S. Berscheid and Pamela C. Regan

Luria, Alexander Romanovich (1902–1977)

Alexander Luria made a distinguished contribution to neuropsychology. He was an expert in aphasia and in the effects of brain injury. His most important theoretical works are *Higher Cortical Functions in Man* and *The Working Brain*.

Joel Redfield

Luscher Color Test

The Luscher Color Test is a projective test that is almost unknown in clinical practice in the United States, although it is widely used in Europe.

The Luscher Color Test, developed by Max Luscher (1970), has a long form and a short form. Both of the forms require that the subject express her preferences for a variety of colors. The test materials consist of color patches, seventy-three patches in the long form and eight patches in the short form.

The essential underlying assumptions for the Luscher Color Test—that color preferences correlate with some significant personality variables—might be credible if not compelling. Luscher's procedures and interpretive principles, however, require more empirical evidence.

Philip A. Goldberg

· M ·

McDougall, William (1871–1938)

William McDougall's theories were based on three assumptions: (1) behavior is purposive or hormic; (2) every individual is endowed with certain purposeful behavioral tendencies called "instincts" or "propensities;" and (3) the entire behavior is determined by instincts or their derivatives, called "sentiments" or "tastes." McDougall formulated his thoughts in terms of a psychophysical reductionism. The basic construct in McDougall's theory is *horme*, the urge to live. McDougall, following in the footsteps of Jean-Baptiste Lamarck, assumed that acquired modes of behavior could be transmitted through genes. His main works are *An Introduction to Social Psychology, An Outline of Psychology,* and *Energies of Men.*

Benjamin B. Wolman

Mahler, Margaret S. (1897–1985)

Margaret S. Mahler's research encompassed three areas: (1) the disturbances of the ego's mastery of motility, (2) severe emotional disturbances in young children and childhood psychoses; and (3) the hypothesis and psychoanalytic observational findings on the symbiotic origin of human existence and the separation-individuation process. She wrote *The Psychological Birth of the Human Infant: Symbiosis and Individuation* (1975) with F. Pine and Bergman.

John Bourke McDevitt

Malpractice in Psychiatry

Malpractice suits now present a much greater problem for psychiatrists than they did 10 or 15 years ago. The most comprehensive source of data on psychiatric malpractice suits is the APA-sponsored Professional Liability Insurance Program. The program has operated since 1984, and it currently provides coverage for approximately 9,000 psychiatrists. According to data from this program, approximately 6% of psychiatrists are named in a malpractice suit in any one year. For the psychiatrist who has been sued once, the chance of being sued a second time rises from 6% to 14% each year, and for the psychiatrist who has been sued twice, the chance of being sued again rises to 21% each year.

Malpractice suits against psychiatrists arise from many different types of clinical situations. The most common single source of claims is the occurrence of an attempted or completed suicide. Such suicide-related claims account for at least 20% of the annual total. Another 20% of claims fall into the general category of complaints of "improper diagnosis and/or treatment." Other sources of malpractice claims account for relatively small numbers of suits, for example, medication side effects, breach of confidentiality, failure to warn third parties of potential harm ("Tarasoff cases"), failure to obtain informed consent for treatment, and improper confinement. Of note is the fact that there are very few claims that arise specifically from the administration of electroconvulsive therapy (ECT).

In years past, undue familiarity was another frequent source of claims. In 1984, for example, 25% of the suits filed were in this category. Since 1985, however, the Professional Liability Insurance Pro-

320

gram has provided coverage only for legal defense in such cases. Insurance coverage is not provided for any damage awards that might be paid as a result of a jury verdict or a settlement. Currently, undue familiarity suits account for only about 1% of the total.

Malpractice claims are filed in response to what is perceived to be an adverse or unsatisfactory outcome. Not every potential claim becomes a malpractice suit. For example, there are far more suicide attempts and completed suicides than there are suicide-related malpractice suits. Some patients—or their families—choose to file suit, while others do not.

Studies have assessed the likelihood of a suit being filed when an adverse outcome has occurred. Likewise, there are studies that have addressed the question of why some patients and families sue while others do not. None of these studies have specifically focused on psychiatric malpractice cases; but the results are, nonetheless, very pertinent to psychiatry. A study published in 1991 provides the most comprehensive assessment of the likelihood of a malpractice suit being filed. In this study, R. W. Brennan and colleagues reviewed approximately 30,000 randomly selected records of admissions to general medical/surgical beds in New York City hospitals. The reviewers identified thousands of incidents that they judged to be indicative of medical negligence. From these thousands of incidents, however, only 50% of the cases filed.

Many patients do not sue even when their care has led to a poor outcome and even when medical negligence may have occurred, and some patients may not be aware of negligence that has occurred, and some may be willing to accept results that they recognize as being of poor quality.

Two major studies have addressed the question of why some patients and families sue while others do not (Hickson et al. 1992). While the focus of these studies was obstetric, gynecologic, and pediatric cases, the results are instructive for all physicians and all mental health providers. A perception of a poor outcome or an injury is a necessary but not a sufficient basis for filing a malpractice suit. Anger toward the physician is a frequent factor, and this anger often arises not because of the patient's dissat-

isfaction with the outcome but rather because of the patient's dissatisfaction with the physician-patient relationship. Patients who sue talk about feeling that their physicians did not care about them, and these patients complain also about a lack of communication with the physicians.

In the case of a completed suicide, when the surviving family members file suit, they are often reflecting their own sense of personal guilt for having failed to stop the suicide. Filing the malpractice suit can be a way for the surviving family members to say that the suicide was not their fault. Even in cases that do not involve suicide, family members can play a major role in bringing about the filing of a suit. Often, the patient may feel comfortable with the medical outcome and with the relationship with the physician, but the suit is filed at the urging of others in the family.

Being sued for malpractice is a traumatic event (Charles and Kennedy 1985). The psychiatrist defendant usually feels unfairly criticized, angry, and embarrassed. In addition, if there was truly a negative outcome, then there is likely to be a sense of guilt and inadequacy. Continuing to practice while involved in a suit can be enormously difficult, especially because the typical suit can take several years to be resolved. What is more, during this time, defendants can feel very much alone with their anxiety and distress, for defense attorneys generally advise that there be no discussion of the case with peers.

Fortunately, most malpractice suits work out well for the defendant psychiatrist. Data from the Professional Liability Insurance Program show that more than three-quarters of all suits are dropped by the plaintiff, dismissed in court, or won by the psychiatrist defendant on a summary judgment. Another 21% of cases are settled out of court, with the program making a payment to the plaintiff on behalf of the insured psychiatrist. No more than 2% of all cases result in a trial; and, of those that do go to trial, four out of five are won by the defendant psychiatrist.

In view of the frequency of malpractice suits against psychiatrists and the enormous problems that they can cause, it is essential that every psychiatrist take active steps toward risk management. Such steps are designed, first, to prevent the occurrence of malpractice suits and, second, to increase the likelihood of prevailing in a suit if one does occur. In a very general sense, risk prevention is synonymous with good-quality care. An example of a specific risk prevention step is the one that is illustrated by the widely known Tarasoff case. This is the step taken by a treating psychiatrist to warn a third party of potential harm that may be inflicted by a patient under the psychiatrist's care.

Another important technique of preventive risk management—and one that is much more frequently needed than is a Tarasoff warning—is the process of obtaining a patient's informed consent for the use of medication. Some psychiatrists are now obtaining written consents for medication use, that is, they have each patient sign a form that sets out the potential side effects of the medication to be used. For the majority of practicing psychiatrists who do not use written consent forms for medication, some other method of obtaining—and documenting—the patient's informed consent is essential. For example, one common technique is that of describing the options available for treatment, explaining the purpose of using the chosen medication, explaining the potential side effects, talking with the patient to be sure that this information is fully understood, obtaining the patient's verbal consent, and then entering a note in the patient's chart. The note is written to document the fact that the patient's consent to take the medication has been obtained and, further, that the consent is informed—that is, based on an awareness and understanding of the purposes of the medication's use and its potential side effects.

The process of obtaining and recording informed consent clearly illustrates two key concepts in risk prevention: communication and documentation. Good communication is a key to establishing good physician-patient relationships. As a result, it is a key to preventing malpractice suits. In psychiatry, there has always been an emphasis on the importance of good communications. Today, however, as psychiatric practice becomes increasingly focused on short-term treatment and crisis intervention, psychiatrists must take particular care to be sure that there is always good communication with their patients, even those who are seen only briefly.

Along with good communication, there must be good documentation. Again, the issue of informed consent illustrates the importance of having adequate documentation. Without documentation of what the patient was told and what the patient's response was, there is no informed consent. As it has been said many times, not only about consents but about other matters as well, "If it is not documented, it did not happen."

Documentation need not be excessively detailed, but there must be enough information in the record to demonstrate key clinical points—and the entries must always be legible. For example, when working with a depressed patient who is potentially suicidal, it is valuable for the record of each patient contact to make reference to the presence or absence of suicidal ideation, intent, and/or planning.

Good documentation certainly will help the legal defense process if a malpractice suit is filed. Good malpractice insurance is the other major contributor to a successful defense. The choice of malpractice insurance is really doubly significant, for the insurance carrier is responsible for selecting the attorney who provides the legal defense.

Malpractice insurance represents one of the most important purchases that psychiatrists must make for their practices. The decision to purchase a particular policy is a complex one. Price (that is, premium level) cannot be the only criterion that is considered. It is essential that the policy be purchased from a company or program that is financially sound. Also, a decision must be made to select occurrence coverage or claims-made coverage. An occurrence policy provides coverage no matter when a suit may be filed, provided that the claim relates to an incident that occurred during the period when the policy was in force. By contrast, a claims-made policy provides coverage only for claims filed during the policy period. When a claims-made policyholder stops purchasing these annual policies, it is necessary to purchase "tail coverage" as protection against any claim that might be filed in subsequent years.

The malpractice insurance scene is one in which there are likely to be many significant changes in the next several years. For example, there is now ongoing discussion in Congress and state legislatures regarding possible changes in the existing legal procedures for handling medical malpractice cases. One focus of these "tort reform" efforts is the approach of placing limits on awards for noneconomic damages, for example, awards for pain and suffering. Another approach is the requirement that large monetary awards be "structured," so that the funds are paid out over time rather than being awarded in a single lump sum.

While some people are promoting changes in the existing legal procedures for handling malpractice suits through tort reform, others are proposing that there be a totally new system for handling these cases. The American Medical Association and others, for example, are proposing a "fault based alternative dispute resolution system" (Johnson et al. 1989). Such a system would continue to require that a plaintiff demonstrate physician error or negligence, but the mechanism for hearing the case would utilize binding arbitration. Another approach that has been recommended is that of "enterprise liability." Under this approach, liability would be assumed not by individual physicians but by hospitals and managed care organizations with which the physicians are associated (Weller et al. 1992).

Alan I. Levenson

Man-Machine Systems

Certain aggregates designed by engineers are known as "man-machine systems," because they consist of combinations of equipment and human beings. The latter operate, maintain, or otherwise use the hardware, computer programs, and documentation that comprise "equipment." Psychologists who call themselves engineering, human factors, or system psychologists examine (1) how the human elements affect the functioning of the system, and (2) how the system and the environment in which it operates affect its human elements.

Analysis
Psychological analysis in systems has dealt almost exclusively with human performance and the effectiveness (including safety) of system operators or maintainers. However, psychologists must also be concerned with other interactions between machines and people—the ways in which the physical system and its components affect the emotions, motivations, and well-being of all of its users. Humanistic concerns about the enjoyment of one's work—and even the availability of work—might influence considerations about "degree of mannedness" even when greater automation makes a system more effective.

Procedures
Psychologists have analyzed and improved the procedures that people use in operating or maintaining complex equipment and have also devised better techniques for "job aids"—handbooks and manuals—that incorporate procedures. Research has assisted the development of techniques for troubleshooting and other procedures in equipment maintenance and for logistical aspects of system maintenance (Parsons 1972).

Training
Most of the training of maintenance or operational personnel in systems aims to provide, through training devices, simulators, and classroom or programmed instruction, the kinds of knowledge and skills needed to perform certain autonomous tasks. The development of training aids, materials, and programs for the variety of such tasks within a system is a major undertaking that should begin early in the system life cycle.

Test and Evaluation
When a test includes operators, psychologists can make sure that these are representative and that human processes, such as learning and fatigue, do not confound the results. When a test includes more than one state of one variable, psychologists with training in experimentation can help establish an appropriate multivariate design to examine the effects of different input loads, physical configurations, and procedures.

H. McIlvaine Parsons

Manifest Anxiety Scale

The Manifest Anxiety Scale (J. V. Taylor 1953) was developed to measure anxiety as a drive as a way of testing hypotheses within the Hullian learning system. The Hullian system (D. Byrne 1974) holds that the strength of a response is a function of the strength of a habit times the strength of the drive minus inhibitory forces. Thus, if anxiety is a drive, the higher the anxiety, the greater the response of a person to a stimulus. This scale was designed to measure the strength of the anxiety drive, although it has been used to measure anxiety in a wide variety of contexts and in studies that have nothing to do with Hullian learning theory.

The scale is composed of fifty true-false items selected from the Minnesota Multiphasic Personality Inventory (MMPI). Split-half reliability of .92 has been reported.

Clifford H. Swensen

Marital Choice: Determinants

The determinants of marital choice may be conveniently separated into two classifications: (1) factors determining a "field of eligibles," and (2) factors determining the choice of partner within a field of eligibles.

The evidence influencing the field of eligibles has been rather apparent throughout history ("birds of a feather flock together"), but quantitative evidence supporting homogamy has been gathered mainly since the end of World War II. It has been found that individuals tend to marry those of the same race, age, education, socioeconomic status, locale, intelligence, attitudes and values, and religion at a greater-than-chance rate.

Although in a general sense individuals marry homogamously, there are two problems with depending on homogamy as the sole determinant of martial choice. First, there may be several marital possibilities with very similar backgrounds. Second, there are always a number of examples of individuals who depart from homogamous norms in one or more important respects. An "old geezer" may marry a "pretty young thing." A white may marry a black, a Jew a gentile, a prince a pauper, and, rather more rarely, an heiress a gasoline attendant.

The theory of complementary needs states that "each individual seeks within his or her field of eligi-

bles for that person who gives the greatest promise of providing him or her with maximum need gratification" (R. F. Winch 1958, 89). However, individuals are drawn together by complementary needs, which are defined as "A's behavior in acting out A's need X is gratifying to B's need Y, and B's behavior in acting out B's need Y is gratifying to A's need X" (93). In practice, Winch expects that a couple should be negatively correlated for a given need (e.g., dominance) and positively correlated for complementary needs (if the man is high on dominance, the woman should be high on submissiveness).

Two basic principles underly the stimulus-value-role theory, first formulated in 1970: (1) marital courtship involves a series of sequential stages, which are labeled "stimulus," "value," and "role," and (2) at any given point in the courtship, its viability is dependent on the equity of exchange experienced.

Bernard I. Murstein

Marital Conflict

Marital conflict is viewed in terms of a manifest and a latent dimension. The manifest dimension involves the issues about which the couple is explicitly concerned. These may include fights over specific matters, like sex or money management.

The latent conflict remains unresolved because it lies beneath the level of conscious awareness and because it is maintained by unrecognized, maladaptive patterns of marital interaction.

The role of the therapist is to assist in the constructive resolution of the latent conflicts. This being done, the manifest issues will be found to have either disappeared or lost their significance. In some instances the marriage may end in a constructive, unembittered divorce, in which each spouse has been strengthened by new self-understanding.

Certain characteristic assumptions about marriage can be made:

1. Marital conflict is inevitable. The goal is not to eliminate differences but to channel their expression along constructive lines.
2. Communication occurs on both verbal and

nonverbal levels. A source of marital friction is an incongruity in the messages being transmitted at these two levels. Incongruities are most likely to result when open expression of differences is inhibited.

3. Spouses frequently differ in their styles of relating. Such differences are to be expected but can be a source of difficulty if the differences are not recognized and each style not accepted as equally valid. The most common stylistic differences represent some variant of the task-versus-socioemotional orientation. One spouse is seen as paying more attention to "getting things done" and "the facts," while the other is thought to be more attuned to the relationship-oriented aspects of marital interchanges.

Kenneth Kressel

Marital and Family Therapy

The nature of the problems in a family is related to many factors, including the evolutionary phase in which the family finds itself. Marital problems may be the focus of concern at any phase. Early in a marriage, problems may focus on new adaptations and the necessity of creating a new home structure. Issues of intimacy and sexuality have to be resolved, and sharing of the mutual workload has to be negotiated. With children, the marital system changes radically, and symptomatic behavior may develop as a reaction to the new stresses.

Eventually, crises connected with physical illness come to each family, and these may put unbearable stresses on the system. A further phase is the aging of the main family members, with the associated problems of retirement, finances, and the illnesses and loneliness that may very well become a continuing part of the total context of the family.

The involvement of the therapist in joint sessions facilitates a more rapid comprehension of relationship difficulties and permits more effective intervention. Cotherapists may help to meet the concern about loss of objectivity on the part of one therapist. This method is also favored by many because it provides a better empathetic and modeling system, especially when male and female cotherapists work together.

The use of couples group therapy has also found wide acceptance, and provides the double benefit of treating the couple as a system while providing an opportunity for experimentation by both partners in forming other relationships, which can be observed and discussed by both.

Multiple family groups may provide many of the advantages of couples groups. In multiple family groups, each family member can make alliances with members of other families and find new ways to resolve old conflicts, and also discover new connections with members of other families in positions similar to her own.

Family therapists are much more active in their therapeutic style than therapists who traditionally see individuals in an analytically oriented model. In addition to this more personally involving style, the family therapist may use any number of special techniques, including paradoxical behavioral methods, role-play and psychodrama, sculpting, home visits, and videotape playback.

Home visits have become another valuable mode of intervening in the family system, but must be kept on a professional basis to enable the therapist to maintain a perspective and avoid being too quickly and too thoroughly caught up in the family system. This latter eventuality renders the therapist powerless as an important influence in intervening in an ongoing family situation, and the old and dysfunctional equilibrium is thereby maintained.

The theoretical position of family therapy is that no one person's behavior can be understood without an understanding of the context in which that person is living, and of the human interactions in which she is involved. By this understanding, then, all therapy can be seen as family therapy, or systems therapy, in that any change in any member person of a system must of necessity result in an alteration in the total system, with effects on all other members.

Ian E. Alger

Marrow, Alfred (1905–1978)

The United States psychologist Alfred Marrow applied Kurt Lewin's method of "action research" to problems of managing industrial organizations and of reducing racial, ethnic, and religious prejudice. His books are *Living without Hate* (1951) and *Changing Patterns of Prejudice* (1963).

Virginia Staudt Sexton

Maslow, Abraham H. (1908–1970)

The United States psychologist Abraham H. Maslow set up a hierarchy of motives, starting with physiological needs. The satisfaction of these needs permits other needs to emerge, such as safety and avoidance of danger. If physiological and safety drives are satisfied, higher needs come into play; for example, belonging and love, followed by the need for self-esteem and self-confidence. The need to do what one can do is called "self-actualization." Maslow noted that self-actualizing people are not free from guilt, anxiety, and conflict, but they are more completely individual and more completely socialized.

Maslow was the founder of humanistic psychology, which is concerned with "creativity, love, self-growth . . . self-actualization, higher values, being, becoming, spontaneity . . . responsibility, psychological health and related concepts." He founded the *Journal of Humanistic Psychology* and the Association for Humanistic Psychology.

S. Stansfield Sargent

Mass Media and Their Influence

Investigators and public authorities have expressed active interest in educational television since the medium rose to popularity in the mid-1950s; the very palpable success of *Sesame Street* stands as clear testimony that the entertainment media can be powerful teachers of cognitive skills.

Content analyses reveal that portrayals of minority groups and women on television are limited and stereotyped and that violence and aggression tend to be the medium's dominant entertainment themes. It has been realistically estimated that the average child will watch the violent destruction of more than 13,400 persons on television entertainment between the ages of 5 and 15, a concern heightened by the fact that most often aggressive acts are portrayed on entertainment television as potent and successful tactics for achieving the protagonist's goals.

Correlational and experimental evidence further converge on the effects of televised aggression by showing that its impact is not limited to stimulating overt aggressive behavior; greater willingness to approve or tolerate the aggressive acts of others, a lowered sensitivity to real-life aggression, expectations of personal victimization, and decrements in cooperative behavior all have been shown to be indirect manifestations of the original input (Drabman and Thomas 1974; Gerbner and Gross 1974; Hapkiewicz and Roden 1971).

According to the *Report of the American Psychological Association Commission on Violence and Youth*, volume I, 1993,

There is absolutely no doubt that higher levels of viewing violence on television are correlated with increased acceptance of aggressive attitudes and increased aggressive behavior. Three major national studies—the Surgeon General's Commission Report (1972), the National Institute of Mental Health Ten Year Follow-Up (1982), and the report of the American Psychological Association's Committee on Media in Society (1992)—reviewed hundreds of studies to arrive at the irrefutable conclusion that viewing violence increases violence. In addition, prolonged viewing of media violence can lead to emotional desensitization toward violence.

Children's exposure to violence in films, television, and popular music, particularly at young ages, can have harmful lifelong consequences. Aggressive habits learned early in life are the foundation for later behavior. Aggressive children who have trouble in school and in relating to peers tend to watch more television; the violence they see there, in turn, reinforces their tendency toward aggression, compounding their academic and social failure. These effects are both short-term and long-lasting: A longitudinal study of boys found a significant relation between exposure to television violence at 8 years of age and antisocial acts—including serious, violent criminal offenses and spouse abuse—22 years later. (33)

Robert M. Liebert

Matching-to-Sample

Matching-to-sample and oddity learning are instances of relational learning paradigms in which the correct response is based upon some relationship among the stimuli present in a display rather than upon their absolute properties. To demonstrate successful solution of such problems, the subject (S) must respond correctly when specific elements of the display are replaced or their reward value reversed. In a typical matching-to-sample experiment, on a given trial a single standard (sample) stimulus is first presented. After one or more responses to the sample, two or more comparison stimuli are presented, one of which, the correct choice, is physically identical to the standard. In simultaneous matching, the sample and comparison stimuli are simultaneously present; in successive matching, the comparison stimuli may be introduced as the sample is terminated (zero delay) or after some interval (delayed matching).

In the more recent literature, delayed matching-to-sample has proved to be a fruitful paradigm in the investigation of short-term memory in animals. Performance is based upon recognition memory, because one of the available comparison stimuli is identical to the standard. A variation of the matching-to-sample procedure, called "symbolic matching" (or conditional matching), provides an analogy to a recall test. With this procedure, the match is based upon an arbitrary association between the sample and the comparison stimuli, rather than upon physical identity; thus, the correct choice requires recall of the value of the standard.

David R. Thomas

Maternal Behavior

Some aspects of maternal behavior have been related to the hormonal changes of childbirth in biological mothers. Among these is postpartum lability. It has been estimated that about 30% of normal mothers experience such emotional upset. So many other factors are confounded with the hormonal changes that accompany giving birth that it is difficult to establish threads of causality between variables.

M. H. Klaus and his coworkers (1970) describe the characteristic pattern of responses that mothers make when they are first presented with their infants. This pattern is especially conducive to infant-mother eye contact, and thus, interaction sequences are highly likely. As M. P. M. Richards (1974) points out, however, psychologists know very little about the effects of different methods of caretaking within the normal range. Nevertheless, the infant's behavior is patterned even during the last months of prenatal life, and these patterns are assigned meaning by the caregiver. Likewise, the infant selectively attends to stimulation that is conducive to communication, as demonstrated by the infant's tendency to attend to faces.

C. Dunn and M. P. M. Richards (1975) reported results from a longitudinal study of sixty-eight home-delivered mother-child pairs in Cambridge, England. They found evidence to suggest that the frequency of affectionate talking by the mother to her baby during the first 10 days of feeding sessions is the most important variable associated with the infant's rate of sucking.

M. D. S. Ainsworth and her coworkers (1974) emphasize the mother's contribution to the quality of the mother-infant relationship in the first year of life. They have found four characteristics of maternal behavior that are significantly related to the quality of these interactions: sensitivity, acceptance, cooperation, and accessibility.

A number of authors have pointed out that research on parenting has emphasized the effects of parent behaviors on the infant and has neglected the effects of infant behavior on the parent. Howard A. Moss's (1967) study clearly shows the effects of babies on their mothers. In this study, boy babies were more irritable and received more response from their mothers than did girls during the third week, but by the twelfth week, the mothers of boys had tired of trying to pacify them and were spending less time responding to them than were the mothers of girls.

The importance of physical contact between child and caregiver, over such other factors as reduction in hunger, forms the basis of John Bowlby's (1958) theory of attachment. The results of H. F. Harlow's research with rhesus monkeys, in which dramatic decrements in later social behavior were shown as a result of having been reared in isolation with a wire mother-surrogate as opposed to a cloth mother-surrogate, have been used to illustrate the importance of intimate physical contact.

Michele Andrisin Wittig

Maternal Employment Effect

The effects of maternal employment are usually not direct but are mediated by other factors. Thus, in addition to the sex of the child, other important aspects of the situation are the mother's attitude about employment, the nature of her child-care arrangements, the amount of strain involved in handling the dual roles of worker and mother, whether employment is full-time or part-time, and a host of other conditions. Positive effects of employment are enhanced when the employment is accompanied by a minimum of conflict and strain for the mother. A very important factor is the age of the child. In general, working mothers, their husbands, and their children tend to have less traditional sex-role concepts and are more likely to approve of maternal employment.

Lois Wladis Hoffman

Mathematics Learning and Instruction

R. M. Gagné (1970) has developed a model for analysis of the different levels of mathematical learning in terms of an instructional hierarchy. The model suggests that if the final skill desired is a problem-solving capability, then the scope and sequence of the mathematics curriculum is determined by a task analysis of the subordinate capabilities prerequisite to the attainment of the given objective. The hierarchical structure of mathematics greatly aids the formulation of the sequence, although the resultant structure of prerequisites is not necessarily universal. Readiness is essentially a function of the presence or absence of prerequisite learning. Thus, mathematics instruction is viewed as the product of effective problem-solving behaviors.

Jean Piaget's developmental research has had a pronounced effect on mathematical learning and instruction. Piaget's (1952) theory of number conservation has directed attention to the stages through which young children pass in arriving at the knowledge of number. Research in the cognitive area of number conservation has changed and broadened the emphasis of mathematics education for young children, from the attainment of narrowly defined mathematics skills to the development of broad intellectual powers.

J. S. Bruner (1966) also views mathematics from the perspective of the inherent processes of learning. The learner begins with the manipulation of materials or tasks in order to present a problem. This problem may take the form of (1) goals to be achieved in the absence of readily discernible means for reaching these goals; (2) contradictions between sources of information of apparent equal creditability; or (3) the quest for structure or symmetry in situations where such order is not readily apparent. The process then becomes more systematic as the learner is led back through the needed associations and concepts to finally derive the appropriate rules for solving the problem.

Jerome C. Bernstein

Maze Learning

In 1902, W. S. Small at Clark University constructed a replica in miniature of the Hampton Court maze and studied the progress of rats learning to find their way through it. This rat-in-maze methodology became the hallmark of the scientific study of learning for half a century. Unfortunately, the method turned out to be a scientific dead end, and it is rarely used these days.

The problem is that maze behavior is quite complex. In just two papers, those on the goal gradient and the habit-family hierarchy, Clark L. Hull dealt with almost three dozen phenomena of such learning. Such complexity led many psychologists to use simpler mazes. Even these have now nearly disappeared from the literature, which is dominated by work with the Skinner box and other simpler methods.

Gregory A. Kimble

Mechanical Aptitude: Measurement Methods

There is no one type of test function that underlies mechanical work to the same extent that general intelligence tests relate to schoolwork. In order satisfactorily to predict a particular mechanical job, a range of different kinds of tests must be used in a battery. Different combinations of tests are usually needed for different jobs.

Intelligence Tests

General intelligence tests tend to be more predictive of how well the individual will do in job training than of how well he will perform subsequently on the job. This is probably due to the fact that the training phase requires more abstract ability. In many cases, the training program involves classroomlike procedures, the reading of materials, and the learning of machine operations. Success at activities of this sort is what intelligence tests predict best.

General intelligence tests tend to be more predictive of success in high-skill than in low-skill jobs. That is, validities are usually higher for jobs such as that of electrical technician or complex machine operator than for jobs such as that of truck driver or furniture mover. The difference in validity is probably due to the increased importance of abstract ability in more highly skilled work. In selecting people for unskilled work, the problem is to set up minimum standards of intelligence rather than to seek persons of high intelligence.

Spatial and Perceptual Tests

One of the best known spatial tests for mechanical aptitude is the Minnesota Paper Form Board Test. This is a printed test in which each item consists of cut-out pieces from a geometrical form, and the subject is required to choose from a number of composite forms what the pieces would look like when put together. It is a useful predictor of grades in shop courses, supervisors' ratings of workmanship, objective production records, and many other measures of mechanical performance..

Mechanical comprehension. Among the most successful tests of mechanical aptitude are those designed to measure the mastery of mechanical principles, or the ability to reason with mechanical problems.

Mechanical information. One of the most useful measures for the selection of skilled and semiskilled workers is a test of information, or knowledge, about tools and machinery.

Analysis of mechanical aptitude tests. A sufficient personnel-selection program usually requires a careful study of the particular industrial setting. The diversity of psychological functions required by different jobs makes it necessary to try out a range of tests to find the one that will work well in practice. Also, it is often necessary to invent and construct tests for particular jobs.

Jum C. Nunnally

Mediation in Learning

The concept of mediation plays a significant role in stimulus-response (S-R) theories, where it is important in the explanation of such "mentalistic" phenomena as thinking, concept formation, and problem solving. For the S-R theorist, the problem with such behavior is that there appears always to be a large ideational gap between the objective stimulus situation and the objective behavior, which reveals that the individual has been thinking, has formed a concept, or has solved a problem. The theoretical contribution of mechanisms of mediation is to bridge this gap.

Gregory A. Kimble

Meditation: Its Clinical Use

Modern westernized forms of meditation are being used in an increasing number of clinical settings as adjuncts to conventional forms of psychiatric treatment. This trend is enhanced as contemporary non-cultic methods of meditation become available and the practice is divested of its esoteric trappings and rituals. Mental health practitioners are thus able to assume a more active role in the management of meditation than was possible when meditation was taught largely by organizations whose instructors were not clinically trained.

Among the clinically based methods, clinically standardized meditation (CSM) (P. Carrington 1979) and respiratory one method (ROM) (H. Benson 1975) are widely used. CSM is designed specifically for use by clinicians and is taught by means of cassette tapes, with the clinician supervising her patient's meditation, either individually or in follow-up group settings, and it comprises a complete training program. ROM is conveyed by means of brief written instructions, which clinicians hand to patients, and does not include full training in the management of the technique.

Meditation is used for pain control by some practitioners. Meditators frequently report that they are able to lessen and sometimes alleviate pain through the use of meditation.

The use of meditation with children is relatively unexplored, although existing reports suggest the desirability of using meditation for behavior problems involving symptoms of tension and/or hyperactivity. For example, while not a meditation technique, Kiddie QR (C. F. Stroebel et al. 1980) is a stress management program widely taught to children ages 3 to 8 in classrooms around the country. The 6-second Quieting Reflex (Stroebel 1976), while derived from the subjective phenomenology of thermal and electromyogram (EMG) feedback, rather than meditation, is being used by many meditators as a quick procedure for beginning their own preferred method of meditating, such as CSM.

Patricia Carrington
Charles F. Stroebel

Meditation as a Therapeutic Agent

Full-scale scientific investigation of meditation has awaited the development of a simple standardized technique suitable for widespread experimental use, because investigators previously could not rely for their subject population on a few practitioners who might take as long as 20 years to master the art of meditation. A simple westernized form of mantra meditation, known as transcendental meditation (TM), developed in 1958 by an Indian monk, Maharishi Mahesh Yogi, fulfills the above criteria and has been used in over 300 experimental investigations on the effects of meditation.

Physiologically, meditation seems to represent a unique state during which the body appears to be in a profound state of rest and where decreased autonomic activity, decreased emotional and sensory reactivity, and decreased muscle tension coincide with a wakeful and alert brain. Changes in the electrical activity of the brain, in the autonomic nervous system, and in somatosensory functions occur during TM, while cardiac output as measured by catheters may be slowed by as much as 25%. Oxygen consumption during TM tends to decrease as much as or more than it does during deep NREM (quiescent) sleep.

Brain waves recorded from well-practiced meditators during TM appear to be characterized by a marked increase in the intensity of alpha wave trains in the central and frontal regions of the brain (although total alpha may not necessarily increase). These may be followed later by bursts of theta waves. Like Zen meditators, TM meditators have been reported to show no habituation to sound and light stimuli administered during meditation. Drowsiness and light sleep also frequently appear in the EEG records of subjects during TM, although in general the meditative state appears to differ from that of both sleep and ordinary rest with eyes closed.

A consistent and reliable change found over time in persons who meditate is a marked reduction in anxiety levels. This finding has been investigated in a number of laboratories, with no failure to replicate. TM seems to reduce anxiety in a majority of those who practice it, although several recent studies indicate that when groups practicing other relaxation techniques are used as controls, similar reductions in anxiety may result from the continued practice of such techniques as progressive relaxation or alpha biofeedback.

Patricia Carrington and Harmon S. Ephron (1976) list the following personality changes noted in meditating patients:

1. *tension reduction*: a general lessening of anxiety, disappearance of inappropriate startle responses, improvement in psychosomatic conditions (e.g., tension headaches, hypertension, insomnias, and hypersomnias), and reduced need for psychotropic medication
2. *energy release*: increased physical stamina, increased creative productivity, and increased productiveness of free associations during the therapeutic session
3. *superego amelioration*: lessened tendencies toward self-recrimination, lessened paranoid tendencies
4. *mood stabilization*: elevation and stabilization of mood in patients with neurotically determined depressions, although not, in their experience, in patients with acute depressive reactions (The latter tended to stop meditating even though they might be showing beneficial results from the meditation.)
5. *availability of affect*: increased affective relatedness to others, increased availability of affect during psychotherapeutic sessions
6. *individuation*: increased sense of separate identity, increased self-assertiveness (the self rather than the expectations of others becoming the point of reference)
7. *antiaddictive properties*: lessening of tendencies toward the abuse of marijuana, alcohol, or cigarettes

Patricia Carrington
Harmon S. Ephron

Melton, Arthur W. (1906–1978)

Arthur Melton's principal interest was experimental design and methodology. The main topics of his research were retroactive and proactive inhibition learning and short-term memory. He was the editor of the *Journal of Experimental Psychology*.

Virginia Staudt Sexton

Memory

Knowledge about the way human memory operates is important for an understanding of how we function. It is difficult to envision how we would function if we had no memory system for representing experiences and events. Without memory we would always live in the immediate present. We would be severely limited in the world of work, unable to function, unable to communicate effectively, and unable to enjoy friends and colleagues. Perhaps the most important loss would be our sense of identity; it is to memory that we owe our sense of personal continuity and our ability to plan for the future. Moreover, memory is essential to the operation of other cognitive processes such as problem solving, reasoning, language, comprehension, and decision making.

Memory Defined

Memory is a complex concept that refers to a number of processes. Memory is not some static entity but a dynamic set of processes with interactions among the processes. Any act of remembering is composed of three components: encoding, storage, and retrieval (Baddeley 1990; Ellis and Hunt 1993). *Encoding* is the process by which we perceive and acquire information. For example, as we read a book we pay attention to the content, focusing on the meaning, and thus encode the gist or main ideas (Kintsch 1974). During encoding some kind of representation is established, sometimes referred to as a memory trace. *Storage* is the maintenance of information, a holding process so that knowledge can be used at a later time. *Retrieval* refers to our ability to access and use stored information. Typically, retrieval involves an active search for stored information; however, in some cases retrieval may be almost automatic, as when we are asked simple questions, such as "What is your mother's name?"

Memory Systems

Memory can be further classified with respect to the types of things remembered. A prominent distinction is that of declarative and procedural memory (L. R. Squire 1987). *Declarative memory* is memory for facts acquired through learning, whereas *procedural memory* is memory for learned skills and procedures. This distinction is based on studies of amnesics who typically show impairments in declarative but not procedural memory. Declarative memory can be further subdivided into episodic and semantic memory (E. Tulving 1983). *Episodic memory* refers to memory for past events in a person's life and is so called because it refers to specific episodes experienced by an individual. *Semantic memory* represents general knowledge of the world. The semantic memory system represents organized information about ideas and facts, such as knowledge of who was the first U.S. president. Notice that semantic memory refers to events that a person did not directly experience but which nevertheless are part of her general world knowledge. The second category, procedural memories, include motor skills, classical conditioning, habituation, and cognitive skills, such as reading.

Explicit and Implicit Memory

An important distinction is that of explicit and implicit memory. *Explicit memory* refers to conscious memory, in which an individual is directed to produce something from memory and is tested by recall or recognition, which are direct tests of memory. *Implicit memory* involves an indirect test, in which memory is assessed by way of a task that does not require an individual to directly consider past experiences. A simple test of recall, such as "What did you eat for breakfast?" is a direct test of explicit memory. In contrast, asking a person to complete a list of word stems, having been shown a list of word pairs during a study session, is an indirect test. In this case, no reference is made to the previously shown word pairs, nor is the test presented as one of memory. What is striking in such tests is that individuals may show strong impairment in direct tests due to a variety of conditions, such as amnesia, whereas little or no impairment appears in the indirect tests. This has suggested to memory theorists

that there may be fundamental differences between memory systems, in which direct tests of memory draw on episodic memory and indirect tests draw on the semantic memory system. Alternative accounts have been proposed based on the idea of task-appropriate processing. Here, it is assumed that differences in implicit and explicit memory reflect differences in the kind of processing that occurs during learning. Regardless of theoretical interpretations, the explicit-implicit memory distinction is a major issue in current memory research (cf. H. L. Roediger 1990; D. L. Schacter 1992).

Working Memory

At one time it was thought that there were two distinct systems of short- and long-term memory, with differences based on the duration of the memory trace, amount of storage capacity, and nature of the memory code or representation. The idea that these two kinds of memory represent different theoretical systems has been generally discredited; however, it is recognized that some sort of system for dealing with the facts of immediate memory or awareness is necessary. Certain events occupy our thought processes at any moment, that is, our active memory, and the concept of working memory has been developed to account for the limitations of active, short-term memory. The idea of working memory has been championed by A. D. Baddeley (1990), and is a system for holding information used for other cognitive work. Working memory does not propose separate principles for short- and long-term memory systems, and all retention is determined by the amount and type of processing devoted to the material, an idea that is called "levels of processing." Baddeley (1990) has proposed two subsystems of working memory: the visuospatial sketchpad, to account for the storage of visual-spatial material, and the articulatory loop, to account for the storage of speech-based material.

Encoding and Retrieval

The analysis of encoding and retrieval in memory has focused on various processes. A number of important processes have been identified, including selective attention, rehearsal, elaboration, semantic processing, imagery, distinctiveness, organization, encoding specificity, cue-dependent retrieval, state-dependent retrieval, and interference. The process of encoding begins with *selective attention*, in which only those features of information that are selected for careful attention are those that are best encoded. *Rehearsal* is important for memory, especially elaborative rehearsal, in which new material being learned is related to existing knowledge. Making information more meaningful by way of *semantic processing* aids retention, as does *mental imagery*. Similarly, both *distinctiveness* and *organization* are important processes in memory, by on the one hand making information more discriminable, and on the other, by providing an organizing structure. Finally, memory depends on the ability to access or retrieve information, which can, itself, be improved by practice (H. C. Ellis 1987; H. C. Ellis and J. M. Hunt 1993).

Conclusion

The study of memory focuses on a large variety of issues and topics. Memory is studied not only with laboratory procedures but also in the real world (L. B. Cohen 1989). Studies of autobiographical memory (K. H. Rubin 1986) help to enrich and supplement findings from laboratory research. Moreover, research on flashbulb memory, self-reference effects, emotion and memory, schemas and memory, memory strategies, memory pathology (such as amnesia), metamemory, eyewitness testimony, spatial memory, children's memory, text processing and memory, inferences, aging and memory, and context effects all attest to the breadth of research topics. These topics also reflect the growing interest in social, emotional, clinical, biological, and developmental factors in memory. This interaction between two areas is nicely illustrated in studies of mood and memory (D. Kuiken 1991) and emotion and memory (B. A. Christianson 1992).

A second characteristic of developments in memory is the rapidity with which new methodologies and theoretical approaches are developed. Memory researchers are not wedded to one technique or paradigm. Similarly, new theoretical developments stemming from connectionistic approaches promise theoretical concepts based on activities of the brain as distinct from computer analogies (D. E. Rumelhart and D. C. McClelland 1986).

Contextualist views are still prevalent. This means that experimental generalizations about memory depend upon a range of contextual factors in memory experiments, including task, instructional, and subject characteristics. Finally, memory continues to occupy center stage in cognitive psychology. The nature of memory representation, how events are encoded and retrieved, and how memory depends upon interpretation of events continue to be of major interest.

Henry C. Ellis

Memory: Psychoanalytic Theory

The most obvious expression of the psychoanalytic theory of memory is found in its attempt to explain not the adequate activity of remembering but the inadequate activity of forgetting as a manifestation of repression. Repression, certainly basic both historically and conceptually in psychoanalytic theory, can be viewed, in part, as motivated forgetting.

Freud claimed that quite often what one forgets turns out to be linked in some way, directly or indirectly, to unconscious ideas significant and painful to oneself. He explained such forgetting as a result of the tendency "to avoid the awakening of pain" through memory.

In forgetting, the method of dealing with such material is its removal from conscious awareness and expression. In other parapraxes, such as slips of the tongue, the prohibited striving asserts itself indirectly by distorting the word or idea in associative connection with it. And the content that does emerge into behavior or consciousness (the slip of the tongue spoken, the incorrect word read, the bungled action carried out) reflects neither complete repression nor complete expression of the prohibited material, but rather a compromise between the two.

L. Luborsky (1964, 1973) uses the psychoanalytic situation to collect systematic data on the particular phenomenon of momentary forgetting, in which one is about to say something, forgets what it is, and then recovers the thought. He reports that, as compared to control segments, segments of the patients' verbalizations preceding instances of momentary forgetting consistently contain evidence of buildup of cognitive disturbance and presence of emotionally laden and conflicted themes; for example, lack of control and competence, as well as transference references.

If forgetting, slips of the tongue, bungled actions, and other parapraxes must be employed to keep repressed ideas and material associatively linked with repressed ideas from overt expression and from gaining access to consciousness, it is only a testimony to the strength and persistence of these repressed ideas. And, indeed, the strength and persistence of repressed instinctual strivings in organizing and utilizing memory are essential features of the psychoanalytic theory of memory. Sigmund Freud (1937) was not merely being metaphorical but really proposing that repressed material could have palpable effects on experience and behavior.

Recent formulations in psychoanalytic ego psychology stress the aspects of thought and of other ego functions that develop and function autonomously and independent of instinctual drive (e.g., H. Hartmann 1950, 1958; H. Hartmann, E. B. Kris, and R. M. Loewenstein 1946). Thus, while they do not dispute Freud's idea that the failure of hallucinatory wish fulfillment can be an impetus to the development of thought, they would point out that the capacity for thought and the development of thought have bases independent of instinctual drive.

The issue of drive versus conceptual organization of memory (D. Rapaport 1951, 1960), if taken beyond the specific question of the relation between drive and memory, raises the general question of how events are stored, organized, and retrieved in memory. Posing the question in these general terms opens the door to considering a wide range of factors.

Morris N. Eagle

Menninger, Karl Augustus (1893–1990)

Karl Menninger's views reflect the influence of Sigmund Freud and of Adolf Meyers. In *The Vital Balance* (1963), he offers a new diagnostic understanding from the perspective of a unitary concept of mental health and illness.

In 1944, the Menninger family reorganized their enterprises into the nonprofit Menninger Foundation, in order to expand their mental health program of education, research, and prevention.

Verne Bennett Horne

Menninger, William C. (1899–1966)

As director of the Menninger Foundation, William C. Menninger applied his psychoanalytic understanding to psychiatric hospital treatment and developed the concept of milieu treatment. Aware of the need for more progressive views in American psychiatry, Menninger spearheaded a group of fellow psychiatrists who, in 1946, organized the Group for the Advancement of Psychiatry, and he became its first chairman. During World War II, Menninger was chief neuropsychiatric consultant to the surgeon general of the U.S. Army.

Roy W. Menninger

Mental Health

The main criteria of mental health are (1) perceiving things the way they are, (2) emotional balance, (3) social adjustment, and (4) achievements consistent with the individual's abilities and opportunities.

Perceiving things the way they are is a highly important criterion of mental health. Successful behavior greatly depends on the ability to perceive oneself and others the way they are; overestimation or underestimation of one's potentialities and of the existing possibilities can lead to serious maladjustment. Facing reality is a crucial issue in life, and to solve a problem one must be aware of what the problem is. The perception of the world is usually distorted in mental disorders, but not as a product of sensory impairment.

Illusions, delusions, and hallucinations are the three levels of losing contact with reality, and are indicators of the degree of mental disorder.

Human behavior is greatly influenced and often controlled by emotions. Pleasure is the healthy reaction to success, and displeasure is the healthy reaction to failure. Mentally healthy individuals react in appropriate ways to stimuli, that is, with joy to success and with sorrow to defeat. Normal emotional reactions are proportionate to their stimuli; a small loss causes a mild emotional reaction, and a grave loss elicits a grave reaction. Mentally healthy individuals endeavor to solve their problems, and their emotional reactions are adjustive.

Social adjustment, that is, the ability to cooperate with others, is the third criterion of mental health. Childhood is a state of dependence on parents and other adults. Adulthood is a state of interdependence. No human being can stay alone, and all human beings must interact with others.

There are four types of social attitude: hostile, instrumental, mutual, and vectorial. A hostile attitude stimulates hurting, harming, and destroying the other person. In an instrumental attitude one expects the other person to help and to take care of one. Mutual relations consist of give and take; one gives help and receives help. A vectorial attitude implies giving without expecting anything in return. Well-adjusted individuals are hostile in self-defense, instrumental in breadwinning efforts, mutual in friendships and marriage, and vectorial in parenthood and in idealistic pursuits.

The relationship between what one can do and what one does is a relevant criterion of mental health. What one can do depends on one's potentialities and one's possibilities. One's potentialities are IQ, the ability to face hardships, and resilience in defeat. Potentialities greatly depend on environment. Even a bright child may not receive adequate guidance and education if he is an orphan, abandoned, or a child of maladjusted parents. When a person has the necessary abilities, and her environment offers the necessary guidance and encouragement to achieving a goal, yet she misses the existing opportunities, some personality defects may be present. Usually, the greater the distance between promise and fulfillment, the lower is the level of mental health.

Benjamin B. Wolman

Mental Health Computer Applications

Patient knowledge, beliefs, attitudes, attributions, and lifestyles, as well as medication packaging, have been suggested as important factors in improving compliance with prescribed treatments. Computers can be programmed to interact with patients to provide information, assess level of understanding, ascertain beliefs and attitudes, and, where appropriate, provide information about alternative beliefs and attitudes. Direct treatment programs are used in the areas of agoraphobia; obsessive-compulsive disorder; and nonpsychotic, nonbipolar, nonsuicidal depression.

While recognizing the threshold or triage problem presented by a new patient, computer programs can quickly screen for the most common disorders and, by branching, follow up in great detail where appropriate. The programs can also be limited in the scope of their work, thus protecting the patient from clinical decisions based on inadequate observation or knowledge.

John H. Greist
Marjorie H. Klein

Mental Health in the Schools

School mental-health programs' most important challenges stem from the fact that their resources cannot meet evident needs. J. C. Glidewell and C. S. Swallow's (1969) survey of school maladjustment incidence studies, done for the Joint Commission on Mental Health of Children (1969), indicates that 30% of American children are experiencing school adjustment problems. And for 10%, those problems are sufficiently serious to require immediate professional help.

In addition to early identification, promising new professional roles, such as the elementary counselor (V. Faust 1968) and the school mental health consultant (L. M. Newman 1967), have been identified, as have a variety of new approaches (e.g., "schools without failure," encounter groups, and behavior modification) to help youngsters cope effectively with the school experience. More systematically, some (E. L. Cowen et al. 1975) have called for school mental-health delivery systems with a combined emphasis on (1) the very young child; (2) widespread screening and early detection of school adjustment problems; (3) use of nonprofessional help-agents to expand the reach of effective services geometrically; and (4) changing professional roles toward such "quarterbacking" functions as education, training, supervision, and consultation, in order to bring meaning and substance to expanded delivery systems.

Emory L. Cowen

Mental Health and Social Psychology in Institutional Settings

The basic reasons for considering mental health as a social issue are:

1. Mental health problems involve a huge number of people; some estimates place the proportion of people presently suffering from some form of mental disorder as high as one in three.
2. The cost of mental illness is very high, not only in human but in social and economic terms. Loss of productivity and waste of human resources must be considered in addition to the direct outlay of capital and operational funds in assessing the total cost.

The constraints of the institutional environment have been shown to have definite adverse effects on patient behavior. J. K. Wing (1968) has demonstrated that the degree of institutional restrictiveness and patient understimulation correlate with the extent to which inmates become socially withdrawn, underactive, silent, and emotionally dulled. Improving the social environment leads to definite changes in these behavior patterns; the "time spent doing nothing" decreases considerably in the patient population. Similar results have been reported in other studies (M. Hunter et al. 1962; E. B. Klein and H. E. Spohn 1962, 1964; B. B. Wolman 1964).

The concept of a total treatment environment, or "therapeutic milieu," originally proposed by Max-

well Jones, has led to the development of several innovative treatment programs (R. B. Ellsworth 1968; C. L. Rausch and H. L. Raush 1968; H. E. Spohn 1958). All of these approaches stress social interaction of patients and staff (with a minimum of status differentiation), a democratic political structure (patient government or participation in making the rules), and the blurring of patient-staff distinctions so that they are likely to stand together on certain issues. Programs to change patient behavior rely primarily on informal group pressure and on systems of positive rewards, which are individualized for each patient.

Leonard Solomon
Henry Wechsler
Bernard M. Kramer

Mental Retardation: Etiology

According to the American Association on Mental Deficiency (AAMD), "mental retardation" refers to subaverage general functioning that originates during the developmental periods and is associated with impairment in adaptive behavior. This definition reflects a specifically developmental approach, which stresses comparisons based on standards appropriate for the child's chronological age and with emphasis on different aspects of functioning at different ages. This definition is stated in terms of general intelligence, which is evaluated together with evaluation in other areas, such as motor skills, academic achievement, self-help skills, vocational skills, social skills, and community adjustment.

The prenatal influences on the fetus that relate to mental retardation arise from the effect on the dividing and differentiating embryonal cells. By the end of the first trimester of pregnancy, the fetal systems, except for the genito-urinary system, are completely differentiated from the ectoderm, mesoderm, and endoderm. For this reason, it is all-important to protect from and prevent any assault on the embryonal cell, via the placenta, that would prevent its proper differentiation and its normal maturation.

Prenatal assaults include untreated infection in the mother, such as syphilis, toxoplasmosis, and cytomegalic inclusion bodies, and viral disease, which can create a fetal meningoencephalitis, in addition to infection of all fetal organs.

The perinatal assaults that lead to retarded mental development are those that create infantile cerebral anoxia of long degree. The trauma of the delivery, infant hemorrhage due to cord abnormalities or clotting disorders, prematurity, postmaturity, and infant respiratory distress of all variations give in common the production of cerebral anoxia by deficient cerebral blood supply or by oxygen desaturation of the circulatory system.

In the postnatal period, the assault on the brain derived from infection, skull trauma, uncontrolled seizures, and toxins and poisons, such as carbon monoxide and lead, can lead to mental retardation either by deprivation of cerebral oxygen supply or by interference with cellular structure and function.

Anatomopathologic and Biochemical Factors in Mental Retardation

A. Primary cerebrocranial developmental defects
   1. Cerebral malformations—e.g., cerebral agenesis, cerebral hypoplasia, cerebral hyperplasia (macrocephaly)
   2. Cranial defects—e.g., craniostenosis, hypertelorism
   3. Congenital ectodermosis—e.g., tuberous sclerosis, cerebral angiomatosis (Sturge-Weber syndrome), neurofibromatosis
   4. Down's syndrome
   5. Familial defect (defective or inferior intelligence in one or both parents and in other siblings)
   6. Undifferentiated cerebrocranial defect, or primary amentia (As our knowledge of cerebral physiology and pathology increases, the number of cases placed in this last category will decline.)
B. Secondary cerebral malformations
   1. Porencephaly—e.g., from trauma
   2. Hydrocephalus—e.g., from congenital anomalies of the central nervous system, intracranial hemorrhage associated with birth trauma or anoxia, or infection of neoplasm

C. Central nervous system abnormalities associated with metabolic defects
   1. Phenylpyruvic oligophrenia
   2. Galactosemia
   3. Congenital hypothyroidism
   4. Hurler's syndrome, dysostosis multiplex
   5. Hepatolenticular degeneration (Wilson's disease)
   6. Reticuloendotheliosis—e.g., Gaucher's disease, Niemann-Pick disease
   7. Maple syrup syndrome
D. Acquired focal or disseminated central nervous system lesions
   1. Post-toxic and infection—e.g., lead encephalopathy, viral encephalitis, kernicterus
   2. Post-traumatic lesions
   3. Posthypoxic lesions
E. Degenerative disorders of the central nervous system
   1. Cerebro-ocular degeneration (Tay-Sachs disease, amaurotic familial idiocy)
   2. Demyelinating encephalopathies
   Margaret Joan Giannini

Mental Retardation: Organic Aspects

It is estimated that 3% of the U.S. population are mentally retarded. This often-quoted estimate is only approximate, because there are no precise data available, except in a few areas of the country. The overwhelming majority (87%) of the mentally retarded fall into the mild category, and the remainder (13%) belong to the moderate, severe, and profound groups.

Phenylketonuria. The majority of patients with phenylketonuria (PKU) are severely retarded, but some patients are reported to have borderline or normal intelligence. Eczema and convulsions are present in about a third of all cases. Electroencephalogram (EEG) is abnormal in about 80%, even in patients without convulsions, showing irregular spike and wave discharges. The majority of patients are undersized and have light complexions and coarse features, and the head tends to be small. Although the clinical picture varies, typical PKU children are hyperactive and exhibit erratic, unpredictable behavior, which makes them difficult to manage. Verbal and nonverbal communication is usually severely impaired or nonexistent.

Cerebromacular degenerations. The cerebromacular degenerations represent a group of disturbances in which there is progressive mental deterioration and loss of visual function. They are all transmitted by an autosomal recessive gene. The four types of cerebromacular degeneration differ as to the age of onset. The earliest one, Tay-Sachs disease, occurs chiefly among Jewish infants, particularly those from Eastern Europe; the others are found in members of all races.

Galactosemia. Galactosemia is transmitted by an autosomal recessive gene. Its metabolic defect consists of the inability to convert galactose to glucose, because of the enzymatic defect of galactose 1-phosphate uridyltransferase.

The clinical manifestations begin after a few days of milk feeding and include jaundice, vomiting, diarrhea, failure to thrive, and hepatomegaly. If milk is not eliminated from the diet, the disease may be fatal within a short time, or it may lead to progressive mental deterioration, associated with cataracts, hepatic insufficiency, and occasional hypoglycemic convulsions.

Goitrous cretinism. Cretinism (congenital hypothyroidism) as a condition associated with mental retardation has been known since antiquity. Throughout modern history up to the middle of the nineteenth century, all forms of mental retardation were considered as variants of this condition.

The classical endemic variety occurs in certain regions as a result of iodine deficiency in the diet. Sporadic athyreosis, congenital absence of the thyroid gland, is the common variety in this country and may be caused by transplacental transmission of immune bodies against thyroid from the mother.

The clinical signs in all varieties include hypothyroidism, goiter (except in athyreosis), dwarfism, coarse skin, disturbances in ossification, hypertelorism, and a large tongue. Mental retardation becomes a part of the clinical picture if the disease is unrecognized and untreated in infancy.

Down's syndrome. Since the classical description of "mongolism" by the English physician Langdon Down in 1866, this syndrome has remained the most discussed, most investigated, and most controversial in the field of mental retardation.

Patients with trisomy 21 (three on chromosome 21 instead of the usual two), who represent the overwhelming majority of Down's syndrome patients, have forty-seven chromosomes, with an extra chromosome 21. The karyotypes of the mothers are normal.

There are over a hundred signs or stigmata described in Down's syndrome, but they are rarely all found in one individual. Among the most frequently encountered are a high cephalic index, epicanthal folds, fissured tongue, dwarfed stature, small rounded ears, strabismus, white speckling of the iris (Brushfield spots), and lax ligaments. The dermal ridges on the palms and soles have a characteristic configuration, which is often diagnostic.

Syphilis. Syphilis in pregnant women used to be a major cause of a variety of neuropathological changes in their offspring, including mental retardation.

Rubella (German measles). This disease has replaced syphilis as the major cause of congenital malformation and mental retardation due to maternal infection. The children of affected mothers may present a number of abnormalities, including congenital heart disease, mental retardation, cataracts, deafness, microcephaly, and microphthalmia.

Erythroblastosis fetalis. This is the most common cause of nonphysiological jaundice and is due to mother-child incompatibility regarding the Rh factor, A or B, or (rarely) Kell, Kidd, and Duffy factors in the blood. The resulting breakdown of the infant's red cells causes bilirubinemia and anemia. Stillbirth due to a generalized edema, hydrops fetalis, occurs in some. In others, kernicterus will develop.

Leon Cytryn
Reginald S. Lourie

Mental Retardation: Overview

The difficulties and misunderstandings surrounding definitions of various disorders of child growth and development and the resultant tragedy of misclassification and mistreatment are readily acknowledged. Ample testimony to the controversy surrounding the labeling of children is found in N. Hobbs (1975).

The actual assessment of an individual's ability to learn new skills and apply this new learning to either old or new problems is rarely done, yet this is what intelligence is allegedly thought to be. Clearly, the person in a deprived environment, regardless of his native intelligence, will be severely limited in the acquisition of new knowledge and the development of new skills. He will probably test as significantly subaverage in general intelligence, remain in or be placed in settings for mentally subaverage individuals, and, in prophecy-fulfilling fashion, continue to perform at a subaverage level on tests of intelligence.

Many environmentally deprived or culturally different individuals have intelligence scores that are just below the average level and have in the past been designated as borderline mentally retarded.

The clinical judgment as to a person's adaptive behavior level is arrived at only after considering the multiple factors that contribute to the development of adaptive behavior. These must include repeated observation of the individual in her natural setting; reports from others who have observed her behavior in other regular settings; recognition of the limitations and opportunities imposed by a given setting, including others in the environment; and consideration of general intellectual functioning from a more structured test situation. When this deficit in adaptive behavior exists concurrently with inadequate intellectual functioning, a second important criterion of mental retardation is fulfilled.

One of the surest ways of preventing an individual's getting an unwarranted and perhaps permanent label is to employ an ongoing evaluation-remediation process of merely tentatively identifying the strengths and weaknesses of the client and then further refining the assessment of these as the client's ability to profit from trial remediation procedures is observed and evaluated.

John H. Meier

Mental Retardation: Social Aspects

Attitudes toward the retarded have not been fixed historically and have undergone major shifts consistent with social and ideological change, as well as fluctuations in popular fads and fashion. Presently, in the United States, there is a strong forward movement to improve the condition of the retarded and to modify social pressures.

James Mercer (1973) calls attention to the destructive social effects of labeling the mildly retarded, with its built-in self-fulfilling prophecy of failure and damage to the self-concept and ego structure of the labeled individual. A social system perspective rather than a clinical one reflecting the medical model is seen as the more valid approach for the mildly retarded.

The consequences for the family of the destructive definition of retardation requires further exploration. The family is, of course, the primary social unit for the continuity and transmission of the values of the culture. Mental retardation complicates severely the family's ability to carry through this goal and to prepare the child for an acceptable and contributing role in society. If labeling the individual as retarded suggests that she will not be qualified to function adequately within society, the family may also be perceived, by implication, as deviant because it has failed one of its major functions.

L. Farber (1968) has found that the level of interaction between the family and the community is influenced by the presence of retardation. Families tend to disengage from community activity and to focus their energy on intrafamily matters. The social mobility of the family is affected, particularly when a severely or moderately retarded child is born early in the marriage. Siblings are influenced in personality and life orientation, and this is more pronounced the closer they are in age to the retarded child.

Social factors assume a major part in understanding the totality of mental retardation. We often measure deficits in societal awareness, attitudes, and commitment to human needs rather than irreversible deficits in the assumed retarded individual.

Lawrence Goodman

Merritt, H. Houston (1902–1979)

H. Houston Merritt's research covered several areas, such as development of diphenylhydantoin (phenytoin) and correlation of morphological and clinical changes in neurosyphilis. Merritt was president of the American Neurological Association, editor-in-chief of *Archives of Neurology*, and editor of the division of neurology of the *International Encyclopedia of Psychiatry, Psychology, Psychoanalysis and Neurology*.

Melvin D. Yahr

Mesmer, Franz Anton (1734–1815)

Franz Anton Mesmer was an early developer of hypnosis. He believed that the power of healing lay in the effects of magnets on body fluids, and he called the new power "animal magnetism." A joint commission of the French Academies of Medicine and Science denied the existence of Mesmeric fluid and attributed Mesmer's influence to the imagination.

John C. Burnham

Meyer, Adolf (1869–1950)

Adolf Meyer's approach to patients was holistic, including the organic, psychological, and social. He was influenced by Darwinian thinking, and according to his conception of psychobiology, he perceived the patient as an organism adapting to an environment. Meyer was critical of Freudians and Kraepelinians.

John C. Burnham

Meynert, Theodore (1833–1892)

The Austrian physician Theodore Meynert considered a number of mental illnesses to be the result of inadequate blood supply to the brain. Depression, he believed, was due to excessive flow of blood in the cerebral vessels. Karl Wernicke and Sigmund Freud were his pupils.

Leo H. Berman

Military Psychiatry

Since World War I, military psychiatry has become established as a regular component of military medicine of the armed forces of the United States and of many other nations. Prior to World War I, mental illness in military personnel was narrowly defined to include mainly severe abnormalities of psychotic proportions. From early reports of the fighting on the Western Front in 1914, there appeared accounts of a new psychiatric disorder in Allied troops, shell shock, which was of such frequency as to constitute a major military medical problem. By 1915–16, Allied medical services clearly recognized that shell shock was entirely a psychological disorder, and the terminology of "war neuroses" came into usage. But by this time, shell shock had achieved fixation and legitimacy as a disease, and thus an inability to function in combat.

Contributions of Military Psychiatry in World War I

In retrospect, World War I provided much of the basis on which the current conceptual and operational framework of military psychiatry has been developed. Major contributions in this regard include:

1. The war offered repeated demonstrations that environmental stress and strain cause mental disorder in so-called normal personnel as well as in those of neurotic or vulnerable predisposition.
2. Treatment of mental illness, particularly the war neuroses, early and near the site of origin, although developed by trial and error, was a logical consequence of the recognition that mental disorder could be caused or precipitated by environmental circumstances.
3. A network of mutually linked and supportive treatment facilities for mental disorders from

front to rear was first established by the American Expeditionary Force medical services.

World War II

The major lesson learned from the psychiatric screening experiences of World War II lies in appreciating the almost insurmountable limitations inherent in any single psychiatric or psychological examination that, prior to induction, attempts to predict future effectiveness or mental breakdown during military service.

The newly built cantonment hospitals of World War II became half-filled with patients having refractory psychiatric syndromes, often including somatic symptoms, to which "gain in illness" had been added. The only solution to the problem seemed to be medical discharge from the army.

Consultation services. Beginning in early 1942, independently and almost contemporaneously, psychiatric outpatient units called "consultation services" were established in various training centers in the United States.

Psychiatric personnel of consultation services worked closely with trainers in aiding the newly inducted soldier to adapt to separation from home, lack of privacy, regimentation, and other changes incident to the transition from civilian to military life. Consultation services not only provided outpatient treatment for referred symptom disorders but participated in the orientation of trainees and in planning the activities of the training program.

Combat psychiatry. In March 1943, during the latter phase of the Tunisia campaign, successful attempts were made to reestablish the World War I forward-type treatment for psychiatric casualties. Cases were held for 2 to 5 days of treatment in a field medical facility near the fighting. Treatment included sedation to insure sleep and rest, ample food, reassurance, and suggestion, along with opportunity to discuss battle experiences. As in World War I, it was found that forward treatment could return a majority of psychiatric casualties to combat duty.

Contributions of Military Psychiatry in World War II

Causation and frequency. It was evident that the continued threat of external danger was an essential element in the causation of combat psychiatric casualties. However, the frequency of psychiatric casualties was related to situational circumstances, which either reduced or enhanced the capacity of combat participants to cope with battle conditions. Most important in this regard was the influence of the small combat group (squad, platoon, or company) or particular members thereof, termed group identification, group cohesiveness, the buddy system, morale, or leadership, which served to sustain the individual in battle. Repeated observations demonstrated that the absence or inadequacy of such sustaining relationships or their disruption during combat was mainly responsible for psychiatric breakdown.

Treatment. It was readily apparent that forward treatment provided prompt relief for fatigue and other physical deficits of psychiatric casualties. However, it was not until recognition of the sustaining group relationships in combat that the significance of treatment near or at the site of origin became fully appreciated. Proximity of treatment to the combat unit tends to maintain relationships and investment in the core group, and motivation to rejoin the combat group is further heightened by improvement in physical well-being because of a respite from combat and recuperative measures of sleep, food, bathing, and the like.

Following the post-Korean War era, military psychiatry continued to elaborate and implement the concepts of social psychiatry. This direction was most likely the result of the momentum developed during wartime. Also, in part, it reflected a nationwide movement toward a community mental health approach. At this time, military psychiatry was preeminent in the establishment and utilization of locally based psychiatric services, which provided intervention rather than distant hospitalization.

In the first two years of the Vietnam War the morale of American armed forces was quite high. But in 1967–69 the military defeat and the decline of public support for the war undercut morale, and drug abuse in the armed forces increased.

As part of military medicine, military psychiatry was born of a need to conserve military manpower from losses due to situationally induced mental disorders.

The contributions of military psychiatry have become gradually incorporated into current changes within the delivery of civilian mental health services, from prolonged care in remote institutions to interventions and treatment by local psychiatric facilities.

Albert J. Glass

Minnesota Multiphasic Personality Inventory

The Minnesota Multiphasic Personality Inventory (MMPI) is the best known and most widely researched psychological inventory in the area of psychodiagnosis and the assessment of psychopathology. Published in the early 1940s, the MMPI has remained essentially unchanged in format since that time, although considerable advances have been made in interpretive methods. The 1972 *Seventh Mental Measurements Yearbook* listed more than 3,000 publications on the MMPI.

The MMPI consists of ten clinical scales and three validity scales (L, F, and K), based on 550 true/false items. Each clinical scale represents one of the major psychodiagnostic categories that were current in the late 1930s. The clinical scales, whose letter abbreviations are given below, are more appropriately known by their numbers (1 through 9 and 0), because a high score on a scale often does not automatically mean identification with that particular patient criterion group. The scales were developed primarily by the empirical method of test construction, a procedure that represented a significant advance for the time in the technology of psychodiagnostic test construction. In its many years of existence, the MMPI has served as a model for the construction of many other psychological assessment devices, and it has also been the major vehicle for research on methodological topics, such as response bias and actuarial versus clinical prediction. The most authoritative reference work on the MMPI is the newly revised two-volume *MMPI Handbook* by A. Dahlstrom, E. E. Welsh, and W. G. Dahlstrom (1972–75).

The MMPI is suitable for ages 16 and over, and is available in three main forms: (1) the card form, in which items are printed on individual cards and are sorted by the respondent; (2) the most common, the booklet form, in which responses are marked on an IBM-style answer sheet and are scored by handscoring stencils or by machine, or can be mailed to a scoring service; and (3) Form R, a newer step-down booklet form with lapboard hard cover. The test takes 40 to 90 minutes to complete, and handscoring the booklet form takes about 10 minutes. Scores are transferred to a profile sheet, which converts them automatically to a normative standard score form (T scores), with mean of 50 and standard deviation of 10, and permits the K correction for defensiveness to be applied. The distributions of nearly all the scales are skewed in the positive direction.

Richard I. Lanyon

Mitchell, S. Weir (1829–1914)

S. Weir Mitchell's neurological practice included a broad spectrum of psychological problems. He became internationally known for his "rest cure," which suggested for psychiatric patients a long period of isolation from persons and surroundings.

Jerome M. Schneck

Modeling in Behavior Modification

Modeling as typically practiced in behavior modification consists of a client observing another individual (i.e., a model) engage in behaviors the client wishes to develop. Without actually performing the observed behavior, the client can learn novel responses or can be induced to perform (or cease to perform) previously acquired responses. An essential ingredient in modeling appears to be covert or representational (verbal or imaginal) processes, which code the modeled material. The representational processes are assumed to guide subsequent performance of the client when external modeling cues are no longer provided.

Motivational processes. Performance of modeled behavior by the observer depends upon external incentive conditions. Favorable consequences provided to the model increase, whereas aversive consequences decrease, the likelihood of observer performance of the modeled behavior.

Modeling has been used to alter a variety of behaviors, including fear and avoidance reactions (including fear of dogs, snakes, heights, water, and taking examinations), obsessions and compulsions, lack of assertiveness, social withdrawal, dependent behavior, interview behavior, and others. Clients treated with modeling have included adults, adolescents, and children in outpatient treatment, as well as institutionalized psychotics, delinquents, and retardates.

Research investigations have successfully developed an effective "modeling package," which includes diverse elements, such as variation of model cues, verbal mediation of modeling stimuli, or guided participation. Moreover, effective treatment variations (e.g., live, film, or covert) lend credence to the potency of modeling as a general therapeutic strategy.

Alan E. Kazdin

Moral Development

Moral development is studied in three separate ways. These approaches are derived from social, developmental, and clinical psychology; they are quite distinct, and this reflects the increasing specialization of psychological research.

The most influential moral development research from a social-psychological perspective is that of Albert Bandura (1971) and his associates (social learning theory). For Bandura, all behavior, including moral conduct, is learned. Each specific form of moral conduct (e.g., telling the truth, keeping one's word, acting altruistically) must be learned separately.

Concerning children's judgments about hypothetical moral dilemmas, Jean Piaget (1964) has found

that the younger ones take no account of an actor's intentions; rather, they make judgments in terms of the amount of damage caused by a particular action. Older children continue to take account of the material consequences of an act, but their judgments primarily take the actor's intentions into account.

L. Kohlberg (1963) has extended this approach to moral development. Having studied the theoretical moral judgments of children from age 10 to early adulthood, he identifies six stages through which these moral judgments seem to evolve. At stage one, morality is defined in terms of the actions that adults reward or punish. At stage two, right and wrong are defined hedonistically, in terms of actions that bring pleasure or pain. At the third stage, decisions are justified in terms of social praise and blame. At the fourth stage, actions are justified by appeals to conventional morality, as represented by the church, state, or government. Persons at stage five justify their actions in terms of social contracts, constitutions, and democratically accepted law. At stage six, actions are justified in terms of universal principles of moral conduct.

Robert Hogan (1973, 1974) describes moral development in terms of three problems that confront every developing child. The major dilemma facing an infant is to secure parental care and nurturance, and to make sense of the world. This is accomplished largely by her allowing herself to be governed by adult rules.

Ultimately, each child must leave the exclusive care of his parents and make his way in a peer group. In the peer group, a child must shed his infantile egocentrism and accommodate himself to a radically expanded set of social norms. This is facilitated by the development of empathy or role-taking ability and by a markedly heightened sensitivity to social expectations, social praise, and blame.

By late adolescence, a child is faced with the problem of establishing a life for herself. This requires reconciling the competing demands of her family and peer group and coming to terms with herself; developing an autonomous lifestyle. This is typically accomplished either through the development of an ideology that rationalizes her intended lifestyle, or through an identification with a "preferred character type," which provides her with an internalized standard for future behavior.

Robert Hogan

Motivation

Motivation describes a hypothetical state invoked to account for discrepancies between the size, intensity, and/or duration of stimulus input, on the one hand, and response or behavior output, on the other. In layman's terms, it is used to explain the "why" of behavior—its determinants and/or the conditions under which it could be expected to recur.

Motivation is not directly observable, but must be inferred to be operative from (1) antecedent manipulations (e.g., deprivation, satiation, stimulation), (2) observations of consequent behavior change or modification (increase, decrease, choice, persistence over time, force, change in effort level), and/or (3) antecedent or postcedent bodily change (neural, endocrine, physiological, psychophysiological).

Some form of motivation construct has been with us since the early Greek philosophers speculated about the nature of man. Over the years, names and descriptions have varied—Hippocrates spoke of humors, René Descartes of passions (of the soul), Charles Darwin of emotions, Arthur Schopenhauer of will, William McDougall and later Konrad Lorenz and Nikolaas Tinbergen of instincts, Sigmund Freud of *Trieb,* R. S. Woodworth and later Clark L. Hull of drive, E. C. Tolman of purpose, Kurt Lewin of valence, Henry A. Murray of needs, etc. In one form or other, all involved explanatory mediating notions intended to account for or explain (1) the energization or invigoration of behavior; (2) the level of behavior intensity and its persistence or sustaining power; (3) the purpose or direction of behavior (choice, preference for or avoidance of goal object); and secondarily, (4) the likelihood, strengthening, weakening, and/or recurrence or cessation of behavior (reinforcement or extinction).

Some motivational concepts are of a "push" type, focusing on the arousal, activation, instigation, or energization of responses, while others are of a "pull" variety, emphasizing goals, direction, purpose, or behavioral outcome; still others describe linkages among initiation, vigor, direction, and degree of persistence of sustained effort, as in the tension-arousal–tension-reduction theories of Freud and of Hull, or in the elegantly detailed sequences of instinctual animal behavior described by ethologists such as Lorenz.

Some mediating motivational processes appear to be primarily biological (emotion, force, drive, instinct, need), others mental (will, wish, feeling, urge, impulse, want, striving, desire, demand), with some of the latter especially goal or future oriented (attitude, plan, motive, incentive, expectation, goal/object, value). Each conception and term carries its own implications, advantages, and limitations.

Until early in the present century, there was more focus on mentalistic than on biological concepts. Early instinct theory was a mix of biological and mental aspects. Later, and through the early 1960s, biologically based drive and instinct models dominated. They assumed some impelling force derived from bodily need and translated into action, which was sustained until such need was reduced or eliminated. As is evident, such concepts are mechanistic or physicalistic, being modeled on the casual sequences of the physical sciences. They are hydraulic in nature, positing an energy well that fills up with continuing deprivation (or some parallel process inducing stimulus increase), with pressure or tension growing until released.

Later forms of drive theory, influenced by evolutionary concepts, saw deprivation as inducing a restlessness leading to response shaping through conditioning or learning, to produce a reduction of need. (Homeostatic theory suggests a physiological basis and explanation for the deprivation-saturation processes.)

Ethological instinct theory has relied on elaborate patterns of innate internal and/or environmental releasers, rather than response shaping through learning, to produce the same need-arousal–need-reduction sequence. Psychoanalytic instinct or *Trieb* theory, though based on clinical rather than experimental data, was likewise biologically based, explicitly hydraulic, and equally mechanistic. While complex defense and channeling processes were hypothesized to account for direction of behavior, and while sometimes intriguing accounts of mental processes were developed and described in great detail, the basic motivational mechanisms of psychoanalytic theory operate in essentially similar fashion to those of other drive and instinct theories.

Positivistic and deterministic thinking in science, along with the concepts of motive in law and theology, reflect the idea of the driven person compelled to an act of good or evil because of some irresistible need that must be satisfied. Dramatically simple and apparently useful as such explanations appeared to be, however, the evidential base for them has failed to hold up.

With the abandonment of drive theory and subsequent attempts to arrive at a comprehensive general theory of motivation, two rather independent lines of development emerged. One abandoned drive-type motivation theorizing and concentrated on explicating the neurological and/or neuroendocrine mechanisms underlying arousal and activation; a second shifted away from biological (and even motivational) explanations in favor of cognitive or mental events as the significant intervening (qua motivational) variables.

Recent authors in the *Annual Review of Psychology* series—on both physiological and cognitive sides—note the decline and later reawakening of interest in motivation per se. So, for example, on the physiological side, W. Timberlake (1993) notes that

> motivation fell out of favor with psychologists because neither deficit nor incentive effects could be tied firmly to physiology, and the relations between deprivation manipulation and behavior differed with both the type of manipulation and the measure of behavior used . . . Motivation became an unnecessary ghost in the machine. (694)

And then concludes,

> To the surprise of many, motivation seems to be making a comeback. (694)

R. G. Geen (1991), on the social side, likewise observes that

. . . motivation was not a popular construct among theorists of social behavior during the 1980s. It was, in fact, seldom identified, even as its effects were described. Instead, motivational processes often had to be inferred from specific behaviors . . . that are more customarily explained in terms not of motivation, but of cognition. (377–78)

Yet, later, after discussing the distinction between deficit and growth motivation and the overlap between explanations of both, Geen concludes,

> Some recent formulations tend to weaken this classic dichotomy . . . The once formidable wall separating motivational and cognitive explanations of behavior may now have been breached. Signs of a rapprochement between cognition and motivation are abundant. . . . (395–96)

Making similar observations in their review of the social foundations of cognition, J. M. Levine, J. W. Resnick, and E. T. Higgins (1993) note that whereas

> cognition as a source of motivation was a fundamental issue in social psychology in the late 1950s and 1960s . . . [more recent research has demonstrated] . . . how motivation can affect the form and substance of cognition as well as the amount of cognitive effort exerted. (587)

These and other current reviews suggest that the 1990s will see further elucidation of neurobehavioral mechanisms and their incorporation into psychological theories of motivation (and vice versa) (W. Timberlake 1993), the integration of cognitive and motivational explanatory concepts, and the reemergence of a comprehensive general motivation theory framework (M. H. Appley 1991).

Such a framework would need to include inputs from a wide range of sources, including those described by Timberlake (1993):

> Motivational systems developed by ethologists . . . inferred from the timing, sequencing and organization of behavior . . . regulatory physiological systems for which control circuitry is inferred from lesions, stimulation, and measurement of hormonal levels and metabolic indicators . . . [the role

of] social contexts of motivation . . . [insights from] optimality and game theory . . . [and] . . . recent work on computer simulation of animals. (694)

and those noted by R. A. Depue and W. G. Iacono (1989) on the neurobehavioral side, including the

> motor/affective (motivational) contribution to . . . active environmental engagement [via the behavioral facilitation . . . system (BFS)] . . . [the "gating" role of] dopamine (DA) activity [in modulating] the flow of motivational information from the limbic system to the motor system [and including the regulation of response strategies requiring cognitive planning]. (470)

Likewise, social facilitation, self-presentation, and related social motives can be shown to have common underlying links to evaluation apprehension, fear of disapproval, social anxiety, and efficacy expectancy (A. Bandura 1988), all parallel to processes seen in other areas of motivation (R. G. Geen 1991, 395).

Finally, we note that control theories, whether focused on self, stress, equilibration, or other regulatory dynamics (M. H. Appley 1991), may have sufficient breadth to include such cognitive motivation concepts as outcome expectations and differential attributions (M. H. Appley 1991; A. Bandura 1991). We foresee the likelihood of still further concordance of views, leading to a comprehensive motivation theory before the end of the 1990s.

Mortimer Herbert Appley

Motor Behavior

An obvious characteristic of human movement is that most of it is volitional and, as such, involves the translation of intent over both function and structure to overt action. Psychologists have invoked a number of descriptions of the way humans plan actions, from which certain commonalities seem extractable: plans are derived from intention; they are general representations of action, not detailed specifications; and they contain some information concerning sequential and temporal characteristics of the act. Unfortunately, these points have

remained empirically elusive, and for the most part, examination of the means by which the spinal cord organizes the functional muscle groupings has been viewed as a potentially more profitable experimental endeavor.

One additional consequence of theoretical considerations is the need to distinguish the levels of the neuraxis at which specific metrical and structural prescriptions are made. Locomotion studies have revealed that increases in running speed are not the result of increased phasing of limb alternation but are rather the result of increases in force application in the stance phase only. These data—in addition to some extracted from investigation of handwriting and other "natural" behaviors—are suggestive that movement duration and spatial relationships remain invariant across varying force applications. It is a rather consistent behavioral finding that limb movements are produced with accuracy on the basis of terminal location rather than on the basis of any time-based specification.

Evidence has promoted the notion that the muscles act at a joint by virtue of their intrinsic, nonlinear vibratory characteristics, so that, regardless of initial location or external perturbations, the limb is capable of achieving the desired equilibrium point (prescribed in terms of agonist and antagonist resting lengths). Accurate stimulated models of limb movement, based on appropriate biological principles, now seem graspable; and these models will bring with them increased theoretical understanding and practical utility.

George E. Stelmach
Barry H. Hughes

Motor Behavior: Social Factors

The "social facilitation phenomenon" refers to both positive and negative effects on a person's behavior as a consequence of the presence of others. Early social facilitation research was equivocal, or so it seemed, until R. B. Zajonc (1965) applied drive theory to this body of research, revealing considerable consistency in the findings. The theory is based on evidence that the presence of passive others is arousing, and that arousal increases the probability of the dominant response being emitted. The dominant response tends to be the correct response in well-learned skills and the incorrect response in skills yet to be acquired. Thus, the presence of others impairs learning but facilitates performance of well-learned skills.

According to Albert Bandura (1969), whether or not observational learning occurs is dependent upon four processes: attentional, retentional, motor reproduction, and motivational. It is obvious that attending to the modeled stimuli and retaining the conveyed information is essential in skill acquisition. Substantial research has shown that social reinforcers are effective in modifying behavior on very simple motor tasks.

Social-psychological research on individual motor behavior has sought to determine unitarily if social factors facilitate or impair learning and performance in terms of speed and accuracy. Current theory intimates that performance of well-learned skills is affected primarily by social motivational factors and that skill acquisition is affected by both, although the informational component has primacy.

I. D. Steiner's (1972) group task taxonomy, which is based on the requirements that task imposes on the group, is helpful in organizing the findings.

Group research has focused on whether group performance can be predicted from knowledge about the ability of individual group members. The answer is dependent upon the nature of the interaction required or permitted by the task. On conjunctive motor tasks, the least proficient member's performance best predicts team performance, while on disjunctive and discretionary motor tasks, group performance is better predicted by the performance of the most proficient member of the group.

Increased communication among all members of a group facilitates performance, particularly on divisible tasks. Communication is important in developing effective group social processes; it is essential in developing and maintaining high levels of cohesiveness and in clarifying group goals to its members. Thus, the communication structure is important in group motivation.

Group cohesiveness is related to increased cooperativeness, better communication, and greater satisfaction within a group. These factors contribute to the general finding that cohesiveness and effective group motor performance are related positively.

Rainer Martens

Motor Development

The human fetus becomes responsive to externally applied cutaneous stimuli at $7\frac{1}{2}$ weeks of age. The receptive field then is appropriately around the "snout" (the perioral region). It then spreads to include the alae of the nose and chin, and by $11\frac{1}{2}$ weeks of age, most of the trigeminally innervated area is stimulus-sensitive. The palms of the hands appear to become receptive at 10 to $10\frac{1}{2}$ fetal weeks of age, and the soles of the feet a little later. These receptive fields continue to enlarge, so that all of the skin is stimulus-sensitive by 32 weeks.

Aside from isolated movements of the head, those of lips and tongue appear as the clearest examples of local reactions in the developing human fetus, and their evolution follows a pattern similar to that of the head. Thus, mouth opening and tongue retraction (along with finger and toe abduction) may appear first as part of the general head-trunk avoiding reaction. At $9\frac{1}{2}$ weeks, stimulation of the lower lip may elicit mouth opening alone. At 12 to $12\frac{1}{2}$ weeks, the mouth will close following stimulation of the lips, and by 17 to 22 weeks, the lips will also protrude and purse. Retraction of the tongue alone may be elicited at $13\frac{1}{2}$ to 14 weeks, and protraction at 33 weeks. The emergence of lip and tongue movements again demonstrates the principles stated earlier; that is, local reactions develop from a total generalized response, and avoiding responses (mouth opening, tongue retraction) precede pursuit (lip pursing, tongue protrusion) movements.

In the neonate, tactile stimulation of the hand elicits only an avoiding response. This consists of abduction and dorsiflexion of the fingers. By 6 weeks of age, the response is more facile and then may be associated with some flexion withdrawal of the whole upper extremity. With maturation of the infant the response begins to show local signature so that at 12 to 20 weeks, the hand may also pronate and supinate to actually "avoid" contact with the stimulus. Pronation appears first and is prepotent.

By 24 to 40 weeks of age, the instinctive avoiding reaction develops in which the hand and arm now make any kind of adroit movement to avoid the tactile stimulus. Visual control is not necessary for production of this reaction.

G. H. Bower's (1974) studies indicate an ability of the very young infant to project and shape the hand to an object in the environment. The infant at this age does not do it as readily as an infant of 5 or 6 months of age, nor certainly as dexterously as an infant of 11 or 12 months of age.

The behavior of the infant herself may also affect the response to input. Some researchers have commented on the role of "state" in determining the facility for elicitation of different types of reflexes. We have observed a similar phenomenon in regard to avoiding and groping reactions. Avoiding reactions can be elicited more easily in the irritable and fussy infant, while groping responses are more easily obtained in the placid and contented infant.

Thomas E. Twitchell

Motor Dexterity: Measurement Methods

Among the oldest motor tests are the pegboards designed to measure arm, hand, and finger dexterity. A typical example is the Stromberg Dexterity Test. The first part of the test requires the subject to place sixty cylindrical blocks into holes as fast as he can. In the second part, the blocks are removed, turned over, and put back in the holes. Another widely used test is the Crawford Small Parts Dexterity Test. In the first part of the test, the subject uses tweezers to place pins in holes and then places a small collar over each pin. In the second part, she puts small screws in place with a screwdriver.

Some tests are designed specifically to test how well the individual can work with tools and small mechanical parts. A typical test of this kind is the Bennett Hand-Tool Dexterity Test. The test requires the subject to remove and replace nuts and bolts as quickly as possible.

Most tests of motor dexterity are highly dependent on speed. Consequently, they prove to be better predictors of jobs in which speed rather than quality is important. There are many jobs in which speed is only a minor consideration. The person who can saw a board quickly does not necessarily have the craftsmanship of the skilled cabinetmaker.

Motor dexterity tests show at best only moderate predictive validity for most situations in which they are used. However, if they are used in conjunction with other ability tests, they often add a small but important increment to the overall validity of the battery. Motor tests tend to be more valid when they are made to resemble the actual machine or instrument featured on the job. Tests designed in this way are called "job miniatures."

Jum C. Nunnally

Motor Learning Theories

Thorndike's Theory

Initial motor-learning theorizing rested most heavily on the traditional stimulus-response (S-R) association theories of learning, which assumed that separate discrete responses and their stimuli are linked for performance either by reinforcement or contiguity. The pioneer of the associative position was Edward Lee Thorndike, whose principle tenet, the law of effect, postulated that an S-R bond was automatically strengthened or weakened as a function of whether the response was followed closely by a rewarding or punishing state of affairs. Thorndike's research interests included motor learning, and in 1927 he employed the motor task of drawing a line a criterion distance to conduct a crucial test of his law of effect. Only persons receiving verbal reinforcement reduced error in relation to the target, and Thorndike interpreted the results as evidence for a connection being strengthened as a result of its consequences. Thorndike subsequently modified his views of learning by playing down the role of punishment in the law of effect and by abandoning the law of exercise (the effect of mere practice alone).

Hull's Theory

The other principal proponent of reinforcement theory was Clark L. Hull (1943), who developed a sophisticated theoretical system, with a series of postulates to explain components of the learning process. Hull assumed that when an organism develops a need it becomes in disequilibrium with its environment, producing a drive within itself. When that need is met, drive reduction or drive stimulus reduction occurs. It is the reduction of drive that is reinforcing to the organism and that causes the response or habit to be learned. Thus, for Hull, learning results from need reduction, which is dependent upon contiguity of stimulus and response closely associated with reinforcement. Of the sixteen postulates formulated within Hull's theoretical framework, it is the constructs of reactive inhibition (Ir) and conditional inhibition (sIr) that appear most relevant to motor learning.

Guthrie's Theory

In contrast to Hull and Thorndike, E. R. Guthrie (1935) found no place for reinforcement in his theory of learning. Guthrie's one law of learning is based on the principle of contiguity, which posits that a combination of stimuli that have accompanied a movement will on their recurrence tend to be followed by that movement. Once the connection has been made by contiguity, no further practice or repetition will strengthen the association. In essence, Guthrie advocates one trial learning, but this is misleading, as he considers a learning situation to contain a multiplicity of S-R bonds. Repetition or drill is therefore necessary to enable the performer to connect all the bonds in the situation.

Tolman's Theory

The main American proponent of perceptual organization as a construct in learning was E. C. Tolman (1932). Combining many Gestaltian concepts, he maintained that behavior is goal directed because the organism uses environmental supports as guides or cues in achieving a goal, developing a general movement pattern rather than a specific response to a set stimulus. Some years later, Tolman anticipated present-day theorists by suggesting that one theory may not be able to adequately account for all forms of animal and human learning.

Associationism and Cognitivism

An important distinction between the learning schools that has particular relevance for motor learning is their conceptualization of the role of feedback

in responding. S-R psychology gives feedback, particularly proprioception, a prominent place in learning, viewing feedback as another stimulus to which responses become conditioned and ultimately learned. This is the basis of William James's (1890) response-chaining hypothesis, but it is a position also found in the later associative theoretical formulations. Additionally, proprioception is given secondary reinforcing powers, making feedback a powerful learning construct within the S-R framework. In contrast, the S-S position holds that once a cognitive map has initiated a motor command, the movement sequence is run off without the requirement of feedback from the periphery. Thus, both the associative and cognitive schools were centralist or open-loop in character. Neither gave response-produced feedback a place in controlling ongoing responding, and this became a growing criticism. S-R psychology emphasized the role of feedback in learning, but the stimulus-response chaining role was very different to that given it by closed-loop conceptions of behavior.

Information Processing

The information-processing theorists' major criticism of traditional learning theory was the latter's persistent attempts to account for behavior simply in terms of an association between a particular stimulus and a specific response.

Adams's Theory

J. A. Adams's (1971) closed-loop theory of motor learning is grounded in the large body of data pertaining to discrete linear positioning movements, and its theoretical constructs are open to operationalization and empirical test. Extrapolating from ideas originally expressed for verbal learning, Adams postulated motor learning to be the product of two independent states of memory, labeled the *memory trace* and the *perceptual trace*. The memory trace acts like a modest motor program, selecting and initiating the response, and its strength is seen as increasing through stimulus-response contiguity over practice trials. After the response has been initiated, the perceptual trace operates as a reference or recognition mechanism, evaluating response-produced feedback from the movement for error detection and correction purposes. This mechanism is defined as a representation of feedback stimuli obtained from past movements, and its strength is a function of the exposure to, and amount of, those feedback stimuli.

Adams's theory has stimulated more empirical studies on motor behavior than all the other closed-loop theories of motor learning combined. This is in large part due to the specific and operational nature of the theoretical constructs postulated.

Motor Program and Efference Copy

The concepts of motor program and efference copy both deny the functional contribution of feedback in motor learning and performance. The motor hypothesis assumes that a prestructured set of muscle commands can determine the full extent of a movement sequence, uninfluenced by response-produced feedback from the periphery. To account for error detection and correction, motor program advocates appeal to the concept of efference copy, which postulates that a higher central system monitors the efferent motor commands issued to a muscle group.

Schema

The concept of schema challenges the way that a movement command and its sensory consequences are stored and chosen, rather than the way that a movement is controlled. The traditional learning theories and more contemporary closed-loop theories all have specific movement commands and consequences uniquely stored in the brain. In contrast, the schema notion suggests it is generalized abstractions of individual movement sequences and their goals that are stored. Again, there is little direct evidence for this position, particularly with respect to motor behavior, but logically it would reduce the storage capacity required of the brain and account for much of the transfer between novel learning situations experienced in everyday activities.

Karl M. Newell

Motor Memory

Long Term

Long-term retention of motor skills has a long history, and there have been a number of reviews (R. A. Schmidt 1972) that summarize the relevant literature and trace its theoretical development. The most striking feature of the long-term retention research is that motor skills are well retained. The prevailing opinion is that memory lost is very rapid in verbal learning, but retention lost is minimal in motor skills.

EXPLANATION OF FORGETTING IN LTM

Much of the work in motor retention concerns mechanisms of forgetting and involves tests of the two theories of forgetting, the trace decay theory and the interference theory. The trace decay theory states that losses in memory occur spontaneously as a function of time and are not affected by other learning. On the other hand, inteference theory explains forgetting through the interaction of other learned habits, which disrupt memory representation. As such, forgetting is a dynamic process and may be of two types: proactive, from items learned prior to criterion learning; and retroactive, from items interpolated between criterion learning and recall.

DISCRETE VERSUS CONTINUOUS TASKS

Consideration must be given to the type of task being studied if one wants to explain some of the differential forgetting found in the motor skill literature. Motor skills may be classified in many different ways: fine or gross, simple or complex, and discrete or continuous. Of particular interest for retention is the discrete-versus-continuous task comparison, because it appears to be one factor that determines the amount of forgetting. When discrete task (e.g., one characterized by a recognizable beginning and ending) is compared to a continuous task (repetitive movements with no definite beginning or ending), differences in retention loss become apparent. Analysis of these tasks reveals that those that are well retained seem not to be dependent upon cognitive decisions concerning what to do in a given stimulus situation but rather to be concerned with making a well-defined movement correctly or quickly.

AMOUNT OF LEARNING

Ability levels. A.V. Carron and Ronald G. Marteniuk (1970) examined the hypothesis that differential forgetting would be evident among subjects differing in initial ability levels. Three layoff intervals were examined (1, 7, 14 days), and there were no differences among the high-, average-, or low-ability groups following the 1- or 7-day layoff. However, a significant difference was present following the 14-day layoff. Inspection of the data revealed that the difference is a result of a slight improvement (reminiscence) in the high-ability group, combined with a forgetting effect for both the low- and average-ability groups. In a follow-up study, Carron (1971) examined the high, low, and average subjects of the previous study after a retention interval of two years. After two years, the high-ability subjects demonstrated less forgetting than the average- or low-ability groups.

Short Term

Short-term memory (STM) is the memory of events that have just been presented; the capacity of this system is thought to be limited. Recall is usually in a matter of seconds and seldom exceeds a minute. The methods employed usually allow strict control of learning periods, intertrial intervals, and difficulty of interpolated information processing. The designation short-term motor memory (STMM) was introduced about 10 years ago, with the overriding theme of making direct comparisons to verbal memory; since that time, STMM has emerged as an area of experimental psychology that possesses its own theoretical orientations, methodological problems, and empirical controversies.

EXPLANATIONS OF FORGETTING

Trace decay. There have been three main explanations of forgetting that have been utilized to explain forgetting in the STMM. Decay theory assumes that when a criterion act is made, a memory trace is formed, which decays spontaneously over retention intervals; thus less discrimination between traces is

possible. As a result, there will be greater error in recall. Because of spontaneous decay, activity prior to learning or interpolated between learning and recall is assumed to be independent of forgetting. In STMM research, it has been found that with unfilled retention intervals, recall gets progressively worse. Due to the type of errors that are generated in movement research, decay interpretations can be fractionalized into two main interpretations: (1) shrinking with time, producing increased undershooting of the recall attempt, and (2) "fading" with time, producing increased variability at recall. Although the evidence is not convincing, it appears that a number of studies have found evidence to support a trace decay interpretation.

Interference. Interference theory views forgetting as a result of competing responses learned either before or after a criterion item that somehow disrupts memory representation. The interference theory is an active theory, because it is based on the dynamic process of experiencing interpolated events and should be contrasted with the passive decay theory (Stelmach 1974).

Directional error shifts at recall have been found by varying the amplitude of the interpolated movement. Other studies have shown that the longer one stays at an interpolated target and the later an interpolated movement is introduced in the retention interval, the greater the error shifts (Stelmach 1974). It has also been shown that response biasing can be reduced by increasing the number of repetitions and by augmenting the feedback of a criterion movement.

Limited processing capacity. The fundamental assumption behind this view is that there is a limit to the amount of information that can be processed in the short-term system. When the amount of information processed exceeds the system's capacity, items are displaced and are lost, because they cannot be transferred to permanent memory. Procedures are used that attempt to occupy the available capacity by requiring performance on the second task.

Some studies have attempted to isolate the information cues utilized in motor memory and document their information-processing requirements. The procedures utilized make either distance or location information unreliable and then require movements either to a terminal location or to a certain distance. Using these procedures, it has generally been found that location information does not decay unless information-processing activity is introduced during the retention interval.

Feedback. To accurately recall a movement requires a memory trace about a past movement and immediately ongoing feedback from the responding limb. The strength of a given trace is thought to be a function of the amount of feedback and the exposure to it. J. A. Adams, E. T. Goetz, and P. H. Marshall (1972), using various combinations of augmented feedback (vision, audition, and heightened proprioception), have demonstrated that forgetting in STMM is related to the amount of feedback available. Augmented feedback yields smaller recall error at immediate recall, and reduces forgetting over periods of delayed recall.

RECOGNITION PARADIGMS

In some experiments, investigators have asked subjects not to recall movements but rather to make a forced choice as to whether the second movement differs from the first. This procedure has been categorized as a recognition paradigm, because the subject has to recognize a movement rather than produce one. Typically, the second response varies from the first by either ±5, ±10, or ±15 degrees, and the recognition score is recorded as a percentage of correct choices given. The results have shown that recognition error increases over time, as with the reproduction method, but that the amount of forgetting is much smaller. Employing identical procedures, others have examined the effects of feedback and practice on the subject's ability to recognize and correct movements. Both have been found to be effective in error detection and correction, provided that vision is one of the feedback channels. These results compare favorably with reproduction measures. While recall and recognition procedures require different behavior on the part of the subject, there appears to be little discrepancy between them, suggesting that they may have identical retention characteristics.

George E. Stelmach

Motor Performance: Attention Demand

In the 1950s and 1960s, experimental psychologists turned to mathematical information theory as a possible framework for describing the time needed to respond to external signals. The notion that humans possess some type of central system with limited capacity was advanced to explain their frequent inability to respond independently to more than one external signal. As a consequence, locating and characterizing decision bottlenecks became a major concern. Attempts to use information theory to specify a fixed human information-processing capacity proved unsuccessful. However, the conceptual and methodological advances made with the information-processing perspective have fostered more detailed and sophisticated study of internal cognitive processes.

Measuring Attention Demands

Continuous tasks (such as tracking), discrete tasks (such as pressing a key in response to a tone), and signal detection tasks (such as detecting a specific letter in a brief visual display) have been used as secondary tasks. Choice of secondary task depends upon the type of primary tasks to be measured. The secondary task should not influence performance on the primary task.

Attention Demands during a Single Movement

A number of movements involve merely the displacement of a limb from one position to another. For example, lifting a cup from the table to one's mouth, pushing a brake pedal, and moving a stylus from a center target to a side target are single movements. A single movement to a target end point has two distinct component phases: (1) the reaction time phase between the signal to respond and response initiation, and (2) the movement phase between response initiation and actual contact with the target endpoint. As a rule, attention demands prove higher during the initiation phase and first portion of the execution phase than during the final portions of the execution phase.

Attention Demands during Continuous Movements
Many skills involve an ongoing continuous movement or patterned sequences of discrete movements. However, both the difficulties inherent in identifying commonalities among these tasks and the problems in identifying and isolating component stages within these tasks have hampered study in this area. Three categories of continuous movements are discussed briefly. Some continuous skills utilize movement patterns or sequences that are repeated periodically; walking, swimming, and bicycling are common examples.

A second category of continuous skill involves patterns of discrete movements made in response to a series of discrete signals. Sight-reading music, typing from a manuscript, and pressing keys in response to a series of lights are examples of such continuous patterns. Attention demands in these tasks reflect the number of possible signals and the time pressure for responding.

A third category of continuous skill includes visually guided behaviors, such as driving a car and pursuit tracking, which require monitoring a changing visual display and making appropriate motor corrections. Manually tracking itself proves attention-demanding, and demands reflect task difficulty.

Application in sports suggests (1) minimizing the attention demands for one's own performance and (2) attempting to maximize demands placed on one's opponents. Presumably, skilled performers have learned to minimize their own attention demands by taking advantage of redundancy and sequential dependencies within a game itself and a specific opponent's style of play. They also generate high attention demands for opponents by minimizing predictability in their own play.

Beth Kerr

Motor Performance: Motivation

Motivation is defined as an internal factor that arouses, directs, and more importantly, integrates a person's behavior. Motivation, like other psychological constructs, is not observed directly but rather is inferred from goal-directed behavior or may even be assumed to exist to interpret behavior.

Motivational constructs, whether they be called drives, needs, or motives, are assumed to underlie behavior, for without them, behavior would either not occur, or if it did, would be random and purposeless.

Learning Theory
Within the framework of learning theory, specifically the punishment paradigm, a series of response-time experiments were undertaken in the early 1950s in the research laboratory of Franklin M. Henry. A drive was created in some of these experiments by the administration of a noxious stimulus or stressor, such as electric shock, loud noise, or bright lights. The onset of the drive stimulus was relevant to the stimulus-reinforcement contingencies.

The effects of motivational transfer were investigated in another series of experiments. Subjects first practiced a coordinated movement, then subsequently practiced a simpler but different movement, and finally were retested on the original coordinated movement. The experimental group differed from the control group in that a stressor was administered for slow responses on the simpler intermediate movement. This manipulation resulted in enhanced performance for the experimental group, while controls failed to exhibit any significant transfer.

Drive Theory
Clark L. Hull's theory postulates that although the individual may be motivated to act (high drive), she may not act unless the habit is sufficiently well established through numerous associations of contiguous stimulus-response (S-R) connections. Any strong stimulus, the reduction of which is reinforcing, should increase the probability of the dominant behavioral response at the time. Early stages of skill acquisition presumably contain dominant responses that are incorrect, whereas later, as the skill is mastered through practice, the dominant response becomes the correct response. Therefore, a positive linear relationship should exist between drive and performance when the correct response is well established.

Another drive theory approach has been to examine motor performance on the same task, with intervals ranging from several hours to several days interpolated between original practice and recall. Using an achievement drive aroused by task instructions, H. J. Eysenck conducted several studies and found that high-drive subjects show greater reminiscence than low-drive subjects on mirror-tracing tasks, but not for reaction-time tasks. Consolidation theory has been used to explain the greater reminiscence of high-drive subjects. This theory maintains that high drive during practice will result in a more "robust" activity trace, resulting in greater long-term memory. Although not examining reminiscence per se, G. Sage and E. V. Bennett have shown support for consolidation theory when subjects were retested one day later on a pursuit rotor. These results and those of other investigators have consistently been obtained only when the administration of electric shock was related or contingent upon past performance.

Activation-Arousal Theory

The most popular motivational framework in which to examine motor performance has been arousal-activation theory. Activation is the degree of energy release of the organism, which varies on a continuum from deep sleep to high excitement. This energy can be measured centrally by means of an electroencephalogram but is more commonly inferred from peripheral measures of arousal, such as muscle tension or heart rate. Whereas many drive theorists assume that behavior is aroused and directed to achieve drive reduction, activation theorists assume that behavior is aroused and directed toward some kind of "balanced" or optimal state.

Another approach to this problem has been to examine motor performance on a variety of motor tasks as a function of trait anxiety. One review indicated that the findings were equivocal, perhaps because trait anxiety only indicates a predisposition to respond with greater arousal, provided the situation encountered is stressful.

Several studies have also found that intermediate levels (e.g., heart rate of 115 and 145 bpm) of exercise-induced activation (EIA) produce faster responses, regardless of whether the task is simple or choice reaction time. However, comparisons between studies prompted B. Gutin (1973) to conclude that motor steadiness tasks requiring consider-

able inhibition are performed at very low levels of EIA, whereas disinhibition tasks (e.g., arm speed) are performed best at very high levels.

Expectancy-Value Theory

The most lucid and applicable formulation of expectancy-value theory for motor performance is in the area of achievement motivation. John W. Atkinson and N. T. Feather (Healey and Landers 1973) have proposed that the environments in which motivation to achieve will be greatest will differ for two theoretical types of individuals: persons predominantly motivated to achieve success (Mas) and those motivated mainly by the fear of success (Maf). Accordingly, the behavior of Mas individuals is said to be a multiplicative function of expectancy for success, incentive for success, and habit strength on the particular task.

Daniel M. Landers

Motor Program

Closed- and Open-Loop Control

There are a number of lines of evidence that criticize the closed-loop notion, but the most important has been the fact that responding to feedback (or error) stimuli requires a great deal of time, making it doubtful that feedback can be used within a movement, especially if the movement is a rapid one. A signal presented to the subject requires from 120 to 200 msec (one "reaction time") before the subject begins to respond to it. Thus, if a signal that the movement is not achieving the environmental goal is presented during the movement, the subject cannot begin to respond to it until at least 120 msec later.

The response to peripheral stimuli, which include stimuli about the correctness of the movement pattern, requires approximately one reaction time to begin. This makes it unlikely that performers monitor stimuli from their moving limbs, initiating corrections if errors in meeting the environmental goal should occur, especially if the movements are rapid (e.g., less than 200 msec).

Role of Feedback

Because of the role of spinal feedback control of motor output, it is probably incorrect to define the motor program as carrying out movement without the involvement of feedback. Rather, the program should be seen as a set of prestructured commands that, when executed, are capable of carrying out all of the movement details, with signals from the environment or moving limb indicating that the pattern of movement chosen should be changed if ineffective, until the program has run its course. Even though the evidence points strongly to a motor-program interpretation, the issue of closed versus open-loop control of movement has not been settled, and a number of theories hold that learning is the development of more effective references of correctness against which feedback is compared during the movement.

Characteristics of the Motor Program

Program running time. A program must run its course for at least one reaction time (or until a very fast movement is completed). This is an ideal minimum, however, and a more realistic minimum is somewhat longer. First, a signal from the environment indicating that the movement pattern should be changed will usually require that enough of the movement has been completed so that an error can arise, lengthening the minimum to one reaction time plus the movement time necessary to produce the error (perhaps as much as 400 msec). In addition, errors can occur in more than one way, and thus the time to react to one of many signals is substantially greater than the reaction time to a single alternative, again increasing the estimate of the minimum program time.

Richard A. Schmidt

Mourning: Psychoanalytic Theory

Sigmund Freud's *Mourning and Melancholia* (1917), first drafted in 1915, goes beyond the ethical explanation of the mechanism of grief and its resolution as compared to the pathological condition of melancholia. Freud calls mourning an affect.

George H. Pollock (1961) has proposed that mourning is an adaptational process, having sequential phases and stages, phylogenetically evolved and present as a reaction to loss, but not solely to object loss. Sigmund Freud (1917) also notes that grief is the reaction to the loss of a loved person. Although reality indicates that the loved object or ideal no longer exists, the mourner initially is unable to withdraw his love or attachment from that which is lost.

John Bowlby (1961) believes that grief is an amalgam of anxiety, anger, and despair following the experience of what is feared to be an irretrievable loss. It differs from separation anxiety, which is experienced when the loss is believed retrievable and hope remains.

Pathological mourning reactions have frequently been equated with depression and, in the older terminology, melancholia. However, the distinction between these two conditions—pathological mourning and the depressive states—may be psychologically and perhaps biologically significant. In pathological mourning we may see various manifestations of defense against mourning; H. Deutsch (1937), for example, describes the absence of grief, and J. Fleming and S. Altschul (1959) describe the activation of the mourning process during psychoanalytic treatment.

G. H. Pollock (1962) studies four loss situations in an attempt to more fully understand the mourning process: (1) adults who have lost one or both parents through death during childhood, (2) adults who have lost one or more siblings through death during childhood, (3) adults who have lost one or more of their children through death, and (4) adults who have lost one or more spouses through death.

The mourning process seems to be a universal adaptive reaction to change and loss, with an outcome of gain and freedom once the process has been completed. Bereavement, the specific reaction to the death of a loved object, is a subclass of the mourning process. The mourning process is a means of reestablishing equilibrium intrapsychically, interpersonally, socially, and culturally.

George H. Pollock

Multiple Personality Disorder

Multiple personality disorder (MPD) is a complex and chronic dissociative psychopathology (Kluft 1987a) characterized by disturbances of memory and identity (Nemiah 1980). The ongoing coexistence of relatively consistent but alternating, subjectively separate identities and recurrent episodes of memory distortion, frank amnesia, or both distinguishes it from other mental disorders. It is currently understood to be a post-traumatic condition that occurs almost invariably as the sequela to overwhelming childhood experiences (Putnam et al. 1986; Spiegel 1984).

Most cultures and societies have had conditions in which another entity is understood to have taken over the mind and body of the afflicted individual (i.e., possession states). When theological paradigms for the understanding of mental disorders were replaced in Europe by what H. F. Ellenberger (1970) describes as the first dynamic psychiatry, a secular expression of many of the same mental structures previously found in possession syndromes began to be reported. Although described earlier by Paracelsus and Petetain, and also by Benjamin Rush, the first attempt to describe a syndrome consisting of these phenomena was made by Eberhardt Gmelin in 1791. A rich but largely forgotten literature on MPD and associated phenomena flourished throughout the nineteenth century. Under Jean-Martin Charcot and Pierre Janet many such patients were identified and treated at the Salpetrière; in the Untied States, Morton Prince, Boris Sidis, and others made noteworthy contributions. However, MPD was dismissed as a subject of importance by the rising tides of psychoanalysis, organic/descriptive psychiatry, and behaviorism. Its study declined to near extinction within a generation.

The current resurgence in interest in MPD has many sources. These include the phenomenological orientation of DMS-III, which distinguishes the dissociative disorders from the hysterias; the impact of feminism in sensitizing the mental health professions to the widespread abuse of women and children; an explosion in the study of post-traumatic stress disorder; interest stimulated by lay books and media attention; the efforts of pioneering teachers, such as the late Cornelia B. Wilbur, M.D.; and finally, the emergence of a modern literature in the 1980s, replete with innovative diagnostic approaches and effective treatment recommendations (Kluft 1991a).

The DSM-III-R diagnostic criteria for MPD are more flexible, less reified, and more consistent with clinical findings than their DSM-III precursors:

A. The existence within the person of two or more distinct personalities or personality states (each with its own relatively enduring pattern of perceiving, relating to, and thinking about the environment and self).

B. At least two of these personalities or personality states recurrently take full control of the individual's behavior. (272)

As of this writing, early drafts of DSM-IV appear prepared to add an amnesia criterion, and may rename MPD "dissociative identity disorder."

The personalities in MPD (alters, alternates) are not separate people. They are alternative ways of configuring aspects of the mental apparatus in relatively stable and enduring manners, which, at least initially, subserve adaptational purposes. J. J. Putnam (1989) conceptualizes the alters as "highly discrete states of consciousness organized around a prevailing affect, sense of self (including body image) with a limited repertoire of behaviors and a set of state dependent memories" (103). Pragmatically, an alter personality is "an entity with a firm, persistent, and well-founded sense of self and a characteristic and consistent pattern of behavior and feelings in response to given stimuli. It must have a range of functions, a range of emotional responses, and a significant life history (of its own existence)" (Kluft 1984a, 23). Alters differ from the various states of mind that all persons experience in that they have different identities, self-representations, and autobiographical memories from one another. Furthermore, one alter will not have a sense of ownership for the actions and experiences of another alter. The non-MPD individual will retain continuity in these four dimensions across widely divergent moods, situations, and behaviors.

Traditionally, the focus has been on the polarized qualities of pairs of alters (e.g., "the good girl" versus "the slut"; "upright citizen" versus "the sociopath"). However, this emphasis on dramatic conflicts fails to address the adaptational functions and strategies the alters subserve and enact. These missions are supported by segregating certain aspects of experience and knowledge from one another in a relatively rule-bound fashion. For example, a young girl subjected to repetitive incestuous abuse may form a number of different personalities: personalities that are unaware of the abuse, so that life within the family can continue in an undisturbed manner and she can preserve affectionate ties to the abuser; male personalities based on the wish that if she were a boy, this would not befall her; sexually welcoming personalities to manage the incest expeditiously and without any resistance that might provoke being beaten into submission; protector personalities based on powerful others to deny future vulnerability; and persecutor personalities based on an identification with the powerful aggressor she can neither fend off nor avoid. The persistence and increasing autonomy of such adaptations over time easily can become dysfunctional MPD. However, the emergence and manifest separateness of the alters is not an inevitable and ongoing concomitant of these purposes and processes.

Furthermore, in most cases the alters come to constitute a system of mind, and many of them have the subjective experience of relating to one another as if they were actual people. Alters may develop a complex inner world with alliances, enmities, and relationships of all varieties. The alters may attempt to influence one another by imposing feelings, impulses, and even actions upon each other. They may offer advice and/or make threats to one another. These expressions are often perceived as verbal hallucinations or vivid thoughts experienced as originating within the head (Kluft 1987b, 1991b). This is why MPD may be quite an active process even in the absence of overt switch behaviors.

Contemporary cases average thirteen to sixteen alters. However, this is deceptive. In most series the mode is three, and the median is eight to ten. In most series, males are less complex than females, averaging about eight in contrast to sixteen to eighteen in women. Furthermore, even in the largest series, cases of extreme complexity (over twenty-five

alters), occurring in 15 to 25% of the patients, unduly inflate the mean (Kluft 1991a).

The personalities' overt differences and disparate self-concepts range from the striking to the minimal. Alters may experience and represent themselves as being of different ages, genders, races, religions, and sexual orientations. They may experience themselves as having different appearances and hold discrepant values and belief systems. Their awareness of one another may range from total to zero. Directionality of awareness is quite common; i.e., A will be aware of B's activities, but B will not be aware of A's (see Kihlstrom 1992; Nissen et al. 1988; Schacter et al. 1989; Silberman et al. 1985). Some may have symptoms not suffered by others. Psychophysiologic differences have been documented (Putnam 1984, 1988, 1991a, 1991b). Differences of visual acuity are well known (Miller 1989). Different handwriting and handedness, voice, vocabulary, accents, speech patterns, and preferred languages are encountered. Facial expressions and movement characteristics may show impressive and rather consistent differences (Kluft et al. 1986). When personalities are creative and have acquired different wardrobes and pursued different interests, their overt differences may be quite distinct.

Personalities may be named or labeled ("anger," "the slut"), or without appellation. The patient usually presents in a host personality (the personality that is out most of the time during a given period of time), which bears the legal name and is depressed, anxious, somewhat neurasthenic, compulsively good, masochistic, and constricted hedonically. It suffers psychophysiologic symptoms and has periods of amnesia or time loss. Frequently encountered personality types are: childlike alters; protectors; helpers-advisors; personalities with distinct affective states; guardians of memories and secrets; memory holders; inner persecutors; anesthetic personalties; expressors of forbidden impulses; avengers; defenders and apologists for the abusers; identifications and introjections; specialized encapsulators of traumatic experiences and powerful affects; very specialized alters; and those that preserve the idealized potential for happiness, growth, and the expression of feelings (Kluft 1991a). However arresting are these differences, they are a more dramatic epiphenomenon than the core of the condition, which is the dissociative adaptation and defensive style (Kluft 1985a). Nonetheless, much of the treatment consists of dealing with these alters' quasi-delusional beliefs in their being separate and autonomous. Because they have different self-structures, different memories, and different (and usually distorted) methods of thought (Fine 1988b), they live in subjectively different realities. Addressing this "multiple reality disorder" (Kluft 1993) is a crucial aspect of their treatment.

Study of the natural history of MPD, long thought a florid and dramatic condition, demonstrates that it is a psychopathology of hiddenness. MPD children as young as 3 have been reported (Riley and Mead 1988). Children present with a plethora of symptoms, which may easily be attributed to other disorders but usually demonstrate some trancelike behavior (Hornstein and Tyson 1991; Kluft 1984c, 1985b). Adolescent females generally present as depressed with somatoform complaints, or with extreme turmoil and alloplastic behavior. Adolescent males often attract attention for aggressive behavior or apparent psychosis (Kluft 1985a). Adult presentations are quite varied; over twenty varieties have been classified, from the most overt to the disguised and subtle (Kluft 1991b).

Approximately 20% of all patients remain overtly MPD on an ongoing basis. Only one-third of these are flamboyant and exhibitionistic; the remainder keep their situation hidden. The remaining 80% do not appear to have overt MPD most of the time, and appear either to have DDNOS or seem without a dissociative diagnosis. However, under stress or other circumstances, their MPD becomes overt during certain "windows of diagnosability." This covertness explains why the average MPD patient spends approximately 6.8 years in the mental health care delivery system before receiving an accurate diagnosis (Putnam et al. 1986).

The etiology of MPD is polyfactorial. The condition occurs when a dissociation-prone child experiences sufficient stress to overwhelm the nondissociative defenses. Personality formation occurs on any of a number of natural substrates with the potential to express "dividedness." This adapta-

tion can become fixed if the child is not protected from further such experiences and/or is not provided with adequate soothing and restorative experiences (Kluft 1984c, 1986b).

Dissociation-proneness appears to have two components: hypnotizability and dissociativity (Carlson and Putnam 1989). The former is quite high in children, and the latter has been observed to increase over time in children with documented abuse (Putnam and Trickett, unpublished data). In the United States and Canada, the most common overwhelming stimulus appears to be antecedent child abuse, reported by as many as 97% of MPD patients (Putnam et al. 1986). Some allegations made by MPD patients have been documented, but this is rarely possible. Fears that recovered "memories" may be confabulated during therapy cannot be completely discounted. However, it is useful to be aware that 38% of women with documented childhood abuse did not acknowledge that abuse when interviewed 17 years later (Williams 1992).

Substrates for multiplicity are inherent in many developmental lines, and in phenomena such as imaginary companionship and introjection among others. In the absence of ongoing hurt, and with compassionate care, some MPD children unify spontaneously (Kluft 1984c).

For many years, the diagnosis of MPD was based on careful exploration of several suggestive signs, or with the use of hypnosis or drug-facilitated interviews. The suggestive signs were "1) prior treatment failure; 2) 3 or more prior diagnoses; 3) concurrent psychiatric and somatic symptoms; 4) fluctuating symptoms and levels of function; 5) severe headaches and/or other pain syndromes; 6) time distortion, time lapses, or frank amnesia; 7) being told of disremembered behaviors; 8) others noting observable changes; 9) the discovery of objects, productions, or handwriting in one's possession that one cannot account for or recognize; 10) the hearing of voices (80% experienced as within the head) that are experienced as separate, urging the patient toward some activity; 11) the patient's use of 'we' in a collective sense and/or making self-referential statements in the third person; 12) the eliciting of other entities through hypnosis or a drug-facilitated interview; 13) a history of child abuse; and 14) an inability to recall childhood events from the years 6 to 11" (Kluft 1991a, 172).

Recently, however, a powerful mental status test specifically designed to explore dissociative experiences has been developed and two structured interviews with over 90% sensitivity and very few false positives have been developed, the Dissociative Disorders Interview Schedule (DDIS; Ross 1989) and the Structured Clinical Interview for the Diagnosis of DSM-III-R Dissociative Disorders (SCID-D) by Marlene Steinberg (1993a, 1993b). Both are amendable to both clinical and research applications. The Dissociative Experiences Scale (DES; Bernstein and F. Putnam 1986) has proven a useful screen for the detection of patients likely to have MPD. Furthermore, Armstrong (Armstrong 1991; Armstrong and R. J. Loewenstein 1990) has solved the vexing problem of making the MPD diagnosis reliably with psychological testing. These new advances have enhanced clinicians' expertise in identifying this long-elusive condition.

The use of these instruments has made it possible to study the epidemiology of MPD, traditionally regarded as a rarity. By screening patient and non-patient populations with the DES and instruments derived from it, and following up patients with suggestive scores with a clinical assessment and/or a DDIS or SCID-D, it has been possible to determine that 3% of the general population in both North America and Europe have scores suggestive of the presence of a major dissociative disorder (Ross 1991; Vanderlinden et al. 1992), and that 3 to 5% of hospitalized psychiatric patients have previously undiagnosed MPD, with still others qualifying for DDNOS (Boon and Draijer, unpublished data; Hornstein and Tyson 1991; Ross 1991; Saxe and van der Kolk, unpublished data). MPD is found outside North America, refuting the argument that it is a North American culture–bound syndrome (e.g., Boon and Draijer [1993] identified seventy-one cases in the Netherlands, using translated versions of the instruments discussed above). Therefore, MPD is a common and widespread psychiatric disorder that has not been recognized as such. In published clinical series, women predominate over men at

ratios of 8 or 9 to 1. However, the reported child cases are approximately 1:1. Much remains to be learned about the recognition of males with MPD (Kluft 1991a).

Treatment

The treatment of MPD ideally should integrate the various alters in the course of resolving the patient's problematic symptoms and difficulties in living. Developing a more harmonious arrangement among the personalities without their necessarily ceding their separateness is regarded as an intermediate goal by most, while some (Watkins and Watkins 1979) regard this as an acceptable outcome. In practice, some patients will refuse to work toward integration, necessitating the latter approach. Some patients are so chaotic that a supportive attempt to enhance their adaptation is essential, at least initially or intermittently.

The treatment of MPD usually proceeds in several overlapping stages, designed to strengthen the patient prior to dealing with painful traumatic material. The following nine-stage outline (Kluft 1991a) is compatible with those offered by B. J. Braun (1986) and F. W. Putnam (1989).

Establishing the psychotherapy involves creating an atmosphere of safety in which treatment frame and the therapeutic alliance are established, and the patient is socialized to the treatment. Next, preliminary interventions facilitate access to the alters, establish safety contracts, foster communication, and maximize symptomatic relief. Then, history gathering and mapping the personality system allows an appreciation of the patient's sense of his or her past, and the rationale of the MPD adaptation. The therapist begins to work with the problems of distressed alters. Only with the patient thus understood and strengthened does the therapist approach the painful past for the metabolism of the trauma. This under way or completed, efforts are made to move toward integration/resolution by sharing and working through the painful material across alters. Then, the alters achieve smooth collaboration (resolution) and hopefully unification (integration). Thereafter, the unified or collaborative individual must learn new nondissociative coping skills, solidify the gains, and complete the process of working through before reaching termination or being placed in a follow-up status.

Treatment usually must involve at least two sessions per week for a period of several years. The use of hypnosis to facilitate treatment has been very successful. Follow-up studies (Coons 1986; Kluft 1984b, 1986a) are flawed because they report the result of neophytes and experts only. Not unexpectedly, the expert-based studies show optimistic results with great stability, and the neophyte-based studies offer a more conservative prognosis. Recent findings (Kluft 1993) demonstrate that MPD patients can be divided by their treatment trajectories into patients who recover rapidly, those who struggle to recovery over a long and rocky road, and a group that may not have the potential to recover except with the most prolonged and heroic therapies. Objective measures of their therapy behavior rather than phenomenologic criteria distinguishes these groups.

Several controversies continue to surround MPD. Many continue to maintain that MPD is a form of hysteria, and that inattention to its manifestations will cause it to wane. Others see it as borderline phenomena gone out of control. Armstrong's data (1991 and unpublished) indicate that the core of MPD is obsessive rather than hysterical or borderline, an observation made earlier by both Richard P. Kluft (1987a) and Ross and Anderson (1988).

Although the natural history of MPD and its covert qualities are well established (Kluft 1985a), many continue to feel that only the most persistently overt cases should qualify for the diagnosis, and that those who think otherwise are overdiagnosing the condition quite severely.

There remains a persistent argument that MPD is largely an iatrogenic condition. Although it is quite easy to induce a subject to mimic MPD phenomena under certain demand characteristics (e.g., Spanos et al. 1985, 1986), there is no published study that documents the creation of a fixed MPD adaptation. The arguments that hypnosis creates or influences the form of MPD have not been sustained; hypnotized and nonhypnotized MPD cohorts have minimal distinctions. The accusation that those with a special interest in MPD unduly influence the condi-

tion's manifestations is countered in a 1989 study by Ross and his colleagues, who found that MPD patients described by "MPD specialists" and Canadian general psychiatrists did not differ in any significant way. In sum, MPD is a naturally occurring disorder and is not an iatrogenic artifact.

Richard P. Kluft

Murphy, Gardner (1895–1979)

Murphy's work in social psychology, personality, creativity, parapsychology, and other areas was open and integrative. He espoused a field theory that emphasized both the biological and the social aspects of behavior. He believed that genetic influences are modified by environmental pressures to produce a self-structure that interprets and acts upon each new situation and also is acted upon and influenced by the situation. Murphy was president of the American Psychological Association, the Society for Psychological Study of Social Issues, and the Society for Psychical Research.

Gertrude Schmeidler

Mythology, Folklore, and Psychoanalysis

Almost from the inception of psychoanalysis, its practitioners have been seriously involved in the study of myths and other forms of folklore, particularly the fairy tale. They studied oral literature, usually without knowledge of the cultures within which it had arisen or that had accepted it by means of diffusion. When their thinking was dominated by the topographical viewpoint or, as it is commonly known, id psychology or libido psychology (Freud 1900, chap. 7; 1915), many psychoanalysts used the study of folklore especially to demonstrate the validity of their recently acquired knowledge concerning unconscious mechanisms and, particularly, symbolism. They sought simultaneously to interpret folklore from its manifest contents and to use the same concepts they had employed in their interpretations to support those concepts.

While the topographical theory continued to prevail in psychoanalytic thinking, most psychoanalytic contributions to folklore continued to have as their major goal the demonstration of the coincidence of the themes and symbols of oral literature in the dreams, fantasies, and transference reactions of their patients.

Psychoanalysts had learned that the themes that are to be found in oral literature arise in the dreams and fantasies of patients who have no knowledge of that literature. Analysts knew, too, that when individuals heard folklore themes, the tales stimulated anxiety and guilt when they reflected cathected unresolved psychic conflicts.

Géza Roheim appears to be the first anthropologist to enter systematic psychoanalytic training in order to learn what field data would be most useful to test analytic ideas cross-culturally and how to amass that information. He had been deeply interested in oral literature from the beginning of his professional work (1913). Folklorists of that time still held generally that keys to understanding folk literature lay with "savages." Roheim (1925, 1974) chose to work especially with the aborigines of Australia.

The myth is a special form of shared fantasy, which serves to bring the individual into relationship with members of her cultural group on the basis of common psychological needs. It can be studied from the point of view of its roles in psychic and social integrations; not only does it assist in alleviating individual guilt and anxiety but it constitutes a form of adaptation to reality; as a form of community illusion, it adds to the cohesion of the social group. Thus, it influences the development of a sense of reality and the superego (J. A. Arlow 1961).

Myths and related phenomena are group-accepted images, which serve as further screening devices in the defensive and adaptive functions of the ego. They reinforce the suppression and repression of individual fantasies and personal myths (D. Eggan 1955). A shared daydream is a step toward group formation and solidarity and leads to a sense of mutual identification on the basis of common needs. Myth makers serve the community alongside poets and prophets, presenting communally acceptable versions of wishes, which therefore were expressed in guilt-laden, private fantasy.

L. Bryce Boyer

· N ·

Narcissistic Alliance

The concept of the narcissistic alliance is predicated on the clinical observation of an omnipresent narcissism and the consequent elaboration of the notion of a narcissistic ontogeny. Although the developmental hypothesis initially arose in the era of the early psychoanalytic preoccupation with instincts and their sequential vicissitudes, the advent of the structural hypothesis and the subsequent clinical and theoretical interest in the ego and its nature as well as its growth and development added a new and enormous enhancement to the developmental notion.

If narcissism is conceptualized as another developmental line, as has been postulated, with its own reflection in structure, with a protected, vulnerable narcissistic frontier or locus of importance, a considerable amount of what one deals with in the immediate clinical context can be more easily understood. It is in this respect that the concept of a narcissistic alliance was elaborated. What we call initial rapport, for example, is certainly one form of the narcissistic alliance.

In this context the narcissistic defenses will once again be mobilized, just as they had been initially in a similarly antitherapeutic fashion. The analyst, then, must be aware of the immediate locus of the danger that confronts the patient and do whatever is necessary to dispel the patient's urgent need of mobilizing militant, narcissistic defenses in this particular area.

The commencement of the narcissistic alliance in an ordinary analysis would antedate the development of a therapeutic alliance as well as the development of the transference neurosis. It would also be clear that during and following the resolution of the transference neurosis, the narcissistic alliance would still remain partly embodied in the therapeutic alliance as its later form, and partly unchanged in its earlier form.

Robert D. Mehlman

National Institute of Mental Health, The

Mental illnesses, which may affect 22% of the population in any given year, exact a $128 billion annual toll in treatment, lost productivity, and other indirect costs—and an incalculable sum in human suffering. The National Institute of Mental Health (NIMH) is the federal agency responsible for research on causes, treatment, and prevention of mental illnesses. It is one of the components of the National Institutes of Health (NIH), U.S. Department of Health and Human Services. From its Rockville, Maryland, headquarters, the institute's extramural programs administer grants and contracts supporting projects by investigators at research centers across the country. In NIMH's intramural program, government scientists directly conduct studies at laboratories on the NIH campus in Bethesda, Maryland, and at other sites in the Washington, D.C., area.

NIMH-supported clinical research addresses the spectrum of mental disorders, with particular focus on serious mental illnesses—schizophrenia, manic-depressive illness, and severe forms of depression, panic, and obsessive-compulsive disorders—which afflict more than 5 million Americans, 2.8% of the adult population. Other studies address epidemiology and delivery of services to the mentally ill. The institute also supports a broad range of basic research in behavioral and neuroscience disciplines.

Among current initiatives are programs targeted at medications development, neuropsychiatric and psychosocial aspects of AIDS, and enhancing scientific infrastructure via innovative applications of information science technologies, brain tissue and gene banks, and the recruitment of more minority and women scientists.

History

Founded in 1946 as one of the original four NIH institutes, the NIMH has played a pioneering role in building the foundations of contemporary neuro- and behavioral science. Over the years, it has also nurtured development of the nation's mental health services systems and professions and parallel federal programs on substance abuse.

The Community Mental Health Centers Act of 1963 provided for an infusion of money for direct grants to help local communities set up comprehensive services, bypassing the overburdened state hospital system. This expanded role brought with it an identity crisis. Even when services accounted for only 8% of its budget in 1964, NIMH had already become the largest NIH institute. By 1967, when services funds surpassed those for research, NIMH's budget dwarfed that of its largest sister institute (the National Cancer Institute) by nearly 2:1. Meanwhile, "Great Society" priorities targeted more NIMH research on social problems, such as poverty, crime, urban problems, and substance abuse; NIMH's portfolio seemed to be losing its focus on mental illness. Many popular ideologies of the era also tended to reinforce a lingering notion of mental illness as fundamentally different from "physical" illness. In 1969, NIMH left the NIH and began a 24-year odyssey.

Yet during this same period, beginning in the early 1960s, a seminal event in the evolution of the mental health sciences was quietly under way: the psychopharmacology revolution. Specific and often dramatic responses of major mental disorders to medications afforded evidence of a biological component, triggering a gradual shift in perceptions; those who had dismissed mental disorders as character flaws or reflections of environmental causes exclusively were forced to reconsider. In meeting the challenge of providing credible assessments of

behavioral/experiential outcomes of both biological and psychological treatments, the mental illness research field pioneered development of methodologies, such as the controlled trial and other innovations now widely adopted throughout medical science.

Another important spinoff of the psychopharmacology revolution came into its own during the 1970s: the explosive growth of neuroscience. Previously autonomous disciplines, such as pharmacology, psychology, and immunology, began forging creative alliances. By 1973, an institute-supported team reported the discovery of the opiate receptor. That same year, NIMH, along with two of its former divisions, which had been reauthorized as the National Institute on Drug Abuse (NIDA) and the National Institute on Alcohol Abuse and Alcoholism (NIAAA), became part of ADAMHA (Alcohol, Drug Abuse, and Mental Health Administration). Shifting political winds, inflation, and the burgeoning demand for services and social problems funding cut into the institute's research investment just as brain science opportunities beckoned. Real dollars for research dropped by 31% from 1969 to 1975, while the NIH institutes grew by an average of 34% during the same period.

A process of refocusing resources on biomedical and mental illness–related behavioral research began in the late 1970s and received added impetus in 1981, when most of the ADAMHA institutes' direct services grants to communities were replaced with block grants to states. During this same period, NIMH's budget for basic studies on social problems was reduced substantially. NIMH reorganized its extramural, or grant-supporting, programs in 1985 to reflect the more focused research mission. With dramatic advances in neuroscience, support for the institute's research programs improved, and research budgets grew. In 1989, Congress and the president declared the 1990s the "Decade of the Brain."

ADAMHA was abolished and NIMH returned to the NIH in 1992. Responsibility for mental health service–related tasks was assigned to the newly created Center for Mental Health Services, within the Substance Abuse and Mental Health Services Administration. NIMH continues to fund services research, however, which provides an essential link between clinical studies and the real world of services delivery, and which enhanced the institute's ability to participate productively in national health care policy reform discussions in the early 1990s.

NIMH's return to the NIH signals a historic shift in views of mental illness, shaped by advances in brain and behavioral research and proven effective treatments. It is now widely recognized that mental illnesses, like most medical problems, involve interactions between biological vulnerabilities and environmental factors. NIMH-supported research examining such interactions has contributed significantly to erasing much of the stigma historically attached to mental illness. This destigmatization has both contributed to and benefited from the emergence during the 1980s of patient/family advocacy groups, which have passionately and persuasively voiced their support for mental health research.

Extramural Programs

NIMH administers some 1,800 grants and contracts supporting research on basic brain and behavior science; prevention, diagnosis, and treatment of mental disorders; epidemiology; and services delivery systems.

Applications are reviewed by the Division of Extramural Activities (DEA), which is charged with ensuring that the institute supports work that offers the greatest promise of furthering knowledge relevant to mental illness. Initial review groups, composed of distinguished scientists from the field, assign each approved grant a numerical score, which is translated into a percentile ranking for funding priority. Ultimate approval authority for funding projects rests with the National Advisory Mental Health Council, the overall advisory board to the institute.

The Division of Epidemiology and Services Research (DESR) manages studies of the frequency of mental disorders and risk factors for their development; prevention of mental illness; violence and traumatic stress; behavioral medicine; and research on the organization, financing, and effectiveness of mental health services. An NIMH-supported multi-site Epidemiologic Catchment Area Study has revealed that more than 20% of the population is

affected by a diagnosable mental disorder in a given year (roughly the same as cardiovascular disorders), including 9% who suffer some disability and 2.8% with severe mental illness.

NIMH's Division of Clinical and Treatment Research (DCTR) supports studies on the causes, pathophysiology, diagnosis, and treatment of major mental disorders. The division also issues the *Schizophrenia Bulletin*, *Psychopharmacology Bulletin*, and *Psychotherapy and Rehabilitation Bulletin*. A recent institute-supported evaluation has found that empirical studies documenting the success rates of treatments for severe mental illness (60–80%) compare favorably to—and even exceed—efficacy rates for most successfully treated "physical" disorders.

NIMH's Division of Neuroscience and Behavioral Science supports fundamental studies and research training in cognition, behavioral, molecular, and cellular neuroscience; neuroimaging and applied neuroscience; personality and social processes; and preclinical psychopharmacology. NIMH has the lead role among a consortium of federal agencies developing a Human Brain Project, which will bring to bear advances in computer/telecommunications to help scientists manage the knowledge explosion in the neurosciences.

Among other activities, the institute is supporting biomedical and psychosocial research on AIDS; nurturing the development of new medications to treat mental illnesses; conducting public education campaigns on depression and panic disorder; expanding research on the mental health needs of women and minority group members; educating teachers and schoolchildren about brain science and the role of animal research; and promoting the exchange of research knowledge ripe for application by professionals in the field.

Intramural Research

The world's largest institution devoted to studies of the brain and mental illness, the NIMH Intramural Research Program (IRP), encompasses 600+ scientists and support personnel working in twenty-four laboratories and branches located on the NIH campus, at the NIH Animal Research Center in Poolesville, Maryland, and at the NIMH Neuroscience Center at Saint Elizabeth's Hospital in

Washington, D.C. Intramural studies represent about 17% of the institute's budget.

In the NIH Clinical Center, more than 200 mental health clinical protocols are under way at any given time, exploring such problems as schizophrenia, Alzheimer's disease, serious mood, anxiety, and eating disorders, childhood disorders, and AIDS. Undergoing tests are new drug treatments and novel environmental interventions, including bright light and sleep/wake cycle shifts for seasonal and circadian mood disturbances.

Elsewhere at NIH, investigators are using molecular genetics probes to explore intracellular signaling systems and have isolated and characterized several important receptors, as well as the brain's own cannabinoids. Developmental psychology researchers are pinpointing how psychopathology in parents may affect children's development and how childhood sexual abuse can predispose for dissociative disorders in adulthood. Studies are also under way on the neural basis of familial behavior in voles and frontal cortex functioning in primates.

At Saint Elizabeth's Hospital in Washington, D.C., NIMH's Neuropsychiatric Research Hospital is focused on studies of schizophrenia. Investigators are bringing to bear the latest scanning technique and a brain bank facility in search of clues to structural and functional brain abnormalities seen in patients. Much of the work has focused on identical twins discordant for the illness. These have recently inspired successful efforts to model hypothesized components of the schizophrenia illness process in rats, including an early limbic-system lesion that produces a delayed onset in young adulthood of symptoms such as hyperreactivity to stress and responsiveness to antipsychotic drugs.

The NIMH IRP has served as a major training ground for research psychiatrists, psychologists, and mental illness–related neuroscience disciplines, and hosts many foreign and domestic guests scientists. The program was recently ranked first among neuroscience programs at the NIH in numbers of papers published and in average citations per paper (1986–1990) by the Institute of Scientific Information Science Indicators Data Base. Worldwide, it ranked second and third respectively in these categories.

NIMH's Future

Ironically, the very pace of research progress has spotlighted concerns about the perceived proximity of neuroscience to such fundamental attributes of the human condition as free will and responsibility. Such fears are amplified in today's climate of scientific illiteracy. A public that does not understand the process of science is vulnerable to an antiscientific agenda of the type embodied today in the animal rights and scientology movements. The growth of these movements is the culmination of trends over the past generation that have attached progressively less priority to investing in the intellectual capital of the nation.

Scientists in the mental health fields will thus increasingly be challenged to take on a public education mission: to interact more effectively with the larger social, political, and human context in which science works. They will be aided in these efforts in this "Decade of the Brain" by the sheer excitement of discovery in the behavioral and brain sciences. Advances in fields such as brain imaging, molecular genetics, and psychoneuroimmunology promise compelling new understanding of human experience and mental illness, which will insure a bright future for NIMH.

Frederick K. Goodwin

Nativism and Empiricism in Perception

The scientific study of perception began in the nineteenth century and proceeded at a rapid pace. In his *Physiological Optics*, Hermann von Helmholtz summarized an enormous body of knowledge, much of which was the result of his own investigations. It was Helmholtz who first formulated clearly the theoretical positions of the innate or intuitive theory of spatial experience on the one hand, and of the empirical theory on the other. The innate theory, he explained, ruled out any further investigations of the origin of spatial perceptions by regarding them simply as a function of hypothetical neural mechanisms assumed to be inborn. Helmholtz, a strong empiricist, claimed that all aspects of perception are determined by experiential factors, including memory, judgment, expectation, and reasoning. Sensations, he maintained, provided only a "sign" for external objects and events, and the interpretation of these signs is learned.

Gestalt. Gestalt psychologists opposed the definition of perception as the interpretation of sensation; they did not consider sensations to be part of phenomenal experience but rather products of artificial analysis. They showed that the effective stimulus for a percept is relational in nature, thus making it unnecessary to refer to past experience. In place of the innate anatomical structures of the nineteenth-century nativist, they substituted the concept of dynamic self-distributing processes in the brain, i.e., sensory organization. These processes of organization are not learned, nor are they products of inherited neural "wiring." Gestalt theories did not deny that past experience plays a role in perception. They insisted, however, that the empiricist provide a plausible account of how a particular perception could be learned.

Hebb's Theory

An empiristic account of the origin and development of form perception was presented by D. O. Hebb in his book *Organization and Behavior* (1949). Hebb was convinced of the validity of empiricism mainly through two lines of evidence. First was the work by A. H. Riesen (1950) on vision in dark-reared chimpanzees and, second, the analysis by M. V. von Senden (1960) of some sixty case reports describing visual experience in congenital cataract patients after surgery.

The middle 1950s saw a surge of research efforts utilizing new methods and new techniques; response indicators were found that made it possible to investigate perception in animal and human infants. R. D. Walk and E. J. Gibson (1961), using the "visual cliff" apparatus, obtained evidence that a wide variety of animal species and human infants could, by the crawling stage, discriminate depth differences. The nativistic position for distance perception was supported in studies with dark-reared rats and animals in the first day after birth. R. L. Fantz (1961) utilized a visual interest test as an indicator and investigated the development of pattern discrimination in the human infant. Reaction to novelty and changes in heart and sucking rates have also served as indicators in studies of infant perception. With a modified discrimination apparatus and training begun at 11 days of age, rhesus monkeys (R. R. Zimmerman and C. C. Torrey 1965) require only 10 days to reach criterion on a form-discrimination task. T. G. R. Bower (1974), in a number of ingenious experiments, has analyzed various aspects of object and space perception in infants.

Carl B. Zuckerman

Need

In ordinary usage, *need* denotes both necessity and want or desire. These obliquely related meanings continue to inform the psychological usage of the term. In their early writings, R. S. Woodworth, Sigmund Freud, and Kurt Lewin use the term to refer to those appetitive necessities whose deficiency or deprivation can be counted upon to produce action that is purposive and goal-seeking.

Kurt Lewin, in his effort to portray the tensionlike character of choice and strategy selection, introduced need (*Bedürfnisse*) as a construct denoting biologically rooted determinants having a quasi-directional (goal-oriented) character, which contributed one element to his equations designed to account for purposive action.

In 1938, Henry A. Murray's *Explorations in Personality* presented a motivational interpretation of personality function that placed the need construct at the heart of the system. It was the array and amalgam of needs that best illuminated the behavior of individuals.

Subsequent theorists have used need in more restricted ways. Abraham Maslow's *Motivation and Personality* (1954) organizes need systems into a functional hierarchy emphasizing the growth dimension of personality, from securing satisfaction of basic deficiency needs to realizing fully the unique capacities of the self. The hierarchy is composed of five classes of needs: physiological, safety, affiliative, esteem, and self-actualization.

The term *need* has also been adopted by theorists who prefer *motive* as their central construct. Following H. A. Murray, David McClelland et al. (1953) use projective measurement to assess the preoccupation of the subject with particular themes of loss or attainment. Systems labeled need achievement (n Ach), need affiliation (n Aff), and need power (n Power) are used to assess motive strength. These scores are then combined with indices of expectancy and value to generate estimate of motivation or action tendency. This use of need as a score label is also found in the Edwards Personal Preference Scale, which uses Murray's list as the basis for a self-report personality measure.

Robert Charles Birney

Neobehaviorism

The term *neobehaviorism* has no clear-cut referent. It has been applied to all behavioristically oriented theorists who became prominent after about 1930: E. R. Guthrie, Clark Hull, B. F. Skinner, and E. C. Tolman, as well as their students and followers. The term has also been used in a more restricted sense, however, to refer to the hypothetico-deductive approach of Hull and was, as such, suggested by Hull himself (1952, 154).

Hull's neobehavioristic position was strongly influenced by the views of John Broadus Watson, "whose ideas about behavior were in the air" at the time of Hull's undergraduate work. Although "inclined to be sympathetic with Watson's views concerning the futility of introspection and the general virtues of objectivity ... [Hull] ... felt very uncertain about many of his dogmatic claims" (Hull 1952a, 153). The objectivism of early behaviorism had partly been a methodological prescription and partly a metaphysical thesis. Methodologically, objectivity in science meant to insist on the intersubjective verification of definitions, procedures, and observations. This stance, however, was sometimes presented along with a denial of the existence of consciousness. For Hull, the existence of consciousness was not to be denied but appeared to be "a problem needing solution" (1937, 30).

Hull's conceptual analysis of learning, trial and error, and rote memorization were also much influenced by the publication of a translation of Ivan P. Pavlov's work on conditioned reflexes in 1927, of which Hull at once began an intensive study (1952a,

154). This led to an extensive review of the then-existent literature (1934), a persistent attempt to interpret all types of learning phenomena in terms of conditioning, and a long series of influential papers in *The Psychological Review*, the major theoretical journal in the field.

A few years before Hull abandoned geometry for "ordinary equations," Tolman had developed R. S. Woodworth's S-O-R formula into a program of theory construction featuring "intervening variables" as a major component of analysis. Hull's adaptation of Tolman's conception led to the systematic theory of the *Principles of Behavior* (1943), a volume that in Hull's own words "was rather different from those commonly offered to psychologists" (1952a, 159).

Amalgamating his own hypothetico-deductive postulate system with Tolman's suggestion to break up the too-complicated input-output function into successive sets of component functions, Hull produced the system described in the *Principles of Behavior* and its elaborations and modifications during the next decade (Hull 1951, 1952).

Tom Verhave

Neuropsychology: Historical Review

The belief that the brain is the chief organ of the mind and of behavior is quite old and is documented in early philosophical writings. Although Aristotle assigned mental functions primarily to the heart, Hippocrates believed the brain to be the organ of intelligence. Galen firmly established the belief that the mind has its seat in the brain. He presumed that sensory impressions enter the ventricles of the brain in the form of humors, and his system represents one of the first attempts to localize mental functions in specific brain structures. In the seventeenth century, René Descartes made more explicit the concepts of mind-body interactions as involving dual systems. Convinced that the brain is the organ of the mind, he chose the pineal gland as the means of interaction between the soul and the brain, because it is the only organ in the brain not duplicated bilaterally. Franz Joseph Gall, a leading anatomist of his time, was the first to recognize the importance of the gray matter of the cerebral hemispheres and its relationship to the fibers of the white matter.

In contrast, P. Flourens, a distinguished French neurophysiologist, undertook experiments that led him to believe in both common and specific action of the different parts of the brain, a theory that emphasizes equipotentiality of response while accepting instances of particular localization of function. These concepts furnished a basis for the neurological views of cerebral action held by those who opposed exact localization.

Aphemia

In 1861, Pierre Paul Broca reported the case of the man with loss of speech or, as Broca put it, loss of the memory for words (aphemia). The man died of an infection shortly after being examined and was later demonstrated to have had tissue destruction in the third convolution of the left frontal lobe. Broca argued that this specific lesion was responsible for the loss of speech, and more generally, that the convolutions of the cerebral cortex can be used to establish exact localization of functions. Previously, there had been uncertainty as to how to distinguish among such small regions of the brain. Broca's discovery stimulated clinical research and resulted in the accumulation of more data tending to support the views of the localizationists. A decade later, Karl Wernicke described a case in which a lesion of the posterior third of the superior temporal gyrus of the left hemisphere caused a disturbance in speech comprehension. Wernicke's conclusion, that the sensory images of speech are localized in this zone of the cortex of the left hemisphere, has become firmly entrenched in the literature. The work of Broca, Wernicke, and others laid the groundwork for a continuing line of investigation on the localization of language.

In experiments reported in 1870, G. Fritsch and E. Hitzig demonstrated the existence of motor centers in the brain. It had long been believed that the tissues of the brain could not be excited by direct stimulation, but these investigators noted eye movements in a patient whose cortex was stimulated electrically. This experiment, which established a series of motor centers in the precentral region of the cerebral cortex, seemed also to validate the general fact of brain centers.

Evolutionary View

During the late 1800s and early 1900s, various views in contrast to the localization and center concepts were promulgated. Jackson, in a series of lectures, rejected exact localization and developed an evolutionary view of higher and lower levels in the nervous system that functioned respectively for more and less complex functions.

In 1902, S. I. Franz, in studies of the frontal lobe, reported that habits lost by destruction of brain tissue could be relearned, although the tissue lost does not regenerate. Such studies moved the pendulum further from exact localization viewpoints. M. Goldstein's concepts of losses of abstract or categorical behavior following brain lesions and Karl S. Lashley's belief in mass action and equipotentiality represented further movements in the same direction.

Manuel Riklan

Neuroses

The diagnosis of neuroses is made on the basis of a variety of symptoms, including anxiety, depression, hypochondriacal preoccupation, conversions, dissociations, preoccupations, and untoward fears. There is a sufficient loss of equanimity, happiness, and satisfactions, and an impairment in personal and social effectiveness. On the other hand, neurotic needs can contribute to individual achievement and, as with anxiety itself, may serve socially constructive purposes. Depressive reactions and obsessive-compulsive reactions are frequently associated with superior intelligence.

The anxiety reactions have been estimated to comprise some 12 to 15% of the neuroses encountered in clinical practice. They may be conveniently distinguished as (1) the acute anxiety attack, (2) the anxiety tension state, and (3) anxiety neurosis. These distinctions help to describe the extent, intensity, and chronicity of the sufferer's symptoms.

Henry P. Laughlin

Nosology: Wolman's System

Benjamin B. Wolman recognizes three major sources of mental disturbance. Some mental disorders have their origin in deficiencies in the organism; they are somatogenic. Somatogenic disorders can be either (1) genosomatogenic, if inherited, or (2) ecosomatogenic, if acquired. It is the remaining category of disorders, (3) sociogenic disorders, upon which Wolman focuses his attention.

Wolman states that three patterns of social interaction can be distinguished, and that imbalance between or distortion of these patterns constitutes sociogenic mental disorder. First, there is the instrumental social pattern, of which the infant-toward-parent interaction is the prototype. In this pattern, the individual is a taker and uses others to satisfy his needs. In normal life, child-parent and business relationships are instrumental. However, the instrumental pattern of relating may become distorted, and a hyperinstrumental pattern of behavior emerges.

The hyperinstrumental type corresponds to what has been called the psychopath or sociopath. Wolman holds that the hyperinstrumental is a very primitive individual whose libido is hypercathected to herself.

The second major pattern is the mutual, which is characteristic of give-and-take relationships, such as friendship and marriage. Normal mutual relationships are characterized by reciprocation and sharing. The abnormal manifestation of this pattern is revealed in the dysmutual mode of relating. The dysmutual is a "love addict," who expects his love to be returned at a high rate of interest. When disappointed, this love turns to hate and self-blame.

Finally, there is the vectorial pattern of interaction, of which the parent-toward-child relationship is the prototype. The vectorial pattern is characterized by giving, by charity, and by dedication to ideals. Schizophrenia is hypervectorial, for example.

Given these three types of abnormal interaction—hyperinstrumental, dysmutual, and hypervectorial—Wolman attempts to relate them to the whole range of neurotic and psychotic disorders by positing a continuum of disorders from neurosis to dementia.

Neurosis, the first level of severity, is characterized by maintenance of ego defenses. Character neurosis occurs when these ego defenses are blended into the personality; latent psychosis occurs when the ego controls begin to fail, but some contact with reality is maintained; manifest psychosis occurs when the ego fails to maintain contact with reality; and dementia occurs when the personality structure collapses.

Wolman has recognized that his classification of three types and five levels of sociogenic disorder omits some of the traditional categories of functional mental disorders, such as paranoia, addiction, and psychosomatic disorder. However, he does not constitute these as separate categories but as symptoms or clusters of symptoms that can occur with any of the three types of sociogenic disorder, differentially serving the patterns and goals of the hyperinstrumental, the dysmutual, or the hypervectorial individual.

Herbert H. Krauss
Beatrice J. Krauss

Nursing, Psychiatric

Master's degree programs in nursing provide the opportunity for specialization, and most schools offer training in adult psychiatry, child psychiatry, mental retardation, and more recently, community mental health and social psychiatry. The course of study is usually 1 to 2 years and includes advanced clinical study as well as courses in education, behavioral sciences, research, and statistics. Many of the clinical programs provide training in interviewing techniques, individual and group psychotherapy, and the skills of supervision.

Doctoral programs in nursing science and nursing education are still being developed. Most nurses who have attained the doctoral degree have entered a program in sociology, education, psychology, or another related field.

Nurses most often function in one of four major roles in regard to patient care:

1. The instrumental role, in which the nurse is primarily responsible for the 24-hour milieu. This role includes the coordination of intraprofessional and interprofessional team efforts

in helping patients toward health. All moment-to-moment contacts with patients are seen as potentially therapeutic in nature. The nurse is the only member of the professional health team who has the experience of hourly physical and emotional care.

2. The collaborative role, in which the nurse functions as a collaborative therapist with the primary therapist of another discipline. In this instance the nurse is able to utilize the awareness of physical and emotional needs of families as, well as those of the identified patients.

3. The nurse-therapist role, in which the nurse functions as the primary therapist for individuals, families, and groups. In this role the nurse is responsible for the direction of the therapeutic process. In order to function adequately in this particular role, the nurse should have advanced training in therapeutic techniques.

4. The community action role, in which the nurse moves within a framework of the local community and larger socioeconomic, political, educational, and health systems for the purpose of bringing about desired changes, which can facilitate health or aid in the treatment and rehabilitation of those who are ill.

As nursing has broadened its educational base and widened its horizons, it has depleted the number of professional nurses that are available for the day-to-day care of hospitalized patients. This has stimulated the development of training programs for the licensed vocational nurse and the psychiatric technician or health services technologist. The organized profession of nursing is moving in the direction of greater participation in the legislative process as it relates to health care.

William E. Stone

·O·

Object Permanence

Genetic Approach

According to Jean Piaget, the notion of object permanence refers to the psychological fact that an object exists in a continuous time and space; that, despite its disappearances from view in a variety of circumstances, it can easily be recovered; and that, when recovered, it will be the same object as when it disappeared. In *The Construction of Reality in the Child* (1954), Piaget proposes that the construction of object permanence is one of the great achievements of the sensorimotor period of development.

In spite of its informality, the essence of Jean Piaget's method is the administration of a variety of tests of increasing complexity. This method has been refined and standardized into test batteries. For example, I. C. Uzgiris and J. McV. Hunt (1974) have constructed the Visual Pursuit and Permanence of Objects series, involving sixteen tasks. A shortened form of this battery was used in a carefully designed study by J. A. Kramer, K. T. Hill, and L. B. Cohen (1975), with babies 5 to 32 months old.

Among objects, persons are a special class, of greater interest to the baby than inanimate objects. Piaget predicts that "person permanence" will be achieved before object permanence in general. This is an important idea in connection with Piaget's general view that when schemata are first established they have a restricted range of application, followed by expansion of the range. To test Piaget's prediction, Bell (1970) has compared inanimate objects with the mother as the hidden object in a battery of tests of search behavior in babies between 8½ and 11 months. In general, Piaget's prediction is confirmed.

In the first investigation of object permanence in animals, Gruber, Girgus, and Banauzizi (1971) use a battery of eight tests similar to Piaget's and show that there is a stagewise development in which 20-week kittens reach a stage of search behavior similar to that of 12-month babies, but that cats probably do not attain the stage of being able to take account of invisible displacements. Vaughter, Smotherman, and Ordy (1972) have found that a 6-month-old squirrel monkey does not respond to the visible concealment of an attractive object by removing the cover, and both the 6- and a 9-month-old monkey searched for an object where it was first concealed rather than where it was last seen being hidden; a 12-month-old and a 30-month-old monkey succeeded in both tasks. Wise, Wise, and Zimmerman (1974) have found a sequence of stages in the rhesus monkey very similar to that described by Piaget for human babies.

Experimental-Perceptual Approach

Inspired by Max Wertheimer's classic work on stroboscopic motion, Gestalt psychologists displayed an early interest in the problem of phenomenal identity. If the stimulus conditions consist of an object displayed at one locus followed by a like object at another locus, what determines that it will be seen as the same object, moving but retaining its identity, rather than as a like object in another place? Thus, the problems of phenomenal identity and of motion perception are inextricably linked. J. W. Ternus's experimental work showed that it is the total dynamic stimulus configuration, not the retinal locus of particular points of stimulation, that determines the perceptual outcome (K. Koffka 1935).

A. Michotte and his collaborators studied phenomenal permanence when objects appear and disappear. When an object disappears it may seem to "go out of existence" or simply to disappear from view—for example, as behind a screen. If a uniform rectangle is projected on a viewing surface and one of its edges remains stationary while the opposite edge moves toward it, the observer does not see the rectangle shrink to zero; rather, he sees it gliding behind a screen. Because no screen is actually present, it is the total dynamic stimulus configuration that generates the phenomenal screen as well as the phenomenal permanence of the disappearing object. If the rectangle has internal structure that remains stationary, or if it has rounded ends, the "screen effect" is lost. A moving object disappearing and then reappearing in another place may seem to have tunneled under or through the intervening medium. L. Knops (1947) has studied the phenomenal variations corresponding to different ways that an object can appear before the subject rather than disappear. Rectangles were either exposed all at once or enlarged over a brief time interval. Among a variety of phenomena observed, if the onset of the stimulus is very sudden, the figure seems to explode from a center (i.e., gamma movement occurs), and it seems to come into existence at that moment. If the stimulus is gradually but rapidly enlarged, it seems to have been previously "there." Depending on the specific stimulus conditions, it may seem to grow, to be revealed by the removal of a screen, or to protrude itself from behind a screen (no screen actually present).

In a review of experimental-genetic findings, P. L. Harris (1975) examines the evidence for the three main hypotheses advanced to account for infants' failures to search for vanished objects in appropriate places: (1) lack of motor skill; (2) lack of specific perceptual-cognitive skills; (3) egocentricity, or the tendency to consider the object as being at the infant's own disposal, or as the product of his own actions. The first of these hypotheses does not imply lack of object permanence, but it has been clearly ruled out by several lines of experimental evidence with human infants and also by the failure of motorically competent mammals, such as kittens, to display object permanence. With regard to the second

hypothesis, the weight of evidence suggests that even when perceptual difficulties are eliminated (e.g., by keeping the displaced object visible behind a transparent screen), the infant may search for the displaced object in the place where he has previously been successful in finding it.

Howard E. Gruber

Obstruction Method

The obstruction method has been widely used since the mid-1920s to make comparative measurements of drive strength. The underlying assumption is that the stronger the drive, the more aversive the stimulation the animal will accept on the way to a goal, and the harder it will work to overcome an obstacle interposed before the goal. The standard obstruction box consists basically of an electrified grid, which must be traversed to contact food, water, a sexually receptive mate, or a female subject's litter, or to initiate intracranial stimulation. The usual measure is the number of traversals during a given period, with a constant (usually moderate) shock intensity.

Frank W. Finger

Occupational Psychiatry

During the 1940s and early 1950s, human relations in industry was associated with three primary schools of thought:

1. *the Elton Mayo school*, with its center at the Harvard Business School and its emphasis on the social system, the clinical approach, and the case method of teaching;
2. *the school of applied anthropology*, associated with Eliot Chapple, William F. White, and Conrad Arensberg, with its emphasis on sound field work and social observations; and
3. *the Kurt Lewin school of group dynamics*, with its center at the University of Michigan and its affiliates at Tavistock Institute of Human Relations in London and the National Training

Laboratories in Washington, D.C., and Bethel, Maine. This school emphasized group process, here-and-now data, and sensitivity training.

Various organizations have instituted a number of creative programs to promote the mental as well as physical health of the worker. These include:

1. increasing individual and group autonomy, resulting in reduced absenteeism and grievances and increased morale and satisfaction (Texas Instruments, AT&T);
2. implementation of flexible work hours (*Gleitzeit*) consisting of (a) a core period of time when everyone must be at work, and (b) a flexible period of time at the beginning and end of each day when employees may arrive and depart at times of their own choosing (Hewlett Packard, Blue Shield of California, John Hancock Insurance Company);
3. the 4/40 work week, designed to increase leisure time and opportunities to take care of personal matters and reduce commuting time (Chicago Zenith Life Insurance Company, New England Deaconess Hospital);
4. executive sabbaticals up to one full year allowing the executive to pursue any field of interest of her own choosing (Xerox Corporation);
5. programs allowing workers to determine their annual salaries and the awarding, periodically, of productivity bonuses. This has resulted in increased profits, even as the company has lowered prices (Donnelly Mirrors Corporation); and
6. educational seminars dealing with drug abuse, alcoholism, stress, and quality-of-life issues (Sun Oil Company, Bell Telephone System, programs at the Harvard Business School).

Barrie Sanford Grieff

Oddity Learning

Oddity learning and matching-to-sample are relational learning paradigms in which the correct response is based on a relationship among the stim-

uli in a display rather than on their absolute properties. To demonstrate successful solution of such problems, the subject must respond correctly when specific elements of the display are replaced or their reward value reversed. In a typical oddity experiment, two circles and a triangle might be presented. The correct choice is the odd stimulus, the triangle.

Because oddity rule learning presumably reflects higher mental processes, it has been widely used as a comparative-developmental tool. It has been determined, for example, that chimpanzees and monkeys perform better on oddity learning than cats and raccoons but not as well as young children. Within the human species, the ability to solve oddity problems seems to develop gradually, with most children succeeding at it by the age of 6 years.

David R. Thomas

Operant Approaches in Behavior Therapy

The first applications of operant conditioning principles to clinical and educational problems were with children and retarded adults. Since the 1950s, successful broad-band treatment programs based largely on applications of operant principles have been documented with psychotic patients, marital problems, autistic children, conduct problems of children in the school and at home, and delinquents (O'Leary and Wilson 1975).

Social reinforcement. A therapist can increase certain client statements (e.g., emotional statements or talk about job stress) by indicating approval of such comments by keen interest in the topic, an understanding nod, or simply an enthusiastic "uh-huh." These findings have significantly contributed to the conceptualization of therapeutic interchange in that they make it clear that therapists can strongly influence their clients' verbalizations—even if inadvertently.

Token reinforcement programs. A token program consists of (1) a set of instructions about the behavior that will be rewarded; (2) a means of making a potentially reinforcing stimulus—usually called a token—contingent upon behavior; and (3) a set of rules governing the exchange of tokens for rewards.

Punishment here refers to the contingent presentation of a stimulus assumed to be aversive. While it is clear that punishment is effective in suppressing self-destructive behavior and in suppressing drinking, punishment should be supplemented by other means of teaching prosocial behaviors. This need for supplemental treatment procedures is most apparent in the modification of addictive behaviors, such as overeating, smoking, and drinking.

Extinction refers to the reduction of behavior as a function of its nonreinforcement or nonreward. Some of the classical demonstrations of extinction involve the removal of attention for undesirable behavior, such as temper tantrums, excessive scratching, and somatic complaints. Anxiety and fearful behaviors have also been reduced by extinction.

While there has been some disagreement about whether modeling and imitation procedures are best explained by operant or by more cognitive principles (Bandura 1971; Gewirtz 1971), modeling procedures have been so central to operant conditioning programs that they have assumed a separate place among the operant intervention procedures.

K. Daniel O'Leary

Operant Behavior

Several research programs have been concerned with the changing dimensional characteristics of individual responses during conventional operant conditioning, extinction, schedules of reinforcement, and manipulation of drive and amount of reinforcement. In addition to recording the customary rate of responding, these studies have measured force, duration, and time integral of force (or effort) for the very same responses entering into the rate computations, as well as for those that do not. Although some work has been done with humans and monkeys serving as subjects, the major theoretical-empirical accounts involve the behavior of rats (J. M. Notterman and D. Mintz 1965) and of pigeons (Rilling, Kramer, and Askew 1970).

The following basic findings have been reported:

1. *Conditioning.* Peak force of response (both for bar pressing and key pecking) tends to be higher than that of the criterion force value. It is substantially higher at the outset of acquisition, but (for rats) decreases monotonically as a function of reinforced responses.
2. *Extinction.* Peak force of bar-pressing response increases dramatically during the first stages of extinction, and then gradually decreases to preconditioning levels.
3. *Schedules of reinforcement.* During *fixed ratio* bar pressing, peak force of response is at its lowest level following the receipt of reinforcement at the end of the cycle. Force magnitude gradually increases with each unreinforced step during a cycle, reaching its maximum value just before the next reinforcement is due.

Force-proportional reinforcement (the greater the force emitted, the greater the number of pellets received) has been shown to shape forces upward, but only when rate of reinforcement is restrained, as when rate of responses is held back through the use of a concurrent, differential reinforcement of low rates schedule.

Band reinforcement is a situation in which the organism is reinforced for emitted forces that fall between an upper and a lower limit.

Peak force of bar pressing increases with hours of deprivation, and decreases with amount of reinforcement. More complex operant phenomena, in which force, duration, time integral of force, and movement are examined as dependent variables, have been reported in the United States and Russia. In general, these studies point to the important influences of proprioceptive and kinesthetic feedback upon the control and emission of motor behavior (Notterman 1973).

Joseph M. Notterman

Organ Modes and Social Modalities in Personality Development

The ego-psychological concepts of organ modes and social modalities were first proposed by Erik Erikson in 1937. His most complete statement of these ideas is contained in the second (1963) edition of *Childhood and Society*. The evolution of these concepts and their significance for psychoanalytic theory have been extensively reviewed by David Rapaport (1956, 1959, 1960).

In normal development, an infant's caretakers respond to her with actions appropriate to the behavioral mode that is dominant at each stage of her development.

The parental response to the child must continuously change as the child grows and changes if a sufficient degree of mutuality is to be maintained to assure what Erikson (1961, 151) terms "cogwheeling" between the generations. The matter is complicated further by the fact that various cultures play upon the psychological needs and organ modes of the infant and small child at various stages of his development with a seeming "unconscious playfulness."

Organ modes contribute to the complex behaviors that Erikson designates "social modalities." The incorporative organ modes that characterize the oral stage of development contribute to the social modality of getting, in the sense of receiving and accepting what is given.

The social modality that characterizes this second oral stage is the modality of taking and holding onto things. But this more aggressive and assertive aspect of the incorporative mode and its associated social modality produces a fateful division of the infant's world and sense of self. In this regard, Erikson (79) notes that when breastfeeding lasts into the biting stage, the child must learn how to suck without biting or else the mother will withdraw the nipple in pain or anger.

The second psychosexual stage of development, the anal stage, is characterized by the retentive mode and also by the eliminative mode—two opposing organ modes that the child must learn to use in an alternating and coordinated manner. These modes give rise to the social modalities of holding on and letting go respectively.

The social modality that characterizes the phallic-locomotor stage is that of "making" in the sense of "being on the make." E. Erikson (1963, 90) notes,

"The word suggests head-on attack, enjoyment of competition, insistence upon goal, pleasure of conquest." [In the boy, the emphasis is on the phallic, intrusive modes; the girl emphasizes "making" by teasing, provoking, and ensnaring, by making herself attractive and endearing.]

Robert B. White

Organization: Sociopsychological Theories

Theories of organization are attempts to model phenomena of human behavior observable in organizational settings. By "organizational setting" or, more simply, organization, is meant a form of human group, "which is often, although not always, large in size, and in which the *fact* of organization is somehow especially striking or salient. . . . Description of their particular structure is therefore generally of more immediate interest than it is in analysis of other social aggregations" (Hollander and Hunt 1976).

The "structure" alluded to in the quotation is a pattern of human interactions. The patterns are both variable and changeable, but it is one apparent function of organizations to stabilize social structures and to control interaction over time, thereby facilitating performance of tasks and achievement of objectives. In fact, these phenomena, and the processes by which they become manifest, constitute the essential domain of organization theory.

Weber

Weberian bureaucracy is a legalistically defined system of organization to which persons are presumed to become attached by an explicit (or implicit) employment contract. Bureaucratic models promote an image of organization typified by such essentials as pervasive specializations of function; hierarchic authority systems; impersonal relationships among members (without favoritism, prejudice, or privilege derived from social positions outside the organization); recruitment and promotion on the basis of ability and knowledge; operation based on universally binding rules and regulations appropriate to the mission of the organization; and "ownership" of organizational positions and their accoutrements or prerogatives by the organization, not the incumbent.

Taylor

For F. Taylor, organization is essentially a pyramidal authority structure, the key to design of which is the *span of control*—the number of subordinates performing standard tasks a single superior can supervise with maximum efficiency for the unit. Taylor thus seeks, and assumes the nature of organization will allow, a rationally differentiated performance system, integrated by a well-defined hierarchic control system, that is subject to evaluation solely on impersonal standards of efficiency.

Mayo and Barnard

By the mid-1930s, Elton Mayo and Barnard each offered views opposed to Taylorism. Without actually relinquishing belief in the fundamental rationality of the organization, they fostered a shift of focus from formal structures and assumptions of impersonal rationality to the characteristics of individual workers, their nonrational emotional nature, and their dispositions toward solidary social affiliation.

Lewin

Eventually drawing on the social-psychological theories of Kurt Lewin, the premises of human relations models are that an arrangement of conditions salutary to satisfying the personal needs and aspirations of workers motivates them to commit time and effort to forging cooperative work groups, which yield productive issue.

D. McGregor and C. Argyris

Akin to personalistic human relations theories of organizations are a group of modern structuralists. Human relations theory stresses the variety of human motivations, the individuality of perception, and the core role of the individual in organization; modern structuralists (e.g., D. McGregor and C. Argyris), while seeming to agree, tend to assume a global personality and hold a powerful, if often implicit, belief in the molding of organizational outcomes by structural forces.

March and Simon

The elements of organizational structure in O. P. March and S. H. Simon's models are largely those of Weber—division of labor, standard work rules, authority systems, etc.—but with greater emphasis upon the internal processes of organization and without the imagery of managerial omniscience. Communication, the patterned flow of information, is here a central concept; coupled with the principle of "uncertainty absorption" (the idea that communication channels and strategies work to make information understandable and explicit), it is elaborated into the source of power and control within the organization.

Katz and Kahn

The theory of D. Katz and R. Kahn pays attention to the diversity of individuals, the realities of organizational structures, the dynamic and partly unpredictable character of intraorganizational processes, and the fact of organizational embeddedness into integrative theories based on the concept of the open social system. The system concept stresses the interdependence of organizational elements and a continuous process of equilibrium-seeking interaction among them that leads to progressive change in the structural and operational properties of the organization.

Raymond G. Hunt

Organization Development

A number of corporations and other organizations have hired applied behavioral scientists as external or internal change agents under the banner of organization development (OD). In some cases, corporations have formed OD groups staffed by professional applied behavioral scientists and located them in personnel offices. In other cases, personnel professionals have acquired the skills and competence to apply OD (Rush 1973). In most cases, OD specialists are concerned with increasing both individual satisfaction and organization effectiveness.

OD is a process by which individuals, groups, and organizations not only solve their problems but learn how to solve problems. Its emphasis and values do not lie in a particular set of ideas about how organizations need to structure themselves or manage themselves.

Michael Beer

Organizers of the Psyche

The term "organizers of the psyche" was first used by R. A. Spitz (1954). He adumbrated, expanded, and further conceptualized this term in 1965. Spitz's conceptualizations about psychic organizers had their inception in his papers on hospitalism, anaclitic depression, and the smiling response. He credits Edward Glover with being the "first among psychoanalysts to introduce the concept of 'critical phases'," anticipating in part the organizer concept.

Psychic organizers represent nodal points in development, sometimes thought of as critical developmental periods. The first psychic organizer emerges at about 3 months and is indicated by the onset of a reliable but automatic smiling response. The smiling response at this developmental stage appears to be part of the built-in, congenital central nervous system (CNS) and neuromotor apparatus, whose time of appearance is under largely (but not exclusively) maturational control. At this time, the infant has emerged from the stage of nondifferentiation which corresponds roughly to Margaret S. Mahler's autistic stage, and also to the undifferentiated state of Heinz Hartmann. It is the beginning of the separation-individuation process, of the differentiation of self from object, of psyche from soma, of separable psychic structures.

The second psychic organizer during normal development is indicated by the onset of stranger-anxiety at about seven months. Again, a shift in development and in the organization of inner and outer experience is indicated. Later research differentiated between stranger-anxiety, with its inception at about 6 to 7 months, and separation-anxiety, with its inception at about 8 to 9 months and its peak somewhat later. It is likely that the 8-months anxiety noted by Spitz represents some combination of both stranger- and separation-anxiety.

The third organizer is the acquisition of semantic communication at about 12 to 15 months. The indicator is the semantic communication for "no." Spitz pointed out in *No and Yes* (1957) that this may take the form of the head-shaking negative gesture for "no" or may take the form of clear communication of "no" in gesture or affective communication.

The onset of dreaming, at about 18 months, is a fourth psychic organizer during infancy. It is quite likely that some form of dreaming, termed "predreams" by David Metcalf, occurs after about age 12 to 16 months, with more primitive "protodreams" taking place between 6 and 12 months. The onset of dreaming, which is manifested by an increase in affective behaviors during sleep and on awakening at about 9 months (night terrors, sleep drunkenness, dream reports with first language), overlaps the period of the transitional object. Thus, at this more complex period in development, evidence of dreaming and attachment to transitional objects are interchangeably indicators of the onset of this fourth organizer, namely, a shift from primary libidinal object constancy to the secondary form, differentiation of primary and secondary process activity, organized mental activity awake and asleep, and the more full and differentiable development of psychic structure with fulfillment now possible in the unconscious and in dreams.

David R. Metcalf

Orienting Reflex

In its most general sense the term *orienting reflex* refers to an unconditioned response to a neutral stimulus (sometimes the conditioned stimulus) in a classical conditioning situation. The orienting reflex has also been called the alpha response (or reflex), the investigatory reflex, the reflex of curiosity, and the "what-is-it?" reflex. As these terms imply, the general reference is to the act of paying attention to events in the environment.

The orienting reflex sometimes undergoes a brief strengthening when it occurs to the conditioned stimulus in a classical conditioning situation. This is the process of alpha conditioning. The more conspicuous property of the orienting reflex, however, is its pronounced susceptibility to habituation. This is biologically important because it provides a mechanism by which the organism ceases to pay attention to repetitive, monotonous, and probably irrelevant stimuli.

In Russian work, the orienting reflex has been the object of considerable experimental attention. This work has concentrated on the complex behavioral and physiological reactions that are associated with various orienting reflexes.

Gregory A. Kimble

· P ·

Pain

Pain, the somatosensory experience, acts as an essential early-warning system that helps the organism to avoid tissue-damaging situations and conditions due to both external stimuli and internal homeostatic abnormalities.

Prominent among pain theories has been a proposition concerning the pain pathways put forth by R. Melzack and P. D. Wall (1965), the so-called gate theory of pain. Their model is especially attractive because it combines much of what is known about the anatomy and physiology of the somatosensory system with known phenomena of pain psychology. It is also a fruitful theory, in that it suggests some new treatments for pain as well as providing an explanation for some of the classic therapies.

Melzack and Wall's hypothesis of a central gating mechanism has faced considerable challenge. R. A. Schmidt (1972) and A. Iggo (1972) have criticized the theory for contradicting certain specific neurophysiological findings involving details of how the gating action might be implemented. M. Feuerstein, Labbé, and Kuczmierczik (1986) developed the specification of pain. They maintain that the specific neurophysiological sensation is the basic element of pain and that it elicits emotional reactions.

According to T. S. Szasz (1982), psychosomatic pain often becomes a method for soliciting help, care, and compassion.

P. D. Wall and J. R. Cronly-Dillon (1960) state that the temporal pattern of the firing of dorsal horn cells in the spinal cord varies as a function of the quality of the stimulus.

Therapy for Pain

Drugs. Pain-alleviating drugs may be classified into several categories. One, the analgesics, consists of those drugs that reduce pain but do not alter the patient's state of consciousness. These include the salicylates, the pyrazolines, pentazocaine, and the para-aminophenols. It is extremely unlikely that specific explanations of their action, still less incontrovertible proof of their efficacy, are likely to be obtained in the near future because of the confounding by possible placebo effects. The action of aspirin (acetylsalicylic acid), the most commonly used analgesic (if not the most commonly used drug of any kind), has been attributed to its ability to inhibit the synthesis of prostaglandins in the bloodstream.

Narcotic agents, the class of drugs including opium and its derivatives (morphine and codeine, among others), and a number of closely related synthetic products, are powerfully effective in reducing sensitivity to pain, but they also alter the level of consciousness in degrees varying from a slight feeling of euphoria or disassociation to total unconsciousness.

Physiotherapy. The common observation that rubbing or tapping can reduce pain is only one example of another class of therapeutic techniques. Various forms of manipulation, massage, and baths have been used for thousands of years as a means of alleviating various kinds of pain.

Hypnosis. Hypnosis and other forms of suggestion or distraction have been successfully used for the alleviation of pain of various kinds, including that produced by phantom limbs and childbirth. The ability of these psychological processes to modulate painful experience is once again evidence of the important role that central cognitive functions play in the experience of pain.

There are several neurophysiological and psychogenic theories of pain, and several drug therapies and psychotherapies are presently used (Wolman 1988).

William R. Uttal

Pair-Bonding and Limerence

Love is both affectional and erotosexual or limerent. Affectional love may be parental, filial, neighborly, or comradely. Erotosexual or limerent love may be either recreational or procreational, each of which may be either connubial or companionate.

Whether sudden or gradual in onset, when limerence is at its peak, the limerent person undergoes subjective and somatic changes similar to those that signify a state of expectancy or anticipation. The cycle of sleeping and waking is altered, as is food intake, thermoregulation, and kinesis. At the approach or thought of the beloved, there are changes in pulse rate, blushing, breathing, swallowing, perspiration, and vocal fluency. Communication with the beloved becomes a prime occupation. Dreams may involve imagery of being together romantically, erotically, and genitally. They may culminate in orgasm with the partner represented in absentia. Awake, attention becomes distracted by preoccupation with considerations of the beloved, even to the point of obsessive rumination that adversely affects work and study.

Limerent attachment to the beloved is possessive and, in varying degree, jealous and intolerant of an actual or suspected rival. The possessive jealousy of limerence may be bilateral, or in other words concordantly shared on a fifty-fifty basis. Pathologically intense, bilateral jealousy may isolate a couple from ordinary socializing, though it may not break their mutual attachment.

Some birds—wild geese and penguins, for example—pair-bond for life and remain exclusive breeding partners. Their pair-bonding dictates that they copulate only with one another. The same does not apply to human beings; human pair-bonding is asso-

ciated with copulation, but not permanently and exclusively with one partner only.

Pair-bondedness can exist without copulation, and copulation can exist without pair-bonding. However, a relationship that is exclusively physical is elusive, if not downright impossible.

Around kindergarten age, children go through a developmental phase of rehearsing limerent pair-bonding in their play. The first manifestation of this rehearsal is with an older person, as in the coquettish and flirtatious play of the little girl with her father, uncle, or another man. Correspondingly, the little boy play-rehearses the escort role with his mother, aunt, or another woman. Two principles are involved: (1) identification with the parent or another adult of the same sex and (2) complementation or reciprocation to the parent or another adult of the opposite sex.

A juvenile crush may begin as admiration and hero-worship of an older person. The bond of identification subsequently extends to become eroticised as a bond of limerence. With or without actual genital eroticism, the relationship of hero-worship typically becomes a rehearsal for the limerent bonding of an eventual age-matched love affair in adolescence.

The old juxtaposition between romantic love—the ideal and unattainable—and carnal lust—the inevitable sin of procreation—has not been fully resolved, the compromise protest that sex in holy matrimony is sacred and beautiful notwithstanding. Love still resides above the belt, and lust below. Love, the madonna, is lyrical, clean, pure, and viewed in public; lust, the whore, is bawdy, dirty, obscene, and hidden in private.

In paraphilia, the juvenile response to developmental thwarting of the mental lovemap selectively impairs neither erotosexual function nor pair-bonding alone, but imposes new constraints on both. The lovemap is redrawn, or altered and distorted, so that the thwarting effect is circumvented. It becomes no longer a lovemap of the ordinary imagery of pair-bonding and its erotosexual component. It is idiosyncratic, and it restricts the number of suitable partners by displacement or inclusion.

In the case of a good match, there is a high probability that the limerent pair-bond will be long-lasting. This rule applies no matter how idiosyncratic, eccentric, or even bizarre the two lovemaps may be.

For those who separate, disillusionment and the erosion of hope may be progressive and the break postponed until, finally, the day of disillusionment dawns. As in possessive jealousy, the reaction then may be destructively punitive, even murderous or suicidal.

John Money

Panic Behavior

Flight behavior in the face of danger is a rational way of responding, and it is not synonymous with panic behavior. What distinguishes flight behavior from panic behavior is the level of adaptivity and rationality of the behavior.

Panic can be defined as a fear-induced flight behavior that further restricts an already limited number of escape routes. Fear and terror become self-perpetuating, and the danger for self and others in the situation is enhanced. Indeed, there may be greater danger from the behavior of the participants than from the threat that precipitated their flight.

Duane P. Schultz

Paracelsus, Theophrastus Philippus Aureolus Bombastus von Hohenheim (c. 1493–1541)

Paracelsus was a controversial Renaissance physician. He believed that mental illnesses could be caused by displaced vital spirits (*mania*), the influence of the moon (*lunatici*), eating and drinking (*vesania*), intestinal worms and blocking, and other natural phenomena. Paracelsus advocated chemical as opposed to herbal remedies to gain control and precision in dosage and effect of medication.

John C. Burnham

Parapsychology

Parapsychology is the scientific study of such topics as extrasensory perception (ESP), psychokinesis (PK), and survival of consciousness after bodily death.

Extrasensory Perception

Extrasensory perception (ESP) is a direct response to thoughts, objects, or events not presented to the sense receptors and not inferable from prior experiences. Its three major subclasses are telepathy (direct response to another's thoughts); clairvoyance (direct response to objects or events); and precognition (direct response to future events). Modern research investigates the conditions that facilitate, inhibit, or misdirect ESP.

Psychokinesis

Psychokinesis (PK) is essentially "action at a distance." Rigorous experimental controls are essential for testing. Dice tests, for example, require that all die faces be called equally often (to compensate for imperfect dice), and that dice be released in an apparatus where they bounce repeatedly (to control for muscular skill). Placement tests require that subjects hope for right and left placement equally often; release be mechanical; equipment be well insulated from vibration; and so on. Temperature tests require insulation from air changes; extremely sensitive recording equipment; and counterbalanced, predetermined sequence for "hotter" and "colder" instructions.

Survival after Death

Survival research investigates claims about ghosts, apparitions, poltergeists, reincarnation, mediumistic messages from the dead, and out-of-body experiences. Research justifies no firm conclusions, because—though it successfully controls against fraud, normal sources of information, and chance success—it cannot control against ESP or PK.

Theory

ESP and PK seem incompatible with classical physics. However, modern physics describes a universe of non-Euclidean spaces with possible direct connections between them, of energy flux rather than static objects, and of possible energy transmission backward in time from future to present. This offers the possibility of reconciling ESP and PK with physical laws. Some suggest that normal consciousness permits perception of the world of classical physics, but "altered states of consciousness" like meditation, which apparently facilitate ESP, permit perception of this non-Euclidean universe.

Gertrude Schmeidler

Parapsychology and Psychiatry

When, in 1882, a group of Cambridge scholars came together to launch the (British) Society for Psychical Research, they initiated the first sustained and systematic effort to separate the genuine from the spurious among the many claims of psychic happenings. They developed vigorous criteria for evaluating spontaneous cases and published their results in proceedings and in a journal that continues to the present time. Their efforts set the pattern for the emergence of the American Society for Psychical Research, at first a branch of the English society, but from 1905 on an independent organization.

Some of the early psychoanalysts, including Sigmund Freud, turned their attention to the question of telepathy and the possible relevance of unconscious psychodynamics as they were beginning to unfold in the psychoanalytic setting (G. Devereux 1953).

J. Eisenbud has written extensively (1970) of the variety of ways that telepathic and precognitive events intrude into the psychoanalytic process. He made explicit use of the telepathy hypothesis in his interpretive exchanges with patients when, at times, more than one seemed to be involved.

J. Ehrenwald implicates the early mother-child symbiosis as the nexus out of which telepathic exchanges evolve.

J. A. M. Meerloo and others regard telepathy as an archaic communication system available for use when other forms of communication are temporarily blocked.

The role psi effects play in dream formation, the

emergence of psi factors in the context of transference and countertransference, the interpretive use of the telepathy hypothesis, the characterologic significance of psi abilities, and the possible role psi effects play in the evolution and manifestation of psychopathology are some of the areas where beginning explorations have taken place and where much more clinical and investigative work will have to be done before a full account can be given of the relevance of psi factors to psychiatry.

Montague Ullman

Pastoral Psychiatry

Pastoral psychiatry is the application of psychiatric expertise to problems commonly encountered in the duties of the clergy. The two great disciplines psychiatry and religion continue to have much in common, and there is ample scriptural precedent for enlightened principles of psychodynamics, psychoanalysis, and psychotherapy, most of them largely the wisdom of practical experience.

Pastoral counselors are urged to place responsibility squarely on the individual client; to insist on full cooperation from family; and to be perpetually on guard against their own psychological defenses, especially those of rationalization, denial, projection, and identification via positive or negative self-involvement. These should warn the counselor about expecting too much or too little, and consequently pursuing only half-hearted or too-diligent measures.

The clergy are habitually at ease with the sick and dying because of their ability to offer hope and comfort through identification with an omniscient and accepting God. Most physicians, including psychiatrists, could benefit from such rules as visiting the patient promptly and frequently, listening more and saying less, eschewing the family's and professional's tendency to avoid painful issues, discussions of estate and family needs, and finding some common meeting ground for reconciling past hopes with present realities and fears.

Calvert Stein

Pavlov, Ivan Petrovich (1849–1936)

After graduation from the Military-Medical Academy in Russia in 1883, Ivan Petrovich Pavlov spent the years 1884 to 1886 in the laboratories of Heidenheim at Breslau and Ludwig in Leipzig. Pavlov developed the "Heidenheim-Pavlov pouch," an exteriorized section of stomach with nerve and blood supply intact. In his early work on digestion, Pavlov worked with dogs that had esophageal fistulae as well as the stomach pouch.

In his earliest work on salivary reflexes to food, Pavlov showed that the mere sight of food elicited salivation. If the dog was allowed to eat the food, the salivation persisted and the reflex was reinforced; if the dog was not allowed to eat the food, the reflex was extinguished. Gradually, Pavlov discovered many important phenomena of conditioning: (1) the acquisition of the conditioned reflexes, (2) extinction, (3) discrimination, (4) spontaneous recovery, and (5) stimulus generalization.

Pavlov's view of neural function was one in which physiological processes were under excitatory and inhibitory control. He differentiated between two forms of inhibition, namely, external inhibition, caused by any novel stimulus, and internal inhibition, which occurs in the absence of unconditioned stimulus. Much of Pavlov's later work involves attempts to understand disordered behavior in terms of conditioning.

Gregory A. Kimble

Peak Experience

Peak experience is a concept originated by Abraham Maslow to designate a type of intense, transitory personal experience in which one tends to lose her feeling of immediate identity and discreteness in the grandeur, awe, and ecstasy of the experience of the moment. The notion of peak experience thus involves a kind of loss or transcendence of the feeling of selfness; it also implies a richness of perceptual experiencing, in which, however, the attitude of the perceiver is one of passive acceptance, rather than of intense, deliberate concentration.

Paul McReynolds

Peer Influences on Socialization

Interaction with peers serves as a "reality check" in terms of the self-concept and in terms of one's social role in relation to agemates. Peer-group evaluation is an honest, and at times harsh, appraisal of the qualities possessed by its members.

Increasingly with age, a disproportionate amount of time is spent with peers as compared with adults. It would follow that the influence of peers increases relative to that wielded by adults. Approval from peers gains in importance as compared with adult approval.

If a child's membership and status in the peer group were of short duration and fluctuated over time, relatively little significance could be attached to the effect of the peer group on its members. However, research has shown that a child's status in the peer group in terms of acceptance and popularity is remarkably stable over time. Moreover, friendship and role patterns are established relatively quickly within a given peer group, and they remain stable. A study of fourth- through eighth-graders has found that friendship choices and sociometric ranking become fairly stable by sixth grade, and there is little change with increasing age thereafter.

Gene R. Medinnus

Perception

Perception is the study of what you comprehend about the world and how you identify objects and attributes in the world: how you spot a squirrel in the woods, identify your friend in a crowd, anticipate the path of a ball in flight, perceive occluded surfaces as complete, see motion in successive still pictures, know the distance of a tree, attend selectively to your friend's voice at a party, etc.

Perception and sensation are separate fields, which are often studied together. Sensation occurs when features in the world stimulate receptors in our eyes, ears, skin, nose, and tongue. Perception is the interpretation of those receptor responses, the interaction of sensation with the brain and the mind.

Johannes Müller's (1826) law of specific nerve energies helps us begin to understand the issues involved. Consider a rose in the garden. Müller made it clear that we cannot be directly aware of the rose, and that the flower does not somehow get inside of us. Rather, those features of the rose to which our sensory systems can respond stimulate our receptors. We never know the rose or anything else directly, we only know the states of our nerves where activity in different nerves indicates different specific things—pain, cold, heat, light, red, etc.

Because different species of animals have different receptor mechanisms, the rose is a different thing for different species. Its shape is different to a bee than it is to us because, among other things, the lenses in bees' eyes are different than ours; the rose is not colored for dogs because they have little color vision; we do not respond to the infrared radiation that a pit viper "sees"; etc. Simply, each animal "sees" selected and distorted aspects of the total rose, and different animals "see" a different rose. The interpretation of the collection of these nervous energies for each organism is its perception of the rose.

Perception has some general rules. It is dynamic; it is based on relations; it organizes complex situations; it produces constancies; and it is selective.

Perception is dynamic. "Taking a picture" with your eye is not the same as taking a picture with your camera. If the camera wiggles, then the picture will be blurred on the film. But, unless your eye wiggles, there will be no picture at all, and you will see nothing. Fortunately, you cannot hold your eye still because of physiological nystagmus, the name for the small, jerky muscle movements that regularly wiggle the eye, causing the image to move across your photoreceptors, the rods and cones at the back of your eye. Whenever this image movement is stopped, which can be done using experimental procedures, people report that the world is dark, even though the eye is still illuminated (Yarbus 1967).

Animals, such as frogs, who do not have these eye movements are functionally blind until something in the world moves. A frog will starve in a sea of frozen flies. Prey animals take advantage of this and other features of motion detection by "freezing" in the presence of predators, thus becoming invisible.

Because our eye movements generate a succession of essentially the same picture on slightly different parts of the eye from moment to moment, an immediate task of perception is to organize these overlapping "snapshots" into the perception of clear and focused objects in a stable world. It does this so well that we are not aware of the dynamic activity taking place.

Perception adjusts for large eye movements as well as for tiny nystagmus movements. When you move your eyes from one place to another, the world sweeps across your retina, and everything appears stable. The reason that the world does not appear to move is because perception automatically corrects for these voluntary changes in eye position. Otherwise, we would be hopelessly confused about the relation between us and the world when we move our eyes and when we walk about.

Relations. Perception is based on relative rather than absolute amounts of receptor and nervous activity. The rose seen in bright sunlight appears essentially the same as when the sky is overcast, even though the amount of light coming from the object may differ by a factor of 10,000 or more in the two situations. Unless the light becomes very dim, the yellow rose appears yellow, and the pages of this book still appear white. If we experienced sensations, rather than relations among them, this would not be the case, because neural activity at the eye is much higher in bright sunlight than in shadow. Perception corrects for the illumination level by calculating differences among all parts of the visual scene (among other processes) such that we "see" the "true" features of the objects rather than the amounts of stimulation that they produce (Wallach 1948; Land 1959). This is called *brightness constancy*. Perception also provides *color constancy* and *size constancy*.

The constancies emphasize the fact that we normally perceive objects as they are, rather than in terms of how they stimulate our receptors. When you see a friend up close and again at a distance, she appears the same size at both places even though she largely filled your eye when close, but covered only a small portion of your retina at a distance. This is because the perception of size is not directly determined by the size of the image on your eye; it is inferred in terms of perceived distance. Apparent size is largely invariant with distance, because perception adjusts its interpretation of size in terms of its prior interpretation of distance.

This fact can be demonstrated by distorting the cues available to the system for judging distance. In A. Ames's distorting room, size judgments are in error. In this room, the windows and floor tiles are trapezoids, with the taller side of each tile farther away than the shorter side by just the right amount, so that each trapezoid forms a square (all right angles) on the retina; when you look into the room through the peephole, all the squares on the back wall are the same retinal size. This provides the visual cue that the left and right sides of the room are at the same distance, even though the left side is actually farther away. The sizes of the people are perceived in terms of these cues. Perception takes priority over knowledge and experience, which are of no help here. Even your mother will appear too large or too small depending on where she is in the room.

Sometimes the natural environment further demonstrates that apparent distance determines apparent size. The moon illusion is an example. When the moon is seen on the horizon, it often appears larger than when it is seen overhead. This occurs even though the moon is the same size at the eye in the two situations; if you photograph the moon at the two places and then measure its size on the film, there is no difference. But the cues for perception are different in the two places. The moon at the horizon is seen beyond a textured world of grass, trees, buildings, roads, etc., which provide cues that the moon is far away (Gibson 1966). Accordingly, perception interprets that the moon must be large because it takes up so much retina at a great distance. For the overhead moon, there are no cues in the empty sky to stimulate a distance response and, just as when you sit in the dark where there again are no distance cues to drive accommodation of the lens in the eye to a far focus, the lens goes toward its resting state, which is to be accommodated for near things. The moon's distance is perceived in terms of this "cue" from accommodation as near, and so it appears small (Lockhead and Wolbarsht 1991).

Aftereffects. Some of the features that are used by perception to provide constancies can be revealed experimentally. Consider motion. If you stare at a waterfall for a while and then look at the grass beside you, the grass will appear to move upward until perception recalibrates for the new visual world. This apparent movement is in the opposite direction to that of the adapted falling water. This motion aftereffect helps to reveal that our ordinary perception of no motion in a stable world is the result of a balance between stimulations of "up" and "down" (and other directions) motion systems. Intuition notwithstanding, the reason that stationary things do not ordinarily appear to move is not the simple fact that their status is perceived directly. Rather, it is because various motion detection systems are stimulated equally and the net outcome is stability. When you stare at the waterfall, the "down" system is stimulated much more than the "up" system and becomes fatigued or adapted. When you now look at the grass, the fatigued "down" system responds less than the opposing "up" system, and the net result is the perception of upward movement.

There are many aftereffects, each pointing to different features of the basic metrics of perception. To see a figural aftereffect, draw a straight vertical line on a sheet of blank paper, and draw a pair of slightly curved, parallel, vertical lines on another part of the page. Now, stare at the curved lines for a minute or two and then look at the straight line. It will momentarily appear to be curved in the opposite direction to the curved lines.

To see a visual afterimage and a color aftereffect at the same time, paint a red disc on a piece of blank paper and stare at the disc for a moment or two; then look at a blank portion of the paper. You will see a disc where there is none (an afterimage), and its color will be green (a color aftereffect). Normally, white stimulates contrasting red and green mechanisms about equally, but here, the red system is somehow adapted, and thus the net response is green. Vision also contrasts yellow-blue and black-white (Hurvich 1981).

Another demonstration of size-distance invariance is available using this afterimage: stare at the disc, brightly illuminated, for perhaps two minutes and then look at a white wall several feet away; the "green disc" will be seen on the wall, and it will appear to be large. A variety of such demonstrations show that perceptual systems adapt to certain dimensions of the world (direction of motion, light level, relative size, red-green difference, orientation, etc.) and that what organisms "see" is differences within these adapted domains (Frisby 1980).

Organization. The physical world is composed of objects in surroundings. To perceive an object as separate from its background, it is necessary to know where the background ends and the object begins. People and animals do this with such ease that we have no sense of how impressive the accomplishment is. Yet the task is so complex that many aspects of it remain impossible for computer systems.

The Gestalt psychologists (Max Wertheimer, Kurt Koffka, Wolfgang Köhler) proposed several principles to account for our ability to separate figure from ground. They labeled these "proximity" (features near each other are seen as grouped), "similarity" (elements that resemble each other tend to be perceived as parts of the same object), "closure" (we tend to see outlines or borders as complete and to ignore gaps), "good continuation" (flowing lines tend to be judged as belonging together more than do lines that form sharp angles), "common movement" (features that move together are seen as belonging to a common object), and "good form" (a loosely specified attempt to further describe object perception). The Gestaltists theorized that these principles of organization operate within a bias for perception to segregate situations into figure and ground, into things and their environments.

Attention. To see an ordinary scene, many sensed features must be organized into the objects and their backgrounds. Sometimes the figure/ground relations in the scene are such that the figure "pops out" of its background and can be attended to quickly. At other times, the figure is difficult to detect; what happens depends on the elements and on how they are arrayed. Explorations of different arrays of elements has helped to reveal figure/ground and attention mechanisms. For example, draw a scattered collection of vertical lines on a piece of paper and, at a random place within the collection, draw a slightly tilted line. On another piece of paper, draw a scat-

tered collection of tilted lines (all the same tilt) plus a vertical line at a random place. You will observe when looking at the two figures that the single tilted line is readily seen; it "pops out" of the vertical lines. However, the single vertical line is rather difficult to detect in the array of tilted lines, it does not "pop out" from the background. Treisman and Gormican (1988) provide many such demonstrations that help us better understand the organization principles used by perception.

Selective attention. Some figure-ground relations are ambiguous. When this happens, attention fluctuates between seeing one and then another part as figure and seeing its opposite part as ground. Sometimes the ambiguity can be controlled by selective attention. Consider a cocktail party where many people are talking at the same time. If you "tune in" to listen to what a man is saying, you are unable to understand what a nearby woman is saying. If you now "tune in" to the woman so that you understand her, you cannot understand the man. This is because you are able to selectively attend to different parts of the auditory frequency spectrum, low for the man or high for the woman. The attended region becomes the figure, and the rest of the sounds become the ground.

Physiological and anatomical correlates. Many facts of perception correlate with anatomy and physiology; only one example is noted here. Contrast information (edges) is processed by different nerve fibers and terminates in other parts of the brain than does color information. Color is primarily processed in the region of the brain involved with high spatial frequency, but it is not processed in the region concerned with location in space, which is a primary process area for contrast information.

Useful reading. Further information about perception is available from many sources, including books by Julian Hochberg (1978), James J. Gibson (1966), Richard Gregory (1966), David Marr (1982), and the journals *Perception* and *Perception and Psychophysics*.

Gregory R. Lockhead

Perls, Friedrich (Fritz) Salomon (1893–1970)

Friedrich Perls was, together with his wife Laura Perls, the cofounder of Gestalt therapy. Perls founded the first Gestalt Institute in New York in 1952. He wrote *Gestalt Therapy Verbatim* (1969), *The Gestalt Approach: Eye Witness to Therapy* (1973), and other books.

Theodore M. Skolnik

Person Perception

Research on person perception has been focused primarily on the question of how people use information about others when making judgments about them and has sought to determine and investigate the cognitive processes influential in making those judgments.

Implicit Personality Theories

Underlying the interest in implicit personality theories is the assumption that each person to some extent attempts to understand the personalities of others, much the same as personality theorists do. Like those theorists, the person utilizes certain categories or units to describe the structures or ingredients of which personalities are composed and develops a conception of the network of relationships that exists among those units.

Procedures for assessing perceived intertrait relationships yield sizable quantities of data when the number of traits used becomes large. Considerable effort has therefore been devoted to applying multivariate methods of data analysis to determine the dimensions that underlie the subject's judgments.

Impression Formation

Research on this topic was stimulated by a classic series of studies published in 1946 by Solomon Asch. A Gestalt theorist, Asch believed that information learned about another person becomes integrated into a unique whole in which the contribution of each item of information to the overall impression is dependent upon the other information known about the person.

Attribution Processes

This research originated in the work of Fritz Heider, who differentiated several possible causes to which a perceiver might attribute another's behavior. For example, if a person has successfully performed some task, an observer might attribute that performance to the actor's ability and/or effort to achieve success. Both of these "personal" attributions involve explaining the behavior in terms of the actor's internal dispositions.

E. E. Jones, H. H. Kelley, and others have analyzed this attribution process in more detail, attempting to delineate the processes mediating between a perceiver's observation of an act and her attribution of that behavior to dispositional or to situational causes. Researchers have examined factors influencing a variety of attributional judgments, including attributions of responsibility for various kinds of acts, the perception of causes for one's success or failure, and attributions of attitudes, abilities, and personality traits to others. This work has also been extended to investigating processes of self-perception, including explanations for one's own behavior and the labeling of one's emotional states.

David L. Hamilton

Person-Situation Interaction

Some researchers have focused increasingly on the social and psychological environments in which people live and function. A first concern in the study of environments has been to classify them into a taxonomy that would include a vast array of variables, such as the weather, the buildings and settings, the perceived social climates, and the reinforcements obtained for behaviors in that situation. Such a classification serves to underscore a fact that has been slighted by traditional trait-oriented approaches to personality: much human behavior depends on environmental considerations, including its physical actualities and its psychosocial interpretations.

When Do Individual Differences Make a Difference?

To understand how the interaction of persons and situations may work, situational variables in the psychological environment may be conceptualized as providing the individual with information; this information influences person variables, thereby affecting how the individual thinks and acts under those conditions. Situations (environments) thus influence behavior by affecting how people encode the situation, the outcomes they expect, the subjective value of those outcomes, and people's competence or ability to generate response patterns.

Conversely, situations are weak determinants of behavior to the degree that they are not uniformly encoded, do not generate uniform expectancies concerning the desired behavior, do not offer sufficient incentives for its performance, or fail to provide the learning conditions required for successful genesis of the behavior.

Walter Mischel

Personal Space and Territory in Humans

Human territorial behavior involves the personalization or marking of a geographical area, and communication that the area is "owned" by a person or group. If a territorial boundary is trespassed, active defense may occur, in which the owner uses a range of protective responses against an intruder, from verbal warnings to physical attack.

Much of the research on personal space was stimulated by Edward Hall, an anthropologist, who has proposed a field of "proxemics," or the study of space as a communication mechanism. Hall hypothesizes four spatial zones:

1. *Intimate distance*, 0–18 inches, where physical contact between people is extensive. At this distance the presence of another person is quite evident, and there is a rich exchange of cues—touch, smell, heat, and detailed visual information. Hall states that such distances are reserved for loved ones or intimates and are not usually sanctioned in public situations.

2. *Personal distance*, $1^{1}/_{2}$–4 feet, still permits rich communication, from the point where people can easily touch one another to where they can interact at about arm's length. This is a transitional zone, where contact can become inti-

mate or formal, and is described by Hall as the distance where lovemaking in the movies begins.

3. *Social distance*, 4–12 feet, is the normal distance for business and public social interaction. Communication richness drops off, although gross visual detail is available, as is some smell, touch, and so forth. Furniture, desks, and interior decor are often arranged to create proximity between people in this zone.

4. *Public distance*, 12–25 feet, is often reserved for formal occasions, for public speakers, or for high-status persons.

Three types of human territories can be identified: primary, secondary, and public territories. Primary territories are owned or exclusively used by a person or group, are under clear-cut control of the occupants, and are central to their lives. In a family home or person's bedroom, it is clear to outsiders who the owner is, and who has control over the place. Such places also play a major role in the person's or group's life. Secondary territories are somewhat less central to the occupant's life, and users have less exclusive control over who has access to the place. The neighborhood bar or the private social club have a blend of limited public availability and some control by regular occupants. Furthermore, in secondary territories, users may shift over time—for example, the afternoon and evening clientele of a bar—and the place is not solely identified as belonging to one group of users. Public territories have a temporary quality, and almost anyone has free access and occupancy rights.

Irwin Altman

Personalistic Psychology

Personalism in psychology views the individual person as the category through which psychology or the mental life is to be understood, hence calling for the reconstruction of psychology with the person as its focal point. Personalistic formulations include the central position accorded the person (e.g., self, ego, or some equivalent term), which is the necessary condition to account for and understand psychological processes, personality being defined in terms of a multiple unity.

Dilthey: The Psyche as a Unity of Composition

Best known for his psychologism, Wilhelm Dilthey sought to establish psychology as the foundation of history and sociology, rather than basing it on metaphysics. His influence reached Edmund Husserl, influencing his phenomenology, as well as influencing Husserl's associate Martin Heidegger, the existentialist. Dilthey, the forerunner of existential psychology, also swayed the thought of Karl Jaspers toward existential psychology. In superseding the existential individual over the rational mind as universal, and stressing the total structure or unity of mental life over the elements of mind, Dilthey became the forerunner of contemporary psychology.

Spranger

Dilthey's student at the University of Berlin, Edward Spranger, applied his teacher's "understanding" psychology to his *Types of Men* (1914), a topological theory of personality. Spranger postulates six types of personality (theoretic attitude, economic attitude, aesthetic attitude, social attitude, political attitude, and religious attitude) corresponding to six kinds of value, grounded in history and culture. He views them as genuine lifestyles or *Lebensformen* (forms of life).

James

Repudiating the notion of a consciousness that is "chopped up in bits," William James preferred to speak of it as a "strain of thought" or a "stream of consciousness," one that flows like a river or stream with states belonging to a "common self."

Calkins

At the turn of the century, Mary Whiton Calkins endorsed a self psychology, defining psychology as "a science of selves." She found inadequate the prevailing definition of psychology as a science of consciousness, because consciousness invariably implies "a somebody-being-conscious," so that perception without a perceiving self or thinking without someone who thinks simply does not exist. Accordingly, psychology must be defined as the "science of the conscious self in relation to its environment" (1909, 1).

Stern

Having defined psychology as "the science of the person as having experience or as capable of having experience," William Stern explained that "the 'person' is a living whole individual, unique, striving toward goals, self-contained and yet open to the world around him; he is capable of having experience" (1938, 70). The person, viewed as a totality, is conceived as a multiplicity of entities integrally contained in a totality as a personal whole. Stern's critical personalism holds to the psychophysical neutrality of being, in which spirit and matter are not dualistic but transcended by a personalistic monism.

Allport

Taking the lead from Stern, Gordon W. Allport developed the psychology of the person as unique and individual; a person whose interests, habits, and traits acquire an independence from their initial motivation, hence becoming motivating in themselves as functionally autonomous. The forces comprising functional autonomy within a person assume an integrative systematic whole, termed the *proprium* (self), a state of "becoming," with its intentional control and ability to achieve goals.

Frankl

Accepting the multiple unity view of personality, Victor E. Frankl (1969) defined "man as unity in spite of multiplicity!" (22). The person, "pulled by values" (will to meaning) is autonomously free to accept or reject them. The "meanings" found in human life are unique to the individual. Logotherapy, predicated on freedom of the will, will to meaning, and meaning of life, emphasizes the noetic dimension.

Rogers

Closely related to the phenomenological psychology of Frankl (but entirely independent of it) is Carl Rogers's phenomenological personalism. The person, struggling between a self-actualizing organism and the self, is initially an aspect of the entire phenomenological field of experience, which acquires an awareness or identification of "I" as a "self-experience."

William S. Sahakian

Personality Development in Childhood

A number of common assumptions underlie most work on the development of personality during the childhood years. One is the belief in the importance of early experiences in shaping future as well as current patterns of reaction. This implies continuity, or consistency over time, in personality traits or interpersonal motives. Longitudinal studies have demonstrated at least modest degrees of consistency from early childhood to later developmental periods in such dispositions as friendly extroversion (versus shy introversion), fearfulness, passivity, and aggression.

In considering personality development during childhood, it is useful to divide this span into two subperiods—early and middle childhood. The critical transition between these two phases comes, at least in modern literate societies, when the child enters school. School entry generally occurs by the age of 6, although many children may have had experience in a kindergarten, nursery school, or group care situation during the preschool years. The immediate social world of the young child consists of parents and siblings (or their institutional surrogates) and other extended family members.

Both cognitive and psychodynamic theories of development suggest that the ability to maintain attachments over increasing intervals of time and space, and thus to tolerate greater separations from the mother figure, are a function of developing internal object representations or images. The original Freudian account of the associated process of identification has been amplified by later psychoanalytic writers and subjected to attempts at empirical verification by social learning theorists.

Much concern has been focused on the possible instigation of aggression in children by violence portrayed on television. Research findings indicate that aggressive media models may indeed influence the acquisition and disinhibition of aggressive responses, but that such effects are highly dependent on the child's emotional adjustment and on previous socialization.

The development of ego functions in the school-age child is expressed in individual differences in cognitive style, in patterning and overall level of intellectual functions, in capacity for delay of gratification, and in tendencies to believe in one's internal capacity to control the environment (versus external control by it).

A number of self-report instruments have been devised to study manifest anxiety among school children, and the findings of these studies indicate that, while higher levels of anxiety may have a potentiating effect on simple conditioning, increased anxiety is disruptive of more complex performances. Anxiety in schoolchildren tends to be negatively associated with social adjustment and self-esteem and to reflect family conflict and rejecting or overly restrictive parental attitudes.

Lucy Rau Ferguson

Personality Theories

Henry Murray notes in his introduction to *Explorations in Personality* (1938, 3),

> Man is to-day's great problem. What can we know about him and how can it be said in words that have clear meaning? What propels him? With what environmental objects and institutions does he interact and how? What occurrences in his body are most influentially involved? What mutually dependent processes participate in his differentiation and development? What courses of events determine his pleasures and displeasures? And finally, by what means can he be intentionally transformed?

Historically, those who accepted Murray's view that personality ought to be the heart of the proper study of psychology have long been disaffected from the academic embodiment of that discipline.

There are good reasons for this. For one, at least until recently, academic psychology took as its archetype what R. W. Sperry (1993) termed *reduc-*

tive or *microdeterministic physicalism*, an episte-mological program remarkably inhospitable to Murray's conceptualization of personality. For another, such a view of personality as Murray's, of necessity must draw heavily from the whole of the human sciences (e.g., anthropology, linguistics, sociology, history, economics, etc.) and humanities, in addition to psychology's academic subspecializations (e.g., learning, differential, social, physiological, developmental, and most recently, cognitive and cognitive neuroscience), clearly a daunting prospect even for those who believe a man's reach should exceed his grasp.

Predictably, given the current status of our own knowledge about people, their development, and what influences them and their interactions, many of what are grandly called personality theories are best viewed as figurations or metaphors. Just as fore-tellable, perhaps, is that the most expansive of these figurations with current weight would originate in the efforts of a few European physicians living in the late nineteenth and early twentieth centuries. Their pragmatic aim was to understand the phenomenology and treat the behavioral anomalies associated with such functional disorders (without known organic etiology) as neurosis (Sigmund Freud, Alfred Adler, Carl Jung) and schizophrenia (Jung).

Humans are driven by their natures to effectively discharge instinctual energy. To do so they must develop stable, accurate internal representations of their own internal behavioral action sequences and of external reality, and learn to coordinate the two effectively. The ability to do so hinges largely upon the successful differentiation of a part of the primi-tive matrix of personality (id) into a reality-oriented, attention-controlling executive function (ego). Under extraordinary but usual conditions of family life (oedipal conflict) a third agency, a functional representation of a parent or parent surrogate, also emerges from the id—the superego. From this time on, the ego arranges to satisfy instinctual demands (largely sexual or aggressive) while maximizing praise from the superego, experienced as pride, and minimizing its censure, experienced as guilt.

Erik Erikson described Freud's theory accurately as emphasizing the inward (the individual and not the group), the downward (the id and not the ego), and the backward (early childhood development and not lifespan development). Many of the psycho-dynamically oriented theorists who followed Freud, largely practicing clinicians, understandably sought to stress those aspects of Freud's theory that they believed he undervalued or neglected. Erikson, for example, sought to highlight the interaction of society and biology in forming personality over the life-span; Freud's daughter Anna, the ego defenses; David Rapaport and R. J. Loewenstein, the ego; Harry Stack Sullivan and Karen Horney, the inter-personal; Horney, Carl Rogers, and H. Kohut. the self; Erich Fromm, the influence on personality formation of the external economic system; the object relations theorists, the internal representation of self and others; and Roy Schafer, the existential qualities of personality. Benjamin B. Wolman, of the neo-Freudians, has offered perhaps the most comprehensive revision of Freud's vision.

With the exception of George Kelly's original psychology of personal constructs, which assumes that each individual must and will create (construe) a "world" adequate to her need to predict and control her future meaningful interactions in it (G. Kelly 1955), no other extent theory of personality rivals in scope and complexity that of Jung, Freud, Adler, and their heirs. Instead, when sweeping claims are advanced about the nature of humans, they stem, as in B. F. Skinner's case, from unwarranted extrapolations of results derived from more limited conceptual frames of reference, such as learning theory. More often, however, modern personality theorists content themselves with more narrow-gauge theories, theories of the middle range.

Arguably, the mid-range conceptualization of personality most indigenous to academic psychology is the Five Factor Model (e.g., Digman 1990). This model has its roots in the work of William Stern, William McDougall, Gordon W. Allport, R. B. Cattell, Hans J. Eysenck, and J. P. Guilford, to mention a few. It was made possible by the invention of the standardized test item, the development of empirical methods of test construction, the formulation of formal test theory, the creation of the construct approach to validation, the evolution of multivariate statistical analysis, and the computer. Put simply, the Five Factor Model posits that within the last decade or so a confluence of research evidence has pointed to the conclusion that the personality might usefully be considered to be composed of five key robust and distinct factors. Some controversy exists about what these should best be named, but the following labels appear to capture the essence of these dimensions to a significant degree: (1) intelligence, (2) conscientiousness, (3) emotional stability, (4) agreeableness, and (5) introversion/extroversion. More puzzling than what they should be called is why only these five factors have emerged so consistently. There is currently no satisfactory explanation for this.

That humans are today's great problem remains as true for us as it was for Murray. Neither psychoanalytic figurations nor the more modest Five Factor Model of personality has convincingly resolved our natures. Increasingly, both seem somewhat stale, representative of an era's end. This may be a reflection of a change of frame of reference that is affecting not only such diverse scientific disciplines as computer sciences, neuroscience, biology, physics, and anthropology but the humanities as well.

R. W. Sperry (1993) was probably right when he announced that a new mode of doing science was in the making, a new paradigm was emergent. He denoted this as the cognitive revolution.

[T]he cognitive revolution represents a diametric turn around in the centuries-old treatment of mind and consciousness in science.... Reconceived in the new outlook, subjective mental states become functionally interactive and essential for a full explanation of conscious behavior.... Reductive microdeterministic views of personhood and the physical world are replaced in favor of a more wholistic, top-down view in which the higher, more evolved entities throughout nature, including the mental, vital, social, and other higher-order forces, gain their due recognition along with physics and chemistry.... In the new synthesis, mental states, as dynamic emergent properties of brain activity, become inseparably interfused with and tied to the brain activity of which they are an emergent property.... A new reciprocal form of casual control is invoked that includes downward as well as upward determinism. (Sperry 1993, 879).

A consensus about what exactly this cognitive revolution entails for personality theories, in particular, has yet to be achieved.

Herbert H. Krauss
Beatrice J. Krauss

Personality Theory: Wolman's System

Benjamin B. Wolman's personality theory is neo-Freudian and psychodynamic. Like many neo-Freudians, Wolman emphasizes the healthy striving of a social, mastering self or ego. In a comprehensive theory, he also retains Freud's emphasis on the difficult balance maintained among aspects of an organism driven by instinctual need and not able to ensure singlehandedly its own survival. While accepting some of Freud's evolutionary constructs regarding motivation to protect the individual's life, and agreeing as to the existence of an unconscious, Wolman centers his theory within a developmental and social context, which pays particular respect to higher levels of organization, that is, humankind's ability to reason, to nurture, and to join forces in social action.

Wolman's system draws heavily on his psychoanalytic clinical experience. His system is built upon a rational/empirical philosophy of science. Wolman believes matter and reality exist independent of a person's social perception, misinterpretation, or "social construction" of events. Theory consists of verifiable relationships between constructs, which can be inferred from empirical facts. He feels it has been demonstrated that an individual's biochemistry can influence thoughts or actions, and thoughts or actions can influence one's biochemistry (Wolman 1988). Personhood is represented more closely in the evolutionary higher functioning of mental processes. All personality issues, therefore, are not reducible to mechanistic chemical or physical processes.

Processes that do not involve higher functions of thought and perception are closer to the unconscious. Wolman sees the conditioning of the viscera, important in emotion, as largely unconscious. Conditioning that relies on speech signals may be closer to an area somewhere between conscious and unconscious, which Wolman terms the "protoconscious." The protoconscious can be described as an awareness without self-conscious control. Wolman believes the protoconscious to be important in mental disorder, dreams, and insight, in which ideas appear to leap to mind. In adopting the concept of the protoconscious, Wolman has rejected Freud's notion of preconscious.

Like Freud, Wolman believes that social reality, and thereby social life, evolves from *cathexis*, investment of energy in one's self and others. Wolman revises Freud's *libido* to a more encompassing lust for life, which grows over the life span to include preservation not only of one's self but of the species. Wolman is heavily influenced by Karen Horney and Harry Stack Sullivan, who emphasize the necessity of other persons' caring, and trust in that caring, for physical and psychological health (Horney 1937; Sullivan 1953). Wolman's idea of lust for life, therefore, concerns desires for survival and interpersonal security (Krauss and Krauss 1977). The lust for life has two arms, Eros and Ares; the first is life promoting, and the second is invested in thwarting objects that threaten life. Eros and Ares can be thought of as love and hostility. Ares is more primitive, and "phylogenetically prior" to Eros. Thus, when an individual is threatened, life functions, such as hunger and desire, may become secondary.

Wolman expands the cathexis concept to include the effects of the investment on the object cathected. Wolman speaks of *interindividual* cathexis to denote, for example, the exchange of energy that occurs when thriving in a child is promoted by nurturance from a parent. Interindividual cathexes can take three dynamic forms: (1) instrumental, when cathexis occurs primarily to satisfy an individual's own needs; (2) mutual, when cathexis occurs so individuals both provide for the other's needs and have their own needs satisfied; and (3) vectorial (the model for which is parenting), when an individual gives energy to meet the needs of another without expectation of need satisfaction in return.

In Wolman's dynamic system, mutuality and vectorialism involve the giving of energy. The giving exercises pathways to further untapped sources of energy, increasing efficiency and utilization of potentialities. Emotional and cognitive accompaniments to giving, therefore, are pride, joy, self-esteem, self-

confidence, and a feeling of power. Likewise, anxiety is the emotional corollary of generally feeling weak and unable to satisfy one's own needs or the needs of others. Depression accompanies "grave" estimations of one's weakness or lack of resources. Wolman believes maladjustment and disorder occur when individuals have unrealistic perceptions of their own power, the resources available to them, or the threats to their safety and survival. People can over- or underestimate their power, resources, or threats. For example, sociopaths tend to believe themselves deprived and threatened, and to attack enemies they perceive as weak.

Realistically, a person's power can be increased by the growth of his own resources or by gaining acceptance from powerful others. Acceptance is particularly important when a person's lack of resources is real, as in the dependency of childhood. As an individual matures, reliance on his own power, with concomitant feelings of confidence and self-esteem, ought to enlarge.

Developmentally, vectorial responses occur later and are more mature than instrumental and mutual responses. However, the mature individual, echoing Horney's concepts of neurosis as rigidity in interpersonal patterns (1937), can be fluidly instrumental, mutual, or vectorial as appropriate. Wolman cites such adult behavior styles as "instrumental in business, mutual in marriage, and vectorial in parenthood" (Wolman 1992, 74).

The giving without receiving of vectorialism poses a problem for any psychology of motivation relying on a hedonic or pleasure-seeking notion of reward. Based on evidence as varied as conditioning studies and historical acts of self-sacrifice, Wolman posits three evolutionary levels of motivation: prehedonic, hedonic, and posthedonic. The first, found in humans and lower organisms alike, concerns associationistic conditioning for which pleasure or pain are irrelevant. For higher organisms, such as mammals, pain often signals danger, and pleasure, safety. Wolman believes that, for human beings, probably the majority of learning experiences are reinforced by pleasure or pain. Pleasure and pain may even supplant survival as motivations, as in the cravings of destructive addictions. With vectorial commitments toward persons or ideals, motivation may become posthedonic. In terms of cathexes, the individual has cathected a beloved or ideal more than the self. Out of empathy, duty, or moral responsibility, it is the suffering or pleasure of the "other" that is protected. Such a motivational style is posthedonic.

Wolman's theory also has an existential component. Realistically, the goal of survival is futile, for, as Wolman states, "All organisms face the same inescapable end" (Wolman 1992, 83). Neither birth nor, to a lesser extent, death is under the individual's control. Rather, the style of the journey between birth and death marks success and health: "The term *self-actualization* implies an adequate use of one's resources toward the attainment of realistic goals" (Wolman 1992, 83). The utilization of resources and the choice of goals may be dependent, to some extent, on the opportunity structure of the immediate environment and the social system within which the individual is embedded, although Wolman believes that societies, like individual personalities, have many elements in common but vary in their structure.

Beatrice J. Krauss
Herbert H. Krauss

Personnel Testing in Business, Industry, and Government

There are many different kinds of personnel tests, and they can be classified along several different dimensions. Among the more important of these are (1) type of administration, (2) format or design, (3) content or subject matter, and (4) basis of interpretation. Two tests developed to achieve the same basic purpose may differ on one or all of these dimensions.

Type of Administration
Group tests. These tests have standardized instructions, which are readily communicable to the examinee. They do not depend upon any interaction between examiner and examinee, and they may even be administered mechanically by tape or cassette recording.

Individual tests. The examiner plays a very impor-

tant role. The basic instructions are standardized, but the examiner has options, which depend on the performance of the examinee.

Format or Design
The majority of tests used by business, industry, and government are paper-and-pencil tests. The examinee is presented with a paper that contains a large number of items intended to elicit his knowledge, belief, attitude, opinion, and so on, with reference to the topic under consideration.

In marked contrast to paper-and-pencil tests are performance tests. These require the use of apparatus or equipment. The equipment varies over a wide range but can be generally classified in one of three categories: (1) basic, including blocks, geometrical forms, mazes, and pictograms; (2) job-related, including nuts, bolts, cogs, tweezers, pins, and rotors; and (3) actual, including typewriters, sewing machines, welding equipment, and trucks. Almost all performance tests are individually administered.

Content or Subject Matter
General learning ability. This is sometimes called general intelligence and is usually measured by an omnibus-type test containing verbal comprehension, verbal reasoning, quantitative reasoning, and spatial visualization items.

Clerical aptitude. A variety of tasks are employed—name checking, number checking, coding, alphabetizing, simple numerical computation, and so forth. All have in common the testing of the ability to handle clerical operations quickly and accurately.

Mechanical aptitude. Items used are most frequently presented pictorially. Concepts involving levers, pulleys, flow, pressure, gravity, and so on, are presented.

Basis of Interpretation
The interpretation of test results may be generally classified in two ways: normative; and clinical, or judgmental. Normative implies objective and quantitative scoring; clinical or judgmental implies subjective evaluations, even though quantitative records may have been kept during the testing process.

The vast majority of tests used by business and industry are sold on a restricted basis by commercial firms, which specialize in this activity.

Charles Paul Sparks

Persuasion

The essence of persuasion is an attack on the audience's existing attitudes. Attitude structures are generally stable, and resistance to change must be overcome. The persuader must find the point at which the message is powerful enough to induce change without causing the recipient to react against the idea of being manipulated.

Attitude change involves changes in beliefs about relevant facts, opinions, the evaluations based upon those beliefs, and response patterns based on the other two components. All of these tend to be stable and to resist being altered. Kurt Lewin identifies three processes of attitude change: unfreezing, changing, and refreezing.

Persuasibility can also be increased by making salient some loyalty or group membership that the audience values. The appropriate norms then come into play to strengthen the persuasive message. Significant changes in such areas as racial prejudice have been obtained by this technique.

Messages have greater effect if the subject is distracted during the presentation. In such cases, the cognitive mechanism is so fully occupied with the two inputs (the message and the distraction) that the internal generation of counterarguments is disrupted. As a result, the subject is less efficient in defending her original attitude structure.

Individuals who are submissive to others are good targets for a persuasive attempt. Thus, people of relatively low status, either generally or in a specific situation and relationship, will be susceptible to sources who are higher in status. Given an understandable message, individuals of low intelligence are more persuasible; so are lower ranking members in a military hierarchy, individuals with low self-esteem, and so on.

In the inoculation design, the persuasive message is viewed as analogous to an infection, and the experimenters "treat" the subject in advance. There are two techniques: strengthening the subject's existing attitudes by giving him supportive messages, and providing counterarguments to refute opposing points. Inoculation does result in less attitude change when, upon a later occasion, propaganda arguments are presented to the subject. Refutational presentations are the more effective, even when they consist of material that differs from the arguments in the actual persuasive message (McGuire 1969).

Peter Suedfeld

Phenomenal Causality and Perception

The impression that one event A causes another event B is a pervasive part of human experience. Simple events, such as the motion of a single object, do not occur in isolation. They are knitted together in a complex web: the motions of both A and B are phenomenally transformed when they become part of the event A → B, and likewise for more complex event structures. The study of impressions of causal relations among objects owes much to the work of A. Michotte (1963).

Social Causation
Fritz Heider (1944) has addressed himself to the role of causal impressions in explaining human conduct. The apparent causes of one person's behavior influence the way that another will respond to her. Heider's ideas have given rise to a large literature on attribution. K. Heider and C. Simmel (1944) created a brief (2½ minutes) film involving three geometrical figures (large triangle, small triangle, circle) moving in and around a rectangular enclosure. Given only very general instructions, subjects described the film in terms of animated beings, usually a connected story, and with a remarkable degree of structural similarity in the stories seen.

Past Experience and Development
Michotte (1963) claims that the phenomenal immediacy of causal impressions, together with their regular dependence on stimulus conditions, demonstrates that they are unlearned, natural perceptual

responses, much as "red" is a perceptual response to certain stimulus wavelengths or relations among such stimuli. But, because he worked only with adult subjects and conducted no training experiments, he did not put this claim to the test. Jean Piaget and M. Lambercier (1958; Piaget 1963) have shown that children up to the age of 7 perceive launching only if there is contact, and not in the case of action at a distance.

The perception of causality may become increasingly differentiated with age and is also influenced by past experience and by the cognitive activity of the subject. Whether there is some irreducible minimum of phenomenal causality that depends only on conditions of stimulation cannot now be said, but almost certainly this question will suffer the same vicissitudes as all other variants of the nativism-empiricism-constructivism debate.

Howard E. Gruber

Phenomenological Psychology

The aim of phenomenological psychology is threefold: (1) to criticize the de facto contexts within which psychology developed; (2) to establish a program for articulating the optimum frame of reference for the evolution of psychology, both as a genuine science and as a profession; and (3) by such a process, to clarify the meaning of psychology and its value for mankind.

Phenomenological Psychology as the Clarification of the Foundations of Psychology as Part of a Philosophical Program

Edmund Husserl, the founder of phenomenology, wanted to found philosophy as a rigorous science, and it was within the context of that project that phenomenology developed. In order to achieve this aim, Husserl needed a method and a region of absolute certitude. The method he arrived at is called the phenomenological attitude, whereby one breaks away from the natural attitude in which objects and events are spontaneously posited as real or unreal. One is present only to the meanings of the objects given in one's own stream of experience, pre-

cisely as they present themselves. Husserl's interpretation of phenomenological psychology is more philosophical, closer to the inspirations of phenomenological philosophy in terms of arriving at methods for determining adequate foundations for the practice of psychology.

Phenomenological Psychology as a Program for Ascertaining Clarified Psychological Praxis

The thoughts of Husserl have been modified by his followers. The person most responsible for interpreting phenomenological psychology in such a way that a genuine psychological program can be established is Maurice Merleau-Ponty. He had a firm grasp of both phenomenological philosophy and empirical psychology, and was more aware of the subtleties and intricacies of psychological praxis than was Husserl. Moreover, because Merleau-Ponty was more concerned with applying phenomenological philosophy than with founding it, he was able to pursue other intentions that proved to be fruitful for psychology.

Amedeo Giorgi

Phenylketonuria

Phenylketonuria is a genetically determined disease characterized clinically by mental retardation and biochemically by the presence of excess phenylalanine and its metabolites in the body fluids.

The main clinical feature is mental retardation. This is usually apparent by the end of the first year of life, although it may be surmised earlier. The degree of mental deficiency varies considerably from case to case, even in the same family. Mental deterioration after childhood is not common. In the majority of untreated children the IQ is below 50, and often in the 20s. However, patients with an IQ above 50 are being reported in increasing numbers, and an occasional untreated phenylketonuric with an IQ in the normal range is on record.

Seizure discharges are present in some 25% of subjects, while abnormalities of encephalogram are seen in a larger number of untreated cases. The finding of hypsarrhythmic pattern is not rare and usually means a poor prognosis. Other and minor neurological disturbances are tremors, muscular hypertonicity, rigid gait, and stooped posture.

Dietary treatment consists of decreasing phenylalanine in the diet. Complete elimination would not be feasible, because phenylalanine is an essential amino acid and is indispensable for life. Low-phenylalanine hydrolysate of protein is available commercially, and carbohydrates, fats, minerals, and vitamins are added.

George A. Jervis

Pheromones

All mammals, including human beings, have areas of the body that produce odoriferous substances. In most mammals, there are specified scent glands in which these strong-smelling exudates are synthesized, while other odors occur as part of normal metabolic processes. Many of these chemical substances are used in communication between species members and even interspecifically.

Chemical Perception

In mammals, chemicals are perceived using three separate methods. The sense of taste allows for the reception of five classes of chemicals, but they must be in solution; this means of perception is thus limited. The olfactory epithelium of the nasal cavity contains receptors leading to the first cranial nerve, which terminates in the olfactory bulb.

Glandular Secretions

Due to the variety of body areas in which scent glands are located, there have evolved a multiplicity of conspicuous behavior patterns associated with the deposition of scent. Typically, the gland is rubbed on an inanimate or animate surface. Hamsters rub the flank gland along vertical surfaces, while rabbits rub the chin gland on conspecifics and conspicuous objects. In some cases, the glandular exudates are not deposited through friction between the gland and a surface but are released directly into the air, such as the stink gland of the skunk.

Urination

The sites preferred for the deposition of scent marks vary from species to species. Often, conspicuous objects in the environment are chosen, such as trees, rocks, and bushes; the same sites may be marked over and over again. In many mammals, such as caviomorph rodents and rabbits, conspecifics are covered in scent, while in some species individuals may redistribute odors on their own bodies.

Transmission of Information

The function of a chemical signal can, in some cases, be assessed by observing the behavioral responses of individuals in the absence of the particular odor. For example, estrous female swine will exhibit the "mating stance" when touched on the back by a human handler; when the odor of a boar is present, 81% of females stand, while only 48% stand in the absence of boar odor. The preputial glands are thought to be responsible for boar sex odor.

Scent and Aggression

In the context of an intraspecific encounter, certain odors may promote certain responses. For example, unfamiliar adult male mice typically fight when introduced. In terms of specific factors controlling scent marking, it has been shown for many mammals that exposure to a novel area (or object) promotes scent deposition. Dogs, cats, gerbils, and hamsters all exhibit increased levels of scent marking when exposed to an unfamiliar territory. As the novelty wears off, there is a decrease in the behavior, but even when animals are fully adapted, scent marking continues as part of the daily activity. In this manner, odor is constantly renewed.

Devra G. Kleiman

Philosophical Psychology

Socrates and his disciple Plato (427–347 B.C.) owed much to the Orphic religious myth of the eternally preexisting and immortal soul and were, therefore, the first scholastic philosophers, using rational argument to justify religious conceptions. Aristotle (384–322 B.C.) rejected the Orphism of his teacher

Plato, seeing the soul as the animating principle of the body, coexistent rather than preexistent, but having one function, intellectual understanding, which transcended everything material. To Aristotle, the supreme human endowment was the creative reason by which humans could govern their emotions, live justly with others, and direct themselves to the contemplative understanding of all reality. Because it was this active intellect, too, that illuminated the sensory world into intelligibility, we have here the perfect statement of Greek intellectualism.

It was not until René Descartes (1596–1650) that a systematic effort to rethink psychology in purely rational terms was attempted. Descartes's revision of psychology as the study of the soul (psyche) was amazingly simple: he abolished soul as an animating principle, replacing it with mind, the essence of which was thinking and whose nature could be comprehended by a kind of mathematical introspection, in which Descartes, the mathematician, was naturally expert. The world of matter was similarly denuded of faculties and forms and reduced entirely to extension, to which God obligingly imparted motion, so that all the processes of nature, including life and the sensorimotor functions of animals, could be explained mechanically. The English took up where Descartes left off, Sir Isaac Newton (1642–1727) providing an almost perfect mathematico-mechanical analysis of the physical world, while the British empiricists (John Locke, George Berkeley, David Hume, David Hartley, and James Mill) between the late seventeenth and the early nineteenth centuries used introspection systematically and inexorably to reduce the Cartesian mind to a mechanical concatenation of images derived from sensory experience.

For all their psychic orientation, both Wilhelm Wundt and Sigmund Freud stood for a kind of mental mechanism. Behaviorism was to attach their psychicism or mentalism, while a new Aristotelianism, that of Franz Clemens Brentano (1838–1917), stressed the dynamic and distinctively nonmechanical quality of mental life and opposed all forms of reductionism and elementarism. Brentano influenced O. Külpe and the Wurzburg school, who did pioneer experimental studies of mental organization, thinking, and volition, and also the philosopher

Edmund Husserl (1859–1938), founder of phenomenology. This minority tradition has had increasing impact in the twentieth century, influencing the holism of the Gestalt school, the hormic vitalism of William McDougall, the eclecticism of R. S. Woodworth and Gordon W. Allport, the self theory of Carl Rogers, and the new psychiatric phenomenology of Ludwig Binswanger and Medard Boss.

Psychologists have also been increasingly concerned with the problems of philosophy of science. H. Feigl (1951), M. Marx (1963), Royce (1972), Stevens (1939), Benjamin B. Wolman and E. Nagel (1965), and others have analyzed the problems of theory formation in psychology and its relationship to formal logic and methodology of science. Clark L. Hull (1943), B. F. Skinner (1945), and others have been influenced by the neopositivist philosophy of the Vienna Circle and P. W. Bridgman's operationism. Robert Plutchik (1963), S. S. Stevens (1939), and others have applied the tenets of operationism to psychological research.

Philosophical issues related to psychology have been of major concern to Jean Piaget (1950, 1957), whose contribution to philosophical issues in psychology covers such diverse areas as logic, epistemology, and ethics. In the collective volume edited by Wolman and Nagel (1965), some authors (P. Griese, T. Kotarbinski, Nagel, Piaget, Wolman, and others) deal with the relationship between psychology and various topics of philosophy, such as mind and body, existentialism, logical analysis, epistemology, and so on, while Royce (1972) has analyzed epistemological and methodological problems of theory formation in psychology.

Raymond J. McCall

Philosophical Psychotherapy

Based on cognitive psychology, philosophical psychotherapy finds its curative effect in the alteration of one's attitude toward life. Philosophical psychotherapy is based on the premise that cognitions, beliefs, and attitudes (that is, one's general philosophical perspective) have a profound effect on emotional and behavioral responses, and that one's style of life, character, and other aspects of personality are significantly influenced by one's *Weltanschauung.*

Philosophical psychotherapy, when used as an adjunct to traditional forms of psychotherapy, often is most effective in those long-term recalcitrant cases that fail to yield when standard forms of therapy alone are used (Sahakian 1980).

William S. Sahakian

Piaget, Jean (1896–1980)

Jean Piaget discovered qualitative differences in persons' thoughts. He elaborated a definite order of periods through which human thought develops: (1) the sensorimotor period, marked by acting and object-related experiences; (2) the preoperational period, marked by being able to hold both symbol and referent in mind; (3) the concrete operational period, characterized by mastering classes, relations, and quantities; and (4) the formal operational period, marked by being able to show flexible, effective thinking.

Piaget performed numerous significant investigations that bear upon epistemology and psychology, such as those that concern the acquisition of concepts like space, geometry, causality, permanence, and conservation, and the development of moral judgment.

Eileen A. Gavin

Piaget's Theory

Jean Piaget spent most of his life trying to integrate two major areas of intellectual pursuit: biology and epistemology. Epistemology is a branch of philosophy concerned with the origin, nature, and limits of knowledge.

Piaget adopted the constructivist's view of knowledge and knowledge acquisition. This is a position that differs radically from the "naive realism" that is the philosophical basis of much of modern-day empiricism and many of the dominant theories of learning and cognition.

Piaget suggests that children do not just respond passively to events occurring in their external environment but, like the scientists who study children, actively construct their views of reality. The developing child is pictured as acting upon objects and actively processing information from both internal and external sources.

One consequence of Piaget's emphasis on this constructivist view of development is that the traditional distinction between self and environment does not exist in his system. This is because the environment is itself internally organized and can never be directly known. Thus, the interaction takes place between the person's own cognitive structures and her perceived environment.

Piaget views intelligence both as a particular instance of biological adaptation and as an extension of it. Adaptation can be described in terms of two complementary processes: assimilation and accommodation. These two processes are present simultaneously in every act and are functionally invariant in that they occur at every developmental level.

Organization and adaptation (assimilation and accommodation) are two general principles of functioning that affect intelligence. These tendencies are possessed by all living biological organisms—and, thus, by all human beings. The particular ways that the individual child adapts and organizes his cognitive structures, however, are dependent upon his experience.

Cognitive structures continually change. They are reorganized as the child adapts (and readapts) to her perceived environment and progresses from lower levels of equilibrium, through states of disequilibrium, to higher levels of equilibrium. These notions are very abstract and general, but they represent the overall framework Piaget brought to the study of the child's intellectual development.

Piaget has described four major periods of intellectual development: the sensorimotor period (birth to approximately $1^1/_2$ or 2 years), the preoperational period (approximately 2–7 years), the concrete-operational period (approximately 7–11), and the formal-operational period (approximately 11–15 years).

Sensorimotor period. During this stage, the infant develops from being heavily dependent on a few heredity-determined reflexes (e.g., sucking, grasping, looking) to a child capable of representing objects and events symbolically (as illustrated by the ability to search for hidden objects, imitate an absent model, or perform acts requiring mental combinations).

The preoperational period. This period can be divided into two subperiods: preconceptual (2 to 4 years) and intuitive (4 to 7) thought. The preconceptual period is a period in which the child goes from the use of actions as representations to enlarging on other means of symbolically representing events. The reasoning of the intuitive phase child is still tied to perceptual relations, and she tends to reason transductively (if A is like B in one respect, then A is like B in all respects) rather than hypothetico-deductively.

The concrete-operational period. The most outstanding feature of concrete-operational thinking is that it is "operational" and reversible. For example, when the intuitive-preoperational child is presented with two identical rows of counters, he may be able to count them and recognize their equality. But, if one row is made longer by spreading the counters out, he says that the longer row has more counters. In the face of (irrelevant) perceived changes, he cannot "conserve" number.

Formal-operational period. During this period (11 or 12 to 15 years), the adolescent acquires thought structures that Piaget describes as second-order operations. That is, she can operate on operations, or propositions, to exhaust all the possibilities in a problem situation. She is able to think in terms of the possible rather than the real and can test out possibilities in a systematic and orderly fashion to determine which possibilities exist in reality. The adolescent can conduct controlled experiments, holding all variables constant but one, to determine the effects of that variable.

Piaget has used the formal language of logic and mathematics to describe the psychological structures that characterize the concrete- and formal-operational stages. He has done this in order to describe the properties of thought at these stages in the precise manner that is so important for communication on a scientific basis.

The uniqueness of Piaget's theory is that he enters the child's world to show how it is different from that of adults. The child's view is perceived not as a wrong view but as a view based on different premises. Piaget has analyzed what those premises are at each stage of development as the child makes her way to adult thinking.

Gerald E. Gruen

Picture Perception

Picture perception uses components of a display as representations. There are several ways this can take place. The components can simply be recognized, or the components can give rise to perceptual effects in the same way that the represented object would if it were present, or both recognition and the perceptual effects can occur.

Approaches

The geometric approach to pictures relies on projective geometry. The fact that light generally travels in straight lines forms the basis of this approach, which emphasizes how light converges to a viewpoint. Using this approach, it is possible to predict, for example, how shape and distance perception would be modified if we observed a photograph from nearer than its appropriate viewpoint.

Research and theory in picture perception has begun to venture beyond the simple sketch or illustration that was the focus for many years. Pictorial devices have been prepared for the blind, finding that outlined and silhouetted objects depicted on flat surfaces can be understood by the blind with little or no training (J. M. Kennedy 1974). Devices for arranging a pictorial impression of brightness analogous to pictorial depth have emerged from research on lines and subjective contours. A number of primates have been tested and found to recognize outlined and photographed objects.

John M. Kennedy

Pinel, Philippe (1754–1826)

In 1792, Philippe Pinel was appointed head physician of Bicetre, and two years later of Salpetrière, where he abolished physical restraint and harsh treatment of patients. Pinel introduced the humanitarian spirit to treatment of mental patients. Pinel's main work is *A Treatise on Insanity* (English edition, 1962).

Leo H. Berman

Platter, Felix (1536–1614)

Felix Platter refused to rule out demonic possession, but he thought that most deviant behavior had physical causes.

John C. Burnham

Play Behavior

Play is an action-oriented, often vigorous, manipulative, or locomotor behavior, whose structure may be highly variable. Play apparently lacks immediate functional consequences, and it is often accompanied by specific forms of nonverbal or verbal communication. Rehearsals of adult activities that occur in play include motor patterns used in hunting, fighting, predator avoidance, tool construction and tool use, and mating, but the consequences of playful activity differ from the consequences of serious performances of the same patterns.

Social (and sometimes even solitary) play interactions in animals are distinguished by persistent or vigorous exercise and experimentation. But even extremely vigorous bouts of play-fighting have never been seen to result in injury or death (despite frequent risk taking and occasional discomfort). How is such vigorous play controlled? Part of the answer is that animals appear to have evolved a special set of postures, gestures, and vocalizations—and perhaps even smells—that serve to communicate playful intent and, thereby, to signal the nonagonistic nature of acts such as hitting or jumping on a conspecific, acts that would otherwise indicate an attack with intent to injure.

Physiological studies of adaptive response to exercise in muscle, bone, and the cardiopulmonary and endocrine systems indicate that without play (or some other appropriate form of vigorous physical exercise) certain body components would never develop adequately but rather would atrophy. Body

components requiring play are those that would otherwise not be frequently exercised until adulthood, namely those somatic systems used by adults for hunting, fighting, escape, and mating.

Robert M. Fagen

Play and Curiosity

Piaget

Jean Piaget made a clear distinction between curiosity and play in his theory of cognition. Curiosity would be one example of what he terms accommodative activity, in which the organism gropes to bring its own responses into accord with the character of environmental stimuli or agents, whereas play would be an example of assimilative activity, in which the organism subordinates the environmental phenomena to its own internal systems of responses, schemata, ideas, fantasies, and so on.

Social Factors

Several researchers have established experimentally that groups manipulated to increase their experience of play subsequently score higher than their controls on creativity tests and in novel associations—which means that though it may be novelty in the environment that gives rise to curiosity, it is play that, in its turn, generates novelty in the organism. In fact, it is possible to argue that play follows when the preceding curiosity leads to accommodative responses at some intermediate degree of discrepancy from those already available in the organism's repertoire, thus bringing play theory into line with the U-shaped functioning discovered in experimental work with exploration.

Structural Aspects

There would appear to be some value in giving central attention to play as a micro–rite of reversal. In play, as in games, the usual control of events is reversed in favor of the players. Play and games contain various levels of reversal, power reversal, role reversal, tactical reversal, reality reversal, and so forth. Playfulness, as contrasted with play, may be defined as a form of rule reversal in which one player constantly changes the rules on the other. But this is only the conative definition of play structure and corresponds to Erik Erikson's stress on play as ego mastery. Play is also cognitive. L. S. Vygotsky defines play as a form of anticipatory formulation. The novelties that are generated in play research are new forms of organization, new forms of synthesis for the player. Erikson defines play as the active creation of models.

Curiosity seems to precede play. It is a form of mastery more relevant to the environment. Play is a form of mastery more relevant to the subjective state of the individual. Tentatively, play could be defined as that subset of voluntary behaviors in which the individual reverses the usual contingencies of power in order to enact a novel formulation of her experience in a vivifying manner. The outcome is greater flexibility, creativity, and optimism. It seems that in human evolution these characteristics have been associated with the need for versatility in novel environments, and that play has potentiated the organism for such versatility. In biological terms, play is a form of adaptive potentiation.

Brian Sutton-Smith

Political Behavior, Nonconventional

Empirical researchers have attempted to avoid definitional problems by ordering political behaviors in Western democracies along a continuum from more to less conventional. A list of these behaviors generally takes the following form (adapted from J. Foster and D. Long 1970; and D. O. Sears and J. B. McConahay 1973):

1. *Private activities:* individual striving, discussion of events with friends, watching campaigns from a psychological and physical distance
2. *Public activities:* voting, signing petitions, writing to officials, writing to newspapers, helping in campaigns
3. *Symbolic (group) activities:* marches to make grievances known, rallies, political organizing
4. *Obstructive group actions:* actions to disrupt governmental or other business, to inconve-

nience others, and to suggest the possibility of violence; sit-ins, boycotts, and strikes
5. *Violent activities:* riots, armed rebellions, revolutions, assassinations, terrorism.

At the individual level, nonconventional political behavior is usually studied by means of survey-interviews of a representative sample of persons residing in the nation, city, or institution under consideration.

The J-curve of rising expectations and gratifications was formally stated by James C. Davies in 1962. As is the case with the relative deprivation theory, it builds upon the frustration-aggression theory formulated by John Dollard and his colleagues in 1939. The J-curve theory proposes that as conditions (particularly economic conditions) get better for people, their expectations keep pace or stay slightly ahead of their actual attainments. At some point, conditions become objectively worse—that is, the conditions curve turns downward so that it would graph like an upside-down J—and this creates an intolerable gap between expectations, which have continued to rise, and gratification, which declines with the decline in objective conditions. This gap between what is wanted and what is received is the source of frustration, which leads to ever more aggressive, nonconventional political activity, and eventually (if the gap is not closed) to violent revolution.

The other theory of nonconventional political behavior is the relative deprivation theory. The psychological version of this theory has been proposed by D. O. Sears and John B. McConahay (1973). A more sociological version has been proposed by T. R. Gurr (1970). In addition to the frustration-aggression theory, the relative deprivation theory draws upon Leon Festinger's social comparison theory, the work on adaptation level of H. Helson, and the work on comparison levels of J. W. Thibaut and H. H. Kelley.

Deprivation is a necessary but not a sufficient condition. So long as the relatively deprived persons blame their deprivation on internal factors (their own inadequacies) or on nonpolitical factors (acts of the deity), the deprivation will not be turned into politically relevant frustrations and grievances. Consequently, a change in attitudes or attributions through interaction with more sophisticated ideologues or through new political socialization is necessary, as well as a state of relative deprivation, in order to produce nonconventional or revolutionary political behavior.

John B. McConahay

Population Control

In the period after 1500, expansion of the population took place. This resulted partly from a reduction in mortality, due to the remission of epidemic diseases—some like leprosy and bubonic plague through natural causes, others like smallpox, cholera, and typhus through the advance of medicine and sanitation. Other contributing causes were a general improvement in climate, expanded commerce, and diffusion of new foodstuffs, such as maize and potatoes. After this expansion, a second stage of the demographic transition occurred, characterized by a decline of the birthrate, at least in the industrialized nations, which led to a balance in birth and death—at a high level of population.

The rapid population increase in the first stage of the demographic transition has resulted for the first time in a threat of worldwide overpopulation; for many reasons the biological balance has been disturbed. The psychological contribution to population control seems to be limited, and its practical applications are most important in helping conduct programs and implementing remedial action.

Kurt W. Back

Postdoctoral Education and Training in Psychology

Postdoctoral education and training in psychology is multifaceted: it can be described as education and training occurring after attainment of the doctoral degree for the purpose of enhancing one's knowledge and/or skills in practice, research, teaching, consultation, or administration.

Need for Postdoctoral Education
The flood of information and knowledge in psychology in recent years has made it obvious that no one person can master knowledge in all of psychology, and that lifelong learning is required to update the particular knowledge and/or skills related to particular specialties.

Retreading
Retreading is a term used to describe those psychologists who wish to change from teaching-research to applied activities in psychology. Postgraduate education and training is sought by individuals with doctorates in other areas of psychology who wish to become clinical psychologists. Such individuals return to a university graduate department or to a professional school of psychology for additional course work and supervised practicum training equivalent to that of the clinical psychologist. Postdoctoral education and training for the development of new knowledge and the updating of knowledge or skills in a particular area of psychology can take many forms. For example, it includes programs of self-study, continuing-education workshops, supervised practice arrangements, research mentorships, sabbatical study, residency programs for specialized practice, and research fellowships.

Postdoctoral Specialty Training
Over the past four decades, postdoctoral education and training in psychology has not been well defined, even though a number of national doctoral education conferences have discussed it at some length. Variability in definition results from the fact that psychology, as a discipline, has been slow to define clearly what constitutes a specialty in psychology. As a result, many postdoctoral education and training offerings have been labeled specialty training, when in fact they may be simply the application of generic knowledge/skills in psychology to a particular population or problem. There are some exceptions. For example, representatives of clinical neuropsychology have conceptualized a body of knowledge and practice skills that must be acquired before one can be recognized as a practice specialist in that area. Postdoctoral training guidelines for this

specialty call for training to last at least 2 years, to provide at least 50% time in clinical service in a hospital setting with neurological or neurosurgical services or both, and to provide at least 25% time in clinical research. Training should provide both didactic and experiential instruction, can be completed only in a clinical health care setting, and is essentially a combination of neurology and psychology. The attainment of the American Board of Clinical Neuropsychology/American Board of Professional Psychology diploma in clinical neuropsychology is the clearest evidence of competence as a clinical neuropsychologist, providing assurance that all education and training criteria have been met. The conceptualization and specificity of guidelines for clinical neuropsychology (and also clinical health psychology) is somewhat advanced in the specificity of its standards for postdoctoral education and training. There is a continuing need for a taxonomy of fields, specializations, subspecializations, proficiencies, and practice and research competencies in psychology.

Program Definition

Mindful of the many ambiguities, delegates representing leadership in postdoctoral education and training as well as graduate education, credentialing, and professional practice convened a National Conference on Postdoctoral Training in Professional Psychology (APPIC 1992) to develop policy and standards for postdoctoral training. The conferees defined the characteristics of a program so that this could be differentiated from ad hoc, temporary, or short-term training arrangements. Recognizing that preparation for licensure and practice was the focus, the conferees agreed that

> the postdoctoral residency in professional psychology is an organized education and training program that follows the receipt of a doctoral degree based upon a program of study in professional psychology.... The postdoctoral residency is advanced education and training based upon sound scientific and professional foundations. Postdoctoral residencies adhere to established standards of education and training as well as provide opportunities for the development of innovative and creative models of professional practice,

program development, teaching, training, and clinical research. (APPIC 1992, 1)

The American Psychological Association is planning to convene a national conference in 1994 to address training issues in research, teaching, and administration and the complementarity of different formats for postdoctoral education and training.

Growth of Postdoctoral Education and Training

The number of postdoctoral training sites has grown rapidly over the years, from about 22 sites in the early 1960s to hundreds of sites currently. Arthur N. Wiens (1993) cataloged over 500 postdoctoral training offerings in 162 U.S. cities in 41 states, and has reported on a preliminary tabulation of 388 sites. The variety of study and research opportunities in postdoctoral education-training and research settings is impressive. A nonsystematic sampling of the database identified fifty applied and research postdoctoral study areas that are available to the postdoctoral trainee.

Need for Public Information

More must be known about the postdoctoral education and training that exists and how to describe it in some rational way that will let the public know something about psychology and the expertise of a given psychologist. It is anticipated that a comprehensive directory of postdoctoral education and training will help to address this public information need. Such a directory would also show the diversity of knowledge in psychology and help to illustrate how psychology's knowledge base has expanded in its first century.

Arthur N. Wiens

Post-Freudian Psychoanalytic Theories

Two strands are prominent amid the many lines of development of psychoanalytic thought: first, the theoretical movement integrating object relations theory with preoedipal development; second, the challenge to metapsychology as a foundation for psychoanalysis. Thus, we find H. Kohut, O. F. Kernberg, Margaret S. Mahler, and H. W. Loewald making major restatements of their theoretical positions.

Stone

L. Stone chides analysts for what he perceives as their paradoxical resistance to change in a field devoted to such ambitious change-oriented goals. He emphasizes the need to adapt analysis so that it might focus its energies more effectively on newer, more complex, and more difficult syndromes. These conditions are embedded in difficult life circumstances and are more perverse and narcissistic in nature.

Kohut (*see* Kohut's Self-Psychology)

Kernberg

O. F. Kernberg defines object relations theory and its place in psychoanalytic theory. He reiterates the position that object relations theory focuses on the processes of internalization of self/other relations commencing in the earliest object psychic states. Kernberg maintains that object relations theory is not of the same order of theory building as the classic metapsychological points of view. The object relations theory occupies an intermediate theoretical space between metapsychological exposition on the one hand and the analyst's immediate clinical understanding of an analysis on the other.

Kernberg emphasizes the presence of unconscious object representations consisting of opposite, contradictory, and conflicting units. These representations underlie manifest areas of neurotic symptoms and character traits. The gradual emergence in an analysis of defense- and impulse-determined object relations may now be managed clinically; the analyst can then remain more neutral, more "analytic," with less regard for oedipal or preoedipal regressive needs of the patient that might seem otherwise to call for analytic parameters.

Parens

H. Parens expands on his own previous attempts to link drive and object relations theory through separation-individuation theory. Parens holds that there is a predetermined unfolding differentiation in the instinctual drives, as psychoanalysts conceptual-

ize the ego and the superego. He postulates that it is an upsurge in aggressive drive activity that thrusts the child from the symbiotic into the separation-individuation phase.

Schafer

R. Schafer's work *A New Language for Psychoanalysis* (1976) raises sharp questions about psychoanalytic metapsychology and invites a good deal of psychoanalytic criticism. This work challenges the basic assumptions of psychoanalysis in much the manner that Stone (1975) had called for. As such, it created an intellectual storm of criticism and advocacy throughout the psychoanalytic literature. Schafer's controversial existential premise is that the person is an agent and, as such, responsible for all that she effects. The person is not, however, responsible for everything that happens to her.

Meissner

According to William W. Meissner (1979), natural-science metaphors permeate Heinz Hartmann's explication of ego functioning. Meissner brings in George Klein's contributions to place Schafer's thinking in a slightly different perspective. He points out how Action language elaborated on Klein's earlier position that psychoanalysis is a science of understanding—of meanings, rationality, and intentionality, rather than biologically derived causalities, vectors, and energies.

Brenner

Charles Brenner (1980) addresses the problem of the confused meanings attached to the term *metapsychology*. He also voices his disagreement with critics who wish to separate psychoanalysis from its base as a "natural science." Brenner reviews Freud's initial definitions and usages of the term *metapsychology*, that is, as a structural theory of the agencies of the psyche and the functioning of the psyche. Brenner feels that Freud's meaning remained constant from the time of the introduction of the term in 1901—that is, the psychology of unconscious mental processes, a synonym for psychoanalytic theory or psychology.

Lampl–de Groot

J. Lampl–de Groot cautions, in working with children, against investing too much attention on ego disturbances and deviations at the expense of the child's primarily instinctual conflicts. Lampl–de Groot has found her perception of the child's inner world, derived from direct work with children, particularly valuable in understanding the normal and pathological vicissitudes of narcissism in adults.

Loewald

In reviewing the Oedipus complex from the point of view of "parricide," parent murder by the child, H. W. Loewald points out that this aspect of the Oedipus complex is the obverse of the castration threat that the father poses to the boy child. Parricide in the psychic realm is a necessary aspect of the oedipal dissolution. The result is that the person becomes responsible for his or her actions. This leads to a recreating of the renounced and mourned oedipal dynamics in nonincestuous love relationships.

T. Wayne Downey

Post–Traumatic Stress Disorder (PTSD)

Theories of Psychological Trauma

In 1893, Sigmund Freud held that neurosis was caused by traumatizing psychic events, characterized by actual sexual violation of a child by an adult. Freud, however, gradually departed from the actualized reality theory as causative agent in favor of a fantasy process theory. Thus, his new position was that children's repressed, affect-charged sights, sounds, and other stimuli associated with the primal scene (or parental sexual encounter) were buried in the unconscious mind, where they created patterns of pathogenic fantasy. The sexual victimization episode, then, was "traumatic" only because the pathogenic fantasy was thrust into consciousness, which mobilized defenses against awareness.

Classical conditioning is learning fear by association. In traumatic situations the sympathetic nervous system is hyperaroused (or "learning primed"), and a population of cues associated with the aversive traumatic event in the surrounding vicinity become conditioned—sounds, persons with specific features, time of year, and atmospheric conditions (such as temperature). Any of these cues can later reactivate dissociated ideas and affects. D. H. Mowrer's two-factor theory predicts that such cues generate instrumental learning—a process to avoid memory- and affect-triggering stimuli.

The cognitive-dynamic theory comes chiefly from E. Horowitz's (1986) information-processing model. He holds that in trauma massive amounts of information (i.e., memories, affects, thoughts, and other trauma-conditioned stimuli) create a psychic overload because the information is in a nonmetabolizable state, which is pathologically organized around avoidance, denial, and numbing to bury affective pain and disorganization. He explains that the trauma information does not match pretraumatic internal models of the self (or cognitive schemas), which sets into motion a "completion tendency" (akin to Sigmund Freud's concept of repetition compulsion). This tendency involves the cognitive processing of the traumatic psychic information that gradually leads to congruence between posttraumatic unstable models and inner stable pretraumatic models of self. Mastery and recovery are facilitated by the biphasic mechanisms of intrusion and numbing.

A psychophysiological theory of post-traumatic stress is postulated by L. de la Pena (1984). He holds that PTSD may be a brain-modulated, compensatory information-augmenting response. Viewing the CNS as an information-processing system, de la Pena postulates that traumatized veterans, having been accustomed to the "information-rich" environment of combat, now experience low levels of arousal as boredom and as sensory deprivation. Such PTSD symptoms as hypervigilance, impulsivity, nightmares, and insomnia are understood as manifestations of "maladaptive information-augmenting mechanisms by which the understimulated, bored brain attempts to rectify its aberrantly low information flow rates to higher . . . levels" (117).

The Diagnosis of Post-Traumatic Stress Disorder

Post-traumatic stress disorder is perhaps best described as a biopsychobehavioral condition due to pervasive alterations and impairments in CNS regu-

TABLE 1
The Biopsychobehavioral Symptoms of PTSD

Biological Symptoms	Psychological Symptoms	Behavioral Symptoms
exaggerated startle response	cognitive confusion	interpersonal isolation and
sleep disturbance/insomnia	dreams and nightmares	schizoidal retreat
circadian rhythm disturbance	dissociative experiences	avoidance of people and
nausea	concentration problems	environmental structures
hyperventilation	memory impairment	reminiscent of the traumatic event
dizziness	concentration deficits	self-destructive behavior
palpitations	catastrophic expectations	impulsivity/"action junkie"
tremulousness	self-abusing ideas	sensation-seeking
	guilt feelings	
	low self-esteem	
	sense of incompetence to live	
	sense of unworthiness of life	
	sense of insecurity and generalized distrust	
	feelings of retaliation	
	rage	
	fear	
	anxiety	
	low tolerance for frustration	
	hypervigilance and irritability	
	impoverished capacity for attachment	
	defensive posture against threat or "return of the dissociated"	
	learned helplessness	
	impoverished capacity for affect tolerance	

lation, in cognitive and perceptual control, and in social functioning. It has been "associated with forensic, social and welfare policy issues . . . [and] has been used successfully in criminal defense" (Orner 1992, 387). The term *trauma* means "wound," and *stress*, an engineering term, refers to tension, strain, and intense pressure, which may come from physical, psychic, and sociocultural forces. Stress responses may be seen on a continuum: instrumental stress, by which is meant stress essential for health and general well-being; detrimental stress, which leads to chronic fatigue syndrome (L. Krupp, W. Mendelson, and R. Friedman 1991) and creates changes that affect health and produce disease progression; and traumatic stress, which leads to a state of emergency-physiological arousal, to a profound sense of persistent threat, and to PTSD.

In the aftermath of trauma, fear-dominated cogni-

tive appraisal mobilizes coping strategies to handle the challenge, threat, or danger experienced by the trauma-surviving person. The effect of stress on the individual's mental and physical well-being was originally documented by Hans Selye (1936, 1956), who defined *stress* as "the nonspecific (that is, common) result of any demand on the body." His "general adaptational syndrome" has set the groundwork for contemporary approaches to understanding the biological-conditioning aspects of PTSD.

Table 1 shows the multidimensional nature of the trauma response.

NATURE AND INTENSITY OF
THE TRAUMATIC STRESSOR
PTSD is a result of a violent assault from natural, technological, or human-engineered stimuli upon a victim's psychological organization and physical integrity. The overwhelming, toxic stimuli, whose

occurrence was too rapid and impact too shocking to integrate at the moment of impact, is called the stressor. The stressor (or criterion A) is necessary for the diagnosis (though not sufficient), because "The nature and intensity of the stressor is seen as the primary etiological factor in individual differences in response to stress" (B. Green et. al. 1985, 407). PTSD can occur at any age, with young children and the elderly being most vulnerable. The causative agent (stressor) may be experienced as mild, moderate, or severe. Human-engineered stressors (e.g., rape, incest, and technological mishaps) appear to be more devastating to the survivor than naturally occurring events (tornadoes, hurricanes, etc.).

In discussing the generic dimensions of the requisite stressor for PTSD, B. Green (1993) highlights the crucial factors that operate singly or in combination to make events traumatic. These are: (1) threat to life and limb; (2) severe physical harm or injury; (3) receipt of intentional injury/harm; (4) exposure to the grotesque; (5) violent/sudden loss of a loved one; (6) witnessing or learning of violence to a loved one; (7) learning of exposure to a noxious agent; and (8) causing death or severe harm to another (138).

People meet the requisite stressor criteria when they are exposed to tragic events, such as war stress (J. O. Brende and E. R. Parson 1985), disasters, criminal assaults (M. Bard and D. Sangrey 1986), terrorism (F. Ochberg 1978), hostage situations, severe burn injuries (D. Patterson et al. 1993), rape and incest (R. Ullman and D. Brothers 1989), hurricanes (R. Scurfield et al. 1993), and interparental murder and community violence.

Criterion A (the stressor) is particularly controversial with regard to DSM-III: "PTSD is an anomaly in DSM III in that it is one of only a few disorders that focus on etiology" (B. Green et al. 1985, 407). N. Breslau and G. Davis (1987) have challenged the validity of linking a specific class of psychological responses with a distinct class of stressors, while others (S. Solomon and G. Canino 1990) question the appropriateness of the requirement that the stressor be "outside the range of usual human experience." Though to date no "gold standard" for PTSD exists due to an absence of general agreement among clini-

cians and social and behavioral scientists on reliable and valid measurement procedures and instruments (R. Gerardi et al. 1989), significant progress has been made in increasing precision in measuring the stressor criterion (T. Keane et al. 1989), and validating the diagnosis of PTSD (T. Keane et al. 1988; K. Nadir et al. 1990; J. Shore 1986; S. Silver and W. G. Iacono 1984).

Overall, the more stressful the event, the more people will be expected to succumb to traumatic responses, and if the stressor gets even more severe all persons will "break down" (F. Hocking 1970).

INTRUSIVE-REEXPERIENCING PHENOMENA

Relived experiences are reminiscent of the original trauma in the form of painful images, memories, ideas, feelings (e.g., repetitive play in children in which aspects of the trauma are reenacted in dreams and behavior), nightmares, and night terror, accompanied by pangs of anxiety, arousal, and related mental disorganization. Intrusive-reexperiencing phenomena are the cardinal and most dramatic features of PTSD, and may be accompanied by a state of altered consciousness and amnesia. M. Horowitz et al. (1980) found that 75% of traumatic stress patients he studied showed intrusive ideation, while S. Madakasira and K. O'Brien (1987) found intrusive reactions in a sample of 116 victims of a natural disaster.

A. McFarlane (1992) theorizes that intrusive ideation may be a marker for predisorder psychological distress rather than evidence of psychopathology. He finds that intrusive-reexperiencing phenomena serve an intervening role between exposure to trauma and the onset of disorder symptomatology.

Freud (1900) believed that the dream is the "royal road" by which the clinician can access the patient's unconscious life. In PTSD, E. R. Parson (1986) notes that dreams are the the royal road to the traumatic event. Freud (1920) was fascinated by the tendency of traumatic dreams and nightmares to reproduce an exact replica of the event as it happened. For Carl Jung, "the typical traumatic affect is represented in dreams as a wild and dangerous animal—a striking illustration of its autonomous nature when split off from consciousness" (quoted in Schwartz 1984, 18).

Alan Brown (1920), Abraham Kardiner (1941), and Sandor Rado (1942) have found that post-traumatic dreams and nightmares are core elements of traumatic neurosis. Kardiner's (1959) clinical observations and research led him to the conclusion that post-traumatic nightmares are "the most universal earmark of the traumatic syndrome," and that "these constant dreams of the failure to consummate successful actions are, in fact, the key to the pathology" (249). One implication for therapy arising out of "the failure to consummate successful actions," in dreams and in life, is the use of cognitive procedures and behavioral programs of care.

AVOIDANCE PHENOMENA

Robert Lifton (1967) uses the term "psychic numbing" for the persistent avoidance and numbing to the external world seen in victims, who have diminished interest in other people, in places, and in things. This adversely affects emotional investments in self, family, friends, community, nation, and, for those seeking assistance, in therapy.

In terms of post-traumatic symptomatology among Holocaust survivors, W. Netherland's (1968) observation of the "robotlike numbness . . . a sordid-looking, emaciated, puppetlike appearance" (67) is a powerful example of constriction and avoidance. Likewise, J. A. M. Meerloo finds that survivors show a numbed demeanor marked by "apathetic indifference, estrangement, and blunting of affects" (67).

M. Horowitz et al. (1980) report that 65% of trauma patients suffer numbing responses, while R. J. McFarlane has found that the "intensity of the intrusive memories" predicted avoidance among a group of traumatized firefighters in Australia. S. Madakasira and K. O'Brien (1987) found that 61% of their sample of tornado victims had memory impairment, and 57% felt estranged (443).

NEUROPHYSIOLOGICAL RESPONSES

A. Kardiner's clinical and scientific observations convince him that "the nucleus of the neurosis [that is, PTSD] is a 'physioneurosis'" (A. Kardiner and

D. Spiegel 1947). CNS-intensive responses accompany PTSD: "Since the brain is the target organ of environmental events, it is through this impact on the brain itself that feelings, thoughts, and behaviors, basic brain functions, are changed" (Ursano et al. 1992, 756). In PTSD, the sense of the world as safe, predictable, and rational is lost; the victim gropes in the "dark terror of insecurity," perpetually geared up for defensive action—an innate preparatory conditioned reflexive stance (Pavlov 1927/1960), Dobbs and Wilson (1960) and Maier and Seligman (1976) have discovered in their work with animal models and with human subjects.

R. Pitman (1993) argues that victims' post-traumatic responses cannot be explained in terms of conditioning alone. He reviewed Adamec's studies using animal models with felines to demonstrate that individual differences in relative strength of defensive responses to external threat are observed from birth, due to specific bias in neural transmission of stimuli to various brain centers.

PTSD sufferers have very little tolerance for psychophysiological arousal. Most studies have found autonomic arousal, and related post-traumatic conditions, such as startle reactions, explosive outbursts, sleep disturbance, cognitive dysfunctions (i.e., memory and concentration problems), rage, irritability, and hypervigilance, to be associated to chronic "adrenergic hypersensitivity" (van der Kolk et al. 1985). For example, S. Madakasira and K. O'Brien (1987) found that 81% of their sample of stressed survivors had startle reactions; 66%, concentration difficulties; 61%, impaired memory; while 68% became distressed at reminders of the disaster.

Physiological reactivity to situations resembling or symbolizing the traumatic event is a widely reported phenomenon in PTSD patients (e.g., E. Blanchard et al. 1983). Other studies have shown significant neurochemical changes in PTSD patients (T. Kosten et. al. 1987; J. Mason et al. 1990) compared to controls in some studies.

ONSET VARIABLES: COURSE OF THE DISORDER

During the chronic stage of traumatic reactions, the victim continues to live in an emotional climate of fear and affective intensity, which is reminiscent of the original event. This pattern may traverse the entire life cycle if viable interventions that aid integration are not available to the patient. The subterranean, latent biopsychic reactions may appear quiescent; however, they often threaten to erupt into affective and actional volatility.

PTSD in Children

The dynamics of PTSD are being applied to the clinical problems of children who suffer the aftermath of violence in the inner cities (E. R. Parson 1993a), kidnapping (L. Terr 1983), sexual victimization (S. Eth and R. Pynoos 1985).

Epidemiology

A national survey of veterans showed that 15% of males and almost 9% of women who served in Vietnam had combat-related PTSD (R. Kulka et al., 1990). When ethnocultural factors were introduced, African-Americans represented almost 20% of the cases and Hispanic-Americans almost 29%. L. Craine et al. (1988) found 66% PTSD prevalence rate among women with a history of sexual abuse, and patients with this history were positive for compulsive sexual behavior, chemical dependency, sadomasochistic sexual fantasy, sexual identity issues, chronic fatigue, and loss of interest in sex. S. Madakasira and K. O'Brien (1987) found that 59% of their sample had acute PTSD in the aftermath of a tornado disaster in northeastern South Carolina.

J. Helzer and associates (1987) found a PTSD prevalence rate of 1 to 2% in the general population. This estimate is believed to be low, particularly when the dramatic and widely reported increase in rates of traumatic injuries through crimes against women and children, motor vehicle accidents (A. Burstein 1989), eyewitness violence trauma in adults (C. Raymond 1988) and in children (E. R. Parson 1993), and others are added.

Associated Diagnoses and Differential Diagnosis

Misdiagnosis of trauma victims may still be a clinical problem in many cases. Psychologists and psychiatrists may confound PTSD with a number of other diagnostic entities. Even when the diagnosis of PTSD is given appropriately to a person, the diagnostician engages in differential diagnostic work. Conditions that create vulnerability to PTSD and those that accompany PTSD when it is truly present include psychiatric conditions such as anxiety disorders, panic disorders, social phobia, adjustment disorders, psychosomatic disorders, somatoform disorders, drug abuse, alcoholism, organic mental syndrome, depression and other affective disorders, passive-aggressive personality, schizoid personality, sociopathic personality, and organic brain syndromes, as well as borderline personality disorder. PTSD has been associated with the other dissociative disorder, multiple personality disorder (MPD) (B. Braun 1993).

Vulnerability

H. Resnick et al. (1992) have found that victims of crime stress may have been vulnerable to development of PTSD because of prior depression. Clinical and research evidence reveals that vulnerability to PTSD derives from a number of sources: biogenetic predisposition; prior traumatization/victimization; early and later severe deprivation in childhood; prior psychiatric illness; poor personality integration; developmental failures or arrests; and nature of available social support system. Pretrauma variables, such as introversion, neuroticism, and family psychiatric illness, were also found to be high risk factors for PTSD in a sample of firefighters (A. McFarlane 1988). Young children and the elderly appear to be particularly vulnerable to the development of PTSD.

Assessing the Trauma Victim

The post-traumatic damage to self processes generated by PTSD requires comprehensibility in assessment to discover the role both pretrauma and trauma factors play in the victim's clinical presentation and general functioning. Assessment begins with establishing rapport with the victim/survivor and a thorough screening to determine the nature of the stressor, degree of exposure, symptomatology, and level of disability. Did the trauma occur a month, 6 months, a year, or 10 years ago or more? Was the trauma person-perpetrated or an act of God? How much toll has chronicity taken upon the basic personality of the victim?

A mental status examination assesses the degree of general mental impairment, to include the presence of hallucinations, delusions, and impaired sensory, perceptual, intellectual, and visual-motor abilities. Assessing the victim's social networks and their density is also important. As symptoms worsen, victims may withdraw in silent hypervigilance, with an irritable mood that can adversely affect marriage, friendships, relatives, and work peers. Therapy may involve strengthening family ties. Assessment procedures include psychodiagnostic instruments such as the Bender-Gestalt and WAIS-R, as well as the projective techniques of the TAT, Rorschach, and the House-Tree-Person. Additionally, the Minnesota Multiphasic Personality Inventory–Post-Traumatic Stress Disorder (MMPI-PTSD) subscale, the Impact of Events Scale (IES; M. Horowitz et al. 1979), and a structured clinical interview schedule such as the Structured Clinical Interview of the DSM III-R (SCID; R. Spitzer et al. 1987) are essential for comprehensibility of assessment.

Management

The clinical management of PTSD involves a form of intervention this author refers to as "intertechnical therapy" (InTT). This refers to the application of multiple theories or schools of psychotherapy integrated into an instrumental set of procedures to address the trauma patient's needs comprehensively (E. R. Parson 1984, 1988). This model, therefore, includes cognitive, psychodynamic, behavioral, and humanistic types of therapy. The approach also incorporates the principles connected to P. Lang's bioinformational theory, which highlights the aligning of the stimulus, response, and cognitive interpretive processes in the immediacy of the treatment. Also important for some victims are occupational and social therapies for disrupted work capabilities and anxious social functioning.

Experience shows that the pervasive traumatic rupturing of self processes requires a broad spectrum of techniques that work together for the victim

or patient (hence, "intertechnical"). Probably no one school of therapy or single set of intervention principles may suffice for trauma victims.

Ideally, prevention of exposure to overwhelming events would forestall the well-known pervasive impairments that attend biopsychic trauma. However, if trauma does strike, the second ideal situation is the beginning of brief therapy or other interventions as early as possible during the initial normal stress-recovery process. The more chronic the disorder, the more problematic the character formations that develop that prevent the ultimate working through of the trauma.

INTERTECHNICAL THERAPY (INTT)
Longitudinal, controlled studies on the effectiveness of therapy and psychopharmacological interventions are few and often inconclusive. Until better studies are available, a few professional therapists have advanced their views on the psychotherapy of trauma victims. InTT is victim-focused and relies heavily upon relational elements of the therapy. The goals of InTT are either to prevent symptoms from reaching the chronic stage or to forestall the downward spiraling from chronic into severe borderline and psychotically malignant forms of PTSD due to excessive biopsychic arousal, "compulsion to repeat trauma" (M. Horowitz 1972), and affective constriction; ameliorate or prevent chronic numbing responses (splitting and related dissociative defenses); and to lay a solid foundation for brief or long-term psychotherapy to work through trauma elements and increase self-esteem.

This model uses specific techniques to address each major symptom of PTSD, and may be applied to the treatment of children with post-traumatic stress disorder (Fredericks 1985; Parson 1993). The model espouses a multiphasic diversiform process. The phases are (1) shielding, (2) stability, (3) exposure, (4) mastery, and (5) reintegration.

Since trauma involves startle, surprise, and intense sensory input and assault, the shielding phase of therapy serves a protective function against overstimulation and promotes a sense of safety and security. This marks the patient's first lesson in "putting affect into words" (Breuer and Freud 1893/1955), which continues throughout the phases of InTT.

Modulation of noradrenergic hypersensitivity is important because it is associated with the dissociative sense of "falling apart."

Safety, as found in an empathic selfobject alliance with the therapist, is geared to controlling the victim's fear, terror, and paranoid apprehensiveness. This phase also employs an introduction to a psychotherapy (pretherapy) subphase that gives patients the opportunity to make informed decisions about beginning therapy (e.g., Omer 1985). This often accelerates positive expectancy and gains in psychological-mindedness (Paolino 1982).

Techniques used derive from psychodynamic theory governing safety elements and affectional bonding (J. Bowlby 1977) in the therapeutic relationship; reassurance; hope; cognitive, behavioral, and drug management of problematic memories; and the patient's struggle for internal calm and need to mobilize hypervigilant defenses (Janis 1958; Janis and Leventhal 1968).

Lithium has been used for post-traumatic impulsiveness and mood dysregulation, while carbamazepine offers relief from dissociative events like flashbacks, and propranolol or clonidine have helped veterans with explosive tendencies. Benzodiazepines have been applied successfully in managing chronic anxiety. For many patients, psychopharmacological therapy helps to make them more amenable to psychotherapy by reducing biopsychobehavioral avoidance mechanisms. InTT espouses the integration of psychodynamic, psychosocial, and neurophysiological processes in treatment (G. Gabbard 1992).

The second phase, stabilization, continues restoring inner sense of stability and coping, a beginning of a sense of mastery over perceived "failure to consummate action" (Kardiner 1959) and over internal eruptions of memory and affects, while increasing self-esteem. Cognitive and behavioral techniques are employed, such as homework assignments, bibliotherapy, psychoeducational procedures, "eye movement desensitization" (EMDR; Shapiro 1989; Wolpe and Abrams 1991), stress management, and altering maladaptive cognition through cognitive restructuring (Beck 1976; Ellis 1962). The patient is to be adequately prepared for phase three, exposure, through a number of cognitive and behavioral techniques (e.g., Keane et al. 1985).

The third phase consists of a number of regressive techniques (J. O. Brende and E. R. McCann 1984) that are essential in InTT technology; for example, meditation, in vivo therapy, or systematic reexposure to traumatic stimuli (through films, other trauma-memory activators, such as the "helicopter ride therapy" [R. Scurfield et al. 1992], imagery, implosive therapy, etc.), self-hypnosis, and hypnotherapy. "Returning to the scene of the trauma," like other regressive techniques (Brende and McCann 1984; Parson 1984), fosters the very needed cathartic discharge that aids psychic integration, ameliorates "malignant memories" (Schwartz and Kowalski 1992), and retrieves "lost emotions" (Brende and Parson 1985; Parson 1993b). Systematic flooding and direct exposure techniques are employed by many practitioners to reduce anxiety across traumatic memories (Fairbanks et al. 1982; P. Boudewyns et al. 1990).

The fourth phase, mastery, involves the primary use of dynamic techniques and cognitive procedures to build self-esteem and self-efficacy (A. Bandura 1977) through self-monitoring (Arnow et al. 1985) and selfobjectal models (in terms of ideals and control). Working through what Krystal (1984) refers to as "human emotional damages" (as a consequence of trauma) involving shame and guilt (Parson 1984; Schwartz 1984; Wong and Cook 1992) helps the patient to achieve a greater capacity for self-responsibility (Globus 1986).

The fifth phase, reintegration, proceeds with dynamic technique to work through pathological identifications, trauma-born narcissism, and varying degrees of dissociative cognitions and affects. As with previous phases, many themes of the trauma will be repetitively reintroduced into the therapy to gain increased insight, mastery, and integration. Freud (1914, 1920) has recognized the importance of thematic-dynamic repetitiveness in therapy to aid integration after trauma, and S. Ferenczi (1924/1980) believes that the "patient must live through the same or a similar phantasy several times till a modicum of insight remains" (71).

Erwin Randolph Parson

Power and Acceptance Theory

The power and acceptance theory of social relations was developed by Benjamin B. Wolman. The theory presents certain aspects of social relations as a function of two determinants: (1) power, defined as the ability to satisfy needs; and (2) acceptance, defined as the willingness to do so. Another term is the concept of "need", which Wolman defines as a "factor necessary for survival" (1974, 151).

Wolman roots power and acceptance theory in a view of child development. The child early distinguishes between people who can satisfy her needs or deprive her of satisfaction (such people have power and are considered strong) and those who can neither satisfy nor deprive her of satisfaction (such people do not have power and are considered weak).

The child further distinguishes between those who are willing to help him (friendly persons) and those who refuse to help him (hostile persons).

Groups can be divided into types on the basis of Wolman's concepts.

1. Instrumental groups (I), in which individuals simply have their needs satisfied by others. Acceptance may be minimally required; a business association is a paradigmatic instance.
2. Mutual groups (M), in which people intend to both give and get power and acceptance; paradigmatic instances are friendship and marriage.
3. Vectorial groups (V), in which people have the objective of satisfying the needs of others. There is an interest in giving without taking; the mother's relation to the child may be considered an example.

Wolman uses the ideas concerning power and acceptance to construct a two-dimensional classification of sociogenic mental disorders. One dimension depends upon the notion that there are levels of mental disorder, beginning with neurosis, extending through character neurosis, latent psychosis, and manifest psychosis, and ending with dementia (collapse of personality structure).

The other dimension, at right angles to the first, consists of three types of mental disorder: hyperinstrumentalism, dysmutualism, and hypervectorialism. The hyperinstrumental type of mentally disturbed individual is a taker, and corresponds to what has often been called a psychopath or sociopath. The hypervectorial type, on the other hand, is giving, even in situations in which people usually take; this type covers all that has been called schizophrenia and related conditions. The third type, the dysmutual, is highly inconsistent in that sometimes he overdoes in giving while at other times he overdoes in taking; a classic instance of this type of disorder is what has been called the manic-depressive.

Harvey London

Power Motivation

David McClelland, in *The Achieving Society* (1961), focuses on high power motivation as a force in a culture that spawns totalitarianism.

Measuring individual differences in the level of power motivation occurs implicitly in three personality scales using objective questionnaire items: the Authoritarianism Scale in *The Authoritarian Personality* (1950) measures agreement with authoritative value statements that express intolerance of dissidents and deviants; the Internal-External Control of Reinforcement Scale (J. B. Rotter 1966) measures a person's feelings of being able to influence her environment; and the Machiavellianism Scale (R. Christie and F. L. Geis 1970) measures preferences for power strategies in interpersonal life.

There have been many social-psychological studies of the situations that arouse power motivation. Jack W. Brehm (1972) reports the arousal of reactance when a person's freedom to decide among alternatives is interfered with by other people. Such interference raises the value of the alternative withheld, an arousal of a primitive power motivation (reactance).

Joseph Veroff

Power, Social

As Sigmund Freud turned his attention to social-psychological variables, social power, explicitly or implicitly, assumed increasing importance in his analyses. Psychoanalytic theory, in turn, contributed toward analyses of power in terms of

1. power and influence occurring without conscious awareness;
2. power and influence as a defense mechanism (for example, the notion of identification with the aggressor as presented by Anna Freud and Bruno Bettelheim); and
3. power and authoritarianism as a personality trait or characteristic.

Alfred Adler first made much of the term, as he focused on the person's "will to power" as a defense against feelings of powerlessness and inferiority. Adler's approach was also adopted by Karen Horney in her analysis of inferiority feelings.

Reinforcement or operant theorists have addressed themselves more specifically to a major variable that affects the probability that a behavior by the agent will lead to a specific behavioral response by the target. They have examined prior patterns of positive and negative reinforcement. A current influence relationship is then a function of whether the agent has rewarded or punished the target for given behavior in the past. The reinforcement approach has a long history in social psychology, going back to Floyd Allport and the imitation studies of Neal Miller and John Dollard and, more recently, Albert Bandura. J. S. Adams and R. K. Romney (1962) have been particularly explicit in applying the B. F. Skinner operant approach to power and authority relationships.

In the study of social power in groups, an important thrust has come from the field-theoretical approach, particularly as developed by Kurt Lewin and, more specifically, by D. S. Cartwright (1965) and J. R. P. French and Bertram H. Raven (1959). This approach emphasizes psychological definition, dynamic analysis in terms of personal needs and tensions, and a comparison of "own" and "induced" forces—the private acceptance of the change by the target versus the continued dependence on the influencing agent.

French and Raven (1959) and Raven (1974) compare six differing types of power, each distinguished in terms of the basis for that power. These types of power can be further grouped according to whether the changed behavior of the target becomes rapidly independent of the agent, and if dependent, whether surveillance by the target is necessary for the change to be maintained. The types of power also differ in terms of attribution for the changed behavior, longevity of change, and the effects on the later interpersonal relationship between target and agent.

1. *Informational power* depends on the persuasive nature of the content of the communication from agent to target and the intrinsic value of the change for the target.
2. *Coercive power* depends for its effectiveness on the agent's ability to mediate punishment for the target, where punishment is threatened if the target does not comply.
3. *Reward power* stems from the agent's ability to mediate rewards, contingent on compliance.

These bases of power do not require surveillance, yet they involve continued dependence of the target upon the influencing agent.

Power may increase one's self-esteem, increase one's prestige in the eyes of third parties as well as the target, and increase feelings of self-efficacy. While it is true that power may increase with higher status, it is also true that power usage may increase status. The exercise of power may lead targets and observers to rate the agent as "strong," and this is often satisfying to the agent (B. B. Wolman 1974).

Bertram H. Raven

Practice and Learning

History of Learning

Building upon the associationistic tradition extending from Aristotle to David Hume, psychological interest in the conditions of practice was crystallized in the eighteenth and nineteenth centuries by the philosophers of English and Scottish empiricism (e.g., David Hartley, Herbert Spencer, and others). Working in the objective tradition of Russian biology, Ivan P. Pavlov and V. M. Bekhterev established the principle of conditioned reflexes through experiments with infrahuman animals trained on elementary tasks in artificial environments.

Edward Lee Thorndike was in the vanguard of this movement, as far as the psychology of learning is concerned. Studying the selective trial-error-and-success behavior of motivated cats, chicks, dogs, fish, and monkeys in some thirty different problem-solving situations, he observed that learned acts appear to be gradually strengthened or weakened as functions of their effects (e.g., success/satisfaction versus failure/annoyance). Skill acquisition, measured by time and error scores, is directly contingent upon feedback events, unmediated by reasoning. Formalized as the law of effect, this empirical generalization may be stated thus: reinforcing or nonreinforcing consequences of an organism's behavior tend, respectively, to increase or decrease the power (e.g., speed, probability) of such activity and, hence, its subsequent learning.

E. R. Guthrie advanced a monistic model of conditioning and learning called the S-R contiguity theory, which represented a clever compromise among Thorndike, Pavlov, and John Broadus Watson. Contiguity is necessary and sufficient to complete the association of R to S in one trial, Guthrie believed. Motivation and reinforcement are less important for habit formation than for behavior; drive maintains activity and determines what movements occur, whereas reward onset simply removes the learner from the stimuli present just beforehand. The last R in a series, therefore, will typically be the one remembered because the changed S protects it from interference. Repetition and reward are required only when the task is complex, involving acts rather than movements, or when learned behavior must be shielded from new associations. Clark L. Hull proposed a pluralistic explanatory system on a grand scale. Known as the S-R reinforcement theory, Hull's system affirms the equal importance of contiguously experienced events in addition to the prin-

ciple of reinforced practice. What is learned, Hull affirms in alliance with Thorndike, is a hypothetical association between an observable S and an overt R, but this habit develops strength gradually, and reward is a necessary condition. To account for the empirical law of effect, he introduces the hypothesis of drive-stimulus reduction as the sine qua non of reinforced habit growth.

From 1945 to the late 1970s, research on the conditions of practice greatly broadened in scope and increased in depth. For the most part, the pursuit of synoptic theories in the classic style of Hull or E. C. Tolman underwent extinction. In its place appeared a few miniature theories or systematic programs of limited applicability (W. K. Estes, N. E. Miller, B. F. Skinner, Kenneth W. Spence, B. J. Underwood) and a veritable explosion of experiments to test specific hypotheses.

Learning and Reinforcement Contingencies

Some psychologists have unearthed further complications in the law of effect. In multiple-choice learning situations—where positive reinforcers are scheduled to occur in a random, unpredictable manner, but with stable average probabilities—subjects tend, with practice, to emit a given disjunctive R in the same percentage of total Rs as the percentage of the total reinforcers that that R can receive.

Learning and Task Characteristics

Although Guthrie, Tolman, and Hull differ on many points, they also believe in the theoretical long-term retention of associations (cognitions, habits), as implied by others since Hartley's time. On this view, which is becoming more credible today, memory is a hypothetically permanent acquired condition of the organism, which is intimately related to learning.

In most psychomotor tasks, speed and accuracy are acquired rapidly during the associative phase, as time and error scores decrease. Tracking, typing, and similar skills usually increase with reinforced practice according to a positive growth function. Thus, the percentage of correct responses ($R\%$) rises with the number of trials (N) from a transfer level (T) and approaches a maximum value (M) at different rates of gain (k). The equation is

$$R\% = M(1 - e^{-kN}) + T$$

Four conventional methods by which the acquisition of verbal skills may be studied are serial, paired-associate, free, and recognition learning. The first two techniques are classical; they are also more structured and better controlled than the last two, largely due to the training and testing methods being continuous. By contrast, in "free" verbal learning, the S items are presented for study either singly or all together, and the trainee must recall or reproduce as many R's as possible in any order after each exposure. Even less demanding is the verbal-recognition procedure, which resembles the free method during the acquisition phase but differs from it when retention is called for, as described above.

Learning and Work Variables

Investigations of the relationships between practice conditions and performance variables and/or effects—like work-rest cycles, R decrements, fatigue, part-versus-whole practicing, vigilance, reactive inhibition, force or information loading, stress, reminiscence, warm-up, time sharing, speed-accuracy tradeoffs, and sustained activity—have been conducted mostly in the domain of psychomotor skills. Three of the classic phenomena of work and rest are practice-distribution effects, reminiscence gains, and warm-up decrements.

Reminiscence, a special kind of heightened recall, is defined technically as a gain in the proficiency of a partially learned R that is attributable to the precurrent conditions of work and rest rather than to extra practice, or even mental rehearsal, during the rest period.

Finally, there is the warm-up phenomenon. This is measured as a dramatically steep and transient further rise in proficiency with practice, which appears during the early phase of each work session, following the initial postrest reminiscence gain. Warming up is needed to overcome the deficit resulting from the immediately preceding rest, hence the term *warm-up decrement*. Skilled musicians and athletes, no less than laboratory neophytes, find that they get "cold" during a break, so when practice is resumed they must spend a little extra time or a few dry-run trials in regaining their optimal performance sets.

That is why baseball hitters and tennis players take practice swings before a game, and why pianists and xylophonists run over their scales before a concert.

Clyde Everett Noble

Praxis Development

Praxis may be defined as an acquired system of coordinated, intentional movements originating during the sensorimotor stage of development, following a course of progressive differentiation and culminating in gestural representation. The acquisition of praxis has long been a subject of interest both to developmental psychologists concerned with symbolic behavior and to neurologists who focus on the clinical significance of the impairment of gestural ability following brain damage.

Early accounts of gestural representation of events or objects consist primarily of naturalistic observations of children engaged in "make-believe" play. The pretended use of an absent object has been noted in children as young as a year and a half.

Jean Piaget (1974) and H. Werner and B. Kaplan (1963) maintain that imitation has its origins in the sensorimotor period of development. However, Piaget speculates that after the sixth stage of sensorimotor intelligence, when imitation no longer requires the presence of a model (i.e., deferred imitation), the imitation becomes internalized. For Werner and Kaplan, this development of deferred imitation is not the end point but only a step in the further development of gestural representation. It is at this point that gesture emerges as a symbolic vehicle. They suggest that, with development, changes occur in accord with the "orthogenetic principle," that is, in the direction of increasing differentiation of the components of the symbol situation.

Five modes of gestural representation have been noted when children are asked to demonstrate the use of a variety of absent playmates. The two modes that typify response of children below the age of 4 years are as follows:

- *deictic behavior*: pointing to the area where the action would take place
- *manipulation of the object of the action*: direct

manipulation of the object of the action without representing the stimulus implement in any way, e.g., rubbing the cheek when asked to show how a razor is used to shave

- *body-part-as-object representation*: the most characteristic mode of representation in 4-year-old children. In this mode, part of the body is recognizably positioned in such a way as to ideally represent the perceptual, formal, and physiognomic properties of the stimulus implement and the characteristic movement that the implement makes; e.g., the index finger, rigidly extended horizontally, vigorously rubs the teeth from side to side as if it were the toothbrush.

Eight-year-old children are noted to position their hand(s) to hold the absent implement, although they are typically unable to use empty space to designate the size of the implement.

By age 12, there is a significant increase in the number of pretended implement-holding responses and a greater articulation of the parts of the implement itself, that is, the length of the implement as well as the diameter of the handle of the implement. In addition, 12-year-old children show an increase in the tendency to represent gesturally, or in pantomime, the context in which the implement would characteristically be utilized.

In normal development a close association exists between symbolic and spatial ability; however, in the dissolution of praxis following brain damage, a dissociation between these components may occur as a function of the cortical area that is damaged. This would suggest that although verbal and gestural behavior may derive from the same sensorimotor substratum, they undergo subsequent, but independent, parallel developmental progressions.

Edith Kaplan

Predatory Behavior

Predation must begin with the locating of prey. For all plant and some animal predators, this involves remaining in one location until a suitable prey approaches (sit-and-wait and filter feeders). The predator then captures and immobilizes the prey, often first luring it closer through the use of structural and behavioral modifications (sign or key stimuli), which make the predator appear to be what it is not. For example, the alligator snapping turtle sits on the bottom of a river with its jaws open, slowly undulating a small wormlike appendage inside its mouth. While they may use such sit-and-wait techniques, animals have an advantage over plants because they can move to areas where the probability of encountering prey is higher; perhaps this is a reason why few plants have become carnivores.

An evolutionary precursor to coordinated group hunting occurs in the coatis, which hunt for small prey, such as lizards, in family bands. While there seems to be no cooperation or sharing, the mere existence of several animals foraging in the same immediate area lessens the probability of a fleeing lizard escaping. Wolves, some other canids, hyenas, and lions combine active location of prey with more or less organized group hunting. Status and social hierarchy, most noticeable in access to the prey after the kill, are intimately involved in these hunts. Organized hunting is often found where the prey is large and potentially dangerous to an individual; however, not all animals killing prey much larger than themselves have evolved organized hunts. Tigers and the large Komodo dragon lizard are clear examples, as are web-building spiders.

The patterning of the behavior components used to overcome and subdue prey are extremely diverse across the animal kingdom. However, there are surprising similarities within and between individuals, and the patterns and topographies are often evolutionarily conservative across genera and families. Hence, the form of predation and its stimulus control, motivation, and neurophysiological correlates are usually sufficient to separate predation from aggression, and modern ethologists abjure the popular confusion between the two (e.g., the "violent" lion). While effective predators often possess "weapons" that make some dangerous to humans (e.g., large cats, poisonous snakes, and spiders), they are often equaled in this respect by vegetarian mammals and invertebrates, who have evolved awesome structures and behaviors used in intraspecific fighting and predator defense. The massive horns of mountain sheep, the tusks of elephants, the kicking of horses, and the stinging of wasps and bees fall into this category. Many predatory animals, because of their lethal weapons, have evolved relatively harmless ritualized forms of combat to settle social disputes. If these are understood, the incidence of injurious encounters with humans can be controlled.

The ontogeny of predatory behavior has often been invoked, and sometimes even studied, in an effort to criticize instinct concepts. If the cat, with all its predatory structural adaptations, is not "instinctively a killer," then the whole notion of innate aggressive behavior is disproven and, with a little social tinkering, the eons of wars and competition will draw to a close. Unfortunately, the ideology involved leads many generally competent minds astray. First, it should be stressed that predatory behavior is not the same as aggression. Second, many animals are born with the behavioral, stimulus, and motivational components of predation already present or maturationally dependent. Young predatory mammals, such as weasels, even before their eyes are open, often respond selectively to odors from prey in the absence of prior experience. Newborn snakes respond to just those prey odors that their species is adapted to eat. Invertebrates and "lower" vertebrates are often viewed (perhaps prematurely) as highly fixed in their prey preferences and predatory behavior. Mammals often do show modifiability, both in the perfection and adaptation of killing sequences and in the relative attractiveness of prey.

Gordon M. Burghardt

Pregnancy: Psychiatric Aspects

Pregnancy is a major developmental transition, which involves biological, psychological, and social changes. During this time and afterward many women may appear more emotionally distressed, but may not meet the criteria for any specific psychiatric illness (Bibring and Valenstein 1976). Mood disorders do occur frequently in the postpartum period in women vulnerable to such conditions, and other mental illnesses may be present during pregnancy and the puerperium (Kumar and Robson 1984; O'Hara 1991; Steiner 1990; Watson et al. 1984).

Mood disorders associated with childbirth have been classified according to severity and timing. "Postpartum blues" is a transient disturbance occurring in 50 to 80% of women, starting within 48 hours of delivery and lasting from a few days to 2 to 3 weeks. It is characterized by emotional lability, anxiety, irritability, crying, insomnia, poor appetite, fatigue, and finally, spontaneous resolution. Women with the most serious blues may go on to develop major depressions. The blues occur cross-culturally, but may be less noticeable in cultures where the new mother is surrounded by supportive family and community members. The etiology is thought to be related to the marked fall in gonadal hormones and role changes. Treatment is usually symptomatic (Gard et al. 1986; Iles et al. 1989; Kuevi et al. 1983; Levy 1987; Pitt 1973; Stein 1982; Stein, Marsh, and Morton 1991).

Postpartum depression is the term used to refer to the mild to moderate depressions that occur in 10% of women in the first weeks to months following the birth of a baby. Diagnosis is based on criteria outlined in the DSM-III-R for major depression. Milder forms are classified as adjustment reaction with depressed mood.

Recent epidemiological studies suggest that occurrence and symptomatology are similar in nonpuerperal controls (O'Hara 1991). As with the blues, etiology is thought to be related to the marked biological changes in the postpartum period, with hormonal effects on central nervous system neurotransmitters interacting with psychosocial stressors in vulnerable individuals who have a past history and family history of depression (Ballinger et al. 1982; Cutrona 1983; George and Sandler 1988; Greenwood and Parker 1984; Handley et al. 1980; Harris et al. 1989). Evaluation must include a careful physical evaluation, including thyroid function. Treatment consists of use of antidepressants, psychotherapy, support groups, and family involvement. Hormones, such as progesterone, have been used in some instances (Dalton 1980), but at this time there are no controlled studies of their effectiveness (Davidson and Robertson 1985; Parry 1992; Pastuszak et al. 1993).

Postpartum psychosis is a relatively rare condition that occurs in 1 to 2 of 1,000 births, usually starting in the first 2 weeks postpartum, but occasionally during the pregnancy (Kendell et al. 1987). These are severe mental illnesses often requiring hospitalization. Seventy-five to 80% are classified as mood disorders, with 60% being depression (Brockington et al. 1981; Gitlin and Pasnau 1989; Kendell et al. 1987). There is thought to be a higher rate of confusion and Schneiderian first-rank symptoms in those with puerperal affective psychoses than in those with nonchildbirth related psychoses (Brockington et al. 1981; Katona 1982). Risk factors include a past history of mental illness, especially bipolar disorder. Women with affective disorders have a 20 to 25% risk of developing a puerperal psychosis (Kendell et al. 1987; Reich and Winokur 1970). Recurrence in subsequent pregnancies is about 34 to 38%, and in nonpuerperal periods, about 50% (Davidson and Robertson 1985; Gitlin and Pasnau 1989). In addition to family history and past history of psychiatric illness, other risk factors may include first pregnancy, cesarean section, and fetal death (Kendell et al. 1987). Etiology is similar to the nonpsychotic major depressions (Handley et al. 1980; Harris et al. 1989; O'Hara 1991). Treatment consists of use of appropriate antipsychotic and antidepressant medications, hospitalization with the baby where possible, and use of electroconvulsive therapy (ECT), which is safer during the pregnancy (Meltzer and Kunar 1985). Patients at high risk for developing puerperal mental illnesses should be followed closely in the first few weeks postpartum with special observation of obsessional thinking, sleep disorder (difficult to judge in new mothers), and feelings of hopelessness and anhedonia. Infanticide and/or suicide are risks in these conditions (Gitlin and Pasnau 1989; Whalley et al. 1982). Schizophrenia may have its onset, exacerbate, or remit during pregnancy and/or the puerperium.

Anxiety disorders, especially those characterized by obsessional thinking about harming the baby, may start during the postpartum period. These may be part of a depressive syndrome or an obsessive-compulsive disorder. Panic reactions may start during pregnancy or after (Crowley and Roy-Byrne 1989; Metz et al. 1988). Treatment with serotonergic reuptake blockers and cognitive therapy may help (Sichel et al. 1993). Disorders of mother-infant rela-

tionship are included in some classifications of puerperal mental disorders. These are delayed attachment, obsessions of hostility to the infant, rejection of the infant, child abuse, and infanticide.

Miriam B. Rosenthal

Prehension in Infancy

Although regularly effective patterns of prehension are uncommon before 4 to 5 months, it has been shown that neonates and very young infants are at times capable of reaching and grasping for objects in space (Bower 1974). Because it is highly unlikely that such behavior could have been learned at this early stage, an innate prehensile program is suggested.

As the development of prehension proceeds, the growth of skill and intention are closely related, and immaturities of one accompany the other. Early, there is slow and uncertain initiation of object reach, together with abortions of reach in midair. Activation responses to visual stimuli, including prolonged gaze, pumping of the arms, and movements of the mouth, frequently fade away or culminate in nonprehensile efforts (e.g., ballistic batting). Reaching, when it occurs, is frequently dysmetric and poorly directed.

Later in infancy, such responses are less common. Beyond 4 to 5 months, infants reach much more promptly and decisively. Movement programs are better related to prehensile objects. In conjunction with smoother movement sequences, infants are more effective in preparing their hands for the requirements of grasp while reaching, and become progressively more capable of retaining objectives in the face of difficulty by altering and restructuring sequences.

Studies of the evolution of contactual and proprioceptive hand and arm reflexes and triggered responses in infancy (T. E. Twitchell 1971) have shown a gradual modification of responses, which could interfere with voluntary prehension (e.g., subsidence of flexor synergy, integration of avoiding reactions), and a gradual development of responses, which might serve it (e.g., fractionation of grasp reflex so that flexion of individual fingers rather than the whole hand is seen; development of the instinctive grasp reaction in which the hand gropes after a retreating tactile stimulus, orients to it, and then grasps it).

Several types of change have been described (J. S. Bruner 1973). With practice, the constituent acts of prehensile programs (e.g., reaching) are modified toward less variability, greater economy and reliability, and freedom from conscious control. Such modularization aids the construction of prehensile sequences.

Deprivation studies present complex problems in extrapolating to normal development but are nevertheless of great interest. Experiments in which 1-day-old monkeys were deprived of the sight of an arm have demonstrated that the opportunity for visual feedback of an actively moving limb during infancy is important for the development of precision in both reaching and grasping (Held and Bauer 1974).

Richard Umansky

Prejudice: Theories

Many researchers have suggested that projection provides the basis for antiblack, anti-Semitic, and other prejudicial attitudes. Support for this view is based on the finding that stereotypes of several very different groups show the same components: a belief that the group is immoral, dirty, and aggressively inclined. The assumption has been, then, that some individuals habitually use projection, and that these personalities exhibit correspondingly greater prejudice.

Situational views of prejudice have examined the particular nature of intergroup relations. Foremost among these theories are those that stress economic or political conflict. For example, in times of economic recession, groups in direct competition with each other for jobs and resources feel heightened hostility. Likewise, in times of war, sentiment against members of the other side runs high, as in the anti–Japanese-American measures of World War II.

Often, the mere perception of a group difference is sufficient to evoke hostility or fear. Donald Hebb has stressed this xenophobic reaction among animals to variations in their species. On the human level, Milton Rokeach has suggested that recognition of an ethnic or racial difference may lead to the assumption of belief dissimilarity, and that it is this assumed belief dissimilarity that generates hostility. A number of researchers have attempted to demonstrate that belief dissimilarity is more influential than racial dissimilarity in manifestations of prejudice.

James M. Jones
Shelley E. Taylor

Prenatal Influences on Personality Development

The research literature describes countless examples of prenatal influence on physical development; fewer studies have been done on the influence on personality and psychological development.

S. A. Mednick and his collaborators (1975) studied the offspring of 200 schizophrenic women in Denmark and found that a history of perinatal birth complications is a good predictor of which offspring will manifest a psychiatric illness later in life. These investigators hypothesize that adverse conditions within the uterine environment (e.g., biochemical defects, toxemia, long labor) can affect a genetically susceptible and vulnerable offspring.

Women in the high-anxiety group evidenced significantly more negative child-rearing attitudes, obtaining higher scores on measures of both hostility and control.

Anthony Davids

Preventive Psychiatry

Preventive psychiatry is an integral part of the professional practice of general or community psychiatry. As an extension of clinical psychiatry, it cannot be relegated to either purely research-oriented specialists or to the nonpsychiatric professionals in community health programs. The theory and practice of preventive psychiatry rest upon the proposition that mental disorders are multifactorial with respect to both etiology and epidemiology.

As a clinician, the community psychiatrist reduces

psychiatric disorders through clinical forms of prevention; in other community situations, he practices primary prevention in ways that are far different from, but essentially not in conflict with, clinical skills.

An operational definition of preventive psychiatry necessitates administrative centralization of a program that embraces a continuum of integrated services. Comprehensiveness and integration obviously involve the vesting of central responsibility in some sort of community health authority.

The idea of prevention would appear to be foreign to such a comprehensive and clinically oriented spectrum of community mental health services, dealing retrospectively with the social concomitants and sequelae of the gravest mental disorders. On the contrary, however, clinical experiences of such depth and breadth provide the kinds of hindsights that focus the attention of inquisitive clinicians upon the history and course of common mental disorders, that is, upon epidemiological questions and considerations, the answers to which provide at least some clues for prognostication and preventive interventions. If every clinician who makes a diagnostic evaluation were obliged also to make a statement about prognosis, the apparent gulf between clinical hindsight and preventive foresight could be appreciably narrowed. At least, this appears to be the first step in the translation of clinical experience into prevention at the tertiary and secondary levels.

Portia Bell Hume

Prison Behavior

The behavior of all those within the confines of a prison is, to a considerable degree, under the controlling influence of physical and social structural variables. Thus, to understand the pathological consequences of the prison experience, it would seem reasonable to focus more on the general kinds of psychopathology that the prison environment produces in incarcerated people than on the kinds of idiosyncratic pathology that some people may bring into prisons.

Interpersonal relationships are characteristically intense because of the physical proximity, lack of

opportunity of "social escapes," and great potential danger or support every inmate and guard offers to every other. However, this intensity is somewhat tempered by the boredom of long periods of time with little or nothing constructive to do and by the insignificance of daily or weekly events.

The marked changes that can be generated in normal individuals by the experience of imprisonment have been studied in a simulation experiment (C. Haney, A. Banks, and P. G. Zimbardo 1973). This research and other comparable studies on the effects of institutions on the behavior of those confined within them point to the powerful forces that total institutions bring to bear in modifying beliefs, perceptions, values, and behavior. Successful and complete adaptation to such regimented, restricting environments is incompatible with a life of relative freedom in the society outside the institution.

Philip G. Zimbardo
Craig Haney

Problem Solving

Thinking may be undirected, as in fantasy and dreams, or directed, as in problem solving. A problem is a situation in which some difficulty must be overcome in order to reach a goal. Problem solving is the process of overcoming that difficulty.

Insight

For several decades during the first half of the twentieth century, the area of problem solving was a battlefield on which the forces of behaviorism and Gestalt psychology fought for supremacy. The behaviorists John Broadus Watson and Clark L. Hull emphasized the role of learning and insisted that all problem solving could be explained in terms of conditioned reflexes. Responses learned in previous situations were generalized to similar stimuli in the present situation. As unsuccessful responses were extinguished, initially weaker responses were elicited, until one of them terminated the problem and was thereby reinforced for the next occurrence of a similar problem. The Gestalt psychologists (Max Wertheimer, Kurt Koffka, and Wolfgang Köhler) admitted that learning was a factor in problem solving, but they distinguished between simple reproductive solutions to familiar problems and the productive thinking inspired by a truly novel problem that requires an unprecedented response for its solution. It is the latter type of problem that is solved by a spontaneous reorganization of the psychological field, which is essentially a perceptual process.

Two-String Problem

The importance of perceptual factors is demonstrated by N. R. F. Maier's (1931) two-string problem. The task here is to tie two strings together, which are hanging from the ceiling too far apart to be reached at the same time. The solution is to tie a pair of pliers to one string and set it swinging, then to grasp the second string and catch the first when it swings back within reach. Most persons were unable to solve the problem without a hint, but when the experimenter brushed against one string so that it began swinging, they solved it shortly thereafter. The perception of the swinging string produces a reorganization of the perceptual field in which the pliers are seen as a pendulum weight rather than as a tool.

K. Duncker (1935) has introduced the term *functional fixedness* to refer to the difficulty of using an object in an unusual way. In one of his experiments, the problem is to fasten three small candles to a door. The solution is to tack three cardboard boxes to the door as platforms for the candles. Everyone solved the problem when the boxes were empty, but when the boxes were used to hold tacks, candles, and matches, respectively, only 43% of the subjects found the solution. The percentage of solutions fell to 14 when the boxes were filled with buttons. The more committed the boxes are to a different function, the less likely they are to be perceived as part of the solution.

Learning

The behaviorists succeeded in demonstrating the importance of learning in problem solving, but to account for their results they had to complicate their explanations by the addition of intervening variables. Unobservable mediating responses and elaborate habit-family hierarchies were postulated to explain productive thinking. The result was to establish a continuum between trial-and-error and insight

and to blur the distinctions between the learning and the perceptual theories of problem solving.

Cognitive psychology is concerned with human information processing, with the questions of how information is encoded, transformed, stored, retrieved, and used. The classic insight problem has been reexamined from this point of view, and functional fixedness has been shown to be a consequence of how an object is coded.

Cognition

G. J. Groen and J. M. Parkman (1972) have devised an information-processing model for the simple problem of adding two numbers that accounts for the following facts:

1. It takes less time to add two digits that are alike than two digits that are different.
2. The time required to add two equal digits does not increase with the size of the digits.
3. The time required to add two unequal digits increases linearly with the size of the smaller digit.
4. The rate of increase in addition time is much less for college students than for children in first grade.

Heuristics

Problems in arithmetic and in deductive logic are solved by algorithms, which are computational rules that guarantee a solution. Heuristics, in contrast, are plausible operations that offer only the *likelihood* of success. One could hardly play chess by considering all the consequences of every possible move, or solve a seven-letter anagram by inspecting all 5,040 permutations of its letters. It is true that when subjects fail to solve an anagram after looking at it for a few seconds, they do begin to rearrange the letters. But if they actually tried to search through every permutation, solution time would be a steeply accelerated function of the number of letters in the anagram. Ira T. Kaplan and T. Carvellas (1968) have observed, however, that as the number of letters increases from three to ten, solution time does not keep pace with the number of possible permutations. In fact, six-, seven-, and eight-letter anagrams are nearly equal in difficulty, which implies that subjects use their knowledge of word structure to guess at the most probable combinations of letters. R. R. Ronning (1965) has shown that the relative difficulty of five-letter anagrams depends on how many permutations are left after those with improbable beginnings have been eliminated.

Computer simulation is a special type of cognitive theory in which the model is a program that is written to process information the way a person does. The General Problem Solver, whose principal heuristic is means-ends analysis, imitates human problem-solving task environments, where a given situation can be compared with a goal situation to discover one or more differences between them, and where there are operators associated with each difference that may be able to eliminate differences of that kind. It can choose chess moves, solve cryptarithmetic problems, and discover proofs in symbolic logic. A. Newell and H. A. Simon (1972) developed the General Problem Solver by asking subjects to think out loud as they solved problems and then writing the program so that it went through the same steps, considered the same alternatives, and found the same solutions as their subjects.

Ira T. Kaplan

Professional Psychologists: Licensing

Statutory credentialing of psychologists and regulation of the practice of psychology is for the protection of the public. All states and the District of Columbia have enacted laws that would accomplish this purpose (Stigall 1983). Historically, the American Psychological Association (APA) and state psychological associations have advocated statutory recognition of the profession because of the legal status thereby accorded to psychologists, and because of the enhanced opportunity to serve the public. The APA has developed model legislation (American Psychological Association 1987) for state licensure of psychologists.

Some laws include a specific definition of *practice* and limit the practice of psychology to persons credentialed as psychologists. These statutes are referred to as "licensing laws." Other jurisdictions either do not attempt to define *practice* or are circular in declaring that the practice of psychology consists in offering services under the title of "psychologist" or some variant thereof. Strictly speaking, these "certification laws" protect only the use of the title; other persons not certified as psychologists may engage in activities commonly defined as the practice of psychology, so long as they do not refer to themselves as a "psychologist" or their activities as "psychological."

The distinction between licensing and certification is not trivial. The 11th U.S. Circuit Court of Appeals ruled Florida's certification act to be unenforceable on constitutional grounds (Freiberg 1992). The court reasoned that restricting persons from calling themselves a psychologist, while at the same time allowing them to practice psychology, abridges the First Amendment right to freedom of speech. The implication of this ruling appears to be that, if there is a compelling public health reason to regulate a profession, the law must go beyond title protection alone.

Most laws are generic in that they credential persons as psychologists, rather than by specialty or subspecialty. This is consistent with the tradition in other learned professions, such as medicine and law. Psychologists are expected to abide by the ethical guidelines of the profession (American Psychological Association 1992), which affirm they are to practice in accordance with their education, training, and experience.

There are notable exceptions to the rule of generic licensing. The state of Illinois licenses only clinical psychologists. Virginia issues separate licenses for psychologists, clinical psychologists, and school psychologists. Nebraska certifies clinical psychologists who meet the requirements for generic licensing and additionally qualify for the specialty certification. A number of states issue credentials as a "health service provider" in psychology, beyond the generic license. Among these are Indiana, Iowa, Kentucky, Massachusetts, Missouri, and Texas.

Certification of school psychologists by the state education agency, with practice limited to the public school setting, is based upon standards different from those typically required for generic licensing as a psychologist. But school psychologists also are credentialed for independent practice on the basis of separate criteria in the states of Colorado, Florida, Ohio, Virginia, and Wisconsin. California offers a similar license for educational psychologists. In all of these jurisdictions, the educational requirement is either the master's or a specialist degree.

Licensing or certification as a psychologist in most states requires a doctoral degree in psychology, successful performance on written and oral examinations, and a period of postdoctoral, supervised work experience. State boards frequently stipulate that the candidate for licensure must have completed an accredited training program or a program that meets equivalency criteria. A listing of professional training programs and internship programs that meet voluntary standards of accreditation is published annually by the APA.

The Examination for Professional Practice in Psychology (EPPP), developed by the Association of State and Provincial Psychology Boards (ASPPB) and independently scored by the Professional Examination Service, is utilized by a majority of state psychology boards. The EPPP is designed to assess mastery of the knowledge base relevant to entry-level practice as a psychologist.

The modal requirement for supervised work experience is 2 years in duration. A number of state boards allow the predoctoral internship to count for 1 year of qualifying experience. Satisfactory completion of the supervised experience may be a condition of eligibility to sit for the EPPP. Oral examinations are developed locally and often cover knowledge of state law and board regulations governing the practice of psychology.

The majority of states provide for only one level of credentialing, i.e., as a "psychologist." A number also allow for credentialing of subordinate providers of psychological services, with limitations as to both title and scope of practice. These service extenders most often are required to function under the supervision of a fully qualified psychologist, or they may be restricted to employment in certain agency settings, or both limitations may apply. Titles such as "psychological associate" or "psychological examiner" are assigned. The educational requirement for credentialing at this level is almost always the master's degree in psychology. Only Vermont and West

Virginia continue to allow persons with subdoctoral training to be licensed as psychologists and practice independently.

All such laws have exemptions that permit unlicensed persons either to call themselves psychologists or to practice psychology under certain circumstances. For example, university faculty who limit their activities to teaching and research may refer to themselves as psychologists within the context of their academic affiliation. Or members of other licensed professions may engage in activities defined as the practice of psychology, provided they do not misrepresent themselves in their professional capacity. Similar exemptions can be found for graduate students and persons working under supervision and for individuals employed in public schools, government agencies, and charitable institutions.

The professional credentialing and regulatory authority of states is vested by law in a board or agency of state government that is charged with carrying out provisions of the relevant statute(s). Besides discharging their examination and licensing functions, state boards are assigned enforcement responsibilities (Stromberg et al. 1988). This may entail disciplinary functions, including revocation or suspension of a license, or it may involve investigation of complaints against persons not licensed as psychologists who are in violation of the law.

Licensing boards are empowered to issue rules interpreting more general statutory provisions. Once officially promulgated, such rules have the force of law and are used by boards in furtherance of their administrative and regulatory responsibilities. Rules address issues such as standards for supervision of unlicensed assistants or candidates for licensure, definitional criteria for subareas of practice, and continuing education (CE) requirements for renewal of license.

The APA Continuing Education Programs Office conducts periodic surveys of state CE requirements. A recent survey (American Psychological Association 1993) found that twenty-eight states require CE for renewal of license, with most specifying a 2-year cycle for documentation of CE credits. State requirements range from 20 credits (Alaska, Massachusetts, and West Virginia) to 100 credits per biennium

(Kansas). Washington State requires 150 credits every 3 years. The modal requirement is 40 CE credits per biennium, or the equivalent thereof.

Members of state boards typically are appointed by the governor, based upon nominations submitted by the state psychological association. Sometimes, nominations are unrestricted and can come from other sources. Public members, as well as psychologists, may be called for in the law. Board members must meet eligibility criteria specified in statute. The term of office is commonly 3 to 5 years.

The majority of state boards are affiliated with the ASPPB, an organization originally formed in 1961 "as a voluntary affiliation of boards engaged in the certification or licensing of psychologists in the United States and Canada." The chief function of this organization is to serve as a clearinghouse for information exchange among state regulatory bodies and, through its committees and annual meetings, to provide a forum for deliberation around issues of common concern. The ASPPB also conducts surveys and develops positions that help to guide state officials in the formulation of regulatory policy. Perhaps the most visible contribution of the association has been the creation and promotion of a standardized national licensing examination, the EPPP.

Tommy T. Stigall

Professional Psychology

The definition of professional psychology has been the root of considerable controversy, particularly in the last 15 years. In 1977, the American Psychological Association (APA) defined the "professional psychologist" as one who has "a doctoral degree from a regionally accredited university or professional school in a program that is primarily psychological, and appropriate training and experience in the area of service offered" (American Psychological Association 1977, 4). For many reasons this definition met with considerable opposition. The assertion that a provider is qualified to practice solely on the basis of prior formal education and supervised training has troubled those responsible for quality control in the practice of professional psychology, and it

is clear that the APA recognizes the inherent weaknesses of this definition. In their specialty guidelines, it is stated that the APA "strongly encourages and plans to participate in efforts to identify professional practitioner behaviors and job functions, and to validate the relation between these and desired client outcomes" (American Psychological Association 1981).

There have been attempts to define more adequately the scope of professional psychology as well as the nature of the graduate education and training programs best suited to train and evaluate students so as to ensure quality and competence. The National Council of Schools and Programs of Professional Psychology (NCSPPP) has played a major role in delineating those areas of knowledge, attitudes, and skills necessary for the practice of professional psychology. The major emphasis has been on the integrative aspect of education and training. The professional psychologist is neither a scientist nor a technician; the hallmark of the professional psychologist is sound judgment—the skillful selection of techniques based on sound knowledge and ethically applied for the individual patient, group, family, organization, or social institution.

Education and Training

It may be argued that currently there are really only two models used to train professional psychologists: the "scientist-practitioner" model and the "practitioner" model, sometimes referred to as the "scholar-professional" model. Because there is a need for professional psychologists who function primarily in practice roles, as well as for professional psychologists who endeavor to advance the scientific knowledge base of the discipline, both models are appropriate and necessary. Furthermore, the criteria used to accredit training programs need to be differentially applied to programs based on the functional relationship they can demonstrate as existing between the program itself and the roles for which they are preparing their students. Generally, scientist-practitioner programs aim to prepare students to do clinical research, and thus should award a doctor of philosophy (Ph.D.) degree. Scholar-professional programs prepare students for professional practice, and should award a professional degree, the doctor of psychology (Psy.D.). The two degrees are to be considered equal in quality; they simply have different objectives and subsequently different emphases in the kind of education and training.

In the last few years, psychology has increasingly turned its attention to the importance of postdoctoral training initiatives in professional psychology. Currently in most states, requirements for licensing include one year of predoctoral internship and one year of supervised postdoctoral training. A number of organizations, including the Association for Psychology Postdoctoral and Internship Centers (APPIC) and the American Board of Professional Psychology (ABPP), are examining this issue very closely. In addition, the newly formed National College of Professional Psychology (NCPP) is especially interested in postdoctoral training, primarily as it relates to postlicensure specialization or proficiency for marketplace consumption. There is also increasing awareness that professional psychology should not be limited to one of the mental health professions. In the political/health policy sense, professional psychology is one of the health professions. This has important implications for training, and psychology training programs are now seeking inclusion under the various Title VII (Health Professions) initiatives.

Professional Practice

There are a host of serious issues facing the professional psychologist in the practice of her craft today. Among the many problems that must be dealt with by the practitioner are the questions of managed care versus integrated care, national health reform, and prescription privileges.

MANAGED CARE VERSUS INTEGRATED CARE

In the last 30 years, the mental health system has evolved from a network of indemnity programs that fostered high quality mental health care into an era of managed care, which is a system of cost control. Managed care has brought with it a number of problems relating to patient access and the quality of care. Until now, corporate America has focused almost entirely on the exorbitant rises in the cost of mental health care. They have relied on insurance companies and managed care firms to rein in costs, but these entities have failed miserably. In addition, some of the cost-control strategies of managed care—frequent-utilization review and inappropriate limited benefits—have hindered access and reduced treatment.

The American Psychological Association Practice Directorate has introduced a new system called "integrated care." This system, which was developed in close collaboration with corporate and labor leaders, integrates reasonable features of managed care with appropriate new quality of care features and depends upon a close ongoing dialogue among psychologists, patients, and payers. Under integrated care, professional psychologists have the responsibility to communicate to the actual payers the most basic understanding of what professional psychology is, what services can be provided, and how effective are the outcomes. Integrated care also argues that long-term care must be made available to patients in need. There is a recognition of the obvious cost implications of making long-term care available; provision is made for utilization review prior to beginning long-term treatment and prior to any inpatient service.

NATIONAL HEALTH REFORM

Professional psychology is vitally concerned with the issue of health care reform and the impact that it may have not only on professional practice but on all areas of psychology. Indeed, warnings have been sounded not only that mental health services are at risk but also that the very existence of professional psychology is in question. Psychologists are now faced with the biggest threat to their livelihood—the very real possibility that mental health, and professional psychology in particular, may be left out of the national health insurance package soon to be developed. One of the main concerns is that, in an effort to reduce health care costs, national health care will incorporate a managed health care approach despite evidence that HMOs have meant low-quality care. The new generation of managed care, labeled "managed competition," would consist of five or six "accountable health plans," which, as megasystems, would exert complete control over all health care. Such a system could present all of the disadvantages of the current managed care programs on a much grander scale.

PRESCRIPTION PRIVILEGES

One of the more controversial issues facing professional psychology today is the question of prescription privileges. Not surprisingly, physicians have generally been strongly opposed to psychologists having these privileges, although there are non-medical practitioners who currently have them, e.g., optometrists and nurse practitioners. What is of greater interest is the fact that a goodly number of professional psychologists are also in opposition. For one thing, these psychologists are fearful that such privileges will bring about a sharp increase in the cost of malpractice insurance. More significantly, many psychologists are against the awarding of prescription privileges because of their fear that this will radically affect the manner in which patients are treated by the professional psychologist. There is a concern that the holistic, humanistic comprehensive approach will be abandoned in favor of the "quick fix" through the use of medication. What is often forgotten in this argument is that the awarding of prescription privileges will also give the professional psychologist the legal right to decide that a patient should be *taken off* medication.

In any event, if legislation regarding this issue is enacted in the future, it will be essential that psychologists be appropriately trained to prescribe psychotropic medications. This probably can be most easily accomplished by having regional training programs, in collaboration with universities and professional schools, prepare interested psychologists for this function.

A Final Word

As professional psychology has expanded its horizons, there have been corresponding problems. There still continues to be disagreement either about the nature of the field or about the kinds of preparation that psychologists should have for professional work. There appears to be some consensus that what professional psychology has to offer in contrast to many other health professions is a scientific foundation for its professional practice. Whether a program

offers a Ph.D. or a Psy.D., and whether that program is in a university or a freestanding professional school, emphasis must be on scholarship *and* practice.

Professional psychologists recognize that they cannot afford to terminate their training with graduation or shortly thereafter. Competent and ethical professional practice requires that one constantly stay abreast of recent developments in the field to ensure the best services to the public. Only by staying alert to the changing winds, by being aware of the legislative pitfalls, and by acting as a lobbying force on behalf of the profession will psychologists be able to satisfy their obligations to the field of professional psychology and maintain the highest standards of practice.

Jules C. Abrams

The Professional Psychology Internship

The internship is an integral part of doctoral training in professional psychology. Long considered the capstone of professional training, the internship is taking on a new role, bridging general doctoral training with specialty postdoctoral training. The internship is required for a doctorate in clinical, counseling, and school psychology. The American Psychological Association accreditation criteria (American Psychological Association 1986) specify that the internship must follow practicum training and precede the granting of the doctoral degree.

Historical Overview

The importance of internship training in the preparation of professional psychologists was recognized at the Boulder Conference (Raimy 1950). However, standards for internship training developed more slowly than did standards for doctoral education in professional psychology. Doctoral programs were accredited by the American Psychological Association beginning in 1948, while internship programs were not accredited until 1956 (American Psychological Association 1992).

The psychology internship grew out of training programs developed by the Veterans Administration and the military following World War II. These training experiences, or internships within the doctoral program (captive internships), initially were the only options for graduate students. As the practice of psychology developed, increasing numbers of training settings became available to doctoral programs. Some graduate programs used these opportunities to put together their own captive internships, which would provide their students with a variety of clinical experiences. At the same time, increasing numbers of independent internship programs formed, offering trainees a diversity of settings and approaches from which to choose.

While the internship remains an integral part of professional education and training, it is no longer the final step before full functioning as a professional. Virtually all North American jurisdictions require a year of postdoctoral supervised practice prior to licensure, in addition to the predoctoral internship (Stigall et al. 1990). Also, the increasing emphasis on specialization brought about by the burgeoning knowledge base in psychology, as well as by market forces, has contributed to the changing role of the internship. The 1987 National Conference on Internship Training in Psychology was the first conference to recognize this change (Belar et al. 1989). The conference document asserts that the internship process, in order to produce practitioners capable of functioning autonomously, should be 2 years in length: 1 year predoctoral and 1 year postdoctoral. While licensure and certification laws require a year of postdoctoral supervised practice, the regulations do not yet require the completion of a formal postdoctoral program. Thus, the internship does remain the last formal training program many psychologists complete.

The internship was conceptualized by the 1987 conference and by the Joint Council on Professional Education in Psychology (Stigall et al. 1990) as being a generalist training experience, which may be followed by a formal postdoctoral program for specialization, or by further advanced training and supervision. This increased emphasis on postdoctoral programs has not detracted from the importance of the internship. Indeed, the internship is a prerequisite to postdoctoral training. Some programs have begun to offer a postdoctoral fellowship coordinated with the internship.

The Association of Psychology Internship Centers, a membership organization of internship and postdoctoral programs, was formed in 1968 to bring order and fairness to the process of offers and acceptances of internship positions. The organization publishes a directory of internship and postdoctoral programs that meet its membership criteria. The membership criteria developed by the organization were adopted by a number of credentialing bodies to define an internship. In 1991 the organization changed its name to the Association for Psychology Postdoctoral and Internship Centers (APPIC) to acknowledge the inclusion of postdoctoral programs in its membership and the organization's increased activity in the postdoctoral area. In recent years, APPIC has become the organization that speaks for the concerns of internship programs in national psychology.

Internships Today

Internships are 1 year full-time or 2 years half-time in an organized training program. There are independent internship centers located in a wide variety of settings, such as hospitals, clinics, mental health centers, prisons, colleges and universities, and schools. There are also captive internship programs, which accept interns from only one doctoral program. Both types of internships are eligible for APA accreditation and for APPIC membership.

Internships are full-fledged education and training programs, offering seminars and didactics in addition to organized clinical experience with supervision. One of the hallmarks of internship training is the increasing responsibility and independence given to the intern across the year. Internships are frequently organized on a rotational system, which allows interns to gain experience in a variety of clinics or units. Many programs have the provision for interns to engage in long-term treatment approaches spanning the whole year, as well as having briefer exposures (rotations) of 3, 4, or 6 months in particular psychological activities. Internship training spans the whole range of services offered by professional psychologists. The following requirements have been proposed for the core curriculum of internships (Belar et al. 1989; Stigall et al. 1990): a variety of methods of both assessment and treatment with diverse populations and presenting problems; research and its applications to practice; professional, legal, and ethical issues; and introduction to supervision and management of psychological services. The Joint Council (Stigall 1990) also adds professional consultation, collaboration with other disciplines, and the development of professional identity and responsibility to its recommended core curriculum.

Independent internship programs select their interns from a national pool of intern applicants. Captive internships, by definition, choose their interns from a single graduate program, university, or professional school. Some internships request or require interviews (in-person or telephone), while others opt to make their choices based upon the application materials alone. Uniform procedures for tendering offers and acceptances of internships, including the date and time of intern notification, are established by the APPIC.

Currently, most internship positions are funded at the local level. The Department of Veterans Affairs (formerly, the Veterans Administration) is an exception to this. It accounts for over 300 nationally funded internship positions in over seventy medical centers. While the VA no longer dominates internship training, slightly over 15% of all funded, APA-accredited internship positions were in VA medical centers in 1992–93 (Klepac and Reynes 1992). In the past, the National Institute of Mental Health also funded significant numbers of interns, but such funding currently accounts for less than 1% of internship positions. Some state governments allot specific funding for internships in state hospitals, universities, or mental health centers, but funding of interns is most often a local decision.

Evaluation and Accreditation of Programs

The American Psychological Association Committee on Accreditation accredits internship programs in professional psychology. Previously, internships were accredited in clinical and/or counseling psychology, but as there are no longer separate internship accreditation criteria for these specialties, this distinction has been dropped (American Psychological Association 1992). The model for the accreditation committee was altered in 1992, creating a body

under the aegis of the American Psychological Association's Board of Educational Affairs, but which is designed to function independently. Members of the committee are nominated by a number of groups representing four domains: graduate departments, training programs (both doctoral programs and internships), practitioners, and the public. APPIC is the nominating organization for the two allotted positions that represent internship programs.

APPIC is not an accrediting agency. It is a membership organization of internship and postdoctoral programs. Still, APPIC does evaluate internship programs, through a paper review. APPIC automatically accepts APA-accredited internships as meeting its membership criteria and reviews all unaccredited programs to ensure that they meet membership criteria prior to listing in the directory. Many of the unaccredited programs listed in the directory are developing programs that may soon obtain accreditation. However, a number of programs have existed for many years without applying for APA accreditation. Programs that are not APA-accredited must present evidence to a review committee every 3 years to show that they continue to meet APPIC membership criteria.

APA accreditation criteria (American Psychological Association 1986) and APPIC membership criteria (Klepac and Reynes 1992) are both focused on assuring a quality internship program. Both sets of criteria aim first at determining that there is indeed a program, rather than simply the availability of supervised practice or on-the-job training. There are many other commonalities in the two sets of criteria: there must be adequate resources available for training, including the presence of appropriately educated and credentialed supervisors; each intern must receive a minimum of 2 hours per week of individual, formal, face-to-face supervision; and there must be opportunity for interaction among interns. The APA criteria are more complex and qualitative in nature than the APPIC membership criteria and emphasize the need for the program to be engaged in an ongoing self-evaluation process.

Increasingly, in professional psychology, educators must be attentive to credentialing requirements in designing education and training programs (Stigall et al. 1990). Most jurisdictions in North America require an internship for eligibility for licensure. Likewise, listing in the National Register for Health Service Providers in Psychology requires an internship. In most instances, internships that are accredited by the American Psychological Association are assumed to meet criteria for licensure or other credentialing. Because most jurisdictions have requirements for internship that are patterned after the APPIC membership criteria, membership in APPIC increases the likelihood that an unaccredited internship will meet credentialing requirements. Thus, in recent years, there has been increasing pressure on graduate students to choose an internship that is APA-accredited or is an APPIC member program. While some graduate students still opt for less formal internship arrangements, they may experience greater difficulties in credential reviews for licensure, National Register listing, and eligibility to take the American Board of Professional Psychology or other specialty board examinations.

Kathie G. Larsen

Projective Techniques

Projective techniques are based on the principle that, when a situation is open to a variety of interpretations, interpretations sometimes differ in accordance with the personalities of people. There is a great deal of everyday experience to support the principle, for example, the individual who, while suppressing his own intense hostility, attributes hostile motives to other people.

The most widely used projective technique is the Rorschach Inkblot Test, which consists of ten inkblots. The individual is asked to tell what she sees on each blot, and for this reason the Rorschach is frequently called a perceptual test.

The Thematic Apperception Test (TAT) is next in popularity to the Rorschach. It consists of pictures of people in different types of social situations. Perhaps more than any other instrument, it is directly concerned with motives. For this reason, the pictures that are used lend themselves to interpretations of motives of aggression, affiliation, security, achievement, and so on.

In applied settings, the evidence is clear that projective techniques have, at most, only a low level of validity in predicting particular criteria. They tend to correlate very little with criteria of vocational success. Projective techniques do a poor job of differentiating normal people from people diagnosed as neurotic.

Although there are some exceptions to the rule, projective techniques tend to have unacceptably low reliability. Although there are arguments about how the reliability of projective techniques should be measured, however it is measured, the typical finding is a reliability around .60, and very few reliabilities as high as .80 are found.

Because the validity of most projective techniques depends on the interaction of examiner, subject, technique, situation, and trait being measured, these techniques are unstandardized and should not be called tests. It obviously is impossible to determine the validity of these myriad possible interactions of examiners and other factors; therefore, it is not possible to know the validity with which projective techniques are employed in particular instances. Although it is not clear that they actually aid interviewing, they certainly cannot be classified as standardized measures of personality traits.

The effective application of projective techniques is exemplified by the work of W. H. Holtzman (1961) and his colleagues on inkblot tests. After careful psychometric work, they constructed alternative forms of an inkblot test, each test consisting of forty-five blots. Homogeneous scales were developed for scoring particular types of responses, such as the tendency to see "good forms" and the tendency to respond to colors. Each subject makes only one response to each blot, and consequently, there is no possibility of variation in that regard influencing results. Instructions and scoring are well standardized, and alternative-form reliabilities of most trait measures are acceptable.

Jum C. Nunnally

Prosocial Development

Central to theories of identification and imitation has been the notion that the warmth of love given the child by the parent will affect that child's similarity to that parent.

Children notice not only whether others help but how others may feel about helping. The evidence, albeit sparse, suggests that children are more likely to imitate a model who shows positive affect. Models who are trying it and liking it are more likely to elicit imitative helping than models who are helping but enjoying it less. Children do learn by vicariously experiencing the contingencies surrounding another's helpful actions.

Mood states have been implicated in affecting helping behavior of both adults and children. B. S. Moore, B. Underwood, and D. L. Rosenhan (1973) have found that children who are asked to recall an event that has made them particularly happy are more likely to donate money to other children than children requested to recall a sad event. Likewise, a child who experiences success on a task is more likely to sacrifice than less successful children.

Studies concerning personal consistency in helping have been primarily in naturalistic settings and have focused upon assessing, often simultaneously, a variety of rather complex behaviors. Children's initiation of social activities, praise giving, reassurance, protection, peer ratings of kindness, and sensitivity to others' feelings are a few of the behaviors indexed.

Socialization practices that may produce the concerned child have been the object of considerable speculation and relatively little exploration. There is some consensus concerning socialization techniques that might facilitate the production of the aiding child. D. Baumrind (1971) has found that parents who could "specify aims and methods of discipline, promoted their own code of behavior, could not be coerced by the child, and set standards of excellence for the child" were the most likely to produce cooperative and helpful children.

James H. Bryan

Protoconsciousness

Sigmund Freud's topographic system of personality suggests three layers, namely the conscious, preconscious, and unconscious (Freud 1949). *Consciousness* is what one is presently aware of. *Preconscious* is what is on one's mind that one is not aware of. The term *unconscious* describes what one is unaware of; dreams, mental symptoms, amnesia, and some errors are unconscious. One of the main tasks of psychoanalytic treatment is to enable the patient to reduce the unconscious conflicts and to become aware of the meaning of her dreams, symptom formation, irrational forgetting, slips of the tongue, and other unconscious phenomena.

The transition from preconsciousness to consciousness does not require outside help. It is a daily occurrence, resembling a transfer of property from one room to another. Preconscious phenomena are easily accessible; they are in the storage room of consciousness. Conscious and preconscious phenomena are actually one and the same thing; preconsciousness is what one was aware of a while ago and what will come back instantly. Thus, the distinction between conscious and preconscious phenomena does not seem to be justified (B. B. Wolman 1992).

There are, however, a great many psychological phenomena that are neither conscious nor unconscious. Consider parapsychology, biofeedback, transcendental meditation, certain imagery phenomena, and altered states of consciousness. All these phenomena belong to a different psychological category, which Benjamin B. Wolman calls "protoconsciousness" (1986).

Lucid dreams are a good example of protoconsciousness. People who experience lucid dreams are asleep and dream. In a lucid dream it seems that one is awake and conscious and asleep and unconscious at the same time. In lucid dreams one is dreaming and is aware of the fact that one is dreaming; therefore, the dream cannot be totally unconscious. Moreover, the dreamer in a lucid dream can reason, remember, and act. The thinking, memorizing, and decision-making processes are definitely conscious, but the unconscious state of sleeping does not interfere with the consciousness. Therefore, lucid dreams have both conscious and unconscious elements. They are neither conscious nor unconscious: they are protoconscious. Lucid dreams can occur in both REM and NREM sleep.

Most parapsychological phenomena, namely clairvoyance and precognition, are neither totally conscious nor totally unconscious. Parapsychological experiences are not conscious, but the person who experiences them is aware of what she experiences. Obviously, telepathy and other parapsychological experiences are protoconscious.

Benjamin B. Wolman

Pseudoconditioning

The process of classical conditioning involves an association between the conditioned stimulus (CS) on the one hand and the unconditioned stimulus (US) or conditioned response (CR) on the other. Certain conditions, however, may produce the appearance of conditioning on a nonassociative basis. The most important of these are sensitization and pseudoconditioning. The latter refers to an increase in the probability of occurrence of the CR to any stimulus as a generalized effect of applications of the US.

Gregory A. Kimble

Psychiatric Interview with Children

Psychiatric interviews with children are active and verbal, whether the child spends the majority of the session in play with the adult as a participant, observer, and commentator, or in conversation that is focused on the problems from which the child (or her parents) is seeking relief.

The psychiatric interview with a child can be useful in all these spheres: fact finding; release and treatment; and educational, organizing, and structuring functions, such as goal setting and prognosis.

Whether in play or in candid discussion of how it feels to be himself in the world, the child derives a feeling of release, of liberation, and of disalienation from the psychiatric interview. If the interviewer can

do nothing else, she should strive to do no harm, at least, and if possible to make the child feel slightly better at the end of the very first hour.

Paul L. Adams

Psychiatric Residency Education

Accreditation

There are nearly 200 residency programs for psychiatric training in the United States. While individual programs may differ significantly when compared to others, all programs in the United States are accredited by a single accreditation body. This is the Residency Review Committee for Psychiatry, which is a component of the Accreditation Council of Graduate Medical Education. The Residency Review Committee (RRC) develops requirements for resident experiences during training, to which all programs must adhere. Programs are reviewed periodically to assure compliance with the requirements of the Residency Review Committee (American Medical Association 1993). The requirements represent expectations for both clinical and didactic experiences. For example, the RRC requires a minimum of 9 months of inpatient experience during residency, suggests that the optimal amount of inpatient experience be 1 year, and prescribes a maximum inpatient experience of 18 months. The outpatient experience is expected to be 1 year in length.

In addition, the RRC prescribes that all residents have an internship year, which includes at least 4 months of primary-care experience delivered in medical, pediatric, or family practice settings, in which the resident has ongoing responsibility for patient care. The RRC also requires 2 months of neurology experience. There are other recommendations for experiences in all subspecialty areas of psychiatry, including child psychiatry, consultation/liaison, geriatrics, forensics, and substance abuse. Further, the RRC requires that residents receive a specific amount of supervision for their clinical experiences. No less than 2 hours a week of supervision time provided by faculty is viewed as acceptable.

The RRC also delineates a variety of areas of

didactic experiences that must be covered. This includes the requirement for educational experiences that cover the major bodies of psychiatric knowledge, such as psychopharmacology, neuroscience, and material on psychotherapies, as well as such issues as cultural impact on psychopathology, and so on.

The RRC also prescribes requirements that involve quality of life and quality of experiences during residency. The RRC requires, for example, that each resident have an office available in which to carry out her clinical activities. The RRC also requires that clinical experiences have increasing levels of responsibility for clinical management as residency progresses.

Recruitment and Selection Process

In the United States, recruitment into psychiatry careers has followed a cyclical pattern, with high rates of interest in the 1960s and 1980s and low rates of interest in the 1970s and so far in the 1990s. At this point, approximately 4% of U.S. medical students enter training in psychiatry. Such training can occur by two routes of entry. Students may enter directly from medical school into an internship year followed by 3 years of residency training. Other students, approximately 30% of all psychiatric trainees, enter at the level of the second year of training following an internship experience or other practice experience in other areas of clinical medicine.

Clinical Rotations

The typical clinical experience for a psychiatric resident in the United States follows a specific sequence. The internship year (the PG-1 year or postgraduate year one) often includes 4 months of primary-care experiences, 2 months of neurology, and 6 months of psychiatric experience. These psychiatric experiences most likely are inpatient-based. The PG-2 year typically includes from 6 to 12 months of further inpatient experience, and may also involve either the beginning of outpatient experiences or subspecialty experiences. The most common subspecialty experiences that are provided during the PG-2 year include consultation/liaison, child psychiatry, or geriatric experiences. The PG-3 year usually involves a focus primarily on ambulatory psychiatry. The major part of the time is spent working with adults, but the program may include experiences in working with children and adolescents as well.

The PG-4 year very often involves significant elective time. Some residency programs provide opportunities for residents to function as chief residents. A chief resident in the United States is defined as one who, in addition to clinical responsibilities, has some administrative responsibility, and teaching and supervising expectations for junior residents and/or medical students as well. On each clinical rotation, residents are expected to be supervised in their clinical work by faculty members.

Didactic Experience

Along with a specific sequence of clinical activities, residents in U.S. programs are provided with a series of seminars and classroom teaching experiences throughout the residency. Some programs start these didactic exercises in the PG-1 year, while others may occur in the PG-2 year to allow those individuals who enter residency training at the PG-2 level to fully experience all of the didactic courses. Courses include principles of interviewing, psychopathology, descriptive psychiatry, various treatment approaches, psychotherapeutic techniques and theories, the neuroscience basis of psychiatry, cultural influences, and so on. Often, a variety of formats is used to transmit specific knowledge. This includes not only classroom teaching or seminar experiences but the use of case conferences, ward rounds, or some other use of the clinical setting.

Evaluation and Certification

Residents are evaluated in both formal and informal ways during the residency years. Most residency programs collect evaluations of clinical competence from supervisors for each of the clinical experiences the resident may have. In addition, information is collected from those faculty who teach seminars. These evaluations are often based primarily on observation and not on formal testing. The RRC, however, does require that there be periodic specific evaluations during residency. The RRC requires a test of cognitive knowledge during each of the 4 years of residency, and a test of clinical competence during 2 of the 4 years of training. Most programs deal with the need for evaluation of cognitive knowledge by use of the Psychiatry Residency in Training Examination. This is a standardized national examination developed by the American College of Psychiatrists, which provides information to the residents and program directors regarding how their knowledge level in a variety of subspecialty areas compares to peers both within their program and nationally.

Assessments of clinical knowledge are conducted primarily through direct observation of a patient interview by the resident and a discussion following the interview with the faculty member regarding the resident's impressions of the patient's psychopathology and suggested treatment approaches. This format mimics one that is used during the certifying exams conducted by the American Board of Psychiatry and Neurology. While the RRC is the evaluation body for residency programs, the American Board of Psychiatry and Neurology is the certifying organization for individual psychiatrists' competence. In order to sit for that examination, a resident must have successfully completed an RRC-approved residency program. The ABPN examination involves two parts, written and oral. The written examination must be successfully completed before a residency graduate is allowed to sit for the oral examination, and both parts must be passed for the resident to be certified by the ABPN. While certification is not a requirement for the practice of psychiatry nationally, a variety of hospitals and local governmental authorities are beginning to increase the desirability of becoming board-certified.

Flexibility and Program Philosophy

Although there is a wide range of clinical and educational experiences prescribed by the RRC in psychiatry, the programs have a great deal of flexibility within this framework, and there is a wide divergence of training philosophy. Some programs focus primarily on a biological model of understanding the etiology of psychiatric illness and on a variety of somatic interventions in treatment. Other programs may focus primarily on an understanding of the psychological etiologies of psychopathology and on psy-

chotherapeutic interventions into treatment. More often than not, however, present-day residency programs are multifocal in their approaches to residency training. In the 1970s, there were great debates regarding which approach to understanding psychiatric illness would predominate, a psychoanalytic approach or a psychopharmacologic approach. These debates, while they still exist in some places, have subsided substantially as psychiatrists have come to realize that no one theoretical perspective is adequate for explaining disordered human behavior and its successful treatment. Rather, a biopsychosocial approach, in which the biological, psychological, and interpersonal aspects of behavior in states of normalcy and pathology are taught, is used. Because of increasing requirements from the RRC, and because of specific theoretical approaches to residency education, there remain unresolved philosophical issues.

Subspecialization

The last 20 years have seen an increase in the number of subspecialty fellowship opportunities for psychiatrists. Child psychiatry fellowships have been in existence for many years, and until recently, child and adolescent psychiatry was the only subspecialty of psychiatry recognized by the Accreditation Council for Graduate Medical Education. However, there are now plans for recognized subspecialty training opportunities in geriatric psychiatry, with opportunities in substance abuse and consultation/liaison psychiatry following close behind. Approximately 15 to 20% of all psychiatric residents choose subspecialty training as an addition to their general psychiatric training. The vast majority of residents pursue training in child and adolescent psychiatry, but with the increase in recognized subspecialty areas of psychiatry it is expected that more and more individuals may choose subspecialty training in geriatrics, consultation psychiatry, substance abuse, and other areas.

Allan Tasman

Psychoanalysis and the Brain

Having begun his career as a neurologist, Sigmund Freud wished from the start to embed his psychological theory in the biological substrate of the brain. In his *Project for a Scientific Psychology* (1895), he attempts to trace his early psychoanalytic discoveries to what was then known of neurology and neuroanatomy. His effort was premature; not enough was known of the brain to explain the workings of the mind.

Freud declared the independence of psychology in a letter to Robert Fliess, but he never gave up hope of bringing mind and brain together. Much of his metapsychology, as he called it, incorporated ideas from the *Project*, elaborated into mental rather than physical processes.

Freud's starting point in the *Project* is the importance of pleasure and pain as motivational factors in mental life. He tries, unsuccessfully, to equate the pleasure and pain experienced in the mind with the activation and inhibition of nerve cells in the brain. The discharge of static electricity from an insulator is the metaphor through which he tries to link these phenomena.

In doing so, he underestimated the role of the depolarization of the nerve cell membrane in the transmission of information across the synaptic contact between one cell and another. As Karl H. Pribram and M. M. Gill (1976) point out, Freud was close to the idea of the nervous system as a network through which information is transmitted via interneuronal signals.

Freud was handicapped by the lack of an information-processing theory to model such a system. The powerful notion of entropy had dominated scientific thought when Freud was a young man. It was not yet clear that living organisms were information-conserving systems, working against the entropic drift of the universe at large.

In his theory of the life and death instincts, Freud (1920) conceptualized the opposing trends of information conservation and entropy as universal forces. But he failed to realize that his theory of psychic energy discharge is more suited to the state of increasing entropy he identifies with the death instinct than to the information conservation of the living.

Freud attributed the functions that bind and synthesize to the life instinct. We now understand these to be processes that conserve and organize information. With the advent of the computer, it has become possible to model systems that begin to approach the complexity of organic processes.

The remarkable advances taking place today in neuroscience have been inspired for the most part by the information-processing approach to biology. New technologies based on computers are creating instruments to measure the small changes that serve as signals in the brain. For instance, with fast computer processing, magnetic resonance imaging can now show how specific areas of brain activation change from moment to moment in real time as we think.

The new sciences of the brain entered psychoanalytic theory in a serious way when Emanuel Peterfreund published *Information, Systems and Psychoanalysis* in 1971. Peterfreund's model was based on the cybernetic theory of regulation by feedback in systems from the simple to the most complex. The model shows that mental and neurophysiological processes can be described in terms of similar dynamisms, even though these dynamisms work at vastly different scales.

This is a clear advance over the psychic energy concept. It works particularly well in Peterfreund's view of the psychoanalytic process as a series of corrections applied over and over again to the analyst's working model of the patient.

A. D. Rosenblatt and J. T. Thickstun (1978) have refined Peterfreund's ideas about the uses of feedback. They subdivide the psychic apparatus into a hierarchy of interacting parts, which they call "motivational systems." Each of these motivational systems has its individual goals, which compete and often conflict with those of the others. Resolution of conflict is the main function at the top level of the system, using feedback and algorithm-like procedures.

Motivational systems added some of the features of artificial intelligence (AI) to the cybernetic model. Classical AI, developed in the 1960s and 1970s, deals for the most part with transformational procedures over a domain of hierarchically ordered symbolic structures. It gives us a model for intelligent behavior in the psychic apparatus as a whole. Traditional psychoanalytic theory assumed such a model but was not able to describe it.

A problem with classical AI is that it is remote from the nuts and bolts of brain physiology. The symbolic structures of classical AI are a late development, both in the evolution of our species and in the growth of the individual person. Brains are relatively inept at doing arithmetic and logic. They are amazingly efficient at the recognition and matching of patterns.

More recently a new form of computer simulation has succeeded in modeling some of the bottom-line elements of brain function. Called "neural networking," "connectionism," or "parallel-distributed processing," this new form of AI promises to fill a large gap. The symbolic structures at the top of the hierarchy can be tied together with the actual functioning of brain cells. Neural networks are simple pattern recognition systems, which can be joined to form hierarchical structures.

Originally proposed by Donald Hebb in 1949, the idea of the neural network has been refined by D. E. Rumelhart and J. L. McClelland (1986) and many others. Many of the original bugs that plagued the early decades of neural network research were worked out in the 1980s. The core of the connectionist model is the modification of synaptic weights by incoming stimuli. Hebb's famous rule states that a synaptic connection between two neurons is strengthened whenever the neurons are stimulated at the same time.

Hebb's rule has had to be modified in various ways to produce effective simulations of neural networks, but it captures the essential point. The modification of synaptic weights is the basis for a continual updating of the properties of a neural network. Feedback flows from neuron to neuron during every cycle of activity. The result is a flexible system of pattern matching, which can locate the unexpected similarities between newly impinging stimuli and those stored in memory.

Like the brain, and unlike the stored programs in a digital computer, simulated neural networks are robust under noisy conditions and even under minor physical damage. They can respond to partial stimuli by recalling the whole stimulus if it has been experienced and stored previously. They can extract similarities from a series of stimuli. They can also generalize from a variety of different but related stimuli.

It is fair to say, in 1993, that the neural network model is possibly the best available to explain the function of connected sets of neurons in the cerebrum and cerebellar cortex. This is true as well of essential supporting structures, like the hippocampus. This is a remarkable finding, because neuronal connections in the brain are many times more complex than they are in computer simulations.

The discovery of dozens of neurotransmitters in the brain only underlines this complexity. One can now begin to plan a program for brain research in the future in which work at every level of organization will contribute to the overall picture.

How does this new picture of the brain affect psychoanalytic theory? First, as D. V. Forrest (1991) has shown, the more psychoanalysts know about the brain, the better they can judge the plausibility of their own theoretical constructs. Freud's hope to embed psychoanalytic theory in biology is much closer to realization now. There are many issues in analytic theory about which we can ask, "Could this really happen in the human brain?" and expect a realistic answer.

We can ask, for example, if psychic energy is purely a metaphor, or else possibly Freud's expression for a quantitative factor that we can describe in more scientific terms. Stanley R. Palumbo (1992) suggests that, for Freud, psychic energy might have been a shorthand term for the summation of synaptic weights in a neural network. Here, the quantitative factor would be relative to the set of possible configurations that lead to the various output states of the network.

We can expect to find that many of Freud's psychological concepts will have neurophysiological counterparts, though differences of scale and structure may make them difficult to recognize at first. This is not to say that the psychological concepts will be reduced to the neurophysiological. There is no theoretical need for the psychological concepts to be derived from the biological. However, there are constraints imposed on the higher-level concepts by the lower.

Psychoanalytic theory will remain free to go

beyond any future theory of brain function, but it will not be free to contradict what we actually know about the brain. Freud worked with a considerable handicap in his lack of knowledge of the biological constraints on a valid psychological theory. What he was able to do in spite of this handicap was truly remarkable.

Many of Freud's concepts may turn out to be a highly condensed shorthand for more complex brain functions. However, his lack of a modern understanding of the brain did lead him into real errors. Sleep research has shown that periods of dreaming begin and end on a fairly rigid biological schedule (E. Aserinsky and N. Kleitman 1953). This clearly contradicts Freud's idea that it is the wish represented in the dream imagery that brings the dream into being.

A fixed and rigid schedule for the onset of dreaming suggests an adaptive function rather than the random expression of wishes (Greenberg and Pearlman 1974; Hawkins 1966). Information-processing constraints on the transfer of new experience into long-term memory suggest that the dream matches new events with events that have been previously stored (Palumbo 1978).

The dream censorship discovered and described by Freud intervenes in the matching of current and past wishes, rather than in the direct expression of repressed impulses. The direct expression of these impulses during dreaming sleep is ruled out by a physiological paralysis of the skeletal muscle system in any case.

This new understanding of dreaming suggests that we take an adaptive view of other forms of unconsciously motivated behavior as well. There are many steps in the processing of what we call an impulse. From the first indication of a biological urge, to the plan or fantasy that attaches the urge to a possibly gratifying action, to the action itself, there will be many transformations and decisions. When we know how these choices are made, by whatever blend of symbol processing and pattern recognition, we will better understand what our patients are trying to tell us.

Knowing that pattern recognition in distributed neural networks is the basic functional mode of the brain will also help us understand how therapeutic change takes place. Freud's idea that insight can be passed in some direct way from consciousness into the depths of the unconscious has never seemed to fit the facts. The neural network model suggests a gradual process in which individual memories are revised and reintegrated to form newer, larger, and more flexible structures.

Stanley R. Palumbo

Psychoanalysis and Education

Sigmund Freud spoke of the psychoanalytic method of treatment as an education to correct the faults of one's childhood that resulted in a neurotic development, which undermined the functions of adaptation and adjustment and led to interfering symptoms. Franz Alexander defined psychoanalytic treatment as emotional reeducation.

The first consequence of Freud's insights was expressed in educational reform movements, which intended to prevent the pathogenic aspects of oppressive education. The themes of that time suggested that the new psychoanalytic pedagogy would uncover the faults of the parents (Pfister) and work for the liberation of the child (Wittels). The interest of the educators centered around the issue of "sexual enlightenment." Psychoanalytically oriented education was a reform movement, often related to revolutionary thoughts concerning the function of education.

The true effect of psychoanalysis in education was felt mostly in some experimental private schools. In central Europe, Anna Freud and Dorothy Burlingham—through their experiments in a small private school—stimulated people like Erik Erikson and Peter Blos, who worked in the school, to contribute so much to educational issues, in such works as *Childhood and Society* and *On Adolescence*, respectively.

A new era began after World War II, beginning with the first edition of the *Psychoanalytic Study of the Child* in America, replacing as it were the *Zeitschrift für Psychoanalytische Pädagogik*. It picked up and completed the threads of prewar endeavors, which, in spite of the war, never quite stopped. Some of these new experiments were forced underground or could be conducted only by pioneers such as Anna Freud and Dorothy Burlingham.

Efforts were started in the United States and in other countries to see psychoanalysis as an additional tool for the educator's armamentarium. Efforts were also made to determine which of the educator's insights were applicable to the therapeutic field.

Some of the attempts at integration have been described by Rudolf Eckstein in his book *In Search of Love and Competence* (1976). Psychoanalysis, following Freud, should inspire child care and education.

Rudolf Eckstein

Psychoanalysis as a Science

Sigmund Freud's scientific work has been presented in six types of propositions. The first four could be classified as synthetic, for they describe facts:

1. *Observable phenomena,* such as masturbation, mutism, homosexuality, thumb sucking, violence, stupor
2. *Introspectively observable phenomena,* such as pain, depression, wish, elation, manifest dream content
3. *Unconscious phenomena,* indirectly accessible to analysis and hypnosis, such as primary processes, reaction formation
4. *Empirical generalization* concerning one or more of the above categories

The last two categories of propositions are not empirical:

5. *Theoretical propositions* (what Freud called *metapsychology*)
6. *Praxeological propositions,* that is, rules of psychoanalytic technique

Psychoanalysis as a theory operates with a complex set of hypothetical constructs and models. For example, the statement that anxiety is a state of tension created by a conflict between the ego and the superego, or the ego and the id, cannot be experimentally or observationally validated. This statement is neither true nor false, because ego and superego are not observable data but hypothetical constructs.

Freud grouped together his theoretical considerations under the heading *metapsychology.* David Rapaport and M. M. Gill (1959) suggest organizing Freud's theory around five metapsychological points of view, namely the dynamic, economic, structural, genetic (developmental), and adaptive.

Benjamin B. Wolman (1977) suggests organizing Freud's theory around seven distinct principles, starting with the philosophical: (1) epistemological realism and (2) monism; then, the methodological: (3) energetism and (4) determinism; and, finally, the substantive principles of (5) economy, (6) pleasure–unpleasure continuum, and (7) constancy.

Being a monist, Freud never gave up hope for a monistic interpretation, which would combine both physical and mental processes in one continuum. But at the present state of scientific inquiry, a radical reductionism must be rejected. Psychology must continue to do what Freud actually did: develop new hypothetical constructs independent of the physical sciences.

Energetism. Freud believed that there is one kind of energy in nature and that all observable actions are either produced by this energy or exist as its variations or transformations. If this holds true in physics, it holds true also in other sciences, such as chemistry, biology, and psychology. This must not be construed in a radical reductionistic vein, for human thoughts are not electrical processes and cannot be reduced to terms of amperes, watts, or volts. Mental processes cannot be reduced to anything that is not mental, but they develop from the same physical source as everything else in the world.

Freud postulated that psychic energy is not an entirely new nor a completely different type of energy. Mental energy is a derivative of physical energy, though no one can really tell how the "mysterious leap" takes place, either from body to mind or vice versa.

Determinism. According to Freud, objective and verified observation is the sole source of knowledge. The results of these observations can be "intellectually manipulated" and put together into a system of generalizations and laws, which then form a system of propositions that explain empirical data. One of these general principles is the principle of causation. Determinism cannot be proven; it must be postulated and corroborated by empirical research.

The economy principle. Freud's theory follows the principle of preservation of energy, and this principle is applied to mental energy. Mental energy can be transformed, released, or accumulated; but it can never disappear entirely. When it is invested into something, this object's representation becomes loaded with a certain amount of mental energy in a manner analogous to that in which bodies become charged with electricity. This process of charging ideas of objects with mental energy was called by Freud "cathexis," and objects in which mental energy was invested were *cathected.* Cathexis can be applied to external objects as well as to one's own organism.

The pleasure–unpleasure principle. Freud followed G. T. Fechner with the idea of pleasure and unpleasure as related to the mental economy of excitation.

The principle of constancy. The principle of constancy serves as the general framework for Freud's theory of motivation. It represents a tension-relief continuum and explains the compulsion to repeat early experiences. The "repetition compulsion" manifests itself in several aspects of human life.

Several theoreticians have tried to reinterpret Freud's theories according to their particular philosophical position, methodological preferences, and conceptual systems borrowed from psychological, biological, and any other studies. Jacob Arlow, Charles Brenner, Gill, R. R. Holt, G. S. Klein, Rapaport, and D. Shakow are among the leading analysts of Freud's theory. New systems based on Freud's work have been developed by Erik Erikson, Heinz Hartmann, B. B. Wolman, and many others (Wolman 1977, 1984).

Psychoanalysis as a technique states what ought to be done in order to obtain certain goals. It is an applied science, a science that does not describe reality but prescribes a course of action. Thus, it is a *praxeology,* a system of aims and means, similar to medicine, education, and political science.

Setting the goals: Teleology. Praxeologies do not set goals arbitrarily. Medical praxeology is an applied science that determines the goals for treatment of diseases. It does not operate in a vacuum; its goals are derived from empirical research and theories. Medicine is based on anatomy, biochemistry, physiology, histology, pathology, and other empirical sciences.

Psychoanalytic praxeology, in its teleological tasks, follows the same reasoning. The immanent goal is mental health, which Freud defined in terms of inner harmony between the id, ego, and superego, with the ego's supremacy. However, this goal could be made more specific and modified according to the sociopsychological needs of particular sectors of populations and cultures. Small wonder that many innovations were proposed (when the center of psychoanalysis moved from Austria to the United States) by Hartmann, Franz Alexander, Lawrence Kubie, Sandor Rado, Erikson, Wolman, and others. All these modifications are based on Freud's idea that the immanent purpose of psychoanalytic treatment is mental health, and all have been influenced, to a certain extent, by the changing times and changing sociocultural climate.

Setting the means: Technology. Every praxeological system must develop definite guidelines as to how its goals can be attained. Without these guidelines or techniques, any praxeology would turn into a mere hortatory system.

Ultimately, praxeological methods (techniques) should be measured by their efficiency, but efficiency itself is not easily measurable, especially in the field of mental health.

Benjamin B. Wolman

Psychoanalysis: Working Through

Sigmund Freud (1914) discovered that interpretation of the unconscious, historical roots of a patient's symptoms, even in the context of affect-laden memory, does not necessarily lead to lasting change. On the contrary, as subsequent psychoanalytically oriented psychotherapists have witnessed, interpretation often leads to increased resistance to understanding. Freud recognized that abreaction alone only leads to temporary symptom relief, because the unconscious psychic conflict, which caused the maladaptive compromise formation, remains intact. A. F. Valenstein (1983) underlines this:

> The analyst, "What about your insights?" The patient replies, "Oh well, I have them. They are on the top shelf of the closet. Someday I might need them."

Working through is tied to the question of what motivates someone to give up old defenses and modes of interaction. This question, in turn, cannot be answered without wondering what the curative factors are in psychoanalytic treatment.

Working through differentiates psychoanalysis from other treatment modalities, because of the intensity with which the working-through process deals with the analysand's resistance to understanding the deepest layers of her unconscious psychological life. Freud (1914) notes, "it [working through] is a part of the work which effects the greatest changes in the patient and which distinguishes analytic treatment from any kind of treatment by suggestion."

Working Through, Resistance, and the Repetition Compulsion

Freud's formulations of resistance reflected the scientific currency of the time, the thermodynamic model. After the conceptualization of the structural model, Freud cataloged five forms of resistance, three stemming from the ego, one from the superego, and one from the id. It was the latter resistance, because of its tenacious compulsion to repeat, that led cognitive insight into a blind alley rather than to freedom from the unconscious conflict.

In *Analysis Terminable and Interminable*, Freud further elaborated on those psychic attributes that inhibit successful analytic work. These include the effects of trauma and constitution, id resistances, adhesiveness of the libido, and the resistances derived from the death instinct. Working through gradually interrupts the ego's attempt to reestablish repression after unconscious conflict has been brought to consciousness by interpretation. This is

an arduous task, because change is mitigated against by the repetition compulsion, which leads to action rather than verbal memory. Freud recognized that, for change to be effective, the patient needs to be in conflict, to experience as ego dystonic both her own resistance and the repetition compulsion: "One must allow the patient time to become more conversant with this resistance with which he has now become acquainted, to work through it, to overcome it, by continuing, in defiance of it, the analytic work . . ." (1914). The repetition compulsion works against remembering by allowing the analysand to perceive the conflict in current terms rather than as a recreation of a past event. In other words, the infantile conflict is seen as real in the context of the transference, rather than as the memory of an intrapsychic conflict.

Later Conceptualizations

Freud raised two important questions that other authors have continued to grapple with: the nature of the resistance to change, and why psychoanalysis takes so long. We can divide the theoretical positions into the structural/conflictual, the developmental, the relational, and the cognitive/biological. Most authors combine these theoretical positions to understand the process of working through.

Otto Fenichel's body of work expands Freud's conception that working through constitutes the protracted interpretation of resistance, which allows the patient to try new solutions to old conflicts. He, like many others, connects working through to mourning. Greenacre (1956) focuses particularly on the special requirements for prolonging the working through of childhood trauma. R. R. Greenson (1965) has emphasized that the analysis of the transference neurosis, which centers on reconstruction, requires an effective working alliance to be worked through. Charles Brenner (1987) argues that the particular resistance that Freud considered central to working through is "the resistance represented by the repetition of childhood wishes in the transference." He then sees working through not as a unique process but as "the analysis of one or another component of psychic conflict."

Many have equated working through with normal development, in which repetition, elaboration, and the maintenance of a background of safety are essential to structural change. Working through is conceptualized as a process through which disturbed developmental arrests are reintegrated in the context of the analytic relationship. P L. Giovacchini (1993) has creatively discussed how, particularly with the disturbed patient, the working through process takes place within a transitional space created by the therapeutic relationship. Here, fantasy and trial solutions can be played with more flexibly than within the more rigid demands of the real world. S. Novey (1962) discusses the question of the time lag between insight and change, particularly emphasizing the rigidity of affective memory as opposed to traditional notions of ego resistance. W. A. Stewart (1963) disagrees with the equation of mourning with working through, suggesting that the object constancy of the analyst and his continued interpretive efforts allow the "relinquishment or transmutation of the unconscious infantile instinctual wishes toward a sublimated ego-syntonic and reality-oriented goal." Valenstein (1983) sees working through as a crucial moment in analysis, where the analysand takes responsibility for translating insight into action. This could be seen as similar to the developmental requirements of adolescence when earlier issues of separation/individuation are integrated into a coherent self-representation. Valenstein also adds the important concept that people are attached to their painful feelings and the defenses and resistances that arise from them, because they are linked to important childhood relationships.

Anna Ornstein (1991) reframes the concept through the lens of self-psychology. Resistance and defense are not seen as aiding the repression of drive wishes—and, therefore, as something to be overcome—but instead as attempts at either protecting the vigor of the self or protecting the self from potential fragmentation. Quoting M. M. Gill, she emphasizes that "while defense is an intrapsychic concept, resistance is an interpersonal one." Working through is the process by which the empathic failures in the self-object transference lead to the repair of childhood failures of empathy, validation, and affirmation.

M. Shane (1979) suggests that "working through

may be postulated as the process of structural development mediated within the analysis by the joint meliorative effects of interpretation and object relations with the analyst." The developmental experience in the analysis takes place not only because childhood relationships are relived in the transference but because the analyst functions as a new object. Although the idea of a new object is not emphasized by Shane, we will elaborate on it to suggest further contemporary views of working through.

The Curative Factor

The debate, crucial to understanding working through, about the curative factors in psychoanalysis centers on what function the analyst plays in facilitating permanent change. The paradigm shift in analysis, in which the analytic experience is considered a two-person endeavor, helps explain why working through takes as much time as it does. The analyst is no longer the outside observer of the patient's psychic reality but a necessary and active participant in the process by which change is mediated. Her actual presence in the process is a determinant of that reality and is viewed as essential for psychic change.

James Strachey's (1934) concepts of the auxiliary superego and the mutative interpretation suggest that the analyst's accepting attitude toward the patient's free associations is a crucial ingredient in the effectiveness of interpretation. He emphasizes that a mutative interpretation must be delivered at the moment of affective urgency and be related to the transference. The effects of such efforts happen over long periods and in small bits, as with mourning.

H. W. Loewald (1960) combines the relational and developmental points of view by suggesting that the analyst becomes a new object to the patient through the process of interpreting transference distortions. This, in turn, allows the patient to rediscover alternative paths of development that had been distorted or unavailable to the child. M. M. Gill, in many articles, has emphasized the centrality of the patient's experience of the here-and-now aspect of the analytic relationship in determining the transference, which helps the patient rediscover these early developmental pathways. Others, such as Robert J. Langs, A. Modell, and E. Schwaber, have elaborated a view of analysis as a two-person endeavor, in which the analyst is always, by the nature of his own particular presence in the relationship, influencing the patient's free associations. Theodore J. Jacobs and M. L. McLauglin have explored the role of enactment in determining the nature of the transference and resistance.

Analytic listening, according to these viewpoints, must incorporate the effects of the analyst, her actions in the relationship, and the patient's experience of the analytic process itself to lead to effective interpretation. Infant research, as a correlate of the analytic process, has also demonstrated the intricately complex ways in which mother and infant function as an interactive system, reaffirming Donald W. Winnicott's notion that there is no such thing as a baby, only a mother/baby relationship.

Working through must also have a neurochemical explanation, because old modes of perception and adaptation are altered by the analytic process. We know that psychic trauma leads to lasting biological changes in the neurochemical structures/pathways of the central nervous system. These changes then predispose one to react as if that traumatic event were reappearing in a misperceived new context. Working through must also be active at the level of similar neurochemical processes. R. M. Galatzer-Levy (1988) offers an analogy from models of artificial intelligence, which suggests that the long time factor is an essential ingredient in working through. The organism needs time and safety to attempt new trial solutions to old problems. Urgent solutions, outside the analytic setting, or when defenses are confronted inappropriately, lead to old but not necessarily optimal solutions. Research on the nature of memory will likely shed additional light on this complex question of what facilitates psychic change.

These ideas would suggest, then, that we do have an increasing understanding of why working through takes as long as it does. The development of permanent new intrapsychic structures requires a unique relationship, as experienced by the patient, where old developmental solutions can be revisited in a new context. In this relationship, new avenues for adaptation can be tested and adopted. Working

through, as now conceived, requires more than an understanding of the resistance against drive derivatives. Working through would include all those processes, unique to the psychoanalytic relationship, whereby insight is transformed into new capacities for perceiving and relating to the world.

Elliot Schildkrout

Psychoanalytic Interaction

The bipersonal field (R. J. Langs 1976) is created by the physical conditions of the analyst's office, the analytic pact, the implicit and explicit ground rules and boundaries of the analytic relationship, and the respective roles and behaviors of the two participants. Any modification in the structure or framework of the field will have a profound influence on both participants and on the therapeutic qualities of the field. The field is essentially bipolar and interactional, with the patient and analyst as its two nodal points; it has an interface that reflects the coalescence of the vectors in the field from moment to moment.

The study of the curative and pathological dimensions of the bipersonal field begins without bias as to which participant is contributing most significantly for the moment to these aspects of the field. It is incumbent upon the participants, generally at different levels of awareness, to make determinations of the therapeutic and disrupted aspects of the field, to validate their assessment, and to then undertake the cure of the disturbing elements.

The bipersonal field concept implies that all disturbances within the analytic situation, and within each of its participants, have an interactional component. This means, for example, that a symptom experienced by the patient has both an intrapsychic and an interactional component and that its determinants are shared by both patient and analyst. Under unusual circumstances, in which the analyst is contributing in a major way to the pathology of the bipersonal field, a symptom experienced within the patient may have as its most central determinant the psychopathology of the analyst—though this conceptualization should not be used to overlook the additional contributions from within the patient. Similarly, countertransference-based symptoms within the analyst have both intrapsychic and interactional determinants.

Embedded in the bipersonal field, the analyst manages and maintains the framework and pursues her efforts to comprehend the unconscious sources of the patient's psychopathology. By adhering to her basic psychoanalytic stance and by offering sensitive, well-timed interpretations, she provides the patient with cognitive insights and reparative identifications.

Robert J. Langs

Psychoanalytic Metapsychology

The concept of metapsychology was first used by Sigmund Freud to mean that the assumptions and formulations of psychoanalytic psychology advanced beyond the limits of conscious experience to explore and explain the unconscious determinants of behavior (Freud 1887–1902, 250).

Freud's early meaning has been considerably modified, both in his later writing and in the development of psychoanalytic theory. Rather than a theory about the forming of psychoanalytic theory, *metapsychology* stands for the highest level of abstraction and integration within psychoanalytic theory itself. It embraces the spectrum from clinical observation and specification of clinical evidences to the highest-level principles of the organization of behavior and experience. Consequently, psychoanalytic metapsychology includes propositions stating the observations, theoretical formulations, and underlying assumptions that are all closely interwoven in the body of psychoanalytic understanding.

The general metapsychological assumptions or points of view have been summarized by David Rapaport and M. M. Gill (1967). While the effect of these formulations may have been to excessively constrain psychoanalytic theorizing and may have left the impression that the focus on the basic assumptions of psychoanalytic theory specifically defined the limits of metapsychology, these formulations still remain basic and more or less definitive.

William W. Meissner

Psychoanalytic Psychotherapy

Psychoanalytic psychotherapy is psychotherapeutic treatment based on the use of psychoanalytic concepts and techniques applied to treatment of an individual with a malfunctioning or disordered personality for whom conventional, classical, orthodox psychoanalytic treatment is contraindicated or inappropriate, either because of real-life circumstances or because of the nature of the individual's psychopathology.

From the beginning that Sigmund Freud made, analysts did not abandon to nonanalysts either the theory or the practice of psychotherapy. In spite of the strong "antidilution" attitudes of Freud, Edward Glover, R. Waelder, and other analysts, a vigorous, dynamic psychology and psychotherapy did develop within and beyond the ranks of psychoanalysts.

A primary consequence of the psychoanalytic point of view in psychotherapy is abandonment of confusing psychiatric nosology as a guideline to technique. Rather, mainstream psychoanalytic psychotherapy is the ordered application of therapeutic techniques to specified aspects of psychological functioning. When a patient appears in the office of an analyst who may choose either to analyze or to do dynamic psychotherapy, the analyst can be guided in his evaluation first by the problem of assessing the potential capability of his own therapeutic capabilities with the therapeutic needs of the patient.

Tarachow

Several models for a broad, psychoanalytic theory of psychotherapy have been formulated since the early 1950s. Two of these have been especially influential and widely accepted. S. Tarachow (1963) proposes a clear theoretical and clinical difference between psychotherapy and psychoanalysis. In this view, every therapy is based on the need of the patient and therapist alike to regard each other as real objects. The analytic situation is created by the imposition of a barrier to reality, or to the mutual urge to act out the real relationship by means of interpretation by the analyst. The therapeutic barrier imposed by the analyst creates the therapeutic task for members of the dyad, as it makes a real situation between them into an as-if situation, which demands attention and comprehension. Analysis is defined as consistent application of the therapeutic barrier.

Dewald

P. A. Dewald's (1964) theoretical base is psychoanalysis, and he concentrates on the variety of approaches of psychotherapy rather than on the differences between therapy and analysis. He makes a distinction between supportive versus insight-directed (expressive) therapy, though with full awareness that such a division cannot always exist in clinical work, for pedagogical reasons.

Internalization

The Menninger Foundation's psychotherapeutic research project conducted a prediction study from 1956 to 1976. From this study, the researchers postulated that the internalization process was the central feature of successful, supportive psychotherapy and also was an important aspect of expressive psychotherapy (L. Horwitz 1975). Symptom relief with some patients in these groups was found to occur without conflict resolution. The researchers concluded that the patient's identification with the therapist, or a wish to please her, had a great deal to do with the improvement. Internalization of a good therapeutic relationship brings about structural change in the patient's internal world of object relationships.

Psychoanalytic psychotherapy can be regarded as requiring more talent and skill, more knowledge and experience, on the part of the therapist than does analysis; yet many or most practitioners regard psychotherapy as easier, simpler, and less technically demanding.

William C. Thompson

Psychoanalytic Situation

To the complex relationship between analyst and patient, authors other than Sigmund Freud (Greenson 1967; Macalpine 1950; Stone 1961, 1967; Zetzel 1970) have added another factor, the analytic setting, and they regard the interrelationship of such components as comprising the "psychoanalytic situation."

Transference

L. Macalpine (1950) disputes the belief that transference manifestations emerge spontaneously from within the neurotic analysand. She hypothesizes that the analytic transference is induced actively in the "transference-ready analysand" by her regressive adaptation to an infantile setting. However, the features of the analytic setting do more than induce regression and the emergence of transference. They contribute to the loosening of defenses, the emergence of fantasies, and the experiencing of wishes more intensely within the safety afforded by restricted motility.

The Patient

E. R. Zetzel (1970) points out that "the analytic process requires of the patient a capacity to regress to a degree sufficient to permit the reopening of conflicts previously closed off by those defenses which represent unconscious automatic responses to signal anxiety" (249–50), without a concomitant regression in basic ego capacities.

R. R. Greenson (1967) states, "The patient is asked: (a) to regress and progress, (b) to be passive and to be active, (c) to give up control and to maintain control, and (d) to renounce reality testing and to retain reality testing" (361).

The Analyst

Ella Sharpe (1950), Greenson (1967), and L. Stone (1961, 1967) have described what psychoanalysis requires of the analyst. Resolution of his own neurotic conflicts; an ability to understand, translate, and communicate unconscious processes; an ability to oscillate between being an involved participant and a detached observer; a capacity for empathy, intuition, compassion, patience, and respect; and a lively interest in and curiosity about people are among the necessary qualities.

S. Joseph Nemetz

Psychoanalytic Technique: Changing Views

The question of technique has been a matter of compelling interest to practicing analysts. Beginning with Sigmund Freud's initial modification of Josef Breuer's hypnotic method, psychoanalysts have continually sought, on the basis of advances in clinical and theoretical understanding, to develop and refine their technique.

Kohut

Heinz Kohut's work focused on the understanding and treatment of a particular group of patients who are characterized by their heightened vulnerability to narcissistic injury. Described as having either narcissistic behavior disorders or narcissistic personality disorders—according to whether the overt manifestations of the psychopathology are reflected primarily in the sphere of actions and behavior or in the patient's mental state—such individuals are regarded as suffering from the same fundamental problem: a weakened and defective self.

Kernberg

Among the most vocal of Kohut's critics is Otto Kernberg (1980). Building on the works of W. R. Bion, W. Ronald Fairbairn, H. Guntrip, and Margaret Mahler, as well as on the classic psychoanalytic approach, Kernberg has been a leading force in developing and explicating the role of object relations theory in psychoanalysis.

Highlighting the role that internalized self and object representations and the libidinal and aggressive drives play in human development and their contribution to the ego organization, Kernberg has emphasized the contribution of object relations theory to psychoanalytic technique.

Mahler

Margaret Mahler's delineation of the separation-individuation process, as it unfolds in infancy and early childhood, has led to the recognition of conflicts that are related to one or another phase of that process. In her view, the analyst's understanding and interpretation of preoedipal conflicts and the way they interdigitate with the conflicts of later child-hood in those cases in which difficulties in the separation-individuation phase have been substantial is essential to progress in analysis.

Resistance

Ernst Kris has shown that the slow, patient, time-consuming work of analyzing resistances whenever they appear fosters the movement of unconscious material toward conscious awareness and is the essential condition for the development of genuine insight. Following Kris's lead, analysts such as Jacob Arlow, Charles Brenner, Hans Loewald, and Milton Horowitz have refined our understanding of the manifold ways in which resistance manifests itself and have clarified the technical problems involved in its management.

Theodore J. Jacobs

Psychoanalytic Theories of Female Personality

Sigmund Freud's studies of female personality began with Anna O. and the first psychoanalytic patients, and led to important discoveries about feminine development. Inferences were drawn from increasingly broad and varied clinical experience. The early psychoanalytic model of female psychology also rested on the discovery of unconscious fantasies associated with libidinal phases and maturational sequences, as well as evolutionary and biological considerations. The foundations of the psychoanalytic psychology of women were summarized by Freud (1931, 1933) in his papers on femininity and later elaborated by Helene Deutsch (1944), M. Bonaparte (1953), and many other analysts.

Feminine character traits were prominently traced to the vicissitudes and elaborations of the female castration complex. For example, feminine modesty could be traced to feelings of unconscious injury and castration; envy, to feeling cheated and deprived of phallic intactness; and vindictiveness, to unconscious vengeful castrating attitudes related to the woman's own fantasied castration.

Modern psychoanalysis considers both the innate and instinctual forces as well as the developmental process and the influence of culture. In uncovering the vast importance of unconscious fantasies and conflicts, particularly of the oedipal phase of development, psychoanalysis also began gradually and systematically to examine normal and pathological lines of development, and to sort out the developmental impact of particular conflicts as well as the developmental challenges and advances leading to mastery and greater maturity.

Adult feminine character transcends simple derivation from the castration complex in an antiquated reductionism. For example, the capacity to be a "good enough mother" is a major developmental achievement, which cannot be simply derived from masochism and penis envy, and which depends upon ego stability and maturity of the total personality.

The menstrual-hormonal cycle—the biological and psychological changes concomitant with menstrual periods and periods of fertility and infertility—are indicative of a feminine psychology that may be uniquely associated with "periodic time and inner space" (E. Erikson 1968). At the same time, how the body is experienced and the reaction to the anatomical differences between the sexes is very much influenced by parental reaction, early object relationships, and multiple innate and developmental factors (Wolman 1975).

Harold P. Blum

Psychobiology

Psychobiology is an organismic conception for research on and treatment of both normal and abnormal behavior, which places emphasis on holistic functioning on the part of an individual within his environment.

Benjamin B. Wolman

Psychoendocrinology

Psychoendocrinology is a field of psychobiology that studies the interrelationship between the endocrine system and behavior; that is, the influence of hormones on behavior and the effect of behavior and

psychological stimuli on the functioning of the endocrine system. Investigations have shown that hormones play a significant role in determining various animal behavior patterns and that the endocrine system and the secretion of many hormones, if not all, are affected by psychological stimuli and states in both animals and humans.

The scope of psychoendocrine research is wide and ever expanding. Among the topics vigorously pursued at present are hormonal factors in sexual behavior, emotions, aggressive behavior, learning, and memory functions; the effect of various forms of stress on the endocrine system; interaction between hormones, neurotransmitters, and psychoactive drugs; hormonal correlates of mental illness and the use of hormones in the treatment of mental and behavioral disorders; psychoetiology of endocrine disorders, sleep, and hormones; and hormonal regulation of homeostatic mechanisms and biological drives. New insights on behavior and endocrine functions are derived from studies on the early influences on ontogenesis of behavior and brain development and on the effects of early experiences on endocrine functions in adult life. The new insights point to (1) the interrelationship between the pituitary gland and the brain; (2) the connection between the hypothalamus and the adrenal cortex; and (3) new techniques, especially the gene-splicing techniques that provide for the production of natural hormones.

Henryk Misiak

Psychohistory

Psychohistory is a contemporary term for the application of psychological insights to historical research. As a process or interaction between the two fields there is no specific origin, but an arbitrary, though reasonable, beginning can be marked in the nineteenth century, when psychology and history emerged in universities as separate disciplines providing postgraduate training and professional careers.

Psychohistory based on psychoanalysis or derived from it has been helpful in detecting lifelong themes or conflicts in individuals and has led to suggestions as to the cause of a particular personality or explanation of behavior otherwise seen as accidental or inexplicable.

Erik Erikson, in his historical study *Young Man Luther* (1958), sought to bridge the gap between individual lives and society by arguing that in the formation of personal identity, culture and personality are amalgamated, and that in child rearing a symmetry develops between what the culture values and expects and the values and lifestyles inculcated in infancy and childhood.

The turmoil of the 1960s and hopes for radical social change imbue the writing of psychohistorians, such as Robert Jay Lifton (1974), who seek to move beyond the study of individuals, however great, to the experiences of large groups sharing some psychological trauma. Survivors of the Hiroshima atomic bomb explosion or concentration camps, for example, possess a "shared theme" in their lives, which continues to modify their outlook and behavior. In the current period of rapid social change, Lifton sees the emergence of "protean man," who has acquired the ability to shift identity, in a not clearly defined way, without necessarily incurring the penalties Erikson had attributed to identity diffusion or identity confusion.

David F. Musto

Psycholinguistics

The relationship between language and the human brain was first described in 1860 by Pierre Paul Broca, who found that speech functions are localized in the frontal lobe of the left hemisphere. The rapid pace with which this faculty develops is evident by the fact that the average 5-year-old child is able to coverse efficiently in his or her native language. A. Noam Chomsky (1965) has developed the theory of transformational grammar. According to Chomsky's nativist theory, language consists of a "hard core" of clarity surrounded by a "continental shelf." Chomsky regards the grammar as directly responsible for the continental shelf because it generates sentences of different grammaticality.

Research on the psychological factors that underlie the use of language has been guided and influenced by the "cognitive revolution" in psychology. This has led to theories regarding the computational framework or cognitive architecture that surrounds the use of language. Computer science has also provided an analogue to the idea of a computational framework in which linguistic structures are called algorithms, and must be balanced against possible representations of those same algorithms. In this instance, language is likened to a computer program. If for example the set of real numbers was defined as the algorithm, the divisibility of every number ending in zero except zero would serve as a representation. Researchers often try to determine what the most frequent representations are for the linguistic structures under study, since as the example suggests, some algorithms may have numerous possible representations. Computer science has also aided research on parallel processing and pattern recognition.

Chomsky's theory of syntactic competence and performance has influenced the concept of a cognitive architecture underlying the use of language. Linguistic structures are said to reside in long-term memory in a symbolic form that can be utilized to interpret incoming language configurations and to generate new outgoing interpretations. Chomsky's argument for a universal grammar implies the existence of such a cognitive architecture within the human brain.

Psychologists generally seek a global understanding of the mental processes that accompany the use of language. To achieve such an objective, experimental research is frequently conducted in the areas of lexical content, semantic content, and syntactic content of language. Lexical research analyzes the words chosen for communication; semantic, the meaning conveyed by what is expressed; and syntactic, the grammatical structure of the phrases and sentences that are used.

Chomsky's influence has also been felt in the effort to relate deep and surface structures to one another. Surface structures are the morphemes, phonemes, and syntax, and the grammatical organization of phrases and sentences. Deep structures are the underlying linguistic components that one converts into written or spoken language. Chomsky and others have proposed "transformational rules of grammar" in an effort to explain how deep structures are transformed into surface ones. Empirical research to test such theories is quite complex, and further collaboration between computer scientists, linguists, and psychologists is needed to enlarge our understanding of how the elements of language are embedded in the human brain.

Benjamin B. Wolman
Paul D. Boyer

Psychological Tests

The use of tests to understand human cognitive and emotional function is one of the oldest and most important contributions of psychology to the applied mental health fields. A psychological test is a standardized technique for obtaining a sample of behavior, which can then be coded or scored to yield quantitative data. These data become valuable to the extent that they accurately describe or predict an individual's operation in important aspects of daily life.

Psychological tests must demonstrate adequate levels of reliability and validity. *Reliability* describes the consistency of the quantitative data if a person is retested with either the same test or an alternative form. *Validity* specifies the relation of the test's data yield to the real-world behavior it attempts to describe or predict. Reliability and validity can be determined, and they place a ceiling on a test's usefulness.

The use of psychological tests raises a variety of ethical and social concerns. These include the professional responsibilities of test users and publishers, the protection of privacy and confidentiality, and the description of any potential for discrimination on the basis of sex or sociocultural status. A. Anastasi (1988) provides a comprehensive discussion of these issues.

A practical way of categorizing psychological tests is in terms of the aspects of human function on which they focus. In broad outline, the spectrum can be divided into the following categories: (1) tests of general cognitive function; (2) tests of specific cognitive operations; (3) tests of interests, values, and attitudes; and (4) tests of personality.

Tests of general cognitive function. One of the earliest uses of psychological testing was to aid in the description of overall intellectual function. Definitions have varied widely, but most current tests of general mental ability describe information-processing efficiency. Using a broad sampling of tasks that make verbal, numerical, and perceptual-spatial demands, tests such as the Wechsler Adult Intelligence Scale—Revised and the Stanford-Binet Intelligence Scale provide a description of "the aggregate or global capacity of the individual to act purposefully, to think rationally, and to deal effectively with his environment" (Wechsler 1944, 3). Within this area of psychological testing, instruments have been developed for use across the life span (Matarazzo 1972; Sattler 1988).

Tests of specific cognitive operations. There are many settings in which information about an individual's function in a specific cognitive area is of value. When the data are used to predict how someone will operate in a particular situation, the tests function as aptitude measures. Achievement testing describes how well a person has acquired specific cognitive skills. Neuropsychological assessment provides information about the operation of specific brain functions.

Aptitude tests are used to aid planning in educational and vocational settings. One commonly used battery is the Differential Aptitude Tests. It provides data about eight specific areas, such as mechanical reasoning, which are useful in predicting academic and vocational success.

Achievement tests are designed to measure how well a person has acquired a specific set of cognitive skills, often as the result of some sort of training program. A number of batteries (e.g., the Stanford Achievement Test) have been developed to cover the areas typically included in elementary and secondary academic settings. Compilations such as the one provided by O. K. Buros (1985) indicate a very large number of tests designed to provide data about specific areas of achievement.

Neuropsychological assessment provides information about the status of brain functions that can be affected by structural damage or deterioration. These descriptions are often useful in indicating the presence, location, and type of problem and in planning appropriate rehabilitation. Among the most widely used neuropsychological batteries are those developed by W. C. Halstead and R. M. Reitan and by Alexander Romanovich Luria.

Tests of interests, values, and attitudes. Information about affinity for particular activities or opinions about particular issues can be of value in a variety of educational, vocational, interpersonal, and social contexts. Interest tests typically provide data about a person's liking for educational or vocational areas. Measures of values and attitudes focus on orientation toward a variety of personal, political, moral, and social issues.

Interest testing is often used to help individuals in their educational or vocational planning. One frequently used interest measure, the Strong Interest Inventory, provides data both about a person's general vocational orientation and the similarity of her preferences to those of individuals successfully working in a wide spectrum of specific occupations. Other common vocational interest tests include the Kuder Occupational Interest Survey and the Jackson Vocational Interest Survey.

Tests of value and attitudes describe a person's orientation toward a variety of economic, social, political, and moral issues. The Work Values Inventory is an example of such a test, furnishing information about the importance a person attaches to different aspects of the world of work. Other instruments provide data about attitudes people have about important aspects of daily life, such as school experience. A large number of scales have been created to describe attitudes toward specific situations, often associated with government or social policy.

Tests of personality. Personality tests describe the relatively enduring features that account for much of the way an individual responds across a variety of situations. Although there is no necessary relationship, personality testing shares much of its history and research base with the investigation of psychopathology.

Objective measures of personality work by presenting individuals with a series of questions for which their answers are limited to choices such as True or False. These responses can then be evaluated in a variety of ways. One approach is to compare an individual's answers to those of some independently identified group, such as schizophrenic inpatients. Another is to generate scores on scales of various aspects of personality, such as conscientiousness or suspiciousness, which have been developed using a variety of content validation, internal consistency, or factor-analytic techniques. The Minnesota Multiphasic Personality Inventory (MMPI-2) is a widely used, primarily pathology oriented multiphasic personality survey that employs scales developed using several of these objective approaches. Examples of objective instruments whose focus is on nonpathological personality operation include the California Psychological Inventory and the Sixteen Personality Factor Questionnaire.

The Rorschach Inkblot Test presents ten moderately ambiguous visual stimuli to which the individual responds with descriptions. These answers can then be coded and interpreted in relation to validity studies, which relate patterns of Rorschach response to a variety of affective, cognitive, and interpersonal features. Other approaches to the Rorschach focus more on response content and utilize specific theories of personality in describing an individual's intrapsychic function.

An example of the projective approach to personality assessment is provided by the Thematic Apperception Test (TAT). Respondents are shown a series of pictures and asked to integrate each into a story that spans some period of time and imagines the thoughts and feelings of its characters. Several systematic approaches have been developed for the use of apperception tests with individuals throughout the life span.

Phillip S. Erdberg

Psychological Treatment of the Physically Disabled

Disability is a relational construct. It properly denotes an interaction between a person and his environment that leads to a performance deemed by relevant parties to be chronically, significantly below standard. The term "disability," therefore, is somewhat elastic. Whether a person has a disability depends not only upon his condition but upon how the environment is made or not made to accommodate to it, what behavior is expected, and how or by whom performance is judged. Because of this, a consensus about disability's demographics has been difficult to obtain.

The National Health Survey, a nationwide survey of households in the United States conducted by the National Center for Health Statistics between 1983 and 1986, found that approximately 14% (based on a population of 231.5 million Americans) of noninstitutionalized residents had an activity limitation (Kraus and Stoddard 1991). Of these individuals, 8.8 million could not perform a major life activity, such as working or keeping house, and an additional 13.6 million could perform such an activity only in a limited fashion.

Using a slightly different metric, the survey found that 21% of noninstitutionalized individuals above age 15 reported functional limitations, many having more than one limitation. Fully 2.5 million people, to cite a few examples, reported not being able to get around inside their home, 2.1 million said they were unable to get in and out of bed unaided, and 2.5 million indicated they could not make their speech understandable to others.

An additional 2 million people live in institutions; about 1.4 million in nursing homes, 250,000 in mental hospitals, 250,000 in facilities for the mentally retarded, and 180,000 in institutions that serve both the frail elderly and the mentally retarded. With the exception of those in facilities for the mentally retarded, the vast majority of residents of institutions are over 65 years old.

Disability is commonly associated with both chronic health conditions and injury. Over 75% of those with multiple sclerosis, for example, experience activity limitations, as do 48% of those with emphysema. Expectably, by any definition, the proportion of those with a disability rises as a function of age. Under 0.4% of persons between ages 5 and 44 need assistance in the activities of daily living; by age 65 and age 85, the percentages are 2.5 and 19.1, respectively.

Those with disabilities constitute a heterogeneous set. As a class, however, disabled individuals living in the United States are far less likely to be formally educated. They are poorer, more limited in social and community participation, less likely to be work-

ing in spite of their desire to do so, and experience less satisfaction with their lives than their counterparts without disabilities (ICD 1986; Krauss and Stoddard 1991).

In the United States, the ascendant clinical paradigm influences others to perceive people with disabilities as being sick and requiring treatment, rather than as persons for whom a disability is but one personal characteristic and who require environmental accommodations and civil rights. Nonetheless, there is little doubt that individuals with disabilities may often greatly benefit from professional psychological interventions.

Systematic investigation of the social and psychological adjustment of those with disabilities is rather recent; less than 50 years has passed since R. G. Barker, D. M. Wright, and M. R. Gonick (1946) produced their seminal *Adjustment to Physical Handicap and Illness: A Survey of the Social Psychology of Physique and Disability*. In the recent past, disabled individuals were usually referred to mental health clinicians for adjustment to disability, depression, and anxiety. Such referrals remain common and to some extent useful; however, increasingly more sophisticated appreciations of the nuances of the human condition are available. As Franklin C. Shontz (1977) has pointed out, (1) psychological reactions to the onset or imposition of a disability need not be uniformly distressing and do not inevitably result in maladjustment; (2) no necessary correlations exist between the physical characteristics of the disability and one's reaction to it; (3) environmental factors (e.g., whether there is accessible transportation) often contribute more to the psychological reactions of people to disability than do personal traits; and (4) of all the factors that affect a person's total life situation, disability is but one, often an important one, but sometimes not.

In addition to the usual nosological considerations (e.g., DSM-IV), clinicians must weigh the significance both impairment and its context have for their clients. In doing so, the following, by no means exclusive, list ought be considered:

1. The meaning context in which disability arises. Clients who receive disabilities in the service of what they consider to be a higher good (sav-

ing someone's life), for example, will likely respond differently than those who receive them through negligence.

2. The time of life when the disability occurs. Unlike those born with atypical physical features, individuals at midlife who sustain a disability display more significant affective disturbances, particularly depressions.

3. The impact the disability has upon a desired lifestyle. To a musician, for example, the loss of a finger may be a greater disaster than the loss of a hand is to a writer.

4. The abruptness of the disability's onset. Adjustment to a disability often takes a different course if the disabling event was sudden and traumatic as opposed to gradual and progressive.

5. The disability's visibility. All visible disabilities produce deviation from socially defined physical perfection. Particular disfigurements may be magnified into a sense of global self-disgust. On the other hand, hidden disabilities (e.g., chronic pain) may deprive a person of the advantages that accrue to those to whom society affords the "sick role," for example, sympathy.

6. The response of others to the disability. Perhaps most importantly, clinicians should understand the meaning a disabling condition has for individuals not only depends on their personalities, but also is a function of the response of others to it. For example, the accommodations their employers make to enable them to keep working; the attitude intimates convey about their worth; the provisions a society makes to ensure their well-being; and so on.

Current treatment techniques are quite varied. Eclectic clinicians will draw on those deemed by both their clients and themselves to be best suited to achieving mutually formulated habilitation and rehabilitation goals. In addition to a selection of individual and group "talking" psychotherapies (e.g., cognitive, psychodynamic, Gestalt), cognitive retraining, meditation, skill training, hypnosis, and an array of behavioral techniques may be drawn

upon, depending upon the particular treatment issue and the skill and orientation of the professionals involved. The client's significant others may also participate (e.g., via family therapy) in the therapeutic program. Peers are playing an increasing role in producing and maintaining positive changes in those with disabilities, whether individually or in support groups. At root, the overarching aim of any treatment regimen is to enable the individual to engage in the most productive, satisfying, and autonomous life possible.

Herbert H. Krauss
Robert Paluck

Psychology and Law

In 1908 Hugo Münsterberg wrote *On the Witness Stand*, in which he assailed the legal profession for not recognizing the positive contribution that psychology could make to the law. Legal scholars, such as John H. Wigmore, responded to Münsterberg by criticizing his unwarranted optimism about the relationship between the two disciplines, claiming that he had oversold what psychology had to offer to the law. And, for nearly six decades after the great Münsterberg-Wigmore debate, the two fields remained virtually isolated from each other.

Since the 1970s, however, we have witnessed an explosion of interest in the relationship between psychology and law. In the 1990s, innumerable books and journals are devoted to the psychology/law interface, interdisciplinary course offerings and graduate training programs have expanded, and national societies (e.g., American Psychology-Law Society/Division 41 of the American Psychological Association, the Law and Society Association) facilitate the interrelationship of the two disciplines.

The Law
Most of the law (i.e., laws, legal systems, legal processes) is based on assumptions about how people act and how their actions can be controlled. When a state enacts a law allowing six-person juries to decide cases in lieu of the traditional 12-member panels, the state is assuming that the quality of justice will be the same, even though the number of

jurors has decreased. When the Federal Food and Drug Administration enacts rules that require warning labels on certain types of products, underlying behavioral and social assumptions are that the label will help consumers select and use products more wisely, and that consumers need this type of protection.

When Congress establishes a legal system, such as by creating a federal administrative agency, to address a perceived social problem or need, it makes numerous assumptions about the optimal method for achieving its goals. A juvenile court is created partially to help the court system respond to the unique concerns posed by delinquent juveniles, with the assumption being that a specialized court will be better equipped than courts of general jurisdiction to understand and address the problems posed in these cases.

To illustrate how assumptions about behavior underlie legal processes, let us consider an individual who is claimed to have a serious mental illness and to be a danger to others. Because of these allegations, this person may become the subject of an involuntary civil commitment petition. Civil commitment law allows the state government to hospitalize such an individual against his will. The law also guarantees these persons due process rights, such as the right to counsel; but do attorneys vigorously defend against commitment of a client who obviously needs treatment? The behavior of the attorneys in the legal context becomes as important as the law that mandated the right to have an attorney.

In some cases, the limits of human capacity must be directly stated to fully understand the validity of the behavioral and social assumptions underlying a law or legal system, thereby providing another reason for the importance of the legal processes component. For example, people have inherent limits in perceiving their environment. The simplest case is where somebody tries to observe an event across the street on a dark night. The ability to perceive may be nonexistent or at least substantially diminished; many factors affect one's perception and memory of events. Yet the law favors eyewitness testimony, assuming that it is inherently accurate.

The behavioral and social assumptions underlying laws, legal system, and legal processes require scrutiny if we are to determine their validity and the appropriateness of the law. Although lawyers are equipped to draft the legal language, they have not been trained either to identify the types of behavioral assumptions we have suggested or to study their validity. Psychologists working within the domain of psychology and law are uniquely qualified for this task.

Psychology

Almost every area of research within psychology, if not every one, has relevant contributions to make to this interaction. For example, cognitive psychologists study the problems of eyewitness and hypnotically induced testimony; developmental psychologists study the impact of divorce and different custodial arrangements on children and ex-spouses; social psychologists study jury decision making; and clinical psychologists study the impact of various court-ordered treatments on mentally disturbed offenders.

Typically, psycholegal research proceeds as follows. The researcher

1. examines the law and identifies the legal issues that warrant consideration or the problem in society the law is designed to address;
2. identifies the behavioral and social assumption(s) underlying the law;
3. reviews the existing theory and research that is directly and indirectly relevant to the validity of these assumptions;
4. conducts new research relevant to these assumptions, if needed;
5. assesses the likelihood that each assumption is valid;
6. determines the appropriateness of the law given the conclusions thus reached; and
7. makes needed recommendations for revision of the law, either to bring it into conformity with the behavioral reality or to suggest to those responsible for implementing or enforcing the law the potential consequences of failing to do so.

This model can be, and has been, modified to accommodate the needs of individual psychological (as opposed to psycholegal) researchers more interested in psychological questions.

Psycholegal and psychological research and theory provide psychologists with the needed information to contribute to the law professionally, and not just scientifically. The most common instance is where psychologists testify as expert witnesses in court. Consider, for example, the clinical or counseling psychologist who is employed by the court or by one of the litigants to evaluate and testify about a defendant who raises an insanity defense; or a psychologist who is asked to testify in a child custody proceeding in order to help the court understand what the emotional consequences of different custodial arrangements would be to children. Professional psychologists have testified on a wide range of issues in both criminal matters (e.g., adult and child sexual abuse, competency, sentencing, death penalty, pornography) and civil matters (e.g., workers' compensation and disability, involuntary civil commitment, product liability, discrimination).

As professionals, psychologists also interact with the law in other ways. Some law enforcement agencies hire psychologists to train new employees on such topics as effective methods of crowd control, interviewing eyewitnesses, handling family disputes, or dealing with alleged offenders with serious mental illnesses or addictions. Other psychologists may be hired by criminal justice agencies to provide assessment, therapy, and counseling to populations who are in direct contact with laws and legal systems (e.g., jail detainees, prisoners, juvenile offenders).

Psychologists also act as evaluator-consultants, using their expertise to evaluate some aspect of the law or advising people within the legal system on how to handle a particular problem. Social psychologists may be called upon to consult with lawyers in selecting a jury or in how best to present physical evidence. Organizational psychologists may provide advice on how best to manage a complex caseload within a court system. Clinical psychologists may work with the FBI to develop criminal profiles of serial killers or cult leaders.

A psychologist may act as a policy analyst for state or federal government. In this role, the professional is concerned with ensuring that lawmakers and administrative agency personnel are making and implementing decisions with a firm understanding of the teachings of behavioral and social science on the relevant topic. When a state legislature is considering changing its test for insanity, a psychologist can synthesize the research available from other jurisdictions that have undertaken similar reforms and present the potential consequences of implementing the new standard.

What is the role of forensic psychology? *Forensic psychology* and *forensic psychiatry* refer to the subspecialties that deal with court-related activities. Because these terms typically refer to psychologists working as experts in the court, or in preparation for a trial, the activities of forensic psychologists or psychiatrists fall under the professional interactions between law and psychology.

One type of professional interaction between psychology and law is the reverse of the above situations—that is, where the law regulates the science and practice of psychology. Just as each way that psychologists aid in the administration of the law results in new questions that require additional psycholegal research, the legal regulation of psychology also raises innumerable researchable assumptions. For example, laws directly regulate the delivery of psychological services (e.g., specifying how psychologists are licensed or certified to practice and how they are permitted to organize their professional business enterprises) and the way clients of professional services enter into the service system, how they are processed through it, and the rights they receive while in it. Research on the assumptions underlying these laws is also needed. For example, if a law mandates that therapists divulge otherwise confidential information that was gained during the course of therapy, will the disclosure or threat of disclosure compromise in some way the ultimate success of the therapeutic endeavor? The law assumes not, or at least that the harm to therapy is far outweighed by the benefit to some third party from the divulgence.

Although many psychologists work in this field without the benefit of a law degree, the importance of understanding the legal environment cannot be overstated. Clinical assessments of alleged mentally disordered offenders, for example, must answer the legal questions posed by the law and the court. Relying solely on psychological knowledge will result in incompetent performance by the psychologist. Thus, the psychology and law field must be recognized as an interdisciplinary enterprise.

Bruce D. Sales
Maureen O'Connor

Psychology of Women

Historically speaking, research on women in psychology only began toward the end of the nineteenth century. This research, almost exclusively performed by men, was replete with gender biases (S. A. Shields 1975). Often, research was changed to fit the prevailing theory on brain size and function. For example, research on the difference in lobe size between males and females was changed to emphasize the parietal lobe over the frontal lobe as being the area with the most developed mental capacities, because women were found to have larger frontal lobes. Such revision in theory served to maintain the premise that males had elevated mental capacities.

Leta Setter Hollingworth was the first psychologist to disprove some of these myths by using empirical research (Hollingworth 1914; Montague and Hollingworth 1914). She argued that social conditions rather than biology could more permanently account for certain male-female differences.

Research on women's issues continued sporadically throughout the first half of the twentieth century, but it was not until the changing and liberating times of the 1960s and 1970s—when more women entered the field of psychology, feminism grew on college campuses, and courses on women were developed—that this interest in women's issues impacted the field of psychology. Finally, in 1973, Division 35, the Psychology of Women, was established by the American Psychological Association.

During the 1970s, the field of the psychology of women expanded at a rapid pace, for scholars were anxious to look at issues that had been ignored. Issues such as aggression, achievement motivation, and maternal instinct were explored. Notable women in the history of psychology were brought to light, some of whom were found to have conducted many of the classic studies of psychology. Although

the studies performed during the 1970s were extremely useful and often groundbreaking, the complexity of the issue of gender was not quite understood. Research often focused on what was wrong with women that they, for example, were not in management positions. Looking at this problem from a social-structural perspective, or examining stereotypes and institutions, was not done until recently.

Margaret Matlin writes, "the reason we study the psychology of women is to explore a wide variety of psychological issues that specifically concern women." Subjects that are looked at can include comparing females to males, with questions such as "What influences in schools incite boys and girls to act differently?" or "Are women and men drastically different?" Other subjects that are often examined are issues that only apply to women, such as menstruation, pregnancy, abortion, childbirth, and menopause. Topics such as rape, sexual harassment, battering, and sexual discrimination and issues such as retirement, career, sexuality, and achievement are examined from a woman's perspective.

By the 1990s, numerous textbooks have been written, and more colleges and universities than ever before offer courses in the psychology of women. Several journals are published specifically to include articles relevant to women, e.g., the *Psychology of Women Quarterly* (published by Division 35 of the APA), *Sex Roles*, and *Women and Therapy*.

Finally, in order more fully to understand and appreciate the intricacies of the psychology of women, the often misunderstood and controversial words *sex*, *gender*, *feminist*, and *sexism* need to be defined. *Sex* is relatively simple, for it only corresponds to those characteristics of a person that are biological in origin (i.e., sex organs or sex chromosomes). *Gender* is a more general appellation that has to do with social categories and assumptions about how women and men behave. It is often used to designate terms such as gender stereotypes, gender roles, and gender comparisons.

The third term of note is *feminist*. A feminist is someone who has values, beliefs, and attitudes that embrace a high regard for women as human beings. Accordingly, a feminist believes that women and men should be equal on an economic, legal, and social basis. It is important to note here that the definition of a feminist includes both women and men.

Another pertinent word is *sexism*. Sexism is a bias or slant against people because of their gender. For example, someone who thinks that women cannot make good engineers is sexist. Sexism can show itself blatantly in the media (i.e., commercials that always portray families with Mother at home in the kitchen waiting for Father to come home from work) and in discrimination. Sexism can also show itself in subtle ways, such as referring to a mature woman as a "girl."

Researchers today acknowledge the complicated nature of questions about the psychology of women and the significance of external influences in our society that determine who women are and what they can do. Currently, research on the psychology of women continues at breakneck speed. The field is becoming more and more interdisciplinary, and it is becoming more challenging.

Florence L. Denmark

Psychologists as Mental Health Service Providers

In the last decade, psychologists have been increasingly recognized as independent health service providers uniquely trained to provide high-quality mental health services. In fact, since the mid-1980s, psychologists have provided more outpatient psychotherapy and psychological diagnostic evaluations than any other doctorally trained mental health profession ("Industry Statistics" 1989).

Statutory Recognition of Psychologists

With the 1989 inclusion in Medicare of psychologists as qualified independent providers, virtually all major publicly funded health care programs recognize psychologists as mental health service providers. This includes the Civilian Health and Medical Program of the Uniform Services (CHAMPUS), under which psychologists may independently diagnose and treat patients, both in the hospital and on an outpatient basis.

Psychologists are similarly authorized to evaluate and treat patients independently under the Federal Employees Health Benefits Program, the Veterans Health Care Expansion Act, and the Civilian Health and Medical Program of the Veterans Administration. The Federal Employees Compensation Act, which provides reimbursement for health services for officers and employees of the federal government, includes the services of "clinical psychologists" under the definition of "medical, surgical, and hospital services."

The Vocational Rehabilitation Act, which requires assessment of persons with both physical and mental handicaps, authorizes psychologists to perform such assessments, consistent with state law and regulations. Also, the Health Maintenance Organization Act, governing all federally qualified health maintenance organizations and mandating coverage of both inpatient and outpatient basic health services, includes psychologists among the providers authorized to provide mental health services.

Finally, psychologists are recognized in both the Federal Rules of Criminal Procedure and the Federal Rules of Civil Procedure. Rule 12.2(c) of the Federal Rules of Criminal Procedure provides for mental examination and expert testimony relating to a mental disease or defect or any other mental condition bearing on the issue of competency. This statute authorizes both psychologists and psychiatrists to perform this function. Similarly, Rule 35 of the Federal Rules of Civil Procedure also includes psychologists among those providers authorized to perform court-ordered mental examinations.

Education and Training

Psychologists receive extensive education and training. The typical training required for independently practicing psychologists includes rigorous academic coursework, relevant research activities, and intensive practical experience leading to the doctoral degree. According to data from the National Research Council (1989), an average of 7.1 years of graduate education and training is taken toward the doctoral degree in psychology.

In addition to coursework and research, training in psychology includes extensive clinical rotations followed by at least one year of full-time supervised internship experience in a hospital, medical center, or clinic. Psychological services mastered in the internship include evaluation, diagnosis, and assessment of the functioning of individuals, groups, and organizations. The services also include preventive and ameliorative interventions that facilitate the functioning of individuals, groups and organizations; consultation and program development; administration and supervision; and the evaluation of psychological services (American Psychological Association 1987).

In addition to receipt of the doctorate, postdoctoral supervised experience is a necessary component of a psychologist's training. All jurisdictions require at least one full year of supervised health service experience after receipt of the doctorate for a candidate to become eligible for licensure.

Licensure in Psychology

In all jurisdictions, the practice of psychology and/or use of the title "psychologist" is regulated by a licensing or certification law. To be licensed for the independent practice of psychology, virtually all states require a minimum of a doctoral degree in psychology from an accredited institution and two years of supervised health service experience, one of which is typically a predoctoral internship. In addition, all states require a candidate for licensure to successfully complete an examination process.

Licensure in psychology is "generic"; that is, all types of practicing psychologists possess the same general license to practice. Each individual's scope of competence, however, is limited to only those activities for which the person is able to demonstrate the requisite education, training, and experience. State boards of psychology are responsible for ensuring that individuals do not practice outside their areas of competence, although boards traditionally have only investigated violations upon complaints registered against licensed psychologists. This generic licensing process has sometimes made it difficult for consumers and third-party payers to identify those licensed psychologists who are qualified to provide mental health services.

In recent years, however, a number of states have enacted "health service provider" (HSP) certification as a supplement to their generic licensure. HSP certification is granted to only those licensed psy-

chologists whose demonstrated education, training, and experience qualifies them to provide clinical or health services.

Future Directions

Although psychologists have tended to be recognized as mental health service providers, their training actually prepares them for service provision in the much broader health care arena. Specialized training in such areas as health psychology, pediatric psychology, rehabilitation psychology, and geropsychology, to name a few, makes psychologists particularly well suited to integrate psychological aspects of patient care with physical care. Now that psychology has established itself more broadly as an autonomous mental health profession, future developments will likely take the form of its broader establishment as an autonomous health care profession.

The trend toward psychology providing a broader range of health services will be furthered by the changes anticipated through national health reform. In particular, the Clinton administration's health care reform proposal, which is expected to provide the core of any changes enacted by Congress, emphasizes a primary-care model (Christianson and Moscovice 1993). In such a system, psychologists will do well to affiliate and collaborate with primary-care physicians (e.g., family practice physicians, internists, pediatricians, obstetricians) on the front lines of health care. Even psychologists practicing in hospitals will be less likely to be focused on traditional mental health services and more focused on the application of psychological intervention strategies to general health care, such as with pediatric oncology programs, cardiovascular disorders, rehabilitation programs, sleep disorders, and gastrointestinal disorders.

Currently, the Center for Substance Abuse Treatment, of the Substance Abuse and Mental Health Services Administration (SAMHSA) has awarded a pilot project to the American Psychological Association to provide linkages between psychologists and family physicians to enhance prevention, assessment, and treatment of alcohol and other drug abuse in rural America (J. G. Hill, personal communication, July 1992). One purpose of the project is to expose psychologists and family physicians to models of collaborative treatment. The data generated from the established psychologist-physician pairs is anticipated to provide further insight into collaboration in a primary care setting.

Another recent development in psychology, with significant implications for the future, has been the creation of a pilot program by the Department of Defense to train licensed clinical psychologists to prescribe psychotropic medication. The goal of this two-year program, which combines academic coursework with practicum training in a medical facility, is to produce a trained and experienced psychologist able to prescribe psychotropic drugs from a limited formulary (Department of Defense 1989). Considerable debate has occurred concerning the pros and cons of incorporating prescribing into psychology's scope of practice (e.g., DeLeon, Fox, and Graham 1991; DeLeon, Greenberg, and Fisher 1990; Fox 1988), and much interest in prescribing both within and without the profession has been generated. A number of states are already exploring legislative amendments to authorize qualified psychologists to prescribe (DeLeon 1992).

Summary and Conclusions

In recent years psychologists have become well recognized as independent mental health service providers in both outpatient and inpatient settings. Practicing psychologists are uniquely trained to provide psychotherapy and assessment for the full range of mental disorders. Psychologists are equally well trained to provide services to a broad range of areas in the health care arena. In the future, psychologists will likely be increasingly recognized as independent health service providers, capable of applying psychological techniques and intervention strategies to the whole range of mental and physical disorders. Psychologists can also be expected to work to expand their scope of practice to include prescription privileges.

Russell Newman

Psychomotor Behavior: Single-Channel Mechanism

The major evidence pertaining to the single-channel model comes from investigations of the phenomenon known as the psychological refractory period (PRP). These have generally involved simultaneous, serial, or continuous presentations of stimuli and a variety of responses, such as a key press, tracking a moving target, or larger movements, such as swinging an arm.

In 1931, C. W. Telford found a delay in the reaction time to the second of a pair of closely spaced stimuli. This delay increased as the intersignal interval (ISI) shortened. Telford called the phenomenon the "psychological refractory period" and attributed it to a central refractoriness that was analogous to the loss of sensitivity found in single nerve fibers immediately following stimulation.

Craik examined the question of whether the lag in tracking a continuously moving target could be explained by the time required for stimuli to pass through the sensory, central, and motor mechanisms. If so, the signals could be received and acted upon continuously, and a smooth tracking response would quickly result. However, he found that instead of pursuing the target in a smooth manner, the unpracticed subject responded to misalignments discontinuously at a frequency of about two per second. Craik noted that this intermittency was not caused by motor limitations, because similar hand movements could be made considerably faster than two per second. Moreover, it was not caused by difficulty in detecting misalignment, because the effect remained when the display was magnified. Craik theorized, therefore, that impairment in activating a response to a new stimulus could result from a time lag caused by the central computing process acting upon a preceding stimulus to produce an efferent discharge.

Craik was aware that with practice a subject could learn to anticipate the future course of the target and thus track more smoothly. Confirmation of this was later provide by E. C. Poulton and by R. M. Gottsdanker. He was also aware that the intermittency period was composed of approximately .3 seconds for the reaction-time delay, with the remainder being the time to perform the actual corrective movement. Corroborative evidence was provided by M. A. Vince's publications of their step-tracking experiments (P. Bertelson 1966), which allowed direct measurement of reaction times (RT) and movement times (MT).

Single-Channel Theory

Craik's idea of the intermittency of the human sensory-motor system soon led to A. T. Welford's advancement of the single-channel hypothesis, which holds that if information from a stimulus arrives while the central mechanisms are busy processing the information from a prior stimulus then it would have to be stored until the central channel became free (Welford 1968). In using reaction time (RT) to estimate the first signal (S_1) channel occupation time, Welford was able to specify that if the second stimulus (S_2) arrived before the end of the reaction time to S_1 (RT_1), then RT to the second signal (RT_2) would comprise a "normal" RT plus the interval between the arrival of S_2 and the end of RT_1. Thus:

$$RT_2 = RT_N + RT_1 - ISI.$$

Another facet of Welford's theory is the phenomenon he called grouping; with very short intersignal intervals (ISIs), the two signals may be treated as one. In Vince's step-tracking experiment, for example, the first response movement was omitted in 20% of the cases under the .05-second ISI condition, 8% under .10 seconds, and very seldom with longer ISIs. Later studies have demonstrated the phenomenon. Welford explained grouping by postulating a "gate" that began closing when the decision center started to operate. He suggested that the gate takes about 80 ms to close, so that any signals occurring within that period would be treated together.

Multichannel Processing

If attention is switched after a fixed interval, multichannel processing would be possible. Direct support was given by F. W. Taylor, P. H. Lindsay, and S. M. Forbes (Welford 1968), who examined the amount of shared capacity processing in auditory and visual discrimination. They quantified the capacity allocated to discrimination by using d^2, which was defined as a measure of discriminatory performance, and found that while the capacity for processing information had a definite limit, parallel processing was possible. Control of this parallel processing was found to require 15% of the total capacity.

Several studies have also found a less-than-unity slope when RT_2 is plotted as a function of the overlap, and often the line begins below the prediction line, thus implying the presence of some residual capacity—which seems to diminish as ISI approaches RT_1. This creates a problem for intermittency theory, which Welford has described in terms of two possibilities, namely: when the first task occupies the channel completely but intermittently (thereby allowing some gaps when the channel is free); or when the occupation is continuous but incomplete (Welford 1968, 134). D. E. Broadbent (1971) favors the idea that, although the channel has a finite capacity, it should be able to handle parallel sets of information, but at a reduced speed.

Response Conflict Theory

The third approach that attributes psychological refractoriness to the effects of S_1 is the response conflict theory, which holds that delays in the selection of the response for execution are caused by a number of competing response tendencies associated with S_1 and S_2 and that the effects on RT_1 and RT_2 depend upon the relative strengths of these tendencies. Therefore, under usual PRP conditions the theory predicts decrements in RT_2 as well as RT_1. In addition, as ISI lengthens the response, conflict should decrease, thereby reducing the corresponding delay in RT_1.

Preparatory State Theories

A second general category of psychological refractory period theories (PRP) considers that delays in RT_2 are due not to the influence of S_1 but to foreperiod effects during ISI. These preparatory state theories regard S_1 as an extra warning signal that initiates a foreperiod prior to the occurrence of S_2. One version is the expectancy hypothesis, which is based on the well-established fact that the probability of occurrence of a signal influences the reaction time to that signal. Thus, the higher the expectancy, the faster the RT.

Later work on the readiness concept has centered on the idea that S_1 may be considered as an extra foreperiod when ISIs are held constant or when no R_1 is required; therefore, RT should be less delayed. However, in his review of studies that test the readiness hypothesis, P. J. G. Keuss (1972) states that although there is general agreement that the mere presentation of S_1 without the requirement of a response to it can facilitate RT_2, there is still some disagreement where conditions have employed constant sets of ISI.

Central Refractoriness

W. G. Koster and R. Van Schuur (1973) have examined the sensitivity hypothesis. They present auditory stimuli ranging from 20–80 dB over 8 ISIs (25–1000 ms) and find that asymptotic levels calculated from individual exponential curves of RT_2 as a function of ISI decrease steadily as the intensity of S_2 increases. This finding is interpreted as favoring the sensitivity model, which is based on recovery of the system following the passage of a signal.

Leslie R. T. Williams

Psychomotor Learning: Warm-up Decrement

The Activity-Set Hypothesis

Richard A. Schmidt and his colleagues (1972) have proposed the activity-set hypothesis, which states that when the subject rests, the activity set is lost—that is, the pattern of adjustment changes—to reflect the activity set appropriate to the "task" of resting. When the subject resumes practice, she performs poorly because of the lost activity set, and it requires a few trials for the pattern of adjustment to be regained. One of the important predictions of this theory is that if a task requiring the same activity set as the criterion task is practiced immediately prior to resumption of practice on the criterion task, the activity set will be reinstated by the secondary task, and warm-up decrement on the criterion task will be reduced or eliminated. Experiments dealing with this prediction form the basis of the support for the activity-set hypothesis.

For example, Schmidt and J. Nacson (1971, experiment 1) used a right-hand force-estimation task (using the hand-gripping muscles) as the criterion task, and twenty trials were provided before a 10-minute rest, after which an additional ten trials were conducted. During the rest, subjects practiced another force-estimation task, but this task used the left hand, a different force, and elbow-flexion activity. When this left-hand task was presented immediately prior to resumption of right-hand practice, warm-up decrement was eliminated, whereas a group without this left-hand task showed the usual large warm-up decrement. As the left-hand task could not be reasoned to increase the habit strength for the criterion task, the interpretation was that the activity set for careful force estimation was lost over rest and, for the group with the left-hand practice, was reinstated prior to right-hand practice, resulting in no warm-up decrement for this group. This supports the notion that warm-up decrement is a loss over rest of the essential adjustments that support a class of similar responses.

Some Characteristics of the Activity Set

In experiments where the activity set was reinstated by practicing a left-hand task of the same class as the criterion task, if the end of left-hand practice was separated from the resumption of criterion-task practice by as little as 40 seconds, the beneficial effects of the left-hand task were nullified; another experiment showed that this effect was nullified if only 25 seconds of rest were provided. It appears that the readjustment is very short-lived and, perhaps, is available to the subject for less than 25 seconds; if practice is not resumed by this time, the warm-up decrement is displayed as usual.

These findings and others, reviewed by Schmidt (1972), suggest that warm-up decrement is caused by a disruption—caused by either rest or performance of a task of a different class than the criterion task—of the essential adjustments that underlie the performance of the task in question.

Richard A. Schmidt

Psychophysical Measurement Methods

In any particular measurement problem, scaling potentially concerns a three-dimensional table of data. On the front face of the cube, one could think of rows as representing stimuli and columns as representing responses to the stimuli. The "slices" of the cube going from front to back represent the responses of different persons to the stimuli. The words *stimuli* and *responses* represent anything that the experimenter does to the subject and anything the subject does in return. Typical things (stimuli) the experimenter does to the subject include having him lift weights, presenting him with spelling words, and showing him a list of foods. Typical responses required for these types of stimuli would be judging which of two weights is heavier, indicating whether or not each word is correctly spelled, or rating how much each food is liked.

Stimuli and People

When one seeks a unidimensional scale of stimuli, the hope is to find a scale that fits the average individual. Thus, a scale developed in this way would be typical of persons as a group, even though it might not perfectly represent the scale that would be obtained by an intensive investigation of any one person. The long-range research purpose in scaling stimuli (rather than persons) is to relate scalings of the same stimuli with respect to different attributes. Thus, after a unidimensional scale has been developed for the perceived loudness of tones, another scaling of the same tones could be made when each tone is accompanied by a light whose intensity is correlated with the intensity of the tone. Scaling of the tones could be made in various applied problems, such as in employing the tones as communication signals. At issue would be mathematical relations between the different scalings of the tones.

Judgments and Sentiments

One of the most important distinctions in measurement theory is that between responses concerning judgments and those concerning sentiments. Judgments include all those instances where there is a correct response. This would be the case, for example, when a child is asked, "How much is two plus two?" This would also be the case when subjects are required to judge which of two tones is louder or which of two weights is heavier. In all these instances there is some veridical comparison for the subject's response, and it is possible to determine whether each response is correct or incorrect.

The word *sentiment* is used to cover all responses concerning personal reactions, preferences, interests, attitudes, and likes and dislikes. An individual makes responses concerning sentiments when she rates boiled cabbage on a seven-step like-dislike rating scale, answers the question, "Which would you rather do, organize a club or work on a stamp collection?" or rank ten actors in terms of her preferences.

Comparative and absolute responses. Another important distinction concerns whether the subject is required to make an absolute response to each stimulus separately or to make comparative judgments or expressions of sentiment among the stimuli. The question, "How long is this line in inches?" for example, would elicit an absolute response. An absolute response is also necessary when the subject is required to rate boiled cabbage on a seven-step like-dislike scale. In both instances the subject responds to each stimulus separately, and he indicates the amount of the attribute in an absolute sense.

Scale for Response

In most types of responses, subjects are required to respond to stimuli in terms of an ordinal, interval, or ratio scale; that is, each subject is required to generate a scale having the properties of one of these three basic types of scales. There are many ways that responses can be obtained with respect to the three types of scales, and each is referred to as a psychophysical method.

Most frequently, subjects are required to operate on an ordinal scale. All the particular methods that can be applied for that purpose are called methods of ordinal estimation. The most straightforward way to do this is by the method of rank order, which, as the name implies, requires the subject to rank stimuli from "most" to "least" with respect to some attribute of judgment or sentiment. A more thorough approach is the method of pair comparisons, in which the subject is required to rank stimuli two at a time in all possible pairs.

For responses concerning interval estimation, one of the most popularly used psychophysical methods is that of equal-appearing intervals. In this method, the subject is instructed to sort the stimuli in such a way as to make the intervals between categories subjectively equal. Thus, if the individual is sorting 100 shades of gray paper from darkest to lightest, she would be instructed to work so that the perceived differences between adjacent categories are equal.

The ratio-estimation methods require subjects to respond to the absolute magnitudes of stimuli. As is true of the interval-estimation methods, there are numerous particular forms of ratio estimation.

Methods for Scaling Stimuli

After responses have been obtained by one of the methods discussed above, the next step is to generate an ordinal, interval, or ratio scale. In the scaling of stimuli, complex models usually are not required for deriving ordinal scales, and the different models used for that purpose usually arrive at the same ordering of stimuli. With the method of rank order, the average ranks would be obtained over subjects, and these would be converted to one overall set of ranks. The final set of ranks would constitute an ordinal scaling of the stimuli for the typical subject.

Scales based on subjective estimates. If the experimenter takes seriously the task required of the subject in giving responses relating to interval scales and ratio scales, it is a simple matter to obtain appropriate scales.

Discriminant models are based on a number of principles and practices.

1. They do not trust subjects to generate interval scales directly, as models based on subjective estimates do.
2. They elicit responses by one of the psychophysical methods relating to ordinal estimates, such as the method of pair comparisons.
3. They assume that the response to any stimulus is not some fixed value, but rather that there is some variability in response to each stimulus.

This variability may be conceptualized in terms of numerous responses by one individual to the same stimuli on different occasions or, more frequently, in terms of the variability among individuals in a group in response to the stimuli.

4. By making assumptions about the distributions of covert responses to each stimulus, percentages of comparative responses are translatable into intervals between the stimuli.
5. It is most frequently assumed that covert errors in response to stimuli are normally distributed, which leads to rather direct computations of interval scales in accordance with the mathematical properties of the normal distribution.

Jum C. Nunnally

Psychophysics: Overview

To understand how the display of environmental flux modulates action, we must investigate, quantitatively if possible, relations among the various forms of environmental energy configurations and human response. This enterprise was christened "psychophysics" by G. T. Fechner in 1860.

The Limen

A first step in psychophysics is to locate the onset of sensibility: the absolute threshold or limen. Fechner provides both data and methods for the assessment of the absolute limen for a variety of sense departments. After Fechner's work, and for the next 50 years, these methods were refined and improved.

TABLE 1

Sense Modality	Absolute Limen (threshold)
Seeing (560 mm)	10^{-6} mL
Hearing (1000 Hz)	10^{-16} watts/cm^2
Touching (1/10 mm hair)	0.1 gm
Smelling (mercaptan, musk)	0.02 ppb, 0.00004 Mg/L
Tasting (NaCl)	0.008 mol
Kinesthetic Movement	0.3°/sec

Estimates made, on a variety of sensory dimensions, of the point at which sensation begins are known with fair precision. Table 1 lists the values of the energy levels for various sense departments at which, by some criterion or other, reactivity to the presence of some stimulating event is observable.

Weber's Law

Weber's law (1834) states that the proportion of the standard stimulus that is necessary to change the observer's judgment by a constant percentage is, in itself, constant and independent of the magnitude of the standard stimulus. This law implies that everywhere on the stimulus continuum a just noticeable difference (JND) is a constant proportion of the magnitude of the stimulus at which the difference is observed. By and large, the law is true for enormous dynamic ranges for most sensory domains. Table 2 shows some representative values of Weber's law constant for a variety of sensory modalities.

TABLE 2

Sensory Modality	Weber's Constant
Seeing (intensity discrimination)	.02
Hearing (intensity)	.05
Hearing (frequency)	.002
Touching (deep pressure)	.015
Smelling (mercaptan)	.005
Tasting (NaCl)	.01

The empirical evidence in support of Weber's law was known to Fechner, who saw in it the possibility of an extension of our knowledge of the human psyche. Fechner's insight was that the truth of Weber's law, combined with the assumption that the subjective magnitude of any JND was the same as any other JND, would yield a scale of subjective magnitude. Subjective magnitudes of stimulus domains could be represented numerically by integrating Weber's law for the stimulus domain.

Signal Detection

When MIT and University of Michigan psychophysicists began to explore a theory of signal detection, they were working from research in electrical engineering. This theory has become a routine part of modern experimental psychology. Briefly, the theory proposes that on each trial the observer's perceptual continuum is stimulated at some point. The point of stimulation depends upon whether the signal was presented on that trial or not. The continuum itself is most frequently stimulated at one point when a signal is present and at a different displaced point when no signal is present, but when noise or other background effects are presumed to be operating.

Experiments generated by the theory of signal detectability have included those designed to elucidate nonperceptual features of the experiment that are important in influencing judgments about perceptual events. A general discussion of these variables is contained in Eugene Galanter (1974).

Scaling Experiments

The second new direction that has been taken by psychophysics is the experimental repudiation of Fechner's theory of measurement as an accurate representation of the psychic effects of stimulus magnitudes. Fechner's law has been replaced by the power function proposed and supported by the experiments of S. S. Stevens and his colleagues (Stevens and Galanter 1957).

Eugene Galanter

Psychosomatic Disorders

The etiologic research of mental disorders is not always capable of giving clear-cut answers. In some instances the causes of a disorder are somatopsychic; a particular disorder can be caused by the body-mind relationship, but in many instances the relationship is much more complicated. For instance, it is my belief that some cases of infantile autism are related to organic causes and are somatopsychic, whereas other cases are caused by parent-child interaction and are sociopsychogenic. Most disorders are a combination of psychosomatic and somatopsychic factors, and my sociopsychosomatic theory of schizophrenia does not exclude the role of genetic and biochemical factors (Wolman 1988).

Current research in biological rhythm and in

altered states of consciousness points to the connection between the impact of unconscious processes on somatic symptoms and to the role of physicochemical factors on psychological symptoms (Wolman and Ullman 1986). Several studies deal with the role of the immune system. The lymphocytes, plasma cells, and macrophages, which are parts of the lymphoid system, and the two immunocompetent B-cells and T-cells play an important role in the functions of the immune physical and mental disorders. The immune system mediates between biochemical and psychological processes and plays a highly important role in somatopsychic and psychosomatic disorders (Wolman, 1988).

Asthma represents a case of a combination of psychosomatic and somatopsychic factors. Asthma attacks are related to an edema of the bronchial wall, to bronchospasm, and to the development of plugs in the bronchial lumina. However, the cause of these symptoms can be physical or chemical or psychological, or a combination of these factors. A chemical irritant, an infection, allergies, dust, and change of temperature can provoke an asthma attack; but an asthma attack can also be provoked by emotional factors, such as fear, frustration, bad news, and depression. Moreover, the predisposition to asthma is often related to parental rejection, parent-child conflicts, and even interparental conflicts (Wolman 1988).

Cardiovascular diseases can be caused by a variety of physical and mental factors. Repeated failures and frustrations, parental rejection, and marital conflict can increase the damage of cardiovascular diseases. Psychological problems can cause a significant reduction in the renal blood flow and increase the arterial blood pressure. Stress can cause myocardial infarction.

R. H. Rosenman and M. R. Chesney (1982) describe two personality types. Type A individuals are ambitious, competitive, and hard-driven, with an excessive sense of urgency of time. They tend to get involved in several vocational and avocational activities, and they are associated with a high prevalence of heart trouble, and specifically with coronary heart disease. Type B individuals are not very active nor competitive, and more of them are in occupations that do not require urgent deadlines. The psycho-

logical traits of Type B people make them less frequently disposed to coronary heart disease.

Many skin diseases are psychosomatic. The nerve endings in the skin are exposed to many adverse stimuli, and skin tends to react to psychological stimuli. Fear and anger often cause flushing and pallor; impatience and shame elicit itching and blushing. Allergies are attributed to a combination of psychological and biochemical causes, and there is a frequent possibility of genetic predisposition of the immune system. Dermatitis is an inflammation of the skin caused by psychological or biochemical factors, or most often by both. Maternal rejection is often the cause of infantile dermatitis, and infantile eczema is often a product of parental inconsistency. Pruritis anogenitalia is usually a product of emotional conflict, and hives (urticaria) are related to allergies. Insecure, anxious, and depressive adolescents tend to develop acne.

Several gastrointestinal diseases are frequently psychosomatic. Anorexia nervosa and bulimia originate in emotional problems such as craving for parental love, disturbance of body image, and low ability to perceive gastric stimuli. Anorectic families stress self-sacrifice, drive, ambition, and achievement. Ulcers occur more often in a certain personality type and are often related to a conflict situation. Obesity can be caused by organic factors, but it is often produced by mental disorders (Wolman 1988).

Benjamin B. Wolman

Psychosomatic Medicine and Psychoanalysis

Sigmund Freud's early papers are sprinkled with references to the intimate relationship between mind and body. In the Dora case (1905) he mentions "conversion" and "somatic compliance."

Freud reserved the concept of conversion to body parts supplied by the sensorimotor system and under the influence of the voluntary nervous system. However, Otto Fenichel (1945) found this too limited, going on to differentiate between organ neuroses and conversion: "One of them is physical in nature and consists of physiological changes caused by inappropriate use of the function in question" (236). For this category of symptoms he preferred the term *organ neurotic*. The other, he stated, "has a specific unconscious meaning, is an expression of a fantasy in a 'body language' and is directly accessible to psychoanalysis in the same way as a dream" (236). This he considered to be conversion.

With his reference to impaired gratification in the child-mother relationship, F. Deutsch (1959) entered into a consideration of separation anxiety and object loss as both early and later triggering stimuli for somatization. This point was elaborated and clinically documented by many.

Franz Alexander (1950), the creator of the Center for the Study of Psychosomatic Disorders at the Chicago Institute for Psychoanalysis, adhered firmly to Freud's view of conversion, but this did not prevent him from going on to the intensive investigation of the psychophysiological response of organs under the control of the autonomic nervous system, thereby contributing perceptive insights into the medical value of psychoanalysis. He also stated that, in theory, because emotional factors influence all body processes through nervous and humoral pathways, every disease is psychosomatic.

A. F. Mirsky (1958) elaborated on Alexander's ideas by detailing a precise study on physiological, psychological, and social determinants in the etiology of duodenal ulcer. He observed that these patients show a relatively high rate of gastric secretion and that the secretory cell mass in such stomachs is greater than in healthy people. Thus he called our attention to the other side of the coin in psychosomatic disorders, that is, the somatopsychic influence in the chain of events involved in somatization.

M. Schur (1955) introduced the concepts of desomatization and resomatization. He referred to the undifferentiated state in infancy when, normally, the responses to a disturbance in homeostasis are diffuse somatic discharge phenomena like vomiting, regurgitation, uncontrolled bowel and bladder function, and lack of coordination in motor response. These are prototypes of somatization on an infantile level.

M. F. Reiser (1966), in an attempt to integrate the psychoanalytic and physiologic theory of psychosomatic disorders, has observed that "features of autonomic nervous system physiology are strikingly similar to, but not necessarily identical with, auto-nomic functions in the neonate and infant" (574). He is of the opinion that some endocrine dysfunction is probably present in all psychosomatic diseases.

J. L. Weil's (1974) neurophysiological model of emotional and intentional behavior delineates the upper limbic-hypothalamic-reticular system of the brain as the mediator for this behavior.

G. L. Engel (1962) has said of the future of medicine, "An important common denominator underlying health and disease is psychological stress, which directly or indirectly determines not only the individual's capacity to cope with other stresses but often his or her exposure to such stresses as well."

Robert A. Savitt

Psychotherapy: Current Research

During the past several decades, psychotherapy research has become well established and made significant advances. Major areas of progress include:

The effectiveness of psychotherapy. Perhaps the most fundamental question posed by the public and researchers relates to the effectiveness of psychotherapy. After literally hundreds of studies and increasingly sophisticated analyses, the following conclusions have become firmly established (M. J. Lambert 1991):

1. Although not everyone benefits from psychotherapy, the evidence supports its general effectiveness. This conclusion seems to hold regardless of the length of therapy, the nature of the problem, the modality, the expertise of the therapist, and many other factors.

2. Patients in so-called placebo control groups do not do quite as well as patients treated by a more-or-less specific form of therapy, but placebo control groups show greater improvement than patients who remain untreated or are assigned to a waiting list.

3. Improvements from psychotherapy are surprisingly durable, although a certain proportion of patients relapse. Therapists and researchers no longer believe that psychotherapy cures "once and for all," and it is now considered entirely

reasonable for patients to seek further therapy when stresses and associated problems recur.

4. A certain percentage of patients—perhaps upward of 10%—either show no improvement or actually deteriorate. Negative effects occur across all modalities. Patient factors play a part, but the role of the therapist has been shown to be of considerable significance. Therapist variables, such as dislike, low empathy, disrespect, and—perhaps above all—subtle pejorative communications play an important role in lack of improvement or deterioration (S. L. Garfield and A. E. Bergin 1986).

Common factors versus specific factors, specific treatments for specific disorders, and mechanisms of change. There has been increasing recognition that factors common in all therapies are critically important contributors to the outcome (J. D. Frank and V. E. Frank 1991). Common factors include, among others, support, reassurance, suggestions, attention, respect, empathy, warmth, positive regard for the patient, interest, and the therapist's commitment to the therapeutic work. These factors appear to be more influential than specific techniques in determining outcomes. The match between patient and therapist variables is another crucially important determinant of treatment outcome.

Although controversy persists that for specific conditions (e.g., phobias and other anxiety disorders, certain sexual problems, and perhaps certain forms of depression) specific treatment approaches may lead to superior outcomes, these effects are obscured by the aforementioned relationship variables.

These findings generally run counter to the contemporary American trend to develop specific treatments for specific disorders, a goal that minimizes personality factors in patients and therapists. There is today a tendency to regard therapist differences, undeniable though they are, as "nuisance variables" or as "error variance." This reasoning ignores what M. J. Lambert (1991) and others have described as "the most potent aspect of therapy: The therapist as a person, that is to say the wisdom and humanity of the therapist" (7). Future research must seek to identify the qualities of particular therapists that make them unusually effective with particular patients. By now there is strong evidence that patient variables carry a very significant weight in determining the progress and outcome of therapy (Garfield and Bergin 1986). Patients who are relatively healthy, have strong adaptive capacities, possess notable ego resources, and are well motivated for therapeutic work have a considerably better prognosis than those who are deficient in these qualities. Patients with longstanding, chronic, and deep-seated personality disorders may generally be expected to profit less from psychotherapy. Moreover, candidates who are likely to do well in one form of psychotherapy are also better candidates for other forms.

Perhaps the most basic question faced by theoreticians, clinicians, and researchers relates to the mechanisms of change in psychotherapy, that is, how personality and behavior change is achieved (H. H. Strupp 1973). Major alternatives, as already noted, are the patient's relationship to the therapist and some form of technical intervention. What may be most therapeutic is the patient's experience of the therapist as a significant other whose feelings, attitudes, and values are "introjected," thus effecting "corrections" of the patient's experience with significant others in her current life.

Sigmund Freud already recognized that it is essential to make the patient a collaborator in the treatment process, a goal that in recent years has gained prominence in practice and research under the broadened heading of the therapeutic alliance. The formation of a good therapeutic alliance early in therapy is an important contributing factor to a good outcome; if a workable therapeutic alliance cannot be developed early in therapy, as may be the case with "difficult" (e.g., negativistic or hostile) patients, the prognosis for a good outcome may be seriously in doubt (D. Hartley and H. H. Strupp 1983).

Of great importance have been advances in neuroscience, together with progress in pharmacotherapy, particularly in the treatment of depression and associated disorders. The growing biological trend in psychiatry has threatened to all but eclipse training for psychiatrists in psychodynamic therapy. Yet, while drug therapy often shows impressive results, it typically cannot deal with interpersonal conflicts and other aspects of patients' maladaptive behaviors, which have traditionally been the concern of psycho-dynamic psychotherapists. Psychotherapy and pharmacotherapy can often be fruitfully combined, which calls for increased collaboration among specialists. As part of this development, there has been a movement by psychologists to obtain prescription privileges, thus far the prerogative of psychiatrists. It seems fairly certain that, with appropriate training, psychologists will eventually be granted the right to enter this arena.

Group therapy. Since its inception in the early 1900s, group therapy has undergone remarkable growth. Approximately 15,000 articles have been published in numerous journals, and in the United States, there are at least eight major journals devoted almost exclusively to group therapy. The majority of group therapists are engaged primarily in clinical work, with relatively few contributing to the theoretical and research literature. Group therapy continues to be in widespread use in a variety of settings. Both short-term group therapies and self-help groups have become popular. More recently, many groups have focused on specific symptoms (e.g., anxiety disorders, bereavement, bulimia, depression). Treatment manuals have likewise come into prominent use.

Group therapy has always been seen as particularly suitable for a range of interpersonal problems, which may not be dealt with directly in individual therapy. Combined treatments have been shown to be more effective than either intervention alone (M. B. Parloff and Dies 1977). Altogether, group therapy has begun to be based on firmer empirical foundations. On the whole, there has been relatively little evidence for differential outcomes in individual and group treatment. Group treatment is, of course, more cost-efficient. On the other hand, knowledge about the complex interactions of psychological factors that influence treatment outcomes remains rather meager.

Marital and family therapy (MFT). MFT has become firmly established on the psychotherapy scene as a viable treatment modality (Gurman and Kniskern 1996). Family therapy has always been

brief and, as such, it fits well with the current thrust for short-term therapy. Thus far, MFT seems to have shunned empirical research, and as in other areas, there has been a significant division between clinicians and researchers. With regard to the study of treatment outcomes, because more than one family member is usually seen, there are greater difficulties in assessing outcomes and in disentangling the factors contributing to change.

Systems therapy. Systems theory views patients in terms of their involvement in their significant life contexts and, in particular, their interpersonal relationships (Ransom 1989). Systems therapy is an application of this conceptual framework to clinical problems. Most practice has been articulated in terms of therapy with couples; however, it can be applied to individuals and larger systems as well. The domain of systems therapy overlaps marital and family therapy but has a distinct flavor. Systems therapy has stressed the ecological impact of therapy, e.g., the reciprocal influences of the therapeutic relationship and the patient's other contemporary relationships. As another example, there are clearly links between depression and its interpersonal contexts; however, systems therapy has yet to evolve a research tradition and become articulated with the main body of psychotherapy research.

Short-term psychotherapy. Along with, and in contrast to, the growing interest in the treatment of more seriously disturbed patients who seem to have outnumbered and replaced the classical neurotic conditions, there has been a powerful emphasis on the briefer forms of psychotherapy, a development that owes much of its impetus to societal pressures for accountability and cost-effectiveness, the steadily increasing demand for mental health services, the sharply rising costs of health care, and the desire of the various mental health professions to meet these needs. As a result, there has been vigorous activity in developing time-limited treatment regimens, with prominent forms being subjected to controlled research.

Most brief treatments share a number of characteristics: (1) promptness of intervention; (2) rapid, early assessment; (3) a quickly established interpersonal relationship from which to obtain therapeutic leverage; (4) management of temporal limitations by the therapist; (5) limitation of therapeutic goals; (6) directive management of the sessions by the therapist; (7) centering the therapeutic content around a dynamic focus or theme; (8) ventilation or catharsis as an important part of most approaches; and (9) flexibility in choice of technique.

Of at least equal importance in determining a good outcome are a set of patient characteristics, such as (1) good previous adjustment, (2) ability to form a productive therapeutic relationship from the beginning of therapy, (3) high initial motivation to work collaboratively with a professional helper, and (4) the relative absence of severe characterological problems, such as extreme dependency, acting out, excessive self-centeredness, and self-destructiveness.

The past decade has witnessed the appearance of treatment manuals. Treatment manuals had their origin in behavioral concepts and techniques that could be specified more easily than psychodynamic ones. However, in recent years, several psychodynamic and interpersonal manuals have been developed and successfully applied (e.g., G. L. Klerman et al. 1984; L. Luborsky 1984; H. H. Strupp 1984). Manuals also permit assessments of the extent to which a therapist "adheres" to a set of techniques, and various measures have been developed for this purpose. Although manuals have moved the field in the direction of greater specificity, the practice of psychotherapy requires the therapist to individualize interventions, which means that considerable individual differences between therapists remain. As-yet-unmeasured qualitative variations in the patient-therapist interaction may override the contributions of technique.

Adherence to a set of techniques, however, is no guarantee that a therapist practices these techniques skillfully. Adherence and skill are by no means identical, with skill being much more difficult to assess than adherence. The measurement of competence and skill has remained a critical but elusive problem that still awaits intensive study. The practice of psychotherapy, like the practice of medicine, remains an art, only certain aspects of which are susceptible to specification and measurement. In particular, the therapist's personality is a critical component of the therapeutic equation. Nonethe-less, in keeping with contemporary trends that stress technique rather than personality variables, it is predictable that treatment manuals will increase in popularity.

Cognitive therapy (CT). Current taxonomies may overestimate the descriptive specificity of mental disorders, which might set limits to the goal of defining specific treatments for specific conditions. The NIMH Treatment of Depression Collaborative Research Program, for instance, found little evidence that interpersonal, cognitive-behavioral, and pharmacological treatments had specific effects on the modalities for which they seemed most directly indicated. Further research is needed on the mechanisms of action of CT for depression, on factors involved in relapse, as well as other areas in which CT is being applied (e.g., panic disorder, eating disorders, personality disorders, etc.).

Behavior therapy. Eclecticism has become a defining characteristic of behavior therapy, which has also been influenced by research in such areas as emotion and neuroscience. Moving gradually in the direction of cognitive and social psychology, there have been integrative efforts of cognitive and behavioral processes. With regard to preferred techniques, efforts to enhance the effectiveness of exposure treatment are bound to continue. This trend may be augmented by the addition of antidepressant drugs.

While various treatments have been shown to be effective, it is necessary to determine which combination of treatments is most effective and cost-effective. Above all, we need to explore further the psychological mechanisms that promote, delay, and sustain therapeutic change. These mechanisms may be largely identical in all forms of therapy, although they may be couched in different languages. Furthermore, there is a need to achieve a better understanding of the processes by which those outcomes are achieved. This requirement is turning the attention of all investigators to process research, which has shown intensified activity.

Training of psychotherapists. In the United States, there has been an enormous influx of individuals entering the broad psychotherapy arena. In psychodynamically oriented programs, reliance continues to be placed on (1) course work, (2) supervision, and (3) personal therapy; in all areas of psychotherapy, however, training and supervision have remained fairly unsystematic, with wide variations in training from program to program. At the same time, competence and skill have remained difficult to define, though progress is being made. Notable advances have come from within cognitive psychology and instructional psychology, both of which have given rise to improved learning technologies, such as interactive videodisc techniques (I. Rock and Williams 1990).

Research design and methodology. Both analog research and clinical trials have received attention from researchers, who have sought to analogize psychotherapy studies to drug treatment research and to make research increasingly generalizable to clinical settings. There has been a growing emphasis on single case designs and the research-informed case study. The latter, in particular, appears to be a valuable strategy in linking traditional designs to the intensive study of single cases (Garfield and Bergin 1986). In evaluating treatment outcomes, meta-analysis has played an increasingly important role. Intended as a systematic way to evaluate a body of literature, an "analysis of analyses," it has gained popularity but has also generated controversy.

Greater collaboration between clinicians and researchers and among researchers of divergent theoretical persuasions is needed. Today, research strategies and designs as well as statistical analyses are carried out at an increasingly sophisticated level (see S. L. Garfield and A. E. Bergin 1986).

Hans H. Strupp

Psychotherapy: Overview

There are at least 400 different types of psychotherapy. All, however, have at least two things in common: (1) the use of verbal techniques aimed at relieving mental distress or of promoting personality change and (2) the establishment of a professional relationship between the carrier of the problem and the helper.

Although modern psychotherapy is about 100 years old, its origins can be traced to much earlier times. The shaman, "witch doctor," and high priest, to whom people in distress brought their problems, were practicing a form of psychotherapy, albeit with a different label. So was Franz Anton Mesmer (F. G. Alexander and S. T. Selesnick 1966), who practiced a form of hypnosis, though he thought that he was using animal magnetism.

Psychodynamic Psychotherapy

Modern psychotherapy can be traced to the work of Sigmund Freud (1963), who developed psychoanalysis, and to the work of experimental psychologists. The therapies that stem from the work of Freud are generally considered to be "psychodynamic." Those that trace their origins to experimental psychology are more likely to be called "cognitive" or "behavioral."

Psychodynamic therapies emphasize the importance of the therapeutic relationship. If progress is to occur, a therapeutic alliance must be established between the patient and the therapist. The alliance is a conscious and rational decision, in which the patient and therapist agree to work together in a harmonious fashion. Both the patient and therapist agree to abide by certain principles during the treatment. Both must accept that the task of therapy will be a mutual exploration of the patient's problems. During treatment, the patient will develop "transference" feelings toward the therapist. The basis of these feelings are early experiences with important figures from the past. Because these feelings are unconscious, they are not within the patient's awareness. The acceptance of transference is an important element in psychodynamic therapy and a key concept in psychoanalysis.

Equally important in psychodynamic psychotherapy is the issue of countertransference, i.e., the therapist's unconscious feelings toward the patient. Therapists must be able to analyze the source of their feelings toward their patients for therapy to be effective.

All psychotherapies have the goal of solving the patient's problems. Psychodynamic therapies try to accomplish this goal by having the patient develop an understanding ("insight") of the reasons for the distress (R. J. Langs 1973). To do so involves making the unconscious conflicts conscious. Hence, a major tool of psychodynamic psychotherapy is interpretation, i.e., helping the patient see the connections between current feelings and behavior and past experience. Interpretations are successful to the degree that they follow from what the patient has said and to the degree that they can be accepted by the patient. Consequently, the process of therapy can be lengthy. It is not unusual for patient and therapist to meet for 50-minute sessions once or more a week for a year.

Psychoanalysis. The most intensive form of psychodynamic psychotherapy is psychoanalysis, which usually involves therapy sessions several times per week, often lasting several years. The patient is asked to recline on a couch and is instructed to say whatever comes into his mind without censoring the material, regardless of how trivial it may seem. This method, free association, is a way of exploring the patient's unconscious. The analysis of dreams is another method of learning about unconscious processes. By interpreting the meaning of the material that the patient produces, the analyst helps the patient develop an understanding of the origin of the feelings and behavior. In psychoanalysis, the patient frequently develops a "transference neurosis," in which the feelings toward the therapist become the major focus of treatment.

Brief dynamic psychotherapy. In an effort to shorten the time involved in psychodynamic therapy, brief models have been developed (Davanloo 1980; Sifneos 1987; Strupp 1984). The main change in these approaches involves the development of a focus—a specific goal—that the therapy will address. The focus is based on a psychodynamic understanding of the patient's conflicts. Because only one focus is chosen, not all the patient's problems will be addressed during the treatment. However, the treatment is time-limited, often involving no more than twenty sessions. Some recent approaches advocate limiting therapy to one session.

Interactional psychotherapy. Interactional psychotherapists (Wolman 1984) accept the importance of transference but emphasize the relationship between the patient and the therapist. In their reactions to patients, therapists must consider the basis of the patient's transference. Consequently, therapists are urged to manipulate the transference. With some patients, the therapist may be active and directive; with others, the therapist may be more neutral.

Therapy consists of three phases. The first involves understanding the basis of the unconscious conflicts. With this new knowledge, the patient needs to define her identity and discover a direction for her life. The goals that she wants to achieve must be based on a realistic appraisal of her abilities. Therapists help their patients in the search for identity, for meaning, and for purpose. Self-acceptance is, therefore, the end point of treatment.

Cognitive-Behavioral Therapy

This approach to treatment is based upon the principles derived from experimental psychology, typically, the psychology of learning. Strictly behavioral techniques have been based upon the principles of operant and classical conditioning. Although John Broadus Watson (Watson and Rayner 1920) and Mary Jones (1924) had demonstrated that a focal fear could be learned and extinguished by pairing an object with a feared response, behavioral therapies had to await the work of Joseph Wolpe (1990) and Hans J. Eysenck (Eysenck and Martin 1987) before receiving wide acceptance. Wolpe demonstrated that focal phobias, such as a fear of heights, could be removed by asking patients to imagine the feared object while it was paired with an incompatible response, such as relaxation. Systematic desensitization, as the method came to be called, continues to be widely applied.

Other methods involved increasing the frequency of positive behavior by reinforcement. Typically, patients' undesirable behaviors are ignored (nonreinforcement) and desirable behaviors receive some type of attention (reinforcement).

The techniques of exposure (P. Boudewyns and W. C. Shipley 1983) have been widely used with anxiety disorder, panic, and obsessive-compulsive disorder. Exposure therapy has many similarities to systematic desensitization in that the patient is usually exposed, through gradual increments, to the anxiety provoking situation. Flooding, a variant of exposure, does not use a graduated method of presenting the feared object but rather presents the most feared aspect of the object and keeps the patient from leaving the scene. If patients are prevented from withdrawing from the situation, the anxiety will diminish. If the exposure is terminated before the anxiety has diminished, flooding can aggravate the condition.

Cognitive therapy (A. T. Beck 1979) assumes that the self-statements that patients make are the root of the distress they experience. These irrational, faulty, and self-defeating statements are thought to be modifiable by behavioral means. Thus, cognitive therapy has become cognitive-behavioral therapy. In pure behavior therapy, as well as in cognitive-behavioral treatment, patients are assigned tasks to do outside the therapy hour.

In contrast to more psychodynamic models, the cognitive-behavioral therapies are usually of brief duration.

Supportive Psychotherapy

Rather than dealing with unconscious processes, supportive therapy (D. Werman 1984) emphasizes conscious material that the patient brings to the session. Very little use is made of interpretation, especially of unconscious conflicts. The emphasis is on strengthening the patient's ability to cope with the environment and on enhancing self-esteem. The focus remains on current problems that the patient presents. Reassurance, suggestion, clarification, and ventilation of feelings are the major techniques used.

Humanistic Therapies

Humanistic therapies (W. C. Tageson 1982) reject both dynamic and cognitive-behavioral models. The basic principle is that people have free will. Because people are free to make choices, it follows that they are responsible for their behavior. Also, they have the capacity to achieve their potential. The task of the therapist is to provide a setting where this potential can be released. Humanistic therapists accept the dynamic view that understanding is basic to the process of growth.

The three major types of humanistic therapy are client-centered (C. R. Rogers 1951), Gestalt (F. S. Perls, R. F. Hefferline, and P. Goodman 1951), and existential (May 1961). Client-centered therapists believe that change occurs when the therapist provides unconditional positive regard and accurate empathy, and is genuine with the patient.

Existential therapists focus on the patient's aliena-

tion and lack of meaning and value. Patients must accept responsibility for themselves. In their practice, many existential therapists use some of the same techniques found in the dynamic therapies.

Gestalt therapy, though accepting the importance of past experience in the development of psychic distress, emphasizes the "here and now." In their treatment, Gestaltists attempt to unify feelings and actions. Many of the techniques of Gestalt therapy have been incorporated into other models of treatment.

Group Therapy

All of the models presented can be delivered either in an individual session with a single patient or in a group setting involving many patients. Group therapy (I. D. Yalom 1985) typically consists of one therapist meeting with six to eight patients once a week for 60 to 90 minutes. Although group therapy was initially a method of providing therapy to many patients at the same time, it has become a recognized modality for the treatment of patients whose problems are in social interactions.

Family Therapy

Family therapy (Nichols and Schwartz 1991) assumes that a patient's problems reside in the family system. Change, therefore, necessitates work with the system, namely, the family. Accordingly, a patient who presents for treatment will be asked to bring the entire family to the session. Despite their emphasis on the system, some family therapists also make use of the theoretical views of the models discussed earlier.

Therapy Outcome

Despite the number of different approaches, it seems that all therapies have similar results. This observation has prompted some investigators to look for common factors in the various models. This interest has spawned the development of a group that is interested in psychotherapy integration (J. C. Norcross 1986). Still others have advocated "technical eclecticism." Some researchers have begun to study therapist variables that might contribute to change. The interaction among therapist variables, patient variables, and the therapeutic process has become a worthwhile area of study.

Psychotherapy works best for the patient who is less disturbed and less chronic; who has a relatively high functioning level and relatively good social support; and who is motivated for change. Thus, psychotherapy is similar to the results for health care in general: the less "sick" the patient, the better the result. More than three-fourths of patients for whom psychotherapy is indicated will probably receive some benefit.

Reuben J. Silver

Punishment: Overview

Aversive stimulation can be arranged so that it occurs contingent upon either the occurrence or absence of an act. In the former case, we say we are trying to discourage that act, and if the subject successfully learns to not perform the act, we call the process passive avoidance learning. In the latter case, we say we are trying to encourage the further occurrence of the act, and if the subject successfully learns to perform the act in question, we call the process active avoidance learning.

Active Stimuli

1. *Operant behavior previously established by the action of rewards.* This type of behavior is eliminated by punishment if the aversive stimulus is intense, is of long duration, and is immediate.
2. *Operant behavior previously established by the action of aversive stimuli.* Active and passive escape and avoidance operants often are intensified by subsequent punishment.

In addition to behavior type or etiology, there are three other major determinants of the effects of a punishment contingency.

1. *Temporal order effects.* If we hold hunger, food reinforcement, and electric shock intensity constant, reversing the order of food

and shock changes the behavior outcome completely.
2. *Discriminative stimulus control.* If the punishment relation is made to hold only under one set of stimulus conditions and never holds under another set, the unwanted behavior is quickly eliminated.
3. *Presence of rewarded behavior alternatives.* If, in the punishment setting, there occur other behaviors that can lead to quick rewards, there is usually a rapid suppression of the punished behavior.

Richard L. Solomon

Punishment and Learning

The effects of punishment on a number of different classes of animal behavior have been investigated. The most commonly studied type is an operant that is maintained by positive reinforcement, such as lever pressing, key pecking, or alley running for food or water reward. In his review, R. L. Solomon (1964) has identified a number of variables that determine the effect of punishment on such behavior. One such variable is the intensity of the punishing stimulus. If punishment is relatively weak, a small amount of suppression may be obtained and the behavior may fully recover once punishment is discontinued. However, as the intensity of the punishing event is increased, response suppression increases and recovery following termination of punishment decreases to the point at which, if fairly strong punishing events are used, no noticeable recovery is observed. Punishment is also particularly effective and permanent if behaviors that are incompatible with the punished response are reinforced.

Consummatory Behavior

Consummatory behaviors, such as feeding, drinking, and sexual behavior, can be shown to be severely disrupted when punished. This disruption may not be short-lived; P. E. Lichtenstein (1950) and others have found that punishment may suppress eating to the point where the animal may starve. Solomon (1964) points out that one would intuitively think that behaviors that are so important to the maintenance of the organism and even the species should not be so susceptible to the effects of punishment. There is, in fact, evidence that suggests that consummatory behavior may be even more sensitive to the effects of punishment than imagined.

Theories

Several theoretical explanations of punishment have been proposed. Among the earliest was Edward Lee Thorndike's (1913) negative law of effect. The negative law of effect asserted that punishment caused "unlearning" of associations between the response and the stimuli that elicited or maintained it. Thorndike (1932) subsequently abandoned this position and instead argued that punishment served to increase alternative behaviors, which compete with the punished response.

A second type of theory of punishment emphasizes the potential instrumental contingencies that are inherent in punishment situations. For example, N. E. Miller and John Dollard (1941) pointed out that any response that is followed by the termination of shock should be strengthened.

O. H. Mowrer (1960) has argued that, under punishment procedures, fear becomes classically conditioned to response-produced stimuli that precede the punishing event. Fear is a conditioned motivation state, the reduction or elimination of which is reinforcing. Since performing the punished response produces stimuli which arouse fear, not making the punished reponse is reinforced because it modifies or eliminates these cues. Thus the punished behavior is suppressed because the animal is reinforced for not performing the response (R. A. Rescorla and R. L. Solomon 1967).

Human Behavior

The issue of whether punishment can effectively modify human behavior is not so clearly resolved. Punishment is most frequently studied in therapeutic settings where the object is to suppress behavior which is socially unacceptable or otherwise harmful to the client or those around him. In general, it would appear that those variables which have been found to be important determinants of the effectiveness of punishment in lower animals also determine

the degree of suppression obtained with humans (A. Bandura 1969; J. M. Johnson 1972). Although well controlled experimental data are scant, it would appear that punishment can substantially reduce or eliminate such behaviors as stuttering, writer's cramp, tremors, self-mutilation, and aggression. Further, in a number of cases, suppression is fairly permanent.

Raymond L. Jackson

Purpose and Purposivism

In the early development of psychology, a strongly mechanistic position—though one with some qualifications—was reflected in the works of René Descartes, Thomas Hobbes, Le Mettrie, and D. Hartley. On the other hand, in the last century, a purposive stance was implied in the development of the concept of will, which implied the existence of purposiveness in behavior. More specifically, Franz Clemens Brentano, James Ward, and others undertook the examination of purpose and intentions in behavior. The first dominant figure in this trend, however, so far as the mainstream of psychology is concerned, was William McDougall (1871–1938), whose views were influenced in part by those of Ward and William James.

McDougall, the first to successfully break way from the conception of psychology as the study of mental contents and to redefine it as the study of behavior, constructed a thoroughgoing purposive system, which he referred to as "hormic psychology" (after the Greek word *hormé*, and previously used by P. T. Nunn to designate an urge in organisms to be guided by given purposes). McDougall considered the existence of purpose in behavior to be self-evident. "Man's life," he said in 1928, "is one long round of purposive strivings, of efforts to attain, to make real, those things which he imaginatively conceives to be good or desirable" (275). McDougall used the word *purpose* to indicate a goal or end toward which a person strives, with the proviso that the person is aware of the goal, that it is *his* goal, and that he desires it and deliberately chooses it.

Unlike other behaviorists of his period, particularly John Broadus Watson, E. C. Tolman was convinced that behavior, in its global or molar sense, is purposive and goal-oriented. Several philosophically oriented psychologists, among them R. Harré, P. F. Secord, W. Day, M. S. Sutherland, Benjamin B. Wolman, and others, are concerned with the concepts of purpose and intention.

Paul McReynolds

Putnam, James Jackson (1846–1918)

James Jackson Putnam organized the American Psychoanalytic Society. Putnam emphasized the duty of doctors to pay attention to the healing of the mind as well as the body, and helped promote social work as a profession.

Leo H. Berman

·Q·

Q-Technique and the Q-Sort

Q-technique is a general methodology developed by Stephenson (1953) for the study of verbalized attitudes, self-description, preferences, and other issues in social psychology, clinical psychology, and the study of personality. A salient principle in Q-technique for the advancement of psychology is that it is more important to make comparisons among different responses (e.g., statements regarding preferences) within subjects than between subjects.

Nature of the Rating Task
The Q-sort also requires subjects to distribute their responses in terms of a fixed distribution, usually an approximately normal distribution. This forces all subjects not only to have the same mean rating but also to have the same standard deviation of ratings and the same curve shape of ratings.

It is best to regard the forced distribution in the Q-sort as an approximation to rank order, a rank ordering in which the number of tied ranks at each point is specified for the subject. The use of an approximately normal distribution rather than some other fixed distribution (e.g., a rectangular distribution) is justified in the general case, because so many things in nature are distributed approximately that way and it fits in with the statistical methods applied to the data.

Stimulus Samples
Psychology, as well as other disciplines, is faced with problems concerning two types of sampling: sampling of people and sampling of stimuli. While psychologists usually are careful to obtain a sufficient number of subjects and carefully assess the statistical error associated with the sample of people, sampling of stimuli (or content) is less controlled.

Types of Stimulus Samples
Two types of content are employed with the Q-sort: random samples and structured samples. In both instances, it is important to realize that the so-called sampling is not done in the same way that one samples from populations of persons. Rather, in sampling material for a Q-sort, one either constructs the materials oneself or borrows them from some available source (e.g., a book containing photographs of statues). The structured sample is one in which the experimenter stipulates the kinds of stimuli that will be included in the content sample in terms of an experimental design.

Analysis of Q-Sort Data
In using inferential statistics with respect to problems of content sampling, as is frequently done with Q-sort data, the experimenter must be aware that it is more difficult to justify the assumptions for such statistics than for those in sampling people. First, there must be a definable population (domain or universe), and it is difficult to define domains of content for Q-sorts. Second, the sampling unit must be defined, and with certain types of content (e.g., statements about psychotherapy or statements relating to personality traits) such definition may be difficult. Third, the stimuli must be either randomly sampled overall (the so-called random sample for Q-sorts) or randomly sampled within specified categories (as in the structured sample for Q-sorts).

Summary

There are advantages and disadvantages to employing the Q-sort rather than other rating methods. First, the Q-sort has certain advantages if one is seeking comparative ratings. For example, Q-sorts take less time than that of the method of rank order and other comparative methods. Second, before the Q-sort is employed, it is important to ensure that sensible comparative responses can be made among the stimuli used in a study. This can be done either with a structured sample that is quite explicit or with a "random" sample that is sensible to other investigators, as is usually the case with ratings of preference for classes of items, such as movie actors or television programs. Third, if the Q-sort is selected as a rating method, various techniques of mathematical analysis may be applied to the data.

Jum C. Nunnally

Quarter-Way House

Within most mental hospitals, especially since the advent of psychotropic drugs, there is a sizable reservoir of chronically ill patients who are sufficiently improved to live in a family setting but who either have no relatives or have relatives who will not accept them into their homes. Typically, the patient has been displaced from the family position he occupied before admission to the hospital, and his proposed release creates a situation so threatening to relatives that they even refuse to permit his placement in a foster home.

New patients are escorted by the supervisor to the quarter-way house. They are greeted by the mother surrogate, introduced to the other members, and shown their rooms, where they may keep all their possessions. They are told about their responsibilities in caring for their rooms and in participating in preparation of meals and housekeeping.

The patient's reintroduction to the community is gradual and designed to keep separation anxiety to a minimum. Initially, he or she accompanies the social worker during a routine call at a foster home where a former patient has been placed.

In the quarter-way house, new identifications and group norms are formed. Staff members, aided by volunteers, help the patients gradually to reacquire the social skills and techniques they will need to live in a community home. Through the support and encouragement the quarter-way house staff gives to patients, social workers are aided in developing a community orientation among the house members.

In mental hospitals, the majority of foster-home placements can be effected directly from the hospital wards. However, the quarter-way house constitutes an effective transitional program for a large group of chronic patients who present great difficulties in extramural placement.

Aaron S. Mason

· R ·

Rado, Sandor (1890–1972)

In Sandor Rado's view, faulty development leads to miscarried repair (defense mechanisms) and to prevalence of emergency emotions (anxiety and unpleasure) over the welfare emotions (love and pride). Rado's main work includes the two-volume *Psychoanalysis of Behavior* (1956, 1962).

John J. Weber

Rank, Otto (1884–1939)

Otto Rank was the first nonmedical analyst to treat patients. In 1912, Rank and Hanns Sachs started the journal *Imago*, and after World War I, Rank was the director of the International Psychoanalytic Publishing House in Vienna. In 1924, Rank published the *Trauma of Birth*; in this book, he introduced a new approach to the genesis of mental development, based on separation anxiety at birth. In the same year, Rank and Sandor Ferenczi published *The Development of Psychoanalysis*, in which they stress the importance of the mother to the infant. According to Rank, by separating from the mother the individual becomes independent and creative; she does this with the help of her will. Rank distinguishes three types of individuals: the neurotic, the average, and the artist.

The goal of Rank's therapy is to help the patient to recognize the all-important personal will and avoid the two kinds of guilt: ethical guilt, due to self-assertion, and moralistic guilt, due to conflict with socially accepted mores.

Samuel Eisenstein

Rape

The problems of victims of sexual assault who are courageous enough to identify themselves as such are notorious. The abuse of the victim by both medical and criminal justice institutions has been amply described, and frequently includes the following beliefs:

1. The rapist is a sexually frustrated man who acts on an uncontrollable urge; thus, rapists are sick and not really responsible for their behavior.
2. Most rapes involve black men raping white women.
3. The fact of prior sexual experience by an unmarried victim is probable evidence of misconduct or provocation on her part; that is, "nice girls don't get raped, and bad girls shouldn't complain."
4. Women are raped because they ask for it by seductive dress and behavior.
5. It is impossible to rape a woman against her will, the corollary being that women actually enjoy rape.

The most significant finding of M. Amir's study is that rape occurs in a context of violence rather than passion, with the purpose of the act to humiliate and debase the victim—the sex act itself is secondary. Rapists are a danger to the community not because they are compulsive sex fiends but because they are violent and aggressive.

The profound impact of rape is best understood in the context of rape as a crime against the person and not against the hymen. Rape is an act of violence and humiliation in which the victim experiences not only overwhelming fear for her very existence but an equally profound sense of powerlessness and helplessness that few other events in her life can parallel.

Emotional responses fall into two major categories, an expressed style and a controlled style. The expressed style is manifested by visible evidence of a massive affective response. The controlled victim appears calm and collected with little external evidence of distress, the apparent calmness reflecting shock, disbelief, and exhaustion. The primary reaction is related to the fear of physical injury, mutilation, and death; that is, the awareness that she could have been murdered. Mood swings are common and include feelings of humiliation, degradation, guilt, shame, embarrassment, self-blame, anger, and fear of another assault.

Medical intervention usually takes place in a hospital emergency setting and has the following goals: immediate care of physical injuries; prevention of venereal disease and pregnancy; and medicolegal examination with documentation by evidence collection for law enforcement.

Elaine Hilberman

Rapaport, David (1911–1960)

David Rapaport was director of the Menninger Foundation School of Clinical Psychology and then director of research. With the assistance of Roy Schafer and Merton Gil, Rapaport published the two-volume *Diagnostic Psychological Testing* (1945–1946). The guiding plan of his life work was to establish psychoanalysis as a general psychology.

Herbert J. Schlesinger

Rating Scales

Rating scales are used widely for the study of personality characteristics, attitudes, values, preferences, and other human impressions. Rating scales are used to measure human impressions in those instances where it is either unfeasible or illogical to attempt measurement in more objective ways.

Graphic and numerical scales. We usually think of rating scales as being presented graphically. In some instances the numbers are defined for subjects, and they write the numbers in spaces opposite the object to be rated instead of having the appropriate numbers marked on a graphic scale. It is customary to refer to these as numerical scales rather than as graphic scales. The issue, however, usually concerns whether there will be numbers employed with a graphic scale or without a graphic scale. Numbers are used as anchors in most rating scales. The numbers must first be defined:

1. completely disagree
2. mostly disagree
3. slightly disagree
4. slightly agree
5. mostly agree
6. completely agree

For several reasons, the use of the graphic scale with numbers is preferable to the use of numbers without the graphic scale. First, because people frequently think of quantities as represented by degrees of physical extension (e.g., by the yardstick and the thermometer), the presence of a graphic scale probably helps to convey the idea of a rating continuum. Second, the graphic scale should lessen clerical errors in making ratings. If the meanings of numbers are given only at the beginning of an inventory and subjects have to remember the meanings as they record the numbers in the blank spaces, they are likely to forget the meanings, for example, to confuse ends of the scale or to assume that 4 means "mostly agree" when it was defined as meaning "slightly agree." The presence of the graphic scale should lessen such errors, particularly if the ends of the scale are anchored by the extremes of the attribute being rated, "completely agree" and "completely disagree," as in the previous example. Third, if subjects write numbers in blank spaces, in some instances, it will be difficult to decipher the numbers. For example, it might prove difficult to tell whether a particular number is 1, 7, or 9. Fewer errors in this regard are made in reading the points marked on graphic scales.

Summative scales. The reliability of summative ratings is directly related to the size of positive correlations among scales. The reliability is high when the correlations are relatively high, and vice versa. The reliability of summative scales also depends directly on the number of items. In addition to the effect of the average correlation between items, the reliability of summative scales also depends directly on the number of items. If there are only half a dozen items in the scale, the reliability obtained from two-step scales might be markedly increased by an increase in the number of scale steps. If, on the other hand, there are over 20 items in the summative scale, it is seldom the case that the reliability is materially increased by the addition of scale steps to the individual scales.

Object Rated

Instead of making ratings of statements relating to attitudes, in some attitude scales, ratings are made of the attitudinal object itself, as would be the case, for example, when the United Nations is rated on a six-point scale bounded by the adjectives *effective* and *ineffective*. When attitudinal objects are rated directly, leniency (as the term applies in ratings of people) would spring from the same sources that it would in ratings of statements. Individual differences in that regard would represent either differences in favorable attitudes toward social objects of all kinds or differences in the tendency to give socially desirable rather than undesirable responses.

Types of Anchors

The definitions of scale steps are referred to as "anchors," and there are different types of anchors that can be employed. Usually, numerical anchors are employed in conjunction with other types. There is no harm in employing numbers on the scale, and they have several distinct advantages. If the meaning of each step on the scale is specified at the beginning of the rating form, as is usually the case, numbers provide an effective means of coordinating those definitions with the rating scales. A second advantage is that numbers on the rating scales constantly remind subjects of the meanings of scale steps. Another advantage of having numbers on the rating scales is that they facilitate the analysis of data, as in placing ratings on cards for computer analyses.

A special type of numerical anchor that is useful in some studies is found on percentage scales. On percentage scales, subjects rate themselves or other people on a continuum ranging from zero to 100%, either in comparison with people in general or in comparison with some special reference group, for example, other students in a particular college.

A second type of anchor, which is widely employed in rating scales, is that concerning degrees of agreement and disagreement, as has been illustrated previously. Where they can be applied, agreement scales are easy to work with. They are easily understood by subjects, and the results obtained from them are rather easily interpreted by researchers. Whereas, superficially, agreement scales might seem to concern judgments rather than sentiments, in attitude scales this is not the case. What an individual does in responding to agreement scales is to indicate her sentiments by agreeing or disagreeing with favorable and unfavorable statements.

Adjectives constitute a third type of anchor for rating scales, as was illustrated previously in the case of scales anchored by valuable–worthless, effective–ineffective, and other pairs of bipolar adjectives. Attitude scales employing bipolar adjectives as anchors are easily constructed and applied to many types of attitudinal objectives. Rating scales employing bipolar adjectives as anchors are said to form a *semantic differential*.

A fourth type of anchor for rating scales concerns comparison stimuli, or product scales, as they are called. A classic example is that of a product scale for the legibility of handwriting. A six-step scale is employed, with each of the numbers 1 to 6 being illustrated with samples of handwriting at different levels of legibility. The samples of handwriting appropriate for the different levels are obtained from the judgments of experts.

Jum C. Nunnally

Rational Emotive Therapy: Ellis's Method

Rational emotive therapy (RET), also called rational behavior therapy (RBT), developed by Albert Ellis (1962), constitutes a system of psychotherapy that consciously and very actively utilizes cognitive, emotive, and behavioral techniques of personality change. Its main assumption is that when humans are upset and invent magical beliefs or ideas about themselves, others, and the world around them, they tend to act in a disturbed or disordered fashion.

RET also uses many emotive methods—for example, unconditional acceptance of the client, rational emotive imagery, and shame-attacking exercises. It also employs most of the major behavioral methods—assertiveness training, operant conditioning, or self-management techniques, and *in vivo* homework assignments.

Albert Ellis

Ray, Isaac (1807–1881)

Isaac Ray was the first great American forensic psychiatrist and a leader in hospital psychiatry.

Leo H. Berman

Razran, Gregory (1901–1973)

Gregory Razran studied little-known Soviet psychophysiological experiments on interoceptive conditioning, semantic conditioning, and the orienting reflex. He wrote *Mind in Evolution: An East-West Synthesis of Learned Behavior and Cognition* (1971); in this book, Razran devised a theory of evolutionary levels of learning modifiability. The first broad category encompasses inhibitory, classical, and operant conditioning. On the next step of the hypothesized evolutionary pyramid are three forms of perceptual learning: (1) several varieties of sensory learning, (2) configuring, and (3) educative learning. At the pinnacle of the hierarchy resides the highest form of learning, closely tied to the evolution of the structured elements involved in language.

Wilma A. Winnick

Reactance Theory

Reactance theory assumes that people believe themselves to have freedoms to engage in specified behaviors. The theory's basic proposition is that when a person perceives that any of her freedoms have been threatened or eliminated, psychological reactance is aroused in her. Reactance is defined as a motivational state that is directed toward the reestablishment of the freedom that has been threatened or eliminated.

Reactance has two general manifestations. As a motivational state, it increases an individual's desire for, or the attractiveness of, the goal that is served by the freedom in question. Even when a freedom has been eliminated, there will be at least a temporary increase in the attractiveness of the activity or goal that has been denied. The second manifestation, which occurs only when a freedom has been threatened but not eliminated, is the attempt by the individual to restore the freedom. In general, freedom may be restored by exercise of it, by attacking the agent responsible for the threat, and by engaging in behaviors that imply that one could exercise the threatened freedom.

In mass persuasion, a communication that tells the audience what conclusion it must draw tends to produce negative attitude change (J. W. Brehm 1966). Similarly, a one-sided argument tends to be less effective when the audience is aware that there are two sides to the issue.

A variety of nonsocial implications of reactance theory have also been studied. When an individual believes he can choose any one of several attractive alternatives and then finds that one of them is unavailable, the unavailable one tends to become more attractive to him. Or, if he discovers that there is a barrier, such as a special tax, to one of the choice items, that item tends to become more attractive. Just the simple act of choice threatens and eliminates freedoms. The thought of having to give up one alternative in order to select another arouses reactance and a consequent tendency for the less-attractive alternative to become more attractive before the choice is made.

Jack W. Brehm

Reaction Time (RT) and Aging

It is important to separate the effects of disease process on reaction time (RT) from the effects of aging within normal limits, especially when comparing RTs across age groups. There is little agreement as to what constitutes "normal" changes in central nervous system function and structure with advancing age and what constitutes a disease process, and there is no set formula for the separation of disease and normal aging other than caution in data interpretation and design of experiments. Functional psychological as well as organic factors may interact with age and RT; for example, nonorganic depression may mimic slowing of response associated with poor physical health.

RT studies indicate that with increasing age individuals become slower in the motor components of response to environmental events. It is highly debatable whether impairment of sensory input can account for RT increases in older individuals. Complex reaction time (responses involving a choice between several alternatives—e.g., classifying sequential stimuli as "same" or "different") shows greater age differences than simple RT. It has been suggested that older subjects require more time to (1) initiate responses, (2) input and identify stimuli, and/or (3) remember what responses are associated with what stimuli.

Jeffrey W. Elias
Wayne E. Watson
Merrill F. Elias

Reaction Time and Choice

Reaction time is typically measured in situations where a signal, such as a light or a sound, is responded to by pressing a key or speaking. It is defined as the time elapsing between the onset of the signal and the initiation of the response. Thus, it includes the times required for activation of the sense organ concerned, for afferent impulses to the brain, for central processes within the brain, for efferent impulses from the brain to the effector organ used to respond, and for activation of this organ to an extent that produces a recordable response.

Reaction Time

Sex. Men are usually found to have faster average reaction times than women.

Occupational level. Some, although not all, studies have found shorter reaction times among those of higher occupational level.

Sense organ stimulated. Tactile stimuli tend to produce faster reactions than auditory, and these, in turn, produce faster reactions than visual stimuli.

Effector making response. Reactions by the hand tend to be faster than those by the foot or by speech. When either of two different hand reactions may be called for, they tend to be faster if they are by different hands than if they are by different fingers of the same hand. Presumably more precise muscular differentiation and control are required in the latter case.

Conditions of testing. Reactions tend to be slower in monotonous conditions, in states of fatigue, or under the influence of sedative drugs or alcohol.

Caution. The more careful the subject, the slower, but at the same time the more accurate, her performance tends to be.

Preparation. Reaction times tend to be shorter if a warning is given about .5 to 2.0 seconds before the signal.

Very short intervals between signals. Reaction time tends to be long to a signal that follows another before the response to the first signal has begun. This is not due to lack of preparedness for the second signal—because if it arrives within about 80 milliseconds of the first, both may be reacted to quickly as if they were a single, complex signal—but rather, appears to be due to the second signal having to wait to be dealt with by the central decision mechanisms until these have finished dealing with the first signal.

Degree of Choice

An important line of research since about 1950 has been on the relationships of reaction time to the number of possible signals and corresponding responses that may occur. Experiments showing that reaction time is longer when there are several possible signals and responses than when there is only one of each were published by F. C. Donders as long ago as 1868, and the progressive rise as the numbers increase was demonstrated by J. Merkel in 1885. The formulation of a lawful relationship between reaction time and degree of choice, and serious attempts to understand the reasons for the rise, were not made until 1952, when W. E. Hick put forward the formulation that has come to be known as Hick's law:

$$\text{Choice Reaction Time} = k \log (n+1)$$

where k is a constant and n is the number of equally probable choices. He suggested that the +1 was due to the need to distinguish not only between the different possible signals but also whether a signal had occurred at all. Hick linked this formulation to information theory, suggesting that the subject gains information, or in other words resolves uncertainty, at a constant rate.

Models of choice reaction. The difference between simple and choice reaction times could be due in part to the fact that preparation can be more complete when there is only one possible signal and response than when there are more than one. However, the progressive rise with degree of choice calls for a further explanation. Modern theories assume that both the evidence from the signal and the activity required to trigger a response have to build up until a criterion point is reached, which is high enough to be only rarely passed by an unusually high instantaneous level of neural noise.

Factors Affecting Parameters

The rise of reaction time with degree of choice is affected by the strategy adopted when ordering a series of subdecisions. The rise is affected much more by the relationships between signals and responses. It is less when these are straightforward—when signals and responses are what is termed *compatible*—than when more complex processes are required to relate the one to the other. Complexity in this sense consists broadly of two types of requirement: spatial transposition and symbolic translation. Influences of these are seen in the fact that reaction is faster when the signals are a row of lights and the responses are made by pressing buttons immediately below them than when the lights form a vertical row

and the buttons a horizontal, or when buttons correspond to digits or other symbols all displayed in the same place or spoken.

Separating Identification of Signal from Choice of Response

Several attempts have been made to measure the times for identification and choice separately. For example, some experimenters have required subjects to respond to signals by moving from a central point to one of several buttons. When these are in widely different directions from the central point, the time taken before leaving it is relatively long, and both identification of signal and choice of response can be assumed to have taken place before any move was made. However, when the buttons are all located in approximately the same direction, the time taken to leave the central point tends to be short.

A. T. Welford

Reading

The earlier work on reading summarized by E. B. Huey in 1908 and the work undertaken later has concerned itself with analysis of the stimulus. Concern for the reader and concern for the materials are not antinomies but focus upon separate aspects of one of humankind's most interesting and complex activities. The public educator is primarily concerned with custodial problems in keeping large numbers of children of varied skills and background together in one classroom under the tutelage of a single teacher. The researcher, on the other hand, is interested in the structure of the materials she deals with.

The message the text contains has come under study partly in reaction to advances in psycholinguistics. The number of statements or "propositions" that a text contains, their logical structure and coherence, the syntactic form of the text and its degree of embedding, and the role of negation and other variables related to logic or to linguistics have increasingly been investigated. A number of measures of "readability" have been devised based on sentence length, frequency of different parts of speech in a sentence, and the like, but no metric has yet successfully quantified the properties of language as to grammatical or linguistic structure generally.

Properties of the Display

Text is presented in many ways, static and dynamic. The stationary printed page is only one variant, if the most common; historically, text was meant as much for monuments as for pages, and it appeared in vertical, horizontal, circular, and other arrays as well (Guarducci 1967). Modern technology allows still other variants, such as temporal superposition of letters and temporal anagrams, among others. In addition to the novelty that such variation creates, the displays enable the investigator to test specific hypotheses about reading, and about the processing characteristics of the visual nervous system.

The simplest test is whether reading can go forward element by element, where "element" means letter, word, or phrase. One study has found that sequential presentation of letters restricts reading rate to about 35 words per minute, or one-tenth the average rate for college freshmen. The reason is that letters have to be presented for about a third of a second each if all the letters or the word they spell are to be identified correctly.

The enormous variety of printing types available speaks both to their imperfection of design and to the varieties of subtle, linguistically extrinsic information that type fonts may convey (Bowman 1968; Updike 1966). Direction of reading, formation of characters, their sequence of presentation, and the timing relations that characterize the sequence all effect what is read (Kohlers 1970).

Properties of the Reader

Skill at reading seems to be only partially correlated with other cognitive and intellectual skills and ranges from limited to exceptional. Even within this domain of "talent" and its statistical distribution, certain facts characterize all readers interpreting marks on a page. Interpreting graphemes in respect to their representation of words, interpreting words in respect to their role in sentences, and interpreting sentences in respect to their place in paragraphs requires in each case that the reader bring to or impose upon the printed signal aspects of knowl-edge and experience that are extrinsic to it but that affect its perception and interpretation. Reading, thus, is always carried out within a frame of reference or context, which is the consequence of the interaction of the signals on the page and the reader's ability to process and interpret them. In this sense, therefore, "comprehension" of text is never a fully measurable quality, because to the degree that each person's history is unique, interpretations, implications, and thus "comprehension" of a passage will differ from person to person. Reading is a cognitive manipulation of symbols; each person's history and experience will induce her to effect that manipulation in a different way. A profound problem for theory is to understand how individuals of different background achieve common understandings from a passage and to evaluate the degree of commonness that is obtained.

Paul A. Kolers

Reasoning and Problem Solving

Reasoning, or to be more specific, deductive reasoning, is that part of the general area of problem solving concerned with logical problems or problems in which logical relations are assumed to be critical. The study of logic in psychology should be differentiated from the study of logic per se. Whereas the latter is the study of formal relations between propositions, the study of logic in psychology emphasizes the issue of how people think.

Types of Tasks Studied

The research of logic has generally been done using problems in which the logical operations are made explicit.

Analysis

Correct answers on these deductive reasoning problems do not tell us much about the process of thinking. In the analysis of such problems, experimenters are generally more interested in the wrong answers. If a particular type of wrong answer occurs frequently, its analysis is important, as it may point to some systematic rule about the way human beings think. For this reason, many syllogistic problems are written as multiple-choice questions, where the correct answer is "none of these conclusions is valid."

Relevant Variables

The subject's motivation or lack of it, her boredom, and her attitude toward the conclusion of a syllogistic argument have all been shown to affect syllogistic reasoning. It has thus been shown that syllogisms for which the conclusion is an emotionally laden topic (as judged by the experimenters) are more prone to error on the part of the subject. It has also been shown that, in general, people will judge conclusions from syllogistic arguments as being valid or invalid depending upon whether or not they agree with the conclusions, regardless of how well that conclusion follows from the logical argument.

A variable that seems to affect problem solving very profoundly is whether the statement or problem is stated in positive or negative terms. It seems that negative information is not used as efficiently or in the same way as positive information, even if the two are logically equivalent.

The grammatical structure, sequence, and wording of a logical problem can also affect its solution, and these variables as well as the ones mentioned above tell something about the nature of human thinking. The specifics of some of these variables can be more efficiently covered in a discussion of the underlying processes affecting thinking.

Underlying Processes

Information-processing time. The span of short-term memory and the amount of information that a subject can handle in a given period of time have also been cited as causing greater difficulty in some problems. Thus, if a subject has to transform information from the negative to the positive, or restructure it into some ordered structure that he has created for the problem, the total information load may approach his capacity and increase errors. It is interesting to note that subjects seem to have to reverse negative statements before they can deal with them.

An important cognitive factor suggested by the research is the type of "logical space" that subjects structure relationships in. Thus, in transitive inference problems it has been found that (1) subjects do better on problems that are stated in an order going from better to worse rather than from worse to better (thus, it is easier to work with "John is better than Mary and Mary is better than Jim" than with "Jim is worse than Mary and Mary is worse than John"), and (2) it is helpful if the first term is an end term (the best or the worst) so that the premise proceeds from an end toward an end. (Thus, "A is better than B, and C is worse than B" was solved more often than "B is better than C, and B is worse than A.")

The assertion that many of the errors in logical reasoning are due to a lack of understanding on the part of the subjects finds support in research, which shows that a little training does much to improve a subject's performance. Logical reasoning, although highly correlated with general intelligence, can be taught.

Aharon H. Fried
Sondra Leftoff

Reconstruction in Psychoanalysis

The term "reconstruction" was first used by Sigmund Freud in 1937 in his paper entitled "Construction in Analysis." In this paper, Freud notes that the goal of reconstruction is to help the patient give up some repressions belonging to her early development and thereby to recollect some early experiences and affects that she has forgotten.

Freud (1937) has pointed out that a correct reconstruction does not always cause the patient to recapture repressed memories, but may merely produce a conviction that the reconstruction is correct; and this conviction will achieve the same therapeutic results as a true recollection. In some instances, a correct reconstruction causes a patient to recapture only a few fragments of memory.

It is not uncommon for a patient to put a great deal of effort into recollecting past events because of his belief that such recollection will cause the symptoms to disappear. This belief usually causes some eventual dissatisfaction with treatment, because the patient's expectations of a magical cure through recollection will not be realized.

Sidney Levin

Regression in the Service of the Ego

Ernst Kris (1952) has proposed the concept of regression in the service of the ego as a temporary, partial, controlled regression. He describes regression in the service of the ego as it operates in wit, in creativity, and in fantasy, and compares such temporary and reversible regressions with the psychotic condition, in which the ego is overwhelmed, and with the process of dreaming, in which the ego yields to the greater control of the primary process in the state of sleep.

Kris describes a controlled and temporary ego regression during inspiration. The integrative or organizational functions of the ego include capacity for self-regulated regression and for control over the primary process. When the ego functions are operative, creativity and passivity may safely combine in an experience of passive receptiveness. The artist retains her ego functions, as regression in the service of the ego influences creative activity by merging primary process with the intact part of the personality.

Gertrude Blanck

Rehabilitation Psychology

Rehabilitation is a set of services and activities designed to help disabled people to achieve optimal adjustment. In the United States there have been two expressions of the specific meanings of rehabilitation. First, as a matter of governmental policy and the law, rehabilitation has been defined as those services needed to return an individual to gainful employment. Second, rehabilitation as a matter of social philosophy has come to be recognized as a "third phase of medical care."

The first normal rehabilitation program in this country was initiated at the Cleveland Rehabilitation Center (1899) and was concerned with the "use of all medical measures which expedite recovery" (Kessler 1950). World War I saw the introduction of a national vocational rehabilitation program for disabled veterans.

Psychologists work for both the public and private systems, in

1. clinical service activities, including assessment, therapy, counseling on an individual and group basis, and consultation and working with staff;

2. research in a variety of fields, including adjustment of physically disabled people, methods of improving adaptation in people with sensory, motor, language, physical, and mental impairments, methods of assessing and improving service delivery, methods of assessing and improving public and employer attitudes and behavior, and studies in the lifestyles of the disabled;

3. administration, in which psychologists occupy different kinds of administrative roles, including direction of individual programs, facilities, and aids in formulation of public policies; and

4. teaching, which may range from lectures and supervision of psychologists to any of the vast number of professions associated with rehabilitation.

Because rehabilitation is highly interdisciplinary, psychologists also are prominent in a number of interdisciplinary professional societies, including the Congress of Rehabilitation Medicine, the National Rehabilitation Association, the American Academy of Cerebral Palsy, the Academy of Aphasia, and the Council for Exceptional Children.

Leonard Diller

Reich, Wilhelm (1897–1957)

Wilhelm Reich is one of the most controversial figures in psychoanalytic history. In 1920, he became the director of the popular Seminar for Psychotherapy. The special interest of this seminar focused on obscure and unknown reasons for failures in analytic technique. Reich's *Character Analysis* (1945) included much material of a nonpsychoanalytic nature. Reich later developed the method of orgone therapy, a "sex economic" approach to psychotherapy. Reich maintained that the object of his research concerned the release of psychic energy bound up in the service of repression of instincts.

Walter Briehl

Reik, Theodor (1888–1969)

Theodor Reik exemplified Sigmund Freud's conviction that the main contribution of psychoanalysis lies outside its medical or therapeutic application. In *Listening with the Third Ear* (1948), Reik indicates that the analyst's own unconscious is in communication with that of the patient. Reik also wrote on problems of crime, confession, and guilt.

Murray H. Sherman

Reil, Johann Christian (1759–1813)

Johann Christian Reil was noted for his work in anatomy of the brain and, later, for his advocacy of psychological therapy in mental illness.

John C. Burnham

Reinforcement

The term *reinforcement* refers to an operation or procedure, the result of that operation, and the underlying process or mechanism responsible for the result. As an operation, reinforcement refers to any procedure that has, as its result, the effect of increasing the rate, probability, vigor, or any other measure of the strength of a response. It also refers to the increase in response strength and is sometimes used to refer to the process that goes on within the organism to produce the increase.

In instrumental conditioning, a change in behavior is produced by a contingency between the subject's responding and a stimulus event. Typically, some arbitrary response (R) is consistently followed by some motivationally significant event (SR), such as the delivery of a food reward to a hungry rat for pressing a bar. The stimulus event is termed the reinforcer, and its presentation following a response is called reinforcement because it has the effect of increasing the probability of (or "reinforcing") the response.

Positive and Negative Reinforcement

Two fundamental procedures of instrumental reinforcement can be identified. In positive reinforcement, response strength increases when presentation of the reinforcer is made contingent upon the response; reinforcers that act in this fashion, examples of which are food, water, and other biological needs, are called *appetitive reinforcers*. In negative reinforcement, response strength increases when removal or cessation of the reinforcer is made contingent upon the response; reinforcers that act in this way (electric shock, extreme cold, or other stimulation that is usually thought of as unpleasant) are termed *aversive reinforcers*.

Six forms of reinforcement can be identified. Two have already been described: positive reinforcement, also called reward training, and negative reinforcement, also called escape training, both of which have the effect of increasing response strength. The third method of increasing response strength is avoidance training, in which presentation of an aversive reinforcer is made contingent on not responding. The three methods of decreasing response strength are *punishment*, where presentation of an aversive reinforcer is made contingent on responding; *omission training*, where presentation of an appetitive reinforcer is made contingent on not responding; and, finally, a procedure known as *time out from reinforcement* (TO), which consists of removal of an appetitive reinforcer contingent upon responding.

Extinction

Because reinforcement theories of learning suppose that response strength is increased by each reinforcement, and because it is reasonable that response strength should be one determinant of response persistence in extinction, considerable attention has been devoted to explaining why intermittent reinforcement should produce greater persistence in extinction. The *dissonance reduction hypothesis* proposes that the partially reinforced subject, after making the response and not finding a reward, experiences dissonance (an incongruity between the present state of affairs and his own behavior), which he reduces by finding other attractive features to the response and whatever it produces (such as entry into the goal box in the case of a rat running down a runway, the experimental situation most studied by researchers of the extinction). Later, in extinction, these attractive features maintain responding. The *frustration hypothesis* suggests that the subject experiences frustration responses and the internal stimuli they produce on unreinforced trials; then, on reinforced trials, these frustration stimuli are associated with responding. In extinction, then, the partially reinforced (PRF) subject has been conditioned to respond in a frustrated state, but the continuously reinforced (CRF) subject has not. The *aftereffects hypothesis* is similar; it proposes that all stimuli produced by nonreinforcement become associated with responding on reinforced trials so that in extinction nonreinforcement elicits responding in PRF subjects. The *discrimination hypothesis* states that CRF subjects discriminate extinction from reinforcement better than PRF subjects, so that CRF subjects quit responding sooner after the initiation of extinction. The *sequential hypothesis* is a synthesis of the aftereffects hypothesis and the discrimination hypothesis, and, in its fullest form, is quite elaborate.

A substantial number of learning theories have emerged in this century, and they can be classified in a variety of ways. One point of distinction between categories of learning theories is whether they assert that reinforcement is a requirement for learning. A number of reinforcement theories of learning exist, and they have all sought to explain how reinforcement works—what makes reinforcers reinforce.

Thorndike

Edward Lee Thorndike stated the first reinforcement theory in 1913, when he asserted that responses followed by a "satisfier" become connected to the stimuli that preceded the response, while responses followed by an "annoyer" become disconnected from the preceding stimuli.

Hull

Clark L. Hull was one of the earliest theorists to propose a theory of reinforcement. He claimed that a stimulus is a reinforcer if it reduces drive. The theory accounts very nicely for the fact that food is a reinforcer only for a hungry animal; if there is no hunger, there is no drive to reduce. Aversive reinforcers work because they create their own drives; that is, shock creates a drive, which is reduced by shock termination.

Later, the theory required a slight modification and became the *drive-stimulus reduction theory*. This theory asserts that reinforcers reduce the internal stimuli produced by drives. Thus, it can account for the immediate effect of food reinforcers even though there is some delay in food being digested. It also accounts for reinforcement with saccharine, a sweet-tasting but nonnutritive substance. Finally, it explains why deprivation states that a subject does not feel, such as asphyxiation by carbon monoxide, are not suitable deprivations for conditioning by reduction.

Premack

D. Premack has devised a different scheme of reinforcement, known as the *prepotent response theory* or response relativity theory. According to Premack, at any given moment there is a hierarchy of response preferences for an animal. Access to a preferred response will reinforce a less-preferred response. Thus, for a hungry animal, eating is a highly preferred response, and the availability of food, which makes eating possible, will reinforce the less-preferred response of bar pressing.

Guthrie

E. R. Guthrie has suggested that the effect of reinforcement is to remove the animal from the stimulus situation in which the response that produced the reward occurred. Thus, because of the reinforcement, the rewarded response is the last response made in the presence of those stimuli. Therefore, when those stimuli are next encountered, they will elicit the response, by the principle of recency.

James P. Rodgers

Reliability of Psychological Measurements

Reliability and Validity

A distinction should be made between test validity and reliability. A test can be highly reliable but not valid for any purpose. For example, the weight of individuals could be used to predict college grades. Whereas weight may be measured very reliably, it would not be valid as a predictor of college grades. However, the opposite is not true—in order for a test to be highly valid, it also must be highly reliable. High reliability is a necessary but not sufficient condition for high validity.

Generalizability

The validity of measures requiring content validity depends upon the extent to which one can generalize the results obtained from one set of items to other items of the same kind. An example is the extent to which the items on a spelling test reflect the results that would be obtained from tests containing different items relating to spelling.

Reliability of measures can also be considered an issue relating to generalizability. Essentially, reliability concerns the extent to which measurements of particular traits are repeatable under the same conditions. Repeatability of measurement is a fundamental necessity in all areas of science.

Reliability concerns the extent to which one can safely generalize from the results obtained by applying a measurement method to people in one situation at one time to the application of the same or a comparable measure of the same trait to the same people in a similar situation at another time. If one can safely generalize in these ways, it can be said that a measure is highly reliable; if not, it must be admitted that there is considerable measurement error in some way related to the nature of the measuring instrument or the way that it is used in.

Attenuation

Measurement error, or unreliability, always works to obscure or *attenuate* any type of scientific lawfulness. Whatever "real" lawfulness there is in nature will appear blurred if relatively unreliable measures are used to chart that lawfulness. An example would be a situation where there is a perfect correlation (r=1.00) between a predictor test and a criterion, such as between a test of scholastic aptitude and grade point averages in college.

Random error works to make an observed relationship less regular than it would be if the randomness were not present. This is why we speak of error, or unreliability, as attenuating, that is, lessening, a correlation. In the previous example, if only a dozen pairs of scores are used, it is possible that the random changes in scores either would leave a correlation unchanged or could, in a very rare circumstance, make the correlation larger.

True Scores

The wider the spread of obtained scores about true scores, the more error is involved in employing the instrument in question. The standard deviation of the distribution of errors for each person would be an index of the amount of error. If the standard deviation of errors were much the same for all persons, which is usually assumed to be the case, one standard deviation of errors could typify the amount of error to be expected.

Reliability Coefficient

A very useful measure of reliability is obtained by correlating the scores on alternative forms of a measure. Alternative forms of a spelling test could be compared by selecting sixty spelling words from fourth-grade readers and randomly dividing them into two thirty-item tests of spelling ability. An alternative form for an existing measure of achievement in arithmetic could be constructed by composing a collection of items that were similar to items in the existing test.

Reliability Estimation

The reliability coefficient consists of the correlation between alternative measures of the same trait and the same people. However, there are a number of different ways that such measures of reliability can be obtained in practice. One method is by the study of internal consistency of the test items. To the extent to which the individual items on a test correlate with one another, the internal-consistency reliability is high.

Jum C. Nunnally

Religion and Psychoanalysis

Religion is regarded in classical psychoanalytic theory as a symbolic repetition of early childhood experience and, thus, as a cultural analogue of the individual phenomena on which the theory is based.

Animism and magic. Many authorities have traced the origin of animism to the need to understand and account for death. In place of this purely cognitive explanation, Sigmund Freud attempted a more comprehensive one: intrapsychic conflict between love and hatred that is intensified by the death of a close relative or friend.

Later work in this area has augmented Freud's explanation by reference to several other elements in the creation of spirits. The extreme characterization of spirits as either idealized and benevolent or utterly destructive and malignant, or both at once, corresponds to the intensity of the extremes of early, especially preoedipal and preverbal, experience.

Totemism and exogamy. The oedipal components of shamanistic practice appear to be grounded in pervasive narcissistic and preoedipal disturbances of the early mother-child relationship. But Freud's contribution to the understanding of religion originated with his treatment of issues from a later period of psychological development, as they are embodied in the practice of totemism. Members of a particular clan believe that they live under the protection of a special totem animal (or plant or even inanimate object), which provides the clan with its name and its hypothetical ancestry.

Freud attempted to draw together the diverse strands of this totemistic complex with a historical reconstruction, the famous "primal horde" theory. In this view, humankind was originally organized in groups dominated by a central male figure who owned all the females of the horde and procreated the children, driving out the sons as they reached maturity. But the exiled brothers finally banded together and, now possessed of the courage and strength that only a group afforded, murdered and devoured the tyrant, thus effecting a magical identification with the feared and envied father and absorbing a portion of his power.

Puberty rites. The most extensively analyzed ritual of primitive religion is the initiation of pubescent boys into the society of adult men. Theodor Reik has provided a comprehensive interpretation of puberty rites. The enactment of separation from the mother of course dramatizes the ritual's ostensible purpose: but this purpose is not as simple as it appears. The fundamental unconscious aim of the rite is the fathers' violent discouragement of the expression of

and their punishment for the young men's incestuous and patricidal wishes.

A fundamental principle of psychoanalytic interpretation is illustrated by its treatment of puberty rites: the end result of a situation reflects the actual intentions of the participants. The mothers weep and wail, and are brusque with their husbands who come to fetch the boys, not for some abstract reason or ceremonial purpose but because they are genuinely, and for good reason, afraid for their sons. The fathers, who masquerade as the boys' protectors against the monster, actually go to extreme lengths to terrify them, and succeed in doing so. The genital operations on the boys—incessantly rationalized by the people and the ethnographers alike as tests of endurance and fortitude—have as their outcome, and thus as their intention, violent mutilation, severe pain in sexual relations, and reduced potency for life, which will always serve as a reminder of the danger of violating the fundamental taboos.

Eastern Religions

Psychoanalytic students of religion have devoted little attention to these religions, despite the sometimes startling availability of underlying fantasies.

Western Religions

Judaism. Psychoanalytic examination of the Old Testament has revealed a latent structure that lies behind and is frequently at variance with the manifest text, the result of tendentious and systematic reediting and falsification imposed on the original by the later priestly hierarchy. The nomadic era of wandering in the desert later recorded in the early books of the Bible involved a complicated religion fashioned out of many diverse elements: totemistic clan organization and consequent polydemonism; dangerous and malevolent spirits appeased only by human sacrifice and symbolic castration; shamanistic ecstasy and the blurring of distinction between shaman and spirit; pervasive magical thinking; and the elimination of the mother as an object of worship and consequent libidinization of the relationship with a divine father.

Christianity. After the abolition by the Jews of child and animal sacrifice, the new religious offshoot of Judaism came to celebrate a human sacrifice as its central mystery, the sacrifice to God the Father of his guiltless human divine son as an atonement for the indelible original sin of mankind. The intolerable burden of guilt that oppressed the Jews was in Christianity magically alleviated by the sacrifice of a scapegoat. Yet although the son is murdered, he not only becomes elevated to the level of God the Father but for all practical purposes actually takes the father's place in the mainstream (Pauline) version. Christianity, the religion of the son, replaces its spiritual progenitor, Judaism, the religion of the father, by exalting the filicidal atonement for a shadowy primal sin into a victory for mankind. From a psychoanalytic viewpoint, this only symbolically identified original sin (eating of the Tree of Life, Knowledge, or Good and Evil in primordial paradise) appears to be a condensation of the two primal oedipal violations for which the Jews suffered such intense guilt: incest with the mother (here, mother of mankind), and the murder and devouring of the father (here represented as the tree totem). The psychological significance of the Jewish iniquity and the Christian original sin is the same.

Retrospect and Prospect

The psychoanalytic treatment of religion has revolved around recurrent and associated cultural themes and patterns of belief and practice that are reminiscent of those reflected in individual psychoanalysis, but has very seldom been based on the role of religion in an individual's life. A person may have motives for his or her beliefs largely unconnected with the psychological functions apparently served by the religious sect to which he or she belongs. Thus, the relationship between private and public or between individual and cultural manifestations of religion is unknown, though in principle knowable.

Charles Ducey

Repression: A Psychoanalytic View

The mechanism of repression consists in the establishment of a countercathexis by the ego. This is possible only after a substantial degree of ego devel-

opment has taken place. Infantile repressions are the basic ones. At one time Sigmund Freud believed that the nature of infantile repressions was unique, and he used the term "primal repression" to designate them. At present we believe that the mechanism is the same for very early repressions as for later ones.

Repression, like all other defense mechanisms, produces a dynamic balance of forces within the mind that may shift from time to time in the direction of either normality or pathology. Repression is called successful when the balance is predominantly in favor of those forces we call "defenses," which act to bar from conscious awareness, from control of motility, and from emotional expression derivatives of the drives or of the superego, generically referred to as the repressed.

Charles Brenner

Resistance in Psychoanalysis

Sigmund Freud (1926) outlined five types of resistance, three of them having their source in the ego, one in the id, and one in the superego. The ego resistances are (1) repression resistances (defense resistance), manifestations of the ego's warding off anxiety associated with unconscious conflict; (2) gain from illness (secondary gain), based on the desire to preserve the real advantage, satisfaction, or relief afforded by the neurosis, and (3) transference resistance, the reanimation of a repression that should only have been recollected. Transference resistance is considered currently to have its sources in the drives (id) and the conscience (superego), as well. Id resistance arises from the pressure of the drives and infantile wishes. Superego resistance "seems to originate from the sense of guilt or need for punishment; it opposes every move toward success, including, therefore, the patient's own recovery through analysis."

Wilhelm Reich (1949) wrote extensively about analysis of resistance, particularly in relation to defenses and to character. He described varieties of neurotic characters, referring to the habitual attitudes and modes of behavior, often egosyntonic, which protect the patient in her usual life and oppose the progress of the analytic work.

R. R. Greenson (1967) has emphasized the importance of analyzing resistance before content and ego before id, and of beginning with the surface, as basic principles though not invariably to be followed. According to Greenson, this rule means that content interpretation will not become effective until the significant resistances have been analyzed.

There are both obvious and subtle pitfalls in an overemphasis on resistance analysis. The patient may feel badgered and harassed; he may feel as if he does not receive sufficient credit for his constructive efforts; the adaptive and expressive aspects of the "resistant" behavior may be overlooked. An embattled analytic impasse may ensue. For example, H. Kohut (1971) and John E. Gedo (1975) have pointed out that early interpretation of idealization of the analyst by the patient as a resistance against acknowledgment of hostile-rivalrous attitudes will result, in patients with narcissistic personality disturbances, in a failure to allow the full-blown emergence of idealizing transferences and may often lead to analytic stalemates.

S. Joseph Nemetz

Reward

Several concepts of reward have been used by psychologists studying learning. Indeed, variations in usage largely have reflected variations in conceptualizing the role of motivation in learning. Common to all usages is the idea that a reward is something that occurs as a consequence of responding—the reward is for doing something—and, implicitly, that reward is an affectively positive (pleasing) stimulus. Early usage stems from the work of Edward Lee Thorndike in animal and human learning and the law of effect. Later usage has reflected both the development of broader theories of reinforcement and the increasing role of incentive as a motivational concept.

Rewards have also been distinguished as stimuli that not only strengthen responding but also may serve as positive incentives, themselves serving to arouse, and become goals of, behavior.

Lawrence R. Boulter

Rivers, W. H. L. (1864–1922)

W. H. L. Rivers started as a physician, then moved to experimental psychology and to cross-cultural studies. Toward the end of his life he was preoccupied with psychotherapy. He took part in the founding of the *British Journal of Medical Psychology*.

Vytautas J. Bieliauskas

Role Theory

The set of interrelated concepts known as *role theory* or *role analysis* provides a general framework for the understanding of social behavior (Sarbin and Allen 1968). The concept of social role, a metaphor derived from the theater, has long been employed in commonsense psychology and in literature as a device for interpreting and illuminating social behavior.

Role theory is primarily concerned with the overt social conduct that validates one's occupancy of a social position—that is, role enactment.

Role expectations clearly influence role enactment. Valid enactment of a social role requires behaving in ways appropriate to the social position, but it would be incorrect to consider role behavior as being rigid and invariant. Role expectations normally indicate permissible limits, beyond which strong social sanctions may result; yet within these boundaries a wide latitude of different behaviors and stylistic variations is acceptable.

One distinctive feature of the role theory formulation should be emphasized: it provides a conceptual bridge linking the individual (role behavior), society (social position), and culture (expectations or norms).

Vernon L. Allen

Rorschach, Hermann (1884–1922)

Rorschach is well known for his projective Inkblot Test, which he published in his book *Psychodiagnostik* (1921).

John C. Burnham

Rorschach Inkblot Method

The Rorschach method is also known as the Rorschach Inkblot Test. It consists of a standard series of ten sizable (page-size) inkblots that represent the stimulus cards of the method. The entire series is presented in a standard sequence, in accordance with the designated numbers (I–X).

Since the major purpose of the Rorschach method is that of obtaining association-interpretations of inkblots, the testing procedure is designed to maximally facilitate such interpretations. At the same time, care is taken to maintain standard conditions for those tested so that the results obtained are comparable across subjects and across examiners.

The most frequently used determinant is that of form (F), the formal characteristics of the blot that match the person's image of an aspect of reality. If the fit between the blot area used and the association content is good, the F is characterized as good form and scored F+. Conversely, if the associated content is formally dissimilar or departs from the actual reality of the defined blot stimulus, then the response is said to be determined by "poor form" and is scored F−. Since the number and variety of responses to the ten inkblots is virtually limitless, and since workers wished to reduce the subjectivity involved in letting the examiner alone determine whether form is good or poor, response lists to the Ws, Ds, and Dds of the Rorschach stimulus material have been compiled. Best known are those of D. N. Hertz, M. Rickers-Ovsiankina, S. J. Beck, and others.

There has been some criticism of the F+ versus the F− dichotomy. Dichotomizing the responses, it is argued, disregards degrees of good and poor form, degrees of "plus" and "minus" quality. A rather sensitive scoring system that regards several stages between plus and minus has been developed by a group of workers at Clark University, under the influence of the late Heinz Werner. This "developmental scoring system" has been especially useful in a number of research projects (Goldfried, Stricker, and Weiner 1971; Rickers-Ovsiankina 1960).

The scoring summary represents the numerical summation of the locations, determinants, and content categories. Included, in addition, are a series of indices that further summarize proportions of categories of response, such as approach, sequence, experience balance, F+ percentage, A percentage, and the median latency time for first response to the cards. Thus, the summary gives a bird's-eye view of the distribution of the several variables and offers the opportunity to translate the specialized Rorschach language into statements concerning personality, based on the hypotheses regarding the meaning of those variables.

Numerous research studies have concerned themselves with the meaning of individual variables, diagnostic precision, prognosis in work situations and psychopathology, and a multitude of other issues related to the Rorschach.

Albert I. Rabin

Rumor Transmission

Descriptions, forecasts, or explanations of events are considered rumors when they are widely circulated and of questionable validity. Rumor research has attempted to determine why there is inaccuracy and why rumors are created and circulated.

Rumor analysts agree that rumors are created and circulated when an emotionally arousing event has not been adequately explained by trustworthy sources. When official sources are seen as untrustworthy (e.g., when a government is known to be censoring the news), those who are seeking clarification will pool their limited data and join their guesses to develop their own explanations (Bauer and Gleicher 1953; Shibutani 1966). In a series of controlled studies, S. Schachter (1959) has shown that people will seek out others who are experiencing the same arousing event in order to obtain cognitive clarity.

Harvey Burdick

Rush, Benjamin (1745–1813)

Benjamin Rush believed that many mental disturbances are due to disease of the brain or vascular system, and therefore advocated bloodletting or various means of tranquilizing, such as a gyrating chair. He is considered to be the first to propound the efficacy of occupational therapy. In 1812 he wrote *Diseases of the Mind*.

Leo H. Berman

· S ·

Sachs, Hanns (1881–1947)

Hanns Sachs was an early member of Freud's inner circle. In 1912 Sachs and Otto Rank founded and became coeditors of the journal *Imago*. In 1939 Sachs founded the *American Imago* and remained its editor with George B. Wilbur. His early writings concerned dream interpretation. Sachs applied analytic theory to sociology and to other fields, such as creative process, artists, and writers. His later papers dealt with the problems of metapsychology, technique, and training.

Sanford Gifford

Sakel, Manfred (1900–1957)

Manfred Sakel introduced and advocated the use of insulin in coma in the treatment of schizophrenia.

Leo H. Berman

Satisfactions and Other Job Attitudes

Job satisfactions are generally defined as affective responses to discriminable characteristics or facets of the task and work environment. These affective responses vary along a like/dislike continuum and reflect a complex process of comparisons between what is experienced on the job; frames of reference that workers have for evaluating what they experience; workers' expectations regarding what is a fair and equitable return for their efforts; and alternatives available to the workers.

Most contemporary methods of assessing job satisfaction have used some form of an attribute checklist on which respondents are asked to indicate whether or not a given attribute—fast-paced—is true of the job or if an attribute—intelligent—is true of the worker's supervisor. Response formats range from a simple yes/no dichotomy to a seven-point scale reflecting the degree to which the attribute is descriptive of the job dimension.

The assessment technique that probably has had the most extensive developmental work and for which we have the most extensive psychometric information is the Job Descriptive Index developed by P. C. Smith and her associates.

Characteristics associated with the tasks performed by workers and environments within which the tasks are carried out have strong, reasonably consistent, and theoretically interesting relationships with reported job satisfactions. The literature relating to satisfaction and other job attitudes is best summarized by emphasizing the ubiquity of individual differences and the moderating effects of environmental and sociocultural variables.

Charles L. Hulin

Schedules of Reinforcement

Schedules of reinforcement refer to rules according to which a reinforcer is presented to an organism. Since the majority of such rules apply only to operant behavior, this discussion will be limited to such behavior, as well as to schedules of positive reinforcement. Continuous reinforcement (CRF) refers to the reinforcement of every response, and extinction (EXT) refers to no reinforcement. Between these two extremes, reinforcers may be scheduled for some but not all responses (partial or intermittent reinforcement).

The delivery of a reinforcer may be made contingent upon the subject's rate of responding. A differential-reinforcement-of-high-rate (DRH) schedule specifies the minimal number of responses per unit of time. The more common differential-reinforcement-of-low-rate (DRL) schedule specifies the minimal acceptable time interval between successive responses. DRL schedules are particularly useful in studying temporal discrimination since they penalize the subject for responding too soon. The delivery of a reinforcer independent of the subject's behavior on a fixed time (FT) or variable time (VT) basis is sometimes used to study operant behavior.

Compound Schedules

Compound schedules of reinforcement are those in which two or more rules operate either concurrently or in sequence. The most common compound schedule is a multiple schedule, an alternating combination of two or more component schedules, each cued by a different exteroceptive stimulus. The component schedules may be the same (e.g., two independent schedules with the same mean interreinforcement interval) or different. A change from a multiple schedule with both components the same to one in which one component schedule is altered is used to study schedule interactions—changes in behavior in the unchanged component. Where different types of schedules are used, stimulus control is reflected by the pattern of responding appropriately to the schedule signaled by the stimulus present at a given time.

A mixed schedule is like a multiple schedule except that the alternating components are not signaled. A chained schedule is one in which two or more (signaled) component schedules are arranged in a fixed sequence with (primary) reinforcement only available in the terminal component. A tandem schedule is like a chained schedule except that the sequential components are not signaled. As in the case of the mixed schedule, the tandem schedule is used primarily as a control condition, in this case to demonstrate the function of the signaling stimuli in a comparable chained schedule. A concurrent schedule is one in which two or more schedules are concurrently in force, each for a different response (e.g., pressing the left lever or the right lever in a rat Skinner box). When the component schedules differ, preference for one over the other may be inferred from differences in the number of responses made on each lever.

David R. Thomas

Schizophrenia: An Adaptive Theory

The model of schizophrenia presented here has been influenced in particular by the formulations of K. Z. Altschule and Karl Menninger. The concept that all organisms exist in equilibria with many other complex interacting systems—living and nonliving—that constitute their environment is not a new one. According to this view, life is a dynamic equilibrium established between an organism and its environment, which equilibrium tends to maintain a relatively constant internal milieu even when the environment fluctuates sharply.

Schizophrenia can be viewed as a compromise in which short-term existence takes precedence over the long-term quality or efficiency of that existence. We can view the acute phase of schizophrenia as the period during which a new steady state is being sought, and the chronic phase as the period in which it has been achieved. Since all steady states have a relative stability, the chronic phase of schizophrenia will be the more difficult one to reverse, and treatment, therefore, should be directed at the acute phase whenever possible. It requires considerable perturbation of a system to disrupt its steady state, and some of the so-called symptoms of acute schizophrenia are nothing more than the phenomena associated with the disruption. It is tempting to speculate that the mobilization of affect in psychotherapy is not the cause of change but rather a barometer of system disturbance; that is, readiness to establish a new steady state.

What is particularly heuristic about this conceptualization of schizophrenia is that it applies to other mental disorders equally well. It allows one to see the behavior of mentally ill people, which society finds unacceptable, as part of their effort to adapt to what they perceive—correctly or incorrectly, consciously or unconsciously—as new circumstances. It takes the symptoms out of the moral context and puts them into the medical realm by making them a part of the human response pattern to a serious new situation. This new situation may exist only in the mind of the individual and not in the environment. Nevertheless, her responses to an altered perception of the environment remains an adaptive effort.

Robert Cancro

Schizophrenia: Comprehensive Psychotherapy

To engage the patient in therapy, the therapist must have a basic attitude of accepting the patient as he is, with his aims in life and values and modes of operating all different from those of the therapist. She must love the patient in his state of decomposition. The patient needs psychotherapeutic objects, and the therapist must provide them across the board in the form of administrator, therapist, ward personnel, and ancillary personnel, and in the form of approaches to the family, whether in casework or family therapy.

The first step in therapy is to be available to the patient as a person who has assets the patient does not have, a person on whom the patient can depend and from whom he or she can borrow ego techniques by imitation. The therapist's calm presence is supportive. The next step consists of making a diagnostic summary, which has little to do with symptoms but rather with the habitual ego techniques the patient uses to negotiate her relationship with the therapist and with other people in her life, in the present and in the past.

With the hallucinated and deluded patient more than with any other, one has to listen for what the patient is *not* saying. The schizophrenic evades the truth of his position, cannot master the realities, and toys with the relevance of his hypotheses. The therapist's ability to face pains of reality without distortion strengthens the patient.

At first the patient may learn to be nonpsychotic only during therapy hours, while remaining psychotic outside therapy. Any regression during therapy, say, from projection to denial, implies the existence of unacknowledged feelings in the relationship, which must be worked out before therapy can continue. The therapist gets her clues as to where the patient is functioning according to the hierarchy of defenses.

As infantile needs interfere with the patient's ego functioning, the therapist must provide supportive measures of sustaining and gratifying the patient. Delusional transference may appear as a sign of the patient's dissatisfaction with the therapist in the extant relationship. When the patient suffers too much pain in the presence of the therapist, she may again resort to the conversion process by distortion, projection, and denial. Supporting conscious awareness of the patient's libidinal and aggressive identifications is the procedure of choice, especially with patients with paranoid, blaming tendencies.

At all times, concern over reality problems takes precedence over inner problems. Unawareness of them will lead to regressions. Gingerly, the therapist deprives and denies complete satisfaction to help the patient understand his or her experience and needs. Gradually the patient and often the therapist experience anxiety about change, which must be acknowledged to him or her. The purpose of the close relationship is to help the patient make a clear image of another person with whom to identify.

Max Day
Elvin V. Semrad

Schizophrenia: Psychoanalytic Views

Interest in the theory and treatment of schizophrenia by analysts has not been comparable to that of the neuroses and character disorders. Sigmund Freud's essentially pessimistic view of schizophrenia, in which he regarded patients as incapable of forming a transference, was a strong deterrent to the clinical investigation of schizophrenia by most psychoanalysts.

Freud (1914) reiterates the two fundamental characteristics of paraphrenia—namely, megalomania and withdrawal of interest from the external world of both people and things. It is here that Freud expresses his rather pessimistic view of the treatment of such patients, believing that the withdrawal of interest could render the patient inaccessible to psychoanalysis.

In his paper on the unconscious, Freud (1915) points out that in schizophrenia there is a withdrawal of instinctual cathexis from object representations. This concept became the basis of the ego deficit theory of Wexler (1975).

Karl Abraham (1908) had more clinical experience with psychotic patients than did Freud. Abraham focused on the libidinal aspects of dementia praecox and particularly pointed up the observation that the patient returns to the period of autoerotism.

Victor Tausk presented his paper *On the Origin of the "Influencing Machine" in Schizophrenia* in 1918. In it he introduces the concept of "loss of ego boundaries" (535), which explains certain phenomena of symptoms in schizophrenia.

Paul Federn's formulations are quite in contrast to those of Freud. Federn (1952) wrote that psychosis is not due to an enrichment of ego cathexis at the expense of object libido; on the contrary, it is due to an impoverishment of the ego cathexis. Similarly, hallucinations and delusions are not restitutional attempts to reestablish contact with the external world but indicative of lesions of the ego itself, which manifest themselves prior to and independently of the ego's loss of interest in the outside world.

W. Ronald Fairbairn (1941) emphasizes the role of object relations early in personality development. He contrasts infantile dependence with mature dependence, and views obsessions and hysteria as defensive against an underlying depressive position. Underlying this depressive position is the schizoid position.

W. R. Bion (1953), using the conceptual mechanism of Melanie Klein relative to the paranoid and depressive positions and projective identification, applies these concepts to schizophrenia. His thesis is that there are sadistic attacks on verbal thought, and this leads to a splitting process that makes it difficult to synthesize in order to achieve a depressive position.

H. A. Rosenfeld (1965) is of the opinion that "psychotic parts of the personality may be split off in very earliest infancy while other parts of the self may develop apparently normally. Under certain circumstances the split off psychotic parts may break through to the surface, often producing an acute psychosis, for example a schizophrenia." (167–68)

Heinz Hartmann (1953) postulates that the pathology underlying schizophrenia is related to the failure of neutralization of aggression. This leads to an inability of the ego to perform its effective defense mechanisms.

E. Jacobson (1954) has followed Hartmann in utilizing the term *self-representations*, and points out that developmentally, during the early preoedipal phase, the good and bad images of the self tend to merge and split with the images of the love objects, with a return to an earlier undifferentiated state occurring whenever the child experiences gratifications, physical contact, and closeness with the mother.

Jacob Arlow and Charles Brenner (1964) apply structural concepts to their explanation of the psychoses. They believe that clinical phenomena are better explained by structural theory. They point out that in psychotic patients the degree of instinctual regression tends to be greater in psychoses, with evidence of prephallic instinctual aims and prephallic wishes. It is unnecessary to assume that a libidinal decathexis has occurred to explain the break with reality. Schizophrenia is only quantitatively different from neurosis.

Harry Stack Sullivan (1953) views schizophrenic experience as having its basis in the massive dissociation of experience due to intense anxiety. As one is growing up, if one experiences intense anxiety, this becomes a part of the "not-me" aspects of the person and remains in dissociation.

The "schizophrenogenic mother" concept has been utilized by Frieda Fromm-Reichmann (1948). She states that "the schizophrenic is painfully distrustful and resentful of other people, because of the severe early warp and rejection that he has encountered in important people of his infancy and childhood, as a rule mainly in a schizophrenogenic mother. During his early fight for emotional survival, he begins to develop the greatest interpersonal sensitivity which remains his for the rest of his life" (163–64).

Under the heading of etiology Harold Searles (1959) has indicated that the central difficulty in schizophrenia relates to impairment in integration and differentiation, with schizophrenic regression being related to the level of early infancy when the infant has not subjectively differentiated from the outer world. He follows Margaret S. Mahler in indicating that the relationship of the infant with the mother never reached a level of symbiotic relatedness.

Silvano Arieti (1968) has divided schizophrenia into four stages. In the first stage, infancy, the child deals with many negative emotions. At the second stage, grammar school, there is no development of basic trust or dialogue with others. At the third phase, adolescence, prepsychotic loneliness and panic occurs. The fourth stage consists of psychotic regression in thinking, impaired volition, and psychotic reality.

Clarence G. Schulz

Schizophrenia: Sociopsychosomatic Theory

Benjamin B. Wolman's theory of schizophrenia provides a developmental, a psychological, an interpersonal, and an organic description of the etiology and course of that pernicious disorder.

Wolman classes interpersonal interaction patterns into three types:

1. those which are primarily *instrumental*, characterized by taking;
2. those which are predominantly *mutual*, characterized by balanced giving and taking; and
3. those which are primarily *vectorial*, characterized by giving.

Because schizophrenia arises when the child, normally a taker, is forced to become a precocious giver, Wolman proposed that childhood schizophrenia be termed *vectoriasis praecocissima*, and schizophrenia that becomes manifest in later life, *vectoriasis praecox*.

Wolman distinguishes among four subtypes of childhood schizophrenia. They are, in order from the most to the least severe:

(1) pseudoamentive, (2) autistic, (3) symbiotic, and (4) aretic. In the pseudoamentive syndrome, "development is stopped before it has the chance to start" (Wolman 1970a, 266). The primary symptoms mimic those of severe mental deficiency. Because of that, it is not uncommon for these pseudoamentive children to be placed in institutions for the severely retarded.

Paralleling the childhood forms of schizophrenia are the schizophrenic syndromes of later life. In paranoid schizophrenia the individual's "regression for survival," though devastating, is, relatively speaking, mild, and paranoid schizophrenia in adults corresponds to the aretic syndrome in children. In a like manner, catatonia may be paired with symbiotic schizophrenia, hebephrenia and simple schizophrenia with childhood autism, and schizophrenic dementia in adults with the pseudoamentia constellation in children.

Wolman suggests ten rules by which the therapeutic interaction ought to be guided:

1. The therapist must provide the patient with unconditional support.
2. The therapist should direct herself toward strengthening the patient's ego.
3. The therapeutic process should be well-modulated. "One step up" is the phrase that should guide the therapist's actions, even if that requires that less dangerous symptoms be supported in order that more dangerous ones be eliminated.
4. The therapist must be both pragmatic and flexible.
5. The therapist must bring herself to the therapeutic interaction.
6. The therapist should aid the patient in testing reality. To do this the therapist must maintain a realistic attitude toward her own abilities and aims.
7. The therapist should avoid interpretations unless she is convinced that they will be therapeutic at the time they are offered: there should be a parsimony of interpretation.
8. The therapist must aim for a realistic management of transference. The therapist must involve herself with the patient's suffering

along with maintaining a professional and vectorial attitude toward the patient.

9. The therapist must exert a strong control over countertransference phenomena.

10. The patient's hostility should be carefully handled. Physical violence should not be permitted or sanctioned.

Herbert H. Krauss
Beatrice J. Krauss

Schlosberg, Harold (1904–1964)

Harold Schlosberg formulated the dual-process theory of conditioning. According to this theory, classical conditioning occurs as a result of the mere contiguous occurrence of the conditioned stimulus (CS) and unconditioned stimulus (US). Operant conditioning entails the operation of the law of effect.

Gregory A. Kimble

School as a Social System

The fact that students are nonvoluntary clients helps establish the condition for substantial tension between the adult and youth subsystems of schools, a tension that influences the characteristics of the informal patterns of association among both teachers and students.

Given the stress evident in teacher-student relationships in all schools, despite the relative isolation of teachers from one another in the performance of their classroom duties (Dreeben 1972), as in the case of students, collegial interaction among teachers tends to generate an informal, or internal, subsystem defensive of adult authority and prerogatives.

The effects of student participation in the social system of the school have been explored in terms of (1) consequences for society as a whole; (2) consequences for the personal development of the individual; and (3) consequences for specific learning on the part of both individuals and groups. For society as a whole, most sociologists see schools serving as agencies of instruction, socialization, custody, and selection.

With regard to the in-school socialization of indi-

viduals, which of course is related to societal objectives, E. Durkheim (1961), R. Dreeben (1968), and T. Parsons (1959) all view schools as places where students learn not only academic subject matter but also behavioral norms appropriate for adult positions or status. Durkheim (1961) has emphasized the opportunity schools provide for training students in self-discipline, in commitment to the common good, and in skills for effective participation in social groups.

David W. O'Shea
Mark B. Ginsburg

School Phobia

School phobia is much more common in the elementary school child. In the adolescent group, school phobia reveals chronic and deeply embedded problems that yield slowly to treatment, and the prognosis is less favorable.

The etiology of school phobia often has been related to separation anxiety. Usually a combination of unresolved dependency and hostility characterizes the relationship between the school-phobic child and his mother, concomitant with a fear of separating from her.

Melvin Sinowitz

School Psychology

School psychology is a specialty concerned with the use of psychological knowledge to promote the cognitive development and mental health of individuals in educational contexts. School psychologists use cognitive, behavioral, and social science along with empirical data to understand the needs of clients, to participate in the design of programmatic approaches to meeting those needs in educational and other settings, and to evaluate the effectiveness of psychological and educational services recommended or provided. Many of the services provided by school psychologists are directly delivered to clients; others are delivered indirectly, through others (e.g. teachers and parents) who influence the lives of students.

At the beginning of the 1990s there were approximately 21,000 school psychology positions in public schools in the United States. Since job sharing is not uncommon among school psychologists, and since school psychologists work in other settings, the number of working school psychologists is currently estimated to exceed 30,000. Few schools do not have a school psychologist assigned to them at least part-time. The National Association of School Psychologists (NASP) has recommended a ratio of 1 school psychologist to 1,000 pupils, with a maximum of four schools served by one school psychologist (NASP 1992). The actual ratio of psychologists to pupils is probably closer to 1 to 2,000.

History

Most school psychologists trace their origins back to Lightner Whitmer, who established the first psychological clinic at the University of Pennsylvania in 1896. This clinic, staffed by multidisciplinary teams, received from schools referrals of children who were having difficulty learning or who had other problems. Whitmer recognized he was among the first applying the new science of psychology to human problems and coined the term "clinical psychology" to describe the work he and his associates were doing in his clinic. Until World War II, clinical and school psychology were very similar fields, both largely serving children and adolescents.

As the field of psychological measurement grew with World War I, school psychologists were among the first to use the new tools developed. Tests such as the Stanford-Binet were used by psychologists working in school districts to help identify and plan for children's individual needs in the same manner as had been done in Whitmer's clinic. School psychologists continued during the 1920s and 1930s to help schools consider individual differences in educational planning and work with exceptional children.

Children whose behavior is disruptive have been referred to school psychologists since the beginning of the century. By the 1920s school psychologists were part of the mental health movement started by Clifford Beers. They utilized psychological counseling as a technique for helping troubled children, and established mental hygiene programs in the schools.

Although school psychologists have always pushed for the individualization of educational planning, the school's response has typically been the compromise of grouping children. In addition to helping select children for special educational programs, school psychologists have been involved historically in programmatic efforts such as instructional grouping, grade-level retention and acceleration, readiness assessment for developmental primary education, and classroom management and disciplinary programs. In recent years, however, an increasing variety of children with special needs has been identified, and the number of special education programs and children served has grown.

As part of the civil rights movement, legislation was passed in the 1970s guaranteeing the right of all children, particularly those with disabilities, to a free and appropriate public education in the least restrictive environment. The definitions and provisions in PL 94-142, the Education for All Handicapped Children Act, created a dramatic growth in the number of school psychologists employed in schools. At the same time, however, it reinforced the connection between school psychology and special education, and heavily influenced the practice of school psychology.

Populations Served and Problems Addressed

As in the past, school psychologists are largely concerned with children of elementary and secondary school age, their families, their teachers, and other direct caregivers, and organizations, such as the school, that serve them. Currently the age range has been extended from birth to adulthood. The growth of preschool and early intervention programs for infants and toddlers, along with the extension downward in age in federal legislation concerning disabled children (Public Law 99-457) has expanded the population eligible for the services of school psychologists.

At the same time, individuals with learning disabilities are now required to be accommodated in higher education, and school psychologists have been working with individuals of any age enrolled in higher education.

Although school psychologists work to promote development by contributing psychological knowledge about learning and the learner, they also respond to signs that the normal development of competence in many areas is at risk. Failure to learn under the typical conditions of instruction and behavior in the classroom, suggesting or reflecting delayed development of social, emotional, or cognitive skills, is often addressed by school psychologists. School psychologists help schools deal with children who have experienced severe stress and crisis during childhood and adolescence, or who evidence signs of mental disorder or specific disabilities that require accommodation.

Settings

Most school psychologists are employed by public school districts. However, school psychologists do practice in hospital settings, correctional institutions, training centers in private industry and human service, or other institutional settings serving children or offering educational programs. School psychologists are found in universities both as teachers and researchers and as practitioners providing services to students. In addition, some school psychologists work in private practice.

Professional Skills, Activities and Methods

School psychologists provide both direct (face-to-face) services to children and families, and indirect services. Direct services include:

Assessment. In order to establish children's needs, school psychologists administer cognitive tests of intellectual functioning, adaptive behavior, educational achievement, and language development. They do assessments of social functioning, emotional development, and perceptual or motor functioning, depending on the reason for referral. Assessment procedures include screening, testing, interviewing, behavioral analysis, observation, and examining work samples or archival information. Data are gathered on the environment as well, to reflect the individual's functioning in an ecological context. Assessment and assessment-related activities occupy much of a typical psychologist's day.

Individual and group counseling. School psychologists also are skilled at individual and group counseling. School psychologists seldom have extended contacts with students and often use brief therapy, or problem-focused techniques. Crisis counseling and intervention is also a common activity of school psychologists. Group work with at-risk students is designed to provide children with coping and stress-reduction strategies. Some school psychologists also work with families in a therapeutic relationship.

Indirect services include:

Consultation and collaboration. School psychologists consult with teachers, parents, and other caregivers. They bring a psychological perspective to a problem-solving process that results in a more creative and sensitive restructuring of the student's environment and interactions with others. The solutions generated by consultation often obviate the need for special education for many children.

Program and Intervention Planning. School psychologists, using information from their needs assessments of children, assist in the planning of specific interventions or of comprehensive programmatic approaches to problems where the intervention is delivered by other professionals. The treatment planning may be for a single intervention for a single child or for a group intervention, such as the creation of a support group for children whose parents are divorcing. Some programs are designed to provide primary prevention of conditions, such as sexual abuse, drug abuse, and teen pregnancy. School psychologists' most common intervention planning is the development of an individual educational plan (IEP) for a child being served in a special education program. In addition to the child level, interventions may be created for schools and school districts under the rubric of organizational development.

Research and evaluation. School psychologists are trained to do research and may help the school district in this regard, but more commonly they work to evaluate the interventions and programs that have been implemented for children. One evaluative role is case management, where services to children and families are coordinated and monitored for effectiveness.

Teaching and supervision. School psychologists may educate teachers, school administrators, parents, and children in particular areas related to psychology, such as classroom management or parenting skills. Academic school psychologists teach at the university level. School psychologists also have supervisory responsibilities for interns, peers, and paraprofessionals working in the school.

The Knowledge Bases of School Psychology

School psychologists have core understandings of the biological and social bases of behavior, individual differences, the history and systems of psychology, research design and statistics, and scientific and professional ethics. In addition, school psychologists draw heavily on learning theory, instructional psychology, developmental psychology, human exceptionality and psychopathology, measurement, community psychology, and social psychology.

In addition to psychology, school psychologists must draw on a knowledge of educational theory and research. They must be cognizant of curriculum, the education of exceptional learners, instructional methods, educational philosophy, the organization and operation of the schools, and school law. Many school psychologists come to the field after teaching careers and draw upon this experience.

Because of the diversity of cultures present in the schools, school psychologists are well grounded in cross-cultural psychology. Cultural sensitivity is central to good test interpretation, counseling, consultation, and evaluation.

Training

The preparation of school psychologists includes extensive course work in the psychological and educational areas outlined above, fieldwork in assessment, counseling, consultation, and other skill areas, and a internship as an apprentice school psychologist.

School psychologists are educated at the graduate level in programs in schools of education (usually with faculty in educational psychology) or in departments of psychology. They are trained at the M.A. or specialist level in programs typically of three years in length, or prepared in doctoral-level programs. The American Psychological Association, which accredits only at the doctoral level, listed in 1992 forty-six accredited programs nationwide. In most states, however, programs need only be accredited by state departments of education, and the NASP directory of training programs lists over 230 programs at all levels nationwide. Because school psychologists work in schools, one outcome of training is an educational credential as a school psychologist granted by a state authority.

School Psychology Organizations

School psychologists belong to local, state, national, and international professional associations. Most states have state associations, which are loosely affiliated with the NASP. This national group accepts membership from individuals credentialed by state agencies and does not distinguish between specialist-level practitioners and holders of the doctorate. School psychologists with doctorates are eligible to join the APA as full members. Within the APA they may join the Division of School Psychology. National and state-level organizations hold conventions and publish newsletters, journals, and other publications.

Specialized school psychology organizations include the International School Psychology Association, the Trainers of School Psychologists, and the Council of Directors of School Psychology Programs. Experienced doctoral practitioners may be examined for a diplomate in school psychology offered by the American Board of School Psychology.

School Psychology Research

A literature in school psychology is well established. The principal journals reporting advances in school psychology are the *Journal of School Psychology*, *School Psychology Review*, *Psychology in the Schools*, and the *School Psychology Quarterly*. Research of interest to school psychologists is published in a variety of journals, but particularly noteworthy are the *Journal of Psychoeducational Assessment* and the *Journal of Educational and Psychological Consultation*.

Summary

School psychology is a well-established field representing a network of mental health practitioners spread throughout the country and world. Because they work in an institution that serves the entire population, they are often an individual's or family's first contact with a mental health provider. School psychology is both applied educational psychology and child psychology practiced in an educational context. School psychologists have a large and important role in primary and secondary prevention of educational and mental health difficulties.

Jonathan Sandoval

Seashore, Carl E. (1866–1949)

Carl Seashore did experimental work in visual accommodation time, sensory perception (pressure and weight), and sensory illusions.

Walter Bernard

Sechenov, Ivan Mikhailovich (1829–1905)

Ivan Mikhailovich Sechenov was a Russian physiologist, the initiator of objectivist psychology in Russia. In 1862 Sechenov discovered mechanisms in a frog brain that inhibit spinal reflexes, normally elicited by the application of painful stimuli to the skin. His 1863 essays, *Reflexes of the Brain*, represent an innovative attempt to establish the physiological basis of psychological processes. All conscious and unconscious acts are viewed as being reflex in nature, that is, determined by external and internal stimuli that activate the central nervous mechanisms, initiating, in turn, motor responses. Motor links may be inhibited (as in thinking) or intensified (as in emotion) by central mechanisms. In 1889 lectures, Sechenov discussed the nervous system as a regulatory mechanism, thus anticipating some of the ideas of cybernetics. Sechenov's work represents a prelude (E. Asratyan's expression) to Ivan Petrovich Pavlov's physiology of higher nervous activity (behavior).

Josef Brožek

Seguin, Edouard (1812–1880)

Edouard Seguin was the pioneer in treatment and training of the mentally defective. In 1837 Seguin began work with Jean Marc Gaspard Itard and subsequently opened his own school. After arriving in the United States in 1852, Seguin developed his methods into a system called the "sense training method." He started with peripheral stimulation, which, he assumed, had central nervous system effect.

John C. Burnham

Selective Attention in Children: Developmental Changes

The domain of selective attention begins with the simultaneous presentation of multiple sensory inputs and ends when one or more (but not all) are selected by the organism for differential processing.

Since the direction of attention, or "what is attended to," is a variable subject to change with appropriate motivational and training contingencies, some control of these factors must be mounted if age changes in relative salience are to be interpreted as developmental changes.

A common experimental task for studying breadth of attention is one in which more than one cue or stimulus attribute can be used to achieve a correct response. Behavioral tests are then performed to determine how many of the simultaneously presented cues have actually been used. Breadth of attention is inferred from the number of redundant, relevant cues the subject has attended to. There are several variants of such paradigms. In one, the incidental-learning design, attention is focused on one of the repeated cues by instructions or training, and measures taken of the extent to which the incidental cues are also learned.

Age changes have been experimentally demonstrated in four related properties of selective attention: (1) direction of attention, (2) breadth of attention, (3) duration and variability of attention, and (4) adjustability of attention.

David Zeaman

Selective Learning

Selective learning is a general term for any form of learning that involves the strengthening of one mode of behavior. It has sometimes been called trial-and-error learning or (rarely) trial-and-success learning. The most important examples with lower animals require the subjects to escape from a puzzle box or learn a maze. At the human level, various experiments on concept formation and problem solving have been conceived in these terms.

Gregory A. Kimble

Self-Actualization

This concept, used explicitly by Kurt Goldstein and Abraham Maslow in their respective descriptions of individual striving for personal "wholeness" and full self-expression, also characterizes the thematic thrust of the motivation-personality theories of Gordon W. Allport, Erich Fromm, Karen Horney, Rollo May, and Carl Rogers. The view, variously expressed, holds that man is basically constructive, accepting, creative, spontaneous, open to experience, self-aware, and self-realizing. It is parental, societal, and cultural controls, through manipulation of rewards and threats of punishment, which inhibit the otherwise natural development of self-expression and self-actualization.

Maslow, as well as Allport, Fromm, and Rogers, distinguished the basic need-gratification or deficiency motivation from self-actualization, "becoming," and growth motivation. Those who achieve the latter level attain freedom from dependence on others, have perceptions less distorted by basic needs, and are able to achieve greater fulfillment in love and in creative experience. Moments of great ecstasy, the true peak experiences of transcendence of time and space, that may occur in love or in mystical, creative, or self-excelling experiences, are possible only for those who are growth-motivated, psychologically healthy self-actualizers. Deficiency-motivated persons are unable to rid themselves of anxiety about need gratification and are thus more conformist and less creatively independent.

Mortimer H. Appley

Self-Concept: Emergence during Adolescence

Adolescence appears to be the period of life during which the individual makes the first serious effort to define the self-concept. It is during this period that the individual comes to a definition of self in order to face a variety of new roles. The adolescent's body is undergoing rapid change in size, form, and function as the capacity for reproduction grows. With sexual maturity comes the need to redefine relationships with agemates of both sexes, especially with the opposite sex. The individual feels pressure from parents, peers, the school, and the community to make decisions about future directions in education and vocation. The individual faces internal and external pressures on several fronts that require self-definition.

Four broadly defined components of self-concept were identified in an investigation conducted on several hundred adolescents of both sexes in grades six through twelve (R. H. Monge 1973). These components were derived from an analysis of descriptions of "My characteristic self (yourself as you most often feel about yourself)" provided by the adolescents. They rated themselves on a set of twenty-one semantic differential scales. The four components were labeled as follows: (a) achievement/leadership, (b) congeniality/sociability, (c) adjustment, and (d) sex-appropriateness of self-concept.

Boys and girls did not differ significantly on their self-ratings on the sex-appropriateness of self-concept component, nor did the boys differ from grade to grade. There was, however, among the girls a trend with increasing age away from the feminine pole (delicate, soft, weak, and sick) and toward the masculine pole (rugged, hard, strong, and healthy). It is likely that girls, as they grow older, increasingly disdain use of the feminine pole adjectives as indicative of an immature, stereotyped kind of femininity more appropriate to the image of "a little girl in a party dress." Girls become increasingly aware that it is permissable for them to apply to themselves the more traditional masculine adjectives and to adopt less traditionally feminine attitudes and behaviors.

Rolf H. Monge

Self-Concept in Post-Freudian Psychoanalysis

The concept of the self as distinct from the ego began to emerge in post–Freudian psychoanalysis under the impact of a developing ego psychology. Heinz Hartmann (1950) saw a necessity for clearly distinguishing between ego and self in order to arrive at a precise definition of narcissism within the framework of structural theory. He therefore defined self in contradistinction to objects; con-sequently, narcissism is self-cathexis, not ego-cathexis. Cathexis of self (more precisely of self-representation) may be located in the id, ego, or superego, and narcissism is actually found in all three.

While largely overlapping with the self concepts that had emerged during the decades of the 1950s and 1960s, H. Kohut's (1971, 1976) evolving psychology of the self was a new departure because it arose from newly recognized and conceptualized configurations of clinical phenomena and because the concept of self, as it began to crystallize, has acquired structure and dimensions of its own that transcend all previous conceptualizations.

The revival in the here and now (of the analytic situation) of the archaic self, which includes part of the environment as a self-object into the totality of its self-experience, Kohut properly terms a "self-object transference" (a more felicitous term than the initial designation of "narcissistic transference"). Now it is the analyst who is the self-object in place of the archaic environment. Absence of the analyst, whether a physical reality or merely a momentary inattentiveness or lapse of empathy, is subjectively apprehended as an incompleteness of the self, with its attending symptomatic manifestations, for example, lowered self-esteem, perhaps even depression, sometimes covered over by anxiety or rage.

The nuclear self is a bipolar hierarchical configuration. It consists at its base of the grandiose-exhibitionistic self with its associated grandiose fantasies, and at its apex, of the idealized parent-imago. In a gradient of energic tension between these poles, the executive functions, talents, and skills actively mediate the flow of self-expressive urges.

The maturation of the self—from the time when a fragile nuclear self first emerges until the time past late latency, around age 8, when this nuclear self has normally achieved an irreversible cohesion—can be viewed along the main dimensions of (a) strengthening the cohesion of its configuration and thus increasing its invulnerability against regression to fragmentation, and (b) the transformation of the archaic nuclear ambitions and ideals into their mature forms, through which the self now expresses its transformed ambitions and ideals, its intentions and goals, the purposes and values of its life.

Serious interference with self-development, whether through failure of the self-object or other cause, results in psychopathology. When trauma prevents consolidation of a nuclear self, psychotic or borderline illness will result. Trauma to an emerged but fragile self before it has achieved adequate cohesion may result in either narcissistic personality disorders, where the most prominent symptomatology is the suffering associated with low self-esteem and where acting-out behavior is not in the foreground, or narcissistic behavior disorders, where acting-out behavior such as perversion, delinquency, or addiction is in the foreground.

Ernest S. Wolf

Self-Control and Behavior Modification

With the advent of behavior modification and its emphasis on functional analysis, researchers began to view self-regulation as a complex acquired skill rather than as an inborn personality strength. Experimental studies began to identify and refine procedures which enhance the individual's ability to control his or her own actions. Evaluative reviews of this research are offered by F. H. Kanfer (1970), Albert Bandura (1971), Michael J. Mahoney (1972), M. R. Goldfried and M. Merbaum (1973), C. E. Thoresen and Mahoney (1974), and Mahoney and Thoresen (1974).

Self-observation, or self-monitoring, appears to be a valuable component in successful self-control (Thoresen and Mahoney 1974). It provides the individual with personal data that assist not only in the initial definition and appraisal of the problem but also in evaluating and revising subsequent self-change strategies.

Self-control strategies have generally focused on producing changes either in the antecedents of a behavior (stimulus control) or in its effects (consequence control). Combinations of these two basic strategies are frequently encountered in clinical self-management.

Self-control research has recognized that the human organism has private monologues to generate cues and consequences that powerfully moderate, and sometimes override, the effects of external variables.

Michael J. Mahoney

Self-Control: Development

Albert Bandura and R. H. Walters (1963) list several modes through which self-control can be displayed: (1) resistance to deviation in situations where there is a temptation to transgress; (2) devaluation of a goal in situations where the goal is not readily accessible or forbidden; (3) capacity to withstand delay or withholding of a social reward; and (4) delay of immediate gratification for a longer-term goal.

Behavior theory views self-control as the manipulation of controlling responses that decrease the probability of the contingent controlled response. This reduction in probability of the controlled response occurs through regulation of the individual's psychological, social, physical, or physiological environment.

Biofeedback
Behavior theory proposes two other mechanisms through which behavior can be self-controlled: respondent control, where autonomic responses in humans can be brought under voluntary control through feedback and reinforcement (e.g., biofeedback), and verbal control of other verbal as well as motor behaviors. Biofeedback has been shown to be effective in such areas as physiological responses, visual acuity, mediation, and behavior therapy (Miller et al. 1973). In a test of contract effects

on self-control, F. H. Kanfer et al. (1974) found that subjects who specifically set a standard of performance are more likely to tolerate an aversive stimulus for the contracted time.

Social Learning
Social learning theory views self-control as avoidance learning and equates self-control with internalization (i.e., behavior that is congruent with internalized norms, rules, or standards). Avoidance learning is the product of the affective conditioning of cognitive and motoric precursers of a response that previously had been punished. Inhibition of the response on future occasions is reinforcing because of anxiety reduction.

Punishment
Experience in rule enforcement, choice of punishment methods, and the child's response to punishment are other factors that influence the effect of punishment in self-control. R. D. Parke (1975) has reported that children who have experienced rule enforcement of another child, and who themselves are punished with a rationale, display more self-control in a temptation situation. Further, children who offer reparation or plead after receiving punishment are more likely to receive a positive response from the disciplinarian, suggesting that children can modify adult behavior in a punishment situation.

The development of self-control necessitates that internalized control of behavior replace external control; that is, the source of reinforcement changes from external to internal. Cognitive factors are influential determinants in this internalization. The specific role of cognition seems to be that of providing a mediational link between the perception of the situation (i.e., stimulus discrimination) and selection of the appropriate response.

Joseph C. Lavoie

Self-Esteem and Social Behavior

Self-esteem is normally conceptualized as an enduring personal characteristic analogous to personality traits. In general, research evidence supports this notion. However, a number of studies indicate that self-esteem does fluctuate as a function of situational factors. Research has shown that individuals with low self-esteem are more influenced by persuasive communication and more conforming in social situations than those with positive self-concepts.

The self-concept appears to be a major determinant of behavior in a variety of situations. While self-esteem can and does fluctuate in response to situational demands, it appears to have considerable transsituational stability.

Robert L. Helmreich

Self: Historical Overview

The self as a self-conscious psyche, as a "thinking thing" (*res cogitans*) peculiarly embodied within a material substance, emerges as the rational "subject" of knowledge with Cartesian rationalism. René Descartes modified and adapted Platonic dualism and Aristotelian functionalism to conform to the strictures of mathematical reasoning and seventeenth-century science. "I think, therefore I am," became the credo for those thinkers who would assign priority to the cogitation of an abstract, ahistorical subject.

Georg Wilhelm Friedrich Hegel, Edmund Husserl, Jean-Paul Sartre, and the existential phenomenologists have carried into our time the project initiated by Plato and the Greeks, refined by Descartes, and systematized by Immanuel Kant, namely, the division of the world of possible knowledge and experience between a rational and self-conscious subject or "transcendental ego" (for Husserl and Sartre) and the objective universe within which actual empirical selves lead their everyday and "prereflective" lives. This notion of the psyche as a self-conscious and rational subject of experience, existing (while earthbound, at least) within an identifiable body (constituting one object among others) presupposes the existence of the subject as a unique and distinguishable individual.

Social science in the twentieth century has contributed two other reformulations of the notion of self: the self in "evolution" and the self as so-cially mediated and linguistically constituted. From nineteenth-century evolutionary biology, modern social psychology and sociology adopted the notion that human beings (like "other animals") are (social) organisms that develop gradually into persons over time. Furthermore, the psyche of a person is basically a "social self," shielding the "social identity" that emerges over the course of the life span, "mirroring" the expectations and behaviors of ("significant") others, crystallizing usually during the crises of late adolescence, and varying in form and function from one society and period of history to another.

Charles P. Webel

Self-Report and Observational Methods

Self-Report Methods

A pioneering self-report inventory was the Personal Data Sheet (R. S. Woodworth 1918), which was used as a means of weeding out emotionally unstable persons from the U.S. Army. There are obvious potential shortcomings of self-report inventories as measures of personality traits, foremost among which is that individuals can lie if they choose to. However, there is no evidence that people actually do strongly distort self-inventories to put themselves in a better light.

Observational Methods

Observations in daily life tend to be superior to the other types of observational methods. Although such ratings frequently suffer because the observer has not had sufficient opportunities to observe the individual in circumstances relevant to the traits being rated, the situation in this regard tends to be much worse in the case of the other observational methods.

Interviews. The interview is a certain type of observational situation. It is seldom used for observing personality traits in general; rather, it is usually restricted to "sizing up" an individual with respect to particular decisions about him, as in a job interview or a psychiatric interview. Usually the interviewer either has never previously met the person being interviewed or has known him only casually.

Because of the small amount of time available to observe the individual (usually less than one hour), interviews make sense only if it can be assumed that (1) the interviewer is particularly talented at observing some important traits, and (2) the purpose of the interview is limited to obtaining information about only a small number of traits. Although the interview does not constitute a valid general tool for the measurement of personality characteristics, it is obviously very useful in obtaining particular information about persons in applied settings.

Behavioral Tests. In some observational situations, directly observable aspects of the subject's behavior are used as measures of personality characteristics. Because the observations concern observable behavior, the situations in which such observations are made are usually referred to as behavioral tests. Like situational tests, behavioral tests consist of contrived situations. One of the earliest and still the best known use of behavioral tests was that of H. Hartshorne, R. May, and F. K. Shuttleworth (1930) in the Character Educational Inquiry. They wanted to measure such traits in schoolchildren as honesty, truthfulness, cooperativeness, and self-control.

When behavioral tests can be employed, they have a number of attractive advantages. The use of actual behavioral products frees the measurement methods from the subjectivity of rating scales. If observations can be made in natural settings where the subject is unaware that he is being tested in any sense, the results are probably more valid.

Jum C. Nunnally

Selye, Hans (1907–1982)

Walter B. Cannon's concept of homeostasis was further developed by Hans Selye, who analyzed the role of emotions and showed how the adrenocortical system reacts to physical and emotional stress.

Benjamin B. Wolman

Semantic Conditioning and Generalization

Words are both physical objects and stimuli with meaning. Serving as conditioned stimuli in classical conditioning experiments, they operate in both ways. Semantic conditioning refers to conditioning in which the aspect of meaningfulness plays a role. The demonstration of this fact usually involves the demonstration of semantic generalization.

Gregory A. Kimble

Semantic Differential

Logic of the Semantic Differential
In spoken and written language, characteristics of ideas and real things are communicated largely by adjectives. Thus, a particular person is characterized as being polite, urbane, timid, and intelligent; and a particular policy in foreign affairs is characterized as being outmoded, rigid, and discriminatory. If it is reasonable to assume that much of "meaning" can be, and usually is, communicated with adjectives, it is also reasonable to assume that adjectives can be used to measure various facets of meaning.

Factors in Semantic-Differential Scales
The numerous factor-analytic studies of semantic-differential scales lead to the conclusion that there are three major factors of meaning involved. The factors do not always have exactly the same content in different studies, and in some studies more than three prominent factors are found. The remarkable fact, however, is that three factors with similar content have occurred in so many analyses under such varied conditions. The most frequently found factor is evaluation, which is defined by pairs of adjectives like the following:

good-bad	honest-dishonest
pleasant-unpleasant	positive-negative
fair-unfair	sweet-sour
wise-foolish	valuable-worthless
successful-unsuccessful	clean-dirty

The second strongest factor that frequently appears in factor analyses of semantic-differential scales is potency. Some of the pairs of adjectives that usually load on that factor are as follows:

strong-weak rugged-delicate
hard-soft large-small
heavy-light masculine-feminine
thick-thin severe-lenient

The third strongest factor that frequently appears is activity. Some pairs of adjectives relating to that factor are as follows:

active-passive quick-slow
tense-relaxed hot-cold
excitable-calm sharp-dull
impetuous-quiet busy-lazy

What the Semantic Differential Measures

The semantic differential mainly measures connotative (or metaphorical) aspects of meaning, particularly the evaluative connotations of objects. For that purpose, it probably is the most valid measure of connotative meaning available. Because of the nature of the instruments, it cannot measure non-connotative associations; for example, from the instrument alone there is no way to learn that "apple" is associated with "orange" or that "New York" is associated with "the United Nations."

Use of Semantic Differential Scales

It is well to employ numbers to designate the steps on semantic-differential scales (e.g., the numbers 1 through 7 to designate the steps on a seven-step scale). Also, the meanings of the numbers should be carefully defined and illustrated in the instructions to the inventory. For example, subjects can be told that, on the scale good-bad, 5 means "slightly good," 4 means "neither good nor bad," 3 means "slightly bad," and so on for the other steps on the scale.

Jum C. Nunnally

Semantic Memory

The description of semantic memory suggests that it must play a role in the understanding of any natural language statement. But thus far semantic-memory research has been more confined than the above would suggest. The research has concentrated on the representations of common class nouns, like *fruit*, *bird*, or *furniture*, and the processes that are applied to them in verifying statements about class membership (e.g., a statement like "An apple is a fruit"). This research has led to a number of theoretical proposals about how meaning is stored in memory. There are two early theories that emphasize the logical structure of semantic memory, then consider findings that show the importance of intuitive or perceived similarity effects in judgments of class membership, and finally consider some models that attempt to encompass both logical and intuitive aspects of semantic structure.

Hierarchical Network Model

The interest in class membership was started by A. M. Collins and M. R. Quillian (1969), who introduced a model in which the logical structure of class relations could serve as an approximation to the structure of semantic memory. This theory, hereafter referred to as the hierarchical network model, assumes that words are represented in semantic memory as independent units (nodes) connected in a hierarchical network by labeled relations.

Predicate Intersection Mode

D. E. Meyers (1970) has proposed a predicate intersection model. This theory assumes a very different type of structural organization for semantic memory. It holds that any class noun is represented in two ways, by the names of all other categories that share exemplars with it, and by the attributes or features that are essential in defining the term.

Size Effect

In view of the above, it is not surprising that many studies have been primarily concerned with the category size effect (or the effect of direct versus indirect superordinates). Some of these experiments have indicated that the effect in question is, at best, severely limited in generality (L. J. Rips, E. J. Shoben, and E. E. Smith 1973; E. E. Smith, E. J. Shoben, and L. J. Rips 1974). In these studies, the category size effect obtains for some categories, but actually reverses for others.

Early theories, the hierarchical network and predicate intersection models, concentrated on the logical rather than intuitive aspects of semantic structure. As a result, these models did not offer any systematic account of why (1) category size effects depend on ratings of semantic relatedness, (2) disconfirmation times depend on subject predicate similarity, and (3) the times needed to confirm superordinate relations depend on typicality ratings. Subsequent theories, the feature comparison and revised network models, have tried to incorporate some intuitive aspects of semantic structure, and consequently can account for more of the existent data. The latter theories, however, may last no longer than their predecessors, for there is still very little known about the psychological representation of semantic knowledge.

Edward E. Smith

Sensation and Perception

Explanation of Perception
There seem to be three different kinds of psychological theories of perception. One, which might be called the stimulus theory, holds that for every kind of perceptual experience there is some feature of stimulation correlated with it. Therefore the focus here is on the first level of analysis. While this psychophysical approach, as it might be called, is undoubtedly correct for certain kinds of perceptual experiences, as for example color or pitch, it is not obvious that it can account for object properties such as size, shape, movement, depth, and the like. The chief proponent of this view, James J. Gibson (1950, 1966), has argued that the relevant stimulation for these properties as well can be isolated and takes the form of a higher-order feature of the incoming stimulation.

A second kind of psychological theory of perception holds that it is not merely the direct transmission of incoming stimulation to the brain that accounts for what we experience, but certain central transformations of that stimulation. This view is best represented by Gestalt theory (W. Köhler 1929; K. Koffka 1935).

The third kind of theory, most closely associated with Hermann von Helmholtz (1867), holds that perception results from a process of cognitive interpretation or inference concerning the proximal stimulus. Such a process is obviously not conscious and, therefore, has been referred to as one of unconscious inference. It is important to note that the genuineness of the experience as perceptual is not questioned. Thus, for example, it can hardly be denied that one has a vivid impression of motion in the case of stroboscopic stimulation.

The Field of Inquiry
Psychophysics. Originally, investigators such as E. H. Weber and G. T. Fechner (1860) were interested in the philosophical question of the quantitative relationship between the physical and psychological domains. Thus Weber asked whether units of sensation and units of physical energy correspond. According to S. S. Stevens (1957), the psychophysical relationship is a power function.

Sensory mechanisms. In the case of vision, it is now known that light quanta falling upon the retina are absorbed by pigments contained in the cells of the retina. Molecules of the pigment, such as rhodopsin, are isomerized by the absorbed quanta. This process in turn causes an electrical change in these cells, which is communicated to other cells farther upstream.

Two important concepts in the matter of sensory coding are *adaptation* and *inhibition*. Continued stimulation of sensory neurons will lead to a diminution in their rate of discharging. Conversely, the absence of such stimulation for a period of time will often lead to an increased sensitivity to subsequent stimulation. These facts have important implications for perceptual experience, as for example the elevation of the absolute threshold following continued exposure to intense light (light adaptation) or conversely, the lowered threshold following a period without such exposure to light (dark adaptation). Stimulation in one region depresses neural activity in an adjacent region. Such *lateral inhibition* has been directly observed in species such as the horseshoe crab by electrical recordings from individual fibers. It has been invoked as an explanatory mechanism to account for a variety of perceptual phenomena such as achromatic color contrast, metacontrast or backward masking, illusions, and aftereffects.

Constancy. The central fact about our perception of objects in the world is that by and large it is veridical, meaning correct rather than illusory. Thus, for example, the size, distance, shape, achromatic color, and condition of rest or motion of an object that we perceive generally corresponds closely with the true size, distance, shape, and other properties of the object that can be ascertained by objective criteria such as measurement. This fact constitutes a problem because the proximal stimulus representing these properties is not constant at all.

According to the theory first formulated by E. Hering (1920) in relation to color constancy, the perception of object properties often depends upon certain stimulus relationships. Thus, for example, whether a surface appears white, gray, or black depends not on the luminance reaching the eye from that surface alone, but on its luminance relative to that of adjacent surfaces.

Relational determination. The perception of properties such as shape is clearly governed by the manner in which the parts of the figure relate to one another. That such relationships are crucial is dramatically demonstrated by the fact that forms can be altered in size and location (transposed) without altering their appearance as shapes, just as a song can be transposed in key without altering the perceived melody.

Organization. We perceive a world consisting of distinct entities, separate and segregated from one another. Yet this organization of the phenomenal world can hardly be said to be supplied by the proximal stimulation, since in vision, for example, that consists of an array of unrelated patches of light of varying luminance and wave length. Therefore, given such ambiguity within the stimulus concerning what in the world is represented, the experience of a specific organization must be understood as an achievement based on some principles of selection and preference within the nervous system of what units of stimulation go with what other units. The Gestalt psychologists raised this problem and sug-

gested a number of principles to account for perceptual grouping and the related phenomenon of figure-ground organization.

Innate determination versus past experience. A fundamental question about perception as we find it in the adult is whether it is the result of some kind of learning based on past experience or whether it is innately determined. This question has been debated since antiquity. Thus, for example, one might ask whether we must learn to perceive form or depth and whether the achievement of perceptual constancy is a product of learning. In contemporary psychology the effort is made to resolve these questions by experimental research.

Irvin Rock

Sensitization

Sensitization may be defined as an increase in response to a repetitive stimulus. Response strength may increase rather than decrease in response to a repetitive stimulus if the stimulus is strong, noxious, or otherwise "significant" to the organism in some way. Some theorists regard dishabituation as simply a specific case of the more general phenomenon of sensitization. Sensitization may be distinguished from the varieties of conditioning, since it does not require any temporal or other association between two stimuli in order to occur. Indeed, if an increase in response to a repetitive stimulus occurs in a classical conditioning paradigm that is not related to the temporal pairing of the unconditioned and conditioned stimuli, it may be termed "pseudoconditioning" or sensitization and is regarded as evidence that the increase in response is not an example of conditioning.

Philip M. Groves

Sensitization-Invigoration Mechanism

One of two motivational mechanisms proposed by Charles N. Cofer and Mortimer H. Appley (1964), the sensitization-invigoration mechanism (SIM) is intended to account for the augmentation in vigor of behavior in the presence of certain stimuli where no evidence of prior learning can be discerned. Modeled on F. A. Beach's sexual arousal mechanism (SAM) the SIM describes the process of arousal and apparent selective sensitivity to certain stimuli observed in hormonally "ready" animals, as contrasted to those in which hormonal levels are low. Maternal behavior, for example, is more likely to be aroused at the sight of rat pups when the female has recently dropped a litter than otherwise. Similarly, nest building, migration, and sexual behavior are more likely to occur, or to occur with greater vigor, in hormonally prepared animals.

Mortimer H. Appley

Sensory Deprivation

The original aim of sensory deprivation research was, as the term implies, to determine the effects of a drastic curtailment of sensory stimulation on human functioning. The original aim met with obstacles from a variety of methodological sources, so that interpretation of findings was difficult. It was nearly impossible to control for each of the many potentially relevant parameters inherent in the complex of conditions.

Gradually it became evident to most investigators that another very troublesome obstacle to unambiguous findings lay in the fact that a subject undergoing sensory deprivation is in a totally altered life situation that affects his self-systems, defenses, fantasies, motivations, and cognitive and interpersonal strategems in a number of ways:

1. Neurologically, by a progressive slowing in mean alpha frequency and with the appearance of marked delta, and, in long-term studies, also of excessive theta wave activity, especially in the temporal lobes;
2. Autonomically, by a decrease in skin resistance (i.e., increased arousal), though with no other consistent differences in heart rate, respiration, temperature, blood pressure, or metabolic rate;
3. Biochemically, by a variable picture: no consistent findings in urinary measures of oxycorticoids and catecholamines (except for subjects

in the respirator setup), but with the finding of certain individual differences between "stayers" and "quitters" in pre-isolation levels of adrenaline and serum uric acid, as well as in urine excretion during deprivation; and
4. Psychologically, by boredom, apathy, and a state of motivational loss that in the realm of thought processes appears as aimless mind wandering, reverie, and fantasy activity, interspersed with periods of sleep and attendant hypnogogic and hypnopompic phenomena.

Certain specific sensory effects, such as lowered thresholds and increased acuity, are also a consistent concomitant of sensory deprivation, which is in keeping with the general sensitivity to minimal and residual stimulation and the stimulus hunger that subjects characteristically show.

Theoretical Formulations

The neurophysiological perspective was originally introduced by Donald Hebb (1955), who saw in these experiments a way of clarifying sensory-cortical interaction. Within this formulation, repetitive, homogeneous, or drastically reduced stimulation is seen as causing the diffuse projection system of the reticular formation—the neurological system deemed essential for "arousal" and organized cortical activity—to become habituated. When this occurs, cortical functioning becomes disorganized, and synchronous firing of cells takes place. The sensory deprivation effects are thus interpreted as a reflection of a general "habituation syndrome."

From the psychoanalytic viewpoint, an intimate relationship between mode of thought and the presence or absence of reality contact is postulated (Rapaport 1958). With diminished reality contact (as in sensory deprivation or sleep) a shift from the secondary process (logical, realistic) to the primary process (drive-organized, developmentally primitive) mode takes place.

The psychological theories have involved a broad cognitive perspective in which constructs derived from information-processing theory play a central role, as well as a general social-psychological approach in which the key concepts evolve around the role of the subject's expectations and the

Comparison of Two Sentence Completion Tests

Variable	Incomplete Sentences Blank (ISB)	Miale-Holsopple Sentence Completion Test (MH)
Purpose of the test	to provide a gross screening device for evidence of maladjustment	to obtain material from which to draw inferences concerning unconscious and semiconscious desires, motives, conflicts, and systems of personality organization
Assumptions underlying test	ISB is a semistructured projective technique in which subject reflects her own wishes, desires, fears, and attitudes; the responses tend to provide information the subject is willing to give, rather than that which she cannot help giving.	MH gives subject opportunity to reveal himself without committing himself; MH meets the primary requirements of the projective method.
Instructions to the subjects	Complete these sentences to express your real feelings. Try to do every one. Be sure to make a complete sentence.	Complete each sentence in whatever way you wish. If you have trouble thinking of a completion to any sentence, put a circle around the number and return to the sentence when you have finished the rest.
Stem structure	unstructured	relatively unstructured
Personal reference	first person or neutral	third-person or neutral except for two first-person stems
Treatment of response	Completions are compared to a manual of sample responses and rated on a seven-point scale for conflict. A summary score of 135 separates adjusted from maladjusted subjects.	No scoring system. The completions provide a basis from which clinical inferences may be drawn.

demand characteristics of the situation. A narrower and more specialized conception posits a specific drive for sensory variation, termed *sensoristatis* (Schultz 1965), and also the notion of an optimal level of arousal that may vary from person to person and which is determined by a number of confluent factors involving constitution, age, learning, recent levels of stimulation, task demands, and diurnal cycling.

Leo Goldberger

Sensory Overload

The term *sensory overload* (sensory overstimulation) designates a situation in which the organism is bombarded by higher-than-normal levels of sensory stimulation, usually in more than one sensory modality. It is the obverse of sensory deprivation (sensory underload), and is similarly classed as a potential stressor.

The scientific interest in sensory overload may be traced to D. Lindsley's proposal (1961) at the 1958 Harvard Symposium on Sensory Deprivation that the conditions of sensory overload, sensory underload, and sensory distortion have a common neurophysiological mechanism, namely, the ascending reticular formation. Lindsley viewed the ascending reticular formation as a kind of barometer for both sensory input and output level, a homeostatic regulator of input-output relations that is subject to an adaptation level. Any deviation from the established level upsets the balance of the regulating system, resulting in a variety of disturbances. Specifically, for the condition of sensory overstimulation from two or more sense modalities (especially a sudden and intense input from afferent and corticofugal sources), Lindsley noted that "blocking of the reticular formation may occur and behavioral immobilization and general confusion may result."

A number of related conceptions and theoretical elaborations have been introduced that have a bearing on sensory overload. Donald Hebb (1955) has proposed a homeostatic theory that views the organism as acting so as to produce an optimal level of excitation; Daniel E. Berlyne (1960) ascribes drive-inducing properties to deviations from an optimum influx of arousal potential; R. Malmo (1959) and many others have written extensively about the notion of a general activation level, which in turn has been related to external sensory input and the inverted U-curve formulation. Under conditions of extreme sensory input, a correspondingly high activation level would ensue, resulting in impaired performance across a variety of tasks.

The findings have varied somewhat from study to study, as a function of the specific stimuli and mode of presentation; nevertheless, they do seem to converge on the conclusion that overstimulation tends to be more aversive than understimulation and that subjects tend to evidence heightened arousal. They report vivid imagery (and occasionally also hallucinatory and delusional processes), body-image distortions, temporal disorientation, and intellectual-cognitive impairments. Significant individual differences have also been noted.

Leo Goldberger

Sensory Preconditioning and Conditioning

This term refers to an experimental procedure designed to determine whether associations can be established between sensory events without the occurrence of a response. The standard method involves three stages of training: (1) two neutral conditioned stimuli (CS), CS_1 and CS_2 (for example, a light and a tone) are presented together for a large number of trials; (2) a response is conditioned to one

of these CSs by pairing it with an unconditioned stimulus (US); and (3) tests are conditioned with the other CS to see whether it will now elicit the conditioned response (CR). If this happens, this means that CS_1 and CS_2 have become equivalent through their earlier pairing and that this has happened without the occurrence of a response.

Gregory A. Kimble

Sentence Completion Tests

Two of the most widely used sentence completion tests are the Incomplete Sentences Blank (ISB), developed by Julian B. Rotter and J. E. Rafferty (1950), and the Miale-Holsopple Sentence Completion Test (MH), developed by J. Q. Holsopple and F. R. Miale (1954).

The sentence completion is above all else a clinical psychological technique. Surveys of practicing clinicians make it clear that sentence completion is a major projective technique, used (as are other such techniques) to answer specific questions about personality and behavior as well as to generate global descriptions of personality organization.

Philip A. Goldberg

Sentence Memory and Comprehension

One of the major research problems of experimental psycholinguistics has been the question of how sentences are understood and remembered. In fact, sentence processes proved to be the natural domain of psycholinguistics partly because sentences have been taken as the unit of theoretical description in linguistics and partly because sentences are convenient psychological objects when one is concerned with how people understand and remember meaningful propositional language. While, initially, there was a focus on the linguistic structures of sentences as variables in sentence processing, it became apparent that sentence process not only depends upon nonlinguistic variables but also needs to be related to models of memory and attention.

"Long-Term" Memory

The question of what type of information is remembered from a sentence has sometimes been connected with distinctions defined by grammatical theory. The possible nature of such a connection, at least a direct one, has become increasingly constrained. The facts of sentence memory rule out any psycholinguistic model of the sentence that does not give prominence to semantics. The development of competing grammatical theories accommodates an increasing set of semantic distinctions. But the connection of such competing theories with the empirical phenomena of sentence memory is exceedingly tentative.

Comprehension

The comprehension of a sentence is a complex psychological event. It both depends on and contributes to long-term memory. Processing mechanisms access word meanings and use relational constraints in comprehending sentences. The processes involved in the immediate understanding of sentences have been studied in a variety of experimental tasks. Comprehension in these tasks refers to brief periods during which some response entails that some working representation of a sentence meaning is achieved. It is not comprehension without memory, but comprehension within or near the limits of immediate memory.

The question of how linguistic strings are analyzed can be considered more generally as a problem of how units are extracted from speech. One possibility is that sentences are recoded into semantic strings with the use of clause structure. A well-known illustration of the use of structure in immediate processing are the "click" experiments of T. G. Bever and others (summarized in Fodor, Bever, and Garrett 1974). Although the source of the effect has not been without dispute, the basic fact now seems established: even when response factors are controlled for, the perceived location of a nonlinguistic signal is displaced toward clause and phrase boundaries.

Significant linguistic units in comprehension are not so different from units of memory. As noted previously, the representation of understood sentences in a long-term memory prominently includes semantic information, and memory experiments suggest some empirical constraints on the representation: that it is abstract, and that it is based on semantic features and semantic relations. The most neutral and perhaps most widely used designation for objects that contain these semantic abstractions is "propositions," a verb plus its related nouns. The propositions of linguistic analysis are, of course, the morpheme content of the "sentoids" of deep structures. While designation and formalization of these abstract objects are open to various interpretations, empirical evidence conveys the conclusion that they are both objects of sentence memory and objects of comprehension work. Memory for sentences is a function of the number of propositions contained in a sentence, as is reading rate. In the case of reading rate, W. Kintsch and J. Keenan (1973) found that for sixteen-word sentences about 1.5 seconds of processing time was required for each proposition. Although the proposition processing rate may vary with text factors (e.g., redundancy), this is a clear evidence that we comprehend and remember ideas, which are both more and less than word strings.

Charles A. Perfetti

Separation and Individuation Phase in Normal Development

In 1955, Margaret S. Mahler introduced into psychoanalytic theory two major hypotheses: that of a universal symbiotic origin of the human condition, and that of the separation-individuation process in the course of normal development.

This process, which takes place, according to Mahler, between approximately the 5th and the 36th month of age, involves the "psychological birth" of the individual. In contrast to the dramatic, clearly observable and well-defined biological birth of the human infant, the psychological birth is a slowly unfolding intrapsychic process—a growing away from the previous undifferentiated relationship with the mother, and toward the differentiation of the self from the mother.

Normal Autistic Phase

During this phase, which lasts from birth to about 1 month of age, the neonate is capable of perceiving little beyond his own body; he seems to live for the most part in a world of inner stimuli, and to function on a purely instinctual basis.

Normal Symbiotic Phase

The normal symbiotic phase reveals the all-important phylogenetic capacity of the human infant to form an emotional tie to the mother, within that "dual unity" that furnishes the soil out of which grow all subsequent human relationships. When a symbiotic phase is satisfactory, it serves as the prerequisite for the infant's successful disengagement from the mother, during the subsequent separation-individuation phase.

The Four Subphases of the Separation-Individuation Phase

The differentiation subphase. At some point in this first subphase, which lasts from about the 5th to the 10th month, a new look of alertness, persistence, and goal-directedness becomes apparent in the infant. This look is a behavioral manifestation of the child's "hatching"; it indicates to us that she has a more permanently alert sensorium, as well as a more consistent sensory investment in the outside world when she is awake. The "birth" of the child as an individual comes about when, as the result of the mother's selective response to her cueing, the child gradually begins to alter her behavior.

The practicing subphase. The central feature of this second subphase, which lasts from roughly the 10th to the 16th month, is the child's elation both in practicing his motor skills and in exploring his steadily expanding environment, human and inanimate. His avoiding of reabsorption into the previous symbiotic orbit with the mother may also contribute to his elated mood.

The rapprochement subphase. In this subphase, which lasts from about the 16th to the 24th month, the mother is no longer "taken for granted" by the child. The acquisition of upright, free locomotion and the beginnings of representational thought cause the toddler to become aware of the finality of her separateness, at the very same time when she has to cope with an ever-expanding and more complex inner and outer reality. Her former obliviousness to the mother's presence is now replaced by an *active approach* behavior—a wish to share her new skills and experiences with the mother, a need for her love, and a constant concern with her whereabouts.

The third subphase demonstrates with particular clarity that the process of separation-individuation has two complementary parts. While individuation generally proceeds rapidly, the child continues to be bothered by her increasing awareness of her separateness; she attempts to cope with this by experimentally moving both away from and toward the mother.

The fourth subphase. During the course of the third year, the toddler becomes more consistently loving, friendly, and cooperative. He is better able than he was earlier to withstand frustration, to delay gratification, and to accept substitute satisfactions. The unfolding of such complex cognitive functions as verbal communication and reality testing, along with pleasure in his attainments and autonomy, contribute to the development on his part of a unified self-image and a beginning measure of self-constancy.

John Burke McDevitt

Separation and Loss in Children

Separation and loss are continuing lifelong experiences and are an integral part of human psychological development. They are intimately intertwined with frustration and gratification, ego development, object relations, superego formation, identification, and other forms of internalization, and are consequently related to all forms of psychopathological development.

At the malignant end of the spectrum of separation and loss are those infants who have been hospitalized or institutionalized before they have developed a highly specific mother-infant attachment, and before object constancy has been achieved. It has been amply demonstrated that, except under very exceptional circumstances, institutions are unable to supply an infant or young child with sufficient interaction with a reliably available object over an adequate period of time to develop a normally cathected mother-infant relationship.

Children who have achieved object constancy (usually during the last half of the first year) in an average expectable environment suffer greater distress on separation from the loved object. At this point the object cathexis no longer attaches automatically to object substitutes even when the child accepts their care, and some investigators feel that aspects of mourning (true object loss) can occur (i.e., decathexis of and identification with the object). Object separation and loss at this stage can result in loss and depletion of the basic self-preservative functions, leading to loss of appetite, failure to thrive, lack of exploratory interests, susceptibility to disease, and interference with the developing self-representation, which is dependent upon libidinization by the love object.

Children who have suffered repeated changes in their love objects develop stable defensive mechanisms against the experience of loss, and they usually defend against adequate new object cathexis.

There is considerable controversy about the ability of children to mourn. Some of the differences in opinion appear to be semantic, but it is agreed that a bereaved child is in a different circumstance from a bereaved adult.

Children have difficulty decathecting love objects and utilize the mechanism of identification in order to reduce the need for painful hypercathexis and decathexis of the lost object. The overuse of more primitive forms of identification, such as primary identification at the oral incorporative and fusion level, can lead to serious developmental arrests.

In older children, loss appears to affect those ego functions that depend upon libidinization by the love object. In the toddler, this includes walking, talking, bladder control, and early sublimatory activities. In the phallic child, it includes control of drive expression, inner and outer reality testing, and the ability to recognize and verbalize painful affects. In general, the most recently acquired functions depend most heavily upon narcissistic supplies from the loved object.

Douglas B. Hansen

Separation and Separation Anxiety

Separation anxiety is part and parcel of need-fulfilling object relationships (Freud 1926). It begins in childhood when infantile object constancy has been established, at the age of 6 to 25 months depending on definition of object representation (Fraiberg 1969), and ends, more or less, usually in late adolescence or adulthood when mature object constancy has been established and need fulfillment more or less ceases.

Separation anxiety may occur in the analysis of adults in two forms: as defensive regression, because of oedipal fears, or as a repetition of preoedipal separation anxiety. The later occurs in cases where the scale is weighted heavily on the side of fixation.

Separation anxiety may occur in relatively undisguised form or may be defended against and, therefore, may be more difficult to recognize. Examples of the former are:

1. *Fear of being alone.* Being alone represents frustration, and (unconscious) aggression against the object representation occurs.
2. *Fear of actual separation from important people.*
3. *Fear of death*, as fear of final separation. This may also have a component in it of punishment for oedipal aggression, i.e., a wish to kill the parent of the same sex.
4. *Fear of frustrating situations*, with the need to cling to and be supported (get advice from or be praised) by the analyst or other parent substitutes.
5. *Tendency to see objects in black and white terms* (good and bad), with little capacity to distinguish shadings in human qualities, frequently combined with outbursts of anger at disappointing objects.

Klaus Angel

Sex Crimes

The emphasis in sex crimes research has centered on the offenders—the etiology of their deviant sexually oriented criminality and the treatment programs developed for their rehabilitation. Psychometric, sociometric, and clinical diagnostic techniques have all been applied to these criminal populations, and typologies of offender groups have been constructed according to their psychopathological, behavioral, and demographic characteristics, in addition to the nature of their criminal activity.

M. Amir's (1971) statistical analysis of the epidemiological nature of the crime reveals that the number of rape events is not significantly associated with the warmer months, as the "thermic theory of crime" would suggest, although multiple rapes (more than one offender) occur more frequently then. Rapes peak on weekends, with the top "risk" hours between 9:00 P.M. and 2:00 A.M. on any day. According to Mintz (1973), "lower class members of society in a crowded inner city, regardless of race, have a high rate of rape arrest" (709). However, rape is a notoriously underreported crime.

A major concern of rape victims is the way that they will be regarded by others. K. Weis and S. S. Borges attribute to the operation of *cognitive dissonance*, or the process that encourages people to search for negative qualities in another that would justify that other's victimization, the responsibility for the generally negative postrape reactions victims encounter from others.

A. W. Burgess and L. L. Holmstrom (1974), on the basis of their experience with rape victims seen at Boston City Hospital in conjunction with the Victim Counseling Program they developed, articulated a two-phase rape trauma syndrome. Disorganization is the dominant reaction in the acute phase, manifested by physical reactions, including disturbances in sleeping and eating patterns, and emotional reactions such as fear, humiliation, guilt, and anger.

Lida Orzeck

Sex Motivation

Patterns of Sexual Behavior

The central features of mammalian copulatory behavior are mounting, vaginal penetration (intromission), and ejaculation by the male. In the female, there is generally some form of postural response that facilitates achievement of intromission. These behaviors on the part of the male and female may or may not be preceded by some form of overt soliciting or courtship behavior.

Physiological Factors Influencing Sex Motivation

In virtually all mammals tested, removal of gonadal hormones results in a reduction of both the frequency and intensity of copulatory activity in the male. In rodent species, male copulatory activity generally ceases entirely within 2 to 3 months after castration. In cats and rhesus monkeys, the decline in male sexual behavior is more gradual. However, the male dog continues to copulate for years after castration, with only a slight decrease in libido. The finding that copulatory behavior in the dog is less affected by castration than is that of the rhesus monkey fails to support the prevalent notion that continued evolution of the neocortex lessens a species' dependence upon gonadal hormones.

In the mammalian female, removal of ovaries leads to an abrupt cessation of sexual activity. The exception here is the human female, where copulation continues in the absence of ovarian hormones. It is suspected that adrenal hormones may play an important role in the sexual activity of the human.

Sexual Arousal Mechanism (SAM)

One of the two hypothetical mechanisms proposed by F. A. Beach to explain the occurrence of sexual behavior in the male rat, the sexual arousal mechanism (SAM), has been considered responsible for the initiation of male sexual behavior. A second mechanism, the intromission and ejaculatory mechanism (IEM; also roughly synonymous with Beach's consummatory mechanism), operates to maintain sexual behavior until ejaculation is achieved.

The SAM has been used to explain individual differences in latency to begin copulating. The proposal of a second mechanism, the IEM, is based upon the observation that certain experimental procedures increase the latency to begin copulation (i.e., interfere with the SAM) but do not interfere with sexual behavior once it is initiated (IEM).

Stimulus and Experimental Factors Influencing Sexual Motivation

Stimulus characteristics of the sexual partner are important to the arousal and the initiation of copulation. While some species, such as the hamster, depend heavily on cues from a single sensory modality, other species utilize cues from several sensory modalities, including behavioral cues from the potential mating partner. In some species, males and females show a preference for particular individuals of their species and will copulate with them more readily than with other individuals.

The cessation of copulation by a normal intact male was once thought to result from fatigue, but more recent evidence indicates that some form of stimulus satiation brings about a cessation of copulation. This conclusion is based upon the observation that males who have ceased copulation with one female will resume copulation if exposed to a different female. While this phenomenon, called the collidge effect, does not occur in all mammalian species, it holds for the majority of species studied. A similar phenomenon has not been observed in females.

Lynwood G. Clemens

Sex Offenders: Treatment

Much of the treatment currently being offered to sex offenders is done under the aegis of special state statutes. These laws, frequently called sexual psychopath laws, usually involve the recommendation of specialized treatment for selected sex offenders following a diagnostic evaluation. The situation is further complicated by the marked differences among the various state statutes dealing with the sex offender. Most of these laws ostensibly incorporate the dual function of treatment for the treatable and continued incarceration for those who do not respond to treatment and who remain a danger to society. Unfortunately, some states that have enacted legislation mandating specialized treatment for sex offenders have failed to provide the requisite diagnostic and treatment capability.

A variety of traditional and nontraditional individual and group psychotherapies have been attempted with sex offenders. A review of articles in the area indicates that reported effectiveness is probably more related to the skills of the therapist than to her specific therapeutic orientation. Individual psychotherapy in a correctional setting, often with an unwilling patient, has its obvious drawbacks. Almost all individual psychotherapy must involve an initial phase devoted to creating a climate that allows the establishment of a therapeutic relationship.

There is evidence that peer pressures for change, along with some of the general factors involved in group therapy, such as universality, catharsis, and group cohesiveness, make group approaches more effective than individual psychotherapy with sex offenders. There are, of course, a vast variety of group therapies.

One promising technique for the treatment of sex offenders is family or couple therapy. Based upon a social systems model, the offender is not seen as a sick individual in a healthy family constellation, but rather the entire family is seen as operating in a dysfunctional or maladaptive fashion. The approach requires that the entire family be treated to establish the requisite social climate for offender rehabilitation.

A number of behavioral techniques used with sex offenders might be classified as social skills training. These include assertiveness training, modeling, and behavioral rehearsal. In essence, these techniques proceed from the base that the individual lacks certain skills necessary for effective social-sexual interactions.

Asher R. Pacht

Sex-Role Stereotypes

Sex-role stereotypes refer to preconceived, simplified assumptions and generalizations about behavior that is expected of males and females solely because they are male or female.

The traditional sex-role stereotypes that place women in a subservient role regardless of their actual role prescription are as common to many cultures as they have been enduring over time. The findings of numerous studies (e.g., Steinmann 1971) done on cross-cultural sex-role perceptions show that almost all groups (including both sexes and various ages) subscribe to the familiar male-superior/female-inferior sex roles. The behavioral enactment and resulting self-perceptions of these roles are shared equally by both sexes.

Daily exposure to rigid sex-role portrayals by the mass media provides steady reinforcement of these stereotypes beyond childhood and throughout life. Helen Franzwa (1975) has detected little change in the feminine stereotype as portrayed in the majority of women's magazine fiction stories from 1940 to 1970. She has analyzed these stories, sampled at five-year intervals, and found that, regardless of year, the heroine is a woman in search of a husband, a woman dependent on her husband, or one whose very existence is defined by her husband and the children he has given her. The unmarried female is depicted as the lonely and unfulfilled spinster, and while the widow or divorcee may seem somewhat independent, she is, in contrast to the men around her, incompetent. Wedding bells mark the happy end to these stories.

Power and other so-called masculine characteristics are given more frequent positive valuations than so-called feminine characteristics, which are less socially desirable. J. K. Broverman and coworkers (1972) have confirmed this, and from data obtained using a 122-item bipolar questionnaire that they developed, they have shown consensus in the existence of sex-different, "masculine"-favored characteristics over groups that differ in age, sex, education, and marital status.

Sex-role stereotypes are undergoing gradual change. Thanks to social and legal progress, many women have successfully joined occupations from which they were excluded for a long time. Today there are very few fields where women do not participate (Wolman and Money 1990).

Florence L. Denmark

Sex Roles and Aging

Studies indicate that men and women who survive to extreme old age (80 and over) are, in the matter of role performance, virtually indistinguishable. Projective data indicate that women, as they age, become more tolerant of their own aggressive, egocentric impulses, while men do the same with regard to their nurturant and affiliative impulses. These data suggest the potential or actual reversal of roles with regard to authority in the family among older married couples.

C. L. Estes
Diane Beeson

Sex Typing

Sex typing is defined as the process by which a person acquires, values, and adopts sex-typed behavior patterns.

The origins of psychological sex differences in sex-typed behaviors are multiple. All behavior is a result of both genetic and environmental influences, because neither operates to produce effects without the other. How they exert their influence is a much more difficult matter to unravel. It is important to appreciate that any statements concerning the degree to which a given trait is heritable must be limited to that trait and the population on which the calculations were done.

A number of psychological theories have been elaborated to explain the mechanisms by which psychological sex differences develop. Social learning theorists appeal to the principles of direct reinforcement, generalization, vicarious reinforcement, and similarity to the model as mechanisms by which an individual learns her sex-appropriate behaviors.

Macoby and C. N. Jacklin (1974) have summarized data that show that modeling, which is a crucial aspect of both social learning and identification theories, is important in the acquisition of a wide variety of behaviors, but that the behaviors thus acquired are not particularly sex typed. Thus, modeling does not play more than a minor role in the development of sex-typed behavior.

Bem (1974) terms persons whose responses are more controlled by situation appropriateness than by sex-role appropriateness as *androgynous*, and has developed a sex-role inventory to assess psychological androgyny. She has validated the inventory by showing that persons whose scores on the scale show them to be either appropriately or inappropriately sex typed display behavioral deficits relative to their more androgynous counterparts (Bem 1975).

Michele Andrisin Wittig

Sexual Behavior: Development

J. Money and A. A. Ehrhardt have attempted to synthesize the results of a broad spectrum of studies from many disciplines regarding human sexuality (Money 1973; Money and Ehrhardt 1972). They propose that the ontogenesis of human sexuality, including what we have distinguished as sex, sex typing, and genital acts, can be compared to a relay race. The developing program for later adult sexuality is first carried in the zygote by the X and Y chromosomes, which determine whether the undifferentiated gonads of the fetus will become testes or ovaries. Once differentiated, the gonads pick up the developmental program. If they are ovaries, the baby becomes female, and if testes, the gonads secrete androgens that virilize the otherwise feminine anatomy of the developing fetus.

At puberty, anatomical and hormonal changes combine with brain dimorphism and previously developed gender identity to produce the final product: the person's adult sexual behavior. This mature phase is often prefigured in adolescents by apparently biologically programmed episodes of "falling in love." Puberty usually does not create sexual object choice but only activates choices already preset in early gender identity.

Richard W. Smith

Sexual Disorders in Females

"Frigidity" has finally been discarded as the blanket diagnosis for all female sexual distress. Sex is no longer something men do to women. Since the publication of *Human Sexual Response* (Masters and Johnson 1966) and *Human Sexual Inadequacy* (Masters and Johnson 1970), we have paid more discriminating attention to how women express and experience their sexuality. Women today expect to be full, active, and responsible sexual partners, entitled to a full range of pleasure. However, a satis-

fying sexual life is not easy to achieve. Good sex requires the harmonious interplay of body and mind within a relationship conducive to sexual expression. So many things can go wrong. No wonder sexual problems are the norm rather than the exception in most women's lives today.

Sexual problems are often caused by cultural imprinting, faulty learning, unresponsive partners, and superficial sources of anxiety, which are amenable to brief, direct, and directive intervention. However, many sexual problems do stem from deep-rooted difficulties not easily influenced by a brief time-limited approach. A sexual problem can symbolically express relationship difficulties or represent a reenactment of a woman's experience growing up within the network of her earliest relationships. Sexual problems are usually not a question of either/or, early or late, deep or superficial, emotional or cognitive, developmental or cultural, biological or learned, organic or psychological, but both and all, and the combinations, proportions, and balances of influences are as varied as the women presenting with the complaints.

Some Observations on Female/Male Differentiation

From the moment of conception, nature, nurture, and culture all contribute to the ongoing *psychosexual* differentiation of the genders.

Women tend to have a firmer, more flexible sense of gender than men. This provides a steadying, organizing influence on a woman's unfolding sexuality. Throughout life she is less threatened by the loss of her sense of being a woman.

Female sexuality has historically been suppressed and inhibited more than male sexuality. Women are socialized into a role that discourages sexual curiosity and exploration; the emphasis in their sex education is on the risks involved.

Women's genitals, except for the vulva, are hidden from view, and they do not visibly move or change. In learning about her sexuality, a young woman has to rely more on vague bodily feelings, proprioceptive sensations, and intellectual learning than her male peers do. Reproductive and sexual functions are inextricably intertwined, not only anatomically but in their mental and emotional representations. So are the excretory functions; they are all "down there." It often takes a long time to sort out the parts and the whole.

Women often first experience sexual feelings in an interpersonal setting, in contrast to most boys, who are initiated into sexual feelings through masturbation. Girls masturbate less, and less often, than boys. It tends to take longer for a woman in our culture to learn to enjoy and to fully appreciate her sexual potential, which, at least as far as orgasmic capacity is concerned, can far exceed a man's. Having attained sexual capacity, women are less vulnerable to its loss, through aging, illness, or medications. (Problems common to postmenopausal women, loss of vaginal lubrication and thinning of the wall of the vagina, are reversible with hormone replacement.)

That a woman can be used against her will as a sexual object and that a woman can take part in the full range of "sexual activity" without being aroused are important variables in terms of sexual control and sexual problems. Traumatic experiences that interfere with optimal sexual development are more common in women, who are the victims of sexual abuse, rape, and incest much more frequently than males.

Many women have experienced dissonance with their sexual development: pregnancy at a very young age, abortions, traumatic relationships, and insensitive spouses, which inhibit, interfere with, and distort their sexual selves. Just as a woman's sense of self tends to mature within the context of relationships (Gilligan 1982), so does her sexuality. The vicissitudes of her intimate relationships are powerful influences on a woman's sexual expression.

Women experience sexual desire differently than men, whose sexuality tends to be more constant, genitally focused, and automatic. A woman's sexual desire tends to be more variable, less insistent, more likely to be suppressed if conditions are not favorable, and to a much greater degree influenced by social and interpersonal factors. How much of this is culturally, how much biologically, determined is still a moot question.

Sexual Dysfunctions

In the *Diagnostic and Statistical Manual of Mental Disorders* (DSM), sexual dysfunctions are diagnosed according to the conceptualization of sexual physiology as triphasic in nature, with a desire phase, an excitement/arousal phase, and an orgasm phase. The diagnosis is related to which phase is interfered with. Over the past 20 years, DSM has undergone several revisions. In the most recent version (DSM-IV draft, 1993) female sexual dysfunctions include:

- Hypoactive Sexual Desire Disorder, defined as "persistently or recurrently deficient (or absent) sexual fantasies and desire for sexual activity. The judgment is made by the clinician, taking into account factors that affect sexual functioning, such as age and the context of a person's life."
- Sexual Aversion Disorder, defined as the "persistent or recurrent extreme aversion to, and avoidance of all (or almost all), genital sexual contact with a sexual partner."
- Female Sexual Arousal Disorder, defined as "persistent or recurrent inability to attain or maintain an adequate lubrication-swelling response of sexual excitement until completion of the sexual activity."
- Female Orgasmic Disorder (Inhibited Female Orgasm) or "persistent or recurrent delay in, or absence of, orgasm following a normal sexual excitement phase. Women exhibit wide variability in the type of intensity of stimulation that triggers orgasm. The diagnosis of Female Orgasmic Disorder should be based on the clinician's judgment that the woman's orgasmic capacity is less than would be reasonable for her age, sexual experience, and the adequacy of sexual stimulation she receives."

The Sexual Pain Disorders include:

- Dyspareunia, defined as "recurrent or persistent genital pain before, during, or after intercourse, that is not caused exclusively by Vaginismus or lack of lubrication."
- Vaginismus, "recurrent or persistent involuntary spasm of the musculature of the outer third of the vagina that interferes with sexual intercourse."

If the symptom is caused by the direct effect of a substance (e.g., street drugs, prescription medication) or a general medical condition, the patient should be diagnosed accordingly as sexual dysfunction due to a general medical condition or substance-induced sexual dysfunction.

All of the above diagnostic categories also include the clause, "The disturbance causes marked distress or interpersonal difficulty."

An additional category, Sexual Dysfunction Not Otherwise Specified, includes dysfunctions that "do not meet criteria for any specific Sexual Dysfunction."

Clinical Approach

Establishing a correct diagnosis is the most important first step in the clinical evaluation of a woman presenting with a sexual complaint. The above diagnoses are inclusive in that they comprehensively cover the range of sexual expression. However, a clinically useful description paradoxically requires both more specificity and more allowance for the fluid, ever-changing quality of women's sexual experience. Specifically, it is necessary to carefully assess each physiological phase—desire, arousal, orgasm—as well as the presence of pain or discomfort and degree of satisfaction with current frequency and quality of sex. We need to learn how the problem first manifested itself, how long it has endured, how pervasive it is (global versus situational) and whether the patient or the partner—or the treating professional!—is the one who designates the condition as a dysfunction. More generally, we need to evaluate how the various problems overlap and interact. Does the patient actually have a sexual dysfunction, or is she suffering from misinformation, lack of experience, anxiety? What comes first: low sexual drive, vaginismus, or a clumsy, inexperienced partner? What is the meaning of the sexual difficulty? How does it affect self-perception, how does it influence the relationship?

Women's sexual concerns tend to cluster around three themes. The first complaint is, "I don't have orgasms" (or the right kind, the right number, in the right place, with the right person). The second theme is: "It hurts when I have sex." The third group of women state, "I'm not interested in sex—not turned on—I don't like sex." Among these women are also those who find sex abhorrent or disgusting.

"I DON'T HAVE ORGASMS."

A woman who has never had an orgasm by any means—intercourse, masturbation, or fantasy—is considered to have primary nonorgasmia. Estimates vary as to how frequent this disorder is, but generally they cluster around 10% of adult women. Some primary nonorgasmic women experience intense levels of sexual arousal, lubricating freely and feeling pleasurable genital sensations, yet do not have orgasmic release. Among these are women who "spectator"—who anxiously monitor their sexual responses, feel tense about their capacity to reach orgasm, or have fears about their adequacy as a sexual partner. Others do not receive enough sexual stimulation to trigger the orgasmic reflex. These women may have partners who, for various reasons, do not or cannot stimulate them adequately. Other women are fearful of losing control, of letting go, fearing the disruptive quality of the imagined orgasm, or they may fear their partner's response to their loss of control, letting shame hold them back. In this group we find women who actually have been experiencing physiological orgasms all along, but have not defined them as such, having expected something more dramatic and earth-shattering than the typical genital muscle contractions. Many of these women, once they relax more fully into the experience, find that their orgasms become deeper, more intensely pleasurable. Some women report very little sensation of any kind in their bodies when sexually stimulated. They may describe vaginal anesthesia or aversion. Many of these women have a history of sexual abuse.

Women who have previously experienced orgasm but no longer do so are considered to have secondary orgasmic dysfunction. This may be due to relationship difficulties or to organic problems, such as disease (diabetes, neurological conditions), medications, or surgical complications. It can also represent a psychological reaction to surgery or illness (abortion, mastectomy, hysterectomy), or to emotional trauma or loss.

Many women report that they can achieve orgasm by direct clitoral stimulation, manually, orally, or with mechanical devices, but that they are unable to reach orgasm through vaginal intercourse. This kind of sexual experience is best not viewed as dysfunctional, but rather as a reflection of not having learned how to obtain adequate stimulation to trigger the orgasm during interpersonal sexual activity. Orgasm is a complex psychophysiological reaction with many components, only one of which is the climactic reflex contractions of the muscles around the vagina that can be measured in the laboratory. How a woman bodily feels these contractions, how she reacts to the sensory input from her skin and from total body contact and pressure, is another aspect. Most important are the expectations, thoughts, memories, and fantasies that are part and parcel of a sexual experience, and to such a large degree color it with pleasure, satisfaction, or frustration.

Many women who have difficulty reaching orgasm can reach high levels of sexual excitement, feeling sexually aroused, with swelling and lubrication of the genitals, but they cannot "let go" into orgasm. Others may have difficulty getting sexually aroused at all, technically falling into a group of sexual dysfunctions called sexual arousal disorders. In actual practice, the diagnostic categories often overlap, as many of these women also subjectively experience a low level of sexual desire.

"SEX IS PAINFUL."

There are roughly three possibilities for pain or discomfort during sexual activity: vaginismus, dyspareunia, and lack of sexual arousal. Vaginismus, in its mildest form—some degree of tension in the muscles guarding the opening of the vagina—is not uncommon among young, sexually inexperienced women. In more severe forms of vaginismus, the spasm of these muscles is so intense that nothing is allowed into the vagina and any attempted entry will cause considerable pain. These women often have a history of painful or forced entry. Vaginismus can be thought of as a conditioned reflex, designed to guard a woman fearful of painful entry, of pregnancy, or of anything entering her body and "getting lost in there." Some of these women may also experience cramplike closures of other body openings, such as the throat or anal sphincter. Vaginismus is generally a relatively easy condition to treat through progres-

sive dilatation and desensitization. Vaginismus may not interfere with sexual arousal. Many women with this disorder are fully orgasmic through other means of stimulation than intercourse.

In dyspareunia it is crucially important to rule out any physical reason for the pain before ascribing it to the rare instance of psychogenic etiology. A careful assessment of when and where the pain occurs is essential. Is it at the moment of penile entry? During penetration? Is it vaginal or deep pelvic pain? Does it subside after intercourse? A careful gynecological examination is a must, to ascertain that there are no infections, lacerations, adhesions, etc. Endometriosis can cause pain during intercourse.

Lack of arousal has to be considered in this context, too. Without sexual excitement and lubrication, the entry of the penis into the vagina and the repeated thrusting motions of intercourse can cause considerable discomfort and irritation.

"I'M NOT INTERESTED IN HAVING SEX."

Hypoactive sexual desire is the most common presenting complaint in sex therapy clinics today; an estimated 40 to 55% of couples receive this diagnosis, generally more women than men (Leiblum and Rosen 1989). The complaints can range from, "I don't want to have sex as often as my partner—although I enjoy it when we do," to "I would give anything to be able to avoid having sex for the rest of my life!" and every variation on the theme in between. A wide variety of factors contribute to the etiology—biological, psychological, and interpersonal. Among the biological factors are hormonal abnormalities, such as androgen deficiency, reactions to medications, illness, and depression. Psychological factors include stress, anxiety, depression—and usually the presence of another sexual dysfunction (Donahey and Carroll 1993). Reactions to past sexual trauma, guilt, and religious prohibition are other common variables. Interpersonal problems are legion, ranging from severe conflict and hostility to lack of trust and intimacy. Some women experience marked changes in sexual interest with their menstrual cycles, often having a heightened interest at midcycle and premenstrually. A sudden change in sexual interest is often relatively easy to treat, but lifelong low levels of sexual interest can be a much more complex problem to deal with, often requiring more extensive psychotherapeutic intervention.

Treatment

After establishing the presence of a specific sexual problem, motivation, responsibility, and capacity for change are evaluated. Any underlying illness (physical or psychiatric) is appropriately evaluated and treated. The role a sexual symptom plays in a relationship is continually assessed. Is the problem symbolic of the relationship? Is it separate from, parallel to, or does it perhaps run counter to the relationship? Is it a symptom that helps a couple stay together or apart?

Is the sexual problem best suited for relationship therapy or for more specific sex therapy? For individual treatment, as a couple, or in a group? Is it a problem that will yield to an educational approach or to supportive counseling—or will it need a more specific treatment modality? Short-term or open-ended? The nature of the problem and the characteristics of the individuals involved, as well as the expertise of the professional, will determine the choice of therapeutic approach. Therapies available today are as varied and heterogeneous as the patients who present for treatment.

Three major theoretical orientations are currently used in the psychotherapy of sexual dysfunctions: cognitive-behavioral, psychodynamic (psychoanalytic, object relations), and systems approaches. These treatments incorporate specific "sex therapy" techniques, pioneered by W. H. Masters and V. E. Johnson, techniques that have been expanded and revised over the years. Some of the basic tenets remain, such as "sex is a natural function." Sex therapy aims to remove any psychosocial roadblocks to free sexual expression. Sex therapy tends to be direct and directive, symptom-oriented and time-limited. It is supportive, educational, and aimed at correcting misinformation. Relief of anxiety, whether from "superficial" or "deep" sources, is of central concern, as is improving communication. Sexual interaction is seen as a form of communication, drawing on primal, nonverbal, bodily expression as well as verbal, rational interaction. The hallmark of sex therapy remains the assigned treatment modules, such as "sensate focus exercises," behavioral prescriptions designed to provide *new* structured experiences, with the power to be emotionally corrective. The clinical challenge in each case is to tailor the treatment to the needs of each particular individual seeking help.

In summary, sexual dysfunction therapy has become increasingly sophisticated and highly individualized, formulated only after thorough medical and psychosocial evaluation of the sexual complaint and flexibly tailored to each individual woman and her relationship. Reported rates of improvement are generally very encouraging, the majority of sexual dysfunctions responding to intervention, at least in the hands of an experienced clinician.

Maj-Britt Rosenbaum

Sexual Disorders in Females: Therapy

Orgasmic Stage

The female orgasm, thought to be under the control of a spinal reflex center, is brought about by strong, rhythmic (at 0.8-second intervals) involuntary contractions of the external third of the vaginal cavity, of the pubococcygeal, bulbar, and perineal floor muscles contracting against the congested, engorged tissues forming the orgasmic platform.

Female sexual responses may be selectively inhibited and disrupted by physical and/or psychological factors, leading to different types of sexual dysfunctions with specific physiological concomitants.

Under the word *frigidity* are subsumed a number of female sexual dysfunctions varying in severity, ranging from total lack of sexual desire and responsivity to sexual stimuli to what may be only the absence of an orgasmic response in an otherwise fully sexually desirous, psychologically motivated, and physiologically responsive female.

Vaginismus is characterized by an involuntary spasm of the lower third of the vaginal cavity's musculature and of the perivaginal muscles. The result is a severe constriction of the vaginal opening, which may entirely impede any attempts at vaginal penetration.

Organic etiology. It is estimated (L. P. Wershub 1959) that approximately 5 to 10% of all the sexual dysfunctions have a demonstrable organic pathology that may involve one or more of the endocrinological, biochemical, and anatomical (vascular, muscular, neurological) systems. However, the figure is thought to be closer to 20% when other factors such as drug ingestion (narcotics, alcohol) or severe psychophysiologic states (depression, psychoses) are taken into account.

Psychological etiology. By far, most human sexual problems are due to psychological causes. In some cases the sexual difficulty is a reflection of an underlying personality psychopathology. However, clinical studies indicate that sexual problems may occur more frequently in individuals who outside the sexual area are symptom-free and are emotionally as well as psychologically functioning competently.

Therapy

Sex therapy begins with sensitively and nonjudgmentally conducted interviews. A detailed assessment of the person's (or the couple's) psychological and emotional development is made. Data are collected on childhood and adolescent sexual practices and parental attitudes toward sexuality. The current lifestyle, interpersonal relationships, patterns of sexual activity, fears, feelings, fantasies, and likes and dislikes about sex are also investigated.

Sex therapy usually combines three major elements:

1. psychodynamic and interpretive elements
2. informational element (giving the patient matter-of-fact information)
3. sexual homework assignments, which may include genital and breast manipulation, as well as intercourse.

Orgasmic Dysfunctions

"Permission" to masturbate starts with the therapist's endorsement and sanctioning of the person's natural right to sexual pleasure. The individual is encouraged to learn about her body, to examine her genitalia, to familiarize herself with the different anatomic structures and with their physiological functions.

W. H. Masters and V. E. Johnson (1970) have reported a treatment success rate of 85.6% with the

primary orgasmic dysfunction and 80.2% with the treatment of coital situational orgasmic dysfunction. Treatment success reaches 90.9% in the therapy of secondary situational masturbatory orgasmic dysfunction.

François E. Alouf

Sexual Disorders in Males

Fetishism. A fetish is an object that is a substitute for something loved or worshiped. Sexual fetishism consists of the utilization of nongenital objects to obtain erotic arousal. Individuals whose preferred or exclusive sexual outlet depends on being aroused by such objects, which for them have a unique erotic appeal, are called fetishists. Various types of objects have been utilized as fetishes. Shoes, boots, corsets, and mackintoshes are referred to with some frequency in the literature.

Transvestism. In this syndrome, the preferred stimulus for sexual arousal is the act or fantasy of wearing female clothing.

Pedophilia. Pedophiles are usually so diagnosed only after they have come to the attention of legal authorities. Sexual offenses against children constitute a significant percentage of criminal sex acts.

Voyeurism. Males arrested for peeping constitute a small percentage of all sexual offenders. The act is typically committed with a strange woman who is unaware of the voyeur's presence.

Exhibition. Exhibitionists almost always have personalities with prominent obsessional features. The sexual symptom has both an impulsive and a compulsive quality often found in other pathological behaviors associated with the obsessional personality, such as compulsive gambling or compulsive eating.

Masochism. In this disorder, sexual arousal occurs as a result of the person's own suffering.

Sadism. Sadistic acts are those in which suffering inflicted upon the object produces sexual arousal in the subject. Individuals fall on a continuum with regard to the intensity with which they experience sadistic states. On the one hand are those who occasionally feel erotically excited by torture or bondage fantasies but who do not introduce sadism into their sexual activity with partners. Such individuals are common among the general population. At the other extreme of the spectrum are lust murderers.

Transsexualism. This is a disturbance of gender identity in which persons biologically of one sex have an intense wish for medical and surgical procedures that would allow them to become members of the opposite sex.

Richard C. Friedman

Sexuality: Freud's Three Essays on the Theory of Sexuality

Oral Phase of Development

This is a period that encompasses approximately the first year and a half of the child's life. The nurturing experience, which is connected with pleasurable oral sensations, is the focus of the oral libidinal experience. The deviations during this phase can lead to an excessive and lasting dependency on outside gratifications. Under certain circumstances, it can lead to precocious independence or to a turning away from object ties.

Anal Phase of Development

The anal phase lasts from about 1.5 to 3 years. During this time, the central nervous system matures to the point where the child can control the anal sphincter; thus, her involuntary functions now become voluntary. The child goes into a period of training of body functions, which is achieved in the social relationship to the mother. Elimination is not only pleasurable but becomes a gift to the mother.

If the conflicts at the anal stage cannot be resolved or are excessive, this will be reflected by various character traits: tidiness, compulsive orderliness or messiness, procrastination, retention or rejection of possessions, and feelings of guilt and ambivalence, including shame or a sense of inadequacy.

Phallic Phase of Development

The phallic phase is centered on genital activity, the heightened erotic sensations of this area, and their impact on gender differentiation. During this period sexual identity takes form, including the child's striving to imitate the same-sex parent, and later,

his striving to replace that parent. The resolution of phallic-phase conflicts permits the establishment of sex identity, a sense of security about body integrity, and an appropriate alliance with the same sex.

Oedipal Phase of Development

This stage, which lasts from about 4.5 to 6 years of age, does not focus on an erogenous zone but rather elevates developmental conflicts to social interaction and the integration of the boy or the girl within a triadic system. The boy's wish to replace the father or the girl's to replace the mother leads now to the anticipation of punishment and guilt and thus consolidates superego formation.

The resolution of the oedipal stage leads to an appropriate relationship with the opposite sex, in which affection and love predominate. At the same time, it allows a close relationship to the same-sex parent. The inability to resolve oedipal conflicts leads to a variety of clinical pictures that are seen as the neurotic carryovers of unresolved conflicts.

Peter B. Neubauer

Sherrington, Charles Scott (1857–1952)

According to Charles Scott Sherrington, reflexes represent the fundamental functional units of the nervous system. Their behavior supports the neuronal (synapse) theory. Sherrington demonstrated and explained the interaction between reflexes with such phenomena as reciprocal inhibition, the startle reflex, and the final common path. Many of the concepts of modern neurophysiology—for example, synaptic potentials and excitatory and inhibitory states—derive from Sherrington's work.

J. Wayne Lazar

Shyness

The middle ground of shyness consists of people whose lack of self-confidence, inadequate social skills, and easily triggered embarrassment produce a reluctance to approach people or enter situations where they cannot readily shrink from the notice of others. This form of shyness is typified by the awkward, socially inept adolescent who cannot ask for a date, a favor, or better service.

Personality trait theorists Raymond Cattell (1965, 1973) and Andrew Comrey (1966) have used questionnaire responses to measure individual differences in the "inherent" trait of shyness. Hans J. Eysenck has subsumed shyness under his studies of introverted and extroverted personality types. But not all shy people are introverted, nor do all extroverts consider themselves not to be shy. For Cattell, "shyness" is one of the popular names used to describe the threctic temperament, which he believes arises from a sympathetic nervous system that is overly susceptible to threat and conflict. Threctic people (such as Emily Dickinson) represent one pole on a continuum that is bounded at the opposite extreme by parmia types, stouthearted, bold, brash, socially aggressive salespersons, competitive athletes, and group therapists—the Teddy Roosevelts, Winston Churchills, and Andrew Jacksons of the world.

Research

Some attention has been directed by speech pathologists toward studying the relationship of shyness to stage fright and speech disorders, such as stuttering. G. M. Phillips and N. J. Metzger (1973) report on a treatment program at Pennsylvania State University to help students overcome communication difficulties arising from the reticent syndrome. In addition, some behavior modification counselors have attempted to extend to the average shy person some of the assertiveness-training programs now being developed for the nonassertive woman.

An extensive self-report questionnaire has been developed, namely the Stanford Shyness Survey (P. G. Zimbardo, P. A. Pilkonis, and R. Norwood 1975), that allows each respondent to define his own experience of shyness in terms of

1. willingness to label oneself dispositionally, or chronically, shy, or merely as temporarily shy in situationally specific contexts;
2. elicitors of shyness among people and situations often encountered;
3. perceived correlates of shyness, including physiological reactions, behavioral manifesta-

tions, cognitive concomitants (thoughts and sensations), and the specific positive and negative consequences associated with being shy; and
4. the desirability, seriousness, and change over time of one's shyness.

Personality Traits

The inner world of shyness is filled with self-consciousness (85%), concern for impression management (67%), concern for social evaluation (63%), negative self-evaluation (59%), thoughts about the unpleasantness of the situation (56%), thoughts about shyness in general (46%), and forms of cognitive distraction aimed at averting all of the above (27%). The dominant physiological reactions reported are: increased pulse (54%), blushing (53%), perspiration (49%), "butterflies in one's stomach" (48%), and a pounding heart (48%).

Whatever the reason people come to label themselves as shy, they seem to react in ways that subsequently confirm and maintain the validity of their labeling process. They come to act more like personality trait theorists than empiricists.

Shyness is a personal, private, and often painful experience, but it is a reflection of social influence and cultural programming rather than individual inadequacy. The prevalence of shyness in a family, school, community, ethnic group, or nation reveals the extent to which people do not feel accepted, valued, and unconditionally loved. Shyness is exaggerated where the cult of ego dominates, where the cultural norms overemphasize competition and individual success.

Philip G. Zimbardo
Paul A. Pilkonis

Signal Detection Theory

Threshold

During the nineteenth and early twentieth centuries, the preferred method for evaluating sensory sensitivity was the so-called threshold, the level of intensity of the stimulus at which the subject just perceives the stimulus. There are two problems with the threshold method. The first is that the threshold, construed as a single stimulus level below which the subject does not perceive the stimulus and above which she does perceive it, does not exist. At very low stimulus intensities, perception is probabilistic. Thus, if a very dim light is flashed repeatedly, on some percentage of occasions the observer will say, "Yes, I see it," and on the complementary percentage of occasions she will say, "No, I don't see it." As the intensity of the light is slowly varied from 0 intensity up to an obviously visible level, the probability of responding "yes" will increase gradually from some low level, not necessarily 0, to 100%. The intensity-probability curve is the *psychometric function*.

The second problem is that the question of motivation reveals itself clearly when one realizes there are two types of error a subject can make in a detection experiment. The first type, called a miss, occurs when the subject says "no" when in fact a physically nonzero stimulus was presented. The second type of error, called a false alarm, occurs when the subject responds "yes" to the presentation of a 0-level stimulus.

Yes-No Experiments

The usual experimental paradigm in signal-detection theory related experiments is the yes-no experiment. On each trial there is a warning, usually in a sensory modality different from the one under study, followed by either the presentation or nonpresentation of a signal. The signal is so weak relative to the background that the subject is to some extent uncertain as to whether it has occurred. If he thinks it has, he indicates "yes," if he thinks not, he indicates "no."

In a given experimental situation varying relative proportions of misses and false alarms can occur. Underlying this statement is the assumption that the total number of errors cannot go below a certain positive number, but that the relative numbers of misses and false alarms are subject to a trade-off so that either one, but not both, can be minimized to an arbitrary extent.

The relative proportion of misses and false alarms that does occur in a signal-detection-theory (SDT) setting is a function not of the subject's sensory abilities but of her motivational state. If one experimenter says to the subject, "It is very important that you detect (and respond appropriately) to every nonzero stimulus," a negative (unpleasant) subjective value has been attached to misses; the subject feels it is a bad thing to miss any nonzero stimuli, so she will be prone to say "yes" when unsure; consequently, many false alarms are bound to occur. On the other hand, the experimenter could say, "Don't say 'yes' unless you are quite sure you've seen the stimulus." In this case, a negative subjective value has been placed on false alarms. The subject will most often say "no" when unsure as to whether the stimulus has appeared, and so a large proportion of misses will obtain. Of course, we can imagine a motivational situation just between these, where an approximately equal percentage of misses and false alarms will tend to occur.

An alternative approach to the measurement of the subject's sensitivity is to utilize the miss–false alarm trade-off as a tool of analysis. The stimulus is first fixed at one value, S_a. On different days the subject is exposed to the following five conditions:

1. false alarms are worth -0.1 cents (the loss of $^{1}/_{10}$ cent per false alarm)
2. false alarms are worth -0.8 cents; misses, -0.02 cents
3. false alarms and misses are both worth -0.05 cents
4. misses are worth -0.08 cents; false alarms, -0.02 cents
5. misses are worth -0.1 cents

Psychoacoustics

Internal noise. In theoretical discussions of pure detection, an "internal noise" is often postulated to substitute, in the derivation of the model, for an externally applied band-limited white Gaussian noise. This is a matter of controversy because it is likely that internal noise is not white, band-limited, or Gaussian.

Verbal experiments. Often, SDT has been used in settings such as verbal memory experiments, where the "stimulus" is actually a class of words, sentences, or whatever. There are several objections here, one methodological. The methodological objection is that by pooling words, information is sacrificed unnecessarily. That is, each word is a unique stimulus; it is an obfuscation to call all words of a certain class one stimulus.

But even if SDT were applied to individual words, it would be inappropriate. Memory may not be a random process at all, or randomness may play a very small part in it. The amount of effort and time expended in the memory search, the length of the list of items, the position of the word in the list, whether the word has been repeated in the experiment, the connotations of the word, and so on all affect its recovery or nonrecovery in a particular setting.

Sensory stimuli. Even in experiments with stimuli of a sensory kind, (e.g., sinusoidal tones), short-term memory effects may intrude, violating the assumption of trial-by-trial independence required by SDT. Theories of so-called sequential effects (J. C. Falmagne, S. P. Cohen, and A. Dwivedi 1975) tell us that the response on a current trial may very well depend on the string of stimuli and responses in the recent past.

John Van Praag

Simulation

Simulation can be provided by means of a mock-up (e.g., of a cockpit, space capsule, or automobile driver station), graphical representation (diagram, picture, or map), synthetic written or spoken messages (transmitted by hand or over a real or pretended telephone or radio channel), imitation radar signals (from imagined aircraft or ships), or computer data and programs. Simulation has been used to investigate the performance of individual operators and entire subsystems and systems (Parsons 1972) in highly complex situations.

Degree of Fidelity

In both training simulation and simulation for design, an all-pervading question arises regarding the degree of fidelity. Any simulation is a mathematical or physical abstraction of the real world. The degree of abstraction is dependent on the purpose to which the simulation findings are to be used. The customary way of determining the fidelity of simulation or the level of abstraction that is satisfactory for

training application is to assess the transfer of training effects against some cost-effectiveness criterion.

Key Ingredients

In addition to the concern for fidelity of simulation, H. M. Parsons (1972) adds the attributes of verisimilitude, reactivity, noise, and time as key ingredients in human-machine design simulations. *Verisimilitude* is subjective realism, which means that the simulation evokes the same behavior from the experimental subjects as the real objects, events, or inputs would, regardless of the extent of the similarity. Verisimilitude, then, is the semblance of reality necessary to elicit the desired responses from the subjects. *Noise* in real-time physical simulation means that somewhere in the system the original inputs to the simulated equipment or operators are distorted to the extent that the correct discrimination and interpretations of the information being transmitted are degraded or prevented. *Time* in any simulation may be represented in real time, fast time, or slow time, or any combination of the three.

Donald A. Topmiller

Single Parenting

Single parenting is defined as a situation in which a parent is raising a child alone, without the partnership of a spouse. Until a quarter of a century ago, it was relatively unusual for a child to be raised by one parent, due to rare events such as the death of a parent, divorce, or a teenage pregnancy not resulting in marriage. Single parenting was viewed as undesirable, both socially and psychologically. It was generally agreed that the lack of a two-parent family would have devastating effects on children, and that single parents were themselves suffering from psychological disturbance.

In the United States, the increase in single-parent families over the past two decades is considered a significant social phenomenon. In 1970, 10% of all families with children under 18 were single-parent families. By 1990, that number had more than doubled, to 25%. In 1990, 31% of all minor children were living with single parents, and 90% of those single parents were mothers. With one-quarter of all families now being headed by a single parent, there has been increased concern about the psychological health, stresses, problems, and needs of such families.

The earlier, more pathology-oriented focus on the single-parent family saw it as a unitary phenomenon with easily defined causation, stresses, and problems. As the sheer number of such families has grown, this focus has given way to an awareness of single families with widely varying causes, problems, and needs. Economic status, race, sex, and type of single-parent family are all factors that define the psychological functioning of single-parent families.

Economic Status

Single parents are markedly poor. As of 1983, 47% of all single mothers lived below the national poverty level in the United States, and the rate was expected to be well above 50% by the 1990s. Even those single mothers who are fully employed have a poverty rate that is two and a half times that of two-parent families. For blacks and Hispanics, the percentage of single mothers who live in poverty is considerably higher. The effects of poverty on family functioning are significant. It is now clear that the economic status of a family, rather than its single-parent status, is predictive of stress and psychological problems in both parents and children, as will be detailed below.

Race and Ethnic Group

Single parenting is more prevalent in black families than in any other social group; it is more prevalent in Hispanic families than among whites. When race and economic level of single parent families are both considered, the devastating effect of poverty is clear. A black or Hispanic single parent with two children is twice as likely as a white single parent to be living below the poverty level.

Membership in black or Hispanic cultures, however, also has ameliorating effects. In both cultures, there tend to exist strong extended-family networks that offer significant practical and psychological support to the single parent. In addition, research on black single parents indicates that they are significantly more likely than whites to see their role as parents as a source of major satisfaction.

Sex

As stated earlier, 90% of all single-parent families are headed by women. However, the number of single-parent families headed by men, while still quite small, doubled between 1980 and 1990. Little is known at present about male-headed single-parent families. Male single parents are somewhat less likely to live in poverty, but if they do, some studies suggest that they are at risk for child abuse. In general, studies show that men appear to find caring for children to be a more significant source of stress and less of a source of pleasure than do women.

Types of Single Parent Families

In families that are headed by a single parent as a result of divorce, separation, or widowhood, parents are likely to remarry, thus making their status as a single-parent family a transitory one. Such families also show signs of significant disturbance in the first few years after attaining single-parent status.

In contrast to such families are those headed by never-married single parents. This group includes all women who choose to have children alone, as well as those men and women who adopt as single parents. In the United States, this group has grown significantly in size in the decade between 1980 and 1990, across all economic, social class, and racial/ethnic groups. This phenomenon might be due to the reluctance of men in a time of economic hardship to take on the responsibility of a family, thus leaving women to go it alone. Increased social acceptibility is also a factor. For some women, increased power and control over life decisions has led to single parenting: in the past decade, single mothers among older professional women have more than tripled.

Sources of Stress

Single parents suffer significantly more stress than do their married counterparts. Stress can come from major life events (such as divorce, death of loved one, job changes, or home changes) or from sources of chronic strain (role demands, isolation, economic worries, etc.). Although major life events are sources of great stress for those who have recently been divorced or separated, it is the stress resulting from chronic strain that has the greatest effect on the single parent. The major sources of such stress are:

(1) income related problems, (2) increased role expectations (taking on the role of mother and father) and role conflict, (3) social isolation and lack of support, (4) concern regarding the quality of child care, and (5) job demands, when such demands call for extreme mental absorption in work. A major factor that can serve to strongly increase or decrease the effect of stress is the single parent's experience of powerlessness. To the extent that a single parent feels powerless to control major aspects of his life, he experiences greater stress and the resultant anxiety and depression.

Lack of control can be felt in both the work and home arenas. If the demands of work are significant and neither coworkers nor employers are particularly sympathetic, a great deal of stress can be experienced. If, in addition, the parent's child care is less than desirable, or if the parent believes that a child's needs demand parental availability, the role conflict between job and parenting is increased. At home, the type of support that may appear to decrease stress can in fact increase it. While a slight majority of single parents have another adult (often a relative) living with them, such a source of practical help can also bring with it a high degree of tension and stress if the parent feels that such help comes with a high degree of dependence and interference attached.

Single parents also feel more lonely and isolated and have less connection with their neighborhood and community. Single parents do not tend to be included in married parents' social networks. In addition, the demands of work and home are so great as to leave little time to establish social networks.

As a result of these stresses, single parents experience significantly more anxiety and depression than do their married counterparts. They use mental health services four times as often as do married parents.

Factors Reducing Stress

Financial security can be the greatest stress reducer for single parents. Even more important than financial security itself, however, is the relative stability of personal income. If a single parent feels that her income level is adequate and predictable, her stress is greatly decreased. A job that is a source of personal satisfaction as well as a source for connection with supportive coworkers leads to decreased stress, an increase in a sense of control over one's life, and an increase in self-esteem. Single parents appear to view the workplace (if its people and policies are supportive) as an alternative to domestic life, a place to establish an identity and connections separate from the parenting role.

Satisfaction with the quality of child care has a strong effect on stress level. Parents who feel that their child is in good hands while they work experience decreased role conflict as well as decreased anxiety.

Supportive relationships can greatly alleviate stress. Although a support network that is task oriented can be useful to the single parent, it is the existence of at least one good and close friendship that is most crucial. Because of the mutuality and level of reciprocity in such a friendship, it leads to much greater stress reduction than does the support of family members (associated to a greater degree with dependence and interference) or the support of formal organizations. A chance to share experience with other single parents is also crucial.

Prevalence of Psychological Problems

PARENTS

Depression is the psychological disorder most frequently cited in single-parent families. Single mothers with low incomes have the highest rate of clinical depression of all parenting groups: some studies cite rates of depression among low-income mothers as high as 59%, with rates highest for single mothers of young children. It is poverty rather than parental status that is the major factor in the high rates of depression.

In addition to depression, single mothers experience more anxiety and lower self-esteem than do married parents. They also feel less satisfaction with their family life. However, there is no evidence that single parents as a group are more pathological than married parents.

In the first two years after divorce, separation, or widowhood, single parents experience significant degrees of depression, helplessness, loneliness, and strain in parent-child relations. These effects are usually transitory, although a significant minority experience continuing difficulties. Single mothers of sons report the greatest level of continued helplessness and parent-child strain.

CHILDREN

On the whole, children of single parents do not show greater level of psychological problems than their two-parent family counterparts if the effects of economic status are controlled. Behavioral problems are significant, however, in recently separated or divorced families and families with a clinically depressed parent. In children of divorce or separation, the first two years after the divorce bring the greatest number of behavioral problems, although problems often persist in boys living with single mothers. Children of clinically depressed parents tend to have a greater incidence of behavioral problems and of depression.

Children from low-income single-parent families are also at high risk for child abuse. It appears that the greatest risk is for children of low-income single fathers. It is likely that the higher prevalence of abuse is due to increased stress and increased isolation in single parents. Because single fathers experience caring for children as more stressful and less of a source of satisfaction, levels of stress may be even higher for this group.

There is some evidence that single mothers tend to have more difficulty gaining compliance from a young child and tend to be more authoritarian. In general, behavioral problems in children are most strongly associated with the single parent's lack of income stability and the lack of close friends.

Children of single parents often perceive themselves as better off and more psychologically healthy than do their parents. This suggests that the parents are at least somewhat successful in keeping their levels of stress, anxiety, and depression from affecting their children's experience of themselves.

Characteristics of Healthy Single-Parent Families

Healthy single-parent families are led by parents who have relatively high self-esteem. The parents have access to supportive friends and coworkers and use this support to relieve stress and receive advice and feedback. There is a high degree of communication between parent and child in healthy single-parent families, and efforts are made to actively solve problems together. The most significant coping strategies for the single parent appear to be taking responsibility for the problem and reappraising the meaning of the problem in a more positive light. These strategies appear to increase the parent's sense that he is in control and has the power to change his situation. Parents in healthy single-parent families have a high sense of competence and control over family life.

Sheila Coonerty

Single-Subject Research

The Two-Sciences Issue

During the nineteenth century, the philosopher Wilhelm Dilthey identified two types of science: *Naturwissenschaft*, which is distinguished by its use of exact, quantitative methods, and *Geisteswissenschaft*, which is qualitative in character and seeks understanding of cultural and historical phenomena. Dilthey's contemporary, W. Windelband, called the natural sciences "nomothetic," meaning that they search for general laws. By contrast, the *idiographic* cultural-historical sciences study specific, unique, and unrepeatable events or individuals.

Benjamin B. Wolman (1981) has pointed out that another underlying issue, traceable to medieval philosophy, is that of realism versus nominalism. Medieval "realists" asserted that universals (e.g., natural laws) are not abstractions but have objective reality. Nominalists argued that only specific objects or events (idiophenomena, in later terminology) are real; universals are mere conveniences or necessities of thought.

K. Goldstein (1939) advocates research on individuals. Goldstein is identified with holism, and he maintains that the careful and complete study of one properly chosen person can reveal universal laws of human nature.

Gordon W. Allport (1962) has proposed the substitution of the words *dimensional* and *morphogenic* for *nomothetic* and *idiographic*. Dimensional traits are commonalities in personality that are found to greater or lesser degrees in all individuals—for example, anxiety, extroversion, dominance, and aging.

Murray Sidman (1960) describes how inferences about learning may be drawn from a sequence of systematically related investigations of single organisms. The logic of Sidman's approach has exerted a powerful influence on procedures used in a veritable flood of single-organism studies of operant conditioning and behavior therapy.

Some confusion in understanding single-organism research may be avoided by applying a distinction between the methodological and the theoretical implications and applications of idiography and nomothesis. By definition, all morphogenic studies of single subjects are methodologically idiographic, but they are not necessarily committed to the theoretically idiographic position that research on individuals cannot yield general (nomothetic) conclusions. In principle, all possible combinations of idiography, nomothesis, method, and theory can be used.

A combination of nomothetic method and idiographic theory is employed when normatively derived (dimensional) tests are used to evaluate individuals. Uniqueness is expected to appear not in an individual's score in any particular dimension but in a distinctive pattern or profile of scores across many scales or subscales. This is the typical approach to evaluation with instruments like the Minnesota Multiphasic Personality Inventory (MMPI).

For those who work in clinical situations, single-subject research carries a power of conviction that large-scale studies do not. A program of operant conditioning that produces quantifiable therapeutic results attracts attention because it has obvious implications for clinical practice.

Franklin C. Shontz

Skill

The most precise definition of *skill* is the qualification to carry out an industrial trade or craft as the result of apprenticeship training. The use of the term in psychology has been broader and covers a wide range of performance that shows an expert quality, acquired in the course of experience or practice, and that may or may not include formal training.

The outstanding characteristic of the "skills approach" is that performance is not viewed merely as response to a stimulus but as a series of observations, decisions, and actions aimed at the achievement of goals. Performance thus has an essential anticipatory character, in that actions are chosen and initiated to meet a situation that is not presently observed but is an extrapolation from the present to the time when the actions will become effective. Therefore, the study of performance needs to take into account not only what actions are taken but also their sequence and timing. These observations, decisions, and actions constitute techniques or methods or, as they are termed, "strategies" by which the performer's capacities are deployed in order to meet the demands of tasks.

Social Skills

Good leadership requires that decisions be based on careful observation of the state and needs of those being led; in face-to-face meetings, motor factors, such as modulation of voice and gesture, are important.

From a psychiatrist's or clinical psychologist's point of view, social skills are important because difficulties in forming human relationships can often be traced to a lack of social skills, which can be remedied by suitable training.

Acquisition of Skill

Improvement of skill with training and practice seems to be due to refinement of strategies rather than to increase of underlying capacities. Limited capacities limit the effects of training, although performance by a person of modest capacities who has been well trained can exceed that of a person with greater capacities who has not. Improvement depends on feedback or "knowledge of results" of previous action. Early in practice this needs to be detailed; but later on, feedback on a broader scale seems to suffice, probably because action has come to be organized into larger units.

A. T. Welford

Skinner, B. F. (1904–1990)

B. F. Skinner developed the theory of radical behaviorism as a basis for the experimental analysis of behavior. Skinner advocated the application of instrumental or operant conditioning procedures to the technology of behavior modification in a wide variety of settings, such as schools, mental hospitals, and correctional institutions. He developed instrumentation, such as the Skinner box, an apparatus that contains a lever that, when pressed, is followed by presentation of a reinforcing stimulus. Skinner also invented a technique for recording responses, called the cumulative record. He suggested that because operant techniques make possible prediction and control of behavior, radical behaviorism offers considerable potential for changing society in a desired direction.

Eileen A. Gavin

Sleep and Dream Research

Sleep Physiology

The physiological characteristics of REM sleep have been found to be so markedly different from those of NREM sleep that early investigators, such as Frederick Snyder, Charles Fisher, and Ernest Hartmann referred to it as a unique state of existence. The manifestations of REM have been conveniently divided into tonic and phasic components. Tonic events are long-lasting changes that are maintained throughout the REM period, such as electroencephalogram (EEG) activation and electromyogram (EMG) suppression.

Neuron firing in areas of the brain, such as the visual cortex and the pyramidal system, is higher in rate during REM than NREM sleep, with REM activity equivalent to that of alert wakefulness. However, in contrast to wakefulness, where neuronal activity is regular and patterned, REM activity occurs in bursts, with periods of relative silence. Through animal ablation studies it has been found that a nucleus located in the pons, one of the most primitive parts of the brain, triggers the REM phase of sleep; when this center is destroyed, REM is abolished.

Heart and respiratory rates and systolic blood pressure show slight increases in average level and marked increases in minute-to-minute variability during REM sleep. The marked irregularity of breathing during REM sleep contrasts sharply with the relatively monotonous stability of respiration during NREM sleep. Increased cerebral blood flow, higher brain temperature, and higher levels of oxygen consumption have also been found during REM periods. In men, in the absence of inhibitory factors, full erection will appear in every REM period, regardless of dream content. The erections must represent some kind of release or stimulation of hypothalamic drive centers.

Sleep Ontogeny

Fifty percent of the average of 16 to 18 hours of sleep per day in the newborn is taken up by REM periods, the percentages being even higher for premature infants. By age two, REM percent drops to 20 to 30% of sleep, a level maintained through most of the life span until extreme old age, when there is a further reduction to 10 to 16% after age 85.

Aging brings the prospect of increased sleep disturbance. Irwin Feinberg found approximately four times as many awakenings lasting five minutes or more in a group of elderly (aged 65 to 96 years) than in a group of young adults (aged 19 to 36 years). The average duration for an awakening in the elderly was 12.8 minutes, while for the young adult it was 4.6 minutes. Although an older person has greater sleep disturbances in the form of less continuous sleep, her total sleep time is not necessarily reduced.

Edwin Kahn
Charles Fisher
Adele Edwards

Sleep and Dreaming

E. Aserinsky and N. Kleitman (1953) and W. C. Dement and N. Kleitman (1957) found (first with infants) that sleep falls into two principal divisions or stages, on the basis of electroencephalogram recordings (EEG), the submental electromyogram (EMG), and eye movements recorded by the electrooculogram (EOG). These sleep stages are called

REM sleep (rapid eye movement) and NREM (non-rapid eye movement) sleep. NREM sleep is generally associated with a slow, fairly regular, and relatively high-voltage EEG; significant muscle tone; regular respirations; and a physiologically steady, somewhat quiescent state.

REM versus NREM

The homeostatic balance between REM sleep, NREM sleep, and the awake state is controlled primarily by humoral mechanisms involving serotonin-norepinephrine balance shifts, centrally mediated via pontine-limbic-hypothalamic-cortical feedback systems.

Nightmares

Night terrors can be triggered in susceptible subjects by abruptly awakening them out of deep, quiet, Stage 4 sleep. Night terrors are rare (incidence is less than 3%), occur early in the night, and are most common in boys during the oedipal period. They are usually followed (i.e., after terrifying arousal from sleep) by intense somatic and autonomic activity. The most common anxiety arousals from sleep are anxiety dreams or REM nightmares.

Dream Development

The stage of nondifferentiation. In the first 3 months of life, no psychic activity proper can as yet be determined. The contributions of many investigators have adumbrated and clarified this fundamental conceptualization.

The stage of protodreams. From 4 to 8 months, a transition is marked from the essentially somatic adaptation of the undifferentiated period to the inception of psychic function. Reports from this period of life mention behavior during sleep and at awakening that lead to the conclusion that protocognitive events, the nature of which is difficult to surmise, are taking place and are experienced by the sleeping infant. Manifestly, at the beginning of this stage, the experience will consist of some form of endogenous sensation mainly related to somatic processes.

The period of predream. The beginnings of verbal communication may make memory traces of verbal representation with a cognitive content available. There is no information of a direct observational nature available on such dreams. There exists, however, a series of behavioral observations that can be interpreted in this sense. The emergence of predreams is predicated on the establishment of primary object-constancy.

Genuine dreams. The beginning of verbally reported dreams occurs at about 18 months, which approximately coincides with Jean Piaget's sixth stage.

Inception of Dreams

The inception of infant dreams has its origins in a primitive confluence of somatopsychic tension states, with evolutionary and maturational connections on one side and experiential, developmental factors on the other. The earliest somatopsychic affect and memory constellations that are the deepest foundations of dreams are not dreams in themselves; they do not yet even have the organization for protodreams; they are necessary but not sufficient for the protodreams, predreams, and eventual dreams of the more mature infant.

It is useful to hypothesize three organizational periods or stages in the natural history of dream development:

1. The protodream, prior to the development of object constancy, and consisting of somatopsychic activity during sleep, evoked perhaps by endogenous sensations.

2. The predream, consisting of some kind of mental activity during sleep, with a quality bordering on visual cognition. This occurs before dreams can be reported, but takes place during and as part of the period of the transitional object.

3. The dream proper, its content verbally communicated and, no matter how "simple and direct," always showing the imprint of the dream work. The dream proper and full verbal communication are circularly related and interdependent. The dream proper is formed with the aid of verbal capacity, verbal skills, and the necessarily connected higher development of the cognitive apparatus. On the other hand, advanced cognitive functioning and the

awake use of symbolization and fantasy depend on the evolving of more complex dream development.

Memory, REM, and Dream

Dreaming is remembered in the same way as is our continuous mental activity during waking. The latter obviously accompanies us uninterruptedly, but by and large, we are unable to recall it; we do not even notice it unless we turn the searchlight of self-observation on it. Like our waking mental activity, these bland, banal dreams accompany mental activity during sleep—as random background noise. Dreams that are remembered are suitable for recall because of the quality and the quantity of affect involved.

David R. Metcalf

Social Disadvantage: Effects on Children

The cumulative effects of environmental deprivation and stigmatization take a particularly critical toll to the extent that a child's self-concept is affected. As R. D. Hess (1970) has pointed out, it is inevitable in a highly competitive society that self-esteem is partially derived from an individual's perception of his ranking or prestige. And to the extent that one feels helpless, dependence on luck rather than effort and feelings of alienation and discouragement begin to emerge.

Children of families who receive public assistance are especially stigmatized by attitudes toward those "on the dole"; the general public resents the parents, particularly if they are able-bodied, for extracting tax dollars from their hard-earned wages, and the children not only because they cost yet more but because they exist at all.

Inadequate medical care, less-than-optimal nutritional intake, exposure to dangers that could potentially cause physical harm and contraction of contagious disease, and the negative effects of overcrowding are among the health-related conditions that are far more prevalent among low-income families than those of the middle class.

Much of the focus of the effects of social disadvantage is on the child's performance level in school. Differences between socially advantaged and disadvantaged children on measures of various cognitive skills have been documented. The reasons offered for the discrepancies tend to fall into two general classes: the cumulative effects of previous deprivations and the nature of the traditional school system.

The dropout rate among socially disadvantaged children is very high as compared to that of the middle class. Yet a vast majority of dropouts have, according to several surveys, the intellectual capability to complete their high school education.

Patricia Keith-Spiegel
Faye D. Siskel

Social Influence

Any social-influence attempt can be analyzed in terms of the independent variable mix of source, message, and channel as it has an impact on the chain of dependent variables, including exposure, attention, and comprehension. Failure to recognize that social-influence research can focus on many different levels of this response chain and can involve many different mixes on the independent variable side can leave the impression that the empirical data are confused or even contradictory.

Through suggestion, a person can be influenced to perceive the world and act in ways that she would not in the normal state: she may be led to hallucinate, seeing objects that are not present; to carry out arbitrary acts for which there is no explicit reason; or to endure higher levels of fatigue than usual, simply because the source suggests such behaviors. Under hypnosis, however, the person will ordinarily not carry out clearly self-destructive or antisocial acts that she would find completely unacceptable in the normal state, unless through suggestion an interpretation is given that the act is excusable.

Social pressure is exercised explicitly or implicitly by the authority figures and peer groups in the person's world. Even if one has only casual regard for the group, and the other members neither insist on conformity nor offer arguments in favor of their position, one tends to adjust one's behavior toward the modal behavior of that group.

The Media
An impressive portion of the U.S. gross national product is devoted to mass media communication.

Coercive Persuasion
Procedures utilized for coercive persuasion seem fairly standardized. The person is exposed to conditions that tend to break down his old ideological system; a new belief structure is suggested; and these new beliefs are reinforced when they occur. During the initial period in captivity, the person is exposed to disorienting and anxiety-arousing conditions: He is frequently but unpredictably interrogated by alternately friendly and severe interviewers, often while suffering from fatigue, natural anxiety, and even malnutrition.

William J. McGuire

Social Learning Theory

The more rudimentary mode of learning, rooted in direct experience, results from the positive and negative effects that actions produce. When people deal with everyday events, some of their responses prove successful, while others have no effect or result in punishing outcomes. Through this process of differential reinforcement, successful forms of behavior are eventually selected, and ineffectual ones are discarded.

Because observational learning entails subfunctions that evolve with maturation and experience, it depends upon prior development. Facility in observational learning is increased by acquiring skill in selective observation, in memory encoding, in coordinating sensorimotor and ideomotor systems, and in judging probable consequences for matching behavior.

Behavior can be increased, eliminated, and reinstated by altering the reinforcing effects it produces. Even subtle variations in the pattern and frequency with which actions are reinforced affect responsiveness. When individuals have been continuously rewarded, they become easily discouraged and give up quickly should their efforts fail. Those who have been reinforced intermittently persist despite only occasional successes.

Vicarious reinforcement introduces judgmental processes into the operation of reinforcement influences. The observed consequences accruing to others provide a standard for judging whether the reinforcements one customarily receives are equitable, beneficent, or unfair.

Self-reinforcement. At the highest level of psychological functioning, individuals regulate their own behavior by the consequences they create for themselves. In this process, people adopt, through precept and example, certain standards of conduct and respond to their own behavior in self-rewarding or self-punishing ways.

Cognitive Control
The widely accepted dictum that behavior is regulated by its effects fares better for anticipated than for actual consequences. In most instances, customary outcomes are good predictors of behavior because what people anticipate is accurately derived from, and therefore corresponds to, prevailing conditions of reinforcement.

Cognitive processes play a prominent role in the acquisition and retention of behavior as well as in its expression. Transitory experiences leave lasting effects by being coded and stored in symbolic form for memory representation. As previously noted, in the process of learning, internal representations of behavior are construed from observed examples and from informative feedback resulting from one's performances. These internal representations then serve as guides to overt action on later occasions. After response patterns become routinized through repeated execution, they are performed without requiring intermediary visualization or thought.

The reciprocal influence between human and environment receives prominent recognition in social learning theory (A. Bandura 1974). Behavior is regulated by its contingencies, but the contingencies are partly of a person's own making.

Albert Bandura

Social Perception: Theories

Functionalism

The functionalist movement can be divided into two groups: the transactional functionalists (S. E. Ames) and the probabilistic functionalists (E. Brunswik). The differences between these positions are minor compared to their basic agreement that the perceiver strives to construct a stable and predictable social world. To accomplish this, the functionalists argue, an individual must infer the nature of a perceived object by unconsciously and immediately judging what physical object would cause the given pattern of stimulation impinging upon her receptors.

The transactional functionalists also argue that an individual's purposes or goals will influence the perceptual process. The perceiver's fundamental goal is to achieve veridical perceptions of his environment. However, for many complex or ambiguous stimuli, especially in the realm of social perception, it is difficult to define exactly what the "correct" perception should be. Which interpretation a given perceiver gives to such stimulus information will depend on what is personally adaptive for him, given his own goals and purposes.

Gestalt

Gestalt psychologists propose that many perceptions are organized and structured at a basic level prior to the possible influence of needs or past experience. Starting from a phenomenological description of experience, these theorists attempt to understand both impression formation and the experience of causality and intentionality as the products of this basic cognitive activity.

In regard to the process of forming an impression of another person, Solomon E. Asch (1952) has argued that an individual organizes the traits of that person to create a "whole," or gestalt. That is, if one person is told that another person is intelligent, skillful, industrious, warm, determined, practical, and ambitious, her final impression of that person will go beyond what a simple addition of those seven traits would determine.

Interactional Theory

According to Benjamin B. Wolman (1992), the impression of another person is greatly influenced by how the other person wishes to be perceived, and how the perceiver and the perceived interact.

William DeJong
Albert H. Hastorf

Social Reinforcement

Social reinforcement, as defined by B. F. Skinner (1953), is not biologically active in a direct sense but derives its reinforcing power from prior association with some element of a social matrix. Thus, it can be considered a secondary reinforcement. To illustrate, food or shock act as primary reinforcements in promoting learning. Praise and reproof are social reinforcements, which also lead to learning.

Primary reinforcement has been found more effective than social reinforcement among retardates, autistic children, normal children who are very young, and severely psychotic patients. Social rewards can be used with such subjects but must be paired frequently with food or punishment to maintain their effectiveness. In contrast, subjects who are capable of complex cognitive function will often learn better with some kind of social reinforcement than with only primary reinforcement.

Bernard Mausner

Social Schemata

The reappearance of cognitive-gestalt approaches to the understanding of human thought and action is occurring in all areas of modern psychology, and social psychology has been a particularly fertile place for the displacement of behaviorism by the perceptual-cognitive theories. Social cognition is currently one of the most active areas of inquiry in social psychology. The investigation of social schemata, therefore, is part of a larger research effort that focuses on underlying cognitive processes through specific topics such as causal attribution, attitudes and beliefs, and social perception.

Charles J. Walker (1976) has found that most

people possess the same social group schemata. People expect groups to be structured with simple vertical and horizontal relations; i.e., they believe groups have authority hierarchies and friendship groupings. Words such as "dominates" or "social-izes" are associated with these schemata.

Research on social structures has revealed that people expect their social groups to possess the mathematical property of linearity. Thus, the investigation of the specific topic of social schemata appears to be unveiling the general nature of cognitive processes.

Charles J. Walker

Social Status

As a concept in group psychology, the social status of an individual has come to mean his worth relative to other group members in contributing to the attainment of group goals. This evaluation of worth must be at least tacitly understood and agreed upon by interacting individuals.

There is a long history of evidence that high-status persons exercise more influence than lower-status persons. While such influence may relate to the capacity of superiors to provide and withhold harm or benefit, it may also stem from their reputation as informed authorities.

A simple status system derives from an implicit contract for maintaining stability and assuring the welfare of interactants in a group relationship. In obtaining or being ascribed high status, one contracts to assume responsibility for maintaining order and for bulwarking the security of members with lesser status.

Small groups composed of members with status inconsistency tend to be troubled by problems of communication and mistrust. In this connection, persons whose status attributes are inconsistent (such as the suddenly wealthy but relatively uneducated businessperson or the deposed politician) experience stress, in that they draw unpredictable and often derogatory responses from others with whom they interact.

It appears that despite the current stress on egalitarian modes of social interaction, orientation to dif-

ferences in status and status striving are inevitably, and often unconsciously, woven into the interpersonal relationships of everyday life.

Marvin A. Iverson

Social Work and Its Role in Psychiatry and Mental Health

Social workers in the mental health arena are typically called psychiatric or clinical social workers. They currently constitute the largest single discipline working in the field of mental health; over 50% of all mental health services in the United States are provided by social workers.

Social workers provide clinical, educational, and administrative services for mental health programs. They also conduct research, evaluate service delivery systems and treatment modalities, and direct quality-assurance programs. Social work education and training, provided on the baccalaureate, master's, and doctoral levels (Edwards 1991), is focused on understanding human behavior from a biopsychosocial perspective and on developing intrapersonal, group, family, and environmental treatment skills.

Generally, social workers assess and treat patients within a social-ecological systems context. That is, social workers typically consider how the immediate environmental climate—including family, neighborhood support systems, employment situation, etc.—as well as the larger community's public policies and laws, impact upon human functioning.

Mental health problems may evolve from biological, psychological, or social difficulties. The role of the social worker is not only to understand the cause of mental dysfunction but also to assess or interpret the client's behaviors from a sociocultural, historical, and ecological or contextual perspective.

Social workers' clinical responsibilities within a psychiatric setting most often include a combination of tasks and activities, such as admissions screening and triage, discharge planning, case management interventions and coordination, patient and family education, social skills training, environmental interventions, and individual, group, and family psychotherapy.

Inpatient hospital programs have traditionally

employed social workers to coordinate and direct discharge planning activities. Many patients do not have the resources, mental capacity, or family support to simply leave a hospital and return to community life. Hospitalization can cause the loss of jobs, housing, savings, and family relationships. It is the social worker's responsibility to ensure that upon leaving the hospital, a patient has an immediate community support network. This may require coordinating and connecting the patient with the public welfare and public housing agencies, community treatment and work training programs, recreational activities, and the like.

In addition to helping patients to meet their concrete survival needs, successful discharge planning must also ensure that the person is psychologically prepared for community life. Mental illness and an extended hospital stay may have reduced the individual's coping skills and ability to communicate appropriately with agencies, peers, and family members. Social workers assess the patient's community perceptions, problem solving and practical life skills, learning or social-cognitive style, social knowledge, goals, family system, and communication skills. From this multidimensional assessment, therapeutic interventions are planned and either conducted or coordinated by the social worker. Further, social workers involved in discharge planning generally provide patients' family members with psychosocial information, as well as information about community resources and assistance in resolving interpersonal problems.

Once patients return to the community, social workers may provide case management services, marriage and family counseling, and/or individual or group psychotherapy. Case management is a comprehensive service intervention that helps individuals cope with community life, resolve crises and unexpected community problems, comply with medical requirements, and remain out of the hospital (Mental Health Resource Program 1993). Social workers conduct ongoing periodic assessments, develop and implement individualized service plans, provide linkage and coordination with community agencies, continually monitor services, and advocate on behalf of patients.

Assessing an agency's environmental climate, service limitations and goals, flexibility, and client-agency fit is also an important social work responsibility. Social work treatment plans often include assertive efforts to educate and inform community agencies about clients' needs, strengths, problems, and unique presentation styles. When appropriate, social workers directly advocate and mediate on behalf of clients.

Most social workers who are involved with psychiatry are trained to offer a variety of child, adult, and family psychotherapies. These may be conducted independently or in conjunction with a larger, more comprehensive treatment plan.

Social workers have traditionally developed and directed social skills and social competence training groups. Requests for these problem-solving and competence-building services have greatly increased as mental health researchers have gained more understanding about the treatment needs of individuals with schizophrenia and other psychotic disorders.

Today, many mental health research and evaluation departments across the nation are administered by doctoral-level social workers. Social workers are also becoming more involved in nationally significant multidisciplinary mental health research. For example, the National Institute of Mental Health's Neuroscience Research Center has extensively involved social workers in studying behavioral changes of individuals with schizophrenia who are on experimental drugs (Grebb et al. 1986). In numerous hospital and university settings, social workers are also involved with the study of the effects of the environment on social and mental development.

Social workers are becoming increasingly involved in quality assurance, program development and evaluation, and administration within mental health. Managed care programs often use social workers to plan and supervise service delivery systems, volunteer programs, and selected nonmedical interventions (such as psychotherapy, psychoeducation activities, and skills training).

The disciplines of neuroscience and neuropsychiatry have greatly expanded the roles of social workers in clinical practice and research. Many mental health organizations use social workers to provide specialized genetic and physical trauma assessments, review children's exposure to lead and other environmental toxins, and counsel or educate families and individuals. Psychiatry has also successfully used social work for educating community agencies and organizations about schizophrenia and other neuropsychiatric problems (Taylor 1987). To meet these new challenges, social work educational programs are incorporating into their curricula more information about genetics, biological development, and neurological functioning.

Edward H. Taylor
Richard L. Edwards

Social Work: Code of Ethics of the National Association of Social Workers

The Code of Ethics of the National Association of Social Workers (1993) sets forth "general principles to guide conduct, and the judicious appraisal of conduct, in situations that have ethical implications" as stated in the preamble. It is further stated that "the following codified ethical principles should guide social workers in the various roles and relationships and at the various levels of responsibility in which they function professionally." The code is then spelled out in six major categories identified by roman numerals, under which are found sixteen subheadings with additional subparagraphs.

I. The Social Worker's Conduct and Comportment as a Social Worker

This category requires the social worker to "maintain high standards of personal conduct in the capacity or identity as social worker." The social worker is also expected to maintain a high degree of competence, and must not permit personal problems to impede his or her professional performance or "jeopardize the best interests of those for whom the social worker has a professional responsibility." The nature of social work as a service profession is explicitly defined with the sentence "The social worker should regard as primary the service obliga-

tion of the social work profession." There follows a requirement of integrity and impartiality, then standards for research.

II. The Social Worker's Ethical Responsibility to Clients

High standards of professional responsibility with regard to clientele are enumerated in this category. Statements of what the social worker should do for clients include "serve clients with . . . the maximum application of professional skill and competence," "apprise clients of their risks, rights, opportunities, and obligations associated with social service to them," and "make every effort to foster maximum self-determination on the part of clients." The social worker is forbidden to "exploit relationships with clients for personal advantage," to "practice, condone, facilitate . . . any form of discrimination," and to "engage in sexual activities with clients." Rules of confidentiality and privacy are found next, beginning with the statement, "The social worker should respect the privacy of clients and hold in confidence all information obtained in the course of professional service." Interaction with clients must be conducted in a manner akin to doctor-patient confidentiality, and confidences should be breached "only for compelling professional reasons." Clients are also to be informed "about the limits of confidentiality in a given situation."

III. The Social Worker's Ethical Responsibility to Colleagues

The first two sentences under this category summarize much of what follows. "The social worker should treat colleagues with respect, courtesy, fairness, and good faith," and "should cooperate with colleagues to promote professional interests and concerns." Further details for interaction with colleagues include activity within a supervisory setting, replacing an absent colleague, arbitrating disputes, or dealing with a colleague who is unable to function properly.

IV. The Social Worker's Ethical Responsibility to Employers and Employing Organizations

The social worker is expected to "adhere to commitments made to the employing organization" and "to improve ... the efficiency and effectiveness of its services." "The social worker should use with scrupulous regard, and only for the purpose for which they are intended, the resources of the employing organization."

V. The Social Worker's Ethical Responsibility to the Social Work Profession

The social worker is expected to "uphold and advance the values, ethics, knowledge, and mission of the profession" and to "protect and enhance the dignity and integrity of the profession" as well as "take action ... against unethical conduct by any other member of the profession." It is also stated that "the social worker should act to prevent the unauthorized and unqualified practice of social work." The value of community service is emphasized, as is the importance of "making social services available to the general public." Keeping abreast of advances in knowledge and practice is deemed a major responsibility to one's profession; hence the social worker is ethically bound to "base practice upon recognized knowledge relevant to social work" and to "critically examine, and keep current with, emerging knowledge relevant to social work."

VI. The Social Worker's Ethical Responsibility to Society

The code concludes by emphasizing a commitment to work for the betterment of the entire society. It is explicitly stated that "the social worker should promote the general welfare of society." This may be done by acting "to prevent and eliminate discrimination" by ensuring "that all persons have access to the resources, services, and opportunities which they require" by promoting "conditions that encourage respect for the diversity of cultures which constitute American society" and by advocating "changes in policy and legislation to improve social conditions and to promote social justice."

Benjamin B. Wolman
Paul D. Boyer

Socialization: An Overview

Socialization deals essentially with the practical problem of how to rear children so that they will become adequate adult members of the society to which they belong.

Psychoanalytic thought has moved away from Freud's explanatory reliance on biological and instinctual factors toward a greater reliance on the importance of social pressures. Uri Bronfenbrenner (1963) refers to this shift in emphasis as the work of Horney, Sullivan, and Erikson.

The purely descriptive study of child behavior, characterized by normative and longitudinal research, is represented by Gesell's studies. Gesell attributed growth and change in psychological processes almost entirely to endogenous regulatory mechanisms.

A particularly important theoretical approach also associated with normative research is that of Jean Piaget and his coworkers. To Piaget, development is a function of an internal process, equilibration, which in turn depends on activity and experience. The child's experience brings out latent contradictions and gaps in her mental structure, and thus acts as a catalyst for inner reorganization. Predominant at times in this reorganization may be an accommodation of an existing structure, modifying it in light of the challenge; predominant at other times may be an assimilation of the challenge itself, bringing it within the scope of the existing structure so that it is no longer a challenge.

Research on socialization has been dominated by an environmentalistic orientation, but there has been a rekindling of interest in genetic and constitutional factors. That the genetic approach can bring new breadth to our thinking can be seen in examining the cross-cultural social anthropological evidence.

Neo-Hullians. Perhaps the most influential group of investigators using a stimulus-response analysis of socialization are the neo-Hullians (e.g. J. Dollard and N. E. Miller, R. R. Sears and his colleagues), whose theoretical ancestry can be traced to Clark Hull.

Bandura and Walters. The social-learning theory of Albert Bandura and R. H. Walters (1963) also notes the importance of external reinforcement in learning. However, these investigators emphasize modeling, imitation, and vicarious learning as somewhat independent of external reinforcement.

Skinner. B. F. Skinner's approach is limited to analysis of the functional relations between discrete responses and stimulus events.

The view that socialization is essentially the habit training of a basically passive organism retains a certain popularity. It is expressed, for example, in efforts to conceptualize the socialization process within a Skinnerian framework, with its emphasis on shaping behavior through the application of external rewards and punishments. Errors following from an extreme passive-child approach are pointed to by John Bell (1965), who notes that the literature on child-rearing practices has been built almost entirely on the assumption of a unidirectional effect from parents to offspring.

Developmentalists have generally viewed development as a positive process. Growth is conceptualized as the continuous emergence of ever-greater adaptive abilities, with the growing child demonstrating and fulfilling this greater potential at successive stages in his development. A group of general personality theorists, including Abraham Maslow, Gordon Allport, and Carl Rogers, have also emphasized positive intrinsic growth tendencies, and these writers are often referred to as self-actualization theorists.

Edward F. Zigler

Socioeconomic Status and Mental Disorders

Thirty-three of the prevalence studies provide at least some data on psychiatric disorders according to one or another indicator of occupation, income, or educational level. The following is a summary of the main findings by Dohrenwend and Dohrenwend.

1. The highest overall rates of functional psychiatric disorder have been found in the lowest social class in twenty-eight out of the thirty-three studies that report data according to indicators of social class.

2. This relationship is strongest in urban settings or in mixed urban and rural settings (nineteen out of twenty studies).

The findings on social class from the epidemiological studies of "true" prevalence have served to raise and reraise the social stress–social selection issue. No research to date has resolved this issue in the sense of assessing the relative importance of the two processes (stress and selection) and the nature of their interaction in relations between social class and various types of psychiatric disorder.

Bruce P. Dohrenwend

Sociology and Psychiatry

One may discern at least three main directions of research within what is called psychiatric sociology, as follows:

Level I   Sociological studies of patients
  A. Sociology of the patient
  B. Social structure and its effects on patients
  C. Social inputs into the one-to-one therapeutic relationship
  D. Diagnostic observations
  E. Mental health professionals
  F. New directions of community mental health services
Level II   Sociological studies of community systems
  A. The formal structure
  B. The informal structure
  C. The "fallout" social isolates
Level III   Sociological studies of mental health in general populations
  A. The core of this research area is to be found in epidemiological investigations.
  B. Longitudinal (life-history) research
  C. Special studies of psychiatric sociology

Leo Srole

Sociology and Psychoanalysis

Totem and Taboo

Early in the development of psychoanalysis, there were efforts to use the knowledge gained from the study of psychopathology to formulate explanations of social behavior. For example, in *Totem and Taboo* (1912) Sigmund Freud attempted to explain structural forms in society (the organization of authority relationships) as mirrors, if not outcomes, of individual libidinal and aggressive development. The fantasies of patricide contained in the Oedipus complex, a universal experience in human development, parallel, if not actual episodes in prehistory, at least collective fantasies that find expression in myth, ritual, and totem worship.

Freud's later study, *Group Psychology and the Analysis of the Ego*, speculates in this second direction. By his focus on identification of group members with one another in their common attachment to leaders and ideals, Freud cleared paths leading to empirical studies of social life, using psychoanalytic theory and interpretations.

Oedipus Complex

Extrapolations from individual development and unconscious mental life to organized social relations depend on the power of a psychological constant, traditionally known in psychoanalysis as the universal Oedipus complex.

The study of social movements, such as revolutionary groups and cults, would seem to require some understanding of how individuals not only address reality but also avoid depressive reactions through action. Insofar as cults provide a rationale for action, along with gratification of preoedipal impulses, the painful feelings and images associated with depression are buffered.

The Family

One model of the family, along which the classical Oedipus complex forms, postulates a high degree of role differentiation between the parents. The mother's role is predominantly "expressive" and concerned with the internal and emotional management of the family. The adult male's role is predominantly "instrumental," and in this capacity the father is the main link between the family and the wider social system: through him the boy adopts his sex role, and the girl her ideal of masculinity and the related cultural symbols and standards. In this model of the family, the father is in effect a "projection" of society, just as the cultural symbols are projections of experiences within the family. The father's role in the resolution of the Oedipus complex helps to break up the boy's dependency on the mother, including his erotic attachment to her, which is countermanded by the incest taboo.

Leadership

The theories of narcissism and the self in psychoanalysis emphasize the ever-present potential for regression, which in turn gives further impetus to the effects of preoedipal development on socialization and social change. Such analytic trends shift attention away from the father, as the mediator between the family and society, to the mother.

Identity Crisis

The contemporary interest in the identity crisis as it affects youth coincides with suggested findings in psychoanalysis of a trend in psychopathology away from the classical symptom neuroses to character neuroses, narcissistic personality disorders, and borderline disturbances. Explaining trends in individual personality configuration, including the typical pathologies, opens a conceptual path to social fact and theory. Historical analyses tend to show that the classical model of the family and the Oedipus complex are not constants but rather variables affected by the wider social structure.

Abraham Zaleznik

Sociopaths

Benjamin B. Wolman describes sociopaths as "narcissistic hyperinstrumentals" (1973). A sociopath is narcissistic in that the primary object of her affection is herself. She is hyperinstrumental in that her primary mode of expressing that affection is through gaining benefits from others to satisfy her own needs.

Wolman describes the adult sociopath as a person

unable to tolerate delay or frustration, lacking in guilt feelings, relatively anxiety-free, lacking in compassion for others, hypersensitive to his own ills, and lacking a sense of responsibility. These symptoms are by-products of a deficient childhood, in which a generalized attitude of "exploit or be exploited" is developed.

The parent–child interactions that would lead to this attitude are (1) deprivation of love and caring, manifested in rejection or neglect, and (2) lack of adequate supervision, manifested in inconsistent or totally absent discipline. The absence of parental affection had dramatic consequences, because the child is deprived of a role model for loving or caring.

This type of person had defective socialization, and thus many authors prefer the term *sociopath*. In the absence of parents with whom she would care to identify, the child develops a very weak superego. Guilt, shame, or blame, if they exist at all, are subverted into two peculiar forms. In the first, the sociopath projects the blame and rage at a hostile world that fails to satisfy her narcissistic and, therefore, all-important needs. In the second, which one could call the depression of sociopaths, she rages at herself for being too weak, too poor, or not shrewd enough to outsmart the world that is against her.

Hyperinstrumental Neurosis

As a rule, sociopaths do not come for treatment because they are dissatisfied with themselves and wish to be changed; they are often hypochondriacs, and the thing they desire is to be relieved from physical pain. Sociopaths on a neurotic level are selfish, dishonest, exploitative individuals, who feel cheated and exploited by others.

Character Neurosis

In this stage of sociopathy, the individual has accepted the symptoms of the neurotic as central to his character and is using the symptoms to attain secondary gains. Other character-neurotic sociopaths may become racketeers, extortionists, or nonviolent criminals.

Latent Hyperinstrumental Psychosis

"The latent psychotic sociopath is frequently aware of his or her murderous impulses and fears that they may lose control and be severely punished" (Wolman 1973, 220).

Manifest Psychosis

On a psychotic level, sociopaths are without goals or aims and seek immediate gratification of whims and wishes without appropriate consideration of the consequences. Drunkards, addicts, bums, and beggars typify the passive form of this disorder; impulsive individuals who rob, cheat, and prey upon the weak represent the aggressive–sadistic form.

Beatrice J. Krauss
Herbert H. Krauss

Somnambulism

Somnambulism, a term derived from the Latin *somnus* (sleep) and *ambulus* (walking), refers to walking and other motor acts occurring while the person remains asleep. Before the age of 6, there are rare reports of sleepwalking. Maximum frequency of occurrence is during pubescence, between 10 to 14 years of age, with decreasing frequency in adulthood.

Not only is there a failure to recall particular acts, but the act itself is not recalled. This is true even if the subject awakens or is awakened, unless the awakening is prolonged and pressed on the subject. As a result, sleepwalking is usually "discovered" or identified for the sleepwalker by someone else.

The laboratory sleep-related studies of sleepwalking have explicated the place of somnambulism in sleep and its lack of relationship to dreaming. Two independent studies have demonstrated that sleepwalking occurs only out of the deepest levels of sleep (Stage 4) and is not associated with the dream phases of sleep, which are identified by an "awake-like" electroencephalogram pattern and rapid eye movements. The electroencephalographic findings are supported by two additional facts. First, there is essentially no recall of dream content by persons on being awakened from somnambulistic episodes. Secondly, sleepwalking can be induced in somnambulistically prone subjects, but only during the deep phases of sleep.

Wilse B. Webb

Space and Psychiatry

Hall defines four classes of space for humans: public, social, personal, and intimate. These may be thought of as space "bubbles" surrounding the individual. Merging the space bubbles of two or more individuals results in physiological, sensory, and psychological changes, the extent depending on the closeness of approach. In other animals there are also gradations, including recognition distance, flight distance, and, in animals that live in bands, a personal space bubble of varying size.

Not all primates display territorial behavior. Within the chimpanzee troop that Jane Goodall studied most intensively, variations of space bubbles were clear. Dominant chimps had a greater space around them, which subordinate chimps feared to penetrate. Dominant animals also had greater freedom of movement than did the lower-ranking animals, including the freedom to penetrate other animals' space bubbles.

Other primates, such as baboons, howling monkeys, and rhesus monkeys, are emphatically territorial. In one famous experiment, conducted by J. A. Carpenter, rhesus monkeys were transported by boat from Southeast Asia to a deserted Puerto Rican island for study. Chaos and anarchy occurred in feeding, mating, and infant care, both on the boat and for a period after being released on the island. Then the monkeys formed stable bands with territories, at which point their behavior returned to normal.

Modern humans use space and deal with territory in ways dictated by the cultures in which they are reared. Because these factors have received little attention in the past, Hall believes that such differences have caused considerable intercultural problems. The differences are not as blatant as those of language and clothing, but furnish discordant cues that remain outside of full awareness.

Human beings shape space, and space shapes human beings. For instance, the Western concept of the family and childhood, as well as modern psychological theories, stems from a change in the use of interior space that occurred just two centuries ago. Prior to that, according to Aries, rooms had no specialized use. A room changed function by adding or removing furniture. There was no privacy in the current sense. Only in the eighteenth century were the words *salle* (room) and *chambre* (bedroom) differentiated in French. At the same time, rooms were given functional names in English, such as *bedroom* and *dining room*. Only after that did modern family life evolve and stabilize.

Territorial behavior in people can be viewed in three categories: individual, small group, and large group. Individual territory begins at home. For example, for each family member, there is a particular bedroom, or bed in a bedroom, or even a particular side of a bed that "belongs" to that family member.

Customs and culture vary considerably, but a common factor is the recognition by the community of family territorial rights. Whether the family is the Western, urban, nuclear one or the prerevolutionary, extended, Chinese one, friends and neighbors honor its rights. Almost universally, the home can be entered only at certain times, by certain people, in certain ways. Permission is necessary to enter, usually restrictions are placed on the mobility of visitors within the family territory.

When considering the large-group aspects of territory in human beings, human intelligence and culture play a crucial role, albeit one of questionable rationality. Only humans will fight to the death over land in which they have no immediate personal interest. It requires an ability to symbolize to propel an Iowa farm boy thousands of miles to engage in a war in totally unfamiliar terrain, in the name of "defense of country."

As the infant grows from toddler to early childhood (ages 2 to 4), adults begin to communicate space norms, and the child begins to learn them. Frequent requests for holding are labeled "babyish," while attempts at conversation at too great a distance elicit demands to come closer and not to shout. Concomitantly, the child is learning about territory, including the clear rights of others compared to her own limited ones.

The pathology of territory may play a direct role in the social pathology of gangs, as well as the hostility that occurs at the edges of different ethnic and racial neighborhoods. The search for "turf" by the urban gang is closely paralleled by the fight by whites to "preserve the neighborhood." More accurately, they both are variations on the theme of territoriality, and, as with deer and chimps, the density of the population seems related to the intensity of aggressiveness.

F. Theodore Reid, Jr.

Spatial Frequencies

The concept of spatial frequencies has become increasingly important in the study of vision. This concept is based on the fact that any complex waveform can be analyzed into a number of elementary sinusoidal waveforms, which, when added together, reproduce the original waveform. The mathematical techniques using this fact are known as Fourier analysis. They have been of use in audition, for example, because they permit the decomposition of complex sounds into their constituent simple harmonic variations in sound pressure level (pure tones). These same techniques have become very prominent in the study of visual processes (T. N. Cornsweet 1970; B. Harris 1975).

Sinusoidal Grating
To fully understand these techniques of analysis of visual scenes, it is easiest to begin by considering one very simple pattern, a sinusoidal grating. A sinusoidal grating is a pattern that looks like a blurry, alternating set of dark and light stripes. In such a pattern, the luminance (light intensity) in the direction perpendicular to the stripes varies sinusoidally, while the luminance in the direction parallel to the stripes remains constant.

Several parameters describing a sinusoidal grating are important. The one of most concern here is *spatial frequency*, that is, the number of cycles of sinusoid per unit distance in the pattern or, equivalently, the number of dark-bar–light-bar pairs per unit distance in the pattern. Spatial frequency and size of bar are inversely proportional to each other, as are the wavelength and frequencies of sound or radio waves. A grating with very narrow bars has a high spatial frequency, while a grating with very wide bars has a low spatial frequency. The *mean luminance* of the grating is the average of the luminance across the whole spatial extent of the grating. The *contrast* of the grating is some measure of the difference between the most-luminous and least-luminous points, usually taken to be half that difference divided by the mean luminance.

Linear Systems
The analysis of visual patterns into spatial frequency components has become important in the study of vision, because it is a natural and fruitful method to use if one is dealing with certain kinds of systems, called linear systems. Some early theories suggested that, at least to a first approximation, the human visual system might be a linear system. By definition, the response of a linear system to a stimulus that equals the sum of component stimuli is exactly equal to the sum of the responses to the component stimuli by themselves (that is, the response to a sum equals the sum of the responses). This is known as the superposition principle.

Channels
Most of the psychophysical experiments that have produced evidence consistent with a model of multiple spatial-frequency channels fall into one of three classes: (1) detection-summation experiments, (2) adaptation (or masking) experiments measuring threshold effects, and (3) adaptation (or masking) experiments measuring suprathreshold effects.

Adaptation Experiments
In adaptation experiments the observer inspects a suprathreshold grating (called the adapting grating) for a relatively long period of time (some minutes) and then looks at another grating (called the test grating). If an individual channel adapts (becomes less sensitive) after a period of being excited, the channels responsive to the adapting grating should be less sensitive after the observer inspects the adapting grating than they were before. But the channels that are not responsive to the adapting grating should be unchanged by inspecting the adapting grating.

A model of multiple spatial frequency channels does predict results, which approximate those actually obtained in a wide range of psychophysical experiments. However, the model cannot account for the fact that different classes of experiments appear to yield descriptions of the channels that are widely divergent. Thus, experiments of Type B suggest channel bandwidths that are much broader than those currently estimated from experiments of Type A. Bandwidths estimated from experiments of Type C are broader still. Moreover, there has been little progress in extending the multiple-channels model to suprathreshold perception.

Norma V. S. Graham

Specialty Practice in Psychology: Guidelines

The *Specialty Guidelines for the Delivery of Services* (American Psychological Association 1980) are among the latest in a series of major policy statements affecting the practice of psychology (issued by the American Psychological Association [APA] between 1974 and 1987). The original *Standards for Providers of Psychological Services* (1974) was approved by the APA Council of Representatives on September 2, 1974. Revisions were issued through 1987.

The APA Council recognized that, once begun, the maintenance of quality assurance procedures is never done. In January 1975, a Committee on Standards for Providers of Psychological Services (COSPOPS) was charged with updating and revising the 1974 policy. In 1976, the committee was charged to limit the scope of the revision to activities ordinarily associated with the professional practice of clinical, counseling, industrial-organizational, and school psychology. In 1977, the APA Council of Representatives voted to adopt the first revision of the original *Standards* (1977).

However, it made its action conditional on the understanding that representatives from the four major specialty areas would be given the opportunity to participate in developing additional sets of standards for specialty practice. This action was prompted by the concerns of many psychologists that the "generic" *Standards* obscured and possibly distorted certain essential differences in orientation and modus operandi among the specialty groups.

APA's First Standards for Specialty Practice

The development of specialty standards entailed more active and far-reaching attempts to involve concerned constituent groups than had attended the preparation of any previous APA policy statement on any subject. Over a three-year period, hundreds of persons identified with each of the four specialty areas contributed directly to the content of the many successive drafts. Their ranks included practitioners, as well as academicians, researchers, trainers, and students.

Largely because most objections had been satisfactorily answered in earlier drafts, the final proposals for specialty standards moved through APA governance without major changes and were ready for review and action by the Council of Representatives at their 1980 meeting in Washington, DC.

The council required that two modifications be made uniformly throughout each of the four proposals:

1. The titles denoting specialty standards would be changed to read *Specialty Guidelines for the Delivery of Services by Clinical* (or Counseling, Industrial/Organizational, School, as appropriate) *Psychologists*.
2. The phrase "minimally acceptable levels" and other obligatory language would be deleted wherever they appeared in the documents. Restating each guideline in simple declarative terms was intended to indicate that the *Specialty Guidelines* were to serve as a set of aspirational statements for psychologists, which would encourage continual improvement in the quality of practice and service.

The council instructed that the next revision of the generic *Standards* (subsequently renamed the *General Guidelines for Providers of Psychological Services*, 1987), also include modifications that incorporated the spirit of the above in order to maintain the association's commitment to quality assurance for the public without unduly compromising its practitioners.

The *Specialty Guidelines* were designed to follow the format and, whenever applicable, the wording of the generic *Standards*. Each specialty volume alerts the reader that publication of the guidelines does not alter the APA's basic position that state licensure/certification should be based on generic, and not on specialty, qualifications. Each explains how the *Specialty Guidelines* serve the public interest by providing potential users and other interested groups with essential information about qualifications and particular services available from each specialty group.

It is observed that all learned disciplines have regarded specialty practice as the natural outcome of increased acquisition of a particular set of knowledge and skills, together with a voluntary limiting of service to a restricted area of practice. Consequently, the *Guidelines* are intended to apply only to those psychologists who voluntarily wish to be designated as specialists.

The APA does serve notice, however, that "following the grandparenting period, psychologists do not put themselves forward as specialists in a given area of practice unless they meet the qualifications" noted for that particular specialty.

Each document affirms that the guidelines have been established as a means of self-regulation to protect the public interest. Each notes that a new Committee on Professional Standards was established in January 1980, charged with keeping the generic *Standards* and the *Specialty Guidelines* responsive to the needs of the public and the profession through systematic review and revision.

The Outlook for Additional Specialty Designation in Professional Psychology

The publication in 1980 of the *Specialty Guidelines for the Delivery of Services* in the four best-known specialties of professional psychology established a precedent for more such action in the future. Already seeking official recognition were groups of psychologists whose practice had concentrated on select problems, settings, populations, or techniques (e.g., rehabilitation, forensics, mental retardation, gerontology, addictions, psychoanalysis, neuropsychology, women, child-clinical, etc.). Each of these special-interest groups had petitioned the APA for recognition as a specialty of psychology. By late 1978, increasing pressures prompted the APA Board of Professional Affairs to convene a Task Force on

Special Criteria, charged with reviewing this matter in depth and returning definitive recommendations for action. In 1980, the task force submitted its final report, "Characteristics and Criteria of a Specialty in Psychology" (APA 1980). Sections of that report are quoted below:

> Specialties grow out of a history and tradition of service, research and scholarship which identify a relationship between an area of need and a body of relevant knowledge and skills within the profession. The Task Force on Specialty Criteria recommends creation of a committee, to be called the Committee on Specialty Designation (CSD), which will recognize specialties in psychology using the following criteria. All of the criteria must be met by any group wishing recognition for a specialty in psychology.

Criteria for Identification of a Specialty

In order to be designated as a specialty in psychology, a group applying to the Committee on Specialty Designation must:

A. Define the specialty in terms of a body of knowledge and a set of skills related to the knowledge base. The skills of this specialty must have demonstrated efficacy for dealing with particular problems, service populations, and settings.

B. Specify the knowledge and skills of the specialty to be acquired through a sequential academic curriculum and a professional training program which include the core knowledge of psychology, but go well beyond it. "Psychologists who wish . . . to add an additional area of applied specialization must meet the same requirements with respect to subject matter and professional skills that apply to doctoral (and postdoctoral) training in the new specialty" (APA 1977, 6).

C. Show the *pattern* of specialty practice to be discriminably different in the aggregate from the *pattern* of practice in other specialties.

D. Identify doctoral programs in regionally accredited institutions in several geographic locations which offer programs in the specialty area.

E. Present standards of practice which define

clearly the range of services and practices for members of that specialty.

The task force recommended that the APA adopt the term "special proficiency" to recognize the mastery of a special skill, special technique, or in-depth knowledge of the unique needs of a specific population or problems of a specific setting. A given special proficiency is not bound to any one specialty of psychology. The task force noted examples of special proficiencies commonly utilized in three major areas of psychological practice. These are:

1. behavior change (e.g., psychoanalysis, hypnosis, group therapy, biofeedback, behavior modification, marriage and family therapy, sex therapy, vocational counseling)
2. evaluation or assessment (e.g., neuropsychological assessment, competency evaluation, program evaluation, market surveys, consumer research, and product evaluation)
3. consultation (e.g., management consultation, organizational development, and consultation to organizations, such as police, schools, military, community agencies, industries, courts, and health facilities)

The criteria finally proposed by the task force emphasized that a specialty of psychology represents an integration of basic knowledge, skills, and practice acquired during extended pre- and postdoctoral preparation for practice within a broad subject matter area of psychology. On the other hand, many of the more circumscribed and focused "special proficiencies" could be subsumed within one or more specialty areas. The task force reaffirmed the APA's position that general providers of psychological services should not be prevented from using the methods or dealing with the populations of any specialty, except insofar as they voluntarily refrained from providing services they were not competent to render (APA 1980).

The issues associated with the development, periodic upgrading, and implementation of the APA's *General Guidelines for Providers of Psychological Services* (1987) and the *Specialty Guidelines for the Delivery of Services* (1980) represent interim stepping stones on the way toward its continuing maturation as a profession. Psychologists are not alone in being held increasingly accountable for the efficacy and quality of the services they provide, and for the adequacy of outcomes obtained by virtue of their interventions. The APA's continuing commitment to develop new, and to revise current, guidelines for practice is the hallmark of a responsible and rapidly expanding profession.

Durand F. Jacobs

Speech and Language: Developmental Disability

Several studies of language acquisition point to a developmental design for language acquisition. The design shows a strong relationship between acquired structures and functions and environmental contexts. From this involvement with the contextual objects, actions, and agents, the child is able to match language and events. The stages through which the child works to acquire progressively more complex grammar may be conceptual as well as linguistic.

The development of a general, standardized test of language has been attempted by a number of test developers. The best known is the Illinois Test of Psycholinguistic Abilities (ITPA). The efforts by D. L. Hedrick and E. M. Prather (1972) have produced a receptive-expressive model designed on a behavioral system. Both tests sample the child's initial level of functioning and determine in subsequent applications the child's progress through the language training program.

J. Hollis, J. K. Carrier, and J. E. Spradlin (1975) relate recepted sensory information (visual, auditory, tactile, and olfactory) and psycholinguistic process information (imitative, nonimitative, constructive, and transformative) with expressed response information (gross motor, signs, writing, and speech). Their design combines C. E. Osgood's language model with a plan for functional intervention.

L. R. Kent et al. have developed a language program for institutionalized, severely retarded nonverbal children from 5 to 20 years of age. The program follows a structured hierarchical sequence of skills and is based on operant conditioning principles. The range of content and applicability of existing language training programs is wide. Some lend themselves to groups in a classroom situation.

Richard L. Schiefelbusch

Spence, Kenneth W. (1907–1967)

Throughout his entire career, Kenneth W. Spence devoted himself to constructing a comprehensive theory of conditioning and other simple learned behaviors. In this effort, Spence was closely associated with Clark L. Hull, whose objectives were similar. Many of Spence's opinions on methodological matters developed out of a long and close association with the positivistic philosopher, Gustav Bergmann. Spence made important contributions to a variety of experimental and theoretical issues, such as learning, discrimination learning, the continuity-noncontinuity issue, anxiety, and conditioning.

Gregory A. Kimble

Spinal Conditioning

Attempts have been made to produce instrumental conditioning in spinal toads, frogs, and rats. In these experiments, the spinal-transected animal is suspended above a water bath. As the hind limb descends to make contact with the water bath, it receives an electric shock, which produces flexion of the limb and disconnects the electric shock. In many instances, the position of the leg is eventually such that the limb is maintained out of the water, thus avoiding the shock. This paradigm may be regarded as an instrumental avoidance conditioning paradigm, and the results of these experiments provide some hope that instrumental conditioning may occur in the isolated spinal cord, and if confirmed, offer another important avenue of investigation for understanding the mechanisms of such conditioning in the spinal animal and insights into the possible mechanisms of similar forms of instrumental conditioning in the intact animal.

Philip M. Groves

Spontaneous Recovery

If, following the extinction of a conditioned response, there is a pause in the experimental procedure, the extinguished response regains some of its strength without further reinforcement. This phenomenon is called spontaneous recovery. The increase in strength follows an increasing negatively accelerated course, which reaches an asymptote in times that different experiments suggest may be anywhere from a fraction of an hour to several hours. Although in some Pavlovian demonstrations the extinguished response appeared to regain full strength as a result of spontaneous recovery, this result is atypical. Usually, the response regains only a fraction of its preextinction strength.

Gregory A. Kimble

Sport Psychology

The relationship between sport and psychology has received increasing attention recently. For many, the application of psychological principles to sports is crucial to the achievement of peak performance. "Ultimately, it's going to come down to what's between their [athletes'] ears," stated Shane Murphy, director of sports science at the U.S. Olympic Training Center (Allman 1992, 50). Although the field has undergone much growth in the past decade, this development has also created considerable ambiguity as to what the field encompasses (Dishman 1983). According to Singer (1989), sport psychology refers to "scholarly, educational, and practical activities associated with the understanding and influencing of selected behaviors of people involved in athletics, physical education, vigorous recreational activity, and exercise" (61). Others focus more specifically on the application of behavioral and psychological principles to optimize athletic performance.

Historical Perspective

Although the notion that mental skills, as well as physical skills, are important in sports has been around for centuries, "sport psychology" emerged in the twentieth century. Early work by A. Griffith

(1926, 1928) introduced the subject in the United States, but it was not actively pursued until 1965, at which time the International Society of Sport Psychology was formed. Over the next two decades, a number of sport psychology organizations were created, including the North American Society for the Psychology of Sport and Physical Activity (NASPSPA, 1967), the U.S. Olympic Committee Registry of Sport Psychologists (1982), the Association for the Advancement of Applied Sport Psychology (AAASP, 1985), and Division 47 (Exercise and Sport Psychology) of the American Psychological Association (1986). Since the 1970s, there has also been a proliferation of texts that address sport psychology. These books serve the needs of many groups, including academicians, clinical sport psychologists, coaches, athletes, and the recreational public. The great majority of the books address utilizing sport psychology to assist individuals and teams in attaining optimal athletic performance.

Current Trends in Sport Psychology

Currently, there are four primary English-language journals that focus exclusively on sport psychology. These include the *International Journal of Sport Psychology*, the *Journal of Applied Sport Psychology*, the *Journal of Sport and Exercise Psychology*, and the *Sport Psychologist*. Other journals that often contain sport psychology–related material include the *Canadian Journal of Sport Science*, *Medicine and Science in Sports and Exercise*, *Perceptual and Motor Skills*, and the *Research Quarterly for Exercise and Sport*.

A great deal of recent research in sport psychology appears to be of an applied nature. Two sport psychology journals are devoted to the dissemination of applied research and practical information (the *Journal of Applied Sport Psychology* and the *Sport Psychologist*). This trend has been useful for examining the relationship between sport and psychology in applied settings. However, there also appears to be a relative dearth of theory-driven studies and a lack of conceptual models for understanding athletic performance and participation. This likely is related to the diversity in the field and to the definitional ambiguity that exists in sport psychology, which may contribute to less-focused research (Rejeski and Brawley 1988).

Domain of Sport Psychology

What then is the domain of sport psychology? Clearly, it is a broad field that shares common interests with psychology, sports science, motor development, and physical education. The diversified nature of sport psychology is seen as both a strength and weakness in the field. As a strength, it appears that many different interests are being served. For example, the AAASP is comprised of three branches: intervention/performance enhancement, social psychology, and health psychology. These subgroups are viewed as providing breadth to the field of sport psychology. However, the diversity may also indicate an identity crisis, reflected by the large number of published articles in the last 15 years that have dealt with professionalization issues (e.g., what is sport psychology? who can call themselves "sport psychologists"?).

There are overlapping areas of interest and expertise for sport psychologists who come from various backgrounds (e.g., clinical or counseling psychologists, physical educators, sports scientists). The question of who is uniquely qualified to provide sport psychology services is related to this overlap and occasionally has been associated with "turf battles." Currently, there are certification provisions being adopted by the AAASP to better define sport psychology and its practitioners. These issues will likely have important implications for sport psychologists because, currently, there are no standardized programs or national guidelines in the United States for the training of sport psychologists. Instead, there are various academic routes for training in sport psychology, including graduate programs in sports science or physical education with emphases in sport psychology at the master's level (and some at the doctoral level). Those trained as psychologists typically seek further training in sports science or focus specifically on working with athletes. This educational process is very different from that in some of the former Eastern-bloc countries, which have established standardized preparation procedures for their sport psychologists. As Singer (1989) points out, given the leadership role that the United States has taken in sport psychology, it seems odd that there is so much internal confusion regarding the nature and goals of the field and the training and qualifications of its practitioners.

As it stands now, the role of the sport psychologist is defined by who is doing the work. At any time, the sport psychologist can be an educator, evaluator/psychodiagnostician, counselor, performance enhancer, researcher, health promoter, and general consultant. However, the prevailing view of the sport psychologist is that of a performance enhancer working in an applied setting. This role typically entails determining an athlete's goals for performance and working with the athlete, coach, or team to overcome weaknesses and further enhance strengths. Common interventions include relaxation training, mental imagery, developing consistent pre-competition plans, distraction control, strategies to overcome errors, and enhancing communication between coach and players.

The field of sport psychology is rapidly growing and has become a legitimate academic activity, as well as a practical application of psychological and behavioral principles to sports. Sport psychology is currently accepted by many as providing an additional advantage to athletes who are striving to reach their potential, thus complementing coaching, physical training, and proper nutrition. However, it clearly is not restricted to performance enhancement; it overlaps with and draws from such fields as clinical and health psychology (e.g., exercise adherence, drug abuse, remediation, and personal growth), kinesiology and movement sciences (e.g., motor learning), and developmental psychology (e.g., child development). This broad knowledge base is indeed a great strength of the field of sport psychology. However, it is likely that the field of sport psychology will only be able to advance as those physical educators, sport scientists, and psychologists (who have an interest in sport and psychology) come together and agree on the nature of the field as well as training and practice guidelines. Active collaborations between organizations such as Division 47 of the APA, the AAASP, and the NASPSPA will prove vital for continued growth.

Robert A. Swoap
James A. Blumenthal

Stanford-Binet Intelligence Test

Alfred Binet pioneered the theory and practice of measuring general ability, by constructing tests to be used with "problem children" in French elementary schools. In his tests developed in 1905–1911, with Theodore Simon, Binet emphasized the ability to make correct judgments, the ability to solve problems, and the ability to understand words and written material.

The original test was only a rough beginning to the measurement of general ability, but it constituted an important first step. Binet's conceptions of how general ability should be measured and the types of items that should be used have dominated most tests of general ability to this day.

The Terman and Merrill Revisions

The most extensive revisions of the Binet-Simon scales were made first by Lewis M. Terman in 1916 and then by Terman and M. A. Merrill in 1937 and 1960. Because their work was done at Stanford University, their revisions were named Stanford-Binet tests. Their work has so extensively revised and extended Binet's tests that it is only out of respect to him that the current form of the test still bears his name.

The 1960 Revision

The 1960 revision of the Stanford-Binet largely involved recombining items and making minor changes in items used previously. Having an alternative form available made it possible to retest children after short periods of time without having the results affected by memory. However, little use was made of form M. Consequently, in the 1960 revision, the best items were selected from both the older forms L and M, and the present form is referred to as "L-M."

Jum C. Nunnally

Startle

Startle to certain types of stimuli appears to be present at birth (sudden noise); other startle responses evolve as a function of neural maturation (blink response to object brought close to the eyes), and others occur as a function of specific experiences of the organism. Thus, it seems that startle responses to some relatively specific stimuli are built into the organism while others are acquired as a function of experience, that is, learned.

Startle responses to repeated stimuli demonstrate decrements in their intensity. This decrement is a type of habituation response and is accounted for by the fact that if a given stimulus occurs a number of times in a reasonably short time span, then the subsequent stimuli are less "unexpected," and the startle response is reduced.

The measurement of startle ranges from simple observations to the use of sensitive devices to record and quantify the finer nuances of startle. The latter may be used to answer questions dealing with the sensitivity of different physiological response systems to startle and its habituation. At the observational level one can observe gross muscular responses; gasps that accompany sudden deep inspiration; eye blinks; stereotyped facial movements; and, under close observation, dilation of the pupil of the eye.

Reduction in startle as measured from muscles appears to be characterized by a rapid reduction of gross muscle responses with inhibition of fine muscle groups evolving considerably more slowly. The facial musculature, including the eyelid, appears to be most sensitive to startle, continuing to manifest heightened output after most other muscles and other response systems no longer manifest any output to a given stimulus.

John A. Stern

Statogram and Statometric Technique

Statogram or statometric technique is a method of measuring interindividual relations in face-to-face groups. The method has evolved in a series of Benjamin B. Wolman's experimental studies, and its rationale has been applied to classification of mental disorders (Wolman 1965).

The Rationale
The underlying conceptual system is related to the way people perceive one another and their motiva-

tion in social relations. According to Wolman's power and acceptance theory, people view each other in two dimensions, namely the strong-weak (power) dimension and the friendly-hostile (acceptance) dimension. The terms *strong* and *weak*, respectively, indicate the ability or lack of ability to satisfy needs. The peak of power is omnipotence and immortality; the bottom of weakness is death. The terms *friendly* and *hostile*, respectively, indicate productive or destructive attitudes.

The power and acceptance theory distinguishes four types of social attitudes, one hostile and three friendly. The hostile attitude leads to hurting, damaging, and, in extreme cases, destroying the object or organism at which it is directed. The friendly attitudes lead to cooperation, helping, and protecting the object or organism toward which they are directed.

Wolman linked the levels of friendliness to the degrees of power. Hostility originates in the fear of being annihilated; threatened organisms fight for survival, and their defensive or offensive aggressiveness stems from fear of death by being eaten (defensive) or of having nothing to eat (offensive). Hungry animals and hungry people fight for survival.

Experimental Studies
In a series of experimental studies, Wolman has developed the statometric method, which measures power, acceptance, leadership, and leadership rating. The statometric power quotient is

$$PQ = \frac{(\Sigma S \times NS - \Sigma W \times NW) \times 100}{(N-1)^3}$$

N is the number of members, $(N-1)^2$ is the maximum possible sum of all scores, NS is the number of members who give positive power ratings, S is the sum of positive scores of power, NW is the number of members who give negative ratings, and W is the sum of these ratings. PQ is the sum of scores actually received, multiplied by the number of people who give them, divided on the maximum possible score, divided on number of members, and multiplied by a hundred. The PQ is the absolute quotient of power. It ranges from -100 to $+100$ in all groups.

The statogram measures attitudes and reflective

social positions within face-to-face groups. Wolman hypothesizes that relationship factors, such as morale, leadership, group cohesiveness, and so on, are greatly influenced by the nature of the group; for example, in an instrumental group, that is, a group comprised of people whose aim is to benefit themselves by their group membership, the most powerful individual is likely to become their leader. In a mutual type of a group, acceptance might be of no less significance than power. In a vectorial group, such as a religious missionary or another group of individuals willing to sacrifice themselves for the sake of their ideals, power and devotion to the goal acquire special significance.

Benjamin B. Wolman

Stimulus-Response Theories in Social Psychology

Stimulus-response (S-R) theories in social psychology tend to use the individual, and not the group, as the major unit of analysis. Regardless of the nature of the particular problem, be it cultural differences or group structure, the S-R analysis will still focus on the behavior of the individual within the collective aggregate and not on the group itself. And, finally, despite important theoretical differences regarding the question of how rewards and punishments work and in definitions of reinforcement, S-R theories make use of the law of effect in their explanations of social behavior.

Albert Bandura (1973) has reconsidered the role of cognitive and "higher mental" processes for a more complete account of human behavior and, thus, appears to be approaching a theoretical position taken earlier by learning theorists, such as Edward C. Tolman (1932) and John Seward (1956), who considered both stimulus-stimulus (S-S) as well as S-R relationships.

Another direction taken by social psychologists as they have continued to explore the phenomena of suggestion and imitation has been to focus on the reality of the group as an entity, which could be studied on its own terms and on group processes. Propositions explicitly phrased in S, O, and R terms have been offered by R. R. Sears (1951), for example, who tackled social interaction, and J. S. Adams and A. K. Romney (1959), who have discussed authority relationships.

Albert J. Lott has attempted to relate group cohesiveness to general behavior theory (A. J. Lott and B. E. Lott 1965) and has defined cohesiveness as that group property that can be inferred from the number and strength of mutual positive attitudes among the group's members.

Perhaps the most significant and potentially far-reaching contribution that S-R theory has made to social psychology has been in the area of attitudes. In 1947, L. W. Doob argued that attitudes should be expected to be acquired in the same way as other habits and should be interpretable in S-R terms.

Research on communication and persuasion, originating with the Yale experiments conducted under the leadership of Carl Hovland, has also been influenced by S-R theory in general and the S-R interpretation of attitudes in particular.

Bernice Lott

Stimulus Substitution

Gregory A. Kimble's stimulus substitution theory is a theory of classical conditioning, the basic process of which is simply that the conditioned stimulus (CS) takes the place of the unconditioned stimulus (US) in the elicitation of the response that gets conditioned. The basic stumbling block for this theory has always been that the unconditioned responses (UR) are almost never identical in any conditioning situation.

Gregory A. Kimble

Stogdill, Ralph M. (1904–1978)

Research on leadership was Ralph M. Stogdill's principal interest. His major volume was the *Handbook of Leadership: A Survey of Theory and Research*.

Virginia Staudt Sexton

Strachey, James (1887–1967)

James Strachey was one of the founding members of the British Psycho-Analytic Society. He was the editor and translator of the *Standard Edition of the Complete Psychological Works of Sigmund Freud.*

M. Masud R. Khan

Structuralism

Structuralism, Edward Bradford Titchener's extension of Wilhelm Wundt's content psychology, emphasizes the organization of facts concerning the generalized, normal, human adult mind, with *mind* defined as the sum total of experience from birth to the present moment. Titchener's aim, like that of Wundt before him, was to analyze experience into its simplest definable components and to determine the mode of connection among these components in the complex forms that experience comes to us. The primary tool of the structuralist is introspection. Titchener's structuralism differs from Wundt's content psychology in many ways, but particularly in that the structural system brings all of the basic categories into play at the level of the attributes.

The structural position, at least in the early period, was basically elementaristic, and in separating meaning from the facts of experience, it set itself in direct opposition to the phenomenological tradition of Franz Clemens Brentano's act psychology and to the Gestalt psychologists, as well as to the American functionalists. The concentration of study on the generalized adult mind also set structuralism in opposition to John Broadus Watson's behaviorism.

Rand B. Evans

Study of Values

The Allport-Vernon-Lindzey Study of Values (1970) was first published in 1931 and has since been reviewed twice. The test was based upon Eduard Spranger's (1928) theory that all humans may be classified into types based upon the values that are preeminent in their lives. Spranger postulated that there are six basic types of people. These types are: (1) the theoretical person, who is primarily concerned with the discovery of truth and order, and with systematizing knowledge; (2) the economic, who is interested in what is useful and practical, and in wealth rather than power; (3) the aesthetic, who is interested in form and harmony, and in the appearance rather than the substance of things; (4) the social, who is altruistic, loves people, and sees people as ends in themselves; (5) the political, who is concerned with personal power, influence, and renown; and (6) the religious, whose highest value is unity, and who is concerned with the creation of the highest and most absolutely satisfying value experience.

Clifford H. Swensen

Suicide: An Overview

The approach of Western civilization to the topic of suicide has been overshadowed by Christian doctrine. Although neither the Old nor the New Testament directly forbids suicide, church elders, perhaps in a move to counteract the excessive penchant for martyrdom and suicide of the early Christians, decreed suicide either a crime or a sin associated with a crime. Saint Augustine (354–430) categorically rejected suicide and labeled it as a crime because it precluded the possibility of repentance and because it violated the Sixth Commandment relating to killing.

Quite apart from its emotional states, suicide manifests three important psychological characteristics.

Transitoriness. The acute suicidal crisis (or period of high and dangerous lethality) is a period of relatively short duration.

Ambivalence. The psychodynamic heart of the suicidal act is ambivalence; the characteristic suicidal sound is the cry for help; the prototypical suicidal act is to cut one's throat and plead for help (and to fantasize rescue and intervention) at the same moment.

Dyadic relationship. Most suicidal events (as is the

case with death in general) are dyadic; that is, they involve two persons. This characteristic of suicide has two phases: the first, during the prevention of suicide, when one has to deal with the "significant other," and the second, in the aftermath of the committed suicide, when one has to deal with the survivor-victim.

Prevention. If one believes that suicidal phenomena are existential, social, psychological, and/or dyadic events, then obviously, primary prevention is enormously complicated—almost tantamount to preventing human unhappiness. Some students of human nature believe that the urge for self-destruction is ubiquitous and perhaps an inevitable price of civilization, if not of life itself.

Postvention. This term refers to actions taken to mollify the aftereffects on a person who has attempted suicide or to deal with the adverse effects on the survivor of a person who has committed suicide. It includes work with the surviving children, parents, and spouses.

Edwin S. Shneidman

Suicide Prevention

Epidemiological studies have identified some groups of persons as notably high suicide risks: (1) the aged, (2) university students, (3) the mentally ill, (4) alcohol- and drug-dependent persons, (5) residents of socially disorganized areas, (6) the socially isolated, (7) offspring from broken homes, and (8) specific occupational groups.

The aged. In the instance of the aged, the broad possibilities of prevention focus upon economic, social, welfare, and medical services to counteract the effects of reduced income, social isolation, loss of occupational and social roles, and declining physical and mental health.

The mentally ill. In Gardner Murphy's study of sixty persons who were under the care of seventy-one physicians within six months or less before committing suicide, the diagnosis of depression was rarely made and seldom treated, and only 40% of the physicians were aware of the suicidal histories of their patients and their high risk.

Alcohol and drug abuse. Alcohol and drug abuse considerably heighten the risk that suicide will be the outcome. At the very least, one would expect that vigorous treatment efforts directed at each of these elements would reduce significantly the danger of suicide.

The vast majority of suicide prevention centers do not provide treatment as such, but they share two very crucial operating principles: around-the-clock help should be available to persons in crisis, and the workers should be able to respond to the person in crisis with competency and resourcefulness. The key to prevention is early recognition and prompt, appropriate intervention (Mathew Ross 1967).

Problems in the hospital management of suicidal patients are often amenable to the observance of fairly overt, straightforward precautions, which include knowing patients' whereabouts at all times; supervised access to potentially dangerous objects; safeguard screens on windows; securing closets, storage, and other areas from patient entry; monitoring of visitors' gift items; and enlisting the assistance of other patients, visitors, and all staff in observation and monitoring.

Mathew Ross

Sullivan, Harry Stack (1892–1949)

Harry Stack Sullivan developed the interpersonal theory of psychiatry, the interpersonal treatment method, and a theory of schizophrenia. In 1933 Sullivan organized the William Alanson White Psychiatric Foundation, and he was also responsible for the foundation's opening of the Washington School of Psychiatry in 1936. Starting in 1938, Sullivan edited the foundation's journal, *Psychiatry.* Sullivan published *Conceptions of Modern Psychiatry* (1947), *The Interpersonal Theory of Psychiatry* (1953), *Schizophrenia as a Human Process* (1962), *The Fusion of Psychiatry and Social Science* (1964), and other books.

Ralph M. Crowley

Sullivan's Interpersonal Theory

Harry Stack Sullivan defined psychiatry as the field of interpersonal relations. He attempted to establish a broad observational platform for the study and treatment of "difficulties in living." He rejected the conventional designation of mental disorder as a disease, except for the outcomes of distinct hereditary components. Sullivan considered the individual not as a fixed entity but rather as a part of a person-to-person encounter. This point of view constitutes a new dimension in the fields of psychiatry and psychoanalysis.

The Interpersonal Dyad

The elaboration of personal experience moves to the foreground of our interest, replacing our former predominant search for intrapsychic conflicts of id and ego forces. Metapsychological constructs as explanatory props recede into the background. In Sullivan's frame of reference, the therapist becomes an integral part of the teamwork between two responsible individuals. A new model emerges, which is more specifically anchored in the therapist's relational participation. It leads to a more open-ended communication, with a personal resonance. The therapist listens to the patient and makes occasional comments about what she has heard, which opens the door for reciprocal observations within the context of the therapeutic situation. There have been significant modifications in the interpersonal dyad since Sullivan's interpersonal point of view, which he presented more than 50 years ago.

Sullivan's interpersonal approach assumes that any method of observation alters the object being observed. Every human being has a repertoire of personal reactions, which depend on reciprocal reactions of others, and these personal reactions can be traced back to early family dynamics (the network of family relationships). As Sullivan said, "People have as many personalities as they have relationships with important others in their life." This important other can be a real person or an eidetic person who had been transposed from the past, as if he were identical to the person encountered in the present. Personality characteristics become evident mainly in an ongoing interpersonal process, which has its roots in the earlier years and which throws its shadow onto the imminent future. This means, of course, that the future as well as the past participate in all human relationships of the present.

It is important to note that within the interpersonal approach the individual is never central in her relationship to the world. The notion of the individual self as a unique individual, a notion highly prized by most people, is considered to be an illusion. The notion that uniqueness is an illusion does not contradict the assumption that each individual has her own internal world, or possesses a native or learned special talent, unique fingerprints, or other special characteristics. Interpersonal theory simply rejects the assumption that the unique individual self has a particular impact on the person-to-person encounter. Instead, interpersonal thinking stresses the manifold unfolding of relatedness that is observable in a me/you encounter. The self is understood as a screen that reflects the impressions and valuations that other people have of us; it reflects the appraisals one has experienced in the eyes of others or that one thinks one has seen in the eyes of others. The self can be considered as that aspect of the personality that is central in experiencing anxiety that stems from the dynamics within the family. Anxiety is important in terms of the self, because it has to do with the perceived opinion of others.

To summarize: There is no longer justification for considering the self as the center of existence. It is likely that the self is not essential to the understanding of human behavior, just as it was erroneous to view the ether as an integral element of the sky.

The Background of Interpersonal Theory

Theories have roots in a variety of sciences. Interpersonal theory builds on the sociological formulations of George Herbert Mead, who wrote the classic text *Mind, Society and Self*. Here, Mead makes it clear that everyone is imprinted by a generalized other; that no one can think of himself without including others in his thoughts; and that language, culture, and society are constantly in a reciprocal relationship where they intermingle with and penetrate one another. Thought, society, and self depend on one another and cannot be separated out. J. M. Baldwin,

C. H. Cooley, and John Dewey had similar thoughts. The philosophical ideology represented by these thinkers is that of pragmatism, which is a typically American ideology. Pragmatism always asks what is best or what works, not why. Others who thought along the same lines are the linguist Edward Sapir, the anthropologist Ruth Benedict, and the philosopher Alfred North Whitehead. Sullivan is the only native American who has significantly contributed to analytic theory, and this is important to remember, because it is responsible for a specific New World cultural view.

The question is often asked whether Sullivan considered himself a psychiatrist or a psychoanalyst. He himself preferred to talk about psychiatry as a more appropriate medium for his multidisciplinary, interpersonal point of view. Sigmund Freud, Mead, and Adolf Meyer were his initial mentors. Their influence was combined with his personal interest in the natural sciences.

Sullivan's leitmotif concerning modern psychiatry was that "in most general terms we are all much more simply human than otherwise, be we happy and successful, contented and detached, miserable and mentally disordered or whatever."

Sullivan's scaffolding for interpersonal psychiatry centers on a dichotomy between satisfaction and security.

Developmental Stages

According to Sullivan, every developmental stage comes to an end when new capabilities have developed, which have been fostered by the fruitful participation of the human environment. The capacity and the readiness of the person and the sensitive encouragement of the environment all come into play so that the new capability can emerge. Maturation is always an interaction between something innate and the encouragement and responsiveness of a sensitive other. It is a time-appropriate combination of inner and outer elements. The following is a very short summary of the developmental stages:

1. *infancy* (up to the second year), until the development of language
2. *childhood* (second to fifth year), until the capacity to play with other children

3. the *juvenile* (sixth to ninth year), playing by the rules, cooperation, and competition, until the capacity for intimacy arises

Stages 1 to 3 include the capacity to love another; the child is totally dependent on her family and is not yet able to freely choose a love object.

4. *prepuberty*, until the development of identity and sexuality. One can see oneself through the eyes of a friend, one can exchange impressions about self and the world, and one can see parents and friends in a different light. Experience is in the syntactic mode, and consensual validation is possible.
5. *puberty,* until the capacity for heterosexual, meaningful experience arises
6. *adult maturity*

The Ecological Principle

Ecology is concerned with the relationship of the organism to its environment in a biological sense; it studies how organism and environment interact and are dependent on one another. Ecology also deals with human relationships to social institutions, with special recognition of the fact that the individual is deeply embedded in his total milieu and that there is a reciprocal relationship between humankind and nature.

The following is an example of the biological aspect of ecology: oxygen is everywhere in the atmosphere, life is totally dependent on it. While one breathes in, oxygen comes into the body, while one breathes out, carbon dioxide leaves the body. There is very little capacity in the body to store oxygen, and life is dependent on the eternal, never-interrupted exchange of oxygen and carbon dioxide. It is impossible to say what is inside and what is outside.

Ecological principle in psychiatry states that every human being needs a continual, never-ending exchange with others in order to remain a human being (this lack is sensory deprivation).

Isolation from meaningful human relationships is similar to severe psychopathology. The necessity for the repeated exchange with others is seen as a basic human requirement—similar to an instinct. If such an exchange is not experienced and felt, loneliness results. Basic human qualities have to be continually renewed in repeated, steady exchanges with a constructive human environment.

The Anxiety Principle

According to Sullivan, anxiety is a totally psychological experience that has no organic basis. It is interpersonal and does not have a biological structure. All other tensions can be resolved through energy transformations, but not the tension of anxiety. To the contrary, anxiety takes precedence over all other tensions and complicates their resolution or deintensification.

In the presence of anxiety, learning from experience is not possible. Anxiety controls awareness in that the important factors that have called out the anxiety remain outside the awareness of the person. That is also the reason why it is impossible to recall the actual events that were experienced under the influence of anxiety. Anxiety isolates the person from all possibility of contacts with others and goes counter to any sense of self-esteem or feeling of interpersonal security. According to Sullivan, anxiety is transmitted by the mother.

The Principle of Similarity

Similarities between human beings are always more important than differences. Something connects people to one another that is stronger than the individual difficulties, and it is this common bond that allows for therapeutic contact.

Mental illness is not an illness but a way of being, the result of relationships to important others that were charged with anxiety. Difficulties in living are due to things that went wrong in relationships to important others in the developmental years. The difficulties can be seen in timing and inadequate judgments in a given situation.

The Tenderness Principle

The word "love" is too often misused. Tenderness is a special sense of care for another person.

The needs of the child elicit tender feelings in the mother, who then can supply the necessary conditions for an anxiety-free mother-child relationship. For instance, when the child is hungry, the mother understands the message of the child. The hunger is expressed as tension by the child, and the mother reacts to the tension with tenderness. The child then reacts to the mother's availability and acceptance of her needs with a healthy appetite, and the mother reacts with a sense of happiness. In other words, the result is a happy chain reaction. The opposite happens when this reaction does not work.

Psychiatric and psychoanalytic theories cannot remain stagnant. They have to be transcended in the long run without necessarily discarding some points of view. Sullivan significantly contributed to the expansion of our way of working in an egalitarian milieu.

Gerard Chrzanowski

Sullivan's Therapeutic Conceptions

Harry Stack Sullivan was very concerned with seriously disturbed patients. He dedicated himself to working with schizophrenic patients. To him, schizophrenia—with few exceptions—was not an illness as such, but a particular human process. His attitude about severe mental disorders can be found in his statement, "Far more than any single act of the therapist it is the general attitude toward the patient which determines his value" (Sullivan 1962). Transference phenomena are also of importance in relieving the introversion of mental life of the patient.

For psychiatric inpatients, Sullivan recommended that the mental hospital should be an educational setting for personal growth for therapists as well as patients, rather than a custodian of personality failure.

According to Sullivan, the purpose of psychiatry is the understanding and facilitation of living. His therapeutic endeavors have predominantly been concerned with multiple manifestations of anxiety. It was his belief that every patient has to be educated to manifestations of anxiety within himself; the quality of the voice, change in theme, hypersensitivity, a particular variety of noninvolvement (apathy), unnecessary argumentativeness, selective inattention, somnolent detachment, and exaggerated anger are all signs of threatening anxiety. Sullivan was convinced that meaningful human contact in the presence of anxiety is essentially impossible, and that it is in the nature of the experience of anxiety that experiences in the presence of anxiety can never be totally conscious. One can only remember what happened prior to the presence of anxiety.

Loneliness takes on particular importance; the need for contact is as basic to human nature as sleep, hunger, thirst, and sexuality. Sullivan believed that meaningful human contact is essential for all human beings and that total aloneness is basically the same as mental illness. Humans have only a limited capacity to "store" experiences of contact. They need repeated exchanges with others to remain human. Isolation from the mainstream of life is at the core of mental disorders.

Anxiety is one of the most frightening experiences. Only loneliness can be more terrifying; loneliness will motivate a person to seek contact with another despite the presence of high anxiety.

The experience of loneliness takes on different forms at different times in the life cycle, and it appears in infants, toddlers, children, and juveniles, and during puberty and adulthood. The necessity of being with others, which when unfulfilled is experienced as loneliness, is seen first in the need to be held and physically touched. A bit later the child wants to play next to and with other children or engage in competitive activity with her friends. Then comes the wish to have a friend, male or female. The next stage leads to the wish for intimacy, then to sexuality, and finally, to cooperation with others for the good of all.

Sullivan was ahead of his time when he stated that, "the acceleration of social progress has become so great that almost every psychiatrist has some occasion to realize that the first viewpoint is too narrow."

Sullivan coined a number of terms that have particular clinical impact, among them *somnolent detachment*. He made a particular distinction between this term and the conventional term *apathy*. Both describe distancing phenomena in interpersonal relatedness. According to Sullivan, apathy is related to essential needs and requirements, while somnolent detachment is a safety device against undesired anxiety in a particular interpersonal setting. The phenomenon of somnolent detachment

can manifest in the patient as well as in the therapist. It can also come to the fore in daily life.

Clara Thompson who had a lifetime friendship with Sullivan, pointed out that Sullivan's first therapeutic contacts were with psychotic patients. He only later became interested in the vicissitudes of neurotic, obsessional, and character disorders.

Sullivan devoted his research and clinical observations to applying psychoanalytic constructs to the therapy of the psychotic. Carl Jung and Eugen Bleuler before him had found psychoanalytic tenets applicable in dealing with the behavior and symbolization of psychotic patients. The general professional viewpoint was that psychoanalysis was not an appropriate method of treatment for psychotic patients. It was erroneously believed that psychotic patients are restricted in following the basic rule of saying what comes to mind and cannot handle transference. Among others, Frieda Fromm-Reichman, a classic psychoanalyst who worked intensively with psychotic patients and in tandem with Clara Thompson, supported Sullivan's clinical approach.

Sullivan and Schizophrenia

Sullivan's perceptivity about schizophrenia as well as his ability as a teacher have been recorded in *A Harry Stack Sullivan Case Seminar: Treatment of a Young Male Schizophrenic* (1976).

Sullivan conducted a five-session seminar for the psychiatric residents at Shepard-Pratt Hospital (1946–47). The emphasis was on a young male schizophrenic who was being treated by Dr. Kwarnes, then a participant resident. The publication of the seminar was added to other posthumous publications, *Schizophrenia as a Human Process* (1962) and *The Fusion of Psychiatry and Social Science* (1964).

The text is somewhat difficult to read, because Sullivan would follow two or three different tracks simultaneously. His main purpose as a supervisor and teacher was to focus on data about a particular sense of communication and participant observation in responding to the patient.

According to Sullivan, in working with deeply troubled patients as well as less troubled ones the procedure of choice is to use not interpretations in the classical style but queries.

Sullivan addressed himself to clinical entities as a frame of reference in therapy. He expressed some reservations about discussing therapeutic approaches in terms of clinical entities, but believed that they do have some purely pragmatic utility.

Sullivan was very much more interested in what can be done about the patient, without particular reference to any specific diagnosis. He preferred an approach based on two frames of reference. The first is the careful viewing of each case in terms of the severity of difficulties in living, with attention to evidence that the patient has demonstrated a capacity to meet difficult or unusually complex situations. Such evidence may prove to be helpful in regard to the prognosis.

The second frame of reference addresses itself to information from the patient about particular assets she possesses, which could open the door to therapeutic opportunities.

Sullivan brought to psychiatry as well as to psychoanalysis a fresh perspective. His compassion for troubled human beings and respect for the underdog were distinct assets.

Gerard Chrzanowski

Summation

A compound stimulus is one that contains two or more stimulus elements (i.e., a compound of light and tone). The term *summation* refers to a procedure in which stimulus elements that are conditioned separately are tested in compound. The summation procedure is typically used to measure excitatory and inhibitory stimulus control.

Summation refers to a procedure in which stimulus elements exhibiting excitatory or inhibitory stimulus control are combined. This combination can produce either suppression or enhancement of the response rate, depending upon the nature of the effects that are being summated. Suppression occurs when inhibitory and excitatory effects are summated; and enhancement occurs when two excitatory effects are summated.

Arthur Gutman

Superego

Although Sigmund Freud alluded to many of the components of the superego almost from the beginning of his theorizing about the human psyche, it was not until about 1923 that he combined them within a single entity, which he called the "superego." The ego was conceived of as a differentiated portion of the id modified through experience with the outer world, and the superego was conceptualized as a portion of the ego that has been further modified by experiences with significant human beings, especially parents and parent substitutes.

The superego is formed through the process of introjection. Introjection is the psychic analogue of ingestion, digestion, and assimilation. It describes the phenomenon by which individuals incorporate parts of the external world into their psyches and make them part of themselves. The superego is a precipitate formed in the ego, which consists of the introjected imagoes of other persons with whom an individual has had an intense interaction. Naturally, the earliest and most significant superego introjects will consist of parent imagoes or those of parent substitutes.

The forerunners of the superego are undoubtedly laid down early in life by the internalization of parental prohibitions, especially with regard to cleanliness training. Through the process of identification, the child essays to be like his parents and to do the things his parents do. Prohibitions are accepted as part of living up to parental standards and ideals. The child begins to experience conflicts between what he would like to do and what he now perceives he "ought" to do.

Along with the dissolution of the Oedipus complex, the parents are abandoned as possible sexual objects and the incest taboo is internalized. Sexual desires directed at other family members must be repressed, and only the affectionate components of love are permitted to find expression. The ego-ideal or superego has the task of effecting these repressions. Indeed, Freud says, it is to that revolutionary event that the superego owes its existence.

The parents are the original obstacles to the realization of oedipal wishes, and the superego falls heir to this task. Freud says that the differentiation of the superego from the ego is one of the most important events in the development of the individual and of culture: "Indeed, by giving permanent expression to the influence of the parents, the superego perpetuates the existence of the factors to which it owes its origins."

Arnold Bernstein

Superstitious Behavior

A reinforcing stimulus (e.g., food for a hungry rat) will strengthen the behavior that it follows. Thus, if the experimenter wants to strengthen the rat's lever press, he will make the food contingent upon this response. However, the reinforcer is, in a sense, fickle, for it tends to strengthen any behavior that it follows, and not just that behavior intended by the experimenter. Superstitious behavior refers to a stereotyped pattern of behavior that emerges as a function of adventitious (i.e., accidental) reinforcement.

Superstitious behavior can be explained as follows. Some will not walk under a ladder, whereas others will. Told that walking under a ladder is dangerous, some will believe it, others not. Thus, those who do not believe it will walk under the ladder and, surprisingly, survive. For those who do believe it, the ladder is a stimulus to be feared. By avoiding the ladder the fear is reduced, and the avoidance behavior is reinforced. Thus, the avoidance behavior is strengthened merely because of belief in avoided calamity by avoiding the ladder.

Arthur Gutman

Surgery and Psychiatry

Diagnosis and the recommendation for surgery evoke three types of stress or threat of stress. The first is loss: loss of time, loss of closeness with family and others, loss of strength and competence, and loss of control of the self, culminating in the feeling of helplessness and need for total care by others. Next is attack on the body from the surgeon's knife, the intruding instruments, tubes, even invisible X-rays, and from drugs and anesthetics, which take

the body away from the possession by the self. Third is restraint—having to stay in the hospital, in bed, possibly strapped to a table, bound by instruments, tubes, catheters, and associated paraphernalia, traction apparatus, and plaster casts.

Postoperative depression is evident in sadness, withdrawal, apathy, facial expression, and other bodily communication, and often in physical pain, which expresses and replaces the emotional pain. This mood is principally a response to loss as a result of the surgical treatment. It may be the loss of a body part, or a strong belief that an important object relationship will be impaired. The sense of irreparable loss may develop from the experience of separation from a parent, spouse, family, work, or friends during the time in the hospital and of feeling alone and abandoned.

In addition to the frightening, nearly fatal stress event, most patients in traumatic surgery present disorganization of mental functioning, an aspect of traumatic neurosis from which the patient must recover by a reorganizing process during surgical treatment. Loss of others in the accident responsible for the patient's injury may be a factor.

James L. Titchener

Sydenham, Thomas (1624–1689)

Thomas Sydenham identified diseases as separate entities. He asserted that hysteria and hypochondriasis are disturbances of the animal spirits, and he established them as afflictions of the mind.

John C. Burnham

Systematic Desensitization

Systematic desensitization is a therapeutic technique for reducing irrational anxiety, which was evolved in its present form by Joseph Wolpe (1958). It is one of the best-known, most widely used, and most intensively researched methods of behavior therapy. The technique involves the following basic procedural elements: training the client in the skill of progressive muscle relaxation; the construction of a hierarchy of increasingly more fear-arousing stimulus situations; and systematically instructing the client to imagine scenes from the hierarchy while deeply relaxed.

Systematic desensitization has been used successfully in treating an impressive diversity of irrational fears and avoidance behaviors, including phobias, compulsions, sexual aversion, psychophysiological disorders, and interpersonal problems.

Systematic desensitization is dependent on the client's cooperation and attention, ability to visualize hierarchy items, and facility in relaxing. Symbolic representation of fear-evoking stimuli cannot be used with clients who do not conjure up sufficiently clear imagery, who fail to react emotionally to imagined scenes, or who experience "runaway imagery," that is, are unable to switch scenes on and off as the procedure requires.

Examples of the efficacy of systematic desensitization include well-controlled comparative outcome research, which has demonstrated that systematic desensitization is significantly more effective than either psychotherapy or attention-placebo treatment conditions in reducing public-speaking anxiety across a variety of behavioral, physiological, and subjective outcome measures.

In another exemplary outcome study of the treatment of outpatient phobic clients, including severe agoraphobics, M. G. Gelder et al. (1973) have found that both systematic desensitization and flooding produce more improvement than a stringent placebo-control treatment condition. Gains were maintained at a 6-month follow-up across multiple outcome measures, without any evidence of symptom substitution. Numerous other controlled studies have established the efficacy of systematic desensitization in the treatment of sexual dysfunction, asthma, acrophobia, and small animal and snake phobias.

G. Terence Wilson

· T ·

Teleology

Most psychologies have either eliminated purpose as a final cause of conduct or have attempted to account for apparent purposiveness in other ways. However, the position of William McDougall was avowedly a purposive psychology. Edward C. Tolman, who called his system a "purposive behaviorism," also saw ends or goals as a most significant basis for conduct. *Purpose*, *goal*, and *intent*, closely related terms, all share something of the meaning of teleology.

Charles N. Cofer

Terman, Lewis M. (1877–1956)

Lewis M. Terman was a pioneer in intelligence and achievement testing in the United States. In 1916, he introduced the Standard Revision of the Binet-Simon scale of intelligence, which was then named the Stanford-Binet Intelligence Test. He also published the National Intelligence Test, the Terman Group Test of Mental Ability, and the Stanford Achievement Tests. Terman's *Genetic Studies of Genius* was published in five volumes (1925–1959).

Richard M. Lerner

Termination of Psychoanalysis

Most of the contributions to the literature on termination advise flexible use of multiple criteria in adaptive, topographical, structural, and transference terms. A multifaceted paradigm for termination criteria could be: Symptoms have been traced to their genetic sources, the investigation yielding insight into the nature of the infantile neurosis; the symptoms have been eliminated or rendered controllable and tolerable; object relations have altered as their burdening transference distortions have been reduced.

Assessment of the state of the transference occupies one of the leading positions among the cluster of criteria. By the time termination is on the analytic agenda, the patient should have become able to relate to the analyst in a realistic, undistorted manner.

The analyst must not confuse "treatment goals," attainable within a reasonable time frame, with "life goals," requiring much longer to achieve (Ticho 1972). The analyst's personal investment in success with a particular patient (worries about stability of outcome, indisposition to part from a particular patient) and fear of having unused treatment time need to be monitored closely to preclude their interfering with termination judgment.

The question is raised as to what to do when patient and analyst do *not* agree that their collaboration should end. In instances when there is a sense of stalemate, there is precedent for intervention by the analyst to unilaterally set a date, hoping thereby to press beyond the stalemate.

During the termination phase, one group of analysts favors "weaning" the patient by decreasing session frequency. Contrariwise, others maintain the fundamental rule until the last minute of the final hour.

During termination, the therapeutic alliance remains as during the earlier period of analysis or shows improvement. Affects related to termination may be of many kinds—anxiety, rage, depression, guilt, sadness, but also relief, joy, and avidity for new experiences. It should be borne in mind that the analyst also experiences some strong affects, such as loss at separation from a patient with whom she has worked with satisfaction. At times, under the stress of termination, transference manifestations in the form of negative, derogatory attacks may be relaxed: the opening of the "exit door" reassures the patient who until then has feared that positive transference affects might become unbearably intense.

L. Rangell (1966) offers two cautions regarding the behavior of the analyst toward his former patient during the posttermination period. One is against undue retention of a now-inappropriate analytic stance. The second, at the opposite pole, is against a premature social relationship, which may register with the ex-analysand as seductively overstimulating.

Stephen K. Firestein

Terrorism: Self-Righteous Violence

At all times and in all civilizations people have craved omnipotence and immortality. The idea of God as the personification of human craving has been imbued with omnipotence and immortality. God does not need food or shelter, nor can he be attacked or hurt; but human beings are vulnerable to hunger, thirst, and hostility. Thus, their main concern is to stay alive. Survival is the main objective of all living matter, and its psychological corollary is the drive for power (defined as the ability to satisfy the basic needs).

Many people are unable and/or unwilling to control their power and act violently. In many cases, violent behavior is an impulsive expression of anger, but often it is a cold and calculated act directed against objects, animals, and people—sometimes against oneself. Not always is it an expression of hatred; people who slaughter cattle do not hate them; they "love" to eat them. Burglars, kidnappers, rapists, muggers, and other violent criminals do not necessarily hate their victims; bank robbers do not resent the banks. Violence can be practiced for gain or for self-aggrandizement.

Obviously, not all violent acts are perpetrated by mentally disturbed individuals, but mental disorder,

being a regressive process, facilitates the rule of Ares and increases the inclination toward violent behavior. Practically, all schizophrenics are inclined to violent behavior directed against themselves or against others. Paranoid schizophrenics tend to believe that someone hates them and/or conspires against them, thus giving them the "right" to defend themselves and/or "punish" their imaginary persecutors.

Some of the worst crimes against humanity were performed under the guise of high moral standards espoused by a rigid superego. This channeling of intrapsychic hostility into social hostility is one of the outstanding symptoms of the schizoid characters, as fear of their own hostility is transformed into a compulsive pursuit of a self-righteous and dictatorial justice. Some self-appointed dictators and terrorist leaders are schizoid types, but some are just selfish and self-righteous sociopaths who exploit others and hate those who resist being exploited.

Sociopaths are cruel to those who fear them, but they are obedient and subservient to those they fear. They torture and mutilate their victims because cruelty enhances their feeling of power. Sociopaths tend to believe that their victims are guilty, and that they are provoked to act in self-defense.

The history of religious and social movements supplies abundant evidence of the widespread tendency to impose one's will upon others. In most cases the imposers successfully practiced brainwashing, and usually their acts of violence were justified by allegedly lofty ideals they themselves seemed to believe in.

People who feel secure, that is, who have a high estimate of their power, are not inclined to overdo in using their power, nor do they have the need to prove that they are strong. People who doubt their strength, however, have the need to overassert themselves and to act aggressively.

People whose lives are hollow tend to follow. People who have nothing to believe in grasp for straws of phony salvation. People who have nothing to strive for blindly follow cult leaders, pseudosaints, and gang leaders, who promise a future paradise. Many young people today seek escape in alcohol and drugs; others join antisocial cults and terrorist groups.

Violent behavior is older than the human race. It

cannot be cured, but it must be restrained. When well-wishing and liberal people unwittingly condone violence, they take part in the destruction of the democratic social and political system and, with it, the entire civilization.

Civilization started when God or wise people said, "Thou shalt not." Whoever allows people to act in an uninhibited manner encourages a Hitler, a Stalin, an Idi Amin, a Khomeini, or anyone else—no matter what their slogans are.

Benjamin B. Wolman

Test Construction

Achievement Tests

The achievement test is the most obvious example of a measure that requires content validity. The term *achievement test* will be used in a general sense to refer to (1) examinations in individual courses of instruction in schools of all kinds and at all levels; (2) standardized measures of achievement used routinely by all the instructors in a particular unit of instruction; (3) commercially distributed tests of achievement used throughout the country. The major part of the test plan is an outline of content for the test that is to be constructed. Because the content validity depends on a rational appeal to an adequate coverage of important content, an explicit outline of content provides a basis for discussing content validity.

In addition to outlining content, the plan should describe the types of items to be employed, state the approximate number of items to be employed in each section and each subsection of the test, and give examples of the types of items to be used. The plan should also state how long the test will take to administer, how it will be administered, how it will be scored, and the types of norms that will be obtained.

Although content validity rests mainly on rational rather than empirical grounds, results from applying an instrument do provide some important types of information. Large-scale investigations are undertaken for important achievement tests. In contrast, the individual instructor may not seek such information at all or may obtain it only incidentally. The first

step in obtaining such information is to administer a large collection of items to a large sample of persons who are representative of the individuals with whom the final test will be employed. To have ample room to discard items that work poorly, there should be at least twice as many items as will appear on the final test.

High-Speed Ability Tests

In their purest form, speed tests consist of items of trivial difficulty. That is, most subjects would get most of the items correct if they were given ample time to perform. By "trivial difficulty" is meant a p value (fraction of subjects getting the item correct) of 0.95 or higher when items are administered under power conditions. One type of item that fulfills this requirement is the simple problem in addition or subtraction.

In a speed test, the average correlation between items is directly related to the amount of time alloted for taking the test. If subjects are given all the time they want, the p values of all items will be either 1.0 or close to that, and consequently the correlations between items will be either zero or close to zero. At the other extreme, if subjects are given practically no time for taking the test, the p values will all be zero or close to zero, and consequently the correlations between items will be near zero on the average. Between these two extremes of time limits, the average p values of items range from zero to 1.0.

As in the construction of all tests, the first step in the construction of a speed test is to develop an item pool. Usually, this is rather easily done because the items on speed tests are generally so simple that it is easy to compose them by the dozens. Constructing a speed test consists almost entirely in finding the time limit that will produce the most reliable distribution of total scores. The amount of experimentation required to find the ideal time limit depends on previous experience with employing time limits with the particular type of item.

Homogeneous Measures of Ability and Personality

The major theory of reliability assumes that each item is a random sample from a specified domain of content. Although the model holds when the domain contains items from different factors, it makes more sense when items from the domain share only one major factor. Eventually, it will be possible to understand the cardinal dimensions of human attributes only when relatively complete factor structures are known for different types of abilities and personality characteristics. The best measures of each factor will be those that correlate highly with one factor and have low correlations with other factors.

One cannot know for sure how many items should be constructed for a new measure until after they are constructed and submitted to item analysis. If the standard is to obtain a test with an internal consistency reliability of .80 (coefficient alpha in the general case, or KR-20 in the case of dichotomously scored items), item analysis might show that the desired reliability can be obtained with as few as twenty items, or that an many as eighty items are required. There are some rules of thumb that can be used to determine the number of items to be constructed. Usually twenty or thirty dichotomous items are required to obtain an internalconsistency reliability of .80.

In gathering data for item analysis, one should administer items under conditions that closely resemble those under which the eventual test will be used. If subjects in the tryout sample are given all the time that they want to complete the items, and one intends to place a severe time limit on the eventual test, an item analysis will probably provide very misleading information.

If items are selected purely in terms of item-total correlations, the success of this method depends on the investigator's ability initially to devise a scoring key that will make the majority of correlations between items positive. In most cases this is easily done.

In most bipolar item domains, it is not necessary to go through the iterative procedure described above. Usually, the investigator can intuit a scoring scheme that will make most correlations between items positive. This is usually easy to do with attitude scales, interest inventories, and most personality inventories. It might be necessary to go through one rekeying of the items, but seldom will it be necessary to repeat the process a number of times.

Jum C. Nunnally

Test Scores, Statistics and Norms

Test results are usually reported in some numerical form, for example, the total number of questions answered correctly on a true-false test. Such numbers are referred to as "raw scores." Raw scores are seldom directly meaningful without some qualification as to how well other persons do or the established standards of performance.

Measures of Variability

Before a particular deviation score can be correctly interpreted, it must be learned how widely the scores are scattered above and below the mean. A deviation score of 2.00 would represent superior performance if all the scores were closely packed about the mean. But, if there were deviation scores going as high as +100 and as low as −100, a deviation score 2.00 would indicate near-average performance. Consequently, in order to properly interpret particular deviations, an index is needed of the amount of variability of scores about the mean.

The range. There are various measures of the amount of variability of scores in a group (also called measures of scatter and measures of dispersion). One very simple index, the range, is obtained by subtracting the lowest score from the highest score.

The average deviation. An index of variability that is dependent on all the scores instead of just two of them and that indicates the position of an individual in a group is the average deviation (AD). As the name implies, it is obtained by finding how much the scores deviate on the average from the mean, as follows:

$$AD = \frac{\Sigma |x|}{N}$$

where the symbol $|x|$ indicates that absolute deviations are being considered, paying no attention to the positive or negative signs.

The standard deviation. The AD has a serious fault: it is based on absolute scores. It is very difficult to work mathematically with absolute scores; consequently, if the AD is used in some of the early statistical work, it severely limits the development of other measures.

An alternative to using either x scores or $|x|$ scores is to work with the squared deviations. These will all be positive, and it also happens that they provide an excellent starting place for the derivation of many other statistics.

The standard deviation and variance can be obtained without actually going through the step of converting from raw to deviation scores, as follows:

$$\sigma^2 = \frac{\Sigma(X\text{-}M)^2}{N}$$

$$\sigma^2 = \frac{\Sigma X^2}{N} - \left(\frac{\Sigma X}{N}\right)^2$$

Norms

The first step in obtaining norms for a test is to define a normative population. What population is defined depends on the interpretations that need to be made of scores. This may be all of the children in the United States (the normative population for most intelligence tests), or all the children in a particular school system (which would offer one basis for interpreting achievement tests).

Standard score norms. Norms are often expressed as either standard scores or transformed standard scores. The performance of the particular person is then compared with the mean score in the normative group and with the standard deviation found in the normative group. Nearly all commercially distributed tests have tables available to translate raw scores directly into standard scores and/or transformed standard scores.

Age norms. It sometimes is desirable to express norms in terms of children's ages. One such set of age norms could be obtained by testing the vocabulary of children at all ages from 4 to 12. For this purpose, a list of 100 words varying in difficulty could be used. The mean score could be obtained for each age group separately.

Quotient scores as norms. The most popular quotient score is the intelligence quotient (IQ), which is obtained as follows:

$$IQ = \frac{MA}{CA} \times 100$$

In this formula, *MA* stands for mental age and *CA* stands for chronological age. The formula shows, for example, that if an 8-year-old child does as well on an intelligence test as the average 10-year-old, he has an IQ of 125. An IQ of 100 is precisely average; above 100 means above average; and below 100 means below average.

Jum C. Nunnally

Testing Ethnic-Minority Children

There are conflicting views regarding the psychological assessment of ethnic-minority children. On the one hand, many authors have pointed out that mainstream assessment instruments (e.g., standardized intelligence tests) are biased against African-American and Latino children (Guthrie 1976; Helms 1992), the two largest ethnic groups in the United States. In contrast, other investigators argue that the available evidence indicates that tests are not biased for ethnic-minority children (Reschly 1978; Jensen 1980; Clarizio 1982). In this review, the evidence to support each position is summarized, and their corresponding assumptions, implications, and potential risks are discussed. In addition, recommendations are offered to address some of the complexities in assessing ethnic-minority children. This brief review draws primarily from the literature regarding the assessment of children's cognitive-intellectual functioning for diagnostic purposes in clinical and educational settings, as this reflects the bulk of the literature in the field. The points may apply to the assessment of other behavioral domains as well.

Evidence

Support for the position that tests are biased against minority children is largely conceptual in nature. The main point is that current tests fail to take into account the sociocultural context of many ethnic-minority children. Recent steps to enhance existing tests for minority children, such as modifying selected test items and including representative samples of African-American and Latino children, are viewed as inadequate in addressing the contextual limitations of the tests. To develop appropriate tests, investigators have been encouraged (a) to define what is normative functioning in specific ethnic groups, (b) to include measures of such behavior in existing tests, and (c) to develop new group-specific tests (J. E. Helms 1992). To date, there is little direct empirical evidence to support this cultural perspective. To test hypotheses generated from this perspective, studies are needed to assess adherence to both mainstream culture and group-specific culture and their relationship to test performance (J. E. Helms 1992). The overrepresentation of African-American and Latino children in special education classes is also used to support the test bias position. The fact that a specific ethnic group is overrepresented in special education classrooms is thought to be a function of biased tests (James Mercer 1979).

The evidence to support the opposing position, that tests are not biased against ethnic-minority children, is derived from direct inquiries of test bias. Studies that have examined the factor structures of cognitive-intelligence tests have found similar factors for African-American, Latino, and Caucasian children, suggesting that the underlying constructs of the tests are similar for each ethnic group. Investigations of predictive validity have also generally failed to find support for test bias. Intelligence test scores predict academic achievement, for example, about the same for the three main ethnic groups (e.g., T. Oakland 1983).

The available evidence is strongest with regard to the no-bias position. The only data to support the notion that tests are biased is limited at best; test bias is only one of many plausible explanations for the overrepresentation of African-Americans and Latinos in special education classrooms. Because the direct inquiries of test bias fail to support its existence, the most reasonable conclusion at this time is that mainstream tests, such as the Wechsler Intelligence Scale for Children (WISC), are not biased against African-Americans or Latinos.

The cultural perspective, however, should not be rejected, despite the lack of any systematic tests of this position. One weakness of test-bias research to date is that investigators have relied exclusively on group-level analyses. To my knowledge, no studies have examined whether test bias occurs for subgroups within ethnic minority groups. For example,

it would be useful to assess the construct validity and predictive validity of mainstream tests for limited-English-speaking Latino children, bilingual English/Spanish children, and monolingual English-speaking Latino and Caucasian children. Some initial steps have been taken in this direction (R. A. Figueroa 1989). Thus, although the available findings indicate that there is no racial or ethnic bias in mainstream tests, such as standardized cognitive-intelligence tests, there remains the possibility that biases may be found for specific subgroups within ethnic-minority groups.

Assumptions, Implications, and Risks of the Test Bias Positions

It is important that practitioners and researchers alike consider key points associated with both test-bias positions. The underlying assumption of each perspective with regard to the cultural specificity and universality of behavior is particularly significant. The view that tests are culturally biased assumes that the meaning of behavior is culture-specific. In other words, to accurately ascribe meaning to behavior, psychologists need to be familiar with the sociocultural context of the observed behavior, in this case, test performance. From this perspective, each group has different sociocultural norms. To identify whether a child has a disability, for example, these specific norms must be used, not some common population norm. Factors related to group-specific norms include cultural values and beliefs and social, economic, and ecological determinants of behavior. Knowledge of the child's context or specific sociocultural norms is viewed as essential to understand the meaning of her test performance. The implication of this approach is that mainstream tests cannot be used in assessing ethnic minority children. It is believed that existing tests should be modified in some fashion to better capture the child's context, or new tests should be developed specifically for a given group. The System of Multicultural Pluralistic Assessment and the translation, partial modification, and standardization of the WISC-R for Puerto Rican Island children and Mexico City children represent examples of modifying existing tests. The development of a projective technique akin to the Thematic Apperception Test for urban ethnic-minority children, Tell-Me-a-Story (R. G. Malgady et al. 1984), is an example of a personality test specifically designed for Latino and African-American children.

The underlying assumption of the no-test-bias perspective is that the meaning of behavior is largely universal. Contextual factors are thought to be of minimal significance. According to this perspective, a low test performance on a given test has the same meaning across groups, regardless of the group's familiarity with the test content or testing format. Tests with a general population norm are judged to provide a useful common metric for nearly all, if not all, groups. Thus, mainstream tests are viewed as valuable in assessing ethnic-minority children. Modifications of existing tests or the development of new tests are not thought to be necessary.

Although the risks of taking either position have not been well documented for children, available studies in the assessment of Spanish-speaking Latino adults suggest that the use of modified or group-specific tests and the use of assumed group-general tests each have their own potential risks (S. R. López and A. Romero 1988; S. R. López and L. M. Taussig 1991). These studies suggest that when using the modified or group-specific tests, children's level of functioning may be overestimated. This may occur because the norms of a specific group may be relatively low as a result of the group's low socio-economic status and educational attainment. For example, the SOMPA has been criticized as having the potential to overestimate children's cognitive functioning, which, in turn, could lead to an under-diagnosis of disability (H. F. Clarizio 1979; D. J. Reschly 1981).

The use of traditional tests has been criticized as having the potential for the opposite type of error, that is, underestimating level of functioning and overdiagnosing disability (e.g., J. R. Mercer 1979). If the culture-specific position is correct, at least with some children, then failure to consider contextual factors and alternative meanings of a child's test performance can potentially lead to judging minority children as lower functioning than they actually are. This is the argument that is typically used when psychological tests are challenged as being culturally biased.

In sum, adherence to either position of test bias or no test bias and the corresponding assumptions and implications is likely prone to systematic error. The critical question is how to reduce the likelihood of potential error. Possibly, practitioners (and researchers) could consider behavior (test performance) from both a culture-specific and a mainstream perspective and, accordingly, use tests from both the culture-specific and mainstream domains. Therefore, if both types of tests result in the same finding of dysfunction or normal functioning, then one can be confident with the consistent results.

Using more than one perspective, however, can lead to conflicting interpretations. For example, mainstream tests may indicate below-average functioning, whereas more modified tests or group-specific tests may indicate average functioning. J. A. Morrison (1988) provides such an example in the assessment of a bilingual Mexican-American boy. The WISC-R results indicated that he was functioning within the "mentally deficient" range (full scale IQ score of 70) and could qualify for an educable mental retardation class. In comparison, the SOMPA results revealed that his estimated learning potential was in the low average range (full scale score of 79), and that, given other assessment data, he would best be placed in a learning handicapped class. There is no standard way to clearly interpret these divergent test results; each case must be considered carefully. As amply demonstrated by Morrison in this case, it is best to use multiple sources of data, such as performance on different tests of similar, related, and different domains (e.g., intelligence, neuropsychological, and emotional domains) and multiple informants (e.g., parents' and teachers' reports). The available evidence from multiple sources can assist the practicing psychologist in carefully considering the usefulness of findings from mainstream and group-specific instruments.

Conclusion

The study of the psychological assessment of ethnic minority children for diagnostic purposes reveals a complex set of issues. Some psychologists view mainstream tests as racially and ethnically biased; others do not. The strict adherence to either perspective, with its assumptions, implications, and potential risks, is likely to do a disservice to children. Instead, multiple perspectives are recommended, specifically the use of both mainstream and group-specific tests. Combined with using multiple methods (see Sattler 1992 for a comprehensive set of guidelines), adhering to mainstream and group-specific approaches will likely enhance the utility and validity of assessing ethnic minority children.

Steven Regeser López

Testing the Mentally Retarded

The focus and purpose of psychological assessment techniques has changed from that of the earlier simplistic assessment of IQ to that of a more analytic effort to determine the assets, and liabilities, of the individual as they relate to specific behavioral repertoires.

Perhaps one of the most salient criticisms of simplistic IQ measures is that assessment is often undertaken solely for administrative purposes and decisions, rather than for remediation or treatment purposes.

To a large extent, the emerging emphasis on behavioral assessment techniques has as its corollary a deemphasis on classification per se. The focus is on an inventory of what exists in the behavioral repertoire; what the developmental potential seems to be for establishing new behaviors consistent with known frameworks for developmental progressions; and what the boundary conditions are that will elicit, shape, and maintain those behaviors contributing to a more adequate behavioral adaptation to the environment and its demands for a variety of behaviors.

Until this point, emphasis has been directed toward the conceptual issues relating to the use of psychological assessment procedures with the mentally retarded, with a concomitant deemphasis upon the more technical aspects of developments relating to test construction, test development, and similar issues. This strategy, it should be remarked, was both conscious and deliberate (J. Sattler 1974).

Allan G. Barclay

Tests, Self-Concept

Evaluative Measures of the Self-Concept

There are a variety of self-concept attitudes, such as self-satisfaction, self-acceptance, self-esteem, self-favorability, the congruence or discrepancy between the individual's ideal self and actual self-concept, and so on. While it is clear that there are substantial differences among these terms—for instance, self-acceptance means respecting one's self, including one's limitations, while self-esteem means pride in one's self, perhaps even believing that one has no limitations—these terms are so intertwined and overlapping in the literature that it is not possible to sort out the differences in any clear-cut fashion. As a consequence, R. C. Wylie (1968) suggests that the generic term *self-regard* be used for all these measures.

In most self-concept research repeated Q-sorts are obtained, and the changes in the self-ideal correlations are used as the dependent measures, for example, in studies of the outcome of client-centered psychotherapy. Increases in these correlations are regarded as indicating greater congruence between the actual- and ideal-self concepts. Such changes can occur either as a result of a change in the actual-self concept in the direction of the ideal, or of a change in the ideal-self concept in the direction of the actual, or of changes in both directions.

Self-Report Inventories

There are a number of self-report personality questionnaires that need to be considered as measures of self-concept, either because the term "self-concept" is part of their title or because the scores yielded by the instrument tend to fit into the phenomenological, humanistic orientation favored by self theorists. Of these, the most widely used would appear to be the Tennessee Self-Concept Test (Fitts 1965), which consists of 100 self-descriptive items, such as "I have a healthy body," "I am a member of a happy family," and so on, 90 of which assess the self-concept and 10 of which are from the MMPI Lie scale and are used to detect dissimulation.

The Personal Orientation Inventory (POI) is a self-report instrument designed to assess attitudes, values, and behaviors stemming from Abraham H.

Maslow's concept of self-actualization. While self-actualization is a rather different concept from that of self-concept, the POI has become a favorite instrument of many phenomenologically and humanistically oriented psychologists, particularly in research attempting to measure the outcome of their therapeutic efforts. The POI consists of 150 paired choice items, such as "I am afraid to be myself—I am not afraid to be myself." In each case the subject is to choose from the offered pair the statement that is the most self-descriptive.

Measurement of the Unconscious Self-Concept

A number of researchers have used the Thematic Apperception Test (TAT) for inferring the subject's self-concept. Similarly, the Rorschach and almost every other projective device have also been used as a measure of some aspect of the self-concept or another.

Leonard D. Goodstein

Teuber, Hans Lukas (1916–1979)

Hans Lukas Teuber's specialties in research were psychophysiology, neurophysiology, and brain sciences. His numerous scientific papers deal with physiological psychology, sensation, perception, and brain function.

Benjamin B. Wolman

Thematic Apperception Test (TAT)

The TAT was developed by Henry A. Murray and others at the Harvard Psychology Clinic in connection with research for *Explorations in Personality* (H. A. Murray 1938). The TAT was designed to measure the *need* and *press* components of Murray's personality theory as part of an intensive study of one "normal" person. The way people respond to TAT cards indicates their attitude to themselves and to significant persons in their lives.

The TAT was quickly absorbed into the clinical psychologist's armamentarium of tests administered to emotionally disturbed or "nonnormal" persons and interpreted within a variety of theoretical for-mats. Examples of interpretation procedures are illustrated by S. Tomkins (1947), E. Shneidman (1951), and M. Stein (1955).

There has been some systematic development and validation of a few need scores, especially the work by David McClelland and others on achievement motivation (1953) and more recently on affiliation and power motivations.

Gradually, an altered mode of practice with the TAT has been replacing the historic and conventional usages (R. H. Dana 1975). This practice begins with different assumptions regarding the purpose of assessment. Within a Newtonian model of science, one person observed another and the inferences obtained by this process were used in decisions made for the assessee.

Richard H. Dana

Therapeutic Alliance

Sigmund Freud (1912) stressed such positive transferences as friendliness, affection, and trust as vehicles of success, especially when analysis is threatened by negative transference manifestations. Humane concern and serious sympathetic understanding are the analyst's contributions to the "analytic pact." With the development of structural theory, these earlier suggestion-fostering elements of the analyst-analysand relationship were recognized as deriving from deeper unconscious libidinal and aggressive motives in both parties.

The total analytic situation or pact contains several elements, all germane to successful work:

1. the patient's reasonable ego, cooperation, desire to get well, and ability to accept the conditions of treatment;
2. the analyst's serious and humane understanding as well as her personal psychological attributes;
3. suggestion; and
4. the emergence of transferences to the therapeutic situation itself.

R. Sterba (1934) and E. Bibring (1937) describe an ego alliance between the patient's reasonable ego and the analyst's analyzing ego. Therein, the analyzable patient splits off his observing and analyzing ego functions from the experiencing aspects of his ego. Introjection of the working analyst is a part of the therapeutic process, in addition to modification of the superego through interpretation. Such an alliance will see the patient through troubled times and allow synthesis of information from his own observing ego and the analyst's interpretations. Otto Fenichel (1941) has similarly stated that, if present, the patient's reasonable ego must be detached from his defensive ego.

E. H. Zetzel (1958), who is credited with first use of the term "therapeutic alliance," locates its origin in pregenital-level dyadic processes mainly involving object relations and reality testing. She states that throughout analysis interpretive attention must be paid to the state of the alliance. Over and above the transference neurosis, a capacity to differentiate objective reality from neurotic distortion must exist, or else analysis cannot begin, nor can subsequent interpretive work be effective.

R. R. Greenson (1967) prefers the term "working alliance" because it places vital emphasis on the patient's capacity to work purposefully in the analytic situation. The patient's unique style of optimal analytic work must be fostered educationally and interpretively, because it is as important as the transference neurosis. In turn, the working style of the patient may be a source of resistance to regression or defensively absorbed into the transference neurosis (e.g., overcompliance).

Greenson maintains that the working alliance is neither transference nor real interaction. As such, an analyst only interpreting and a patient only associating, to the neglect of proper appreciation of the total real participation of both parties, will hamper development of the transference neurosis.

Anna Freud (1954), in discussing L. J. Stone's reference to the "real personal relationship" between analyst and patient versus the "true transference reactions," states, "Such a distinction coincides with ideas I have always had on this subject. . . . As far as the patient has a healthy part of his personality, his real relationship to the analyst is never submerged."

M. Kanzer (1975) has cautioned that until these concepts are understood in terms of child development and structural adaptive perspectives, they are liable to the usual pitfalls of pragmatic, intuitive, nonanalytic lapses in technique. In particular, he questions the practice of simply confessing real mistakes by the analyst as if this could take the place of analyzing such mistakes. Jacob Arlow (1975) sees Zetzel's focus on pregenital primitive relationship difficulties and Greenson's emphasis on the current real relationship as preoccupation with historically outdated technical problems involving overreliance on the positive transference. He questions the authenticity of "adultomorphic retroprojections of events in the mental life of the child during the first few months of life" as correlative to the transference of the adult patient.

Interest in the nontransference aspects of the total analyst-analysand relationship has existed since the early work of Freud. Efforts to clarify this area of interaction have been variously labeled "ego alliance" (R. Sterba 1934); "therapeutic alliance" (E. H. Zetzel 1956); "working alliance" (R. R. Greenson, 1967); the "rational transference" (O. Fenichel 1941); and "mature transference (L. J. Stone 1961, 106).

Edward H. Knight

Therapeutic Misalliance

One of the most frequent disturbances of the therapeutic alliance is best conceptualized as a result of a pathogenic interaction between the patient and analyst, termed the *therapeutic misalliance* (R. J. Langs 1975). The therapeutic alliance is the conscious and unconscious agreement on the part of the patient and analyst to join forces in effecting symptom alleviation and characterological changes for the patient through insight and other constructive means, which promote structural change and conflict resolution. Therapeutic misalliances are, therefore, interactions between these two participants that are designed either to undermine these goals or to achieve symptom modification, however temporary, on some other basis.

The Motives for the Development of Therapeutic Misalliances

For the patient, the search for sectors of misalliance with her analyst stems from the hope for maladaptive relief from anxiety and guilt related to her intrapsychic conflicts and pathogenic introjects. Through the development of a misalliance, she is able to momentarily validate her distorted view of the world in a manner that justifies the maintenance of her psychopathology. In developing an interaction of this type with her analyst, the patient is able to gratify a variety of inappropriate instinctual needs and to reinforce a wide range of superego pathology.

The analyst's motives for accepting or initiating a misalliance are not unlike those within the patient. They stem from his inevitable residuals of unmastered anxiety and guilt, neurotic and maladaptive defensive needs, and unresolved searches for inappropriate gratification. One important factor is the analyst's reactions to the stringencies of his analytic role and the extraordinary renunciation that it entails. In addition, any type of countertransference difficulty may be translated into this type of pathogenic interaction with the patient.

Despite the many temporary gains for both patient and analyst derived from a sector of misalliance, there are powerful motives within each of them to modify and resolve such interactions and to restore a proper therapeutic atmosphere.

The Vehicles through Which Misalliances Are Effected

The patient's attempts to create sectors of misalliance with the analyst develop along two lines: efforts to modify the framework of the analytic relationship and attempts to involve the analyst in pathogenic interactions. The former is an extremely common and relatively unrecognized vehicle for the development of misalliances.

The second means, through which the patient involves her analyst in sectors of misalliance, is based on unconscious components of the analytic interaction through which the two share defenses and inappropriate gratifications.

For the analyst, too, there are two main ways in which she evokes or participates in misalliances with patients: through modifications in the framework and through countertransference-based interventions and interactions with the patient. The unconscious utilization of modifications and deviations in technique is perhaps one of the most widely and erroneously rationalized means through which analysts have created sectors of misalliance with their analysands.

In her interaction with the patient, the analyst has ample opportunity to develop both gross and subtle sectors of misalliance. They stem from a wide range of countertransference-based behaviors that have seductive, hostile, defensive, and provocative qualities.

The Analytic Resolution of Therapeutic Misalliance

The unconscious development and conscious analytic resolution of sectors of misalliance is one characteristic of a viable analytic process. The analysis of the unconscious perceptions, fantasies, memories, and introjects that contributed to the patient's participation in a misalliance provides crucial insights into core genetic experiences, fantasies, and conflicts related to the patient's psychopathology. At the same time, the conscious and unconscious realization that the analyst has been able to recognize, modify, and analyze a misalliance provides the patient with an important opportunity for positive identification with him. In addition, the insightful resolution of such experiences offers the analyst an opportunity for self-analytic work and gain; while such endeavors are not the basic province of the patient's analysis, their inevitable occurrence affords the analyst a special opportunity for inner change in his work with patients. The working through of this type of shared interactional pathology is one of the most important means through which a truly viable therapeutic alliance is established and reinforced during the course of an analysis.

Robert J. Langs

Therapeutic Regression

Sigmund Freud's notion of topographical regression was dictated by his model of the psychic apparatus, in which regression consists in the excitation moving in a backward direction from the motor and toward the sensory end, where it finally affects the perceptual system. This regressive movement, opposite to the normal progressive movement within the psychic apparatus, ultimately produces hallucinatory forms of wish-fulfillment rather than a seeking and finding of satisfaction in reality. Shifting this perspective into the terms of a more contemporary structural model, following Anna Freud (1965), we can say that regression occurs in all parts of the tripartite mental apparatus, in id, ego, or superego.

The consideration of regression in a therapeutic context requires an understanding of its developmental reference points. The course of libidinal development is expressed in terms of the cathexis of objects and the quality of object relationships. Both libidinal and aggressive drive components progress from one developmental level to the next and, thus, are directed to phase-specific objects, which serve their respective needs at each stage.

The most common set of fixation points, which carry with them the most intense investment of libidinal and aggressive cathexes, are found in the oedipal situation. In the classical configuration, the relatively intense libidinal cathexis of the opposite-sex parent and the relatively intense aggressive cathexis of the same-sex parent sets up a context of fixation, which becomes relatively difficult to resolve and absorb in the progressive movement of developmental exigencies. Consequently, it is the failure to resolve and integrate these oedipal fixations, together with their component elements of castration anxiety and penis envy, that is found to be typically involved in the core conflicts of neurotic pathology. For most neurotic patients, this danger is remote because the relative stability of their ego and superego structures permits them to tolerate such regression while maintaining an effective therapeutic alliance with the analyst.

As the patient's resistances stiffen, the regression is correspondingly stalemated. Consequently, especially in the earlier phases of the analysis, when the regressive movement is beginning to take hold, the analyst's attention and the major focus of the analytic work is taken up with the analysis of resistances. As each layer of resistance is worked through, the repressive barrier is diminished and the potentiality is mobilized for further regression.

The regression in the analytic setting is induced specifically for therapeutic purposes. Thus, the analytic process seeks an optimal degree and kind of regression that will serve the therapeutic purposes most aptly. The amount, degree, pacing, and depth of regression are all issues that must be judged in relationship to the needs, pathology, and capacity of each individual patient.

William W. Meissner

Thinking

According to Donald O. Hebb (1958), an initial indication of thoughtful behavior is a temporal delay between stimulus and response, indicating an interposed mediational process (as opposed to the immediacy of response characteristic of reflexive behavior). Further, internal mediating processes are indicated by flexibility and variety of response in the presence of the same stimulus (the absence of the stimulus-bound quality of reflexive behavior). Finally, thoughtful behavior is characterized by temporal sequencing and integration of future events, which occur through internal mediational factors only and do not depend on continuous sensory input for organization.

Concept Identification

Most experimental studies have been on attribute learning, in which the rule is specified at the outset (usually a simple affirmative rule), and the subject must learn to identify the relevant attribute and its appropriate value. In rule learning experiments, the relevant attributes are known and the rule for their combination must be learned. The subject attempts to discover the attribute or the rule by guessing, for each stimulus pattern presented, whether it is or is not an example of the classification principle (i.e., she states, for each example, whether she believes it is a positive or a negative instance of the principle). Her response to the first pattern is, of course, a guess. But she can utilize the feedback she receives after each guess, telling her whether she was right or wrong in her response (referred to as confirming and infirming evidence) to guide her in discovering the correct rule or attribute.

Concept Attainment

A second area of research interest has been on the subject factors involved in concept attainment. Here, the experimenter is interested in individual differences in performance, both as a function of previous experimental history and of previous personal history.

G. H. Bower and T. R. Trabasso (1964) have provided an early formal version of the hypothesis model, which was a focus for much of the research in this area during the 1960s. They suggest that a subject randomly samples a single hypothesis from a set of possible hypotheses and maintains that hypothesis until an error is made. He again randomly samples from the set of all possible hypotheses, maintains this until he makes an error, and continues until he samples the correct hypothesis (win-stay, lose-shift strategy). Final success is an all-or-none phenomenon, in which a subject is in either the presolution or the solution state.

Underlying Processes

Memory. Bower and Trabasso sought to determine what is learned about the stimuli in a concept-attainment task. They propose a no-memory model, in which a subject has no memory for previously tested and rejected hypotheses, or any relevant stimulus attributes other than those available in the last instance. Support for this view comes from experiments in which a subject who was in a presolution state for one concept was shifted to a new concept without being informed of this.

Strategies. J. S. Bruner, J. J. Goodnow, and G. A. Austin (1956) developed a set of ideal strategies that one could use in dealing with both selection and reception tasks. They used these as a basis for comparison with individual performance, to determine how an individual actually approaches problems and how she compares with the ideal in doing this. These experimenters were concerned with styles of problem solving and the factors involved in these different styles.

There appears to be strong evidence for some kind of hypothesis-testing model of concept attainment, and that subjects can maintain more than one hypothesis simultaneously.

Transfer in Rule Learning

L. E. Bourne (1967, 1973) and his associates (Dodd et al. 1971) studied transfer effects in concept-attainment tasks. They found that pretraining on a variety of rule-learning tasks improves the learning of the most difficult rules. The greater the variety of rule-learning tasks encountered, the larger the positive transfer effect. It appears that with training, a subject can learn formal logic strategies for dealing with rule learning, strategies based on logical truth tables. In using truth tables, one notes whether a given feature is present or absent in a given exemplar.

Sondra Leftoff
Aharon H. Fried

Thirst

Thirst is a strong motivation to seek, obtain, and consume water, which derives from the physiological need of the organism for water. With regard to human consumption of fluids, the critical aspect of this definition is the basis for thirst in bodily dehydration, because social, psychological, and other nonhomeostatic influences also may provide humans with a strong motivation to drink liquids.

Body fluid, essentially a dilute saline solution, accounts for more than half of body weight. Much of that water is located within tissue cells and provides the fluid matrix necessary for their function. Another functionally significant, albeit relatively small, portion of the body fluid is the blood plasma contained within the circulatory vessels. Water moves freely throughout the body by osmosis across cellular and capillary membranes and thereby permits all body fluids to be in osmotic equilibrium.

There are two natural stimuli for thirst. Because they arise from dehydration of separate body fluid compartments, the resultant water intakes are not equally capable of rehydration. For example, when pure water is lost, water consumption by thirsty animals proceeds until body fluid concentrations and volumes have been restored, whereupon the stimulus for thirst disappears and drinking stops. When the volume of blood plasma is decreased, however, what is needed is not water but a relatively dilute saline solution. If only water is consumed, then it does not repair the circulatory deficits but instead is distributed evenly throughout the body fluid so as to maintain osmotic equilibrium in all tissues. Further drinking is soon inhibited, despite the continued presence of plasma volume deficits, due to the osmotic dilution of body fluid that results from the accumulation and retention of ingested water.

Basic physiological mechanisms tend to conserve body fluids and thereby minimize the occurrence and degree of dehydration. Nevertheless, a need for water develops periodically and becomes manifest in thirst. Two conditions that trigger thirst have been identified, one related to an increase in the concentration of body fluid and the other to a decrease in the volume of blood plasma. When thirst is due to the former, water consumption dilutes body fluids towards normal levels and thereby removes that stimulus for thirst; when thirst is due to the latter, water and salt must be consumed together for plasma volume deficits to be restored. The mechanisms by which these dehydrational stimuli are translated within the brain into motivated activities remain obscure.

Edward M. Stricker

Thompson, Clara (1893–1958)

In 1941, Clara Thompson, Karen Horney, and Eric Fromm left the New York Psychoanalytic Institute and, together with Harry Stack Sullivan and Frieda Fromm-Reichman, founded the William Alanson White Institute. Thompson presented her ideas on changing concepts in psychoanalysis in papers on Sandor Ferenczi, Sullivan, and Fromm. Thirteen of her thirty-five papers deal with women and their problems.

Earl G. Witenberg

Thomson, Godfrey (1881–1955)

Godfrey Thomson developed the First Northumberland Mental Test, later to become known as the Moray House Test. He wrote *The Factorial Analysis of Human Ability* (1937–38), in which he put forth his "sampling theory." Thomson conducted large-scale research on demographic variables and realized that a different culture demands a different test, rather than a translation of an existing test.

Vytautas J. Bieliauskas

Thorndike, Edward Lee (1874–1949)

Edward Lee Thorndike's findings supported C. Lloyd Morgan's law of effect and suggested the law of practice, which emphasizes the association of animal movements that are organized by "successful acts." Thorndike denied the similarity of animal and human association.

J. Wayne Lazar

Titchener, Edward Bradford (1867–1927)

Edward Bradford Titchener was the leader of the "structuralist" school of psychology in America. Titchener's primary professional goal was to establish psychology as a science as firmly as physics or chemistry. Titchener was interested in determining the structure of mind, that is, in analyzing mind into its constituent elements, and in determining the laws of combination of these elements. In his view, the tool of psychology is introspection—a careful and rigorous observation of the experience produced by stimuli presented to the subject under carefully controlled conditions. Titchener's main works are *Experimental Psychology: A Manual of Laboratory Practice* (1901–5), *A Textbook of Psychology* (1910), and *Systematic Psychology: Prolegomena* (1928).

Thomas C. Cadwallader

Tolman, Edward Chase (1886–1959)

Edward Chase Tolman's basic concept was that of *sign-gestalt expectation*—a proposition on the part of the learner that given such and such a sign (cue), following such and such a behavior route (doing so and so) will lead to such and such a significate (a changed state of affairs). Tolman's theory was developed within the context of maze learning in the white rat; what the rat learns (sign-gestalt expectations) could also be defined as a knowledge (cognition) of what leads to what in the maze. In the studies of latent learning, rats ran mazes without reward, then the reward was introduced. *Purposive Behavior in Animals and Men* (1932) is Tolman's major book.

Gregory A. Kimble

Topographic Model in Post-Freudian Theory

Most authors have noted that, in actual practice, those behaviors that represent compromise formations (such as dreams, parapraxes, or isolated neurotic symptoms) continued to be explicated in accord with the topographic model. Certain exponents of ego psychology decried this reliance on a theoretical tool they regarded as outmoded and inadequate. This point of view found its most emphatic spokesmen in Jacob Arlow and Charles Brenner (1964). Other authors (e.g., Kubie 1966) saw these facts as evidence of the limitations of the structural tripartite model as a universal explanatory framework.

The merits and limitations of both theories were reviewed by M. M. Gill (1963), whose ultimate conclusions echoed Sigmund Freud's position of 1938. With respect to the topographic theory itself, Gill began a process of revision, later continued by R. R. Holt (1967) and P. Noy (1969).

One attempt to delimit the appropriate field of application of the topographic model was made by John E. Gedo and A. Goldberg (1973). They held that the various alternative models of the mind proposed by Freud and his successors are not necessarily mutually exclusive, and they maintained that

the topographic model had been devised to illuminate functioning at one particular developmental level.

John E. Gedo

Touch

Although the sense of touch is mediated by the skin, the largest and most extensive sense "organ," the receptors responsible for transducing the various forms of mechanical and thermal energy to produce its varied sensations have thus far been inadequately identified, largely because of the complexity of the skin itself. Within the three major layers of skin tissue (epidermis, dermis, and subcutaneous tissue) lies an extensive array of structures: muscle tissue, blood vessels, free nerve endings, mucous ducts, and hair follicles, to mention a few.

Sensory Nerves
The sensory nerves from cutaneous receptors enter the central nervous system through the dorsal roots of the spinal cord. Of the thirty-one pairs of spinal roots, sensory nerves enter all but the topmost pair. The population of cutaneous nerves entering at any one level belongs to those receptors within a certain defined area of the skin surface. This area is known as a dermatome, and although there is a good deal of overlap in the innervation pattern across spinal levels, methods such as dorsal root section or injections of stimulants or anesthetics and clinical observations (concerning the extent of the skin affected in nerve block traumata, for example) have allowed mapping of these areas. It is within the spinal cord that a division occurs in the conduction pathways for the touch modalities.

Topography
Spatial discrimination varies across the body, as do sensitivities to pressure and vibration. Both the localization of a single punctate stimulus and the spatial resolving power of the skin, as reflected by the ability to discriminate two points of stimulation from one another, have been employed as measures of the acuity of touch.

Simple pressure as a stimulus for touch actually requires the existence of a gradient of tissue displacement in order to be an effective stimulus. This fact is simply demonstrated by the pattern of touch evoked by dipping a finger into a container of mercury. It is only at the interface where a gradient exists that the sensation of pressure is present. In addition, pressure thresholds are a function of the area of the stimulator, and indeed, stable thresholds often require the use of fine hairs or needles as the stimulators.

Pacinian Corpuscles

One particular population of cutaneous receptors, the Pacinian corpuscles, demonstrates electrophysiological activity that mirrors the activity of stimulus failure. This receptor population responds only to changes in pressure, and not at all to static deformation.

Thermal Stimuli

Thermal stimuli interact with the physical structure of the skin to produce temporal lags in, and attenuation of, temperature changes. In addition, the complex thermoregulatory mechanisms of the body tend to resist the local changes produced by the experiment. However, with stimulators such as temperature cylinders or Peltier effect transducers, devices that are capable of maintaining relatively constant temperatures, the surface of the human skin can be mapped psychophysically for temperature "spots." A dual mechanism for thermal touch sensations is suggested by such a mapping, because it commonly demonstrates poor coincidence between cold and warm sensitive points.

Adaptation to nonpainful thermal stimuli between 15° and 42°F occurs rapidly and extensively, as is apparent in everyday experience. Cold or warm water initially produces the appropriate sensation, the magnitude of which rapidly decreases. If an increase or decrease in temperature is produced, it may again be felt. Further adaptation will occur, of course, if this stimulus level is maintained.

Roger W. Cholewiak

Tourette, Gilles de la (1859–1904)

Gilles de la Tourette was Jean-Martin Charcot's pupil. He studied *tic convulsif*, later called Tourette's syndrome.

Elaine Shapiro
Arthur K. Shapiro

Toxic Psychoses

Mental symptoms associated with misuse of drugs and medications or related to metabolic disorders, nutritional deficiencies, or infections are not in themselves specific to a particular chemical substance. Abnormal behavioral responses depend not only on the toxic agent but also on conditions under which the person is subjected to the agent. Personality, past experience, age, and other attributes of the individual, as well as the intensity, duration, and type of the intoxication, are significant factors in determining the clinical picture. The following are only a few examples.

Bromides

Acute bromide intoxication. Although acute fatalities from bromides are rare, there are reports of death ascribed to the ingestion of a single, large dose of bromide or taking large amounts over a period of days.

Chronic bromide intoxication. M. Levin has pointed out that bromide psychoses are not all similar, and he has listed four varieties: simple bromide intoxication, delirium, hallucinosis, and transitory schizophrenia associated with paranoid symptomatology.

Simple bromide intoxication. This condition is characterized by progressive dullness, sluggishness, forgetfulness, and irritability as bromide accumulates in the nervous system. The pupils are irregular and may become sluggish and even fixed to light. There are tremors, unsteadiness of gait, and general incoordination, with slowing of speech.

Delirium. Characteristic manifestation of bromide delirium is disorientation. The patient suffers some weeks with simple intoxication and then may become confused as to time. There may be disturbances of mood, restlessness, apprehensiveness, inability to sleep, delusions, and hallucinations.

Barbiturates

Symptoms. Simple intoxication with barbiturates results in acute and chronic symptoms somewhat similar to those in alcohol intoxication—dullness, sluggishness, sleepiness, slowness of speech and understanding, impaired memory, and disturbances in thought processes and judgment.

Belladonna Alkaloids

Psychotic manifestations of overdose of atropine may be observed with doses of 10 mg and more and are associated with burning and dryness of the mouth, difficulty in deglutition and speech, and intense thirst.

Oxygen

Oxygen lack. There is evidence of very strong sensitivity of the higher cerebral centers to oxygen lack. Not all parts of the brain are equally affected by hypoxia: those regions with the highest metabolic rates succumb first, and those with the lowest rates last. During a slow, progressive hypoxia, precise contact with the environment is first lost. There then follows motor restlessness, succeeded by muscle spasms, convulsive episodes, disturbances of heart action, and failing respiration.

Carbon dioxide. Up to 10% concentration in air of carbon dioxide appears to act as a respiratory and cardiovascular stimulant, but above this critical level the respiratory depressant effects of the gas begin to appear. Exposure to 5–6% has been found to cause mental depression, ataxia, dizziness, and fatigue.

Carbon monoxide. Because carbon monoxide acts to reduce the oxygen-carrying capacity of the blood, the signs and symptoms of carbon monoxide intoxication are those of oxygen lack, particularly of the central nervous system. After acute carbon monoxide poisoning, there may be permanent brain damage.

Metals

Mercury. Chronic mercurialism may result from exposure to small amounts of mercury over extended periods of use in industrial situations.

Chronic mercury poisoning may be characterized by disturbances of the alimentary tract, renal damage, anemia, high blood pressure, and peripheral neuritis. The central nervous system may be involved, with tremors varying in degree from slight tremor of the hand, eyelids, or tongue to marked generalized tremors and shaking.

Ebbe Curtis Hoff

Trait Theory and Genetics

The complexity of the behavior patterns defined in trait theory makes it unlikely that a researcher would discover qualitative differences among individuals, which might be attributed to the action of a single gene. Thus, methods most frequently employed are derived from the theory of the genetics of continuous traits and rely on the observation of the covariance of relatives. Heritability estimated from the correlation among individuals of a single degree of relationship requires the assumption that the effect of the shared environment is zero. While this may not seem unreasonable for siblings who have been separated at birth, it may be difficult to defend for twins or full siblings reared together.

Both the wealth and variety of evidence collected on various measures of IQ leave little doubt concerning an important genetic contribution to individual differences. The biases in the methods most frequently employed suggest that the heritability of this trait may be somewhat less than the .70–.80 often estimated for American and northern European populations. Evidence for a genetic contribution to population differences is much more fragmentary and tentative. A detailed consideration of the evidence and the issues is presented by J. Loehlin et al. (1975).

Efforts in behavioral genetics are not limited to the investigation of hereditary factors. The method of J. K. Haseman and R. C. Elston was applied to data from monozygotic (MZ) twins, dizygotic (DZ) twins, and full siblings on the High School Personality Questionnaire, the Culture-Fair Intelligence Scale, and the High School Objective-Analytic Personality Battery. Of particular interest were the estimates of common environmental covariance estimated from MZ and DZ twins and from MZ twins and full siblings.

Available data are derived primarily from small-sample investigations, broadly distributed across both traits and methods. Large-scale researches, either underway or nearing completion, promise to expand both the scope and the quality of our knowledge of hereditary influences on psychological traits.

Studies of the genetic correlations among elements of behavior promise to provide data on the biological structure underlying the relationships among variables. The parallel analysis of environmental correlations will provide a comparison of the structure conditioned by environmental factors.

Thomas W. Klein

Traits

Theories

The work on individual differences inspired by Francis Galton and James McKeen Cattell led to a measurement emphasis that has been ever since a major facet of the approach. The idea of variability and measured variability leads naturally to concern over what is measured and how it is measured. Added impetus, though emphasizing cognition, came from the appearance of the Binet-Simon scales of intelligence in 1905 and the psychometric and factor-analytic thrust given by Charles Spearman's two-factor theory of intelligence.

A second major influence was the growing theoretical concern for attributes of a person that could be used for both descriptive and theory-building purposes. The majority of these early conceptualizations came from abnormal psychology. Here is seen the influence of Sigmund Freud, Carl Jung, Ernest Kretschmer, and William McDougall.

A trait is an attribute of a person. That is, it describes an aspect of a person. Initially, these were descriptions of behavior (e.g., reckless, stubborn) and sometimes of mental states (e.g., depressed). Even at this primitive stage it becomes apparent that we are talking about an *inferred* characteristic. Thus, if an individual is observed to take risks in a variety of situations where the penalty for error may be severe and choice of less hazardous alternatives is ready to hand, we characterize such a person as "reckless."

Quantification

The quantification of traits has characterized the scientific development of trait theory. There seemed good reason to believe that although all factors derived in personality research might not prove useful, at least the major traits of personality should be accounted for and the level of conceptualization removed from that of the isolated response or test score to the level of inferred variables, namely the latent traits. In 1957, Cattell described fidelity, consistency, structural relations, and relevance as source traits.

- *Fidelity* is a quantitative statement concerning the extent to which the variance of the measure may be attributed to the trait.
- *Consistency* is the extent to which a trait may be measured with equivalent fidelity over change in population, general circumstances of the testing situation, and variation in administration (e.g., sex of the administrator).
- *Structural relations.* Traits are hypothetical elements in a theory. They are not viewed, within most theories, as being independent isolates but as forming parts of meaningful equations. Thus, evidence of relation between a trait and other traits should be mandatory.
- *Relevance.* To be a satisfactory element in a theory, a trait should show solid positive evidence in all four of the above areas. Fidelity and consistency are essentially psychometric attributes; they set minimum standards and indicate where more research needs to be carried out. Structural relations and relevance are of more theoretical concern and indicate, given appropriate measurement properties, the extent to which a trait has a place in a theoretical system.

Measurement

Self-description. It is in this domain that most effort has been expended in terms of technology. The questionnaire, for example, from the time of R. S. Woodworth's Personal Data Sheet (1919), has been the subject of much psychometric effort. The comparative ease with which a questionnaire can be constructed and its properties known has certainly assisted in this.

The verbal content of the scales may also have led to a form of law of diminishing returns in terms of trait variance, and the majority of traits of major concern are probably present among the more well known personality inventories: the Guilford-Zimmerman Temperament Survey; Cattell's Sixteen Personality Factors Questionnaire; Jackson's Personality Research Form; the Comrey Personality Scales; the Eysenck Personality Inventory; and the Minnesota Multiphasic Personality Inventory.

Morphology. From Hippocrates to the present century, several attempts have been made, to link body build to personality. A very large number of measures, and combinations of measures, can be obtained.

Motor-perceptual and performance measures. Included within this very large class are such projective tests as the Rorschach and the Thematic Apperception Test (TAT). Other measures include Herman A. Witkin's Rod-and-Frame Test and the Porteus Mazes. The trait of field independence (Witkin) or simply "independence," as it has been called by others, is an example of a trait derived from such measures.

John D. Hundleby

Transcendental Meditation and Psychiatry

Transcendental meditation may be a very useful technique for moderating the widespread tendency of individuals in Western culture to live as if in a state of perpetual crisis, in which minimal stimulation produces an emergency response too much of the time. As a means of dealing with this Western "stress syndrome," transcendental meditation appears to be the most effective of the general relaxation techniques. It can be taught to psychiatric patients with a wide variety of illnesses, and appears to add a significant positive therapeutic impact to the overall treatment program.

Bernard C. Glueck

Transcultural Psychiatry

Cultural psychiatry is a branch of social psychiatry, which is concerned with the cultural aspects of etiology, frequency and nature of mental illness, and the care and aftercare of the mentally ill within the confines of a given cultural unit. The term *transcultural psychiatry*, which is an extension of cultural psychiatry, denotes that the vista of the scientific observer extends beyond the scope of one cultural unit into another, whereas the term *cross-cultural* is applied to comparative and contrasting aspects of psychiatry in any of the areas named.

In all major societies or cultures, patients have been found who exhibit the classical pictures of schizophrenia, depression, paranoia, and senile psychosis. Yet culture-determined differences in the frequency and nature of symptoms are known to occur.

Preferences for forms of psychotherapy transculturally depend on differences in etiological views and on cultural and ideological differences.

Eric D. Wittkower

Transfer of Training

The learning of a skill is never an isolated event, because the way that a new skill is learned depends in part upon the activities that preceded it. The effect of previous learning on the acquisition of skill at a subsequent task is known as transfer of training (or transfer of learning). Research is most often concerned with the effect of learning a first task (A) on the subsequent learning of a different task, or of a different version of the same task (B). A related issue is the effect of learning task B on the retention of the skill acquired in task A. The effect of A on B is the strict concern of transfer, from which the effect of B on A is normally distinguished as *retroaction*.

Experimental Design

Several different measures of transfer have been proposed. For many purposes, one of the formulas of the R. M. Gagné, H. Foster, and M. E. Crowley (1948) type may be used. These measures all express the transfer difference between experimental group performance on task B and control performance on task B as a percentage of the total learning attainable on B. The primary intention is to provide for some degree of comparability between transfer measures made on tasks with different learning curves. The amount of attainable learning of B, which forms the baseline, may be supplied in advance, if there is a known perfect score. However, in most psychomotor skills a perfect score does not exist, and the baseline is estimated by subtracting the control group initial score from their asymptote or final learning score.

Some of the earliest experimental work on transfer was concerned with psychomotor skills, in the form of "bilateral transfer" or "cross-education." The German laboratories of the later nineteenth century noted that skills learned with the left hand were transferred almost intact to the right hand, although formal studies using control groups did not appear until much later.

Transfer Theories

By the 1930s and 1940s, the emerging picture was of positive transfer varying as a function of stimulus similarity between tasks A and B (and amount of task-A learning), with a tendency toward negative transfer when the response elements differed. Since World War II, the work has been marked by an increased sophistication in the specification of input, output, and feedback variables, and an increase in the number of studies that analyze rather than ascertain the effects of transfer.

Negative Transfer

Understanding negative transfer is crucial to the explication of transfer relationships. It is necessary for the subject to differentiate between the responses required by task A and by task B, in order to inhibit the practiced task-A responses when the available cues indicate that task-B responses are appropriate. Because negative transfer will arise from poor differentiation, it follows that the interference should tend to increase as response similarity increases.

Task Difficulty

The special problem of task difficulty emerged when several studies showed better transfer from difficult to easy tasks than in the reverse direction. Early attempts at explanation relied on the concept of optimal zones in the task variables affecting skilled performance. Transfer was thought to be better in the difficult-to-easy direction, from outside to inside an optimal zone, than from within the zone to the more difficult conditions outside the zone.

Dennis H. Holding

Transference: Freudian and Post-Freudian Concepts

The phenomenon of transference, one of Sigmund Freud's (1912) central psychoanalytic concepts, was based on the repetition compulsion, echoed the displacement of affective investments from one idea to another as in the dream work, and drew on unconscious libidinal attachments from the infantile level directed to the analyst as a new and significant object in the analytic relation. In this classic view, transference was based on libidinal instinctual dynamics and worked by displacement from the past to the present.

In subsequent years, the concept of transference underwent a transformation that broadened its connotations to include every emotional connection to the analyst, that extended the transference model to encompass the range of psychopathology addressed by psychoanalysis in its widening scope, and that began to pay increasing attention to the diversity of developmental levels from which transference components derive. We can survey these developments in terms of transference variants and mechanisms.

Transference Variants

In addition to the classic form of transference based on libido, transferences can be based on aggressive and narcissistic derivatives; other variants include so-called self-object transferences, transitional relation transferences, and finally, neurotic and psychotic transferences. Variations of these transference forms may appear in highly individuated combinations and relative degrees of intensity, varying according to the developmental history and pathological organization of the patient's personality structure.

Libidinal transferences tend to follow the classic model and usually occur in a milder form as positive transference reactions. They are derivatives of phallic-oedipal, libidinal impulses and may be permeated to varying degrees by pregenital influences. Generally, they do not cause any particular difficulties and may not even require interpretation if they contribute to the gradual development of the therapeutic alliance. Freud's recommendation was that they call for interpretation only when they serve as a resistance.

They may take a more extreme form, however, becoming a major source of resistance (H. P. Blum 1973; P. L. Giovacchini 1975b). Erotic transferences are often seen in borderline or psychotic patients, usually in connection with regression. Such transferences are intense, tenacious, resistant to interpretation, tend to draw the analyst into forms of joint acting out, and frequently are acted out outside the analysis (H. P. Blum 1973). Erotic transferences usually reflect a loss of the discrimination between fantasy and reality and an impairment of reality testing. They may be mingled with primitive forms of idealization and form a significant contribution to a transference psychosis.

Aggressive transferences can take the form either of negative transference or a more pathological paranoid transference. Negative transferences can be seen in patients at all levels of psychopathology, but may be the predominant form of transference expression in borderline patients (O. F. Kernberg 1968, 1976, 1984). Some therapists would maintain that the degree of the patient's propensity for negative transference is a measure of his potential unanalyzability (P. L. Giovacchini 1975a). Such patients tend to see the therapeutic relationship in terms of power and victimization, regarding the therapist as omnipotent and powerful, while the patient experiences himself as helpless, weak, and vulnerable (W. W. Meissner 1981; T. H. McGlashan 1983).

The paranoid transference is an extreme expression or intensification of a negative transference. While in the negative transference the therapist may be seen as powerful and the patient as weak, in a paranoid transference the therapist will be seen as threatening, persecuting, or controlling, or as trying to exercise sadistic domination over the patient (O. F. Kernberg 1984). A paranoid transference may emerge suddenly, usually in response to some action or intervention on the therapist's part that suggests some lapse in empathy or understanding. Paranoid transferences also may become delusional and involve significant regressive failures in reality testing, so that the paranoid attitude becomes in fact part of a transference psychosis.

Narcissistic transferences were delineated by Heinz Kohut (1971). Kohut saw the narcissistic transferences as variations of the patterns of projection of archaic narcissistic configurations onto the therapist. They can be thought of as based on projections of the narcissistic introjects, both superior and inferior (Meissner 1978, 1981). Thus, the therapist comes to represent either the grandiose self or the idealized parental imago. Activation in the therapy of the omnipotent and idealized object leads to the formation of an idealizing transference in which all power and strength are attributed to the idealized object, leaving the subject feeling empty and powerless when separated from that object. The transference thus represents an attempt to achieve union with the idealized object in order to regain narcissistic equilibrium.

The patterns of idealization may reflect different levels of developmental attainment. Idealizing transferences may reflect developmental disturbances in the idealized parent imago, particularly at the time of the formation of the ego ideal by introjection of the idealized object. In its more archaic expressions, narcissistic idealization may take the form of global, mystical, or religious concerns, linked with all-inspiring qualities that seem somewhat diffuse and vague and not attached to a single admired figure. In such cases, the revived narcissistic equilibrium can be experienced as a sense of omnipotence and omniscience, combined with feelings of aesthetic and moral perfection. These feelings can be sustained as long as the patient can maintain a sense of union with the idealized therapist. Through this connection with the sustaining and idealized object, symptoms related to the narcissistic disequilibrium are modified, particularly affective disturbances of depression, shame, or inferiority, as well as disturbances in work capacity or hypochondriacal preoccupations (H. Kohut 1971). This pattern of idealization may give way to the opposite pattern of devaluation of the therapist (G. Adler 1970, 1985; Kernberg 1970; Myerson 1974), in which the sense of narcissistic inferiority and worthlessness is attributed to the therapist, thus reinforcing the patient's superiority and grandiosity (Adler 1970; Myerson 1974; Meissner 1981, 1986).

In some individuals the narcissistic fixation leads to the development of the grandiose self. The reactivation in analysis of the grandiose self provides the basis for the formation of the mirror transference. H. Kohut (1971) has described three forms of these: the archaic merger transference, a less archaic alter-ego transference or twinship, and the mirror transference in the narrow sense. In the most primitive merger transference, the analyst is experienced only as an extension of the subject's grandiose self, and thus becomes the repository of the patient's grandiosity and exhibitionism. In the alter-ego or twinship transference, activation of the grandiose self leads to the experience of the narcissistic object as similar to the grandiose self. In this variant, the object as such is preserved but is modified by the subject's perception of it to suit the subject's narcissistic needs, that is by assuming that the analyst is either like or similar to herself, or that they are similar in psychological makeup. In this type of transference, then, the reality of the analyst or therapist is modified by a projection of some aspects of the patient's grandiose self onto the object.

In the most mature form of mirror transference, the analyst is experienced as a separate person, but nonetheless one who becomes important to the patient and is accepted by him only to the degree that he is responsive to the narcissistic needs of the reactivated grandiose self. Kohut appeals here to the model of the gleam in the mother's eye, which responds to and mirrors the child's exhibitionism; correspondingly, the analyst's function is to admire and reflect the grandiosity and exhibitionism of the patient.

Self-object transferences also derive from Kohut's (1971, 1977, 1984) self psychology. The self-object involves an investment of the self in the object so that the object serves a self-sustaining function that the self cannot perform for itself—whether it is a question of maintaining fragile self-cohesion or in regulating self-esteem. The essential idea is that the nuclear self, defined in exclusively narcissistic terms (Kohut 1971), is continually at risk of fragmentation, disorganization, enfeeblement, or chaos, but that this inner state of fragility and vulnerability is protected and masked by a complex array of defenses. This state of affairs is the result of developmental failures in which the child's need to establish an autonomous self was denied or negated by the unempathic intrusions of parental self-objects (Kohut and E. S. Wolf 1982), resulting in primary disorders of the self.

The relationship between the patient and the therapist as the empathic self-object plays a specific role in the therapeutic process. In a sense, speaking teleologically, the patient's psyche makes the therapist a functional self-object in order to facilitate the processes of growth and structuring of the self. The self-object then serves to evoke and sustain the patient's self-organization and self-experience. G. Adler (1980) describes self-object transferences as "transferences in which the analyst and patient are variably fused along a complex continuum in which the analyst performs certain functions for the patient which are absent in the patient and which require the presence and functioning of the analyst for the patient to feel whole and complete" (547). This conceptualization is cast less in terms of object relations, that is, in terms of the interpersonal relationship between the self and its object, and more in terms of the intrapsychic experience of the self-object relationship, that is, the relationship between the self and its experienced object imagoes.

Self-object transferences reflect the underlying need-structure that the patient brings to the therapeutic relationship, based on the predominant pattern of self-object deprivation or frustration and the corresponding seeking for the appropriate form of self-object involvement. In these terms, a number of configurations have been described (Kohut and Wolf 1978, 1982). The understimulated self lacks vitality and is plagued by feelings of emptiness, boredom, and apathy, and thus seeks stimulation and even excitement or thrills as a means of warding off the pain of inner deadness. The overstimulated self struggles with intense ambition and fantasies of greatness, which force it to inhibit its capacity for productive or creative effort, or cause it to draw back from contexts in which they may become the center of attention or admiration. Such individuals thus find little satisfaction in external success. The intensity of their own exhibitionistic and grandiose wishes and fantasies is frightening and inhibiting. The overburdened self sees the world as potentially hostile and dangerous and thus reacts with hypersensitivity and feels easily attacked and vulnerable. At times, this pattern of reaction may even approach paranoia. The fragmenting self, on the other hand, frequently becomes disorganized and loses a sense of coordination in various aspects of her behavior and functioning. In the face of often trivial narcissistic deprivation, trauma, or disappointment, she loses a sense of her own internal cohesion and integration. Such states of fragmentation may often manifest themselves in hypochondriacal symptoms and preoccupations.

Some of the descriptions of self-object need represent efforts to translate the patterns of transference interaction based on narcissistic dynamics into the perspective of the relationship between self and self-object. Thus, mirror-hungry personalities express their need for mirroring in efforts to evoke attention, recognition, admiration, and approval from the object as a way of countering their inner sense of worthlessness, devaluation, and diminished self-esteem. Similarly, ideal-hungry personalities seek out objects whose power, beauty, prestige, intelligence, or other admirable qualities correspond to their need to attach themselves to the idealized object. Such patients can feel good about themselves and maintain a sense of inner equilibrium and cohesion only insofar as they are connected to these idealized objects. However satiating of such need the attachment to the object may be, the underlying neediness and emptiness will inevitably reassert itself and lead to dissatisfaction with the currently idealized object and a renewed search for another such object.

Variations on the mirroring transference theme include the alter-ego-hungry personality, who seeks a relationship with the object who can serve as a twin and whose conforming appearance, opinion, or

values confirms and sustains the integrity of the self. At a more pathological level, the merger-hungry personalities attach themselves to the object with such intensity that the boundaries between their own identity and that of the object become confused and lead to states of merger in which the subject is no longer able to discriminate his own thoughts or wishes or feelings from those of the object. The merger transference reconstitutes the fusion with the self-object of early development, akin to the earliest narcissistic union with the mother, in which the putative object shows no initiative or autonomy of its own but exists solely as an extension of the self. Such patients often expect that the therapist will know their most private thoughts and feelings without their saying anything about them. In such circumstances, any separation or autonomy of the object becomes intolerable and even devastating. In contrast, the contact-shunning personality is forced to avoid any significant involvement with objects as a way of defending itself from the underlying intense need for the object. These individuals tend to be exquisitely sensitive to rejection, but on a deeper level struggle with the basically schizoid fear of engulfment and destruction in the union with the object.

In these transferences, the classical meaning of transference has undergone radical modification. Rather than displacements from earlier object-relational contexts, the patient brings to bear a need based in her own deficient capacity and defective character structure—a need to involve the object in a dependent relationship in order to complete or stabilize her own psychic integration. What is "transferred," if anything, is rather a defect or lack resulting from developmental experience with unempathic or unresponsive objects.

Transitional relatedness offers an additional transference model, based on the analysis of Donald W. Winnicott's (1953) notion of the transitional object. The transference in more primitive character structures is regarded as a form of transitional object relation in which the therapist is perceived as outside the self, but is invested with qualities from the patient's own archaic self-image (A. Modell 1963). The intensity of this experience can vary considerably, ranging from relatively high levels of maintained reality testing to the opposite level of transference psychosis, reflecting the patient's inherent need for more primitive transitional involvement not only with people but often with things. Within the transitional relationship, the subject utilizes magical thinking to create a secure sense of being protected by an omnipotent maternal presence (Feinsilver 1983). The form of transitional relatedness seems to have a significant degree of overlap with the previously described self-object transferences and would be subject to some of the same qualifications.

Transference neurosis was originally regarded as the form of transference developing in analysis that expressed repressed infantile instinctual wishes (infantile neurosis) and became a source of resistance to remembering in the analytic process (Freud 1912). Freud thought the transference neurosis could replace the infantile neurosis and thus provide the focus for analytic treatment. Contemporary opinion is divided as to its importance and centrality, whether it forms to the extent Freud thought, and whether it is necessary for successful analysis—for some it remains an essential vehicle for analytic interpretation and resolution of the transference, while for others it may never develop or, to the extent that it does, may play a less central role in the process of cure (Panel 1991).

Transference psychosis occurs when the failure of reality testing leads to a loss of self-object differentiation and the diffusion of self and object boundaries (O. F. Kernberg 1968). The metaphors of fusion and merger are used to describe this phenomenon, as in the narcissistic merger transference. Such mirroring may reflect an attempt to refuse with an omnipotent object as a defense against underlying fears of vulnerability and powerlessness. The fused dyad has been invested with omnipotent powers (T. H. McGlashan 1983) to preserve the patient's fragile sense of self, but may also include negative transference, in which fusion carries the threat of engulfment and loss of self that may precipitate a paranoid transference reaction (H. F. Searles 1985).

These are regressive transference psychoses in which reality testing fails so that the line between fantasy and reality is blurred, and the difference between transference and the real person of the therapist is obscured (P. L. Giovacchini 1987).

The therapist is experienced, not as *like* the past object, but as *identical* to it (Wallerstein 1967). The resulting transference psychosis reflects the emergence of delusional material in the transference.

Transference Mechanisms

Understanding transferences requires some exploration of the underlying mechanisms and their dynamic interactions. I will focus here on three mechanisms that contribute to transference formation, namely, displacement, projection, and projective identification.

Displacement is the basic mechanism of the classic transference paradigm, in which an object representation derived from any level or combination of levels of the subject's developmental experience is displaced to the new object in the therapeutic relationship. The object representation is imposed on the new object, namely, the analyst or therapist, so that he now comes to be invested with the affective burdens and connotations that were inherent in the old object relationship. Displacement is the basic mechanism for libidinally based transferences, both positive and erotic, as described above. By and large, displacement transferences play a dominant role in neurotic disorders, in which phallic-oedipal dynamics tend to play a dominant role in the transference; as one moves further down the psychopathological spectrum, such phallic-oedipal derivatives tend to be absorbed in and overwhelmed by more primitive concerns of separation, abandonment, idealization, dependence, and merger.

Projection tends to play a more prominent role in the formation of transferences in more primitive character disorders, while displacement transferences tend to play a less significant part (W. W. Meissner 1981, 1984, 1988). Projections are derived from the configuration of the introjects, which constitute part of the core internalizations of the patient's self-structure. Consequently, the effect of the projective or externalizing transference is to make the therapist represent a part of the patient's own self-organization (H. F. Searles 1984). Whether in the more specific forms of projection or in more general forms of externalization, the transference projections may not simply be based on intrapsychically derived distortions but may have a reality component insofar as they correspond to aspects of the therapist's or analyst's actual traits or behaviors, which become exaggerated by the patient's pathological needs (R. Langs 1978–79; H. F. Searles 1978–79). The connection with the actual traits of the therapist may involve countertransference elements, but may also relate to her real characteristics, exclusive of transferential considerations.

The projection of elements derived from the aggressive introject provides the basis for both negative and paranoid transference reactions (Giovacchini 1975b; Kernberg 1966, 1968, 1984). By the same token, the projection of the elements of the victim-introject allows the patient to assume the hostile, sadistic, or aggressive position in which he becomes the aggressor to the therapist's victim. These patterns are usually defensively and reciprocally linked, so that when the patient is in the aggressive position it usually represents a defense against underlying fears of weakness, powerlessness, and vulnerability. By the same token, when he occupies the victim position, this can be considered to be defending against underlying fears of his own destructiveness, hatefulness, and power. Similar patterns can take place around narcissistic issues involving introjective configurations of narcissistic superiority and inferiority. When the superior narcissistic elements are projected, the result is a form of idealization of the object, just as, when the inferior aspects are projected, the result is a corresponding devaluation of the object and enhancement of the grandiose self.

The projective dynamics in the self-object transferences are somewhat obscure, but it seems more likely that these forms of transference tend to draw or pull the object or the environment into a position of meeting the pathological needs of the self. Thus, in the various forms of self-object transference, the therapist can be drawn into the process of responding to the needs of the self without necessarily becoming herself an object of specific projection on the part of the patient. If anything is projected it would be an infantile wished-for imago, one that was lacking earlier in the patient's experience. While the transitional transference enjoys a considerable degree of overlap with self-object transferences, the projective element tends to be somewhat more explicit as the self-contribution to the transitional

phenomenon. Even though the transitional object and the resulting transitional relationship are not constituted solely by the projection, the object as experienced by the patient nonetheless represents an amalgamation or combination of the objective attributes of the real object, namely the therapist, and the subjectively derived projective content. This view of transitional relatedness leaves open the question of the degree to which the real attributes of the therapist correspond to or even contribute to the shaping of the transference.

Projective identification is often appealed to as a constitutive mechanism of transference, particularly in the Kleinian perspective. Confusion arises from the failure to clearly distinguish between projection and projective identification (Meissner 1980, 1987). Melanie Klein's view of projective identification comes out of the linkage between projection and introjection, mechanisms that she saw operating in constant interaction in a variety of developmental contexts. She argues that the projection of impulses or feelings into another person brings about an identification with that person, based on the attribution to that other of one's own qualities, that becomes the basis for a certain form of empathy and connection with the object. Thus, by implication, the notion of projective identification adds to the basic concept of projection the notes of diffusion of ego boundaries, a loss or diminishing of self-object differentiation, and inclusion of the object as part of the self.

Later elaborations of the notion of projective identification have translated it from a one-body context into a two-body context. The mechanisms come to apply to an interaction between two subjects, one of whom projects something onto or into the other, whereupon the other introjects or internalizes what has been projected. Instead of the projection and identification taking place in the same subject, the projection takes place in one and the internalization in the other (H. Segal 1957; J. S. Grotstein 1981). This latter usage has served as a basis for an extensive extrapolation of the concept of projective identification to apply to object relations of all sorts, including transference (H. Segal 1977).

William W. Meissner

Transference Neurosis

Freud used the term *transference neurosis* in two ways. Nosologically, the transference neuroses include hysterical and obsessive-compulsive conditions, and refer to those patients capable of establishing a transference with the analyst. These disturbances are distinguished from the narcissistic neuroses, which refer to patients who are not able to form such relationships and, therefore, Freud felt, are not amenable to psychoanalytic treatment. Technically, "transference neurosis" is the term Freud utilized to designate the revival, under certain specific conditions, of the infantile neurosis in the analytic situation.

Victor Calef (1971) has summarized the salient elements of the transference neurosis in the following seven points:

1. The infantile neurosis is revived.
2. The illness is new, concentrated upon the relationship to the doctor, and created out of the frustrated demand for love.
3. The symptomatology is dynamic, shifting, and changing in nature, not static.
4. Energy is displaced and transformed; the mechanisms of regression and repetition are essential to the development of the transference neurosis.
5. The old symptoms of the adult neurosis lose their libidinal force.
6. The transference situation in the transference neurosis is not identical and does not describe in a one-to-one manner the nature of the infantile relationships, which have become transferred.
7. Eventually the transference neurosis itself becomes involved in a resistance to treatment; however, its management permits the undoing of repression and is the central issue of treatment; this differentiates analysis from other forms of treatment.

Victor Calef
Edward M. Weinshel

Transference Resistance

Sigmund Freud's description of transference resistance appears in his technical paper "The Dynamics of Transference" (1912). Here he observes that, early in treatment, one finds generally a positive transference, which is predominantly conscious and which expresses itself in friendly or affectionate feelings.

As the analytic work progresses, however, and as the effects of the analytic regression take hold, this situation changes. As the analytic work comes closer to the neurotic conflicts, the resistances increase, and specific transference resistances are mobilized.

The negative transference forms the other dimension of the transference resistance. The negative aspects of transference are usually found side by side with more positive aspects, reflecting the underlying ambivalence of the patient's object relations. While ambivalence is a normal phenomenon, Freud observes that its titer seems to be increased in neurotic people.

While the resistances against the transference take place essentially outside of the transference dynamics—either prior to or subsequent to the emergence of the transference—resistances also occur within the transference and between transference elements. Such resistances may take the form of defensive configurations.

Clinical work with transference resistances, as with all resistances, entails their recognition, clarification, and ultimately, interpretation. This work allows for the full emergence of the transference neurosis and its resolution. The conceptual evolution within psychoanalysis has generated a certain diversity in therapeutic approaches. In Freud's terms, the transference was viewed as the attachment of repressed instinctual fantasies to the analyst. But with the development of a structural approach, the superego began to play a more significant role in the understanding of transference dynamics. As the introjected derivative of the oedipal situation, the transference distortion was seen in terms of the projection of aspects of the superego to the person of the analyst. Consequently, the analyst was viewed not only as an object of displaced infantile incestuous or ambivalent fantasies but, in addition, as a substitute by projection for the prohibiting parental figures who had been more or less definitively internalized as the superego.

The divergence of conceptual views has had its impact on the therapeutic approach to transference resistances. Ego psychologists, who tend to emphasize the role of the ego and the analysis of defenses, tend to follow Freud's view that analysis should proceed from surface to depth and regard material produced early in the analysis as reflecting defensive processes and resistances rather than displacements to the analyst of early instinctual fantasies. In this view, the transference neurosis emerges only after ego defenses have been sufficiently analyzed and undermined to mobilize infantile elements.

Negative transference resistances often have a paranoid cast, which may be difficult to unearth, may be well defended by the patient, and may reflect a deep level of underlying mistrust. Such patients often stir up acute paranoid responses in the face of the analytic regression, or may persist in a more or less chronic but low-grade masochistic position, in which the analyst is seen in hostile, judgmental, or critical terms. The latent paranoid defense and the submissive masochistic transference may also be in the service of the defense against positive but threatening affects. If the negative therapeutic response goes unanalyzed, it may eventuate in a negative therapeutic reaction. Edward Glover (1972) has identified this as a form of "superego resistance" in which guilt-motivated persistence of symptoms serves as a form of self-punishment. A. A. Modell (1971) has stressed the role of unconscious guilt, specifically in terms of preoedipal determinants and their inherent relationship to envy and narcissistic deprivation. Similar dynamics have been described by A. F. Valenstein (1973) in discussing the role of attachment to painful feelings in the negative therapeutic response.

As in the case with transference neuroses, so also in the analysis of narcissistic transferences the analyst does not inhibit the spontaneous mobilization of transference elements. Interpretation begins only when the transference manifestations become a transference resistance. Heinz Kohut has suggested that it is characteristic of the narcissistic transference resistance that it leads not so much in the direction of fulfillment of infantile wishes as toward attempts at retreating from them. Consequently, he emphasized the need for working through other aspects of the transference resistance in order to allow sufficient mobilization of narcissistic transference elements.

William W. Meissner

Transpersonal Psychology

The task of transpersonal psychology is concern for transpersonal processes, values, and states; unitive consciousness; metaneeds; peak experiences; ecstasy; mystical experience; being; essence; bliss; awe; wonder; transcendence of self; spirit; sacralization of everyday life; oneness; cosmic awareness and play; individual and species-wise synergy; meditation; spiritual paths; compassion; transpersonal cooperation, realization, and actualization; and related concepts and activities.

The history of Western psychology, before the emergence of transpersonal psychology, reveals little enduring interest in the study of experiences that appear to have spiritual, religious, or cosmic significance. Three important exceptions may be noted. The first is William James's interest in religiosity and mysticism, expressed in his Gifford lectures on natural religion, delivered in 1901 to 1902 at the University of Edinburgh, and published as *Varieties of Religious Experience* (1958).

The second historical exception is Carl Jung's theory of personality, particularly its concepts of the collective unconscious and the self. Special emphasis is placed on these aspects of Jung's theory because they permeate the transpersonal movement, although references to Jung are surprisingly lacking in much of its literature.

The third exception to Western psychology's general lack of interest in transpersonal processes is the general field of parapsychology (Wolman 1977). Studies of clairvoyance, telepathy, psychokinesis, and precognition have gained scientific recognition mainly because the pioneer, J. B. Rhine (who began the experimental study of parapsychology at Duke University in 1927), demanded that research reported in the *Journal of Parapsychology* meet the highest standards of scientific respectability.

Franklin C. Shontz

Treatment of Mental Disorders: Issues in the Philosophy of Science

Empirical sciences are presented in a series of statements called propositions. Formal logic distinguishes two classes of propositions, namely, analytic and synthetic. Analytic propositions are mere definitions; synthetic propositions are statements of fact, and as such they are the backbone of all empirical sciences.

Human behavior, normal and abnormal alike, can be described in four types of synthetic propositions; (1) overt, observable behavior (e.g., psychomotor phenomena, epileptic seizures, etc.); (2) introspectively observable behavior (e.g., pain, delusions, etc.); (3) inferable data, nondirectly observed (e.g., repressed wishes, psychosomatic causes of overt symptoms, etc.); and (4) generalizations of any of the first three propositions.

It can be easily proven that none of these categories apply to the treatment of mental disorders, whether it is practiced by a neurosurgeon, psychiatrist, clinical psychologist, or any other professional, or whether the treatment method is physical, chemical, or psychological. For instance, the proposition "Epilepsy is a disease transmitted by a single recessive gene" is either true or false, but the proposition "Epilepsy should be treated by thorazine" is neither true nor false; it is a good or bad recommendation.

Treatment of mental disorders is practiced by medically trained psychiatrists, clinical psychologists, and other mental health professionals. Medicine, like education, engineering, and agriculture, is an applied science—a system that devises actions based on empirical science. Such a system of devices is called praxeology (Kotarbinski 1965).

Praxeological propositions are neither true nor false. They describe ends and means, goals, and methods leading toward the achievement of the goal. Every praxeological system, such as agriculture, education, engineering, and medicine, is comprised of two parts. The first part deals with goal setting, and it is called teleology (from the Greek *telos*). The second part deals with methods and means, and it is called technology (Wolman 1949).

Healing praxeologies lean heavily on the various empirical disciplines that deal with the human organism. These disciplines determine the concept of health, and thus enable praxeology to set health as the immanent goal of medicine. To protect health and restore it whenever it has been damaged or lost is the immanent goal of medical praxeology.

Praxeological technology studies the various methods and their efficiency. Ultimately, the treatment method can be validated or invalidated depending on its results.

Benjamin B. Wolman

Triage Service in Psychiatry

Triage is a French military word that originally meant the rapid evaluation, sorting, and treatment of battle casualties. Minor injuries are treated at once on the scene, while more severe injuries are quickly evaluated and provided only with necessary first aid and sent behind the lines to more suitable treatment centers.

The ideal of psychiatric triage is in a general hospital in the heart of the community served. This should be an emergency room service or an acute admission ward. The general hospital enables related physical problems to be simultaneously evaluated and treated.

In situations of few staff and many patients, psychiatric triage provides high-quality patient evaluation and treatment. This is effected by having highly trained staff evaluate every new case at a central facility.

David J. Muller

Tuke, Daniel Hack (1827–1895)

Daniel Hack Tuke wrote extensively about medical care. He was one of the founders of the Aftercare Association in Great Britain. His main works were *A*

Manual of Psychological Medicine (with John Buckwill, 1858) and *Dictionary of Psychological Medicine* (1894).

John C. Burnham

Tuke, Samuel (1784–1857)

In 1813, Samuel Tuke published *Descriptions of Retreat* (about the York Retreat) and explained the principles of kindness, minimum physical restraint, activity programs, and moral treatment of mental patients. His main work is *Description of the Retreat,* *an Institution New York for Insane Persons of the Society of Friends, Containing an Account of Its Origins and Progress, the Modes of the Treatment, and a Statement of Cases* (1864).

John C. Burnham

Tuke, William (1732–1822)

William Tuke founded the York Retreat and initiated reforms in the treatment of the mentally ill in Great Britain and elsewhere in the world.

John C. Burnham

· U ·

Ukhtomsky, Alexei Alexeivich (1875–1942)

Alexei Alexeivich Ukhtomsky was a disciple of Ivan Mikhailovich Sechenov and of N. E. Vedensky. He was responsible for the theory of Dominanta, meaning that spots of the motor cortex, if successfully stimulated, take control of near and far points of the nervous system and draw them together.

Gustav Eckstein

· V ·

Valence

This concept was introduced by Kurt Lewin (1951) to refer to the attractiveness or repulsiveness of an activity or the expected consequence of an activity in the psychological environment of an individual. His conceptual analysis of motivation, conflict, and action (first summarized in 1938) was guided by the analogy provided by the post-Galilean physics of motion. The valence $Va(G)$ that an object or activity G possesses for a person at a given time is attributed to the state of need in the person (t_g) and upon the perceived nature of the object or activity:

$$V(a)=f(t_g, G)$$

If $Va(G)$ 0, a positive valence, then the magnitude of psychological force $(F_{P,G})$, the impetus to action, will be positive and produce approach behavior. If $Va(G)$ 0, the valence is negative. Then the psychological force that is produced is represented as

$$F_{P,-G,}$$

a force to avoid an activity or the expected negative consequence of an activity.

John W. Atkinson

Validity of Psychological Tests

Validity is a matter of degree rather than an all-or-none property, and validation is an unending process. Whereas measures of length and of some other simple physical attributes may have proved their merits so well that no one seriously considers changing to other measures, most measures should be kept under constant surveillance to make sure they are behaving as they should. New evidence may suggest modifications of an existing measure or the development of a new and better approach to measuring the attribute in question (e.g., anxiety, intelligence, or the temperature of stars).

Predictive Validity

The term *prediction* is used in a general (and ungrammatical) sense to refer to functional relations between an instrument and events occurring before, during, and after the instrument is applied. Thus, a test administered to adults could be used to make "predictions" about events that occurred in their childhood.

Up to about 1950, it was frequently said that the validity of a measure was indicated by the correlation between the measure and its criterion. Actually, predictive validity (criterion-related validity) usually is not the most important standard for judging the worth of measures employed in basic research.

Content Validity

There are many examples of measures that require content validity. All achievement tests require content validity, as would be the case, for example, with a comprehensive measure of progress in school up to the end of the fourth grade or a comprehensive measure of the extent to which men had performed well in a school for electronics technicians in the armed forces.

Some forms of empirical evidence are helpful in judging content validity. For example, at least a moderate level of internal consistency among the items within a test would be expected; that is, the items should tend to measure something in common. This is not an infallible guide, however, because with some subject matters it is reasonable to include material that taps somewhat different abilities.

Construct Validity

To the extent that a variable is abstract rather than concrete, it is spoken of as being a *construct*. Such a variable is literally a construct in that it is something that the scientist puts together from her own imagination, something that does not exist as an isolated, observable dimension of behavior. A construct represents a hypothesis that a variety of behaviors will correlate with one another in studies of individual differences or will be similarly affected by experimental treatments.

Issues regarding construct validity boil down to a number of conclusions. First, it must be realized that many forms of psychological measurement cannot be assessed for their usefulness primarily by methods relating to predictive validity and content validity, this typically being the case with measures employed in basic research. Second, many of the construct names that populate psychological theories are not very precise semantically (e.g., intelligence or anxiety).

Jum C. Nunnally

Values Measurement

Values concern sentiments, along with attitudes, interests, and other human preferences. As the term will be used here, values concern preferences for "life goals" and "ways of life," in contrast to interests, which concern preferences for particular activities.

In contrast to measures of interests, measures of values are seldom used in applied activities; instead, they are usually employed in basic research in sociology and social psychology.

Jum C. Nunnally

Values and Value Systems

A common definitional element in philosophical and economic treatment of the problem of human values is behavioral selectivity, or the lack of indifference of the person for distinct outcomes or states of affairs. Theories about human selectivity are both prescriptive (normative) and descriptive.

Theories of moral development in contemporary social psychology have been heavily influenced by the interactionist positions of Jean Piaget and George Herbert Mead. The direction of moral development is commonly characterized as being from egocentrism to a concern with larger and larger social entities and also from the concrete to the abstract. L. Kohlberg has provided evidence that this sort of developmental progression is characteristic of a wide variety of cultures.

Among the theoretical and empirical issues that provide a focus for contemporary research on values, the following five questions may serve as prominent examples:

1. *The problem of multidimensionality of values (or utilities).* Economists and decision theorists have commonly assumed that in principle all values are commensurable—that is, some common scale of values may be used to compare any set of valued objects, for example, hours of work and articles of consumption.
2. *The translation of individual to collective preference patterns—Arrow's paradox.* Preference rankings exhibited by individuals have been shown to produce certain paradoxes when grouped together.
3. *The problem of value-expectancy interactions.* Game theorists and decision theorists conventionally assume that outcome values and outcome likelihoods vary independently of each other—that is, the subjective probability associated with the occurrence of the event is supposed to be some function of the relative frequency of the occurrence of that event in the past (plus generalizations from other events).
4. *The issue of unconscious motives or values.* A good portion of conventional goal-directed

behavior does not require recourse to unconscious values or motives for explanation.

5. *The problem of the equivocal relationship between preference behavior and values.* Daniel E. Berlyne has developed a clear operational distinction between the pleasingness of stimuli and their interestingness. His studies, in the general area of experimental aesthetics, show that subjects rate simple, symmetrical, and low-information value stimuli as pleasant, but that they prefer to spend time looking or listening to stimuli that are relatively more complex and rich in information—more interesting.

Karl E. Scheibe

Vandalism

It is important to recognize that vandalism is often purposeful and carries a message of political, social, or psychological value from the perpetrator of the act to the society. Secondly, vandalism ought not to be discounted by attributing it to the immaturity of juveniles; it can occur at all socioeconomic and age levels in any society that engenders feelings of powerlessness and anonymity in its citizens.

The extent of vandalism in a given society may be seen as an index of the degree to which the social cohesion that binds individuals into a community is being warped. As such, it is a bellwether of the breakdown in social trust and respect that can eventually be transformed into the violent destruction of other people as well as of their property. Therefore, vandalism must be recognized for the serious social psychological issues it poses to any society, not merely for its obvious economic consequences.

Philip G. Zimbardo

Vigilance and Motivation

Vigilance has become a major topic in behavior research because it offers a genuinely important applied problem easily transferred to the controlled conditions of the laboratory for study. The fact that performance in vigilance tasks is reliably affected by variation in stimulus, task, environmental, social, and personality parameters also makes it an attractive vehicle for study of many problems in behavior theory.

Signal Detectability
Research. Four classes of variables that could affect vigilance by increasing or decreasing motivation can be identified: dynamic characteristics of stimuli; incentives, including knowledge of results; environmental conditions or changes; and observer temperament. Each class will be considered with respect to detection level and performance decrement over time.

The effects of environmental conditions and living schedule on vigilance appear to be, like those for other behaviors, extremely complex. The evidence does suggest that if the deviation from normal is sufficiently great, or the truly critical variables are identified and varied, substantial detrimental effects result. Sleep deprivation and noise-exposure effects offer the prime examples insofar as vigilance is concerned. If sleep deprivation is substantial and performance is measured throughout the circadian cycle, vigilance level declines and there is a vigilance decrement with time at work at the expected points in the cycle. Noise at levels to at least 80 db often improves performance in vigilance tasks.

George Moeller

Vincent Curve

The Vincent curve is a method for constructing learning curves for the results of experiments where subjects are run to some fixed criterion of performance. Such procedures create a problem because different subjects will take different numbers of trials to meet the criterion. If data were plotted trial by trial, there would be different numbers of subjects and different individuals at many data points. In order to avoid this problem, the data are plotted as a function of a fraction of the number of trials required by each subject, most commonly tenths of the total.

Gregory A. Kimble

Violence and Youth

The Summary Report of the American Psychological Association Commission on Violence and Youth (1993) defined youth as the period from preschool through college, ages 3 through 22. The report admits that "no definitive answer yet exists that would make it possible to predict exactly which individuals will become violent" (17). Psychologists seek a unified theoretical model that would include both nature and nurture. However, a child's level of aggression among her agemates appears to be an important factor that indicates her future aggressive behavior: "Children who show a fearless, impulsive temperament very early in life may have a predisposition for aggressive and violent behavior" (18).

Family background plays a significant role in antisocial and violent behavior. Interparental interaction and abusive parental discipline play a significant role in the development of violent behavior in the offspring. Moreover, it may also interfere with academic and social life in school. Children who are aggressive and violent tend to share common experiences.

The APA Commission reviewed several contributing factors, including socioeconomic experience, prejudice, and discrimination. The attitude of the mass media to violence, and their impact on youth violence in particular, is a significant factor. The commission also found that poverty is an important determinant of violence, whereas race is not. Prejudice and discrimination against ethnic groups undermines their self-confidence and self-esteem, and contributes to anger and violence. The commission reported that the United States has the highest rate of violence of any industrialized country. Moreover, the way the "American mass media present image after image reflecting the violence in society in some cases may exploit or contribute to it" (24). Access to firearms, involvement with alcohol and drugs, participation in antisocial groups, and exposure to violence in mass media are experiences that are a "trajectory toward violence."

The APA Commission explored possible programs for intervention. Effective intervention programs are based on an understanding of sociocultural and developmental factors that lead to antisocial behavior, and which develop strategies that are efficient in changing human behavior. A positive intervention in early childhood can reduce antisocial and aggressive behavior at the present time and in years to come. The commission recommends 1) "home visitor" programs that include prenatal and postnatal family counseling, 2) preschool programs, and 3) school-based primary intervention programs for children and adolescents.

The commission strongly recommends psychological research that should identify effective intervention programs "that address the continuum of prevention, early intervention, and rehabilitation."

Benjamin B. Wolman

Visual-Motor Information

Present-day cognitive psychology is returning to its earlier awareness of the need to relate human performance to cognitive processes.

Visual motor organization (VMO) lies along a continuum, the two endpoints of which are sensory and perceptual. "Sensory VMO" depends mainly on the speed and accuracy with which exteroceptive and kinesthetic information can be conjointly processed during the development of skill. The same is true for "perceptual VMO," but—in addition—the acquisition of skill is abetted by the greater possibility of being able to synthesize information more readily, and thereby to plan. "Synthesizing" implies the combining of different sources of information such that the result transcends the entering components, even though it depends upon them. "Planning" implies taking advantage of whatever coherence or predictability may exist in a situation.

Joseph M. Notterman

Visual Sensitivity

The most common procedure for specifying the visual system's sensitivity is to determine the intensity (number of quanta/unit area/unit time) needed to produce a sensation of light. In determining this intensity, called the threshold intensity, procedures called psychophysical methods are used.

Ambient Light

When the ambient light level is changed, the visual system's sensitivity does not immediately adjust to the new level. If ambient light is increased, the adjustment is quite rapid, a fraction of a second for small changes and only a few minutes for an extreme change from darkness to high light levels. However, if ambient light is decreased, the adjustment can be quite slow.

Measurement

There are measures of visual sensitivity concerned with visual capabilities other than the simple detection of light. The eye is very good at discriminating spatial details; this ability is referred to as visual acuity. The acuity of the visual system is measured in terms of the minimum size (expressed in minutes of visual angle) of some aspect of a test object that can be detected or recognized by an observer.

Intensity of Light

The measures of spatial and temporal acuity described above are concerned with defining and measuring the limits of visual capability. Recently, the eye's sensitivity to a range of temporal and spatial frequencies has been obtained. The general approach is one borrowed from the engineer's concept of a modulation transfer function. For a given frequency of temporal alternation or spatial frequency of an acuity grating, the time or space average intensity is held constant and the depth of modulation or contrast is decreased until the observer can no longer detect the fluctuation or spatial grating. With this procedure, the visual system's sensitivity to a range of frequencies, under various conditions, can be measured.

Donald C. Hood

Visually Controlled Movement

Higher mammals, including human beings, are deficient at birth and proficient as adults in the visual coordination of movement. Substantial experimental investigation has been devoted to the conditions underlying the adult achievement. Evidence arises from two principal sources: adaptation studies using adult human subjects exposed to optical rearrangement of vision, and developmental studies of neonatal animals, usually cats, reared with limited exposure to the environment.

A. H. Riesen and his colleagues at the University of Chicago presented the first studies that directly implicated movement in the acquisition of normal perceptual capacities. Riesen (1958) had earlier noted that kittens reared in the dark show significant deficits in performance of visually guided movement when first brought into light. Riesen later discovered that comparable deficits follow rearing with exposure in light limited to periods when the kitten is restrained in a holder. Hein and Held suggested that the essential deprivation for a restrained animal was elimination of opportunity to link body movements with their normal visual consequences while moving about in light.

Feedback

Previous experiments emphasized the role of motor-visual feedback (1) in determining which of a number of independent components of visual-motor coordination would develop, and (2) in the adjustment of selected components of visually coordinated movement to prismatic displacement of vision. However, the performance of visually controlled movement implies integrated action among the component subsystems. The finding that visually guided locomotion in the kitten is prerequisite to the development of visually guided reading indicates that the sequence of acquisition is constrained.

Alan Hein

Vitalism

Vitalism is the idea that a special principle distinguishes living organisms from inorganic substances. It can be traced to Aristotle but was given special prominence when it was espoused by the great German physiologist Johannes Müller.

The principle was also espoused by Hans Driesch, among others. Driesch offered four proofs of vitalism: (1) his work on sea urchins showed that any cell could develop into a whole organism; the cells were thus equal in potential or equivalent with respect to the organic principle or development; (2) the facts of inheritance—no machine can reproduce itself; (3) there is an evaluative use of past experience by living organisms; and (4) memory and creation of novelty are seen in organic life but not in inorganic substances.

Charles N. Cofer

Voluntary Behavior

History

In nineteenth-century faculty psychology, intentional behavior was said to be a function of the will and to occur because of the operation of this mental category. The concept of volition failed to survive the objectivist psychological revolution of the early twentieth century for the following reasons:

1. The notion that behavior can be explained by assignment to a category is empty of scientific value.
2. The assignment to a faculty of the mind raised all the problems associated with mentalism.

The theory of ideomotor action concerns the stimuli responsible for voluntary behavior. William James maintained that these stimuli exist and that they are images of the consequences of the act—what it would feel like to raise an arm, what the visual consequences of looking to the right might be, and so on. Given such an image, James maintained, voluntary behavior is as automatic as any other.

Scattered Experimental Work

The sparse history of investigation of voluntary processes includes one line of work in a most unlikely context—human eyelid conditioning. In these experiments, subjects are conditioned to blink to some neutral stimulus, which is paired with an effective unconditioned stimulus (US), most often a puff of air delivered to the cornea. In experiments of this type, two response forms can be identified. One, a voluntary form, is a large response of short latency and long duration. The other, a conditioned form, is a smaller response with a longer latency and a brief duration. Although the segregation of subjects on the basis of response form is not absolute, it is possible to identify some individuals whose responses are predominantly voluntary and others whose responses are predominantly conditioned.

Another line of work involving the basic procedures of conditioning that relates to voluntary behavior is that on the operant conditioning of visceral responses initiated by Neal Miller (1969). Although Miller's interpretation of his results seems likely to be incorrect, this should not lead to a depreciation of the value placed on this work. In these experiments, Miller and his associates made the receipt of reinforcing brain stimulation contingent upon the occurrence of some interval response (heart rate, blood pressure, bowel distention) in curarized rats. The purpose of curarization was to eliminate responses of the skeletal musculature that might mediate the response of interest. In a series of experiments, Miller and his associates showed that these latter responses could be manipulated by the procedures of operant conditioning or brought under voluntary control independently of skeletal mechanisms.

Other Properties of Voluntary Acts

The classical writings on voluntary behavior contain other leads to investigation, sometimes bolstered by a limited amount of experimental work. One of these relates to William James's account of the history of a voluntary act, the proposal that a voluntary act is never voluntary the first time that it occurs.

Gregory A. Kimble

·W·

Wagner von Jauregg (Wagner-Jauregg), Julius Ritter (1857–1940)

Julius Ritter Wagner-Jauregg was the first psychiatrist to win the Nobel Prize. The award was for his malarial fever treatment of general paralysis (syphilitic paresis). In 1887, he noticed that psychoses sometimes improve in patients who have had intercurrent infectious diseases.

John C. Burnham

Watson, Goodwin (1899–1976)

Goodwin Watson published several books in social psychology, among them *Social Psychology: Issues and Insights* (1966).

Virginia Staudt Sexton

Watson, John Broadus (1878–1958)

John Broadus Watson is the father of behaviorism. Initially, Watson adopted conventional psychological concepts to describe his animal research. His 1913 paper "Psychology as the Behaviorist Views It" may be regarded as the launching point of the behaviorist movement. *Behavior: An Introduction to Comparative Psychology* (1914) expresses Watson's early position. Watson argued that if psychology was to be a science, it had to emulate other sciences in studying publicly observable phenomena. Watson argued that only objective methods be used, such as systematic observation—preferable experimenta-

tion—in contrast to the subjective method of introspection. Among Watson's secondary points was the statement that the goal of psychology was prediction and control of behavior. Watson's views evolved over the years, and the most radical of his positions were his metaphysical behaviorism, his materialistic monism, and his radical environmentalism.

Thomas C. Cadwallader

Wechsler, David (1894–1981)

David Wechsler developed several intelligence scales. The first edition of the *Measurement of Adult Intelligence* was published in 1939. During World War II, he devised the Army Wechsler Scale and, later, the Wechsler Intelligence Scale for Children (WISC). In 1955, a revision of the Wechsler–Bellvue (W–B), titled the Wechsler Adult Intelligence Scale (WAIS), appeared. Wechsler revised the WISC, developed the Wechsler Pre-School and Primary Scale of Intelligence (WPPSI) and completed a revision of the WAIS. In his last years, Wechsler worked on a scale for use for the elderly, called the Wechsler Intelligence Scale for the Elderly (WISE).

Allen Jack Edwards

Wechsler's Intelligence Tests

David Wechsler began his work on the measurement of general ability with the development of an adult test, which is frequently used with students aged 15 and older. The presently used form is called the Wechsler Adult Intelligence Scale (WAIS; Wechsler 1955). The WAIS consists of the following eleven subtests:

I WAIS: Verbal Scale
1. General information
2. General comprehension
3. Arithmetical reasoning
4. Similarities
5. Digit span
6. Vocabulary
II WAIS: Performance Scale
7. Digit symbol
8. Picture completion
9. Block design
10. Picture arrangement
11. Object assembly

Children's Scale

A separate scale is available for children, which is called the Wechsler Intelligence Scale for Children (WISC). The first version appeared in 1949. A revised edition was published in 1974 and is designated WISC-R. The WISC-R is used for children and adolescents aged 6–17, and the WAIS is used for all older age groups. The WISC-R is very similar to the WAIS, the major difference being that the WISC-R contains material more appropriate for, and more interesting to, younger people. The subtests of the WISC-R are as follows:

Verbal Scale
1. General information
2. General comprehension
3. Arithmetic
4. Similarities
5. Vocabulary
   Alternate: Digit span
   Performance Scale
6. Picture completion
7. Picture arrangement
8. Block design
9. Object assembly
10. Coding
    Alternate: Mazes

IQs on the WISC-R are determined in the same general manner as on the adult test. As in the adult form, IQs can be obtained separately for total scale, verbal scale, and performance scale.

Jum C. Nunnally

Wernicke, Karl (1848–1905)

Karl Wernicke published the first comprehensive description of cerebral localization. Wernicke viewed mental disorders as diseases of the brain. He demonstrated the dominance of one hemisphere of the brain, and described the Wernicke syndrome and Wernicke encephalopathy.

Leo H. Berman

Wertheimer, Max (1880–1943)

Max Wertheimer was one of the founders (with Wolfgang Köhler and Kurt Koffka) of Gestalt psychology. He investigated perceptual grouping or organization, such as proximity, similarity, symmetry, and closure. He termed these organizational phenomena *Gestalten*, and emphasized their outstanding features in perception, which he called the law of Prägnanz.

Frank Wesley

Weyer, Johannes, (c.1516–1588)

Johannes Weyer wrote a memorable criticism of the Inquisition. He suggested that mental illness was often involved in cases where people were accused of witchcraft.

John C. Burnham

White, William Alanson (1870–1937)

William Alanson White was one of the early American psychoanalysts. White was the president of the First International Congress of Mental Hygiene and one of the editors of the *Journal of Nervous and Mental Disease* and of the *Psychoanalytic Review*. In 1933 Harry Stack Sullivan organized the William Alanson White Psychiatric Foundation in honor of White.

White was instrumental in bridging the gap between psychoanalysis and academic psychiatry.

Benjamin B. Wolman

Winnicott, Donald W. (1896–1971)

Donald W. Winnicott's approach to psychoanalysis was influenced by his clinical work with children. His main works were *Through Pediatrics to Psycho-Analysis* (1958) and *Therapeutic Consultations in Child Psychiatry* (1971).

M. Masud R. Khan

Witkin, Herman A. (1916–1979)

Herman A. Witkin's interests and research focused on the relationship between cognition and personality, examined from experimental, social, cross-cultural, and developmental perspectives. His two major volumes are *Personality through Perception: An Experimental and Clinical Study* (1954) and *Psychological Differentiation: Studies of Development.*

Virginia Staudt Sexton

Wolman, Benjamin B. (1908–)

Benjamin B. Wolman's scientific contribution includes the relationship between psychology and philosophy of science; the sociopsychological theory of instrumentalism (taking), mutualism (giving and taking), and vectorialism (giving) in behavior; personality theory with the new concepts of we-ego and vectorial ego; the sociopsychosomatic theory of mental disorders; and psychoanalytic psychotherapy based on interaction between doctors and patients. In 1970 Wolman organized the International Organization for the Study of Group Tensions, and he is its president and editor of the organization's journal. In the years 1977 to 1983, Wolman edited the thirteen-volume *International Encyclopedia of Psychiatry, Psychology, Psychoanalysis and Neurology.*

Paul D. Boyer

Word Association

The word association method was one of the earliest projective techniques. It was popularized by Carl Jung, and for a while was a widely used clinical assessment technique.

There are several standard lists available, the oldest being the Kent-Rosanoff Free Association Test. Clinicians who use this method either construct their own stimulus word lists or modify existing lists to increase the sensitivity of the technique for a particular subject. Flexibility is one of the word association method's strongest clinical features.

Philip A. Goldberg

Work Motivation

Contemporary views of work motivation can be roughly classified as primarily content oriented or as primarily process oriented. Content theories attempt to specify what it is that motivates people at work. Process theories, on the other hand, are more concerned with how behavior is energized and the nature of the interactions among the variables, which are important to understanding motivated behavior.

The most basic of the process theories is the S-R one, which views behavior as resulting from a combination of drive and habit strength. Drive is held to result from internal forces initiating behavior; habit strength, from stimulus-response connections built up from prior reinforcement experience. Thus, in broad outline, the two variables of drive and habit strength interact to determine the extent and direction of behavior.

Expectancy theories go further, to allow for purely cognitive or symbolic manipulation of stimulus-response connections. That is, the patterning of activities is not based just upon habits learned through reinforcement experiences but upon the individual's beliefs or expectations regarding the probability of various outcomes from behavior.

Equity theory is another process system of work motivation, which builds upon concepts of cognitive dissonance to explain the dynamics of behavior. The theory contends that individuals assess their current situation—for example, levels of pay—in terms of the ratio of their inputs (effort) to outcomes (actual pay) in comparison with relevant others.

John R. Hinrichs

Work Therapy

Work therapy is an ancillary procedure designed to fill the daily vacuum of the psychiatric patient's day, which otherwise consists of taking some pills, being part of a group psychotherapy session (where this exists), or individual psychotherapy once or twice weekly. Work therapy is aimed more at becoming a matrix for the "free-floating" psychotic state, at serving as a support, and at blocking any efforts at withdrawal, detachment, or retirement into an inner fantasy world. The mentally ill are only too prone to detach themselves from the group, and this has serious antitherapeutic potential. Work becomes therapeutic for a mentally ill patient when she manipulates neutral objects in a nonthreatening social field (the workshop).

Work therapy is an action phenomenon, as opposed to inaction. It has a realistic incentive—pay, as opposed to tokenism. At least for the chronic patient, it presents some hope, though small, of rehabilitation and eventual discharge. It has been consistently maintained that the workshop be a planned, realistically oriented activity, making socially relevant demands on the patient.

The supply of work is limited to the shop's ability to function competitively in the open market. Generally, the types of contracts available are those from industries that function on a very thin profit margin and where the labor costs are crucial to their survival.

Herman C. B. Denber

Wundt, Wilhelm (1832–1920)

Wilhelm Wundt published *Foundations of Physiological Psychology* in 1874. In 1879, he established in Leipzig the first university institute of experimental psychology. He defined psychology as the science of immediate experience, with consciousness its main subject matter.

Frank Wesley

· Y ·

Yerkes, Robert M. (1876–1956)

Robert M. Yerkes wrote widely on the behavior of many species. In addition, he helped to bring Ivan Petrovich Pavlov's work to the attention of American science, and pioneered in the development of devices designed to aid in the investigation of the behavioral capacities of lower animals.

Gregory A. Kimble

Yerkes-Dodson Law

The original version of this principle stated that the optimal intensity of shock motivation varies inversely with the difficulty of the discrimination to be learned. Easy discrimination problems can be learned under intense shock, while more difficult discriminations are best learned under more moderate levels of shock. A later version substituted degree of learning (habit strength) for difficulty of discrimination. In this version, the law will be manifest if, with a given degree of prior training, the quality of performance is observed to increase and to decrease as the intensity of the motivating conditions increases. It is presumed that the optimal level of motivation will increase as training (and thus habit strength) is increased.

Edward L. Walker

Yoked Control

Yoked control is an experimental design intended to control for the effects of the mere occurrence of some event (usually a reinforcer) as opposed to the effect of a contingency between a response and the same event. In this method subjects perform in pairs. An experimental subject can obtain or avoid an event by making a specified response. The yoked-control subject experiences the event as frequently as the experimental subject and on the same schedule. Usually, this is accomplished by electrical circuitry, which makes the event occur for the two individuals simultaneously. An alternative method is to retain a record of when the event occurs for the experimental subject so that it can be administered to the yoked subject on the same schedule at some later time.

Gregory A. Kimble

· Z ·

Zeigarnik Effect

The Zeigarnik effect refers to the tendency of a person to recall a greater proportion of interrupted than of completed tasks. Bluma Zeigarnik (1927), a student of Kurt Lewin, investigated Lewin's field theory assumption that an intention to perform a task creates a state of psychic tension persisting until task completion. If performance is interrupted, the unresolved tension will be reflected in a heightened tendency to recall the interrupted task. John W. Atkinson has demonstrated experimentally that task recall is determined both by a subject's characteristic motivation and by situational factors affecting ego involvement.

John P. Sabini
Charles Philip Smith

Zener, Karl Edward (1903–1964)

In the field of conditioning, Karl Edward Zener was best known for pioneer work on salivary conditioning in the dog. In these studies, Zener conditioned salivary responses to a bell but, departing from the Pavlovian tradition, took motion pictures of the animals and analyzed the complexities revealed in these filmed records. Zener's contribution is represented in "The Significance of Behavior Accompanying Salivary Secretion for Theories of the Conditioned Response" (1937).

Gregory A. Kimble

Bibliography

Abramson, L. Y., M.E.P. Seligman, and J. D. Teasdale (1978). "Learned Helplessness in Humans: Critique and Reformulation." *Journal of Abnormal Psychology* 87: 49–74.

Acitelli, L. K. (1992). "Gender Differences in Relationship Awareness and Marital Satisfaction among Young Couples." *Personality and Social Psychology Bulletin* 18: 102–10.

Ader, R. (1981). *Psychoneuroimmunology.* New York: Academic Press.

Adler, A. (1928). *Menschenkenntnis.* Leipzig: Verlag S. Hirzel.

——— (1929). *Problems of Neuroses.* London: Paul Kegan.

——— (1930). *The Education of Children.* New York: Greenberg Publishers.

——— (1939). *Social Interest.* New York: G. P. Putnam's.

——— (1951). *Practice and Theory of Individual Psychology.* New York: Humanities Press.

Adler, G. (1980). "Transference, Real Relationship, and Alliance." *International Journal of Psychoanalysis* 61: 547–58.

——— (1985). *Borderline Psychopathology and Its Treatment.* New York: Aronson.

Adler, L. L., ed. (1977). "Issues in Cross-Cultural Research." *Annals of the New York Academy of Sciences* 285.

———, ed. (1982). *Cross-Cultural Research at Issue.* New York: Academic Press.

———, ed. (1989). *Cross-Cultural Research in Human Development: Life-Span Perspectives.* New York: Praeger.

———, ed. (1994). *International Handbook on Gender Roles.* Westport, CT: Greenwood Press.

Adler, L. L., and H. E. Adler (1990). "Matching to Sample by Atlantic Bottlenose Dolphins (*Tursiops Truncatus*): Chinese Characters and English Words." *Annals of the New York Academy of Sciences* 602: 113–26.

Adler, L. L., and U. P. Gielen, eds. (1994). *Cross-Cultural Topics in Psychology.* Westport, CT: Praeger.

Ainsworth, M.D.S. (1989). "Attachments beyond Infancy." *American Psychologist* 44: 709–16.

Ainsworth, M.D.S., M. Blehar, E. Waters, and S. Wall (1978). *Patterns of Attachment: A Psychological Study of the "Strange" Situation.* Hillsdale, NJ: Erlbaum.

Allender, J. (1991). *Imagery in Teaching and Learning.* New York: Praeger.

Allman, W. F. (1992). "The Mental Edge." *U.S. News & World Report,* August 3, pp. 50–56.

American Medical Association (1993). "Special Requirements for Residency Training in Psychiatry." *Graduate Medical Education Directory 1993–1994.* Chicago: Author, pp. 121–26.

American Psychiatric Association (1989). *Task Force Report: Treatment of Psychiatric Disorders* (vol. 3), (regarding sexual disorders in females). Washington, DC: Author, pp. 2237–415.

——— (1992). *1991–92 Annual Report of the Professional Liability Insurance Program Sponsored by the American Psychiatric Association.* Washington, DC: Psychiatrists' Purchasing Group.

——— (1993). *Task Force on DSM-IV: DSM-IV Draft Criteria.* Washington, DC: Author.

——— (1994). *Diagnostic and Statistical Manual of Mental Disorders IV.* Washington, DC: Author.

American Psychological Association (1977). *Standards for Providers of Psychological Services.* Washington, DC: Author.

——— (1980a). *Specialty Guidelines for the Delivery of Services by Clinical Psychologists.* Washington, DC: Author.

——— (1980b). *Specialty Guidelines for the Delivery of Services by Counseling Psychologists.* Washington, DC: Author.

——— (1980c). *Specialty Guidelines for the Delivery of Services by Industrial-Organizational Psychologists.* Washington, DC: Author.

——— (1980d). *Specialty Guidelines for the Delivery of Services by School Psychologists.* Washington, DC: Author.

——— (1981). "Specialty Guidelines for the Delivery of Services: APA Committee on Professional Standards." *American Psychologist* 36: 639–81.

——— (1987a). "Model Act for State Licensure of Psychologists." *American Psychologist* 42: 696–711.

——— (1987b). *General Guidelines for Providers of Psychological Services* (rev. ed.). Washington, DC: Author.

——— (1992a). *Bylaws of the American Psychological Association.* Washington, DC: Author.

——— (1992b). "Ethical Principles of Psychologists and Code of Conduct." *American Psychologist* 47: 1597–628.

American Psychological Association Committee on Accreditation (1992). "APA-Accredited Predoctoral Internships for Doctoral Training in Psychology, 1992." *American Psychologist* 47: 1637–52.

American Psychological Association Committee on Accreditation and Accreditation Office (1986). *Accreditation*

Handbook. Washington, DC: American Psychological Association.

American Psychological Association Continuing Education Programs Office (1993). *Survey of Mandatory Continuing Education Requirements for Renewal of Licensure*. Washington, DC: Author.

Ammerman, R. T., and M. Hersen, eds. (1990). *Treatment of Family Violence: A Sourcebook*. New York: Wiley.

Anastasi, A. (1988). *Psychological Testing* (6th ed.). New York: Macmillan.

Anderson, J. R. (1985). *Cognitive Psychology and Memory*. New York: W. H. Freeman.

——— (1990). *The Adaptive Character of Thought*. Hillsdale, NJ: Erlbaum.

Anderson, M. (1992). *Intelligence and Development: A Cognitive Theory*. Cambridge, MA: Blackwell.

Appley, M. H. (1983). "Motivation Theory: Recent Developments." In B. B. Wolman, ed., *International Encyclopedia of Psychiatry, Psychology, Psychoanalysis and Neurology* (Progress Volume), pp. 279–83. New York: Aesculapius.

——— (1991). "Motivation, Equilibration, and Stress." In R. A. Dienstbier, ed., *Perspectives on Motivation: Nebraska Symposium on Motivation, 1990*. Lincoln: University of Nebraska Press, pp. 1–67.

Appley, M. H., and C. N. Cofer (1964). *Motivation, Theory and Research*. New York: Wiley.

Appley, M. H., and R. A. Trumbull (1986). "Development of the Stress Concept." In M. H. Appley & R. A. Trumbull, eds., *Dynamics of Stress: Physiological, Psychological, and Social Perspectives*. New York: Plenum, pp. 1–18.

Armstrong, J. (1991). "The Psychological Organization of Multiple Personality Disordered Patients as Revealed in Psychological Testing." *Psychiatric Clinics of North America* 14: 533–46.

Armstrong, J., and R. J. Loewenstein (1990). "Characteristics of Patients with Multiple Personality and Dissociative Disorders on Psychological Testing." *Journal of Nervous and Mental Disease* 178: 448–54.

Aron, A., E. N. Aron, and D. Smollan (1992). "Inclusion of Other in the Self Scale and the Structure of Interpersonal Closeness." *Journal of Personality and Social Psychology* 63: 596–612.

Asarnow, J. R., and S. Bates (1988). "Depression in Child Psychiatric Inpatients: Cognitive and Attributional Patterns." *Journal of Abnormal Child Psychology* 16: 601–15.

Association of Psychology Postdoctoral and Internship Programs (1992). *National Conference on Postdoctoral Training in Professional Psychology: Policy Statement. Ann Arbor, Michigan, October 27–31, 1992*. Washington, DC: Author.

Association of State and Provincial Psychology Boards and the National Register of Health Service Providers in Psychology (1993). *Doctoral Programs Meeting Designation Criteria*. Washington, DC: Authors.

Axsom, D. (1989). "Cognitive Dissonance and Behavior Change in Psychotherapy." *Journal of Experimental Social Psychology* 25: 234–52.

Baddeley, A. D. (1990). *Human Memory: Theory and Practice*. Needham Heights, MA: Allyn and Bacon.

Bagnozzi, R. P. (1993). "Assessing Construct Validity in Personality Research: Applications to Measures of Self-Esteem." *Journal of Research in Personality* 27: 49–87.

Baker, E., M. Freeman, and S. Clayton (1990). *Cognitive Assessment of Subject Matter: Understanding the Marriage of Psychological Theory and Educational Policy in Achievement Testing*. Los Angeles: UCLA Press.

Ballinger, C. B., D.S.G. Kay, G. J. Naylor, and A.H.W. Smith (1982). "Some Biochemical Findings during Pregnancy and after Delivery in Relation to Mood Change." *Psychological Medicine* 12: 549–56.

Balsom, P., and C. Dempster (1980). "Treatment of War Neuroses from Vietnam." *Comprehensive Psychiatry* 21: 167–75.

Bandura, A. (1969). *Principles of Behavior Modification*. New York: Holt, Rinehart and Winston.

——— (1977). "Self-Efficacy: Toward a Unifying Theory of Behavioral Change." *Psychological Review* 84: 191–215.

——— (1986). *Social Foundations of Thought and Action: A Social Cognitive Theory*. Englewood Cliffs, NJ: Prentice Hall.

——— (1988). "Self-Efficacy Conception of Anxiety." *Anxiety Research* 1: 77–98.

Bard, M., and D. Sangrey (1986). *The Crime Victim's Book* (2nd ed.). New York: Brunner/Mazel.

Barlow, D. H., and J. A. Cerny (1988). *Psychological Treatment of Panic*. New York: Guilford.

Barlow, D. H., M. G. Craske, J. A. Cerny, and J. S. Klosko (1989). "Behavioral Treatment of Panic Disorder." *Behavior Therapy* 20: 261–82.

Baron, M., and J. Rainer (1988). "Molecular Genetics and Human Disease: Implications for Modern Psychiatric Research and Practice." *British Journal of Psychiatry* 152: 741–53.

Baucom, D. H., and N. Epstein (1990). *Cognitive-Behavioral Marital Therapy*. New York: Brunner/Mazel.

Baum, A., and P. B. Paulus (1987). "Crowding." In D. Stokols & I. Altman, eds. *Handbook of Environmental Psychology* (vol. 1). New York: Wiley, pp. 533–70.

Bayer, R. (1987). *Homosexuality and American Psychiatry*. New York: Basic Books.

Beach, S. R. H., and K. D. O'Leary (1992). "Treating Depression in the Context of Marital Discord: Outcome and Predictors of Response of Marital Therapy versus Cognitive Therapy." *Behavior Therapy* 23: 507–28.

Beach, S. R. H., E. E. Sandeen, and K. D. O'Leary (1990). *Depression in Marriage*. New York: Guilford.

Beck, A. T. (1976). *Cognitive Therapy and the Emotional Disorders*. New York: International Universities Press.

Beck, A. T., A. Freeman, and associates (1990). *Cognitive Therapy of Personality Disorders*. New York: Guilford.

Beck, A. T., A. J. Rush, B. F. Shaw, and G. Emery (1979). *Cognitive Therapy of Depression: A Treatment Manual*. New York: Guilford.

Belar, C. D., L. A. Bieliauskas, K. G. Larsen, I. N. Mensh, K.

Poey, and H. J. Roehlke (1989). "The National Conference on Internship Training in Psychology." *American Psychologist* 44: 60–65.

Berardo, F. M. (1990). "Trends and Direction in Family Research in the 1980s." *Journal of Marriage and the Family* 52: 809–17.

Berg, I. (1976). "School Phobia in the Children of Agoraphobic Women." *British Journal of Psychiatry* 128: 86–89.

Berg, M. D. (1977). "The Externalizing Transference." *International Journal of Psychoanalysis* 58: 235–44.

Berk, R. A., E. A. Boyd, and K. M. Hamner (1992). "Thinking More Clearly about Hate-Motivated Crime." In G. M. Herek and K. T. Berrill, eds., *Hate Crimes: Confronting Violence against Lesbians and Gay Men.* Newbury Park, CA: Sage, pp. 123–43.

Bernstein, E., and F. W. Putnam (1986). "Development, Reliability, and Validity of a Dissociation Scale." *Journal of Nervous and Mental Disease* 174: 727–35.

Berry, J. W., Y. H. Portinga, M. H. Segall, and P. R. Dasen (1992). *Cross-Cultural Psychology: Research and Applications.* New York: Cambridge University Press.

Berscheid, E. (1985). "Interpersonal Attraction." In G. Lindzey and E. Aronson, eds., *The Handbook of Social Psychology* (3rd ed., vol. 2). New York: Random House, pp. 413–84.

———— (1994). "Interpersonal Relationships." *Annual Review of Psychology* 45: 79–129.

Bibring, G., & A. Valenstein (1976). "Psychological Aspects of Pregnancy." *Clinical Obstetrics and Gynecology* 19: 357–71.

Biller, H. B. (1974). *Paternal Deprivation.* Lexington, MA: Heath.

Birtchnell, J. (1993). "Does Recollection of Exposure to Poor Maternal Care in Childhood Affect Later Ability to Relate?" *British Journal of Psychiatry* 162: 335–44.

Blake, D., K. Weathers, D. Kaloupek, G. Klauminzer, & T. Keane (1989). *Clinician Administered PTSD Scale (CAPS).* Boston: National Center for PTSD, DVA Medical Center.

Blanchard, E., L. Kolb, T. Pallmeyer, and R. Gerardi (1983). "A Psycho-Physiologic Study of Post-Traumatic Stress in Vietnam Veterans." *Psychiatric Quarterly* 54: 220–28.

Blanck, G., and R. Blanck (1974). *Ego Psychology: Theory and Practice.* New York: Columbia University Press.

Blum, H. (1980). "The Value of Reconstruction in Adult Psychoanalysis." *International Journal of Psycho-Analysis* 61: 39–52.

Blumstein, P., and P. Kollock (1988). "Personal Relationships." *Annual Review of Sociology* 14: 467–90.

Bock, P. K., ed. (1994). *Psychological Anthropology.* Westport, CT: Praeger.

Bond, M. H., ed. (1988). *The Cross-Cultural Challenge to Social Psychology.* Newbury Park, CA: Sage.

Bongar, B., & L. E. Beutler, eds. (1994). *Foundations of Psychotherapy: Theory, Research, and Practice.* New York: Oxford University Press.

Boon, S., and N. Draijer (1993). "Multiple Personality Disorder in the Netherlands: A Clinical Investigation of 71 Cases." *American Journal of Psychiatry* 150: 489–94.

Borkenau, P., and B. Muller (1992). "Inferring Act Frequencies and Traits from Behavior Observations." *Journal of Personality* 60: 553–73.

Bornstein, M. H., and M. E. Lamb, eds. (1992). *Developmental Psychology: An Advanced Textbook* (3rd ed.). Hillsdale, NJ: Erlbaum.

Bornstein, R. F. (1989). "Exposure and Affect: Overview and Meta-Analysis of Research, 1968–1987." *Psychological Bulletin* 106: 265–89.

Borysenko, J. (1988). *Minding the Body, Minding the Mind.* New York: Bantam Books.

Bouchard, T. J., Jr., and P. Propping, eds. (1993). *Twins as a Tool of Behavior Genetics.* New York: Wiley.

Boudewyns, P., L. Hyer, and M. Woods (1990). "PTSD among Vietnam Veterans: An Early Look at Treatment Outcome Using Direct Therapeutic Exposure." *Journal of Traumatic Stress* 3: 359–68.

Boudewyns, P. A., and R. H. Shipley (1983). *Flooding and Implosive Therapy: Direct Therapeutic Exposure in Clinical Practice.* New York: Plenum.

Bourg, E. F., R. J. Bent, J. McHolland, and G. Stricker (1989). "Standards and Evaluation in the Education and Training of Professional Psychologists." *American Psychologist* 44: 66–72. (The National Council of Schools of Professional Psychology, Mission Bay Conference.)

Bower, G. H. (1985). "How Might Emotions Affect Learning?" In S. A. Christianson, ed., *Handbook of Emotion and Memory.* Hillsdale, NJ: Erlbaum, pp. 3–31.

Bowlby, J. (1973). *Separation: Anxiety and Anger.* New York: Basic Books.

———— (1977). "The Making and Breaking of Affectional Bonds, I: Aetiology and Psychopathology in the Light of Attachment Theory." *British Journal of Psychiatry* 130: 201–10.

Braun, B. G. (1986). "Issues in the Psychotherapy of Multiple Personality Disorder. In B. G. Braun, ed., *Treatment of Multiple Personality Disorder.* Washington, DC: American Psychiatric Press, pp. 1–28.

———— (1993). "Multiple Personality Disorder and Post-Traumatic Stress Disorder: Similarities and Differences." In J. P. Wilson and B. Raphael, eds., *International Handbook of Traumatic Stress Syndromes*, pp. 35–48. New York: Plenum.

Bray, D. W., and associates (1991). *Working with Organizations and Their People.* New York: Guilford.

Braye, C. (1993). "Clinicopathological Studies of the Dementias from an Epidemiologic Viewpoint." *British Journal of Psychiatry* 162: 439–46.

Breckler, S. J., and E. C. Wiggins (1991). "Cognitive Responses in Persuasion: Affective and Evaluative Determinants." *Journal of Experimental Social Psychology* 27: 180–200.

Brehm, J. W., and E. A. Self (1989). "The Intensity of Motivation." *Annual Review of Psychology* 40: 109–32.

Brende, J. O. (1981). "Combined Individual and Group Therapy for Vietnam Veterans." *International Journal of Group Psychotherapy* 31: 367–78.

Brende, J. O., and L. McCann (1984). "Regressive Experiences in Vietnam Veterans: Their Relationship to War, Post-

Traumatic Symptoms and Recovery." *Journal of Contemporary Psychotherapy* 14: 57–75.

Brende, J. O., and E. R. Parson (1985). *Vietnam Veterans: The Road to Recovery.* New York: Plenum.

Brenner, C. (1985). "Countertransference as Compromise Formation." *Psychoanalytic Quarterly* 54: 155–63.

———— (1987). "Working Alliance, Therapeutic Alliance, and Transference." *Journal of the American Psychoanalytic Association* 27: 137–58.

Breslau, N., and G. Davis (1987). "Post-Traumatic Stress Disorder: The Stressor Criterion." *Journal of Nervous and Mental Disease* 175: 255–64.

Brockington, I., K. Cernik, E. Schofield, et al. (1981). "Puerperal Psychosis." *Archives of General Psychiatry* 38: 829–33.

Brownell, K. D. (1989). *Learn to Eat.* Dallas, TX: Brownell & Hager.

Bruner, J. S. (1990). *Acts of Meaning.* Cambridge, MA: Harvard University Press.

Buikhuisen, W., and S. A. Mednick, eds. (1988). *Explaining Criminal Behavior: Interdisciplinary Approaches.* Leiden, the Netherlands: E. J. Brill.

Burgess, A. W., and L. L. Holstrom (1986). "The Rape-Trauma Syndrome." *American Journal of Psychiatry* 143: 64–68.

Burns, D. D. (1980). *Feeling Good: The New Mood Therapy.* New York: Morrow.

Buros, O. K. (1985). *The Ninth Mental Measurements Yearbook.* Highland Park, NJ: Gryphon Press.

Burstein, A. (1988). "Post-Traumatic Stress Disorder in Victims of Motor Vehicle Accidents." *Hospital and Community Psychiatry* 40: 295–97.

Cacioppo, J. T., R. E. Petty, and L. G. Tassinary (1989). "Social Psychophysiology: A New Look." *Advances in Experimental Social Psychology* 22: 39–91.

Caporeal, L. R., and M. B. Brewer (1991). "Reviving Evolutionary Psychology: Biology Meets Society." *Journal of Social Issues* 47(3): 187–95.

Carey, S. (1985). *Conceptual Change in Childhood.* Cambridge, MA: MIT Press.

Carlson, E. B., and F. W. Putnam (1989). "Integrating Research on Dissociation and Hypnotizability: Are There Two Pathways to Hypnotizability?" *Dissociation* 2: 32–38.

Carver, C. S., and M. F. Scheier (1981). *Attention and Self-Regulation: A Control Theory Approach to Human Behavior.* New York: Springer-Verlag.

Cash, T. F. (1990). "The Psychology of Physical Appearance: Aesthetics, Attributes, and Images." In T. F. Cash & T. Pruzinsky, *Body Images: Development, Deviance, and Change.* New York: Guilford, pp. 51–79.

Chapman, M. (1988). *Constructive Evolution: Origins and Development of Piaget's Thought.* New York: Cambridge University Press.

Charles, S. C., and E. Kennedy (1985). *Defendant: A Psychiatrist on Trial for Medical Malpractice.* New York: Free Press.

Chomsky, N. (1959). "A Review of B. F. Skinner's *Verbal Behavior.*" *Language* 35:26–58.

———— (1965). *Aspects of the Theory of Syntax.* Cambridge, MA: MIT Press.

———— (1970). *The Acquisition of Syntax in Children from 5 to 10.* Cambridge, MA: MIT Press.

Chopra, D. (1989). *Quantum Healing: Exploring the Frontiers of Mind/Body Medicine.* New York: Bantam Books.

———— (1991). *Unconditional Life: Mastering the Forces That Shape Personal Reality.* New York: Bantam Books.

Christianson, S. A., ed. (1992). *Handbook of Emotion and Memory.* Hillsdale, NJ: Erlbaum.

Chrzanowski, G. (1977). *Interpersonal Approach to Psychoanalysis: A Contemporary View of Harry Stack Sullivan.* New York: Gardner Press.

———— (1982). "Interpersonal Formulations of Psychotherapy: A Contemporary Model." In J. C. Anchin & D. J. Kiesler, eds., *Interpersonal Psychotherapy.* New York: Pergamon.

Churchland, P. M. (1988). *Matter and Consciousness: A Contemporary Introduction to the Philosophy of Mind* (rev. ed.). Cambridge, MA: MIT Press.

Clarizio, H. F. (1979). "In Defense of the IQ Test." *School Psychology Digest* 8: 79–88.

———— (1982). "Intellectual Assessment of Hispanic Children." *Psychology in the Schools* 19: 61–71.

Clark, D. M. (1989). "Anxiety States: Panic and Generalized Anxiety." In K. Hawton, P. M. Salkoviskis, J. Kirk, and D. M. Clark, eds., *Cognitive Behavior Therapy for Psychiatric Problems: A Practical Guide.* Oxford, England: Oxford University Press.

Clark, M. S., and G. M. Williamson (1989). "Moods and Social Judgments." In H. Wagner and A. Manstead, eds., *Handbook of Social Psychophysiology.* New York: Wiley, pp. 347–70.

Cohen, G. (1989). *Memory in the Real World.* London: Erlbaum.

Collier, G. (1993). *Social Origins of Mental Ability.* New York: Wiley.

Conduct Problems Prevention Research Group (1993). "A Developmental and Clinical Model for Prevention of Conduct Disorders: The FAST Track Program." *Development and Psychopathology* 4: 509–27.

Conn, D., A. Grek, and J. Sadavoy, eds. (1989). *Psychiatric Consequences of Brain Disease in the Elderly.* New York: Plenum.

Coons, P. M. (1986). "Treatment Progress in 20 Patients with Multiple Personality Disorder." *Journal of Nervous and Mental Disease* 174: 715–21.

Costello, C. G., ed. (1993). *Symptoms of Schizophrenia.* New York: Wiley.

Council for the National Register of Health Service Providers in Psychology (1993). *National Register of Health Service Providers in Psychology.* Washington, DC: Author.

Cowly, D., and P. Roy-Byrne (1989). "Panic Disorder during Pregnancy." *Journal of Psychosomatic Obstetrics and Gynecology* 10: 193–210.

Craighead, L. W., W. E. Craighead, A. E. Kazdin, and M. J. Mahoney, eds. (1994). *Cognitive Behavioral Interventions:*

Principles, Issues and Applications. Needham, MA: Allyn & Bacon.

Craighead, W. E. (1990). "There's a Place for All of Us." *Behavior Therapy* 21: 3–23.

Craighead, W. E., L. W. Craighead, and S. Ilardi (1994). "Behavior Therapies in Historical Perspective." In B. Bongar and L. E. Beutler, eds., *Foundations of Psychotherapy: Theory, Research, and Practice.* New York: Oxford University Press.

Craine, L., C. Henson, J. Collier, and D. Maclean (1988). "Prevalence of a History of Sexual Abuse among Female Psychiatric Patients in a State Hospital System." *Hospital and Community Psychiatry* 39: 300–304.

Crowell, D. H., I. M. Evans, and C. R. O'Donnell, eds. (1987). *Childhood Aggression and Violence: Sources of Influence, Prevention, and Control.* New York: Plenum.

Crump, L. (1987). "Gestalt Therapy in the Treatment of Vietnam Veterans Experiencing PTSD Symptomatology. In W. Quaytman, ed., *The Vietnam Veteran: Studies in Post-Traumatic Stress Disorder.* New York: Human Sciences Press, pp. 90–97.

Curran, W. J., A. L. McGarry, and S. A. Shah, eds. (1986). *Forensic Psychiatry and Psychology: Perspectives and Standards for Interdisciplinary Practice.* Philadelphia: Davis.

Cutrona, C. E. (1983). "Causal Attributions and Perinatal Depression." *Journal of Abnormal Psychology* 92: 161–72.

Dalton, K. (1980). *Depression after Childbirth.* Oxford, England: Oxford University Press.

Davanloo, H. (1980). *Short-Term Dynamic Psychotherapy.* New York: Aronson.

Davidson, J., and E. Robertson (1985). "A Follow-Up Study of Post-Partum Illness, 1946–1978." *Acta Psychiatrica Scandinavica* 71: 451–57.

Dawkins, R. (1989). *The Selfish Gene* (2nd ed.). Oxford, England: Oxford University Press.

"Definition and Description of Clinical Psychology Adopted (1990) Jointly by the Division of Clinical Psychology (12) of the American Psychological Association and the Council of University Directors of Clinical Psychology" (1991). *Clinical Psychologist* 44: 5–11.

De Fries, J. G., R. Plomin, and D. W. Fulker (1994). *Nature: Nurture during Middle Childhood.* Cambridge, MA: Blackwell.

DeLeon, P. H., R. E. Fox, and S. R. Graham (1991). "Prescription Privileges: Psychology's Next Frontier." *American Psychologist* 46(4): 384–93.

Denmark, F. L., and M. Paludi, eds. (1994). *Handbook on the Psychology of Women.* Westport, CT: Greenwood Press.

de Montigny, C., and G. Cournoyer (1987). "Lithium Addition in Treatment of Resistant Depression." In J. Zohar & R. H. Belmaker, eds., *Treating Resistant Depression.* New York: PMA Publishing.

Denny, E. B., and R. R. Hunt (1992). "Affective Valence and Memory in Depression: Dissociation of Recall and Fragment Completion. *Journal of Abnormal Psychology* 101: 575–80.

Depue, R. A., and W. G. Iacono (1989). "Neurobehavioral Aspects of Affective Disorders." *Annual Review of Psychology* 40: 457–92.

Dewsbury, D. A. (1990). *Contemporary Issues in Comparative Psychology.* Sunderland, MA: Sinauer.

Dienstfrey, H. (1991). *Where the Mind Meets the Body: Type A, the Relaxation Response, Psychoneuroimmunology, Biofeedback, Neuropeptides, Hypnosis, Imagery and the Search for the Mind's Effect on Physical Health.* New York: HarperCollins.

Digman, J. M. (1990). "Personality Structure: Emergence of the Five Factor Model." *Annual Review of Psychology* 41: 417–40.

Dishman, R. K. (1983). "Identity Crises in North American Sport Psychology: Academics in Professional Issues." *Journal of Sport Psychology* 5: 123–34.

Donahey, K. M., and R. A. Carroll (1993). "Gender Differences in Factors Associated with Hypoactive Sexual Desire." *Journal of Sex and Marital Therapy* 19: 25–40.

Duck, S. W., ed. (1988). *Handbook of Personal Relationships: Theory, Research and Interventions.* Chichester, England: Wiley.

Dunkin, M. J., and J. Barnes (1986). "Research on Teaching in Higher Education." In M. C. Wittrock, ed., *Handbook of Research on Teaching,* pp. 754–77. New York: Macmillan.

Dunnette, M. D., and L. M. Hough, eds. (1990–93). *Handbook of Industrial and Organizational Psychology* (4 vols.). Palo Alto, CA: Consulting Psychologists Press.

Eagly, A. H., and S. Chaiken (1992). *The Psychology of Attitudes.* San Francisco: Harcourt Brace Jovanovich.

Eaves, L. J., H. J. Eysenck, and N. G. Martin (1989). *Genes, Culture, and Personality: An Empirical Approach.* London: Academic Press.

Elliott, S. N., and J. C. Witt, eds. (1986). *The Delivery of Psychological Services in Schools: Concepts, Processes, and Issues.* Hillsdale, NJ: Erlbaum.

Ellis, A., and W. Jordan (1987). *The Practice of Rational-Emotive Therapy.* New York: Springer-Verlag.

Ellis, H. C., and R. R. Hunt (1993). *Fundamentals of Cognitive Psychology.* Madison, WI: Brown and Benchmark.

Endicott, J., and R. Spitzer (1978). "A Diagnostic Interview: A Schedule for Affective Disorder and Schizophrenia." *Archives of General Psychiatry* 35: 837–44.

Erikson, E. H. (1958). *Young Man Luther.* New York: Norton.

——— (1968). *Identity: Youth and Crisis.* New York: Norton.

Estes, W. K. (1991). "Cognitive Architectures from the Standpoint of an Experimental Psychologist." *Annual Review of Psychology* 42: 1–28.

Eth, S., and R. Pynoos (1985). "Developmental Perspective on Psychic Trauma in Childhood." In C. R. Figley, ed., *Trauma and Its Wake.* New York: Brunner/Mazel.

Evans, J. St. B. T. (1989). *Bias in Human Reasoning: Causes and Consequences.* Hove, England: Erlbaum.

Evans, R., V. Sexton, and T. Cadwallader, eds. (1992). *The American Psychological Association: A Historical Perspective.* Washington, DC: American Psychological Association.

Eysenck, H. J. (1991). "Personality, Stress, and Disease: An Interactionist Perspective." *Psychological Inquiry* 2: 221–32.

Eysenck, H. J., and I. Martin, eds. (1987). *Theoretical Foundations of Behavior Therapy*. New York: Plenum.

Eysenck, M. W. (1992). *Anxiety: The Cognitive Perspective*. Hillsdale, NJ: Erlbaum.

Fairbanks, J., and T. Keane (1982). "Flooding for Combat-Related Stress Disorder: Assessment of Anxiety Reduction across Traumatic Memories." *Behavior Therapy* 13: 499–510.

Fairbanks, J., R. McCaffrey, and T. Keane (1985). "Psychometric Detection of Fabricated Symptoms of Post-Traumatic Stress Disorder." *American Journal of Psychiatry* 142: 501–10.

Fairburn, C. G., R. Jones, R. C. Peveler, R. A. Hope, and M. O'Connor (1993). "Psychotherapy and Bulimia Nervosa: Longer Term Effects of Interpersonal Psychotherapy, Behavior Therapy, and Cognitive Behavior Therapy. *Archives of General Psychiatry* 50: 419–28.

Falco, K. (1991). *Psychotherapy with Lesbian Clients*. New York: Brunner/Mazel.

Feather, N. T. (1991). "Human Values, Global Self-Esteem, and Belief in a Just World." *Journal of Personality* 59: 83–106.

Fehr, B., and J. A. Russell (1991). "The Concept of Love Viewed from a Prototype Perspective." *Journal of Personality and Social Psychology* 60: 425–38.

Feighner, J. P. (1983). "The New Generation of Antidepressants." *Journal of Clinical Psychiatry* 44(2): 49–55.

Feinsilver, D. B. (1983). "Reality, Transitional Relatedness, and Containment in the Borderline." *Contemporary Psychoanalysis* 19: 537–69.

Feksi, A., et al. (1984). "Maternity Blues and Hormone Levels in Saliva." *Journal of Affective Disorders* 6: 351–55.

Figueroa, R. A. (1989). "Psychological Testing of Linguistic-Minority Students: Knowledge Gaps and Regulations." *Exceptional Children* 56: 145–52.

Fincham, F. D., and T. N. Bradbury, eds. (1990). *The Psychology of Marriage: Basic Issues and Applications*. New York: Guilford.

Fine, C. G. (1988a). "The Work of Antoine Despine: The First Scientific Report on the Diagnosis of a Child with Multiple Personality Disorder." *American Journal of Hypnosis* 31: 33–39.

———— (1988b). "Thoughts on the Cognitive-Perceptual Substrates of Multiple Personality Disorder." *Dissociation* 1(4): 5–10.

Fink, M. (1979). *Convulsive Therapy: Theory and Practice*. New York: Raven Press.

Finklehor, D. (1994). "The International Epidemiology of Child Sexual Abuse." *Child Abuse Neglect* 18(5): 409–17.

Flavell, J. H. (1963). *The Developmental Psychology of Jean Piaget*. Princeton, NJ: Van Nostrand Reinhold.

———— (1985). *Cognitive Development*. Englewood Cliffs, NJ: Prentice-Hall.

Foa, E., and M. Kozak (1986). "Emotional Processing of Fear: Exposure to Corrective Information." *Psychological Bulletin* 99: 20–35.

Foa, E. B., B. O. Rothbaum, D. S. Riggs, and T. B. Murdock (1991). "Treatment of Post-Traumatic Stress Disorder in Rape Victims: A Comparison Between Cognitive-Behavioral Procedures and Counseling." *Journal of Consulting and Clinical Psychology* 5: 715–23.

Fordham, M. (1970). *Children as Individuals*. New York: C. G. Jung Foundation.

Forrest, D. V. (1991). "Mind, Brain and Machine: Object Recognition." *Journal of the American Academy of Psychoanalysis* 19: 555–77.

Fowler, R. D. (1990). "Report of the Chief Executive Officer." *American Psychologist* 45: 803–6.

———— (1993). "Report of the Chief Executive Officer." *American Psychologist* 48: 727–36.

Fox, R. E. (1988). "Prescription Privileges: Their Implications for the Practice of Psychology." *Psychotherapy* 25(4): 501–50.

Frances, A. J., H. Pincus, and T. A. Widiger (1990). "DSM-IV Work in Progress." *American Journal of Psychiatry* 147: 1439–48.

Frank, J. D., and J. B. Frank (1991). *Persuasion and Healing* (3rd ed.). Baltimore: Johns Hopkins University Press.

Frederick, C. (1985). "Children Traumatized by Catastrophic Situations." In S. Eth and R. Pynoos, eds., *Post-Traumatic Stress Disorder in Children*. Washington, DC: American Psychiatric Press.

Freiberg, P. (1992). "Florida Law Offers No Protection of Title." *APA Monitor*, April, pp. 1, 25.

French, J. L., ed. (1993). "The History of School Psychology." *Journal of School Psychology* 31(1): 1–235. (Special issue.)

Freud, S. (1952). "Project for a Scientific Psychology." In J. Strachey, ed., *The Standard Edition of the Complete Psychological Works of Sigmund Freud* (vol. 1). London: Hogarth Press, pp. 281–397. (Original work published 1895.)

———— (1953). "The Interpretation of Dreams." In J. Strachey, ed., *The Standard Edition* (vol. 4). London: Hogarth Press. (Original work published 1900.)

———— (1955)."Beyond the Pleasure Principle." In J. Strachey, ed., *The Standard Edition* (vol. 18). London: Hogarth Press. (Original work published 1920.)

———— (1959). "Inhibitions, Symptoms, and Anxiety." In J. Strachey, ed., *The Standard Edition* (vol. 20). London: Hogarth Press. (Original work published 1926.)

Friedman, M. (1988). "Toward Rational Pharmacotherapy for Post-Traumatic Stress Disorder: An Interim Report." *American Journal of Psychiatry* 145: 281–85.

Friedman, R. C. (1988). *Male Homosexuality*. New Haven, CT: Yale University Press.

Friedman, R. C., and J. Downey (1993). "Neurobiology and Sexual Orientation: Current Relationships." *Journal of Neuropsychiatry* 3(2): 131–53.

Friedman, R. M. (1986). "The Psychoanalytic Model of Male Homosexuality: A Historical and Theoretical Critique." *Psychoanalytic Review* 4: 483–519.

Frisby, J. (1980). *Seeing*. Oxford, England: Oxford University Press.

Fuller, R. W., and D. T. Wong (1987). "Serotonin Reuptake

Blockers In Vitro and In Vivo." *Journal of Psychopharmacology* 7: 365–435.

Gabbard, G. (1992). "Psychodynamic Psychiatry in the 'Decade of the Brain.'" *American Journal of Psychiatry* 149: 991–98.

Galatzer-Levy, R. M. (1988). "On Working Through: A Model from Artificial Intelligence." *Journal of the American Psychoanalytic Association* 36: 125–52.

Gallistel, C. R. (1990). *The Organization of Learning.* Cambridge, MA: MIT Press.

Gard, P. R., et al. (1986). "A Multivariate Investigation of Postpartum Mood Disturbance." *British Journal of Psychiatry* 148: 567–75.

Gardner, H. (1985). *The Mind's New Science: A History of the Cognitive Revolution.* New York: Basic Books.

Gardner, M. R. (1983). *Self Inquiry.* Boston: Little, Brown.

Garton, A. F. (1992). *Social Interaction and the Development of Language and Cognition.* Hillsdale, NJ: Erlbaum.

Gathercole, S. E., A. D. Baddeley (1990). "The Role of Phonological Memory in Vocabulary Acquisition: A Study of Young Children Learning New Names." *British Journal of Psychology* 81: 439–54.

Geen, R. G. (1991). "Social Motivation." *Annual Review of Psychology* 42: 377–99.

Geller, E. S., L. Paterson, and E. Talbott (1982). "A Behavioral Analysis of Incentive Prompts for Motivating Seat Belt Use." *Journal of Applied Behavior Analysis* 15: 403–15.

Gelso, C. J., and B. R. Fretz (1992). *Counseling Psychology.* Fort Worth: Harcourt Brace Jovanovich.

George, A., M. Sandler (1988). "Endocrine and Biochemical Studies in Puerperal Mental Disorders." In R. Kumar and I. F. Brockington, eds., *Motherhood and Mental Illness, vol. 2: Causes and Consequences.* London: Wright, pp. 78–112.

Gianutsos, J. G., and J. M. Notterman (1987). "Individual Differences in the Ability to Use EMG-Derived Visual Feedback." *Perceptual and Motor Skills* 64: 927–34.

Gibbs, N. R. (1993). "The Father." *Time,* June 23, p. 53.

Gill, M. (1979). "The Analysis of the Transference." *Journal of the American Psychoanalytic Association* 27: 263–88.

Gilligan, C. (1982). *In a Different Voice: Psychological Theory and Women's Development.* Cambridge, MA: Harvard University Press.

Ginsburg, H. P., and S. Opper (1988). *Piaget's Theory of Intellectual Development* (3rd ed.). Englewood Cliffs, NJ: Prentice-Hall.

Giovacchini, P. L. (1975a). *Psychoanalysis of Character Disorders.* New York: Aronson.

——— (1975b). "Self-Projections in the Narcissistic Transference." *International Journal of Psychoanalytic Psychotherapy* 4: 142–67.

——— (1987). "The 'Unreasonable' Patient and the Psychotic Transference." In J. S. Grotstein, M. F. Solomon, and J. A. Langs, eds., *The Borderline Patient: Emerging Concepts in Diagnosis, Psychodynamics, and Treatment* (vol. 2). Hillsdale, NJ: Analytic Press, pp. 59–68.

——— (1993). *Borderline Patients, the Psychosomatic Focus, and the Therapeutic Process.* Northvale, NJ: Aronson.

Gitlin, M. J., and R. O. Pasnau (1989). "Psychiatric Syndromes Linked to Reproductive Function in Women." *American Journal of Psychiatry* 146: 1413–22.

Gittelman, R., ed. (1986). *Anxiety Disorders of Childhood.* New York: Guilford Press.

Globus, G. (1980). "On 'I': The Conceptual Foundation of Responsibility." *American Journal of Psychiatry* 137: 417–22.

Gold, M. S., et al. (1987). "The Contribution of Blood Levels to the Treatment of Resistant Depression." In J. Zohar and R. H. Belmaker, eds., *Treating Resistant Depression.* New York: PMA Publishing.

Goldberger, L., and S. Breznitz, eds. (1993). *Handbook of Stress: Theoretical and Clinical Aspects.* New York: Free Press.

Goldstein, G., and M. Hersen, eds. (1990). *Handbook of Psychological Assessment* (2nd ed.). Elmsford, NY: Pergamon.

Goldstein, M. Z., ed. (1989). *Family Involvement in Treatment of the Frail Elderly.* Washington, DC: American Psychiatric Press.

——— (1990). "Evaluation of the Elderly Patient." In D. Bienenfeld, ed., *Verwoerdt's Clinical Geropsychiatry* (3rd ed.), pp. 47–58. Baltimore: Williams and Wilkins.

——— (1991). "Family Therapy." In J. Sadavoy, L. W. Lazarus, and L. Jarvik, eds., *Comprehensive Review of Geriatric Psychiatry.* Washington, DC: American Psychiatric Press, pp. 513–25.

——— (1993). "Elder Abuse and Neglect." In H. I. Kaplan and B. J. Sadock, eds., *Comprehensive Textbook of Psychiatry* (6th ed.). Baltimore: Williams and Wilkins.

Gomez-Palacio, M. M., E. R. Padilla, and S. Roll (1983). *Escala de inteligencia Wechsler para nivel escolar.* Mexico City: El Manual Moderno.

Goodwin, F. K., A. J. Prange, Jr., R. M. Post, G. Muscattola, and M. A. Lipton (1982). "L-Triiodothyronine Converts Tricyclic Antidepressant Non-Responders to Responders." *American Journal of Psychiatry* 139: 334–38.

Gottesman, I. I. (1991). *Schizophrenia Genesis: The Origin of Madness.* New York: Freeman.

Gottesman, I. I., and J. Shields (1982). *Schizophrenia: The Epigenetic Puzzle.* Cambridge, England: Cambridge University Press.

Green, B. (1993). "Identifying Survivors at Risk: Trauma and Stressors across Events." In J. P. Wilson and B. Raphael, eds., *International Handbook on Traumatic Stress Syndromes.* New York: Plenum, pp. 135–43.

Greenberg, R., and C. Pearlman (1974). "Cutting the REM Nerve." *Perspectives in Biology and Medicine* 17: 513–21.

Greenwood, J., and G. Parker (1984). "The Dexamethasone Suppression Test in the Puerperium." *Australian and New Zealand Journal of Psychiatry* 18: 282–84.

Grotstein, J. S. (1981). *Splitting and Projective Identification.* New York: Aronson.

Groth-Marnat, G. (1990). *Handbook of Psychological Assessment* (2nd ed.). New York: Wiley.

Grove, W. M., and D. Cicchetti, eds. (1991). *Thinking Clearly about Psychology,* vol. 2, *Personality and Psychopathology.* Minneapolis: University of Minnesota Press.

Groves, P. M., and G. V. Rebec (1988). *Introduction to Biological Psychology* (3rd ed.). Dubuque, IA: Wm. Brown.

Gruber, H. E., and E. B. Wallace, eds. (1989). *Creative People at Work: Twelve Cognitive Case Studies*. New York: Oxford University Press.

Grusec, J. (1992). "Social Learning Theory and Developmental Psychology: The Legacies of Robert Sears and Albert Bandura." *Developmental Psychology* 28(5): 776–86.

Grusec, J. E., and H. Lytton (1988). *Social Development: History, Theory, and Research*. New York: Springer-Verlag.

Guthrie, R. (1976). *Even the Rat Was White*. Boston: Little, Brown.

Gutkin, T. B., and C. R. Reynolds, eds. (1990). *The Handbook of School Psychology* (2nd ed.). New York: Wiley.

Habermas, J. (1979). *Communication and the Evolution of Society*. Boston: Beacon Press.

——— (1988). *On the Logic of the Social Sciences*. Cambridge, MA: MIT Press.

Hacking, I. (1991). "Double Consciousness in Britain, 1815–1875." *Dissociation* 4: 134–46.

Handley, S. L., et al. (1980). "Tryptophan, Cortisol and Puerperal Mood." *British Journal of Psychiatry* 136: 498–508.

Harlow, H. F. (1958). "The Nature of Love." *American Psychologist* 13: 673–85.

Harris, B., et al. (1989). "The Hormonal Environment of Post-Natal Depression." *British Journal of Psychiatry* 154: 660–67.

Hartley, De. D., and H. H. Strupp (1983). "The Therapeutic Alliance: Its Relationship to Outcome in Brief Psychotherapy." In J. Masling, ed., *Empirical Studies of Psychoanalytic Theories* (vol. 1), pp. 1–37. Hillside, NJ: Analytic Press.

Hass, R. G., et al. (1991). "Cross-Racial Appraisal as Related to Attitude Ambivalence and Cognitive Complexity." *Personality and Social Psychology Bulletin* 17: 83–92.

Hatfield, E., and R. L. Rapson (1987). "Passionate Love/Sexual Desire: Can the Same Paradigm Explain Both?" *Archives of Sexual Behavior* 16(3): 259–78.

Hatfield, E., and S. Sprechner (1986). "Measuring Passionate Love in Intimate Relationships." *Journal of Adolescence* 9: 383–410.

Hawton, K., et al., eds. (1989). *Cognitive Behavior Therapy for Psychiatric Problems: A Practical Guide*. Oxford, England: Oxford University Press.

Hebb, D. O. (1949). *The Organization of Behavior*. New York: Wiley.

Helms, J. E. (1992). "Why Is There No Study of Cultural Equivalence in Standardized Cognitive Ability Testing?" *American Psychologist* 47: 1083–101.

Hendrick, C., ed. (1989). *Close Relationships: Review of Personality and Social Psychology* (vol. 10). Newbury Park, CA: Sage.

Hendrick, C., and S. Hendrick (1986). "A Theory and Method of Love." *Journal of Personality and Social Psychology* 50: 392–402.

——— (1989). "Research on Love: Does It Measure Up?" *Journal of Personality and Social Psychology* 56: 784–94.

Herman, J. L. (1992). *Trauma and Recovery*. New York: Basic Books.

Herrans, L. L., and J. M. Rodriguez (1992). *Escala de inteligencia Wechsler para niños—revisada*. San Antonio, TX: Psychological Corporation, Harcourt Brace Jovanovich.

Herrnstein, R., and C. Murray (1994). *The Bell Curve: Intelligence and Class Structure in American Life*. New York: Free Press.

Hersen, M., A. E. Kazdin, and A. S. Bellack, eds. (1991). *The Clinical Psychology Handbook* (2nd ed.). New York: Pergamon.

Hersen, M., and D. H. Barlow, eds. (1976). *Single-Case Experimental Designs: Strategies for Studying Behavior Change*. New York: Pergamon.

Higgins, E. T., ed. (1990). *Handbook of Motivation and Cognition: Foundations of Social Behavior* (vol. 2). New York: Guilford.

Hilgard, E. R. (1987). *Psychology in America: An Historical Survey*. San Diego: Harcourt Brace Jovanovich.

Hillman, J. (1972). *The Myth of Analysis*. New York: Harper & Row.

——— (1975). *Re-visioning Psychology*. New York: Harper & Row.

Hintzman, D. (1990). "Human Learning and Memory: Connections and Dissociations." *Annual Review of Psychology* 41: 109–39.

Hochberg, J. (1978). *Perception*. Englewood Cliffs, NJ: Prentice-Hall.

Hochheimer, W. (1969). *The Psychotherapy of C. G. Jung*. New York: C. G. Jung Foundation. (Excellent summary of Jungian therapy.)

Holland, P., and H. Wainer (1993). *Differential Item Functioning*. Hillsdale, NJ: Erlbaum.

Hollon, S. D., R. J. DeRubeis, M. D. Evans, M. J. Wiemer, M. J. Garvey, W. M. Grove, and V. B. Tuason (1992). "Cognitive Therapy and Pharmacology for Depression: Singly and in Combination." *Archives of General Psychiatry* 49: 774–81.

Horney, K. (1937). *The Neurotic Personality of Our Time*. New York: Norton.

——— (1939). *New Ways in Psychoanalysis*. New York: Norton.

——— (1945). *Our Inner Conflicts*. New York: Norton.

——— (1950). *Neurosis and Human Growth*. New York: Norton.

Hornstein, N. L., and S. Tyson (1991). "Inpatient Treatment of Children with Multiple Personality/Dissociative Disorders and Their Families." *Psychiatric Clinics of North America* 14: 631–48.

Horowitz, M. (1986). *Stress Response Syndromes* (2nd ed.). London: Aronson.

Horowitz, M., N. Wilner, and Alvarez (1979). "Impact of Events Scale: A Measure of Subjective Distress." *Psychosomatic Medicine* 41: 209–18.

Howard, A., G. Pion, G. Gottfredson, P. Flatteau, S. Oskamp, S. Pfafflin, D. Bray, and A. Burstein (1986). "The Changing

Face of American Psychology." *American Psychologist* 41: 1311–27.

Howell, W. C. (1993). "Engineering Psychology in a New World." *Annual Review of Psychology* 44: 231–63.

Hullin, R. P. (1980). "Minimum Serum Lithium Levels for Effective Prophylaxis." In F. N. Johnson, ed., *Handbook of Lithium Therapy*. Baltimore: University Park Press.

Huntington's Disease Collaborative Research Group (1993). "A Novel Gene Containing a Trinucleotide Repeat That Is Expanded and Unstable on Huntington's Disease Chromosomes." *Cell* 72: 971–83.

Hurvich, L. (1981). *Color Vision*. Sunderland, MA: Sinauer.

International Center for the Disabled (1986). *The ICD Survey of Disabled Americans: Bringing Disabled Americans into the Mainstream*. New York: International Center for the Disabled.

Isay, R. A. (1989). *Being Homosexual*. New York: Farrar, Strauss, Giroux.

Jacobs, T. (1986). "On Countertransference Enactments." *Journal of the American Psychoanalytic Association* 34: 289–307.

——— (1992). *The Use of the Self: Countertransference and Communication in the Analytic Situation*. New York: International Universities Press.

Jacobson, N. S., and G. Margolin (1979). *Marital Therapy: Strategies Based on Social Learning and Behavior Exchange Principles*. New York: Brunner/Mazel.

Jahoda, G. (1992). *Crossroads Between Culture and Mind: Continuities Change in Theories of Human Nature*. London: Harvester Wheatsheaf.

Jankowiak, W. R., and E. F. Fischer (1992). "A Cross-Cultural Perspective on Romantic Love." *Ethnology* 31: 149–55.

Jarvik, L. F., and C. H. Winograd, eds. (1988). *Treatment for the Alzheimer Patient*. New York: Springer.

Jefferson, J. W., J. S. Greist, D. L. Ackerman, and J. A. Carroll (1987). *Lithium Encyclopedia for Clinical Practice*. Washington, DC: American Psychiatric Press.

Jensen, A. R. (1980). *Bias in Mental Testing*. New York: Free Press.

Johnson, B. T., and A. H. Eagly (1990). "Involvement and Persuasion: Types, Traditions, and the Evidence." *Psychological Bulletin* 107: 375–84.

Johnson, K. B., et al. (1989). "A Fault-Based Administrative Alternative for Resolving Medical Malpractice Claims." *Vanderbilt Law Review* 42: 1365–1407.

Jones, E. E. (1986). "Interpreting Interpersonal Behavior: The Effects of Expectancies." *Science* 234: 41–46.

Jordaan, J. P., R. A. Myers, W. L. Layton, and H. H. Morgan (1968). *The Counseling Psychologist*. Washington, DC: American Psychological Association.

Joseph, B. (1983). "On Understanding and Not Understanding: Some Technical Issues." *International Journal of Psycho-Analysis* 64(3): 291–98.

Joyce, P. R., and E. S. Paykel (1989). "Predictors of Drug Response in Depression." *Archives of General Psychiatry* 46: 89–99.

Jung, C. G. (1953). *Two Essays on Analytical Psychology* (Bollingen series, vol. 7). Princeton, NJ: Princeton University Press.

——— (1956). *Symbols of Transformation* (Bollingen series, vol. 5). Princeton, NJ: Princeton University Press.

——— (1959). *The Archetypes and the Collective Unconscious* (Bollingen series, vol. 9). Princeton, NJ: Princeton University Press. (See vol. 20, *Index*, for reference to terms used.)

——— (1964). *Civilization in Transition* (Bollingen series, vol. 10). Princeton, NJ: Princeton University Press.

Jussim, L. (1991). "Social Perception and Social Reality: A Reflection-Construction Model." *Psychological Review* 98: 54–73.

Kagehiro, D. K., and W. S. Laufer, eds. (1992). *Handbook of Psychology and Law*. New York: Springer-Verlag.

Kalat, J. W. (1992). *Biological Psychology* (4th ed.). Belmont, CA: Wadsworth.

Kalff, D. (1971). *Sandplay: Mirror of a Child's Psyche*. San Francisco: Browser Press.

Kanizsa, G. (1990). "Subjective Contours." In I. Rock, ed., *The Perceptual World*. San Francisco: Freeman, pp. 155–63.

Kaplan, H. I., and B. J. Sadock (1991). "Psychiatric Interview, History, and Mental Status Examination." In *Synopsis of Psychiatry* (6th ed.). Baltimore: Williams & Wilkins, pp. 193–204.

Kaplan, H. S. (1983). *The Evaluation of Sexual Disorders: Physiological and Medical Aspects*. New York: Brunner/Mazel.

Katona, C. (1982). "Puerperal Mental Illness: Comparisons with Nonpuerperal Controls." *British Journal of Psychiatry* 141: 447–52.

Katzell, R. A., and J. T. Austin (1992). "From Then to Now: Development of Industrial-Organizational Psychology in the United States." *Journal of Applied Psychology* 77: 803–35.

Katzell, R. A., and R. A. Guzzo (1983). "Psychological Approaches to Productivity Improvement." *Personnel Psychology* 38: 468–72.

Kazdin, A. E. (1978). *History of Behavior Modification: Experimental Foundations of Contemporary Research*. Baltimore: University Park Press.

Kazdin, A. E. (1994). "Antisocial Behavior and Conduct Disorder." In L. W. Craighead, W. E. Craighead, A. E. Kazdin, and M. J. Mahoney, eds., *Cognitive Behavioral Interventions: Principles, Issues and Applications*. Needham, MA: Allyn & Bacon.

Kazdin, A. E., and G. T. Wilson (1978). *Evaluation of Behavior Therapy: Issues, Evidence, and Research Strategies*. Cambridge, MA: Ballenger.

Kaufman, J., and E. Zigler (1987). "Do Abused Children Become Abusive Parents?" *American Journal of Orthopsychiatry* 57: 186–92.

Keane, T., P. Malloy, and J. Fairbanks (1984). "Empirical Development of an MMPI Subscale for the Assessment of Combat-Related Post-Traumatic Stress Disorder." *Journal of Consulting and Clinical Psychology* 52: 888–91.

Keefe, F. I., and J. C. Beckham (1994). "Behavioral Medicine." In L. W. Craighead, W. E. Craighead, A. E. Kazdin, and M. J. Mahoney, eds., *Cognitive Behavioral Interventions:*

Principles, Issues and Applications. Needham, MA: Allyn & Bacon.

Kelly, G. A. (1955). *The Psychology of Personal Constructs.* New York: Norton.

Kelly, J. A., J. S. St. Lawrence, H. V. Hood, and T. L. Brasfield (1989). "Behavioral Intervention to Reduce AIDS Risk Activities." *Journal of Consulting and Clinical Psychology* 57: 60–67.

Kendell, R., J. Chalmers, and C. Plaz (1987). "Epidemiology of Puerperal Psychoses." *British Journal of Psychiatry* 150: 662–73.

Kendell, R. E. (1985). "Emotional and Physical Factors in the Genesis of Puerperal Mental Disorders." *Journal of Psychosomatic Research* 29: 3–11.

Kendzierski, D. (1990). "Decision Making versus Decision Implementation: An Active Control Approach to Exercise Adoption and Adherence. *Journal of Applied Social Psychology* 20: 27–45.

Kernberg, O. F. (1976). "Technical Considerations in the Treatment of Borderline Personality Organization." *Journal of the American Psychoanalytic Association* 24: 795–829.

——— (1984). *Severe Personality Disorders: Psychotherapeutic Strategies.* New Haven: Yale University Press.

Kihlstrom, J. F. (1992). "Dissociation and Conversion Disorders." In D. J. Stein and J. E. Young, eds., *Cognitive Science and Clinical Disorders.* New York: Academic Press, pp. 247–70.

Kintsch, W. (1988). "The Role of Knowledge in Discourse Comprehension: A Construction-Integration Model." *Psychological Review* 95: 163–82.

Klauber, J. (1987). *Illusion and Spontaneity.* London: Free Association Books.

Klein, M. (1948). *Contributions to Psychoanalysis.* London: Hogarth Press. (Original work published 1921–45.)

——— (1963). *Our Adult World and Other Essays.* New York: Basic Books.

——— (1975). *Love, Guilt, and Reparation.* London: Hogarth Press. (Original work published 1935.)

Klepac, R. K., and R. L. Reynes (1992). *Internship and Postdoctoral Programs in Psychology.* Washington, DC: Association of Psychology Postdoctoral and Internship Centers.

Klerman, G. L., M. M. Weissman, B. J. Rounsaville, and E. S. Chevron (1984). *Interpersonal Psychotherapy of Depression.* New York: Basic Books.

Kluft, E., J. Poteet, and R. P. Kluft (1986). "Movement Observations in Multiple Personality Disorder: A Preliminary Report." *American Journal of Dance Therapy* 9: 313–46.

Kluft, R. P. (1984a). "An Introduction to Multiple Personality Disorder." *Psychiatric Annals* 14: 19–24.

——— (1984b). "Treatment of Multiple Personality Disorder: A Study of 33 Cases." *Psychiatric Clinics of North America* 7: 9–29.

——— (1984c). "Multiple Personality in Childhood." *Psychiatric Clinics of North America* 7: 121–34.

——— (1985a). "The Natural History of Multiple Personality Disorder." In R. P. Kluft, ed., *Childhood Antecedents of Multiple Personality,* pp. 197–238. Washington, DC: American Psychiatric Press.

——— (1985b). "Childhood Multiple Personality Disorder: Predictors, Clinical Findings, and Treatment Results." In R. P. Kluft, ed., *Childhood Antecedents of Multiple Personality.* Washington, DC: American Psychiatric Press, pp. 168–96.

——— (1986a). "Personality Unification in Multiple Personality Disorder: A Follow-Up Study." In B. G. Braun, ed., *Treatment of Multiple Personality Disorder.* Washington, DC: American Psychiatric Press, pp. 29–60.

——— (1986b). "Treating Children Who Have Multiple Personality Disorder." In. B. G. Braun, ed., *Treatment of Multiple Personality Disorder.* Washington, DC: American Psychiatric Press, pp. 79–105.

——— (1987a). "An Update on Multiple Personality Disorder." *Hospital and Community Psychiatry* 38: 363–73.

——— (1987b). "First-Rank Symptoms as a Diagnostic Clue to Multiple Personality Disorder." *American Journal of Psychiatry* 144: 293–98.

——— (1991a). "Multiple Personality Disorder." In A. Tasman and S. M. Goldfinger, eds., *The American Psychiatric Press Annual Review of Psychiatry,* vol. 10, pp. 161–88. Washington, DC: American Psychiatric Press.

——— (1991b). "Clinical Presentations of Multiple Personality Disorder." *Psychiatric Clinics of North America* 14: 605–29.

——— (1993). "Treatment Trajectories in the Treatment of Multiple Personality Disorder. *Dissociation* 6.

Knoff, H. M., and G. M. Batsche (1987). "The Revised Credentialing Standards of the National Association of School Psychologists: Implications for Independent Practice in School Psychology." *Professional Practice of Psychology* 8(1): 7–17.

Koffka, K. (1931). *Growth of the Mind.* New York: Harcourt Brace.

——— (1935). *Principles of Gestalt Psychology.* New York: Harcourt Brace.

Kohlberg, L. (1984). *Essays on Moral Development: The Psychology of Moral Development* (vol. 2). New York: Harper & Row.

Kohler, W. (1947). *Gestalt Psychology.* New York: Liveright.

Kohut, H. (1977). *Restoration of the Self.* New York: International Universities Press.

——— (1984). *How Does Analysis Cure?* New York: International Universities Press.

Kohut, H. S., and E. S. Wolf (1982). "The Disorders of the Self and Their Treatment." In S. Slipp, ed., *Curative Factors in Dynamic Psychotherapy.* New York: McGraw-Hill, pp. 44–59.

Kolb, L. (1987). "A Neuropsychological Hypothesis Explaining Post-Traumatic Stress Disorders." *American Journal of Psychiatry* 144: 989–95.

Kosten, T., et al. (1987). "Sustained Urinary Norepinephrine Elevation in Post-Traumatic Stress Disorder." *Psychoneuroendocrinology* 12: 13–20.

Kraus, L. E., and S. Stoddard (1991). *Chartbook on Work Disability in the United States: An InfoUse Report.* Washington, DC: U.S. National Institute on Disability and Rehabilitation Research.

Krauss, H. H., and B. J. Krauss (1977). "Nosology: Wolman's System." In B. B. Wolman, ed., *International Encyclopedia of Psychiatry, Psychology, Psychoanalysis & Neurology*, vol. 8. New York: Aesculapius, pp. 86–88.

Krosnick, J. A., and D. F. Alwin (1989). "Aging and Susceptibility to Attitude Change." *Journal of Personality and Social Psychology* 57: 416–25.

Kruschke, J. K. (1992). "ALCOVE: An Exemplar-Based Connectionist Model of Category Learning." *Psychological Review* 92: 22–44.

Kübler-Ross, E. (1969). *On Death and Dying*. New York: Macmillan.

Kuevi, V., R. Causon, A. F. Dixson, et al. (1983). "Plasma Amine and Hormone Changes in Postpartum Blues." *Clinical Endocrinology* 19: 39–46.

Kuiken, D., ed. (1991). *Mood and Memory*. Newbury Park, CA: Sage.

Kulka, R., W. Schlenger, and J. Fairbanks (1990). *Trauma and the Vietnam Generation*. New York: Brunner/Mazel.

Kumar, R., and K. Robson (1984). "A Prospective Study of Emotional Disorders in Childbearing Women." *British Journal of Psychiatry* 144: 35–47.

Kunda, Z. (1990). "The Case for Motivated Reasoning." *Psychological Bulletin* 108: 480–98.

Kurtines, W. M., and J. L. Gewirtz, eds. (1991). *Handbook of Moral Behavior and Development*, vol. 1, *Theory*; vol. 2, *Research*; vol. 3, *Application*. Hillsdale, NJ: Erlbaum.

Kwarnes, R. G., ed. (1976). *A Harry Stack Sullivan Case Seminar: Treatment of a Young Male Schizophrenic*. New York: Norton.

Lacan, J. (1977). *Ecrits*. New York: Norton.

——— (1981). *The Four Fundamental Concepts of Psychoanalysis*. New York: Norton.

——— (1988). *The Seminar of Jacques Lacan: Book I, Freud's Papers on Technique, 1953–1954*. London: Cambridge University Press.

Lambert, M. J. (1991). "Introduction to Psychotherapy Research." In L. E. Beutler and M. Crago, eds., *Psychotherapy Research*. Washington, DC: American Psychological Association, pp. 1–11.

Lang, P. (1979). "A Bio-Informational Theory of Emotional Imagery." *Psychophysiology* 16: 495–512.

Langs, R. J. (1978). "Responses to Creativity in Psychoanalysis." *International Journal of Psychoanalytic Psychotherapy* 7: 189–207.

——— (1981). "Modes of 'Cure' in Psychoanalysis and Psychoanalytic Psychotherapy." *International Journal of Psychoanalysis* 62: 199–214.

Lanning, K. (1991). *Consistency, Scalability, and Personality Measurement*. New York: Springer-Verlag.

Laufer, R. S., and E. R. Parson (1985). *The Laufer-Parson Guilt Inventory*. New York: International Policy Research Institute.

Lave, J. (1990). *Cognition in Practice: Mind, Mathematics and Culture in Everyday Life*. New York: Cambridge University Press.

Lazarus, R. S. (1993). "From Psychological Stress to the Emotions: A History of Changing Outlooks." *Annual Review of Psychology* 44: 1–21.

Leahy, R. L., and A. T. Beck (1988). "Cognitive Therapy of Depression and Mania." In A. Georgotas & R. Cancro, eds., *Depression and Mania*. New York: Elsevier.

Leiblum, S., and R. Rosen (1989). *Principles and Practice of Sex Therapy: An Update for the 1990s*. New York: Guilford.

Leone, P. E., ed. (1990). *Understanding Troubled and Troubling Youth*. Newbury Park, CA: Sage.

Levine, J. M., L. B. Resnick, and E. T. Higgins (1993). "Social Foundations of Cognition." *Annual Review of Psychology* 44: 585–612.

Levine, S. (1992). *Sexual Guide: A Clinician's Guide*. New York: Plenum.

Levy, V. (1987). "The Maternity Blues in Postpartum and Postoperative Women." *British Journal of Psychiatry* 151: 368–72.

Lewicki, P. (1986). *Nonconscious Social Information Processing*. New York: Academic Press.

Lewinsohn, P. M., et al. (1990). "Cognitive-Behavioral Group Treatment of Depression in Adolescents." *Behavior Therapy* 21: 385–401.

Lewis, J. L., and G. Winokur (1982). "The Induction of Mania: A Natural History Study with Controls." *Archives of General Psychiatry* 39: 303–6.

Lifton, R. J. (1987). *The Future of Immortality*. New York: Basic Books.

——— (1990). *The Genocidal Mentality: Nazi Holocaust and Nuclear Threat*. New York: Basic Books.

Lindzey, G., and E. Aronson, eds. (1985). *The Handbook of Social Psychology* (3rd ed.). Reading, MA: Addison-Wesley.

Linehan, M. M. (1993). *Cognitive-Behavioral Treatment of Borderline Personality Disorder*. New York: Guilford.

Livingston, R. (1987). "Sexually and Physically Abused Children." *Journal of the American Academy of Child and Adolescent Psychiatry* 26: 413–15.

Livingstone, M. S., and D. H. Hubel (1987). "Psychophysical Evidence for Separate Channels for the Perception of Form, Color, Movement, and Depth." *Journal of Neuroscience* 7(11), 3416–68.

Lockhead, G., and M. Wolbarsht (1991). "Toying with the Moon Illusion." *Applied Optics* 30: 3504–7.

Loewenstein, R. J. (1991). "An Office Mental Status Examination for Complex Chronic Dissociative Symptoms and Multiple Personality Disorder." *Psychiatric Clinics of North America* 14: 567–604.

Lopez, S. R., and A. Romero (1988). "Assessment of the Intellectual Functioning of Spanish-Speaking Adults: A Comparison of the EIWA and WAIS." *Professional Psychology: Research and Practice* 19: 263–70.

Lopez, S. R., and I. M. Taussig (1991). "Cognitive-Intellectual Functioning of Impaired and Nonimpaired Spanish-Speaking Elderly: Implications for Culturally Sensitive

Assessment." *Psychological Assessment: Journal of Consulting and Clinical Psychology* 3: 448–54.

Luborsky, L. (1984). *Principles of Psychoanalytic Psychotherapy.* New York: Basic Books.

Lyons, J., and T. Keane (1992). "Keane PTSD Scale: MMPI and MMPI-2 Update." *Journal of Traumatic Stress* 5: 111–18.

Madakasira, S., and K. O'Brien (1987). "Acute Post-Traumatic Stress Disorder in Victims of a Natural Disaster." *Journal of Nervous and Mental Disease* 175: 286–90.

Maier, S., and M. Seligman (1976). "Learned Helplessness: Theory and Evidence." *Journal of Experimental Psychology* 105: 3–46.

Main, M., N. Kaplan, and J. Cassidy (1985). "Security in Infancy, Childhood, and Adulthood: A Move to the Level of Representation." *Monographs of the Society for Research in Child Development* 50: 66–104.

Mahoney, M. J., A. E. Kazdin, and N. J. Lesswing (1978). "Behavior Modification: Delusion or Deliverance?" In C. M. Franks and G. T. Wilson, eds., *Annual Review of Behavior Therapy, Theory, and Practice,* vol. 2. New York: Brunner/Mazel, pp. 11–40.

Malgady, R. G., G. Costantino, and L. H. Rogler (1984). "Development of a Thematic Apperception Test (TEMAS) for Urban Hispanic Children." *Journal of Consulting and Clinical Psychology* 52: 986–96.

Marlatt, G. A., and J. R. Gordon, eds. (1985). *Relapse Prevention.* New York: Guilford.

Marmor, J., ed. (1980). *Homosexual Behavior: A Modern Reappraisal.* New York: Basic Books.

Marr, D. (1982). *Vision.* San Francisco: W. H. Freeman.

Martinez, J. L., Jr., and R. P. Kesner (1991). *Learning and Memory: A Biological View.* New York: Academic Press.

Maruish, M. E., ed. (1993). *The Use of Psychological Testing for Treatment Planning and Outcome Assessment.* Hillsdale, NJ: Erlbaum.

Massaro, D. C., and N. Cowan (1993). "Information Processing Models: Microscopes of the Mind." *Annual Review of Psychology* 44: 383–425.

Masters, W. H., and V. E. Johnson (1966). *Human Sexual Response.* Boston: Little, Brown & Co.

——— (1970). *Human Sexual Inadequacy.* Boston: Little, Brown & Co.

Mathis, B. C., R. J. Menges, and J. H. McMillan (1977). "Content and Boundaries of Educational Psychology." In D. J. Treffinger, J. K. Davis, and R. E. Ripple, eds., *Handbook on Teaching Educational Psychology.* New York: Academic Press, pp. 25–43.

Matlin, M. W. (1993). *The Psychology of Women.* (2nd ed.). Orlando, FL: Harcourt Brace Jovanovich.

Matoon, M. (1992). *Jungian Psychology after Jung.* St. Paul, MN: Anda Divine. (Monograph.)

May, M. L., and D. B. Stengel (1990). "Who Sues Doctors? How Patients Handle Medical Grievances." *Law Society Review* 24: 105–20.

Mayes, A. R. (1988). *Human Organic Memory Disorders.* New York: Oxford University Press.

McCann, L., and L. Pearlman (1990). "Vicarious Traumatization: A Framework for Understanding the Psychological Effects of Working with Victims." *Journal of Traumatic Stress* 3: 131–50.

McCord, J., ed. (1992). *Facts, Frameworks, and Forecasts: Advances in Criminological Theory, Vol. 3.* New Brunswick, NJ: Transaction Publishers.

McCrae, R. R., and O. P. John (1992). "An Introduction to the Five-Factor Model and Its Applications." *Journal of Personality* 60: 175–215.

McDougall, J. (1979). "Primitive Communication and the Use of Countertransference." In L. Epstein and A. Feiner, eds., *Countertransference.* New York: Aronson.

McFarlane, A. (1988a). "The Aetiology of Post-Traumatic Stress Disorders Following a Natural Disaster." *British Journal of Psychiatry* 152: 110–21.

——— (1988b). "The Longitudinal Course of Post-Traumatic Morbidity: The Range of Outcomes and Their Predictors." *Journal of Nervous and Mental Disease* 176: 30–39.

——— (1992). "Avoidance and Intrusion in Post-Traumatic Stress Disorder." *Journal of Nervous and Mental Disease* 180: 439–45.

McGlashan, T. H. (1983). "Omnipotence, Helplessness, and Control with the Borderline Patient." *American Journal of Psychotherapy* 37: 49–61.

McKhann, G., D. Drachman, and M. Folstein (1984). "Clinical Diagnosis of Alzheimer's Disease: Report of the NINCDS-ADRDA Work Group Under the Auspices of Department of Health and Human Services Task Force on Alzheimer's Disease." *Neurology* 34: 939–44.

McLaughlin, J. T. (1981). "Transference, Psychic Reality and Countertransference." *Psychoanalytic Quarterly* 50: 639–64.

——— (1991). "Clinical and Theoretical Aspects of Enactment." *Journal of the American Psychoanalytic Association* 39: 595.

McLaughlin, M. L., M. J. Cody, and S. J. Read (1992). *Explaining One's Self to Others: Reason-Giving in a Social Context.* Hillsdale, NJ: Erlbaum.

McLeer, S. V., E. Deblinger, and D. Henry (1992). "Sexually Abused Children at High Risk for Post-Traumatic Stress Disorder." *Journal of the American Academy of Child and Adolescent Psychiatry* 31: 875–79.

McReynolds, P. (1989). "Diagnosis and Clinical Assessment: Current Status and Major Issues." *Annual Review of Psychology* 40: 83–108.

Meichenbaum, D. H. (1975). "Self-Instructional Methods." In F. H. Kanfer and A. P. Goldstein, eds., *Helping People Change: A Textbook of Methods.* New York: Pergamon, pp. 357–91.

Meissner, W. W. (1978). *The Paranoid Process.* New York: Aronson.

——— (1980). "A Note on Projective Identification." *Journal of the American Psychoanalytic Association* 28: 43–67.

——— (1981). *Internalization in Psychoanalysis.* New York: International Universities Press.

——— (1984). *The Borderline Spectrum: Differential Diagnosis and Developmental Issues.* New York: Aronson.

——— (1987). "Projection and Projective Identification." In J.

Sandler, ed., *Projection, Identification, Projective Identification*. Madison, CT: International Universities Press, pp. 27–49.

———— (1988). *Treatment of Patients in the Borderline Spectrum*. Northvale, NJ: Aronson.

Meltzer, E., and R. Kumar (1985). "Puerperal Mental Illness, Clinical Features and Classification: A Study of 142 Mother and Baby Admissions." *British Journal of Psychiatry* 147: 647–54.

Mercer, J. R. (1979). *SOMPA: System of Multicultural Pluralistic Assessment Technical Manual*. New York: Psychological Corporation.

Mercer, J. R., and J. F. Lewis (1977). *System of Multicultural Pluralistic Assessment*. New York: Psychological Corporation.

Metz, A., D. Sichel, and D. Goff (1988). "Postpartum Panic Disorder." *Journal of Clinical Psychiatry* 49: 278–79.

Miller, J. G., D. M. Bersoff, and R. L. Hardwood (1990). "Perceptions of Social Responsibilities in India and in the United States: Moral Imperatives or Personal Decisions?" *Journal of Personality and Social Psychology* 58: 33–46.

Miller, J. L., and P. D. Eimas (1995). "Speech Perception: From Signal to Word." *Annual Review of Psychology* 46: 467–92.

Miller, S. D. (1989). "Optical Differences in Cases of Multiple Personality Disorder." *Journal of Nervous and Mental Disease* 177: 480–86.

Miller-Jones, D. (1989). "Culture and Testing." *American Psychologist* 44: 360–66.

Millon, T. (1991). "Classification in Psychopathology: Rationale, Alternatives, and Standards." *Journal of Abnormal Psychology* 100: 245–61.

Mills, D. H., A. M. Wellner, and G. R. VandenBos (1979). "The National Register Survey: The First Comprehensive Study of All Licensed/Certified Psychologists." In C. A. Kiesler, N. A. Cummings, and G. R. VandenBos, eds., *Psychology and National Health Insurance: A Sourcebook*. Washington, DC: American Psychological Association, pp. 111–28.

"Mind and Brain." (1992). *Scientific American* 267(2). (Special issue.)

Modell, A. (1984). *Psychoanalysis in a New Context*. New York: International Universities Press.

Montgomery, B. M., and S. Duck, eds. (1991). *Studying Interpersonal Interaction*. New York: Guilford.

Moreau, D. L., M. Weissman, and V. Warner (1989). "Panic Disorder in Children at High Risk for Depression." *American Journal of Psychiatry* 146: 1059–60.

Morrison, J. A. (1988). "Rudy Garcia: A SOMPA Case Study." In R. Jones, ed., *Psychoeducational Assessment of Minority Group Children: A Casebook*, pp. 79–107. Berkeley: Cobb & Henry.

Mosak, H. H. (1973). *Alfred Adler: His Influence on Psychology Today*. Park Ridge, NJ: Noyes.

Mueller, J. H. (1992). "Anxiety and Performance." In A. P. Smith and D. M. Jones, eds., *Handbook of Human Performance*. London: Academic Press, pp. 127–60.

Murphy, K. R., and F. E. Saal, eds. (1990). *Psychology in Organizations: Integrating Science and Practice*. Hillsdale, NJ: Erlbaum.

Mussen, P. H., ed. (1988). *Carmichael's Manual of Child Psychology*. New York: Wiley.

National Association of School Psychologists (1992). *Professional Conduct Manual*. Silver Spring, MD: Author.

Nadir, K., R. Pynoos, and J. Fairbanks (1990). "Children's PTSD Reactions One Year after a Sniper Attack at Their School." *American Journal of Psychiatry* 147: 1526–30.

Nelson, J. C., and J. B. Bowers (1978). "Delusional Unipolar Depression: Description and Drug Treatment." *Archives of General Psychiatry* 35: 1321–28.

Nelson, J. C., et al. (1982). "Desipramine Plasma Concentration and Antidepressant Response." *Archives of General Psychiatry* 39: 1419–22.

Newell, A. (1990). *Unified Theories of Cognition*. Cambridge, MA: Harvard University Press.

Newell, K. M. (1991). "Motor Skills Acquisition." *Annual Review of Psychology* 42: 213–37.

Nichols, M. P., and R. C. Schwartz (1991). *Family Therapy: Concepts and Methods*. New York: Allyn & Bacon.

Nies, A., and Robinson, D. S. (1982). "Monoamine Oxidase Inhibitors." In E. S. Paykel, ed., *Handbook of Affective Disorders*. New York: Guilford.

Nissen, M. J., et al. (1988). "Memory and Awareness in a Patient with Multiple Personality Disorder." *Brain and Cognition* 8: 117–34.

Norcross, J. C., ed. (1986). *Handbook of Eclectic Psychotherapy*. New York: Brunner/Mazel.

Notterman, J. M. (1987). Comments as discussion evaluator of the "Art of Psychoanalysis as a Technology of Instruction." J. E. Gedo, presenter. Panel discussion conducted at the meeting of the American Academy of Psychoanalysis, New York.

Notterman, J. M., and H. N. Drewry (1993). *Psychology and Education: Parallel and Interactive Approaches*. New York: Plenum.

Oakland, T. (1983). "Concurrent and Predictive Validity Estimates for the WISC-R IQs and ELPs by Racial-Ethnic and SES Groups." *School Psychology Review* 12: 57–61.

Ochberg, F. (1986). "The Victim of Violent Crime." In L. Radelet, ed., *The Police and the Community*. New York: Macmillan.

Offerman, L. R., and M. K. Gowing, eds. (1990). "Organizational Psychology." *American Psychologist* 45: 95–283. (Special issue.)

O'Hara, M. W. (1987). "Post-Partum Blues, Depression, and Psychosis: A Review." *Journal of Psychosomatic Obstetrics and Gynecology* 7: 205–27.

O'Hara, M. W., J. Schlechte, D. Lewis, and M. Varner (1991). "Controlled Prospective Study of Postpartum Mood Disorders: Psychological, Environmental and Hormonal Variables." *Journal of Abnormal Psychology* 100: 63–73.

O'Hara, M. W., J. Schlechte, D. Lewis, and E. Wright (1991). "Prospective Study of Postpartum Blues: Biologic and Psychosocial Factors." *Archives of General Psychiatry* 48: 801–6.

O'Hara, M. W., M. W. Varner, and S. R. Johnson (1986). "Assessing Stressful Life Events Associated with Childbearing: The Peripartum Events Scale." *Journal of Reproduction and Infant Psychology* 4: 85–98.

O'Keefe, D. J. (1990). *Persuasion: Theory and Practice.* Newbury Park, CA: Sage.

O'Leary, K. D., and P. H. Neidig (1993). "Treatment of Marital Violence." Paper presented at meeting of the Association for the Advancement of Behavior Therapy, Atlanta, GA. (Available from K. D. O'Leary, Department of Psychology, State University of New York–Stony Brook, Stony Brook, NY.)

O'Leary, K. D., and S. G. O'Leary (1977). *Classroom Management: The Successful Use of Behavior Modification* (2nd ed.). New York: Pergamon.

Omer, H. (1985). "Fulfillment of Therapeutic Tasks as a Precondition for the Acceptance in Therapy." *American Journal of Psychotherapy* 39: 175–87.

Oparin, A. I. (1957). *The Origins of Life on Earth.* New York: Academic Press.

Orner, R. (1992). "Post-Traumatic Stress Disorders and European War Veterans." *British Journal of Clinical Psychology* 31: 387–403.

Ornstein, A. (1991). "The Dread to Repeat: The Working-Through Process in Psychoanalysis." *Journal of the American Psychoanalytic Association* 39: 377–98.

Orvashel, H. G., and M. M. Weissman (1986). "Epidemiology of Anxiety Disorders in Children: A Review." In R. Gittelman, ed., *Anxiety Disorders of Childhood.* New York: Guilford.

Ott, J. (1991). *Analysis of Human Genetic Linkage.* Baltimore: Johns Hopkins University Press.

Oyama, O., and F. Andrasik (1992). "Behavioral Strategies in the Prevention of Disease." In S. M. Turner, K. S. Calhoun, and H. E. Adams, eds., *Handbook of Clinical Behavior Therapy* (2nd ed.). New York: Wiley, pp. 397–413.

Pallmeyer, T., E. Blanchard, and L. Kolb (1986). "The Psychophysiology of Combat-Induced Post-Traumatic Stress Disorder in Vietnam Veterans." *Behavior Research and Therapy* 24: 645–52.

Palumbo, S. R. (1978). *Dreaming and Memory: A New Information-Processing Model.* New York: Basic Books.

Palumbo, S. R. (1992). "Connectivity and Condensation in Dreaming." *Journal of the American Psychoanalytic Association* 40: 1139–59.

Paolino, T. (1982). "Some Capacities Required to Be a Psychoanalytic Psychotherapist." *Journal of Contemporary Psychotherapy* 13: 3–16.

Paris, S. G., and B. K. Lindauer (1982). "The Development of Cognitive Skills during Childhood." In B. B. Wolman and G. Stricker, eds., *Handbook of Developmental Psychology.* Englewood Cliffs, NJ: Prentice-Hall, pp. 333–49.

Parloff, M. B., and R. R. Dies (1977). "Group Psychotherapy Outcome Research," 1966–1975. *International Journal of Group Psychotherapy* 27: 281–320.

Parrot, A., and L. Bechhofer, eds. (1991). *Acquaintance Rape: The Hidden Crime.* New York: Wiley.

Parson, E. R. (1984). "The Reparation of the Self." *Journal of Contemporary Psychotherapy* 14: 4–56.

——— (1988). "Post-Traumatic Self Disorders." In J. P. Wilson, Z. Harel, and B. Kahana, eds., *Human Adaptation to Extreme Stress: From the Holocaust to Vietnam.* New York: Brunner/Mazel.

——— (1993a). "Inner City Children of Trauma: Urban Violence Traumatic Stress Response Syndrome and Therapists' Responses." In J. P. Wilson and J. Lindy, eds., *Countertransference in the Treatment of Post-Traumatic Stress Disorder,* n.p., n.p.

——— (1993b). "FC Trauma Technology. *Report to the William Joiner Center.* Boston: University of Massachusetts.

——— (1993c). "Post-Traumatic Narcissism: Healing Traumatic Alternations in the Self Through Curvilinear Group Psychotherapy." In J. P. Wilson and B. Raphael, eds., *International Handbook of Traumatic Stress Syndromes.* New York: Plenum.

Pastuszak, A., et al. (1993). "Pregnancy Outcome Following First Trimester Exposure to Fluoxetine (Prozac)." *Journal of the American Medical Association* 269: 2246–48.

Patterson, D., J. Everett, C. Bomvardier, K. Questad, V. Lee, and J. Marvin (1993). "Psychological Effects of Severe Burn Injuries." *Psychological Bulletin* 113: 362–78.

Paul, G. L., and R. J. Lentz (1977). *Psychosocial Treatment of Chronic Mental Patients.* Cambridge, MA: Harvard University Press.

Paykel, E. S., E. M. Emms, J. Fletcher, and E. S. Rassaby (1980). "Life Events and Social Support in Puerperal Depression." *British Journal of Psychiatry* 136; 339–46.

Peebles, M. J. (1989). "Post-Traumatic Stress Disorder: A Historical Perspective on Diagnosis and Treatment." *Bulletin of the Menninger Clinic* 53: 274–86.

Pepler, D. J., and K. H. Rubin, eds. (1991). *The Development and Treatment of Childhood Aggression.* Hillsdale, NJ: Erlbaum.

Perfetti, C. (1989). "These Are Generalized Abilities and One of Them Is Reading." In L. B. Resnick, ed., *Knowing, Learning and Instruction: Essays in Honor of Robert Glaser.* Hillsdale, NJ: Erlbaum.

Perkins, D. N. (1995). *Outsmarting IQ: The Emerging Science of Learnable Intelligence.* New York: Free Press.

Perls, F. S. (1969). *Gestalt Therapy Verbatim.* Lafayette, CA: Real People.

Pervin, L. A., ed. (1990). *Handbook of Personality Theory and Research.* New York: Guilford.

Piaget, J. (1932). *The Moral Judgment of the Child.* London: Routledge & Kegan Paul.

——— (1952). *The Origins of Intelligence in Children.* New York: International Universities Press.

——— (1954). *The Construction of Reality in the Child.* New York: Basic Books.

——— (1970). *Science of Education and the Psychology of the Child.* New York: Orion Press.

——— (1971). *Genetic Epistemology.* New York: Columbia University Press.

——— (1973). *To Understand Is to Invent the Future of Education.* New York: Grossman.

Piaget, J., and B. Inhelder (1958). *The Growth of Logical Think-

ing from Childhood to Adolescence. New York: Basic Books.

Piattelli-Palmarini, M., ed. (1980). *Language and Learning: The Debate Between Jean Piaget and Noam Chomsky.* London: Routledge & Kegan Paul.

Pitman, R. (1993). "Once Bitten, Twice Shy: Beyond the Conditioning Model of PTSD." *Biological Psychiatry* 33: 145–46.

Poland, W. (1986). "The Analyst's Words." *Psychoanalytic Quarterly* 55: 244–71.

Popper, K. R. (1972). *Objective Knowledge: An Evolutionary Approach.* Oxford, England: Oxford University Press.

Povinelli, D. J. (1993). "Reconstructing the Evolution of the Mind." *American Psychologist* 48: 493–509.

Pratkanis, A. R., S. J. Breckler, and A. G. Greenwald, eds. (1989). *Attitude Structure and Function.* Hillsdale, NJ: Erlbaum.

Pribram, K. H., and M. M. Gill (1976). *Freud's Project Reassessed.* New York: Basic Books.

Pruet, K. (1984). "A Chronology of Defensive Adaptations to Severe Psychological Trauma." *Psychoanalytic Study of the Child* 39: 591–612.

Pulaski, M. A. (1971). *Understanding Piaget: An Introduction to Children's Cognitive Development.* New York: Harper & Row.

Putnam, F. W. (1984). "The Psychophysiological Investigation of Multiple Personality Disorder." *Psychiatric Clinics of North America* 7: 31–39.

———— (1988). "The Switch Process in Multiple Personality Disorder and Other State-Change Disorders." *Dissociation* 1(1): 24–32.

———— (1989). *The Diagnosis and Treatment of Multiple Personality Disorder.* New York: Guilford.

———— (1991a). "Recent Research on Multiple Personality Disorder." *Psychiatric Clinics of North America* 7: 489–502.

———— (1991b). "Dissociative Phenomena." In A. Tasman and S. M. Goldfinger, eds., *The American Psychiatric Press Annual Review of Psychiatry* (vol. 10). Washington, DC: American Psychiatric Press, pp. 145–60.

Putnam, F. W., et. al. (1986). "The Clinical Phenomenology of Multiple Personality Disorder: Review of 100 Recent Cases." *Journal of Clinical Psychiatry* 47: 285–93.

Quitkin, F., A. Rifkin, and D. F. Klein (1979). "Monoamine Oxidase Inhibitors: A Review of Antidepressant Effectiveness." *Archives of General Psychiatry* 36: 749–60.

Ramsey, T. A., and J. Mendels (1980). "Lithium in the Acute Treatment of Depression." In F. N. Johnson, ed., *Handbook of Lithium Therapy.* Baltimore: University Park Press.

Ransom, D. C. (1989). "Development of Family Therapy and Family Theory." In C. N. Ramsey, ed., *Family Systems in Medicine.* New York: Guilford.

Rapee, R. M., and D. H. Barlow, eds. (1991). *Chronic Anxiety, Generalized Anxiety Disorder, and Mixed Anxiety Depression.* New York: Guilford.

Reed, S. K. (1988). *Cognition: Theory and Application* (2nd ed.). Pacific Grove, CA: Brooks/Cole.

Rejeski, W. J., and L. R. Brawley (1988). "Defining the Bound-

aries of Sport Psychology." *The Sport Psychologist* 2: 231–42.

Reschly, D. J. (1978). "WISC-R Factor Structures among Anglos, Blacks, Chicanos, and Native American Papagos." *Journal of Consulting and Clinical Psychology* 46: 417–22.

———— (1981). "Evaluation of the Effects of SOMPA Measures on Classification of Students as Mild Mentally Retarded." *American Journal of Mental Deficiency* 86: 16–20.

Resnick, H., D. Kilpatrick, C. Best, and T. Kramer (1992). "Vulnerability-Stress Factors in Development of Post-Traumatic Stress Disorder." *Journal of Nervous and Mental Disease* 180: 424–30.

Resnick, J. W. (1991). "Finally, a Definition of Clinical Psychology: A Message from the President, Division 12." *The Clinical Psychologist* 44: 3–11.

Resnick, L. B., J. M. Levine, and S. D. Teasley, eds. (1991). *Perspectives on Socially Shared Cognition.* Washington, DC: American Psychological Association.

Resnick, P., and M. Schnicke (1992). "Cognitive Processing in Therapy for Sexual Assault Victims." *Journal of Consulting and Clinical Psychology* 60: 748–56.

Rettig, S. (1990). *The Discursive Social Psychology of Evidence: Symbolic Construction of Reality.* New York: Plenum.

Richardson-Klavehn, A., and R. A. Bjork (1988). "Measures of Memory." *Annual Review of Psychology* 39: 475–543.

Rieber, R. W., ed. (1989). *The Individual, Communication and Society: Studies in Emotion and Social Interaction.* New York: Cambridge University Press.

Rieder, R. O., and Kaufman (1988). "Genetics." In J. A. Talbott, R. E. Hales, and S. C. Yudofsky, eds., *Textbook of Psychiatry.* American Psychiatric Press, pp. 33–65.

Rikels, K., and E. Schweitzer (1990). "Clinical Overview of Serotonin Reuptake Inhibitors." *Journal of Clinical Psychiatry* 51(12): 9–12.

Riley, R. L., and J. Mead (1988). "The Development of Symptoms of Multiple Personality Disorder in a Child of Three." *Dissociation* 1(4): 41–46.

Robinson, J. P., P. R. Shaver, and L. S. Wrightsman, eds. (1991). *Measures of Personality and Social Psychological Attitudes.* San Diego, CA: Academic Press.

Rock, I. (1975). *An Introduction to Perception.* New York: Macmillan.

Roediger, H. L., III (1990). "Implicit Memory: Retention without Remembering." *American Psychologist* 45: 1043–56.

Roitblat, H. L., T. G. Bever, and H. S. Terrace, eds. (1984). *Animal Cognition.* Hillsdale, NJ: Erlbaum.

Rosenberg, R. N., S. B. Prusiner, S. DiMauro, R. L. Barchi, and L. M. Kunkel, eds. (1993). *The Molecular and Genetic Basis of Neurological Disease.* Boston: Butterworth-Heiman.

Rosenblatt, A. D., and J. T. Thickstun (1978). "Modern Psychoanalytic Concepts in a General Psychology, Pts. 1–2." *Psychological Issues Monographs* 42–43. New York: International Universities Press.

Rosenthal, R., and L. Jacobson (1968). *Pygmalion in the Classroom.* New York: Holt, Rinehart & Winston.

Rosenzweig, M. R., ed. (1992). *International Psychological*

Science: Progress, Problems, and Prospects. Washington, DC: American Psychological Association.

Rosenzweig, M. R., and A. L. Leiman (1982). *Physiological Psychology.* Lexington, MA: D. C. Health.

Ross, C. A. (1989). *Multiple Personality Disorder: Diagnosis, Clinical Features, and Treatment.* New York: Wiley.

——— (1991). "Epidemiology of Multiple Personality Disorder and Dissociation." *Psychiatric Clinics of North America* 14: 503–17.

Ross, C. A., and G. Anderson (1988). "Phenomenological Overlap of Multiple Personality Disorder with Obsessive-Compulsive Personality Disorder." *Journal of Nervous and Mental Disease* 176: 295–99.

Ross, C. A., and G. R. Norton (1989). "Effects of Hypnosis on the Features of Multiple Personality Disorder." *American Journal of Clinical Hypnosis* 32: 99–106.

Ross, C. A., G. R. Norton, and G. A. Fraser (1989). "Evidence against the Iatrogenesis of Multiple Personality Disorder." *Dissociation* 2: 61–65.

Routh, D. K. (1991). "The Section on Clinical Child Psychology: A 30-Year Retrospect and Prospect." *The Clinical Psychologist* 44: 33–37.

——— (1994). *Clinical Psychology since 1917: Science, Practice and Organization.* New York: Plenum.

Rubin, D. C., ed. (1986). *Autobiographical Memory.* Cambridge, England: Cambridge University Press.

Rumelhart, D. E., and J. L. McClelland, eds. (1986). *Parallel Distributed Processing.* Cambridge, MA: MIT Press.

Rush, A. J., A. T. Beck, M. Kovacs, and S. D. Hollon (1977). "Comparative Efficacy of Cognitive Therapy and Pharmacotherapy in the Treatment of Depressed Outpatients." *Cognitive Therapy and Research* 1: 17–37.

Sales, B. D., ed. (1994). *Specialization in Psychology.* New York: Plenum.

Samuels, A. (1985). *Jung and the Post-Jungians.* London & Boston: Routledge & Kegan Paul.

Sandler, A. M. (1977). "Beyond Eight-Month Anxiety." *International Journal of Psychoanalysis* 58: 195–207.

Sandler, J. (1976). "Countertransference and Role Responsiveness." *International Review of Psychoanalysis* 3: 32–37.

Sattler, J. M. (1992). *Assessment of Children* (4th ed.). San Diego: J. M. Sattler.

Scanzoni, J., et al. (1989). *The Sexual Bond: Rethinking Families and Close Relationships.* Newbury Park, CA: Sage.

Schacter, D. L. (1992). "Understanding Implicit Memory: A Cognitive Neuroscience Approach." *American Psychologist* 47: 559–69.

Schatzberg, A. F., et al. (1987). "Recent Studies on Selective Serotonergic Antidepressants: Trazodone, Fluoxetine, Fluvoxamine." *Journal of Clinical Psychopharmacology* 7: 445–95.

Schwaber, E. (1981). "Empathy: A Mode of Analytic Listening." *Psychoanalytic Inquiry* 1: 357–92.

——— (1983). "A Particular Perspective on Analytic Listening." *Psychoanalytic Study of the Child* 38: 519–46.

——— (1990). "Interpretation and the Therapeutic Action of

Psychoanalysis." *International Journal of Psychoanalysis* 71: 229–40.

Schwartz, E., and J. Kowalski (1992). "Malignant Memories: Reluctance to Utilize Mental Health Services after a Disaster." *Journal of Nervous and Mental Disease* 180: 767–72.

Schwartz-Salant, N. (1989). *The Borderline Personality.* Wilmette, IL: Chiron.

Schwebel, N., and J. Raph, eds. (1973). *Piaget in the Classroom.* New York: Basic Books.

Scurfield, R., S. Kendershine, and R. Pollard (1990). "Inpatient Treatment for War-Related Post-Traumatic Stress Disorder: Initial Findings of a Long-Term Outcome Study." *Journal of Traumatic Stress* 3: 185–201.

Scurfield, R. M., et al. (1993). "Stormy Weather, Speedy Action: VA Responds to Hurricane Iniki." *VA Practitioner*, March, pp. 45–52.

Searles, H. F. (1984). "Transference Responses in Borderline Patients." *Psychiatry* 47: 37–49.

——— (1985). "Separation and Loss in Psychoanalytic Therapy with Borderline Patients: Further Remarks." *American Journal of Psychoanalysis* 45: 9–27.

Sedler, M. J. (1983). "Freud's Concept of Working Through." *Psychoanalytic Quarterly* 52: 73–98.

Segal, H. (1973). *Introduction to the Work of Melanie Klein.* London: Hogarth.

——— (1977). "Countertransference." *International Journal of Psychoanalytic Psychotherapy* 6: 31–37.

Selye, H. (1976). *The Stress of Life.* New York: Brunner/Mazel.

Shane, M. (1979). "The Developmental Approach to 'Working Through' in the Analytic Process." *International Journal of Psychoanalysis* 60: 375–82.

Shapiro, F. (1989). "Efficacy of the Eye Movement Desensitization Procedure in the Treatment of Traumatic Memories." *Journal of Traumatic Stress* 2: 199–223.

Shaw, R. R. (1991). "Concepts and Controversies about the Transference Neurosis: Panel Discussion." *Journal of the American Psychoanalytic Association* 39: 227–39.

Sherry, D. F., and D. L. Schacter (1987). "The Evolution of Multiple Memory Systems." *Psychological Review* 94: 439–54.

Shields, S. A. (1975). "Functionalism, Darwinism, and the Psychology of Women: A Study in Social Myth." *American Psychologist* 30: 739–54.

Shiffrin, R. M., and W. Schneider (1977). "Controlled and Automatic Human Information Processing, II: Perceptual Learning, Automatic Attending, and a General Theory." *Psychological Review* 84: 127–90.

Shimamura, A. P., T. L. Jernigan, and L. R. Squire (1988). "Korsakoff's Syndrome: Radiological (CT) Findings and Neuropsychological Correlates." *Journal of Neuroscience* 8: 4400–410.

Shontz, F. C. (1977). "Six Principles Relating Disability and Psychological Adjustment." *Rehabilitation Psychology* 21: 207–10.

Shore, J., E. Tatum, and W. Vollmer (1986). "Psychiatric Reactions to the Mount St. Helen's Experience." *American Journal of Psychiatry* 143: 590–95.

Sichel, D., et al. (1993). "Postpartum Onset of Obsessive Compulsive Disorder." *Psychosomatics* 34: 277–79.

Siegel, B. (1986). *Love, Medicine and Miracles.* New York: Harper & Row.

Sifneos, P. E. (1987). *Short-Term Dynamic Psychotherapy: Evaluation and Techniques.* New York: Plenum.

Silverman, M. (1987). "The Myth of the Perfectly Analyzed Analyst." In E. Slakter, ed., *Countertransference.* New York: Aronson.

Simon, H. A. (1990). "Invariants of Human Behavior." *Annual Review of Psychology* 41: 1–19.

Singer, R. N. (1989). "Applied Sport Psychology in the United States." *Journal of Applied Sport Psychology* 1: 61–80.

Slawson, P. (1991). "Psychiatric Malpractice: Recent Clinical Loss Experience in the United States." *Medicine and Law* 10: 129–38.

Smith, C. P., ed. (1992). *Motivation and Personality: Handbook of Thematic Content Analysis.* Cambridge, England: Cambridge University Press.

Smith, I. L., R. K. Hambleton, and G. A. Rosen (1988). "Content Validity Investigations of the Examination for Professional Practice in Psychology." *Professional Practice of Psychology* 9(1): 43–80.

Smith, M. L., G. V. Glass, and T. L. Miller (1980). *The Benefits of Psychotherapy.* Baltimore: Johns Hopkins University Press.

Snow, R. E., and J. Swanson (1992). "Instructional Psychology: Aptitude, Adaptation, and Assessment." *Annual Review of Psychology* 43: 583–626.

Spanos, N. P., J. R. Weekes, and L. R. Bertrand (1985). "Multiple Personality: A Social Psychological Perspective." *Journal of Abnormal Psychology* 94: 362–76.

Spanos, N. P., J. R. Weekes, E. Menary, and L. R. Bertrand (1986). "Hypnotic Interview and Age Regression Procedures in the Elicitation of Multiple Personality Symptoms: A Simulation Study." *Psychiatry* 49: 298–311.

Sperry, R. W. (1993). "The Impact and Promise of the Cognitive Revolution." *American Psychologist* 48: 878–85.

Spiegel, D. E. (1977). "Antisocial Behavior: An Overview." *International Encyclopedia of Psychiatry, Psychology, Psychoanalysis & Neurology* (vol. 2). New York: Van Nostrand Reinhold, pp. 64–71.

——— (1984). "Multiple Personality as a Post-Traumatic Disorder." *Psychiatric Clinics of North America* 7: 101–10.

Spreen, O., and E. Strauss (1991). *A Compendium of Neuropsychological Tests.* New York: Oxford University Press.

Squire, L. R. (1987). *Memory and Brain.* New York: Oxford University Press.

Squire, L. R., and M. Frambach (1990). "Cognitive Skill Learning in Amnesia." *Psychobiology* 18: 109–17.

Stein, G. (1982). "The Maternity Blues." In I. F. Brockington and R. Kumar, eds. *Motherhood and Mental Illness.* San Diego, CA: Academic Press, pp. 119–54.

Stein, G., A. Marsh, and J. Morton (1981). "Mental Symptoms,

Weight Changes, and Electrolyte Excretion in the First Post Partum Week." *Journal of Psychosomatic Research* 25: 295–408.

Stein, T., ed. (1993). "Changing Perspectives on Homosexuality." In J. M. Oldham, M. Riba, and A. Tasman, eds., *Psychiatry.* Washington, DC: American Psychiatric Press.

Steinberg, M. (1993a). "Structured Clinical Interview for the Diagnosis of DSM-III-R Dissociative Disorders (SCID-D)." Washington, DC: American Psychiatric Press.

——— (1993b). "Interviewer's Guide to the Structured Clinical Interview for the Diagnosis of DSM-III-R Dissociative Disorders (SCID-D)." Washington, DC: American Psychiatric Press.

Steiner, M. (1990). "Postpartum Psychiatric Disorders." *Canadian Journal of Psychiatry* 35: 89–95.

Sternberg, R. (1988). *The Nature of Creativity: Contemporary Psychological Perspectives.* New York: Cambridge University Press.

Sternberg, R. J., and M. L. Barnes, eds. (1988). *The Psychology of Love.* New Haven, CT: Yale University Press.

Sternberg, R. J., and A. E. Beall (1993). *Perspectives on the Psychology of Gender.* New Haven, CT: Yale University Press.

Stigall, T. T. (1983). "Licensing and Certification." In. B. D. Sales, ed., *The Professional Psychologist's Handbook.* New York: Plenum, pp. 285–337.

Stigall, T. T., E. F. Bourg, P. M. Bricklin, A. L. Kovacs, K. G. Larsen, R. P. Lorion, P. D. Nelson, A. R. Nurse, R. W. Pugh, and A. N. Wiens (1990). *Report of the Joint Council on Professional Education in Psychology.* Baton Rouge, LA: Joint Council on Professional Education in Psychology.

Stout, C. E., ed. (1996). *The Integration of Psychological Principles in Policy Development.* Westport, CT: Praeger.

Stricker, G., and J. Gold (1993). *Comprehensive Handbook of Psychotherapy Integration.* New York: Plenum.

Stromberg, C. D., et al. (1988). *The Psychologist's Legal Handbook.* Washington, DC: Council for the National Register of Health Service Providers in Psychology.

Strupp, H. H. (1973). "On the Basic Ingredients of Psychotherapy." *Journal of Consulting and Clinical Psychology* 41: 1–8.

Strupp, H. H., and J. L. Binder (1984). *Psychotherapy in a New Key: A Guide to Time-Limited Psychotherapy.* New York: Basic Books.

Sullivan, H. S. (1953). *The Interpersonal Theory of Psychiatry.* New York: Norton.

——— (1954). *The Psychiatric Interview.* New York: Norton.

——— (1956). *Clinical Studies in Psychiatry.* New York: Norton.

——— (1962). *Schizophrenia as a Human Process.* New York: Norton.

Suls, J., and T. A. Wills, eds. (1991). *Social Comparison.* Hillsdale, NJ: Erlbaum.

Suomi, S. J. (1986). "Genetic, Maternal, and Environmental Influences on Social Development in Rhesus Monkeys." In B. Chiarelli and R. Coruccini, eds., *Primate Behavior and Sociobiology.* Berlin: Springer-Verlag.

Super, D. E. (1980). "Transition from Vocational Guidance to

Counseling Psychology." In J. M. Whiteley, ed., *The History of Counseling Psychology*. Belmont, CA: Wadsworth, pp. 16–24.

Tageson, W. C. (1982). *Humanistic Psychology: A Synthesis*. Homewood, IL: Dorsey Press.

Tasman, A., and J. Kay (1987). "Setting the Stage: Residency Training in 1986." In C. Nadelson and C. Robinowitz, eds., *Training Psychiatrists for the 90s*. Washington, DC: American Psychiatric Press, pp. 49–59.

Taylor, C. (1989). *Sources of the Self*. Cambridge, MA: Harvard University Press.

Terr, L. (1983). "Chowchilla Revisited: The Effects of Psychic Trauma Four Years after a School Bus Kidnapping." *American Journal of Psychiatry* 140: 1543–50.

Tesser, A., and D. P. Cornell (1991). "On the Confluence of Self Processes." *Journal of Experimental Social Psychology* 27(6): 501–26.

Tesser, A., and P. Shaffer (1990). "Attitudes and Attitude Change." *Annual Review of Psychology* 41: 479–523.

Thomas, R. M. (1992). *Comparing Theories of Child Development* (3rd ed.). Belmont, CA: Wadsworth.

Thompson, R. J., Jr. (1991). "Psychology and the Health Care System: Characteristics and Transactions." In J. J. Sweet, R. H. Rozensky, and S. M. Tovian, eds., *Handbook of Clinical Psychology in Medical Settings*. New York: Plenum, pp. 11–25.

Timberlake, W. (1993). "Animal Behavior: A Continuing Synthesis." *Annual Review of Psychology* 44: 675–708.

Tobach, E., H. E. Adler, and L. L. Adler (1973). "Comparative Psychology at Issue." *Annals of the New York Academy of Sciences* 223: 1–198.

Tonkin, M., and H. J. Fine (1985). "Narcissism and Borderline States: Kernberg, Kohut, and Psychotherapy." *Psychoanalytic Psychology* 2: 221–39.

Torem, M. (1990). "Covert Multiple Personality Underlying Eating Disorders." *American Journal of Psychotherapy* 44: 357–68.

Treisman, A., and S. Gormican (1988). "Feature Analysis in Early Vision: Evidence from Search Asymmetries." *Psychological Review* 95: 15–48.

Tulving, E. (1983). *Elements of Episodic Memory*. New York: Oxford University Press.

Tuma, J., ed. (1985). *Proceedings: Conference on Training Clinical Child Psychologists*. Section on Clinical Child Psychology, Division of Clinical Psychology, American Psychological Association.

Tunks, E., & A. Bellissimo (1991). *Behavioral Medicine Concepts and Procedures*. New York: Pergamon.

Tuokko, H., T. Hadjistavropoulos, J. A. Miller, and B. L. Beattie (1992). "The Clock Test: A Sensitive Measure to Differentiate Normal Elderly from Those with Alzheimer's Disease." *Journal of the American Geriatric Society* 40(6): 579–84.

Turner, J. C. (1991). *Social Influence*. Pacific Grove, CA: Brooks/Cole.

Turner, S. M., K. S. Calhoun, and H. E. Adams, eds. (1992). *Handbook of Clinical Behavior Therapy* (2nd ed.). New York: Wiley.

Tybout, A. M., and N. Artz (1994). "Consumer Psychology." *Annual Review of Psychology* 45: 131–69.

Ullman, R., and D. Brothers (1988). *The Shattered Self*. Northvale, NJ: Analytic Press.

Valenstein, A. F. (1983). "Working Through and Resistance to Change: Insight and the Action System." *Journal of the American Psychoanalytic Association* 31: 353–74.

van der Kolk, B. (1987). *Psychological Trauma*. Washington, DC: American Psychological Association.

van der Kolk, B., and van der Hart (1989). "Pierre Janet and the Breakdown of Adaptation in Psychological Trauma." *American Journal of Psychiatry* 146: 1530–40.

Van Hasselt, V. B., and M. Hersen, eds. (1992). *Handbook of Social Development: A Lifespan Perspective*. New York: Plenum.

Vaux, A. (1988). *Social Support: Theory, Research, and Intervention*. New York: Praeger.

Vygotsky, L. (1986). *Thought and Language*. Cambridge, MA: MIT Press.

Watkins, J. G., and H. H. Watkins (1979). "Theory and Practice of Ego State Therapy: A Short-Term Therapeutic Approach." In H. Grayson, ed., *Short-Term Approaches to Psychotherapy*. New York: National Institute for the Psychotherapies and Human Sciences Press, pp. 176–220.

Watson, J. P., S. A. Elliott, A. J. Rugg, and D. I. Brough (1984). "Psychiatric Disorder in Pregnancy and the First Postnatal Year." *British Journal of Psychiatry* 144: 453–62.

Wedding, D. (1990). *Behavior and Medicine*. St. Louis: Mosby Year Book.

Wehr, T. A., and F. K. Goodwin (1979). "Rapid Cycling in Manic-Depressives Induced by Tricyclic Antidepressants." *Archives of General Psychiatry* 36: 555–59.

Weiler, P. C., et al. (1992). "Proposal for Medical Liability Reform." *Journal of the American Medical Association* 267: 2355–58.

Weiner, B. (1990). "History of Motivational Research in Education." *Journal of Educational Psychology*. 82(4): 616–22.

Weiner, I. B. (1992). "Current Developments in Psychodiagnosis." *Independent Practitioner* 12: 114–19.

Weisse, C. A. (1992). "Depression and Immunocompetence: A Review of the Literature." *Psychological Bulletin* 111: 475–89.

Weissman, M. M., J. F. Leckman, K. R. Merikangas, G. D. Gammon, and B. A. Prusoff (1984). "Depression and Anxiety Disorders in Parents and Children." *Archives of General Psychiatry* 41: 845–52.

Wellman, H. H. (1990). *The Child's Theory of Mind*. Cambridge, MA: MIT Press.

Wellner, A. M., ed. (1978). *Education and Credentialing in Psychology*. Washington, DC: Steering Committee on Education and Credentialing.

Werman, D. (1984). *The Practice of Supportive Psychotherapy*. New York: Brunner/Mazel.

Wertheimer, M. (1945/1959). *Productive Thinking*. New York: Harper.

Wertsch, J. V. (1988). "L. S. Vygotsky's 'New' Theory of Mind." *American Scholar*, winter, pp. 81–88.

Whalley, L., D. Roberts, J. Wentzel, et al. (1982). "Genetic Factors in Puerperal Affective Psychoses." *Acta Psychiatrica Scandinavica* 65: 180–93.

Whitmont, E. (1969). *The Symbolic Quest.* New York: C. G. Jung Foundation. (Excellent summary of analytical psychology.)

Whorf, B. L. (1956). *Language, Thought, and Reality.* Cambridge, MA: MIT Press.

Wickens, C. W. (1992). *Engineering Psychology and Human Performance* (2nd ed.). New York: HarperCollins.

Widiger, T. A., and T. J. Trull (1991). "Diagnosis and Clinical Assessment." *Annual Review of Psychology* 42: 109–33.

——— (1992). "Personality and Psychopathology: An Application of the Five-Factor Model." *Journal of Personality* 60: 363–93.

Wiens, A. N. (1993). "Postdoctoral Education-Training for Specialty Practice: Long Anticipated, Finally Realized." *American Psychologist* 48: 415–22.

Williams, H. G. (1983). *Perceptual and Motor Development.* Englewood Cliffs, NJ: Prentice-Hall.

Wolman, B. B. (1985). *Interactional Psychotherapy.* New York: Van Nostrand Reinhold.

———, ed. (1985). *Handbook of Intelligence.* New York: Wiley.

——— (1987). *The Sociopathic Personality.* New York: Brunner/Mazel.

——— (1988). *Psychosomatic Disorders.* New York: Plenum.

——— (1989). *Dictionary of Behavioral Science* (2nd ed.). New York: Academic Press.

——— (1992). *Personality Dynamics.* New York: Plenum.

Wolman, B. B., and J. Money, eds. (1993). *Handbook of Human Sexuality* (2nd ed.). Northvale, NJ: Aronson.

Wolman, B. B., and G. Stricker, eds. (1994). *Anxiety and Related Disorders: A Handbook.* New York: Wiley.

Wolpe, J. (1958). *Psychotherapy by Reciprocal Inhibition.* Stanford, CA: Stanford University Press.

——— (1990). *The Practice of Behavior Therapy.* New York: Pergamon.

World Health Organization (1994). *Mental Disorders: Glossary and Guide to Their Classification in Accordance with the Tenth Revision of the International Classification of Diseases.* Geneva, Switzerland: Author.

Wurmer, J. (1987). "From Explanation to Prediction and Prevention: Future Implications of a Performance Theory for Antisocial Behavior." In *Assessment for Decision: Rutgers Symposia on Applied Psychology* (vol. 1), pp. 280–82. New Brunswick, NJ: Rutgers University Press.

Wyschogrod, E., ed. (1973). *The Phenomenon of Death.* New York: Harper & Row.

Yates, A., and T. Musty (1988). "Erroneous Allegation of Molestation by Preschool Children." *American Journal of Psychiatry* 145: 989–92.

Zuckerman, M. (1991). *Psychobiology of Personality.* Cambridge, England: Cambridge University Press.

Zung, W. W. K. (1983). "Review of Placebo: Controlled Trials with Bupropion." *Journal of Clinical Psychiatry* 44(2): 104–14.

Index

Abortion, 1
Abraham, Karl, 1
    on schizophrenia, 496
Abreaction, 1–2
Abstinence, 2–3
Acceptance theory, power and, 19
Acculturation, 3
Achievement motivation, 3
Achievement tests, 3–5, 448
    construction of, 567
    professional uses of, 5
    survey vs. diagnostic, 4
    types of, 4–5
    validity of, 4
Ackerman, Nathan, 212
Acquired immunodeficiency syndrome.
    See AIDS (acquired immunodefi-
    ciency syndrome)
Act, pure stimulus, 7
Acting out, 5–6
    hate and, 242
Action for Mental Health, 118
Activation-arousal theory, motor perfor-
    mance and, 354
Active imagination, 300
Activity, spontaneous, 6–7
Activity drive/deprivation, 6
Activity set theory on psychomotor
    learning, 459
Activity theories, illusion and, 273
Act psychology, 7
Adam, J. A., motor learning theory of,
    349–50
Adaptation, sensory coding and, 509,
    547
Adaptation-level (AL) theory of motiva-
    tion, 7–8
Adaptations vs. parameters in adolescent
    psychoanalysis, 15
Adaptive behavior measurement, 8
Adaptive theory of schizophrenia,
    494–95
Adler, Alfred, 9, 248
    on group therapy, 236–37

theory of, 9–11
    treatment method of, 11–13
Adolescence
    adjustment to, 13–14
    family and mental health of, 211
    homosexuality in, 254
    hospital therapy in, 261–62
    identity crisis in, 14, 544
    psychoanalysis in, 15
    psychopathology in, 14–15
    psychotherapy for juvenile delin-
    quents in, 301–2
    runaway behavior in, 16
    self-concept in, 503
    violent behavior in, 598
Adorno, T. W., 61, 272
Adults
    affiliation among, 17
    intelligence and learning in, 16
    separation anxiety in, 516
Aesthetics, curiosity, exploration, and,
    143–44
Affect(s). *See also* Emotion(s)
    S. Freud's theory on, 17
    isolation of, as defense mechanism,
    152
    C. Jung on, 297
    therapeutic aspects in psychoanaly-
    sis, 17
Affective functions of auditory commu-
    nication, 58
Affective psychoses, genetics and, 228
Affiliation, interpersonal, 17
Age
    conditioning and, 123–24
    constraints of, on learning, 78
    mental retardation and mental,
    311–12
Aged. *See also* Aging
    dementia in, 154–56
    depression in, 157, 230–31
    hypochondriasis in, 21, 231
    organic brain syndromes in, 22–23,
    230

psychotherapy with, 18
    suicide prevention for, 557
Aggression
    in children, 18, 390
    in human beings, 18–19
    political behavior and, 402–3
    power and acceptance theory on, 18
    psychoanalytic theory on, 19–20
    scent and, 397
Aggressive transferences, 585
Aging, 20. *See also* Aged
    convalescence and, 20–21
    cross-cultural psychology and, 142
    geriatric psychiatry and, 230–31
    intelligence, learning, and, 16
    learning, problem solving, and, 21
    nonorganic disorders and, 21–22
    organic mental disorders and, 22
    organic psychoses and, 22–23
    physiological aspects of, 23
    reaction time and, 479–80
    sensation and perception related to,
    23–24
    sex roles and, 519
    sexuality and, 24
    skill and, 24–25
    theories on, 20
Aichhorn, August, 25
AIDS (acquired immunodeficiency syn-
    drome), 148, 254, 264–67
    clinical course of HIV infection and,
    265–66
    epidemiology of, 264–65
    risk and prevention of, 265
    stigma and denial in epidemic of,
    266–67
Alcohol abuse
    antisocial behavior and, 41
    suicide prevention and, 557
Alcoholism in adolescence, 15
Alexander, Franz, 25
Alienation, 25–26
Allee, Warder Clyde, 26
Allelomimetic behavior, 26

Allport, Gordon W., 26
    on functional autonomy of motives, 224
    personalistic psychology of, 389
Allport-Vernon-Lindzey Study of Values, 556
Altered states, psychoanalytic research on, 127–28
Altruism
    development of, 26–27
    helping behavior and, 27
Altruistic surrender as defense mechanism, 151–52
Alzheimer's disease, 27, 154–55
American Board of Professional Psychology (ABPP), 27–30
    National Register of, 243–46
    need for specialty certification in psychology and, 30
    organizational structure of, 29
    pursuit of specialty certification and, 29–30
American Medical Association (AMA), 195
American Psychiatric Association (APA), 31–32, 194
American Psychological Association (APA), 32–35
    central office, 33–34
    child psychology and, 99
    divisions and state associations, 33
    ethical principles and code of conduct by, 193–94
    governance and structure of, 33
    internship program accreditation by, 429–30
    membership, 32–33
    origins, 32
    priority issues, 34–35
    professional licensing and, 423–25
    report on youth and violence from, 598
    specialty practice guidelines, 548–50
American Psychological Society (APS), 35–36
Amitriptyline, 158
Amoxapine, 160
Amphetamine dependence and treatment, 179
Amygdala system, 85–86
Anaclitic depression in infants, 62
Analyst-patient interaction, 442–43
    acting out and, 5
    communicative interaction, 116–17
    countertransference, 134–37
    K. Horney on, 256–58
    C. Jung on, 298, 300

listening process and, 315
    psychoanalytic situation and, 444
    rule of abstinence and, 2–3
    therapeutic alliance and, 573–74
    therapeutic misalliance and, 574–75
    transference (*see* Transference in psychoanalysis)
Analytic psychology, 295–301
    theory, 295–98
    therapy based on, 298–301
Anchors, rating scale, 478
Androgeny, C. Jung's concept of, 299
Angell, James R., 36
Animals
    activity drive/deprivation in, 6
    age constraints on learning, 78
    allelomimetic behavior in, 26
    autoshaping in, 64–65
    comparative psychology of, 120–22
    contact need in, 129
    early experience in, 181
    ethology and, 196–97
    hedonic theories of motivation in, 246
    hoarding in, 250
    homing behavior in, 252
    imprinting of, 78, 120–21, 196
    innate releasing mechanisms in, 282–83
    learning sets and, 312–13
    maze learning by, 233, 328–29
    pair-bonding in, 380–81
    predatory behavior in, 417–18
    protocooperation in, 26
    punishment and learning in, 471–72
    sex motivation in, 517–18
    spinal conditioning of, 551
    territorial behavior in, 546
Animism, 154, 487–88
Anokhin, Pyotr Kusmich, 37
Anorexia nervosa, 37, 106
Anthropology
    psychiatry and, 37–38
    psychoanalysis and, 38
Antidepressant drugs, 158–59
Antigone principle, 39
Antisocial behavior, 39–42
Anxiety
    A. Adler on, 13
    aging and, 21
    cardiovascular disease and, 89
    in children, 42–43, 377, 390, 515–16
    cognitive-behavior therapy for, 105–6, 111–12
    conditioning and, 43
    fear, depression, and, 43–44
    K. Horney on avoidance of, 259–60

measurement of, 190, 323–24
    psychoanalytic theory on, 44
    separation, 42–43, 377, 516
    H.S. Sullivan on, 560, 561
    theory and research on, 44–45
    therapy for (*see* Systematic desensitization)
Apathy, H.S. Sullivan on, 561
Aphasia in infants, 63
Aphemia, 368
Appetitive reinforcers, 485
Applied behavior analysis, 103–4
Appraisal and coaching of personnel, 45
Approach-avoidance conflict, 125–26
Aptitudes and aptitude testing, 45–46, 448
    of artistic aptitude, 48–49
    of mechanical aptitude, 329
Aquinas, Thomas, 49–50, 207
Archetypes, C. Jung on, 296, 297
Archives of the History of American Psychology, 46
Argyris, C., on organizations, 376
Arieti, Silvano, 12, 46
    on schizophrenia, 497
Aristotle, 2, 49, 120, 207, 397–98, 599
Arlow, Jacob, on schizophrenia, 496
Arrow's paradox, 596
Art and psychoanalysis, 47, 315–16
Artificial intelligence, 435–36
Artistic aptitude, methods of measuring, 48–49
Art therapy, 47
Asch, Solomon E., 538
Aspiration
    expectancy and, 198–99
    level of, 313–14
Assertion training, 104
Assertiveness training
    in classrooms, 67
    in structured group therapy, 68
Associationism, 49–50
    educational psychology and, 183
    motor learning and, 349
Asthma, 463
Attachment, 167
    J. Bowlby's theory of, 317, 328
    of infant with father, 212
    of infant with mother, 327–28
Attention
    conditioning and, 51
    habituation of, in infants, 239–40
    motor performance and, 352–53
    selective, in children, 502
Attention research in social psychology, 51–52

Attitudes
cognitive dissonance theory and, 55, 107–8
ideology, belief systems, values, and, 272–73
on jobs, 493
toward mentally retarded, 339
opinions and, 53–55
persuasion and change in, 395
research on attention and, 51–52
theories of development and change in, 52–53
Attraction, interpersonal, 55–56
Attribution theory, 56–58
attributional bias and error, 58
causality and, 57
commonsense attributional principles, 57–58
individual differences and, 57
self-perception and, 58
Auditory communication, 58–59
Auditory psychophysics, 59–60
Auditory space perception, 60–61
Augustine, St., 207, 556
Authoritarianism, 61, 272–73, 413
Authoritarian Personality, The (Adorno, et al.), 61, 272, 413
Authority and control in organizations, 129
Autism, infantile, 61–62, 515
differential diagnosis of, 62–63
Autistic children, therapy for, 63
Automatic vs. controlled model of human information processing, 269
Autonomic conditioning, perceptual factors in, 63–64
Autonomic nervous system, 79, 89
emotions and, 191
Autoshaping, 64–65
Aversion therapy, 65
Avoidance learning, 214
Avoidance procedure, Sidman's, 65
Avoidance training, 284–85
Avoidant disorder in children, 42

Balance theory, 52, 66, 107, 110
Balint, Michael, 66
Bandura, Albert
on moral development, 343
on self-control, 505
self-efficacy theory of, 104–5
on socialization, 542–43
social learning theory of, 104–5, 166
Barbiturates, toxic psychoses from, 581
Bargaining theory on coalition formation, 102

Barnard's model of organizations, 376
Bateson, Gregory, 66
Baye's rule on opinion modification and decision making, 149–50
Beard, George Miller, 67
Beaunis, Henri, 67
Beck, Aaron T., cognitive therapy model by, 110–12
Behavior. *See also* Social behavior
adaptive, 8
aggression in children, 18, 390
altruistic, 26–27
antisocial, 39–42
attitudes and, 54–55
coronary artery disease and, 89
culture and, 570–71
development, sexual, 520
on history as study of, 249
instinctive patterns of, 283
interpersonal, 290–91
maternal, 327–28
measurement of adaptive, 8
motor, 346–47
nonconventional political, 402–3
operant, 374
panic, 381
play, 401
predatory, 418
in prison, 421
psychomotor, 24–25, 457–59
reactance theory of, 479
runaway, in adolescents, 16
sex-typing of, 519–20
of spontaneous activity, 6–7
superstitious, 563
violent, and youth, 598
voluntary, 600
Behavioral approaches to personality and psychopathology, 69–70
Behavioral assessment in behavior therapy, 70
Behavioral ecology, 71
Behavioral medicine, 71–72
Behavioral rehearsal, 104
Behavioral test as observational method, 507
Behaviorism
classical, 72–73
educational psychology and, 183–84
functionalism and, 224
neobehaviorism, 367
operant, 73
on personality and psychopathology, 69–70
B. F. Skinner and theory of, 534
J. B. Watson and theory of, 601
Behavior modification

classroom techniques of, 67
with mentally retarded and psychotics, 67
modeling in, 342–43
self-control and, 504–5
Behavior therapy, 467
behavioral assessment in, 70
cognitive-behavior therapy, 103–7
desensitization (*see* Systematic desensitization)
emotions and, 188
in groups, 68–69
operant approaches to, 373–74
overview of, 68
on personality and psychopathology, 69–70
Bekhterev, Vladimir M., 73
Beliefs, 142
ideology, values, attitudes, and systems of, 272–73
reasoning and, 142–43
Belladonna alkaloids, toxic psychoses from, 581
Bem, Daryl, 55
Bennett Hand Tool Dexterity Test, 348
Beritov Beritashvili, Ivan S., 73
Berne, Eric, 74
Bernfeld, Siegfried, 74
Bertalanffy, Von Ludwig, 74
Bibring, E., 163
Bilateral electroconvulsive therapy (ECT), 130
Bilingualism, 74
Binet, Alfred, 74, 553
Binet-Simon intelligence scale, 74
Biochemical factors in metal retardation, 337
Biochemistry of learning and memory, 75–77
catecholamines and, 77
cholinergic functions in, 76
macromolecular events in, 75–76
serotonin and, 76–77
Biofeedback, 77–78
development of self-control and, 505
Biological constraints on learning, 78
Biological drives, 78–79
Biological maturation, educational psychology and, 185
Biological psychology, 79
Biological rhythms, 6, 82
in animals, 121
Bion, W. R., on schizophrenia, 496
Biopsychology, 79–82
Biorhythms, 82
Birth order, A. Adler on, 10–11

Bleuler, Eugen, 82
Blindness in infants, 62
Blocking, 51
Bloomfield, L., 173
Blos, Peter, on adolescent individuation phase, 169
Blum, H., 137
Body temperature, maintenance of, 81
Borderline personality disorder, 83
    A. Adler's therapy and, 13
Bowlby, John, 164, 167
    attachment theory of, 317, 328
Brain, the
    aging and, 23
    amygdala, 85–86
    biopsychology and, 79, 80–81
    language and, 83–85
    limbic system of, 77–78, 81
    mental retardation and cerebro-macular degenerations, 338
    motivation, emotion, and, 85–86
    neuropsychology and, 367–68
    perception by (see Perception)
    psychoanalysis and discoveries about human, 435–37
    response of, to isolation and sensory deprivation and, 293
Brenner, Charles, 136
    psychoanalytic theory of, 405
    on schizophrenia, 496
Brentano, Franz Clemens, 86, 398
    act psychology of, 7
Breuer, Josef, 86
    catharsis and, 1–2
BRIAAC (Behavior Rating Instrument for Autistic and Atypical Children), 62–63
Brief dynamic psychotherapy, 469
Brigham, Amariah, 86
Brill, Abraham Arden, 87
Broca, Pierre Paul, 87, 368
Brogden, Wilfred John, 87
Bromides, toxic psychoses from misuse of, 580–81
Brown, P. L., 64
Bühler, Charlotte, 87
Bulimia, 37, 106
Bupropion, 160
Burns, David, 111
Burrow, T. L., on group therapy, 236
Business. See also Industry; Organizations
    appraisal and coaching of personnel in, 45
    consumer psychology and, 128
    job analysis in, 294–95

occupational psychiatry and, 372–73
    organization development and, 376–77
    personnel testing in, 394–95
    psychology in industry and, 278–80
Bykov, Konstantin Mikhailovich, 87
Bystander intervention, 87

Calef, Victor, 590
California Psychological Inventory, 88
Cannon, Walter Bradford, 88
Carbon dioxide and carbon monoxide poisoning, 581
Cardiovascular diseases, psychosomatic aspects of, 89, 463
Carmichael, Leonard, 89
Carus, Carl Gustav, 120
Catecholamines in learning and memory, 77
Catharsis, 1–2, 86
Cathexis, 393
Cattell, James McKeen, 90
    trait theory of, 90–91
Cattell, R. B., 287
Causality and perception, 395–96
Chaining in operant conditioning, 183
Character analysis, 91
Character neurosis, 545
Charcot, Jean-Martin, 91
Chemoreception, 91–92, 397
Chiarugi, Vincenzo, 92
Chicago Psychoanalytic Institute, 25
Child abuse, 92–95
    definitions and nature of, 92–93
    effects of, 94–95
    epidemiology of, 93–94
    infantile autism and, 62–63
    multiple personality disorder and, 358
    treatment for, 95
Childbirth, mood disorders and, 418
Child development, 164–68
    anxiety and, 43, 377
    cognition and, 166, 185, 308–9
    curiosity and, 143
    emotions and, 167
    E. Erikson's psychosocial phases of, 169
        table, 168
    A. Freud's concept of, 95
    language, speech, and, 165, 308–9, 377, 550–51
    in morality, 166–67, 343
    perception and, 165
    personality and, 390 (see also Personality development)

phase-specific tasks in, 168
    table, 169
    J. Piaget on, 399–400
    praxis development in, 416–17
    prosocial development, 431
    selective attention and, 502
    separation and individual phase in, 169, 514–15
    social competency and, 122–23
    social development and, 167–68
    H. S. Sullivan on interpersonal relations and, 559
    B. Wolman on power and acceptance theory in, 413
Child psychiatry, 95–96, 248, 432
Child psychology, clinical, 98–99
Child-rearing practices, cross-cultural psychology and, 141
Children. See also Child development; Infants
    abuse of, 92–95
    aggression in, 18
    anxiety in, 42–43, 377, 390
    autism in, 61–63
    curiosity in, 143
    deviational, 169–70
    drawings of, 141
    divorce, effects of, on, 176–77
    emotional disturbances in, and role of school psychologist, 190
    fathers and, 212–13
    grandparents of, 233–34
    K. Horney on anxiety in, 259–60
    imaginative development in, 273–74
    independence in, 276
    individuality, emergence of, in, 277–78
    information processing in, 281–82
    intelligence testing of, 286–87, 602
    moral development in, 343–44
    peer influences on, 383
    post-traumatic stress disorder, 410, 411
    psychiatric interview with, 432
    psychological effects of facial and body deformity in, 204
    psychological problems of, in single-parent families, 532
    schizophrenia in, 63, 497–98
    selective attention in, 502
    separation and loss in, 42–43, 515–16
    social disadvantage, effects of, on, 536
    socialization of, 210, 542–43

testing of ethnic-minority, 569–72

violent behavior in, 598

Chlorpramine, 158

Choice, reaction time and, 480–81

Cholinergic enzymes in learning and memory, 76

Chomsky, A. Noam, 96, 174, 447–48

Christianity, psychoanalytic examination of, 488–89

Chromosomal abnormalities, 228

Circadian rhythms, 82
in animals, 121

Civil commitment, 218

Civil competencies, 218

Classical behaviorism, 72–73. *See also* Behaviorism

Classical conditioning, 124–25
cognitive-behavior therapy and applications of, 104
cognitive factors in, 108–9
H. Eysenck on neuroses and, 69–70
instrumental conditioning vs., 283
interoceptive conditioning as, 290
interstimulus interval function in, 292
learning as, 311
orienting reflex in, 377–78
pseudoconditioning, 432
stimulus substitution in, 555
work of I. Pavlov in, 383

Classical studies and psychoanalysis, 96

Classification, nosology, and taxonomy of mental disorders, 96–97

Classroom
behavior modification in, 67
cognitive style in, 109
power, acceptance, and discipline in, 310–11
as social system, 97–98

Clinical and statistical prediction, 101–2

Clinical child psychology, 98–99

Clinically standardized meditation (CSM), 330

Clinical psychology, 99–101. *See also* Psychology

Closed- and open-loop control in motor program, 354–55

Closure, creativity and, 138

Coalition formation, 102

Cocaine, 102

Code of conduct, psychologists', 193–94

Code of ethics, social workers', 541–52

Coercive power, 414

Cognition
in animals, 121–22

in children, 166, 185, 308–9
cross-cultural psychology and, 141
habituation of attention and, 240
intelligence and, 102–3
language and, 308–9
motor learning and, 349
problem solving and, 422
in social learning, 537
thinking and, 576–77

Cognitive-behavior therapy, 103–7
psychotherapy and, 469–70

Cognitive consistency theories, 52, 66, 107

Cognitive dissonance theories, 107–8, 110
attitudes and, 55, 107–8
crime victims and, 517
decision making and, 150
expectancy and, 108
interpersonal attraction and, 56

Cognitive factors in classical conditioning, 108–9

Cognitive map, 109

Cognitive style in classrooms, 109

Cognitive theories
education and, 184
of emotion, 188
of morality, 166
in social psychology, 109–10

Cognitive therapy, 110–12, 467
A. Adler's, 11–13
cognitive assessment, 110
cognitive specificity, 110–11
intervention strategies, 111–12
marital, 112
outcome evaluation, 112

Collective behavior, 112–13

Collective unconscious, C. Jung on, 296

Collins, A. M., 508

Color constancy, 113–14

Color vision, 114–15
aging and, 24
Luscher Color Test and, 318–19

Communication
auditory, 58–59
in clinical psychotherapy, 115–16
theory of, 116

Communicative interaction in psychoanalysis, 116–17

Community mental health, 117–18

Community mental health centers, 117–18
for aged, 146
legislation on, 118–19

Community Mental Health Centers Act of 1963 and 1970, 118–19, 240

Community psychology, 119–20

Comparative psychology, 120–22

Competence motivation, 186

Competence to stand trial, 217

Competency, 122–23

Competition and cooperation, 130

Comprehension, sentence memory and, 513–14

Compulsive disorders, aging and, 21

Computer(s)
applications of, to mental health, 335
discourse processing and modes related to, 174–75
human information processing and, 267–69
information processing theory related to, applied to brain and psychoanalysis, 435–36

Computer-aided instruction (CAI), 183–84

Computerized testing, 123

Concept attainment, thinking and, 577

Concept identification, thinking and, 576–77

Conditioned Reflex Therapy (Salter), 68

Conditioned stimuli (CS), 124

Conditioning
age and, 123–24
antisocial behavior as failure of, 40
anxiety and, 43
attention and, 51
autonomic, 63–64
classical (*see* Classical conditioning)
counter-, 134
discrimination reversal in, 176
dual-process theory of, 498
generalization in, 226
higher order, 125
individual differences in, 276–77
instrumental (*see* Instrumental conditioning; Operant conditioning)
interoceptive, 290
interpersonal attraction and, 56
semantic, 507
sensory, 513
spinal, 551
spontaneous recovery of extinguished response in, 551

Cones (eye), 115

Confinement, isolation and, 292–93

Conflict, 125–26
marital, 324–25

Conflict management in industry, 126–27

Conflict resolution, 126
Conformity, theories of, 127
Connectionist law, 183
Connoly, John, 127
Consciousness
	protoconsciousness and, 431–32
	psychoanalytic research on, 127–28
Consistency theories (balance and dissonance), 52, 66, 107, 110
Constancy
	S. Freud's principle of, 439
	sensory coding and, 510
Construct validity of psychological tests, 596
Consumer psychology, 128
Contact need, 129
Content psychology vs. act psychology, 7
Content validity of psychological tests, 595–96
Contrast mechanisms, 129
Control and authority in organizations, 129
Convalescence, aging and, 20–21
Conversion as defense mechanism, 152
Convulsive therapy, 129–30
	for depression, 161–62
Cooperation and competition, 130
Coping psychology, 130–31
Coronary artery disease, 89
Correlational analysis of psychological tests, 131–32
Council for the National Register of Health Service Providers, 243–46
Counseling psychology, 132–34
	clientele of, 134
	functions of, 133–34
	history of, 132–33
	organizations for, 134
	philosophy of, 133
	preparation for, 134
	settings of, 133
Counterconditioning, 134
Countertransference, 134–37
Covariation principle in attribution theory, 57–58
Creativity, 138–39
	four steps of, 138
	Gestalt psychology and, 138
	in groups, 139
	methods of measuring, 137–38
	psychoanalytic studies on, 139
	psychology of artists and, 316
	stimulation of, 138–39
Cretinism, mental retardation and, 338
Crime
	origins of criminality and, 217–18

post-traumatic stress disorder in victims of, 410
	sex-related, 476–77, 516–17, 518
Criminal justice system
	forensic psychiatry and, 216–18, 453
	role of psychologists in, 313, 452–54
Criminal responsibility (insanity defense), 217
Crisis intervention, 139–40
Cross-cultural psychology, 3, 140–42
Crowd behavior, 112–13, 151
Crowding, effects of population density and, 156
Cultural estrangement, 25
Cultural psychiatry, 3, 140–42, 583
Culture
	behavior and, 570–71
	thought and, 142–43
Curiosity
	development of, in children, 143
	exploration, aesthetics, and, 143–44
	play and, 401–2

Darwin, Charles R., 79, 120
	on human emotions, 187
	theories of, 145
Daseinsanalyse, 197–98
Day health centers for elderly, 146
Day hospitals, 145
Deafness in infants, 62
Death, 146–47
	S. Freud on drive or instinct toward, 19, 146, 223
	C. Jung on, 299
	relationship between physician and dying patient, 179–80
	survival after, 381
"Death and dying," 147–48
Decision making, 149–50
Decision theory in social psychology, 150
Deculturation and disinhibition, 150–51
Defenses and defense organization, 151–53
Delay of reinforcement, 153
Delirium, 153–54, 580–81
Delirium tremens (DTs), 154
Delusions, 154
Dementia in elderly, 22, 23, 154–56
	evaluation, assessment, and diagnosis of, 155–56
	treatment and approaches to, 156
Denial, 131
Density and crowding, effects of population, 156
Depersonalization, 156–57
Depression
	A. Adler on treatment of, 12

in adolescence, 15
	aging and, 21
	anaclitic, and infantile autism, 62
	anxiety, fear, and, 43–44
	cognitive-behavior therapy for, 105, 110–12
	mania and, 163–64
	postpartum, 418
	psychotherapy for, 157–58
	in single parents, 531–32
	somatic therapies for, 158–62
	B. Wolman's view, 162, 393
Descartes, René, 50, 80, 397
Desipramine, 158
Determinism, S. Freud's theory and, 438–39
Deutsch, Helene, 164
Developmental psychology, 164–68. See also Child development
Developmental tasks, phase-specific, 169
Deviational children, 169–70
Dewald, P. A., 444
Dewey, John, 170, 224
	functionalism and progressive education of, 183
Diagnostic and Statistical Manual of Mental Disorders, 170–71
	Third Edition (DSM-III), 39, 42, 170, 171, 172, 408
	Fourth Edition (DSM-IV), 170–71, 172, 356
Diagnostic tests, 4
Diamond model of movement conformity, 127
Differential diagnosis, 171–73
Dilthey, Wilhelm, 173
	on history and psychology, 248–49
	personalistic psychology of, 389
Direct coping, 130–31
Disabled persons. See also Mentally ill; Mentally retarded
	learning disabilities, 312
	psychological treatment of physically, 449–51
	social behavior and deformed children, 204
	in speech and language skills, 550–51
Discounting principle in attribution theory, 57–58
Discourse structure and discourse processing, 173–75
Discrimination in operant conditioning, 183
Discrimination learning, 175–76
Discrimination reversal in conditioning, 176

Discrimination training, 226
Disease
　Alzheimer's, 27
　asthma, 463
　cardiovascular, 89, 463
　Graves', 234
　mental retardation and, 338
　phenylketonuria, 396–97
　psychosomatic disorders, 462–63
Disgust, 176
Disinhibition, 150–51
Displacement, 152, 588
Dissociative identity disorder, 356
Dissonance theory, 52, 107. *See also* Cognitive dissonance theories
Divorce, psychological aspects, 176–77
Dix, Dorothea Lynde, 117, 177
Dogmatism, 61
Dollard, J., 69
Dora case, 5
Down's syndrome, mental retardation and, 338
Doxepin, 158
Drawings
　children's, and cross-cultural psychology, 141
　human figure, 263–64
Dreams and dreaming, 534–36
　A. Adler on, 11
　brain research and, 437
　in children, 377
　development of, 535
　inception of, 535–36
　C. Jung on, 300–301
　lucid dreams, 431–32
　memory, REM, and, 536
　nightmares, 535
　REM vs. NREM sleep and, 535
Dreikurs, Rudolf, 177
Driesch, Hans, 599–600
Drive(s), 177
　biological, 78–79
　S. Freud's theory of instinctual, 222–23
　C. Hull's theory of, and motor performance, 353–54
Drug(s)
　cocaine, 102
　effect of, on synaptic pathways, 81
　hallucinogens, 241–42
　for pain therapy, 379
　psychologist's privilege to prescribe, 427, 457
　toxic psychoses from misuse of, 580–81
　for treatment of depression, 158–62

Drug abuse
　of amphetamines, 179
　antisocial behavior and, 41
　of hypnotic sedative drugs, 178–79
　suicide prevention and, 557
Drug abuse rehabilitation, 177–79
Drug addiction
　in adolescence, 15
　antisocial behavior and, 41
　S. Rado on, 163
　treatment for, 177–78
Drug problems and school pyschologist, 179
Duncker, K., 422
Dying patients and physicians, 179–80
Dynamic psychology, 180

Early experience, 181
　mild mental retardation and, 181–82
Eating disorders, 37
　cognitive-behavior therapy for, 106
Ecology
　behavioral, 71
　of groups, 235–36
　H. S. Sullivan's interpersonal theory and, 556–60
Economic hypothesis, Sigmund Freud's, 221
Economic status
　effects of lowered, on children, 536
　mental disorders and, 543
　single parenting and, 530
Economy principle, Sigmund Freud's, 439
Education. *See also* Educational psychology
　achievement tests in, 4–5, 448
　classroom as social system, 97–98
　classroom behavior modification, 67
　classroom discipline, 310–11
　cognitive style in, 109
　individualized instruction in, 283
　in mathematics, 328
　mental health in, 335–36
　postdoctoral psychological, 403–4
　preschool/day-care, with mentally retarded persons, 181–82
　programmed instruction, 183–84
　progressive, 183
　psychoanalysis and, 437–38
　school as social system, 498
　school psychologists and emotionally disturbed children, 190
　school psychology in, 498–502

Educational psychology, 182–86
　associationism and E. Thorndike's connectionist law, 183
　behaviorism and B. F. Skinner, 183–84
　cognitive psychology and education, 184
　definition and influence of values on, 182
　S. Freud on education and, 184
　functionalism and J. Dewey's progressive education, 183
　future of, in United States, 185–86
　Gestalt psychology and insight thinking, 184
　operation on different types of information and, 184–85
Effect, law of, 309
Effectance motivation, 186
Efference copy, 350
Ego, the
　S. Freud's concept of, 221–22
　C. Jung on, 297–98
　regression in service of, 484
Ego and Mechanisms of Defense, The (A. Freud), 151
Ego involvement, 186
Elderly. *See* Aged; Aging
Electroconvulsive therapy, 129–30, for depression, 161–62
Electromagnetic spectrum, 114
Ellis, Albert, rational emotive therapy of, 478–79
Emergency management in psychiatry, 186–87, 592
Emergency theory, emotions and, 190
Emotion(s)
　antisocial behavior and control of, 41
　anxiety, 43–44
　autonomic physiology of, 191
　brain, motivation, and, 85–86
　depression, 43–44
　development of, in children, 167
　disgust, 176
　emergence theory of, 190
　fear, 43–44
　hate, 242–43
　hopelessness, 255
　love, 317–18
　measurement of, 190–91
　pair-bonding and limerence, 380–81
　theories of, 187–89
Emotional disturbances in mentally retarded, 189
Emotionally disturbed children and school psychologists, 190

Emotions Profile Index (EPI), 190–91
Empiricism in perception, 365–66
Encoding process in memory, 331, 332–33
Enculturation, 140
Endocrine system
    biopsychology and, 79, 81
    relationship between behavior and, 446
Energetism, S. Freud's theory and, 438
Environment
    human factors and design of, 263
    intelligence and, 286
    K. Lewin's field theory and, 215–16
    person interaction with, 387–88
    psychoanalytic, 444
Environmental psychology, 191–92
Epidemiological research in social psychiatry, 192–93
Equipotentiality, K. Lashley's principle of, 80
Equity theory on work motivation, 603–4
Erikson, Erik Homburger, 193, 391, 447
    on developmental tasks, 169
    table, 168
    on personality development, 374–75
Escape training, 284
Ethical hedonism, 246
Ethical principles
    applied to genetics, 229
    medical and psychiatric, 194–96
    for psychologists, 193–94
    for social workers, 541–42
Ethnic minority
    single parenting and, 530
    testing children from, 569–72
Ethological motivation theory, 196
Ethology, 120, 196–97
Evolution, theory of
    biological psychology and, 79
    neuropsychology and, 368
Exhibitionism, 525
Existential analysis (Daseinsanalyse), 197–98
Existential psychology and therapy, 198
Expectancy and aspiration, 198–99
Expectancy theory on work motivation, 603
Expectancy value theory and motor performance, 354
Experience
    early, 181
    effects of, on causality and perception, 395–96
    innate determinism vs. past, in perception, 510
    mental retardation and, 181–82

peak, 383
    subjective, in conditions of sensory deprivation, 292–93
Experimental design, 199–200
Experimental neurosis, 200
Experimental psychology, 80, 200–201
Explicit memory, 332
Exploration, curiosity and, 143–44
Exposure therapy, 469–70
Extinction of response, 201, 485–86
    spontaneous recovery after, 551
Extrasensory perception (ESP), 381
Extrinsic motivation, 201–2
Eye, color vision in, 113–15. See also Vision
Eysenck, Hans J., 202
    on beliefs and ideology, 273
    on neuroses and conditioning, 69–70
Eysenck's Personality Inventory (EPI), 202
Eysenck's trait theory, 202–3

Facial and body deformity in children, psychological effects of, 204
Factor analysis of psychological tests, 204–6
    J. Cattell's trait theory and, 90–91
Faculty psychology, 207
Failure, tendency to avoid, 207
Failure to thrive, in infants, 62
Fairbairn, W. Ronald, 207–8
    on schizophrenia, 496
Family
    anorexia nervosa and, 37
    in etiology of mental disorders, 208–10
    influences of, on socialization, 210
    mental health and, 210–11
    single parent, 211, 529–32
    sociology and psychoanalysis of, 544
Family therapy, 95, 212, 325, 466, 470
Fathers and children, 212–13
Fatigue and motor performance, 213
Fear
    anxiety and, 43–44
    as motivation, 213–14
Feature detection, 214–15
Federn, Paul, 215
    on schizophrenia, 496
Feedback
    ethology and notion of, 196
    motor memory and, 352
    motor program and role of, 355
    in visually controlled movement, 599
Feeling, 85. See also Emotion(s)

Feeling Good (Burns), 111
Females
    in adolescence, 13–14
    homosexuality in, 254–55
    maternal behavior in, 327–28
    psychiatric aspects of abortion in, 1
    psychiatric aspects of pregnancy in, 418–19
    psychoanalytic theories of personality in, 445–46
    psychology of, 454–55
    sex-role stereotyping of, 518–19
    sexual disorders in, 520–25
Feminism, 454–55
Fenichel, Otto, 163, 215
Ferenczi, Sandor, 91, 215
Festinger, Leon, cognitive dissonance theory of, 55, 107–8, 110
Fetishism, 525
Fetishism (Freud), 146
Fetus. See also Infants; Neonates
    motor development in, 347–48
    personality development and prenatal influences on, 420
Feuchtersleben, Ernst Freiherr Von, 215
Field theory, 215–16
Fillmore, C., 174
Five Factor Model of personality, 391–92
Flavell, J. H., 185
Flooding, 469–70
Flournoy, Theodore, 216
Fluency, measurement of verbal, 137–38
Fluoxetine, 160
Fluvoxamine, 160
Folklore, mythology, and psychoanalysis, 360–61
Forensic psychiatry and psychology, 216–18, 453
Forgetting, explanations for, 351–52. See also Memory
Form perception, 218–19, 366
Foster homes for mentally ill, 219
Fourier, Jean-Baptiste, 59
Fractional anticipatory goal response, 219
Frank, J. D., on goals and level of aspiration, 314
Frankl, Victor E., personalistic psychology of, 389
Franz, Sheperd Ivory, 219
Free association and psychoanalytic method, 220
Freud, Anna, 6, 15
    on child development, 95
    on repression, 151
    work of, 220
Freud, Sigmund, 220, 248, 398. See

also Post-Freudian psychoanalytic theory; Psychoanalysis; Psychoanalytic theory
on abreaction and catharsis, 1–2, 86
on acting out, 5
affect theory of, 17
on anxiety, 44
on the brain and psychoanalysis, 435
classical studies and work of, 96
on consciousness, 431
on death drive/instinct, 19, 146, 223
on defense and repression, 151, 489
on depression, 163, 164
on dreams vs. art and literature, 315–16
economic hypothesis of, 221
on education, 184
ego concept of, 221–22
on emotions, 187–88
free association method of, 220
id concept of, 272
on instinctual drives (libido), 17, 19–20, 207–8, 222–23, 270
organ neurotic concept of, 463–64
on reconstruction, 483
on resistance, 489
on rule of abstinence, 2–3
on schizophrenia, 495–96
scientific propositions and principles of, 438–39
sexuality theory of, 526
structural model of, 222
superego concept of, 562–63
topographic model of, 223
on totem and taboo, 38
on transference, 584–89
on transference neurosis and transference resistance, 590–91
on working through, 439–42
Fromm-Reichmann, Frieda, 223
on schizophrenia, 496
Frustration, 223–24
aggression and, 18–19
political behavior and, 402
Functional autonomy of motives, 224
Functional fixedness, 422
Functionalism, 224
educational psychology and, 183
as social perception theory, 538
Functional theory on attitude change, 53
Fundamental interpersonal relations orientation (FIRO), 290–91
Furniture placement in psychotherapy settings, 115

Galactosemia, mental retardation and, 338

Ganser syndrome, 225
Gardner, J. E., 137
Gender, 454, 519–20
Gender differences, 166
Gender identity, 225
adolescent self-concept and, 503
Gender roles
aging and, 519
cross-cultural psychology and, 141–42
stereotyped, 518–19
General adaptation syndrome, 225–26
Generalization decrement, 226
Generalization in conditioning, 226, 507
Genetic counseling, 229
Genetics
animal behavior and, 196–97
antisocial behavior and, 40–41
intelligence and, 286
mental disorders and, 209–10
object permanence and influence of, 371
personality development and, 226–27
psychopathology and, 227–29
trait theory and, 581–82
Genius, 230
Geriatric psychiatry, 230–31
Gero, G., 163
Gestalt psychology, 231–32
on creativity, 138
educational psychology and, 184
on form perception, 218–19
isomorphism and, 231
learning and, 232
on object permanence, 371–72
perception and, 231–32, 366, 386
as social perception theory, 538
thinking, problem solving, and, 231–32
Gestalt qualities, C. F. von Ehrenfels on, 7
Gestalt therapy, 232–33
Gilligan, C., 166
Glandular secretions, pheromones and, 397
Glover, Edward, 233
Goal gradient, 233
Goal response, fractional anticipatory, 219
Goals, level of aspiration and, 313–14
Goldstein, Kurt, 233, 503
Gordon, W. J. J., 138
Government, personnel testing in, 394–95
Grandeur, delusions of, 154
Grandparenthood, 233–34

Graphic and numerical rating scales, 477
Graphic art, measuring aptitude in, 48–49
Graves Design Judgment Test, 48–49
Graves' disease, emotional factors in, 234
Grief reaction, 157, 163, 355
Griesinger, Wilhelm, 234
Groddeck, Georg, 234–35
Group(s)
cohesiveness of, 235
creativity and, 139
goals and aspiration studies of, 314
preferences of, 235
relations between, 289
Group dynamics, 235
Group ecology, 235–36
Group homes, 236
Group therapy, 68–69, 236–37, 466, 470
Guilford, J. P., on structure of intellect, 237–38, 288
Guilford-Zimmerman Temperament Survey (GZTS), 238
Guthrie, E. R.
on reinforcement, 486
theory of learning by, 311, 349, 415

Habit, 239
Habit-family hierarchy, 239
Habituation, 239
of attention in infants, 239–40
Hacinski test, 155
Halfway houses, 240
Hall, G. Stanley, 241
Hallucinations, 241
sensory deprivation and, 292
Hallucinogens, 241–42
Harlow, Harry F., 121, 129, 312
Harlow, Margaret K., 121, 129
Hartmann, Heinz, 242, 504
on schizophrenia, 496
Haslam, John, 242
Hate, 242–43
Hausmann, M. F., on goals and level of aspiration, 314
Health care reform, psychology practice and impact of, 426–27, 456
Health services in psychology, register of, 243–46
Healy, William, 248
Hebb, Donald O., 288
on neural networks, 436
theory of form perception by, 219, 366
on thinking, 576–77
Hedonic theories of motivation, 246
Hedonism, psychological, 246
Hegel, Georg Wilhelm Friedrich, 146

Heidegger, Martin, 147, 197
Heider, Fritz, 57
    balance theory of, 56, 107, 110
Heimann, P., 135, 136
Heinroth, Johann Christian August, 247
Hierarchical network model of semantic
    memory, 508
Helmholtz, Hermann Ludwig Ferdinand
    von, 80
    on perception, 365–66
    on stages of creativity, 138
Helping behavior, 27
Helplessness, 247
Herbart, Johann Friedrich, 247
Heredity. See Genetics
Heroine, 177–78
Heuristics, problem solving and, 422–23
Hilgard, Ernest R., 247
Historical research, application of psy-
    chological insight to, 446–47
History, psychoanalytic, 250
History and psychology, 248–49
History of psychiatry, 247–48
Hoarding, 250
Hoffer, Willi, 250
Hogan, Robert, on moral development,
    343
Holism, 250
Holtzman Inkblot Technique (HIT),
    250–51
Homeostasis, 251–52
    basic processes of, 252
    feedback circuits and maintenance
    of, 81
    psychological, 252
    role of external cues in, 251–52
    work of W. B. Cannon on, 88
Homicide as psychiatric emergency,
    186–87
Homing, 252
Homophobia, 253, 254
Homosexuality, 252–55
Hopelessness, 255
Hoppe, F., on goals and aspiration levels,
    314
Hormic psychology, 255–56, 320
Hormones, 81
Horn Art Aptitude Inventory, 49
Horney, Karen, 248, 256
    psychoanalytic technique of, 256–58
    theory of, 258–61
Hospitals
    day and night, 145
    psychiatric units of, 262
    therapy of adolescents in, 261–62
Hostile human relations, B. Wolman on,
    162, 369, 393

Hostility, 19
Hovland, Carl I., 263
Hue constancy (color), 114
Hull, Clark L., 263
    effect of anxiety on conditioning
    and theory of, 43
    goal-gradient hypothesis of, 233, 263
    on habit, 239
    on hypothetico-deductive method,
    271
    incentive factor and, 275
    motor learning theory of, 348–49,
    353–54
    neobehaviorism of, 367
    on pure stimulus act, 7
    on reinforcement, 486
    on socialization, 542
    theory of learning by, 311
Human(s)
    aggression in, 18–19
    early experience in, 181
    existential psychology and charac-
    teristics of, 198
    personal space and territory in, 388
    sex motivation in, 517–18
    space and territory concepts in,
    546–47
Human factors, 263
Human figure drawing, 263–64
Human immunodeficiency virus (HIV),
    264–67. See also AIDS (acquired
    immunodeficiency syndrome)
Human information processing (HIP),
    267–69
Humanistic psychology, 269, 326
Humanistic psychotherapy, 470
Hume, David, 50
Humorous laughter, 309
Hunger, 269–70
    instincts and, 270
Husserl, Edmund, 396, 398
Hygiology, 133
Hyperinstrumental neurosis, 545
Hypertensive disease, behavioral mecha-
    nisms in, 89
Hypnosis, 270–71
    for pain relief, 379–80
Hypochondriasis, aging and, 21, 231
Hypothetical-deductive method, 271

Id, role of, in psychoanalytic structural
    theory, 272
Idealizing transferences, 585–86
Ideation, delusional, 154
Identification as defense mechanism, 152
Identification function of auditory com-
    munication, 58

Identity crisis, 14, 544
Ideology, belief systems, values, attitudes
    and, 272–73
Illinois Test of Psycholinguistic Abilities
    (ITPA), 550
Illness, behavioral medicine for, 71–72
Illusions, 273
Imagery, psychoanalytic research on,
    127–28
Imagination, childhood development of,
    273–74
Imipramine, 158
Immune system
    aging and, 230–31
    biopsychology and, 79, 81–82
Implicit memory, 332
Impotence therapy, 274–75
Imprinting, 78, 120–21, 196
Incentive and learning, 275
Incentive factor, 274
Incentive theory of motivation, 275–76
Independence, in children, 276
Individual differences in conditioning,
    276–77
Individuality, emergence of, 277–78
Individualized instruction, 283
Individual psychology
    A. Adler's, 9–13
    R. Dreikurs as proponent of, 177
Industrial mental health, 278
Industry. See also Business; Organi-
    zations
    conflict management in, 126–27
    job analysis in, 294–95
    occupational psychiatry in, 372–73
    organization development in, 376–
    77
    personnel appraisal and coaching
    in, 45
    personnel testing in, 394–95
    psychology in organizations and,
    278–80
Infants. See also Children; Neonates
    attachment of, to fathers, 212–13
    autism in, 61–62
    cognition in, 185
    conditioning of, 124
    development of emotions in, 167
    development of object permanence
    in, 371–72
    development of perception in, 165
    dreaming by, 535–36
    emergence of individuality in, 277–
    78
    habituation of attention in, 239–
    40
    intelligence testing of, 286–87

maternal behavior and, 327–28
motor development in, 347–48
object permanence awareness in, 371–72
organizers of the psyche in, 377
perception in, 281
personality development in, 280–81
prehension in, 419–20
separation-individuation phase in development of, 169, 514–15
smiling response in, 377
startle response in, 553–54
Information, educational psychology and operation on different types of, 184–85
Informational power, 414
Information processing
  in children, 281–82
  in humans, 267–69
  motor learning theory and, 349
Informed consent for treatment, 320, 322
Ingenieros, José, 282
Ingratiation, 282
Inhibition, sensory coding and, 509–10
Innate determinism vs. past experience in perception, 510
Innate releasing mechanism in animals, 282–83
Insanity defense in criminal trials, 217
Insight
  creativity and, 138
  problem solving and, 421–22
Insight thinking, 184
Instinct(s), 196
  A. Adler on, 9
  hunger and, 270
  motivation and, 344
Instinctive behavior patterns, 283
Instinctoid needs, 9
Instinctual drives (libido), Sigmund Freud's theory of, 17, 19–20, 207–8, 222–23, 270
Institutions, 450
  mental health and social psychology in, 336
Instruction. *See also* Education
  computer-aided, 183–84
  individualized, 283
  mathematics, 328
Instrumental conditioning, 283–85. *See also* Operant conditioning; Reinforcement
  cognitive-behavior therapy and applications of, 103–4
  reinforcement and, 484–86
  spinal conditioning in, 551
Instrumental human relations, B. Wol-

man on, 162, 369, 393, 413, 497, 544, 545
Instrumental learning, 69
Integrated care in mental health, 426
Intellect, J. P. Guilford's structure of, 237–38
Intellectual abilities, individual differences in, 285–86
Intelligence
  in adults, 16
  J. Cattell's trait theory on, 90
  cognition and, 102–3
  genius and, 230
  heredity, race, environment, and, 286
  individual differences in, 285–86
  theories of, 287–88
Intelligence tests, 74, 448, 553
  developmental changes and, 286–87
  mechanical aptitude and, 329
  mentally retarded and, 572
  Stanford-Binet, 448, 553
  D. Wechsler's, 448, 601–2
Intention, antisocial behavior and, 41
Interactional psychotherapy, 469
Interactional theory of social perception, 538
Interactions, psychoanalytic, 442–43. *See also* Analyst-patient interaction
Interactive function of auditory communication, 58
Interests
  S. Freud on withdrawal of, 495–96
  methods of measuring, 288–89
  testing of, 289, 449
Intergroup relations, 289
  prejudice and, 420
International relations and psychiatry, 290
Internships in psychology, 427–30
Interoceptive conditioning, 290
Interpersonal affiliation, 17
Interpersonal attraction, 55–56
  love and, 317–18
Interpersonal behavior, 290–91
  isolation and, 293
Interpersonal relations
  A. Adler on, 10–11
  development of, 167–68
  love and, 317–18
  in prisons, 421
  H. S. Sullivan's theory on, 558–60
  B. Wolman on, 162, 369, 393, 413, 497

Interpersonal theory, H. S. Sullivan's, 558–60
  anxiety principle of, 560
  background on, 558–59
  developmental stages and, 559
  ecological principle of, 559–60
  interpersonal dyad in, 558
  similarity principle of, 560
  tenderness principle of, 560
Interpretation of Dreams, The (Freud), 96, 146
Interpretive process in psychoanalysis, 291–92
Interstimulus interval function, 292
Intertechnical therapy (InTT), 411–12
Interviews as observational method, 506–7
Introjection as defense mechanism, 152
Investigatory behavior, 143–44
Isocarboxazid, 159
Isolation
  confinement and, 292–93
  as defense mechanism, 152
Isolation of affect, as defense mechanism, 152
Isomorphism, Gestalt psychology and, 231

Jacobson, E., 163
  on schizophrenia, 496
James, William, 294, 591
  on human emotions, 187
  personalistic psychology of, 389
Janet, Pierre, 294
Jaspers, Karl, 147, 294
Jenkins, M. A., 64
Job analysis, 294–95
Job satisfaction, 493
Johnson, William H., studies on sexuality by, 274, 524, 525
Joint Commission on Mental Illness and Health, 31, 118
Jones, Ernest, 295
Judaism, psychoanalytic examination of, 488
Judgment theory on attitude change, 53
Jung, Carl Gustave, 248, 295
  analytic theory of, 295–98, 591
  therapy of, 298–301
Juvenile delinquents, psychotherapy of, 301–2

Kahlbaum, Karl Ludwig, 303
Kahn, R., on organizations, 376
Kallmann, Franz J., 303
Kant, Immanuel, 207, 303

Katz, D., on organizations, 376
Keller, F. S., 183–84
Kelley, Harold, 57
Kelman, Harold, 303
Kernberg, O.
    on psychoanalytic technique, 445
    psychoanalytic theory of, 405
Kierkegaard, Soren, 147
Kimble, Gregory A., 555
Kinesics, 116
Kinesthesis, 303–4
Kinsey, A. C., studies on sexuality by, 253
Kirchhoff, Theodore, 56, 304
Klein, Melanie, 135, 163, 305
    contribution of, to psychoanalysis, 305
Knauber Art Ability Test, 49
Koffka, Kurt, 305
Kohlberg, L., 166
    on moral development, 343
Köhler, Wolfgang, 184, 306
Kohut, Heinz, 306
    on psychoanalytic technique, 445
    self psychology of, 306–7, 504
Konorski, Jerzy, 307
Kraepelin, Emil, 307
Krafft-Ebing, Richard, 307
Kretschmer, Ernst, 307
Kris, Ernst, 445, 484
Kubie, Lawrence, 307
    on instincts, 270
Kübler-Ross, Elisabeth, 147–48
Kuder Preference Record, 289

Lacan, Jacques, 147, 308
Lampl-de Groot, J., psychoanalytic theory of, 406
Language. See also Linguistics
    autism and child developmental disorders in, 63
    bilingualism and, 74
    brain and, 83–85
    cognitive development and, 308–9
    developmental disabilities in child speech and, 550–51
    development of, in children, 165, 377
    disabilities in speech and, 550–51
    psycholinguistics, 447–48
    sentence completion tests, 513
      table, 512
    sentence memory and comprehension, 513–14
    word association, 603
Lashley, Karl S., 80
Latent learning, 309

Laughter, 309
Law. See Legal system
Law of effect, 283, 309
Leadership, 280, 310
    power, acceptance, and, 310–11
    sociology and psychoanalysis of, 544
Learned helplessness, 247
Learning
    in adults, 16
    aging and, 21
    avoidance, 214
    biochemistry of, 75–77
    biological constraints on, 78
    classical theories of, 311
    discrimination, 175–76
    Gestalt psychology and, 232
    habit and, 239
    incentive and, 275–76
    instrumental, 69
    latent, 309
    law of effect and, 183, 309
    matching-to-sample and, 327
    of mathematics, 328
    maze, 233, 328–29
    mediation in, 329
    among mentally retarded, 311–12
    motivational role of fear in, 213–14
    motor performance, motivation, and, 353–54
    oddity, 327, 373
    omission, 284
    practice and, 414–16
    in problem-solving, 422
    psychomotor, 416, 459
    punishment and, 471–72
    rule learning, 185, 577
    selective, 502–3
    theory of, on attitude change, 52–53
    theory of motor, 348–50
    theory of social (see Social learning theory)
    Vincent curves and, 597
Learning disability, 312
Learning set, 312–13
Legal system, 451–54
    forensic psychiatry and, 216–18, 453
    role of psychologists in, 313, 452–54
Lerner, Karl Edward, 313
Lesbians, 254–55
Level of aspiration, 313–14
Lewerenz Tests in Fundamental Abilities of Visual Art, 49
Lewin, Bertram David, 163, 315
Lewin, Kurt, 315
    field theory of, 215–16
    organizational theory of, 376
    valence concept of, 595

Libidinal transferences, 585
Libido theory (instinctual drives), Sigmund Freud's, 17, 19–20, 207–8, 222–23, 270
Licensing of psychologists, 423–25
Lie detection, 315
Lie therapy, 117
Life space, Kurt Lewin on, 215–16
Life-span development, cross-cultural psychology and, 141
Light, sensitivity to, 598–99. See Vision
Likert scale, 53–54
Limbic system, 77–78, 81
Limerence, 380–81
Lindsley, D. B., 188
Linguistic function of auditory communication, 58
Linguistics, 447–48. See also Language
    brain, language, and, 83–85
    N. Chomsky on, 96, 174, 447
    discourse structure and discourse processing in, 173–75
    psycholinguistics, 447–48
    semantic conditioning and generalization, 507
    semantic differential, 507–8
    semantic memory, 508–9
Listening process in psychoanalysis, 315
Literature and psychoanalysis, 315–16
    mythology and folklore, 360–61
Lithium, 161
Little, M., 135, 136
Liver, hunger sensations and, 269
Locomotion exploration, 143–44
Locus of Control Scale, 316–17
Loewald, H. W., psychoanalytic theory of, 406
Loneliness, H. S. Sullivan on, 561
Long-term memory (LTM), 350, 514
Lorenz, Konrad, 120
    on innate releasing mechanism, 282–83
    on instinct and hunger, 270
Loss
    in children, 42, 515–16
    depression following, 157–58
    mourning and, 355
Love, 317–18
    mating and, 56
    pair-bonding and, 380–81
Lucid dreams, 431–32
Luria, Alexander Romanovich, 318
Luscher Color Test, 318–19

McClelland, David, 413
McDougall, William, 320

hormic psychology of, 255–56
purposivism of, 472
McGregor, D., on organizations, 376
Magic, 487–88
Mahler, Margaret S., 320, 497
  on psychoanalytic technique, 445
  on separation-individuation developmental phase, 169, 514–15
Males
  in adolescence, 13–14
  homosexuality in, 252–54
  impotence therapy for, 274–75
  sex-role stereotyping of, 518–19
  sexual disorders in, 525–26
Malpractice in psychiatry, 320–23
Managed care in mental health, 426
Management education, 278
Mania, psychoanalytic theories on depression and, 163–64
Manifest anxiety scale, 323–24
Man-machine systems, 323
Maprotiline, 160
March, O. P., on organizations, 376
Marital and family therapy, 325, 466, 470
  cognitive-behavior therapy, 106, 112
  group therapy for, 237
Marital choice, determinants of, 324
Marital conflict, 324–25
Marrow, Alfred, 326
Masculine protest, A. Adler on, 11
Maslow, Abraham H., 326
  on peak experiences, 383
  on self actualization, 503
Masochism, 525
Mass action, K. Lashley's principle of, 80
Mass media, influence of, 326–27, 537
Masters, Virginia, studies on sexuality by, 274, 524, 525
Matching-to-sample, 327
Maternal behavior, 327–28
Maternal employment effect, 328
Mathematics learning and instruction, 328
Mating and love, 56
Mayo, Elton, on organizations, 376
Maze learning, 328–29
  goal gradient in, 233
Meaninglessness, 25
Measurement. *See also* Test(s)
  of adaptive behavior, 8
  of anxiety, 323–23
  of artistic aptitude, 48–49
  of attitudes, 53–54
  of creativity, 137–38
  of emotions, 190–91

of interests, 288–89
of mechanical aptitude, 329
of motor dexterity, 348
of personality and attribution, 57
psychophysical, 460–61
rating scales, 477–78
reliability of psychological, 486–87
of semantic differential, 507–8
statogram and statometric technique in, 554–55
of values, 596
of variability, 568–69
Mechanical aptitude, methods of measuring, 329
Mechanoreceptors, 303–4
Media, influence of, 326–27, 537
Mediation in learning, 329
Medicine
  behavioral, 71
  ethical principles in, 194–96
  psychosomatic, 463–64
  surgery and psychiatry, 563
Meditation
  clinical uses of, 330
  psychiatry and transcendental, 583
  as therapeutic agent, 330–31
Megalomania, 495
Meier Art Judgment Test, 48
Meissner, William W., psychoanalytic theory of, 405
Melton, Arthur W., 331
Memory, 331–33
  biochemistry of, 75–77
  definition and processes of, 331
  dreams, REM sleep, and, 536
  encoding and retrieval in, 332–33
  explanations for failure of, 351–52
  explicit and implicit, 332
  long-term, 351, 514
  motor learning and, 349–50
  of motor skills, 350–52
  psychoanalytic theory on, 333–34
  semantic, 508–9
  sentence, 513–14
  short-term, 351
  systems of, 332
  thinking and, 577
  working, 332
Menninger, Karl Augustus, 334
Menninger, William C., 334
Mental disorders. *See also* Psychopathology; Psychoses
  in adolescence, 14–15
  aging and, 21–23, 230–31
  classification, nosology, and taxonomy of, 96–97, 170–71
  crisis intervention for, 139–40

deculturation and disinhibition, 150–51
differential diagnosis of, 171–73
family in etiology of, 208–10
genetics and, 227–29
in mentally retarded, 189
multiple personality disorder, 356–60
neuroses, 368
philosophy of science and treatment of, 592
post-traumatic stress disorder (PTSD), 406–12
in pregnancy, 418–19
psychosomatic, 462–63
schizophrenia (*see* Schizophrenia)
in school children, 190
sexual, 520–26
social processes causing, 192–93
sociopathology, 544–45
treatment of deviational children, 169–70
B. Wolman on levels of, 162
Mental health, 334–35
  community, 117–19
  computer applications related to, 335
  family and, 210–11
  in industry, 278
  managed vs. integrated care in, 426
  national health reform and, 426–27, 456
  register of services in, 243–46
  in schools, 335–36
  social issues related to, 336
  social work and, 539–41
  H. S. Sullivan on treatment of, 560–62
Mental health centers, community, 117–18
  legislation on, 118–19
Mental health service providers. *See also* Psychiatrists; Psychologists
  national register of, 243–46
  nonprofessional, 119
Mental Health Study Act of 1955, 118
Mental Health Systems Act of 1980, 119
Mentally ill. *See also* Mental disorders; Psychopathology
  deinstitutionalization of, 31–32
  foster homes for, 219
  group homes for, 236
  halfway houses for, 240
  quarter-way houses for, 475
  reforms in care of, 117–18
  suicide prevention for, 557

Mentally retarded
    behavior modification with, 67
    emotional disturbances in, 189
    learning among, 311–12
    testing of, 572
Mental retardation, 336–39
    adaptive behavior as classification of, 8
    early experience and mild, 181–82
    etiology of, 336–37
    infantile autism and, 63
    organic aspects of, 337–38
    overview of, 338–39
    social aspects of, 339
Mercury poisoning, 581
Merritt, H. Houston, 340
Mesmer, Franz Anton, 340
Metacommunication, 115
Metals, toxic psychoses from, 581
Metapsychology, psychoanalytic, 438, 443
Meyer, Adolf, 340
Meyers, D. E., 508
Meynert, Theodore, 340
Military psychiatry, 340–42
Mill, James, 50
Miller, M. E., 69
Mind-body connection, 71, 80
Minimum power theory on coalition formation, 102
Minnesota Multiphasic Personality Inventory (MMPI), 342, 449
Minnesota Vocational Interest Inventory, 289
Mitchell, S. Weir, 342
Mitchell-Bateman, Mildred, 1
Mobs, 113, 151
Modeling
    antisocial behavior and, 40
    in behavior modification, 342–43
Monoamine oxidase inhibitors (MAOIs), 159–60
Mood states
    helping behavior and effect of, 431
    in pregnancy and childbirth, 418–19
Moral development, 343–44
Moral reasoning, cross-cultural psychology and, 141
Moreno, J. L., on group therapy, 236
Morgan, C. Lloyd, 120
Morrow, J. P., 288
Motivation, 344–46
    achievement, 3
    adaptation-level theory of, 7–8
    brain, emotion, and, 85–86
    J. Cattell's trait theory on, 90
    effectance, 186

ethological theory of, 196
extrinsic, 201–2
fear as, 213–14
hedonic theories of, 246
homeostasis and theory of, 252
incentive and, 275–76
motor performance and, 353–54
power, 413
sensitization-invigoration mechanism (SIM) and, 510–11
sex, 517–18
theory of ethological, 196
thirst as, 577–78
vigilance and, 597
B. Wolman on levels of, 393
work, 603–4
Motivation Analysis Test, 90
Motives, functional autonomy of, 224
Motor action, educational psychology and, 184–85
Motor behavior, 346
    social factors in, 346–47
Motor development, 347–48
Motor dexterity, methods of measuring, 348
Motor learning
    kinesthesis and, 304
    theories of, 348–50
Motor memory, 350–52
Motor performance
    attention demand and, 352–53
    fatigue and, 213
    kinesthesis and, 304
    motivation and, 353–54
Motor program, 350, 354–55
Mourning
    in children, 516
    psychoanalytic theory on, 355
Movement
    fetal and infant motor development, 347–48
    kinesthesis and perception of, 303–4
    locomotion exploration, 143–44
    motor behavior, 346–47
    motor dexterity, 348
    motor learning, 304, 348–50
    motor memory, 350–52
    motor performance, 213, 304, 352–54
    motor program, 354–55
    object permanence and perception of, 371–72
    praxis development, 416–17
    visually controlled, 599
    visual-motor information and, 598
Müller, Johannes, 599

Multiple personality disorder, 356–60
    characteristics of, 356–58
    diagnosis of, 358–59
    etiology of, 358
    treatment of, 359–60
Murphy, Gardner, 360
Murray, Henry, 390
Musical aptitude, measurement of, 48
Mutual human relations, B. Wolman on, 162, 369, 393, 413, 497
Mythology, folklore, and psychoanalysis, 360–61

Narcissistic alliance, 362
Narcissistic personality and behavior, 306–7
Narcissistic transferences, 585, 586
National Association of Social Workers, 541–42
National health reform, psychology practice and impact of, 426–27, 456
National Institute of Mental Health, 362–65
    extramural programs, 364
    future of, 365
    history of, 117, 363–64
    intramural research, 364–65
National Mental Health Act of 1946, 117
National Register of Health Service Providers in Psychology, 243–46
Nativism in perception, 365–66
Need, 366–67
Negative reinforcement, 284, 485
Negative transfer, 584
Negligence, antisocial behavior as, 41
Neobehaviorism, 367
Neonates. *See also* Fetus; Infants
    conditioning of, 123–24
    motor development in, 347–48
    prehension in, 419–20
    startle response in, 553–54
Nervous system. *See also* Brain
    biopsychology and, 79–81
    effects of tricyclic antidepressants on, 158–59
Neural networks, 436
Neurasthenia, 67
Neurologists, achievement tests used by, 5
Neurons, all-or-none law applied to, 80
Neuropsychiatric disorders, genetics and, 229
Neuropsychology, historical review of, 367–68
Neuroscience, 80
Neuroses, 368
    A. Adler on, 12, 13

character, 545
depressive, 157
J. Dollard and M. E. Miller on, 69
experimental, 200
H. Eysenck on, 69–70
S. Freud on actual, 44
K. Horney on, 259–61
hyperinstrumental, 545
C. Jung on, 299–300
H. Kohut on self and, 307
in mentally retarded, 189
symptoms of, in children, 169
transference, 588, 590
B. Wolman on, 162, 545
Neurotransmitters, 80–81, 436
Newcomb, T. M., 56
Newton, Isaac, 398
Nightmares, 535
Nonconventional political behavior, 402–3. See also Terrorism
Nonorganic disorders among aged, 21–22
Normlessness, 25
Nortriptyline, 158
Nosology, 96–97, 369
Nowlis Mood Checklist, 190
Nursing, psychiatric, 369–70

Obesity, 106
Objective fatigue, 213
Object permanence, 371–72
Object relations theory, 405
Observational methods, self-report and, 506–7
Obstruction method, 372
Occupational psychiatry, 372–73
Occupational therapy, 262
Oddity learning, 327, 373
Oedipus complex, 96, 544, 562
Ohio Vocational Interest Survey (OVIS), 289
Olfaction, 92
Omission learning, 284
On Death and Dying (Kübler-Ross), 147–48
Operant behavior, 374
Operant behaviorism, 73
Operant conditioning. See also Instrumental conditioning
in behavior therapy, 373–74
B. F. Skinner's extension from, to programmed instruction, 183–84
Opiate addiction and treatment, 177–78
Opinions, attitudes and, 53–55
Organic brain syndrome (OBS), 22, 23, 154, 230

Organic mental disorders among aged, 22
Organization development (OD), 376–77
Organization of sensory information, 510
Organizations. See also Business; Industry
control and authority in, 129
psychology of industry and, 278–80
sociopsychological theories on human behavior in, 375–76
"Organizers of the psyche," 377
Organ modes and social modalities in personality development, 374–75
Orienting reflex, 144, 377–78
Overanxious disorder in children, 42
Overshadowing, 51
Overstimulation, 512–13
Overtraining reversal effect (ORE), 51
Oxygen, toxic psychoses from lack of, 581

Pain, 379–80
behavioral medicine for, 71–72
meditation and control of, 330
modes of, 86
theories of, 379
therapy for, 379–80
Pair-bonding and limerence, 380–81
Palliative coping, 130–31
Panic behavior, 381
cognitive therapy for, 106, 111–12
Panic disorders, cognitive-behavior therapy for, 106
Paracelsus, Theophrastus Philippus Aureolus Bombasatus von Hohenheim, 381
Parameters vs. adaptations in adolescent psychoanalysis, 15
Paranoid transferences, 585
Parapsychology, 381–82, 591–92
psychiatry and, 382
Parasympathetic nervous system (PNS), 191
Parens, H., psychoanalytic theory of, 405
Parent-child interactions
A. Adler on, 10
development of altruism and, 26–27
leading to sociopathy, 545
maternal behavior and, 327–28
prosocial development and, 431
social development and, 167–68
socialization and, 210
symbiotic psychosis and, 62
Parenting
achievement motivation and, 3
child socialization and, 210, 542–43

effects of maternal employment, 328
by fathers, 212–13
by mothers, 327–28
schizophrenogenic mother, 496
single, 529–32
Paroxetine, 160
Passionate Love Scale, 317
Pastoral psychiatry, 382
Pavlov, Ivan Petrovich, 175, 200, 383
Pavlovian conditioning. See Classical conditioning
Peak experience, 383
Pedophilia, 525
Peer influences on socialization, 383
Perception, 383–86, 509–10. See also Sensation
aftereffects of, 385–86
aging and, 509–10
attention and, 386
auditory space, 60–61
autonomic conditioning and, 63–64
causality and, 395–96
chemoreception, 91–92, 397
constraints on, and learning, 78
development of, in infants and children, 165
dynamism of, 384
explanation of, 509
feature detection, 214–15
field of inquiry in, 509–10
of form, 218–19
Gestalt psychology and, 231–32, 366, 386 (see also Gestalt psychology)
hallucinations as errors in, 241
homeostasis and, 251–52
of hunger, 269
in infants, 281
of movement (kinesthesis), 303–4
nativism and empiricism in, 365–66
object permanence and motion, 371–72
organization of, 386
person, 387
physiological and anatomical correlates of, 386
picture, 400
psychophysics of, 461–62
relativity of, 384–85
signal detection theory on, 527–29
theories of social, 538
of touch, 579–80
vision (see Vision)
Perceptual tests and mechanical aptitude, 329
Perls, Friedrich (Fritz) Salomon, 387
Persecutory delusions, 154

Personalistic psychology, 388–90
Personality
    behavioral approaches to, 69–70
    multiple, 356–60
    psychoanalytic theories of female,
        445–46
    types of (see Personality types)
Personality development
    in childhood, 390
    cross-cultural psychology and, 141
    emergence of individuality and,
        277–78
    E. Erikson on organ modes and
        social modalities in, 374–75
    genetic influences on, 226–27
    in infants, 280–81
    M. Klein on, 305
    prenatal influences on, 420
Personality disorder. See also Mental
        disorders
    antisocial behavior and, 41
    borderline, 83
    multiple personalities in, 356–60
Personality tests, 57, 88, 202, 238, 342,
        449
    construction of, 567–68
Personality theories, 390–92
    A. Adler's individual psychology,
        9–11
    H. Eysenck's trait theory, 202–3
    W. R. Fairbairn's, 207–8
    Five Factor Model, 391–92
    person perception and, 387
    B. Wolman's, 392–94
Personality types
    authoritarian, 61, 272–73, 413
    cardiovascular disease and, 89, 463
    shy, 526–27
Personalized System of Instruction (PSI),
        183–84, 283
Personal Orientation Inventory (POI),
        572–73
Personal space
    group ecology and general systems
        theory on, 236
    psychiatry and, 546–47
    territory and, in humans, 388
Personnel
    appraisal and coaching of, 45
    testing of, in business, industry, and
        government, 394–95
Person perception, 387
Person-situation interaction, 387–88
Persuasion, 395
    coercive, 537
Phase theory on auditory space percep-
        tion, 60–61

Phenelzine, 159
Phenomenal causality and perception,
        395–96
Phenomenological psychology, 396
Phenylketonuria, 396–97
Pheromones, 397
Philosophical psychology, 397–98
    associationism, 49–50
    classical studies and, 96
    existential analysis, 197–98
    existential psychology and therapy,
        198
    faculty psychology, 207
    phenomenological, 396
Philosophical psychotherapy, 398–99
Philosophy, human struggle with death
        in, 146–47
Phobia, 13
    school, 498
Photoreceptors, 114
Physically disabled, psychological treat-
        ment of, 449–51
Physicians, dying patients and, 179–80
Physiological psychology, 80
Physiotherapy for pain relief, 379
Piaget, Jean, 399
    on accommodation and instinct, 270
    on cognitive development in chil-
        dren, 166, 185, 308–9
    on development of imagination,
        273–74
    on intelligence, 288, 399
    on moral development, 343
    on object permanence, 371
    on play and curiosity, 401
    theory of, 399–400, 542
Picture perception, 400
Pinel, Philippe, 400–401
Plato, 49, 207, 397
Platter, Felix, 401
Play and curiosity, 401–2
Play behavior, 401
Pleasure-unpleasure principle, Sigmund
        Freud's, 439
Plutchik, Robert, theory of emotions by,
        189
Political behavior, nonconventional,
        402–3
Polygraph and lie detection, 315
Population control, 403
Positive reinforcement, 485
Postdoctoral education and training in
        psychology, 403–4
Post-Freudian psychoanalytic theory,
        404–6
    on acting out, 6
    on self-concept, 504

topographic model in, 579
    on transference, 584–89
Post-traumatic stress disorder (PTSD),
        406–12
    biopsychobehavioral symptoms of,
        407 table
    in children, 410, 411
    cognitive-behavior therapy for,
        105–6
    diagnosis of, 406–10
    epidemiology of, 410
    management of, 411–12
    theories of psychological trauma
        and, 406
    victim assessment, 410–11
    vulnerability to, 410
Power
    leadership, acceptance, and, 310–11
    social, 414
    theory of acceptance and, 413
Powerlessness, 25
Power motivation, 413
Practice and learning, 414–16
Praxeology, 439
Praxis development, 416–17
Preconditioning, sensory, 513
Predatory behavior, 417–18
Predicate interaction mode of semantic
        memory, 508
Prediction
    clinical vs. statistical, 101–2
    validity of psychological tests for,
        595
Preference behavior and values, 597
Pregnancy, psychiatric aspects, 418–19
Prehension in infancy, 419–20
Prejudice, theories of, 420
Premack, D., 486
Prenatal influences on personality devel-
        opment, 420
Preparatory state theories, 458–59
Prepotent response theory, 486
Preschool day-care intervention with
        mentally retarded, 181–82
Prescription privileges, psychologists',
        427, 457
Preventive psychiatry, 420–21
Pride system, Karen Horney's, 260
Prisons
    behavior in, 421
    psychologists working in, 313
Problem solving, 421–23
    aging and, 21
    cognition and, 422
    Gestalt psychology and, 231–32
    heuristics and, 422–23
    insight and, 421–22

learning and, 422
reasoning and, 482–83
two-string problem, 422
Problem-solving training, 104
Professional psychologists, licensing of, 423–25. *See also* Psychologists
Professional psychology, 425–27
Professional psychology internship, 427–30
Programmed instruction, 183–84
Progressive education, J. Dewey's, 183
Projection, 152, 588–89
Projective identification, 589
Projective techniques, 430
Prosocial development, 431
Prosodics, 84
Protoconsciousness, 431–32
Protocooperation, 26
Protriptyline, 158
Pseudoconditioning, 432
Psyche
    C. Jung's concept of, 295–98
    organizers of, 377
Psychiatric emergency, 186–87
Psychiatric interview with children, 432
Psychiatric nursing, 369–70
Psychiatric residency education, 432–34
Psychiatric units in hospitals, 262
Psychiatrists
    achievement tests used by, 5
    education of, 432–34
    malpractice suits against, 320–23
    professional associations of, 31–32
Psychiatry
    anthropology and, 37–38
    child, 95–96, 248, 432
    communication in, 115–16
    cultural, 3, 140–42, 583
    differential diagnosis in, 171–73
    emergency management in, 186–87
    epidemiological research in social, 192–93
    ethical principles in, 194–96
    forensic, 216–18, 453
    geriatric, 230–31
    history of, 247–48
    international relations and, 290
    malpractice in, 320–23
    military, 340–42
    occupational, 372–73
    parapsychology and, 382
    pastoral, 382
    preventive, 420–21
    social work and, 539–41
    sociology and, 543

space concept for humans and, 546–47
surgery and, 563
transcendental meditation and, 583
transcultural, 583
triage service in, 592
Psychoacoustics, signal detection theory and, 528–29
Psychoanalysis. *See also* Freud, Sigmund
    acting out in, 5–6
    of adolescents, 15
    affects and, 17
    analyst-patient interaction (*see* Analyst-patient interaction)
    anthropology and, 38
    art and, 47
    the brain and, 435–37
    classical studies and, 96
    communicative interaction in, 116–17
    education and, 437–38
    free association and, 220
    K. Horney's technique of, 256–58
    interpretive process in, 291–92
    M. Klein's contribution to, 305
    listening process in, 315
    literature and, 315–16
    mythology, folklore, and, 360–61
    as psychodynamic psychotherapy, 469
    psychosomatic medicine and, 463–64
    reconstruction in, 291, 483
    religion and, 487–89
    resistance in, 291, 440, 445, 489–90
    rule of abstinence in, 2–3
    as science, 438–39
    self-concept in post-Freudian, 504
    sociology and, 544
    termination of, 565–66
    therapeutic alliance in, 573–74
    therapeutic misalliance in, 574–75
    therapeutic regression in, 575–76
    transference in, 291, 444, 584–89
    treatment goals vs. life goals in, 565
    working through and, 439–42
Psychoanalytic history, 250
Psychoanalytic interaction, 442–43
Psychoanalytic metapsychology, 443
Psychoanalytic psychotherapy, 443–44
Psychoanalytic research
    consciousness, altered states, and imagery, 127–28
    on creativity, 139
Psychoanalytic situation, 444
Psychoanalytic technique, 445

Psychoanalytic theory. *See also* Post-Freudian psychoanalytic theory
    on aggression, 19–20
    on antisocial behavior, 40
    on anxiety, 44–45
    the brain and, 435–37
    creativity and, 139
    on defenses and defense organization, 151–53
    on depression and mania, 163–64
    of female personality, 445–46
    after S. Freud, 404–6
    S. Freud's, 221–23 (*see also* Freud, Sigmund)
    K. Horney's, 256, 258–61
    on memory, 333–34
    on mourning, 355
    on power, 414
    on repression, 489
    on schizophrenia, 494–97
    as science, 438–39
    on self-concept, 504
    topographic model in post-Freudian, 579
    on transference, 584–89 (*see also* Transference in psychoanalysis)
Psychobiology, 446
Psychodynamic psychotherapy, 468–69
Psychoendocrinology, 446
Psychohistory, 446–47
Psychokinesis (PK), 381
Psycholinguistics, 96, 447–48
Psychological hedonism, 246
Psychological homeostasis, 252
Psychological refractory period (PRP), 457–59
Psychological tests, 448–49. *See also* Test(s); Testing
    correlational analysis of, 131–32
    factor analysis of, 204–6
    validity of, 595–96
"Psychological theories" on coalition formation, 102
Psychological treatment of physically disabled, 449–51
Psychologists, 423–30, 455–57
    achievement tests used by, 5
    education and training of, 403–4, 425–26, 455–56
    ethical principles of, 193–94
    future directions for, 456–57
    internships of professional, 427–30
    in legal and criminal justice systems, 313
    licensing of, 423–25, 456
    as mental health service providers, 455–57

Psychologists (*cont'd*)
  national register of, 243–46
  postdoctoral education and training
    for, 403–4
  professional associations of, 27–30,
    32–36
  professional practice by, 426–27,
    456–57
  in schools (*see* School psychologists)
  specialty certification for, 29–30
  specialty practice of, guidelines for,
    548–50
  statutory recognition of, 455
  training in child psychology for,
    98
Psychology
  act, 7
  biological, 79
  biopsychology, 79–82
  child, 98–99
  classical, systematic, and contempo-
    rary, 49–50
  clinical, 99–101
  communication in, 115–16
  community, 119–20
  comparative, 120–22
  consumer, 128
  coping, 130–31
  counseling, 132–34
  cross-cultural, 3, 140–42
  developmental, 164–68
  differential diagnosis in, 171–73
  dynamic, 180
  education and (*see also* Education;
    Educational psychology)
  environmental, 191–92
  existential, 198
  experimental, 200–201
  faculty, 207
  Gestalt (*see* Gestalt psychology)
  guidelines for specialty practice in,
    548–50
  history and, 248–49
  holistic, 250
  hormic, 255–56, 320
  humanistic, 269
  internships in, 427–30
  law and, 451–54
  managed vs. integrated care in, 426
  personalistic, 388–90
  phenomenological, 396
  philosophical, 397–98
  postdoctoral education and training
    in, 403–4
  professional, 425–27
  rehabilitation, 484

  school, 498–502
  of self, H. Kohut's, 306–7
  social (*see* Social psychology)
  specialty practice in, 548–50
  sport, 551–53
  transpersonal, 591–92
  of women, 454–55
Psychomotor behavior
  aging and, 24–25
  single-channel mechanism of,
    457–59
Psychomotor learning, warm-up decre-
    ment in, 416, 459
Psychopathology. *See also* Mental disor-
    ders
  in adolescence, 14–15
  behavioral approaches to, 69–70
  cross-cultural psychology and, 142
  genetics and, 227–29
  C. Jung on, 298
  H. Kohut on self and, 306–7
  multiple personality disorder, 356–
    60
  of self, 306–7
  sociopaths as, 544–45
Psychophysical measurement methods,
    460–61
Psychophysics, 461–62
  auditory, 59–60
  of perception, 509
Psychoses
  A. Adler on, 12
  aging and organic, 22–23
  behavior modification and, 67
  delusions and, 154
  disinhibition and, 150
  drug misuse and toxic, 580–81
  genetics and affective, 228
  postpartum, 418–19
  symbiotic, 62–63
  transference, 588
Psychosomatic disorders, 462–63
Psychosomatic medicine and psycho-
    analysis, 463–64
Psychotherapy, 464–71
  with aged, 18
  behavior, 467
  for borderline personality disorder,
    83
  cognitive, 467
  cognitive-behavioral, 469–70
  common and specific factors in,
    465–66
  communication in, 115–16
  current research in, 464–68
  for depression, 157–58

  effectiveness of, 464–65, 470–71
  group, 236–37, 466, 470
  humanistic, 470
  hypnosis in, 270–71
  for juvenile delinquents, 301–2
  marital and family, 466, 470
  overview of, 468–71
  philosophical, 398–99
  psychoanalytic, 443–44
  psychodynamic, 468–69
  rational emotive therapy, 478–79
  research design and method in, 468
  for schizophrenia, 495
  short-term, 466–67
  supportive, 470
  systems, 466
  training in, 467–68
Puberty rites, 488
Punishment, 471, 485
  aggression in children and, 18
  development of self-control and,
    505
  instrumental conditioning and, 284,
    374
  learning and, 471–72
Pure stimulus act, 7
Purpose and purposivism, 472–73
Putnam, James Jackson, 473

Q-technique and Q-sort, 474–75
Quarter-way house, 475
Quillian, M. R., 508

Race
  intelligence and, 286
  single parenting and, 530
Racker, Heinrich, 136
Rado, Sandor, 163, 476
Rank, Otto, 476
Rapaport, David, 164, 477
Rape, 476–77, 517
Rating scales, 477–78
Rational emotive therapy, Albert Ellis's
    method of, 478–79
Rationalization as defense mechanism,
    152
Ray, Isaac, 479
Rayleigh, J. W. S., 60
Razran, Gregory, 479
Reactance theory, 479
Reaction formation as defense mecha-
    nism, 152
Reaction time (RT)
  aging and, 479–80
  choice and, 480–81
Reading, 481–82

Reasoned action, theory of, 55
Reasoning
  beliefs and, 142–43
  problem solving and, 482–83
Recognition paradigms, memory and, 352
Reconstruction in psychoanalysis, 291, 483
Regression, 575–76
  as defense mechanism, 152
  in service of ego, 484
Rehabilitation psychology, 484
Reich, Anne, 135
Reich, Wilhelm, 91, 484
Reid, Thomas, 207
Reik, Theodor, 485
Reil, Johann Christian, 485
Reinforcement, 485–86
  behavior therapy and, 373–74
  delay of, 153
  extinction of response after removal of, 201, 485–86
  incentive factor in, 275
  learning and, 415
  positive and negative, 485
  schedules of, 493–94
  social, 373, 538
Reinforcer, secondary, 125
Reinforcer-induced constraints on learning, 78
Relational determination, sensory coding and, 510
Relaxation, illness and, 72
Releasing functions of auditory communication, 58
Reliability of psychological measurements, 486–87
Religion
  pastoral psychiatry and, 382
  psychoanalysis and, 487–89
Remembering, Repeating, Working Through (Freud), 5
Reminiscence, learning and, 416
REM sleep, 535, 536
Repetition compulsion, 440
Repression, 489
  as defense mechanism, 152
  S. Freud on, 151
  memory and, 333
Research
  on antisocial behavior, 42
  on anxiety, 44–45
  on consciousness, altered states, and imagery, 127–28
  on creativity, 139
  current, in psychotherapy, 464–68

experimental design in, 199–200
  at National Institute of Mental Health, 364–65
  single-subject, 532–33
  on sleep and dreams, 534
  in social psychiatry, 192–93
  on values, 596–97
Resistance in psychoanalysis, 291, 445, 489–90
  transference, 590–91
  working through and, 440
Respiratory one method (ROM), 330
Response conflict theory, 458
Reticular activating system (RAS), 188
Retreading, 403
Retrieval process in memory, 331, 332–33
Reward, 490
Reward power, 414
Reward training, 284
Rivers, W. H. L., 490
Rogers, Carl
  on group therapy, 237
  personalistic psychology of, 389–90
Rokeach, Milton, on authoritarianism, 273
Role theory, 490
Romanes, George J., 120
Rorschach, Hermann, 491
Rorschach Inkblot Method/Test, 430, 449, 491
Rosenfeld's theory of schizophrenia, 496
Rotter, Julian B.
  on goals and level of aspiration, 314
  locus of control scale and social learning theory of, 316–17
Rottner, Julian, 57
Rottner scale, 57
Rubinfine, David L., 164
Rule learning
  educational psychology and, 185
  thinking and transfer in, 577
Rumination in infants, 62
Rumor transmission, 491–92
Runaway behavior in adolescents, 16
Rush, Benjamin, 492

Sachs, Hanns, 493
Sadism, 525–26
Safeguarding devices, A. Adler on, 10
Sakel, Manfred, 493
Salter, Andrew, 68
Sandler, J., 136, 164
Satisfaction, job, 493

Scent, pheromones and perception of, 397
Schafer, R., psychoanalytic theory of, 405
Schank, R., 174–75
Schedules of reinforcement, 493–94
Schema
  motor learning and concept of, 350
  social, 538–39
Schilder, P., on group therapy, 236
Schizophrenia, 494–98
  adaptive theory on, 494–95
  in adolescence, 14
  aging and, 22
  comprehensive psychotherapy for, 495
  genetics and, 227–28
  in infants and children, 63, 497–98
  psychoanalytic views of, 495–97
  social processes causing, 192–93
  sociopsychosomatic theory, 497–98
  H. S. Sullivan on treatment of, 560, 561–62
Schlosberg, Harold, 498
School(s)
  mental health in, 335–36
  as social system, 498
School phobia, 498
School psychologists
  certification of, 423–24
  drug problems and, 179
  emotionally disturbed children and, 190
  training of, 501
School psychology, 498–502
  history, 499
  knowledge bases of, 501
  organizations for, 501
  populations served and problems addressed by, 499–500
  professional skills, activities, and methods in, 500–501
  research on, 501–2
  settings for, 500
  training in, 501
Science. *See also* Research
  psychoanalysis as, 438–39
  treatment of mental disorders and issues in philosophy of, 592
Searles, Harold, 147
  on schizophrenia, 497
Seashore, Carl E., 502
Seashore Measures of Musical Talents, 48
Sechenov, Ivan Mikhailovich, 502
Seguin, Edouard, 502

Selective attention in children, developmental changes and, 502
Selective learning, 502–3
Self
depersonalization of, 156–57
historical overview on views of, 506
C. Jung on, 297–98
H. Kohut's psychology of, 306–7
turning against, as defense mechanism, 152
Self-actualization, 326, 394, 503, 573
Self-concept
in adolescence, 503
in animals, 122
antisocial behavior and, 40
ego involvement and, 186
emergence of, in adolescence, 503
illness and, 72
in post-Freudian psychoanalysis, 504
tests of, 572–73
unconscious, 573
Self-control
behavior modification and, 504–5
in children, 18
cognitive-behavior therapy and, 105
development of, 505
Self-efficacy, A. Bandura's theory of, 104–5
Self-esteem and social behavior, 505–6
Self-estrangement, 26
Self-help, cognitive therapy and, 111–12
Self-object transferences, 586–87
Self-perception
attribution theory and, 58
theory and attitudes on, 55
Self-regard, 572
Self-reinforcement, social learning and, 537
Self-report
on emotions, 190–91
inventories based on, 572–73
observational methods and, 506–7
Self-representations, 496
Self-sacrifice (Antigone principle), 39
Selye, Hans, 507
on general adaptation syndrome, 225–26
Semantic conditioning and generalization, 507
Semantic differential, 507–8
Semantic memory, 174, 508–9
Sensation, 509–10. See also Perception
aging and, 23–24
of hunger, 269–70
psychophysics of, 461–62

signal detection theory and, 527–29
touch and, 579–80
Sensitization, 510
Sensitization-invigoration mechanism, 510–11
Sensoristatis, 512
Sensory deprivation, 292–93, 511–12
Sensory limitations in auditory communications, 59
Sensory mechanisms, perception and, 509–10
Sensory overload, 512–13
Sensory preconditioning and conditioning, 513
Sentence completion tests, 513
table, 512
Sentence memory and comprehension, 513–14
Separation and individuation phase in normal child development, 169, 514–15
Separation and loss in children, 515–16
Separation and separation anxiety, 42–43, 377, 516
Serotonin
role of, in learning and memory, 76–77
specific drugs as reuptake inhibitors, 160
Sertraline, 160
Sex crimes, 516–17
rape as, 476–77, 517
treatment for perpetrators of, 518
Sex differences, 166
gender identity and, 225
Sex hormones, 81
Sexism, 455
Sex motivation, 517–18
Sex offenders, treatment of, 518
Sex roles
aging and, 519
stereotyping of, 518–19
Sex therapy, 524, 525
Sex typing, 519–20
Sexual abuse of children, 93, 94–95
Sexual arousal mechanism (SAM), 517
Sexual assault, 476–77, 516–17
Sexual behavior
development of, 520
patterns of, 517
Sexual disorders in females, 520–24
clinical approach to, 522–24
gender differences and, 520–21
sexual dysfunctions, 521–22
therapy for, 524–25
treatment of, 524
Sexual disorders in males, 525–26

impotency therapy, 274–75
Sexuality
aging and, 24
S. Freud's essays on theory of, 526
homosexuality, 252–55
Shaping in operant conditioning, 183
Sherrington, Charles Scott, 526
Short-term memory (STM), 351
Shyness, 526–27
Sidman, Murray, 65
Sidman's avoidance procedure, 65
Signal detection theory, 527–29
psychophysics and, 462
vigilance, motivation, and, 597
Sign-gestalt expectation, 579
Similarity, H. S. Sullivan's principle of, 560
Simon's model of organizations, 376
Simulation, 529
Single parenting, 529–32
characteristics of healthy, 532
economic status and, 530
family types, 530
psychological problems associated with, 531–32
race, ethnic group, and, 530
stress reduction in, 531
stress sources in, 530–31
Single-subject research, 532–33
Situation. See also Environment
interaction between person and, 387–88
psychoanalytic, 444
Skill, 533
acquisition of, 533
aging and, 24–25
social, 533
transfer of, 583–84
Skin, perception of touch in, 579–80
Skinner, B. F., 56, 534
on emotions, 188
operant behaviorism and, 73
operant behaviorism extended to programmed instruction by, 183–84
on socialization, 543
on social reinforcement, 538
theory of learning by, 311
Slavson, Samuel, on group therapy, 236–37
Sleep
dreaming and, 534–36 (see also Dreams and dreaming)
ontogeny of, 534
physiology of, 534
REM and NREM, 535, 536
Sleepwalking (somnambulism), 545

Smell, sense of, 92
Smiling response, in infants, 377
Social behavior
    allelomimetic, 26
    antisocial behavior and, 39–42
    auditory communication as, 58–59
    bystander intervention as, 87
    child face and body deformity and, 204
    play as, 401
    power and acceptance theory of, 413
    role theory and, 490
    self-esteem and, 505–6
Social causation, 395
Social Class and Mental Illness, 192
Social competency, 122–23
Social conditions, A. Adler on human development and, 10–11
Social development in infants and children, 167–68
Social disadvantage, effects of, on children, 536
Social exchange theories on interpersonal attraction, 56
Social facilitation phenomenon, 346–47
Social influence, 536–37
Social isolation, 25–26
Socialization, 542–43
    family influences on, 210
    peer influences on, 383
    prosocial development and, 431
Social learning theory, 537
    cognitive-behavior therapy and, 104–5
    locus of control scale and, 316–17
    moral development in children and, 166
    on personality and psychopathology, 70
    J. B. Rotter's, 316–17
    on self-control, 505
Social modalities and organ modes in personality development, 374–75
Social perception, theories of, 538
Social power, 414
Social psychiatry, epidemiological research in, 192–93
Social psychology
    attention research in, 51–52
    cognitive theories in, 109–10
    decision theory in, 150
    mental health and, in institutional settings, 336
    stimulus-response theories in, 555
Social reinforcement, 373, 538

Social schemata, 538–39
Social skills, 104, 533
Social status, 539
Social system
    classroom as, 97–98
    school as, 498
Social work
    code of ethics for, 541–42
    role of, in psychiatry and mental health, 539–41
Sociobiology, 121
Socioeconomic status
    effects of disadvantaged, on children, 536
    mental disorders and, 543
Sociology
    psychiatry and, 543
    psychoanalysis and, 544
Sociopaths, 544–45, 566
    psychiatry of law and term, 217
Sociopsychological theories of organization, 375–76
Sociopsychosomatic theory of schizophrenia, 497–98
Socrates, 397
Somnambulism, 545
Somnolent detachment, H. S. Sullivan on, 561
Space, personal
    group ecology and general systems theory on, 236
    psychiatry and, 546–47
    territory and, in humans, 388
Space perception, auditory, 60–61
Spatial frequencies, vision and, 547–48
Spatial tests and mechanical aptitude, 329
Spearman, Charles, 285, 287
Specialty practice in psychology, guidelines for, 548–50
Speech and language, developmental disability in, 550–51
Speed tests, construction of, 567
Spence, Kenneth W., 551
Sperry, R. W., 392
Spinal conditioning, 551
Spinoza, Benedict de, 50
Spitz, René A., 164
Splitting, as defense mechanism, 152
Spontaneous activity, 6–7
Spontaneous recovery, 239, 551
Sport psychology, 551–53
    current trends in, 552
    domain of, 552–53
    historical perspective on, 551–52
Spranger, Edward, personalistic psychology of, 389

Stage models of human information processing, 268–69
Standardized tests, 4–5
Stanford-Binet Intelligence Test, 448, 553
Startle, 553–54
Statogram and statometric technique, 554–55
Status, social, 539
Stereotypes, sex-role, 518–19
Stern, William, personalistic psychology of, 389
Stimulus deprivation in infants, 62
Stimulus-response theories in social psychology, 555
Stimulus substitution, 555
Stogdill, Ralph M., 555
Stone, L., psychoanalytic theory of, 405
Strachey, James, 556
Strategies, thinking based on, 577
Stress
    anxiety and, 44–45
    general adaptation syndrome and, 225–26
    meditation for reduction of, 583
    post-traumatic stress disorder, 406–12
    single parenting and, 530–31
Stromberg Dexterity Test, 348
Strong, E. K., 288
Strong-Campbell Interest Inventory (SCII), 289
Structuralism, 556, 578
Structural model, Sigmund Freud's, 222
    ego and, 221–22
    id and, 272
Studies on Hysteria (Freud), 2, 220, 221
Study of values, 556
Sublimation as defense mechanism, 152
Suicide, 556–57
    A. Adler on, 12–13
    characteristics of, 556–57
    malpractice cases and, 320
    as psychiatric emergency, 186–87
Suicide prevention, 557
Sullivan, Harry Stack, 248, 557
    interpersonal theory of, 558–60
    on schizophrenia, 496
    therapeutic conceptions of, 560–62
Summation, 562
Summative rating scales, 477–78
Superego, Sigmund Freud's concept of, 562–63
Superstitious behavior, 563
Supportive psychotherapy, 470
Surgery and psychiatry, 563

Survey tests, 4
Sydenham, Thomas, 563
Symbiotic psychosis, 62
Symbol, C. Jung on, 296
Sympathetic nervous system (SNS), 191
Synaptic pathways, 80–81
Synectics, 138–39
Systematic desensitization, 563–64
  in classrooms, 67
  cognitive-behavior therapy and, 104, 105
  in structured group therapy, 68
Systems design, auditory communication and, 58, 59
Systems therapy, 466

Tarachow, S., models of psychotherapy by, 443–44
Tarasoff cases, 320, 322
Tasks
  difficulty and transfer of, 584
  discrete vs. continuous, in motor skills memory, 350–51
  learning and characteristics of, 415–16
  Zeigarnik effect, in recall of, 606
Taste, 91–92
Tausk, Victor, on schizophrenia, 496
Taylor, F., on organizations, 376
Taylor Manifest Anxiety Scale (MAS), 190
Teleology, 439, 565
  A. Adler on, 9–10
Television, impact of, 326–27
Temperament, 167
  J. Cattell's trait theory on, 90
  H. Eysenck on, 202
  Guilford-Zimmerman survey of, 238
Temperature, perception of, 580
Tenderness, H. S. Sullivan's principle of, 560
Tennessee Self-Concept Test, 572
Terman, Lewis M., 565
Termination of psychoanalysis, 565–66
Territorial behavior and personal space in humans, 388
Terrorism, 402, 566–67
Test(s). See also Intelligence tests; Measurement; Psychological tests; names of individual tests
  achievement, 3–5, 448
  aptitude, 45–46, 448
  construction of, 567–68
  of creativity, 137–38
  cultural bias in, 570–71
  for diagnosis of autism, 62

interest inventories, 288, 289
  personality, 88, 202, 238, 342, 449
  personnel, 394–95
  projective techniques, 430
  scores, statistics, and norms for, 568–69
  of self-concept, 572–73
  sentence completion, 513
    table, 512
  survey vs. diagnostic, 4
Testing
  computerized, 123
  of ethnic-minority children, 569–72
  of mentally retarded, 572
Teuber, Hans Lukas, 573
Thematic Apperception Test (TAT), 430, 449, 573
Therapeutic alliance, 573–74
  in adolescent psychoanalysis, 15
Therapeutic misalliance, 574–75
Therapeutic regression, 152, 484, 575–76
Therapist-patient relationship, A. Adler on, 11–12. See also Analyst-patient interaction
Thermal stimuli, 580
Thinking, 576–77. See also Cognition
  culture and, 142–43
  Gestalt psychology and, 231–32
  insight and, 184
  language and, 74
Thirst, 577–78
Thompson, Clara, 578
Thompson, Silvanus, 60
Thomson, Godfrey, 578
Thorndike, Edward Lee, 120, 578
  law of effect in associationism by, 183, 309
  motor learning theory of, 348, 415
  on reinforcement, 486
Thought. See Cognition; Thinking
Threat, anxiety and, 44–45
Threshold, perceptual, 527–28
Thurstone, L. L., 288
Thyroid potentiation, 161
Tinbergen, Nicholaas, 120, 121
Titchener, Edward Bradford, 556, 578
Token reinforcement programs, 373–74
Tolman, Edward Chase, 579
  cognitive map of, 109
  on emotion, 188
  theory of learning by, 311, 349
Tomkins, Silvan
  on beliefs and ideology, 273
  theory of emotions by, 188
Topographic model
  S. Freud's, 223
  in post-Freudian theory, 579

Torrance Tests of Creative Thinking, 137
Totalitarianism, 413
Totemism, 488
Touch, 579–80
Tourette, Gilles de la, 580
Toxic psychoses, 580–81
Training, transfer of, 583–84
Trait anxiety, 276
Traits, quantification and measurement of, 582–83
Trait theory, 582
  J. Cattell's, 90–91
  H. Eysenck's, 202–3
  genetics and, 581–82
Transcendental meditation, 330
  psychiatry and, 583
Transcultural psychiatry, 583
Transference in psychoanalysis, 291, 444, 584–89
  counter-, 134–37
  C. Jung on, 300
  mechanisms of, 588–89
  variants of, 584–88
Transference neurosis, 590
  in adolescence, 15
Transference resistance, 590–91
Transfer of training, 583–84
Transpersonal psychology, 591–92
Transsexualism, 526
Transvestism, 525
Tranylcypromine, 159
Trazodone, 160
Treatment of mental disorders, 592. See also Mental disorders
Triage service in psychiatry, 592
Tricyclic antidepressants (TCAs), 158–59
Trimipramine, 158
Truth therapy, 117
Tuke, Daniel Hack, 592–93
Tuke, Samuel, 593
Tuke, William, 593
Turiel, J. C., 167
Turning against self as defense mechanism, 152

Ukhtomsky, Alexei Alexeivich, 594
Unconditioned stimuli (US), 124–25
Unconscious, C. G. Jung on concept of collective, 296
Unconscious motives and values, 596–97
Undoing, as defense mechanism, 152–53
Urination, pheromones and, 397
Utilities, multidimensional values as, 596

Valence, 595
Validity of psychological tests, 595–96

Value-expectancy interaction, 596
Values and value systems, 596–97
    Allport-Vernon-Lindzey Study of, 556
    in educational psychology, 182
    ideology, belief systems, and, 272–73
    issues in contemporary research on, 596–97
    measurement of, 596
    moral development and, 596
Vandalism, 597
Vectorial human relations, B. Wolman on, 162, 369, 393, 413, 497
Ventromedial hypothalamic (VMH), 269
Vernon, P. E., 288
Vicarious functioning, K. Lashley's principle of, 80
Vigilance and motivation, 597
Vincent curve, 597
Violence, 151
    in media, 326–27, 390
    rape and sexual assault as, 476–77, 516–17
    terrorism as self-righteous, 566–67
    youth and, 598
Vision
    aging and, 23–24
    color, 24, 113–15, 318–19
    contrast mechanisms, 129
    cross-cultural psychology and, 141
    development of, 165
    feature detection and, 214–15
    sensitivity of, 598–99
    sensory mechanisms of, 509–10
    spatial frequencies in, 547–48

Visually controlled movement, 599
Visual-motor information, 598
Visual sensitivity, 598–99
Vitalism, 599–600
Vocational Interest Blank (VIB), 288
Voluntary behavior, 600
Von Ehrenfels, Christian Freiherr, on Gestalt qualities, 7
Von Wolff, Christian, 207
Voyeurism, 525

Wagner von Jauregg (Wagner-Jauregg), Julius Ritter, 601
Wallach, H., color vision studies of, 113–14
Walters, R. H.
    on self-control, 505
    on socialization, 542–43
Warm-up decrement, 416, 459
Washburn, Margaret Floy, 120
Watson, Goodwin, 601
Watson, John Broadus, 72, 103, 367,
    on behaviorism, 601
    on emotion, 188
Weber, M., on organizations, 375–76
Wechsler, David, 285, 287, 601
Wechsler's intelligence tests, 448, 601–2
Wender, Louis, on group therapy, 236
Wernicke, Karl, 602
Wertheimer, Max, 602
    on form perception, 218–19
Weyer, Johannes, 602
White, William Alanson, 602–3
Wilson, E. O., 121
Wing Standardized Tests of Musical Intelligence, 48

Winnicott, Donald W., 603
Witkin, Herman A., 603
Wolman, Benjamin, 603
    Antigone principle of, 39
    in childhood autism and schizophrenia, 63
    nosology system of, 162, 369, 393
    personality theory of, 392–94
    on protoconsciousness, 431–32
    psychoanalytic principles of, 438
    on schizophrenia, 497–98
Women, psychology of, 258, 454–55. *See also* Females
Woodworth, R. S., 177
    on dynamic psychology, 180
Word association, 603
Work and Values Inventory, 289, 449
Working memory, 332
Working through in psychoanalysis, 439–42
Work motivation, 603–4
Work therapy, 604
Work variables, learning and, 416
Wundt, Wilhelm, 398, 604

Yerkes, Robert M., 120, 605
Yerkes-Dodson Law, 605
Yes-no experiments on signal detection, 528
Yoked control, 605
Youth, violence and, 598. *See also* Adolescence

Zeigarnik effect, 606
Zeitgebers, 82
Zerner, Karl Edward, 606